Legal Recognition of Same-Sex Partnerships

A Study of National, European and International Law

Edited by
ROBERT WINTEMUTE
School of Law, King's College,
University of London
and
MADS ANDENÆS
British Institute of International and Comparative Law,
London

OXFORD – PORTLAND OREGON
2001

Hart Publishing
Oxford and Portland, Oregon

Published in North America (US and Canada) by
Hart Publishing c/o
International Specialized Book Services
5804 NE Hassalo Street
Portland, Oregon
97213-3644
USA

Distributed in the Netherlands, Belgium and Luxembourg by
Intersentia, Churchillaan 108
B2900 Schoten
Antwerpen
Belgium

Hart Publishing Ltd is a specialist legal publisher based in Oxford, England. To order further copies of this book or to request a list of other publications please write to:

Hart Publishing Ltd, Salter's Boatyard, Oxford OX1 4LB
Telephone: +44 (0)1865 245533 or Fax: +44 (0)1865 794882
e-mail: mail@hartpub.co.uk
WEBSITE: http//www.hartpub.co.uk

British Library Cataloguing in Publication Data
Data Available
ISBN 1 84113–138–5 (paperback)

Typeset by Hope Services (Abingdon) Ltd.
Printed and bound in Great Britain on acid-free paper by
Biddles Ltd, www.biddles.co.uk

Foreword

THE LAST QUARTER of the twentieth century saw a dramatic increase in the number and power of organised gay and lesbian social and political movements. This was accompanied by the systematic assertion, through legal strategies and challenges, of gays' and lesbians' rights to dignity and to full and equal citizenship. Decriminalising lesbian and gay sexual expression has been an indispensable first preoccupation; and in many jurisdictions (though still too few) this has been achieved. But for many, the scholarly and political focus has shifted to the quest for full and equal recognition of same-sex partnerships. Lesbians and gay men are demanding the right to form legally protected families, to receive benefits equal to those afforded state-sanctioned unions, and, in many cases, the equal right to marry.

The implicit premise of these claims was given clarion expression recently in the Constitutional Court of South Africa. Justice Ackermann stated for a unanimous Court that lesbians and gays in same-sex partnerships "are as capable as heterosexual spouses of expressing and sharing love in its manifold forms", and "likewise as capable of forming intimate, permanent, committed, monogamous, loyal and enduring relationships; of furnishing emotional and spiritual support; and of providing physical care, financial support and assistance in running the common household". Finally, gays and lesbians:

> "are capable of constituting a family, whether nuclear or extended, and of establishing, enjoying and benefiting from family life which is not distinguishable in any significant respect from that of heterosexual spouses".[1]

But on whose terms—and on what basis—is recognition to be gained? Are our relationships to be recognised only if they are in all respects, save for the gender of our partners, indistinguishable from traditional heterosexual marriages? Or are we to assert an entitlement to self-definition and autonomy that will lead to distinctive forms of union? If the latter, just how far should the boundaries of convention be pushed?

The call for full and equal recognition of same-sex partnerships has forced lesbian and gay communities to examine the nature of their demands and to re-evaluate their positions in societies that are often quite hostile to their demands. This has on occasion resulted in fundamental conflict within such communities themselves, sowing seeds of division amongst political activists, community-based organisations and those who just want to be like everyone else. At the heart of the conflict is the difficult choice often facing lesbian and gay people:

[1] *National Coalition for Gay and Lesbian Equality* v. *Minister of Home Affairs*, 2000 (2) SA 1 (Constitutional Court) at 32–3 (para. 53).

"equality" on society's terms, or continued marginalisation. At the heart of the conflict is the danger of being forced to accept an undignified position of compromise: denial of the reality of lived experiences and the expression of diversity and difference.

Legal formalism and a rights discourse uncritical of existing patterns of systematic discrimination and injustice have formed the backdrop to such divisive developments. A legal culture built on tradition and continuity does not easily revisit old assumptions, prejudices or practices, but more often justifies the present by appealing to the past, looking forward without learning from the mistakes of yesterday. It is in such legal cultures that lesbian and gay people seeking legal protection for their families may be forced to appeal to an argument of sameness, to dismiss difference and to deny the richness of diversity.

Recent developments do give cause for hope. The rights discourse is shifting, with formalism giving way to emphasis on the claims of substantive equality. This is not to suggest that formal equality is trivial. That would be wrong, since the attainment of formal equality represents a very real gain for those previously denied it. But it is to recognise a goal beyond that of only formal equivalence. In the words of Justice Albie Sachs, again of the Constitutional Court of South Africa:

> "What becomes normal in an open society, then, is not an imposed and standardised form of behaviour that refuses to acknowledge difference, but the acceptance of the principle of difference itself, which accepts the variability of human behaviour."[2]

In *Legal Recognition of Same-Sex Partnerships: A Study of National, European and International Law*, Robert Wintemute and Mads Andenæs have brought together the writings of many respected jurists, academics, legal practitioners and activists from Latin America, Asia, Australasia, North America, Europe, the Middle East and Africa. This book is a thought-provoking, substantial and much needed contribution to the debate on same-sex partnerships. At issue is the right of lesbian and gay people to family life, the scope and content of the right, and its legal recognition and protection.

The importance of the book lies first in its simultaneous reflection of unity and diversity. But it lies also in the way it brings the once marginalised into the mainstream. In effect, this book constitutes an international coming-out of legal thought and scholarship. In doing this so emphatically, proudly and authoritatively, it serves as a powerful addition to a growing body of comparative legal studies. From theory to practice, from justification to critique, the book works its way through the complex and often intricately interconnecting relationships between law, legal process and social change.

The essays in the book offer no simple solutions. The book however raises many questions. And it serves as a much-needed resource just when the highest courts of many countries are grappling with rapidly evolving conceptions of life

[2] *National Coalition for Gay & Lesbian Equality* v. *Minister of Justice*, 1999 (1) SA 6 (Constitutional Court) at 68–9 (para. 134).

partnerships and family life, attempting to make sense of the true implications of a commitment to substantive equality and to a new world order based on respect for and promotion of a culture of fundamental human rights. But it is also more than this: it is a testimony to the struggles waged by ordinary lesbian and gay people as they claim what the law has no right to deny them. It is a collection of battles lost and won, a documentation of the lives of those who—for far too long—have been excluded from history.

In our newfound optimism, however, we must not forget that for most lesbian and gay people throughout the world, the legal recognition of same-sex partnerships is still a prize perhaps not yet even open for discussion. South Africa, whose Constitutional Court has produced perhaps the most limpid affirmations of gay and lesbian equality, has neighbours whose leaders denounce us in demeaning and often threatening language. In many countries, gays and lesbians are still beaten and imprisoned and even killed for expressing love. Our families are still torn apart by legal systems that equate homosexuality with child abuse. Many of us continue to be forced into marriages against our wills; and our rights to freedom and security, health care, employment, housing and social services are insufficiently recognised. As Justice Ackermann, again, noted:

> "The denial of equal dignity and worth all too quickly and insidiously degenerates into a denial of humanity and leads to inhuman treatment by the rest of society in many other ways."[3]

While we continue to push boundaries, and to advocate for and claim our rightful places in society, let us remember that, for as long as lesbian and gay people face oppression anywhere, we cannot but regard our hard won freedoms as fragile, and only partial.

The Hon. Justice Edwin Cameron
Judge of the Supreme Court of Appeal, South Africa
Acting Justice, Constitutional Court of South Africa, 1999–2000

[3] *Supra* n.1, at 28 (para. 42).

Acknowledgments

THIS BOOK IS based on "Legal Recognition of Same-Sex Partnerships: A Conference on National, European and International Law", Centre of European Law, School of Law, King's College, University of London, 1–3 July 1999. The first person I must thank is my honorary co-editor Mads Andenæs, the former Director of the Centre of European Law (now Director of the British Institute of International and Comparative Law), without whose inspiration and support the conference would not have been organised, and this book would not have been published. Over a drink in late July 1998, two of Mads's ideas (a conference on the new Nordic and Dutch registered partnership laws, and a conference on the recent transsexual and lesbian cases in the European Court of Justice) fused with my own desire to organise an international conference on lesbian, gay, bisexual and transgendered legal studies, inspired by the work of such pioneering conference organisers as Leslie Moran ("Legal Queeries", Lancaster University, 1995), Daniel Borrillo ("Homosexualités et Droit", Université de Paris X (Nanterre), 1997), Didi Herman and Carl Stychin ("Gender, Sexuality & Law", Keele University, 1998), and Stephen Whittle ("Transgender Agenda", Exeter College Oxford, 1998).

The conference could not have taken place without a generous financial contribution from the Centre of European Law, for which I would like to thank Mads Andenæs, Piet Eeckhout and Richard Whish. Additional funding from Yves Saint Laurent Couture, the School of Law Research Committee (King's College London), the Butterworths Fund for European Exchanges (Society of Public Teachers of Law, United Kingdom), and the Equal Opportunities Officers of the General Council of the Bar (England and Wales) was greatly appreciated, and allowed a number of speakers to attend. Christine Copping and Andrea Cordwell James (Centre of European Law), and Thomas Formond (doctoral candidate, Université de Paris X), made the conference run smoothly.

Around 135 chairs, speakers and other participants came from the United Kingdom and two dozen other countries: Australia, Austria, Belgium, Brazil, Canada, China (Hong Kong), Denmark, Finland, France, Germany, Hungary, India, Ireland, Israel, Italy, Japan, Luxembourg, the Netherlands, New Zealand, South Africa, Spain, Sweden, Switzerland, and the United States. In particular, I would like to thank the judicial chairs and speakers for their individual contributions, as well as their lively debate on "The Judicial Role in Protecting Human Rights": Lord Slynn of Hadley (House of Lords; former Judge and Advocate General, European Court of Justice; President of the Centre of European Law), Judge Deborah Batts (United States District Court, Southern District of New York), Mr. Justice Edwin Cameron (then of the High

Court, Johannesburg), Judge Michael Elmer (Maritime and Commercial Courts, Copenhagen; former Advocate General, European Court of Justice), Justice Michael Kirby (High Court of Australia), Justice Claire L'Heureux-Dubé (Supreme Court of Canada), and Dr. Pieter van Dijk (Council of State, Netherlands; former Judge, European Court of Human Rights). Madame Noëlle Lenoir (then of the Conseil Constitutionnel, France) had hoped to attend but was unable to do so. Thanks too to Cherie Booth QC for joining the panel on "Litigation Under European Community Law". On behalf of all the conference participants, I would like to express our condolences to the families of distinguished human rights barrister Peter Duffy QC (8 August 1954–5 March 1999), and Judge Federico Mancini of the European Court of Justice (23 December 1927–21 July 1999), who had accepted invitations to chair or speak.

Further thanks are owed to all the contributors to this book for their hard work in producing their chapters, and their patience throughout the editing process; to Dean Anthony Kronman, Deputy Dean Kate Stith, and Associate Dean Mike Thompson at Yale Law School for the excellent facilities that allowed me to complete the editing during a sabbatical visit; to Bill Eskridge for being an extraordinary host; to Brian Bix, Jennifer Brown, Harold Koh, Judith Resnik, Reva Siegel, Kenji Yoshino and Stéphane Garneri (doctoral candidate, Université d'Aix-en-Provence) for stimulating and helpful conversations; to my secretary at King's, Catherine Calder; and to Hannah Young at Hart Publishing.

Finally, I would like to thank my partner for his support, in sickness and in health, in pre-conference stress and on post-conference holiday, with virtually no legal recognition, since 1989. And I would like to dedicate this book to same-sex partners throughout the world who refuse to accept that the bus can go by without stopping, or that they must sit at the back once they are allowed to board.

Robert Wintemute
Senior Research Associate
Yale Law School
New Haven, Connecticut, U.S.A.
8 May 2001

Contents

PART II NATIONAL LAW

Section A—United States

Section B—Canada

Section C—Africa, Australasia and Latin America

PART IV INTERNATIONAL LAW

Introduction

ROBERT WINTEMUTE*

> "These constitutional challenges have in common the assertion that the right to marry without regard to the sex of the parties is a fundamental right of all persons and that restricting marriage to only couples of the opposite sex is irrational and invidiously discriminatory. We are not independently persuaded by these contentions and do not find support for them in any decisions of the United States Supreme Court. The institution of marriage as a union of man and woman, uniquely involving the procreation and rearing of children within a family, is as old as the book of Genesis. . . . [T]here is a clear distinction between a marital restriction based merely upon race and one based upon the fundamental difference in sex." *Baker* v. *Nelson*, 191 N.W.2d 185 at 186–7 (Minnesota Supreme Court, 15 October 1971), appeal dismissed for want of a substantial federal question, 409 U.S. 810 (U.S. Supreme Court, 10 October 1972).

> "A marriage can be contracted by two persons of different sex or of the same sex".[1] ("*Een huwelijk kan worden aangegaan door twee personen van verschillend of van gelijk geslacht.*") Article 30(1), Book 1 of the Civil Code of the Netherlands, as amended by the Act on the Opening Up of Marriage of 21 December 2000, in force on 1 April 2001.

THE CONFERENCE ON which this book is based opened on 1 July 1999, three days after the thirtieth anniversary of the Stonewall riots in New York in 1969,[2] twenty-four days after the tenth anniversary of the enactment of Denmark's registered same-sex partnership law in 1989,[3] and seven days before the introduction in the Dutch Parliament of the bill on the opening up of civil marriage to same-sex couples.[4] During the first twenty years of the post-Stonewall lesbian, gay, bisexual and transgendered equality movement, legal recognition of same-sex partnerships was not a priority in most industrialised democracies. Although a few brave couples, such as Jack Baker and James

* Reader, School of Law, King's College, University of London.

[1] Translated by Kees Waaldijk. See chap. 23, App. II.

[2] 27–28 June 1969. See Martin Duberman, *Stonewall* (New York, Dutton Signet, 1993).

[3] Law on Registered Partnership (*Lov om registreret partnerskab*), 7 June 1989, nr. 372. See Lund-Andersen, chap. 21.

[4] 8 July 1999. See Waaldijk, chap. 23, App. II.

McConnell of *Baker* v. *Nelson*,[5] sought marriage licenses in the early 1970s, the focus of most litigation and lobbying was securing the right of lesbian, gay and bisexual[6] individuals to engage in private sexual activity without fear of criminal prosecution, and to be open about their sexual orientations in the workplace, without fear of dismissal or other discrimination, including in the armed forces.

However, as these goals began to be achieved in more and more jurisdictions during the 1980s and early 1990s, lesbian, gay and bisexual[7] individuals began to dare to imagine the possibility of equality, not only for themselves as individuals, but also for their relationships with their partners. Two "shots heard round the world" helped make relationship recognition *the* burning legal and political issue for the lesbian, gay and bisexual minority in more and more industrialised democracies by 1999. The first shot was the adoption of a registered partnership law in Denmark in 1989 that permitted same-sex couples to acquire almost all of the legal rights and obligations of married different-sex couples. The first shot inspired the second,[8] applications for marriage licenses in Hawaii in 1990 by Ninia Baehr and Genora Dancel, Tammy Rodrigues and Antoinette Pregil, and Pat Lagon and Joseph Melillo. The rejection of their applications led to the Hawaii Supreme Court's historic decision in *Baehr* v. *Lewin* in 1993 that the denial of marriage licenses to same-sex partners was prima facie sex discrimination, which violated the Hawaii Constitution unless it could be justified by a "compelling state interest".[9]

The specific purpose of the conference and of this book has been to examine an issue that jurisdictions around the world are increasingly forced to address: whether and to what extent to recognise in law (both by granting rights and imposing obligations), and to require private parties to recognise, partnerships or couple relationships formed by two men or two women, or by two persons who are both legally (but not factually) male or female. In the Foreword and in the forty-two chapters and two introductions that follow, an international team

[5] *McConnell* v. *Anderson*, 451 F.2d 193 at 196 (8th Circuit 1971), upheld the subsequent denial of a job to McConnell: "[T]he prospective employee demands, as shown . . . by the marriage license incident, . . . the right to pursue an activist role in implementing his unconventional ideas concerning the societal status to be accorded homosexuals and, thereby, to foist tacit approval of this socially repugnant concept upon his employer". See also *Re North & Matheson* (1974), 52 D.L.R. (4th) 280 (Manitoba County Court).

[6] Lesbian, gay and bisexual individuals have often neglected the concerns of transgendered individuals, especially with regard to ensuring that they are protected by anti-discrimination legislation, whether the ground is "sex" or "sexual orientation" or "gender identity". By making the sexes of individual partners irrelevant, legal recognition of same-sex partnerships can provide solutions to common legal problems faced by same-sex couples, and by different-sex couples considered legally "same-sex" because one partner is transgendered. However, it does not address the need of many transgendered individuals for legal recognition of their gender identity. See Whittle, chap. 39.

[7] In Europe, transgendered individuals have been the pioneers in litigating before the European Court of Human Rights for the right to marry and for parental rights for non-genetic parents. See Whittle, chap. 39; Wintemute, chap. 40.

[8] W N Eskridge, Jr., *Equality Practice* (New York, Routledge, forthcoming in 2001).

[9] 852 P. 2d 44, clarified, 852 P.2d 74. See Wolfson, chap. 9.

of forty-seven judges and legal scholars analyse the theoretical, historical, legal, political and social aspects of this issue under the national (including federal, state, provincial, regional or local) law of twenty-three countries[10] (the United States, Canada, South Africa, Australia, New Zealand, Brazil, Japan, China, India, Israel, Denmark, Sweden, the Netherlands, Belgium, France, Spain, Italy, Switzerland, Austria, Hungary, Germany, Ireland, and the United Kingdom), under European law (European Community law and the European Convention on Human Rights), and under international law (United Nations human rights law).

With some assistance from the contributors, readers will be able to compare the different jurisdictions for themselves.[11] They will note both the great similarity in the legal problems faced by same-sex partners (with regard to employment benefits, social security, pensions, housing, services, immigration, taxation, inheritance, property division and support obligations when relationships break down, parental rights, and access to civil marriage), and the fascinating diversity of legal responses to these problems, resulting from the very different constitutional, historical, social and political contexts in each jurisdiction. In the Conclusion, drawing on the work of the contributors, I will attempt to categorise and rank developments throughout the world as of 2001, and to predict the course of developments over the next five to ten years. Readers who would like an overview, to assist them in deciding which chapters to read, might wish to jump to the Conclusion after the Introduction (and then return to the middle!).

The broader purpose of the conference and of this book has been to bring together judges and academic and practising lawyers interested in the field of sexual orientation, gender identity and law, to share ideas and information and to make contacts. Although there are many people working in this field around the world, lesbian, gay, bisexual and heterosexual, transgendered and non-transgendered, most of us are relatively isolated. Those of us working in universities are often lucky to have a single colleague with similar interests. In some countries, research in this area is not seen by universities as legitimate scholarship, or as suitable for doctoral candidates aspiring to an academic career. I hope that this book will not be seen as only about same-sex partnerships, but also as a collection of international and comparative scholarship on sexual orientation, gender identity and law, especially from countries about which little has been published in English.

It has not been a purpose of the conference or of this book to provide a forum for those who are opposed to any form of equality for lesbian, gay, bisexual and

[10] It was not possible to include chapters on three countries with legislation on same-sex partnerships (Iceland, Norway and Portugal), or on two countries with pending bills on same-sex partnerships (the Czech Republic and Finland). Developments in these countries will be mentioned in the Conclusion.

[11] Cross-references have been added to facilitate this. "See Bell, chap. 37" means see the chapter by Bell in this book.

transgendered individuals, or for couples consisting of two persons of the same sex (factually or legally), or who argue that because civil marriage has always been different-sex only in a particular jurisdiction, it can never change. A book about discrimination against racial, ethnic or religious minorities, or against women, would be unlikely to include chapters by persons advocating discrimination against these groups, or arguing that tradition requires the maintenance of certain forms of discrimination. The traditional view, largely derived from the doctrines of dominant religions, that only married different-sex couples are deserving of legal recognition, has powerful exponents who have no trouble making their voices heard.[12]

The contributors to this book share a common starting point: that tradition and religious doctrines are not decisive on questions of secular law reform; and that lesbian, gay, bisexual and transgendered individuals are generally entitled to equal treatment with heterosexual individuals. Their disagreements, and the robust debate regarding same-sex marriage in the Theoretical Perspectives section and elsewhere in the book, relate to the forms of equality that are desirable or feasible. Should same-sex couples be granted equal treatment with unmarried different-sex couples, the right to contract civil marriages, or separate legal frameworks? Or should any preferential (or disadvantageous) recognition of anyone's partnership or couple relationship by the law be abolished?

[12] See e.g. "Family, Marriage and 'De Facto' Unions" (Pontifical Council for the Family, dated 26 July 2000, released on 21 Nov. 2000), http://www.vatican.va/roman_curia/pontifical_councils/family, paras 23, 47: ". . . 'de facto unions' between homosexuals are a deplorable distortion of what should be a communion of love and life between a man and a woman . . . The bond between two men or two women cannot constitute a real family and much less can the right be attributed to that union to adopt children . . . To recall . . . the grave error of recognizing or even making homosexual relations equivalent to marriage does not presume to discriminate against these persons in any way . . . [M]aking de facto unions equivalent to the family . . . is an evil for persons, families and societies." See also (same URL) "Declaration of the Pontifical Council for the Family regarding the Resolution of the European Parliament dated March 16, 2000, making de facto unions, including same sex unions, equal to the family" (17 March 2000) ("This Resolution represents a grave and repeated attack on the family based on marriage. . . . Every society is solidly based on this marital union because it is a necessary value. To deny this fundamental and elementary anthropological truth would lead to the destruction of the fabric of society. . . . [T]he great majority of European families . . . now see themselves unjustly considered as equal to this type of 'union' through the Resolution. . . . Lawmakers, therefore, and in particular Catholic members of parliaments, should not favor this type of legislation with their vote because it is contrary to the common good and the truth about man and is thus truly unjust."); *Catechism of the Catholic Church*, No. 2357, http://www.vatican.va/archive/ccc/index.htm (Part 3, Section 2, Chapter 2, Article 6, II. The Vocation to Chastity) ("Basing itself on Sacred Scripture, which presents homosexual acts as acts of grave depravity, tradition has always declared that 'homosexual acts are intrinsically disordered'. They are contrary to the natural law. . . . Under no circumstances can they be approved."); Congregation for the Doctrine of the Faith, "Letter to the Bishops of the Catholic Church on the Pastoral Care of Homosexual Persons" (1 Oct. 1986), http://www.vatican.va/roman_curia/congregations/cfaith/index.htm, paras. 3, 9, 10 ("Although the particular inclination of the homosexual person is not a sin, it is a more or less strong tendency ordered toward an intrinsic moral evil, and thus the inclination itself must be seen as an objective disorder. . . . The Church . . . is really concerned . . . about those who may have been tempted to believe [the] deceitful propaganda [of the pro-homosexual movement]. . . . When . . . homosexual activity is . . . condoned, . . . neither the Church nor society at large should be surprised when . . . irrational and violent reactions increase.").

One dictionary defines "recognise" as "[a]cknowledge the existence, legality, or validity of, esp[ecially] by formal approval or sanction; accord notice or attention to; treat as worthy of consideration . . .".[13] *Legal Recognition of Same-Sex Partnerships* is about whether or not the law is willing to acknowledge a social fact. Loving, lasting, mutually supportive relationships between two men and between two women, or between two persons who are legally (but not factually) of the same sex, exist and have existed in many countries for many years.[14] A good example is that of James Egan and John Nesbit, two gay pensioners who had been living together as a couple for over forty-six years when their equality claim was rejected by the Supreme Court of Canada in 1995.[15] This book is about when, and to what extent, the law will "open its eyes"[16] to the reality and dignity of these relationships.

[13] *The New Shorter Oxford English Dictionary*, Vol. 2 (Oxford, Clarendon Press, 1993).

[14] In Canada, the 2001 Census (Question 6) uses for the first time the categories "Common-law partner (opposite-sex)" and "Common-law partner (same-sex)" to describe the relationships of persons living together.

[15] See *Egan* v. *Canada*, [1995] 2 SCR 513. See also Casswell, chap. 11; Lahey, chap. 12.

[16] See J Millbank, "If Australian Law Opened Its Eyes to Lesbian and Gay Families, What Would It See?", (1998) 12 *Australian Journal of Family Law* 99.

1

Same-Sex Relationships: An Australian Perspective on a Global Issue

THE HON JUSTICE MICHAEL KIRBY AC CMG*

A CHANGING LEGAL ENVIRONMENT

THE CONFERENCE ON which this book is based, held in London on 1–3 July 1999, could not, and would not, have happened even a few years ago. The attendance of many senior judges from a number of countries would have been unthinkable. Same-sex relationships were the outward manifestation of impermissible emotions. Such emotions, or at least the physical acts that gave them expression, were criminal in many countries. If caught, those involved would be heavily punished, even if their acts were those of adults, performed with consent and in private. Needless to say, such laws, whether enforced or not, led to profound alienation of otherwise good citizens, to serious psychological disturbance when people struggled to alter their natural sexual orientation, to suicide, blackmail, police entrapment, hypocrisy and other horrors.

It is fitting that, as the modern criminalisation of homosexual conduct largely derived from the laws of England, and had been copied faithfully throughout the British Empire (even in places where the previous developed law had made no such distinctions), leadership in the direction of reform should eventually have come from the United Kingdom. The Wolfenden Report[1] and the reform of the law which followed[2] became the model whose influence gradually spread throughout the jurisdictions of the Commonwealth of Nations, or at least

* Justice of the High Court of Australia. Commissioner of the International Commission of Jurists. In 1999, the author included in his entry in *Who's Who in Australia* details of his relationship with his partner of thirty years, Johan van Vloten. Such entries had not been previously included in the publication. This fact was noted in due course by sections of the media in Australia with entirely predictable results.

[1] *Report of the Committee on Homosexual Offences and Prostitution,* Cmnd. 247 (London, HMSO, 1957) (chaired by Sir John Wolfenden).

[2] Sexual Offences Act 1967 (England and Wales). The Sexual Offences (Amendment) Act 2000 removed discrimination from the age of consent in sexual offences in the whole United Kingdom in Nov. 2000.

amongst the old Dominions. Some of the more autocratic societies within the Commonwealth have recently rediscovered the sodomy offences and utilised them against political critics.

The Wolfenden reforms in England, and their progeny, both responded to and stimulated changes in community opinion about homosexual conduct. These changes, in turn, have influenced social attitudes to people who are homosexual, bisexual or transgender in their sexual orientation. Once the lid of criminal punishment and social repression was lifted, people came to know their gay and lesbian fellow citizens. They came to realise that, boringly enough, they have all the same human needs as the heterosexual majority. The needs for human love, affection and companionship; for family relationships and friendships; for protection against irrational and unjustifiable discrimination; and for equal legal rights in matters where distinctions cannot be positively justified.

A measure of the continuing erosion of public opposition to legal change in this area, and of strong generational differences in attitudes to such subjects, can be seen in a recent survey conducted in the United States of America.[3] Accepting that country as probably the most conservative on this subject amongst the Western democracies, what is notable in the comparison with the results of a similar survey conducted thirty years ago is the strong shift towards acceptance of the legalisation of homosexual relations (then 55 per cent; now 82 per cent), and the strong support amongst younger people for legalising homosexual relations. Similar surveys in other Western countries, including my own, indicate identical and even stronger shifts in public opinion.

Significantly, the principal reason given in the American survey by those personally opposed to homosexuality is "religious objections" (52 per cent). Yet even amongst the major religions in many Western countries, there has been a cautious shift to recognition of the need for change. Many commentators on the Pope's visit to the United States in January 1999 remarked on the "sharp generational polarisation" on issues such as homosexuality, premarital sex and the ordination of women priests.[4] In Australia, some thoughtful commentators within the Catholic Church (now the largest religious denomination in the country) have begun to talk of sexuality beyond the absurd proposition that would insist upon acceptance of sexual orientation but prohibit all of its physical and emotional manifestations. Thus Bishop Patrick Power in Canberra, Australia has called for Christian "solidarity with the poor, the marginalised, the oppressed".[5] He said: "[There] is a very real difficulty for the Church in

[3] See *Washington Post*, 26 December 1998 at A12 (survey conducted by the *Washington Post*, Kayser Family Foundation, and Harvard University).

[4] G Niebuhr, "In US Pontiff to look to the new generation" *International Herald Tribune*, 26 January 1999, at 2. For parallels between discrimination against women and against homosexuals, see M Nussbaum, *Sex and Social Justice* (New York, Oxford University Press, 1998).

[5] Citing *Instrumentum Laboris* No. 3. Bishop P Power, "Marginalised People: In Society and in the Church", address to the Oceania Synod of Bishops, 1998.

terms of its credibility in the wider community. Some members of the Church community and hierarchy appear to act quite cruelly towards people such as single parents, homosexuals, divorced and remarried couples, former priests and religious."

The advent of the Human Genome Project and the likelihood that, in many cases at least, sexual orientation is genetically determined, make it totally unacceptable to impose upon those affected unreasonable legal discrimination or demands that they change. It was always unacceptable; but now no informed person has an excuse for blind prejudice and unreasonable conduct. If we are talking about the unnatural, demands that people deny their sexuality or try to change it, if it is part of their nature, are a good illustration of what is unnatural. An increasing number of citizens in virtually every Western democracy are coming inexorably to this realisation. People are not fools. Once they recognise the overwhelming commonalities of shared human experience, the alienation and demand for adherence to shame crumbles. Once they reflect upon the utter unreasonableness of insisting that homosexuals change their sexual orientation, or suppress and hide their emotions (something they could not demand of themselves), the irrational insistence and demand for legal sanctions, tends to fade away. Once they know that friends and family, children, sisters or uncles, are gay, the hatred tends to melt. In the wake of the changing social attitudes inevitably come changing laws: in both statutes made by Parliaments and common law made by judges.

Virtually every jurisdiction of the common law is now facing diverse demands for the reconsideration of legal rules as they are invoked by homosexual litigants and other citizens who object to discrimination. To some extent the standards of change have been set by regional bodies such as the European Court of Human Rights,[6] and international bodies such as the United Nations Human Rights Committee.[7] In the past, litigants to prosecute cases involving these issues could not be found. This was because of various inhibitors: the risk of criminal prosecution; the fear of social or professional stigmatisation; the desire to avoid shame to oneself or the family. Now that these controls are removed, it must be accepted that courts and legislatures will face increasing demands that legal discriminations be removed and quickly. The game of shame is over. Reality and truth rule. Rationality and science chart the way of the future. The same thing happened earlier to laws and practices which showed discrimination on the grounds of race and gender. The same opposition was mooted in the name of religion, of nature and of reason. No one of value believes the myths of racial or gender inferiority anymore. There is no reason to believe that it will be different in respect of discrimination on the ground of sexuality.

[6] *Dudgeon* v. *United Kingdom* (1981) 4 European Human Rights Reports (EHRR) 149; *Norris* v. *Republic of Ireland* (1988) 13 EHRR 186; *Modinos* v. *Cyprus* (1993) 16 EHRR 485.

[7] *Toonen* v. *Australia* (1994) 1 International Human Rights Reports 97.

Sometimes litigants will be able to invoke a national charter of rights, as has happened in Canada.[8] Sometimes their cases will involve very large questions as in a case in New Zealand.[9] At other times they will involve something as tedious as the construction of the Rent Act, as occurred recently in England.[10] Australia has not been immune from these developments.

THE AUSTRALIAN CONSTITUTIONAL SETTING

In order to approach Australian legal developments it is necessary to appreciate the nature of the Australian federation. The Constitution divides the lawmaking power in Australia between the Commonwealth (the federal polity) and the States. Generally speaking, as in the United States of America, if a legislative power is not expressly granted by the Constitution to the federal Parliament, it remains with the States. The result of this arrangement, again speaking very generally, is that large areas of private law—and especially of criminal law—are left to State lawmaking. The federal Parliament, outside the Territories where it enjoys plenary constitutional powers,[11] has tended to be concerned in matters of lawmaking with subjects of national application and in federally specified areas.

This general description must be modified by appreciation of three important developments which have gathered pace in recent decades. First, the federal Parliament, encouraged by expansive decisions on the grants of federal constitutional power, has extended its legislation into areas which almost certainly were not expected to be regulated federally when the Constitution was enacted in 1900.[12] Thus, by the use of tax incentives, a large framework of federal legislation has recently been enacted governing the law of superannuation (contributory pensions) in Australia.[13]

Secondly, although Australia is now almost alone in that it does not have either a comprehensive constitutional charter of rights, nor a statute-based guarantee of fundamental civil entitlements, much anti-discrimination legislation has been enacted, including at the federal level. Some of this has been

[8] *Egan* v. *Canada* [1995] 2 SCR 513; *M* v. *H* [1999] 2 SCR 3. See generally Robert Wintemute, "Discrimination Against Same-Sex Couples: Sections 15(1) and 1 of the Charter: *Egan* v. *Canada*", (1995) 74 *Canadian Bar Review* 682, "Sexual Orientation Discrimination as Sex Discrimination: Same-Sex Couples and the Charter in *Mossop, Egan* and *Layland*", (1994) 39 *McGill Law Journal* 429.

[9] *Quilter* v. *Attorney-General* [1998] 1 NZLR 523.

[10] *Fitzpatrick* v. *Sterling Housing Association Ltd* (1999), [2001] 1 AC 27 (HL).

[11] Australian Constitution, s. 122.

[12] For example, in *Re Wakim, ex parte McNally* (1999) 93 ALJR 839 at 850, McHugh J remarked that the "marriage" power in the Australian Constitution (s. 51(xxi)) might today "or in the near future" mean "a voluntary union for life between two *people* to the exclusion of others", so as to permit the Parliament of the Commonwealth to "legislate for same-sex marriages".

[13] *Attorney-General of the Commonwealth* v. *Brechtler* (1999) 73 Australian Law Journal Reports 981 at 993–6 (High Ct of Aust).

supported by the federal power to make laws with respect to external affairs. International treaties to which Australia has subscribed have become a means of supporting the constitutional validity of federal legislation outside traditional federal fields. It was in this way, in reliance upon Australia's obligations under the International Covenant on Civil and Political Rights that the federal or Commonwealth Parliament enacted the Human Rights (Sexual Conduct) Act 1994. That Act was adopted in response to the decision of the United Nations Human Rights Committee in *Toonen* v. *Australia*.[14] That decision found that the sodomy laws of Tasmania, the sole Australian State then to retain such laws, imposed an arbitrary interference with Mr Toonen's privacy in respect of his adult, consensual, private sexual relationship with his partner. Following a decision of the High Court of Australia in favour of Mr Toonen and his partner, upholding the constitutional viability of the proceedings,[15] the Tasmanian Parliament repealed the offending provisions of the Criminal Code. It has since enacted a non-discriminatory offence which makes no distinction on the basis of sexuality.

Thirdly, there has been a rapid growth in the number and importance of federal courts and of federal jurisdiction in Australia over the past twenty years. This has been, in part, a response to the general enlargement of federal law, the growth of the federal bureaucracy, the expansion of federal administrative law rights,[16] and the need for effective judicial supervision to bring the rule of law into every corner of federal administration in Australia.

There are six States in Australia. There are also two mainland Territories (the Northern Territory of Australia and the Australian Capital Territory) which have been granted substantial self-government under federal legislation. Accordingly, outside the areas regulated directly by federal law in Australia, there are eight significant legal jurisdictions. All have their own separate statutory regimes dealing with the vast array of private law matters, local administrative law and most matters of criminal law. It is beyond the scope of this chapter to review the legislation in each of the eight sub-national Australian jurisdictions. I will concentrate therefore on the State of New South Wales, which is the most populous State in Australia.

CHANGES IN STATE LEGISLATION

As in most jurisdictions which inherit statutes going back to much earlier colonial times, a large number of enactments of the New South Wales Parliament (and some of them not so old) reflect discrimination against homosexual

[14] *Supra* n.7.

[15] *Croome* v. *Tasmania* (1997) 191 Commonwealth Law Reports 119.

[16] Administrative Appeals Tribunal Act 1975 (Commonwealth); Administrative Decisions (Judicial Review) Act 1977 (Commonwealth).

citizens. This has been called to notice by the Anti-Discrimination Board.[17] The examples are many and found in every corner of the law—even unexpected corners. Thus, the Stamp Duties Act 1920 (NSW) provides that, if a share of a jointly owned property is sold by one party in a heterosexual relationship following the end of that relationship, and if so ordered by a court, the remaining partner may be exempted from paying stamp duty. There is no such entitlement to exemption for a same-sex partner. Similarly, the Superannuation Act 1916 (NSW) contains a definition of "spouse", in relation to a death benefit, which has the consequence that, where a contributor to a superannuation scheme dies without leaving a legally recognised "spouse" (or, in some cases, children), the deceased contributor's estate will receive only a refund of contributions without interest. This involves less favourable treatment for partners of the same sex and some others who are less likely to have a lawful "spouse" or child.

The Adoption of Children Act 1965 (NSW) provides that a court can make an adoption order in favour of a married couple or, in certain circumstances, to a man and a women in a de facto relationship. Such an order cannot be made in favour of persons in a same-sex relationship, whatever its duration and whatever the exceptional circumstances of the case. The Evidence Act 1995 (NSW) contains certain legal privileges in respect of opposite-sex couples which are not extended to same-sex partners. The New South Wales Anti-Discrimination Board has repeatedly submitted to the State Parliament and Government that the legislation of the State needs to be changed to afford wider recognition to relationships involving same-sex partners and persons in non-traditional and/or extended family relationships. Because of the growing numbers of persons in a variety of human relationships who fall outside the protection of the present law, reform of the law is needed. The first, partial and limited reforms took place in 1998 and 1999.

The Equal Opportunity Tribunal established by the Anti-Discrimination Act 1977 (NSW) is empowered to hear complaints in certain circumstances where a person claims to have suffered discrimination on the ground of his homosexuality. Such complaints are now regularly taken to the Tribunal. In 1995, it found that a health fund which had refused to allow the complainants a "family" or "concessional" rate was guilty of unlawful discrimination. The complainants were two males bringing up the son of one of them. They had joint bank accounts, joint ownership of a motor vehicle and a joint mortgage. Although the couple did not fit within the "spouse" relationship under the rules of the fund, they did come within the "family" relationships as defined. They were entitled to the concessional rate. An appeal by the fund to the Supreme Court of New South Wales failed.[18]

As a background to what now follows, it is appropriate to say that such studies as have been conducted in Australia to sample the opinion of same-sex

[17] New South Wales Anti-Discrimination Board, Newsletter, *Equal Time*, Feb. 1999.
[18] *NIB Funds Limited* v. *Hope*, 15 Nov. 1996, Supreme Court of New South Wales (unreported).

partners seem to indicate that the majority surveyed (80 per cent) do not consider that marriage or marriage equivalence is desirable in their cases.[19] However, they do want the discrimination removed and legal protections against discrimination provided. At least in New South Wales, the legislators are responding.

In 1998 the Same-Sex Relationships (Compassionate Circumstances) Bill 1998 (NSW) was introduced into the New South Wales Parliament, to meet what were described as "urgent areas of need which relate to wills, family provision and hospital access" for same-sex partners.[20] The purpose of that Bill, a Private Member's measure, was to pick up on a commitment given by the State Premier to the President of the AIDS Council of New South Wales prior to the election in which his party achieved Government in 1995. That commitment was:

> "Labor is committed to reform of legislation around same-sex relationships so that same-sex partners have the same rights and responsibilities as heterosexual *de factos* when their partner is hospitalised or incapacitated. We will also ensure that same-sex partners are not discriminated against in the operation of the will and probate and family provisions".[21]

This measure was not enacted as the Government cancelled the allocation of time to Private Members for the remainder of the parliamentary session. Several other Private Member's Bills or related topics also lapsed when the New South Wales Parliament was dissolved for a State election held in March 1999.

The new State Parliament, which convened after the re-election of the Australian Labor Party Government led by Mr Carr, moved quickly to enact the Property (Relationships) Legislation Amendment Act 1999 (NSW). The Bill for that Act was introduced into the Legislative Council by the State Attorney-General (Mr J W Shaw QC). It was passed by that Chamber by 37 votes to three. In the Legislative Assembly, it was passed without division. The debates were notable for enlightened views expressed by members of both Houses and both sides of politics, although there were also expressions of prejudice and ignorance.[22] Mr Shaw described the legislation as "historic", which for Australia it certainly is. He went on:

> "In an open and liberal society, there is no excuse for discrimination against individuals in our community based on their sexual preference. To deny couples in intimate and ongoing relationships within the gay and lesbian community the same rights as heterosexual *de facto* couples is clearly anomalous".[23]

[19] S Sarantakos, "Legal recognition of same-sex relationships", (1998) 23 *Alternative Law Journal* 222, and "Same-Sex Marriage: Which Way to Go?", (1994) 24 *Alternative Law Journal* 79.

[20] C Moore MP (NSW), *Media Release*, 20 October 1998.

[21] Letter by the Hon R Carr MP to the President, AIDS Council of NSW, 22 February 1995. See "Statement by Ms Clover Moore MP to the Legislative Assembly of New South Wales" in *New South Wales Parliamentary Debates* (Legislative Assembly), 22 Oct. 1998, at 59.

[22] See J Millbank and W Morgan, chap. 14.

[23] See *New South Wales Parliamentary Debates* (Legislative Council) 13 May 1999, 228; 26 May 1999, 36.

A speech by a National Party member of the Lower House, representing a rural electorate and a party sometimes described as conservative (Mr Russell Turner MP), was specially striking:

> "Generally, they [people in same-sex relationships] have faced life, they have been through agonies and they, in a lot of instances, are probably far better adjusted than many married couples who are living in a state of acceptance by the community, the church, and the laws of this country".[24]

The legislation broadly assimilated same-sex partners within the De Facto Relationships Act 1984 (NSW), which has been renamed the Property (Relationships) Act—itself a sign of how common *de facto* relations of all kinds are in Australia today.[25]

The thrust of the New South Wales Act is to allow for court orders adjusting property relations on the termination of a domestic relationship. The rights affected include real and personal property rights, such as rights of inheritance upon intestacy, taxes in relation to property transfers between partners, insurance contracts, protected estates, family provision (following inadequate testamentary provision), and State judges' pensions. Non-property rights are conferred in relation to human tissue and medical treatment decisions, coroner's inquest participation, decisions about bail for arrested persons, guardianship and other mental health decisions, rights in retirement villages and accident compensation.

A multitude of New South Wales Acts are amended by the 1999 Act to impose on same-sex couples the same obligations to disclose interests as would exist in the case of spouses. Areas acknowledged as still requiring attention include adoption, foster parenting and superannuation for State government employees. The New South Wales Legislative Council's Standing Committee on Social Issues (chaired by Ms Jan Burnswoods MLC) has a reference from the New South Wales Parliament on relationships law reform. The Chair has called for submissions on the ways in which the Property (Relationships) Amendment Act 1999 does not adequately address legal concerns necessary to remove residual legal discrimination. Another matter on the list for the future in New South Wales may be the age of consent laws which, as in England (where reform took place in November 2000), discriminate between sexual activity that is male-male (18 years), male-female (16 years) and female-female (16 years).

Following the New South Wales legislation, the Parliament of the State of Queensland enacted broadly similar legislation. However, so far no other Australian State or Territory Government has indicated its intention to

[24] See *New South Wales Parliamentary Debates* (Legislative Council), 1 Jun. 1999, 740 at 741. Subsequently the Leader of the National Party was reported as predicting that there would be "no more watering down our opposition to indulgent and selfish gay rights laws", in *Sydney Morning Herald*, 19 June 1999, at 11.

[25] J Millbank and K Sant, "A Bride in Her Every-day Clothes: Same Sex Relationship Recognition in NSW", (2000) 22 *Sydney Law Review* 181.

follow.[26] A new government in Victoria has committed itself to examining the New South Wales model, which one New Zealand commentator has rejected as not going far enough.[27] On a national level, the importance of the New South Wales and Queensland Acts should not be exaggerated. But they are significant and symbolic. In a Federation such as Australia, reforms enacted in one jurisdiction tend, in time, to influence developments in others. Once it was South Australia that led the way in such matters (including decriminalisation of homosexual acts and the enactment of anti-discrimination legislation). This time it has been New South Wales.

Even before the 1999 reforms were adopted, legislation was enacted by the New South Wales Parliament which provided an interesting model to afford protection to people in same-sex relationships under State law. Thus, the Workers' Compensation Legislation Amendment (Dust Diseases and Other Matters) Act 1998 (NSW) contained, in Schedule 6, a number of amendments to the Workers' Compensation (Dust Diseases) Act 1942 (NSW). Amongst those changes is a new definition of "*de facto* relationship" in s. 3(1) of the 1942 Act. The redefinition is broad enough to encompass same-sex relationships:

> "*De facto relationship* means the relationship between two unrelated adult persons:
> (a) Who have a mutual commitment to a shared life, and
> (b) Whose relationship is genuine and continuing, and
> (c) Who live together, and
> who are not married to one another."

This provision allows for definitional flexibility as social considerations develop and change. Much work remains to be done. But significant reforms have been accepted in Australia's most populous State. A model has been provided for the rest.

CHANGES IN FEDERAL LEGISLATION

The Australian Constitution, celebrating its centenary in 2001, is one of the four oldest documents of its kind still in operation in the world. When adopted, it did not contain a general Bill of Rights, such as became common in the post-independence constitutions of other countries of the Commonwealth of Nations. There is therefore no precise equivalent to the Bill of Rights in the United States Constitution, or the Charter of Rights and Freedoms in the Canadian Constitution, to stimulate and facilitate challenges to discriminatory provisions in federal law. Generally speaking, in such matters Australians must rely on the Federal, State and Territory Parliaments and Governments to secure changes. Only rarely can the aid of the courts be enlisted.

[26] Queensland, Property Law Amendment Act 1999; Industrial Relations Act 1999, Sched. 5, definitions of "spouse" and "discrimination". But see Millbank and Morgan, chap. 14, n. 90.

[27] DF Dugdale, "Same-Sex Relationships" (Feb. 2000) *New Zealand Law Journal* 3.

Under the Australian Constitution, one matter upon which the federal Parliament enjoys legislative power is "immigration and emigration".[28] Since 1984, in part because of lobbying by the Gay and Lesbian Immigration Task Force (GLITF), changes have been introduced into Australian migration law and practice which have expanded the rights of entry into Australia of persons in same-sex relationships.

The main breakthrough occurred in 1985 when Mr Chris Hurford was Minister for Immigration. Upon his instructions, regulations and practices were adopted which, to a very large extent, removed discrimination and provided for the consideration of applications for migration to Australia largely (but not entirely) on an equal footing.

Entry into Australia of non-residents is governed by the Migration Act 1958 (Commonwealth) and the regulations made under that Act. The regulations now provide for visa subclasses to permit the entry into Australia of people in "interdependent" relationships. This is the adjectival clause which has been adopted to describe same-sex partners. The relevant Australian visa classes are 310 and 301. They permit migration to Australia of a person sponsored by his or her partner. Comparable visas to allow change of status within Australia are visa classes 826 and 814.[29] The two categories mirror, in turn, those applying to persons seeking entry to Australia on the basis of a *de facto* heterosexual relationship.

The annual migration programme (RAM) for Australia contains an allocated number of places available to persons in the "interdependent" categories. In comparison with the total size of Australia's migration programme, the numbers are very small. For the financial year 1996–97, 400 places were reserved for "interdependency visas".

Some discrimination remains in migration law and practice. Thus, for heterosexual *de facto* relationships and "interdependency relationships", the partners must be able to prove a twelve months committed relationship before being eligible to proceed with the application. In the case of heterosexual relationships, this precondition can be overcome, quite simply, by marriage, an event substantially within the control of the persons themselves. A similar short-cut is not available to same-sex couples. In countries which still criminalise, prosecute or stigmatise persons who establish a same-sex household, proof of twelve months cohabitation, especially with a foreigner, may be difficult or even impossible. Provision is made for waiver of this requirement in compelling circumstances.

A second important omission from current immigration law is that persons from overseas, who are not Australian or New Zealand citizens and seek either

[28] Australian Constitution, s. 51(xxvii). The Commonwealth also enjoys power with respect to naturalisation and aliens (s. 51(xix)) and external affairs (s. 51(xxix)).

[29] D Bitel, "Recognition of Same-Sex Relationships in Australian Immigration Law", unpublished paper presented to International Bar Association Conference, Vancouver, September 1998, at 3. See especially the federal Migration Regulations, reg. 1.09A ("Interdependent relationships").

to migrate or enter Australia temporarily, are unable to include in their application as members of their family unit (and thus bring with them) persons with whom they presently reside in a same-sex relationship in their country of origin. GLITF has made representations for the amendment of the law in this regard. However, the Minister has indicated that a same-sex partner of an applicant for immigration must apply for a visa in their own right if they wish to enter Australia with their partner. Only a person in a same-sex relationship with an Australian citizen (or a permanent resident or an eligible New Zealand citizen) is able to apply for an interdependency visa for migration to Australia, sponsored by the Australian partner.[30]

Notwithstanding these defects, it is clear that Australian immigration law is comparatively enlightened on this subject. As yet, only a few countries (eg, the United Kingdom, the Netherlands, Belgium, Iceland, Norway, Denmark, Sweden, Finland, Australia, New Zealand, South Africa and Canada) have a policy of recognising same-sex relationships for immigration purposes. In the case of the United Kingdom, only in October 1997 did the Immigration Minister announce a "concession" whereby most couples legally unable to marry, including same-sex partners (a category formerly rejected), would be recognised for purposes of immigration to the United Kingdom.[31]

In the field of refugee law, Australia is a party to the 1951 Refugees Convention, which is incorporated into domestic law.[32] One of the categories of persons entitled to enjoy refugee status is one who:

> "owing to a well-founded fear of being persecuted for reasons of . . . membership of a particular social group . . . is outside the country of his nationality and is unable or, owing to such fear, is unwilling to avail himself of the protection of that country".

The possibility that in some countries homosexuals and others in same-sex relationships would be so categorised has been recognised in a number of decisions in Australia and the United Kingdom.[33] In Australia, for at least five years, both the Department of Immigration at the primary level and the Refugee Review Tribunal, have granted refugee status to both male and female homosexuals who could establish a well-founded fear of persecution in their country of nationality.[34] Various difficulties arise in such a case, because of views

[30] GLITF (NSW), *Same-Sex Couple Discrimination for Independent and Business Visa Applications*, submission to the Australian Human Rights and Equal Opportunity Commission (Jun. 1997).

[31] W Gryk, "The Recognition of Unmarried Relationships Under British Immigration Law—An Evolving Process?", unpublished paper presented to International Bar Association Conference, Vancouver, 16 September 1998, at 2.

[32] Migration Act 1958 (Commonwealth), s. 4(1).

[33] Cf. *Applicant A* v. *Minister for Immigration and Multicultural Affairs* (1997) 190 Commonwealth Law Reports 225 at 304 (n.296). See also *R* v. *Immigration Appeal Tribunal, ex parte Shah* [1999] 2 Weekly Law Reports 1015 at 1044 per Lord Millett ("[g]iven the hostility encountered by all homosexuals in such a society and the obvious problems the applicant would have in satisfying his tormenters of his own sexual abstinence, I doubt that the difficulty [of establishing that a fear of persecution was well founded] would be a real one").

[34] Bitel, *supra* n. 29 at 4–5.

sometimes taken in the Tribunal concerning the need for applicants to prove their sexual orientation, and because of a paucity of information about the persecution of homosexuals in some countries. Australia has developed policies for the group "women at risk". There may be a need for similar supportive programmes for homosexual refugees and also for their same-sex partners.[35] Many of them are at serious risk in their countries of origin or temporary residence.

Superannuation in Australia is now largely regulated by federal laws. The Senate Select Committee on Superannuation of the Australian Parliament reported in September 1997.[36] The Committee put forward "as a general proposition" a proposal earlier made to it, in the context of a review of superannuation: that persons without defined dependants (such as a widow, widower or eligible children) should have an entitlement under federal law to nominate a beneficiary, so that they would not lose entirely the benefit of entitlements which would otherwise accrue to them were they in a currently eligible relationship. The Senate Committee recognised that the present provisions were a "discrimination against those . . . not in a recognised relationship".[37] The Committee held back from making a recommendation that provision should be made for the "nomination of a dependant" because of reconsideration of the current structure of the scheme established by the Act.[38] However, as in the case of the Parliamentary Scheme, applicable to federal politicians, the Committee recommended[39] that the rules under which the benefits were paid "should be reviewed to ensure that they are in accordance with community standards".

A Private Member's Bill,[40] introduced into the House of Representatives of the federal Parliament by an Opposition member, seeks to remove discrimination against same-sex couples in the sphere of superannuation. Earlier, a larger measure was introduced into the Australian Senate,[41] also by an Opposition Senator. It was referred to the Senate Legal and Constitutional References Committee. In December 1997, that Committee tabled a report recommending that couples or partners should be protected by superannuation entitlements

[35] Cf. Bitel, *ibid.* at 5.

[36] Australian Parliament, Senate Select Committee on Superannuation, *The Parliamentary Contributory Superannuation Scheme and the Judges' Pensions Scheme*, 25th Report (Canberra, September 1997).

[37] *Ibid.* at para. 4.6.

[38] *Ibid.* at para. 4.7.

[39] *Ibid.* Recommendation 4.1.

[40] Superannuation (Entitlements of Same-Sex Couples) Bill 1998. Although the member introducing the Bill (Mr A Albanese MP) gave the Second Reading Speech for the Bill on 7 June 1999, the Bill has not yet been enacted. The speech followed shortly after a report of the Australian Human Rights and Equal Opportunity Commission, *Superannuation Entitlements of Same-Sex Couples* (June 1999), was tabled in the Federal Parliament by the Attorney-General. The Commission found that present Australian superannuation law was in breach of two international conventions to which Australia is a party, the ICCPR and the ILO Discrimination (Employment and Occupation) Convention. In August 2000, the conference of the Australian Labor Party (ALP) adopted as party policy the removal of discrimination against same-sex couples in the context of superannuation. The ALP is the main Opposition Party.

[41] Sexuality Discrimination Bill 1995.

regardless of their sexuality or gender. Neither of the foregoing Bills has yet attracted the support of the Australian Government. In March 2000, a further Private Member's Bill identical to the one that had stalled in the House of Representatives, was introduced into the Australian Senate in the hope of advancing consideration of its proposals in the Parliament. It remains under consideration.

However, the Australian Government has introduced the Superannuation Legislation (Commonwealth Employment) Repeal and Amendment (Consequential Provisions) Bill 1998 (Cth). This proposes amendments to superannuation and like legislation to deal with a number of situations, including one where an "eligible person", who was party to a superannuation scheme, dies without leaving a spouse or child to whom pension payments are made. According to the Bill, in such a situation, there will be payable to the legal personal representative of the deceased person an amount equal to the total of the minimum amounts which the federal authorities would have had to contribute to a complying superannuation fund for the benefit of an "eligible person".

The discrimination in the field of superannuation and like benefits[42] has become more noticeable as other federal legislation, and legislatively encouraged moves in Australia, have come to recognise and protect the "employment packages" of persons governed by federal law. Nowadays, it is much more common to look to a person's total employment "package" rather than just their base salary. Where there is a significant differentiation in superannuation and like benefits, unconnected with the quality of their professional performance and concerned only with their private domestic arrangements, unjust discrimination can be seen in sharp relief.[43] According to news reports, politicians of most political alignments in Australia have begun to perceive the serious injustice which is worked by current superannuation and like laws in the case of persons living in stable same-sex relationships.[44]

Recently, an Australian Ambassador, presenting his credentials to the Monarch of the country to which he was accredited by Australia, took along his same-sex partner. Such relationships are legally recognised in that country,

[42] An example in the Australian armed forces is the Veterans' Entitlements Act 1986 (Commonwealth), s. 5E(2), which defines "a member of a couple" as a person who is legally married or "living with a person of the opposite sex . . . in a marriage-like relationship". This definition was used to deny Edward Young a war widower's pension after the death of his partner of thirty-eight years, Lawrence Cains, who was a World War II veteran. After the federal Human Rights and Equal Opportunity Commission declined to inquire into his complaint (on 23 Dec. 1999), Mr Young submitted a communication to the United Nations Human Rights Committee on 26 April 2000. See Helfer, chap. 41.

[43] See D McCarthy, "Superannuated", 182 *Brother–Sister* (Melbourne) 15 April 1999, at 7.

[44] C Pearson, "Saving not such a super idea for same-sex couples", *Australian Financial Review*, 3 May 1999, at 19. Cf. the motion of Ms Leane Burke MP (Prahran) in the Victorian Parliament, adopted by the Victorian conference of the Liberal Party of Australia, which urged the Federal Government to "ensure same-sex partners are given equality of treatment with respect to superannuation payments as those given to opposite-sex *de facto* partners". See also J McKenzie, "Super Boost for Equality Campaign", 182 *Brother–Sister* (Melbourne) 15 April 1999, at 3.

where the action of the Ambassador would have been unremarkable. Yet the diplomat and his partner had to suffer the indignity in Australia of a tabloid headline reducing his serious professional career to the insult: "Three Queens in One Palace".[45] Yet it took more courage and honesty for the Ambassador to do as he did than to continue with pretence. It took more courage and integrity than the anonymous by-line writer exhibited in the newspaper concerned. And it must be acknowledged that the Australian Department of Foreign Affairs and Trade has, in this respect, observed a non-discriminatory policy. The certified agreement adopted by the Australian Department of Foreign Affairs under the Workplace Relations Act 1996 (Cth)[46] states:

> "The conditions regarding the official recognition of *de facto* relationships for the purpose of the conditions of service apply regardless of sexual preferences".

Similar statutory "certified agreements" have been adopted by other federal departments and agencies in Australia. In practice, this means that for most benefits of office (but not yet superannuation), same-sex partnerships enjoy equal status for employment benefits in the federal public service in Australia. Thus, in the Australian foreign service, benefits include: airfares to and from posting; the payment of supplementary living allowances as a couple whilst overseas; the payment of other incidental allowances on the same basis where an entitlement arises (eg clothing allowances); and the payment of health cover by the Federal Government for both partners during the posting. It is necessary to have the relationship officially recognised by the relevant Department before the partners proceed to the posting, by the provision of a statutory declaration with accompanying evidence. But these and other benefits are closely similar to those of any other non-married *de facto* partner. The achievement of such entitlements and practices evidences a commitment by those in charge to the principle of non-discrimination in the matter of sexuality and federal public employment.

The Parliament of Australia in respect of its members, and in some areas of its legislative responsibility, has begun to act. The Executive of the federal Government in Australia has quite properly moved, in respect of its officers, to abolish discrimination in employment benefits, and to exercise its powers under delegated legislation in a non-discriminatory way. Even the federal Judicature in Australia has begun to provide benefits of domestic and international travel for non-married partners of federal judges of whatever sex. But the federal Judges' Pensions Act 1968 remains resolutely unchanged.[47]

[45] *Daily Telegraph* (Sydney), 26 February 1999, at 7.

[46] Australia Department of Foreign Affairs and Trade, Certified Agreement, 1998–2000.

[47] Cf. C Stychin, "*Grant*-ing Rights: The Politics of Rights, Sexuality and the European Union", (2000) 51 *Northern Ireland Legal Quarterly* 281 at 282, 300.

THE JOURNEY OF ENLIGHTENMENT

There are other changes which are occurring in the statutory regimes governing the benefits of same-sex partners in Australia.[48] The changes are occurring bit by bit and piece by piece. This is what happened earlier with racial and gender discrimination. It is still happening in those fields. The end of unfair discrimination has not yet been achieved. Australia, like other countries, is on a journey of enlightenment. It has taken important steps; but many more remain to be taken, as Jenni Millbank and Wayne Morgan point out in chapter 14. It seems likely that progress towards the removal of discrimination which cannot be rationally justified, will continue. As a people generally committed to equal justice for all under the law, I have confidence that the Australian legal system, and those who make the laws in Australia, will, in due course, eradicate unfair discrimination on the basis of sexuality. The scales are dropping from our eyes. Injustice and irrational prejudice cannot survive the scrutiny of just men and women.

It can only be in the interests of society to protect stable and mutually supportive relationships and mutual economic commitment. It is against society's interests to penalise, disadvantage and discourage them. Australia is accepting this truth. There remain stubborn opponents. Much reform remains to be carried out. And beyond Australia, there is a world of discrimination and oppression to be shamed and cajoled into reform by Australia's just example.

[48] See Australia Remuneration Tribunal, Determination No 2 of 1998, Members of the Parliament—Travelling Allowance, para. 2.8: "A senator or member may nominate to the Special Minister of State one nominee as eligible to receive travel privileges under this entitlement, and, subject to any procedural rules made by the Special Minister of State, may vary that nomination from time to time."

PART I
THEORETICAL PERSPECTIVES

Introduction

Theoretical Perspectives

DAVID AJ RICHARDS*

LIBERAL CONSTITUTIONAL DEMOCRACIES increasingly acknowledge that claims of gays and lesbians are based on fundamental constitutional rights that are, in turn, grounded in respect for human rights required by arguments of justice. Two kinds of argument have been prominent: first, arguments appealing to basic liberties (including that to an intimate life); second, arguments for an equal respect free of irrational prejudices (like racism and sexism) that dehumanise and degrade. For example, the European Court of Human Rights has found laws criminalising gay sex to be unconstitutional violations of applicable guarantees of the right to respect for private life;[1] and the United States Supreme Court, which had earlier declined (five to four) to hold comparable laws unconstitutional,[2] later found state constitutional provisions, that forbade all laws protecting gays and lesbians from discrimination, an unconstitutional violation of the right to be free of dehumanising prejudice.[3] The present volume examines the relatively recent elaboration of these arguments to justify various forms of legal recognition of same-sex partnerships. The five essays in Part I (on theoretical perspectives) focus, in particular, on whether these arguments justify claims for such recognition and, if so, on what terms. The authors (Nicholas Bamforth, Chai Feldblum, Davina Cooper, Janet Halley, and William Eskridge) are among the most thoughtful and probing advocates for the constitutional and human rights of gays and lesbians. The authors apparently concur that some form of legal recognition of same-sex partnerships is in order, but three of them (Cooper, Halley, and Eskridge) disagree sharply about the preferred form such legal recognition should take.

Nicholas Bamforth offers a compelling normative argument of liberal political and constitutional theory for reconceiving both the main arguments for gay rights (the right to respect for private life and the right against unjust prejudices) in terms that constitutionally require legal recognition of same-sex partnerships. His argument proceeds in three stages. First, critically building on the previous theories of Richard Mohr and David Richards, he identifies the interests expressive of

* Edwin D Webb Professor of Law, School of Law, New York University.

[1] See *Dudgeon* v. *United Kingdom* (1981) 4 EHRR 149 (Court).
[2] See *Bowers* v. *Hardwick*, 478 US 186 (1986).
[3] See *Romer* v. *Evans*, 517 US 620 (1996).

sexual orientation as aspects of the underlying human right to intimate association, a right that persons may pursue in the empowering terms of autonomously reflective reasonable standards and judgments expressive of conviction. Second, equal respect for this basic human right requires that its exercise not be subject to dehumanising prejudices that, in their nature, cannot be reasonably justified in terms of compelling secular purposes (as opposed to purposes acceptable only in sectarian terms). Third, opposition to expanding the right to intimate life beyond decriminalisation to recognition of same-sex partnerships (by new natural laws theorists) rests, on critical examination, on such sectarian terms; such opposition appeals to sectarian arguments that fail to treat gays and lesbians as persons, degrading them in terms of stereotypes of sexuality and gender that dehumanise. Both the right to respect for private life and the right not to be subjected to unjust prejudice, properly understood, thus require legal recognition of same-sex partnerships.

Bamforth's claim for his argument may be questioned along two dimensions: its alleged originality and its failure to address the question of gender stereotypes. With respect to the former, his argument is surely much closer to the theorists he criticises both in spirit and substance, than he allows.[4] And his argument against sectarianism would surely have been strengthened by dealing with the ways in which the force of such sectarianism in modern politics is motored by reactionary and unprincipled attempts to limit the scope of a considerable constitutional achievement: the condemnation of the expression of unjust gender stereotypes through law. The right not to be dehumanised on grounds of unjust gender stereotypes extends, as a matter of principle, to all persons (men and women, heterosexual and homosexual). The popularity of sectarian appeals to truncate the principled scope of this right (not extending it to gays and lesbians) unjustly both expresses and reinforces sexism.[5]

Bamforth powerfully establishes at least a normative presumption of equality in the legal treatment of same-sex and opposite-sex intimate relations; Chai Feldlbum agrees, but urges that such arguments normatively address the underlying normative goods to which all persons (whatever their sexual orientation) have a basic human right. Neither Bamforth nor Feldblum explores how, on balance, such equality should be understood. Both Davina Cooper and Janet Halley offer reasons for resisting an interpretation of this presumption in terms of same-sex marriage (as opposed to other forms of legal recognition of same-sex partnerships); William Eskridge criticises their reasons.

Davina Cooper offers a general argument for reconceiving the case for gay/lesbian rights in terms of a normative paradigm of equal power. Cooper resists, on the one hand, construing the case for gay/lesbian rights in terms of a

[4] See, for example, DAJ Richards, *Identity and the Case for Gay Rights: Race, Gender, Religion as Analogies* (Chicago, IL, University of Chicago Press, 1999).

[5] See, for extensive elaboration of this point, DAJ Richards, *Women, Gays, and the Constitution: The Grounds for Feminism and Gay Rights in Culture and Law* (Chicago, IL, University of Chicago Press, 1998).

model of group equality that fails to do justice to the internal complexity of the group in question; on the other hand, she urges that the model of equality (focusing, as it does, on individual persons) be appropriately contextualised, in terms of a normative ideal of equal power over resources and structures that will allow persons to interpret and weight these abstract goods, according to their different convictions and preference orderings. Importantly, these resources and structures include normative and epistemological principles about how to conduct intimate life in public and private life. In Cooper's view, egalitarian assessment must be extended to these principles, ensuring that all persons are guaranteed the requisite equal power to determine and shape these principles, consistent with their diverse convictions and preference orderings. It is from this perspective that Cooper interrogates developments in legal recognition of same-sex partnerships. The concern is that some of these developments may uncritically enforce on all gays and lesbians precisely the normative and epistemological conventions that some of them may and should resist, as inconsistent with their right to equal power over these issues in light of their convictions and preference orderings. Cooper urges careful normative thought about different ways of implementing legal recognition of same-sex partnerships. We should, she argues, prefer those options that are more consistent with an appropriate concern for equality in both public and private life, and for the legitimate normative diversity that such concern requires.

Janet Halley is concerned not, as Cooper is, with normative political theory, but with certain allegedly problematic moves in the rhetoric of certain American advocates of same-sex marriage, in particular, arguments made by Evan Wolfson and William Eskridge. These arguments start from admirable normative premises calling for equal recognition of the intimate relations of heterosexuals and homosexuals, but then interpret such recognition in terms of something much more problematic, namely, the disciplinary normalisation of same-sex intimate relations according to the dominant model of heterosexual marriage. Halley observes that not all developments in recognition of same-sex partnerships thus combine recognition with normalisation; she points, for example, to the "*pacte civil de solidarité*", recently adopted in France,[6] which, at least in one of its proposed (though not adopted) forms, would have afforded not a substitute for marriage, but an alternative institutional arrangement available to same-sex and cross-sex couples, without regard to the nature of their emotional bond and without any assumption that it is erotic. The proposed French arrangements, for Halley, would have admirably denormalised marriage, and yet afforded appropriate legal recognition for same-sex intimate life. Halley concludes by examining characteristically American appeals to the basic right of marriage, which, she argues, use the rhetoric of rights in ways that conceal, and thus fail reasonably to assess, their costs in terms of regulation of same-sex intimate life. Any adequate political theory of these matters must,

[6] See D Borrillo, chap. 25.

Halley urges, responsibly take into account the entailments of regulation required by arguments for rights. We should bring normative political theory to bear on an honest assessment of both rights and regulation: are the benefits worth the burdens?

William Eskridge's argument examines the criticism of arguments for same-sex marriage (as the preferred model for legal recognition of same-sex partnerships) offered by advocates, like Davina Cooper and Janet Halley, of the rights of gays and lesbians. Eskridge questions these arguments both in terms of their appeal and in terms of the consequences to which they appeal. Such postmodernist arguments are, Eskridge suggests, academically elitist, obscure and insular; they are barely intelligible to most gays and lesbians, and they thus fail to take seriously the human issues of respect for their basic rights that matter to most gays and lesbians. More importantly, such arguments appeal to certain consequences that would allegedly follow from legal recognition of same-sex marriage.

But, the consequences in question are, at best, speculative. Eskridge describes the range of legal developments in the recognition of same-sex partnerships, and questions whether these developments (including that of same-sex marriage) have had or are likely to have the undesirable consequences predicted by Cooper, Halley and others. If anything, consequentialist arguments could plausibly be mustered to exactly the opposite effect, namely, that legal recognition of same-sex partnerships (including same-sex marriage) would address the very roots of both sexism and homophobia. Eskridge puts this latter point, ironically, in postmodernist terms. Legal recognition of same-sex partnerships effectively degenders marriage, that is, critically addresses the unjust construction of intimate relations in terms of conventional stereotypes of gender hierarchy. Legal recognition of same-sex partnerships legitimates gender performances that critically subvert the entrenchment of unjust gender stereotypes as the terms of both public and private life. To this extent, legal recognition of such partnerships addresses the very roots of homophobia in dehumanising stereotypes of gender and sexuality enforced through law. On this view, recognition of same-sex marriage would have consequences (limiting the force of homophobia) from which all gays and lesbians (partnered and unpartnered) would profit immeasurably.

There is one argument that should reasonably be added to Eskridge's defensive and offensive armory. If the movement for legal recognition of same-sex partnerships rests, as Bamforth and Feldblum powerfully argue, on an argument of basic human rights, then consequences may not even be relevant, at least in the way that Eskridge appears willing to concede. Human rights have a normative force in constitutional argument that imposes on the state a very heavy burden of compelling secular justification, before such rights may be abridged. If the arguments of new natural law are clearly inadequate to meet this burden, postmodernist arguments (at least understood as grounds for truncating the availability of same-sex marriage) may be even less weighty. Why should any gay or lesbian couple be forbidden marriage on grounds that would reasonably be rejected as compelling reasons for forbidding straight couples from marrying? A distinction without a difference in this domain smacks of homophobia, assuming a rationalisation in stereotypes that it cannot reasonably justify. We need perhaps to remind ourselves of the important distinction between the different standards applicable to our political and constitutional morality, and those relevant to our personal moral lives. One may be personally moved, as I am, by some of the postmodernist arguments of Cooper and Halley not to want to define one's long-term passionately loving homosexual attachments (endlessly renegotiated and reaffirmed on the basis of intensely mutual personal need) in terms of the frigid stereotypes of ascribed roles implicit in conventional marriage, and yet find their arguments quite inadequate as compelling public reasons that justify limiting the right to marriage to heterosexual intimate life.

If this is true, the case for same-sex marriage (as the preferred form of legal recognition of same-sex partnerships) may be stronger than even Eskridge, perhaps its strongest contemporary proponent, supposes.[7] In the United States, we have had ample historical experience with the normative consequences of according a stigmatised minority, African Americans, separate but allegedly equal access to public and private institutions. Such treatment culturally dehumanised whole classes of persons, in ways that we now condemn as the unjust cultural construction of racism. We have had extensive historical experience about how and why abridgment of the right to intimate life played so important a role in the cultural construction of the dehumanising stereotypes of ethnic difference, unjustly used to support and sustain political racism. If our constitutional condemnation of anti-miscegenation laws[8] is to racism what denial of any rights to intimate life of homosexuals is to sexism and homophobia, as I and others now believe it is,[9] then we must scrutinize with concern forms of legal recognition of same-sex partnerships that enforce separate but equal in the domain of sexual orientation. The exclusion of same-sex partnerships from full legal recognition constructs the dehumanisation of homosexuals, as if they could no more have loving and humane intimate lives than could animals. If the strategic price we are paying for some forms of legal recognition of same-sex partnerships implicates such continuing complicity with the very terms of our dehumanisation, we may be paying a price in the terms of our human dignity that we cannot and should not, as a matter of fundamental principle, justify or suppose to be justifiable.

[7] I am indebted for these reflections to conversations with Yuval Merin, a graduate student at New York University School of Law, whose doctoral dissertation makes an argument along these lines.

[8] Anti-miscegenation laws prohibiting black–white marriages existed in the United States until *Loving* v. *Virginia*, 388 US 1 (1967).

[9] See Richards, *supra* n.5; Koppelman, chap. 35.

2

Same-Sex Partnerships and Arguments of Justice

NICHOLAS BAMFORTH*

IN DEBATES CONCERNING the legal recognition of same-sex partnerships, arguments of justice are important at two levels. The first, and deeper, level consists of arguments from the realms of political and legal philosophy. One characteristic of liberal societies is a commitment to the notion that—given the law's inherently coercive potential—individual laws must have a sound normative justification in order to be regarded as morally legitimate. Laws affording meaningful legal protection to those in same-sex relationships may well involve coercion: hostile employers might be required to extend the availability of employment benefits to same-sex as well as opposite-sex partners of their employees,[1] for example, while unwilling housing associations might be obliged to allow same-sex as well as opposite-sex partners to succeed to the tenancies of properties.[2] A defensible normative justification must therefore be provided for such laws, deriving from our background theories of justice and political morality—that is, from theories concerning (respectively, although the two are often interlinked) the rightful allocation of entitlements amongst members of liberal societies *in general*, and the ways in which the political institutions of such societies should act.[3]

Arguments at the second, shallower, level relate to the constitution of the society in which legal recognition of same-sex partnerships is sought. Such recognition might, depending upon the constitution in issue, occur either via legislative intervention or via judicial decision-making. For such intervention to be regarded as legitimate in terms of *that particular* constitution, however, it must be shown to fall within the proper constitutional powers of the legislature or court in question. Arguments at the second level therefore concern questions of constitutional law and interpretation.

* Fellow in Law, Queen's College, University of Oxford.

[1] Contrary to the result in Case C-249/96, *Grant* v. *South-West Trains* [1998] ECR I-621.

[2] A result achieved in English law by statutory interpretation: see *Fitzpatrick* v. *Sterling Housing Association* [1999] 3 WLR 1113.

[3] See further Nicholas Bamforth, *Sexuality, Morals and Justice* (London, Cassell, 1997), especially ch. 1.

Considerable interaction between the two levels is, of course, possible. In a society with a written constitution, arguments of legal and political philosophy may well inform a court's interpretation of provisions of that constitution; and in a society without a written constitution, such arguments can still inform a court's judgment on an issue which is of constitutional significance in that it concerns the powers of government institutions and/or the rights of individuals.[4] Equally, a court's interpretation of a *particular* constitutional provision—concerning, for example, privacy—may usefully illustrate the strengths or weaknesses of arguments for legal recognition of same-sex partnerships based on a *general* philosophical defence of the right to privacy. The two levels of argument can nonetheless be meaningfully separated: for, while the first level can be applied to liberal societies in general,[5] the second level will vary according to the constitutional provisions of *each* society. For example, only some liberal societies give explicit constitutional protection to privacy rights—but a philosophical defence of privacy rights might still be used to justify amendments to the constitution of a society which did not openly protect them.

This chapter will consider arguments of justice at both levels. It will do so by analysing the strengths and weaknesses of three possible philosophical arguments for legal recognition of same-sex partnerships—namely respect for privacy, equality, and autonomy/empowerment—and of the 'new natural law' arguments which have been used to oppose such recognition.[6] Cases in which courts have interpreted particular constitutional rights to privacy, equality and dignity (a near sibling of autonomy) will play an important role in this analysis. It should be noted that the philosophical and constitutional arguments which can be and have in practice been used to justify legal recognition of same-sex partnerships have all initially been used to justify the creation of legal protections (for example against employment discrimination) for *individuals* who are lesbian or gay. It will therefore be important to see how far each argument can satisfactorily be extended into the partnership context.[7] The chapter will not deal, specifically, with gay liberationist or queer theory arguments.[8] For, while such arguments can usefully highlight shortcomings in the use of law and legal

[4] This assumes that a society can still be said to have a constitution even though it lacks a written constitutional instrument. Arguments to the contrary appear to be specious, given that courts are still required, in such a society, to set precedents concerning the powers and rights of the government and of citizens, and the legislature can still pass statutes concerning these issues. The real issue in such a society is not that there is no constitution, but that the constitutional rules are not explicit.

[5] I discuss the cultural limits of such arguments in Bamforth, *supra* n.3 at 112–24.

[6] See further Bamforth, *supra* n.3, chs. 4, 6, 7.

[7] In the context of legal protections for individuals, it is sometimes claimed that a person's sexual orientation is in some sense fixed ("immutable"), and that it is unjustifiable for the law to penalise activity resulting from a factor which is beyond individual control. This argument is weak as a general matter (see Bamforth, *supra* n.3 at 203–6), and is wholly unhelpful in the present context given that a person's decision to enter into a settled sexual/emotional relationship with a particular partner can hardly be described as predetermined.

[8] See further Bamforth, *supra* n.3 at 220–9. For useful analysis of queer theory and law, see C Stychin, *Law's Desire: Sexuality and the Limits of Justice* (London, Routledge, 1995).

rights in countering social oppression, they can range in their aims from the deconstruction through to the overthrow of existing power structures and social categories. A purely deconstructionist analysis is, by its very nature, unlikely to be of assistance in constructing normative philosophical or constitutional arguments of any sort, while those concerned to overthrow existing social categories are likely to view the use of law as at best a tactical weapon in their struggle, something to be used on a pragmatic basis only. Ultimately, normative analysis of the appropriate role of law is unlikely to play a large part in this project.

RESPECT FOR PRIVACY

Since 1957, respect for privacy has been one of the most prominent arguments—at both the philosophical and constitutional levels—for granting substantive legal protections to lesbians and gays. The classic formulation of this argument was contained in the 1957 Wolfenden Committee Report, which recommended the partial decriminalisation of male homosexual relations in the United Kingdom.[9] The Committee asserted that the criminal law should not intervene in the private lives of citizens any further than was necessary to:

> "preserve public order and decency, to protect the citizen from what is offensive or injurious, and to provide sufficient safeguards against exploitation and corruption of others, particularly those who are specially vulnerable because they are young, weak in body or mind, inexperienced, or in a state of special physical, official or economic dependence".[10]

This meant that:

> "[u]nless a deliberate attempt is made by society, acting through the agency of the law, to equate the sphere of crime with that of sin, there must remain a realm of private morality and immorality which is, in brief and crude terms, not the law's business".[11]

Private, consensual sexual acts between adult males fell, according to the Committee, within this protected realm. In subsequent years, respect for privacy has been a central argument in many of the key constitutional cases concerning lesbian and gay issues (including partnership rights),[12] and one might therefore try to argue that same-sex partnerships deserve legal protection because they fall within the protected realm of privacy.

[9] *The Report of the Committee on Homosexual Offences and Prostitution*, Cmnd. 247 (London, HMSO, 1957).

[10] *Ibid.* paras.13–14.

[11] *Ibid.* para. 61.

[12] In relation to individual rights, see e.g. *Dudgeon* v. *United Kingdom* (1981) 4 EHRR 149; *Norris* v. *Ireland* (1989) EHRR 187; *National Coalition for Gay and Lesbian Equality* v. *Minister of Justice* [1999] 1 SA 6; *Smith and Grady* v. *United Kingdom* (2000) 29 EHRR 493; *Lustig-Prean and Beckett* v. *United Kingdom* (2000) 29 EHRR 548.

Despite their popularity, however, respect-for-privacy arguments contain three important weaknesses, the third of which is particularly acute in the context of same-sex partnerships. The first weakness is that, as Judith Jarvis Thomson has suggested, "[p]erhaps the most striking thing about the right to privacy is that nobody seems to have any very clear idea what it is".[13] In philosophical terms, privacy has been variously interpreted as meaning that certain physical spaces—usually the home—should be free from legal regulation, that certain activities or relationships should remain unregulated by law and that certain types of personal information should be protected from revelation.[14] The bald assertion that the law should be concerned to protect a person's privacy cannot tell us with any precision therefore which activities or areas of life should in fact be protected. Further detail is always needed to explain why these, rather than any other, areas and activities deserve protection. To explain the merits of a *particular* definition of privacy, any such account, if it is to avoid circularity, must usually also be framed in terms of values which lie *behind* the notion of privacy itself.[15] In consequence, demands for the legal protection of privacy are really demands for the protection of the value(s) underpinning and explaining a particular definition of privacy, begging the question why we do not simply refer to those values rather than using privacy as a cover.[16]

This problem can be highlighted by considering two privacy-based arguments which have been advanced in relation to same-sex sexual acts. The first is Richard Mohr's analysis of US law.[17] Mohr uses a privacy argument to oppose laws which prohibit same-sex sexual acts, but rests this argument on a dignity-based analysis. Mohr interprets respect for privacy as meaning that certain activities—sexual acts—should be protected, as opposed (for example) to physical spaces.[18] He argues that sexual activity by its very nature excludes all but the participants, for whom ordinary perceptions of the rest of the world

[13] "The Right to Privacy" (1975) 4 *Philosophy and Public Affairs* 295 at 295.

[14] Compare S Warren and L Brandeis, "The Right to Privacy" (1890) 4 *Harvard Law Review* 193; C Fried, "Privacy", (1968) 77 *Yale Law Journal* 475; Ruth Gavison, "Privacy and the Limits of Law", (1980) 89 *Yale Law Journal* 421; D Richards, *Sex, Drugs, Death and the Law: An Essay on Human Rights and Overcriminalization* (Totowa, Rowman & Littlefield, 1982). For general criticism of the definitions of privacy, see D Bedingfield, "Privacy or Publicity? The Enduring Confusion Surrounding the American Tort of Invasion of Privacy", (1992) 55 *Modern Law Review* 111; K Thomas, "Beyond the Privacy Principle", (1992) 92 *Columbia Law Review* 1431.

[15] In practice, this is likely to depend upon whether the account in question is of a perfectionist or anti-perfectionist nature. See further Bamforth, *supra* n.3 at 208 *et seq*.

[16] If privacy is simply used in its own right as the foundation of a claim, a theorist is still likely to run up against the argument that they have failed to supply an adequate normative basis for their explanation of *why* some things are public and others private. For such a critique of R Dworkin's "Liberal Community", (1989) 77 *California Law Review* 479, see Bamforth, *supra* n.3 at 212–4.

[17] R Mohr, *Gays/Justice: A Study of Ethics, Society, and Law* (New York, NY, Columbia University Press, 1988). Although Mohr seemingly implies that his analysis is of a philosophical character, in reality it is more an interpretation of privacy under US constitutional law coupled with certain philosophical observations.

[18] *Ibid*. at 104–6. Mohr thus claims that sexual activity between consenting adults in "cruising areas" (parks, toilets, etc.) to which the public have access potentially can be protected as private because they fall within his activity-related definition of privacy.

diminish during intercourse. Sexual acts are thus, Mohr claims, inherently private.[19] Furthermore, sexual activity plays a fundamentally important role in most people's lives.[20] Mohr suggests that the "basic [moral] evil" of laws prohibiting same-sex sexual acts is that "they are an affront to dignity".[21] This is because they fail to respect a person as a "chooser—a subject conscious of herself as an agent with plans, projects, and a view of her own achievements".[22] Given that anti-sodomy laws do not treat a lesbian or gay person's desires, plans, aspirations and values as worthy of the same level of social care as that accorded to a heterosexual person's, they also violate the entitlement to equal respect, together with the entitlement to respect as a moral agent—which requires that one is judged according to individual merits or accomplishments rather than by reference to "irrelevant features" such as sexual orientation.[23] In a similar vein, Mohr claims that it may be justifiable to create laws protecting lesbians and gays against discrimination since discrimination fails to show respect for persons as equals.[24]

Several flaws can be identified in Mohr's account. For one thing, his philosophical argument is vague and his definition of dignity rather loose. Mohr does not acknowledge, for example, that people can have very different views about what constitutes an "irrelevant feature" when assessing or characterising someone in moral terms. Many conservatives *do* believe that a person's lesbian or gay sexual orientation is a relevant reason for treating them unfavourably. We can argue that this view is wrong, but this is not the same as being able to demarcate in a morally neutral way, as Mohr seems to believe is possible, which human characteristics are "relevant" and which are not. Furthermore, Mohr fails to explain how his notion of "entitlement to equal respect" would work, for there are plainly *some* human desires, plans and aspirations—for example, a plan to become a mass murderer—which can rightly be treated less favourably than others. For present purposes, however, the central flaw in Mohr's account is that while his arguments are dressed up in the constitutional language of privacy, this is simply a vehicle for the deeper notion of respect for human dignity, which acts as the true driving force behind his opposition to anti-sodomy laws. Privacy is, for Mohr, merely the *label* under which dignity is promoted in the area of sexual activity.

A similar point can be made about the privacy argument advanced by David Richards. Richards claims that respect for privacy rests on a basic moral vision of people as autonomous and entitled to equal respect.[25] Autonomy turns on the idea that people have a range of capacities enabling them to act on and to

[19] *Ibid.* at 100–4.
[20] *Ibid.* at 109–12.
[21] *Ibid.* at 57.
[22] *Ibid.* at 58.
[23] *Ibid.* at 59.
[24] *Ibid.* at 141–51.
[25] Richards, *supra* n.14, chs. 1, 2, especially at 33–4. See also L Henkin, "Privacy and Autonomy", (1974) 74 *Columbia Law Review* 1410.

develop plans of action in their lives,[26] and Richards argues that each person's capacity for autonomy should be viewed as being of equal value.[27] Respect for privacy is:

> "intended to facilitate the exercise of autonomy in certain basic kinds of choice that bear upon the coherent rationality of a person's life plan . . . . Certain choices in life are taken to bear fundamentally on the entire design of one's life, for these choices determine the basic decisions of work and love, which in turn order many of the subsidiary choices of human life".[28]

Richards argues that sexual autonomy is central to the idea that a person is free, given that sexuality has a powerful role as an independent force in a person's imaginative life and general development.[29] The absence of any form of love—of which sexual affection may be a crucial ingredient—would make a person's life empty, deformed and twisted. Richards suggests that the profoundly personal and intimate nature of sexual activity thus demands privacy[30] (thereby interpreting privacy, like Mohr, as something applicable to certain activities[31]). The importance of autonomy within this argument means that one's sexual self-definition must be allowed to extend to the sex of the person(s) with whom one has intercourse.

Viewed in the round, it is not entirely clear whether Richards is claiming that sexual autonomy is a positive moral good which must be protected for its own sake or, more negatively, that the state should not intervene to regulate areas where people should make their own choices concerning moral goods.[32] Either way, the general tenor of his argument is to identify autonomy as the key issue, with privacy serving as the label under which autonomy ought to be protected constitutionally. In both Richards's and Mohr's accounts, privacy therefore serves a similar role, perhaps reflecting the more general philosophical uncertainty about whether privacy should be seen as a specific good in itself (and if so, why), or whether it should be seen as the label given to a set of distinct goods which are simply grouped together for convenience's sake.[33] At the constitutional law level, this uncertainty must, furthermore, survive the South African

[26] Richards, *supra* n. 14 at 8.

[27] *Ibid.* at 9.

[28] *Ibid.* at 50.

[29] *Ibid.* at 53.

[30] *Ibid.* at 52–3.

[31] *Ibid.* at 38.

[32] Richards seems to be claiming that he holds the second, narrower position: *ibid.* at 8–9, and, more broadly, Richards's article "Kantian Ethics and the Harm Principle: A Reply to John Finnis", (1987) 87 *Columbia Law Review* 457. *Cf.*, however, R George, *Making Men Moral: Civil Liberties and Public Morality* (Oxford, Clarendon Press, 1993) at 139–60.

[33] Cf. Thomson, *supra* n.13 at 313; Thomas Scanlon, "Thomson on Privacy", (1975) 4 *Philosophy and Public Affairs* 315; J Reiman, "Privacy, Intimacy, and Personhood", (1976) 6 *Philosophy and Public Affairs* 26; Fried, *supra* n.14; J Eichbaum, "Towards an Autonomy-Based Theory of Constitutional Privacy: Beyond the Ideology of Familial Privacy", (1979) 14 *Harvard Civil Rights–Civil Liberties Law Review* 361; J Rubenfeld, "The Right to Privacy", (1989) 102 *Harvard Law Review* 737.

Constitutional Court's reassertion in *National Coalition for Gay and Lesbian Equality* v. *Minister of Justice* of the value of privacy arguments as a vehicle for justifying the decriminalisation of same-sex sexual acts.[34] Ackermann J defined the right to privacy protected by section 14 of the South African Constitution as "a sphere of private intimacy and autonomy which allows us to establish and nurture human relationships without interference from the outside community".[35] Although he attacked the common law offence of sodomy as violating the constitutional rights to equality, dignity *and* privacy, he also described opposition to the idea that discrimination against gay men should be prohibited on the ground of privacy *alone* as "understandable".[36] And, while Sachs J opposed the notion that privacy should be treated as the "poor relation" of equality[37] and called for a broad interpretation of the right to privacy,[38] he went on to suggest that the "*motif* which links and unites equality and privacy, and which, indeed, runs right through the protections offered by the [South African] Bill of Rights, is dignity",[39] implying that privacy, even at a constitutional level, can be treated as a label for a deeper moral or constitutional value.

The second weakness of privacy arguments is that they do not necessarily entail the claim that there is anything morally worthwhile about same-sex sexual acts or emotional relationships. Richard Mohr's account *does* appear to see such sexual acts as involving a moral good in their own right,[40] but many supporters of the decriminalisation of homosexual acts in Britain and Canada in the 1960s were careful to stress their personal disapproval of such acts.[41] Furthermore, new natural law theorists such as John Finnis, who are hostile to same-sex sexual acts or relationships *themselves* argue that the law should (grudgingly) refrain from prohibiting such acts so long as they occur in private.[42] As such, respect for privacy arguments cannot be guaranteed to make a terribly strong or positive defence of same-sex sexual acts or relationships.[43] Kendall Thomas has thus argued that in US constitutional litigation "the rhetoric of privacy has historically functioned to perpetuate the oppressive politics of the 'closet': privacy is the ideological substrate of the very secrecy that

[34] *Supra* n.12.

[35] *Ibid.* at para. 32.

[36] *Ibid.* at para. 31.

[37] *Ibid.* at para. 115.

[38] *Ibid.* at para. 116.

[39] *Ibid.* at para. 120.

[40] The tone of chs. 2 to 4 of Mohr's *Gays/Justice*, *supra* n.17, seems generally to support the view that there is a moral good, although p.4 is rather vague.

[41] See further G Kinsman, *The Regulation of Desire: Sexuality in Canada* (Montreal, Black Rose, 1987) at 164–72; S Jeffery-Poulter, *Peers, Queers and Commons: The Struggle for Gay Law Reform from 1950 to the Present* (London, Routledge, 1991) at 81–2; A Grey, *Quest for Justice: Towards Homosexual Emancipation* (London, Sinclair-Stevenson, 1992) at 125–6.

[42] See *infra*, text accompanying nn. 68–111.

[43] See M Sandel, "Moral argument and liberal toleration: Abortion and homosexuality", (1989) 77 *California Law Review* 521 at 537; E Cameron, "Sexual Orientation and the Constitution: A Test Case for Human Rights", (1993) 110 *South African Law Journal* 450 at 464.

has forced gay men and lesbians to remain hidden and underground".[44] As such, it may be preferable to base a claim for legal recognition of same-sex partnerships on some more positive argument.

The third weakness is that respect for privacy arguments can generate artificiality: given the limitations already discussed, it is only by severely stretching our idea of what *counts* as private that we can use privacy to justify prohibiting discrimination in the workplace or the public arena.[45] Excessive stretching of the concept of privacy is likely to undermine its plausibility as a normative basis for protecting lesbians and gays from discrimination, for privacy would have to be used in situations to which it is unsuited. If we are not to stretch privacy, however, then it seems doomed—in the manner highlighted by Ackermann J—to be an additional argument which is used simply to reinforce broader concepts such as equality and autonomy. This difficulty is particularly acute in the context of same-sex partnerships since, while having a same-sex partner might be felt to be an aspect of a person's private life, *legal registration* of that partnership—whether through marriage or some other ceremony—*necessarily* adds a public element to the situation. It is not for nothing that one popular argument for granting legal recognition to same-sex partnerships is that this would give them legitimacy by allowing them to receive an 'official' stamp of approval—neatly highlighting the "public" element this would involve.

On balance, therefore, respect-for-privacy arguments are not terribly strong, at least unless used with other arguments such as equality and autonomy. Furthermore, the public element which is necessarily involved in the legal *recognition* of same-sex partnerships makes such arguments particularly unhelpful in this context. Alternative arguments will, in consequence, be needed.

EQUALITY

Despite the longer-term popularity of respect for privacy, most political demands for legal protections for lesbians and gays have been expressed—since the mid-1980s—in the language of equality (and, at the philosophical level, have relied on the concept of equality).[46] Broadly speaking, equality arguments maintain that lesbians and gay men should not, because of their sexual orientation, be treated any less favourably than heterosexuals since the two groups are of

[44] Thomas, *supra* n.14 at 1510.

[45] In constitutional terms, this may sometimes be the only route open to a court—as, for example, in *Lustig-Prean and Beckett* v. *UK supra* n.12—but this is not a tactic which should readily be adopted in philosophical argument. For background discussion in relation to the European Convention on Human Rights, see R Wintemute, *Sexual Orientation and Human Rights: The United States Constitution, the European Convention, and the Canadian Charter* (Oxford, Clarendon Press, 1995) at 130–1.

[46] See, e.g., J D'Emilio, *Making Trouble: Essays on Gay History, Politics, and the University* (New York, NY, Routledge, 1992) at 182; HC Deb., 21 Feb. 1994, Col.97 (Tony Blair MP); HC Deb., 21 Feb. 1994, Col.110 (Chris Smith MP) .

equal moral worth. Equality arguments have three strengths. First, they are easy to understand and have a clear, emotive appeal.

Secondly, they tackle head-on the weaknesses of respect-for-privacy arguments. On the one hand, equality arguments entail the strong claim that lesbian and gay sexuality—or some specified aspect of it—is just as good, morally-speaking, as heterosexuality; otherwise, such arguments could provide no justification for treating the two as equals. They thus avoid the second weakness of privacy arguments. On the other hand, equality arguments can, in their strongest form, be used to justify a wide range of legal protections for lesbians and gays: indeed, they can potentially be used to justify the removal of *any* form of unfavourable treatment which is not meted out to heterosexuals. Analytically, equality arguments can be used to justify the removal of hostile criminal laws, the prohibition of employment discrimination against lesbians and gays, and the creation of partnership rights for same-sex couples. They thus avoid the third weakness of privacy arguments.

Thirdly, the range of potential applications of equality arguments highlights a further advantage, at least in the present context. Such arguments can in principle be used just as easily to demand legal protection for same-sex couples as for individuals. This is because, in order to determine that unequal treatment has occurred, it is no more difficult to compare a same-sex couple with an opposite-sex couple than it is to compare an individual lesbian or gay man with an individual heterosexual. Equality arguments can thus promote consistency between cases involving individuals and couples.

However, equality arguments have two weaknesses of their own. The first is specific to the context of same-sex partnerships. Even if equality arguments can in principle be used to justify the granting of partnership rights, the case law suggests that courts are reluctant for constitutional reasons to allow equality-based claims which involve the status of same-sex partnerships, as opposed to claims involving the entitlements of individual lesbians or gay men (although this depends upon the constitution in question and there are counter-examples[47]). The reason for this reluctance is usually that it is felt that matters relating to same-sex partnerships are sufficiently "controversial" that they should be left to the legislature.[48] However, this apparent weakness of equality arguments perhaps relates more to form than to substance, given that judicial reticence,

[47] See the South African Constitutional Court's decision in *National Coalition for Gay and Lesbian Equality* v. *Minister of Home Affairs* (2 Dec. 1999), <http://www.concourt.gov.za/archive.html>, paras. 55 *et seq* (Ackermann J).

[48] For example, in *Grant*, *supra* n.1, the European Court of Justice characterised the case (arguably inaccurately) as turning on the legal status of same-sex partnerships, and proceeded to declare that the matter was one for the legislature to tackle (at paras. 24, 29–36, 48). And, while the Canadian Supreme Court found that members of same-sex couples should be able to claim financial support in *M* v. *H*, [1999] 2 SCR 3, Cory J. stressed that the case essentially concerned the rights of individuals rather than any broader question concerning the rights of same-sex couples in general (paras. 53–55). See also the critique of the House of Lords' decision in *Fitzpatrick*, *supra* n.2, in SM Cretney and FMB Reynolds, "Limits of the Judicial Function" (2000) 116 *Law Quarterly Review* 181.

however expressed, is more likely to be caused by the subject-matter of the case, namely same-sex partnership rights, than by the nature of the argument used in support of the recognition of such rights.

The second, more fundamental difficulty is that equality arguments are question-begging, in a fashion analogous to many respect-for-privacy arguments.[49] For to say that two persons (or couples) are morally equal, we need to explain *why*, in normative terms, they deserve to be viewed in this way.[50] The concept of equality cannot, in and of itself, provide us with an answer—for at root, the term "equality" is simply a descriptive label telling us *that* two persons (or couples) deserve analogous treatment, rather than *why* such treatment is merited.[51] We need to find an argument deeper than equality and involving some distinct scale of value in order to answer the "why" question.[52] As Joseph Raz has suggested:

> "we only have reason to care about inequalities in the distributions of *goods* and *ills*, that is of what is of value or disvalue for independent reasons. There is no reason to care about inequalities in the distribution of grains of sand, unless there is some other reason to wish to have or avoid sand".[53]

In relation to the legal entitlements of lesbian and gay individuals or couples, such a reason can only be found in a deeper justification for granting legal protection, suggesting that it is that justification which should—in the interest of clarity—be used in the first place.

This does not mean, however, that there is no role whatever for equality arguments. Given their popularity and clear, emotive appeal it may well be felt that it is useful to employ such arguments, so long as they are seen as a purely rhetorical flourish reinforcing a coherent, independent and deeper argument for the legal recognition of same-sex partnerships, and for legal protections for indi-

[49] Apart from what I have termed the "why" question (see text accompanying the footnotes following this one), arguments concerning the legal rights of individual lesbians and gay men can also beg a "what" question, in the sense that it is unclear whether it is same-sex sexual acts or lesbian/gay/bisexual sexual identities which are being declared to be the moral equivalents of heterosexual acts or identities, (see Bamforth, *supra* n.3 above at 238–50). However, the "what" question has a clear answer in relation to partnership rights, in that the relevant comparison in this context is plainly between same-sex and opposite-sex couples. Such an answer might, though, in itself highlight a shortcoming of equality arguments: for it would presumably be desirable to use a similar argument to justify legal recognition of same-sex partnerships and legal protections for individual lesbians and gay men—otherwise one risks the possibility of discontinuity between two related contexts, and consequent intellectual incoherence. A way forward may, nonetheless, have been identified by the South African Constitutional Court in *Minister of Justice*, *supra* n.12. See further Angelo Pantazis's useful analysis "How to Decriminalise Gay Sex", (1999) 15 *South African Journal of Human Rights* 188 at 191–2.

[50] See further J Raz, *The Morality of Freedom* (Oxford, Clarendon Press, 1986), ch. 9; P Westen, "The Empty Idea of Equality", (1982) 95 *Harvard Law Review* 537.

[51] This argument is developed further in Bamforth, *supra* n.3 at 250–8.

[52] *Cf.*, however, B Williams, "The Idea of Equality", ch.6 in P Laslett and WG Runciman (eds.), *Philosophy, Politics and Society (Second Series)* (Oxford, Basil Blackwell, 1962); T Nagel, *Mortal Questions* (Cambridge, Cambridge University Press, 1979), ch.8.

[53] Raz, *supra* n.50 at 235. See also Westen, *supra* n.50, especially at 542, 547–8, 557.

vidual lesbians and gay men. For if the term "equality" has a strong political appeal, there is no harm in using it as a campaigning slogan *if* it is made clear that it is no more than that.[54] Furthermore, if a deeper argument for legal protection works successfully, it is likely to produce some sort of social equality—provided that "equality" is understood as the loose, statistical label which roughly *describes* that end-result (in the same sense in which members of a society might loosely be described as "content" or "prosperous", socially-speaking), rather than as the normative justification for getting us to that position. Equality may therefore be a more promising argument than respect for privacy, but a still stronger argument will plainly be necessary in order reliably to justify the legal recognition of same-sex partnerships.

AUTONOMY/EMPOWERMENT

It is submitted that the most coherent argument for affording individual lesbians and gay men legal protections against social hostility and for recognising same-sex partnerships is based on the concepts of autonomy and empowerment.[55] For this argument acknowledges the crucial role of sexual expression and emotional feelings to our well-being as humans, and also seeks to rely openly on the central value—whether this is described as "autonomy" or "dignity"—which in fact underpins (but is often, as we have seen, hidden behind) most respect-for-privacy and equality arguments.

The autonomy/empowerment argument divides into two parts, the first of which consists of the claim that sexual/emotional desires, feelings, aspirations, and behaviour[56] are of central importance for human beings. Sometimes, people value and desire sexual acts just as sexual acts; on other occasions, the value of such acts stems from their role as a central means of communicating and experiencing reciprocal affection and desire within a broader emotional relationship. For most adults, sexual freedom of action is thus important as a means (one of the most powerful means of expressing affection within an emotional relationship) or as an end (sexual communion and pleasure). In either case, the relevant freedom is of fundamental importance to those involved: as HLA Hart observed in his defence of the Wolfenden Committee's proposals, sexual impulses play a strong part in each person's day-to-day life, and their suppression can affect

[54] See also S Epstein's discussion in "Gay Politics, Ethnic Identity: the Limits of Social Constructionism", in Edward Stein (ed.), *Forms of Desire: Sexual Orientation and the Social Constructionist Controversy* (New York, NY, Garland, 1990) at 289 *et seq*.

[55] See further Bamforth, *supra* n.3 at 158–67 where it is suggested that the autonomy/empowerment argument rests on a broadly social democratic theory of justice and political morality. Obviously those who do not share such a theory might not find this argument appealing but, if so, they will need to find a way of containing the difficulties in the other arguments discussed if they are to present a coherent case for legal protection for lesbian or gay individuals or same-sex partnerships.

[56] For further definition, see R Wintemute, *supra* n.45 at 6–10.

"the development or balance of the individual's emotional life, happiness, and personality".[57] A person's sexual tastes, and sexual and emotional encounters and relationships, are, respectively, often among the most centrally personal characteristics and experiences they have. It would otherwise make little sense to regard such matters—as most of us do—as being not merely private but *intimate*. For the word "intimacy" might be felt to capture far better than the word "privacy" the uniquely personal nature of sexual/emotional matters, and their connection with a person's autonomy or dignity.

Two factors help explain the intimate nature of sexual acts. The first is the unparalleled degree of human interdependence involved in any sexual encounter, whether that encounter occurs on a casual basis or as part of a committed sexual/emotional relationship. While this interdependence becomes deeper and more emotional when the relationship between the participants is of a committed nature, any consensual sexual act involves a level of reciprocity and exchange—sometimes purely physical, sometimes also spiritual—which is not found in other areas of life. Indeed, people often judge the quality of a sexual encounter according to the extent to which such elements are discernibly present within it; for sexual encounters are inherently mutual rather than individual events.[58] Whether a sexual act occurs on a casual basis or as part of a committed relationship, it entails a deep level of human interdependence quite unlike that found in other co-operative activities.

The second factor is that sexual tastes—in terms of what we think makes someone a desirable sexual partner, or what makes something a pleasurable sexual act—vary almost infinitely, and each person's tastes and fantasies go to the very heart of what it is, for them, to be the particular human being that they are. The notion of sexual orientation, in the sense of the sex of the person(s) to whom one is attracted, is just one aspect of this. Within the basic parameters of their sexual orientation, people are often able to conceptualise their ideal sexual tastes and fantasies more clearly than other types of taste or aspiration. Each person's conception of sexuality is, in its way, unique and central to them. Taken together, these two factors suggest that a person's understanding of what is, for them, desirable sexual and/or emotional contact should—with one important limit, relating to consent—be respected by the law. It also follows that, subject to this limit, each person's understanding of their sexual identity deserves respect, as do the sexual and/or emotional relationships in which they engage, an argument which applies both to individual lesbians and gay men and to those engaged in same-sex relationships. The consent-related limit to this principle is that sexual acts and sexual/emotional relationships deserve respect only insofar as the participants have freely consented to participate (and to participate in the way that they have) in the act or relationship concerned. For

[57] *Law, Liberty, and Morality* (Oxford, Oxford University Press, 1963) at 22.

[58] *Cf.*, however, the view of the new natural lawyers, see *infra*, text accompanying nn. 68–111. The argument presented here would explain why masturbation is generally seen as an inferior activity to sex—for the former is a solitary compensation for the absence of the latter, mutual activity.

without free choice, the second factor explaining the intimacy of sexual acts and the value of sexual activity is missing.

Philosophically, these ideas can be gathered together under the idea of a moral entitlement to autonomy. RA Duff has suggested that respect for a person as an autonomous subject requires respect for their integrity as a sexual agent, able to decide for themselves who to take as sexual partners.[59] Duff uses this moral argument to justify the criminal law's prohibition of rape, and it can be used just as strongly to explain why a person's sexual fantasies, aspirations and behaviour, together with their sexual/emotional relationships, should be respected by society and—where relevant—by the law. Lack of consent to a sexual act destroys the underlying reason for protection, namely respecting people as autonomous sexual agents. If autonomy is to be taken seriously, however, then each individual's appreciation and definition of what is, for them, a valuable sexual act or sexual/emotional relationship must—within the limits of consent—be respected.[60]

The second part of the autonomy/empowerment argument reinforces the first (dealing with the importance of "intimacy") by considering the effects of laws and social practices which treat lesbians and gays, whether as individuals or as members of partnerships, in a hostile and discriminatory fashion. Laws and social practices which target any social group as a recipient deserving of unfavourable treatment could be said to objectify members of that group: the members, unlike non-members, are stigmatised as being undeserving of full consideration as human beings because of a characteristic or characteristics which they are assumed to possess by virtue of their actual or perceived group membership. A group will typically be singled out for hostile treatment where some element of social sensitivity or controversy attaches to it. The consequent objectification can be powerfully dehumanising, in that it can disempower people in an acute and sometimes total fashion—as where a person is subjected to severe physical attack because of their actual or perceived group membership.

Of course, it cannot always be wrong to single out particular groups for unfavourable treatment. We might well say that any reasonable theory of justice and political morality would authorise, within appropriate limits, the punishment of a group of self-identified torturers or child molesters. However, unfavourable treatment of members of a group, whether socially or at the hands of the law, can be classified as improper discrimination where they are treated as objects rather than subjects due to their group membership, *provided that* membership of that group should, according to our theories of justice and political morality, properly be regarded as morally neutral or positive.[61] It is in order

[59] RA Duff, *Intention, Agency and Criminal Liability: Philosophy of Action and the Criminal Law* (Oxford, Blackwell, 1990) at 167–73.

[60] This has implications for the range of consensual sexual acts which should be allowed. For a practical application of this argument, see N Bamforth, "Sado-Masochism and Consent" [1994] *Criminal Law Review* 661.

[61] See, e.g., Mohr, *supra* n.17 at 58.

to draw this distinction clearly that both parts of the autonomy/empowerment argument are necessary. The first part identifies a moral good, sexual autonomy, which is threatened by hostile laws or social practices. From the standpoint of sexual autonomy people are entitled to be considered as sexual subjects rather than objects, an entitlement which is violated by laws which single out lesbian or gay individuals or couples for unfavourable treatment, thereby failing to protect them as choosing, feeling human subjects (bringing into play the second part of the argument). By granting legal protection we are, in consequence, both helping to combat objectification and disempowerment *and* protecting the moral good associated with freely-chosen sexual behaviour, conceptions of sexuality, and sexual/emotional relationships.

Of course, evidence is needed to sustain the claim that laws which regulate lesbian or gay sexuality in a hostile fashion, or which fail to grant appropriate legal protections (including partnership rights), actually *encourage* objectification and disempowerment.[62] A number of examples, both social and legal, can be cited. One powerful social example is the *Report of the Secretary's Task Force on Youth Suicide*—a nationwide survey commissioned by the United States Department of Health and Human Services.[63] The Report (published in 1989) concluded that young lesbians and gay men were two to three times more likely to attempt suicide than other young people in the USA; that lesbian and gay youth suicides may comprise up to 30 per cent of youth suicides in the United States each year; and that young lesbians and gay men often faced extreme physical and verbal abuse, rejection and isolation at the hands of their families and peers. By way of an explanation, the Report suggested that laws which prohibited same-sex sexual acts or singled out lesbians and gays for hostile treatment could cause particular misery to lesbian and gay teenagers by reinforcing their lack of self-esteem and the notion that it was socially acceptable for them to be attacked. Courts have also been sympathetic to the notion that hostile laws can have an adverse social impact. In *Norris* v. *Ireland*, in which the European Court of Human Rights concluded that an Irish law prohibiting consensual same-sex sexual acts violated Article 8 of the European Convention on Human Rights, the Court accepted that, even though the applicant had never actually been prosecuted for consenting homosexual activity, the mere existence of such a law—carrying with it the constant risk of prosecution—caused social anxiety, guilt and depression.[64] The South African Constitutional Court has recently been even more blunt. In ruling that it was unconstitutional for national immigration law to deny non-South African same-sex partners of

[62] For discussion of the social impact of law more generally, see Bamforth, *supra* n.3, ch. 8.

[63] See *Volume 3: Prevention and Interventions in Youth Suicide* (U.S. Department of Health and Human Services, 1989). This volume also contains reports of empirical work conducted by an official commission of inquiry in Massachusetts, and by the National Gay and Lesbian Task Force. Thomas, *supra* n.14 especially at 1485–6, develops the theory that laws which criminalise same-sex sexual acts legitimise anti-gay violence.

[64] *Supra* n.12.

South African citizens the same immigration rights as opposite-sex partners, Ackermann J. (for the Court) asserted in *National Coalition for Gay and Lesbian Equality* v. *Minister of Home Affairs* that:

> "The message [of the denials] is that gays and lesbians lack the inherent humanity to have their families and family lives in . . . same-sex relationships respected or protected. It serves in addition to perpetuate and reinforce existing prejudices and stereotypes. The impact [of the law] constitutes a crass, blunt, cruel and serious invasion of their dignity".[65]

The autonomy/empowerment argument can thus cater for both same-sex partnership rights and rights for individuals, and might be felt to avoid the other problems affecting the respect for privacy and equality arguments. Two possible objections to it must, however, be considered.[66] The first is that, in employing notions such as choice and consent, the argument wrongly assumes that these notions are unproblematical and easy to apply.[67] Difficult questions are, after all, involved in determining whether we can ever make an entirely free choice, whether a choice has been freely made in a given fact-situation, and so on. In the context of sexual activity and relationships, however, this objection could be said to be somewhat facile. For, while ideas of choice and consent may well be undermined by definitional uncertainty at a *general* level—and while a given individual's life may, because of their economic circumstances, education, health, etc., involve little choice all-things-considered—there are nonetheless *specific* points in just about everyone's life when decisions have to be made about matters of immediate and personal concern which, *relative to that person's circumstances*, do involve a clear choice. A good example would be what one eats for dinner within one's available budget. A person with little money and no education about dietary matters is likely, objectively-speaking, to have a poor set of options at this point—but, within their budgetary constraints, they do still have to make a positive choice *between* the options available to them.

[65] *Supra* n.47 at para. 54.

[66] David Richards' sympathetic questioning of the argument of this chapter "along two dimensions" (Introduction to Part I, text to n.4) can be dealt with relatively quickly. First, this chapter stakes no particular "claim to originality" in relation to the arguments of justice which are considered. The point is to analyse the strengths and weaknesses of arguments which appear to the author to be in general circulation. My book *Sexuality, Morals and Justice*, *supra* n.3, can, I hope, claim to be an original contribution insofar as it compares arguments of privacy, equality, immutability, gay liberation/queer theory and autonomy/empowerment *specifically* in relation to lesbian and gay rights claims, but I should immediately acknowledge that it has since been joined by David Richards' useful work *Identity and the Case for Gay Rights: Race, Gender, Religion as Analogies* (Chicago, University of Chicago Press, 1999), to which I pay tribute. Secondly, I agree with Richards' observation that gender stereotyping is closely connected with social disempowerment (I have sought to develop this point further myself, at least in relation to the comparative case law, in "Sexual Orientation Discrimination After *Grant* v. *South-West Trains*", (2000) 63 *Modern Law Review* 694) and might be used as specific evidence in support of the more general argument of this chapter.

[67] See D Herman's review of *Sexuality, Morals and Justice*, [1998] *Public Law* 689.

Sexual activity and sexual/emotional relationships generate similar specific choices. Regrettably, sexual coercion is widespread. Nonetheless, in the absence of physical, moral, social or economic coercion—and however little choice an individual may have in other areas of their life—people still regard themselves as having to make a choice when deciding whether to accept someone's sexual proposition, or an invitation to a romantic dinner, or a marriage proposal, or when deciding whether to make any of these suggestions or invitations to another person themselves. As with a choice concerning meals, the options on offer may not be particularly promising, but a choice is still required and in the absence of coercion, it would be patronising to those involved to argue any differently. Indeed, more *concentrated* choices are likely to be made concerning sexual acts and sexual/emotional relationships—given their intimate subject-matter—than would be made concerning meals and other non-intimate matters. It may also be fair to say that the concepts of choice and consent are likely to have far *greater* resonance for lesbians and gay men than for heterosexuals, given that in acknowledging their sexual orientation so many have had to make a *conscious* decision to brave prevailing currents of social hostility. In consequence, the first objection would seem to lack foundation in the context of sexual activity and sexual/emotional relationships.

The second objection is more fundamental. This objection—which, in relation to same-sex partnerships, could also be aimed at equality and some respect-for-privacy arguments—has been developed by a group of theorists known as "new natural lawyers", who maintain that same-sex sexual acts and relationships are inherently immoral. It will be suggested in the next section of this chapter, however, that this objection should be rejected; unless one shares the new natural lawyers' profoundly Roman Catholic view of the world, their argument is unappealing.

NEW NATURAL LAW

The new natural lawyers' views are encapsulated in the writings of John Finnis, Robert George and others.[68] Finnis, George and their supporters argue that same-sex sexual acts are wrongful because they violate the basic good or goods inherent in marital sexual acts of a potentially procreative variety. Indeed, *any* sexual act apart from vaginal intercourse between a married opposite-sex couple is wrongful according to this view, as is masturbation.[69] This conclusion is, of course, diametrically opposed to the first part of the autonomy/empowerment argument considered above. The new natural lawyers go on to claim that

[68] See, principally, J Finnis, "Law, Morality, and 'Sexual Orientation' ", (1993–4) 69 *Notre Dame Law Review* 1049; R George, *In Defense of Natural Law* (Oxford, Clarendon Press, 1999), especially chs. 8 (with G Bradley), 9 (with P Lee), 11, 15, and 16. For general discussion of what is "new" about this type of natural law theory, see George, *In Defense of Natural Law*, chs. 1 and 2.

[69] For a general summary, see George, *ibid*. at 161–2, 215.

while the criminal law should not completely prohibit private consensual sexual acts between persons of the same sex, the law can properly seek to discourage people from engaging in such acts and should not recognise same-sex partnerships.

As Finnis acknowledges, this argument requires us to confront an underlying question, namely "[w]hat is wrong with homosexual conduct?".[70] In answering this question, Finnis's (and the other new natural lawyers') methodology is based on his broader natural law theory, according to which natural law principles derive from indemonstrable, pre-moral propositions.[71] Finnis suggests that there is a set of basic goods—life, knowledge, play, aesthetic experience, friendship, practical reasonableness, and religion—which everyone uses in determining what they should do, regardless of their actual conclusions, and which are self-evident, intrinsic values which need no demonstration and which are desirable for their own sake.[72] The basic goods are thus categorised as pre-moral and objective. To be free and responsible, however, a person must be able to make rational choices about which basic goods to pursue and when. This, according to Finnis, is done using the requirements of practical reasonableness, which provide criteria for distinguishing between ways of acting which are morally right and morally wrong.[73] A decision concerning the basic goods therefore acquires moral force by *being* practically reasonable (and is immoral if it is not).[74]

The new natural lawyers argue that sexual acts between persons of the same sex go against a basic good or goods, and are therefore wrongful when evaluated from the standpoint of practical reasonableness. There may be some uncertainty, however, as to which basic goods are involved. Finnis initially appears to talk of heterosexual marriage as involving *two* basic goods—the production of children, as part of the basic human good of life, *and* the good of friendship, through the amalgamation of the lives of the marriage partners. However, he also talks of these as *aspects* of the marriage partners' shared common good *of marriage*,[75] implying that the common good of marriage is *itself* a basic good in addition to the list discussed above.[76] Robert George and Gerard Bradley favour this latter interpretation, and suggest that:

> "the intrinsic point of sex in any marriage, fertile or not, is, in our view, the basic good of marriage itself, considered as a two-in-one-flesh communion of persons that is consummated and actualized by [sexual] acts of the reproductive type. Such acts alone

[70] *Ibid.* at 1055

[71] *Natural Law and Natural Rights* (Oxford, Clarendon Press, 1980) at 29, 33.

[72] *Ibid.* at 22, 85–97.

[73] *Ibid.* at 23, 103.

[74] *Ibid.* at 101. For further details, see pp. 103–26.

[75] See, generally, Finnis, *supra* n.68 at 1064–7.

[76] Finnis suggests, in *Natural Law and Natural Rights*, that the list of seven basic goods is not exhaustive (*supra* n.71 above at 90–2). For the treatment of marriage as a basic good, see *supra* n.68 at 1070–1.

> among sexual acts can be truly unitive, and thus marital; and marital acts, thus understood, have their intelligibility and value intrinsically".[77]

Procreation is not, therefore, itself the point of marital sex; rather, children conceived during marital intercourse participate in the good of their parents' marriage.[78]

Finnis applies his view of the basic goods (however interpreted) to suggest that, "[t]he union of the reproductive organs of husband and wife really unites them biologically", allowing them to experience their "*real common good—their marriage* with the two goods, parenthood and friendship, which . . . are the parts of its wholeness as an intelligible common good".[79] Biological union must involve, Finnis argues, at least the possibility of procreation, and therefore entails "the inseminatory union of male genital organ with female genital organ". Even if this does not result in conception on most occasions when it occurs, it nonetheless unites husband and wife "biologically because it is the behavior which, as behavior, is suitable for generation".[80] In a similar vein, Patrick Lee and Robert George suggest that:

> "In reproductive activity the bodily parts of the male and the bodily parts of the female participate in a single action, coitus, which is oriented to reproduction (though not every act of coitus is reproductive) . . . Coitus is a unitary action in which the male and the female become literally one organism".[81]

A properly unitive sexual act must thus be the *type of act* which is, in general, capable of generating children between spouses—so even within marriage, acts of oral and anal sex go against the basic goods. Marriage is also, on this view, confined to opposite-sex partners.[82]

George and Bradley seek to reinforce these arguments by suggesting that another basic good (integrity) is also relevant. They claim that:

> "In choosing to perform non-marital orgasmic acts, including sodomitical acts . . . persons necessarily treat their bodies and those of their sexual partners (if any) as means or instruments in ways that damage their personal (and interpersonal) integrity; thus, regard for the basic human good of integrity provides a conclusive moral reason not to engage in sodomitical and other non-marital sex acts".[83]

According to this argument, the body may not be treated as a mere instrument without damaging a person's integrity as a unity of body, mind and spirit—and non-marital sexual acts and masturbation involve using the body in this way.[84] For George and Bradley believe that such acts are typically performed for pleasure.

[77] George, *supra* n.68 at 14.
[78] *Ibid*. at 141–2.
[79] Finnis, *supra* n.68 at 1066 (emphasis added). See also George, *supra* n.68 at 146–7, 168–70.
[80] Finnis, *supra* n.68 at 1066, n.46.
[81] George, *supra* n.68 at 168.
[82] Finnis, *supra* n.68 at 1067; see also George, *supra* n.68 at 161.
[83] George, *supra* n. 68 at 139.
[84] *Ibid*. at 147–51.

But pleasure (including sexual pleasure) cannot in itself provide a coherent moral basis for engaging in sexual activity, since it is an instrumental rather than a basic good.[85] Instead, the value of pleasure depends on the moral quality of the acts in which it is sought—hence "to simply instrumentalize intercourse to pleasure . . . is to vitiate its marital quality and damage the integrity of the genital acts even of spouses".[86]

George and Bradley suggest that it is for this reason that Finnis claims that attempts to promote the goods involved in marriage by any type of orgasmic non-marital sex are "simply an illusion".[87] In making this claim, Finnis argues that:

> "Reality is known in judgment, not in emotion, and *in reality*, whatever the generous hopes and dreams and thoughts of *giving* with which some same-sex partners may surround their sexual acts, those acts cannot express or do more than is expressed or done if two strangers engage in such activity to give each other pleasure, or a prostitute pleasures a client to give him pleasure in return for money, or (say) a man masturbates to give himself pleasure . . . there is no important distinction in essential moral worthlessness between solitary masturbation, being sodomized as a prostitute, and being sodomized for the pleasure of it".[88]

Whatever commitment partners of the same sex may feel towards one another, their union "can do no more than provide each partner with an individual gratification"—something which involves each in treating their bodies as instruments, conduct which "dis-integrates each of them precisely as acting persons".[89]

As mentioned above, the new natural lawyers do not believe that the law should be used to prohibit completely same-sex sexual activity. Rather, Finnis suggests that the law should seek to discourage such acts, which should not be prohibited if they occur in private.[90] For, while the state can monopolise the legitimate use of force—through law—it should not coerce people in matters of belief,[91] or in relation to private acts of virtue and vice (in this case, sexual activity).[92] Nonetheless, the common good of society would be overlooked if:

> "laws criminalizing private acts of sodomy between adults were to be struck down . . . on any ground which would also constitutionally require the law to tolerate the advertising or marketing of homosexual services, the maintenance of places of resort for homosexual activity, or the promotion of homosexualist 'lifestyles' via education and

[85] *Ibid.* at 141–2, 149, 162–7.
[86] *Ibid.* at 149.
[87] Finnis, *supra* n.68 at 1065. The point is discussed in George, *supra* n.68 at 148.
[88] Finnis, *supra* n.68 at 1067.
[89] *Ibid.* at 1066–7.
[90] *Ibid.* at 1070–1; see also Finnis's "Is Natural Law Theory Compatible with Limited Government?", in R George (ed.), *Natural Law, Liberalism and Morality* (Oxford, Clarendon Press, 1996). An analogous recognition of the limits of legal enforcement can be found in George, *supra* n.68 at 152–3.
[91] Finnis, *supra* n.68 at 1072.
[92] *Ibid.* at 1073–4, 1075–6.

public media of communication, or to recognize homosexual 'marriages' or promote the adoption of children by homosexually active people, and so forth".[93]

George and Bradley assert, seemingly for similar reasons, that the state can legitimately refuse to recognise same-sex partnerships.[94]

The new natural lawyers' arguments and conclusions are thus radically inconsistent with the autonomy/empowerment argument discussed above. It is submitted that their case can be rebutted, however, for it contains two related and, for present purposes, fundamental flaws.[95] The first is that the new natural lawyers' arguments appear to be circular *unless* it is acknowledged that they rest clearly on theological foundations. This is important since Finnis himself appears anxious to *deny* that his arguments are of a theological character. For he claims that he seeks to present "reflective, critical, publicly intelligible and rational" arguments for his conclusions concerning same-sex sexual acts and relationships,[96] and assumes that his arguments can provide a negative answer to the rhetorical question whether:

> "the judgment that [homosexual conduct] is morally wrong [is] inevitably a manifestation . . . of purely religious, theological, and sectarian belief which can ground no constitutionally valid determination disadvantaging those who do not conform to it?"[97]

A similar theme seems to run through George's work.[98] The new natural lawyers are, in consequence, faced with an unpalatable choice: they can either continue to claim to be offering a non-sectarian, constitutionally-oriented argument against legal recognition of same-sex partnerships (a claim which can be rebutted by analysis of their writings) or they can acknowledge that new natural law arguments plainly *do* depend for their analytical force upon a conservative version of Roman Catholic theology which, as we will see, is likely to prove unappealing to many.[99]

The true basis of new natural law arguments can be demonstrated by considering both the sources used by Finnis and George and the content of their substantive arguments. In relation to sources, Finnis certainly refers to the works of Socrates, Plato and Aristotle,[100] but Catholic teachings are used as authority for much of his argument, including the central parts considered here. For example, Finnis uses Catholic teachings to support his views concerning the place of sexual intercourse within marriage;[101] he acknowledges (as does George) that his

[93] Finnis, *supra* n.68 at 1076.

[94] George, *supra* n.68 at 139, 153.

[95] For more general criticism, see Bamforth, *supra* n.3 at 150–90.

[96] Finnis, *supra* n.68 at 1055

[97] *Ibid.*

[98] This seems to be an underpinning theme of *In Defense of Natural Law*, *supra* n.68.

[99] For a general illustration of these convictions, see Finnis's *Moral Absolutes: Tradition, Revision and Truth* (Washington, DC, Catholic University of America Press, 1990).

[100] Finnis, *supra* n.68 at 1063; see, more generally, the argument at 1055–63.

[101] *Ibid.* at 1063–76.

arguments about the "wrongfulness" of many sexual practices are an application of the theory developed by Germain Grisez in his work on moral theology;[102] and, in discussing the common good which the state is empowered and required to foster, Finnis bases his argument on the stipulations of the Second Vatican Council.[103] Meanwhile, having initially presented his arguments in non-sectarian terms, George later produces what appear to be just the same arguments as examples of the Catholic Church's teachings about sexual morality.[104]

More fundamentally, it is difficult to see how Finnis's and George's claims can make sense *in substance* as philosophical arguments unless their theological basis is acknowledged. The new natural lawyers' claims about sex and marriage provide a good example. A committed, monogamous same-sex relationship need not (as a question of fact) lack the companionship and mutual and exclusive commitment which Finnis claims are part of the good of marriage. For Finnis, George and Bradley, however, same-sex relationships involve disrespect for the basic goods because of the *inherently* marital nature of sex (from which flows their argument concerning dis-integrity). But the problem here is that, taken at face-value, their argument descends into self-justifying circularity. Finnis and his supporters would effectively be saying that a sexual/emotional relationship between partners of the *same* sex is morally inappropriate because sexual acts should only be performed between partners of the *opposite* sex who are married. When asked why this is, they would talk about the "intrinsic point" of marital sex, which can (again, why?) be the only "truly unitive" sexual act in view of the inherent nature of coitus. Presented in this way, their argument is self-referential and littered with unexplained references to what is "intrinsic", "real", or part of "reality". It can offer us no clear *normative* justification for claiming that morally legitimate sexual activity is confined to vaginal intercourse between opposite-sex spouses (and for defining marriage as being confined to persons of the opposite sex). It can only do this once we acknowledge that the reason *why* certain things are "intrinsic" or "real" is, for the new natural lawyers, to be found in Roman Catholic teaching concerning sexual morality.

We are thus left with the impression that Finnis's and George's claims—about "reality" or about the rightful purpose of sex—make little sense as reasoned arguments unless one shares their conservative Catholic theology. Despite Finnis's claim to be advancing a non-sectarian argument, an acknowledgement that his argument is sectarian is implicit in his comment (made in an earlier piece of work) that:

> "The . . . absoluteness of the properly . . . specified norm excluding adultery is found in the constant Christian tradition, from the beginning, against abortion, suicide, fornication, homosexual sex, and blasphemy and disclaimer of the faith. The tradition is massively solid".[105]

[102] *Ibid.* at 1063. See also the footnotes in George, *supra* n.68, chs. 8, 9.
[103] Finnis, *supra* n.68 at 1073.
[104] Compare George, *supra* n.68, chs. 8, 9, and pp. 290–4.
[105] Finnis, *supra* n.99 at 8–9.

Robert George concedes the point still more clearly. He and Gerard Bradley acknowledge that, given the indemonstrability of their claims, they might be "simply wrong in believing that marriage, as a one-flesh communion of persons, is possible".[106] George also acknowledges that:

> "It is entirely understandable that someone whose self-understanding is formed in accordance with the characteristically modern conception of human nature and the human good would be dubious about the proposition that there are morally compelling reasons for people who are not married, who cannot marry, or who, perhaps, merely prefer not to marry, to abstain from sexual relations . . . . The alternative conception of human nature and its fulfilment articulated in the natural law tradition (and embedded in one form or another in historic Jewish and Christian faith) enables people who critically appropriate it to understand themselves and their sexuality very differently".[107]

Thus, while the new natural lawyers claim to be providing an argument of general appeal against the legal recognition of same-sex partnerships, they fail in this objective since their argument actually rests on narrow, theological foundations. Without such foundations, their argument is circular. Once the foundations are acknowledged, however, the new natural lawyers' argument is likely to appeal only to those who share their religious convictions.

This brings us to the second flaw, which is that the new natural lawyers' argument is indeed likely to lack general appeal. For, as David Richards has argued, Finnis's:

> "moral terrain is a pre-Reformation world of self-evident moral truths that takes seriously neither the injustice and irreparable breakdown of that world nor our corresponding moral and political needs to construct a basis for community founded not on unbelievable moral certainties but on the common threads of reasonable belief and action on which free persons can base civility and the toleration of equal respect".[108]

Richards goes on to suggest that "even on their own sectarian terms", Finnis's writings in this area are "remarkably free of any close attention to history, to facts, or to ethically sensitive concern for persons as individuals".[109] This would appear to be borne out by the arguments we have considered. For, if Finnis and George are correct, then all sexual acts apart from vaginal sex between opposite-sex spouses count for nothing; they are morally "worthless" and involve the participants in pursuing an "illusion". This entails a condemnation of *all* sexual activity involving lesbians and gays (even those who are in the most committed sexual/emotional relationships), *all* sexual activity involving heterosexuals who are unmarried (even if they are in committed sexual/emotional relationships) and *all* sexual activity other than vaginal intercourse involving heterosexual couples who are married, as well as *all* acts of masturbation. Indeed, George is

[106] George, *supra* n.68 at 145.
[107] George, *supra* n.68 at 284.
[108] Richards, *supra* n.32 at 471.
[109] *Ibid*. at 468.

willing to accept this conclusion even though he believes "that genuine homosexual orientation exists".[110]

The new natural lawyers are, in short, prepared to dismiss the most personal and intimate feelings of many millions of people because of their failure to match up to a set of pre-ordained, absolute moral rules which make little sense unless one subscribes to a particular brand of conservative theology. Religious believers are entitled morally to disapprove of other people's sexual activity, but it is quite another thing to use this disapproval in order to justify the legal regime which Finnis and George are advocating. If the merits of such a regime seem obvious to Finnis and George, it is only because of their unquestioning and inflexible conservative theology. Their disregard for the feelings and experiences of so many human beings—which are valuable and important to their holders—implies a complete lack of concern for the diversity of human experience and a blind determination to fit the world into a prescribed 'reality', as constructed according to their religious beliefs.[111] This being so, it is submitted that the new natural lawyers cannot provide an effective answer to the autonomy/empowerment argument.

CONCLUSION: THE PRACTICAL ROLE OF ARGUMENTS OF JUSTICE

Of the three philosophical arguments which might be used in support of granting legal recognition to same-sex partnerships, it has been asserted that the third argument, that of autonomy/empowerment, is clearly the strongest. Furthermore, the flaws in the new natural lawyers' case against legal recognition (and other forms of legal protection for lesbians and gays) are such that their arguments are unappealing unless one shares their particular religious beliefs. Autonomy/empowerment should, on this basis, be advanced as the main philosophical argument of justice in favour of according legal recognition to same-sex partnerships, whether or not this is tied to the promotion of equality as a social goal. At the philosophical level, this argument can therefore be used to inform political debate, and particularly (in countries without a written constitution) debates about whether the legislature should grant statutory protection to same-sex partnerships.

However, the constitutional provisions in force in any given society may compromise the extent to which autonomy can be of use. If, for example, there is no specific *constitutional* right to autonomy (or its near sibling, dignity) in the society concerned, it may be necessary to frame claims for legal recognition of same-sex partnerships, whether this is to be achieved through litigation or legislation, in terms of the constitutional rights which *are* recognised. To do otherwise would be excessively purist, and in practice it may not involve the complete

[110] George, *supra* n.68 at 281.

[111] See S Macedo's similar criticisms in "Homosexuality and the Conservative Mind", (1995) 84 *Georgetown Law Journal* 261 at 284–5, 292–3.

abandonment of autonomy since, as we have seen, many respect-for-privacy and equality arguments could in fact be said to have their roots in autonomy or dignity. Finally, in the case of litigation, it is fair to expect that any court's perception, of how far the constitution or rules it is required to interpret allow it to make decisions which may be perceived as being of a "controversial" or "progressive" nature, is likely to affect its willingness, in litigation concerning same-sex partnerships, to make decisions which grant substantive protections to same-sex couples in the absence of legislative intervention. In consequence, the arguments of justice which are in play can either be curtailed by judicial concern for constitutional principles such as the separation of powers (however this is interpreted), or can be used to justify the adoption by the court of a "progressive" stance even in the face of such concerns. Arguments of justice, at both levels, are thus central to claims for the legal recognition of same-sex partnerships.

3

The Limitations of Liberal Neutrality Arguments in Favour of Same-Sex Marriage

CHAI R FELDBLUM*

INTRODUCTION

THERE ARE MANY ways one can talk about the desire on the part of gay couples to get married. The most common approach, used by political liberal advocates of same-sex marriage, is to argue that marriage is a "right" that should be made available to same-gender couples, on the same grounds as it is made available to opposite-gender couples. An assessment of whether marriage is a normative good, or of the potential moral consequences of gay couples achieving the right to marry, is either ignored or relegated to a marginal place in such discussions.

By contrast, the most common approach used by opponents of same-sex marriage is to argue that if marriage is made available to same-gender couples, the institution of marriage will be radically redefined and the moral foundations of society will be irrevocably shattered. The moral normative good of marriage, and the inherent incapacity of gay couples to embody such a moral normative good, stands at the very core of this concern and argument on the part of opponents of same-sex marriage.

There is a third, less common, approach to same-sex marriage articulated by some gay rights advocates. These advocates engage directly with the question of whether marriage for same-gender couples is a normative good and with the societal implications of gay people achieving the right to marry.

I believe it is useful— indeed critical—that a discussion of marriage for same-gender couples include a discussion of the normative moral good or harm of marriage, and of the potential moral consequences of gay couples achieving the right to marry. But I do not believe engaging in such a discussion must necessarily lead to the complete embrace or rejection of a traditional view of marriage. Indeed, a key intellectual benefit of engaging in such a conversation is that

* Professor of Law, Georgetown University Law Center. Many thanks to Lisa Mottet for helping me excerpt this piece from a longer paper on the "Normative Good of Same-Sex Marriage".

it allows us (indeed forces us) to question, consider, and analyse what we believe to be the normative good of marriage. The understanding of the normative good that might result from such an exploration may be conservative, radical, progressive—or some combination of the three.

In this chapter, I explore how liberal neutrality principles have dominated the discourse of most advocates of same-sex marriage, and how such principles are explicitly or implicitly rejected by those who oppose same-sex marriage. In particular, I explore the presence and ramifications of such principles in the discourse of Members of Congress debating the Defense of Marriage Act. While I leave to a longer version of this chapter an argument for the normative good of marriage, this chapter lays the foundation for that conversation.

LIBERAL NEUTRALITY ARGUMENTS

The most common way political advocates discuss the effort to achieve same-sex marriage is to talk about equality, fairness, and the simple "right to marry". In an early advocacy piece, entitled "Why Gay People Should Seek the Right to Marry", Tom Stoddard made the following point:

> "First, and most basically, the issue is not the desirability of marriage, but rather the desirability of the *right* to marry. That I think two lesbians or two gay men should be entitled to a marriage license does not mean that I think all gay people should find appropriate partners and exercise the right, should it eventually exist".[1]

Using the terminology of simple equality is commonplace in the political discourse surrounding efforts to achieve recognition of marriage for same-gender couples. A good example is the Marriage Resolution, circulated by the Marriage Project of the Lambda Legal Defense and Education Fund and endorsed by a range of organisations. This Resolution states:

> "Because marriage is a basic human right and an individual personal choice, RESOLVED, the State should not interfere with same-gender couples who choose to marry and share fully and equally in the rights, responsibilities, and commitment of civil marriage".[2]

This resolution has been endorsed by religious organisations, civil rights organisations, and individuals. The resolution itself commits the endorsers to no particular view on the normative good of marriage, nor does it explicitly commit the endorsers to a view that gay relationships and gay sex are normative goods. Rather, it states a simple principle of neutral equality: marriage is a basic

[1] T Stoddard, "Why Gay People Should Seek the Right to Marry," in WB Rubenstein (ed.), *Sexual Orientation and the Law* (St.Paul, MI, West Publishing, 1997) at 716, 720 (reprinting OUT\LOOK, Fall 1989, at 8).

[2] Lambda Legal Defense and Education Fund, *Marriage Resolution* <http://www.lambdalegal.org/cgi-bin/pages/documents/record?record=142>.

human right and the State should allow any two people who wish to exercise that right to do so.

This emphasis on choice and equality as essential bases for extending a right to marry to gay couples is repeated by advocates of marriage for same-sex couples in both academic writings and in the mainstream press. Evan Wolfson, a tireless, intelligent, and forceful proponent of extending equal marriage rights to gay couples,[3] made this point clearly in an article addressing the "intra-community critique" of seeking the right to marry:

> "The court [in *Baehr* v. *Lewin*] grasped what many even in our own community have not: the fundamental issues in these cases are choice and equality, not the pros and cons of a way of life, or even the 'right' choice".[4]

A key component of the equality argument is an emphasis on the myriad functional benefits marriage brings to heterosexual couples, and the concomitant denial of such benefits to similarly-situated gay couples.[5] The range of benefits dependent on marriage are recounted to emphasise the unfairness of denying gay people the *choice* to enter the status of marriage, should they so desire.[6] The equality being denied, in other words is the denial of an important, substantive right.

Advocates who emphasise equality as a basis for justifying marriage of same-gender couples are not unaware of the tremendous transformative potential—to the institution of marriage itself and to the status of gay people—that inheres in same-gender couples achieving the right to marry. For example, Evan Wolfson acknowledges "marriage's central symbolic importance in our society and culture", and not only recognises, but applauds, the "transformational potential of gay people's inclusion . . . in marriage".[7]

[3] Evan Wolfson established and is the director of the Marriage Project at the Lambda Legal Defense and Education Fund. He was until April 2001 also co-counsel in the case of *Baehr* v. *Lewin*, which achieved preliminary success in challenging the denial of marriage licenses to same-gender couples in Hawaii. See *Baehr* v. *Lewin*, 852 P.2d 44, clarified, 852 P.2d 74 (Hawaii Supreme Court 1993); Wolfson, chap. 9.

[4] E Wolfson, "Crossing the Threshold: Equal Marriage Rights for Lesbians and Gay Men and the Intra-Community Critique", (1994–5) 21 *New York University Review of Law and Social Change* 567 at 580.

[5] For example, David Chambers has documented the extensive economic and social benefits that accrue through the status of marriage. See DL Chambers, "What If? The Legal Consequences of Marriage and the Legal Needs of Lesbian and Gay Couples", (1996) 95 *Michigan Law Review* 447 at 452–485. Others have also emphasised the practical benefits marriage can provide gay couples. See, e.g., Wolfson, *supra* n.4 at 580 n.55.

[6] See WN Eskridge, Jr., *The Case for Same-Sex Marriage: From Sexual Liberty to Civilized Commitment* (New York, Free Press, 1996) at 67 ("[W]hen the state denies lesbian and gay couples a marriage license, it is not just denying them a simple, one-shot right to marry. Rather, the state is also denying those couples dozens of ongoing rights and privileges that are by law associated with marriage").

[7] Wolfson, *supra* n.4, at 580, 597. One aspect of the transformative potential, to which Wolfson refers, is the dramatic challenge same-gender marriages pose to the strict gender roles and power differentials that often occur within opposite-gender marriages.

But Wolfson and his co-counsel did not argue, before the courts in *Baehr*, that the government should provide marriage licenses to same-gender couples in *order* to convey approval of gay relationships and gay conduct. Presumably, they would never make such an argument. These lawyers argued, in response to the State of Hawaii's claim that recognising same-sex marriages will be harmful to children and society, that same-sex marriages are indeed good—for both the couples involved and for their children.[8] But this line of argument is different from arguing that the *reason* the government should recognize same-sex marriage in the first place is in *order* to signal approval of same-sex relationships.

Advocates engaging in such arguments are not being disingenuous. The analysis these advocates use comports with a widely-accepted form of liberal political theory that believes political discourse should be concerned with "rights," not with conceptions of the "good". According to this view, by dint of our living in a pluralist society, individuals in our society will necessarily hold divergent normative and moral beliefs. Thus, the role of government is to ensure that individual rights, within this pluralist society, are adequately safeguarded—and not to take action that affirmatively advances one moral, normative view of "the good" over others.[9]

Under this view, governmental actions may, of course, serve as a catalyst for substantive, social change. Indeed, advocates of liberal neutrality may even applaud such changes as consistent with their own personal, normative views of the good. But such advocates would never assert that the legitimate *reason* for the government to have taken the action in the first place was *in order* to achieve the particular normative end that happened to be consistent with their personal conception of the good. Rather, the legitimate reason for the government's action—and indeed, the *only* legitimate reason for governmental action—is to ensure *equality* among its citizens.[10]

[8] *Baehr* v. *Miike*, 1996 WL 694235 at *9–12 (Hawaii Circuit Court 1996) (summarising testimony of plaintiffs' witnesses that "gay and lesbian parents and same-sex couples are as fit and l oving parents as non-gay persons and different-sex couples", and noting the opinion of one of plaintiff's witnesses that "allowing same-sex couples to marry would have a positive impact on society and the institution of marriage"). See *supra* n.3.

[9] See J Rawls, *Political Liberalism* (New York, Columbia University Press, 1993) at 173–211; R Dworkin, *Taking Rights Seriously* (Cambridge, Harvard University Press, 1977) at 90–100; BA Ackerman, *Social Justice in the Liberal State* (New Haven, Yale University Press, 1980) at 349–78. For commentators who have analysed political liberal theory in the context of same-sex marriage, see C Ball, "Moral Foundations for a Discourse on Marriage for Same-Sex Couples: Looking Beyond Political Liberalism", (1997) 85 *Georgetown Law Journal* 1871 (analysing theories of political liberalism offered by Rawls and Dworkin); MC Regan, "Reason, Tradition, and Family Law: A Comment on Social Constructionism", (1993) 79 *Virginia Law Review* 1515 at 1518 (noting that "neutrality liberalism" requires the state to be "neutral among different conceptions of the good life").

[10] I recognise that using the term "equality" is a simplification of the more nuanced approaches that have been developed within political liberalism. Nevertheless, I believe the term captures generally the essential theme of political liberalism.

Note, for example, Wolfson's official response to the State's argument that "allowing same-sex couples to marry conveys in socially, psychologically, and otherwise important ways approval of non-heterosexual orientations and behaviors":[11]

> "This pernicious asserted State interest is neither 'compelling' nor legitimate. It is not for the State to approve or disapprove of 'non-heterosexual orientations and behaviors'; indeed, under our constitutional scheme, the State has no business dictating an orthodoxy or ideology of superiority or subordination, whether in creed, religion, sexual orientation, gender or race. The State has even less business enforcing its approval by stigmatizing a particular group or class, branding its members second-class citizens, or denying their right to marry and participate equally in society".[12]

Thus, Wolfson's response to his opponents is not "yes, your feared result is exactly the result we want government to advance on our behalf." Rather, his response is that government must act neutrally with regard to all its citizens.[13]

A similar view of the state is articulated by William Eskridge. How, Eskridge asks, should the state "deal with people who dislike each other?"[14] Eskridge's answer is straightforward:

> "In my view, the state should neither encourage nor tolerate intergroup discrimination. The only productive way is to tell each group that the state will treat both with strict equality and will not tolerate intrusions by one group into the other's liberties".[15]

This view of the state underlies Eskridge's response to the argument that allowing same-gender couples to marry would represent governmental approval or endorsement of the underlying gay relationship. Eskridge rejects this "stamp-of-approval argument",[16] as he calls it, by observing that "the state is not a bit choosy about who can marry," and that anyone from convicted rapists and child molesters to deadbeat dads are routinely given marriage licences by government clerks.[17] Eskridge's conclusion is that:

> "It is fanciful to think that the state's issuance of a marriage license is a signal of anything beyond the couple's ability to fill out a form. A church's decision to bless a marriage typically has normative significance as to the particular marriage, but the state's decision to issue a license does not".[18]

[11] Wolfson, *supra* n.4 at 577.

[12] *Ibid.* at 577 n.45 (citations omitted).

[13] In fairness to Wolfson, and to other litigators, such individuals are operating within a legal system that they (and most others) understandably perceive to be premised on liberal neutrality principles. Hence, it is not surprising that the legal arguments that litigators who wish to win their cases use match those principles well.

[14] Eskridge, *supra* n.6 at 8, 51–2, 88.

[15] *Ibid.* at 190.

[16] *Ibid.* at 105.

[17] *Ibid.* at 106–7 ("However evil, perverted, or incompetent you might be, the clerk will still give you the marriage license, because the clerk and the state do not care about your character, morality, or competence").

[18] *Ibid.* at 105.

This discourse of liberal neutrality, which views equality as both the reason to seek the status of marriage, as well as the sole legitimate reason for government to grant such status to same-gender couples, is agnostic on whether marriage itself is a normative good. Nor does this discourse require a normative view on the goodness of the relationship of the same-gender couple, including any sex such a couple might engage in. Such assessments are irrelevant. The very basis of the discourse assumes that members of the public, and the legislators they elect, might well view gay couples and gay sex with disgust, repulsion, or simple discomfort. But that is all of no matter. Under this theory, the governmental action of granting a marriage license to a same-gender couple signals no more approval of the act of gay sex or the group of gay couples, than the governmental action of granting a marriage license to a convicted rapist signals approval of the act of rape or the group of rapists.

There is a variant of liberal neutrality discourse which does not appear to be as agnostic on the normative good of marriage. Many supporters of same-sex marriage who engage in liberal neutrality discourse seem to have little difficulty in accepting, either implicitly or explicitly, the background societal view that marriage itself is a normative good. These supporters, however, do believe the state must remain resolutely neutral on whether *homosexuality* is a normative good. This variant of liberal neutrality discourse is quite common among non-gay, political supporters of same-sex marriage.[19]

Of course, it should come as no surprise to observers of the American political scene that arguments based on liberal neutrality dominate the discourse when a minority seeks to secure rights from a dominant majority. Such arguments resonate deeply with the American people. There is an inchoate, yet real, sense in this country that America is a land of freedom, equality, and fairness. Many Americans believe (or seem to want to believe) that an essential element of our country's history, integrity, and even legacy is our commitment to fairness and equality for all our citizens, despite our differences and diversity.[20]

There is an additional perceived strength in the arguments of liberal neutrality. Framing the debate as a fight for "equal marriage rights", rather than as a fight dependent in any way on endorsement of the underlying same-sex relationships, allows supporters of marriage for gay people to sidestep any difficult questions that may arise regarding the morality of gay sex and gay relationships. Such an outcome is perceived to be welcome if advocates are unsure how a majority of the public might feel about the morality of gay people or gay sex.

My assertion is not that advocates who employ liberal neutrality arguments do so *because* they are afraid of the majority's views of gay people and gay sex.

[19] Indeed, the signatories to the Marriage Resolution circulated by Lambda probably fall into this category.

[20] See JR Pole, *The Pursuit of Equality in American History* (Berkeley, University of California Press, 1993) at 1–97; RJ Harris, *The Quest for Equality* (Baton Rouge, Louisiana State University Press, 1960) at 1–23. See also CR Feldblum, "Sexual Orientation, Morality, and the Law: Devlin Revisited" (1996) 57 *University of Pittsburgh Law Review* 237 at 298–304 (discussing reasons why people use neutrality arguments).

Most advocates employ such arguments because they intuitively believe these are the appropriate arguments to use in our democratic republic. And they certainly have a distinguished roll-call of political theorists to back them up in such a belief.[21] My assertion is simply that such advocates are not *dismayed* by the fact that the political discourse they use (and which they believe everyone else is, or should be, using) allows—indeed requires—governmental actors to sidestep any normative assessments about gay people and gay sex.

THE REALITY OF LEGISLATIVE DEBATE

In 1996, the United States Congress entered the debate on same-sex marriage with consideration and passage of the Defense of Marriage Act (DOMA).[22] DOMA was brought up for consideration several months before the Presidential election in November 1996, and was presented as a necessary defensive maneuver in light of the ongoing litigation in Hawaii which presaged the recognition of same-sex marriages.[23]

The first section of DOMA amended the statutory provision implementing the "full faith and credit" clause of the Constitution and provided that no state would be required to give effect to a same-sex marriage were such a marriage to be recognized in another state.[24] The second section provided that, any time the term "marriage" appeared in federal law, it would mean "only a legal union between one man and one woman as husband and wife", and that any time the term "spouse" appeared, it would mean only "a person of the opposite-sex who is a husband or a wife".[25] Thus, upon passage of DOMA, even if the law of a particular state recognized spouses of the same sex, federal law would not.

The main argument levied against DOMA by opponents of the legislation was that the legislation was "political" and gratuitous. The opponents' rationale was that there was no immediate danger that any state would recognize marriage between same-sex couples in the near future.[26] Moreover, if legislators truly cared about defending marriage and the American family, there were

[21] See *supra* n.9.

[22] Introduced as HR 3396 in the United States House of Representatives and S 1740 in the United States Senate, the Defense of Marriage Act ("DOMA") was signed by President William Clinton on September 21, 1996 as Pub L 104 199, 110 Stat. 2419 (1996).

[23] See 142 *Congressional Record* S12015 (daily ed. 30 Sep. 1996) (statement of Sen. Abraham); 142 *Congressional Record* H7441 (daily ed. 11 July 1996) (statement of Rep. Canady) ("It appears that gay rights lawyers are soon likely to win the right for homosexuals to marry in Hawaii, and that they will attempt to 'nationalize' that anticipated victory under force of the Full Faith and Credit Clause of the U.S. Constitution").

[24] Defense of Marriage Act, Pub L 104–199, s. 2(a), 110 Stat. 2419, 2419 (1996) (amending 28 USC s. 1738).

[25] *Ibid*. s. 3(a), 110 Stat at 2419 (amending 1 USC s. 7).

[26] The only State that had moved toward such recognition was the State of Hawaii. *Baehr* v. *Lewin*, see *supra* n.3, was pending in the trial court during the DOMA debate. Even if the State were to lose at both the trial and appellate levels, a final ruling in the case—and hence, the reality of same-sex marriage—would not have been realized for a minimum of one to two years.

numerous other social and economic changes Congress could enact—everything from health care reform to violence prevention—that would be more effective in helping families survive than would passage of DOMA.[27] Thus, clearly, the sole reason DOMA was being pushed forward in the months prior to the November 1996 election was to force President Clinton to make a difficult political decision, to force other Democrats who had indicated support for gay equality to take a difficult political stance as well, and generally to create a "wedge issue" in the upcoming election.[28]

The attack on the political motivations of DOMA supporters was consistent with the primary message gay and lesbian political groups were presenting to Members of Congress. For example, press releases and statements from the Human Rights Campaign (HRC), a political advocacy group on gay and lesbian issues, emphasized the political motivation behind introduction and consideration of DOMA, and the legislation's irrelevance to the many pressing economic and social issues facing the country. Stickers prepared by HRC, and worn by sympathetic lobbyists during hearings and votes on DOMA, read: "Don't They Have Anything Better to Do?"[29]

The political argument against DOMA was supplemented by prudential and constitutional concerns. One argument was that the first section of DOMA, which allows a state to ignore same-sex marriages recognised in another state, was unnecessary because all states were already allowed, under accepted legal doctrines, to ignore marriages from other states that violated their public

[27] See 142 *Congressional Record* at S10112 (daily ed. 10 Sept. 1996) (statement of Sen. Boxer) ("I can truly say if we want to defend marriage, we should be discussing ways that truly help lift the strains and stresses on marriage."); at S10107 (statement of Sen. Kerry) ("If this were truly a defense of marriage act, it would expand the learning experience for would-be husbands and wives. It would provide for counseling for all troubled marriages, not just for those who can afford it. It would provide treatment on demand for those with alcohol and substance abuse. . . It would guarantee day care for every family that struggles and needs it. . . ."); 142 *Congressional Record* at H7273 (daily ed. 11 July 1996) (statement of Rep. Schroeder) ("I had an amendment [to DOMA] saying 'The real defense of marriage would be to say at the Federal level you don't give benefits to the next marriage until the person who left that marriage has dealt with the first one in a property settlement based on fault.' . . . If we really want to defend marriage in this country, then say to people, when you make that commitment, you have to mean that commitment. And even if you want to leave that commitment, you may be able to leave it physically, but you cannot shed it economically.").

[28] See 142 *Congressional Record* at H7272 (daily ed. 11 July 1996) (statement of Rep. Moakley) ("This issue . . . divides our country when we should be brought together; and frankly, it appears to be a political attempt to sling arrows at President Clinton."); at H7277 (statement of Rep. Woolsey) ("Mr. Speaker, welcome to the campaign headquarters of the radical right. You see, knowing that the American people overwhelmingly rejected their deep cuts in Medicare and education, their antifamily agenda and their assault on our environment, the radical right went mucking around in search of an election year ploy [DOMA] to divide our country."); at H7278 (statement of Rep. Frank) ("No one in the world believes this [legislation] is not political."); 142 *Congressional Record* at S10115 (daily ed. 10 Sept. 1996) (statement of Sen. Mikulski) ("We should recognize the politics behind this debate. It is an effort to make Members of Congress take an uncomfortable vote. It is an effort to put the President and Democrats on the spot, and at odds with a group of voters who have traditionally supported the President and the Democratic Party.").

[29] Sticker on file with author. I served as a legislative consultant to the HRC from 1993 to 1998, and was serving in that capacity during HRC's efforts to oppose DOMA. I was thus significantly involved in crafting various legal/political materials opposing DOMA.

policy.[30] A second argument was that, even assuming States might be required under the federal Constitution's Full Faith and Credit Clause to recognise same-sex marriages from other States, Congress did not have the constitutional power to pass a statute effectively allowing States to ignore such marriages.[31] Indeed, reading the "effects" language of the Full Faith and Credit Clause as granting Congress such authority—which is what supporters of DOMA were urging[32]—would create, according to the opponents of the bill, a horrific precedent for Congress.[33]

The charge against DOMA was, thus, dominated by attacks on the political motivations of the bill's supporters, and by legalistic arguments regarding the lack of necessity, unconstitutionality, and precedential harm of DOMA.[34] There was little, if no, argument that marriage was a normatively good status that government should encourage same-gender couples to achieve, just as it encourages opposite-gender couples to marry, or that gay relationships are a

[30] See, e.g., testimony of Professor Cass Sunstein before the Senate Judiciary Committee, 11 July 1996 (reprinted in 142 *Congressional Record* S10112 (daily ed. 10 Sept. 1996)) ("The two Restatements [of Conflicts] show that it is long-standing practice for interested states to deny validity to marriages that violate their own public policy"). Evan Wolfson was displeased with this argument because, from his perspective, it was an open question whether States could invoke a "public policy" exception against recognition of same-sex marriages from other States. Many Members of Congress opposing DOMA, however, perceived the argument that the bill was "unnecessary" as an equally (if not more) compelling argument than the fact that the bill might be "unconstitutional."

[31] See, e.g., Letter from Professor Laurence H Tribe to Rep. Edward M. Kennedy 1–2 (24 May 1996) ("[M]y conclusion is unequivocal: Congress possesses no power under any provision of the Constitution to legislate any such categorical exemption from the Full Faith and Credit Clause of Article IV.") (on file with author); 142 *Congressional Record* S10102 (daily ed. 10 Sept. 1996) (statement of Sen. Kennedy) (noting that both Professor Tribe and "conservative constitutional scholar Cass Sunstein" believe DOMA to be unconstitutional); 142 *Congressional Record* at H7485 (daily ed. 12 July 1996) (statement of Rep. Frank) ("Congress cannot grant a power to the States which, under the Constitution, the Congress itself does not have or control.").

[32] Art. IV, s. 1 of the US Constitution states: "Full faith and credit shall be given in each state to the public acts, records, and judicial proceedings of every other state. And the Congress may by general laws prescribe the manner in which such acts, records, and proceedings shall be proved, and the effect thereof." See 142 *Congressional Record* at S10101 (daily ed. 10 Sept. 1996) (statement of Sen. Lott) ("No one should doubt that Congress does have the authority to act. The same article of the Constitution that calls for 'full faith and credit' for State court decisions also gives Congress the power to decide how that provision will be implemented. . . . 'And the effect thereof.' Those words make clear what the Framers of the Constitution intended").

[33] See, e.g., Letter from LH Tribe, *supra* n.31, at 3–4 ("[T]he proposed measure would create a precedent dangerous to the very idea of a *United* States of America. For if Congress may exempt same-sex marriage from full faith and credit, then Congress may also exempt from the mandate of the Full Faith and Credit Clause *whatever* category of judgments. . . .") (emphasis in original); Feldblum, "The 'Defense of Marriage Act': A Constitutional Problem", (prepared on behalf of HRC, Summer 1996) at 2 (on file with author) ("Once Congress decides that sentence two of the Full Faith and Credit Clause gives it the power to create a "*Some* Full Faith and Credit" Clause, Congress must expect a range of interest groups to line up, clamoring for Congress to exercise this new-found power.") (emphasis in original).

[34] While arguments about political motivations are not liberal neutrality arguments *per se*, these arguments did allow opponents of DOMA to move their part of the debate away from a conversation about the normative value of same-gender relationships and on to a conversation about political grandstanding.

normative good that government should support and encourage by making the institution of marriage available to gay couples.

Actually, opponents of DOMA never stated that marriage itself was *not* a normative good. Indeed, most opponents of DOMA agreed, either implicitly or explicitly, with proponents of DOMA that marriage for opposite-gender couples was an important societal institution that the government should support.[35] But opponents of DOMA never argued that marriage was a normative good the state should support, *and* that the love between same-gender couples was a normative good the state should equally support—for example, through ensuring such couples access to the important and good institution of marriage. Thus, the arguments presented by most opponents of DOMA fit the second variant of liberal neutrality discourse I describe above.

Lest the reader presume I was an innocent bystander during the development of these legalistic arguments on DOMA, let me be clear. As a legal consultant to the Human Rights Campaign, I was an active participant in developing and shaping the legal arguments opposing DOMA. And the memos I produced for the legislative debate focused primarily on the unconstitutionality of the legislation, not on the normative good of either marriage or same-sex relationships.[36] In one set of "talking points" regarding DOMA, I did state that "[t]he *moral* position is to validate the effort of two people [of the same sex] to commit themselves to each other in a caring, loving, and responsible manner," and "[t]hat's why marriage is a good thing—*for everybody*".[37] But I quickly followed those statements with the assertion that "one can be *strongly* against the right of two people of the same sex to marry—and still be *strongly* against the so-called "Defense of Marriage Act", based on constitutional and prudential reasons.[38]

The constitutional and prudential arguments that legal scholars, including me, made repeatedly to Congress were thus reflected in the Congressional debate on DOMA. By contrast, arguments about the normative moral good of same-sex relationships were hardly made either by advocates or by Members of Congress. Indeed, the prudential and constitutional arguments against DOMA that we offered to Congress allowed Members to state, simultaneously, that they did not support same-sex marriage and yet they opposed DOMA. As Senator John Kerry (D-MA) observed:

[35] See *supra* n.27 and accompanying text.

[36] See Feldblum, *supra* n.33 (noting Congress lacks constitutional authority to amend the Full Faith and Credit Clause to allow states to ignore judgments and proceedings that would otherwise deserve full faith and credit); Feldblum, "The 'Defense of Marriage Act': A Host of Problems", (prepared on behalf of HRC, Summer 1996) (on file with author) (noting both unconstitutionality and lack of necessity of DOMA); Feldblum, "Talking Points on DOMA," (prepared on behalf of HRC, Summer 1996) (on file with author) (providing several arguments against DOMA).

[37] Feldblum, "Talking Points", *supra* n.36 at 2 (emphasis in original). I am convinced that the only reason my political talking points ever included such a statement in the first place is because of the academic work I had done, reflecting on the possible limitations of liberal neutrality discourse. See Feldblum, *supra* n.20; see also Feldblum, "The Moral Rhetoric of Legislation", (1997) 72 *New York University Law Review* 992.

[38] Feldblum, "Talking Points", *supra* n.36 at 2 (emphasis in original).

"I am not for same-sex marriage . . . I will vote against this bill, though I am not for same-sex marriage, because I believe this debate is fundamentally ugly, and it is fundamentally political, and it is fundamentally flawed".[39]

Not surprisingly, the few references to gay relationships made by opponents of DOMA that included some recognition of the normative good of same-gender relationships came from the three openly gay Members of Congress who referred to their personal relationships. For example, Congressman Studds used his personal relationship as the basis for a pitch for fairness and equality to his colleagues:

"For the last six years, as many Members of this House know, I have been in a relationship as loving, as caring, as committed, as nurturing and celebrated and sustained by our extended families as that of any Member of this House. My partner, Dean, whom a great many of you know and I think a great many of you love, is in a situation which no spouse of any Member of this House is in. . . . The spouse of every Member of this House is entitled to that Member's health insurance, even after that Member dies. . . . That is not true of my partner. The spouse of every Member of this House knows that if he or she is predeceased by their spouse . . . they have a pension. I have paid every single penny as much as every Member of this House has for that pension, but my partner, should he survive me, is not entitled to one penny. I do not think that is fair. . . I do not believe most Americans think that is fair".[40]

Similarly, Congressman Barney Frank talked about his personal relationship in his effort to understand why Members of Congress believed marriages between opposite-gender couples needed to be "defended" against recognition of marriage for same-gender couples:

"This is the most preposterous assertion of all, that marriage is under attack. . . . How does the fact that I love another man and live in a committed relationship with him threaten your marriage? . . . What is attacking you? You have an emotional commitment to another man or another woman. You want to live with that person. You want to commit yourselves legally. I say I do not share that commitment. I do not know why. That is how I was born. That is how I grew up. I find that kind of satisfaction in committing myself and being responsible for another human being who happens to be a man, and this threatens you"?[41]

[39] 142 *Congressional Record* at S10107 (daily ed. 10 Sept. 1996) (statement of Sen. Kerry). Several other Members of Congress made the same point. See, e.g., at S10117 (statement of Sen. Feinstein) ("I personally believe that the legal institution of marriage is the union between a man and a woman. But, as a matter of public policy, I oppose this legislation [because] . . . it set[s] a very bad precedent . . . and it is unnecessary."). See also at S10113 (statement of Sen. Boxer) ("This vote isn't about how I feel on the issue of gay marriage.").

[40] 142 *Congressional Record* at H7277–78 (daily ed. 11 July 1996) (statement of Rep. Studds).

[41] *Ibid.* at H7278 (statement of Rep. Frank). Congressman Steve Gunderson also referred to his personal relationship, although in a statement inserted in the Congressional Record, and not read out loud: "I have a 13 year relationship with my partner. Yet, while some of my congressional colleagues are in their second or third marriage—their spouse receives the benefits of their health insurance and automatically receives their survivor benefits should that occur. Why should they be given these benefits, when my partner—in a relationship much longer than theirs—is denied the same?" 142 *Congressional Record* at H7492 (daily ed. 12 July 1996) (statement of Rep. Gunderson).

Although Congressmen Studds, Frank, and a few others talked about the value and commitments of same-gender relationships, their statements were still situated primarily in the context of liberal neutrality arguments. For example, Congressman Studds talked about the *unfairness* of his partner, Dean, being denied benefits. Studds did not tell his colleagues they needed to approve of his relationship with Dean, or that they needed to consider his relationship with Dean to be a normatively good thing, in order for them to vote with him against DOMA. Simple *fairness* for all couples, regardless of the normative goodness of the underlying relationships of those couples, was the sole justification proffered for voting against DOMA.[42]

Indeed, the best reflection of this approach was Congressman Barney Frank's response to the repeated charge by DOMA supporters that granting marriage licenses to same-sex couples would signal approval by the government of such couples' homosexual conduct. Congressman Frank asked and answered the following in response to that charge:

> "What kind of almost totalitarian notion is it to say that whatever Government permits, it sanctions and approves? . . . Does civil law, by allowing you to divorce and remarry, say, good, we approve of that, we sanction your walking out on that marriage and starting a new one? No, what civil law says is, in a free society that is a choice you can make".[43]

Frank did allow there was a "role for morality in Government." But Government's "moral duty" according to Frank, was "to protect innocent people from those who would impose on them. That is a very important moral duty".[44] Thus, under this view, strict maintenance of government neutrality,

[42] Indeed, Congressman Gunderson pointed out that, as a "traditionalist," he had been "fully prepared to reach out to my colleagues in reaffirming the institution of marriage as we know and understand it [as a union between a man and a woman]." 142 *Congressional Record* at H7492 (daily ed. 12 July 1996). Gunderson noted, at H7492, that he went to Congressman Henry Hyde, Chairman of the House Judiciary Committee, and to Speaker Newt Gingrich and said: "I am willing to join with you in reaffirming the definition of marriage, though I am a gay man [in a 13-year relationship]. All I ask in return is that you remove the 'meaness, prejudice, and hatred' surrounding this issue."

The only comment by a Member of Congress that included an endorsement of the normative good of marriage, and an apparent endorsement of same-sex relationships, was made by Congressman Meehan (D-MA). Meehan's comment, at H7486, contained both an equality, rights-based argument and a normative goods argument—and was spurred by a personal reflection:

> "I have been thinking a lot about this legislation this week because tomorrow I am getting married. . . . I can't imagine that my fiancé and I could make such a momentous decision to wed—and then have the Government step in and say no, you can't do that. I can't imagine that two people who simply want to exercise a basic human right to marry, a right our society encourages, could be denied. . . . Our society encourages and values a commitment to long-term monogamous relationships—and we honor those commitments by creating the legal institution of marriage. If we then deny the right of marriage to a segment of our population, we devalue their commitment without compelling reasons, but simply because we don't like their choice of partners. We can't have it both ways".

[43] *Ibid.* at H7483 (statement of Rep. Frank).

[44] *Ibid.*

and a resulting assurance that all citizens will be treated with strict equality by governmental actions, is the core moral duty and achievement of the state.[45]

Despite strenuous efforts by opponents of DOMA to move the political debate on the legislation away from normative moral questions regarding same-sex relationships, supporters of DOMA operated almost exclusively on the plane of normative judgments—and indeed, filled in a few normative views on behalf of opponents of DOMA. One of the chief sponsors of DOMA in the House of Representatives, Congressman Charles Canady (R-FL) had this to say:

> "All of this rhetoric [opposing DOMA] is simply designed to divert attention from what is really at stake here. . . . It is an attempt to evade the basic question of whether the law of this country should treat homosexual relationships as morally equivalent to heterosexual relationships. That is what is at stake here. . . .
>
> Should the law express its neutrality between homosexual and heterosexual relationships? . . . Should this Congress tell the children of America that it is a matter of indifference whether they establish families with a partner of the opposite sex or cohabit with someone of the same sex? Should this Congress tell the children of America that we as a society believe there is no moral difference between homosexual relationships and heterosexual relationships? Should this Congress tell the children of America that in the eyes of the law the parties to a homosexual union are entitled to all the rights and privileges that have always been reserved for a man and a woman united in marriage?
>
> To all these questions the opponents of this bill say yes. They say a resounding yes. They support homosexual marriage. They believe that it is a good thing. They believe that opposition to same-sex marriage is immoral.
>
> Those of us who support this bill . . . reject the view that the law should be indifferent on such matters, and in doing so I think it is unquestionable that we have the overwhelming support of the American people".[46]

A "resounding yes" from the opponents of DOMA on these questions? A resounding silence would be closer to the truth. As noted, most opponents of DOMA found a myriad of reasons to vote against the bill, all of which had absolutely *nothing* to do with sending any message to the children of America that "homosexual marriage" is a "good thing." And, to the extent that some opponents of DOMA, such as Congressman Frank, did engage with the issue of morality and approval, it was merely to rebut the political theory assumption underlying the questions posed by Congressman Canady—that a decision by a government to grant marriage licenses to a group of people would necessarily indicate support or approval by the government of such a group.

[45] Rawls articulates such government neutrality as a "political conception of justice" which is "itself a moral conception. . . . [I]t is affirmed on moral grounds, that is, it includes conceptions of society and of citizens as persons, as well as principles of justice." Rawls, *supra* n.9 at 147.

[46] 142 *Congressional Record* at H7491 (daily ed. 12 July 1996) (statement of Rep. Canady). See also 142 *Congressional Record* at S10114 (daily ed. 10 Sept. 1996) (statement by Sen. Coats) ("Government cannot be neutral in this debate over marriage. . . . [W]hen we prefer traditional marriage and family in our law, it is not intolerance. Tolerance does not require us to say that all lifestyles are morally equal.").

While supporters of DOMA were thus both indignant and graphic during the legislative debate regarding the assault same-sex marriages would pose to traditional morality,[47] they were less clear as to *why* such marriages constituted such an assault. That is, while many speakers either assumed or stated that homosexuality was unnatural and immoral, they provided few clues as to *why* gay sex, or a gay relationship, *is* inherently immoral.

For many speakers, the assault that homosexuality and same-sex marriages posed to traditional morality was so intuitively obvious that they recoiled from the need to even explain it. Indeed, they viewed the fact that they were required to explain this obvious truth as evidence itself of the moral decay in society.[48]

Some Members of Congress did attempt to provide reasons why a marked distinction exists between heterosexual marriages and same-sex unions. Senator Robert Byrd explained that: "[O]ut of same-sex relationships, no children can result. Out of such relationships, emotional bonding often times does not take place". Senator Lauch Faircloth explained that: "Same-sex unions do not make strong families. Supporters of same-sex marriage assume that they do. But that assumption has never been tested by any civilized society".[49]

"Reasons" of this sort, however, are simply restatements of the fact that Senator Bryd and Senator Faircloth strongly believe there are marked distinctions between heterosexual marriages and same-sex unions. Not only are such reasons ultimately unpersuasive when critically analysed in the light of empirical data,[50] but Members of Congress who open the debate to a serious discus-

[47] See, e.g., 142 *Congressional Record* at H7482 (daily ed. 12 July 1996) (statement of Rep. Barr) ("[A]s Rome burned, Nero fiddled, and that is exactly what the gentlewoman and others on her side [opposing DOMA] . . . would have us do. Mr. Chairman, we ain't going to be fooled. The very foundations of our society are in danger of being burned. The flames of hedonism, the flames of narcissism, the flames of self-centered morality are licking at the very foundations of our society: the family unit").

[48] See 142 *Congressional Record* at S10108 (daily ed. 10 Sept. 1996) (statement of Sen. Byrd) ("That we have arrived at a point where the Congress of the United States must actually reaffirm in the statute books something as simple as the definition of 'marriage' and 'spouse' is almost beyond my grasp."); at S10117 (statement of Sen. Faircloth) ("It defies common sense to think that it would even be necessary to spell out the definition of 'marriage' in Federal law."); at S10104 (statement of Sen. Nickles) ("The fact that some may even consider this legislation controversial should make the average American stop and take stock of where we are as a country and where we want to go."); at S10114 (statement of Sen. Coats) ("It is amazing to me . . . and disturbing that this debate should even be necessary. I think it is a sign of our times and an indication of a deep moral confusion in our Nation").

[49] 142 *Congressional Record* at S10109 (daily ed. 10 Sept. 1996) (statement of Sen. Byrd), at S10117 (statement of Sen. Faircloth). As William Bennett observed in an editorial included in the Congressional Record by Congressman Smith from Texas: "To say that same-sex unions are not comparable to heterosexual marriages is not an argument for intolerance, bigotry, or lack of compassion. . . . But it is an argument for making distinctions in law *about relationships that are themselves distinct*." 142 *Congressional Record* at H7495 (reprinting William J. Bennett, "Not a Very Good Idea," *Washington Post*, 21 May 1996)) (emphasis added). Bennett's reasons for the distinctness appeared to be that same-sex unions are inherently non-monogamous, and that it was well known that children are best reared by a mother and a father.

[50] Empirical assertions about differences between same-gender and opposite-gender unions have, in fact, not been borne out by any reliable research. See, e.g., SM Duffy and CE Rosbult, "Satisfaction and Commitment in Homosexual and Heterosexual Relationships", (1986) 12 *Journal*

sion of such reasons ultimately undermine their argument that homosexual conduct simply *is* immoral.[51] Ironically, forcing a rational conversation about morality is probably the *last* thing opponents of same-sex marriage should want to do.

One possible coherent position against same-sex marriage would be one that relied exclusively on religious faith. Indeed, a few Members of Congress did rely on Biblical principles to justify their vote in favor of DOMA.[52] But most members of Congress invoked notions of upholding "morality" and the "foundations of society" as their reasons for passing DOMA, and not the need to adhere to any particular verse in the Bible. The reason for their approach is not difficult to discern. Legislators perceive that, as a constitutional matter, they need to have some reason, apart from solely the dictates of a particular religion, for the passage of a piece of legislation.[53] In contrast, arguments about "morality" are perceived by legislators to be legitimate, secular "reasons" for legislative action, as distinct from arguments derived solely from religious precepts and faith.[54] But

of Homosexuality 1; LA Kurdek and JP Schmitt, "Relationship Quality of Partners in Heterosexual Married, Heterosexual Cohabiting, Gay, and Lesbian Relationships", (1986) 51 *Journal of Personality and Social Psychology* 711; DP McWhirter and AM Mattison, *The Male Couple* (Englewood Cliffs, NJ, Prentice-Hall, 1984); P Blumstein and P Schwartz, *American Couples: Money, Work, and Sex* (New York, NY, Morrow, 1983); AP Bell and MA Weinberg, *Homosexualities: A Study of Diversity Among Men and Women* (New York, NY, Simon and Schuster, 1978). Citing a study performed at UCLA, Eskridge notes that gay and straight couples show no differences in "measures of love, compatibility, closeness of the relationship, and satisfaction of the relationship." Eskridge, *supra* n.6 at 109 (citing LA Peplau and SD Cochran, "Sex Differences in Values Concerning Love Relationships", (paper presented at the Annual Meeting of the American Psychological Association, Sept. 1980)).

[51] As conservative commentator Florence King observes: "In a media-saturated society teeming with talk-show producers casting dragnets over think tanks, proponents of gay marriage win merely by being scheduled. By contrast, the conservative instinctively recoils from analyzing eternal verities. . . . In the final analysis he believes in the sanctity of marriage 'just because.' " 142 *Congressional Record* at H7494 (daily ed. 12 July 1996) (reprinting Florence King, "The Misanthrope's Corner", *National Review*, 3 June 1996). Louis Michael Seidman has observed that as soon as believers in given truths begin to engage in liberal reasoning, they necessarily undercut their assertion that "it just IS this way." See LM Seidman, "This Article is Brilliant/This Article is Stupid: Positive and Negative Self-Reference in Constitutional Practice and Theory", (1998) 46 *University of California at Los Angeles Law Review* 501 at 560 (analysing debate between Stephen Macedo and Robert George on homosexuality).

[52] See, e.g., 142 *Congressional Record* at H7486 (daily ed. 12 July 1996) (statement of Rep. Buyer) ("We are a nation . . . based on very strong Biblical principles. . . . God laid down that one man and one woman is a legal union. . . . that God-given principle is under attack. . . . We as a Federal Government have a responsibility to act and we will act."; 142 *Congressional Record* at S10111 (daily ed. 10 Sept. 1996) (statement of Sen. Bryd) ("Let us make clear that we . . . affirm our trust in the divine approbation of union between a man and a woman . . . for all time.").

[53] The First Amendment to the US Constitution prohibits Congress from making any law "respecting an establishment of religion". Statutes that have as their sole purpose the promotion of religion violate the Establishment Clause of the First Amendment. See *Stone* v. *Graham*, 449 U.S. 39 (1980) (holding unconstitutional a state statute requiring copy of Ten Commandments to be posted on public classroom walls).

[54] Given the US Supreme Court's decision in *Bowers* v. *Hardwick*, 428 U.S. 186 (1986), these legislators are probably not wrong in their constitutional assessment. *Hardwick*, 428 U.S. at 196 ("The law . . . is constantly based on notions of morality."). Some commentators believe the Supreme Court significantly revised its view of the interrelationship between public morality and law in its

if religious beliefs cannot be the sole basis on which to establish the immorality of an action, the question remains as to *why* homosexual conduct *is* immoral. That question was never clearly answered by supporters of DOMA, nor were such supporters ever directly challenged to answer such a question by opponents of DOMA.

Much of the debate on DOMA thus fell into two predictable discourses, with each side contesting or evading the premises on which the other discourse was based. Supporters of DOMA believed an essential role for government was to preserve the moral fiber of the country, and that endorsement of heterosexual marriage as morally superior to same-sex unions was a critical component of that role. This group could not imagine anyone legitimately contesting their moral view of the harm posed to society by acceptance of homosexuality. Opponents of DOMA, by contrast, largely avoided the underlying question of the role of government and morality, focusing instead on the fact that the bill was politically motivated, unconstitutional, and unnecessary. While this group never contested the view that marriage itself was "good", it viewed the morality of the underlying issue (same-sex marriage) as essentially irrelevant—and, indeed, contested the view that government sent any moral messages through the granting of marriage licenses.

There was one Senator who opposed DOMA, Charles Robb from Virginia, who explicitly acknowledged the moral dimensions of the legislative choice before Congress. Robb's lengthy statement thus stood out, as both unusual and compelling, in the legislative debate. Robb observed:

> "[A]t its core, marriage is a legal institution officially sanctioned by society through its Government. This poses the dilemma of whether a society should recognize a union which the majority either can't relate to or believes is contrary to established moral tenets or religious principles. We find ourselves again at the intersection of morality and Government, a place where some of our most divisive and complicated social issues have torn at us throughout our history as a Nation".[55]

In addressing this dilemma, Robb confessed that "the true issue which confounds and divides us . . . is how we feel about intimate conduct we neither understand nor feel comfortable discussing." He noted that, over time, he had come to the understanding that "the clear weight of serious scholarship has concluded that people do not choose to be homosexual, any more than they choose their gender or their race". This was critical to Robb's subsequent moral analysis:

> "[I]mmorality flows from immoral choices. But if homosexuality is an inalienable characteristic, which cannot be altered by counseling or willpower, then moral objec-

decision in *Romer* v. *Evans*, 517 U.S. 620 (1996). It seems more likely to me, however, that the *Romer* Court simply had a different view of the relevant morality to take into account in that case. Feldblum, "Based on a Moral Vision," *Legal Times*, 29 July 1996, S31 (noting the "compelling vision of justice and morality" animating the Court's analysis).

[55] 142 *Congressional Record* at S10122 (daily ed. 10 Sept. 1996) (statement of Sen. Robb).

tions to gay marriages do not appear to differ significantly from moral objections to interracial marriages".[56]

While Robb acknowledged that "social mores can and should guide our Government," he viewed the vote on DOMA as requiring legislators to "choose between conflicting moral judgments." As Robb put it: "Many believe homosexuality is immoral, but many also believe that discriminating against people for attributes they cannot control is immoral".[57]

Ultimately, Robb did not make an argument for the normative moral goodness of same-sex relationships. Rather, like other Members, he concluded his argument by saying: "[Y]ou don't have to be an advocate of same-sex marriages to vote against the Defense of Marriage Act. You only have to be an opponent of discrimination".[58] Yet, in the body of his speech, Robb had already acknowledged that deciding whether discrimination against a group was *justified* or not itself required *normative moral* assessments and choices.[59] Thus, Robb's speech bridged, to some extent, the legislative discourses: he acknowledged the moral dilemma that a vote on DOMA posed, and then challenged the moral assessment that had been made by DOMA supporters.[60]

In the House of Representatives, Senator Robb's honesty was matched by that of Congressman Henry Hyde (R-Ill.). Unlike most supporters of DOMA, Congressman Hyde did not assert there was an inevitable, societal view on the immorality of homosexual conduct. Rather, Congressman Hyde observed:

> "[T]his is one of the most uncomfortable issues I can think of to debate. It is something I really shrink from because there is no gentle easy way, if we are to be honest and candid, to discuss the objections to same-sex marriage, the disapprobation of homosexual conduct, without offending and affronting *an ever-widening group of people who have come to accept homosexual conduct*".[61]

For his part, Congressman Hyde had no intention of abandoning the view that homosexual conduct was morally wrong. As Congressman Hyde summed up the debate:

[56] *Ibid.*

[57] *Ibid.* at S10123.

[58] *Ibid.*

[59] "Other [Senators supporting DOMA] admit that they intend to discriminate, but they believe that discrimination here is justified. They justify their prejudice against homosexuals by arguing that homosexuality is morally wrong—thereby assuming it is not a trait but a choice, and a choice to be condemned." *Ibid.* at S10122.

[60] This approach is similar to what I raised for consideration in the context of the debate on the Employment Non-Discrimination Act, a bill that would prohibit discrimination based on sexual orientation in employment: "What do we lose, and indeed what might we gain, if we answered [Congressman] Poshard's question with a response that acknowledged his moral dilemma, but then challenged him on the legitimacy of the moral views that gave rise to the dilemma in the first place?" Feldblum, "Moral Rhetoric of Legislation," *supra* n.37 at 1005.

[61] 142 *Congressional Record* at H7500 (daily ed. 12 July 1996) (statement of Rep. Hyde) (emphasis added).

"It is appropriate that Congress define marriage. You may not like the definition the majority of us want, but most people do not approve of homosexual conduct. They do not approve of incest. They do not approve of polygamy, and they express their disapprobation through the law. It is that simple. It is not mean spirited. It is not bigoted. It is the way it is, the only way possible to express this disapprobation".[62]

Ultimately, both chambers expressed overwhelming agreement with Congressman Hyde's conclusion. The Defense of Marriage Act passed by a vote of 342–67 in the House of Representatives and by 85–14 in the Senate.[63]

AN ALTERNATIVE VISION

The debate on DOMA highlights the lengths that advocates for gay rights will go to avoid a normative discussion of the morality of sexual relationships between people of the same gender. It is difficult to say that such an approach, relying on principles of liberal neutrality, is necessarily unrealistic.[64] Indeed, it is probably unrealistic to expect anything *other* than such an approach by most federal and state legislators today. There is a legitimate reason why the legal materials I developed for DOMA drew heavily on principles of liberal neutrality. At this point, that is the discourse advocates of gay rights in the political world feel most comfortable deploying.

But it is fair to ask if such an approach is ultimately ineffective.[65] To argue that the governmental act of granting marriage licenses and benefits to same-sex couples carries with it no moral message at all is, I believe, ultimately unpersuasive. Congressman Canady was wrong that opponents of DOMA had answered his questions about the messages to be sent to the children of America with a "resounding yes". But he was not far off in assessing the normative impact that governmental recognition of marriage for same-sex couples might well have in practice.

Moreover, Congressman Hyde correctly noted that the debate was now made more difficult for individuals in his position because of changing societal views on the appropriateness of *homosexual conduct*. Such views have changed in society because of the presence of individuals, in all walks of life, who are open and honest about being gay, lesbian, or bisexual—and who have not hidden the fact that their particular sexual orientation usually includes (if they are lucky) a sexual and emotional relationship with a person of the same gender.[66]

[62] 142 *Congressional Record* at H7501.

[63] 142 *Congressional Record* at H7501 (Roll Call vote 316), 152 *Congressional Record* at S10129 (daily ed. 10 Sept. 1996) (vote no. 280).

[64] Compare Ball, *supra* n.9 at 1879.

[65] *Ibid*. This, in my mind, is the question Michael Sandel posed so provocatively, and persuasively, in his article exploring the "limits of toleration." See M Sandel, "Moral Argument and Liberal Toleration: Abortion and Homosexuality", (1989) 77 *California Law Review* 521 at 537.

[66] Several episodes of the NBC television comedy, Ellen, which aired during the fall of 1997 with a lead character who had recently "come out" as a lesbian, were a dramatic example of the average American being exposed to the everyday life—including the dating life—of a gay person.

Thus, personal knowledge and experience of gay people who are living quite ordinary lives, including quite ordinary sexual lives, have changed the views of many in the public about the appropriateness of gay conduct. What the debate on DOMA teaches us is that the *majority's* view on the appropriateness of gay conduct might well need to change as well before a representative body of the public will vote to recognize same-sex marriages. That is, in order to be successful in convincing a legislator to vote for same-sex marriage, that legislator must *first* be convinced that gay sexual conduct is, from a moral perspective, normatively *different* from sexual conduct he or she continues to believe is morally wrong (such as incest or polygamy).

Advocates who wish, nevertheless, to continue to base their arguments solely on liberal neutrality principles, in order to gain the advantage of sidestepping normative assessments about gay people and gay sex, must realize that any advantage necessarily depends on *all* governmental actors agreeing that liberal neutrality principles *are* the principles that should govern decision-making by the state. If, by contrast, a significant number of lawmakers make legislative decisions based on their personal normative and moral assessments, the fact that advocates of liberal neutrality can cleverly sidestep such assessments may mean nothing more than that such advocates have retreated from the battlefield on which the real war is being waged. Indeed, the DOMA debate is an excellent example of legislators engaging in normative assessments as a basis for their ultimate vote.[67]

I do not believe it is realistic to expect advocates of gay equality in the political arena to shift immediately to a battlefield of normative assessments. There are few legislative champions currently willing to venture onto such a battlefield, and one must do battle with the champions one has. Moreover, there are substantive advances that have been achieved, and can be achieved in the future, using the reasoning and rhetoric of simple equality.[68] At a most basic level,

[67] A second problem with the liberal neutrality approach is that it may rest on an incoherent principle—that it is possible for government to *be* neutral. One could argue that whenever the state chooses to act, or chooses *not* to act, in an area of socially contested views, it is taking a position on behalf of one view over another. For example, if the state chooses to issue marriage licenses to same-gender couples, it is not acting neutrally with regard to a socially contested view of marriage, any more than if it chooses *not* to issue such licenses.

[68] For example, endorsement of liberal arguments based on equality and fairness is demonstrated by the relative success of the Employment Non-Discrimination Act, which would have banned sexual orientation discrimination in employment, but failed to pass the Senate in 1996 by only one vote. See 142 *Congressional Record* at S10139 (daily ed. 10 Sept. 1996) (Roll Call 281). See also P Freiberg, "Wilson Handed a Bitter Defeat: University Regents Approve Benefits for Employees", *Washington Blade*, 28 Nov. 1997, at 14 (discussing extension of domestic partnership benefits to University of California employees). In response to Governor Pete Wilson's assertion that the University's extension of domestic partnership benefits would "treat something less than a marriage as, essentially, marriage," Regent Ward Connerly (of anti-affirmative action fame) responded: "I too support the institution of marriage—I've been married 34 years. But I would submit to you there are values that transcend marriage—the value of equality, the value of individual liberty, the value of letting people have the right to pursue happiness on their own terms, not ours." *Washington Blade* at 14.

principles of political liberalism ensure that voices of a minority group can be *heard* and respected in political discourse.[69]

But gay advocates should be aware of the limitations of the battlefield on which they are fighting. I believe governmental recognition of same-sex marriage will be difficult to achieve based solely on principles of toleration and fairness. In all likelihood, such recognition will require an explicit acknowledgment of a clash of moral principles, and a persuasive argument as to why gay relationships are as morally positive for individuals and for society as are heterosexual relationships.

[69] R West, "Universalism, Liberal Theory & the Problem of Gay Marriage", (1998) 25 *Florida State University Law Review* 705 at 711 ("I am certain a commitment to liberalism, universalism, and individualism is necessary to provide a floor for these arguments [that individual rights can result in societal goods]; without such a commitment, there is just no reason for these arguments to be heard, much less honored or heeded.")

4

Like Counting Stars?: Re-Structuring Equality and the Socio-Legal Space of Same-Sex Marriage

DAVINA COOPER*

INTRODUCTION

SINCE THE 1980s, political support and acceptance of same-sex relationships has rapidly garnered strength. By the late 1990s, developments included the striking down of sex-discriminatory spousal laws,[1] local domestic partnership provisions by cities and firms, and the introduction of state-recognised, registered partnerships.[2]

Yet the past decade has also witnessed opposition and anatagonism to lesbian and gay spousal recognition.[3] Hostility has come not only from the Right, but also from lesbian and gay communities who oppose same-sex marriage on the grounds that it promotes neither equality nor freedom. Many of these arguments are well-known and have been extensively rehearsed: for instance, the feminist claim that the historically patriarchal function and property associations of marriage render it incapable of offering a route to liberation or equality.[4] Others

* Professor, School of Law, Keele University. Thanks to Didi Herman and Morris Kaplan for their helpful comments. The discussion of proper place and the public/private, although not in relation to spousal recognition, also appears in D Cooper, "'And You Can't Find Me Nowhere': Relocating Identity and Structure Within Equality Jurisprudence", (2000) 27 *Journal of Law and Society* 249.

[1] S Boyd, "Family, Law and Sexuality: Feminist Engagements", (1999) 8 *Social and Legal Studies* 369.

[2] H Bech, "'Marriage' and 'Homosexuality' in 'Denmark'", in K Plummer (ed.), *Modern Homosexualities* (London, Routledge, 1992); R Halvorsen, "The Ambiguity of Lesbian and Gay Marriages: Change and Continuity in the Symbolic Order", (1998) 35 *Journal of Homosexuality* 207; B Søland, "A Queer Nation? The Passage of the Gay and Lesbian Partnership Legislation in Denmark, 1989", (1998) 5 *Social Politics* 48.

[3] See J Goldberg-Hiller, "Hawaiian Wedding Song: Same-Sex Marriage and the Politics of Sovereignty in Hawai'i", (paper presented at the American Law and Society Association Annual Conference, Chicago, May 1999).

[4] C Smart, *The Ties that Bind: Law, Marriage and the Reproduction of Patriarchal Relations* (London, Routledge & Kegan Paul, 1984) at 146; P Ettelbrick, "Since When is Marriage a Path to Liberation?" in R Baird and S Rosenbaum (eds.), *Same-Sex Marriage: The Moral and Legal Debate* (Amherst, NY, Prometheus Books, 1997) .

oppose, or express ambivalence about, lesbians and gay men demanding spousal recognition on other grounds. These include fears of sexual and cultural assimilation; objections to the privileging of couples; a belief that marriage represents a misguided conception of how to create enduring kinship relations; the privatisation of welfare within the couple, thus relieving the state of responsibility to support unemployed/elderly/disabled persons;[5] and the belief that visibility will equal increased state surveillance, regulation and control.

In the context of these contrasting positions, this chapter explores the pursuit of spousal recognition (SR) for same-sex couples, focusing on the implications of its introduction for a politics of equality. SR has been advocated on various grounds, including those of privacy and respectability; however, a key basis for demanding SR is that it offers a route to, and symbol of, gay equality—whether in terms of opportunities, recognition, freedom or satisfaction. Conventionally interpreted as a group equality demand, SR parallels a series of "analogous" historical demands by groups seeking parity with dominant forces. As such, it takes its place within a "multicultural" paradigm of equality.[6] But while this paradigm is highly influential, I want to argue for a way of engaging with SR beyond the parameters of multiculturalism, in other words, to adopt an approach that decentres the group as equality's primary concern.

My reasons for doing so are several. As theorists have argued in other contexts,[7] group equality models tend to treat groups as discrete, bounded classes with shared interests, identities and concerns. To the extent that problems of classification are identified (what is it to be Jewish, Black, lesbian, or female for example?), these are seen as problems at the group's margins. This model of groups has three major problems. First, it cannot deal adequately with the multiple social positionings most people find themselves in. Secondly, it assumes (without necessarily meaning to) that groups such as lesbians and gay men are immutable. Thus, gay equality aims to benefit a distinct pre-existing group, gays, instead of aiming to benefit all those whose lives at different points have gay elements. Thirdly, to the extent that separate communities can be identified, group equality tends to treat intra-group equality as less significant—groups become black boxes entitled to parity vis-à-vis others, while their own internal practices often remain neglected.

If the group does not form a useful unit for equality claims, what alternatives are available? One approach is to focus on individual equality in ways reminiscent of traditional liberalism. Thus, in the context of same-sex marriage, if two individuals wish to marry or institutionalise their relationship, sexual orientation should not pose an obstacle (providing it does not generate recognisable forms of harm). However, this version of negative equality of opportunity is far

[5] See Boyd, *supra* n.1.

[6] C Calhoun, "Nationalism, Political Community and the Representation of Society", (1999) 2 *European Journal of Social Theory* 217.

[7] E.g., D Herman, "Are We Family?: Lesbian Rights and Women's Liberation", (1990) 28 *Osgoode Hall Law Journal* 789; Calhoun, *supra* n.6.

from satisfactory.[8] Liberal equality paradigms, with their emphasis on the individual as both the object of equality and author of its achievement, tend to divorce equality from society. Extracting agency from the social, liberal individualism does not deal with why someone would want to marry—treating it simply as a personal taste preference. This fails to recognise the social construction of desire and interests as well as the social roots, implications and symbolic meanings of marriage and recognised coupledom. In addition, equality becomes a matter of levelling. Theoretically this could be levelling up or down. However, in the case of liberal equality paradigms, it tends to be in the direction of the dominant norm. Thus, gays should have marriage, the poor should have televisions. In this way, the norms of the status quo are not just maintained but also reinforced and legitimised in the process.

This last point suggests a more fundamental problem facing equality as a political paradigm than simply the limitations of an individual-oriented model. If we take the question of transport, would equality exist if everyone had access to cars and the financial means to drive them (i.e., get insurance, buy petrol etc.)? Moreover, regardless of equality, would this be advisable? One response is to argue that equality is only *one* normative principle—it cannot do all the work—and needs supplementing with other principles such as justice, environmentalism, and social responsibility. While I have some sympathy with this approach, I also want to argue that equality is more than a formalistic, quantitative paradigm—a matter of ensuring we all have the same "amount". However, this requires a more *social* conception: that interprets equality as the contestation of social relations of inequality far more generally. Thus, if we remain with the car example, the pursuit of equality also asks us to consider how car-driving is linked to the construction of masculine desires; the impact of pollution and road building on future generations; and the geographical intersection of social relations and practices of class and ethnicity with the location of housing, leisure activities and employment.

I therefore want to argue for an approach which, by-passing the middle terrain of group agency, looks two ways: on the one hand, to individuals; on the other, to the social inequalities and asymmetries that pattern and organise our society. While the first functions as a broad, normative aspiration or vision, the second provides us with a political, strategic focus. Before going on to locate this discussion in the context of spousal recognition, let me briefly set out these two approaches to equality. The individual approach I am taking is based on a notion of equality of power.[9] Deploying a "generative" conception of power, equality of power's claim is that all people should have the same level of capacity to shape their environment, whether discursively, by means of resources, or by recreating or disrupting disciplinary structures.[10]

[8] See also Calhoun, *supra* n.6 at 221.

[9] See D Cooper, *Power in Struggle: Feminism, Sexuality and the State* (Buckingham, Open University, 1995).

[10] See also *ibid.* at ch.8.

Equality of power encompasses other conceptions of equality such as equality of resources, but also goes beyond them. First, it includes engaging with technologies which currently allow some people to generate effects or outcomes that others are denied. These include systemic forms of power based on position and location in relation to, for instance, the law and family, as well as discourses which legitimate or rationalise current social relations. Here engagement requires more than the simple redistribution of resources. Equality of power also asserts an active, participatory vision of equality that includes not only the pursuit of personal goals and interests, but also involvement in economic, political and social decision-making processes. This contrasts with other models of equality which treat people as principally concerned with consumption, eg, achieving an equal capacity to shop or travel.[11]

Equality of power offers a more radical conception of equality than many other approaches. However, as anything but a loosely imagined aspiration, it quickly reveals its limitations.[12] As I have outlined above, an individual-centred model of equality, divorced from the social, cannot stand alone. Equality is not an arithmetic formula that, once arrived at, simply requires to be installed, with society downgraded to a simple problem of operationalisation. At the same time, if we focus on social structures at the expense of individuals, equality becomes meaningless. The reason for challenging social inequalities derives, I would argue, from people's ethical entitlement as living human beings to equal participation and benefits from society. Thus, we need to hold on to the individual subject, while recognising that both inequality and equality are quintessentially social concerns. But if the primary political strategy is to challenge social inequalities, what exactly does this mean? While the concept of social inequalities (or relations) tends to stand in as short-hand for relations of class, gender, race etc., I want to use it in a more expansive way to refer to the organising principles that structure societies.

Organising principles (OPs), as I am using the term, refer to the complex, multifarious, material/ideological patternings whose differently condensed forms across time and space enable us to identify societies—both nesting and overlapping. OPs operate in two ways: as interpretive frameworks, they are "read off" from social relations and practices; at the same time, they structure and are (re)produced by social practice. Thus, OPs are far from static. While in modern, liberal, western democracies, they include legitimacy, capitalism, gender, and non-participative democracy, what counts as an OP as well as the particular character it takes is constantly open to change and revision.

I have discussed the workings of OPs in more detail elsewhere.[13] In the rest of this chapter, I want to focus on what this framework can offer when analysing equality in relation to same-sex spousal recognition. To do so, I need to intro-

[11] Cf. R Dworkin, "Foundations of Liberal Equality", in S Darwall (ed.), *Equal Freedom* (Ann Arbor, MI, University of Michigan Press, 1995) at 225.

[12] See Cooper, *supra* n. 9.

[13] *Ibid.*

duce at this point a vital element. OPs, as the list above reveals, can refer to quite different things. The key distinction I wish to make for the purpose of my analysis is between *social* OPs (such as gender, race, age, and sexuality) which are fundamentally concerned with inequality—that is asymmetries of power are at their heart; and *normative-epistemological* OPs. These latter refer to forms of social patterning or order that in their dominant form compress the space between social interpretation and vision. In other words, how society seems is also how it should be. Examples of normative-epistemological OPs include: the rule of law; representative democracy; and legitimacy.

In the context of discussing equality, the tendency is to focus on one particular *social* OP. This approach has been criticised by those who emphasise the social significance of "multiple oppression" or "intersectionality". In other words, we are not solely women, Black or middle-class, for example. However, I want to go beyond this approach to argue that equality strategies must consider not only other "vectors" or "indices" of social inequality, but also the role played by normative-epistemological OPs. These are important to sustaining the status quo. Through normative-epistemological OPs, a society is presented as being, with minor exceptions or flaws, the best it can be. While these principles may not be hegemonic in the sense of generating widespread support or commitment, their authority and influence comes from their congruence with social structures and practices.

But what has this to do with spousal recognition? I want to argue that the political consequences of institutionalising same-sex relationships depends, at least in part, on the intersection between spousal recognition and normative-epistemological OPs. This has several possible aspects. First, the encounter may render same-sex spousal recognition illegitimate or absurd; alternatively, it may absorb same-sex marriage into the status quo (as many feminists fear). Secondly, spousal recognition may unpick, challenge or revise the normative-epistemological principles it encounters. Normative-epistemological principles validate the status quo, but they can also help to entrench new hegemonies. In this latter role, the is-ought is reversed. In other words, rethinking what OPs such as the rule of law, justice, "proper place" and legitimacy can mean enables us to look critically at their current functioning. The third possibility is that the encounter between OPs and socio-legal reform provides a contingent, mediated space for lesbian and gay political agency, with the potential to take the impact and meaning of the encounter in a range of different directions. In the discussion below, I want to suggest that all three developments are occurring. However, given my concern with strategy, I want to emphasise the possibilities for political agency and argue that the ramifications of spousal recognition for equality depend on how it is argued for, implemented, and inhabited; while at the same time recognising that these strategic interventions are mediated and overdetermined by wider social processes and changes.

SEXUALITY AND "PROPER PLACE": DISRUPTION AND REVISION

My focus in the following discussion centres on two normative-epistemological OPs: "proper place" and the "public/private". After briefly setting each out, I turn to explore the way in which they intersect the drive for lesbian and gay spousal recognition. Both proper place and the public/private emphasise the structuring role played by space at a physical but also metaphorical level. The OP proper place—with its cultural and social division between that which is in and out of place—highlights the ways in which inequality is linked to cultural and physical forms of differentiation and segregation.[14]

De Certeau distinguishes, in his analysis, place from space in a way that I do not follow in my discussion here.[15] However, his conception of place is useful in its emphasis on order and discrete relational positions. Within modern western societies, we can see proper place operating in conjunction with other organising principles to separate activities and peoples into hierarchically related, albeit mutually constitutive, spaces.[16] The power of the "proper" in relation to social change is threefold: it works to delegitimise certain reorganisations of persons, practices and identities into new spaces or combinations; offers a powerful device for criticising and condemning the new; and through its capacity to keep social phenomena apart, defuses and contains challenges. Fundamentally, the notion of the proper is a deeply and thoroughly internalised structuring device in western, liberal societies. Indeed, for children, learning what goes where is a key early lesson that also functions as a measuring rod of cognitive/ emotional "normality".

At the same time, the notion of *spatial* differentiation as a significant organising principle at the turn of the century may seem, to some degree, counter-intuitive. In many ways, spaces appear more culturally diverse and heterogeneous; from a gender perspective, men and women seem less confined to separate spheres, and lesbian and gay sexual expressions more visible than even two decades ago. At the same time, there is a countervailing tendency for spaces to become more ordered, efficient and mono-functional. This does not require us to contrast today with a golden age of spatial anarchy, but rather to attend to current impulses to continue the segregation and disciplining of particular acts and identities. In line with a policy rhetoric of equal opportunities, this impulse tends not to focus on status or those characteristics discursively constituted as immutable. Nevertheless, the alternative policy emphasis on activities and personal presentation has ramifications for socially identified constituencies. For instance, in Britain, the Blair government of the late 1990s has been associated

[14] See M de Certeau, *The Practice of Everyday Life* (Berkeley, CA, University of California Press, 1984) at 117; T Cresswell, *In Place/Out of Place* (Minneapolis, MN, University of Minnesota Press, 1996).

[15] de Certeau, *supra* n.14.

[16] E.g., see S Razack, "Race, Space and Prostitution: The Making of the Bourgeois Subject", (1998) 10 *Canadian Journal of Women and the Law* 338.

with a stream of statements and policies that targeted working-class children and those who are homeless, mentally ill, travellers or refugees as potentially "out of place" in urban centres and residential areas, as jeopardising, through their behaviour and demeanour, orderly, respectable city streets.

For lesbians and gay men, the ideologies and practices of proper place are very apparent in the spatial regulation of sexual identities and activities. As Gill Valentine, a leading geographer in the area of sexuality, suggests:

> "[A] kiss is not just a kiss when it is performed by a same-sex couple in an everyday location. . . . The heterosexuality of the street is . . . an insecure appearance that has to be maintained by regulatory regimes".[17]

At its most overt, this takes the form of excluding certain activities, interactions, and identities. While the boundaries of propriety and appropriate conduct are often explicit, with clear penalties or punishment if breached, boundaries may also function more covertly.[18] Embarrassment or evasion may be used to denote "inappropriate" conversations or behaviours; but commonly even these signals prove unnecessary. Most lesbians and gay men have a sufficiently strong sense of heterosexual norms to govern themselves—presenting those forms of conduct or appearance that seem required.

Yet, sexual inequality is not just about exclusion, and lesbians and gay men are not simply despatialised. One argument is that the "proper" works here to banish homosexuality to the private domain of home and intimate relations. However, the sexualisation of space is far more complex. Certain city areas have historically been associated with sex work and with gay male sexual activity. Moreover, at the turn of the twenty-first century, certain kinds of lesbian and gay presentations are acceptable in some leisure, occupational, and civic spaces. At the same time, *lesbian* neighbourhoods, workplaces and leisure venues, in particular, tend to be located in less prestigious or more risky locales. Hetherington[19] argues that marginal identities are attracted to marginal spaces, but this is not purely an issue of collective agency; economic, social and political inequalities also play a central role.[20]

The subordination of lesbian spaces also functions more symbolically. Within the dominant heterosexual imaginary, lesbian spaces remain, despite social liberalisation, the still largely unknowable, hazardous spaces that exist beyond, but also define the boundaries of, acceptable female behaviour. One more concrete portrayal of lesbian space can be found in the media's representations of the Greenham Common Women's Peace Camp in the 1980s.[21]

[17] G Valentine, "(Re)negotiating the 'Heterosexual Street': Lesbian Productions of Space" in N Duncan (ed.), *BodySpace* (London, Routledge, 1996) at 154.

[18] *Ibid.*

[19] K Hetherington, *Expressions of Identity* (London, Sage, 1998).

[20] E.g., see T Rothenberg, "'And She Told Two Friends': Lesbians Creating Urban Social Space" in D Bell and G Valentine *Mapping Desire* (London, Routledge, 1995).

[21] Cresswell, *supra* n. 14; S Roseneil, *Disarming Patriarchy: Feminism and Political Action at Greenham* (Buckingham, Open University, 1995); A Young, *Femininity in Dissent* (London, Routledge, 1990).

Greenham provides an excellent example of the way "proper place" was used by the media to construct the peace camp and its inhabitants according to a matrix of dangerous, infectious womanhood.

Greenham Peace Camp also demonstrates, as Cresswell argues, the way in which "proper place" is a disputed concept.[22] While the media and local residents claimed it was the women that were out of place in a conservative, rural locality, the protestors asserted that that role was filled by the US military base. Thus, the notion of what is proper is clearly contingent and open to change. While to some degree this can occur through symbolic forms of activism and argument, change does not emerge smoothly from rational debate; material processes are also central to revisioning and, more importantly, to transforming society's OPs.

Wider social changes have enabled lesbians and gay men in recent years to challenge, transgress and resist the content and authority of proper place, and to envision and create alternative geographies. Examples include the transient disruption and recoding of what is proper through direct action, demonstrations and marches. Here city landscapes are appropriated and transformed according to a gay, cultural logic. A more permanent re-creation of who and what is "in place" is apparent in the evolution of lesbian and gay neighbourhoods. In addition, the discursive strategy of reading spaces against their cultural grain to draw out covert lesbian and gay meanings, more commonly associated with literary and cinematic texts, demonstrates the ways in which the proper can be rendered both ambiguous and permeable.

Yet, if we accept that proper place, as it currently operates, works generally to legitimatise and naturalise the physical and metaphorical division and segregation of identities, activities, and discourses in ways that sustain inequalities of power,[23] two options emerge. The first is to weaken "proper place" as an OP; the second is to redefine it. Weakening the structural significance of proper place—through constant transgressions of its order—is in turn also likely to generate far more of a spatial overlap of diverse activities and peoples.[24] While hierarchies might continue to function *within* spaces, heterogeneity would, arguably, weaken hierarchies *between* spaces, as activities and people bearing different degrees of status co-existed instead of being spatially segregated. What happens *within* particular spaces, however, highlights the way in which "proper place" is not simply about geographical allocation. It also concerns "knowing one's place"—understanding and submitting to hierarchically differentiated rules and norms. Even spaces encompassing different activities and people can function in precise, disciplinary ways, particularly where strong norms of differentiated, appropriate conduct are internalised.

22 *Supra* n.14.

23 See also de Certeau, *supra* n. 14 at 38.

24 See D Cooper, "Regard Between Strangers: Diversity, Equality and the Reconstruction of Public Space", (1998) 18 *Critical Social Policy* 465.

Can the structuring significance of proper place, then, be meaningfully reduced, or does this require a level of social transformation currently impossible to contemplate? Demotion also raises the question: how? In this chapter, I wish to avoid the idealist claim that argument and debate alone can eradicate problematic OPs; in the case of proper place, enormous material changes would be required if its significance was to be lessened. It may therefore be more useful to consider whether the content and meaning of proper place are more open to adjustment or change. The lesbian and gay strategies identified above aim to achieve this in two ways: first, to include lesbians and gay men within the prevailing meaning of "proper"; second, to redefine proper more generally in egalitarian, inclusive ways. One interpretation of proper place might be that of cultural and social diversity—that the "good space" bears a complex mixture of overlapping social codes and meanings. Another interpretation might be space that is just, fair or equal. From this perspective, it would be those strategies and practices *challenging* egalitarian norms that would appear out of place.

RE-STRUCTURING PUBLIC AND PRIVATE

The second spatial OP I wish to consider concerns the relationship between public and private. Within liberal discourse, the public/private divide often functions as a subset of proper place, providing a central binary division for locating where activities are appropriate. This understanding, however, has been extensively criticised at both a normative and analytical level by a range of feminist theorists. While the approach I adopt has benefited from feminist critiques, it nevertheless offers a somewhat different "take". It is a perspective that shares some parallels with that of Peter Steinberger,[25] who argues for a revised approach to the terms public and private, oriented around manners or styles of action. In particular, he suggests that public manners be equated with impartiality, accountability and judgment. I have several disagreements with Steinberger's approach, particularly his understanding of the difference between public and private; however, my approach shares a desire to avoid seeing public and private as separate physical spaces.

Elsewhere, I have discussed the possibility of rethinking public space as a process of making space public.[26] Instead of seeing public space as a physical container for particular activities, we can see it as the geographical dimension of public-building—by which I mean the development of a collective identity as strangers sharing equal regard.[27] Development of such an identity co-exists in

[25] P Steinberger, "Public and Private", (1999) 47 *Political Studies* 292.

[26] Cooper, *supra* n. 24.

[27] While there are many situations in which people encounter each other as strangers, the best examples of public-formation are either when an event or common concern draws people together (eg, a show, demonstration or sudden crisis) or where "unthreatening" individuals play this role (eg, the conversation starter at the bus stop or shop). However, both of these sets of circumstances

an interconstitutive but uneasy dynamic vis-à-vis a public relationship to place. For this latter suggests the possibility of places in which all people feel like strangers. But is this possible? Can places generate comprehensive sensations of strangeness?[28] In asking this, I do not assume the negative connotations usually attached to strangeness. Outsiderness can be associated with excitement, challenge, fascination and learning as well as alienation. While it is hard to imagine spaces that are completely unfamiliar to everyone, a more common example is spaces which contain a mixture of symbols and meanings with which no one entirely identifies: a process perhaps most common in multi-cultural, inner-city neighbourhoods. Because no one sees the space as fully theirs, everyone's spatial identifications are more ambivalent and, potentially, detached.

The installation of diverse, overlapping symbols that speak to different constituencies also facilitates social interactions as strangers. But what does it mean to relate *positively* as strangers? It does not mean pretending that people are our kin; rather it is about seeing a value in relating to, and being present as, strangers. At the same time, we cannot treat everyone identically. Just as spaces cannot alienate everyone, so it would be absurd to say we must show no more intimacy with a partner than to a stranger, or that all spaces should be accessible, equally, to everyone. First this ignores the value of different spaces functioning differently. It also underestimates the importance of a sense of belonging and control, not necessarily over all spaces at all times, but certainly in some contexts. Finally, it forgets the ways in which the creation of a "public" (as strangers sharing equal regard) requires familiarity—being at home—with this underlying (public) norm. Thus, the conception of public requires, and is rooted within, private norms of belonging and familiarity.[29]

Using the term "private" to denote relations both to space and to others based on familiarity and "at-homeness" may seem at first glance a typical liberal construction. However, the approach I am taking is different in several respects. First, the concept of private does not denote a specific place such as the home or domestic sphere. Rather, it identifies a particular set of norms: feelings of belonging, "comfortability", and knowing, derived from familialising practices, symbols, and physical structures. Thus, while the parental home may feel, for instance, a non-private place for many lesbians and gay men, in a context of non-recognition or acceptance of their sexuality,[30] certain neighbourhoods

demonstrate very limited publics: first, because they operate within contexts in which strangers are often divided into the safe and the risky, with the latter associated with danger or distaste; second because people meet as unequals due to OPs of gender, class, ethnicity and age.

[28] While many spaces alienate large numbers, this is arguably because they are organised around the interests or cultural symbols of an elite.

[29] Cf. Calhoun, *supra* n.6, who argues, "Publics . . . are arenas in which people speak to each other at least in part as strangers. This need not mean that they have never met, but that they are not bound by dense webs of common understanding or shared social relations."

[30] See L Johnston and G Valentine, "Wherever I Lay my Girlfriend, that's my Home: The Performance and Surveillance of Lesbian Identities in Domestic Environments", in D Bell and G Valentine (eds.), *Mapping Desire* (London: Routledge, 1995).

might feel far more familial given the visibility of similar-looking men and women, "knowing" exchanges (eg, smiles) with passers by, and the presence of alternative venues, bookshops, bars etc.[31] Indeed, we see this substitution very clearly in gay discourse about "families of choice" or "feeling at home" in lesbian neighbourhoods.

Second, what follows from this is that there is no clear division between those spaces in which public norms prevail and those organised around private norms; most spaces incorporate a combination of the two. The nature of the balance and relationship between co-existing public and private norms in particular spaces is constantly evolving, however, and frequently the subject of dispute. For instance, is the exchange of body-fluids in the street acceptable? And if not, why not? Leaving to one side questions of convention, is it because permitting intimate interactions undermines more generally people's relations and interactions as strangers in a place where this form of interaction should prevail?

These issues highlight the ways in which the relationship between, as well as the interpretation of, public and private can work to reinforce or undermine structural inequalities. I would suggest that in Britain at the turn of the twenty-first century, the reinforcing of inequality is articulated to the predominance of norms of belonging, familialism, and home, that is to private norms over public ones, within civil and political life. Here I am arguing against the conventional feminist, but also liberal, position that political, nation-state activity is concerned with, and articulates, public norms. For we can see the institutional pervasiveness of private norms in the popular discourse of social inclusion, which is largely about incorporating people within community—as belonging—the good stranger reinscribed in the familial trope of kin.

Yet, the prevalence of private norms might not matter if such norms challenged social inequalities. The trouble is that the private norms prevailing in Britain today largely reflect established cultural and social interests, reinforcing, in turn, the exclusion and alienation of others. Hegemonic private norms, whether articulated to practices within the street or home, reflect a sensibility and form of organisation based on discipline, consumption, limited responsibility, and a zero-sum conception of belonging. This has particular implications for those defined as outsiders by virtue of their ethnicity, sexuality or class; indeed the private—or what I would like to call "akinship": organising people according to their apparent similarities, consanguinity and social ties of belonging—reinforces the constitution of them as such.

What I am suggesting then is two-fold. First, the public/private as an OP can sustain inequalities through its division of norms and modes of being: one way of behaving on the street, another in the home or office. At the same time, the problem does not simply lie in requiring particular activities, sensibilities or discourses within specific locations, an articulation I have argued, that is partial,

[31] Valentine, *supra* n. 17 at 150; cf. Calhoun, *supra* n. 6 at 222. Obviously, how "at home" different lesbians, for instance, feel will depend on other factors such as class, ethnicity, etc. It will also vary depending on mood, i.e., feeling at home at certain times but not at others.

contested and contingent. Equally significant is the way both public and private are organised. Public can mean relations of superficial politeness, formality, and alienation. It can also identify (and create) excitement, challenge, and regard—the responsibility, pleasure and interest strangers can share. Private too, as I have suggested, can take both reactionary and more progressive forms. Thus, while equality strategies may, in part, be concerned with shifting the balance from private to public norms—since belonging and "at-homeness" may be inherently exclusionary—they can also work with the prevailing private orientation that exists to generate "at-homeness" based on *different* norms and relations. For instance, the installation of disparate cultural symbols within urban neighbourhoods, rather than being read defensively along a zero-sum matrix of belonging, can provide a device for facilitating "at-homeness" amongst diverse, overlapping minorities.

REGULATING PARTNERSHIPS

So far, I have argued that proper place and the public/private distinction both work to sustain inequality through exclusions, hierarchies of who or what is proper, and the prevalence of relations of belonging based upon racialised, heterosexual norms. At the same time, both OPs can be reconfigured differently and, as such, work against social inequalities. I now wish to both develop and concretise this analysis by focusing on lesbian and gay attempts to achieve partnership equality through the institutional recognition of their relationships. As I suggested at the beginning of this chapter, the demand for recognition has had many successes—as governments have introduced same-sex partnership schemes and courts have redefined the meaning of terms such as "spouse".[32]

In the rest of this chapter, I want to consider these developments in terms of the potential challenge they pose to structural inequality. From the perspective of equality of power, lesbian and gay marriage can be seen as a progressive venture.[33] First, it gives lesbians and gay men access to some of the same benefits as heterosexuals.[34] Secondly, by doing so, it allows them to pursue their own conceptions of the good life.[35] Yet, framing equality according to a group-based paradigm, as I argued earlier, is also problematic. Deployed in this context, it can essentialise lesbian and gay identity and desires—that is posit a common, shared, "homosexual" core; assume equality means bringing lesbians and gays "up"—bestowing upon them the freedom and entitlements heterosex-

[32] Spousal recognition may be imposed by courts *ex post facto*, on same-sex couples and unmarried heterosexual couples, which is different from a couple choosing to enter a marriage/registered partnership.

[33] M Kaplan, "Intimacy and Equality: The Question of Lesbian and Gay Marriage", (1994) 25 *Philosophical Forum* 333.

[34] E.g., see D Chambers, "What If? The Legal Consequences of Marriage and the Legal Needs of Lesbian and Gay Male Couples", (1996) 95 *Michigan Law Review* 447.

[35] E.g., see Søland, *supra* n. 2.

uals possess; and cut lesbian and gay equality off from other social relations and organising principles, both in terms of what equality means, and the implications of its pursuit.

In contrast, if our starting point is the way in which social and normative-epistemological OPs generate inequalities that include, but are not limited to, the disregarding of gay and lesbian relationships, different strategies emerge. Clearly, one way of dealing with the heterosexual character of family policy is to extend spousal recognition to same-sex partners, but other strategies exist also, particularly once we take into account the interface between relationship recognition, OPs of age, ethnicity, and class, and wider questions of social responsibility. In the following discussion of same-sex spousal recognition (SR)—a term I use broadly to encompass the range of ways in which lesbian and gay relationships receive governmental, civic and commercial recognition—my focus is the implications SR poses for equality. To pursue this analysis, I situate same-sex partnership recognition within the normative-epistemological principles outlined above. Does SR keep lesbians and gay men in their place or allow them to enter the place of the dominant other? Does it create new forms of exclusion and impropriety? And what impact does it have on the balance between public and private norms? Do same-sex marriages facilitate relations between strangers or simply reinforce private norms of familiarity? And, if the latter, are these private norms transformed, in any way, in the process?

CREATING A SATELLITE SPACE

> "The space of a tactic is the space of the other. Thus it must play on and with a terrain imposed on it and organized by the law of a foreign power".[36]

In attempting to incorporate lesbian and gay relationships within the proper place of the conjugal relationship, spousal recognition raises several possibilities: first that a single space will be opened up and extended—that of the institutionally recognised relationship; second, that we will witness the creation of a new, narrowly defined and disciplined space—one that joins existing satellites already encircling the conjugal, heterosexual couple; or third, that same-sex SR will constitute a troubling space with the potential to destabilise more traditional forms of social ordering. While outcomes depend, at least in part, on the actual form SR takes, SR does appear to solidify the spatial boundaries of the domestic/romantic partnership,[37] mobilising a framework in which social and economic benefits, responsibilities and rights are organised around the (gendered) couple, with each individual bearing their own "complementary" place. While many gay, pro-marriage couples feel that they can avoid the internal

[36] de Certeau, *supra* n. 14 at 37.

[37] Such solidification may occur partly through re-legitimising the spousal space, by removing from it an increasingly perceived form of discrimination.

divisions and allocations that heterosexual marriages engender, the creation of a shared, pure, stable space comes through fairly explicitly in some of the comments of more conservative SR advocates. Metaphorical broom in hand, they present themselves as intent on sweeping out the immature, high-risk and contagious elements that threaten to sully the creation of a respectable homosexual space.[38]

The rigidifying of boundaries and the inequities this creates for certain forms of personal status and relations is, perhaps, an obvious consequence of creating a new socio-legal category. The constituencies explicitly excluded are clear: the very young, single people, those in non-romantic or non-coupled relationships, as well as those who refuse to "opt in" either because they have nothing to gain or because they feel alienated by this new, official space. Thus, perhaps the more interesting question is to what extent can SR also work against such solidification? Can it challenge the hierarchical distribution and segregation of people, identities, and activities? I want to consider here two possible options. First, SR might function as a location from which to challenge the inequalities generated by the privileging of the conjugal relationship. Second, the space of SR might itself be a space of constant transgressing. In other words, a space that thrives on challenging its own legitimacy. While neither of these options are evident in the current drive for relationship recognition, which, with some exceptions, models itself on the paradigmatic heterosexual spouse, four more critical strategies are imaginable. These strategies do not reject the demand for SR but attempt to link this demand to a politics that challenges both the privileging of relationships (and spousal relationships in particular) and the protection and solidification of certain socio-legal and cultural spaces.

Strategy One: Examining the Wider Social Consequences

This first strategy, paralleling similar proposals in relation to lesbian and gay rights regimes more generally, focuses on the arguments made in support of institutional recognition. In particular, it poses the possibility of advocating SR while, at the same time, refusing to undermine other kinds of relationships (eg, friends, neighbours) or personal statuses (eg, as single). For one of the problems with the pursuit of SR is the way in which claims for marriage and registered partnerships (implicitly or otherwise) trivialise, infantalise or subordinate other relationships. Following Kaplan's line of argument,[39] these other relations might include the fleeting sexual encounter with an unknown other—usually pitted as the antithesis of the conjugal couple—as well as friendship networks.

The creation of a non-hierarchical relationship discourse does not mean, however, indefinitely expanding the borders of what counts as being in its

[38] E.g., see C Dean, "Gay Marriage: A Civil Right", (1994) 27 *Journal of Homosexuality* 111.

[39] M Kaplan, *Sexual Justice: Democratic Citizenship and the Politics of Desire* (New York, NY, Routledge, 1997) at 237–8.

proper place, for an equality strategy also needs to consider the implications of promoting certain statuses or practices on other aspects of the social. We can see a similar dilemma in arguments that lesbians and gays are "in place" in the military. While clearly discrimination is present in bans on homosexual armed forces staff, a wider equality strategy has to consider whether the arguments being made also legitimise a coercive military structure which works to defend and promote international inequalities. Tensions over inclusion illustrate the problems of focusing on groups rather than OPs. While a group-based approach to equality means "raising" those with less (here excluded gays), a more structural approach that focuses on challenging *social* OPs requires us to consider a range of strategies in terms of their respective feasibility and possible implications.

Strategy Two: Implementing to Dismantle Hierarchies

The second strategy concerns the actual operationalisation of partnership recognition. Can SR be *implemented* in a way that helps to dismantle relationship hierarchies, pluralising who and what constitutes the proper locus for particular powers, rights and obligations? I want to briefly outline three approaches to operationalising institutional recognition that have been adopted by governments and employers:[40] contract, opting in, and regimes of default. By organising the "proper" in different ways, they have different implications for relationship hierarchies. The first approach, contract, has the potential to escape pre-given categories of recognition. It identifies an approach in which individuals decide whom they wish to designate as the proper recipient of various benefits and decision-making powers. This might be their intimate partner, it might be someone else, or they may choose to spread benefits and powers across different parties. The state or company then recognises as proper those parties who have fulfilled the necessary criteria of recognition.[41]

The second approach, opting in through marriage or registered/domestic partnership, retains many contractual elements.[42] Kaplan and others have advocated opting in over individual contracts on the grounds that it is more financially accessible: an "off the rack" procedure that does away with the need for

[40] See also M Eichler, *Family Shifts: Families, Policies, and Gender Equality* (Oxford, Oxford University Press, 1997).

[41] The problems with this approach parallel those identified more generally in relation to contracting: ie, individualism, voluntarism, unequal bargaining power, rigidity, reductionism, transaction costs, and "predictivism" (an assumption that the future can be known and managed through a prior contract).

[42] Scandinavian registered partnerships have been criticised for emphasising the contractual nature of the relationship rather than the couple's contribution to society or their expression of a permanent, deep commitment, Halvorsen, *supra* n.2 at 216; Søland, *supra* n. 2. For this reason, Sullivan and others have advocated lesbian and gay marriage instead, A Sullivan, "Virtually Normal", in R Baird and S Rosenbaum (eds.), *Same -Sex Marriage: The Moral and Legal Debate* (Amherst, NY, Prometheus Books, 1997).

expensive, time-consuming multiple contracts.[43] At the same time, opting in may not be comprehensive; for instance, it may exclude parental powers—lesbians and gay men not being deemed a proper place for children. It thus tends to co-exist with both contract and default regimes. While opting in retains some degree of choice—we can determine whom our partner is and whether we wish to participate—such choice will be circumscribed to exclude "improper" selections, such as biological relations, children, and multiple partners.

The third approach, the default regime, takes away this latter element of choice: we cannot choose for our partners not to count. Instead, governments, courts and (to a lesser degree) employers allocate benefits, powers and obligations according to publicly determined conceptions of appropriateness. This may be on the basis of particular relationships (eg, common law marriages, long-term same-sex partnerships) or according to other criteria, such as "best interests". This third approach has the potential for a more radical, collective revisioning of "proper place". For instance, it can avoid the individualist, predictive, and voluntarist assumptions particularly apparent in contract, allowing responsibilities to be spread more widely, such as through extending tortious duty of care principles to new parties. At the same time, given that many governments are more conservative than social movements on these issues, the creation of statutory regimes may do little to challenge relationship hierarchies. Thus, it may be, at least in the first instance, that contract—with its widest element of choice and capacity for differentiation—provides the best way of blurring relational boundaries, challenging the notion that only certain relationships—for example, the intimate spousal partnership—constitute the proper location for particular benefits and powers.[44]

Strategy Three: Inhabiting New Socio-Legal Spaces

My third strategy for contesting conventional conceptions of proper place and the inequalities it sustains and legitimises focuses on the way the socio-legal spaces of SR are *inhabited* once in operation. Do lesbians and gay men enter these spaces, for example, through marriage and commitment ceremonies in too sombre and respectful a manner? Would greater levity, parody, pastiche or the explicit incorporation of non-heterosexual elements help to sustain SR as spaces that are not proper places? In other words, as spaces in which the "out of place" functions less as the constantly feared intruder—and thus boundary marker—and more as the one whose entry is permitted and even celebrated.

[43] Kaplan, *supra* n. 33 at 353.

[44] Even if contract is given a pre-eminent position as a way of facilitating innovation, default regimes and processes of opting in may also be needed to deal with the limitations and problems of a contractually-based method. The application of contract here assumes that benefits and responsibilities can be passed to another; clearly, whether such secondary rights, powers, and duties exist is an equally important and politically contested topic.

Examples might include drag weddings, staged non-monogamous commitments, serial registered partnerships, celebratory divorces.

In posing this strategy, with its clear echoes of a poststructuralist queer transgressive politics,[45] three difficulties immediately emerge. First, why would people enter into an institutionalised arrangement if they disagreed with it? Even if registering a relationship was being done for pragmatic reasons, it is unlikely participants would have any interest in its simultaneous parody. Arguably such forms of parody occur in response to being excluded, thus inclusion quickly tempers any transgressive motivation. Second, the creation of "improper" conjugal performances may appear to pose a purely oppositionalist perspective in which the "out of place" is valorised regardless of what it entails. This tension returns us to the issue raised above: namely whether certain activities and identities, such as the eroticisation of violence, adult-child sexual relationships, explicit non-commitment (and forms of emotional "betrayal") are legitimately out of place. At the same time, notions of proper place with their disciplining and ordering of practices and identities largely function today to legitimate, stabilise and sustain a non-egalitarian status quo. Dis-order therefore may be beneficial, at the same time, recognising that such dis-order can take many forms. Transgression does not operate according to a binary system in which a monistic order of propriety faces its singular antithesis. Given that the form of dis-order is not pre-given, reflection and choice are both possible and essential. Finally, the third danger in attempting to disrupt the creation of a proper, legitimate space is that it risks trivialising and ridiculing lesbian and gay relationships, whilst leaving other "marital" relationships unblemished. Indeed, by undermining satellite forms, the heterosexual "original" may end up strengthened and further naturalised.

Strategy Four: Alliances with Radical Heterosexuals

It is in response to this that I turn to my fourth strategy: occupying the space of SR in order to challenge and contest the heterosexual spousal form. One form this might take is alliances with radical heterosexuals. While SR might encourage heterosexuals to feel that marriage is modernising and thereby becoming less politically problematic, the development of registered partnerships, in particular, poses an alternative that heterosexuals might wish also to enter. This echoes political tendencies amongst heterosexual feminists—which have to some degree come and gone—to forego marriage, given their critique of its gendered history and connotations. Thus, progressive heterosexuals might evacuate their own proper, and largely privileged, place to enter the satellite, subordinate space of lesbian and gay and other relationships outside marriage.

[45] See H Brooks, "Doing Things with Sex" in C Stychin and D Herman (eds.), *Sexuality in the Legal Arena* (London, Athlone Press, 2000).

Or they might evacuate marriage for a legal arrangement that, partly in recognition of the often temporary status of romantic relationships, displaces the covalence between sexual intimacy and legal rights and duties, thereby putting pressure on the state to organise social welfare in ways that decentre sexually intimate partnerships.

EGALITARIAN PRIVATE NORMS WITHIN A HIERARCHICAL PUBLIC

So far, I have discussed the interface between proper place and SR, in the context of strategies for pursuing relationship equality. I now want to turn to my second normative-epistemological OP. In my earlier discussion, I suggested that, despite variation in the balance between public and private norms, private norms of familialism, kinship and belonging tend to be privileged in western, liberal nation-states today. This has clear implications for equality. The private poses a way of structuring inequality according to a nexus of familiarity/home in which distance correlates with lowered obligations. In an asymmetrical world, this reinforces and legitimates inequalities between nations and regions. But how does this relate to same-sex spousal recognition? Does gay marriage reinforce private relations according to a descending spiral of commitment?

Within the socio-legal space of the same-sex spouse, private norms are privileged in several ways. Leaving to one side the more conventional conception of privacy, which institutional recognition may make possible in the sense of fortifying legal walls against outside scrutiny (although not in all respects), spousal recognition emerges in a social and cultural context in which meaningful life is seen to depend on our intimate relations.[46] From a different perspective, Andrew Sullivan argues that SR facilitates acceptance and, hence, belonging within wider kinship structures.[47] Quintessentially then, spousal recognition is not about relating equally and positively towards strangers, except in as much as the spousal partner has shifted from legal stranger to kin.[48]

A central criticism that can be made then of same-sex marital status, and the nexus it constructs between romantic relationships and legal/economic/social rights and obligations, is that it tips the balance further away from relations between strangers. Christine Pierce[49] makes this argument explicit when she suggests:

> "Unfortunately, priority rankings among various kinds of claims are determined by the cultural maps worked out by individual societies, and nearness and kinship are

[46] See generally K Weston, "Forever is a Long Time: Romancing the Real in Gay Kinship Ideologies", in S Yanagisako and C Delaney (eds.), *Naturalizing Power: Essays in Feminist Cultural Analysis* (New York, Routledge, 1995) and Kaplan, *supra* n. 39 at 209.

[47] Sullivan, *supra* n.42 at 129.

[48] R Mohr, "The Case for Gay Marriage", in R Baird and S Rosenbaum (eds.), *Same-Sex Marriage: The Moral and Legal Debate* (Amherst, NY, Prometheus Books, 1997) at 92.

[49] C Pierce, "Gay Marriage", (1995) 26 *Journal of Social Philosophy* 5 at 12–13.

> real and important . . . it is important for the sake of creating new sentiments to press for gay marriage so that lesbians and gay men can become visible as . . . families, and kin".

From the private-oriented space of spousal recognition, the stranger is an outsider to whom entry is barred. Indeed, entry in the form of a "marriage of convenience", whether heterosexual or now possibly homosexual, comprises a form of cheating or transgression that fundamentally reneges on the familial character of the conjugal space.

The private orientation of spousal recognition has a number of implications for equality. At an abstract level, it reinforces the idea that little is owed to the stranger *qua* stranger; responsibility is rather to family and kin. More concretely, while the introduction of spousal provisions may distribute economic resources within conjugal-type relationships, in accordance with prevailing, proper conceptions of the economics of intimate relations, it does not challenge wider economic and class inequalities. Indeed, as Boyd[50] and others have argued, judicial and political support for same-sex spousal recognition is in part due to their desire to further privatise social welfare.[51] Yet, while private norms of familial responsibility may be mobilised to sustain public inequalities, they can also be articulated to more progressive practices and relations. As I suggested earlier, the existence of private norms is inevitable; thus the question is what private norms are being advocated? It is in this respect that proponents' arguments that the institutionalisation of lesbian and gay relationships can generate recognition for more progressive familial values may be most pertinent. Same-sex spousal recognition may pose a way of giving legitimacy and publicity, and of reinscribing spousal relationships more generally, according to norms that assert greater spousal/familial democracy and a fairer, more equal gender division of labour.[52]

So far, I have suggested that same-sex spousal recognition may—if not strengthen—then at least reflect a shift towards private rather than public norms. While this appears, at first glance, self-evident, there is another perspective, one that sees spousal recognition as fundamentally concerned with the stranger or outsider. Regardless of whether intimate relationships gain institutional recognition, they tend to be acknowledged by friends and some family members. Therefore, the value of institutionalisation may be less about acceptance from close kin, than about the acceptance that comes from those at a distance. As Morris Kaplan argues, recognition for lesbian and gay spouses is

[50] *Supra* n. 1.

[51] See generally M Barrett and M McIntosh, *The Anti-Social Family* (London, Verso, 1982) at 134.

[52] B Cox, "A (Personal) Essay on Same-Sex Marriage", in R Baird and S Rosenbaum (eds.), *Same-Sex Marriage: The Moral and Legal Debate* (Amherst, NY, Prometheus Books, 1997); J Weeks et al. "Partners by Choice: Equality, Power and Commitment in Non-Heterosexual Relationships", in G Allan (ed.), *The Sociology of the Family* (Oxford, Blackwell, 1999); though see S Oerton, "'Queer Housewives?': Some Problems in Theorising the Division of Domestic Labour in Lesbian and Gay Households", (1997) 20 *Women's Studies International Forum* 421.

largely concerned with impacting upon third party behaviour through the obligations placed upon them.[53] Who then are these third parties?

In terms of their relationship to organising principles of class and authority in particular, such strangers are not in the main subordinate or marginal subjects but those with political and economic power. It is the government, large corporations, legal system, mass media and health-care system who are hailed in the institutionalisation of lesbian and gay relationships.[54] For it is these entities whose power to bestow or recognise inheritance rights, pension entitlements, insurance benefits, ownership of property, and medical decision-making is at stake. We might therefore argue that a major limitation of spousal recognition (shared with many rights-based claims), from an equality perspective, is that it looks to, and thereby helps reproduce, the authority and legitimacy of the Establishment. It is a demand by lesbians and gay men that the Establishment hail them, not as they have been traditionally hailed, as sick, sinful or marginal people, but rather as respectable (property-owning) citizens of the polity.

Is this shift an empowering one? While some see it as affirmatory—rendering it possible for lesbians and gay men to participate within the public sphere and relate to others as equals—to critics it represents the articulation of a subordinate political relationship that sustains the status quo. But do lesbians and gay men have a meaningful choice? Why should they accept less than others as a result of ignoring, or adopting an oppositionalist stance towards, the state? These questions in turn raise wider concerns about the modern, liberal state: namely, can it be benevolent? Or is the state essentially damaging, such that any deepening of one's relationship to it (assuming this is what spousal recognition involves) will be inevitably harmful?

As with the debates over rights, this dichotomy may be part of the problem. Arguably, it is possible to do three things simultaneously: recognise the problematic character of the state; recognise that the state can change; and attempt to pursue reforms or innovations through state structures. Yet, paralleling my comments above, this requires that lesbian and gay activists make visible the

[53] *Supra* n. 33.

[54] I want to enter two caveats or exceptions to this. First, in some court decisions defining lesbians and gay men as (potential) spouses, the party who must confer the benefit is in fact the partner, who claims a legal strangeness the court refuses to uphold. Whether over alimony or child support, courts have here imposed a familial, interdependent frame, against the claims of the partner that she is "just a friend" (see also S Gavigan, "A Parent(ly) Not: Can Heather Have Two Mommies?" in D Herman and C Stychin (eds.), *Legal Inversions: Lesbians, Gay Men, and the Politics of Law* (Philadelphia, Temple University Press, 1995); Boyd, *supra* n.1). My second caveat is that my argument so far has focused too exclusively on one space: the satellite space of the registered partnership. If we consider, however, the impact of same-sex spousal recognition on the metaphorical space of heterosexual marriage, a different set of public norms are given voice. From the perspective of the hetero-spousal, socio-legal space, the new aliens in the midst are not the Establishment but the lesbian and gay couples who have been brought within recognised conjugal regimes. Whether these strangers are treated with parity and respect depends in part on the terms of their entry. And whether this goes any distance to shifting the focus, away from the introspective norms of spousal space to more public-oriented norms, depends on the impact such entry has on relations between strangers more generally.

politically ambivalent character of the state in the claims they make upon it. This means consciously avoiding the discursive production of a sanitised central power that, through SR, lesbians and gay men aspire to bind themselves to. It also involves arguing that the state—contrary to popular discourse—is not a public domain but intimately concerned with relations of belonging and "at-homeness". Thus, if SR is to be integrated within a more public orientation, and a progressive one at that, what is required is not the creation of a state-centred, couple-based citizenship but the far more difficult process of reorienting the gaze and obligations of the spousal "unit" towards dispossessed outsiders.

CONCLUSION

I want to conclude with three points. First, this chapter has brought together three concepts (equality of power, organising principles, and same-sex spousal recognition) in order to explore the impact of lesbian and gay marriage and registered partnerships on the pursuit of equality. Broadly, my argument has been that it is not enough to focus on gays as a group or set of individuals who have been granted less. While the individual capacity to impact and to exercise power equally is important, this makes little sense outside of a structural understanding of social relations. Moreover, it is through engaging with such social relations that individual equality is pursued (albeit in a constantly changing form).

Adopting this more structural approach, and drawing on the concept of social and normative-epistemological organising principles, a central theme of this chapter has been the importance of recognising the intersections between different forms of social inequality, as well as the way in which they interact with legitimised forms of social ordering. If same-sex SR constitutes a consciously chosen political strategy, its impact on other social relations, and on other OPs is important. While SR has been criticised for reinforcing inequalities amongst lesbians and gays, less attention has been paid to its impact on OPs such as proper place and the public/private, which are not linked definitionally to social inequality in the way that gender and sexuality are, but which nevertheless help to sustain, validate and order a presently unequal society.

Secondly, despite the insistence of many protagonists that contributors to the debate take a clear position, either for or against gay spousal recognition, I want to argue for a more equivocal response. The effects of SR on embedded, enduring social inequalities appear ambiguous once we broaden the field of our enquiry away from a narrow, group-based conception of gay equality to incorporate wider social relations; it is also too early to say what the longer-term impact of same-sex SR will be, on gay equality, heterosexual coupledom and wider social patterns. To judge SR as being the wrong strategy for generating equality runs the risk of assuming too high a level of political agency amongst gay marriage proponents. SR is a historically embedded development. It is a product not only of the increasing shift towards formal gay equality witnessed in many countries over the past three decades, but also of less positive developments: in particular, the failure to develop more collective forms of commitment and responsibility, in fields such as health, poverty, transport, and migration. Thus, critics on the left are wrong to attack lesbians and gay men for developing a conjugal gaze and imaginary. While I would agree that as an aspiration it seems a rather limited one, spousal recognition is foremost a response rather than a cause of wider social shifts.

But, and this is my final point, criticising the voluntarist assumptions of some SR opponents should not be taken to mean that political agency is impossible or irrelevant. In this chapter, I have suggested that the approaches activists and others might take—and are taking—can make a difference to whether same-sex SR contests or reinforces current conceptions of "proper place", conservative understandings of familiarity and at-homeness, and a disregard for less powerful constituents. In addition, I want to suggest that both the pursuit of, and debates around, same-sex SR provide an invaluable spring-board into wider discussions about the distribution of responsibility. While many on the left (gay and straight) see spousal recognition as boring or irrelevant, the questions it raises intersect with issues that progressive and radical forces have been debating and struggling over for decades. Attempts to expand the category of recognised intimate partners, in the context of wider forms of privatisation and other global shifts, thus provide us with a very welcome opportunity to revisit the question: should responsibility for ourselves and others be structured according to a spectrum of emotional, geographical and relational proximity?

The potential SR poses as a site of struggle is not simply a discursive one. As I have sought to demonstrate in the final sections of the chapter, it is in the strategies, tactics and choices of activists, policy-makers and citizens, in the way in which the institutionalisation of new relationships is pursued, operationalised and lived out, that more radical forms of equality are facilitated, pre-figured or closed down. Thus, against the "nayes" and "ayes" of disputants in debates over spousal recognition, I want to suggest that we dismantle the binary divide around which debate has formed in favour of an approach towards SR that encompasses five things: an approach, first, that is politically pragmatic, nuanced, and inclusionary; second, that centres those who seem least powerful; third, that sustains the pressure for collectivised forms of responsibility; fourth, that attracts those who are not lesbians or gay men into new institutional arrangements; and, finally, that avoids fetishising, fortifying or overloading romantic coupledom.

5

Recognition, Rights, Regulation, Normalisation: Rhetorics of Justification in the Same-Sex Marriage Debate

JANET HALLEY*

IN THIS CHAPTER, I examine some of the rhetorical forms in which pro-gay advocates in the United States justify lifting the current de facto, if not always de jure, ban on same-sex marriage. At the moment, by my count, we in the US have four basic modes of justification for same-sex marriage.[1] Two are explicit: Recognition and Rights. Each of these modes of justification is typically proposed as simple and internally coherent, but each is actually internally heterogeneous, and moreover each disguises while depending on a supplementary rhetoric of justification. That supplementary rhetoric is sometimes Regulation, and it is almost always Normalisation. I think this hidden complexity makes the project of seeking same-sex marriage normatively much more dubious than it might appear. At the very least, I hope to persuade those who seek this goal to do so with more frankness about their implicit endorsement of Regulation and Normalisation.

I will proceed by spelling out, first, some relationships between Recognition and Normalisation and, second, some relationships between Rights, Regulation, and Normalisation.

* Professor of Law, Harvard Law School. Thanks for assistance with this essay to Wendy Brown, Judith Butler, Richard T Ford, Roberta Krueger, Nancy Rabinowitz, members of the Stanford Law and Humanities Seminar, and new and old friends at Hamilton College. For help in construing recent changes in French law, thanks to Judith Butler, Angela Carter, Allison Danner, Didier Eribon, and Robert Wintemute. For library assistance nonpareil, thanks to Paul Lomio and the Stanford law librarians. And for financial assistance, thanks to the Robert E Paradise Faculty Scholarship at Stanford Law School and to Ric Weiland.

[1] Typically, state marriage statutes in the US did not limit capacity to marry along the dimension of sex: they were silent on the very point that is crucial to this volume. Increasingly, however, as political pressure for same-sex marriage has emerged, state statutes and state constitutitional amendments, as well as the federal Defense of Marriage Act, explicitly limit access to marriage, or inter-sovereign recognition of foreign marriages, to cross-sex couples.

RECOGNITION AND NORMALISATION

In an essay entitled "From Redistribution to Recognition?", Nancy Fraser identifies the politics of sexuality as, classically, a politics of recognition. She distinguishes it sharply from the politics of the working class, which she describes as, classically, a politics of redistribution. I emphasise the terms she uses that are characteristic of recognition discourse:

> "Gays and lesbians suffer from heterosexism: the *authoritative* construction of norms that privilege heterosexuality. . . . The remedy for the injustice, consequently, is *recognition*, not redistribution. Overcoming homophobia and heterosexism requires changing the *cultural valuations* (as well as their legal and practical expressions) that privilege heterosexuality, deny *equal respect* to gays and lesbians, and refuse to recognize homosexuality as a *legitimate* way of being sexual".[2]

According to Fraser, economic harms suffered by sexual minorities are derivative of their primary harm, which is "quintessentially a matter of recognition".[3] Even when economic remedies are sought, they must be evaluated for their effectiveness in undoing the harm of disrespect.

Now I think it is true that the legal refusal of same-sex marriage, in a world in which cross-sex marriage is not only permitted but applauded, deprecates same-sex relationships—devalues them, delegitimates them. This derogation is the target of the Recognition justification of same-sex marriage, and it draws upon an etymology of the term "re-cognition": the law should *re*-cognise same-sex relationships, should *re*-think them. Not bad or indifferent, but good.

That seems very simple, but there are elements in same-sex marriage Recognition rhetoric that are problematic. This rhetoric derives much of its appeal from representing those who engage in same-sex relationships as the unequivocal agents of the normative projects of these relationships; and from appearing, when they turn to the public and the state, to ask for so little. I will consider each of these in turn.

First, these arguments posit that same-sex relationships already exist in the real world in a marriage-like form: extending recognition to them won't change the landscape of relationships or our ideas of their value very much. Thus, in his 1994 article "Crossing the Threshold," Evan Wolfson describes marriage as a private relationship which the state merely blesses. Marriage, Wolfson indicates, is:

> "not a mere dynastic or property arrangement; and it is not best understood as a tool or creature of the state or church. . . . [T]oday marriage is first and foremost about *a*

[2] N Fraser, "From Redistribution to Recognition?: Dilemmas of Justice in a 'Postsocialist' Age" in N Fraser, *Justice Interruptus: Critical Reflections on the "Postsocialist" Condition* (London, Routledge, 1997), at 18–19.

[3] *Ibid.*, at 18.

> *loving union between two people who enter into a relationship* of emotional and financial commitment and interdependence, two people who seek to make a public statement about their relationship, sanction*ed* by the state, the community at large, and, for some, their religious community".[4]

The "loving union" comes "first"; the state's role is retrospective and grammatically passive. Similarly, Wolfson stipulates that the premier interest which people have in marriage is the "public affirmation of emotional and financial commitment and interdependence".[5] In this formulation, the couple's interdependence *precedes* and is metaphysically *independent of* its *affirmation*. The couple made itself what it is; and made itself good; all that the public and the state need to do is assent to this *fait accompli*.

But the bid for recognition is actually much more complex than that, inasmuch as the moment the bid is made, the agency of same-sex couples promptly becomes double bound. To seek recognition is to concede the authority of those whose regard is sought. Consider an analogy involving a teacher, a student, and an examination. We normally think of the teacher as having all the power: she can stipulate that the student cannot have something he wants very much without taking the examination and performing according to the teacher's scale of values on it. But at the same time, the student, by taking the examination, concedes the legitimacy and authority of the professor who grades it. The student bestows on the teacher the power to evaluate and rank her. Similarly, a movement that seeks public recognition of its personal relationships concedes that the power to bestow value on them lies in the public. And a movement that seeks *state* recognition of its personal relationships concedes that the power to evaluate and rank them lies in the *state*.

The "recognition gesture" thus places the state not only in second but also in first place. The state originates the terms on which the couple can be thought of as good. Seeking Recognition may begin as a project in which the couple is the subject, but it becomes a project in which it is an object. The couple mixes its subjectivity with subjection the moment it makes its bid for recognition.

Second, the implicit claim that recognition of same-sex marriage is a small change in norms, merely redesignating already-existing relationships now deemed "bad" as "good", is similarly unsimple. Recognition of same-sex marriage would reposition marriage quite substantially—would *normalise* it. The link between Recognition and Normalisation was suggested by Arnie Kantrowitz, who said in 1983 that: "The right to chose marriage is the ultimate normalisation of relations between gay and non-gay society".[6] "Normalisation" in this formulation appears to be nothing more than the recognition effect designated by Fraser and sought by Wolfson. But by framing his goal as the realignment not just of values but of two

[4] E Wolfson, "Crossing the Threshold: Equal Marriage Rights for Lesbians and Gay Men and the Intra-Community Critique" (1994) 21 *New York University Review of Law and Social Change* 567 at 579 (emphasis added).

[5] *Ibid.*, at 580.

[6] *Ibid.*, at 583 n.68 (Wolfson quoting Kantrowitz).

"societies," Kantrowitz also invoked another sense of the term normal, the one in play when your doctor says to you, expecting you to be relieved, "Your blood pressure is normal". She means not only "it's good", but also "it's average"— indeed "it's good *because* it's average". She declares a *relationship* between your blood pressure and everyone else's, a relationship that bestows value on your blood pressure by withholding it from that of other, imagined, patients.[7]

A similar ordering of *all* sexual relationships might be what we get out of legal recognition of same-sex marriage. As Claudia Card[8] and Michael Warner[9] argue, the achievement of same-sex marriage would erase the same-sex/cross-sex distinction currently drawn precisely at the borders of marriage, leaving in stark relief those borders themselves. Marriage itself would not merely continue to bestow positive recognition: it would become more *average*. And if same-sex couples respond to this change by marrying, the married/unmarried distinction would become simpler and more powerful as a mode of social ordering. Unmarried adults, and their sex lives, would become *weirder*. That would be a powerful effect of Normalisation in the sense of *ordering the population around a mean*, and it is an implicit goal of the apparently far less ambitious rhetorical project of "mere" Recognition.[10]

[7] In the essay he contributes to this volume, William N Eskridge, Jr uses the term "normalisation" in a way that entirely misses the conceptual novelty of the work of Michel Foucault and Georges Canguilhem that he cites and that I depend on here. (See Eskridge, chap. 6, n.10 and accompanying text.) "Normalisation" in this use is not the generation and imposition of some consolidated idea of good behavior or good values, the coercive herding of more and more people into the normalcy defined by that behavior or those values; it is the ever-shifting, provisional ordering of a social, conceptual, and ethical field around a distinction—say, married/unmarried; or a range of distinctions—say, wife/mistress/girlfriend; or a standard—say "room temperature" or "illness" or "reasonableness." It is the temporal negotiation all across the social field—within the domain of the "normal" and beyond it—of the determinative and ethical value of the relevant distinction, range of distinctions, or standard. In Eskridge's more conventional use of the term "normalisation," valuation precedes social ordering: someone or something decides that X conduct is good and uses power to coerce more people to do X for that reason. In Canguilhem's and Foucault's use of the term, ethical value may or may not emerge as an effect of the ordering of the field; may attach itself anywhere in it at different times; and may be entirely absent from the process. Modern medicine posits that the blood pressure that most seemingly healthy people have most of the time is "good": the average is deemed to be good. Some religions posit that ascetic or ecstatic experiences that can be undertaken only by an elite are "best": the average there is not necessarily bad, but it's not best. There is nothing "simple" about "normalisation" so understood. (See Eskridge, chap. 6, two sentences in text following n.29.). In the following paragraphs, Eskridge purports to take substantial hits on my argument (and Michael Warner's argument, which inspires mine) that marriage normalises, but he is really not talking about our arguments at all. See M Warner, *The Trouble with Normal: Sex, Politics, and the Ethics of Queer Life* (New York, NY, Free Press, 1999), ch. 2 ("What's Wrong with Normal?") at 41–80, and ch. 3 ("Beyond Gay Marriage") at 81–147.

[8] C Card, "Against Marriage and Divorce" (Summer 1996) 11(3) *Hypatia* 1.

[9] See Warner, *supra* n.7.

[10] DAJ Richards and W Eskridge, in essays included in this volume, attribute to me positive "consequentialist" arguments—that is, confident statements about *what will happen* if same-sex marriage is legally available. (See Richards, Introduction to Part I, pp. 27–9; Eskridge, chap. 6, text accompanying nn. 8, 23.) I don't think I have been read very carefully. "Might be" is not "will be"; "Of course things could go the other way" is not a statement of *what will happen*. Eskridge carries the error further, attributing to me a warning that the eventualities I draw up are to be avoided on some normative theory or other. (See Eskridge, chap. 6, p. 123.) I am assessing the contours

Of course things could go the other way: recognition of same-sex marriage might lend new momentum to the long-running erosion of the specialness of marriage. No longer privileged by restriction to *some* unions and deprived of its power to send the message that those unions are particularly good, marriage might become less, not more, meaningful. Cross-sex couples could lose interest in marriage as a result, opting to cohabit rather than marry. Pro-marriage voting strength could erode; the social consensus that it is worthwhile to devote public and private resources to "support marriage" could break up. If this happens, rather than a convergence of same-sex with cross-sex couples in maintaining the centrality and thus the normalising power of marriage, "mere" Recognition will have contributed to the end of marriage's centrality as a mode of social ordering. In that sense, Normalisation is not necessarily implicit in Recognition. But the two can be detached in this way only by positing a "what if" scenario that denies one of the key premises of Recognition rhetoric: that it asks for so little. The end of marriage as social conservatives want to know it is not "so little".

I would note also that not all Recognition projects seek the same strong Normalisation. The recent legislative struggle that produced the French PaCS (*Pacte Civil de Solidarité*) provides several examples of Recognition projects that would not have normalised in the strong way that U.S. same-sex marriage efforts, if successful, would likely do. The original proposal, presented by Senator Mélenchon in 1990, would have been open to any two persons regardless of their sexes or of the nature of their relationship.[11] The next legislative proposal narrowed access one tick: ascending and descending relatives could not enter into the relation with one another.[12] Later still came in legislative proposals that required that the pair be *a couple*. The actual legislation promulgated in 1999 limits access to the PaCS to unrelated adults who are not married or bound by any other PaCS, who have a common legal residence (but not necessarily a single domicile) and who intend by their registry of a PaCS to formalise the economic interdependency of their "*vie commune*".[13]

This process of limiting access to the PaCS to relationships that are ever-increasingly marriage-like was culminated within days of passage of the legislation, in a decision of the *Conseil constitutionnel* which construed the new law to require *sexual* attachment as an essential element of the PaCS relation.[14]

of arguments here, not of realities yet unknown; and as I say in my last paragraph, I'm not sure how one would select among the myriad normative theories for assessing marriage. It remains an open question for me, for instance, whether same-sex couples with a queer project for their sexual or political lives—couples whose members might currently find it difficult to indicate their dissent from the valuation of marriage as a human and social good—might discover a crucial resource in their ability to *refuse* marriage. Producing oneself as weird can be precisely what one values.

[11] See Borrillo, chap. 25, at n. 11 and accompanying text. I am indebted to Daniel Borrillo for his careful legislative history of the PaCS.

[12] *Ibid.*, at n. 12 and accompanying text.

[13] Loi no. 99–944 du 15 novembre 1999 relative au pacte civil de solidarité, <http://www.legifrance.gouv.fr/html/frame_jo.html>.

[14] Decision No. 99-419 DC (9 Nov. 1999), <http://www.conseil-constitutionnel.fr/decision/1999/99419/index.htm>.

Indicating that "*la vie commune*" anticipated by the PaCS legislation did not extend to a mere commonality of interests or mere cohabitation of two people, the *Conseil* held that the PaCS is available only to those who intend to lead "*une vie de couple*". And what is "*une vie de couple*"? Apparently it is "*une vie sexuelle*". The *Conseil* insisted on this narrowing of the PaCS because the legislation, by barring blood relatives and those who are already married from obtaining PaCS status, "*a déterminé les composantes essentielles*" of the relation. The court apparently thought that nonincestuousness and nonpolygamy were "essentially" sexual limits. This interpretation is of course not the product of strictly logical thought. The danger that blood relatives might form PaCSs in order to formalise incestuous relations is not the only reason to bar them from the status: it is equally plausible that the evil to be avoided is that they would strip resources otherwise available to other family members by giving formal priority to a duty of support running only between the parties to the PaCS. And the danger that those who are already married would elevate an adulterous relationship to formal dignity by means of a PaCS is not the only reason to bar them from the status: it is equally plausible that the evil to be avoided is allowing married people to assume a duty to shift resources from their marital families to their PaCS, franc-for-franc to the detriment of the former. And even if the evil to be avoided was a sexual one, that does not make sexual attachment an essential element of the PaCS in general, but rather a risk foreseen for some particular PaCS relationships. The logic of the *Conseil constitutionnel* hangs together only if we add a premise not admitted to in its opinion: that marriage is not merely *a* but *the* paradigm of intimate adult commitment.

In parsing the successive accretion of marriage-like status rules limiting access to the PaCS, it may be helpful to distinguish marriage *substitutes* from marriage *alternatives*. The early proposals sponsored by the left were, I would suggest, marriage *alternatives*. They would have permitted individuals—whether in mere *pairs* or in *couples*, but above all, *not the state*, to determine the substantive content of particular PaCS relationships. These proposals would have bestowed recognition on same-sex couples and cross-sex couples without regard to the nature of their emotional bond and without any assumption that it was erotic: as long as the pair was ready to assume mutual responsibility for one another's daily needs and debts, the relationship would have been available. It could have been assumed by priest and housekeeper, two business partners, two roommates, two friends.

By contrast, the PaCS legislation as construed by the *Conseil constitutionnel* is a marriage *substitute*. With the sole exception that same-sex couples can avail themselves of it, it has the access rules of marriage. It accords a pared-down list of the substantive rules of marriage as well. In both respects, it resembles nothing on the U.S. scene so much as Domestic Partnership, which is consistently imagined as a marriage substitute, a way of bestowing a few sticks in the marriage bundle on couples the members of which are willing to attest that they live in a marriage-like relationship: monogamous, sexual, domestic, economically interdependent, and long-term.[15]

Even though marriage alternatives *are* Recognition projects, they are much less likely to normalise marriage, and much more likely to denormalise it, than marriage substitutes. To be sure, marriage substitutes have some denormalising force. Even as construed by the *Conseil constitutionnel*, the PaCS, like American Domestic Partnership when it is equally available to cross-sex and same-sex couples, may render marriage a little bit less paradigmatic. Under both regimes, marriage no longer normalises all sexual relationships: the marriage substitute does too, and since marriage and the marriage substitute are different in other ways (the latter is easier to dissolve, less loaded with traditional expectations, free of religious jurisdiction, etc.), introduction of the latter significantly diminishes the hegemonic posture of marriage. But let us imagine that the PaCS had remained available without any stipulation that it accommodates only "*une vie de couple*" or, indeed, without any requirement that the two people engaging in the relation *be* "a couple." That would have denormalised marriage in another, perhaps more significant way. As pairs with different modes of mutual dependency adopted the PaCS form, they would have pluralised it. The PaCS itself would have resisted normalisation.[16] Unfortunately we won't have an opportunity to observe how this would have affected marriage, but here are two examples of what I think we'll be missing. Wouldn't it have occurred to more people than it does now to question whether friendship deserves the same level of commitment which is now captured for sexual relationships by marriage and its substitutes? Mightn't it have occurred to more people that the PaCS, with its individually tailored duty of support and easy exit rules, could sustain linked relationships and could therefore do without its current monogamy rules? In short, wouldn't marriage and the marriage paradigm have come in for some serious normative competition? Wouldn't the power of marriage to arrange the field of adult intimacy have wobbled from its center?

We in the U.S. will achieve none of this by seeking same-sex marriage. Indeed, the complex pattern of competing normalisations that emerges from the

[15] For example, Stanford University defines a Domestic Partner as

> "the partner of an eligible employee or retiree who is of the same sex, sharing a long-term committed relationship of indefinite duration with the following characteristics:
> —Living together for at least six months
> —Having an exclusive mutual commitment similar to that of marriage.
> —Financially responsible for each other's well being and debts to third parties. . . .
> —Neither partner is married to anyone else nor has another domestic partner.
> —Partners are not related by blood closer than would bar marriage in their state of residence".

Stanford University, "Enrollment Information for Same-Sex Domestic Partners."

[16] For an argument that denormalisation would be better furthered in the U.S. not by marriage substitutes like Domestic Partnership, but by marriage alternatives modeled on forms of association currently recognised in contract and corporate law, see Martha M. Ertman, "Marriage as a Trade: Bridging the Private/Private Distinction," (2001) 36 *Harvard Civil Rights—Civil Liberties Law Review* 79.

addition of the PaCS to French law, and that would have emerged from the formation of actual multiformed PaCSs within French society if the legislation had not been narrowed so dramatically, throws a sharp emphasis on the much more binary pattern that will prevail if US advocates of same-sex *marriage* achieve their goal.[17]

RIGHTS, REGULATION AND NORMALISATION

Rights are an exceedingly rich mode of justification for all kinds of things in the US—indeed, sometimes it appears to be the only language of justification in which we can speak to one another. The particular form that they take in US pro-same-sex-marriage argumentation is nicely exemplified by the second "interest" that Wolfson says people have in marriage: "*access* to legal and economic *benefits and protections*".[18]

When we say "rights of marriage," we frequently fold together, as Wolfson does here, the right *to* marry and the rights *of* marriage. This is a perfectly legitimate thing to do: from the perspective of candidates for marriage it makes sense, in that they want the former because it bestows the latter; and from the perspective of the US Supreme Court it made sense on a theory that, inasmuch as the latter are fundamental, the former must be as well.[19] But the very nature of the "right" in question is somewhat complex, in ways that will be clearer if we tease apart the right to marry and the rights of marriage, and some of their subsidiary elements.

There are, as far as I can tell, four basic forms of the argument that same-sex marriage is justified by a right to marry. The four asserted rights are:

1. The right to select one's marital partner without interference from the state;

[17] Morris Kaplan argues that the Recognition project avoids Normalisation and in fact may contribute to the multiplicity and accessibility of sexual intimacies and intensities that do not resemble marriage. He is not able to specify how this result would be delivered, however. His argument that "[a]t bottom the demand for recognition of same-sex partnerships is a demand to acknowledge the validity of lesbian and gay forms of life" (MB Kaplan, *Sexual Justice: Democratic Citizenship and the Politics of Desire* (London, Routledge, 1997) at 235, emphasis added) is simply incorrect. At least as it has been made in the U.S., it is a demand for acknowledgment of the validity of a *particular form* of lesbian and gay life: monogamous, sexual, domestic, economically interdependent, and long-term lesbian and gay life—that is, *marriagelike* lesbian and gay life. And second, his argument that seeking recognition of same-sex marriage is a form of civil disobedience (rather than an implicit concession that the state has legitimate power to bestow value on sexual relationships) is too ideal to have more than speculative importance. He is unable to define a single tactic, aside from violating sodomy statutes in the context of a public celebration of a same-sex couple's commitment to one another, that could meet the definition of civil disobedience, and he concedes (at 228–9) that the very people likely to seek marriage would be the last to undertake such a performance precisely because their monogamous, domestic, etc., sexual normativity would object strongly to it. Seeking recognition of same-sex marriage may be *dissent*, but it is dissent from the state's refusal to say it values lesbian and gay couples.

[18] Wolfson, *supra* n.4, at 580.

[19] See *Zablocki* v. *Redhail*, 434 US 374 at 386 (1978).

2. The right to choose marriage as the form for one's intimate relationships;
3. The right to be free from discrimination on the basis of some improper ground (gender, sexual orientation) in gaining access to marriage; and
4. The fundamental right *of* marriage.

These are not all the same thing, either in the law that they elaborate, or in the rhetoric of justification they invoke. I have ranked them in an order that emphasises a key discontinuity: the "right to select one's marital partner without interference from the state" and "the right to chose marriage as the form for one's intimate relationships" are deeply individualist and even libertarian in their framing (the former more so than the latter), while "the fundamental right *of* marriage" describes the marital relationship as a thoroughgoing engagement in a basic social form.

This discontinuity is endemic in invocations of marriage rights. Compare Kantrowitz's rights talk with that of the U.S. Supreme Court in its most-often-quoted definition of marriage. Kantrowitz asserted:

> "If it is *freely chosen*, a marriage license is as fine an *option* as sexual license. All *I* ask is the right to *choose for myself*".[20]

This speaker is a bold loner, the liberal individual *par excellence*—but it is also the speaker whom we have just heard asking for an "ultimate normalization". This tension between the individual and the social should come as no surprise: after all, the act of marrying cannot be done alone. On the sociability of marriage, consider the US Supreme Court's characterisation of marriage in *Griswold* v. *Connecticut*, a 1965 decision holding that married couples have the right to use contraceptives:

> "Marriage is a *coming together* for better or for worse, hopefully enduring, and intimate to the degree of being sacred. It is an *association* that promotes *a way of life*, not causes; a *harmony* in living, not political faiths; a *bilateral loyalty*, not commercial or social projects. Yet it is an *association* for as noble a purpose as any involved in our prior decisions".[21]

Of course this is a rights-*of*-marriage decision, but this passage has been crucial in right-*to*-marry analyses, and for an obvious reason: if marriage is a fundamental form of human association, access to it is also fundamental; it is a fundamental right. But note that, in this formulation, marriage is not a *choice of mine*; it is an *association of us*. The couple replaces the individual as the subject of marital rights.

Here we have a shift that is buried in much US same-sex rights-claiming, when advocates assert the rights of "individuals *and couples*" to choose

[20] A Kantrowitz, "Till Death Do Us Part: Reflections on Community", *The Advocate* (Los Angeles), March 1983, at 27 (emphasis added).

[21] *Griswold* v. *Connecticut*, 381 U.S. 479 at 486 (1965) (emphasis added).

marriage.[22] The conflict elided in this formulation remains immanent at the moment a couple—or, the two individuals in it—decide to get married, but it is extremely salient when the couple—or, one of the two individuals in it—decides to divorce. We have in the US today, for example, a system of unilateral divorce by either spouse: a spouse who wishes to oppose a divorce in the hope of "saving the marriage" *will not prevail* against a spouse willing to testify that the marriage has irretrievably broken down. Alternatively, consider the succession of subjects in three important reproductive decision-making cases: we go from *Griswold*, which recognises the right of the marital *couple* to use contraceptives; to *Eisenstadt* v. *Baird*, which extends that right to unmarried individuals on the ground that the US Constitution regards married couples not as a unit but as *two rights-bearing individuals*;[23] to *Planned Parenthood of Central Missouri* v. *Danforth*, which holds that when a wife wants to elect an abortion which the husband opposes, the state may not require the wife to preserve the husband's potential child.[24] These gripping scenarios involving one spouse's unilateral control over matters central to the marriage are probably never imagined on wedding day, but they are implicit in it, and thus in any right of a couple—or the individuals in it?—to *have* a wedding day.

Over and above that rift, there is the further one between the rights of the individual and the couple on one hand, and the rights of the whole community with respect to their marriage on the other. The latter are eerily suggested in a passage from *Loving* v. *Virginia*, a 1967 US Supreme Court case holding that the states could not ban interracial marriage. One reason for that holding: marriage is a *fundamental right* in the sense that everyone has an interest in its nondiscriminatory availability:

> "To deny this fundamental freedom on so unsupportable a basis as the racial classifications embodied in these statutes . . . is surely to deprive *all* the State's citizens of liberty without due process of law".[25]

All citizens of the state are *actually* injured when *some* of them are punished for engaging in an interracial marriage. Here we see another hint, perhaps even stronger than the one sounded in *Griswold*, that "marriage rights" vastly overflow any individualist framing, placing individuals, couples and the broad totality of "the social" into a convergence that must bear within it the potential for

[22] Evan Wolfson provides the following "Marriage Resolution" promulgated by Lambda Legal Defense and Education Fund, Inc., and other pro-gay, pro-same-sex-marriage groups:

> "Because Marriage is a basic human right and an individual personal choice, RESOLVED, the State should not interfere with same-gender *couples who choose* to marry and share fully and equally in the rights, responsibilities, and commitment of civil marriage".

E Wolfson, "Why We Should Fight for the Freedom to Marry: The Challenges and Opportunities that Will Follow a Win in Hawaii" (1996) 1 *Journal of Gay, Lesbian, and Bisexual Identity* 79 at 82 (emphasis added).

[23] 405 US 438 (1972).

[24] 428 US 52 at 67–72 (1976).

[25] 388 US 1 at 12 (1967).

tension. And there is always a key conceptual tension. The interest of "all the State's citizens" in *your* marriage places almost excruciating pressure on the idea of marital *rights*. If rights are liberties, if they are classically the freedoms of individuals to act without state interference, entering into a relationship with every "citizen of the State" can only problematically be the content of a right.

The language of rights and freedom in U.S. same-sex marriage justification frequently runs up against this problematic, only to suppress it. Tropically, this occlusion takes the form of claims that marriage is a plastic social form always ready to receive the impressions of our wishes. In his book *The Case for Same-Sex Marriage*, William N Eskridge, Jr., insists that "marriage is a prepolitical form of interpersonal liberty", even as he acknowledges that it "is a creature of law and generates many legal ripple effects".[26] But ultimately he refutes the idea that the marital form has liberty-constraining functions: "Neither history nor the Bible nor the imperative of procreation establishes what marriage *must* be, as a matter of law. Marriage is an important legal construction, and it is what we *make* it to be".[27] Similarly, Evan Wolfson argues that marriage "is socially constructed, and thus transformable"[28]: "the fundamental issues in the [right-to-marry] cases are choice and equality, not the pro's and con's of a way of life, or even the 'right' choice".[29] But Wolfson has just told us that, according to the US Supreme Court in *Griswold*, marriage is fundamental precisely *because* it promotes *a* way of life.

More rarely (because the actual concrete incidents of marriage are so rarely important in same-sex marriage justifications),[30] the occlusion of Regulation by Rights occurs on the terrain of the couple's—or its individuals'?—control over the marital form. David Chambers, in his 1996 article entitled "What If?: The Legal Consequences of Marriage and the Legal Needs of Lesbian and Gay Couples",[31] considers the possibility that same-sex marriage would constrain, not foster, the liberty of gay men and lesbians. It is rare to find anyone even asking the question. For Chambers, the danger to gay liberty is mitigated by the increasing availability of antenuptial agreements and other contractual inroads on marriage as a rigidly state-defined status. And so he ultimately concludes that the specific terms of marriage are increasingly subject to determination by

[26] WN Eskridge, Jr., *The Case for Same-Sex Marriage: From Sexual Liberty to Civilized Commitment* (New York, Free Press, 1996) at 132.

[27] *Ibid*., at 160 (emphasis in original).

[28] Wolfson, *supra* n.4, at 589.

[29] *Ibid*., at 580.

[30] In 1996, Chambers noted that "[i]n the vigorous public discussion [on same-sex marriage], few advocates address at any length the legal consequences of marriage. William Eskridge, for example, devotes only six of the 261 pages in his fine new book, *The Case for Same-Sex Marriage*, to the legal consequences, and his, with one exception, is the longest discussion I can find". D Chambers, "What If?: The Legal Consequences of Marriage and the Legal Needs of Lesbian and Gay Couples" (1996) 95 *Michigan Law Review* 447 at 450. My research has not divulged anything that would allow me to amend this observation. The legal sequelae of marriage just don't matter much in this rhetorical field.

[31] *Ibid*.

particular couples: as long as that is true, the constraints are at once sporadic and, most likely, loosening. That being so, Chambers concludes, marriage represents a net gain in liberty for gay men and lesbians.

Chambers is utterly unique in the pro-same-sex-marriage literature, as far as I know, in acknowledging without cavil that marriage is a form of regulation.[32] But his cost/benefit analysis is a bit skewed to enhance his liberty-wins outcome. His own recitation of the specific legal consequences of marriage includes several terms that are *utterly unalterable* by the parties to particular US marriages: first, any criminal prohibition of either partner's engagement in sex with a third person (adultery laws); second, any employer rules against married couples working in the same workplace (anti-nepotism policies); third, the duty of support, at least to the extent of paying third parties out of one's own assets for a spouse's "necessary expenses"[33] and, in community property states, of depleting the marital "community" to pay *any* debts incurred by a spouse during the marriage; fourth and fifth, exit from the marriage only by death or divorce, with the state taking jurisdiction over each and often imposing substantive requirements when it gains this control. There are at least three more that are so widely taken for granted—so hidden in plain sight—that even Chambers doesn't isolate them. The first two are rigid, though silent, substantive bans: one, marriage to one-and-only-one person at a time (no polygamy or polyandry); and two, no "term" marriage contracts (no "5-year renewable" marriage; no "marriage for tonight"). The third arises from the state's plenary, but at any given moment perhaps unexercised, power to "construct" the marital form. The state can change the basic rules of marriages currently under way without providing a special exit for those who do not consent to the change. It has done so in my lifetime: the adoption of no-fault divorce drastically changed the terms of millions of ongoing marriages, pervasively, it appears, to the disadvantage of wives. States could reinstate a requirement of fault for divorce today without consulting the wishes of married individuals or couples beyond what is necessary to pass normal legislation and without "grandfathering in" their current access to no-fault divorce.[34]

[32] *Ibid.*

[33] Note that, because medical care above and beyond that covered by insurance or social welfare programs is deemed "necessary," this obligation can be catastrophic for unlucky spouses.

[34] Eskridge misreads this argument in the essay he contributes to this volume. He attributes to me a point I do not make: that "same-sex marriage will invite increased state attention to queer people or their relationships". (See Eskridge, chap. 6, p. 123.) For Eskridge, "same-sex marriage" and "gay marriage" are interchangeable, and would be the place where the state could find "queer people". (See Eskridge, pp. 117, 120, 124, 125, 127.) But for me, the term "gay" and the term "marriage" have such divergent referential objects that I could not sensibly use them in Eskridge's formulation. "Gay" (to me) designates an historical project of producing erotic subjects of a certain sort; marriage is a legally enforced relationship with access and exit rules and substantive legal and cultural content. To say that marriage, or marriages, or a marriage, could be gay, jumps a very complex conceptual divide separating and joining the *production of subjects* from and to the *institutional forms that law provides for human sociability*. I avoid the term "gay marriage" because I think crossing back and forth across that divide is hard, detailed work—hard work that is presumed away by the term. And I don't think that recognising "gay marriage" as Eskridge conceptualises it would have any necessary meaning for "queer sexuality." I say "queer" in order *not to say* "gay"; if possible, "queer" should float free of homosexual identity with all its particularities; I think some

Moreover, the rights of marriage are not always "of the couple" but rather, often, lie *against* one spouse. It is charming to call these elements of marriage "duties," "obligations", and "civilised commitment"—but let's face it: the rights of spouse against spouse are also what we must mean when we say "the rights of marriage". If I marry you, I can sue you for divorce (as no one else can); can make you divide the property that the state deems us to "share" under the order of a court; and can often (in the US) seek to introduce evidence of your marital fault to tilt the rules or the judge's discretion in my direction. As Chambers concludes, "at divorce and death, states impose on married couples a prescriptive view of the appropriate financial relationship between them".[35] And even though many of the specific terms of that prescription can be bargained away by the spouses in a prenuptial agreement or waived in a will (as Chambers is relieved to point out), that bargaining and giving away will happen in the

same-sex sex is not queer and some cross-sex sex is queer; the excitement of having the term queer available arises in part from the open edge it offers people, without reference to the same-sex-ness or cross-sex-ness of any particular element of erotic life, to know, think, act or feel something about oneself and others in sexual ways that seem now to be unknowable, unthinkable, unactable, unfeelable. On my use of the term "queer," "gay marriages" would not necessarily harbor more or less "queerness" than what Eskridge would call "straight marriages." It appears that, when Eskridge and I talk about sexuality, we have very different conceptual (not to mention political and erotic) projects going.

Eskridge also inaccurately attributes to me a claim that recognition of same-sex marriage "will instigate a state mobilisation around sex-negative regulations" (Eskridge, *supra*, p. 125): I make no such claim. Continuing the critique, he inaccurately attributes to Michel Foucault (and, it appears, to Michael Warner and me) the view that "nothing happens as a direct result of top-down stimuli (including laws); social change occurs from the bottom up" (Eskridge, *supra*, p.125). These are crude formulations which no one well trained in postmodern theory would avow, and that have no purchase in the work of Foucault, Warner, or me (hubristic catalogue). Taken together with misreadings noted above, these errors may seem small. But they rob Eskridge's refutation of my argument of the bite he wishes it to have.

Eskridge is right of course to identify me as a person who argues that he and other gay centrists who seek legal recognition of same-sex marriage fail to deal forthrightly with the regulatory dimensions of marriage. Eskridge's essay in this volume is a good example of what I am objecting to. He wishes to refute my assertion that same-sex marriage would offer to same-sex couples a regulatory form with intensities and invasiveness that are distinctive and that would be new to them; I am wrong on this point, he says, because the state also regulates nonmarital "households," producing a symmetry that renders an extension of the regulatory domain of marriage to include same-sex relationships no extension of regulation at all. (See Eskridge, *supra*, p. 123.) But the analogous regulatory regimes that he identifies as appearing on either side of the marriage/not-marriage distinction are not necessarily *the same* or *as regulatory*. Surely if avoiding state regulation is your goal, you will use different words in answering the question "Would you want exit from your relationship to be by divorce or by the terms of a cohabitation agreement?" You might also have very different answers on either side. Nor does Eskridge engage the many ways that marriage produces regulatory effects, not only on the married couple, but through one spouse on another, and ultimately through the couple on the entire social array—ways which I detail in this paragraph and in the following ones. Teaching family law has given me deep respect for the particularities of marriage and the complex ways in which *some* of its elements are mimicked (not copied) by regulatory practices applicable outside the marital relationship; but it has also borne in upon me again and again that marriage in the United States remains a unique legal form of human sociability. It *is* discrimination; no discrimination, no marriage. And I think ultimately Eskridge would not disagree; he seeks a marriage right precisely because marriage is unlike unmarriage.

[35] Chambers, *supra* n.30, at 479.

shadow of the law (as Robert Mnookin and Lewis Kornhauser's classic article advises us).[36] Indeed, even the crudest application of economic modeling techniques to this process reveals the possibility that *any* important—or trivial!—decision in the marriage may be affected by these supposedly waivable endpoint rules.[37] The rights of spouse against spouse can be a source of diffuse, infinitesimal regulation of the marriage by a public that need not be visibly present.

Finally, even the most unequivocally beneficial of the marital rights recognised in the US—for instance, the spousal immigration and naturalisation preference, the federal command that employers must provide people with short leaves to care for their ill spouses, the eligibility to depend on a spouse's social security benefits, the exemption from federal and often state gift and estate taxes—depend on the state for their very meaning. They are not "rights" to be free from state interference à la the right of free speech: by contrast, they intrinsically involve a relationship with the state. Nor are they like other rights to enter legally enforceable relationships—for instance, the right to contract or to make a decision to procreate; by contrast, the state sets almost all the terms of these rights of marriage, while married people merely *receive* them. (The decision to exercise the right is, formally, distinct from design and receipt of the right itself.) It is far more apt to think of marriage in this aspect as a license. Here, as when the state stipulates that only X, Y, or Z type of entity can run a charter school or sell legal services, the state creates a warp in the distribution of some social good and then requires that only license holders can partake of it. But licenses aren't really about rights: they are instead a form of *regulation*.

Moreover, the regulatory effects of these marital "rights" extend way beyond the relationship of the licensed pair to the state. The four examples I just gave—the immigration and naturalisation preference, mandated availability of caretaking leave, social security dependency eligibility, and gift and estate tax exemption—allocate benefits to spouses on an assumption that each marriage is a mutual aid society. My family law professors at Yale, John Simon and Jay Katz, cannily described this aspect of US marriage as a private welfare system. The features I have just named transfer goods from some "public"—whether that is the pool of dispreferred potential immigrants, the employer, all participants in the social security system, or all those competing for state tax proceeds—to the marriage in order to subsidise the spouses' mutual duty of support. Other rules insist on specific transfers *within* the marriage: for example, social welfare programs, both public ones like Social Security and private ones like college scholarship programs, take both spouses' incomes into account in determining the eligibility of one of them for need-based subsidies. All of these rules posit that the *marriage* is primarily liable for its *members'* welfare.

[36] Robert Mnookin & Lewis Kornhauser, "Bargaining in the Shadow of the Law: The Case of Divorce" (1979) 88 *Yale Law Journal* 954.

[37] For some not-so-crude, indeed quite arresting, examples, see GS Becker and KM Murphy, "The Family and the State" (1988) 31 *Journal of Law and Economics* 1; S Lundberg and RA Pollak, "Bargaining and Distribution in Marriage" (Fall 1996) 10 *Journal of Economic Perspectives* 139.

This liability survives the marriage, moreover, as we see in divorce and probate rules requiring that spouses who have passed out of the marriage, either by divorce or death, continue to bear a unique responsibility for the former spouse's support. Taken together, these private-welfare-system rules are deeply distributive in their function. They say to married people: *You*, not *we*, will support *you*. And thus they also say to *un*married people: We will not support you; *you are on your own*.[38]

Thus the social totality is implicated in the marital form. Rights have led to Regulation, and Regulation (like some aspects of the much more demure project of Recognition) has led to Normalisation. Is regulation of this kind a bad thing? Is normalisation of this kind a bad thing? These are hard questions. Every resource known to ethical philosophy, every theory of the state, every model of justice, offers a different way of approaching them. The purpose of this chapter is not to decide those questions or to argue that one or the other understanding of ethics, the state, or justice is the right one to use in answering them. My point instead is that we can't begin that work without an honest, beady-eyed understanding of *what marriage is*. And to that end, I would invoke two procedural norms which I think ought to guide us: "honesty is the best policy" and "be careful what you ask for." I rely on them to say: recognition and rights arguments depend on regulation and normalisation arguments; and it is bad to have a debate over the social value of lifting the ban on same-sex marriage that fails to acknowledge—indeed, that typically hides—these entailments.

[38] Thus Fraser's model of the relationship between Recognition and economic redistribution in gay rights claiming is, at least in the instance of marriage rights, mistaken. As I indicated above, see *supra*, text accompanying nn.3–4, Fraser regards Recognition as a distinct remedy that has merely consequential impacts on economic distribution. But claiming to have a right to marry (or to have one's same-sex relationship recognised through legal marriage) *is* claiming a certain place in the private welfare system managed through marriage; and it *is* claiming a right to avoid another place in it.

6

The Ideological Structure of the Same-Sex Marriage Debate (And Some Postmodern Arguments for Same-Sex Marriage)

WILLIAM N ESKRIDGE, JR*

STATE RECOGNITION OF same-sex partnerships as marriages is a sensible idea that is simultaneously radical and conservative. It is sensible because it insists on formal equality in state treatment of same-sex and different-sex couples.[1] It is radical because marriage between two people of the same sex challenges the conceptions of marriage and gender roles held by most Americans: a woman cannot be a wife unless partnered with a man, her husband; a man cannot be a husband unless partnered with a woman, his wife. It is conservative because it accepts the value of marriage—interpersonal commitment in particular—and offers it as a positive aspiration for gay and lesbian couples.

As the case for same-sex marriage has gained some support among fair-minded people and inspired an increasing number of jurisdictions to provide formal recognitions of same-sex partnerships, a fierce debate has been joined. Given its simultaneously radical and conservative ramifications, same-sex marriage has drawn fire from both right and left. *Traditionalist* critics consider same-sex marriage too radical and insufficiently attentive to the unique value of

* John A Garver Professor of Jurisprudence, Yale Law School. I am most appreciative of helpful and learned comments on earlier drafts of this chapter from Robert Wintemute and Edward Stein. Joshua Stehlik, Yale 2001, provided helpful research assistance.

[1] For a sampling of the rich literature setting forth legal and political arguments for same-sex marriage, see WN Eskridge, Jr, *The Case for Same-Sex Marriage* (New York, NY, Free Press, 1996); MB Kaplan, *Sexual Justice: Democratic Citizenship and the Politics of Desire* (New York, NY, Routledge, 1997); RD Mohr, *A More Perfect Union: Why Straight America Must Stand Up for Gay Rights* (Boston, MA, Beacon Press, 1994); S Sherman (ed.), *Lesbian and Gay Marriage: Private Commitments, Public Ceremonies* (Philadelphia, PA, Temple University Press, 1992); M Coombs, "Sexual Dis-Orientation: Transgendered People and Same-Sex Marriage", (1998) 8 *UCLA Women's Law Journal* 219; MC Dunlap, "The Lesbian and Gay Marriage Debate: A Microcosm of Our Hopes and Our Troubles", (1991) 1 *Law and Sexuality* 62; ND Hunter, "Marriage, Law, and Gender: A Feminist Inquiry", (1991) 1 *Law and Sexuality* 9; E Wolfson, "Crossing the Threshold: Equal Marriage Rights for Lesbians and Gay Men and the Intra-Community Critique", (1994–95) 21 *New York University Review of Law and Social Change* 567.

different-sex marriage, long recognised in western history. *Progressive* critics consider same-sex marriage an insufficiently radical challenge to oppressive traditions and too accommodating to mainstream values. Notice how the traditionalist and progressive critiques mirror one another.

Likewise, the specific responses made by the differently situated critics reflect parallel universes: traditionalist justifications for continued exclusion perversely mirror progressive justifications for much greater inclusion. For example, both kinds of critics object that formal equality for lesbian and gay couples would *normalise* lesbian and gay couples. Such normalisation would assertedly promote homosexuality, which the traditionalist finds an inferior condition,[2] or standardise gay lives around committed coupling, which many progressives find too confining.[3] As to the argument that same-sex marriage would extend useful state benefits to same-sex couples and would encourage commitment, the critics bemoan the *regulatory effects* of such a move. Traditionalists say it would undermine the state's effort to encourage different-sex marriage,[4] while progressives say it would introduce too much state involvement in some, and perhaps many, gay and lesbian relationships.[5] Naysayers fault the gender-role argument for same-sex marriage through strategies of *denial*: traditionalists deny that natural gender roles should be sacrificed,[6] while some progressives deny that same-sex marriage will have any such effect.[7] Table 1 maps the arguments for same-sex marriage and the mirror-image responses by traditionalist and progressive critics.

Table 1 is just a starting point for thinking about the underlying structure of the same-sex marriage debate. The case for same-sex marriage starts with the principle of formal equality: similarly situated people (and couples) should presumptively be treated similarly.[8] Critics of same-sex marriage generally deny that same-sex couples are situated similarly to different-sex couples, but also direct much of their analyses on the bad consequences formal equality would generate, both for their own constituencies and for the country as a whole. Defenders respond that same-sex marriage would not necessarily have such malignant consequences. Mark this irony. Although the case for same-sex

[2] See RA Posner, *Sex and Reason* (Cambridge, MA, Harvard University Press, 1991), at 311.

[3] See PL Ettelbrick, "Since When Is Marriage a Path to Liberation?", (Fall 1989) 6 *OUT/LOOK* at 8–12, reprinted in WN Eskridge, Jr. and ND Hunter (eds.), *Sexuality, Gender, and the Law* (Westbury, NY, Foundation Press, 1997), at 817–18.

[4] See The Ramsey Colloquium, "The Homosexual Movement: A Response by the Ramsey Colloquium", (March 1994) 41 *First Things*.

[5] See N Duclos, "Some Complicating Thoughts on Same-Sex Marriage", (1991) 1 *Law and Sexuality* 31 at 52–5.

[6] See J Finnis, "Law, Morality, and 'Sexual Orientation'", (1994) 69 *Notre Dame Law Review* 1049 at 1051–3.

[7] See ND Polikoff, "We Will Get What We Ask For: Why Legalizing Gay and Lesbian Marriage Will Not 'Dismantle the Legal Structure of Gender in Every Marriage'", (1993) 79 *Virginia Law Review* 1535.

[8] See Eskridge, *supra* n.1, at 123–82, for the formal argument, and at 183–91, for a functional argument supporting the importance that formal equality has and should have in our polity.

Table 1: Arguments For and Against Same-Sex Marriage

Case For Same-Sex Marriage	Traditionalist Arguments Against Same-Sex Marriage	Progressive Arguments Against Same-Sex Marriage
Formal Equality: Same-sex couples ought to be treated the same as different-sex couples.	*Normalisation*: Equal treatment would normalise homosexuality, which is either bad or, at least, not as good as heterosexuality.	*Normalisation*: Equal treatment would normalise gay couples, denigrate uncoupled gays, or contribute to the standardisation of same-sex relationships.
Regulatory Benefits: Marriage recognition would assure gay couples of tangible benefits, as well as reinforcement of interpersonal commitment.	*Regulatory Costs*: Legitimating an alternative "lifestyle," same-sex marriage would undermine different-sex marriage.	*Regulatory Costs*: Introducing the state into same-sex partnerships, same-sex marriage would undermine the liberty of lesbians, gay men, and bisexuals.
Critique of Gender Roles: Same-sex marriage would help erode rigid gender roles (woman=wife and child-rearer; man= husband and breadwinner) within marriage.	*Denial*: Woman's natural role is to be married to a man, and vice-versa. (Woman's natural role is to bear children in the context of marriage to a man.) The state cannot change that.	*Denial*: State recognition of same-sex marriages would have scant effect on gender roles. (It would further marginalise the most radical gender-benders.)

marriage centrally focuses on the idea of formal equality, the debate appears to the casual observer to be overwhelmingly *consequentialist*. What would be the consequences of formal equality? Not good for straight people say traditionalist opponents. Nor for queer people say progressive opponents. That pretty much covers the population.

Although the debate appears to be consequentialist, no one actually knows the consequences, especially the long-term consequences, of state recognition for same-sex marriage. That hardly seems to matter when the debate also concerns an institution so freighted with cultural significance as marriage. Thus, a second—and more fundamental—feature of the same-sex marriage debate is that it is *abstract and ideological*. The consequentialist features of the debate are about theoretical and symbolic consequences more than actual and tangible consequences. Accordingly, people's positions are driven by their underlying institutional and theoretical commitments, and few people are really open to changing their minds, at least in the short and medium term. Roughly speaking, the underlying theoretical stances are these: *premodern* theories about natural gender roles inspire the most dedicated traditionalist opposition; *modern* liberal theories emphasising individual freedom of choice are the mainstay of same-sex marriage proponents; *postmodern* theories stressing oppressive cultural constraints on liberal freedom of choice inspire most of the progressive opponents of same-sex marriage.

A third feature of the same-sex marriage debate is its *rhetorical asymmetry*. Although the most dedicated traditionalist opponents are inspired by premodern natural law-type theories, they realise that their position must also be defended along modernist lines as well, because such arguments are the lingua franca of public discourse in modern democracies. Hence the debate between same-sex marriage proponents and traditionalist opponents tends to be, ostensibly, liberal and rights-oriented. This works to the disadvantage of opponents, because their modernist arguments are pretexts for their natural law position. Their argument that same-sex marriage would hurt children raised in such households has been witheringly reviewed by the modernist experts in child psychology, and their other arguments fare no better.[9] Nonetheless, their position prevails in most places because of old-fashioned homophobia and residual nervousness about change from the most robust premodernist baselines.

In contrast, the progressive critics of same-sex marriage slight modernist liberal argumentation and insist on postmodern starting points. Our identities are contingent and always in the process of formation. That process is one of struggle and resistance. It can be obstructed or distorted by modernist as well as premodernist discourses; while the latter deny human subjects any freedom from their received social role, the former promise freedom but deliver norms of standardisation and responsibility that are just as confining. The liberal ideal of formal equality has little relevance for such critics, except as something to be deconstructed. For one example, consider this familiar deconstructive move: formal equality for a minority group presents itself as improving the status of the group, but that improvement rests upon the minority's acquiescing in the norms of the majority; such acquiescence is acceptable to that portion of the minority that is already most like the majority (thus the subgroup with the higher status anyway); ergo, formal equality has the consequence of debasing the minority, insofar as its people give up part of their uniqueness, and of splitting the minority into those advantaged by assimilation and those who find themselves even more marginalised.

Because the main debate is with traditionalists, proponents of same-sex marriage have not only devoted little attention to the debate within progressive, particularly queer, communities, but have also generally responded to the postmodern questions with the same modernist answers they provide in the main debate. The progressive critics, in turn, deny the legitimacy of liberal arguments

[9] *Ibid.*, at 87–122; WN Eskridge, Jr., *Gaylaw: Challenging the Apartheid of the Closet* (Cambridge, MA, Harvard University Press, 1999) at 271–92.

and make their own arguments in abstract terminology that is sometimes incomprehensible to most bisexuals, lesbians, gay men, and transgendered people. For example, supporters of same-sex marriage respond to traditionalist arguments that marriage both has been, and should be, different-sex in nature by showing how similarly same-sex couples fit the relevant modern policy goal of marriage— commitment to one another in a unitive partnership. Progressive critics jump on this response as proof that the same-sex marriage movement seeks to normalise all queer people around the minority who prefer marriage-like arrangements. The same dynamic repeats itself in connection with the regulatory costs and gender-role arguments. Table 2 is another mapping of the same-sex marriage debate along this structural dimension.

Table 2, and the dynamic it illustrates, ought to concern all pro-gay and pro-queer thinkers. Progressive same-sex marriage proponents, such as Nan Hunter and I, realise that we need to be more attentive to the arguments of critics, such as Paula Ettelbrick and Nancy Polikoff. Any failure of mutual engagement

Table 2: The Argument Flow in the Same-Sex Marriage Debate

Traditionalist Starting Point: Conservative Arguments for Keeping the Status Quo	The Gaylegal Response: Liberal Arguments for Same-Sex Marriage Recognition	The Progressive Critique: Why Liberal Gay Arguments Are Not Queer
Difference. The pro-creative goal is essential to marriage. "Homo-sexuals" don't belong, unless they convert to heterosexuality.	*Sameness*. The unitive goal of marriage is one that same-sex couples can enjoy just as much as different-sex couples.	*Difference*. The sameness argument marginalises most queer people. Normalising around marriage is statist, coercive, and ignores more radical strategies.
Status. "Homosexual marriage" would under-mine "real" marriage, an institution already under siege from liberalising state "reforms" such as no-fault divorce.	*Choice*. Gay marriage is no threat to the institution. It is unfair not to allow same-sex couples to have access to the state benefits and duties of marriage.	*Status*. Buying into state-sanctioned marriage under-mines our capacity for sexual choice: state recognition obscures other ways of human coupling and may even invite meddling in the sex lives of queer people.
Role Fixity. Husband and wife are essential roles in marriage, and they can only be filled by man and woman, respectively.	*Role Flexibility*. Rigid gender roles are neither necessary nor just in modern society. Same-sex marriage would challenge, and perhaps undermine, this premise of sexism.	*Role Fixity*. Although rigid gender roles are bad, same-sex marriage will do little to undermine them. It may reinforce the outlaw roles ascribed to some queer people.

misses opportunities to learn useful things about the best path toward reform. Moreover, there are ramifications of this nonengagement in the mainstream debate. Not only do progressive critiques mirror (in a weird way) traditionalist critiques of same-sex marriage, but traditionalist opponents episodically seize upon the progressive critiques, to show that same-sex marriage proponents are misrepresenting the consequences of same-sex marriage; this traditionalist strategy, in turn, presses proponents into more assimilative, and allegedly anti-queer, rhetorical strategies. This is not a good dynamic, and I want to resist its pull. In the remainder of this chapter, I shall tease out the differences among traditionalist (premodern), liberal (modern), and progressive (postmodern) discourses about same-sex marriage. Among other things, this shows the deep conceptual error traditionalists make when they seek to expropriate postmodern arguments for their own reactionary purposes. More importantly, I want to suggest ways the same-sex marriage movement should attend to progressive critiques, and to pose some provisional postmodern arguments in favor of same-sex marriage.

THE NORMALISATION ARGUMENT

Different deployments of the term *normal* help us understand the different stances in the same-sex marriage debate. For the traditionalist, the normal is what history or religion tells us is natural for the human subject; most traditionalists insist that the only natural (and therefore only normal) marriage roles are those of husband engaged in procreative intercourse with his wife. Hence, same-sex marriage is abnormal, and treating it as normal is an abomination. Modernists are more flexible: each person has her own individual needs, and we all ought to be able to choose what is normal for ourselves. What is normal for me might be abnormal for you, and the liberal state ought to accommodate diversity of tastes. Some postmodernists maintain that there is a subtext to the ostensibly pro-choice liberal text in the regulatory state, namely, the modernist tendency to limit choice or to encourage preferred choices through a process of normalisation.[10] Rather than dictating a person's choices through insistence on natural law roles, the state participates in a social process whereby the statisti-

[10] On normalisation as a conforming feature of modernism and its obsession with standard deviations, see Michel Foucault, *Discipline and Punish: The Birth of the Prison* (Alan Sheridan translator) (New York, Vintage, 1979 [original, 1975]) at 182–84; Georges Canguilhem, *The Normal and the Pathological* (Carolyn R. Fawcett translator) (New York, Zone, 1989 [original, 1966]). Janet Halley's contribution to this volume (Halley, chap. 5, n.7) reads these sources differently than I do but misreads the argument I make in the text. For example, I do not maintain that normalisation necessarily entails valorisation of the "average"; all I read Foucault and Canguilhem to say is that normalisation can have consequences by constraining perceived choice or by exercising a gravitational pull on decisions. Nor does this section address Halley's own version of the normalisation argument, which is in my view different from those of Ettelbrick and Polikoff and Warner but came to my attention too late in the drafting process for me to address in detail.

cal norm exercises a gravitational pull on people to conform, and most comply without thinking. According to such postmodernists, this is a coercive process.

Paula Ettelbrick first advanced a rudimentary version of the normalisation objection in the same-sex marriage literature, and Nitya Duclos and Nancy Polikoff (among others) have developed it along postmodern feminist lines.[11] The concern has several dimensions. The main one is that state recognition of same-sex marriage would be a strong signal valorising only those kinds of relationships among gay people—and thereby marginalising lesbian couples who choose not to marry, gay men who prefer multiple partners, and bisexual and gay people who for various reasons are not coupled. Ettelbrick and Duclos also worry that the people left behind will be disproportionately gay women, people of color, and working class folks.[12] Finally, there is a general concern that same-sex marriage would deradicalise the gay rights movement, deflecting attention and activism away from more worthy queer projects.

The standard liberal response to these arguments looks to the preferences of sexual minorities in the United States. Popular polls say that most bisexuals, lesbians, and gay men want to have the right to marry.[13] This reflects the social fact that most gay people are not as radical in their aspirations as Polikoff and Ettelbrick; it probably is the case that most gay people want to be normalised—especially if normalisation means greater toleration and acceptance within their families, workplaces, and communities. This is not a satisfactory answer from a postmodern point of view. The current preferences of gay people, progressives maintain, reflect the triumph of normalisation, not truly unconstrained choice. Some postmodernists would maintain that the main effect of normalisation is that it limits choice by constraining people's ability to imagine other ways of structuring their relationships. Because sexual and gender nonconformists have never been given unconstrained choices in our society, there is no telling what their ideal choices would actually be. The role of progressive activists is to insist that more real choices be available, and this is an idea that I recommend to everyone involved in the same-sex marriage movement.

In evaluating the normalisation objection, it is productive to think about how same-sex marriage might fit into the overall struggle for legal and social

[11] See Ettelbrick, *supra* n.3; Polikoff, *supra* n. 7. See also Duclos, *supra* n.5, at 35–52.

[12] See Ettelbrick, *supra* n.3, at 12 (*Sexuality, Gender, and the Law* at 818). There is no empirical basis for accepting—or rejecting—this proposition, and there is no good reason in theory why gays of color, lesbians, and working class gays would not marry. Most of the plaintiffs in the reported cases are from one of these groups; lesbian couples in particular have been found by social scientists to derive greater satisfaction than gay male or straight couples from committed relationships; working class and interracial couples would find the protective benefits of marriage particularly useful—although Duclos, *supra* n. 5, at 54–5, is right to say that many of the burdens of marriage, such as disqualification from some social benefit programs, would fall disproportionately on indigent gay people.

[13] The most ambitious polls to this effect, published in the August 1994 (gay men) and August 1995 (lesbians) issues of *The Advocate*, were self-selected and therefore cannot be generalised. Nonetheless, most intellectuals assume their results to reflect the preferences of ordinary bisexuals, gay men, and lesbians.

toleration, and even acceptance, of gay or queer people. Same-sex marriage could be desirable from a progressive point of view if it would, in the long term, contribute to greater social acceptance of gay people and other sexual nonconformists— not just married gay couples. Here is the logic of this possibility. Driven by strong emotions, homophobia is resistant to logical argumentation and can be exacerbated by angry confrontation; like other kinds of prejudice, it is intensified when its objects are perceived as threats to the homophobe's cherished values.[14] Social scientists have found that the homophobe is most likely to adjust his attitudes if someone close to him—especially a family member or a coworker—comes out to him *and* engages him personally by showing him that the gay person and the straight person have much in common, including shared values.[15] As a public declaration of commitment, same-sex marriage is not only necessarily a coming out experience, but is also the coming-out of the gay pair as a couple, reaffirming the same kind of values husbands and wives exchange in mainstream society. Every same-sex marriage—whether sanctioned by the state or not—stimulates a dialectic within families, workplaces, and communities. While the typical reaction to such coming out is avoidance or even rejection, the ongoing conversations following a gay marriage can and frequently do change people's attitudes about the couple and about gay people generally. That this is a painfully slow process should not obscure the fact that this is the only process that reliably operates to diminish homophobia.

It is also erroneous to assume (as I once did) that the struggle for same-sex marriage necessarily or practically precludes the creation of other institutions for recognition of same-sex unions. As the same-sex marriage movement in Europe suggests, the compromises that proponents make on the path toward same-sex marriage will create new institutional norms for thinking about human relationships. Responding to demands for same-sex marriage, the Netherlands' Parliament enacted a law recognising registered partnerships, granting almost all of the rights, benefits, and obligations of marriage but not the name. Unlike the pioneering Danish statute, the Dutch law made registered partnerships available to different-sex as well as same-sex couples, and about a third of the Dutch registrants have been different-sex couples. Like the laws in Sweden and other countries, the Netherlands' new statute did not disturb laws recognising specified rights and responsibilities between cohabiting same-sex as well as different-sex couples. When the Dutch government in 1999 introduced a bill to recognise same-sex marriages in the Netherlands, the bill left the new registered partnership institution in place; it remains available for different-sex

[14] See G Haddock, et al., "Assessing the Structure of Prejudicial Attitudes: The Case of Attitudes Toward Homosexuals", (1993) 65 *Journal of Personality and Social Psychology* 1105. Critique of social science studies of prejudice can be found in C Kitzinger, *The Social Construction of Lesbianism* (London, Sage, 1987), at 153–77.

[15] See GM Herek and JP Capitanio, "'Some of My Best Friends': Intergroup Conflict, Concealable Stigma, and Heterosexuals' Attitudes Toward Gay Men and Lesbians", (1996) 22 *Personality and Social Psychology Bulletin* 412.

as well as same-sex couples even after same-sex marriage was recognised in 2001.[16] In 1999, the French government created the new *pacte civil de solidarité* (PaCS), which allows couples to assume mutual responsibility for one another's debts and needs and which is available to couples of all sorts—including different-sex as well as same-sex couples.[17] As in the Netherlands, this new institution did not entail the abolition of others already in place for cohabiting couples.

The United States has just offered an example of this phenomenon. In *Baker* v. *State*,[18] the Vermont Supreme Court ruled that the state could not discriminate against same-sex couples in its provision of benefits and obligations for committed unions. The court instructed the legislature to adopt a law equalising the benefits and obligations accorded same-sex and different-sex unions. After an intense and illuminating public debate, the Vermont legislature adopted an equalisation statute.[19] Vermont created a new institution similar to the European registered partnerships. Same-sex couples can enter into *civil unions*, which carry the same benefits and obligations as marriage. More intriguingly, the same statute created another new institution, somewhat like the French PaCS. Different-sex as well as same-sex couples in Vermont can become *reciprocal beneficiaries*, whereby each has the express right to make decisions for the other if she or he is incapacitated, and each has an implicit responsibility to act in the interests of the other partner.[20] The new reciprocal beneficiary law is limited to partners already related to one another by blood or adoption (and ineligible for a marriage or civil union) and so is not aimed at romantic partners, as the French PaCS law is, but it certainly introduces a new legal institution for recognising close relationships. Like the French PaCS, the Vermont reciprocal beneficiary idea offers both same-sex and different-sex couples legal possibilities that did not exist before lesbian and gay liberals agitated for state recognition of same-sex marriage. These laws argue strongly against the suggestion that state recognition of same-sex marriage means that the state will normalise all of its regulations around marriage and marriage alone.

The same-sex marriage movement is part of a larger evolution in the way the state regulates human coupling. Today in Vermont, Sweden, the Netherlands, and France—and tomorrow in many other jurisdictions—couples of all kinds will have a *menu of options*, with state-provided protections and obligations for each option:[21]

[16] For an account of the same-sex marriage movement in the Netherlands, see Waaldijk, chap. 23.

[17] See Borrillo, chap. 25.

[18] 744 A.2d 864 (Vermont Supreme Court 1999), which can be viewed at <http://www.leg.state.vt.us/baker/baker.cfm>. See Bonauto, chap. 10; WN Eskridge, Jr, *Equality Practice* (New York, NY, Routledge, forthcoming in 2001).

[19] See An Act Relating to Civil Unions (H. 847), 2000 Vermont Statutes No. 91 (adopted 26 Apr. 2000), which can be viewed at *ibid.* or <http://www.glad.org>.

[20] See *ibid.*, s. 29.

[21] The list in the text is an expansion of Eskridge, *supra* n.1, at 77–80. See also Kaplan, *supra* n.1.

—*Dating*, where law in western countries intervenes only to protect against torts or crimes.
—*Cohabitation*, during which the law in most western countries will also enforce implicit and quasi-contractual obligations of one partner to another.
—*Reciprocality*, whereby the law recognises the ability of one partner to make decisions on behalf of, and the responsibility to make them in the interests of, an incapacitated partner. Vermont's reciprocal beneficiaries law reflects this regime; the French PaCS law does this but goes beyond it, to the next level.
—*Cohabitation Plus*, which also entails certain "unitive benefits" (such as pension benefits, decisionmaking capacity, etc.) as a matter of law for couples that have either registered or cohabited for a specified period of time. France, Hungary, the Netherlands, Sweden and Canada (federal level, Ontario, Québec and British Columbia) offer this regime to same-sex as well as different-sex couples.
—*Registered Partnership*, which entails all or almost all the same benefits and obligations of marriage, but not the name. Although pioneered in Denmark and other Scandinavian countries as an alternative only for same-sex couples (as is the Vermont civil unions law), the Netherlands offers registered partnerships to different-sex couples as well.
—*Marriage*, with all its attendant regulatory duties and benefits, discussed below.

Perhaps surprisingly, the same-sex marriage movement and its traditionalist opponents have generated a series of social experiments in various states which not only provide different options for couples who do not desire to marry, but provide different models for state recognition of relationships. Thus the struggle for same-sex marriage has directly benefitted couples of all sorts—including couples who would not marry even if they could do so. What about the unpartnered or multiple-partnered gay person? No one really knows what effect the same-sex marriage movement will have for them. If it contributes to greater toleration and regulatory diversity, it might help all gays. If it further embeds marriage as the only, or most worthy, partnering strategy, it might hurt many gays. However, it is ironic, but possibly telling, that the same-sex marriage movement has achieved visibility and modest success at precisely that point in time when marriage has weakened as a normalising force. On the one hand, this undermines the suggestion that same-sex marriage will marginalise uncoupled lesbians, gay men, and bisexuals. As a single person well-accepted by my "married" lesbian, gay, and bisexual friends, I am not as pessimistic as the happily coupled Ettelbrick that normalisation will ostracise people like me. On the other hand, there are postmodern and gay-friendly reasons to lament the decline of marriage and commitment as normative aspirations, as I shall argue below. Nonetheless, the normalisation concern should remain relevant for the gay rights movement, and its leaders have an obligation to push the state to be responsive to the needs of nonmarried gay people, even after same-sex marriage has become a legal as well as social fact in their respective countries.

THE REGULATORY COSTS ARGUMENT

Nitya Duclos first detailed many of the ways in which legally recognised marriage imposes costs on the partners that may be particularly unwelcome to lesbian and gay couples, especially those who are not middle class.[22] She did not maintain that the regulatory costs are prohibitive, just that they complicate the formal equality argument for same-sex marriage. Her point remains relevant and important. Janet Halley warns that potential state interventions in same-sex marriages include enforcement of adultery and anti-nepotism rules, and of support duties; breaking up entails a potentially devastating operation of expensive state divorce procedures.[23] If the point of Halley's list is to emphasise the distinctive regulatory features entailed in state recognition, it is a reiteration of Duclos' heavily documented argument. This is a widely accepted idea. My book on same-sex marriage, for example, emphasised the ways that state-sanctioned marriage creates a particular regulatory regime; my book was distinctive in arguing that the obligations of marriage can serve the positive goal of reinforcing commitment. Morris Kaplan, David Chambers, and other writers have developed this idea as well.

If the point of Halley's list is to sound an alarm that same-sex marriage will invite increased state attention to queer people or their relationships, it is overstated. A list of potential state interventions into the lives of same-sex couples married to one another is no more impressive than one detailing the potential state interventions into the lives of cohabiting but unmarried same-sex couples: enforcement of sodomy rules and of contractual or quasi-contractual agreements of support; arbitration of disputes within the household; protection of the rights of blood family members to make decisions for an incapacitated partner and to inherit his possessions if he or she dies without a will; enforcement of the rights of an outside biological parent to children raised in the household; and so forth. The same-sex marriage debate ought not to lose track of the fact that the state pervasively—even if for the middle class it is most of the time just potentially—regulates households, married or not. Some of the state's intrusions (like interfering with childrearing) are more likely to occur in nonmarital households; others (like divorce proceedings) are more likely in marital households.

An even more aggressive variation on Duclos' caution is the argument that the organised demand for same-sex marriage enables, and even encourages, the state to continue to nose around in the lives of unmarried, as well as married, sexual minorities. According to Michael Warner, "as long as people marry, the state will regulate the sexual lives of those who do not. It will refuse to recognize the validity of intimate relationships—including cohabiting partnerships—

[22] See Duclos, *supra* n.5, at 52–5. For a balanced assessment, see DL Chambers, "What If? The Legal Consequences of Marriage and the Legal Needs of Lesbian and Gay Male Couples", (1996) 95 *Michigan Law Review* 447.

[23] See Halley, chap. 5, pp. 108–11.

between unmarried people".[24] Note the extravagant causal claim and the dubious factual assertions. The second quoted sentence is erroneous: states like Canada, the Netherlands, France, Sweden, and Vermont now recognise cohabiting partnerships as well as marriages, and proposals for gay marriage in those and other jurisdictions generally have not suggested that recognition for cohabiting partnerships be revoked.[25] The first quoted sentence is true but incomplete and inconsequential. There is no inevitable connection, nor does the author demonstrate one, between continued state recognition of marriage and state regulation of extramarital sexual behaviors. Even as increasing numbers of straight people postpone or avoid marriage, the state not only remains intent on regulating everyone's sexual lives, but some of its regulations are either new or are more vigorous than ever before—such as rules against rape, including same-sex rape; unwelcome sexual touching short of rape; sexually harassing conduct in the workplace or at school; sexual relations between an authority figure and a patient, student, etc.; and sexual interactions between adults and minors. Indeed, the state's assertive regulation of private sex lives has entered married people's bedrooms even more dramatically than those of unmarried people. In my lifetime, all the states in the United States have revoked or limited the exemption married men traditionally enjoyed against prosecutions for raping their wives, most states have created programs to police other kinds of sexual violence and abuse by one spouse against another, and many states prosecute molestation of children by their fathers and stepfathers more aggressively than ever before.[26]

Katharine Franke offers a fascinating parallel that might be read to suggest gay people have something to fear from state-sanctioned marriage. In an ongoing historical study, Franke is showing that recognition of slave marriages after the American Civil War was often the occasion for the state to impose its conceptions of sexual fidelity and monogamy on unions that had been more flexibly organized before the law entered the picture.[27] Should queer communities expect similar consequences from state recognition of their unions? I doubt it,

[24] M Warner, "Normal and Normaller: Beyond Gay Marriage", (1999) 5 *GLQ: A Journal of Lesbian and Gay Studies* 119 at 127.

[25] The second sentence quoted in the text also says that the state will refuse "to grant them the same rights as those enjoyed by married couples." This is either false or substantially false as to Denmark, whose registered partnership law accords same-sex couples pretty much all the benefits and obligations given to different-sex married couples, and as to Vermont, whose new civil unions law assures exact equality of benefits and obligations for same-sex unioned couples as for different-sex married couples. (A caveat: the Defense of Marriage Act, Public Law No. 104–109, 110 Stat. 2419 [1996] assures that same-sex couples in civil unions will not be accorded the same federal benefits and obligations as different-sex married couples, but there is nothing Vermont could have done about that.) The Netherlands has eliminated the main legal distinction, namely adoption rights, between registered partners and married couples (at least for Dutch children). See Waaldijk, chap. 23.

[26] On advances and limits, see generally P Gilmartin, *Rape, Incest, and Child Sexual Abuse* (New York, NY, Garland Publishing, 1994).

[27] See KM Franke, "Becoming a Citizen: Reconstruction Era Regulation of African American Marriages", (1999) 11 *Yale Journal of Law and the Humanities* 251.

because the normative force of marriage is waning today, just as it was waxing in the late nineteenth century. Consider also the extraordinarily different contexts of state recognition of slave marriages in the 1860s and of gay marriages in the 2000s. Unlike slave unions, which were wholly outside the law in the American south before 1865, gay unions in the 1980s and 1990s have often been recognised as cohabiting relationships, domestic partnerships, and registered partnerships in other countries and parts of the United States—without any sign that recognition has stimulated any other kind of state nosiness. Indeed, state recognition of same-sex unions has not been possible until the state let up on its suppression of queer sexualities—once again unlike the situation in southern states after the Civil War. Finally, the nineteenth century state enforced fornication and adultery laws (the main mechanisms for oppression of former slaves) vastly more than the state does today; the main state mechanism for invading the families of sexual nonconformists today is to take away custody or visitation rights to their children. Same-sex marriage would offer no greater state opportunities for that kind of discipline than the current regulatory regime and, if anything, would offer a little more security for lesbian and gay couples to protect their childrearing rights. Although posing an intriguing parallel, Franke's study has no strong implications for the same-sex marriage debate.

More broadly, the postmodern critique of causal thinking engenders scepticism about the fears of critics, like Warner, that same-sex marriage will instigate a state mobilisation around sex-negative regulations. A postmodern insight is that nothing happens as a direct result of top-down stimuli (including laws); social change occurs from the bottom up, as a multitude of discourses and power exchanges go on simultaneously.[28] This insight undermines the ability of postmodernists to make consequentialist arguments, including some of the normalisation arguments discussed in the previous section, as well as Warner's sexual repression argument here.[29] Thus, a thoroughgoing postmodernist should not be surprised that the decline of state-sanctioned marriage among straight people, and the willingness of the state to recognise nonmarital unions (the menu sketched above), have occurred at the same time that the state is increasingly attentive to the sex lives of everyone—including married people! The topography of state activity is much more complex than simple normalisation and sexual repression arguments make it out to be. To put it too simply (still), the eruption of public discourse about, and increasing toleration of, individuated sexual variety has contributed to counterdiscourses about the harms that "sexuality unbound" poses to vulnerable people—employees, children, spouses, single mothers, and so on. The same-sex marriage movement plays little if any role in this complicated dynamic.

[28] E.g., M Foucault, *Introduction*, vol. 1 in *The History of Sexuality* (Robert Hurley translator) (New York, NY, Pantheon Books, 1978 [original, 1976]); PM Rosenau, *Post-Modernism and the Social Sciences: Insights, Inroads, and Intrusions* (Princeton, NJ, Princeton University Press, 1992).

[29] Critiques of causal thinking can also apply to my anti-prejudice strategy in the previous section, even though my account is carefully contextual.

The postmodern critique of causal thinking ought to add a note of sobriety to the overheated same-sex marriage debate. All sides overstate—some writers hysterically so—the ability of the state to normalise people around state-sponsored goals. Whether one's preferred goal is civilised commitment (proponents of same-sex marriage), sexual liberty (some progressive opponents), or even compulsory heterosexuality (traditionalist opponents), the state's endorsement will not advance that goal in a linear way, and might even undermine the goal. On the other hand, the state together with other institutions can have some effect on social norms, and the symbolic importance of state recognition or nonrecognition of same-sex marriages is sufficient to sustain enthusiasm for the various perspectives discussed in this chapter.

There is value in the critical focus on the regulatory implications of marriage for lesbian, gay, and other queer families. We should consider not just the risks and benefits of a strategy that involves the state, but we should also consider the worthiness or utility of the values we want the state to endorse, at least symbolically. From the beginning of this debate, I have maintained that interpersonal commitment is a valuable thing for the state or queer communities to endorse. I have traditionally emphasised modernist arguments for that proposition: the aspiration of mutual emotional as well as sexual dependence on, and commitment to, the welfare of another human being is what most gay people think they want, produces great personal satisfaction, and completes them as human beings.[30] Traditionalist and progressive critics of same-sex marriage have left this argument relatively unchallenged, but would like for it to be irrelevant in light of their normalisation arguments. Apart from the problems with normalisation arguments against same-sex marriage, I now add this postmodern argument in favor of interpersonal commitment.

One condition giving rise to postmodern thinking is the ways in which the communications and transportation revolutions have allowed us to be fluid and many-sided. Postmodernity has enabled the *protean self* to emerge for large numbers of people, who assume different identities in the many different contexts they face, and whose personal fluidity reflects the fluidity and disruptions of their social and political environments.[31] The protean self is most available to westerners with money and mobility, and such people have a range of choices unprecedented in human history, but that very multiplicity and fluidity has yielded a self that is fractured and nostalgic as well as protean. In a world of multiple identities and wide choices, the fractured self yearns for human connections that last—history and genealogy, ethical and religious traditions, and

[30] See L Kurdek and JP Schmitt, "Relationship Quality of Partners in Heterosexual Married, Heterosexual Cohabiting, and Gay and Lesbian Relationships", (1986) 51 *Journal of Personality and Social Psychology* at 711, for a sample of the empirical literature which supports the proposition in the text. See also SL Nock, *Marriage in Men's Lives* (New York, NY, Oxford University Press, 1998).

[31] See RJ Lifton, *The Protean Self: Human Resilience in an Age of Fragmentation* (New York, NY, Basic Books, 1993), at 1–12. See also KJ Gergen, *The Saturated Self: Dilemmas of Identity in Contemporary Life* (New York, NY, Basic Books, 1991).

intimate bonds, including and particularly longstanding bonds of family.[32] This yearning is ambivalent, as the protean self both aspires to and fears the stability and reliability offered by interpersonal commitment. As Mitt Regan has argued in detail and from postmodern premises, there is presently no western institution that better captures the hopes and fears of the fractured selves of gay people, as well as straight people, than the institution of marriage.[33] Although the protean self ensures that marriages are no longer "till death do us part," the romantic desire to marry maintains a postmodern hold on Americans and other westerners.

THE GENDER-ROLE ARGUMENT

Nan Hunter maintains that same-sex marriage "could also destabilize the cultural meaning of marriage. It would create for the first time the possibility of marriage as a relationship between members of the same social status categories".[34] Drawing from evidence I compiled, Nancy Polikoff smartly responded that most of the historical examples of culturally or legally recognised same-sex marriages did not destabilise gender roles within the marriages or the societies in which they were located.[35] But the historical evidence I compiled simply demonstrated that same-sex unions had been recognised as marriages in other cultures, which refuted the traditionalists' factual claim that same-sex marriage is an oxymoron. Reflecting the dominance of men in pre-industrial societies, the large majority of the marriages I surveyed were male–male marriages which did ape male–female marriages. None of my examples, however, fit the situation in western culture today: industrialisation and technology have freed women and men to rethink gender roles, and same-sex marriage exploits that cultural opening. As traditionalists insist, same-sex marriage would be a dramatic shift in the way western culture thinks about marriage—and, I should submit, gender roles. Prior historical evidence is not dispositive as to that issue, although Polikoff's argument is cogent insofar as it shows that gender roles will change slowly at most.

More important, the gender-role argument does not depend upon the possibility that same-sex couples will actually abandon the traditional division of labor (breadwinner, housekeeper) within marriage. In a woman-woman marriage where tasks are divided up along traditional lines, a woman will be doing the accustomed male role of working outside the home. In a man-man marriage

[32] See Lifton, *ibid.* at 120–4; MC Regan, Jr., *Family Law and the Pursuit of Intimacy* (New York, NY, New York University Press, 1993), at 69–88.

[33] See Regan, *ibid.* at 119–22 (argument for gay marriage).

[34] Hunter, *supra* n.1, at 11. See L Duggan and ND Hunter, *Sex Wars: Sexual Dissent and Political Culture* (New York, NY, Routledge, 1995), at 101–6.

[35] See Polikoff, *supra* n.7, at 1538, drawing from WN Eskridge, Jr., "A History of Same-Sex Marriage", (1993) 79 *Virginia Law Review* 1419–514.

where tasks are divided up along traditional lines, a man will be doing the accustomed female role of keeping house. It is this symbolism that represents the deeper challenge to traditional gender roles. Progressive critics of same-sex marriage have no answer to this argument, other than to marginalise it as a strategy whereby "same-sex marriage in this culture might slightly improve things, if not for queers, then, indirectly, for women married to men".[36] Shouldn't queer progressives be happy to advance the indefensibly subordinate role of women in our society, whatever women's choices? Isn't it a squalid postmodernism that considers only "what's in it for us" and does not care about larger progressive goals? In any event, there are postmodern theoretical reasons to consider the symbolism more broadly significant.

Judith Butler says that gender is a social construction, and one whose binariness is a key feature of compulsory heterosexuality. Butler further maintains that gender is:

> "performative—that is, constituting the identity it is purported to be. . . . There is no gender identity behind the expressions of gender; that identity is performatively constituted by the very 'expressions' that are said to be its results".[37]

Under this view, the symbolism of two women married to one another is potentially significant, for every day and in public view at least one of the women will be performing in ways that everyone knows do not fit with women's traditional roles. Although the marriage ceremony itself is a powerful bit of western choreography, it is the day-by-day choreography that makes same-sex marriage potentially most destabilising of gender roles. If Butler and Rich are right that gender is the linchpin of compulsory heterosexuality, the destabilisation over discursive time ought to contribute to the destabilisation of anti-gay, and perhaps also anti-queer, attitudes and regulation.

The destabilisation can even occur once same-sex marriage becomes part of public discourse, without any legal action. Queer people of all kinds have been given opportunities to be heard and "seen" in ways not possible before the same-sex marriage debate hit the western world. Mary Coombs provides a dramatic example of how this can happen. She demonstrates that many of the pioneers and activists of same-sex marriage in western culture have been and are transgendered people.[38] Many male-to-female transsexuals are married to women before and after their sex change therapies and operations. Has their sex changed? Their gender? Their sexual orientation? Were these people heterosexual before and homosexual after their operations? If the state insists on their heterosexuality and that their marriages are not same-sex marriages after their

[36] Warner, *supra* n.24, at 147.

[37] J Butler, *Gender Trouble: Feminism and the Subversion of Identity* (New York, NY, Routledge, 1990), at 24–5. I do not know Butler's views regarding same-sex marriage. Her work, *The Psychic Life of Power: Theories in Subjection* (Stanford, CA, Stanford University Press, 1997), suggests she might be sceptical.

[38] See Coombs, *supra* n.1, at 242–65.

operations, as courts in England and the United States have generally held,[39] the legal system has yielded a wonderful pastiche of gender: a woman is married to a person with female sex organs, female hormones, female attire, but whose male chromosomes enable the state to pretend that she is filling the male sex role so that the marriage can still be considered different-sex. Priceless. Iterated in various venues and discussed widely, scenarios like this have interjected a little bit of queer consciousness into mainstream discourse. This is normalisation with an edge.

Postmodern critics make much more interesting arguments against same-sex marriage than premodern or modern critics do, but there are surprisingly many postmodern points to be made in favor of the idea, too. Table 3 outlines that debate and concludes this chapter.

Table 3: Postmodern Arguments For and Against Same-Sex Marriage

Modernist Arguments For Same-Sex Marriage	Postmodern Arguments Against Same-Sex Marriage	Postmodern Arguments For Same-Sex Marriage
Formal Equality: Same-sex couples ought to be treated the same as different-sex couples.	*Normalisation*: Equal treatment would normalise marriage and married couples, closing off possibilities of expanded options and possibly denigrating unmarried people.	*Destabilisation*. The same-sex marriage movement has generated experiments expanding options for state recognition of nonmarital unions and has brought queer voices into this public discourse.
Regulatory Benefits: Marriage recognition would assure gay couples of tangible benefits, as well as reinforcement of interpersonal commitment.	*Regulatory Costs*: Marriage recognition would introduce the state into same-sex unions, which would undermine the liberty of lesbians, gay men, and bisexuals.	*Causal Caution*: Both sides overstate the effects of same-sex marriage. The state is already and always present in relationships. Even the obligations of marriage reinforce interpersonal commitment.
Critique of Gender Roles: Same-sex marriage would help erode rigid gender roles (woman=wife and child-rearer; man= husband and bread-winner) within marriage.	*Denial*: State recognition of same-sex marriages would have scant effect on gender roles. (Even if it did, what good does that do for queers?)	*Performativity*: The choreography of woman-woman marriage would be a daily deconstruction of rigid gender roles, and of compulsory heterosexuality as well.

[39] See *ibid*., at 244–57 (discussing the cases).

PART II

NATIONAL LAW

Section A—United States

7

Legal Recognition of Same-Sex Partners Under US State or Local Law

ARTHUR S LEONARD*

INTRODUCTION

TO UNDERSTAND THE law concerning legal recognition of same-sex partners in the United States, one must understand the peculiar structure of US law and government. The US has fifty state jurisdictions, as well as the District of Columbia (our quasi-self-governing capital city), and other legal entities with bodies of local law, such as Puerto Rico and the US Virgin Islands. A body of federal law sits atop the state and local structures. Decisions in state courts and enactments of state legislatures are, of course, binding only within their own states, but state appellate decisions have some force as persuasive precedents in other states, and principles of comity (as well as constitutional requirements of "full faith and credit") require in many instances that states provide some recognition to the legislation of other states in certain contexts. That means that while each state decision creates binding legal precedent only in the court's own state, and each state or local law will directly apply only in that limited jurisdiction, what the state courts and legislatures do can have important ramifications beyond their borders.

Much of the law that affects the everyday lives of people in the United States is state and local law, which pervasively regulates family life and lays the foundation for workplace law and economic relations. The federal government is limited to the legislative powers enumerated in the Constitution, dealing with issues of national scope; by contrast, the state governments are considered to have general "police" powers to enact laws for the protection of public safety, health and morals and to regulate the ongoing relationships between the people residing within their boundaries. Thus, what the state legislatures and state

* Professor of Law, New York Law School; Editor, Lesbian/Gay Law Notes, http://www.qrd.org/www/usa/legal/lgln. The writer acknowledges the assistance and financial support of New York Law School for his participation in the conference and a faculty research grant to underwrite work on this chapter.

courts have to say about marriage, child custody, distribution of assets after death, commercial transactions and the like will be of primary concern for anybody inquiring about the legal status of same-sex couples, even though one must also take account of the potential impact of federal law where it may apply.

There has been plenty of litigation over recognition of same-sex couples in the state courts. Most of this is not planned in some grand strategy for social change but rather arises out of the everyday life of gay people. These cases take in an extraordinary range of issues, only a few of which can be discussed in detail here. To the general public in the US, domestic partnership may appear to be mainly about health insurance, but many of the litigated cases have had nothing to do with that. The great variety of subject matter shows that same-sex partnerships are about much more than two people living together; indeed, the fact of domestic partnership permeates the life of its participants.

Litigants seeking recognition of their relationships have by no means prevailed in all of these cases. The results are about equally divided between wins and losses, although rather more of the former in recent years. In this chapter, I will first give a cursory overview of the litigation results to date in a variety of areas, and then touch in more detail on three court decisions of major import. I will not deal with litigation about the right to marry, which will receive extensive treatment in chapters nine and ten, but rather will focus on legal recognition of same-sex partners outside the context of marriage. Neither will I address legal recognition of same-sex partners in the context of litigation about children concerning adoption, custody or visitation, which will be addressed in chapter 8.

Following the discussion of judicial recognition, I will mention some other ways that same-sex couples have achieved recognition under state and local law, either through voluntary adoption of policies by executives and legislatures, or through collective bargaining by labor union representatives of public employees. Recognition of same-sex partners by private entities obtained through collective bargaining or by direct negotiation (for example, through employee representation committees) is beyond the scope of this discussion, but it is noteworthy that hundreds of employers in the United States have voluntarily extended recognition to same-sex partners of their employees without government compulsion,[1] and that businesses providing goods and services to the public are increasingly taking account of non-marital partners when such status is relevant to a particular customer policy.

[1] See BNA Daily Labor Report (2000 No. 123, 26 June, p. B-2/3): "According to Kim Mills, Education Director of Human Rights Campaign, 99 companies on the Fortune 500 list have domestic partnership policies, as do 513 other private sector companies (including nonprofits and unions), 110 colleges and universities, and 88 state and local governments."

SUMMARY OF LEGAL DEVELOPMENTS

Employee Benefits Claims

These cases involve claims that employees are entitled to have benefits coverage for their same-sex partners in the same way that other employees have benefits coverage for their legal spouses. I will discuss the most successful lawsuit in this area, *Tanner* v. *Oregon Health Sciences University*,[2] in detail below. To date, litigation results have been mixed, with many more losses than victories for benefits claimants,[3] and it appears that legislation will be a more effective route to achieving domestic partnership recognition in relation to employee benefits.

Estates and Trusts Matters

In 1993, a New York appeals court rejected the attempt by the alleged surviving partner in a gay male relationship to assert the claim of a surviving spouse to an elective share of the estate, overriding the decedent's testamentary disposition. The court refused to accept the argument that failing to recognise a same-sex surviving partner would violate the constitutional requirement of equal protection of the laws.[4] Similarly, the Court of Appeals in the state of Washington recently refused to extend a common-law right of surviving heterosexual partners in a "meretricious relationship" to a surviving same-sex partner who was attempting to use the doctrine to establish intestate succession rights to real

[2] 971 P.2d 435 (Oregon Ct. of Appeals 1998) (state constitutional equal protection requirement mandates extension of health benefits eligibility to same-sex partners of public employees).

[3] See *Funderburke* v. *Uniondale Union Free School District No. 15*, 676 N.Y.S.2d 199 (N.Y. Supreme Ct. Appellate Div. 1998), leave to appeal denied, 92 N.Y.2d 813 (N.Y. Ct. of Appeals 1999); *Hinman* v. *Dept. of Personnel Administration*, 213 Cal. Rptr. 410 (Calif. Ct. of Appeal 1985) (rejects benefits claim); *Phillips* v. *Wisconsin Personnel Commission*, 482 N.W.2d 121 (Wis. Ct. of Appeals 1992) (rejects benefits claim); *Ross* v. *Denver Dept. of Health & Hospitals*, 883 P.2d 516 (Colo. Ct. of Appeals 1994) (rejects benefits claim); *Rutgers Council of AAUP Chapters* v. *Rutgers University*, 689 A.2d 828 (N.J. Superior Ct. Appellate Div. 1997) (rejects benefits claim); and see *Rovira* v. *AT&T*, 817 F.Supp. 1062 (S.D.N.Y. 1993) (denied benefits claim asserted under federal employee benefits law); cf., *Gay Teachers Assoc'n* v. *Board of Education*, 585 N.Y.S.2d 1016 (N.Y. Supreme Ct. Appellate Div. 1992) (recognising cause of action for benefits; not an ultimate disposition on the merits); *Univ. of Alaska* v. *Tumeo & Wattum*, 933 P.2d 1147 (Alaska Supreme Ct. 1997) (accepting benefits claim, but decision prospectively reversed by legislative amendment of marital status discrimination law). The Vermont Labor Relations Board ruled that the employees of the University of Vermont were entitled under their collective bargaining agreement, which prohibited sexual orientation discrimination, to have coverage for their same-sex partners: *Grievance of B.M., S.S., C.M., and J.R.*, No. 92–32 (4 June 1993). Private arbitrators rejected domestic partnership benefits claims in *American Assoc'n of Univ. Professors, Kent State Chapter & Kent State Univ.*, 95–1 ARB (CCH) Para. 5002 (1994), and *Marion City Schools & Marion Education Assoc'n*, 111 Lab. Arb. (BNA) 134 (1998).

[4] *In re Matter of Cooper*, 592 N.Y.S.2d 797 (N.Y. Supreme Ct. Appellate Div. 1993), appeal dismissed, 624 N.E.2d 696 (1993).

property.[5] However, in a case where refusal to grant legal recognition actually benefitted the surviving same-sex partner, the Louisiana Court of Appeals ruled that the surviving partner was not a "concubine". A law limiting the amount that a person could bequeath to a concubine thus did not apply in a pending will contest between a surviving partner named as a beneficiary and members of the deceased's legally recognised family.[6] And in a dispute over disposition of a body, a New York court ruled that a surviving gay life partner had standing as a representative of the decedent's wishes in a dispute over the funeral and burial arrangements.[7]

Dissolution of Relationships

In one of the earliest attempts to attain recognition of a partnership in the context of a break-up, in 1984, a Pennsylvania appellate court rejected a gay man's attempt to have a property disposition made under a statute governing the distribution of assets on the dissolution of a marriage.[8] An Ohio appellate court issued a similar ruling a decade later.[9] In a 1996 decision, the South Carolina Supreme Court refused to impose a constructive trust or recognise an equitable lien in favor of one partner upon the break-up of a long-term lesbian relationship, finding inadequate evidence that the partner retaining the assets had made the kinds of commitments that would justify such action.[10] Courts are divided over whether formerly-married gay persons should lose entitlement to alimony or maintenance payments from their former spouses when they begin cohabiting with a new partner of the same sex, but the majority favor allowing alimony to continue, on the ground that the new relationship has no legal status imposing a support obligation on the same-sex partner.[11]

[5] *Vasquez* v. *Hawthorne*, 994 P.2d 240 (Wash. Ct. of Appeals 2000).

[6] *In re Bacot*, 502 So.2d 1118 (Louisiana Ct. of Appeal), *certiorari* denied, 503 So.2d 466 (Louisiana Supreme Ct. 1997).

[7] *Stewart* v. *Schwartze Bros.-Jeffer Memorial Chapel, Inc.*, 606 N.Y.S.2d 965 (N.Y. Supreme Ct. Queens Co. 1993). There is an unpublished Massachusetts court decision to similar effect. See *Clarke* v. *Reilly*, Mass. Superior Ct., No. 87–0939 (May 5, 1988), reproduced in edited form in AS Leonard *et al.*, *AIDS Law and Policy: Cases and Materials* (Houston, TX, John Marshall Publishing Co., 1995) at 483.

[8] *DeSanto* v. *Barnsley*, 476 A.2d 952 (Penn. Superior Ct. 1984). In 1999, a panel of the Superior Court rejected an attempt by a gay man to escape the *DeSanto* precedent by attempting to describe the case as a distribution of assets on termination of a business partnership, in *Mitchell* v. *Moore*, 729 A.2d 1200 (Penn. Superior Ct. 1999).

[9] *Seward* v. *Mentrup*, 622 N.E.2d 756 (Ohio Ct. of Appeals 1993).

[10] *Doe* v. *Roe*, 475 S.E.2d 783 (S.C. Supreme Ct. 1996).

[11] *Gajovski* v. *Gajovski*, 610 N.E.2d 431 (Ohio Ct. of Appeals 1991) (alimony may continue); *People ex rel. Kenney* v. *Kenney*, 352 N.Y.S.2d 344 (N.Y. Supreme Ct. N.Y.County 1974) (alimony may continue); *Van Dyck* v. *Van Dyck*, 425 S.E.2d 853 (Georgia Supreme Ct. 1993) (alimony may continue); *contra*, *Weisbruch* v. *Weisbruch*, 710 N.E.2d 439 (Illinois Appellate Ct. 1999) (same-sex couple can be found to be in conjugal relationship, thus terminating alimony entitlement).

Housing Rights

In perhaps the most significant recognition of same-sex partners, New York's highest court found that a surviving same-sex partner could be considered a family member entitled to successor tenant status in a rent-controlled apartment in New York City in 1989.[12] A New York appellate court subsequently extended the logic of this decision to a federal rent subsidy program.[13] However, when a same-sex couple sought to obtain jointly a homeowners liability insurance policy, a New York court found that the insurer was not required to sell to them as a couple.[14] And another New York court found no violation when a university refused to allow a medical student to live with her same-sex partner in university housing provided to married students.[15]

Domestic Violence Laws

Several Ohio courts have ruled that same-sex partners may have the benefit of court protection under statutes intended to protect cohabitants from domestic violence, but a Pennsylvania court has taken the contrary position.[16]

Public Benefits Laws

A New York court held that the same-sex partner of a crime victim could not apply for compensation to a public crime victim compensation board, even though a spouse of a crime victim is entitled to compensation under similar circumstances.[17] But a California court ruled that when a man died from work-related causes, his surviving same-sex partner could be entitled to a death benefit under the state's workers compensation law.[18] And the highest court in

[12] *Braschi* v. *Stahl Assocs. Co.*, 543 N.E.2d 49 (N.Y. Ct. of Appeals 1989). Since *Braschi*, lower New York courts have generated a body of decisions attempting to determine successorship claims where the nature of the relationship is disputed by the landlord.

[13] *Evans* v. *Franco*, 668 N.Y.S.2d 26 (N.Y. Supreme Ct. Appellate Div. 1998).

[14] *Eisner* v. *Aetna Casualty & Surety Co.*, 534 N.Y.S.2d 339 (N.Y. Supreme Ct. N.Y. County 1988). In a similar decision, a California court ruled that an insurance company could refuse to sell liability insurance to a same-sex couple seeking coverage for their jointly-owned truck, in *Beaty* v. *Truck Insurance Exchange*, 8 Cal. Rptr. 2d 593 (Calif. Ct. of Appeals 1992).

[15] *Levin* v. *Yeshiva University*, 691 N.Y.S.2d 280 (N.Y. Supreme Ct. N.Y. County 1999), affirmed, 709 N.Y.S.2d 392 (N.Y. Supreme Ct. Appellate Div. 2000). But see *infra* n.83.

[16] *State* v. *Yaden*, 692 N.E.2d 1097 (Ohio Ct. of Appeals 1997); *State* v. *Linner*, 655 N.E.2d 1180 (Ohio Municipal Ct. 1996); *State* v. *Hadinger*, 573 N.E.2d 1191 (Ohio Ct. of Appeals 1991); *contra*, *D.H.* v. *B.O.*, 734 A.2d 409 (Pa.Super.Ct. 1999). In an unpublished decision, *State* v. *Baker*, Florida Circuit Judge Ficarrotta, Hillsborough County, ruled on 23 June 1999 that the state's domestic violence law applied to a same-sex couple.

[17] *Secord* v. *Fischetti*, 653 N.Y.S.2d 551 (N.Y. Supreme Ct. Appellate Div. 1997).

[18] *Donovan* v. *Workers' Compensation Appeals Board*, 187 Cal. Rptr. 869 (Calif. Ct. of Appeal 1982).

Massachusetts ruled, in a case that would undoubtedly be precedential for same-sex partners, that the unmarried opposite-sex domestic partner of a worker would be entitled to unemployment compensation benefits if she had to leave her job when her partner relocated to take a new job.[19]

Tort Claims

Although most US jurisdictions will allow a claim for emotional distress damages on behalf of a person who witnesses a severe injury to a close family member caused by the intentional or negligent acts of another, a California court refused to allow such a claim by a same-sex partner.[20] Conversely, a trial court in the District of Columbia ruled that a surviving partner could bring a damage claim under the District's wrongful death statute as "next of kin" of the deceased.[21]

Miscellaneous

A federal court ruled in Pennsylvania that a same-sex partner would be entitled to visit her incarcerated partner as if she were a spouse.[22] A California court ruled that a photographer had violated the civil rights of a same-sex couple by refusing to include their picture in a high school reunion memory book that featured pictures of class members with their spouses.[23] A Minnesota court ruled that the same-sex partner of a woman severely injured in an automobile accident should be appointed her legal guardian, despite the opposition of the injured woman's parents, on the ground that the two women constituted a "family of affinity".[24] On the other hand, a New York court rejected the claim that a same-sex partner can assert an evidentiary privilege to protect conversations with the partner in the same way that the law recognizes such a privilege for spouses.[25] Also, federal courts have rejected an attempt by a same-sex couple to file a joint bankruptcy petition, to obtain legal recognition for immigration purposes, or to file joint income tax returns.[26]

[19] *Reep* v. *Commissioner of Dept. of Employment & Training*, 593 N.E.2d 1297 (Mass. Supreme Judicial Ct. 1992).

[20] *Coon* v. *Joseph*, 237 Cal. Rptr. 873 (Cal. Ct. of Appeal 1987).

[21] *Solomon* v. *District of Columbia*, 21 Fam. L. Rep. (BNA) 1316 (D.C. Superior Ct. 1995). See also *Smith* v. *Noel*, [Sept. 2001] *Lesbian/Gay Law Notes*, supra n.* (San Francisco Superior Ct., 27 July 2001). Compare *Raum* v. *Restaurant Assocs., Inc.*, 675 N.Y.S.2d 343 (N.Y. Supreme Ct. Appellate Div.), appeal dismissed, 92 N.Y.2d 946 (N.Y. Ct. of Appeals 1998) (state may exclude unmarried partners from bringing a wrongful death action).

[22] *Doe* v. *Sparks*, 733 F.Supp. 227 (W.D.Penn. 1990).

[23] *Engel* v. *Worthington*, 23 Cal. Rptr. 2d 329 (Calif. Ct. of Appeal 1993).

[24] *In re Guardianship of Kowalski*, 478 N.W.2d 790 (Minn. Ct. of Appeals 1991).

[25] *Greenwald* v. *H & P 29th Street Assoc'n*, 659 N.Y.S.2d 473 (N.Y. Sup. Ct. App. Div. 1997).

[26] *In re Allen*, 186 Bankruptcy Reporter 769 (Bankr.N.D.Ga. 1995); *Adams* v. *Howerton*, 673 F.2d 1036 (9th Cir.), *certiorari* denied, 458 U.S. 1111 (1982); *Sullivan* v. *Immigration and*

THREE SIGNIFICANT CASES

In this section, I will discuss three significant state court appellate rulings on claims for recognition of their families by same-sex couples. The cases illustrate three specific routes for judicial decision-making: common law adjudication, statutory or regulatory construction, and constitutional interpretation. In each case, the claimants were seeking the courts' acceptance of the reality of family life as a justification for abandoning formalistic rules based on the legal construct of marriage. In two of the three cases, the claimants were successful. Ironically, the successful cases were those seeking expansive interpretations of statutory or constitutional texts, while the failure came in a common law case where one might think the court would have the most leeway to make an adjustment to existing law.

Braschi v. *Stahl Associates Co.*

Braschi v. *Stahl Associates Co.*[27] is a 1989 New York decision concerning housing rights. Rental housing is such a scarce commodity in New York City that there has been some form of rent regulation almost continuously since World War II. Landlords eager to get rent increases must look to evictions for breach of lease or to vacancies due to the death or leaving of a tenant. Regulations provide that if a rent-regulated tenant dies or leaves, members of his or her family who are living in the apartment have a right to take over the tenancy, depriving the landlord of the benefits of vacancy.[28] If a landlord retakes possession of a rent-controlled apartment, he can raise the rent to market rates before taking a new tenant.

Under such a regime, lack of recognition for same-sex partners could work a significant hardship if partners did not originally rent an apartment as a couple, and there was no legal obligation for landlords to accept unrelated persons as joint tenants. Furthermore, in many cases the living situation consisted of a legal tenant having invited a prospective partner to move in under the guise of a "roommate", not wishing to discuss the nature of the relationship with the landlord. Indeed, until the legislature acted to guarantee the right of tenants to have unrelated roommates, overruling a Court of Appeals decision that allowed a landlord to evict a tenant for taking in an unrelated roommate, tenants would

Naturalization Service, 772 F.2d 609 (9th Cir. 1985); *Mueller* v. *Commissioner of Internal Revenue*, T.C. Memo 2000–132, 2000 Westlaw 371545 (U.S. Tax Ct. 12 April 2000); cf. the proposed Permanent Partners Immigration Act of 2001, H.R. 690, <http://thomas.loc.gov/home/c107query.html>.

[27] 74 N.Y.2d 201, 543 N.E.2d 49 (N.Y. Ct. of Appeals 1989).

[28] N.Y.C. Rent and Eviction Regulations, 9 NYCRR 2204.6(d). The regulation provides that the landlord may not dispossess "either the surviving spouse of the deceased tenant or some other member of the deceased tenant's family who has been living with the tenant".

have had reason to fear revealing to their landlords that they were living with unrelated roommates.[29] When a same-sex partner who was the legal tenant in a regulated apartment died, the survivor sometimes could negotiate a deal with the landlord to remain or become the legal tenant, but the rent demanded might be exorbitant. And, of course, a landlord might claim that surviving partners had no entitlement to continued residency and thereby move to evict them.

This was what happened in *Braschi*. Leslie Blanchard and Miguel Braschi, a same-sex couple, had lived together in Mr Blanchard's rent-controlled apartment in Manhattan for over ten years when Blanchard died from AIDS in 1986. The landlord wanted to evict Braschi. Braschi wanted to stay in his decade-long home and sought an injunction and declaration of entitlement to become Blanchard's successor as a rent-controlled tenant. Braschi sought legal recognition as a member of Blanchard's family. He presented evidence about the nature of their relationship to the trial court, which found that the relationship "fulfills any definitional criteria of the term 'family'". The landlord won a reversal in the NY Appellate Division, which concluded that the term "family," not expressly defined in the regulation, applied only to "family members within traditional, legally recognized familial relationships". The Appellate Division placed specific reliance on the Roommate Law's proviso that roommates would not automatically acquire any right to continued occupancy in the event of a tenant's death or vacating of the apartment.[30]

The New York Court of Appeals, the state's highest court, was divided on the appeal. With one of the seven members abstaining, three judges endorsed an opinion that adopted a functional definition of family and applied it to Blanchard and Braschi, a fourth concurred in the result on different grounds, and two dissented.

The plurality opinion, by Judge Vito Titone, was the first in the US to accord legal status to same-sex partners, although it was not by its terms so limited, and unmarried opposite-sex partners have also benefited from the ruling. Titone held that where the key term—here, "family"—was not expressly defined, the "general purpose" of the statute should guide the court in adopting a definition that would "effectuate the statute". Here, the purpose was to prevent the "sudden eviction" of somebody from an apartment upon the death of their co-resident family member, and to "forestall profiteering, speculation and other disruptive practices" arising from the tight rental market.[31] Titone stated:

> "[T]he term family, as used in [the regulation], should not be rigidly restricted to those people who have formalized their relationship by obtaining, for instance, a marriage certificate or an adoption order. The intended protection against sudden eviction

[29] The Court of Appeals decision was *Hudson View Properties* v. *Weiss*, 450 N.E.2d 234 (1983), overruled by the legislature through the enactment of NY Real Property Law section 235-f, which provides, *inter alia*, that roommates do not automatically acquire "any right to continued occupancy in the event that the tenant vacates the premises."

[30] 74 N.Y.2d at 206–207.

[31] *Ibid*. at 209–10.

should not rest on fictitious legal distinctions or genetic history, but instead should find its foundation in the reality of family life. In the context of eviction, a more realistic, and certainly equally valid, view of a family includes two adult lifetime partners whose relationship is long term and characterized by an emotional and financial commitment and interdependence".[32]

The court said that the determination whether a person would qualify as a family member should be made on a case-by-case basis, and mentioned as factors for courts to consider: "the exclusivity and longevity of the relationship, the level of emotional and financial commitment, the manner in which the parties have conducted their everyday lives and held themselves out to society, and the reliance placed upon one another for daily family services". The court emphasized that "the presence or absence of one or more of [these factors] is not dispositive since it is the totality of the relationship as evidenced by the dedication, caring and self-sacrifice of the parties which should, in the final analysis, control".[33] Significantly, the court did not mention any sexual relationship between the parties, and in citing lower court rulings to document how these factors had been used, included cases involving both same-sex and opposite-sex partners, as well as cases where the familial relationship included children being raised by adults to whom they were not legally related.[34]

Concurring in the result, Judge Joseph Bellacosa opposed adopting any specific definitional formula, finding that this would intrude on the function of the legislature, but instead suggested that, in light of the purpose of the regulation, in each case the court should decide on equitable grounds whether the surviving resident should be covered by the regulation.[35]

The dissenters, of course, charged the majority with usurping the role of the legislature, undermining the operation of the rent control system, and adopting an interpretation that conflicted with the policy adopted in the Roommate Law and the state's intestacy laws.[36] They also objected that there would be "serious practical problems" created by the decision, since it would require a case-by-case inquiry into the nature of the relationship between people living together and a "subjective determination in each case of whether the relationship was genuine, and entitled to the protection of the law, or expedient, and an attempt to take advantage of the law", leading to potentially inconsistent results and difficulties for landlords in knowing who was entitled to protection.[37]

[32] *Ibid*. at 211.

[33] *Ibid*. at 212–13.

[34] Cases cited included *Athineos* v. *Thayer*, New York Law Journal (25 March 1987), at 14, col. 4 (Civil Ct.), affirmed, NYLJ (9 Feb. 1988), at 15, col. 4 (Appellate Term) (orphan never formally adopted but lived in family home for 34 years); *2–4 Realty Assocs*. v. *Pittman*, 137 Misc. 2d 898, 902 (two men living in a "father-son" relationship for 25 years); *Zimmerman* v. *Burton*, 107 Misc. 2d 401, 404 (unmarried heterosexual life partners); *Rutar Co*. v. *Yoshito*, No. 53042/79 (Civil Ct.) (unmarried heterosexual life partners); *Gelman* v. *Castaneda*, NYLJ (22 Oct. 1986), at 13, col. 1 (Civil Ct.) (male life partners).

[35] 74 N.Y.2d at 214–216.

[36] *Ibid*. at 216–224.

[37] *Ibid*. at 221–222.

The decision had a happy sequel. Representatives of groups that had filed *amicus* briefs met with state housing department officials and got them to amend the regulations to codify the decision for all regulated apartments. Landlord groups challenged the legality of the expanded regulations, but their suit was rejected by the courts.[38] The tenant succession regulations have not always provided relief for petitioners, who sometimes have difficulty showing that their relationship qualified as "familial", but at least they are given the opportunity, rather than being presumed to have no basis for a legal claim. Perhaps more significantly, the *Braschi* ruling has provided a policy statement upon which subsequent New York courts could rely when confronting new questions involving legal recognition of same-sex families. It has been cited prominently by the Court of Appeals in allowing a same-sex partner to adopt her partner's child,[39] and by a lower appellate court upholding New York City's enactment of a far-reaching domestic partnership ordinance.[40]

Coon v. *Joseph*

The second case, *Coon* v. *Joseph*,[41] was a 1987 decision of the California First District Court of Appeal, an intermediate appellate court. It arose from a 1984 incident on a San Francisco city bus. Gary Coon and his partner, Ervin, attempted to get on the bus. According to Coon's complaint, the bus driver, Michael Joseph, refused to let Coon get on the bus but allowed Ervin on the bus, only to verbally abuse him and strike him in the face. Coon claimed that on observing this abuse of his partner, he suffered severe emotional distress. Coon sued the bus driver and the city, seeking damages for intentional and negligent infliction of emotional distress, municipal negligence in hiring and supervising Mr. Joseph, and violation of Coon's civil rights.[42]

California has recognised a tort action for serious emotional distress suffered by a person who observes a substantial injury inflicted on somebody with whom they have a close, personal relationship. In its leading case, *Dillon* v. *Legg*,[43] the California Supreme Court listed three requirements: (1) that the plaintiff was at the scene of the incident; (2) that the shock resulted from direct emotional impact upon the plaintiff from contemporaneous observance of the incident; and (3) that the plaintiff and the victim were closely related. Most California courts (and courts in other states with similar rules) have limited

[38] *Rent Stabilization Assoc. of N.Y.C., Inc.* v. *Higgins*, 630 N.E.2d 626 (N.Y. Ct. of Appeals 1993).

[39] *Matter of Jacob*, 660 N.E.2d 397 (N.Y. Ct. of Appeals 1995).

[40] *Slattery* v. *City of New York*, 697 N.Y.S.2d 603 (N.Y. Supreme Ct. Appellate Div. 1999), appeal dismissed, 94 N.Y.2d 897 (N.Y. Ct. of Appeals 2000) (rejecting challenge to validity of New York City domestic partnership ordinance on preemption grounds).

[41] 192 Cal. App. 3d 1269, 237 Cal. Rptr. 873.

[42] 192 Cal. App. 3d at 1272.

[43] 703 P.2d 1 (Calif. Supreme Ct. 1985).

liability to cases where the plaintiff was a parent, spouse or child of the victim. Sometimes persons engaged to be married have been included, but there were California cases excluding siblings or cousins. Coon relied heavily on the prior court of appeal decision *Ledger* v. *Tippitt*,[44] in which the court allowed recovery by an unmarried opposite-sex partner with whom the victim was raising their child.

The trial court found that a same-sex relationship would not qualify, and the majority of the court of appeal panel agreed, in an opinion by Judge Scott. The court majority found that even though Coon described his relationship with Ervin as intimate, stable, and emotionally significant, and that the two men had been living together as "exclusive life partners" for a year, "the inclusion of an intimate homosexual relationship within the 'close relationship' standard would render ambivalent and weaken the necessary limits on a tortfeasor's liability mandated by *Dillon*. We view the establishment of a clear and definite standard limiting liability to be of great importance".[45] Judge Scott wrote that "to include the 'emotionally significant', 'stable', and 'exclusive' relationship pled by appellant as a 'close relationship' . . . would invite inconsistent results because recovery would be dependent upon the personal, completely subjective viewpoints of the trier of fact".[46] As to the *Ledger* case upon which Coon relied, Scott found it "inapposite", asserting that "[t]he complaint here does not allege facts establishing a 'de facto' marital relationship recognized in *Ledger*. Nor could such allegation be made because appellant and Ervin are both males and the Legislature has made a determination that a legal marriage is between a man and a woman".[47] Thus, the court found that it would not be within the reasonable scope of foreseeable injury by a negligent tortfeasor that the man observing an injury to a male victim would be in a close relationship with the victim and thus be likely to experience great emotional distress. Concurring, Judge Barry-Deal emphasised that the place for Coon and others similarly situated to seek relief was the legislature.[48]

Judge White disagreed. "In a contemporary society (and particularly in San Francisco)", wrote White, "it is foreseeable a homosexual relationship might exist. Such a relationship may be significant enough to meet the third *Dillon* requirement".[49] White rejected the majority's assertion that this would produce inconsistent results due to the "subjective viewpoints" of juries and judges, commenting that "the courts have been determining for some time whether a particular relationship constitutes a significant one", and citing as the main example the *Ledger* case.[50] However, White concurred in the result, finding that

[44] 210 Cal. Rptr. 814 (Calif. Ct. of Appeal 1985).
[45] 192 Cal. App. 3d at 1275.
[46] *Ibid*. at 1276.
[47] *Ibid*. at 1277.
[48] *Ibid*. at 1277–1279.
[49] *Ibid*. at 1284.
[50] *Ibid*. at 1283.

Coon's allegations did not depict a serious enough injury to warrant awarding damages for bystander liability.[51]

The *Coon* decision, which predated *Braschi* by two years, involved very similar considerations. Something happens to one member of a same-sex couple, and the other member suffers an injury or might incur a future injury as a result, under circumstances where the law would provide some protection or relief had the partners been legal spouses. Should the law extend that protection or relief to same-sex partners whose relationship is spousal in character, due to their emotional and financial interdependence and shared residence? In *Braschi*, applying a flexible approach in light of the regulatory purpose, the court effectuated that purpose by adopting a broad interpretation of the term "family", which was not specifically defined in the applicable regulations, with dissenters arguing, among other things, that case-by-case determinations would lead to uncertainty and inconsistent results. In *Coon*, the court, fearing uncertainty and inconsistent results, insisted on a formal line based on existing legally-recognised relationships, provoking a dissent arguing that it would effectuate the purpose of the legal rule to take a case-by-case approach based on the reality of modern family life—an approach one would think intuitively attractive to a court ruling on a common law claim.

Tanner v. *Oregon Health Sciences University*

For many people in the US, a central issue for legal recognition of same-sex couples is access to the economic employment benefits that legal spouses of employees receive in most workplaces. In the US, the government does not directly finance medical and dental services to the general population. While the poor, the physically and mentally disabled, and the elderly can participate in government welfare or insurance programs, everybody else is on their own. For many US workers, employment-related insurance is the main source of coverage for their medical expenses. And it is customary, whether in the public or private sector, for employers to cover not only the employee but also the employee's spouse and children. Employees may have to make an extra contribution for spousal and child coverage, but the amount is less than it would cost to purchase equivalent coverage on the market.

Obtaining legal recognition for same-sex partners in this context has become a central goal of the movement for lesbian and gay rights in the US Although some employers have extended recognition for this purpose voluntarily or through collective bargaining with labor unions, and many municipal and a few state employers have done so voluntarily through legislation or executive action, it has also become the subject of litigation. There are substantial barriers to the plaintiffs. The federal Employee Retirement Income Security Act

[51] 192 Cal. App. 3d at 1284–85.

(commonly referred to as ERISA) preempts all state or local laws that relate to or affect employee benefit plans concerning health insurance or pension rights of private sector employees. Consequently, state or local laws banning sexual orientation, sex or marital status discrimination can provide no assistance in private sector cases, and state and local legislatures are precluded from passing statutes requiring such coverage by private employers. ERISA preemption does not apply to the public sector, however, so almost all the litigation (and state and local legislation) has involved public employees. If the federal courts were to accept the argument that failure to extend benefits to cover same-sex domestic partners constitutes sex discrimination, it would be possible for many private sector employees to sue for benefits under Title VII of the federal Civil Rights Act of 1964, which forbids discrimination on the basis of sex in terms and conditions of employment in all private sector workplaces with 15 or more employees, and which is not preempted by ERISA. But most US courts seem disinclined to accept the sex discrimination theory.[52]

Most partnership benefits suits have been unsuccessful. The first victory was a lawsuit that was favorably settled short of a decision on the merits, *Gay Teachers Association* v. *Board of Education of the City of New York*,[53] which resulted in the extension of benefits to New York City employees in 1993. A lawsuit against the University of Alaska succeeded at the trial level, but was overturned when the state legislature amended the marital status discrimination statute upon which the case was based.[54]

The first case to produce an extensive appellate opinion upholding the benefits claim on the merits is *Tanner* v. *Oregon Health Sciences University*,[55] a 1998 decision by the Oregon Court of Appeals. Three lesbian employees of a government-funded University sued on two theories: first, citing a state civil rights law prohibiting discrimination on the basis of an employee's sex or the sex of any other person with whom the employee associates;[56] second, citing the privileges and immunities clause of the Oregon Constitution, which prohibits the state from granting privileges or immunities not equally belonging to all citizens.[57] The trial court agreed with both theories, and the state appealed.

[52] *DeSantis* v. *Pacific Telephone & Telegraph Co.*, 608 F.2d 327 (9th Cir. 1979) is the first of many appellate cases holding that Title VII's ban on sex discrimination may not be construed to forbid discrimination on the basis of sexual orientation. However, in litigation over the right to same-sex marriage, the Hawaii Supreme Court has accepted the argument that failure to afford same-sex couples the same rights as opposite-sex couples could constitute sex discrimination in violation of its state constitution. See *Baehr* v. *Lewin*, 852 P.2d 44 (Hawaii Supreme Court 1993); Koppelman, chap. 35. In *Baker* v. *State of Vermont*, 744 A.2d 864 (Vermont Supreme Court 1999), only one of the justices followed the *Baehr* court's logic, the remainder of the court using other theoretical approaches to find that same-sex couples were constitutionally entitled to the same rights and benefits of marriage as opposite-sex couples. See Bonauto, chap. 10.

[53] 585 N.Y.S.2d 1016 (N.Y. Supreme Ct. Appellate Div. 1992).

[54] *Univ. of Alaska* v. *Tumeo & Wattum*, 933 P.2d 1147 (Alaska Supreme Ct. 1997).

[55] 971 P.2d 435 (Oregon Ct. of Appeals 1998).

[56] Oregon Revised Statutes section 659.030(1)(b).

[57] Oregon Constitution, art. I, s. 20.

The state had argued that its denial of benefits was not predicated on the sex or sexual orientation of anybody, but was based on marital status, a ground not covered by the civil rights law. In response, Presiding Judge Landau observed that drawing a line based on marital status had a disparate impact on same-sex partners, who were denied the right to marry under state law. Oregon's civil rights law affords both disparate treatment (direct discrimination) and disparate impact (indirect discrimination) claims. Furthermore, the statute banned discrimination based on the sex of a person with whom the employee associates, a concept directly applicable to this case. The court found that the civil rights law bans discrimination against same-sex couples; thus, failure to cover domestic partners would violate the law if not for another provision creating a "safe harbor" defense: "it is not an unlawful employment practice for an employer . . . to observe the terms of a . . . bona fide employee benefit plan, such as a retirement, pension or insurance plan, which is not a subterfuge to evade the purposes of this chapter". The court found no evidence that the state adopted its benefits plans intending to discriminate against gay people, so the safe harbor applied and the statutory claim was rejected.[58]

Turning to the state constitution, the court invoked a 1981 Oregon Supreme Court decision holding that Article I, Section 20, of the Oregon Constitution "forbids inequality of privileges or immunities not available upon the same terms, first, to any citizen, and second, to any class of citizens".[59] In common with federal courts construing the equal protection clause of the US Constitution, the Oregon courts have distinguished between "suspect" classes and other classes, and applied strict scrutiny to government policies affecting the former. The court described "suspect" classes as those defined by characteristics that "are historically regarded as defining distinct, socially-recognized groups that have been the subject of adverse social or political stereotyping or prejudice", and that:

> "if a law or government action fails to offer privileges and immunities to members of such a class on equal terms, the law or action is inherently suspect and. . . may be upheld only if the failure to make the privileges or immunities available to that class can be justified by genuine differences between the disparately treated class and those to whom the privileges and immunities are granted".[60]

The court found that gay people are members of a "suspect class" in light of the Oregon precedents.

> "Sexual orientation, like gender, race, alienage, and religious affiliation is widely regarded as defining a distinct, socially recognized group of citizens, and certainly it is beyond dispute that homosexuals in our society have been and continue to be the subject of adverse social and political stereotyping and prejudice",

[58] 971 P.2d at 441–444.

[59] *State* v. *Clark*, 291 Or. 231, 237, 630 P.2d 810 (1981).

[60] 971 P.2d at 445–446.

wrote Judge Landau for the court.[61] The court found that the parties had not presented any justification based on sexual orientation for disqualifying same-sex partners from participating in employee benefit plans. The court pointed out that Oregon's privileges and immunities clause is concerned not just with disparate treatment but also with disparate impact, so the use of marital status as a basis for determining eligibility was constitutionally invalid because it disproportionately disqualified gay partners from obtaining benefits that are available to opposite-sex partners through marriage. Consequently, the plaintiffs won on their constitutional claim, and all public employers in Oregon are now obligated to extend spousal benefit eligibility to same-sex partners of their employees.[62]

Could this result be replicated in other states? Idiosyncratic statutory and constitutional language and methodology may work against it, but the idea that laws banning marital status discrimination (which exist in more than 20 states) might be used to compel public employers to extend benefits to their employees' same-sex partners should be helpful. And the Oregon Court of Appeals' determination that laws that discriminate against unmarried couples have a disparate impact on (discriminate indirectly against) same-sex partners, because such partners cannot marry, and that such disparate impact works a deprivation of equal protection of the laws, creates a persuasive precedent that might be expected to provide a convenient argument for courts in other states inclined to take on the urgent task of eliminating a gross social inequity.

LEGISLATIVE RECOGNITION FOR SAME-SEX PARTNERS

Political advocacy for lesbian and gay rights in the United States is strongest at the municipal level, so it is not surprising that cities and towns are among the first to have agreed through local legislation to extend some degree of recognition to same-sex partners living or working within their borders.[63] Advocates for the extension of such recognition have had to face a variety of arguments, including that recognition for same-sex couples but not unmarried opposite-sex

[61] *Ibid.* at 447.

[62] *Ibid.* at 447–448. The government did not appeal to the Oregon Supreme Court and amended regulations to comply with the decision. See Oregon Administrative Rules Compilation, chs. 102 and 103 (Public Employee Benefits Board rules on Eligibility, etc.).

[63] It is virtually impossible to provide a complete list of such jurisdictions, as there is no centralised reporting and publishing of municipal law in the United States. However, various organisations specifically interested in this issue attempt to keep current tabulations, e.g., the American Association for Single People (http://www.unmarriedamerica.com), the National Gay and Lesbian Task Force (http://www.ngltf.org), and Human Rights Campaign (http://www.hrc.org). A recent report asserted that as of the beginning of 2000, there were 41 municipal governments that had set up some form of domestic partnership registry and 83 municipal governments that were providing some type of employment benefit for domestic partners of their employees: Wayne van der Meide, *Legislating Equality: A Review of Laws Affecting Gay, Lesbian, Bisexual and Transgendered People in the United States* (NGLTF Policy Institute, Washington, DC, 2000), at 6 (http://www.ngltf.org/library/index.cfm).

couples would violate constitutional equality principles, or that recognising unmarried couples as legal entities would undermine the institution of traditional marriage. Some jurisdictions, rejecting the former argument, have extended recognition only to same-sex couples, accepting the proposition that the continuing bar against same-sex marriage leaves same-sex couples uniquely deprived of the benefits of recognised family status,[64] while others have accepted the first argument and have decided to recognise same-sex couples only within the broader context of an inclusive recognition of all non-marital couples. In at least one municipality, Austin, Texas, the city council's decision to adopt the more inclusive approach may have contributed to its subsequent overturning through a referendum promoted by local religious leaders, who argued that extending recognition to unmarried heterosexual couples severely undermined the state interest in supporting legal marriages between persons of the opposite sex.[65]

Municipal ordinances vary as well in the extent to which they confer tangible benefits on those couples whose relationships they recognise. In some jurisdictions, same-sex couples can register with the municipality and obtain some form of certification, but no further benefit comes with that action. At the other extreme is New York City, where a comprehensive domestic partnership ordinance that was enacted in 1998 adopted the general policy that the city would treat registered domestic partners the same as married couples for all purposes of municipal law and regulations.[66] Most frequently, however, the municipal domestic partnership ordinance will treat registered partners as equivalent to spouses for purposes of specific public employee benefits programs and personnel policies, and perhaps for purposes of visitation with inmates in correctional institutions or patients in municipal hospitals and similar institutional settings.[67]

However, municipalities have limited legislative powers in the US, and the extent of those powers varies from state to state and even between municipalities within some states, depending upon how the state's constitution and enabling statutes deal with the distribution of power as between state and local government. While New York City has broad authority to legislate on matters

[64] *Cleaves* v. *City of Chicago*, 68 F.Supp. 2d 963 (N.D. Ill. 1999) (rejecting claim that same-sex only city domestic partnership benefits plan violates equal protection). See also Conclusion, p. 765, n.11.

[65] See, generally, *Bailey* v. *City of Austin*, 972 S.W.2d 180 (Tex. Ct. of Appeals 1998) (after repeal of partner benefits ordinance, individuals who had been receiving benefits could maintain promissory estoppel action to seek order continuing benefits).

[66] For a summary of the provisions of the New York City ordinance, see AS Leonard, "Mayor Giuliani Proposes His Domestic Partnership Policy", (May/June 1998) 4 *City Law* 49 (Center for New York City Law, New York Law School). In addition to adopting the general policy, the ordinance amended numerous provisions of the New York City administrative code specifically to insert the term "domestic partner" in the list of individuals covered by the provisions. See New York City Local Law No. 27 of 1998, http://leah.council.nyc.ny.us/law98/int0303a.htm. Portions of this ordinance are codified in various parts of the New York City Administrative Code. The definitional section can be found at 3 Admin. Code of N.Y.C., chapter 2, subchapter 3 "Domestic Partnership".

[67] For a summary of such benefits plans as of January 2000, see van der Meide, *supra* n.63.

of general welfare so long as it does not adopt any policies specifically prohibited by or contrary to those mandated by state law,[68] some cities' legislative power is very limited by contrast.

Opponents of the domestic partnership concept have instigated litigation in many jurisdictions challenging the legitimacy of municipal domestic partnership ordinances, and have been successful in some cases in getting the courts to declare the measures invalid.[69] The most frequent basis for such invalidation has been that the state had preempted the issue of municipal employee benefits by adopting a statute defining who was eligible to receive such benefits, and specifically limiting eligibility to members of a municipal employee's legally recognised family as sanctified by traditional state law principles.[70] In at least one case, however, a municipality whose domestic partnership ordinance was declared invalid on this basis (Atlanta, Georgia) made a careful study of the grounds for the court's decision and enacted a new ordinance carefully and successfully tailored to avoid the problems the court had identified.[71] In many recent cases, courts have found ways to get around these arguments and sustain the extension of benefits.[72]

In light of the limitations of municipal legislative authority, achieving domestic partnership legislation on the state level has become an important goal of advocates for legal recognition of same-sex partners. In one state, New York, such advocacy was partially successful for reasons having more to do with politics than the merits of the issue. Governor Mario Cuomo, seeking re-election in a close race and concerned that the lesbian and gay voters, if sufficiently motivated, might provide the winning margin, responded to a longstanding request to consider negotiating domestic partnership benefits with the unions representing state employees with a convenient signal of willingness shortly before the election. Although the governor was narrowly defeated for re-election, his successor agreed to ratify the domestic partnership benefits that were negotiate,

[68] See *Slattery*, *supra* n.40.

[69] See, generally, RC Miller, "Validity of Governmental Domestic Partnership Enactment", 74 *American Law Reports* 5th 439 (1999).

[70] *Lilly* v. *City of Minneapolis*, 527 N.W.2d 107 (Minn. Ct. of Appeals 1995; review denied 1995) (state law preempts municipal partnership benefits ordinance); *accord*, *City of Atlanta* v. *McKinney*, 454 S.E.2d 517 (Georgia Supreme Ct. 1995); *Arlington County, Virginia* v. *White*, 528 S.E.2d 706 (Virginia Supreme Ct. 2000). In *Connors* v. *City of Boston*, 714 N.E.2d 335 (Mass. Supreme Judicial Ct. 1999), the court held that the mayor of Boston lacked authority to extend benefits by executive order to domestic partners of municipal employees.

[71] *City of Atlanta* v. *Moran*, 492 S.E.2d 193 (Georgia Supreme Ct. 1997) (finding new ordinance valid under principles used to invalidate old ordinance in *McKinney*, *ibid*.).

[72] *Crawford* v. *City of Chicago*, 710 N.E.2d 91 (Illinois Appellate Ct.), appeal denied, 720 N.E.2d 1090 (Illinois Supreme Ct. 1999); *Slattery*, *supra* n.40; *Schaefer* v. *City and County of Denver*, 973 P.2d 717 (Colo. Ct. of Appeals 1998; certiorari denied, 1999); *Moran*, *ibid*. See also (not officially published) *Godley* v. *Cities of Chapel Hill and Carrboro* (North Carolina Superior Court, Orange County, Hudson, J., May 8, 2000); *Concerned Citizens of Broward County* v. *Broward County* (Florida Circuit Court, Broward County, Andrews, J., April 30, 1999); *Jacks* v. *City of Santa Barbara* (California Superior Court, Santa Barbara County, Dec. 17, 1998).

and even to extend them to state executive branch employees who were not covered by collective bargaining contracts.[73]

By contrast, state legislative extension of benefits was achieved in Hawaii and Vermont by different routes (see chapters 9 and 10.) In Hawaii, a same-sex marriage lawsuit[74] provoked extensive debate in the state legislature about providing some mechanism short of marriage to meet the equity claims of same-sex couples. What emerged was a Reciprocal Beneficiary Law,[75] under which Hawaiian adults living in partnerships that could not be eligible for marriage (whether same-sex or opposite-sex) could become "reciprocal beneficiaries" entitled to recognition for certain purposes specified in the statute, including employee benefits eligibility for partners of public employees in the state. In Vermont, an arbitration decision pertaining to domestic partnership benefits claims under a collective bargaining agreement governing employees of the state university led the state government executive to negotiate similar benefits for other state employees.[76] Subsequently, the legislature responded to the state Supreme Court's 1999 decision in same-sex marriage litigation by passing a Civil Union statute, creating an institution parallel to marriage for same-sex partners (and a distinctly lesser, reciprocal beneficiary institution carrying very limited tangible consequences for relatives ineligible for a marriage or civil union).[77] The Vermont civil union law goes the furthest of any US legislation to make available to same-sex couples a legal status akin to marriage. Indeed, the statute extends to same-sex partners who become "civilly-united" according to its terms every right, benefit and responsibility of marriage that the state can confer.

By early 2000, seven states and the District of Columbia had adopted some form of recognition for same-sex partners. In addition to New York, Hawaii, and Vermont, the state of California had adopted a partnership registry system and extended benefits to partners of state employees,[78] and limited benefits had

[73] "Cuomo Decides to Extend Domestic-Partner Benefits", *N.Y. Times* (29 June 1994) B5; "State Plans to Extend Benefits to Gay Couples", *Buffalo News* (29 June 1994); "New Cuomo Plan Offers Insurance Benefits to 'Significant Others'", 1994 Westlaw 3342928 (17 September 1994); "A Look at Gov. George Pataki's First 100 Days", 1995 Westlaw 6723166 (7 April 1995).

[74] In *Baehr* v. *Miike*, 1996 Westlaw 694235 (Hawaii Circuit Ct. 1996), on remand from *Baehr* v. *Lewin*, 852 P.2d 44 (Hawaii Supreme Ct. 1993), a Hawaii trial court found that the refusal to grant marriage licenses to same-sex couples violated the ban on sex discrimination in the state constitution. The legislative activity described in the text occurred as the state lodged its appeal of this ruling in the state supreme court.

[75] 1997 Hawaii Session Laws, Act 383 (effective 1 July 1997); Hawaii Revised Statutes, e.g., section 572C-4, http://www.capitol.hawaii.gov/Site1/archives/docs 2001. asp#hrs.

[76] See SN Averill, "Comment, Desperately Seeking Status: Same-Sex Couples Battle for Employment-Linked Benefits", (1993) 27 *Akron Law Review* 253 at 263–4.

[77] 2000 Vermont Acts and Resolves, Act 91 (26 April 2000) (http://www.leg.state.vt.us/baker/baker.cfm).

[78] 1999 California Statutes chapter 588 (A.B. 26), http://www.leginfo.ca.gov/statute.html, codified at Calif. Family Code Div. 2.5 (establishing Domestic Partnership Registry), Calif. Health & Safety Code sec. 1261 (recognising registered partners for purposes of hospital visitation), Calif. Government Code art. 9 (extending eligibility for employee benefits to domestic partners of state employees).

been made available by executive action of the governors in Delaware and Massachusetts. In Oregon, as noted above, the *Tanner* decision mandated extension of benefits to state employees. The District of Columbia's legislative council adopted a registration and benefits program, but Congressional action blocked implementation of the benefits program by forbidding the District from spending any of its budget on benefits for unmarried partners of its employees.[79]

Where state laws must fall short at present, whether they extend to same-sex marriage or some parallel institution under a different name such as "civil union," is in providing the full panoply of rights that the federal government extends to marital partners in the US; the federal government has much to say about the incidents of marriage, despite the reservation to the states of the initial authority to establish the requisites for marriage within their own jurisdictions.

In 1996, in one of the grossest examples of legislation specifically enacted to pander to voters during a heated national election, the Congress passed and President Bill Clinton signed the so-called Defense of Marriage Act, a statute intended to relieve states of any obligation under the federal constitution to afford legal recognition to lawful same-sex marriages (in the event that any state should legally authorise such marriages to be performed) and to exclude any such marriages from being recognised for the purpose of any federal law or policy.[80] While it is customary in the United States for federal agencies and courts to look to state law to determine whether somebody is married for purposes of federal law, the federal courts had previously made clear that the question whether somebody is considered married for purposes of such federal functions as immigration and naturalisation would be determined as a matter of federal law.[81] The Defense of Marriage Act codifies the judicial view. Although it is likely that challenges to both aspects of the Act will take place if a state actually allows same-sex partners to marry, it is also possible that the constitutionality of the Act will be implicated with the passage of laws such as those of Hawaii and Vermont: "reciprocal beneficiaries" or "civilly-united" partners could attempt to achieve recognition of their state-recognised familial status under federal immigration, tax or other legal regimes in which spousal status can be crucial, or to compel other states to recognise their partnerships as carrying "extraterritorial" force.

Discussion of legislation as a vehicle for attaining recognition of same-sex partners would not be complete without mention of a relatively new device that has been adopted by several cities on the West Coast of the United States: municipal ordinances making extension of employee benefits to same-sex partners of employees a prerequisite to eligibility to contract with the municipality to provide goods or services. San Francisco pioneered this device and, after it

[79] See van der Meide, *supra* n.63, at 85.

[80] U.S. Public Law 104–199, codified at 1 US Code section 7 and 28 U.S.C. section 1738C (1996).

[81] *Adams* v. *Howerton*, 673 F.2d 1036 (9th Cir.), certiorari denied, 458 U.S. 1111 (1982); *Sullivan* v. *Immigration & Naturalization Service*, 772 F.2d 609 (9th Cir. 1985).

had partially survived an initial court challenge on grounds of federal preemption,[82] Seattle and Los Angeles moved to adopt it as well. San Franciscans estimated that several thousand private sector employers, including many located outside the city, had adjusted their employee benefits programs in order to retain or bid on contracts with the city. While the last word has not been said judicially on the viability of such municipal laws and their extra-territorial reach, advocates for partner recognition have begun to lobby in other major cities, including New York, for the adoption of similar ordinances, which could accomplish circuitously what ERISA-preemption prevents state and local governments from doing directly.

CONCLUSION

Litigation for recognition of same-sex partnerships arises spontaneously from the increasing eagerness of gay people to live together openly, voluntarily assuming responsibilities of loyalty and emotional and financial support that are legally imposed on married couples. While the multitude of legal concerns arising from partnered living might be solved simply by allowing same-sex couples to marry, it is unlikely that that this will be achieved soon in the US, and the appropriateness of requiring the full panoply of rights and obligations of legal marriage for any partnership that desires context-specific recognition is questionable. Many heterosexual couples live together without marriage, which testifies to the widespread belief that marriage is not the best situation for every couple. Society needs to consider how best to reinforce non-marital relationships that fill a large share of the societal needs for which marriage currently provides a limited response.

Consequently, litigating for recognition of same-sex partners within specific limited contexts will continue to be an important strategy in the United States,[83] even as more states take the intermediate steps exemplified in Vermont, Hawaii, California, and New York City, of passing statutes extending some of the rights of marriage to unmarried domestic partners, or the ultimate step of letting same-sex couples marry. In addition, legislation, collective bargaining, and negotiation all remain routes within which same-sex partners in the United States may seek to obtain some form of recognition for their partnerships.

[82] *Air Transportation Assoc'n* v. *City of San Francisco*, 992 F. Supp. 1149 (N.D. Cal. 1999); *S.D. Myers* v. *City of San Francisco*, 253 F.3d 461 (9th Cir. 2001) (finding no ERISA preemption of municipal ordinance limiting eligibility for city contracts to companies that provide domestic partnership benefits for employees; but finding partial preemption under Airline Transportation Act of any requirement that an airline extend benefits bearing significant economic cost). See [Summer 2001] *Lesbian/Gay Law Notes*, supra n.*.

[83] On 2 July 2001, the New York Court of Appeals reversed and remanded *Levin*, *supra* n.15, applying the same disparate impact analysis as the *Tanner* court. See http://www.courts.state.ny.us/ctapps/decision.htm; [Summer 2001] *Lesbian/Gay Law Notes*, supra n.*.

8

Lesbian and Gay Couples Raising Children: The Law in the United States

NANCY D POLIKOFF*

LESBIAN AND GAY couples in the United States who wish to raise children find that their options depend primarily on the state in which they live. The development of policy and law affecting gay and lesbian parents has been shaped by the distinct place of family law within the US federal system. Embedded in the US Constitution is the principle that some aspects of life are governed by state law, determined in each state and not subject to federal uniformity. Family law is one such area. Although Congress passes much legislation that affects families, it cannot determine the standards that courts apply to family disputes, including those involving child custody and visitation. Thus, campaigns to recognise the ability of lesbians and gay men to provide happy and healthy homes for children have been fought primarily at the state level, one state at a time. Determinations are made by state legislatures or, more commonly in the custody and visitation arena, by state appeals courts. With the smallest of exceptions, child custody and adoption decisions from a state's highest court cannot be appealed to the US Supreme Court, making each state's highest court the final word for parents and prospective parents in that state.

The most dramatic consequence of this aspect of the struggle on behalf of gay and lesbian parents is the lack of uniformity among states. Crossing the border from Virginia to the District of Columbia, or from Missouri to Illinois, for example, can mean the difference between losing and retaining custody or being able to adopt as a gay or lesbian couple.[1] Dramatic affirmations of lesbian and

* Professor of Law, Washington College of Law, American University.

[1] This does not mean that a lesbian or gay parent may easily move and thereby take advantage of better laws. In a custody dispute, the state in which the child has been living for the previous six months is likely to be the one that has jurisdiction to hear the case. If a lesbian mother moves with her children to a state with more favorable custody laws, she cannot file for custody there for six months. During that time, if her husband or ex-husband files in the state where the family lived, the mother will be forced to litigate there. In the area of adoption, many states have residency requirements. A couple is able to take advantage of better state laws by moving to a new state but may have to wait a year before being able to adopt in the new state.

gay parenting are irrelevant beyond the borders of the state where they are pronounced; conversely, vitriolic rejection of lesbian and gay childrearing in one state has no bearing in any other state.

A word of caution is also in order about the distinction between formal law as reflected in court decisions and informal law as practiced by individual trial court judges. Family court judges have enormous discretion to make custody and visitation determinations, and they are usually affirmed on appeal. There is no way to know the number of custody and visitation disputes that have been resolved by trial judges, both in favor of and against gay and lesbian parents, and have never been appealed. In states where the case law is generally good for gay and lesbian parents, there is often plenty of room for a judge opposed to gay and lesbian parenting to decide against gay and lesbian parents. Likewise, in states where case law is bad for gay and lesbian parents, there is often room for a sympathetic judge to mitigate the effects of what looks like negative precedent. Thus the life of an individual gay or lesbian parent can be determined not only by state law but by the individual judge assigned to the case.

Disputes about lesbians and gay men raising children arise in two different contexts. The first and most frequent context concerns the ability of a lesbian or gay man who was once heterosexually married and who had children within that marriage to retain custody of the children at the time of divorce or at a subsequent time, especially if he or she lives with a partner. The second context involves planned lesbian and gay families, those in which a lesbian or gay couple wishes to embark on parenting together. The issues confronting this type of family include qualifications for adoption and foster parenting, access to means of alternative reproduction, ability of a lesbian or gay man to adopt his or her partner's child, and the way courts settle disputes about parental rights and responsibilities. This chapter addresses both of these contexts in turn.

CHILDREN BORN DURING HETEROSEXUAL RELATIONSHIPS

Although a parent's homosexuality was explicitly acknowledged in a handful of reported custody and visitation disputes in the United States going back to 1952,[2] cases began appearing more frequently in the early and mid 1970s, as the women's liberation movement and changing attitudes towards divorce made it easier for all women to leave marriages, and as the gay liberation movement enabled significant numbers of gay men and lesbians to embrace an identity they had earlier been taught to despise. By this time, courts had adopted a gender-neutral "best interests of the child" standard for determining custody, a standard leaving enormous discretion in the hands of trial court judges.

During this time, there were both successes and failures in custody disputes, and early court decisions revealed a dynamic specifically relevant to lesbian and

[2] See e.g. *Commonwealth* v. *Bradley*, 91 A.2d 379 (Penn. Superior Court 1952).

gay couples wishing to raise children: judges might be willing to give custody or unrestricted visitation to a single lesbian or gay parent whose homosexuality would be less visible to the children, but a parent living with a partner could be required to choose between keeping her children or keeping her partner relationship. In one highly publicised case in 1972, a lesbian couple in Seattle, Washington was permitted to keep custody of six children between them but was ordered not to live together. The women set up apartments across the hall from one another, went back and forth between the two apartments, and embarked upon a public campaign to undo the restriction placed on them. They interested a doctor at the University of Washington in their family, and he helped the university get a grant to make a movie, "Sandy and Madeleine's Family", which included Margaret Mead articulating a supportive position. Local lesbians rallied in support of the women, and their organising spawned the Lesbian Mothers National Defense Fund, the first grass roots organisation in the United States dedicated exclusively to the rights of lesbian mothers. In 1974, the women's ex-husbands took them back to court claiming violations of the order not to live together and asking for a change of custody. Their petition was denied, and the trial court lifted the restriction on Sandy and Madeleine's cohabitation.

This happy ending was not often duplicated; it was more common for a judge to find the home created by a lesbian mother and her partner abnormal, immoral, or harmful to the children. Gay fathers, who were usually in court seeking unrestricted visitation with their children, often faced court orders that their partners could not be present when they saw their children, and that their children could never visit the homes they shared with their partners.[3]

Custody and visitation disputes between a lesbian or gay parent and her or his ex-spouse have given judges a perfect opportunity to express disapproval of childrearing by lesbian and gay couples. In these cases, there is a heterosexual parent, often remarried, offering to care for the children. A judge who might be willing to leave a happy, healthy child with a single gay or lesbian parent may embrace the opportunity to remove the child from a home the parent shares with a partner. For example, a 1980 Missouri decision changing custody from a lesbian mother to a heterosexual father compared the presence of the mother's partner around the children to the presence of "a habitual criminal, or a child abuser, or a sexual pervert, or a known drug pusher".[4] A 1985 Virginia decision held that a gay parent living with a partner was always an unfit parent.[5] Ten years later, that same court upheld a trial judge's order removing custody of a

[3] Discussion of early lesbian and gay custody disputes can be found in RA Basile, "Lesbian Mothers I", (1974) 8 *Women's Rights Law Reporter* 3; ND Hunter and ND Polikoff, "Custody Rights of Lesbian Mothers: Legal Theory and Litigation Strategy", (1976) 25 *Buffalo Law Review* 691; RR Rivera, "Our Straight-Laced Judges: The Legal Position of Homosexual Persons in the United States", (1979) 30 *Hastings Law Journal* 798.

[4] *N.K.M.* v. *L.E.M.*, 606 S.W.2d 179 at 183 (Missouri Court of Appeals 1980).

[5] *Roe* v. *Roe*, 324 S.E.2d 691 (Virginia Supreme Court 1985).

child from his lesbian mother, Sharon Bottoms, and prohibiting any visitation in the home Sharon shared with her partner or in her partner's presence. The child was placed instead with Sharon's mother, Kay Bottoms.[6] This case garnered national media attention, much of it favorable to Sharon, but six years later the child is still with his grandmother, and efforts to lift the restriction on visitation in the presence of Sharon's partner continue to be unsuccessful.

Recent appellate court decisions from a number of states, mostly in the South, continue this dynamic of disapproval, especially of a lesbian or gay parent who lives with a partner. In a 1998 Alabama case, custody was transferred from a mother who had raised her daughter with her partner for six years to a father who had remarried, in spite of the opinion of the child's therapist recommending that custody remain with the mother. The court explicitly condemned the mother for establishing "a two-parent home environment where their homosexual relationship is openly practiced and presented to the child as the social and moral equivalent of a heterosexual marriage". The court cited the state's criminal sodomy statute and a statute requiring that sex education in schools emphasise that, "homosexuality is not a lifestyle acceptable to the general public and that homosexual conduct is a criminal offense under the laws of the state".[7] Then the court concluded that the mother was exposing her daughter "to a lifestyle that is neither legal in this state, nor moral in the eyes of most of its citizens". Although an expert testified concerning the many studies supporting the positive mental health of children raised by lesbian mothers, the court adopted the position that, "the degree of harm to children from the homosexual conduct of a parent is uncertain. . .and the range of potential harm is enormous".[8]

Because of the state-by-state nature of US family law, these cases represent only one end of the spectrum. At the other end are states in which appellate courts have reversed trial court orders either transferring custody from a gay or lesbian parent living with a partner, or putting restrictions on visitation that would not allow the partner to be present around the children. In 1985, the Alaska Supreme Court reversed a trial judge who had changed custody from a lesbian mother living with her partner to a heterosexual father living with his new wife. The court ruled that a mother's lesbian relationship should be considered only if it negatively affected the child and that it was "impermissible to rely on any real or imagined social stigma attached to the mother's status as a lesbian".[9] A 1998 opinion from the highest court in Maryland overturned a trial judge's order that a gay father's partner be prohibited from being present during the father's visitation, and that the children could never spend the night at the home their father shared with his partner.[10] The Maryland opinion cited

[6] *Bottoms* v. *Bottoms*, 457 S.E.2d 102 (Va. 1995).
[7] Alabama Code s. 16–40A-2(c)(8).
[8] *J.B.F.* v. *J.M.F.*, 730 So. 2d 1190 at 1195–6 (Alabama Supreme Court 1998).
[9] *S.N.E.* v. *R.L.B.*, 699 P.2d 875 at 879 (Alaska Supreme Court 1985).
[10] *Boswell* v. *Boswell*, 721 A.2d 662 (Maryland Court of Appeals 1998).

similar positive decisions from California, Illinois, Oregon, Pennsylvania, and Washington.[11]

Although today, at the turn of the twenty-first century, childrearing by out gay men and lesbians has become increasingly common, and although young gay men and lesbians have an increasing number of positive images and role models that allow them to affirm their sexual orientation, large numbers of adults still do not come out as gay or lesbian until after they marry and have children within those marriages. When those marriages end, or subsequently, when the gay or lesbian parent wants to build a family life with a same-sex partner and to include the children in such a family, he or she is vulnerable to an ex-spouse, or even other relatives, who may seek to change custody or impose restrictions on visitation. The life stories of such lesbian and gay parents look strikingly like those of their counterparts in earlier decades, and their fate continues be determined more than anything else by the states in which they live and the judges who hear their cases.

PLANNED LESBIAN AND GAY FAMILIES

Issues of adoption and foster parenting by gay men and lesbians in the U.S. first surfaced in the 1970s, primarily in the context of gay teenagers whose parents would not allow them to live at home. Shortly after its founding in 1973, the National Gay Task Force, in conjunction with New York City child welfare agencies, developed a network of gay foster homes for homeless gay teenagers who were not functioning well in city group homes. Although the extent of such programs is not well documented, New York's was not the only one. In 1974, a Washington state judge approved the placement of a gay teenager with gay foster parents. A year later, however, another Washington state judge denied such a placement, siding with the child's father, who opposed it. In spite of favorable testimony from social workers, juvenile parole officers, a psychiatrist, and a psychologist, the judge reasoned that "substituting two male homosexuals for parents does violence not only to the literal definition of who are parents but offends the traditional concept of what a family is".[12]

There is no record of an adoption by an openly gay or lesbian parent during the 1970s. It is likely, however, that gay men and lesbians who were not open were able to adopt. Every state permits single adults to adopt, and state adoption agencies would have happily approved a single parent, especially for a hard-to-place child or for a child related to the adopting parent, such as a niece or nephew, whose parents died or were otherwise unable to raise the child.

[11] See *In re marriage of Birdsall*, 243 Cal. Rptr. 287 (California Court of Appeal 1988); *In re Marriage of Pleasant*, 628 N.E.2d 633 (Illinois Appellate Court 1993); *In re Marriage of Ashling*, 599 P.2d 475 (Oregon Court of Appeals 1979); *Blew* v. *Verta*, 617 A.2d 31 (Pennsylvania Superior Court 1992); *In re Marriage of Wicklund*, 932 P.2d 652 (Washington Court of Appeals 1996).

[12] These cases are discussed in Rivera, *supra* n.3 at 907–8.

By the late 1970s, numerous factors coincided to launch a new form of open lesbian and gay parenthood not tied to heterosexual marriage. The gay rights movement enabled many young adults to embrace, rather than reject, their sexual orientation. Men and women who, in an earlier period, would have married out of convention, fear, or denial, no longer necessarily took such a path. While it may have initially appeared that parenthood would never be an option for such men and women, other cultural and medical phenomena soon resulted in a new frame of mind. Specifically, births of out-of-wedlock children no longer carried the stigma they did in earlier decades, and medical technology opened the possibilities for conception without sexual intercourse. At some point in the late 1970s, therefore, open lesbians in significant numbers began contemplating planned motherhood, primarily using alternative insemination as the means of conception.

Although there are accounts of decisions by lesbian couples to raise children together as far back as 1965, this form of planned motherhood probably first took hold in the San Francisco area about 1978. Word spread through pamphlets describing alternative insemination. Women who could not find doctors or sperm banks that would service lesbians, or any unmarried woman, learned how to do the procedure themselves with semen obtained from a willing donor.[13]

Lesbians considering motherhood chose adoption as well as alternative insemination. Although many private adoption agencies would work only with married couples, others were open to single parents. Public agencies, often entrusted with finding homes for hard-to-place children, almost always accepted applications from single men and women. Lawyers advised adoption applicants not to lie but also said that it was not necessary to volunteer information that was not asked. Many social workers, privately supportive of gay adoption but concerned about unsympathetic judges, asked no questions that would require revealing sexual orientation so that they could write reports that portrayed a lesbian or gay applicant simply as a single parent. Although only one state, Florida, banned adoption by gay men and lesbians, in a statute enacted in 1977,[14] few prospective adoptive parents wanted to risk rejection by judges empowered to grant or deny adoptions. Most, therefore, described themselves without reference to their sexual orientation.

In the mid-1980s, sustained national attention to the suitability of lesbians and gay men raising children emerged in the context of foster parenting. Many

[13] Unlike some European countries, no state in the United States has a ban on alternative insemination of lesbians or unmarried women. This does not reflect support for lesbian childbearing. Rather, it reflects the fact that the provision of semen by sperm banks or private doctors is not a state-regulated enterprise. A lesbian who can pay for the procedures, and who can find a doctor or sperm bank who will work with her, has access to such services. Conversely, a lesbian who cannot afford such care, or who has no provider near her who will service her, has no legal recourse and will be forced to achieve conception by other means.

[14] Florida Statutes ch. 63.042, s. 3: "No person eligible to adopt under this statute may adopt if that person is a homosexual."

states, chronically short of foster homes, licensed lesbian and gay foster parents beginning in the mid-1970s, a practice supported by both the American Psychological Association and the National Association of Social Workers. But in May, 1985, neighbors of a gay couple in Boston who served as foster parents went to the local newspaper, the Boston Globe, to express their disapproval. The ensuing publicity, in print media and on television, sparked widespread debate about gay men and lesbians raising children. The Massachusetts Department of Social Services removed the children from the home, and the lower house of the Massachusetts legislature voted to prohibit children's placement in lesbian and gay homes, explicitly defining homosexuality as a threat to children's well being. Although that bill did not become law, Massachusetts changed its policy, issuing regulations that made it almost impossible for lesbians and gay men to become foster parents.[15] In the wake of that controversy, in 1986 the New Hampshire legislature enacted a law prohibiting both adoption and foster parenting by lesbians and gay men.[16]

Despite setbacks such as those in Massachusetts and New Hampshire, across the country the number of gay and lesbian families in which, from birth, a child had two parents of the same gender continued to grow throughout the 1980s. Lawyers in states thought to be favorable towards lesbian and gay parenting developed theories using existing adoption statutes to ensure that both partners would be the legal parents of the children they were raising together.

Lawyers coined the term "second-parent adoption" to describe the equivalent of a step-parent adoption, in which a biological (or legally adoptive) parent's partner adopts his or her child. The term "joint adoption" was used to designate adoption of a child by both members of a couple, a practice unheard of earlier unless the couple was legally married. The first second-parent adoption was granted in Alaska in 1985, and within months there were others in Oregon, Washington, and California. All these were granted by trial court judges without written opinions, making them of limited precedential value. The adoption decrees were circulated among a small group of legal advocates who used them to help develop the law in an increasing number of jurisdictions. Although law review articles first discussed these cases in 1986, there was no reported opinion granting a second-parent adoption until 1991.

Other reported decisions came shortly thereafter. The highest courts of New York, New Jersey, Vermont, Massachusetts, Illinois, and the District of Columbia have approved such adoptions and instructed trial judges to grant them under the same best-interests-of-the-child standard used in all

[15] For extensive discussion of the people involved in the Massachusetts foster care controversy, see L Benkov, *Reinventing the Family* (New York, NY, Crown, 1994) at 86–98; N Miller, *In Search of Gay America* (New York, NY, Harper & Row, 1989) at 121–30.

[16] New Hampshire Revised Statutes Annotated ss. 170-B:4 (adoption), 161:2(IV) (fostering); upheld in *Opinion of the Justices*, 530 A.2d 21 (New Hampshire Supreme Court 1987); repealed by 1999 New Hampshire Laws ch. 18.

adoptions.[17] Final appellate courts in only three states, Wisconsin, Colorado and Connecticut, have rejected such adoptions, in decisions narrowly construing their adoption statutes.[18] Trial courts in more than a dozen other states have granted such adoptions, and in some counties, such as those in the San Francisco Bay area, there have probably been thousands over the last fifteen years.

The success of second-parent adoptions is largely attributable to the context in which they arise and the limited role of the judge in any individual case. A petition to make a non-biological mother a legal parent to the child does not ask a judge to express any opinion about lesbian and gay parenting generally; it simply asks the judge whether the child will be better off with one parent or with two. There is no heterosexual parent vying for the child, who will be raised in a lesbian home regardless of the parents' legal status. In that context, the decision is usually easy for a judge. Also, the judges who hear adoption petitions often are the same judges who, in other cases, hear allegations of abuse and neglect and see children whose lives have been destroyed by myriad factors. The judge who granted the first second-parent adoption in New York put it this way:

> "Today a child who receives proper nutrition, adequate schooling and supportive sustaining shelter is among the fortunate, whatever the source. A child who also receives the love and nurture of even a single parent can be counted among the blessed. Here this court finds a child who has all of the above benefits and two adults dedicated to his welfare, secure in their loving partnership, and determined to raise him to the very best of their considerable abilities. There is no reason in law, logic or social philosophy to obstruct such a favorable situation".[19]

When a couple seeks to adopt a child together, they usually want a joint adoption, in which they will both be the child's legal parents. Most agencies that permit individual lesbians and gay men to adopt do not permit such joint adoptions, reasoning that marriage is a prerequisite for joint adoption and that therefore no unmarried couple may jointly adopt. Couples are unlikely to challenge such a policy for fear that no child will be placed with them, and thus most children adopted into lesbian and gay families have, in the eyes of the law, only one parent. If the state permits second-parent adoption, the couple can achieve legal status for both parents through a two-step process, first an adoption by one of them and later a second-parent adoption.

[17] *In re M.M.D.*, 662 A.2d 837 (District of Columbia Court of Appeals 1995); *In re Petition of K.M and D.M.*, 653 N.E.2d 888 (Illinois Supreme Court 1995); *In re Adoption of Tammy*, 619 N.E.2d 315 (Massachusetts Supreme Judicial Court 1993); *In the Matter of the Adoption of Two Children by H.N.R.*, 666 A.2d 535 (New Jersey Supreme Court 1995); *In the Matter of Dana*, 660 N.E.2d 397 (New York Court of Appeals 1995); *In re Adoption of B.L.V.B.*, 628 A.2d 1271 (Vermont Supreme Court 1993).

[18] *In re T.K.J.*, 931 P.2d 488 (Colorado Supreme Court 1996); *In re Adoption of Baby Z.*, 724 A.2d 1035 (Connecticut Supreme Court 1999); *In re Angel Lace M.*, 516 N.W.2d 678 (Wisconsin Supreme Court 1994). These courts have not based their decisions on the sexual orientation of the parents, but rather on an interpretation of the adoption statutes as precluding adoption by any two unmarried persons, or by the partner of a parent, unless that partner is the parent's husband or wife.

[19] *In re Adoption of Evan*, 583 N.Y.S.2d 997 at 1002 (New York Supreme Court 1992).

Michael Gallucio and Jon Holden faced such a prospect when the New Jersey state agency placed with them a drug-addicted, lung-damaged, HIV-positive, three-month-old foster child, Adam, and then told them two years later that it would approve only one of them as an adoptive parent. Michael and Jon knew that New Jersey approved second-parent adoptions, and the agency told them they could go through that procedure, but they did not want the extra expense or the gap during which Adam would have only one legal father. In a class action suit filed by the American Civil Liberties Union (ALCU), Michael and Jon challenged the state's regulations. The judge granted Michael and Jon their joint adoption. The state agency had nothing but praise for the care the couple had provided the child, and the judge found that the adoption was both legally permissible and in the child's best interests. Two months later, the state and the ACLU reached a settlement in which the state agreed to evaluate gay and lesbian, as well as unmarried heterosexual, couples by the same criteria used to evaluate married couples. Although the settlement was widely reported, incorrectly, as making New Jersey the first state to permit joint adoption by gay couples, the case did make New Jersey the first state with a written policy from its child welfare agency requiring equal treatment for gay and heterosexual prospective adoptive parents.[20]

Michael Gallucio and Jon Holden could pursue their case with the confidence that, whatever the outcome, New Jersey would not remove Adam from their home. The state agency knew they were gay when Adam was placed with them, and this fact had not kept them from being licensed as foster parents. Throughout the 1990s, lesbians and gay men became increasingly visible as foster parents for the growing number of abused, neglected, and abandoned children in state social service systems. In settlement of a law suit, Massachusetts in 1990 abandoned its regulations that made placement of a child with gay or lesbian foster parents almost impossible. A 1994 Florida court decision struck down that state's unwritten policy against licensing gay and lesbian foster parents.[21] In 1996, an Iowa gay male couple were named foster parents of the year by the state's Foster and Adopted Parents Association. They were nominated by their 17-year-old foster son, and over the preceding seven years they had fostered 13 children, one of whom they had adopted.[22] What began in the 1970s as

[20] See *Holden* v. *New Jersey Dept. of Human Services, Div. of Youth and Family Services*, No. C-230-97 (N.J. Superior Court Chancery Div., 17 Dec.1997) (consent judgment ordering that the DYFS repeal and no longer enforce DYFS policy stating that "in the case of unmarried couple cohabiting, only one person can legally adopt a child"). Prior to the Gallucio and Holden case, New Jersey had adopted regulations on adoption by lesbian and gay individuals. See New Jersey Administrative Code, title 10, s. 10:121C-2.6(a): "The Division shall allow any adult to apply to be an adoptive parent regardless of age, race, color, national origin, disability, gender, religion, sexual orientation or marital status." See also s. 10:121C-4.1(c): "The Division shall not discriminate based on the adoptive parent's race, age, sex, disability, marital status, sexual orientation or religious beliefs; however, these factors may be considered in determining whether the best interest of the child would be served by a particular placement for adoption."

[21] *Matthews* v. *Weinberg*, 645 So. 2d 487 (Florida District Court of Appeal 1994).

[22] "Gay Couple Top Foster Parents", *Des Moines Register*, 1 June 1996, at 1.

advocacy for licensing of gay foster parents to meet the needs of gay teenagers unwanted by their parents and ill-served by other placements such as group homes, had been broadened by the 1990s—and by the boom in planned gay and lesbian families—to include the desires and abilities of lesbians and gay men to help meet the desperate need for placements for children in state care.

Progress in the area of second-parent and joint adoption has also been possible in the United States because of our common law tradition and the role of judges in the interpretation of statutes. Most states do not have adoption statutes written specifically with planned lesbian and gay families in mind. Under principles of statutory interpretation, however, judges may apply the wording of statutes to cases before them, even if the specific application of the statute was not contemplated by the legislature. Thus, some courts have reasoned that a statute permitting "any person" to adopt a child, coupled with a rule of construction that considers the singular tense interchangeable with the plural under most circumstances, should be interpreted to permit any two people, even if not married, to jointly adopt.[23] Other courts have permitted second-parent adoptions by analogising to step-parent adoptions, which are specifically covered by statutes.[24]

These forms of statutory construction are less likely to be used in civil law countries, where joint and second-parent adoption is generally dependent upon the legislature enacting affirmative statutes for that purpose. That does not mean that state legislatures have no role in the United States. All of the court decisions approving joint and second-parent adoptions for lesbian and gay parents have interpreted state law as permitting such adoptions. A state legislature could respond to such a decision by enacting a statute prohibiting such adoptions. To date, no legislature in a state whose courts permit joint or second-parent adoption has done this. Indeed in Vermont, one of the first states whose supreme court approved such adoptions, a revision of the adoption statutes in 1995 codified the court decision.[25] In 2000, the Connecticut legislature enacted a statute permitting second-parent adoption in response to a 1999 court decision that such adoptions were not permitted under the existing adoption code.[26]

Inexorably, the formation of lesbian and gay families with children has been followed by the dissolution of some of those families. When a second-parent or joint adoption has not taken place, these dissolutions have presented courts with two options—to recognise planned lesbian and gay families and modify family law principles to protect the interests of parents and children in such families, or to maintain a rigid definition of parenthood that often fails to recognise

23 This was part of the reasoning in *In re M.M.D.*, *supra* n.17.

24 An example of this type of reasoning is found in *In re Adoption of B.L.V.B.*, *supra* n.17.

25 Vermont Statutes Annotated, title 15A, s. 1-102(b): "If a family unit consists of a parent and the parent's partner, and adoption is in the best interest of the child, the partner of a parent may adopt a child of the parent. Termination of the parent's parental rights is unnecessary in an adoption under this subsection."

26 Connecticut General Statutes Annotated, sections 45a-724, 45a-731, as amended by 2000 Connecticut Legislative Service Public Act 00-228.

the reality of children's actual relationships with parenting figures. Courts, sometimes claiming that legislative language gave them no choice, have usually taken the latter option. In most states that have faced the issue, courts have refused to look beyond biology or the legal status conferred by formal adoption.

Disputes about parenthood have arisen primarily in two contexts. The first is a claim by a non-biological parent to continue a relationship with a child when she and the child's biological parent separate. The second is a claim by a biological father, usually a semen donor, who demands legal parental status in disregard of an agreement with the lesbian couple that he would not assert formal parental rights based on biology.

These cases initially posed a dilemma for gay and lesbian legal organisations. The National Center for Lesbian Rights (NCLR), for example, had a policy of not representing one lesbian against another. Yet it became apparent early on that in lesbian breakups, the parent with the legal status was using doctrine designed to protect parents from outsiders, such as relatives or temporary child care providers, for the purpose of excluding from the child's life a former partner who had functioned as the child's parent. Even if the legally unrecognised mother stayed home with the child, or if the child called both women "Mommy", or had the last name of the legally unrecognised mother, or asked to live with, or at least visit, the person s/he clearly considered another parent, courts rejected such claims under a narrow definition of parenthood tied to a heterosexual paradigm of family. Thus NCLR reexamined its policy and determined, as did other gay legal organisations, that it would advocate upholding the family deliberately formed by the couple and their children and oppose a legal parent's attempts to write the legally unrecognised parent out of the child's life.

This advocacy has been largely unsuccessful. Appellate courts in California and New York, the states with the largest number of planned lesbian and gay families, have both closed the door on all claims by non-biological mothers,[27] and recognised the claims of semen donors.[28] Claims on behalf of non-biological mothers have also been rebuffed in Ohio, Texas, Tennessee, and Florida.[29] In 1995, a Wisconsin Supreme Court decision permitted such parents to request visitation rights but not custody, even if the non-biological parent was the child's primary caretaker.[30] Recent successes, however, might be evidence of a trend towards greater recognition of two-mother lesbian families. In 1999, the

[27] *Z.C.W.* v. *Lisa W.*, 84 Cal. Rptr. 2d 48 (California Court of Appeal 1999); *Curiale* v. *Reagan*, 272 Cal. Rptr. 520 (California Court of Appeal 1990); *Alison D.* v. *Virginia M.*, 572 N.E.2d 27 (New York Court of Appeals 1991).

[28] *Jhordan C.* v. *Mary K.*, 224 Cal. Rptr. 530 (California Court of Appeal 1986); *Thomas S.* v. *Robin Y.*, 618 N.Y.S.2d 356 (New York Supreme Court Appellate Division 1994).

[29] *Music* v. *Rachford*, 654 So. 2d 1234 (Florida District Court of Appeal 1995); *Liston* v. *Pyles*, 1997 Ohio App. LEXIS 3627 (Ohio Supreme Court 1997); *White* v. *Thompson*, 1999 Tenn. App. LEXIS 629 (Tennessee Supreme Court. 1999); *Jones* v. *Fowler*, 969 S.W.2d 429 (Texas Supreme Court 1998).

[30] *In re H.S. H.-K.*, 533 N.W.2d 419 (Wisconsin Supreme Court 1995).

Massachusetts Supreme Judicial Court upheld a grant of visitation rights to a non-biological lesbian mother, giving her the status of "de facto parent".[31] In 2000, a Maryland appeals court approved awarding visitation to a non-biological mother using a best interests of the child standard, although it upheld the trial court's determination that, under the particular facts in the case, visitation was not in the child's best interests.[32] The most far-reaching decision came in 2000 from the New Jersey Supreme Court, when it held that a non-biological lesbian mother who met specified criteria could request both custody and visitation rights and would be judged on an equal footing with a biological mother.[33]

The most extreme example of a biological mother's attempt to write a non-biological mother out of her child's life occurred in North Carolina in 1997. In 1993, in Washington state, Shifra Erez gave birth to a child and consented to the child's second-parent adoption by her partner, Aviva Starr. The adoption was granted under Washington law. The couple and their child moved to North Carolina in 1995 and separated in 1996. Erez left their daughter with Starr, who filed a petition for custody. Erez responded by asking the court to find that Starr's adoption of the child was contrary to the public policy of North Carolina and should therefore not be recognised by a North Carolina court. She argued that North Carolina courts would not have granted the second-parent adoption and that North Carolina did not recognise same-sex marriages. Although the North Carolina judge upheld the Washington adoption, the case illustrates the lengths some individual gay men or lesbians are willing to go to use legal arguments, even blatantly homophobic ones, to negate an already vulnerable planned gay or lesbian family.

In almost every state, the rigid definition of parenthood that excludes a legally unrecognised (non-biological *and* non-adoptive) lesbian mother includes not only the biological mother, but also the biological father. Lesbians who use anonymous semen donors through their doctors or through sperm banks are protected from paternal claims, but those who have chosen known donors, who are often gay men, are vulnerable to a paternity claim by the donor that could lead to court-ordered visitation rights or even a transfer of custody. When the intent of the parties at the time of conception has been clear, the lesbian and gay legal organisations have argued that the parties' agreement should be carried out, but they have again been thwarted by the dominant heterosexual paradigm. The rights and responsibilities of parenthood cannot be contracted away, and therefore courts will refuse to enforce agreements, even if written, that the semen donor will not claim legal parental status. This doctrine stems partly from the laudable goal of ensuring that heterosexual fathers will be unable to walk away from their obligation to financially support their children. But the

[31] *E.N.O.* v. *L.M.M.*, 711 N.E.2d 886 (Massachusetts Supreme Judicial Court 1999).

[32] *S.F.* v. *M.D.*, 751 A.2d 9 (Maryland Court of Special Appeals 2000).

[33] *V.C.* v. *M.J.B.*, 748 A.2d 539 (New Jersey Supreme Court 2000). See also *Rubano* v. *DiCenzo*, 759 A.2d 959 (Rhode Island Supreme Court 2000).

doctrine reflects a larger theme in the contemporary contest over "family values". At a time when policy makers can blame all social ills on single mothers and the lack of fathers in the lives of children, the courts are unlikely to affirm the ability of a lesbian couple, or indeed any unmarried woman, to raise a child alone if there is a man clamoring for the right to parent. Thus courts have almost uniformly embraced semen donors' claims to the rights of fatherhood.[34] This ideological conflict between recognition of the inherent worth of a variety of family structures and dogmatic adherence to the supremacy of a childrearing model with one mother and one father, forms the core of the policy disputes over lesbian and gay parenting into the twenty-first century.[35]

The number of planned lesbian and gay families skyrocketed in the United States in the 1990s, bringing unprecedented visibility in the media, in schools, in churches and synagogues, and in the courts. In November 1996, Grammy award winning-singer Melissa Etheridge appeared on the cover of *Newsweek* with her pregnant partner, Julie Cypher. Dozens of articles appear in daily newspapers each year, in such places as Dayton, Ohio, Sarasota, Florida, and Greensboro, North Carolina, as well as all major cities, describing local lesbian and gay families and their children. News coverage has included the relatively recent phenomenon of gay fathers raising biologically-related children born to a surrogate mother, a practice which captured the attention of the major national media with the opening in 1996 of a Los Angeles-based agency devoted exclusively to matching prospective gay fathers with surrogate mothers.[36]

With this visibility has come an increased number of heterosexual allies, people in positions of power able to influence mainstream organisations, as well as ordinary people whose children become friends with children of gay and lesbian parents, thereby learning about gay and lesbian families in ways that break down myths, stereotypes, and fear. In 1995, the American Psychological Association issued *Lesbian and Gay Parenting: A Resource for Psychologists*, a review of 43 empirical studies and numerous other articles that concluded that "[n]ot a single study has found children of gay and lesbian parents to be

[34] The exception is *Leckie* v. *Voorhies*, 875 P.2d 521 (Oregon Court of Appeals 1994), in which the court denied a semen donor's paternity petition. Oregon has a statute stating that semen donors do not have parental rights, and the semen donor in that case had signed an agreement waiving parental rights. Some state statutes preclude a donor from asserting paternity if the insemination is performed by a doctor. Lesbians who self-inseminate are not protected by these statutes. See *C.O.* v. *W.S.*, 639 N.E.2d 523 (Ohio Court of Common Pleas 1994); *Jhordan C.* v. *Mary K.*, *supra* n.28.

[35] The ideological underpinnings of the right wing so-called "family values" movement and the impact of that movement on lesbian and gay families, is well analysed in J Stacey, *In the Name of the Family: Rethinking Family Values in the Postmodern Age* (Boston, MA, Beacon Press, 1996).

[36] The legal status of surrogate motherhood, the process whereby a woman gives birth to a child conceived through insemination for the purpose of providing a man with a biological child, like all other matters discussed in this chapter, varies dramatically from state to state. In some states, surrogacy agreements are unenforceable. In others, the practice is permitted as long as the surrogate is not paid. Some states permit the practice but restrict its use to married couples, excluding single men whether they are heterosexual or gay. For a review of state statutes, see MJ Hollandsworth, "Gay Men Creating Families Through Surro-Gay Arrangements: A Paradigm for Reproductive Freedom", (1995) 3 *American University Journal of Gender & the Law* 183.

disadvantaged in any significant respect relative to children of heterosexual parents".[37]

With increased visibility, however, has come increased political volatility. Legislatures have had more opportunities to debate lesbian and gay parenting, and their reactions have been primarily hostile. In 1999, Arkansas passed a regulation prohibiting foster parenting by lesbians or gay men.[38] In 2000, Utah prohibited adoption by anyone cohabiting (residing and having a sexual relationship) with another person outside of marriage, leaving single lesbians and gay men, but not those living with partners, able to adopt.[39] Also in 2000, Mississippi prohibited "[a]doption by couples of the same gender".[40] Many of the arguments against same-sex marriages in state legislatures, during debates on bills denying legal recognition to such marriages, have included hostile references to lesbians and gay men raising children.

On the positive side, however, in 1999 New Hampshire repealed its ban on foster parenting and adoption by gay men and lesbians.[41] With a Democratic governor and a legislature that in 1997 had outlawed discrimination based on sexual orientation in employment, housing, and public accommodations, New Hampshire had a different atmosphere than it had a decade earlier, when the ban was enacted and one legislator argued that lesbians and gay men wanted to "raise their own meat" to sexually molest. Upon signing the 1999 repeal, Governor Jeanne Shaheen commented that foster and adoptive families would now be selected based on fitness, "without making prejudicial assumptions". In 2000, the Connecticut legislature gave lesbian and gay families a victory when it enacted a statute explicitly permitting second-parent adoption.[42]

CONCLUSION

The state-by-state nature of family law in the United States has always produced a checkered legal and political climate for lesbian and gay parents. This remains as true today as it was in the 1970s. The story of the last thirty years is the story of advances followed by repercussions. The present assault on lesbian and gay parenting, exemplified by an increasing number of states considering bans on adoption or foster parenting, is taking place in the context of unprecedented numbers of gay men and lesbians choosing to be parents. The public nature of

[37] American Psychological Association, *Lesbian and Gay Parenting: A Resource for Psychologists* (Washington, DC, 1995) at 8, http://www.apa.org/pi/parent.html.

[38] See "Board Adopts Ban on Gay Foster Parents", *Arkansas Democrat-Gazette*, 24 March 1999, at B-3.

[39] Utah Code Annotated ss. 78-30-1(3)(b), 78-30-9(3), as amended by 2000 Utah Laws ch. 208, ss. 5, 7.

[40] Mississippi Code Annotated s. 93-17-3(2), as amended by 2000 Mississippi Laws (Senate Bill 3074).

[41] *Supra* n.16.

[42] *Supra* n.26.

the debate about childrearing by lesbians and gay men has drawn opposition from the religious right, and from secular groups espousing "family values" ideology that glorifies heterosexual marriage and blames all social ills on marital dissolution (or non-formation) and the absence of fathers in the lives of children. On the other hand, this public debate has garnered the support of the principal mainstream organisations committed to positive outcomes for children—the American Psychological Association, the National Association of Social Workers, and the Child Welfare League of America. Because of the US federal system, there will never be only one law concerning lesbian and gay childrearing. Rather, there will continue to be 51 separate legislative battlefields, each requiring its own local strategy, and hundreds of appellate judges and thousands of trial judges, all of whom must be educated. While ground is being and will be lost in some states, lesbians and gay men continue to raise children, even in states without friendly legal climates, and there is no evidence that this trend is letting up.

9

The Hawaii Marriage Case Launches the US Freedom-to-Marry Movement for Equality

EVAN WOLFSON*

ALTHOUGH SAME-SEX COUPLES had sought the freedom to marry from the very beginning of the modern gay rights movement, American courts in the 1970s were willing to rubberstamp anti-gay discrimination.[1] Couples were routinely denied civil marriage licenses—no matter how long they had been together, no matter how committed their relationships, and no matter how much they (and their children) needed the legal, economic, and social support that comes with civil marriage.[2] Lesbian and gay movement organisations did little to challenge the continuing exclusion of same-sex couples from the basic human right, the important personal choice, and the legal protections, responsibilities, and commitment that civil marriage represents. All that changed in the early 1990s, with a groundbreaking case in Hawaii.[3]

In December 1990, three same-sex couples in Hawaii asked for civil marriage licenses, which were denied in April 1991. Their attorney, Dan Foley of the Honolulu law firm of Partington & Foley, filed a legal case that rocked the world. The lower court rebuffed the couples, but on 5 May 1993, the Hawaii Supreme Court ruled that the denial of licenses constituted prima facie sex

* Freedom-to-Marry Project, New York (formerly Director, Marriage Project, Lambda Legal Defense and Education Fund, New York). Lambda is the leading US national legal rights organisation for lesbians and gay men. Wolfson served as co-counsel in the Hawaii marriage case and coordinates and promotes efforts nationwide to win the freedom to marry.

[1] See E Wolfson, "Crossing the Threshold: Equal Marriage Rights for Lesbians and Gay Men and the Intra-Community Critique", (1994) 21 *New York University Review of Law and Social Change* 567 at 568. On the history of discrimination and change in the institution of marriage, see W Eskridge, *The Case for Same-Sex Marriage* (New York, NY, Free Press, 1996); EJ Graff, *What is Marriage For?* (Boston, MA, Beacon Press, 1999).

[2] On the consequences of being denied the freedom to marry, see, e.g., J Wriggins, "Marriage Law and Family Law: Autonomy, Interdependence, and Couples of the Same Gender", (2000) 41 *Boston College Law Review* 265; CW Christensen, "If Not Marriage? On Securing Gay and Lesbian Family Values by a 'Simulacrum of Marriage'", (1998) 66 *Fordham Law Review* 1699; DL Chambers, "What If? The Legal Consequences of Marriage and the Legal Needs of Lesbian and Gay Male Couples", (1996) 95 *Michigan Law Review* 447.

[3] See Wolfson, *supra* n.1, at 572–81.

discrimination, in violation of the state constitutional guarantee of equal protection.[4] For the first time ever, a court declared that lesbian and gay couples in love were entitled to a day in court, to challenge their exclusion from the central social and legal institution of marriage.

From the moment the Hawaii Supreme Court issued its landmark ruling in 1993, the challenges and opportunities loomed large.[5] Gay legal groups began beating the drum, urging other national gay organisations, state and local groups, and allies to seize the moment to educate the public, organise against right-wing attacks, and do the necessary cultural and political work that must accompany legal advances for true social change. For the first time ever, a broad swath of the gay national and local groups came together around a single statement of belief, the Marriage Resolution,[6] and began meeting regularly to coordinate and promote efforts through the National Freedom to Marry Coalition.

Of course, the 1993 ruling did not order the issuance of marriage licenses or strike down the marriage law. All the Hawaii Supreme Court did was what courts are supposed to do: turn to the government and say, if you are going to discriminate, you have to have a reason. The Court sent the case back to the lower court to give the government a chance to show that "reason" (a "compelling state interest") or stop discriminating.

Despite this measured judicial step, right-wing anti-gay groups went on the attack. The backlash began even before anyone had lashed, that is, before any court had examined the government's reason, indeed, before any state had permitted same-sex couples to wed. In 1995, anti-marriage bills were introduced in three state legislatures to codify the de facto reality that, in all fifty states, same-sex couples were denied marriage licenses, and to declare the radical proposition that the prospective lawful marriages of same-sex couples would be denied equal treatment under law, should they cross the wrong state border. With waves of anti-marriage legislation introduced across the country every year since 1995, these anti-marriage activists sought to make America a "house divided" in which couples could be legally married in some states but no more than roommates in the eyes of the law if they traveled through, worked in, or visited another state.[7]

[4] *Baehr* v. *Lewin*, 852 P.2d 44, clarified on grant of reconsideration in part, 852 P.2d 74 (1993). For all the decisions in the *Baehr* case, see "Marriage Project", <http://www.lambdalegal.org/cgi-bin/pages/issues/record?record=9>.

[5] See Wolfson, *supra* n.1; "Marriage Project", *ibid.*

[6] "Because marriage is a basic human right and an individual personal choice, RESOLVED, the state should not interfere with same-gender couples who choose to marry and share fully and equally in the rights, responsibilities, and commitment of civil marriage." See "Marriage Project", *ibid.* See also E Wolfson, "Why We Should Fight for the Freedom to Marry: The Challenges and Opportunities That Will Follow a Win in Hawaii", (1996) 1 *Journal of Gay, Lesbian and Bisexual Identity* 79 at 82–3; Evan Wolfson, "How to Win the Freedom to Marry", [Fall 1997] *Harvard Gay and Lesbian Review* 29.

[7] For materials on the right's anti-marriage campaign and activities in the states, see "Marriage Project", *supra* n.4.

In February 1996, most of the "usual suspects" in the right-wing anti-gay set gathered in Iowa, shortly before the presidential caucuses, to announce an all-out state-by-state campaign against gay people's freedom to marry. These right-wing opponents decided to inject the question of civil rights for lesbians and gay men into presidential election-year politics. They sought thereby to whip up their troops and scare politicians who had just begun to experience the emerging public discussion of how the denial of civil marriage harms real-life families.

In addition to a spate of state-by-state anti-marriage bills, these anti-gay groups prompted Republican legislators in Congress to introduce a federal anti-marriage measure, the so-called "Defense of Marriage Act" or DOMA.[8] Inserting the federal government into marriage for the first time in U.S. history, the so-called DOMA created a radical federal caste system of first-class and second-class marriages.[9] Under DOMA, if the federal government likes whom you marry, your first-class marriage gets a vast array of legal and economic protections and recognition from federal statutes.[10] But if the federal government does not like whom you marry, your second-class marriage is denied federal recognition, protection, and benefits in all circumstances. Additionally, DOMA purported to authorise states to discriminate against the lawful marriages of same-sex couples validly celebrated in other states—an unprecedented attempt to transform the Constitution's full faith and credit clause[11] into a "some faith and credit" clause at the whim of Congress. For all its radical sweep and dubious constitutionality, however, DOMA did not "ban" same-sex couples from marrying; rather, it represented a concession by our enemies that gay people seem likely to win the freedom to marry, and thus they wish to discriminate against the soon-to-be lawful marriages.

In America, we should not have second-class citizens, and we should not have second-class marriages. Hearkening back to the not-so-long-ago ugly days of discrimination against those who chose to marry the "wrong" kind of person (such as interracial or interfaith couples) and the days when Americans had to "go to Reno" (Nevada) just to get a civil divorce, these state and federal anti-marriage bills are unconstitutional, divisive, wrong, and cruel. They will be challenged once couples are allowed to legally marry in some state, as the civil rights struggle to win the freedom to marry advances.[12]

[8] Codified as 1 United States Code section 7, 28 U.S.C. s. 1738C. See Feldblum, chap. 3.

[9] E Wolfson and M Melcher, "DOMA's House Divided: An Argument Against the 'Defense of Marriage Act' ", (1997) 44 *Federal Lawyer* 31.

[10] In a report prepared at the request of Congress six months after the vote to discriminate against gay people's marriages, Congress was informed that the federal anti-marriage law excluded same-sex couples from over 1049 ways in which federal law addresses marital status. Report No. OGC-97-16 (31 Jan. 1997), http://www.gao.gov (GAO Reports, Find GAO Reports).

[11] The Full Faith and Credit Clause, United States Constitution, Article 4, section 1, is a prime engine of federal unity and interstate comity, as well as a protection for the expectations of American citizens and couples as they travel or do business throughout the country. *Supra* n.9, at 31–3.

[12] On DOMA's unconstitutionality, see *supra* n.9; A Koppelman, "Dumb and DOMA: Why the Defense of Marriage Act is Unconstitutional", (1997) 83 *Iowa Law Review* 1; L Kramer, "Same-Sex

Unsurprisingly, anti-marriage measures, such as DOMA, those adopted by state legislatures, and the ballot initiatives (referendums) launched by right-wing groups when some state legislatures rejected their discriminatory bills, have been used to attack gay individuals and families far beyond the domain of marriage itself.[13] Even more significantly, the anti-marriage measures are not just an attempt to erect additional legal barriers against equality, they represent the right-wing's effort to squelch the emerging and vital discussion about gay people's freedom to marry and the meaning of equality. In that, they have failed. As religious denominations, politicians, news media, community leaders, and the public continue to debate civil marriage, civil unions, and gay inclusion, a Wall Street Journal/NBC poll reported in September 1999 that two-thirds of all Americans now believe that gay people will win the freedom to marry (and the sky will not fall).[14] The latest Associated Press poll showed only 51 per cent opposed.[15]

Meanwhile, in Hawaii, the Supreme Court's 1993 ruling led to a full trial on the justifications for discrimination. After extensive testimony and briefing, Judge Kevin Chang held that the state had failed to show even a single valid reason for denying lesbian and gay couples the opportunity to make the legal commitment of marriage.[16] That historic ruling represented the first, and still the only, time that a court has recognised that same-sex couples, too, have the freedom to marry and ordered *full* equality for lesbians and gay men.[17] The

Marriage, Conflict of Laws, and the Unconstitutional Public Policy Exception", (1997) 106 *Yale Law Journal* 1965; M Strasser, *Legally Wed: Same-Sex Marriage and the Constitution* (Ithaca, NY, Cornell University Press, 1997). Apart from the unconstitutionality of discrimination against lawfully married couples simply because they are gay, refusal to "recognise" couples' marriages as they travel from state to state "aconstitutionally" contravenes settled expectations and standard approaches toward interstate respect for marital status. See Bonauto, chap. 10, nn.135, 137, 141 (articles by Wriggins, Cox).

[13] As of Sept. 2000, thirty-three state legislatures had adopted anti-marriage measures. In three other states (Alaska, California, Hawaii), voters had approved anti-marriage ballot measures or constitutional amendments. See "2000 Anti-Marriage Bills Status Report", http://www.lambdalegal.org/cgi-bin/pages/documents/record?record=578. On 7 Nov. 2000, 70% of Nebraska voters ratified the most sweeping anti-marriage measure to date, Nebraska Constitution, Art. I, s. 29: "Only marriage between a man and a woman shall be valid or recognized in Nebraska. The uniting of two persons of the same sex in a civil union, domestic partnership, or other similar same-sex relationship shall not be valid or recognized in Nebraska".

[14] See "Optimism Outduels Pessimism", *Wall Street Journal*, 16 Sept. 1999, at A10.

[15] "Poll Is Mixed On Gay Marriage", *Newsday*, 1 June 2000. While showing only 51% opposition to equal marriage rights, the poll also reported that a majority support providing gay couples the components of marriage, such as inheritance, health insurance, and social security benefits. As in all such polls, young people were significantly more supportive of equality in marriage.

[16] *Baehr* v. *Miike*, Civ. No. 91–1394, 1996 WL 694235 (Hawaii Circuit Court, 3 Dec. 1996). See also SA Marcosson, "The Lesson of the Same-Sex Marriage Trial: The Importance of Pushing Opponents of Lesbian and Gay Rights to Their 'Second Line of Defense' ", (1996–97) 35 *Journal of Family Law (University of Louisville)* 721.

[17] Following the landmark Hawaii trial court ruling, a court in Alaska held that the choice of a life partner in marriage is fundamental, and therefore that the state must show a compelling state interest in order to exclude same-sex couples from the freedom to marry. *Brause* v. *Bureau of Vital Statistics*, No. 3AN-95-0562 CI., 1998 WL 88743 (Alaska Superior Court, 27 Feb. 1998), "Marriage Project", *supra* n.4. Before an appeal could be heard, right-wing groups pushed through a constitutional amendment, ratified by voters on 3 Nov. 1998, which blocked the courts' ability to hold the

judge stayed his order that the licenses issue pending an appeal to the State Supreme Court.

Knowing that they had failed to show a good reason for discrimination, the opponents of equality remained unrelentingly determined to thwart an independent judiciary's review of the exclusion from marriage. They poured millions of dollars into the state to pressure the legislature and the electorate into adopting a constitutional amendment that had the radical aim of removing the marriage law (and its discriminatory different-sex restriction) from judicial review under the equal protection guarantees of the Hawaii Constitution.[18] The Hawaii Supreme Court subsequently ruled that its hands were tied, because the amendment "[took] the statute out of the ambit of the equal protection clause of the Hawai'i Constitution", at least as regards marriage licenses, and dismissed the case.[19] Thus ended the famous "Hawaii marriage case" that had once seemed the likeliest vehicle for ending sex discrimination in civil marriage, much as *Perez* v. *Lippold* in California had begun the nation's journey toward ending race discrimination in civil marriage.[20]

state to its obligation to show a reason before discriminating against gay people. See Alaska Constitution, Art. I, s. 25: "To be valid or recognized in this State, a marriage may exist only between one man and one woman." See also Wriggins, *supra* n.2, at 291–92 n. 176.

[18] For the amendment, ratified by a vote of 69% to 29% on 3 November 1998, see Appendix to this chapter. See also State of Hawaii, *Report of the Commission on Sexual Orientation and the Law* (1995), <http://www.hawaii.gov/lrb/rpts95/sol/soldoc.html> (recommending that the legislature allow same-sex couples the freedom to marry, or "a universal comprehensive domestic partnership act that confers all the possible benefits and obligations of marriage for two people, regardless of gender"). The negotiations that led to the constitutional amendment also resulted in a 1997 law allowing same-sex couples, and other pairs legally prohibited from marrying, to register as "reciprocal beneficiaries" and receive some of the legal and economic protections and obligations of marriage (more than are accorded gay and lesbian couples in any other U.S. jurisdiction, except now Vermont). See Hawaii Revised Statutes, e.g., section 572C-4, <http://www.capitol.hawaii.gov/site1/archives/docs2001.asp#hrs>. See also B Burnette, "Hawaii's Reciprocal Beneficiaries Act", (1998–99) 37 *Brandeis Journal of Family Law* 81.

[19] *Baehr* v. *Miike*, 994 P.2d 566 (Table)(9 Dec. 1999). Even while declaring that it could no longer order the issuance of licenses, the Court did not foreclose litigation for the full and equal rights and benefits accompanying marriage (apart from the status itself). And in a pivotal footnote, the Court declared that sexual orientation discrimination warrants strict scrutiny under the Hawaii Constitution. See Appendix to this chapter; "Marriage Project", *supra* n.4. The Court did not explain how the 1998 constitutional amendment, granting the legislature a power which it had not exercised prior to the Court's decision, could retroactively validate the different-sex-only marriage law. See M Strasser, "*Baehr* Mysteries, Retroactivity and the Concept of Law", (2000) 41 *Santa Clara Law Review* 161.

[20] 198 P.2d 17 (1948). In *Perez*, a four-to-three majority made the California Supreme Court the first American court ever to strike down the long-standing prohibitions on interracial marriages—which, like same-sex couples' marriages, were condemned as contrary to the definition of marriage or divine will, likely to lead to a parade of horribles (i.e., bestiality, incest, polygamy, and the downfall of society), and best left to the mercy of legislatures rather than courts. It took another nineteen years following that breakthrough before the US Supreme Court struck down race discrimination in marriage across the country, in the best named case ever, *Loving* v. *Virginia*, 388 U.S. 1 (1967). Just as we ended race discrimination in civil marriage, so will we see an end to sex discrimination in civil marriage, as more and more fair-minded people come to see that there is no good reason for excluding gay and lesbian couples from the commitment, responsibilities, and support we seek to share.

Even though the Hawaii case failed to bring us all the way to the breakthrough we still hope to see soon, it served as a historical vehicle that launched an important, necessary, and continuing national discussion. It laid the foundations for the next major affirmative freedom-to-marry case and the ensuing civil union legislation in Vermont, as well as for states to come, pushed mainstream politicians and others into an "all but marriage" position in support of gay inclusion and rights, and left us far ahead of where we were when it started. Thanks to the Hawaii case and the ongoing freedom-to-marry movement it sparked, the idea of gay people getting married has gone from an "oxymoron" ridiculed by our opponents, or a dream undiscussed by non-gay people (and most gay people, too), to a reality waiting to happen.

As my friend and litigation partner, Mary Bonauto, shows in the next chapter, within just seven years of the Hawaii Supreme Court's initial ruling, we have seen the creation of civil unions, that is "gay marriages", on US soil. While "gay marriage" is not good enough (we want "marriage", full equality, not two lines at the clerk's office segregating couples by sexual orientation), the progress and possibilities remain astonishing. Full equality and inclusion shimmer within reach. Now it is up to us—gay and non-gay alike—to do the reaching, and the reaching out.

APPENDIX

The following is the opinion of the Supreme Court of Hawaii in *Baehr* v. *Miike*, 994 P.2d 566 (Table)(9 Dec. 1999):

Summary Disposition Order

Pursuant to Hawaii Rules of Evidence (HRE) Rules 201 and 202 (1993), this court takes judicial notice of the following: On April 29, 1997, both houses of the Hawaii legislature passed, upon final reading, House Bill No. 117 proposing an amendment to the Hawaii Constitution (the marriage amendment). See 1997 House Journal at 922; 1997 Senate Journal at 766. The bill proposed the addition of the following language to article I of the Constitution: "Section 23. The legislature shall have the power to reserve marriage to opposite-sex couples." See 1997 Haw. Sess. L. H.B. 117 s.2, at 1247. The marriage amendment was ratified by the electorate in November 1998.

In light of the foregoing, and upon carefully reviewing the record and the briefs and supplemental briefs submitted by the parties and amicus curiae and having given due consideration to the arguments made and the issues raised by the parties, we resolve the defendant-appellant Lawrence Miike's appeal as follows:

On December 11, 1996, the first circuit court entered judgement in favor of plaintiffs-appellees Ninia Baehr, Genora Dancel, Tammy Rodrigues, Antoinette Pregil, Pat Lagon, and Joseph Melillo (collectively, the "plaintiffs") and against Miike, ruling (1) that the sex-based classification in Hawaii Revised Statutes (HRS) s.572-1 (1985) was "unconstitutional" by virtue of being "in violation of the equal protection clause of article I, section 5 of the Hawaii Constitution," (2) that Miike, his agents and any person acing in concert with or by or through Miike were enjoined from denying an application for a marriage license because applicants were of the same sex, and (3) that costs should be awarded against Miike and in favor of the plaintiffs. The circuit court subsequently stayed enforcement of the injunction against Miike.

The passage of the marriage amendment placed HRS s.572-1 on new footing. The marriage amendment validated HRS s.572-1 by taking the statute out of the ambit of the equal protection clause of the Hawaii Constitution, at least insofar as the statute, both on its face and as applied, purported to limit access to the marital status to opposite-sex couples. Accordingly, whether or not in the past it was violative of the equal protection clause in the foregoing respect, HRS s.572-1 no longer is.[21] In light of the marriage amendment, HRS s.572-1 must be given full force and effect.

The plaintiffs seek a limited scope of relief in the present lawsuit, i.e., access to applications for marriage licenses and the consequent legally recognized marital status. Inasmuch as HRS s.572-1 is now a valid statute, the relief sought by the plaintiffs is unavailable. The marriage amendment has rendered the plaintiffs' complaint moot. Therefore,

IT IS HEREBY ORDERED that the judgment of the circuit court be reversed and that the case be remanded for entry of judgment in favor of Miike and against the plaintiffs.

IT IS FURTHER ORDERED that the circuit court shall not enter costs or attorneys' fees against the plaintiffs.

DATED: Honolulu, Hawaii, December 9, 1999.

[21] [note 1 in opinion] In this connection, we feel compelled to address two fundamental misapprehensions advanced by Justice Ramil in his concurrence in the result that we reach today. First, Justice Ramil appears to misread the plurality opinion in *Baehr* v. *Lewin*, 74 Haw. 530, 852 P.2d 44, reconsideration and clarification granted in part, 74 Haw. 650, 875 P.2d 225 (1993) [hereinafter, "*Baehr I*"], to stand for the proposition that HRS s.572-1 (1985) defines the legal status of marriage "to include unions between persons of the same sex." Concurrence at 1.

Actually, that opinion expressly acknowledged that "rudimentary principles of statutory construction renders manifest the fact that, by its plain language, HRS s.572–1 restricts the marital relation to a male and a female." *Baehr I*, 74 Haw. at 563, 852 P.2d at 60. Second, because, in his view, HRS s.572-1 limits access to a marriage license on the basis of "sexual orientation," rather than "sex," see concurrence at 1 n.1, Justice Ramil asserts that the plurality opinion in *Baehr I* mistakenly subjected the statute to strict scrutiny, see id. at 2–3. Notwithstanding the fact that HRS s.572-1 obviously does not forbid a homosexual person from marrying a person of the opposite sex, but assuming arguendo that Justice Ramil is correct that the touchstone of the statute is sexual orientation, rather than sex, it would still have been necessary, prior to the ratification of the marriage amendment, to subject HRS s.572-1 to strict scrutiny in order to assess its constitutionality for purposes of the equal protection clause of article I, section 5 of the Hawaii Constitution. This is so because the framers of the 1978 Hawaii Constitution, sitting as a committee of the whole, expressly declared their intention that a proscription against discrimination based on sexual orientation be subsumed within the clause's prohibition against discrimination based on sex. See Stand. Comm. Rep. No. 69, in 1 Proceedings of the Constitutional Convention of Hawaii of 1978, at 675 (1980). Indeed, citing the foregoing constitutional history, Lewin conceded that very point in his answering brief in *Baehr I* when he argued that article I, section 6 of the Hawaii Constitution (containing on express right "to privacy") did not protect sexual orientation because it was already protected under article I, section 5. Lewin could hardly have done otherwise, inasmuch as his proposed order granting his motion for judgment on the pleadings in *Baehr I* contained the statement that "undoubtedly, the delegates (to the convention) meant what they said: Sexual orientation is already covered under Article I, Section 5 of the State Constitution."

10

The Freedom to Marry for Same-Sex Couples in the United States of America

MARY L BONAUTO[1]

WHY THE FREEDOM TO MARRY MUST BE PART OF FAMILY AND EQUALITY LITIGATION—A LITIGATOR'S PERSPECTIVE

Marriage and Other Routes to Family Recognition

FOR THOSE WHO believe that there should be no privileged places from which gay, lesbian, bisexual and transgendered people should be excluded, marriage is a badge of full and equal citizenship. Whether or not an individual chooses to participate in the institution is a different issue from having the choice—as a free and equal citizen—to marry the person of his or her choice. Securing equality under law and access to the same protections and responsibilities which non-gay Americans take for granted—and in the process expanding the conception of "family"—all animate the freedom-to-marry movement in the United States.

Ever since the Stonewall Riots in 1969, at least some gay and lesbian people staked their claims for equal citizenship on seeking the right to marry. In the 1970s cases of *Baker* v. *Nelson*, *Jones* v. *Hallahan* and *Singer* v. *Hara*,[2] plaintiffs invoked evolving notions of constitutional privacy and equality to argue that the State had no excuse for carving gay and lesbian couples off from a fundamental right described as "one of the vital personal rights essential to the orderly pursuit of happiness by free men".[3] Although the courts were dismissive (in the

[1] Civil Rights Director, Gay and Lesbian Advocates & Defenders (GLAD, a New England-wide litigation group seeking equal justice under law for gay men, lesbians, bisexuals, transgendered people and people with HIV, http://www.glad.org), and co-counsel, with Beth Robinson and Susan Murray (partners at the law firm of Langrock, Sperry & Wool, Middlebury, Vermont), in *Baker* v. *State of Vermont*. Thanks to Gary Buseck, Jennifer Levi, Evan Wolfson and Beth Robinson for reviewing earlier drafts of this chapter.

[2] *Baker* v. *Nelson*, 191 N.W.2d 185 (Minnesota Supreme Court 1971), appeal dismissed, 409 U.S. 810 (1972); *Jones* v. *Hallahan*, 501 S.W.2d 588 (Kentucky Court of Appeals 1973); *Singer* v. *Hara*, 522 P.2d 1187 (Washington Court of Appeals 1974).

[3] *Loving* v. *Virginia*, 388 U.S. 1 at 12 (1967) (striking down Virginia's ban on interracial marriage).

words of one commentator, "it was as preposterous for a man to argue that he had a right to marry another man as it would be for him to argue that he had a right to get pregnant"[4]), the battle was joined.

Others have documented how the legitimate preoccupation with AIDS, and feminist and other critiques of marriage, combined to elevate concerns other than marriage through the 1970s and into the 1980s.[5] The 1986 United States Supreme Court decision in *Bowers* v. *Hardwick*,[6] a nadir for gay people, compounded the difficulty. Ruling that a state may criminalise intimate sexual relations between two men despite evolving notions of personal autonomy, the Court declared, "no connection between *family*, marriage, or procreation on the one hand and homosexual conduct on the other has been demonstrated. . . ."[7]

Although marriage cases disappeared from the legal landscape for a time, both marriage and family-recognition litigation soon came back with great force.[8] Numerous personal tragedies, and legal indifference to those tragedies, made what constitutes "family" a defining rights issue. Gay and lesbian families were injured and disrespected every time (and with the advent of AIDS illnesses and deaths, there were many more times) a person was excluded from medical decisionmaking for his or her partner by the "real" family; when a person could not be by his or her partner's side in the hospital; when a deceased's remains were disposed of by the "real" family in ways contrary to the deceased's wishes; when a surviving partner was dispossessed of his or her own belongings by a deceased partner's family members; when a partner could not automatically inherit from his or her deceased partner; when a will was challenged by a family member for "undue influence".[9] From these tragedies came the realisation

[4] DL Chambers and ND Polikoff, "Family Law and Gay and Lesbian Family Issues in the Twentieth Century," (1999) 33 *Family Law Quarterly* 523 at 525.

[5] WN Eskridge, *The Case for Same-Sex Marriage* (New York, NY, Free Press, 1996), at 57. The intra-community debate about the desirability of seeking marriage continues. See e.g. Richards, Introduction to Part I; chaps. 2 to 6, 20, 42. Some of those previously associated with an anti-marriage position are now more supportive of seeking the freedom to marry. See e.g. PL Ettelbrick, "Would Vermont's Civil Union Law Be Good For Other States?", *Washington Times*, 19 June 2000, at 40. But for either gay people or anti-gay extremists to insist on marriage's immutability or essentialism ignores its well-documented historical evolutions. Feminist objections to marriage, for example, have transformed marriage into an institution of formal (if not actual) equality. African-Americans who were once denied marriage because they were slaves are of course now fully free to marry. See N Cott, *Public Vows: A History of Marriage and the Nation* (Cambridge, MA, Harvard University Press, 2000). See also EJ Graff, *What Is Marriage For?* (Boston, MA, Beacon Press, 1999).

[6] 478 U.S. 186 (1986).

[7] *Ibid.*, at 191 (emphasis added).

[8] Most of the cases rejecting marriage rights for same-sex couples since 1980 have been based on federal constitutional claims. See *Storrs* v. *Holcomb*, No. 80174, New York Supreme Court, Appellate Division, Third Department (24 Dec. 1997) (dismissing case on procedural grounds); *Dean* v. *District of Columbia*, 653 A.2d 307 (D.C. Court of Appeals 1995) (rejecting statutory and federal constitutional claims); *Adams* v. *Howerton*, 486 F.Supp. 1119 (Central District of California 1980) (a same-sex marriage valid under state law would not confer spousal status under federal immigration law), affirmed, 673 F.2d 1036 (9th Circuit), certiorari denied, 458 U.S. 1111 (1982).

[9] See e.g. Jeffrey G. Sherman, "Undue Influence and the Homosexual Testator", (1981) 42 *University of Pittsburgh Law Review* 225; GM Torielli, "Protecting the Nontraditional Couple in Times of Medical Crisis," (1989) 12 *Harvard Women's Law Journal* 220.

that the fight to name intimate gay and lesbian relationships as existing, good, important and familial in nature must be part of the lesbian and gay civil rights struggle.

Domestic Partnership and Second-Parent Adoption

The approaches in fighting for recognition of our families as "legal families" are richly varied. One of the most visible efforts has been the phenomenon known as "domestic partnership". It is a status which recognises unmarried couples and their children as a "family" for certain limited purposes. Since US residents have no access to uniform or universal health care coverage, many seek "domestic partnership" plans at work in order to provide health insurance benefits for their partners, just as employers provide benefits to employees' spouses. Other monetary and non-monetary benefits may be provided as well, such as when cities and towns allow a domestic partner access to school records of a child of the partnership, or when an employer provides access to bereavement leave and leave to care for an ill partner. It is justly framed as an issue of "equal pay for equal work": absent domestic partnership, a lesbian employee of twenty years can secure no benefits for her partner of twenty years, but a new employee can automatically secure benefits for her husband of two weeks. This approach envisions workplace benefits allocated on the basis of an existing family relationship rather than by marital status alone.[10] Beyond private employers, several state and local governments have implemented domestic partnership plans for their employees.[11] Without a doubt, this movement for workplace equity also transforms the awareness of the non-gay world about the existence of same-sex relationships, and provides a new cultural vocabulary for understanding same-sex loves: "partner" has come to replace "roommate," "friend" and "companion".

A second major focus has been on "second-parent adoption", a process which secures the relationship of a child to both of his or her lesbian or gay parents (or unmarried non-gay parents), rather than just to the biological or initial adoptive

[10] To qualify for domestic partnership, an employee usually must attest under oath to certain facts: that the parties live together, that their relationship is exclusive, and that they are financially interconnected. See JP Baker, "Equal Benefits For Equal Work? The Law of Domestic Partnership Benefits," (1998) 14 *The Labor Lawyer* 23.

[11] As of Aug. 2000, 18% of all employers (including automakers DaimlerChrysler, General Motors and Ford), 102 of the Fortune 500 companies, and fifty-three per cent of all high-tech firms provided health insurance benefits to domestic partners. See *The State of the Workplace for Lesbian, Gay, Bisexual and Transgendered Americans 1999 and 2000* (Washington, DC, Human Rights Campaign, 1999 and 2000), <http://www.hrc.org> (WorkNet, Publications), at 25–6, 31 (2000 ed.). In the public sector, ninety state or local governments or agencies provided health benefits to the domestic partners of employees. See *The State of the Workplace, supra,* at 28 (2000 ed.). Several of the states do so as a result of litigation. See Leonard, chap. 7. Local governments may provide benefits to non-employees as well, for example by permitting registered domestic partners access to a partner who is in a municipal jail or hospital.

parent. Unlike some countries with registered partnership laws, second-parent and joint adoption are increasingly common in the United States.[12] Second-parent adoption entitles the adopting parent to a full legal relationship with the child, without ever terminating the rights of the existing parent. The result is not only that the child has two legal parents—but also that there is an indirect recognition of the relationship of the parents. Two same-sex partners have now been recognised as both being legal parents to their children through adoption by the highest courts of five states and the District of Columbia,[13] by trial judges in approximately another fifteen states,[14] and through legislative or executive action in three states.[15]

Domestic partnership and second-parent adoption are two of the brightest and most important lights of the movement for recognition of same-sex families. While both are vital, they are also limited. A small minority of employers offer domestic partnership benefits.[16] Gay employees have to out themselves to their employer to take advantage of the benefits, not an insignificant hurdle given that only twelve states and the District of Columbia forbid discrimination in employment on the basis of sexual orientation.[17] Furthermore, employees must pay income tax on the value of domestic partnership benefits, whereas married spouses do not.[18] Most pension and retirement plans either are unavailable to same-sex partners, or limit the options of gay employees who wish to provide for their partners.[19] Similarly, second-parent adoption is a step in the right direction, but it does not offer complete recognition to a family. Nor is it available where a former spouse or biological parent refuses to relinquish rights, or even widely available in over 80 per cent of the states. Without such adoptions, children have no legal tie to the other "non-legal" parent when the couple separates or the legal parent dies.[20]

[12] See Polikoff, chap. 8.

[13] *Ibid.*, at nn.17–18.

[14] See Report of the American Bar Association, Resolution 109B, at 10–11 and nn. 20, 24 (8 Feb. 1999).

[15] See Polikoff, chap. 8, at nn.20, 25, 26 (Vermont, New Jersey and Connecticut).

[16] See *supra* n.11.

[17] California, Connecticut, Hawaii, Maryland, Massachusetts, Minnesota, Nevada, New Hampshire, New Jersey, Rhode Island, Vermont, Wisconsin.

[18] See e.g. Internal Revenue Service, Private Letter Ruling 9717018 (25 April 1997); PLR 9231062 (7 May 1992). An employee of a domestic partner may be able to exclude the value of benefits from income if the partner is also a tax dependent. Internal Revenue Code, section 152.

[19] See Leonard, chap. 7; J Wriggins, "Kinship and Marriage in Massachusetts Public Employee Retirement Law: An Analysis of the Beneficiary Provisions, and Proposals for Change," (1994) 28 *New England Law Review* 991.

[20] See Polikoff, chap. 8; N Polikoff, "This Child Does Have Two Mothers: Redefining Parenthood to Meet the Needs of Children in Lesbian Mother and Other Non-Traditional Families," (1990) 78 *Georgetown Law Journal* 459. The issue of how families should or may handle the issue of continued contact between a "non-legal parent" and their child dominates the docket of the gay legal organisations and has become an issue of major concern in the community. See GLAD, "Protecting Families: Standards for Child Custody in Same-Sex Relationships," (1999) 10 *University of California Los Angeles Women's Law Journal* 151.

There are myriad other family-related issues to which health insurance benefits, domestic partnership, and second-parent adoption do not speak.[21] While advocates will continue their efforts to ensure that the law respects the many forms of families which exist, "marriage" will remain for the foreseeable future a key factor dividing the "haves" from the "have-nots" in the overwhelming majority of interactions between a couple or family and the state and other institutions, and for claims between the couple or within the family. Absent marriage, same-sex families are automatically deprived of an astonishing array of protections, benefits and responsibilities afforded by the state, and by the many institutions which imitate the state scheme.[22]

Common-Law Marriage

Compounding the difficulty for litigators and policy-makers in the United States is the lack of recent tradition in using concepts of "common-law" or "de facto" marriage to recognise unmarried heterosexual relationships as akin to married families. This factor distinguishes developments in Canada, Australia and several European countries, which have recently allowed both same-sex and different-sex couples to partake of some of the benefits and responsibilities of married pairs. In the nineteenth century, states moved to eliminate "informal" marriages and overwhelmingly required statutory marriages.[23] Only a very few states authorise common-law marriage, and these states discourage it. This reality deprives litigators in the US of an argument applied forcefully to legal schemes in countries which recognise both married and unmarried heterosexual couples as meriting legal protection: the criterion for benefits and protections is no longer marriage but the impermissible criterion of sexual orientation. By contrast, in the United States, benefits typically remain conditioned upon one's marital status regardless of sexual orientation.[24]

Discrimination and Functional Interpretation Arguments

Short of seeking marriage, litigators in the United States have two major tools for seeking rights and protections: (1) discrimination arguments premised upon

[21] See Wolfson (chap. 9, n.1), at 604–8.

[22] See Chambers (chap. 9, n.2).

[23] See e.g. M Grossberg, *Governing the Hearth: Law and the Family in Nineteenth Century America* 64–102 (Chapel Hill, NC, University of North Carolina Press, 1985). Courts have explicitly rejected common-law marriage claims by same-sex couples. See *DeSanto* v. *Barnsley*, 476 A.2d 952 (Pennsylvania Superior Court 1984).

[24] A rare exception is *Vasquez* v. *Hawthorne*, 994 P.2d 240 (Washington Court of Appeals 2000) (gay couple could not take advantage of equitable device allowing unmarried couples to inherit from their partners without a will), where discrimination based on sex and sexual orientation is being argued before the Washington Supreme Court.

constitutional equal protection clauses or anti-discrimination legislation; and (2) arguments for broad and functional interpretations of statutory terms such as "spouse" and "family", or common law equitable principles.

The gist of a discrimination argument is that providing benefits only to married spouses is discriminatory on the basis of sexual orientation, since same-sex couples who have no access to civil marriage will always be excluded from the benefit. There have been a few victories by governmental employees seeking health insurance benefits through their jobs using this approach, and that trend may continue.[25]

Aside from the difficulty of litigating benefit-by-benefit, protection-by-protection, to date most courts have refused to apply the anti-discrimination provisions in a way which would compel equal treatment of same-sex families and married families. In most cases in which a member of a lesbian or gay couple has sought health insurance, or family leave benefits to care for an ill partner, from a government employer, the courts have ruled that the denial of benefits is not because the employee is gay or lesbian, but because the employee is unmarried.[26]

This is no sleight of hand, the courts explain, because unmarried heterosexual employees and unmarried gay employees are being treated alike. Neither is eligible for spousal-type benefits. Accordingly, there is no unlawful discrimination. The factor distinguishing one class from another is marriage: unmarried gay people must be compared to unmarried heterosexuals rather than to the class of married persons. When litigators point out the obvious—that the comparison of same-sex couples to unmarried different-sex couples is unfair because gay people do not presently have the option of legal marriage—the courts have answered that any concerns about the "perceived unfairness of the state's marital laws . . . is for the legislature [to address] and not the courts".[27]

The second approach posits that the statutory terms "spouse" and "family", and words of like import, should be construed using a functional definition of those terms, rather than automatically assuming that they connote relationships of blood, adoption or marriage. For example, New York State's highest court ruled that the surviving partner of a deceased man was a "family" member entitled to remain in the deceased's rent-controlled apartment under New York City's rent control ordinance.[28] In a Minnesota case, involving a woman who fought a seven-year court battle against her partner's family to be named the legal guardian of her partner, the court described the two women as a "family of affinity, which ought to be accorded respect".[29]

[25] See Leonard, chap. 7.

[26] *Ibid.*

[27] *Phillips* v. *Wisconsin Personnel Commission*, 482 N.W.2d 121 at 127 (Wis. Ct. of Appeals 1992).

[28] *Braschi* v. *Stahl Assocs. Co.*, 543 N.E.2d 49 (N.Y. Ct. of Appeals 1989). See Leonard, chap. 7.

[29] *In re Guardianship of Kowalski*, 478 N.W.2d 790 at 797 (Minn. Ct. of Appeals 1991). This case was even more important culturally than legally and was a key factor in galvanising the lesbian

Apart from statutes, equitable doctrines and the common law can be applied flexibly to provide protection to a broader array of families than has been customary. A Massachusetts court declared a lesbian the "de facto" parent of the son whose birth she planned and whom she raised, even though they had no biological or adoptive relationship, and despite the biological mother's objection to the continuation of the relationship.[30] Contemporary conceptions of "parenthood" are evolving to support families who share commitment, caretaking and support, while lacking traditional legal relationships.

Overall, however, the wins are exceptions. When litigators argue not that the statutory term "spouse" is discriminatory, but that it should be interpreted to include same-sex partners as the functional equivalent, courts nonetheless consider the merits of the marriage exclusion. But they do so by applying unhelpful principles of statutory construction, rather than examining the more forceful constitutional arguments against such an exclusion. A New Jersey appellate court observed in a fashion typical of these cases:

> "in dealing with statutory and contract interpretation, we have not been disposed to expanding plain language to fit more contemporary views of family and intimate relationships".[31]

Those same rigid rules of statutory construction were used recently by an appellate court in Illinois to hold that a woman was not entitled to take an automatic spousal share of her deceased partner's estate. Andrea Marie Hall and Regina Pavone lived together for eight years, during which they had a private wedding ceremony. They combined all finances, and Regina supported Andrea's son and mother. When Regina argued that she should be treated as a spouse for purposes of intestate succession after Andrea's death, the court did not address the constitutionality of the couple's exclusion from marriage, but simply used this exclusion to justify a further exclusion from intestate succession. According to the court, "it is clear from the alleged facts that the relationship did not meet the statutory requirements for a valid marriage", i.e., a union of one man and one woman. Second, the court distinguished away cases allowing people to inherit as spouses, even when the statutory requirements were breached in some way, because in those cases people believed in good faith that they were married. By contrast here, "although petitioner Hall may have subjectively believed that the ceremony and exchange of vows and rings constituted a marriage between themselves, they nonetheless knew that the marriage was not legally recognized". Finally, the court also justified its refusal to treat their

community's emphasis on securing family recognition in the 1980s. See N Hunter, "Sexual Dissent and the Family", *The Nation*, 7 Oct. 1991, at 60.

[30] *E.N.O.* v. *L.M.M.*, 711 N.E.2d 886 (Massachusetts Supreme Judicial Court), cert. denied, 120 Sup. Ct. 500 (1999). See Polikoff, chap. 8.

[31] *Rutgers Council of AAUP Chapters* v. *Rutgers University*, 689 A.2d 828 at 831 (N.J. Superior Ct. Appellate Div. 1997).

relationship as equivalent to a marriage for purposes of intestacy because that would resurrect common-law marriage.[32]

One final litigation note concerns the federal government. Except when constitutional violations are involved, the fifty states and not the federal government are the gatekeepers of marriage. The states issue marriage licenses, and the federal government of the United States, with rare exceptions, honors those state determinations as to who is married. This changed with the passage of the *federal* "Defense of Marriage Act" in 1996 which now provides a *federal* definition of marriage as "the union of one man and one woman as husband and wife" for all *federal* laws and programs.[33]

Although a litigant could challenge the denial of marriage rights, or one of the myriad (state or federal) rights, protections and responsibilities of marriage, as inconsistent with the United States Constitution's guarantees of equal protection and due process, most claimants (such as those in Hawaii, Alaska and Vermont) have preferred to invoke state constitutions. Aside from the incoherence of much of federal equal protection law, there is also a widespread perception that the United States Supreme Court is loath to make a decision which is at odds with the law of the majority of the states, or to order them to do something which none or few of them yet authorises.[34]

In sum, litigators can and will continue to bring factually compelling cases with sympathetic plaintiffs seeking particular responsibilities, benefits or protections, and seeking broader conceptions of what counts as a family. Each of these cases has been educational, making gay people more real—both as individuals and as families—and illustrating the diversity of family forms existing in the United States. But until same-sex couples and gay and lesbian people have the freedom to choose to enter into civil marriage (barring a global reconstruction of the way the state interacts with families), the overwhelming majority of benefits, protections and responsibilities of marriage, and the badge of equal citizenship, will be out of reach.

AFTER HAWAII, A SECOND CHANCE IN VERMONT

Why did a rural state associated with dairy farms, and the third smallest population in the country, end up at the cutting-edge of equality for same-sex couples in the United States? Many have pointed to its history of firsts:[35] it was the first state to outlaw slavery; the first state to allow all men to vote; the first state in

[32] *In re Estate of Andrea Marie Hall*, 707 N.E.2d 201 at 204–5 (Illinois Ct. of Appeals 1998).

[33] See Feldblum, chap. 3; Wolfson, chap. 9.

[34] See Wolfson, chap. 9, n.13. See also Eskridge, *supra* n.5, at 154–9 (the US Supreme Court took its lead from the states in striking down interracial marriage bans and passed up several opportunities before *Loving* to invalidate the measures).

[35] See Bonauto, Murray and Robinson, "The Freedom to Marry for Same-Sex Couples: The Opening Appellate Brief of Plaintiffs Stan Baker et al. in *Baker et al.* v. *State of Vermont*," (1999) 5 *Michigan Journal of Gender and Law* 409 at 426 and n. 67 (hereafter, "Opening Brief").

which an appellate court permitted second-parent adoptions; the first state to pass legislation codifying the right to second-parent adoption[36]; one of the few states that never had a ban on interracial marriage; and one of the first states to have comprehensive anti-discrimination protection for gay people in employment and housing,[37] and provide domestic partnership benefits for state employees.[38]

No doubt those factors were important, but others were at work too. In 1995, attorneys Beth Robinson and Susan Murray formed a group called the Vermont Freedom to Marry Task Force, whose sole goal was to talk to other Vermonters about why marriage matters, and why same-sex couples should be included within it. The group was formed in anticipation of a ruling authorising civil marriage for lesbians and gay men in Hawaii. Task Force members went to meetings with their neighbors, where they often showed their home-made video[39] of same-sex couples in Vermont talking about their relationships. They also traveled to county fairs and attempted to engage their fellow citizens on this issue at the Task Force booth.

The *Baker* v. *State of Vermont* Litigation[40]

In 1997, after three same-sex couples from the same county were denied marriage licenses by their respective town clerks, they filed suit. To many, especially within Vermont, it seemed to be the right time and the right place—the next logical step to assure comprehensive protections for families.

The Plaintiff Couples

The plaintiffs are the heart of the story. As much as *Baker* v. *State* is a case about gay people and same-sex families, it is also a personal narrative of the plaintiffs and their families. Stan Baker and Peter Harrigan have considered themselves a couple since the early 1990s. They decided they wanted to marry because of their respect for their parents and their parents' marriages, and because they believe marriage is a good model for a relationship. Holly Puterbaugh and Lois Farnham have been together since 1973, have fostered several children, and have

[36] 15A Vermont Statutes Annotated section 1–102 (b) (1999).

[37] 21 V.S.A. s. 495 (1999); 9 V.S.A. s. 4503 (1999).

[38] *B.M., S.S., C.M. & J.R.* v. *Univ. of Vermont*, Vt. Labor Relations Board, No. 92–32, 16 V.L.R.B. 207, 220 (1993).

[39] "The Freedom to Marry: A Green Mountain View" (17 minutes), Vermont Freedom to Marry Task Force, <info@vtfreetomarry.org>.

[40] *Baker* v. *State of Vermont*, No. 51009–97 CnC, slip opinion (Chittenden Superior Ct., 19 Dec. 1997), http://www.vtfreetomarry.org/opinion121997.html (hereinafter, *Baker Trial*); *Baker* v. *State of Vermont*, 744 A.2d 864 (Vermont Supreme Court 1999), http://www.leg.state.vt.us/baker/baker.cfm (hereinafter, *Baker*). See Symposium, (Fall 2000) 25 *Vermont Law Review*; WN Eskridge, Jr, *Equality Practice* (New York, NY, Routledge, forthcoming in 2001).

raised an adopted daughter who recently left for college. They want to marry to secure protection for their family. Nina Beck and Stacy Jolles became a couple in 1990 and participated in a Jewish religious ceremony celebrating their union in 1991. They decided to get involved in the *Baker* litigation for the sake of their son, believing it damaging for him to grow up in a world where his parents' relationship to each other was not recognised.

The Common Benefits Clause: An Equality Provision with an Eighteenth-Century Name

At the centre of the plaintiffs' claims was the Vermont Constitution's Common Benefits Clause (Chapter I, Article 7), part of the original 1777 Constitution:

> "That government is, or ought to be, instituted for the common benefit, protection, and security of the people, nation or community, and not for the particular emolument or advantage of any single person, family, or set of persons who are a part only of that community"; . . .

Although antiquated in terminology, this provision has been described by the Vermont Supreme Court as a living promise unconstrained by eighteenth-century standards,[41] and is Vermont's version of the equality provisions found in the federal and all state constitutions.

The case started with simple facts about civil marriage: (1) it exists in and is licensed by the State of Vermont; (2) it is a legislative creation, even if for some it also has religious meanings; and (3) it is both a special status and a gateway to hundreds of rights, responsibilities and protections under state law. This led to three major constitutional claims in the case.[42]

The Fundamental Right to Marry

First, the couples argued that they enjoy a fundamental right under the Vermont Constitution to marry the "person of their choice". This language comes from *Perez* v. *Lippold*, the 1948 California interracial marriage ruling which set out the framework for understanding civil marriage as the freedom to marry the person of your choice without state interference.[43] The echoes of *Perez* are evident in the later United States Supreme Court decisions finding marriage to be a fundamental right under the US Constitution.[44] As with other fundamental

[41] *Brigham* v. *State*, 962 A.2d 384 at 397 (1997).

[42] Both the trial court and the Supreme Court rejected the plaintiffs' argument that the marriage statutes' gender-neutral language permitted them to marry. *Baker Trial*, *supra* n.40, at 4–7; *Baker*, at 868–9. All of the arguments are set out in Bonauto, et al., *supra* n. 35; Bonauto, Murray and Robinson, "The Freedom to Marry for Same-Sex Couples: The Reply Brief of Plaintiffs Stan Baker et al. in *Baker et al.* v. *State of Vermont*," (1999) 6 *Michigan Journal of Gender and Law* 1 (hereafter, "Reply Brief").

[43] 198 P.2d 17 (California Supreme Ct. 1948).

[44] *Loving*, *supra* n.3; *Zablocki* v. *Redhail*, 434 U.S. 374 (1978); *Turner* v. *Safley*, 482 U.S. 78 (1987).

rights, marriage cannot be denied without a compelling state interest which is narrowly tailored to the classification. Here, the couples argued, there is no reason to carve them off from the fundamental right to marry, declared by the US Supreme Court in *Loving* v. *Virginia* in 1967 to be "essential to the orderly pursuit of happiness by free men."[45]

Understanding that the State would argue that only male-female marriage is fundamental, the plaintiffs focused on substance rather than form, asking why certain rights are deemed fundamental. For example, *Roberts* v. *U.S. Jaycees* explained why marriage and some other relationships are accorded constitutional protection.

> "Family relationships by their nature involve deep attachments and commitments to the necessarily few other individuals with whom one shares not only a special community of thoughts, experiences and beliefs, but also distinctly personal aspects of one's life".[46]

Deep attachments and commitments are the defining parameters for family protection; just as those parameters encompass marriage, childbirth, and raising and educating children, they include the plaintiffs' family relationships.

The State, and especially its *amici curiae*, raised the specter of how to limit the fundamental right of marriage if same-sex couples were included, as though the State's power to defend any distinctions in marriage would be eviscerated if it could not justify this particular discrimination. While the State may discriminate when it has a compelling interest to do so, the plaintiffs argued that no such interest had been demonstrated with respect to the exclusion of same-sex couples. Moreover, the "slippery slope" fears of polygamous and incestuous marriages were the same canards relied upon by the dissenting opinion in *Perez*, and by the State of Virginia in *Loving* (both interracial marriage cases)—and were no more true now than then.[47]

Sex and Sexual Orientation Discrimination

The second major argument asserted by the plaintiffs was that withholding marriage licenses is sex and sexual orientation discrimination, which cannot be justified by the State. As in *Baehr* v. *Lewin*,[48] the plaintiffs made a formal sex discrimination argument that paralleled the race discrimination argument in *Loving* v. *Virginia*. If one's choice of marital partner is circumscribed by one's sex (as with one's race in *Loving*), then the State is engaging in sex discrimination. In *Baehr*, the Hawaii Supreme Court accepted this argument, holding that the state's marriage scheme discriminated on the basis of sex and must be

[45] *Loving*, *ibid*. at 12. The state constitutional counterpart of this argument was successful with a trial judge in Alaska in *Brause*, Wolfson, chap. 8, n.18: "the choice of a life partner is personal, intimate, and subject to the protection of the right of privacy."

[46] 468 U.S. 609 at 618–20 (1984).

[47] Reply Brief, *supra* n.42, at 33–4.

[48] 852 P.2d 44 (Hawaii Supreme Court 1993). See Wolfson, chap. 9; Koppelman, chap. 35.

justified by a compelling state interest. The plaintiff couples argued that the same must be true in Vermont.

As in *Loving*, the State predictably argued the "equal application rule", i.e., that there is no discrimination as between men and women: all men are forbidden from marrying someone of the same sex, and all women are so forbidden. The answer then, as now, is that the right to be free from discrimination is an individual right, not a group right.[49] As Martin Luther King, Jr. famously remarked, "races do not marry; individuals marry".[50]

The couples' substantive sex discrimination argument actually derived from the State's defenses, i.e., that men and women are different biologically, culturally, physically and psychologically—and that marriage requires a union of those differences. In reply, the couples pointed to cases condemning broad generalisations about the sexes and about gender roles as a basis for limiting individual choice on the basis of gender, even when those generalisations may be rooted in empirical observation.[51]

Closely related to the formal and substantive sex discrimination arguments was the claim that by prohibiting men from marrying men, and women from marrying women, the State was essentially barring gay and lesbian individuals and couples from marrying.[52] Classifications based on sexual orientation, the plaintiffs argued, merit exacting review from the courts because they are irrelevant to any proper legislative goal, and single out a group historically subjected to discrimination. In sum, any law which purports to distinguish gay and lesbian families, on the basis of generalisations about the ability of gay and lesbian persons to form, nurture, and maintain cohesive families that serve the same functions in our society as other families, is as flawed as laws that once excluded women from educational opportunities on the basis of women's claimed inferiority.

Absence of a Legitimate Basis

The third prong of the couples' case was simply that there is no legitimate or sensible reason for the exclusion of same-sex couples from civil marriage. However much latitude the legislature has to pass laws, at a bare minimum, citizens in Vermont have the right not to be disadvantaged or set apart by laws which have no reasonable relationship to a legitimate public purpose. Under this analysis—which bears some resemblance to federal rational basis review but is not identical to it—the plaintiffs argued that there is no valid reason for the State to exclude same-sex couples from civil marriage, and that the reasons advanced by the State were not rationally related to the exclusion.

[49] Reply Brief, *supra* n.42, at 11–2.

[50] Martin Luther King, Jr., "Stride Toward Freedom", in Washington (ed.), *A Testament of Hope* 478 (New York, Harper Collins, 1986).

[51] Reply Brief, *supra* n.42, at 13–17.

[52] Opening Brief, *supra* n.35, at 465–6.

The crux of the State's defenses rested on procreation and biology. Time and again the State charged that marriage had been linked to procreation historically, and that same-sex couples cannot reproduce without the assistance of "third parties".[53] The couples responded that the right to marry is not, and constitutionally cannot, be derived from the ability to procreate, especially where married couples enjoy a constitutional right to use contraception.[54] Common sense and experience also show that there are many married but childless couples—whether from choice or circumstance.[55] Moreover, two people beyond their childbearing years can meet, fall in love, and decide to spend their final days together without the slightest hope of procreating, yet still enjoy a constitutionally protected marriage. Finally, two of the three couples, like many other gay and lesbian people, are actually raising children, thereby undermining the State's assumption that parenting requires unassisted procreation.[56]

The Trial Court's Dismissal

The trial judge dismissed the case in December 1997, rejecting the couples' arguments about fundamental rights, and sex and sexual orientation discrimination.[57] Focusing solely on whether there was any legitimate reason for the discrimination, the judge rejected six of the seven proffered reasons for discrimination as "absurd", "speculative" or entirely lacking in common sense. Nonetheless, on the basis that the State has an interest in "furthering the link between procreation and child rearing" and that marriage furthers that link, the judge felt constrained to dismiss the case under what she described as a deferential standard of review. The couples then appealed to the Vermont Supreme Court, which heard oral argument on 18 November 1998.

The Vermont Supreme Court's Ruling

On 20 December 1999, in *Baker* v. *State of Vermont*,[58] the Vermont Supreme Court asked: "May the State of Vermont exclude same-sex couples from the benefits and protections that its laws provide to opposite-sex married couples?"[59] The answer of all five judges was "no". For the first time, a final appellate court in the United States had held that same-sex couples are

[53] *Baker*, *supra* n.40, at 881.

[54] *Griswold* v. *Connecticut*, 381 U.S. 479 (1965); *Eisenstadt* v. *Baird*, 405 U.S. 438 (1972).

[55] During the oral argument before the Vermont Supreme Court, Justice Morse asked: "Can we constitutionally ban marriage for infertile couples?"

[56] Opening Brief, *supra* n.35, at 437–42; Reply Brief, *supra* n. 42, at 22.

[57] *Baker Trial*, *supra* n.40, at 17.

[58] *Baker*, *supra* n.40.

[59] *Ibid.*, at 867.

constitutionally entitled to all of the protections and benefits provided through law to opposite-sex married couples.[60]

The Court explicitly declined to reach the issue of whether or not same-sex couples are constitutionally entitled to the civil marriage licenses plaintiffs had sought. Instead, the Court characterised the case as one focused upon the consequences of official exclusion from the statutory benefits, protections and security incident to a marriage under Vermont law, noting that "some future case may attempt to establish that—notwithstanding equal benefits and protections under Vermont law—the denial of a marriage license operates per se to deny constitutionally protected rights".[61]

Common Benefits Clause vs. *Fourteenth Amendment*

As in any case raising equal protection claims under a state constitution, the Court first turned to the federal Fourteenth Amendment in order to compare the standards and methods of analysis with those in Vermont. Noting that the Vermont provision pre-dated the federal charter and that the two provisions differ "[h]istorically and textually", the Court determined that, despite a similarity of purpose, the approach in Vermont is "broadly deferential to the legislative prerogative to define and advance governmental ends, while vigorously ensuring that the means chosen bear a just and reasonable relation to the government objective".[62] In addition to determining the legitimacy of a law's purpose and its relationship to that purpose, the Court added, "the justifications demanded of the State may depend upon the nature and importance of the benefits and protections affected by the legislation".[63] In short, while not stating that Vermont's common benefits analysis is any different from its federal counterpart, it acknowledged that "Article 7 would require a 'more stringent' reasonableness inquiry than was generally associated with rational basis review under the federal constitution".[64]

Analysis Under Common Benefits Clause

The Court then examined "the language of the provision in question, historical context, case-law development, the construction of similar provisions in other state constitutions, and sociological materials".[65] Those sources assist with the main task in interpreting the Common Benefits Clause.

> "[O]ur duty is to discover the core value that gave life to Article [7] . . . Out of the shifting and complicated kaleidoscope of events, social forces, and ideas that culminated

[60] *Ibid.*, at 867, 886.

[61] *Ibid.*, at 886.

[62] *Ibid.*, at 870, 871.

[63] *Ibid.*, at 871.

[64] *Ibid.* See also *ibid.*, at 870 ("While the federal amendment may . . . supplement the protections afforded by the Common Benefits Clause, it does not supplant it as the first and primary safeguard of the rights and liberties of Vermonters".)

[65] *Ibid.*, at 873.

> in the Vermont Constitution of 1777, our task is to distill the essence, the motivating ideal of the framers. The challenge is to remain faithful to that historical ideal, while addressing contemporary issues that the framers undoubtedly never could have imagined".[66]

Two principles controlled. One was a "principle of inclusion" in which the "vision of government [was one] that afforded every Vermonter its benefit and protection and provided no Vermonter particular advantage".[67] Equality, the other animating value, meant "equal access to public benefits and protections for the community as a whole".[68] The concept of equality which dominated the thinking of the framers was not "civil rights for African-Americans or other minorities" but "equal access", with any differences among people reflecting "differences of capacity, disposition, and virtue, rather than governmental favor or privilege".[69]

With those principles identified, the Court stated a more specific test under Article 7. Stated simply, the Court must "ascertain whether the omission of a part of the community from the benefit, protection and security of the challenged law bears a reasonable and just relation to the governmental purpose".[70] In addition,

> "consistent with the core presumption of inclusion, factors to be considered in this determination may include: (1) the significance of the benefits and protections of the challenged law; (2) whether the omission of members of the community from the benefits and protections of the challenged law promotes the government's stated goals; and (3) whether the classification is significantly underinclusive or overinclusive".[71]

Common Benefits Clause Applied to Marriage

Applying the specific test under the Common Benefits Clause, the Court found that the "part of the community" disadvantaged by the marriage laws is "anyone who wishes to marry someone of the same sex".[72] After exploring the State's asserted purposes, the Court concluded that, "in light of history, logic, and experience, . . . none of the interests asserted by the State provides a reasonable and just basis for the exclusion of same-sex couples from the benefits incident to a civil marriage license under Vermont law".[73]

The principal purpose articulated by the State in defense of the marriage laws was the State's interest in furthering the link between procreation and parenting. The Court acknowledged that the States had an interest in promoting

[66] *Ibid*., at 874.
[67] *Ibid*., at 875.
[68] *Ibid*., at 876.
[69] *Ibid*.
[70] *Ibid*., at 878–9.
[71] *Ibid*., at 879.
[72] *Ibid*., at 880. The Court rejected the sex discrimination argument and the analogy to *Loving*, pointing out that men and women are equally disadvantaged by the marriage statutes. *Ibid*., at 880 n.13.
[73] *Ibid*., at 886.

permanent commitments between couples for the security of their children, and that the State had done so in the past through marriage. But the Court found this rationale "significantly underinclusive", both because the current laws benefit many couples who neither intend to have or are capable of having children, and because many children are being raised by same-sex parents.[74]

> "To the extent that the state's purpose in licensing civil marriage was, and is, to legitimize children and provide for their security, the statutes plainly exclude many same-sex couples with respect to these objectives. . . . [and] exposes their children to the precise risks that the state argues the marriage laws are designed to secure against".[75]

In a related vein, the State argued that excluding same-sex couples from marriage:

> "promotes a 'perception of the link between procreation and child rearing' and that to discard it would advance the notion that mothers and fathers . . . are mere surplusage to the functions of procreation and child rearing".[76]

The fact that same-sex couples have children with the assistance of reproductive technology was not a persuasive justification for exclusion from marriage, because the majority of consumers of such technology are married infertile couples.[77] "Accordingly, there is no reasonable basis to conclude that a same-sex couple's use of the same technologies would undermine the bonds of parenthood, or society's perception of parenthood".[78]

Having identified the logical flaws in the State's justifications, the Court acknowledged that a government classification may still be upheld in some cases, even though it fails to extend protection to all who are similarly situated.[79] Here, however, the State did not argue that its drawing the line at different-sex couples was legitimate because of either pragmatism or administrative convenience.[80] Moreover, the plaintiffs' interests were considerable, both because marriage has historically been an important right which "significantly enhances the quality of life in our society",[81] and because the benefits and protections incident to a marriage license "have never been greater".[82]

The Court also rejected the other defenses raised by the State. "Childrearing" could not be viewed as a justification in light of the fact that the legislature had not favored opposite-sex parents over same-sex parents.[83] The notion that Vermont's marriage laws were adopted to maintain uniformity with the laws of

[74] *Ibid.*, at 881.
[75] *Ibid.*, at 882.
[76] *Ibid.*
[77] *Ibid.*
[78] *Ibid.*
[79] *Ibid.*, at 882–3.
[80] *Ibid.*, at 883.
[81] *Ibid.*, citing *Loving*, . . . *supra* n.3, at 12 ("[t]he freedom to marry has long been recognized as one of the vital personal rights . . .").
[82] *Ibid.*, at 883.
[83] *Ibid.*, at 885.

other states was belied by the fact that Vermont's laws do not conform to those of other states in the areas of first-cousin marriages and the approval of second-parent adoptions.[84] Finally, the State could not justify its different treatment of same-sex couples based on "the long history of official intolerance of intimate same-sex relationships," both because "animus" against a class is not "a legitimate basis for continued unequal application of the law", and because "recent legislation plainly undermines the contention".[85]

The Court's conclusion[86] charted the common ground between the plaintiffs and all Vermonters.

> "The extension of the [Constitution] to acknowledge plaintiffs as Vermonters who seek nothing more, nor less, than legal protection and security for their avowed commitment to an intimate and lasting human relationship is simply, when all is said and done, a recognition of our common humanity".[87]

The Remedy

Rather than order the issuance of marriage licenses to same-sex couples, the Court deferred to its sister branch of government and held that the legislature must have the first opportunity to remedy the constitutional violation identified by the Court.

> "Whether this [remedy] ultimately takes the form of inclusion within the marriage laws themselves or a parallel 'domestic partnership' system or some equivalent statutory alternative, rests with the Legislature".[88]

The Court also retained jurisdiction of the case to facilitate the plaintiffs' return to court if the legislature failed to act in a reasonable time.[89]

Anticipating objections to its decision, the Court stressed that it had the power and responsibility to decide the case ("[o]ur constitutional responsibility to consider the legal merits of issues properly before us provides no exception for the controversial case"[90]), and that the issue turned on the secular benefits

[84] *Ibid.*

[85] *Ibid.* (repeal of fellatio statute, enactment of non-discrimination and hate crimes laws).

[86] In a concurring opinion, Justice John Dooley argued that the Court should have distinguished between civil rights cases and economic cases, and that sexual orientation is a suspect classification under Vermont law. *Ibid.*, at 889–97. In a concurring opinion, Justice Denise Johnson accepted the sex discrimination argument. She also dissented on the remedy, concluding that the Court should have ordered the issuance of marriage licenses once it had identified the constitutional violation. *Ibid.*, at 897–912.

[87] *Ibid.*, at 889.

[88] *Ibid.* The Court cited but did not endorse the Danish and Norwegian registered partnership laws, as well as the report of the Hawaii Commission on Sexual Orientation and the Law (Wolfson, chap. 9, n.18). *Ibid.*, at 886–7. The Court preferred a legislative solution because: "A sudden change in the marriage laws or the statutory benefits traditionally incidental to marriage may have disruptive and unforeseen consequences. Absent legislative guidelines defining the status and rights of same-sex couples, consistent with constitutional requirements, uncertainty and confusion could result." *Ibid.*, at 887.

[89] *Ibid.*, at 889. See also *ibid.*, at 887 (absent legislative grant of benefits, plaintiffs may petition the court for "the remedy they originally sought," i.e., marriage licenses).

[90] *Ibid.*, at 867.

and protections offered married couples, rather then "the religious or moral debate over intimate same-sex relationships".[91]

Proceedings in the Vermont House of Representatives[92]

House Judiciary Committee

On 4 January 2000, just fifteen days after the Supreme Court's ruling, House Judiciary Committee Chair Thomas Little sent a memorandum to his ten colleagues, detailing the process he hoped would guide their deliberations in crafting the first legislative response to the decision. Representative Little charted a course whereby the Committee would hear several weeks of testimony, before making a decision as to which path to pursue: equality in marriage or a "parallel" system. History may well judge that the eleven committee members—from all parts of the State, evenly split between Republicans and Democrats (with one Progressive), and including two retired state troopers, the one openly gay member of the Legislature, three lawyers, and several Roman Catholics—fulfilled their responsibilities admirably.

In accordance with Vermont tradition, the first witnesses were Beth Robinson and Susan Murray, two of the co-counsel in the *Baker* case. They stressed that the issue facing the Legislature was about protecting real people and real families in the Vermont community, and not about religious marriage.[93] Over the next several weeks, the Committee explored the history of marriage,[94] Vermont's marriage and family laws, the economic implications of including same-sex couples in marriage or a domestic partnership system, constitutional guidelines for crafting its response, international systems for recognising same-sex relationships, the experience of Hawaii, the nature of domestic partnership plans in the United States, the federal Defense of Marriage Act, competing religious views about how the legislature should proceed,[95] and issues of how other states would treat couples under whatever scheme the legislature might develop.

[91] *Ibid.*, at 867.

[92] Much of the legislative history can be found at <http://www.leg.state.vt.us/baker/baker.cfm>.

[93] Murray and Robinson, "Summary of Key Points" (11 Jan. 2000).

[94] One witness who was described as "invaluable" by Committee Chair Little was Nancy Cott, Professor of History and American Studies, Yale University. Contrary to the often repeated claim that marriage has been the same for five thousand years, Professor Cott explained that the history of marriage in the western world and the United States has been a history of change. Many of the changes to marriage were as or more "radical" in their day than marriage of same-sex couples is today. See Cott, *supra* n.5.

[95] Testifying in support of the freedom to marry were the Episcopal Bishop of Vermont, the highest ranking official of the United Church of Christ in Vermont, and a Rabbi (Conservative). In opposition appeared the Roman Catholic Bishop of Vermont along with several Evangelical Protestant pastors.

Numerically, more opponents of equality for same-sex couples testified than supporters, with the former advocating a constitutional amendment to undo the effect of the *Baker* decision.[96]

Public Hearings

The emotional response to the *Baker* decision rose steadily, with active grass-roots efforts on both sides.[97] Emotion swelled when the combined House and Senate Judiciary Committees took testimony from the public on two winter evenings.[98]

Lesbian and gay individuals and couples and families were front and centre in the discussions, explaining that they wanted marriage both for practical purposes and to erase their sense of second-class citizenship. Some had stories of hardship and mistreatment to tell, including being denied access to partners in hospitals or medical settings, even when they had the proper paperwork. Parents came forward and urged the Committees to allow the benefits and protections of marriage to flow through them to their children. Non-gay supporters of equal marriage rights viewed the issue as one of civil rights and basic fairness, and reassured the Committees that their own families would not be threatened by recognition of lesbian and gay families. Many clergy and people of faith testified for the freedom of gay people to choose civil marriage too, arguing that the Bible does not forbid it and that human compassion and dignity demand it. At the second hearing in particular, a number of young people spoke and explained that they saw this as a basic issue of discrimination and fairness.

At both hearings, the opponents made it crystal clear that they were unalterably opposed to both domestic partnership and marriage. Many testifying in opposition quoted from the Bible and urged the Legislature to do nothing or amend the Constitution. Some even urged impeachment of the Supreme Court justices. The other arguments mustered by opponents attacked the idea that this was a civil rights issue, drew analogies to the "natural world" to suggest that gay people are unnatural, claimed that legislative action would put Vermont on the slippery slope toward polygamy and other destabilising changes to marriage,

[96] One opponent, David Orgon Coolidge (Marriage Law Project, Catholic University, Washington, DC), conceded that if the Committee believed that the relationships of same-sex couples deserve equality (which he did not), then the Legislature should grant them access to marriage. Author's telephone conversation with Beth Robinson and Susan Murray.

[97] Both sides hired professional lobbyists. The Vermont Freedom to Marry Action Committee was the clearinghouse for supporters of *Baker*. Opposition groups included "Take It to The People", "Who Would Have Thought, Inc.", "Vermonters for Traditional Marriage", and "Loyal Opposition" (the political action arm of anti-abortion activist Randall Terry).

[98] The hearings were held on the evenings of 25 January and 1 February 2000. The first hearing was broadcast on Vermont Public Radio; the second on Vermont Public Television.

and voiced fears that Vermont would face divine retribution if it provided rights to same-sex couples.[99]

Drafting a "Civil Rights Act for Gay and Lesbian Families"

The turning point for the House Judiciary Committee arrived on 9 February 2000 when it took a straw poll and decided to focus its drafting efforts on a parallel system, rather than end discrimination in the marriage statutes. Some members referred to their upcoming task as drafting a "civil rights act for gay and lesbian families."[100]

This approach was a blow to Vermont's freedom-to-marry advocates, who had worked toward the simple and obviously equal solution of amending the marriage statutes. After about a week of internal consultations, the Action Committee gave a cautious nod of approval to the approach as a pragmatic step toward marriage—while never accepting anything short of full equality in civil marriage as sufficient or right. The group's support also remained conditioned on ensuring that the final bill was a truly parallel system without further compromises.

Disappointed as the freedom-to-marry advocates were, it was also clear that the House Judiciary Committee had been moved by the hearings and were drafting a law the likes of which had never been seen in the United States. The Committee's very first statement of findings included these bold words:

> "Notwithstanding social and cultural discrimination, many gay and lesbian Vermonters have formed lasting, committed, intimate and faithful relationships with persons of their same sexual orientation. These couples live and work together, raise children together, care for family members together, and participate in their communities together, just as do couples who are married under Vermont law. . . . The state has a strong interest in promoting stable, strong and lasting families, including families based upon a same gender couple".[101]

While the bill went through several drafts, ultimately the committee settled on the term "civil union" to describe the status of the new institution, and made it parallel to marriage in virtually every way (entrance requirements, exit requirements, and treatment of spouses in a civil union or marriage).

[99] Slogans in opponents' newspaper advertisements included "Homosexual Union is Not a Civil Right. Homosexual Behavior Hurts Everyone" and "Supreme Court v. God". At the second hearing, the Roman Catholic Church convened a rally on the State House steps.

[100] Eight members supported domestic partnership in lieu of marriage. Critically, all members adamantly opposed a constitutional amendment or any other effort to reverse the Court's historic ruling for equality.

[101] House Jud. Com., "Draft for discussion purposes, Preamble/Findings of the General Assembly" (2 Feb. 2000).

Debate and Votes in the House of Representatives

On 29 February 2000, the House Judiciary Committee approved "An Act Relating to Civil Unions", now known as House Bill 847, by a 10–1 vote, thereby clearing the way for a vote by the 150 members of the House of Representatives.[102] The bill needed to pass by a majority vote two times before it could be forwarded to the State Senate, and proposed amendments had to be voted upon first. The Civil Unions Bill passed on its second reading in the House on 16 March 2000 by a vote of 76–69.

Roughly twelve amendments were offered in the course of the two-day debate.[103] Virtually all of the hostile amendments were defeated. Efforts to delay the bill or withdraw it and put the issue to a popular vote, were defeated.[104] Attempts to dilute the bill by reducing the number of protections or equating same-sex couples with unmarried blood relatives, were defeated. A definition of marriage as the union of a man and a woman was added, since that is how the Supreme Court had interpreted the existing marriage statutes in *Baker*. Bans on recognition of marriages of same-sex couples from other states, as well as a direct "prohibition" of marriage for same-sex couples, were defeated as well.[105] One of the last amendments to be defeated, accompanied by a blistering attack on gay people by its sponsor, would have required both parties to a civil union to be either HIV-positive or HIV-negative.[106] A so-called "freedom of conscience" provision, which would have allowed town clerks to opt out of their obligation to certify civil unions, was also rejected. Once the amendments had all been considered, debate focused on the Civil Unions Bill itself.

What emerged from the debates was the enormous courage and conviction of the Representatives voting for the bill. What was less visible, but equally important, was the leadership of House Judiciary Committee members, especially Thomas Little, in answering objections and keeping the bill on track.

Representative Diane Carmolli, a member of the Judiciary Committee and a life-long Roman Catholic, voted in favor and said she thought this was "the first time the church has turned its back on families—on children and families".[107] Another member of the Committee, Rep. William Lippert (the only openly gay member of the legislature), rose late in the first day "to put a human face on this bill". He went on to address opponents: "We can argue about whether these are civil rights or other rights, but they are rights I don't have right now and almost everyone else in this chamber does".[108] Rep. Mary C. Mazzariello, came out as the mother of two lesbian daughters, a fact that had not been known by her

[102] The lone dissenter, Rep. Bill MacKinnon, favored marriage over civil unions.
[103] On the first day, an amendment permitting same-sex marriage was defeated 22–125.
[104] These included efforts to call a Constitutional Convention (not authorised under Vermont law) and send the issue to a State-wide Advisory Ballot Question in the November 2000 elections.
[105] The recognition ban was defeated 55–89; the direct prohibition was defeated 62–83.
[106] Rep. Nancy Sheltra's virulence backfired; the amendment was defeated 2–136.
[107] Rutland *Herald* (16 March 2000), at 1, 4.
[108] *Ibid.*, at 1, 10.

colleagues. Describing her daughters' and her family's pain over their inability to "fit the mold," she asked her colleagues to "make Vermont a leader in the preservation of family life".[109] Last but certainly not least, at a particularly tense moment in the debates, Rep. Francis Brooks of Montpelier, the only African-American in the House, said: "I can't sit here and be reminded of various acceptable ways of telling other people, 'No, you're not quite there'". He talked about his own struggle not to be viewed as different by other people, and concluded, "I guess if I could say anything to anyone is to say please consider the human being that you have decided to place a stigma on".[110]

Proceedings in the Vermont Senate

After the House vote, the Senate Judiciary Committee commenced hearings and deliberation on the bill. In addition, since constitutional amendments may commence only in the Senate and only in specified years,[111] the Committee came under intense pressure to scuttle the entire House effort. Opponents of the House bill and supporters of a constitutional amendment began a public relations campaign claiming that the Civil Unions Bill was in fact marriage.

Witnesses began testifying on 22 March 2000, with Robinson and Murray testifying on the meaning of the *Baker* decision. Five of the six plaintiffs appeared with them. Nina Beck talked to the Committee about how her religious marriage to her partner Stacy Jolles in 1991 had sustained them through the joys and difficulties of eight years together, including the death of one of their sons. The Committee also heard from Rep. Little, representatives from the Attorney General's office, law professors, faith groups, and members of the public. Attempting to mollify those who criticised the legislature for not taking into account the sentiments of "the people," the Committee held interactive television public hearings to allow Vermonters to testify from their home towns.

After concluding its hearings and making minor changes to the House bill, the Senate Judiciary Committee approved it by a four to two vote. All eyes then turned to the thirty members of the Senate on 18 and 19 April for two important votes: first, on proposed constitutional amendments hostile to equality for lesbian and gay families; and second, on the Senate Judiciary Committee's version of the Civil Unions Bill.

The first set of votes addressed the constitutional amendment proposals. Proponents of the amendments insisted that the voters had a right to decide this issue directly at the ballot box, while opponents of the amendments defended the justness of the *Baker* ruling and praised the wisdom of the Constitution's framers for attempting to protect minorities from the tyranny of the majority.

[109] *Washington Blade*, 17 March 2000, at 1, 16.
[110] *Ibid.*
[111] Vermont Constitution, Ch. II, s. 72.

While some proponents argued for majority rule, others invoked anti-gay stereotypes and doomsday predictions.[112] Opponents of changing the Constitution argued that the purpose of the constitutional amendment process was not to provide a referendum process, but to remedy a defect in the Constitution. If the people are unhappy that the majority of Senators believe the *Baker* decision is correct, they argued, then the people may speak at the ballot box in November 2000 when the senators would be up for re-election. Many talked about how change often inspires fear: Senator Anne Cummings used the example of how her own grandparents had had stones thrown at them on the way to Roman Catholic Mass because their religion was strange to other Vermonters at that time.

In the final tally, the effort to amend the Vermont Constitution by defining marriage as the union of one man and one woman failed (13–17)—far short of the two-thirds majority necessary to commence the amendment process. Another proposed constitutional amendment, which would have defined marriage as male-female only and would have prevented the Supreme Court from ordering that the benefits and protections of marriage be conferred on anyone other than male-female couples, also failed (9–21). The latter constitutional amendment, if carried through the whole legislative process and ultimate voter ratification, would have overruled the *Baker* decision.[113]

With the constitutional amendment proposals defeated, debate began on the Civil Unions Bill itself. Senate Judiciary Committee Chair Richard Sears began the discussion with a review of the court ruling, the positions of the various players, and the observation that most Vermonters did not have a strong feeling one way or another. Nearly every Senator spoke at least once and the extent of soul searching was evident. None of the Senators were openly gay or lesbian. A number of supporters acknowledged that they had not wanted to think about these issues and that they had to "get beyond the easy answers". Several also acknowledged having acted on anti-gay bias in the past, but that this process, including the receipt of vicious hate mail, had "allowed them to walk in the shoes of another person". Senator Sears, like other Senators, received mail stating he would go to hell for supporting civil unions. Sears analogised himself to the character of Huck Finn in Mark Twain's novel. He invoked a passage in which Huck is afraid to help the slave Jim escape because Huck will be damned to hell, but then decides "to go ahead and be damned to hell".[114]

Some answered specific charges of opponents. Countering the claim that the bill is about sex, Senate President Peter Shumlin talked about a lesbian family he knows:

[112] Supporters of the constitutional amendments claimed that gays are not worthy of protection because they do not contribute to society through reproduction and have sexual practices distasteful to the great majority of Vermonters.

[113] Under Vermont law, opponents cannot even commence the constitutional amendment process again until 2003. See *supra* n.111.

[114] Author's Senate notes (19 April 2000).

> "Their relationship is about a lot more than sex. It's about raising children, working in the school system, watching each other grow old and get sick—about all those decisions we make as families. We should embrace that long term commitment".[115]

Many Senators acknowledged that neither the voters nor religious groups were united on this issue. Senator Ben Ptashnik, whose parents were imprisoned at a Nazi labor camp in Buchenwald, along with other Jews, gays and gypsies, spoke tearfully of how the fear and hatred sown by some religious entities can lead to the kind of dehumanisation of people which allows things like the Holocaust to happen.[116] Others pondered what qualities are necessary for a good marriage, while others quoted from constituents' letters.[117]

Several Senators said they had spoken with their children, who saw the Civil Unions Bill, or even marriage, as the fair thing to do. Senator Mark MacDonald, an eighth grade social studies teacher, analogised his being drafted during the Vietnam War "to do what was moral" to his vote in favor of the Civil Unions Bill. His thinking about how he would explain his vote against it to his students ultimately persuaded him to vote for the bill. The bill passed by a 19–11 vote on the morning of 19 April.

The Governor, a long-time supporter of a partnership-style "compromise", signed the bill into law in a private ceremony with his staff on 26 April 2000. In a later message to media, he stated,

> "I think [the bill] is a courageous and powerful statement about who we are in the state of Vermont. I believe what the Legislature has crafted speaks to the notion that the founding fathers of this state put in the Constitution in 1777, that all people are created equal. I believe it speaks to the notion, with the common benefits clause that the court cited, that all people are created equal and that no one group of Vermonters will get more benefits or fewer benefits than any other group of Vermonters".[118]

Content of the Civil Unions Law

The Civil Unions Law, most of which became effective on 1 July 2000, is unique in the United States.[119] It provides a system for entering into civil unions which

[115] Author's Senate notes (18 April 2000).

[116] *Ibid.*

[117] The following letter was read by Senator James Leddy: "I am a seventy-eight year old Catholic mother of eight. This is not about statistics or Biblical interpretation. It is about a farm family and a son who announced twenty-six years ago that he is gay. What could we do? Cast him out or accept him instantly? Patronize him or love him? We brought up our eight children with the same value system. Did we do something wrong? Our son would not choose emotional and cultural persecution. He was just plain born gay. I can only say that God blessed us with eight children. And God made no mistake when he gave us our gay son". *Ibid.*

[118] "Healing begins now, Dean says after signing bill," Rutland *Herald*, 27 April 2000.

[119] See "An Act Relating to Civil Unions", Act 91 of 2000, http://www.leg.state.vt.us/baker/baker.cfm. In section 1, the Legislative Findings constitute an explicit declaration of the existence and value of same-sex families:

is parallel to the system for entering into marriages. Same-sex couples[120] may apply to town clerks for a civil union license, have that license certified by a judge, justice of the peace, or willing member of the clergy, and then receive a civil union certificate.[121] Parties to a civil union in Vermont will be treated as spouses under the law and must end their relationship in the family courts under the laws governing divorce proceedings.[122] Two general provisions in the Law make major substantive changes to other areas of law:

> "Parties to a civil union shall have all the same benefits, protections and responsibilities under law, whether they derive from statute, administrative or court rule, policy, common law or any other source of civil law, as are granted to spouses in a marriage".[123]

> "A party to a civil union shall be included in any definition or use of the terms 'spouse', 'family', 'immediate family', 'dependent', 'next of kin', and other terms that denote the spousal relationship, as those terms are used throughout the law".[124]

Among the hundreds of rights and responsibilities conferred by the Law are: (a) the right to be treated as legal next-of-kin, including preferences for guardianship of and medical decision-making for an incapacitated partner, automatic inheritance rights, the right to leave work to care for an ill spouse, hospital visitation, and control of a spouse's body upon death; (b) the right to be treated as an economic unit for state (but not federal) tax purposes, including the ability to transfer property to each other without tax consequences, to have greater access to family health insurance policies, and to obtain joint insurance policies and joint credit; (c) equalisation in the worker's compensation and public benefits laws; (d) parental rights; and (e) the right to divorce and to a procedure for ascertaining property division, child custody and support.[125] Discrimination against parties to a civil union is considered marital status discrimination,[126] and broad non-discrimination prohibitions require insurers to make available policies which treat parties to a civil union like married spouses.[127]

"(7) The State has a strong interest in promoting stable and lasting families, including families based upon a same-sex couple. (8) Without the legal protections, benefits and responsibilities associated with civil marriage, same-sex couples suffer numerous obstacles and hardships. (9) Despite long-standing social and economic discrimination, many gay and lesbian Vermonters have formed lasting, committed, caring and faithful relationships with persons of their same sex. These couples live together, participate in their communities together, and some raise children and care for family members together, just as do couples who are married under Vermont law".

[120] *Ibid.*, s. 3 (codifed as 15 Vermont Statutes Annotated section 1202(2)) (parties must "[b]e of the same sex and therefore excluded from the marriage laws").

[121] *Ibid.*, s. 5 (18 V.S.A. chapter 106)

[122] *Ibid.*, s. 3 (15 V.S.A. ss. 1204(d), 1206).

[123] *Ibid.*, s. 3 (15 V.S.A. s. 1204(a)).

[124] *Ibid.*, s. 3 (15 V.S.A. s. 1204(b)).

[125] *Ibid.*, s. 3 (15 V.S.A. s. 1204(e)) (non-exclusive list of benefits and responsibilities).

[126] *Ibid.*, s. 3 (15 V.S.A. s. 1204(e)(7)). A representative from the Vermont Attorney General's Office agreed that discrimination against parties to a civil union is also discrimination based upon sexual orientation.

[127] *Ibid.*, s. 18 (8 V.S.A. s. 4063a). See also *ibid.*, s. 17 (8 V.S.A. s. 4724(7)(E)).

Another innovation in the Law, inspired in part by legislation in Hawaii and in part by a wish to acknowledge another constituency among Vermont's families, was the new category of "reciprocal beneficiaries", who would become eligible for certain benefits available to spouses.[128] Unlike parties to a civil union, reciprocal beneficiaries need only present a notarised declaration to the Commissioner of Health to either declare or terminate their relationship. Reciprocal beneficiaries must be at least eighteen, related by blood or adoption (and therefore barred by the consanguinity laws from entering into a civil union or marriage), and not presently married or a party to a civil union.[129]

The Civil Unions Law also established a Review Commission, whose members are charged with educating the public about the new law, collecting information about "the implementation, operation and affect" of the law and how "other states and jurisdictions" treat Vermont civil unions, and reporting its findings to the legislature.[130] In a sign that this category of family could grow in future years, the Review Commission will also examine whether the reciprocal beneficiary status should be expanded and conferred greater rights and responsibilities.[131]

RECOGNITION OF SAME-SEX CIVIL UNIONS AND MARRIAGES BY OTHER STATES AND THE FEDERAL GOVERNMENT

Much has already been written about whether other states would treat as a marriage the marriage of a same-sex couple licensed and certified by the first state to do so (which many had expected would be Hawaii). The same question now arises with respect to civil unions in Vermont, where a new legal institution has been created that parallels civil marriage. The question becomes whether a civil union, as a legislatively-created status equivalent to marriage, must be treated like a marriage under other states' laws dealing with the benefits, protections and responsibilities of marriage. (See Conclusion, p. 769.)

The starting point for this analysis is the Civil Unions Law itself. The law's sheer breadth and scope supports the claim that a civil union should be viewed as the equivalent of civil marriage for the purposes of the benefits, protections and responsibilities afforded by civil marriage.[132] The statutory construction provision further requires that: "[t]his act shall be construed broadly in order to secure to eligible same-sex couples the option of a legal status with the benefits and protections of civil marriage".[133] The law's express purpose matches its substance and rules of construction, by clarifying that same-sex couples receive

[128] "An Act Relating to Civil Unions", Act 91 of 2000, ss. 29–38 (15 V.S.A. ch. 25). The statutory rights for which reciprocal beneficiaries qualify include hospital visitation and decision-making about medical treatment, anatomical gifts, and disposition of remains.

[129] *Ibid.*, s. 29 (15 V.S.A. s. 1303).

[130] *Ibid.*, s. 40.

[131] *Ibid.*, s. 40(d)(4).

[132] *Ibid.*, s. 3 (15 V.S.A. s. 1204 (a)).

[133] *Ibid.*, s. 39.

a new legal status by entering into a civil union.[134] Even with this powerful legislation on their side, the extent of the protections and respect afforded to couples joined in a Vermont civil union, after returning to or moving to another state, remains uncertain, but will unfold over time with loved ones, in places of worship, in communities, in workplaces, in legislatures and in the courts.

Legal argumentation aside, individuals and families are well-advised to proceed cautiously before litigating. Some states and private parties will likely recognise civil unions as a matter of common sense and with no further compulsion. This seems especially likely in the case of insurers and other businesses with offices in Vermont, who will have an incentive to maintain good relations. But discrimination will also inevitably occur. At that point, the couple may decide to absorb the discrimination, understanding that recognition and equal treatment are long-term civil rights concerns. Alternatively, the couple can consult a knowledgeable attorney about pressing for recognition through negotiation or litigation. It is important that the first few cases be filed in the states with the strongest legal basis for assuring equal treatment and recognition, and in matters which are well-developed factually.

The two major approaches governing the legal effect due to marriages (or civil unions) are: (1) non-constitutionally based arguments; and (2) constitutionally-based arguments. Since courts will not reach constitutional questions where another basis exists for resolving a question, the starting point is the non-constitutional approaches.

Non-Constitutional Approaches to Recognition

Setting aside for the moment the complicating factor of state laws purporting to bar respect of a same-sex marriage (or civil union) licensed and certified by another state,[135] the overwhelming rule in each American jurisdiction for many years has been that a marriage validly entered into in the place of celebration will be valid elsewhere.[136]

In some states, the simplest method for resolving this issue is contained in the state's own statutory scheme, which requires recognition of valid marriages licensed outside the forum state.[137] For example, several states have adopted the

[134] *Ibid.*, s. 2(a) ("to respond to the constitutional violation found by the Vermont Supreme Court in *Baker* v. *State*, and to provide eligible same-sex couples the opportunity to 'obtain the same benefits and protections afforded by Vermont law to opposite-sex couples' as required by Chapter I, Article 7th of the Vermont Constitution").

[135] These laws are subject to challenge under state and federal constitutional principles. See Wolfson, chap. 9, n.12; Jennifer Wriggins, "Maine's 'Act to Protect Traditional Marriage and Prohibit Same-Sex Marriages': Questions of Constitutionality Under State and Federal Law", (1998) 50 *Maine Law Review* 345.

[136] Richman and Reynolds, *Understanding Conflict of Law*, 2d ed. (New York, NY, Matthew Bender, 1993), s. 116, at 362.

[137] See BJ Cox, "Same-Sex Marriage and Choice of Law: If We Marry in Hawaii, Are We Still Married When We Return Home?", [1994] *Wisconsin Law Review* 1033 at 1066.

Uniform Marriage and Divorce Act (UMDA), which contains specific language validating foreign, out-of-state marriages.[138] UMDA-inspired laws in other states accomplish the same result.[139] Exceptions and non-recognition laws squarely conflict with the UMDA's policy goal of validating marriages.[140]

Absent a recognition statute, courts will likely turn to conflict of laws principles to determine whether to apply the law of the state certifying the marriage, and therefore recognise the marriage or civil union, or alternatively apply local law (or the law of some third state) and refuse to recognise the relationship.[141] Most states have selected one of four basic choice-of-law principles: (1) the First Restatement rule of *lex loci celebrationis*;[142] (2) the Second Restatement rule of applying the law of the state with the "most significant relationship to the spouses and the marriage";[143] (3) governmental interest analysis, which applies the law of the state with the strongest interest;[144] and (4) Leflar's choice-influencing considerations, which augur for the "better rule of law" and acknowledge the substance of the issue to be decided.[145]

Constitutional Approaches to Recognition

There are four major constitutional arguments favoring recognition of marriages (and arguably civil unions) of same-sex couples from state to state.[146] A full discussion of each of these approaches is well beyond the scope of this chapter.

First, non-recognition violates the Full Faith and Credit Clause, the Privileges and Immunities Clause, the right to travel and other federalist provisions of the United States Constitution.[147] The framers of the US Constitution deliberately

[138] UMDA, s. 210, 9 Uniform Laws Annotated 176 (1987).

[139] Cox, *supra* n., 137 at 1066–7 & nn. 185–202.

[140] *Ibid.*, at 1070–4. "Marriage evasion" statutes, withholding recognition when a state's citizens travel out-of-state to evade local law prohibiting a particular marriage, are a complicating factor but not an insurmountable barrier. *Ibid.* at 1074–1082.

[141] See A Koppelman, "Same-Sex Marriage, Choice of Law, and Public Policy," (1998) 76 *Texas Law Review* 921; BJ Cox, "Same-Sex Marriage and the Public Policy Exception in Choice-of-Law: Does It Really Exist?", (1996) 16 *Quinnipiac Law Review* 105; Note, "In Sickness and In Health, In Hawaii and Where Else?: Conflict of Laws and Recognition of Same-Sex Marriages," (1996) 109 *Harvard Law Review* 2038; TM Keane, "Aloha, Marriage? Constitutional and Choice of Law Arguments for Recognition of Same-Sex Marriages," 47 *Stanford Law Review* 499 (1995); Cox, *supra* n. 136, at 1083–117.

[142] *Restatement of Conflict of Laws*, s. 121 (1934).

[143] *Restatement (Second) of Conflict of Laws*, s. 283(1) (1971).

[144] B Currie, *Selected Essays on the Conflict of Laws* (Durham, NC, Duke University Press, 1963), at 90. But see L Kramer, "Interest Analysis and the Presumption of Foreign Law", (1989) 56 *University of Chicago Law Review* 1301.

[145] RA Leflar, "Choice-Influencing Considerations in Conflicts Law," (1966) 41 *New York University Law Review* 267.

[146] Many of the same arguments apply to recognition and equal treatment of marriages and civil unions by the federal government. See Wolfson, chap. 9, nn. 9, 12.

[147] US Constitution, Article IV, s. 1: "Full faith and Credit shall be given in each State to the public Acts, Records, and judicial Proceedings of every other State. And the Congress may by

sought to bind the separate states into one nation through the various federalist provisions.[148] Each of these provisions prohibits a state from pursuing policies that subvert national unity, by discriminating against interstate or out-of-state entities or activities. The goal of national unity inevitably requires barring parochial state policies inimical to that goal.[149] With respect to Full Faith and Credit, a civil union or marriage qualifies under each prong of the Clause: it is an "act" because it is performed by a public official or agent and occurs pursuant to a statutory scheme; a "record" because the civil union or marriage certificate is a public record; and a "judicial proceeding" because a marriage or civil union is a great deal like other judgments, and in some cases, is performed by judicial officials or agents.[150] The US Supreme Court has also recently clarified that there is no general public policy exception to the command of Full Faith and Credit.[151]

Second, the recognition of marriages or civil unions based on the respective sexes of the spouses, i.e., recognising the marriage of a woman to a man but not the marriage of a woman to a woman, is impermissible sex discrimination which cannot be justified absent an exceedingly persuasive justification.[152] Many states treat equally common-law and other marriages of persons from out-of-state, even when the forum state would not have licensed and certified the marriage itself. Failure to extend the same treatment and rules to same-sex couples may violate equal protection guarantees (in the case of a governmental actor), or state and federal non-discrimination laws (in the case of both governmental and private entities).

Third, denial of recognition to valid marriages of same-sex couples is not reasonably related to any legitimate state interests, and is likely to be based on the impermissible purpose of disadvantaging same-sex couples for its own sake.[153]

Finally, marriage (and arguably, the status conferred upon entering a civil union) is a fundamental right that may not be abridged absent a compelling state interest narrowly tailored to the classification at issue. Here, the question is whether a state may void the marriage or civil union of a couple who are already legally united under the laws of another state, and not whether the forum itself must permit same-sex couples to marry or enter into a civil union within the forum state. That a couples' marriage partakes of a "basic civil right" cannot be doubted.[154] Voiding an existing marriage creates unique hardships beyond

general Laws prescribe the Manner in which such Acts, Records and Proceedings shall be proved, and the Effect thereof." See also Article IV, s. 2; Amendment XIV, s. 1.

[148] *Sutton* v. *Lieb*, 342 U.S. 402 (1952).

[149] See e.g. *Saenz* v. *Roe*, 119 S.Ct. 1518 (1999).

[150] *Supra* n.119, s. 5 (18 V.S.A. ss. 5164, 5167).

[151] *Baker* v. *General Motors*, 118 S.Ct. 657 (1998).

[152] Opening Brief, *supra* n.35, at 459–65; Reply Brief, *supra* n.42, at 8–17; Koppelman, chap. 35.

[153] Opening Brief, *ibid.*, at 436– 459; Reply Brief, *ibid.*, at 22–38; Eskridge, *supra* n.5, at 88–122; Strasser (chap. 9, n.12), at 71–99.

[154] *Supra* n.44. See also WN Hohengarten, "Same-Sex Marriage and the Right of Privacy", (1994) 103 *Yale Law Journal* 1495.

those experienced by denial of permission to marry in the first place. It undermines the reliance the couple has justifiably placed on their marital status under the law of the state in which they were married, or in which they entered into a civil union. It invites chaos by imposing conflicting marital statuses on the couple in different states—married or civilly united in one state but not across the border. It throws into disarray the spouse's rights in their property and their rights and responsibilities regarding their children. In effect, non-recognition of an existing marriage or civil union divorces the couple against their will by operation of law within the borders of the non-recognising state, without even providing the process and legal certainty inherent in divorce proceedings. In addition, any legitimate state interest that might conceivably be served by not permitting same-sex couples to marry becomes even weaker where recognition of pre-existing marriages or civil unions is concerned. Indeed, no legitimate reason exists for negating a couple's fundamental right to marry solely because they are of the same sex.

CONCLUSION

Within the gay, lesbian, bisexual and transgender community, the advent of civil unions can be seen as a prism refracting different sentiments about how to achieve family recognition and equal treatment. For those who wish to build new family-oriented institutions, or for those who simply want no part of marriage's history as an oppressive institution, the *Baker* decision and civil unions provide a different model for providing security to families.[155] The civil unions law is a breathtaking advance for gay and lesbian people and same-sex families, which will transform the legal status of participants from "legal strangers" to legal next-of-kin.[156] In this way, Vermont's law is akin to the "Registered Partnership" laws in Denmark, Norway, Sweden, Iceland and the Netherlands. These laws have provided substantial protections and reassured the people of those countries that doing so is good public policy. And with couples from all states entering into civil unions, for the first time in the United States, Americans will meet same-sex couples who have a marriage-like legal status. They will be able to evaluate for themselves whether those protections have hurt their own families or "destroyed marriage," or on the other hand, whether same-sex families are now simply facing less discrimination and enjoying more security and peace of mind. In short, they will see that the sky has not fallen.

At the same time, for those who seek equality across the board, the fact that the civil unions law is not marriage, and is a separate institution from marriage, smacks of "separate" and "unequal." There is something undeniably stigmatis-

[155] See *supra* n. 5.

[156] But see A Sullivan, "State of the Union: Why 'civil union' isn't marriage," *The New Republic*, 18 May 2000, at 18.

ing about being excluded from the cultural status and word "marriage." The notion that the Vermont legislature had to create a separate institution, albeit one that parallels civil marriage in virtually every way, can be viewed as a capitulation to homophobia, i.e., gay people are not good enough to be included in civil marriage.[157] While the Vermont Supreme Court and state legislature went further than any other state to date in proclaiming and effectuating the basic equal citizenship rights of gay people, both lacked the wherewithal to declare that there is one standard of justice for all Vermonters which demands inclusion of same-sex couples within marriage.

It cannot be doubted that the debates surrounding inclusion of same-sex couples within civil marriage prompted a more far-reaching discussion than has existed in recent years about the state's role in supporting or not supporting particular families. For those who welcome such discussions, the marriage debates have propelled the discussion into new territory. Moreover, by explicitly including reciprocal beneficiaries within the legislation and extending certain rights to such persons, the legislature reached out to protect even more families who choose to so acknowledge their relationships.[158]

As always, the struggle for equality for gay and lesbian citizens is a long-term one. In the words of Beth Robinson,

> "We're finally on the bus. We have a legal status. But we're at the back of the bus. If I know Vermonters, then as the bus rolls along, the passengers will get to know one another. And as they chat, they will swap seats. And the distinctions will fall away".[159]

This is not to say there will be no discomfort to the status quo. In the words of the former slave Frederick Douglass:

> "If there is no struggle, there is no progress. Those who profess to favor freedom, and yet deprecate agitation . . . want crops without plowing up the ground, they want rain without thunder and lightning. They want the ocean without the awful roar of its waters".[160]

[157] In his memoir, civil rights hero John Lewis describes his shock and disappointment when certain African-Americans accepted a "compromise": formerly segregated lunch counters would begin a partial integration by serving blacks separately in designated sections of the formerly whites-only restaurant. "We couldn't believe that this was their proposal. . . . Couldn't they see that this was not about sandwiches and salads. It was not about being allowed to sit separately at a counter. It was about nothing less than being treated exactly the same as the white people with whom we shared citizenship in this country". John Lewis, *Walking with the Wind* (New York, NY, Simon & Schuster, 1998), at 113.

[158] The reciprocal beneficiaries provisions show how attempts to change comprehensively the ways in which the state interacts with families may in fact be aided by inclusion of gay and lesbian people in the existing marriage system.

[159] Author's conversation with Beth Robinson.

[160] Foner and Taylor (eds.), *Frederick Douglass: Selected Speeches and Writings* (Chicago, IL, Laurence Hill Books, 1999), at 367.

Section B—Canada

Introduction

Same-Sex Partnerships in Canada

THE HON JUSTICE CLAIRE L'HEUREUX-DUBÉ*

THIS IS AN opportune time to consider the recognition of same-sex relationships in Canadian law. In May 1999, the Supreme Court's judgment in *M* v. *H.*[1] was released, where our court, in an 8–1 judgment, held that denying members of same-sex couples access to Ontario's spousal support legislation was a violation of the guarantee of equality without discrimination contained in the *Canadian Charter of Rights and Freedoms*. The majority of the Court emphasised the significant pre-existing disadvantage experienced by gays and lesbians, and pointed out that exclusion from legal regimes such as the Ontario *Family Law Act* contributes to their marginalisation and invisibility to the law. As noted by Cory and Iacobucci JJ., writing for the majority,

> "The exclusion of same-sex partners . . . promotes the view that M., and individuals in same-sex relationships generally, are less worthy of recognition and protection. It implies that they are judged to be incapable of forming intimate relationships of economic interdependence as compared to opposite-sex couples, without regard to their actual circumstances. As the intervener EGALE submitted, such exclusion perpetuates the disadvantages suffered by individuals in same-sex relationships and contributes to the erasure of their existence".[2]

This judgment reflected developments in Canadian equality law that have taken place over the past several years. In the recent case of *Law* v. *Canada (Minister of Employment and Immigration)*,[3] our Court emphasised a conception of equality that focuses on the *effects* of legislation on individuals or groups differentially treated by government action, and found that equality rights are violated when the human dignity of the claimant is affected. The Court unanimously emphasised the role of s. 15 of the *Charter* in protecting those who are vulnerable, disadvantaged, or marginalised, as well as the importance of a contextual analysis that focuses on the perspective of those affected by legislative distinctions. Writing for the Court, Iacobucci J. emphasised the importance of a purposive approach to s. 15 of the *Charter* and defined that purpose broadly, as follows:

* Justice of the Supreme Court of Canada.

[1] [1999] 2 SCR 3.

[2] *Ibid.* at para. 73.

[3] [1999] 1 SCR 497.

"the purpose of s. 15(1) is to prevent the violation of essential human dignity and freedom through the imposition of disadvantage, stereotyping, or political or social prejudice, and to promote a society in which all persons enjoy equal recognition at law as human beings or as members of Canadian society, equally capable and equally deserving of concern, respect and consideration".[4]

This goal of making our society one where everyone is treated with the same consideration and respect is what underlies the importance of ensuring that our law does not marginalise, exclude, or devalue individuals in same-sex relationships. Indeed, recognising the equality rights of members of same-sex couples is part of the larger goal that all minorities and disadvantaged groups must receive the equal protection and benefit of the law without discrimination.

The Court's judgment in *M.* v. *H.* was the culmination of several years of considerable change in Canadian law and society's treatment of same-sex relationships. Only six years earlier, in *Mossop* v. *Canada*,[5] a majority of our Court held that it was incorrect for the Canada Human Rights Commission to find that the denial of bereavement leave to a gay man to attend the funeral of his partner's father, when he would have been entitled to such leave had his partner been female, was discrimination on the basis of family status. In 1995, a majority of the Court, in *Egan* v. *Canada*,[6] found that it was acceptable for the government to deny pension benefits to members of same-sex couples when they were given to opposite-sex cohabiting couples.

However, more recent cases have led to successful claims by those in same-sex relationships. In the spring of 1998, the Court released its decision in *Vriend* v. *Alberta*.[7] The Alberta government had explicitly refused to include discrimination on the basis of sexual orientation in its human rights legislation. The Court unanimously held that this was a violation of equality rights and read into the legislation protection against sexual orientation discrimination. The majority emphasised the harm that discrimination in society causes to gays and lesbians, and that the message sent by the legislation was that gays and lesbians were not worthy of recognition or protection under the province's laws. The judgment in *M.* v. *H.* built closely upon this important development in equality rights.

Changes have not come only at the Supreme Court level. In lower courts across the country, when gays and lesbians have challenged legislation that gives benefits to opposite-sex cohabiting couples but not members of same-sex couples, nearly all courts have allowed these claims. Definitions of "spouse" that exclude members of same-sex partnerships have been consistently overturned. The most significant examples in recent years include the Ontario Court of Appeal's judgment in *Rosenberg* v. *Canada*,[8] where the Court held that the fail-

[4] *Ibid.* at para. 88(4).
[5] [1993] 1 SCR 554.
[6] [1995] 2 SCR 513.
[7] [1998] 1 SCR 493.
[8] (1998) 158 DLR (4th) 664.

ure of the Income Tax Act to give tax exemptions to private pension plans that included benefits for same-sex spouses violated equality rights, and the decision of the Ontario Court Provincial Division in *Re K. & B.*,[9] where the Court held that the failure to allow members of same-sex couples to adopt each other's children was also a violation of equality rights. In short, recognition of the equality rights of members of same-sex couples is coming about quickly, and legal changes are dramatic.

However, changes in the legal status of lesbians and gays have not come about without considerable social and political controversy and upheaval. Indeed, gay and lesbian rights have led to some of the most heated disputes in the Canadian media and political arena that this country has seen in recent years, and these have led to considerable discussion about the judicial role in overturning legislation. The debates that followed the judgments of the Supreme Court in *Vriend* and *M.* v. *H.*, in particular, were heated. However, recent public opinion surveys suggest that, contrary to what many suggest, the public is generally supportive of extending rights to members of same-sex couples. A recent opinion poll indicated that 56 per cent of Canadians support our Court's decision in *M.* v. *H.*; that 53 per cent of Canadians support permitting same-sex marriages; and that 63 per cent of Canadians believe that those in same-sex relationships should be entitled to spousal benefits.[10] This indicates that courts are attuned to society's changing attitudes to same-sex partnerships and equality rights generally, and that Supreme Court judgments on issues of equality *do* reflect the values of ordinary Canadians.

The last five years have seen a tremendous change in the recognition of the legal status of same-sex relationships in Canadian law and, more generally, in the approach taken to equality rights by the courts. In the next two chapters, Donald Casswell and Kathleen Lahey reflect on the manner in which these changes have come about and the consequences of these developments for the future. They also reflect on the advantages and disadvantages of recognition of same-sex relationships through court decisions, rather than through legislative change. We have made much progress in recognizing equality rights within the law in a short period of time. Perhaps the debate should now be about where we are going and how we will get there. How can we ensure that we continue to make progress in the recognition of equality rights, not only for those in same-sex relationships, but for all those in Canadian society who have been disadvantaged and marginalised within our legal system.

[9] (1995) 125 DLR (4th) 653.

[10] "Most in poll want gay marriages legalized" *The [Toronto] Globe and Mail*, 10 June 1999, A1.

11

Any Two Persons in Canada's Lotusland, British Columbia

DONALD G CASSWELL*

INTRODUCTION

THE LOTUS OF Greek mythology was a magical plant whose berry, when eaten, induced luxurious languor and euphoric forgetfulness. The appellation "Lotusland" thus connotes any place of indolent enjoyment and well-being. Canadians sometimes call our western-most province, British Columbia, "Lotusland". Those of us who live in British Columbia take "Lotusland" quite seriously. After all, we enjoy snow-capped mountains, the spectacular Pacific coastline, beautiful cities and a reputation for a relaxed lifestyle. Other Canadians think that British Columbians are just smug and tend to use "Lotusland" somewhat dismissively.

Whatever the comparative benefits of living in British Columbia as opposed to elsewhere in Canada, British Columbia has certainly been "Lotusland" for lesbian and gay Canadians in terms of legal recognition of same-sex partnerships. In particular, British Columbia was the first jurisdiction in Canada to enact legislation recognising same-sex partnerships in such important areas as medical services, pensions, and family relations law. Developments in 1999 and early 2000, however, challenged British Columbia's position as the Canadian leader in legally recognising same-sex partnerships.

On 20 May 1999, the Supreme Court of Canada delivered its landmark eight-to-one decision in *M.* v. *H.*[1] The case involved former lesbian partners, one of whom, after they had separated, sued the other claiming support and a division of property. The Court held that the definition of "spouse" applicable to partner support in Ontario's Family Law Act was unconstitutional because it included unmarried opposite-sex partners but not same-sex partners.[2] While the Court's decision strictly applies only to this particular definition of "spouse", it

* Professor of Law, University of Victoria, Victoria, British Columbia, Canada. I would like to thank Ena Ackerman (LL.B., U.Vic., 2001) and Allison Fieldberg (LL.B., U.Vic., 2001) for their valuable research assistance. Of course, any errors or omissions in this chapter are entirely my responsibility.

[1] [1999] 2 S.C.R. 3 (S.C.R. available at http://www.lexum.umontreal.ca/csc-scc/en/index.html).
[2] Revised Statutes of Ontario 1990, chapter F.3, section 29.

has tremendous precedential significance with respect to all definitions of "spouse" and, indeed, all other family relationship signifiers, in all Canadian legislation. In response to the Court's ruling, the federal and several provincial governments said that they would examine their legislation generally to determine whether amendments to recognise same-sex partnerships were required.[3] Indeed, in late 1999 and 2000, Ontario, British Columbia, and the federal government all enacted omnibus legislation in response to *M. v. H.*[4]

Earlier, on 10 June 1999, the Québec National Assembly, under the leadership of the Parti Québécois government, had already enacted omnibus legislation to provide that same-sex partners have the same legal status, rights and obligations as unmarried opposite-sex partners.[5] Québec thus became the first province to enact omnibus legislation recognising same-sex partnerships. Moreover, it is worth emphasising that the Québec National Assembly passed this legislation unanimously and had given it preliminary approval on 19 May 1999, the day before *M. v. H.* While British Columbia is Canada's "Lotusland," Québec is indeed "*la belle province*".

However, on 20 July 2000, British Columbia regained its national leadership position with respect to same-sex partnership recognition when, as considered below, the British Columbia government went to court to challenge the exclusion of same-sex partners from the right to marry legally.

The primary purposes of this chapter are to summarise the current state of British Columbia law concerning recognition of same-sex partnerships and to speculate on how British Columbia law may develop in this regard in the future. First, however, I briefly provide some context concerning Canadian law which may be of interest to non-Canadian readers.[6]

SOME CONTEXT CONCERNING CANADIAN LAW

Legislative jurisdiction

The Constitution of Canada provides that legislative jurisdiction is shared between the federal and provincial governments.[7] (The federal government has delegated some of its legislative jurisdiction to the three territories.) The federal Parliament has exclusive legislative jurisdiction with respect to some matters;

[3] See, eg, CBC News, 21 May 1999, "Most premiers ready to make changes after same-sex ruling", <http://cbc.ca/news>(Search, "same-sex ruling").

[4] Amendments Because of the Supreme Court of Canada Decision in *M. v. H.* Act, Statutes of Ontario 1999, chapter 6; Definition of Spouse Amendment Act, 2000, Statutes of British Columbia 2000, ch. 24; Modernization of Benefits and Obligations Act, Statutes of Canada 2000, ch. 12.

[5] An Act to amend various legislative provisions concerning de facto spouses, Statutes of Québec 1999, chapter 14.

[6] I have considered lesbian and gay equality claims more comprehensively in DG Casswell, *Lesbians, Gay Men, and Canadian Law* (Toronto, Emond Montgomery Publications Limited, 1996).

[7] Constitution Act, 1867, 30 & 31 Victoria, ch. 3 (U.K.), as amended.

the provincial legislatures have exclusive jurisdiction with respect to other matters; and with respect to still other matters, the federal Parliament and the provincial legislatures share jurisdiction. In many cases, therefore, the federal and provincial levels of government must necessarily cooperate in enacting constitutionally valid legislation.[8]

In particular, relevant to the constitutionality of legislation concerning domestic partnership or same-sex marriage, the federal Parliament has exclusive legislative jurisdiction concerning "marriage and divorce", and the provincial legislatures have exclusive jurisdiction concerning "solemnization of marriage in the province" and "property and civil rights in the province".[9] The case law interpreting these provisions of the Constitution is complex. However, two points are generally accepted. First, the Constitution provides for overlapping legislative authority. Second, the federal Parliament has legislative authority with respect to the capacity to marry, that is, with respect to who can or cannot marry.[10]

Canadian Charter of Rights and Freedoms

The Canadian Charter of Rights and Freedoms[11] includes the following provisions:

> "Section 1. The Canadian Charter of Rights and Freedoms guarantees the rights and freedoms set out in it subject only to such reasonable limits prescribed by law as can be demonstrably justified in a free and democratic society".
> "Section 15(1). Every individual is equal before and under the law and has the right to the equal protection and equal benefit of the law without discrimination and, in particular, without discrimination based on race, national or ethnic origin, colour, religion, sex, age or mental or physical disability".
> "Section 32. This Charter applies . . . to the Parliament and government of Canada . . . and . . . to the legislature and government of each province. . . ."

The Charter came into force on 17 April 1982, except for the equality guarantees of section 15, which came into force on 17 April 1985. The Constitution provides that any law that is inconsistent with the Charter is of no force or effect.[12] The Supreme Court of Canada has interpreted this provision as enabling courts to strike down unconstitutional legislation or effectively amend

[8] See generally, PW Hogg, *Constitutional Law of Canada* (Scarborough, Ontario, Carswell, 1996 with regular loose-leaf updates).

[9] Constitution Act, 1867, *supra* n.7, ss. 91(26), 92(12), and 92(13).

[10] See, *In Re Marriage Legislation in Canada*, [1912] A.C. 880 (Privy Council); *Hellens* v. *Densmore*, [1957] S.C.R. 768.

[11] Enacted as Part I of the Constitution Act, 1982, being Sched. B of the Canada Act, 1982 (U.K.), ch. 11.

[12] Constitution Act, 1982, *ibid.*, s. 52.

it by "reading in" or "reading down," that is, adding words to or deleting words from the legislation as enacted.[13]

The Charter has been the single most important development in Canadian legal history. In a recent Supreme Court of Canada decision, Justice Iacobucci stated that the Charter had resulted in "a redefinition of our democracy"[14] and that:

> "When the Charter was introduced, Canada went, in the words of former Chief Justice Brian Dickson, from a system of Parliamentary supremacy to constitutional supremacy . . . . Simply put, each Canadian was given individual rights and freedoms which no government or legislature could take away. However, as rights and freedoms are not absolute, governments and legislatures could justify the qualification or infringement of these constitutional rights under s. 1".[15]

Parliamentary supremacy is, however, not entirely dead. Section 33 of the Charter permits the federal Parliament or a provincial legislature to enact legislation which expressly declares that it will operate "notwithstanding" that it may, or even patently does, violate certain provisions of the Charter. The equality rights guaranteed by section 15 are among those provisions of the Charter which may be overridden using the section 33 "notwithstanding clause". A declaration enacted pursuant to section 33 only has effect for five years, but may be re-enacted. Section 33 has only very rarely been invoked, and only once in the context of lesbian and gay rights.

In 2000, the Alberta legislature, reacting in horror to *M.* v. *H.*, amended the Alberta Marriage Act to define "marriage" as "a marriage between a man and a woman" and to declare that the Act operated notwithstanding the Charter.[16] Invoking section 33 of the Charter does protect the Act from Charter scrutiny. However, the Act's definition of "marriage" is nevertheless clearly *ultra vires* the Alberta legislature since, as mentioned already, legislation relating to the capacity to marry is within the legislative jurisdiction of the federal Parliament. Thus, I have no doubt that a court would hold that this restrictive definition of "marriage" is of no force or effect. The Legislature also added a preamble to the Marriage Act which states, in part, that "marriage is an institution the maintenance of which in its purity the public is deeply interested in" and that this "principle", and other "principles" listed in the preamble, are "fundamental in considering the solemnization of marriage".[17] A statute's preamble has no independent legal effect but can be considered by a court in interpreting the statute. I make two comments concerning the Alberta Marriage Act's preamble. First, the Legislature's reference to the "purity" of marriage, with the necessary impli-

[13] *Schachter* v. *Canada*, [1992] 2 S.C.R. 679.

[14] *Vriend* v. *Alberta*, [1998] 1 S.C.R. 493 at 564.

[15] *Ibid.*, at 563.

[16] Marriage Act, Revised Statutes of Alberta 1980, ch. M-6, sections 1(c.1) (definition of "marriage"), 1.1(a) (Charter override), as amended by Marriage Amendment Act, 2000, Statutes of Alberta 2000, ch. 3, ss. 4, 5.

[17] Marriage Amendment Act, 2000, *ibid.*, s. 2.

cation that marriage would be polluted by including lesbians and gay men, is a shockingly outrageous insult to lesbians and gay men. Second, the reference to "solemnization of marriage" is a patently self-serving and pathetic attempt constitutionally to legitimate legislation which any first-year law student would know is clearly *ultra vires*.

Section 15 of the Charter made possible the tremendous advance in lesbian and gay legal rights and, in particular, the recognition of same-sex partnerships that has occurred in Canada in the last decade or so. "Sexual orientation" is not included in the grounds of prohibited discrimination enumerated in section 15. However, the crucially important words, "in particular", which precede the enumerated grounds made everything possible for lesbian and gay people claiming equality. In 1989, the Supreme Court of Canada relied upon these words in unanimously holding that section 15 afforded protection against discrimination, not only on the basis of its enumerated grounds, but also on the basis of grounds that were analogous to those enumerated grounds.[18] In 1995, the Supreme Court of Canada unanimously held, in *Egan* v. *Canada*, that sexual orientation was an analogous ground of discrimination under section 15 and, therefore, discrimination on the basis of sexual orientation was prohibited under the Constitution.[19] The remaining hurdles for lesbian and gay equality-seekers in any particular case are to convince the court that, first, the impugned legislation or other government action discriminates on the basis of sexual orientation and, second, that such discrimination is not justified.[20]

Human rights legislation

The federal government and all provincial and territorial governments have enacted human rights legislation, which in most jurisdictions is concerned mainly with prohibiting discrimination. In British Columbia, the Human Rights Code[21] prohibits discrimination on the basis of sexual orientation in accommodation, employment, tenancy premises, purchase of property, membership in trade unions or occupational associations, publications, and access to services and facilities customarily available to the public. Sexual orientation was first included in the Code as a prohibited ground of discrimination in 1992.[22] However, as with Charter analysis, the Code's prohibition against sexual

[18] *Andrews* v. *Law Society of British Columbia*, [1989] 1 S.C.R. 143. *Andrews* did not involve a claim based on sexual orientation discrimination, but rather a claim based on discrimination against non-citizens.

[19] [1995] 2 S.C.R. 513.

[20] For example, the gay claimants in *Egan* v. *Canada* ultimately lost by a narrow five-to-four decision of the Supreme Court. For analysis of *Egan* v. *Canada*, see, Robert Wintemute, "Discrimination Against Same-Sex Couples: Sections 15(1) and 1 of the *Charter*: *Egan* v. *Canada*," (1995) 74 *Canadian Bar Review* 682.

[21] Revised Statutes of B.C. 1996, ch. 210.

[22] Human Rights Amendment Act, Statutes of B.C. 1992, ch. 43.

orientation discrimination does not in itself guarantee recognition of same-sex partnerships in particular situations. Discrimination on the basis of sexual orientation must be established in the context of any specific claim, including claims to recognition of same-sex partnerships.

By the mid-1990s, the federal and most provincial and territorial governments had amended their human rights legislation to include sexual orientation as a prohibited ground of discrimination, or were at least in the process of doing so. A notable exception was the province of Alberta, whose Progressive Conservative government had specifically refused to amend Alberta's human rights legislation to prohibit discrimination on the basis of sexual orientation. This refusal was challenged, and, in 1998, the Supreme Court of Canada unanimously held, in *Vriend* v. *Alberta*,[23] that the omission of sexual orientation as a prohibited ground of discrimination in Alberta's human rights legislation violated section 15 of the Charter. The Court ruled that sexual orientation should be "read into" the legislation.

An important point must be emphasised for non-Canadian readers. As section 32 of the Charter, set out above, makes clear, the Charter applies only to government action, not private action. (The practical difficulty in drawing this distinction may be ignored for present purposes.) Human rights legislation, on the other hand, applies to both government and private action. Therefore, what *Vriend* effectively did, via the Charter, was to prohibit discrimination on the basis of sexual orientation by both government and private actors. Needless to say, this legal development has been controversial. However, along with other lesbian and gay Canadians, I find myself shouting, "hurray for the Charter and the Supreme Court of Canada".

CURRENT RECOGNITION OF SAME-SEX PARTNERSHIPS IN BRITISH COLUMBIA

Overview

There are approximately 500 statutes in British Columbia, about a quarter of which have something to do with spousal or family status. A mere decade ago, not one of them recognized same-sex partnerships. Today, many do and, in view of *M.* v. *H.*, it is reasonable to expect that eventually all will do so. This truly dramatic change in the law in such a short time has come about because of the Charter, the decisions of the Supreme Court of Canada referred to above, and the lesbian- and gay-positive provincial government currently in office.

The New Democratic Party (NDP) was elected in 1991 to form British Columbia's government and re-elected in 1996. To say that this government has been lesbian- and gay-positive is an understatement. The NDP government does not just have openly gay members both in Cabinet and on its backbenches

[23] *Supra* n.14.

(although not quite as many as Britain's 1997–2001 Labour government!). It was also the first government in Canada to recognise same-sex partnerships in legislation dealing with medical services, family relations, and pensions. (Interestingly, several judicial "firsts" recognising same-sex partnerships also occurred in British Columbia courts, as noted below.)

British Columbia's legislation recognising same-sex partnerships did not, however, come about solely because of the NDP government's lesbian- and gay-positive policy. In introducing legislation recognising same-sex partnerships, the government was responding to court decisions which had indicated that such recognition was the constitutionally right thing to do. However, government is entitled to credit, in several instances, for having amended British Columbia legislation based on court decisions in other provinces, without waiting for decisions of British Columbia courts or the Supreme Court of Canada.

The British Columbia Legislature has used two techniques to recognise same-sex partnerships. First, in adoption legislation, privileging of "spouses" has been abrogated, with legal rights being afforded instead to any two persons. Second, numerous statutes have now been amended to include same-sex partners in their definitions of "spouse". Two different formulae had until 2000 been used by the Legislature in extending definitions of "spouse" to include same-sex partners. As an example of the first formula, the Medicare Protection Act had for several years defined "spouse" as follows:

> " 'Spouse' with respect to another person means a resident who is married to or is living in a marriage-like relationship with the other person and, for the purposes of this definition, the marriage or marriage-like relationship may be between persons of the same gender".[24]

The second formula, and the more commonly used definition of "spouse" extended to include same-sex partners, refers only to a "marriage-like relationship" and omits reference to the possibility of "marriage" between same-sex partners. A typical example of such a definition of "spouse" is the following in the Family Relations Act:

> " 'Spouse' [includes] a person who . . . lived with another person in a marriage-like relationship . . . and . . . the marriage-like relationship may be between persons of the same gender".[25]

In British Columbia, legally-recognised marriage is presently limited to opposite-sex partners. Therefore, the first formula for an extended definition of "spouse", which included the possibility of "marriage" between same-sex partners, appears to have been intended to permit recognition under British

[24] Revised Statutes of B.C. 1996, ch. 286, s. 1; originally enacted by Medical and Health Care Services Act, Statutes of British Columbia 1992, ch. 76, s. 1; repealed and replaced by Definition of Spouse Amendment Act, 2000, *supra* n.4, s. 26.

[25] Revised Statutes of B.C. 1996, ch. 128, s. 1, as amended by Family Relations Amendment Act, 1997, Statutes of B.C. 1997, ch. 20, s. 1.

Columbia law of same-sex marriages which were legally valid under the law of another country, state, or province. It is more difficult, however, to speculate why the British Columbia Legislature used this formula only somewhat exceptionally, rather than consistently, in enacting extended definitions of "spouse" to include same-sex partners. Further, it is not a case of the first formula having been "tried" and then quickly and consistently abandoned, since it was used as recently as 1997 in family relations legislation, as noted below.

A flurry of legislation dealing with same-sex partnership recognition was enacted by the British Columbia legislature in 1999 and 2000, most notably the Definition of Spouse Amendment Act, 1999 ("the 1999 Act"),[26] and the Definition of Spouse Amendment Act, 2000 ("the 2000 Act").[27] These Acts included same-sex partners in the definitions of "spouse" in various statutes which had already been extended to include unmarried opposite-sex partners. The result was to treat same-sex partners equally with unmarried opposite-sex partners and, in many but not all cases, equally with married spouses. The 1999 Act amended five provincial statutes and the 2000 Act, more comprehensive omnibus legislation, amended 35 statutes, including the five which had already been amended by the 1999 Act.[28]

In the 2000 Act, the legislature settled on the second formula mentioned above for extended definitions of "spouse" and abandoned the first formula. Thus, all extended definitions of "spouse" in British Columbia legislation now define "spouse" as a person who is, or was, "married to another person" or "living and cohabiting with another person in a marriage-like relationship, including a marriage-like relationship between persons of the same gender". In some cases, the living and cohabiting together must additionally have existed for some specified minimum period of time. There is no reference to the possibility of "marriage" between same-sex partners.

It is important to emphasise and contrast the way in which British Columbia's omnibus legislation recognised same-sex partnerships with the methods used in the Québec, Ontario, and federal omnibus legislation. As indicated, British Columbia's legislation included same-sex partners in extended definitions of "spouse". The Québec and federal legislation grouped same-sex partners and unmarried opposite-sex partners together as "de facto spouses"[29] or "common-law partners" respectively, but not as "spouses". Interestingly, an incidental

[26] Definition of Spouse Amendment Act, 1999, Statutes of B.C. 1999, ch. 29.

[27] Definition of Spouse Amendment Act, 2000, Statutes of B.C. 2000, ch. 24.

[28] After enacting the 1999 Act, but before proclaiming it in force, the British Columbia government decided to enact more comprehensive omnibus legislation in response to *M.* v. *H.* Proclamation of the 1999 Act was therefore delayed until after the enactment of the 2000 Act, which, among other things, repealed and replaced parts of the 1999 Act. Proclamation of both Acts was coordinated, and they came into force in various stages in 2000 (Definition of Spouse Amendment Act, 2000, *ibid.*, s. 41; B.C. Regulation 280/2000). Thus, provisions of the 2000 Act amending the five statutes already dealt with in the 1999 Act in some cases do not refer to the root Acts actually being amended, but rather to the relevant provisions of the 1999 Act, which in turn lead eventually to the Acts being amended.

[29] In French, "*conjoints de fait*".

effect of the federal legislation was to "demote" unmarried opposite-sex partners, who previously had been included in various extended definitions of "spouse". Ontario's legislation created a separate category altogether for "same-sex partners" alone, while leaving unmarried opposite-sex partners in various extended definitions of "spouse".[30] M., the plaintiff in *M.* v. *H.*, applied to the Supreme Court of Canada for a rehearing concerning remedy, intending to argue that the Ontario legislation's differential treatment of same-sex partners and unmarried opposite-sex partners did not satisfy the Court's May 1999 order. On 25 May 2000, the Court dismissed her application without reasons.[31]

I turn now to a consideration of some principal examples of how British Columbia law does, or does not, recognise same-sex partnerships.

Employment benefits

As indicated above, British Columbia's Human Rights Code prohibits discrimination on the basis of sexual orientation in both public and private sector employment. Court decisions in the early to mid-1990s interpreted the meaning of "discrimination on the basis of sexual orientation" in both employment-related and non-employment-related fact situations.[32] As a result of these decisions, employers and labour arbitrators became increasingly convinced that failure by an employer to provide the same employment benefits to its employees' same-sex partners and their families, as were provided to its employees' opposite-sex partners and their families, constituted "discrimination on the basis of sexual orientation." Therefore, many public and private sector employers in British Columbia began to provide the same benefits to their employees' same-sex partners and their families as they provided to their employees' opposite-sex partners and families. In particular, the British Columbia government, as an employer, has extended equal employment benefits to its employees' same-sex partners and their families. Trade unions deserve credit for having been particularly instrumental in working toward amendment of collective agreements to provide equal employment benefits to their lesbian and gay members.

The trend in British Columbia, and in Canada generally, is toward extending employment benefits to employees' same-sex partners and their families. Indeed, the decision of the Supreme Court of Canada in *M.* v. *H.*, while on its facts not involving employment benefits, has in my opinion certainly made it clear that comprehensive provision of equal employment benefits will ultimately be legally required. In British Columbia, certain benefits, namely, medical

[30] See Lahey, chap. 12.

[31] See <http://www.lexum.umontreal.ca/csc-scc/en/bul/2000/html/00–05–26.bul.html> (Rehearing)(No. 25838).

[32] Very important decisions in this regard were, *Haig* v. *Canada* (1992), 94 D.L.R.(4th) 1 (Ontario Court of Appeal), and *Egan* v. *Canada*, *supra* n.19. *Egan* did not involve an employment-related claim, but rather federal social security benefits.

services coverage and pensions, are already comprehensively dealt with in legislation, as will be seen below.

Pensions

In 1998, the definition of "spouse" in British Columbia's legislation regulating public sector pension plans was amended to include same-sex partners.[33] This legislation regulated the pension plans of members of the Legislative Assembly, college instructors, municipal workers, members of the provincial public service, and teachers. In enacting this legislation, the British Columbia government was responding to the 23 April 1998 decision of the Ontario Court of Appeal in *Rosenberg* v. *Canada (Attorney-General)*.[34] The Court had held that the definition of "spouse" in the federal Income Tax Act,[35] which applied to registration of pension plans for income tax purposes and was limited to opposite-sex partners, was unconstitutional and ordered that a reference to same-sex partners be "read into" the definition. On 22 June 1998, the last possible day for the federal government to decide whether to seek leave to appeal *Rosenberg* to the Supreme Court of Canada, it announced that it was accepting the decision of the Ontario Court of Appeal and would not seek leave to appeal. Meanwhile, the British Columbia government had already proceeded to amend the public sector pension plans legislation and the amending legislation came into force on 30 July 1998. British Columbia thus became the first jurisdiction in Canada to comprehensively amend its public sector pension legislation to provide that same-sex partners were eligible to receive spousal pension benefits.

In 1999, the British Columbia Legislature enacted legislation which similarly included same-sex partners in the definition of "spouse" in all private pension plans in which an employer contributes to employee pension funds.[36] Thus, if an employer contributes to funds in support of any spousal pension benefits provided to its employees, it must include same-sex partners in the definition of "spouse". The only alternative is to provide no spousal pension benefits at all to employees, an alternative which is hardly realistic in British Columbia's current employment benefits context. In a News Release dated 2 June 1999, the Minister

[33] Pension Statutes Amendment Act (No. 2), 1998, Statutes of B.C. 1998, ch. 40, amending: Legislative Assembly Allowances and Pension Act, Revised Statutes of B.C. 1996, c. 257, s. 1; Pension (College) Act, R.S.B.C. 1996, c. 353, s. 1; Pension (Municipal) Act, R.S.B.C. 1996, c. 355, s. 1; Pension (Public Service) Act, R.S.B.C. 1996, c. 356, s. 1; Pension (Teachers) Act, R.S.B.C. 1996, c. 357, s. 1. The latter four statutes were subsequently repealed and replaced by the Public Sector Pension Plans Act, S.B.C. 1999, c. 44, which in turn was subsequently amended by the Definition of Spouse Amendment Act, 2000, S.B.C. 2000, c. 24.

[34] (1998), 158 D.L.R.(4th) 664 (Ontario Court of Appeal).

[35] Revised Statutes of Canada 1985 (5th Supplement), ch. 1, s. 252(4).

[36] Pension Benefits Standards Amendment Act, 1999, Statutes of B.C. 1999, ch. 41, amending Pension Benefits Standards Act, Revised S.B.C. 1996, c. 352, which was subsequently amended by Definition of Spouse Amendment Act, 2000, S.B.C. 2000, c. 24.

of Labour indicated that this change would apply to more than 1,000 pension plans registered with the British Columbia Superintendent of Pensions.[37]

Social assistance

British Columbia legislation provides that a person's eligibility for social assistance is determined not only by their own financial situation, but also by that of their "dependants" and "families".[38] In practice, those administering social assistance take into account the financial situation of an applicant's "household". The legislation does not recognise same-sex partners as "spouses". However, pursuant to administrative policy, persons who live together in a "marriage-like relationship" are treated as "spouses". In particular, persons who self-identify as same-sex partners living in a "marriage-like relationship" will be treated as spouses and, therefore, members of the same "household" for social assistance purposes.[39] This is an example of a situation in which recognition of same-sex partnerships may work against the financial self-interest of same-sex partners.

Medical services coverage

In 1991, shortly before the NDP government was elected, the British Columbia Supreme Court held in *Knodel* v. *British Columbia*[40] that the omission of same-sex partners in the definition of "spouse" in medical services legislation violated the Charter. (The former Social Credit government had defended the restrictive definition of "spouse" which excluded same-sex partners.) The Court ordered that same-sex partners be included in the definition of "spouse". This was the first court decision anywhere in Canada requiring a statutory definition of "spouse" to include same-sex partners. The NDP government did not appeal from this decision and amended the medical services legislation accordingly.[41]

[37] Province of British Columbia, Ministry of Labour, *News Release re Bill 58, 2 June 1999, Spousal Pension Change Shows Commitment to Equity.*

[38] B.C. Benefits (Appeals) Act, Revised Statutes of B.C. 1996, chapter 25; B.C. Benefits (Child Care) Act, R.S.B.C. 1996, c. 26; B.C. Benefits (Income Assistance) Act, R.S.B.C. 1996, c. 27; B.C. Benefits (Youth Works) Act, R.S.B.C. 1996, c. 28; Disability Benefits Program Act, R.S.B.C. 1996, c. 97.

[39] Information provided to author by persons working in the administration of the British Columbia benefits program.

[40] (1991), 58 B.C.L.R.(2d) 356 (British Columbia Supreme Court).

[41] Medical and Health Care Services Act, Statutes of B.C. 1992, ch. 76, s. 1 (now the Medicare Protection Act, *supra* n.24).

Hospital visitation, treatment decisions, advance directives concerning health and personal care

Pursuant to legislation enacted in 1993 and in force since February 2000, a person is able to make treatment decisions on behalf of their incapacitated same-sex partner.[42] Similarly, a person may appoint their same-sex partner as their proxy to make decisions concerning their personal or health care in the event they become incapacitated.[43]

Partnership breakdown: custody of and access to children, child support, partner support, property and pension division, domestic contracts

British Columbia's statutory family relations law is set out, primarily, in the Family Relations Act and the Family Maintenance Enforcement Act.[44] In legislation enacted in 1997 and proclaimed in force in 1998, the British Columbia Legislature amended these Acts to include same-sex partners in their definitions of "spouse".[45] British Columbia thus became the first province to amend its family relations legislation to include same-sex partners in the definition of "spouse". Interestingly, even though both statutes were amended at the same time, the Legislature amended the definition of "spouse" in the Family Maintenance Enforcement Act using the formula which contemplated same-sex marriage, whereas the definition of "spouse" in the Family Relations Act was limited to marriage-like relationships. (As already noted above, the definition of "spouse" in the Family Maintenance Enforcement Act was subsequently amended in 2000 and is now limited to referring to "marriage-like relationships".) In enacting these inclusive definitions of "spouse," the British Columbia Legislature was responding to the 18 December 1996 decision of the Ontario Court of Appeal in *M. v. H.*,[46] which had held that the definition of "spouse" in Ontario's Family Law Act with respect to partner support was unconstitutional, since it included unmarried opposite-sex partners but not same-sex partners. As noted above, that decision was subsequently affirmed by the Supreme Court of Canada.

[42] Health Care (Consent) and Care Facility (Admission) Act, Revised Statutes of B.C. 1996, chapter 181, originally enacted as S.B.C. 1993, c. 48 (in force 28 Feb. 2000), and subsequently amended by Definition of Spouse Amendment Act, 2000, S.B.C. 2000, c. 24.

[43] Representation Agreement Act, Revised Statutes of B.C. 1996, ch. 405, originally enacted as S.B.C. 1993, c. 67 (in force 28 Feb. 2000), and subsequently amended by Definition of Spouse Amendment Act, 2000, S.B.C. 2000, c. 24. The delay in proclaiming this legislation (and the consent Act, *ibid.*) in force was for reasons unrelated to recognition of same-sex partnerships.

[44] Family Relations Act, *supra* n.25; Family Maintenance Enforcement Act, Revised Statutes of B.C. 1996, ch. 127, as amended by Definition of Spouse Amendment Act, 2000, S.B.C. 2000, c. 24.

[45] Family Relations Amendment Act, 1997, *supra* n.25; Family Maintenance Enforcement Amendment Act, 1997, Statutes of B.C. 1997, ch. 19.

[46] (1996), 142 D.L.R.(4th) 1, affirmed by Supreme Court of Canada, *supra* n.1.

The following are some key aspects of British Columbia family relations law. With respect to custody of and access to children, child support, and partner support, same-sex partners have access to the same judicial remedies as married or unmarried opposite-sex partners. With respect to property or pension division, on the other hand, the situation is somewhat more complex. The starting point is that the provisions of the Family Relations Act concerning property and pension division apply only to married spouses. Thus, neither same-sex partners (who cannot marry) nor unmarried opposite-sex partners have access to the remedies provided for in the Act concerning property and pension division. However, the Act further provides that "spouses" who are not married may agree that the provisions of the Act governing property and pension division apply to them.[47] Same-sex partners who have lived together for two years in a "marriage-like relationship" are "spouses" under the Act and, therefore, may enter into such an agreement, which is then judicially enforceable. The Legislature obviously thought that, while certain relationship-dependent rights and obligations should flow automatically from living in a "marriage-like relationship" (such as custody, access and support rights and obligations), access to remedies concerning property and pension division should not apply, unless the parties to the marriage-like relationship (whether same-sex or opposite-sex) specifically agree that that should be the case.

Even in the absence of a property and pension division agreement, however, all is not lost for a former same-sex partner who is left in a financially disadvantaged position after separating from their partner, and who claims a division of property against them. They may claim the common law judicial remedy of a constructive trust. Indeed, a 1986 decision of the British Columbia Supreme Court, *Anderson* v. *Luoma*,[48] was the first reported Canadian case in which a constructive trust was imposed on a former same-sex partner.

I make two final comments. First, even before British Columbia's family relations legislation was amended specifically to provide for domestic contracts between same-sex partners, the British Columbia Supreme Court had held that, at common law, such a contract was judicially enforceable.[49] Indeed, the 1991 decision of the British Columbia Supreme Court in *Sleeth* v. *Wasserlein*,[50] in which the court enforced a separation agreement settling the financial affairs of a lesbian couple, was the first Canadian case in which a domestic contract between same-sex partners was judicially enforced.

Second, while division of property agreements between same-sex partners were enforceable at common law, the statutory provisions concerning such agreements facilitate making and enforcing them. For example, enforcing a contract for support at common law was exceedingly difficult, if not impossible. In

[47] Family Relations Act, *supra* n. 25, s. 120.1.

[48] (1986), 50 R.F.L.(2d) 127 (B.C. Supreme Court); see, also, *Forrest* v. *Price* (1992), 48 E.T.R. 72 (B.C.S.C.).

[49] *Anderson, ibid.*; *Sleeth* v. *Wasserlein* (1991), 36 R.F.L.(3d) 278 (B.C.S.C.).

[50] *Ibid.*

particular, a court might not specifically enforce a contract under which one party was bound to make continuous payments to another, since that would require constant supervision by the court.[51]

Adoption

The British Columbia Adoption Act provides that a child may be adopted by "one adult alone or two adults jointly".[52] Thus, joint adoption of an unrelated child by same-sex partners is permitted. The Act further provides that an adult "may apply . . . to jointly become a parent of a child with a birth parent of the child".[53] "Birth parent" is defined as a "birth mother" or "birth father", which in turn are defined as a child's "biological mother" or "biological father". "Biological mother" and "biological father" are not defined. The Act thus clearly allows for step-parent (or "second-parent") adoptions of a same-sex partner's child, except in two situations.

First, given the array of reproductive technologies now available, determining who are a child's "biological mother" and "biological father" might be problematic in some cases. For example, if A's egg was fertilised *ex utero* using B's sperm, the fertilised egg was put into C's womb and there grew into D, and C gave birth to D, how many "biological" parents would D have? In particular, would C be a "biological mother" of D, presumably together with A? Or would she be a legal mother of D, albeit not a "biological mother"? Or would she simply be a legal "stranger" *vis-à-vis* D? In other situations, however, determining who was a "biological mother" or "biological father" would not be difficult. For example, a woman—whether lesbian or heterosexual—who secured fertilisation of her own egg, through insemination or otherwise, and then gave birth herself would clearly be a "birth parent", as would a man—whether gay or heterosexual—who provided sperm for fertilisation.

Second, a situation far more likely to cause practical difficulty, a parent's partner—whether a married spouse, an unmarried opposite-sex partner, or a same-sex partner—cannot adopt their partner's child if their partner became the child's parent through adoption. This treatment of adoptive parents, their children and their partners seems to invite Charter challenge.

The amendments to the Adoption Act to permit joint adoption of a child by same-sex partners, and most step-parent adoptions by same-sex partners, were enacted in 1995 and came into force in 1996. British Columbia thus became the

[51] See *Anderson* v. *Luoma* (1984), 14 D.L.R.(4th) 749 (B.C.S.C.) (report of application for interim support, as distinguished from reasons for judgment at trial, cited *supra* n.48); in *M.* v. *H.*, *supra* n.1, at paras. 119–124, Justice Iacobucci explained more generally why both the law of contract, and equitable common law remedies such as a constructive trust, are unacceptable alternatives to spousal support obligations under family relations legislation.

[52] Revised Statutes of B.C. 1996, ch. 5, ss. 5, 29, originally enacted by Adoption Act, S.B.C. 1995, c. 48, ss. 5, 29.

[53] *Ibid.*, s. 29.

second province, after Québec,[54] to amend its adoption legislation effectively to permit such adoptions. In enacting this legislation, the British Columbia Legislature was responding to the 24 May 1995 decision of the Ontario Provincial Court in *Re K. & B.*,[55] which had held that the provisions of Ontario's adoption legislation which restricted step-parent adoption to opposite-sex partners[56] were unconstitutional, and ordered that same-sex partners be "read into" the legislation's definition of "spouse".

Access to alternative insemination treatment

In 1995, the British Columbia Human Rights Council (now the Human Rights Commission) held that a lesbian couple, who had been refused alternative insemination treatment by a physician because they were lesbians, had been discriminated against on the basis of sexual orientation in violation of the British Columbia Human Rights Act (now the Human Rights Code). The Council reasoned that the prohibition against discrimination on the basis of sexual orientation with respect to access to services customarily available to the public, afforded same-sex partners the same access to alternative insemination treatment as afforded opposite-sex partners. In 1996, the British Columbia Supreme Court affirmed this decision.[57]

Wills and estates

Under British Columbia law, a person has always been able to appoint their same-sex partner as their executor under their will and to designate their partner as a beneficiary under their will. This was, however, certainly not a manifestation of same-sex partnership recognition, since a person could appoint any legal "stranger" as their executor or beneficiary.

Until very recently, on an intestacy, a same-sex partner was not recognised as a spouse, or indeed any other family member, of their deceased partner. They were not, therefore, entitled to inherit any of their deceased partner's estate. In 1999, the British Columbia Legislature amended British Columbia's estates administration legislation to include same-sex partners in the definition of "spouse". [58] Therefore, on an intestacy, a same-sex partner inherits the statutorily specified spouse's portion of their deceased partner's estate.

[54] See Québec Civil Code, article 546, Statutes of Québec 1991, ch. 64 (in force on 1 Jan. 1994).

[55] (1995), 125 D.L.R.(4th) 653.

[56] Child and Family Services Act, Revised Statutes of Ontario 1990, ch. C.11, ss. 136(1), 146(4).

[57] *Potter* v. *Korn* (1995), 23 C.H.R.R. D/319 (B.C. Human Rights Council), application for judicial review dismissed, *Korn* v. *Potter* (1996), 134 D.L.R.(4th) 437 (B.C. Supreme Court).

[58] Estate Administration Act, Revised Statutes of B.C. 1996, ch. 122, as amended by Definition of Spouse Amendment Act, 1999, S.B.C. 1999, c. 29, s. 4, which was repealed and replaced by Definition of Spouse Amendment Act, 2000, S.B.C. 2000, c. 24, s. 11.

Similarly, until very recently, a same-sex partner who had been financially dependent upon their partner, but who was inadequately provided for in their partner's will or indeed not provided for at all, did not have access to the statutory remedies providing for the variation of wills ("dependant's relief"), in situations in which a spouse or child who had been financially dependent upon a deceased was not adequately provided for in the deceased's will. In 1999, the British Columbia Legislature amended British Columbia's wills variation legislation to include same-sex partners in the definition of "spouse".[59] Therefore, a same-sex partner who was financially dependent upon their deceased partner, and who was not adequately provided for in their partner's will, may apply for judicial variation of the will to make adequate provision for them.

Marriage

British Columbia's Marriage Act refers to "persons intending to marry" and is not on its face limited to opposite-sex partners.[60] However, court decisions have held that, at common law, marriage is limited to opposite-sex partners, and further that the common-law limitation does not violate the Charter.[61] It is important to emphasise that these were lower court decisions only—no provincial Court of Appeal nor the Supreme Court of Canada has yet considered a claim by same-sex partners to the right to marry.

In 2000, the federal Parliament affirmed the common-law limitation of marriage to opposite-sex partners. The Modernization of Benefits and Obligations Act, the federal omnibus legislation enacted to recognise same-sex partnerships, defined "marriage" as "the lawful union of one man and one woman to the exclusion of all others".[62] Most of the Modernization of Benefits and Obligations Act, including the definition of "marriage", came into force on 31 July 2000, and other provisions of the Act came into force in stages in 2001. This definition of "marriage" is clearly *intra vires* the federal Parliament, since it deals with capacity to marry. However, it may still be unconstitutional and of

[59] Wills Variation Act, Revised Statutes of B.C. 1996, ch. 490, as amended by Definition of Spouse Amendment Act, 1999, S.B.C. 1999, c. 29, s. 17, which was repealed and replaced by Definition of Spouse Amendment Act, 2000, S.B.C. 2000, c. 24, s. 13. See also *Grigg* v. *Berg Estate*, [2000] B.C.J. No. 36 (B.C. Supreme Court, 11 Jan. 2000, original reasons for judgment), [2000] B.C.J. No. 1080 (B.C.S.C., 31 May 2000, supplementary reasons for judgment), which held, before the amendment to the Wills Variation Act came into force, and applying the Supreme Court of Canada's reasoning in *M.* v. *H.*, that omission of same-sex partners and unmarried opposite-sex partners in the Wills Variation Act was unconstitutional. The court ordered that the extended definition of "spouse" then contained in the Definition of Spouse Amendment Act, 1999 be read into the Wills Variation Act, but suspended its declaration for one month to give the government an opportunity itself to bring the extended definition into force.

[60] Revised Statutes of B.C. 1996, ch. 282, s. 16.

[61] *North* v. *Matheson* (1974), 52 D.L.R.(3d) 280 (Manitoba County Court); *Layland* v. *Ontario (Minister of Consumer and Commercial Relations)* (1993), 104 D.L.R.(4th) 214 (Ontario Divisional Court).

[62] Modernization of Benefits and Obligations Act, *supra* n.4, s. 1.1.

no force or effect if a court—and, ultimately, the Supreme Court of Canada—determines, first, that it violates the Charter's guarantee of equality and, second, that the violation cannot be justified under section 1 of the Charter. The federal "one man and one woman" definition of "marriage" now affirms the common-law exclusion of lesbians and gay men from marriage. It is important to emphasise that Parliament did not invoke section 33 of the Charter in enacting this restrictive definition of "marriage".

By far the most important news in 2000 on the "marriage front" occurred, however, in British Columbia. On 20 July 2000, the British Columbia government filed a petition in the Supreme Court of British Columbia seeking a declaration that the limitation of marriage to same-sex partners violated the Charter, could not be justified, and was of no force or effect.[63] Essentially, British Columbia wants court authorisation to start issuing marriage licences to same-sex partners under the provincial Marriage Act. British Columbia's support for same-sex marriage is truly historic. The federal government has responded in support of the common-law exclusion.

BRITISH COLUMBIA LAW INSTITUTE'S RECOMMENDATIONS

As indicated above, the Supreme Court of Canada delivered its decision in *M.* v. *H.* on 20 May 1999. Later the same day, the British Columbia government announced that it would introduce omnibus legislation to amend all British Columbia statutes to recognise same-sex partners in the same way as unmarried opposite-sex partners.

A template for such omnibus amending legislation was already in place. Following upon the 1997 amendments to British Columbia's family relations legislation, referred to above, the British Columbia government asked the British Columbia Law Institute, an independent law research and reform body, to review British Columbia's statute law and to make recommendations concerning changes necessary to recognise "non-traditional family relationships", including same-sex partnerships. On 19 March 1999, the Institute issued its *Report on Recognition of Spousal and Family Status*.[64] The Institute comprehensively reviewed all provisions in British Columbia legislation denoting a spousal or family relationship. Full consideration of the Institute's recommendations is beyond the scope of this chapter. I will only very briefly summarise two of the Institute's recommendations which have particular salience for present purposes.

[63] See, eg, "B.C. wants to legalize same-sex marriages", *Vancouver Sun* (21 July 2000). See also *Peter Cook & Murray Warren* v. *B.C. (Ministry of Health)*, Case No. 2000234 (B.C. Human Rights Commission, filed 17 July 2000) (B.C. Human Rights Code challenge to refusal to issue marriage license).

[64] See <http://www.bcli.org/pages/projects/rrsfs/contents.html>.

First, the Institute recommended enactment of a Domestic Partner Act, under which any two adults could register a "domestic partner declaration" stating that they were "domestic partners". In particular, same-sex partners could register as domestic partners. Under the Act, domestic partners would have the same legal status, rights and obligations as married spouses. While the provisions of the Act as recommended by the Institute would obviously be available to people living in marriage-like relationships, the Act would not, however, be restricted to people living in such relationships. The Institute said that, in its opinion, domestic partnership legislation would fall within the province's constitutional jurisdiction with respect to "property and civil rights in the province".

Second, the Institute recommended amendments to 88 British Columbia statutes to, among other purposes, recognise same-sex partners living in marriage-like relationships in the same way as unmarried opposite-sex partners living in marriage-like relationships. In this regard, the Institute recommended an extended definition of "spouse" which did not include reference to the possibility of "marriage" between same-sex partners. However, the amendments would allow for recognition of a same-sex marriage recognised in another country, state or province. The Institute's *Report* specifically set out precise recommended wording for amendments to all 88 statutes in draft Bill form.

If the Institute's recommendations concerning enactment of a Domestic Partner Act and omnibus amending legislation were followed, British Columbia family relations law would recognise three forms of personal partnership, namely:

1. "married spouses", a status limited under marriage law to opposite-sex partners;
2. "domestic partners", who would have the same legal status, rights and obligations as married spouses, and who could be same-sex partners, opposite-sex partners, or any other two persons; and,
3. persons recognised in certain situations as "spouses" because, as a matter of fact rather than formal agreement, they live in a marriage-like relationship, who may be same-sex partners or opposite-sex partners and who would have many, but not all, of the rights and obligations of married spouses and domestic partners; in particular, significant differences with respect to division of property would continue, on the reasoning that partners who live in a marriage-like relationship but who have not married or registered as domestic partners have not made a voluntary commitment sufficient to justify the application of the division of property rules applicable to married spouses and domestic partners.

The obvious and fatal flaw in this organisation of personal relationships is the acceptance and perpetuation of heterosexual privilege fundamentally inherent in preserving "married spouse" status as an option available only to opposite-sex partners. As indicated, British Columbia has enacted omnibus legislation to recognise same-sex partnerships, albeit not as comprehensively as the Institute had recommended. On the other hand, I submit that the British Columbia government was right in not enacting domestic partnership legislation along the lines suggested by the Institute, and instead choosing courageously to challenge the limitation of marriage to opposite-sex partners.

THE ULTIMATE PARTNERSHIP RECOGNITION GOAL FOR LESBIANS AND GAY MEN: SAME-SEX MARRIAGE

In *M.* v. *H.*, Justice Cory. emphasised that the case "ha[d] nothing to do with marriage *per se*" and, in particular, that "there [was] no need to consider whether same-sex couples can marry".[65] Similarly, Justice Iacobucci stated: "I wish to emphasize . . . that . . . [t]his appeal does not challenge traditional conceptions of marriage".[66] These clear statements were insufficient to allay the worst fears of some homophobes. For example, in the federal House of Commons, the opposition Reform Party (now the Canadian Alliance Party) said that they were worried that the Liberal government might be planning to legally recognise same-sex marriage. The opposition forced debate on a resolution stating that "marriage is and should remain the union of one man and one woman to the exclusion of all others, and that Parliament will take all necessary steps . . . to preserve this definition of marriage in Canada". On 8 June 1999, with government support, the House of Commons adopted this resolution by a vote of 216 to 55. It is important to emphasise that this resolution, while symbolically important, had no legal effect. The next day, however, a survey was released indicating that 53 per cent of Canadians favoured extending legal marriage to same-sex partners.[67] (In British Columbia, 54 per cent supported same-sex marriage, while in Québec, the figure was 61 per cent.) Canadians are clearly more enlightened on this issue than our politicians. As already indicated, in 2000, the Canadian Alliance opposition, again with government support, ultimately succeeded in having a "one man and one woman" definition of marriage written into federal legislation. However, significantly, Parliament did not "take all necessary steps . . . to preserve this definition of marriage in Canada", since it chose not to invoke section 33 of the Charter.

The Canadian Alliance opposition's response to *M.* v. *H.* came as no surprise. Marriage is the inner sanctum of heterosexual privilege. As lesbian and gay equality claims move closer to that inner sanctum, homophobes become increasingly threatened. However, same-sex marriage is the ultimate goal necessary to achieve equal recognition of same-sex partnerships. As long as lesbians

[65] *M.* v. *H.*, *supra* n.1, at paras. 52, 55.

[66] *Ibid.*, at para. 134.

[67] Angus Reid Group survey for The Globe and Mail and CTV, conducted between 25 May and 30 May 1999, that is, shortly after the Supreme Court of Canada's decision in *M.* v. *H.* See *Globe and Mail*, 10 June 1999, A1.

and gay men are excluded from statutorily-recognised marriage, we are effectively told by our governments that we are not as worthy of state recognition as our fellow citizens who happen to be heterosexual. Of course, some lesbians and gay men regard marriage as an oppressive institution, particularly for women, based on sexism and heterosexism, and have absolutely no desire to claim access to it. (Many heterosexuals share this view.) Further, access to marriage does not involve the same financial and other urgency as did access to pensions, adoption, estates law, and a whole host of other forms of same-sex partnership recognition, considered above. However, some lesbians and gay men do want to marry, and others at least want the right to choose whether or not to marry.

British Columbia's challenge to the limitation of marriage to opposite-sex partners may take five to seven years ultimately to be determined by the Supreme Court of Canada. In my opinion, there is no doubt that the Court will hold that limiting marriage to opposite-sex partners constitutes discrimination on the basis of sexual orientation in violation of section 15 of the Charter, and that the violation cannot be justified under section 1. In the meantime, it must be emphasised that domestic partnership legislation, such as the Domestic Partner Act recommended by the British Columbia Law Institute, while certainly meritorious in intent, is not sufficient to achieve full partnership recognition equality for lesbian and gay people with heterosexuals as long as we are denied access to marriage. In my opinion, the British Columbia government should be lauded for boldly challenging the limitation of marriage to opposite-sex partners, rather than choosing the more timid option of enacting domestic partnership legislation while same-sex partners remained excluded from the option of marrying.

Alternatively, however, pending a determination of the constitutionality of excluding same-sex partners from marriage, if the British Columbia government really aims to rid the province of legislation which perpetuates discrimination against lesbian and gay people, it could repeal British Columbia's Marriage Act and replace it with domestic partnership legislation that applies equally to both same-sex and opposite-sex partners. Marriage could then be dealt with solely by religious and other groups who would be free to determine whether they recognise only same-sex marriages, only opposite-sex marriages, or both. The obvious political difficulty for the government in repealing the Marriage Act would be that it would clearly be seen to be taking away the most visible and highly prized manifestation of government-sanctioned heterosexual privilege. Daring to do that in order to achieve partnership recognition equality for lesbian and gay people would take real courage indeed, and is probably not a politically realistic option, even for a government as courageous as British Columbia's.

CONCLUSION

As I have indicated, British Columbia has been the undisputed leader in Canada in recognising same-sex partnerships. While legal developments in 1999 and early 2000 briefly challenged that leadership position, British Columbia is once again at the forefront, this time by challenging the last legal refuge of heterosexual privilege, namely, the limitation of marriage to opposite-sex partners.

If, as I believe, the Supreme Court of Canada ultimately determines that limiting marriage to opposite-sex partners is unconstitutional, then the federal and provincial governments would be forced to co-operate to decide whether to statutorily recognise same-sex marriage, get out of the marriage business altogether, or preserve heterosexual privilege by invoking section 33 of the Charter. Perhaps by the time these decisions are necessary, public support for same-sex marriage will have risen above 1999's 53 per cent level, thus enabling other governments to join with British Columbia's in doing the constitutionally right thing and recognizing same-sex marriage.

In the meantime, Canadian lesbians and gay men can take heart in British Columbia's leadership in recognising our personal relationships and, therefore, us. After all, British Columbia *is* Canada's Lotusland!

POSTSCRIPT

Even in Lotusland, occasional setbacks on the road to equality for lesbians and gay men can happen. On 16 July 2001, British Columbia's newly elected Liberal government withdrew the province's court petition supporting same-sex marriage.[68] However, the British Columbia Supreme Court hearing of two similar petitions commenced on 23 July 2001.[69]

[68] "B.C. quits same-sex challenge . . .", *Vancouver Sun* (17 July 2001).

[69] "Same-sex couples launch court action", *Vancouver Sun* (24 July 2001). See Lahey, chap. 12, n.21; DG Casswell, "Moving Toward Same-Sex Marriage", (2001) *Canadian Bar Review* (forthcoming).

12

Becoming "Persons" in Canadian Law: Genuine Equality or "Separate But Equal"?

KATHLEEN A LAHEY*

INTRODUCTION

CANADIAN PARTICIPANTS ARRIVED at the King's College conference on queer relationships in July 1999 in a state of elation over the remarkable breakthroughs in the legal status of lesbian and gay relationships in Canada that had taken place over the preceding year. After more than two decades of judicial and legislative intransigence, litigation launched under the Canadian Charter of Rights and Freedoms had resulted in numerous pivotal rulings that had extended Charter equality guarantees to lesbian women and gay men. They were particularly heartened by the 20 May 1999 decision of the Supreme Court of Canada in *M.* v. *H.*[1], in which the Court had resoundingly declared that excluding lesbian and gay couples from a legislative definition of "spouse" that included cohabitants of the "opposite sex" unjustifiably violates the equality guarantees of the Charter.

Canadian queers are considerably more subdued now. Amidst the rapid legislative changes generated by these judicial decisions, what could be described as reactionism has now set in. Each jurisdiction that has purported to codify these court rulings by passing comprehensive legislation relating to lesbian and gay couples has actually introduced new segregated legal categories for queer couples as they have recognised them. At the same time, these new statutes have invariably left some important legal issues unresolved.

Three trends in the overall legal status of lesbian and gay couples have converged to produce this result. First, there is a very strong trend toward

* Professor, Faculty of Law, Queen's University, Kingston, Ontario. I would like to thank the British Columbia Foundation for Legal Research for the research funding that made this study possible. For more detailed information on the constitutional and fiscal implications of federal relationship recognition legislation (Bill C-23), see "The Impact of Relationship Recognition on Lesbian Women in Canada: Still Separate and Only Somewhat 'Equivalent' ", to be published in 2001 by Status of Women Canada http://www.swc-cfc.gc.ca.

[1] [1999] 2 S.C.R. 3 (S.C.R. available at http://www.lexum.umontreal.ca/csc-scc/en/index.html).

increasing judicial recognition of lesbian women and gay men as full "persons" in Canadian law. Both the *M.* v. *H.* decision of 1999 and the *Vriend* v. *Alberta*[2] decision of 1998 eradicated key legal incapacities that had been imposed on lesbian women and gay men by virtue of their sexuality. *M.* v. *H.* established that lesbian and gay couples cannot be excluded from the category of common-law spouses, and *Vriend* established that lesbian women and gay men cannot be denied the protection of anti-discrimination provisions in human rights legislation on the basis of their sexuality. The Supreme Court of Canada adopted the language of constitutional personhood in concluding that such legal incapacities violate the equality provisions of the Canadian Charter of Rights and Freedoms, and this trend can also be discerned in numerous lower court decisions.

Second, inclusion of lesbian and gay couples in the category of "opposite-sex cohabitants" or common-law spouses has ignited vocal opposition to the possibility that marriage rights might be extended to queers. Unlike the United States, where cohabitants have few if any legal rights or obligations, recognition of common-law spouses has grown by leaps and bounds in Canada since 1974, with the result that, in many jurisdictions, they have many of the same rights and obligations as those historically assigned only to married couples. However, even in Canada, non-married cohabitants do not have the same property rights as those enjoyed by married couples (rights in the family home, forced shares of net family property, inheritance rights, dependent's relief). Inclusion of lesbian and gay couples in the category of common-law spouses has not had any effect on the denial of those incidents of marriage to lesbian and gay couples. And unlike heterosexual couples, lesbian and gay couples cannot gain access to those property rights by choosing to get married.

The third trend that can be seen in Canada in the last few years is the growing gap between the nature of judicial orders in discrimination cases and the nature of legislative remedies. Whereas courts have tended to extend full equality to lesbian and gay couples, legislatures that have addressed relationship issues have tended to extend only partial equality to lesbian and gay couples. This has been done either by creating new segregated classes of relationships, or by extending only some relationship rights to lesbian and gay couples, or both. Some legislative schemes are more inclusive than others, but no jurisdiction has fully extended all the rights and obligations of non-married cohabitants to lesbian and gay couples, nor has any jurisdiction extended any of the core incidents of marriage to either heterosexual or queer cohabitants.

In addition to judicial decisions, I will discuss in detail four of the five Canadian jurisdictions that have developed statutory schemes partially recognising lesbian and gay couples: Ontario, Québec, Canada, and Nova Scotia.[3] My contention in this chapter is that only if the *courts* in Canada are left to give expression to the full concept of constitutional personhood, is it likely that les-

[2] [1998] 1 S.C.R. 493.
[3] For a detailed discussion of British Columbia, see Casswell, chap. 11.

bian and gay couples will attain full and genuine equality under the Charter of Rights. The more the provincial and federal *legislatures* have intruded into this area of law, the more partial and discriminatory relationship recognition has become. Perhaps because this new generation of legislation springs from continuing reluctance to extend genuine equality to lesbian and gay couples, it has come to resemble the racist "civil rights" legislation passed by southern United States in the mid-1800s, and the European registered partnership statutes passed in the 1980s and 1990s.

CONSTITUTIONAL PERSONHOOD

"Person" is one of the most basic categories of legal functioning in Euro-Canadian discourse. Indeed, the pivotal role of the *"Persons" Case*[4] in identifying the directions for constitutional, human rights, and other law in Canada reveals that the concept of "person" is absolutely basic to any notion of equality, human dignity, or full legal capacity in North American jurisprudence.

The legal history of the concept of "person" confirms this primacy. The law of persons crystallised in Roman civil law, where it was used to maintain hierarchies of privilege. "Citizens" of the Roman state were considered to have all the powers to act that could be recognised in law: they could sue and be sued; they could act as witness and juror in legal proceedings; they could enter the state and demand to remain there; they enjoyed protection from violence and the rights of free movement and political expression; they could vote, hold public office, and access public services; and they enjoyed all the private law rights of contract, property ownership, marriage, and custody of children.

During the first millennium C.E. of European history, these classical incidents of legal personality were exported and deployed to maintain hierarchies of privilege. Beginning with the Visigothic Code (c. 450 C.E.), the incidents of legal personality were suspended for Jewish persons who refused to convert to Christianity, and, at around the same time, "sodomy" was criminalised. During the second millennium C.E., legal capacity was manipulated in similar ways: in English law relating to minors, incompetent persons, Jewish persons, and married women; in North American law in the slave codes and "Black codes" of the southern states, and in laws relating to Aboriginal persons, immigrant Chinese workers, and Japanese internment; in German laws of the Third Reich relating to Jewish persons, other ethnic minorities, and sexual minorities; and in South African apartheid laws.

During the last 150 years, constitutional, international, and domestic legal instruments have been devised to block such political abuses of legal capacity, and were initially intended to restore full legal capacity to members of such

[4] *Reference as to the meaning of the word "persons" in section 24 of the British North America Act, 1867*, [1928] S.C.R. 276, reversed by *Edwards* v. *A.G. Canada*, [1930] A.C. 124 (Privy Council) (*"Persons" Case*).

disadvantaged groups by invalidating incapacitating laws. Constitutional "equality" as initially guaranteed in the Fourteenth Amendment to the United States Constitution had two specific purposes: to render invalid legislative classifications that negatived the legal capacities of former slaves, and to protect federal programs designed to ameliorate the conditions of freed slaves from charges that they were constitutionally invalid.[5] While the focus of such provisions may appear to have shifted to the protection of "human dignity" in the last fifty years, the subject-matter of twentieth-century anti-discrimination statutes closely tracks the original US civil rights statutes of the 1860s that gave rise to the Fourteenth Amendment: both types of provisions were intended to secure the basic elements of legal status, and to ensure access to the necessities of life, in order to protect unpopular minorities from discrimination.[6]

I think of constitutional personhood as encompassing those incidents of legal personality that members of disadvantaged groups must obtain if they are to be able to compete for genuine substantive equality, without being artificially encumbered or disadvantaged in that competition. Constitutional personhood is, in a sense, the ultimate jurisprudential measuring stick, against which groups such as sexual minorities can assess their ability to deal with the very real and pervasive effects of social prejudice in everyday life.

BEFORE THE CHARTER OF RIGHTS

Until the Charter of Rights began to exert some influence on the legal status of Canadian sexual minorities in the mid-1980s, lesbians and gays had only partial legal personality, and the legal capacities of transgendered and transsexual people were denied, except to the extent that they were able to meet strict statutory requirements relating to "sex change" surgery and identity. One of the presumptions used to maintain the disadvantaged status of sexual minorities in the jurisprudence of this era was the "heterosexual presumption", applied by courts when interpreting legislation that on its face made no reference to sexuality or to the sex/gender of those in relationships. Beginning with marriage cases, courts developed this presumption by linking judicial findings that partners of the same legal sex did not have the biological capacity to reproduce with the concept of legal capacity, thus concluding that lesbian and gay couples lacked the legal capacity to form legally-recognised relationships.[7]

[5] While the Fourteenth Amendment does not mention race or slavery specifically, it was formulated by the reconstructionist Congress after the Civil War in order to put the abolition of slavery in the Thirteenth Amendment into effect, despite political resistance. See also *Constitution of the United States of America: Analysis and Interpretation*, 88th Congress, 1st session, Senate Document No. 39 (Washington, D.C., Congressional Record, 1964), at 63–65.

[6] For an extended discussion of these developments, see Kathleen A. Lahey, *Are We "Persons" Yet? Law and Sexuality in Canada* (Toronto, Univ. of Toronto Press, 1999), ch. 4.

[7] *Corbett* v. *Corbett*, [1970] 2 All E.R. 33, relied upon in *Re North and Matheson* (1974), 52 D.L.R. (3d) 280 (Manitoba County Court).

By the mid-1970s, Canadian legislatures had already begun to buttress this heterosexual presumption against the day that courts might be persuaded that lesbian and gay partners are "persons" too, by replacing statutory references to common-law spouses with the phrase "cohabitant of the opposite-sex".[8] This "opposite-sex movement" affected growing numbers of federal statutes, and the timing alone, with the first lesbian and gay marriage challenges being launched, suggests that the new phrase was intended to head off claims that sexuality-neutral marriage statutes did not prohibit lesbian and gay couples from marrying.[9] By the late 1970s, the cumulative effect of this kind of thinking had also resulted in judicial rulings that deprived lesbian women and gay men of protection under Canadian and US anti-discrimination statutes. At that time, complaints had been laid by lesbian women and gay men under the heading of "sex" discrimination, but the courts had concluded that discrimination on the basis of sexuality was really discrimination on the basis of "sexual orientation"—which of course was not covered by those statutes.[10]

The overall position in pre-Charter legal doctrine was thus one of marked discrimination against all sexual minorities. Not only were transsexual and transgendered persons conflated with "homosexuals", and the term "bisexual" was used as an oblique way to refer to gay men, but sexual minorities found that they were denied a wide range of personal and relationship rights in Canadian law: legal remedies for homophobic harassment and other forms of discrimination; immigration as individuals, partners, or refugees; financial support or division of assets on relationship breakdown; child custody or access; employment benefits for cohabiting partners; and legal capacity to marry.

SHIFTING THE DISCOURSE: THE CHARTER OF RIGHTS

The equality guarantees in section 15(1) of the Charter of Rights finally made it possible for lesbian women and gay men to break through the presumptions and prejudices that had resulted in these pervasive denials of the legal personality of sexual minorities. The Charter has affected this picture in three important ways. First, the open-ended language used to describe the groups protected by the equality provisions of the Charter induced some legislatures to insert "sexual

[8] The first such definition of "spouse" was enacted in 1974: Statutes of Canada (S.C.) 1974, chapter (c.) 8, section (s.) 3(7), amending the War Veterans Allowance Act, now Revised S.C. (R.S.C.), c. W-3. This was followed by omnibus legislation that made the same amendment to numerous other federal statutes.

[9] The federal government addressed the issue of sexuality obliquely—while enacting legislation responding to the recommendations of a royal commission on the status of women—instead of opening up the rarely-amended federal statute that directly regulates capacity to marry. Repeated attempts to obtain archival materials that might shed some light on this choice have, to date, revealed nothing. However, it could well be that, at the time, the federal government did not want to make *any* reference to sexuality in statute law.

[10] See eg *Re Board of Governors of the University of Saskatchewan and Saskatchewan Human Rights Commission* (1976), 66 D.L.R. (3d) 561 (Saskatchewan Court of Queen's Bench).

orientation" clauses into anti-discrimination statutes. Ontario in 1986 was the first to follow Québec's pre-Charter 1977 example. During the mid-1980s, there was a wave of Charter "compliance" law reform activity which largely centred on sex/gender "compliance", but the Ontario legislature concluded that the Charter required that lesbian women and gay men receive protection from discrimination as well.

Second, after the Supreme Court of Canada adopted a substantive approach to defining "equality" when applying section 15(1) of the Charter in *Andrews* v. *Law Society of British Columbia*[11] in 1989, the definition of "discrimination" developed in that case was used in key lower court decisions to displace the heterosexual presumption.[12] This in turn enabled courts to conclude that denial of both personal and relational rights on the basis of sexuality violated section 15(1) of the Charter.

These two effects combined powerfully in the pivotal 1992 decision of the Ontario Court of Appeal in *Haig and Birch* v. *Canada*,[13] in which the court read "sexual orientation" into the federal anti-discrimination act. Bolstered by this development, the human rights tribunal that heard *Leshner* v. *Ontario*[14] in 1992 was able to strike down the statutory opposite-sex definition of "spouse" in Ontario's anti-discrimination legislation and require the employee benefit package offered to provincial employees to provide survivor pensions to same-sex partners of employees. Since 1992, lesbian women and gay men have enjoyed increasing success in litigating both as individuals and as couples in the courts.

Although the result in *Egan and Nesbit* v. *Canada*[15] has remained a disappointment, in that five of nine judges of the Supreme Court of Canada believed in 1995 that discrimination against lesbian and gay couples in federal income support programmes was "demonstrably justifiable", three other Supreme Court decisions have moved beyond that result. In *Miron* v. *Trudel*,[16] the Supreme Court concluded that restricting insurance benefits to married couples discriminated against cohabiting opposite-sex couples. In *Vriend*, the Court confirmed that the personal right of access to anti-discrimination machinery to remedy discrimination could not be denied on the basis of sexuality. And in *M.* v. *H.*, which involved both personal and relationship issues, the Court concluded that lesbian partners have the personal right to judicial determination of support rights and the relational right of support when the facts support such claims.

[11] [1989] 1 S.C.R. 143.

[12] The first of these cases was *Veysey* v. *Correctional Services of Canada* (1989), 29 F.T.R. 74 (Federal Court, Trial Division), affirmed on different grounds (1990), 109 N.R. 300 (Federal Court of Appeal).

[13] (1992), 94 D.L.R. (4th) 1.

[14] (1992), 92 C.L.L.C. D/184 (Ontario Human Rights Tribunal).

[15] [1995] 2 S.C.R. 513.

[16] [1995] 2 S.C.R. 418.

JUDICIAL RECOGNITION OF CONSTITUTIONAL PERSONHOOD

The third effect of the Charter has been to support judicial restoration of the legal personality of lesbian women and gay men as courts have "read out" discriminatory language and have declined to "read in" language that creates classifications based on sexuality in legislation. This little-noted effect of the Charter can be seen in the way in which courts have framed their orders when remedying discrimination.

Courts have clearly preferred, when framing these orders, to eliminate all legislative classifications based on sexuality or the sex of partners. In this regard, judicial orders under the Charter bear a very close resemblance to the order in the famous Privy Council decision in the 1929 *"Persons" Case*, in which the court declined to read the Canadian constitution "as if" the word "persons" excludes women. Beginning with the Federal Court of Appeal decision in *Veysey*, interpreting "common-law partner" in a prison's "Private Family Visiting Program" as including a same-sex partner,[17] the courts have declined to read sexuality-neutral provisions "as if" they exclude lesbian and gay couples.

When statutory provisions have been facially discriminatory, by referring to sexuality or sex, courts have crafted declarations that have achieved the inclusive effect described above by first removing all expressly discriminatory terms. Thus, for example, when statutory provisions have defined "spouse" as including only cohabitants of the "opposite sex", courts have used their power under the Charter to "strike down" or "read out" terms like "opposite sex". They have then been able to read the remaining sexuality-neutral language as including lesbian and gay couples. When sex-specific terms like "husband and wife" have been "read out", sex-neutral phrases such as "two persons" have been "read in" in their place.[18]

Only when the grammatical construction of the provision in question has made it impossible to eliminate discriminatory language by reading out, reading in, or reading sexuality-neutral language neutrally, have the courts inserted additional sexuality-specific classifications into statutes that have been challenged under the Charter. For example, in *Rosenberg* v. *Canada (Attorney General)*,[19] the court had to add the phrase "or of the same sex" to the definition of "spouse". Because of the way in which the extended definition of "spouse" had been formulated in section 252(4) of the Income Tax Act, mere removal of the phrase "of the opposite sex" would have affected not only the definition of cohabitant, but also the definition of formal marriage. Since the Charter challenge had focused only on the cohabitant aspect of the definition of "spouse", the court was understandably reluctant to frame an order that would include lesbian and gay couples in the definition of married spouses. Thus in

[17] See *Veysey*, *supra* n. 12.

[18] See eg *M.* v. *H.* (1996), 142 D.L.R. (4th) 1 (Ontario Court of Appeal).

[19] 158 D.L.R. (4th) 664 (Ontario Court of Appeal).

cases in which it has been grammatically impossible to simply read the offending words out of the statute, courts have departed from their clear preference for neutral language that eliminates sexual classifications and have created what appear to be new sexuality-based classifications. Whichever method is used in their remedial orders, Canadian courts have established a strong record of fashioning remedies that reflect the full constitutional personhood of lesbian women and gay men.

LEGISLATIVE RECOGNITION: NEW FORMS OF DISCRIMINATION

As "opposite sex" legislative definitions of deemed "spouse" have been judicially corrected to include lesbian and gay cohabitants, some legislatures have begun to enact statutes that recognise lesbian and gay relationships. On a political level, these statutes fall into two distinct categories. On the one hand are the statutes that arise from a sympathetic desire to ameliorate the status of lesbian and gay couples and their families. I would put the changes that have been enacted in British Columbia in successive stages of legislation since 1995,[20] and the changes wrought by Bill 32 in Québec in 1999, into this category. On the other hand are the statutes that are motivated more by a desire to keep lesbian and gay couples out of the legal category of "spouse" at all costs, even if that means extending many of the rights of heterosexual cohabitants to queer couples. Bill 5 in Ontario (1999), federal Bill C-32 (2000), and Nova Scotia Bill 75 (2000) fall into this category.

Whatever the political motivations behind these changes might be, these legislative regimes all have two things in common. First, all of these new legislative structures perpetuate discrimination on the basis of sexuality to some extent or another. None of them can be considered to fulfil the mandate of section 15 of the Charter in the way that judicial remedies for violations of section 15 have, for none of these statutes has eradicated all legislative classifications based on sexuality in those jurisdictions. All of them create new legislative classifications in one way or another even as they may extend some of the rights and obligations of cohabitants to queer couples. The differences among these five sets of provisions are really just differences in degree.

Second, none of the five legislative regimes extend any of the core incidents of marriage to lesbian and gay couples (except, in Nova Scotia, through the segregated device of registered domestic partnerships), while all five jurisdictions continue to deny lesbian and gay couples the right to marry.[21] For both these

[20] See Casswell, chap. 11.

[21] In 2000, Charter challenges were filed seeking access to formal marriage in three provinces: (1) in British Columbia, *In the Matter of Applications for Licences by Persons of the Same Sex Who Intend to Marry*, No. L001944 (challenge to federal law brought by the B.C. Attorney General, whose standing was upheld by Brenner C.J. on 8 Jan. 2001, http://www.courts.gov.bc.ca/jdb-txt/SC/01/00/2001BCSC0053.htm), *Egale Canada Inc., et al.* v. *Attorney General of Canada, et al.*, No. L002698, *Dawn Barbeau & Elizabeth Barbeau, et al.* v. *Attorney General of B.C.*,

reasons, it can be seen from Table 1 (pp. 246–48) that even the five jurisdictions that have enacted legislative provisions relating to lesbian and gay couples still discriminate on the basis of sexuality, especially when queer couples are compared with married couples.

The classical incidents of legal personality can be broken down into two basic categories: individual or personal rights, and relational rights. Rights to identity or status rights such as the right to be gay or transsexual without suffering reprisals such as loss of employment are essentially personal rights, whereas rights that touch on the legal status of relationships can be classified as relational rights. From this perspective, the classical rights to sue and be sued, act as witness or juror, enter the state, take up citizenship, enjoy protection from violence, and enter into contracts, including employment contracts, can be considered to be personal or identity rights. Rights to marry and have custody of children are relational rights, as are any rights that depend upon being able to marry or have custody of children.

As the *Vriend* case demonstrated, sexual minorities will not have full personal or status rights until they can have recourse to legal remedies for discrimination of every kind. Thus the fact that two jurisdictions—the Northwest Territories and Nunavut—still have not included "sexual orientation" in their human rights codes means that sexual minorities in those parts of Canada still have no ability to seek legal redress for employment discrimination, denial of housing or public services, and other basic necessities of life. Nor do they have full contractual rights in those jurisdictions, because employment contracts that extend family benefits to workers can still exclude employees with lesbian and gay partners from the scope of those benefit plans.[22]

And despite the stunning decision in *M.* v. *H.*, nowhere in Canada do sexual minorities who are involved in relationships with persons of their same legal sex have the right to one of the most fundamental incidents of full legal personality—the right to marriage. Denial of the right to marry carries with it denial of every other right that is restricted to married couples—the rights conferred by marital property regimes, the status of natural parent of a spouse's child (even though lesbian and gay partners can become parents through step-parent

et al., No. L003197 (B.C. Supreme Court, Vancouver); (2) in Ontario, *Hedy Halpern & Coleen Rogers, et al.* v. *Attorney General of Canada, et al.*, No. 684/00 (Ontario Superior Court of Justice (Divisional Court), Toronto); (3) in Québec, *Michael Hendricks & René Leboeuf* v. *Linda Goupil (Minister of Justice of Québec), et al.*, No. 500–05–059656–007 (Québec Superior Court, Montréal). The Toronto case will be heard with *Metropolitan Community Church of Toronto* v. *Attorney General of Canada, et al.*, No. 39/2001 (demanding that the Registrar General of Ontario register two same-sex marriages performed at the Church on 14 Jan. 2001). See also Casswell, chap. 11, pp. 231, 235.

[22] Lesbian and gay couples in the NWT and Nunavut could, of course, file claims of sexual orientation discrimination and rely on *Vriend* to obtain an order requiring that "sexual orientation" be read into these human rights codes. However, such challenges have not yet been brought, nor are they likely to be in the near future. Queer existence remains relatively invisible in both jurisdictions, and access to the legal process is similarly constrained: as of 2001, there is only one lawyer in the whole of Nunavut, which spans three time zones.

Table 1: Selected Legal Capacities of Lesbians and Gays in Canada (under legislation enacted as of 30 April 2001)

	Anti-discrim. legislation includes "sexual orientation"	Anti-discrim. legislation: same-sex partners in definition of "marital status"	Capacity to marry (fed., Qué., Alta. have statutes with man-woman definitions)	Automatic inheritance rights if same-sex partner dies intestate	Dependent's relief (right of same-sex partner to challenge will if inadequate provision)
Federal	X	not added to definition	man-woman definition	provincial issue	provincial issue
Ontario	X	"same-sex partnership status"	federal issue		
Québec	X	not a "civil status"	federal issue (man-woman definition)		
British Columbia	X	no definition; arguably included by case-law	federal issue	X	X
New Brunswick	X	no definition	federal issue		
Prince Edward Island	X	no definition	federal issue		
Nova Scotia	X	not in definition	federal issue	if registered domestic partner	if registered domestic partner
Newfoundland	X	no definition	federal issue		
Manitoba	X	no definition	federal issue		
Saskatchewan	X	no definition	federal issue		
Alberta	*Vriend*	not in definition	federal issue (man-woman definition)		
Yukon	X	no definition	federal issue		X
Northwest Territories	if *Vriend* applies	no definition	federal issue		
Nunavut	if *Vriend* applies	no definition	federal issue		

	Share of family home or other family property on relationship breakdown (*)	De facto parent-child relationships recognised	Adoption	Employment benefits for same-sex partner	Pension benefits for surviving same-sex partner
Federal	provincial issue	X	provincial issue	federal public sector employees	federal public sector employees; all federal pension programmes
Ontario		X	co-parent can "step-parent" adopt partner's biological child; joint adoption not clear	provincial public sector employees; all provincially-regulated private sector employees	provincial public sector employees; all provincially-regulated private pension plans
Québec			joint adoption probably available	all employees	all public and private pension plans
British Columbia	property division rules apply only if both partners agree	de facto parent deemed a "step-parent"	can adopt jointly or as "step-parent"	all employees	all public and private pension plans
New Brunswick					
Prince Edward Island					
Nova Scotia	if registered domestic partner	not clear		if registered domestic partner or (by case-law) if public sector employee	if registered domestic partner or (by case-law) if public sector employee

Table 1: *cont.*

	Share of family home or other family property on relationship breakdown (*)	De facto parent-child relationships recognised	Adoption	Employment benefits for same-sex partner	Pension benefits for surviving same-sex partner
Newfoundland					
Manitoba				provincial public sector employees	provincial public sector employees
Saskatchewan				provincial public sector employees (and some private sector)	
Alberta			can adopt as "step-parent"		
Yukon					
Northwest Territories					
Nunavut					

adoption), and a wide array of statutory and private law rights ranging from tax credits and deductions to insurance benefits and pension rights as a survivor or as a former spouse. (Even the list of rights and responsibilities that apply to registered domestic partners in Nova Scotia remains limited.)

The expansion of the legal consequences of non-married cohabitation over the last twenty-five years has blurred the effects of denial of marriage rights to lesbian and gay couples, as they have been given limited access to the category of legally-recognised cohabitation. However, it is still true that nowhere in Canada do non-married cohabitants have *all* the legal rights and responsibilities of married couples, while everywhere they remain totally barred from the one incident of non-married cohabitation that makes cohabitation a "free" state for opposite-sex couples—the right to choose to marry if they are not legally incapacitated by prior marriage or mental competence.

As Table 1 demonstrates, the total bar on marriage, the limited recognition of relational rights, and the denial of most of the core incidents of marriage lead to the conclusion that lesbians and gays do not possess the full legal capacities of those in heterosexual relationships. Thus they still do not have access to the same rights and responsibilities as heterosexual couples, even when they want to. Lesbian and gay couples accordingly cannot provide as fully for their partners or children as can heterosexuals. With the exception of Nova Scotia, none of the rights listed in Table 1 becomes available until after the statutory period of cohabitation has been satisfied (from one to three years, depending on the jurisdiction).

In the remainder of this chapter, I take a closer look at the current legal status of lesbian and gay couples under the statutory provisions that have been enacted in four of the five jurisdictions that have taken this route.

Ontario Bills 167 (1994) and 5 (1999)

Ontario has been the site of many successful Charter challenges to legislation that discriminates against lesbian and gay couples. Like relationship recognition litigation elsewhere in Canada, these cases have challenged the exclusion of lesbian and gay couples from the legislative category of "opposite-sex" cohabitants that has been used to expand the term "spouse".

Table 2 sets out the impact of this litigation on lesbian and gay couples. With the exception of the items relating to emergency consent, where a 1992 amendment to consent to treatment legislation extended the right to consent to a partner's medical treatment in emergencies to lesbian and gay couples, all the items under the heading "same-sex cohabitants" have been extended to lesbian and gay couples as the result of litigation.

In 1993, the Ontario Law Reform Commission published a report that recommended adoption of European-style registered partnership legislation.[23]

[23] *Report on the Rights and Responsibilities of Cohabitants Under the Family Law Act* (Toronto, Ontario Law Reform Commission, 1993).

This recommendation was not greeted with enthusiasm, largely because Ontario lesbians and gays had realised by then that they had already achieved superior rights, in relation to family formation, parent-child relationships, access to alternative conception, and anti-discrimination protection, as the result of judicial declarations.

Bill 167

In 1994, the left-of-centre New Democratic Party government introduced the first major bill designed to move beyond the case-law and bring equality to lesbian and gay couples across the board. Bill 167 (the Equality Rights Statute Law Amendment Act, 1994) initially included lesbian and gay couples in the term "cohabitant" and therefore in expanded definitions of "spouse", for the purposes of nearly sixty statutes. It also included lesbian and gay couples in gender- and sexuality-neutralised definitions of "marital status", "family", and "next of kin" wherever they were being given the same rights and responsibilities as opposite-sex cohabitants.

Bill 167 was intended to create a two-tiered concept of "spouse", by including lesbian and gay couples in the category of "cohabitants" deemed to be spouses, while continuing to reserve some legal rights and responsibilities only for spouses who were married couples. These "for married couples only" provisions included the right to marry, matrimonial property rights to the family home and other family property, the presumption that a married partner is the natural parent of children born during the marriage (even if there is no biological connection), and income tax provisions.

Despite the free vote promised on this bill, and despite the reservation of key rights and responsibilities to married couples, right-wing opponents of Bill 167 vociferously demanded that lesbian and gay couples be removed entirely from the expanded definition of "spouse" and that their cohabitation be recognised in some other manner. Last-minute changes to the bill were never released because it was defeated so decisively on 9 June 1994. But according to government statements, lesbian and gay couples would have been denied the ability to adopt children jointly, other "marital rights" were to be withdrawn, and some form of registered domestic partnership legislation was under consideration as a way to create a separate statutory classification into which to place queer couples.

M. v. *H.*

After Bill 167 was defeated, it began to look like litigation was the preferred route to relationship recognition, as court after court removed or expanded opposite-sex definitions of "cohabitant" in extended definitions of "spouse" in provincial legislation. This litigation culminated in May 1999 with the decision of the Supreme Court of Canada in *M.* v. *H.*, which declared that definitions of "spouse" that included opposite-sex cohabitants but not same-sex cohabitants were unconstitutionally discriminatory.

Unfortunately, the Supreme Court's order in *M.* v. *H.* did not go nearly as far as had the order of the Ontario Court of Appeal, which had constitutionally corrected the definition of "spouse" by reading out "a man and woman" and reading in "two persons".[24] In contrast with the Ontario court, the Supreme Court gave the provincial government six months to revise the legislation itself, instead of revising it for the province. The Court agreed to that variation in its remedial order, because the province had convinced the Court that it was in a better position to sort out statutory inconsistencies created by declaring the definition of "spouse" in Part III (Support Obligations) of the Family Law Act to be discriminatory while the definition in Part IV (Domestic Contracts) remained unchallenged. Thus the Court left the resolution of those inconsistencies to the province.

Bill 5

Instead of just reconciling the inconsistencies between Parts III and IV of the Family Law Act, however, the province took advantage of the Supreme Court's order by completely rewriting the definition of "spouse" to exclude lesbian and gay couples in every Ontario statute that uses that term. A massive piece of legislation—Bill 5—was introduced and rushed through all three readings and assent within 24 hours. Entitled "An Act to amend certain statutes because of the Supreme Court of Canada decision in *M.* v. *H.*",[25] Bill 5 redefined "spouse" to refer only to married couples and cohabitants of the opposite sex, and created a new legislative category—"same-sex partners"—into which it places cohabitants of the "same sex". Bill 5 made this change to some 400 sections in over sixty statutes in Ontario.

Bill 5 thus replaces the former two-tiered definition of "spouse" (married couples and opposite-sex cohabitants) with a three-tiered system in which opposite-sex cohabitants are expressly included in many definitions of "spouse", while lesbian and gay couples are given many—but not all—of the rights and responsibilities of opposite-sex cohabitants in the new third category of "same-sex partner". The result is three classes of relationships:

(1) married couples;
(2) opposite-sex cohabitants, who continue to be deemed to be "spouses" in over seventy statutes; and
(3) "same-sex partners", who appear in some sixty-five statutes.

The provisions from which opposite-sex cohabitants are excluded relate to the core incidents of marriage: matrimonial home provisions and sharing of family

[24] (1996), 142 D.L.R. (4th) 1.
[25] S. Ontario (S.O.) 1999, c. 6.

property on relationship breakdown, inheritance rights on death without a will, and forced shares of the estate on death despite the provisions of the will. Lesbian and gay partners are excluded from all those provisions, and, as well, have been excluded from roughly a dozen statutes that give opposite-sex cohabitants the same rights and responsibilities as married couples (e.g., provisions relating to municipal taxation and provincial income taxation.)

As Table 2 (pp. 254–56) indicates, the separate classification of "same-sex partner" carries with it far fewer rights and responsibilities than those extended to either married or cohabiting heterosexuals. In addition, lesbian and gay couples can no longer lay complaints for discrimination on the basis of "marital status" before the Ontario Human Rights Commission; they can only complain of discrimination based on "same-sex partnership status". This term remains undefined and may attract a very different level of protection.

Bill 5 does extend some "new rights" to lesbian and gay couples: rights under the Coroners Act (making funeral arrangements, demanding an inquest), rights to compensation for victims of crime, the right to bring a negligence action after the death of a partner (wrongful death suits), the right to take advantage of the support payment enforcement system run by the province, the right to share rooms in nursing homes and rest homes, and the power to direct organ donations. If Bill 5 had not been passed, it seems likely that courts, if prompted by litigation, would have extended all these rights to lesbian and gay couples in light of the Supreme Court's decision in *M.* v. *H.*, and would not have departed from prior remedies to create a new class of "same-sex partners" in order to do so. Because of Bill 5, these "new rights" are not spousal or cohabitant rights, but for lesbian and gay couples, are the rights of "same-sex partners".

The provincial government gained the support of some members of lesbian and gay organisations for Bill 5 by pointing out that this legislation created "instant equality" for lesbian and gay couples in Ontario, and saved couples from having to litigate each statutory definition separately (or in some form of omnibus action). However, political practice has since demonstrated that this short-term advantage may well be overshadowed by the discriminatory impact of the separate category "same-sex partner". Relying on several cases that refused to uphold segregated governmental classifications for lesbian and gay couples,[26] *M.* filed for a rehearing as to remedies before the Supreme Court, asking that the province be ordered to formulate a constitutionally acceptable method of extending cohabitant rights to lesbian and gay couples. After this application for rehearing was rejected, the province of Ontario began amending administrative forms such as those used to initiate family property and custody

[26] These cases have included *Dwyer* v. *Toronto (Metropolitan)*, [1996] O.H.R.B.I.D. No. 33 (Ontario Human Rights Tribunal); *Canada (Attorney General)* v. *Moore and Akerstrom*, [1996] C.H.R.D. No. 8 (Canadian Human Rights Tribunal), affirmed (1998), 55 C.R.R. (2d) 254 (Federal Court Trial Division); *Brillinger* v. *Brockie*, [2000] O.H.R.B.I.D. No. 3 (Ontario Human Rights Tribunal) (*obiter*).

proceedings to force lesbian and gay couples to identify themselves not as "cohabitants," but as "same-sex partners". The long-term implications of this development remain unclear.

Québec Bill 32 (1999)

The overall status of lesbian and gay couples in Québec law is a combination of the very different levels of recognition of non-married cohabitants in the Québec Civil Code,[27] and in other Québec statutes. The Civil Code, which regulates marriage, filiation and succession, has very few references to non-married cohabitants,[28] and most of the provisions of the Code relating to adult relationships are expressly focused on marriage only. A few provisions of the Code are framed in terms that suggest that cohabitants might fall within them (provisions relating to joint adoption, joint annuities, and insurable interests), and those provisions are so generally expressed that there is no reason why lesbian and gay couples should not fall within them, even if this was not intended. For example, Article 546 provides that "[a]ny person of full age may, alone or jointly with another person, adopt a child".

In other Québec statutes, the status of both opposite-sex couples and lesbian and gay couples is completely different from that found under the Civil Code. Most other statutes that mention marriage also apply to non-married cohabitants. These types of statutes generally relate to government action, programmes, or benefits such as health services, the Québec Pension Plan, workplace standards, and automobile insurance standards.

This bifurcated model sets up a dual regime in which only the state of formal marriage gives rise to what are ordinarily understood as marital rights or responsibilities between the spouses under the Civil Code, while formal marriage or long-term cohabitation can give rise to rights or responsibilities between the couple as a whole and the government under other Québec statutes. The result is minimal rights for cohabitants under the Civil Code, and substantially equal rights for cohabitants under the rest of Québec law.

The Charter of Human Rights and Freedoms of Québec,[29] which was the first human rights code in Canada to prohibit discrimination on the basis of "sexual orientation" in 1977, has had little impact on the position of lesbian and gay couples in Québec. Exceptionally, in 1994, a Human Rights Tribunal ruled that

[27] S. Québec (S.Q.) 1991, c. 64.

[28] Exceptional references to "concubinaries" ("*concubins*") can be found in Articles 555 (consent to adoption limited to particular persons) and 1938 (right to take over a lease of a dwelling). In this respect, the Québec Civil Code is not unlike the French Civil Code, which refers to "*concubins*" or "*concubinage*" only in a few places, e.g., Articles 283, 285–1, 311–20, 340–4, 515–8. In both Québec and France (unlike, e.g., Ontario), non-married cohabitants live in a "free union" or "*union libre*", in the sense that they do not have financial support obligations regardless of how long they cohabit. See Borrillo, chap. 25.

[29] R.S.Q., c. C-12, s. 10.

Table 2: Ontario: Rights and Obligations of Married Couples, Opposite-Sex Cohabitants, and Lesbian and Gay Couples

	Married couples ("spouses")	Opposite-sex cohabitants ("spouses")	Lesbian and gay couples ("spouses" before Bill 5)	Lesbian and gay couples ("same-sex partners" under Bill 5)
FAMILY LAW:				
capacity to marry	X	X		
emergency consent for partner	X	medical	medical (1992)	medical
share of family home or other property on relationship breakdown	X			
elective and default property regimes	X			
equitable remedies for division of property	not needed	X	X (continues after Bill 5)	
marriage/cohabitation agreements	X	X		X
financial support obligations (alimony)	X	X	*M. v. H.*	X
child support obligations and custody/access rights (biological and non-biological parents)	X	X	case-law	X
filiation (status of partner who is not a genetic parent)	spouse deemed a natural parent	cohabitant deemed a natural parent	de facto parent (continues after Bill 5)	
second-parent adoption	X	X	*Re K.* (1995), 125 D.L.R. (4th) 653	X

joint adoption	X	X	case-law	possibly covered by "any two individuals" if court finds in best interests of child
inheritance rights on intestacy	X			
joint annuities	X	X		
insurable interest (eg., in life of partner)	X	X	case-law in some circumstances	X
protection of family assets against partner's creditors	X	X		X
HUMAN RIGHTS CODE: included in "marital status"	X	X	some protection through "sexual orientation"	"same-sex partnership status" protected
pension benefits for partners covered	X	X	*Dwyer*	X
PUBLIC LAW: public health insurance coverage for partner	X	X	X	X
access to alternative conception	X	X	X (continues after Bill 5)	
worker's compensation (eg., death benefits for surviving partner)	X	?		X

Table 2: *cont.*

	Married couples ("spouses")	Opposite-sex cohabitants ("spouses")	Lesbian and gay couples ("spouses" before Bill 5)	Lesbian and gay couples ("same-sex partners" under Bill 5)
provincial tax provisions (some confer benefits, some impose tax penalties)	X	X		
exemption from taxes imposed on transfer of vehicle to partner	X	X	X (continues after Bill 5)	
automobile insurance coverage	X	*Miron* v. *Trudel*	doubtful	X
public sector employment benefits for partner	X	X	X	X
survivor benefits for partner under public sector employment pensions	X	X	X	X
welfare benefits and student assistance (partner's income considered in calculating need)	X	X		X
OTHER:				
enforcement of child support orders	X	X		X
information re partner's death	X	X		X
conflict of interest because of partner (and disclosure)	X	X		X

a campground that described itself as a "family" service could not exclude a lesbian couple.[30] However, this ruling has had no impact on the status of lesbian and gay couples under either the Civil Code or general Québec statutes.

This is the context in which omnibus Bill 32, enacted in June 1999,[31] sought to change the legal status of lesbian and gay couples. Bill 32 amended twenty-eight Québec statutes by extending the category of cohabitation ("*conjoints de fait*" or "de facto spouses", or similar language) to lesbian and gay couples, but did not make any changes to the Civil Code. Thus lesbian and gay couples have approximately the same status as opposite-sex cohabitants in Québec: they have none of the many rights and responsibilities that attach to married couples, but they have many of the rights and responsibilities that apply to cohabitants. These changes were made by deleting sexuality-specific terms (such as "husband" or "wife") from cohabitation provisions and replacing them with sexuality-neutral provisions (such as "two persons who live together. . ."), or by adding "of the same sex" to opposite-sex provisions.

Although it now looks as if Québec law relating to couples has two tiers, it is really a three-tier system, because lesbian and gay couples do not have all the rights and responsibilities of opposite-sex cohabitants. The biggest difference between lesbian and gay couples and opposite-sex couples is that they do not have the all-important right of choosing which regime they will fall under—the marital regime of the Civil Code or the general cohabitant regime, mainly found in other Québec statutes. The three regimes are as follows:

(1) marriage under the Civil Code, with all its rights and responsibilities;
(2) opposite-sex cohabitation, with the right to choose to acquire the rights and responsibilities under the Civil Code through formal marriage;
(3) lesbian and gay cohabitation, with many of the rights of opposite-sex cohabitants, but no right to marry in order to acquire marital rights/responsibilities.

There are other differences which arise as the result of the incomplete extension of the rights of cohabitants to lesbian and gay couples. Despite the long list of provisions amended directly or indirectly by Bill 32 to include lesbian and gay couples, there are still many Québec statutes that are either expressly limited to opposite-sex couples, or use sexuality-neutral language (eg., "*conjoint*" or "spouse") that does not clearly guarantee that it will apply to lesbian and gay couples. There are also several provisions that appear to continue to apply only to married couples: only married couples can obtain reciprocal enforcement of maintenance orders; only married couples are declared by the Charter of Human Rights and Freedoms of Québec to be subject to the principle of equality of rights and obligations "in the marriage"; and only married couples are subject to some conflict of interest provisions.

[30] *Trudel et Commission des droits de la personne du Québec* v. *Camping & Plage Gilles Fortier Inc.*, [1994] J.T.D.P.Q. no. 32 (Québec Human Rights Tribunal).

[31] An Act to amend various legislative provisions concerning de facto spouses, S.Q. 1999, c. 14.

A few cohabitant provisions have not yet been clearly extended to lesbian and gay couples; in addition to some conflict of interest provisions, hunting and fishing rights in James Bay are extended only to "legitimate spouses".[32] And Québec statutes still use the term "*conjoint*" or "spouse" without defining it. Because of the continuing uncertainty surrounding a November 1998 decision on queer survivor benefits under pension plans,[33] it is not clear whether this term will apply to lesbian and gay couples, or whether the government will oppose attempts to apply it to queer couples. Examples of provisions using "*conjoint*" or "spouse" are: the right to receive information on the death of a spouse; the allocation of Aboriginal land rights to spouses; electoral enumeration definitions of "spouse"; substituted service of documents in some legal proceedings; and provisions imposing burdens such as conflict of interest clauses, disclosure of conflict of interest requirements, and anti-avoidance provisions.

The current status of lesbian and gay couples in Québec under the Civil Code and other Québec statutes (as amended by Bill 32) is outlined in Table 3 (pp. 260–1). This table should be read with some caution. In addition to the uncertain impact of Bill 32 on the many provisions that remain unamended (some twenty-eight in all), it is not clear how the Supreme Court of Canada decisions in *Miron* v. *Trudel* and *M.* v. *H.* might affect opposite-sex cohabitant access to the rights and obligations of marriage, or lesbian and gay cohabitant access to the categories of "married couple" or "cohabitant", where these terms have not been extended expressly.

Federal Bill C-23 (2001 and Beyond)

The jurisdiction of the federal government in Canada is very different from that of the provinces. Under the Constitution of Canada, the provinces have jurisdiction over such matters as contract, tort and property law, family law (including the solemnisation of marriage), and most employment issues, while the federal government has jurisdiction over such matters as criminal law, immigration, banking, capacity to marry, divorce, and employment in the federal government or its agencies and federally-regulated industries.

Despite the seeming separation of provincial and federal jurisdictions, there are many areas of overlap between them. Sometimes this overlap is quite limited, as in immigration law, where the federal government creates its own policies on family reunification and does not make much reference to provincial law in implementing them. Sometimes this overlap is considerable, as in taxation law, where the provisions of federal tax law incorporate provincial law by

[32] This provision is no doubt aimed at limiting customary and treaty rights of the Cree in Québec. It is not clear whether this phrase would include opposite-sex cohabitants.

[33] *Québec (Commission des droits de la personne et des droits de la jeunesse)* v. *Québec (Procureur général)* (13 Nov. 1998), No. 500–05–036134–979 (Québec Superior Court, Montréal, Vaillancourt J.).

reference, and then the provinces incorporate federal income tax law as a whole by reference (Québec excepted). Thus, in autonomous areas of federal law, the federal government writes its own statutory and regulatory definitions of terms such as "spouse" and "child". In areas that are intertwined with provincial law, the federal government has tended to develop definitions of "spouse" and "child" that begin with some basic principles but then can be expanded by reference to provincial definitions.

One area of jurisdiction that is particularly overlapping and even confused is jurisdiction over marriage. Although jurisdiction over capacity to marry is considered to be a federal matter, until the enactment of Bill C-23, federal legislation made no mention of sexuality in relation to marriage. Federal marriage legislation had only been concerned with degrees of consanguinity and solemnisation in some contexts. In contrast, some provinces have legislated in relation to some aspects of capacity such as prior marriage, mental capacity, and age of consent. Such legislation has been upheld to the extent that it can be connected to the province's jurisdiction over "solemnisation" of marriage.

Over the last twenty-five years, the federal government has gradually expanded "spouse" to include opposite-sex cohabitants in a wide variety of circumstances. Beginning with amendments to the War Veterans Allowance Act in 1974, the federal government reduced the number of years of cohabitation required to establish de facto or common-law marriage from seven to just one or two. Also beginning in 1974, Parliament systematically inserted the requirement that cohabitants be of the "opposite sex". Until Bill C-23, most federal statutes used some expanded form of "spouse" that was expressly limited to couples of the opposite sex.

The federal government has been extremely slow to recognise both the individual and relationship rights of queers. In 1992, the Ontario Court of Appeal held in *Haig and Birch* that the Charter required that "sexual orientation" be read into the Canadian Human Rights Act. Only in 1996 did the federal government carry out its 1986 promise to add "sexual orientation" to the Act.[34] Revenue Canada had to be ordered to stop administering the Income Tax Act as if its sexuality-neutral provisions excluded lesbian and gay couples.[35] The federal government has promised new immigration regulations for years, but still refuses to include lesbian and gay partners in the category of "spouse". The current bill before Parliament would admit lesbian and gay partners as "common-law partners" (and members of the "family class"), replacing the policy that has existed since 1994 of admitting them as non-family on discretionary "compassionate" grounds.[36] The federal government amended sentencing laws

[34] S.C. 1996, c. 14.

[35] *Moore and Akerstrom*, *supra* n.26.

[36] Immigration and Refugee Protection Act, Bill C-11, passed by House of Commons on 13 June 2001 s. 12(1): "A foreign national may be selected as a member of the family class on the basis of their relationship as the spouse, [or] common-law partner . . . of a Canadian citizen or permanent resident." The definition of "common-law partner" will be set out in regulations, and could require a minimum cohabitation period of one year.

Table 3: Québec: Rights and Obligations of Married Couples, Opposite-Sex Cohabitants, and Lesbian and Gay Couples

	Married couples ("*conjoints*" or "spouses")	Opposite-sex cohabitants ("*conjoints de fait*" or "de facto spouses")	Lesbian and gay couples ("*conjoints de fait*" or "de facto spouses" under Bill 32)
CIVIL CODE:			
capacity to marry	X	X	
emergency consent for partner	X	medical	medical
share of family home or other family property on relationship breakdown	X		
elective and default property regimes	X		
marriage/cohabitation agreements	X	X	
financial support obligations (alimony)	X		
child support obligations and custody/access rights (biological and non-biological parents)	X	X	
filiation (status of partner who is not a genetic parent)	spouse deemed a natural parent	cohabitant deemed a natural parent	
second-parent adoption	X		
joint adoption	X	X	X
inheritance rights on intestacy	X		
joint annuities	X	X	
insurable interest (eg, in life of partner)	X	?	?
protection of family assets against partner's creditors	X		

QUÉBEC CHARTER OF HUMAN RIGHTS:			
included in "civil status"	X		limited protection through "sexual orientation"
pension benefits for partners covered	X		
ADDED TO PUBLIC LAW BY BILL 32:			
public health insurance coverage for partner	X	X	X
access to alternative conception	X	X	X
worker's compensation (eg, death benefits for surviving partner)	X	X	X
provincial tax provisions (some confer benefits, some impose penalties)	X	X	X
exemption from taxes on transfer of vehicle to partner	X	X	X
automobile insurance coverage	X	X	X
public sector employment benefits for partner	X	X	X
survivor benefits for partner under public sector employment pensions	X	X	X
welfare benefits and student assistance (partner's income considered in calculating need)	X	X	X
EXCLUDED FROM BILL 32:			
enforcement of child support orders	X		
information re partner's death	X	X	?
conflict of interest because of partner (and disclosure)	X	some	?

to treat homophobic hatred as an exacerbating factor,[37] but then declared itself legally unable to address hate speech recently imported from the United States.

This governmental resistance was supported by the 1995 Supreme Court of Canada decision in *Egan and Nesbit*, in which a five-to-four majority of the Court concluded that exclusion of lesbian and gay couples from the extended opposite-sex definition of "spouse" in federal social assistance legislation was constitutionally permissible. However, the Supreme Court decisions in *Vriend* and *M.* v. *H.* have subsequently changed the litigation climate considerably.

In *M.* v. *H.*, the Supreme Court concluded that an Ontario extended opposite-sex definition of "spouse" violated the Charter equality guarantees. In *Rosenberg*, the Ontario Court of Appeal ruled that, notwithstanding a similar extended opposite-sex definition of "spouse" in the federal Income Tax Act, lesbian and gay employees were constitutionally entitled to survivor benefits under their employers' registered pension plans. In *Moore and Akerstrom*, the Federal Court (Trial Division) concluded that the federal government's proposal to segregate lesbian and gay employees in separate employment benefit plans was constitutionally impermissible. The combined effect of *M.* v. *H.*, *Rosenberg*, and *Moore and Akerstrom* brought the federal government to the realisation that it would only be a matter of time before it would be ordered to include lesbian and gay couples in extended definitions of "spouse" throughout federal legislation. Each of these three decisions arose out of challenges to the "opposite-sex" definition of "spouse" that has been so extensively incorporated into federal and Ontario legislation, and all three delivered the same message: excluding lesbian and gay couples from extended opposite-sex definitions of "spouse" is discriminatory, and is not saved by giving them equivalent rights in segregated categories.

Since *Egan and Nesbit* was decided in 1995, the federal government had displayed a decided preference for extending rights to queer couples—when it had to—on a segregated basis. Thus, it was not surprising that, when the government's long-promised "omnibus" bill to recognise queer couples was introduced in 2000, it did so by removing lesbian and gay couples from the legal category of "spouse" completely. Bill C-23, the Modernisation of Benefits and Obligations Act,[38] accomplished this by repealing twenty-five years' worth of extended opposite-sex definitions of spouse—which had treated opposite-sex cohabitants and married couples as equivalent in the majority of federal enactments—and creating two new categories: "spouses", now reserved for married couples only, and "common-law partners", to which both opposite-sex and "same-sex" couples who meet statutory criteria have been moved.[39] Section 1.1 of Bill C-23 also

[37] Criminal Code, R.S.C., c. C-46, s. 718.2(a)(1), inserted by S.C. 1995, c. 22.

[38] S.C. 2000, c. 12. See Casswell, chap. 11, p. 230.

[39] The test of "common-law" partnership is living conjugally for one year or having a child together. "Having a child together" is not defined, but federal legislation consistently defines "child" by looking to de facto parentage, which is factually dependent on actual care of a child.

purports to define "marriage", for the first time in a federal statute, as man-woman-only: "For greater certainty, the amendments made by this Act do not affect the meaning of the word 'marriage', that is, the lawful union of one man and one woman to the exclusion of all others".[40]

On a substantive level, it is clear that the overriding legislative purpose of the abandonment of the extended opposite-sex definition of "spouse" is to remove queer couples from statutory association with married couples and to segregate them—along with heterosexual cohabitants—in the new (old) category of "common-law partner". This can be seen from the changes made to the Income Tax Act: Bill C-23 has repealed the existing definition of "spouse"[41] and has reenacted it word for word as the definition of "common-law partner".[42] The substantive tests for the existence of a common-law relationship have not been changed at all. Only the name of the category has been changed. The definition of "spouse" that had been constitutionally corrected in the *Rosenberg* decision has been repealed completely, and "spouse" has once again become an undefined term in the Income Tax Act. The net result of these technical changes, which have been carried out in a similar fashion in all the other amended statutes, is that all non-married couples have now been segregated from married couples in a new statutory category called "common-law partners".

This change is intended to make it look as if the federal government perceives marriage to be a "unique" institution, that heterosexual and queer cohabitants are different from married couples, and that all cohabitants are being treated "equally" by classifying them together as "common-law partners". Superficially, it may appear that the government has replaced the three-tier set of categories that discriminated against lesbian and gay couples with a new, "equal", two-tier system. In reality, Bill C-23 has merely replaced one three-tiered system with another three-tiered system. The three new categories are these:

(1) "spouse," reserved for married couples only;
(2) "common-law partners" of opposite sexes, who have substantially the same rights and responsibilities they had when they were classified as "spouses," including the capacity to marry; and
(3) "common-law partners" of the same sex, who are unequal to both spouses and opposite-sex common-law partners: they do not have

[40] Svend Robinson MP's private member's Bill C-264, given first reading on 14 Feb. 2001, would add the following provision to the Marriage (Prohibited Degrees) Act, S.C. 1990, c. 46: "A marriage between two persons is not invalid by reason only that they are of the same sex." Because jurisdiction over capacity to marry is federal, provincial man-woman-only definitions of marriage are arguably *ultra vires*. See Québec, Civil Code, S.Q. 1991, c. 64, article 365; Alberta, Marriage Act, R.S. Alberta (R.S.A.), c. M-6, s. 1(c)(1), as amended by S.A. 2000, c. 5. S. 1.1 of the Alberta Act invokes the override provision of the Charter (s. 33). But see S.C. 2001, c. 4, ss. 4–5 (federal man-woman-only definition added to Québec Civil Code). See also *Recognizing and Supporting Close Personal Relationships Between Adults: Discussion Paper* (Ottawa, Law Commission of Canada, May 2000), http://www.lcc.gc.ca/en/themes/pr/cpra/paper.html.

[41] Income Tax Act, s. 252(4), enacted effective for the 1993 taxation year.

[42] Income Tax Act, s. 248(1), as of 1 January 2001.

> "marital status" under the Canadian Human Rights Act;[43] they do not have the legal capacity to marry; and Bill C-23 continues to withhold several significant legal rights and responsibilities that are extended to opposite-sex common-law partners.

In light of the Supreme Court of Canada decision in *Miron* v. *Trudel*, which established that opposite-sex common-law couples cannot be denied spousal rights without justification, and *M.* v. *H.*, which established that lesbian and gay couples cannot be denied the rights of opposite-sex cohabitants without justification, it seems unlikely that this new three-tiered scheme will pass constitutional muster. However, it places the burden squarely on lesbian and gay couples to challenge it in the courts.

On a substantive level, the federal government has gone to a great deal of effort to make it look as if lesbian and gay couples will now have all the rights and responsibilities of heterosexual cohabitants, and that the real and meaningful line of division is the distinction between cohabitants and married couples. But this is simply not true. Two of the most important areas of litigation since section 15 of the Charter came into effect have been the unequal age of consent rules for sexual activity in criminal law, which impose a higher age of consent for anal intercourse than other sexual contact,[44] and the refusal to permit lesbian and gay Canadians to sponsor their partners for immigration purposes. Both of these forms of discrimination disparately impact lesbian and gay couples. Neither of these forms of discrimination have been redressed in Bill C-23—the federal government had indicated that it "preferred" to deal with both of them when it later re-examined those areas of law. Nor does Bill C-23 extend the non-compellability of disclosure of marital communications in legal proceedings to lesbian and gay or opposite-sex cohabitants.

Table 4 (pp. 266–7) outlines the overall impact of Bill C-23 on the status of lesbian and gay couples. Although there is now greater equivalence between the three classes of relationships listed above, there are still extremely important areas of continuing discrimination. And just as importantly, it appears that the government is actually willing to backtrack on the constitutionally-mandated equality of heterosexual cohabitants in order to carve out a new non-marital status that it obviously hopes will withstand Charter challenge. The net result is an evident lack of respect for the feelings or dignity of either lesbian and gay or heterosexual cohabitants.

[43] This is a significant omission, because the last Supreme Court of Canada decision that considered whether lesbian and gay couples have any form of "marital status" (or "family status") ruled clearly that they do not. See *Attorney-General of Canada* v. *Mossop*, [1993] 1 S.C.R. 554.

[44] The higher age of 18 for anal intercourse (vs. 14 for all other sexual contact) in s. 159 of the Criminal Code has been struck down as discrimination, violating section 15(1) of the Charter and not justifiable under s. 1, in *R.* v. *M.(C.)* (1995), 98 C.C.C. (2d) 481 (Ontario Court of Appeal), and *R.* v. *Roy* (1998), 125 C.C.C. (3d) 442 (Québec Court of Appeal). Yet the federal government has declined to appeal these decisions to the Supreme Court of Canada, or take steps to repeal the higher age, and prosecutions continue. See *Lucas* v. *Toronto Police Service Board* (2000), 51 O.R. (3d) 783 (Ontario Superior Court of Justice).

MARRIAGE AND REGISTERED PARTNERSHIPS

As the five jurisdictions (Ontario, Québec and Canada, discussed above; British Columbia, discussed in chapter 11; and Nova Scotia, discussed below)[45] have formulated and debated their lesbian and gay cohabitant bills, one of the points that has nearly disappeared from sight is that, despite *Miron* v. *Trudel*, there is still a big divide between married couples and opposite-sex cohabitants, and another big divide between opposite-sex cohabitants and lesbian and gay cohabitants.

The biggest difference between married and unmarried heterosexuals is that married couples have full rights to share the family home and family property, rights to intestate succession and forced shares of each other's estates, dependent's relief, and presumptions of "natural" parentage of children born during the marriage even when one spouse is not a biological parent (for any reason at all). Across the country, with only a few exceptions,[46] these rights are reserved exclusively for married couples, and have not been extended to unmarried opposite-sex couples, even when they cohabit for lengthy periods of time, raise children, and support each other.

Although unmarried opposite-sex couples may be barred from marriage by a prior undissolved marriage, religious belief, or other impediment, by virtue of their heterosexuality they have the legal capacity to choose to marry, and thus to gain access to the core incidents of marriage listed above. The divide between heterosexual and queer cohabitants is threefold: as cohabitants, queers do not enjoy any of the core incidents of marriage; in no jurisdiction do they enjoy all

[45] The Family Services Act, R.S. New Brunswick (R.S.N.B.), c. F-2.2, s. 112(3), as amended by S.N.B. 2000, c. 59, imposes spousal support obligations on "[t]wo persons, not being married to each other, who have lived together . . . continuously for a period of not less than three years in a family relationship in which one person has been substantially dependent upon the other for support". Alberta's Child Welfare Act, S.A. 1984, c. C-8.1, s. 65(3), as amended by S.A. 1999, c. 26, which expressly permits step-parent adoption, was applied to a lesbian couple in *Re "A"* (1999), 181 D.L.R. (4th) 300 (Alberta Court of Queen's Bench). See also App. I, p. 776 (piecemeal reforms in Newfoundland and the Yukon). On 2 April 2001, in *Re Sand (Estate)*, http://www.albertacourts.ab.ca/jdb/monthqb.htm, the same trial court held that legislation granting intestate succession rights to a "spouse", but not to a same-sex partner, violates section 15 of the Charter. Perras J. declared the legislation invalid, subject to a suspension of nine months to allow the Alberta government to amend it. The Alberta government announced that it would not appeal, and that it would conduct a review of all legislation on spousal rights. See *Edmonton Journal* (4 April 2001). For 2001 omnibus legislation in Manitoba and Saskatchewan (not included in Table 1), see App. I, p. 776.

[46] For exceptions regarding property division, intestacy and dependent's relief, see Table 1 (British Columbia, the Yukon and Nova Scotia). The presumption that a lesbian or gay cohabitant is a "step-parent" in B.C. uses segregating language and falls short of establishing them legally as a "natural parent" (a legal term), thus withholding important inheritance and other rights from children with whom a parent-child relationship has been established through the cohabitation of the parents. B.C. law on parentage reserves the category of "natural parents" for the birth mother and her husband or male cohabitant, even when donor insemination is used and the husband or male cohabitant is not the genetic father of the child. In contrast, the lesbian cohabitant of a birth mother and the gay cohabitant of a birth father are recognised, but are instead classified as "step-parents", a term previously reserved for an adult who assumes the role of parent sometime after the birth of a child.

Table 4: Canada (Federal Level): Rights and Obligations of Married Couples, Opposite-Sex Cohabitants, and Lesbian and Gay Couples

	Married couples ("spouses")	Opposite-sex cohabitants (formerly "spouses", now "common-law partners")	Lesbian and gay couples ("spouses" before Bill C-23)	Lesbian and gay couples ("common-law partners" after Bill C-23)
FAMILY LAW:				
capacity to marry	X	X		
division of pension on divorce	X	X		X
filiation (status of partner who is not a genetic parent)	parent	de facto parent	de facto parent	de facto parent
protection of family assets against partner's creditors	X	X		X
federal child support guidelines (minimum amounts of support in each province)	X	X		X
HUMAN RIGHTS ACT:				
included in "marital status"	X	X	some case-law	
PUBLIC LAW:				
limits on eligibility for unemployment insurance of partner working in family business	X	X		X
federal tax benefits and burdens	X	X	tax-exempt health, pension survivor benefits	X

public sector employment benefits for partner	X	X	X	X
public sector employee pension benefits for surviving partner	X	X	X	X
Canada Pension Plan survivor and death benefits	X	X	mixed tribunal rulings	X
welfare benefits (eligibility tests look to partner's income)	X	X		X
right of non-citizen partner to immigrate	X	X (if partner marries citizen or permanent resident)	admitted on compassionate grounds but inconsistent	
OTHER:				
Aboriginal legislation	X			removed after protest by Aboriginal groups
disclosure of marital communications not compellable	X			
conflict of interest because of partner (and disclosure)	X	some	if factual conflict, in some contexts	X
identification of couples by sex/sexuality in census	X	X	beginning in 2001	

the rights of heterosexual cohabitants; and they do not have the legal capacity to bridge those divides by choosing to marry.

Given the choice between the strategy of suing under the Charter for the right to marry *versus* the strategy of seeking legislative relief from these forms of discrimination, it would again appear that lesbian and gay couples could expect to obtain fuller relief from courts than from legislatures. I draw this conclusion for three reasons. First, European legislation that is intended to bridge the divide between married and queer couples is consistently discriminatory in form. "Registered partnerships" do offer a method of memorialising lesbian and gay relationships, but they are entirely separate from marriage in form and legal effect, and, while they do extend access to some of the core incidents of marriage to registered partners, they invariably withhold others. In addition, no jurisdiction that permits registration of partnerships permits completely equal joint adoption, joint custody of children, or access to artificial insemination by lesbian and gay couples. Attempts to redress these forms of discrimination have, to date, failed.[47]

Second, Canadian proposals for registered partnership legislation continue this pattern of discrimination. As the Ontario government attempted to save Bill 167 from defeat in 1994, it promised to jettison joint adoption rights, claiming that it was moving closer to a European-style registered partnership system. And the 1999 British Columbia Law Institute (BCLI) domestic partnership proposals, which would offer queer couples a "choice" between registered and unregistered partnerships, intended to parallel the heterosexual choice between marriage and cohabitation, would still generate a hierarchy of relationship categories based on sexuality.[48] Third, the first registered partnership system to be enacted in Canada—Nova Scotia Bill 75[49]—clearly contains numerous discriminatory provisions. This makes it clear that, despite the weight of judicial authority across the country, there is some sense even on the part of lesbian and gay communities that enactment of some discriminatory partnership legislation is better than attempting to obtain judicial redress for discrimination.

[47] See Lahey, *supra* n.6, ch. 11, for an overview of the main forms of discrimination found in registered partnership provisions. In 2000, the Vermont legislature enacted the most comprehensive registered partnership statute found anywhere (see Bonauto, chap. 10), but it is still discriminatory. "Civil unions" are available only to same-sex couples, who are still prohibited from marrying, and the administration of the civil union legislation remains entirely separate from the administration of marriage laws. Licenses, registration books, ceremonies, and vital statistics are all segregated. Paradoxically, even the Netherlands legislation, which opened civil marriage to lesbian and gay couples on 1 April 2001, contains some discriminatory provisions relating to parental presumptions and adoption. Some European countries, such as Denmark, Iceland, the Netherlands, and Sweden, have recently begun to amend, or are considering amending, their registered partnership legislation to eliminate discriminatory provisions relating to custody, adoption, and reproductive technology. But no jurisdiction has eliminated them all. See Waaldijk, chap. 23; Lund-Andersen, chap. 21; Ytterberg, chap. 22.

[48] *Report on Recognition of Spousal and Family Status*, British Columbia Law Institute (Vancouver, British Columbia Law Institute, 1999), http://www.bcli.org/pages/projects/rrsfs/contents.html.

[49] Law Reform (2000) Act, Statutes of Nova Scotia 2000, c. 29 (Royal Assent, 30 Nov. 2000; in force on 4 June 2001, except for income tax provisions, in force on 1 Jan. 2001).

Nova Scotia Bill 75 and the BCLI domestic partnership proposals both reflect the growing difficulty of reconciling continued denial of marriage rights to lesbian and gay couples with the more recent prohibition on discrimination between opposite-sex cohabitants *versus* married couples, and the prohibition on discrimination between lesbian and gay cohabitants *versus* opposite-sex cohabitants. In addition, the older policy solution—ascribing spousal treatment to cohabitants—has now given rise to a small but important group of Charter challenges, in which unmarried heterosexuals have successfully challenged this ascribed spousal treatment on constitutional grounds, where it involves the imposition of unchosen burdens.[50]

What lies at the heart of this conflict in policy directions, of course, is the concept of "choice". As heterosexual cohabitants are establishing that they have the right to choose *not* to be treated as spouses, lesbian and gay couples are attempting to establish that they have the right to choose *to become* spouses by marriage. Both the BCLI proposals, and the new Nova Scotia registered partnership statute, attempt to head off both these types of challenges by creating new types of relationships that do give lesbian and gay couples some choices, but still fall short of giving them all the choices available to heterosexual couples.

The main elements of the Nova Scotia partnership legislation are outlined in Table 5 (pp. 270–1). As amended by Bill 75, Nova Scotia law now provides for five categories of relationships: marriage; registered domestic partnership; unregistered domestic partnership (where a domestic-partnership declaration is signed but not registered); common-law partnership (after one or two years of cohabitation); and short-term unrecognised cohabitation (of less than one or two years). A registered domestic-partnership declaration grants to the partners, "as between themselves and with respect to any person", certain of the rights and obligations of spouses.[51] An unregistered domestic-partnership declaration is effective "as between the parties . . . to confer on each of them the status, rights and obligations of domestic partners", but is only evidence of a domestic partnership vis-à-vis third parties.[52] There would seem to be a strong incentive to register a domestic-partnership declaration once it is signed, given the greater certainty that it will be enforceable against third parties. Apart from the provincial Income Tax Act (to which has been added the category "common-law partner" now found in the federal Income Tax Act), registered (and possibly unregistered?) domestic partners have all the rights and obligations of common-law partners, plus additional rights relating to intestate succession, property division, probate and dependent's relief.

As with federal Bill C-23, opposite-sex cohabitants have been removed from the category "spouses" and are now classified, along with lesbian and gay

[50] See *R.* v. *Rehberg* (1994), 111 D.L.R. (4th) 336 (Nova Scotia Supreme Court); *Falkiner* v. *Ontario*) (1999), 188 D.L.R. (4th) 52 (Ontario Superior Court of Justice, Divisional Court).

[51] *Supra* n.49, s. 45, adding Part II (Domestic Partners), including s. 54(2), to the Vital Statistics Act.

[52] *Ibid.*, adding s. 54(3).

Table 5: Nova Scotia: Rights and Obligations of Married Couples, Opposite-Sex Cohabitants, and Lesbian and Gay Couples

	Married couples ("spouses")	"Registered domestic partners" (opposite-sex or same-sex) (added by Bill 75)	"Common-law partners" (opposite-sex or same-sex) (added by Bill 75, or other legislation or case-law)
FAMILY LAW:			
capacity to marry	X	heterosexual partners only	heterosexual partners only
emergency consent for partner	X		
share of family home or other property on relationship breakdown	X	X	
elective and default property regimes	X	X	
equitable remedies for division of property	not needed	not needed	X
marriage/cohabitation agreements	X	X	X
financial support obligations (alimony)	X	X	X
child support obligations and custody/access rights (biological and non-biological parents)	X	X	X
filiation (status of partner who is not a genetic parent)	spouse deemed a natural parent (rebuttable)		not clear
second-parent adoption	X		
joint adoption	X		
inheritance rights on intestacy	X	X	
joint annuities	X		X

insurable interest (eg., in life of partner)	X	X	X
protection of family assets against partner's creditors	X	X	X
HUMAN RIGHTS CODE:			
included in "marital status"	X		
PUBLIC LAW:			
public health insurance coverage for partner	X		X
access to alternative conception	X		X
worker's compensation (eg., death benefits for surviving partner)	X		
provincial tax provisions (some confer benefits, some impose tax penalties)	X	X (indirectly through Bill C-23 and federal tax legislation)	X
exemption from taxes on transfer of vehicle to partner	X		
automobile insurance coverage	X	*Miron* v. *Trudel*	*Miron* v. *Trudel*
public sector employment benefits for partner	X	X	X
survivor benefits for partner under public sector employment pensions	X	X	X
welfare benefits and student assistance (partner's income considered in calculating need)	X		
OTHER:			
enforcement of child support orders	X	X	X
information re partner's death	X		
conflict of interest because of partner (and disclosure)	X		

couples, as "common-law partners". In amended legislation to which common-law partners have been added, they will receive spousal treatment, but not spousal status. Similarly, "domestic partnership" is also a segregated legal category used in parallel with "marriage". Many of the rights and responsibilities of spouses are extended to domestic partners, but they gain access to them *qua* "domestic partners" and not *qua* "spouses".

The discriminatory impact of this new system of classifications arises both from the establishment of segregated legal categories, into which lesbian and gay couples now fall, as well as from the fact that lesbian and gay couples have consistently fewer choices of regimes and of rights/responsibilities than do heterosexual couples:

(1) *heterosexual cohabiting couples have all five choices:* marriage, registered domestic partnership, unregistered domestic partnership, common-law partnership, short-term unrecognised cohabitation.
(2) *lesbian and gay cohabiting couples have four of those five choices:* registered domestic partnership, unregistered domestic partnership, common-law partnership, short-term unrecognised cohabitation;
(3) *only opposite-sex couples can obtain relationship recognition even if they do not wish to cohabit:* they may still choose to marry;
(4) *non-cohabiting lesbian and gay couples cannot obtain any form of relationship recognition:* they cannot marry, and domestic partnership (registered or unregistered) and common-law partnership require actual cohabitation.

Not only do lesbian and gay couples in Nova Scotia still lack the *choice to marry* that all cohabiting and non-cohabiting opposite-sex partners have, registered domestic partnerships are clearly intended to have lesser status than marriage. Unlike spouses, who must divorce before they can remarry, domestic partners can marry while the domestic partnership (registered or unregistered) is still in existence. Unlike a marriage, a domestic partnership (registered or unregistered) can be terminated unilaterally, if the partners have lived separately for one year or if one partner marries.[53] Not surprisingly, Bill 75 does not accord parental status to non-genetic registered domestic partners .

Although Bill 75 is festooned with new types of relationships and an increased number of apparent choices, it still relegates lesbian and gay couples to third-class relationship status. Even their registration would bring with it fewer real choices and rights, for they would never, on this scheme, be permitted the choice of marriage. Indeed, Bill 75 strengthens the marriage bar by forcing couples who wish to acquire some of the most basic rights and responsibilities of marriage to acquiesce in separate accommodation.[54]

[53] *Ibid.*, adding ss. 55(1), 57. Termination by marriage occurs by operation of law as soon as one partner's certificate of marriage is registered.

[54] The BCLI proposals for registered domestic partnership are roughly similar to Bill 75 in Nova Scotia. See Casswell, chap. 11.

THE FUTURE OF QUEER PERSONHOOD

State control over marriage is really state control over relationships. The extent of state control over relationships depends on state assignment of legal status to relationships. The Canadian state is obviously in an expansive phase of relationship regulation, and has been since the end of World War II.

The state's motives for increasing the scope of its regulation of relationships is quite different from people's motives for entering into regulated relationships. In the Roman Empire, the state's interest was in maintaining and increasing the size of the "citizen" class, in the face of increasing reliance on non-citizens to defend the borders of the empire, and in providing productive labour. Couples entered into heterosexual marriage because various tax penalties, state benefits, inheritance rules, and confiscatory property rules were devised to induce members of the citizen class to marry heterosexually, have children with each other, and leave their property to their children, instead of to friends or intimate same-sex partners. Indeed, the whole concept of "legal capacity" was also designed to delineate "citizens" from non-citizens.

In Canada, the state's motives are also predominantly regulatory. Identification of cohabiting couples appears to be high on the list of priorities, and the Canada Customs and Revenue Agency has made it perfectly clear that it intends to use both its civil and criminal powers to compel disclosure of relationship status, even if non-disclosure does not result in tax reduction. As one of its employees stated recently: "You wanted it, you fought for it, you won it, you are equal now. Deal with it". Non-disclosure will most often be motivated by a desire to optimise social assistance benefits, such as the national child benefit, child care expense deductions, the Goods and Services Tax credit, and other benefits delivered through the tax system. State recognition of queer relationships will compel disclosure. This, in turn, will reduce the number of claimants to these types of benefits and simultaneously empower the state to "privatise" social welfare costs whenever it can prove cohabitation.

This is not a new dynamic. Nor is the use of separate legal categories and registries to carry it out new. Before the United States Civil War, African slaves were not permitted to marry, and their children were not in law their own children. After the Emancipation Proclamation, one of their new "civil rights" was the right to marry. This "right" was no choice, however. Former slaves were forced to register their marriages upon pain of criminal penalty. Registration was carried out by the Freedman's Bureau, which was also responsible for allocating social assistance and relief to former slaves. Freedman's benefits were distributed in light of marital status, calibrated by the "colour" of each partner, and even former relationships had to be reported. Registries were used to keep track of the children of former slaves, and state laws stipulated that children "in need" were to be removed from their parents.[55]

[55] For an example of these "civil rights" provisions and "child welfare" laws, see Laws of Mississippi, 1865, c. IV, s. 1, c. V, s. 1.

Out of the separate marriage registries of the Freedman's Bureau, the "certificates of racial composition" of African-American marriages kept by both state and local registries, and the criminal penalties for non-registration of cohabitation, grew the degrading "separate but equal" doctrine of the Fourteenth Amendment equal protection clause, and with it the "anti-miscegenation" laws that persisted until 1967 to segregate African-Americans in completely separate systems of marriage.

The legislation that has been enacted or proposed in Canada for the recognition of lesbian and gay marriages bears a remarkable resemblance to those old separate systems of the post-Civil War states. Recognition is compulsory, and is not a choice. Disclosure of the relationship to the state is compulsory, and non-disclosure is subject to civil and criminal penalties.[56] Legal status is extended to lesbian and gay couples in a variety of ways, but it is always a lesser status and a segregated status. Even when registration is offered, as in Nova Scotia since June 2001, it is still clearly a lesser status and is carefully segregated as well.

This is not the relationship recognition given to full and unquestioned constitutional persons. This is the form of relationship recognition that is reserved for subjected and regulated classes, who are expected to be so eager for the benefits of recognition that they will comply voluntarily, even eagerly. This is the form of relationship recognition that demonstrates that in Canada, at least, lesbian and gay couples are still really at the beginning of the road to full and genuine equality.

As with the racial liberation movement that began in the early 1800s on this continent, marriage rights undoubtedly will be the last segregation. It took one hundred and one years, after the first race civil rights statute was passed in the United States in 1866, to bring the principle of constitutional personhood to bear on the "miscegenation" statutes that had swept thirty-five states in the first half of the twentieth century. It was not until 1967 that the religious objections to inter-racial marriage which had justified those statutes were rejected, as the US Supreme Court began to apply the equal protection clause of the Fourteenth Amendment to those statutes.[57]

I am not suggesting that lesbian and gay couples should be marrying, should want to marry, or should give marriage any kind of primacy. But I am suggesting that the creation of segregated legal structures, that parallel but do not touch existing marriage legislation, merely changes the way in which the simple right to marry continues to be denied. Like roping off sections of law school classrooms for Black Americans,[58] or paying to send Black university students to another state for their education,[59] setting up registered domestic partnership legislation segregates same-sex couples from other cohabiting couples in struc-

[56] The same statements are true of heterosexual cohabitation, with the difference, however, that it is only lesbian and gay couples who have no other alternative to such ascribed status.

[57] *Loving* v. *Virginia*, 388 U.S. 1 (1967).

[58] See eg *McLaurin* v. *Oklahoma State Regents*, 339 U.S. 737 (1950).

[59] See eg *Missouri ex rel. Gaines* v. *Canada*, 305 U.S. 337 (1938).

tures that are not so much equal as they are predominantly separate. The fact that other pairs of adults (siblings, friends, tennis partners), who may see some benefit in claiming the rights of married couples, may be permitted to join this segregated class (as under the BCLI proposals) does not disguise its essential nature. Indeed, including them actually trivialises the effort it has taken to gain recognition for same-sex couples, as part of the process of gaining full personhood for sexual minorities in Canada.

The developments in Canadian law relating to sexuality have held out a beacon of hope to those in countries whose constitutions have yet to embrace people characterised by their sexualities or gender identities. But the reality is that it has taken the entire weight of the Charter of Rights equality guarantees, the progressive *Andrews* test of discrimination, the careful consideration of many judges, and the efforts of a whole generation of litigants and lawyers to achieve but partial restoration of the constitutional personhood of Canadian queers. Despite all this, the most basic of all relational capacities—the legal capacities to marry and acquire full recognition of parental status[60]—remain the most denied and most partial of all.

[60] See *Re Nova Scotia (Birth Registration No. 1999-02-004200)*, [2001] N.S.J. No. 261 (Quicklaw) (N.S. Supreme Ct., Fam Div., 28 June 2001) (exclusion of same-sex couples from second-parent adoption violates Charter).

Section C—Africa, Australasia and Latin America

13

Politics, Partnership Rights and the Constitution in South Africa . . . (and the Problem of Sexual Identity)

CRAIG LIND*

INTRODUCTION—BACKGROUND LAW AND POLITICS

THE BILL OF Rights chapter in the Constitution of the Republic of South Africa is more explicit in its condemnation of discrimination against lesbians and gay men than almost every other national constitution in the world. It was the first specifically to outlaw discrimination on the ground of "sexual orientation".[1] For that reason alone, South Africa could have been expected to be among the first nations, if not the first, to see the emergence of formal equality for lesbians and gay men in family law.[2] But that has not been so.

THE EXPLICIT PROTECTION OF EQUALITY

Section 9 of the final Constitution provides as follows:

> "(1) Everyone is equal before the law and has the right to equal protection and benefit of the law. . . .
> (3) The state may not unfairly discriminate directly or indirectly against anyone on one or more grounds, including race, gender, sex, pregnancy, marital status, ethnic or social origin, colour, sexual orientation, age, disability, religion, conscience, belief, culture, language and birth.

* Lecturer, School of Legal Studies, University of Sussex.

[1] See Constitution of the Republic of South Africa Act, No. 200 of 1993, s. 8(2) (interim Constitution) (in force on 27 April 1994); Constitution of the Republic of South Africa, Act No. 108 of 1996, s. 9(3) (final Constitution) (adopted by the Constitutional Assembly on 8 May 1996, amended by the Assembly on 11 Oct. 1996, signed by President Nelson Mandela on 10 Dec. 1996, in force on 4 Feb. 1997). See also final Constitution s. 35(2)(f)(i) (right of detained person to communicate with their "spouse or partner").

[2] At the informal level, weddings have been celebrated in South Africa (as elsewhere) for quite some time: see C Lind, "Sexual Orientation, Family Law and the Transitional Constitution", (1995) 112 *South African Law Journal* 481.

(4) No person may unfairly discriminate directly or indirectly against anyone on one or more grounds in terms of subsection (3). National legislation must be enacted to prevent or prohibit unfair discrimination.
(5) Discrimination on one or more grounds listed in subsection (3) is unfair unless it is established that the discrimination is fair".

Two limitations should be noted. One is to be found in the section establishing the right itself. "Fair" discrimination is permissible. The other is to be found in section 36, which provides:

"(1) The rights in the Bill of Rights may be limited only in terms of law of general application to the extent that the limitation is reasonable and justifiable in an open and democratic society based on human dignity, equality and freedom, taking into account all relevant factors, including—
(a) the nature of the right;
(b) the importance of the purpose of the limitation;
(c) the nature and extent of the limitation;
(d) the relation between the limitation and its purpose; and
(e) less restrictive means to achieve the purpose".

Since its enactment, several writers have taken the view that the equality provision of the South African Constitution could, and should, be interpreted to give effect to full equality for South Africa's lesbians and gay men in the realm of family law.[3] The argument was made that real equality demanded that lesbians and gay men should be able to marry partners of their choice and so attract all the privileges of that most privileged of family relationships. Each contributor to the "debate" seems to be of the opinion that the limitations clause could not be used to justify continued discrimination against lesbians and gay men without distorting the purpose of the protection granted in the equality clause. Obviously, there seems to be a distinct one-sidedness to the "debate" on the issue in South Africa. No academic writer seems to have argued explicitly (in South African legal journals, at least) that the privileges of marriage should not be extended to lesbians and gay men.

THE POLITICAL STRATEGY

While the academic writers' arguments could be seen to have laid the groundwork for an inevitable legal challenge to the exclusive heterosexuality of marriage, which could quite conceivably have succeeded, the quest for full marriage rights through the courts has not been pursued in South Africa. Indeed, in the

[3] See Lind, *ibid.*; "Focus on Same-Sex Marriage (special issue)", (1996) 12 *South African Journal of Human Rights* 533; Lorraine Volhuter, "Equality and the Concept of Difference: Same-Sex Marriages in the Light of the Final Constitution", (1997) 114 *South African Law Journal* 389; Elsa Steyn, "From Closet to Constitution: The South African Gay Family Rights Odyssey" in J Eekelaar and T Nhlapo (eds.), *The Changing Family: Family Forms and Family Law* (Oxford, Hart Publishing, 1998) at 405.

first four years of the existence of the equality clause (from April 1994 to April 1998), remarkably little use was made of the courts to achieve family rights[4] for lesbians and gay men. That is not to say that it was not recognised that the existence of a constitutional right to equality had the potential to free family law from its heterosexual traditions.[5] But something did impede its formal use in the achievement of that end. As a result, the limitations that have restricted family rights to heterosexual couples continue, in large measure, to apply in South Africa. Legal marriage remains unavailable to lesbians and gay men[6] and the common law on parental status remains unchanged.[7] At the level of activist politics surrounding the equality provision and the idea of lesbian and gay marriage, enthusiasm seems also to have been slow to develop. Only late in 1998, some five years after the enactment of the inclusive equality clause, was a public rally held to promote lesbian and gay family recognition in South Africa.[8]

The appearance of apathy, however, is deceptive. Closer examination of both legal and political activism in South Africa reveals a deliberate and disciplined strategy for the achievement of family equality for South Africa's lesbian and gay population. While some battles are now being fought (and won) in courts and tribunals, these are merely the outcomes of much lower-keyed struggles, which have often been of long duration and were always likely to achieve more than could have been achieved by an outright assault on marriage (or even some lesser family rights) in the courts. It is probably accurate to assume that the direct cause of the more subtle lobbying approach adopted in South Africa had its roots in the process by which sexual minorities were protected in the interim constitution itself.

South African society, it is generally acknowledged, is not morally progressive. In this it is not unlike the societies of its nearest neighbours in Africa, including Zimbabwe, Namibia and Swaziland. And it is telling that in each of those countries (and most recently, also in Kenya and Uganda), national leaders have chosen to express homophobic sentiments in order to revive their

[4] Indeed, no substantive rights for lesbians and gay men were achieved through litigation during this period.

[5] See T Mosikatsana, "Gay/lesbian adoptions and the best interests standard: A critical analytical perspective", [1996] *Acta Juridica* 114, and "The Definitional Exclusion of Gays and Lesbians from Family Status", (1996) 12 *South African Journal of Human Rights* 549.

[6] But numerous religious and other social ceremonies are being held to celebrate their marriage-like status. And there are social instances of "divorce" being reported in the local and international gay press.

[7] Represented most starkly and most derisively in the decision in *Van Rooyen* v. *Van Rooyen* 1994 (2) SA 325 (Witwatersrand High Court). See P de Vos, "The Right of a Lesbian Mother to Have Access to Her Children: Some Constitutional Issues", (1994) 111 *South African Law Journal* 687; Mosikatsana, *supra* n.5; E Bronthuys, "Awarding Access and Custody to Homosexual Parents of Minor Children", (1994) 3 *Stellenbosch Law Review* 298. It should be noted that the Law Commission is currently engaged in a program of research aimed at reform of the law relating to children in South Africa.

[8] "Recognise our Relationships" Rally, St George's Cathedral, Cape Town, 22 November 1998.

popularity amongst their people.[9] Whether or not the population actually embraces these anti-gay and anti-lesbian outbursts remains untested. But it is clear that forceful, enthusiastic, very public, and often repeated expressions of homophobia have done these leaders no harm.

If moral conservatism is the order of the day in these nations, it seems surprising that the rights of sexual minorities were thought important enough to protect in the interim constitution at all. And yet they were. The cause was almost certainly the result of the synthesis of two kinds of power at play in South African politics in the early 1990s. The first was the influential positions held by particular members of the lesbian and gay community (and their friends and supporters) within the African National Congress (ANC) and other political parties negotiating the interim constitution.[10] The other was the prominent role played by lesbian and gay lawyers (and their friends and supporters) in the transition to democracy (both as draftsmen and as people promoting a just constitution for South Africa).[11] In other words, the protection was won by a subtle lobbying process, which relied on elite relationships within the powerful bodies responsible for negotiating and drafting the interim constitution. It did not attempt to publicise itself more generally, nor did it rely on general "public" pressure. Indeed, publicity would almost certainly have undermined the attempt to achieve the object of constitutional protection.[12]

Because of the personal dynamics that saw the protection of minority sexualities in the interim constitution, it was not inconceivable that a democratically elected body, which was less influenced by elites within South African society, would see the matter of equality differently. The relative unimportance of sexual diversity as a feature of South African life to the mass of people, and consequently its unimportance as constitutional doctrine, suggested that one of two things could, quite conceivably and quite easily, have happened in the process of drafting the final constitution. In the first place, the inclusion of sexual orientation protection in the equality clause could have reoccurred by simple oversight. The clause could have been left intact without reconsideration, by virtue of its insignificance as a topic of negotiation when so many more serious constitu-

[9] See N Hoad, "Tradition, Modernity and Human Rights: An Interrogation of Contemporary Gay and Lesbian Rights Claims in Southern African Nationalist Discourses", (1998) 2(2) *Development Update* 32 at 33–4.

[10] Jara and Lepinsky, "Forging a Representative Gay Liberation Movement in South Africa", (1998) 2 *Development Update* 44. See too M Gevisser, "A Different Fight for Freedom: A History of South African Lesbian and Gay Organisation from the 1950s to 1990s" (especially at 52 ff), and S Nkoli "Wardrobes: Coming Out as a Black Gay Activist in South Africa", both in Mark Gevisser and E Cameron (eds.), *Defiant Desire: Gay and Lesbian Lives in South Africa* (London, Routledge, 1995).

[11] See, for example, E Cameron, "Sexual Orientation and the Constitution: A Test Case for Human Rights", (1993) 110 *South African Law Journal* 450; K Botha and E Cameron, "Sexual Privacy: Considerations on Parity, Policy and Enforcement in a Changing South Africa", [1993] *South African Human Rights and Labour Law Yearbook*; Lind, *supra* n.2; "Focus", *supra* n.3.

[12] See R Louw, "Gay and Lesbian Sexualities in South Africa: From Outlawed to Constitutionally Protected", in Moran, Monk and Beresford (eds.), *Legal Queeries: Lesbian, Gay and Transgender Legal Studies* (London, Cassell, 1998).

tional problems needed resolution. Alternatively, the issue could have been used (as it has been used in Zimbabwe, Namibia and Swaziland) as a distraction from more intransigent political and constitutional problems. If it were clear that the vast majority of the population had no sympathy with sexual minorities, ousting them from the protection of the constitution could have appealed to popular sentiment and been used as a mechanism for undermining opposition to (or at least distracting opposition from) more contentious constitutional issues.[13]

The fear of many lesbian and gay activists was, therefore, that the protection that had been won in the interim constitution could easily be lost during its renegotiation. If South African society was not a society in which minority sexualities were at least neutrally regarded, there was no reason to think that a democratic body representing the interests of the electorate would adopt the same generous, progressive attitude towards the protection of their rights. And if the society was not positively predisposed to protect lesbian and gay sexuality, only a subtle, quiet strategy would achieve the extension, into the final constitution, of the protection won in the interim document.

For that reason a cautious strategy was formalised in the objects of the National Coalition for Gay and Lesbian Equality (NCGLE), which was set up by a number of lesbian and gay organisations in South Africa in 1994 to oversee the implementation of the equality clause of South Africa's interim constitution.[14] The aims of the Coalition give a clear indication of the priorities of the organisation and, consequently, some idea of the strategy to be adopted in achieving its goals. These were to:

> "3.1. promote equality before the law for all persons, irrespective of their sexual orientation[,] in the Constitution of the Republic of South Africa and to secure the specific inclusion of sexual orientation as a ground for non-discrimination in the [final] Constitution;
>
> 3.2. reform and repeal laws that discriminate on the basis of sexual orientation, including the decriminalisation of same-sex conduct;
>
> 3.3. promote and sponsor legislation to ensure equality and equal treatment of people in respect of their sexual orientation;
>
> 3.4. challenge by means of litigation, lobbying, advocacy and political mobilisation, all forms of discrimination on the basis of sexual orientation;
>
> 3.5. promote an understanding and commitment within the gay, lesbian and transgendered communities of human rights and sustainable social development; and
>
> 3.6. continue to train and to develop a representative leadership on the basis of nonracism and nonsexism". [15]

Clearly, the NCGLE did not, in the immediate aftermath of the implementation of the interim constitution, see as its priority the use of the courts to demand instant equality for lesbians and gay men. A more complex strategy

[13] See Hoad, *supra* n. 9.

[14] Representatives of some 41 organisations gathered at a meeting in Johannesburg on 3 December 1994 and launched the NCGLE: see Jara and Lepinsky, *supra* n.10. The NCGLE is now the Lesbian and Gay Equality Project, <http://www.q.co.za/equality/index.htm>.

[15] See Louw, *supra* n.12.

was selected. Simply put, a very public, aggressive demand-driven strategy was thought likely to undermine chances both of obtaining real equality and, perhaps more importantly, of sustaining equal protection for people irrespective of their sexual orientation.

The result was a strategy to achieve legal recognition of lesbian and gay family relationships as quietly as possible. To this end specific rights, in the particular contexts of specific spousal benefits, were sought from specifically targeted agencies, organisations and individuals. Instead of pursuing marriage and thereby acquiring all at once, the Coalition set out to acquire so many of the attributes of marriage for lesbians and gay men that the acquisition of marriage itself would ultimately be rendered irrelevant, or would be easy (since it would involve only a slight material gain for lesbians and gay men beyond what they had already achieved by that stage). This strategy was both pragmatic and ideological: pragmatic, because achieving individual family rights was likely to be easier than achieving an entire collection of rights, previously denied to lesbians and gay men, all at once; and ideological because it acknowledged that serious criticism (most significantly, feminist) of the institution of marriage itself made the idea of lesbian and gay marriage unattractive to many (if not most) lesbian and gay political activists.[16]

In the years since the adoption of the interim constitution, therefore, the NCGLE has involved itself in a series of activities that have been aimed at achieving equal family rights for lesbians and gay men. It has negotiated directly with government (in the case of immigration rights) and with private individuals and corporations (in the contexts of pensions and medical aid schemes). It has also lobbied Parliament (concerning new legislation on fairness in employment and reform of the law on medical aid schemes) and the South African Law Commission (in the context of plans for the reform of children's welfare and recommendations about pension benefits sharing). It has also approached the courts and tribunals where lobbying has proved to be inadequate as a means of achieving the family rights sought.

In most of the rest of this chapter, an attempt will be made to elaborate some examples of the diversity of approaches adopted by the NCGLE, in its efforts to extend the boundaries of family law to cover lesbian and gay families.

Immigration

Like most western societies, South Africa's immigration law allows relatively easy access to immigrant status to the foreign spouse of a South African citizen.[17] The same immigration facility was not available to the same-sex partners

[16] See e.g. P Ettelbrick, "Since When Is Marriage a Path to Liberation" in S Sherman (ed.), *Lesbian and Gay Marriage: Private Commitments, Public Ceremonies* (Philadelphia, PA, Temple University Press, 1992); Didi Herman, "Are We Family?: Lesbian Rights and Women's Liberation", (1990) 28 *Osgoode Hall Law Journal* 789.

[17] See Aliens Control Act, No. 96 of 1991, s. 25(5).

of South African citizens. In May 1997, however, after some negotiations between the NCGLE and the Department of Home Affairs, an agreement was reached which allowed foreign same-sex partners of South African citizens to be admitted to the country using an "unusual circumstances" discretion contained in section 28(2) of the Aliens Control Act (1991). The agreement was understood to be temporary, operating only until the Act could be amended to comply with the constitutional guarantee of equality. Lesbian and gay partners, the NCGLE had argued to the Department and the Department had appeared to accept, should be treated like spouses under the legislation, and their exclusion from the benefits available to spouses therefore contravened the provision of the Constitution requiring the equal protection of all irrespective of their sexual orientation.

The arrangement worked successfully for about seven months. A steady trickle of applications from same-sex partners of South African citizens was received, and the partners were, in each case, allowed to remain in the country on the basis of this agreement. However, in November 1997, the NCGLE received a letter from the Department of Home Affairs stipulating that, as applications from same-sex couples had become routine, their circumstances could no longer be considered to be "unusual" under the rules creating the Minister's discretion. Foreign individuals in same-sex relationships with South African citizens would, therefore, no longer be given exceptional leave to remain in the country. At least one foreign partner was served with deportation papers on the basis of this change in policy.

The government seemed no longer to accept that the Aliens Control Act contravened the Constitution and effectively announced an intention to renege on its undertaking to ensure that the legislation was appropriately amended. Because of the threat to deport several foreign partners of South African lesbians and gay men, the NCGLE brought an action in the High Court. On appeal, in *NCGLE* v. *Minister of Home Affairs*,[18] the Constitutional Court upheld NCGLE's claim that the offending section of the Act was unconstitutional. Ackermann J (speaking for the unanimous court) followed the robust approach he and Sachs J had adopted in the "Sodomy Case",[19] and held that the provision contravened both section 9 (equality) and section 10 (dignity) of the Constitution:

> "[49] . . . The impact of section 25(5) is to reinforce harmful and hurtful stereotypes of gays and lesbians. . . .
>
> "[53] . . . The subsection . . . in effect states that all gay and lesbian permanent residents of the Republic, who are in same-sex relationships with foreign nationals, are

[18] (2 Dec. 1999), 2000 (2) SA 1, <http://www.concourt.gov.za/archive.html>, affirming 1999 (3) SA 173 (Cape High Court). What may seem odd about the government's decision to defend this action is that, in March 1999 (some five months before argument before the Constitutional Court), the Cabinet had approved a white paper which proposed that new immigration legislation should provide for a ministerial discretion that would allow same-sex couples to be treated as spouses: *White Paper on International Migration*, ch. 7, para. 14(2) (March 1999), <http://www.polity.org.za/govdocs/white_papers/migration.html>.

[19] *NCGLE* v. *Minister of Justice* (9 Oct. 1998), 1999 (1) SA 6 (Constit. Ct.).

not entitled to the benefit extended by the subsection to spouses married to foreign nationals in order to protect their family and family life. This is so stated, notwithstanding that the family and family life which gays and lesbians are capable of establishing with their foreign national same-sex partners are in all significant respects indistinguishable from those of spouses and in human terms as important to gay and lesbian same-sex partners as they are to spouses.

[54] The message and impact as clear. Section 10 of the Constitution recognises and guarantees that everyone has inherent dignity and the right to have their dignity respected and protected. The message is that gays and lesbians lack the inherent humanity to have their families and family lives in such same-sex relationships respected or protected. It serves in addition to perpetuate and reinforce existing prejudices and stereotypes. The impact constitutes a crass, blunt, cruel and serious invasion of their dignity. The discrimination, based on sexual orientation, is severe because no concern, let alone anything approaching equal concern, is shown for the particular sexual orientation of gays and lesbians.

[59] . . . It is true . . .that the protection of family and family life in conventional spousal relationships is an important governmental objective, but the extent to which this could be done would in no way be limited or affected if same-sex life partners were appropriately included under the protection of section 25(5). There is in my view no justification for the limitation in the present case and it therefore follows that the provisions of section 25(5) are inconsistent with the Constitution and invalid".[20]

Not only did the Constitutional Court confirm the High Court's decision as to the unconstitutionality of the provisions dealing with "spouses" in the Aliens Control Act, it also provided the applicants with a more secure remedy (under section 172 of the final Constitution). Ackermann J was characteristally blunt:

"The real question is whether, in the circumstances of the present matter, reading in would be just and equitable and an appropriate remedy".[21]

After holding that suspending a declaration of unconstitutionality would not necessarily achieve a just (or constitutionally permissible) result, he ordered that the words "or partner, in a permanent same-sex life partnership" be read into the subsection after the word "spouse".[22] He reiterated his view that parliament could, if it chose to, refine the court's redrafting by an appropriate legislative amendment (subject to the constitutional guarantees which would be protected by the court).

The government responded to this judgment in February 2000 with the publication of an Immigration Bill.[23] For the purposes of immigration the new legislation will, if enacted, define "spouse" as "a person who is party to a marriage, or a customary union, or to a permanent relationship which calls for cohabitation and mutual financial and emotional support, and is proven with a

[20] *Home Affairs*, *supra* n.18, at paras. 49, 53, 54, 59.

[21] *Ibid.* at para. 70.

[22] *Ibid.* at para. 86. The issue of different-sex partners who do not wish to marry was not before the Court. *Ibid.* at para. 87.

[23] Government Gazette, Vol. 416, No. 20889, Notice 621 (15 Feb. 2000): <http://www.polity.org.za/govdocs/notices/2000/not0621.html> (s. 1(xxxix)).

prescribed affidavit substantiated by a notarised contract". If legislation along these lines is passed, South Africa will have moved another step closer to the recognition of lesbian and gay marriage. In some legislation, at least, same-sex partners will have entered the realms of one of the two family relationships which tradition has regarded as its most important.

Medical Aid Schemes

In South Africa, the state takes very little responsibility for the medical treatment of citizens. This has meant that Medical Insurance, or Medical Aid Schemes, usually contracted through employers, have become an important source of funding for medical treatment. These schemes invariably extend their benefits to members of the family of an employee. However, "family" has, traditionally, been defined heterosexually in these schemes.

The advent of the equality clause in the Constitution made it possible for a challenge to be launched against the exclusive privileging of heterosexuality in these schemes. Between 1994 and 1998, the NCGLE, in the course of some negotiating, managed to convince a number of large employers to amend their definitions of "family" in their medical aid schemes so as to include families based on same-sex relationships.

In the one unsuccessful negotiation, the court stepped in to cure the deficiencies of the scheme's exclusive privileging of heterosexual relationships. In *Langemaat* v. *Minister of Safety and Security*,[24] the Transvaal High Court ruled that the definition of a dependant in the Police Force's Medical Aid Scheme (PolMed) violated the constitutional protection of equality. By providing that a dependant was "the legal spouse or widow or widower or a dependant child", the definition unfairly discriminated against people on the basis of their sexual orientation. Roux J. held that the stability and permanence of same-sex relationships was no different from that of married couples and that both types of union deserved respect and protection.

Since that case was decided, the Medical Schemes Act (No. 131 of 1998) has been passed to regulate medical aid schemes in South Africa (and in particular to protect the interests of members of medical schemes). In section 1, a dependant has been defined broadly to include a "spouse or partner. . .". Furthermore section 24(2)(e) prohibits the registration of a medical scheme which unfairly discriminates on the ground of sexual orientation (amongst others). It is, therefore, clear that lesbians and gay men will be admitted to the same protection in this respect as members of heterosexual families are.

Pension Funds

As in many (if not all) western jurisdictions, pension funds in South Africa make provision for the members of the family of the beneficiary of the fund. Family,

[24] 1998 (3) SA 312 (Transvaal High Court).

once again, has traditionally been defined heterosexually. And once again the equality clause has been argued to have ushered in an era of potential change. However, that potential was, initially at least, undermined by a 1998 South African Law Commission discussion paper on the sharing of pension benefits.[25] The discussion paper (which included a draft Division of Retirement Fund Benefits on Divorce Bill) proposed that benefits should continue to be limited to spouses in a pattern along the lines of traditional marriage. Same-sex relationships, and even heterosexual long-term cohabitation relationships (which it referred to as "shacking up" arrangements),[26] were excluded. The explanatory note accompanying the proposal explained that "the development of our law has not reached the stage where such relationships are recognised as marriages in the true sense".[27]

The NCGLE responded by suggesting that the personal views of the author of the discussion document had been allowed to dictate its terms, despite their inconsistency with the trend in family law to bring the variety of personal relationships in society within its ambit (and, in particular, into line with the provisions of the equality clause of the Constitution). It pointed to a number of recent cases,[28] statutes,[29] bills,[30] and other government consultation documents[31] which had explicitly broadened the scope of "family", "spouse", and "domestic relationship" so as to provide for the wider variety of families that existed in South African society. While the Law Commission's work on pensions is, as yet, incomplete, it seems probable, given the trend being established in much new law regulating family life in South Africa, that the NCGLE's strategy will work to achieve legislation on pension sharing on separation which will take into account a greater variety of family relationships than the discussion document envisages, including lesbian and gay relationships.

On another front, the NCGLE has been remarkably successful. It has managed to enlarge the nature of family relationships which are afforded protection under particular pension schemes established in terms of the Pension Funds Act of 1956. Under the 1956 Act, the Pension Funds Adjudicator is required to adjudicate in matters where pension fund administrators are alleged to have failed to operate their schemes in accordance with the Act. The Adjudicator has gone on to hold that he must also adjudicate in matters in which pension fund admin-

[25] *Sharing of Pension Benefits* (Project 112), Discussion Paper 77, <http://www.law.wits.ac.za/salc/discussn/dp77.html>.

[26] *Ibid.*, at para. 4.1.2.2.

[27] *Ibid.*

[28] See e.g. *Fraser* v. *Children's Court of Pretoria North* 1997 (2) SA 261 (Constitutional Court); *Harksen* v. *Lane* 1998 (1) SA 300 (Constit. Ct.) and, perhaps most significantly in this context, *Langemaat*, *supra* n.24.

[29] See e.g. Basic Conditions of Employment Act, No. 75 of 1997, section 27(2)(c)(i) (providing for family responsibility leave in the event of the death of a "spouse or life partner").

[30] See e.g. Domestic Violence Bill, No. 75 of 1998, clause 1(vi), which became Domestic Violence Act, No. 116 of 1998, s. 1 (vii)("domestic relationship").

[31] See e.g. Department of Welfare, *White Paper on Social Welfare*, Government Gazette No. 16943 (2 Feb. 1996).

istrators are alleged to have operated their schemes in defiance of the requirements of the Constitution.[32]

On several occasions, the NCGLE has assisted employees claiming that the administrators of their pension funds have violated the 1956 Act and the Constitution, by failing to provide benefits for their same-sex partners where the same benefits would have been provided for married couples or unmarried heterosexual cohabitants. In *Martin* v. *Beka Provident Fund*,[33] the adjudicator (Professor John Murphy) agreed with the arguments presented by the NCGLE, and followed the trend towards a purposive interpretation of the 1956 Act and the Constitution which he had established earlier. He held that the exclusion of same-sex partners from the class of persons entitled to enjoy a spouse's pension, in the particular pension scheme under consideration, violated section 9 of the Constitution. Professor Murphy went on to require the fund in question to amend its definition of marriage to remove the discrimination inherent in it, and to comply with the requirements of section 9 of the Constitution. He reiterated a view he had expressed earlier that:

> "A . . . purposive and contextual interpretation . . . reveals that the purpose of the legislature in enacting the provision was to broaden the category of persons entitled to share in death benefits by including persons involved in relationships which the law traditionally does not accept as constituting legal dependency. The provision has the progressive aim of recognising that modern society is tolerant of relationships besides the nuclear family arrangements sanctioned by the common law. The test in this regard is whether the parties lived in a relationship of mutual dependence and ran a shared and common household".[34]

In the light of this decision it seems clear that, to a large extent, lesbian and gay couples have already achieved parity with heterosexual couples in the context of pension rights at the time of the death of one of the partners. And despite an inauspicious beginning, it does not seem too unrealistic to predict that a similar, positive result will be achieved when new legislation on pension splitting (when relationships end in separation) is enacted.

The future

It seems that substantial parity between lesbian and gay and heterosexual relationships in South Africa can be predicted with relative confidence.[35] Complete

[32] See e.g. *Martin* v. *Beka Provident Fund*, Case No. PFA/GA/563/99 (8 June 1999), http://www.fsb.co.za/pfa/martin.htm ("I am obliged to give effect to the value contained in section 9 of our Bill of Rights"); *Low* v. *BP Southern Africa Pension Fund*, Case No. PFA/WE/9/98 (2 Dec. 1998), <http://www.fsb.co.za/pfa/low.htm> "[C]onstitutional scrutiny of the rules of pension funds and their decisions clearly falls within my jurisdiction").

[33] *Ibid.*

[34] See *TWC* v. *Rentokil Pension Fund*, Case No. PFA/KZN/129/98 (26 Oct. 1998), <http://www.fsb.co.za/pfa/chapman.htm>.

[35] See Revenue Laws Amendment Act, No. 59 of 2000, s. 1(1), amending Estate Duties Act, 1955, s. 1: "'spouse', in relation to any deceased person, includes a person who . . . was the partner of such person . . . in a permanent same-sex life relationship". See also App. I, p. 778.

parity is also possible. The long-awaited reform of the Marriage Act 1961 is pending. If it includes gender-neutral references to the partners to a marriage relationship, the courts may already be predisposed to interpreting these references as permitting lesbian and gay partners to marry. If, on the other hand, gender-specific language is used to limit marriage to heterosexual relationships, the constitutional battle for same-sex marriage is likely to be at least as difficult as it has proved to be in the USA and Canada.[36]

QUESTIONS OF CULTURE AND IDENTITY

This chapter has, until now, eschewed the need to concern itself with the problematic nature of sexualised identities, either generally or in their specifically (southern) African context. Political and legal struggles for the partnership rights of lesbians and gay men have been taken to be easily understood to apply to an easily identifiable class of persons. Indeed, much of the work done to have protection from discrimination on the basis of sexual orientation inserted into the Constitution was based on that assumption.[37]

In this final section, a number of concerns will be raised about the nature of sexual identity in South Africa. In particular, it is suggested that the political and legal strategies that have been chosen to protect the sexual choices of individuals have had, and will continue to have, a constitutive effect on the sexual identities of South Africans. Given that those strategies have been predominantly "western", it seems the nature of sexual identity in South Africa is being deliberately channelled so as to replicate western sexual identity. In that way it is also avoiding any tendency towards a more consciously African notion of meaning associated with sexual conduct and desire.

The Social Construction of Sexuality

As has already been suggested, southern African society is generally considered to be morally conservative. The deprecation of people displaying "deviant" sexualities has become a viable political rallying call in southern and more recently central Africa. Clearly it is thought that political capital can be made by the simple assertion that "homosexuality" is "unAfrican" and ought, on that ground, to be wiped out in Africa.

At one level, of course, this assertion is almost entirely uncontentious.[38] The development of a homosexual personal identity is, largely, a modern Western cultural phenomenon.[39] However, the (historical) absence of "homosexuality"

[36] See chaps. 9–12.

[37] See Cameron, *supra* n. 11.

[38] See Hoad, *supra* n.9.

[39] See M Foucault, *The History of Sexuality: Volume 1, An Introduction* (London, Penguin, 1978; transl. R Hurley); J Weeks, *Sex, Politics and Society: The Regulation of Sexuality Since 1800*, 2d ed. (London, Longman, 1989).

(as identity) in Africa does not imply that same-sex sexual conduct has not been practised in Africa, nor does it mean that that conduct was entirely devoid of social meaning. Our failure to understand what that meaning might have been (historically), and might have become (contemporarily), says more about our lack of historical and anthropological inquisitiveness in the context of Africa than about its non-existence.

From the little research that has been done into same-sex sexual practices (and sexual relationships) in southern Africa, it does seem to be clear that both same-sex sexual conduct, and the relationships which sometimes resulted, did give rise to social understandings and forms of behaviour.[40] However, the nature of the personal identities that are associated with these social meanings is much less clear or, at least, much less clearly like the social meanings that have come to be associated with same-sex sexual conduct in the West.[41]

Given the serious dearth of information on the historical roots and meanings of same-sex sexual conduct in traditional African societies, it seems entirely plausible to imagine a past in which it occurred. It is possible, for example, that that conduct occurred, without significant social antagonism, against a backdrop of heterosexual family relationships formed for social propagation purposes (procreating, rearing and supporting children into an appropriate adulthood). In these circumstances, African societies would have had no need for sexualised identities. Conduct could have been accepted, without anguish, provided that the desire which fuelled it did not disrupt the performance of necessary social roles (protector of children, provider for families, social leadership, etc.).

In a society which adhered to values like this, the protection of a "homosexual person" in legal regulation would have seemed anomalous. No such person would have existed. Those who had same-sex sexual desire would have satisfied their desire with relative ease, and because no social significance was associated with the conduct, no identity (no label) would have been necessary to define those who engaged in it.

Unfortunately, this imagined history (which could, no doubt, be established by the appropriate research), can be no more than a history. That the African world was once so does not suggest that a reversion to that world is necessary. The social world has moved on. And the norms prevailing today in southern Africa are those constructed by an African society dramatically altered, particularly by its western colonial past (which infiltrated every facet of life). Thus, while African homosexuality may not have developed if the European colonial powers had not plundered the continent, the fact of European dominance in

[40] See e.g. the analysis done of mine hostel sexual practices and relationships by TD Moodie (with V Ndatshe), *Going for Gold: Men, Mines and Migration* (Berkeley, CA, University of California Press, 1994). See too Z Achmat, "Apostles of Civilised Vice: Immoral and Unnatural Vice in South African Prisons and Compounds, 1980–1990", (1993) 19 *Social Dynamics* 92; T Dirsuweit, "Sexuality and Space: Sexual Identity in South African Mine Compounds and Prisons", (1998) 2 *Development Update* 107.

[41] See Hoad, *supra* n.9.

Africa cannot be removed simply by the desire that it ought not to have happened. All of African culture has been touched by western influence. And part of the consequence of that influence has been, in the context of this chapter, the rise in the significance of formal legal regulation and human rights protection and the creation of sexualised identities. It is submitted, then, that the creation of European sexualised identities in (principally white) Africa was bound to affect the sexual practices and ultimately the identities of black men and women, who began to reflect on their sexual desire in ways similar to those of white lesbians and gay men. Other western influences—like industrialisation, capitalism, mass urbanisation, and class structure[42]—were all likely to contribute to the creation of African sexualised identities, influenced by, but yet different from, western sexualities.

Law and Social Construction

What may be significant about the constitutional protection of equality on the basis of sexual orientation in South Africa is that it is was born when the nature of sexualised identities in (significantly, perhaps, black) South Africa had achieved very little measure of uniformity (or at least visibility).[43] While it is possible to trace the development of an African parallel to western sexual identity (by reference to the development of a bar culture in the townships, for example),[44] it may be that the very project of tracing that particular history is prechosen by a view of how minority sexual identities came to be established in western societies.[45] The desire to find African lesbians and gay men and the resulting failure to consider that sexualised identities might have been substantially different in African culture, may have given rise to a failure to recognise that they may not, largely, have been there to be found at all; same-sex sexual conduct may have had radically different social meanings and consequences which may have made an identity associated with it entirely unnecessary.

In these circumstances, the protection of sexual identity which was found to be necessary at the time of constitutional drafting seems to be plausibly "unAfrican". The identity that needed protection was largely white (and probably middle-class). What is instructive now, however, is the extent to which the constitutional protection itself has been responsible for the creation of a visible, vibrant sexualised identity.[46] The political and legal struggles around section 9

[42] See P de Vos, "On the Legal Construction of Gay and Lesbian Identity and South Africa's Transitional Constitution", (1996) 12 *South African Journal of Human Rights* 265.

[43] See Jara and Lepinsky, *supra* n.10.

[44] See Gevisser, "A Different Fight", *supra* n.10.

[45] See e.g. J Weeks, *Coming Out: Homosexual Politics in Britain from the Nineteenth Century to the Present* (London, Quartet, 1977), and *Sex, Politics and Society*, *supra* n.39, for a history of British (and, perhaps by extension European and American) homosexuality.

[46] See Jara and Lepinsky, *supra* n.10. Cf. O Phillips, "Zimbabwe" in West and Green (eds.), *Sociolegal Control of Homosexuality* (New York, NY, Plenum Press, 1997).

have created (and are creating) the identity which in the West seemed to precede self-asserting political and legal action.

While this development is enormously beneficial to those who have a Western bent (white lesbians and gay men and African men and women who have adopted a similar identity), it may, at the same time, be undermining an older tradition of sexual tolerance, where sexual conduct and desire is of little concern to society and consequently has nothing like the same significance to social life as "sexual orientation" is beginning to have in South Africa. Simply put, the binary division between homosexual and heterosexual identities is being established in South Africa in a way in which legal and social repression have traditionally been seen to establish that binary division in the West. Given that the object of the political and legal struggles is to undermine that division, it may seem odd that it should be coming so vibrantly to life now.

CONCLUSION

South Africa is beginning to recognise that same-sex sexual relationships are family relationships which deserve the protection that other family relationships are given in law.[47] While the progress that is being made, from the perspective of lesbians and gay men, is positive, it has been suggested in this chapter that there may be circumstances in which the active desire to promote the rights of lesbians and gay men may undermine the sexual tolerance at which it is aimed, by unravelling whatever traditions of tolerance may exist in African culture. A more conscious attempt to discover traditions of tolerance in Africa may be necessary to bring about more effectively the transformation at which the Constitution is aimed.

[47] On 7 August 2001, the Pretoria High Court began hearing constitutional challenges by lesbian judges Anna-Marie De Vos and Kathy Satchwell to legislation restricting both second-parent adoption and judicial employment benefits to spouses. The Natal Witness (8 Aug. 2001), http://www.witness.co.za/wit_4judges20010808.htm.

14

Let Them Eat Cake and Ice Cream: Wanting Something "More" from the Relationship Recognition Menu

JENNI MILLBANK* AND WAYNE MORGAN**

INTRODUCTION

THE NOTION OF "same-sex marriage" is quite alien to Australia. Although the issue of relationship recognition for those outside the heterosexual "norm" is certainly hotly debated, the particular Australian legal and social context have shaped the strategies employed by activists in unique ways. The recognition of same-sex relationships may be a "global" issue, but we should not assume that the strategies employed, for example, in the USA, can be uncritically transposed and used in a different cultural context.

Australia is completely unlike the USA, and many other countries, in that it has extensive legal recognition of heterosexual unmarried relationships. With very few exceptions, cohabiting heterosexual partners are on a par with married spouses in terms of their legal rights and obligations.[1] The process of rethinking the rights and liabilities that attach to relationships, and of shifting toward recognition of heterosexual cohabitees, began in New South Wales in the late 1970s and early 1980s. In 1983, the NSW Law Reform Commission recommended the creation of a new legislative property division regime for heterosexual de facto couples (which federal family law could not regulate for constitutional reasons), as well as their inclusion in around a dozen other areas

* Senior Lecturer in Law, University of Sydney.
** Senior Lecturer in Law, Australian National University, Canberra.

[1] The major exception is access to property distribution regimes on relationship breakdown, which are governed by state and territory law if the couple is unmarried, and federal law if they are married. See R Graycar and J Millbank, "The Bride Wore Pink . . . To the Property (Relationships) Amendment Act 1999", (2000) 17 *Canadian Journal of Family Law* 227. The following abbreviations will be used: New SouthWales (NSW), Victoria (Vic.), Queensland (Qld.), South Australia (SA), Western Australia (WA), Tasmania (Tas.), Australian Capital Territory (ACT), Northern Territory (NT).

of law.[2] These recommendations were implemented the following year, and in subsequent years, cohabiting heterosexual couples were included in all NSW laws as spouses. Through the late 1980s and early 1990s, the inclusion of heterosexual cohabitees in the laws of other Australian jurisdictions spread so as to be virtually universal now.[3] This recognition was presumption-based, and operated from the premise that such couples were married "in fact", if not in law; hence "de facto spouses" became an accepted legal and social concept.

This context is vital in understanding the range of relationship recognition options available in Australia, in which marriage or marriage-like "opt-in" registration systems are not viewed as paradigmatic. It is also important to note that Australia has a federal system of government, with many powers that affect relationships—such as inheritance laws—controlled by states. While states often deliberately mirror each others' provisions for consistency, there is considerable variation across states in many areas of "relationship law" as to who is included and how, as well as a long history of piecemeal law reform.

In the first part of this chapter, Wayne Morgan discusses the process of court-based attempts at same-sex relationship recognition in Australia, and why these judicial challenges have been largely doomed to failure. These failures, the lack of any real constitutional ability to challenge legislation on equality grounds, and the very limited scope for community-based amicus briefs or intervention in individual litigation, has led to a greater focus on legislative rather than judicial activity in Australia—a marked contrast to Canada and the US. In the second part of this chapter, Jenni Millbank examines one such campaign for legislative change which has recently led to significant reforms in NSW.

RELATIONSHIP RECOGNITION IN AUSTRALIAN CASE LAW: THE MAINTENANCE OF HETEROSEXUAL PRIVILEGE

Case analysis in any area of sexuality is not a simple process. It is not enough simply to look at the outcome in such cases, to see if lesbians and gay men have won or lost. It is not enough to engage in a traditional legal analysis of the judgments, restricting comment to the logic and legal consistency of the judicial pronouncements. In sexuality case analysis, it is also important to examine questions of identity formation in the judicial text. How do judges understand and construct notions of "sexuality"? How do judges go about maintaining a

[2] NSW Law Reform Commission (NSWLRC), *De Facto Relationships, Report 36* (Sydney, NSWLRC, 1983). The report is identified as the beginning of a process of legal change in this area for the reason that it was the first coherent and public reform project. It led to the De Facto Relationships Act 1984 (NSW) (which gave courts power to divide property using a guided discretion, if the couple had lived together for two years, or had a child or would otherwise face hardship), and to the inclusion of heterosexual de facto couples in legislation on joint adoption, inheritance and accident compensation.

[3] See J Millbank, "If Australian Law Opened Its Eyes to Lesbian and Gay Families, What Would It See?", (1998) 12 *Australian Journal of Family Law* 99.

system of heterosexual privilege in the face of increasing demand for the recognition of other forms of identity and relationships? A focus on such questions brings into sharp relief the "politics" surrounding the institution of marriage and other forms of recognition. Although it is now a hackneyed debate, the question of which forms of relationship recognition will best destabilise heterosexual privilege has not (and perhaps cannot) be resolved.[4]

In keeping with these theoretical points, I am not just interested in the "outcomes" achieved by sexual outsiders in their judicial battles to be included within heterosexual privilege. In any event, the "outcomes" in terms of victories for sexual outsiders have been few indeed in Australian case law.

Apart from outcomes, I am interested in how far (if at all) the cases break down the privilege of heterosex. What images do the legal texts transmit?[5] I argue that even in the few cases where non-heterosexual relationships are recognised, the privilege of heterosex is also validated and the current hierarchies of gender and sexuality are maintained. This is demonstrated by a (necessarily brief) review of the court and tribunal challenges made to heterosexual privilege in Australia. Here, I discuss three sites of conflict surrounding relationships: first, the general area of "relationship rights"; secondly, transsexuality; and finally, anti-discrimination law.

Relationship Rights: Custody, Property and Everything Else

The area of Australian case law where sexual outsiders have, perhaps, had most success in terms of "outcomes" is in the general area of "relationship rights" or "family" law. These areas in Australia show a mixed record in dealing with lesbian and gay families.[6] In all areas (custody, adoption, rights of carers, property division, intestacy and wills, state and private pensions or superannuation, and immigration), heterosexual privilege has been attacked but largely maintained. Again, because of the particular Australian context, most gay and lesbian efforts have focused on legislative reform.

Lesbians and gay men have had most success in child custody disputes. Of course, such disputes are of many different types, e.g. between straight men and lesbians once in a relationship with them, or between same-sex partners (usually lesbians), and the different contexts influence the judicial pronouncements. The Australian system of family law has been more open to lesbian and gay claims

[4] See R Robson, *Sappho Goes to Law School* (New York, NY, Columbia University Press, 1998), ch. 10; L Duggan, "Queering the State", (1994) 39 *Social Text* 1.

[5] There can be little doubt that it is not just heterosexuality per se, but particular forms of heterosex which are privileged by the law. A hierarchy is set up, and at the apex of that hierarchy is a model of heterosexuality based upon monogamous coupledom, lifelong commitment, and the production of off-spring. This model has historically been dependent on the subordination of women for its functionality. This model has also been privileged in law, above all others, through the legal mechanism of marriage: a state-sanctioned civil contract with significant practical and social effects.

[6] See generally, Millbank, *supra* n.3.

than some other comparable jurisdictions (e.g. the United States).[7] But the Australian system still discriminates, even in this area. This is seen in the scrutiny to which sexual outsiders are subject in the Family Court (by counsellors and judges), and in the way judges determine what is in "the best interests of the child".[8] In other words, in custody disputes between homo and hetero, homos still have to jump through hoops not required of their heterosexual counterparts (despite formal statements by the Family Court that *sexuality per se* is not relevant).

It is also still true to say that, generally speaking in Australian family law, any non-biological parent has very few (if any) rights or support obligations. This is the context of *W* v. *G*,[9] where the biological mother of a child born in a lesbian relationship sued the non-biological mother for child support. No relevant legislation applied to this situation, but the equitable doctrine of promissory estoppel was used to award a lump sum payment, on the basis that the non-biological mother had made a "promise" to parent.[10] Joint adoption is impossible for lesbian or gay *couples* in Australia. Lesbians and gay men can adopt as unmarried *individuals*, but the demand for adoptions and the agencies' preference for married or unmarried hetero couples makes this practically impossible as well.

In property disputes between married or hetero de facto partners, division is handled by legislative schemes in most Australian jurisdictions.[11] In the absence of statutory regimes, same-sex partners must apply to the various Supreme Courts for division of property according to equitable principles. There have been such cases,[12] but they are expensive, slow and the outcome is uncertain. The outcome also depends on the level of homophobia of the particular judge.

Generally speaking in Australian succession law, same-sex partners are not included under intestacy legislation and are often subject to challenge if their partner has left a will naming them as principal beneficiary.[13] There have been some legislative reforms in the Australian Capital Territory to deal with this unfairness,[14] and the comprehensive reforms in NSW (discussed below) will

[7] Millbank, *supra* n.3 at 121. See also M Bateman, "Lesbians, Gays and Child Custody: An Australian Legal History", (1992) 1 *Australian Gay and Lesbian Law Journal* 46; J Millbank, "Lesbian Mothers, Gay Fathers: Sameness and Difference", (1992) 2 *Australian Gay and Lesbian Law Journal* 21; J Millbank, "Lesbians, Child Custody and the Long Lingering Gaze of the Law" in S Boyd (ed.), *Challenging the Public/Private Divide: Feminism, Law and Public Policy* (Toronto, University of Toronto Press, 1997).

[8] Millbank, *supra* n.3, at 121–2.

[9] (1996) 20 Fam LR 49 (NSW Supreme Court).

[10] See J Millbank, "An Implied Promise to Parent: Lesbian Families, Litigation and *W* v. *G*", (1996) 10 *Australian Journal of Family Law* 112.

[11] See *supra* n.1.

[12] See e.g. *Harmer* v. *Pearson* (1993) 16 Fam LR 596 (Queensland Court of Appeal), and *W* v. *G*, *supra* n.9, discussed in J Millbank, "Law's Conscience and Same-Sex Couples: When Is Property a Common Currency?", (1998) 3 *Sister in Law* 19.

[13] Millbank, *supra* n.3, at 107.

[14] See *infra* n.62.

also now equate same-sex couples with heterosexual de facto couples in succession law in that jurisdiction.

Spouses' benefits under both state and private pension (superannuation) schemes have also become controversial. Superannuation funds in Australia (governed by federal law)[15] are huge in terms of their economic and political clout and cover an ever-growing proportion of the population.[16] Under these schemes, spouses are entitled to a range of benefits, but only if hetero. This situation was challenged in the 1995 case of *Brown* v. *Commissioner for Superannuation*.[17] Mr Corva, who was a Commonwealth (federal) employee, died. His surviving partner of 10 years, Mr Brown, tried to claim the pension benefit that would have been available to a "spouse". The claim was rejected on the basis of the definition given to that term, i.e., consistently with the discrimination cases outlined below, "spouse" was given a heterosexist definition. The fund's decision was upheld "reluctantly" by the Administrative Appeals Tribunal (AAT). Mr Brown then complained to the Human Rights and Equal Opportunity Commission (HREOC) who, in light of the AAT finding and limits on its own jurisdiction, dismissed the complaint. Federal reform in the area of pension funds is supposed to be on the agenda, but it has not seen the light of day yet.[18]

Finally, in the area of immigration, which is governed by federal law, Australia has an "interdependency" category under which entry is permitted to the partners of lesbian or gay residents or citizens.[19] The numbers admitted under this category have varied with the policies of successive governments, although cases in the Immigration Review Tribunal have broadened the meaning of the "interdependency" category, making entry easier.[20] This ease has been more than countered, however, by reforms under the current government, which have tightened the criteria. For example, proof of one year of cohabitation is now required.[21] Such cohabitation can be virtually impossible for many lesbian or gay couples separated by citizenship.

[15] Superannuation Industry (Supervision) Act 1993 (Commonwealth or Cth) (SISA).

[16] Employers have an obligation under federal law to pay superannuation contributions into funds on behalf of their employees.

[17] (1995) 21 AAR 378 (Administrative Appeals Tribunal).

[18] In 1996, a Senate Select Committee on Superannuation recommended that the SISA be reformed to include same-sex couples. Because HREOC could not provide a remedy to Mr Brown, it instigated its own inquiry and released a report to the same effect in 1999. See *Superannuation Entitlements of Same-Sex Couples: Report of Examination of Federal Legislation (HRC Report No. 7)* (Sydney, HREOC, 1999), http://www.hreoc.gov.au/human_rights/gay_lesbian/index.html>. In April 2000, a majority of the Senate Select Committee on Superannuation and Financial Services recommended that a private member's Superannuation (Entitlement of Same Sex Couples) Bill be passed, after a public inquiry in which only five of the 360 submissions received opposed the Bill. Despite this overwhelming support and the support of the superannuation industry, the Government members of the Committee wrote a dissenting report based upon the five (religious) submissions opposing the Bill. The blatant homophobia of the Prime Minister Howard and the federal Coalition Government (see discussion of IVF below) mean that the Bill will not be passed.

[19] Migration Regulations 1993 (Cth), visa classes 305 for temporary residency and 814 for permanent residency.

[20] Millbank, *supra* n. 3, at 115.

[21] *Ibid.*

Thus, it can be seen that lesbians and gay men have had some relative success in the area of "relationship rights". In the absence of legislative reform, however, it remains true that lesbian and gay families are not treated equally with their heterosexual counterparts. This subordinating hierarchy of value placed on different types of relationships is seen even more clearly in the cases concerning transsexuality and the anti-discrimination cases.

Transsexuality

Transsexuals in Australia have brought cases challenging their classification according to their designated biological sex at birth. Some of these claims have been successful; however, there have been no cases in which the issue of transsexual marriage has been litigated. This is probably because judges have made very clear obiter statements that seek to preserve the sanctity of heterosexual unions and their privilege from any incursion by transsexuals.

Australian law on transsexuality begins with the English case of *Corbett*,[22] and the finding that, at least for the purposes of marriage, "sex is determined at birth".[23] There has been some progression beyond this in Australian cases, in that courts and tribunals have recognised the claims of male-to-female transsexuals to be regarded as female after "full" reassignment.[24] This magnanimous recognition by the law, however, has very strict limits. The cases make clear that, even after reassignment, the individual cannot fall within the legal definition of "spouse" and cannot legally marry.[25] Andrew Sharpe has analysed these cases, showing the way in which they concentrate on the subject's capacity to simulate heterosexual intercourse.[26] In their focus on biological sex and questions of anatomy, these cases confirm the dominance of the male/female binary opposition and the privilege of heterosex. And in these cases, the judges have made it plain that "special considerations" surround marriage and their judgments in no way open that door.[27]

There have been legislative reforms in three Australian jurisdictions: South Australia, the Northern Territory and NSW.[28] However, the federal nature of

[22] *Corbett* v. *Corbett* [1970] 2 WLR 1306.

[23] *Ibid.* at 1324.

[24] See *In the Marriage of C and D (falsely called C)* (1979) 35 FLR 340 (Family Court of Aust.); *R* v. *Harris & McGuiness* (1989) 17 NSWLR 158 (NSW Court of Criminal Appeal); *Dept of Social Security* v. *HH* (1991) 13 AAR 314 (Administrative Appeals Tribunal); *Dept of Social Security* v. *SRA* (1993) 118 ALR 467 (Federal Court of Aust.).

[25] See, in particular, *Harris* and *SRA*, *ibid.*

[26] A Sharpe, "The Transsexual and Marriage: Law's Contradictory Desires", (1997) 7 *Australasian Gay and Lesbian Law Journal* 1.

[27] In Australia, "marriage" is legislatively defined by federal law as the union of a man and a woman. See Marriage Act 1961 (Cth); Family Law Act 1975 (Cth). In both *Harris*, *supra* n.24, at 189, and *SRA*, *supra* n. 24, at 495, the Courts stated that their decisions had no application to the law of marriage.

[28] Sexual Reassignment Act 1988 (SA); Transgender (Anti-Discrimination and other Acts Amendment) Act 1996 (NSW); Births, Deaths and Marriages Registration Amendment Act 1997 (NT).

the Australian jurisdictions, and the fact that Commonwealth legislation takes precedence, means that the states and territories cannot alter the legal definition of marriage. Hence, the legislative reforms have gone no further than the court cases. They give general recognition to the new sex of the post-operative transsexual, but not for the purposes of marriage. As stated above, the meaning of "marriage" under federal law has not been directly tested by a transsexual claimant (pre- or post-operative), and it is possible that the words "man and woman" in federal legislation could be interpreted as allowing a transsexual to marry. It is doubtful, however, whether any Australian court would give such an interpretation, and there is no prospect of federal legislative reform.[29]

Anti-Discrimination Law

Anti-discrimination law in Australia is a growing field. All jurisdictions (except Western Australia which has none, and the Commonwealth which has very limited protection) prohibit discrimination based on some variant of "sexuality".[30] Gay men and lesbians have attempted to use anti-discrimination law to attack their exclusion from benefits which hetero couples enjoy. Many of these cases come to an end in confidential conciliation, and their results are not known.[31] There are only five cases that have gone to the tribunal stage and hence have produced published reasons: two in NSW, two in the federal jurisdiction, and one in Queensland. Only one has been successful. All five cases confirm the privilege which hetero coupledom continues to enjoy.

[29] But see the surprising obiter comments of McHugh J in *Re Wakim; Ex parte McNally* (1999) 163 ALR 270 at 286 (High Court of Australia):

> "[I]n 1901 'marriage' [in the Constitution] was seen as meaning a voluntary union for life between one man and one woman to the exclusion of all others. . . . [A]rguably 'marriage' now means, or in the near future may mean, a voluntary union for life between two *people* to the exclusion of others."

[30] See NSW, Anti-Discrimination Act 1977 (male or female "homosexuality"; "transgender"); SA, Equal Opportunity Act 1984 ("sexuality": heterosexuality, homosexuality, bisexuality, transsexuality); ACT, Discrimination Act 1991 ("sexuality": heterosexuality, homosexuality including lesbianism, bisexuality; "transsexuality"); Qld., Anti-Discrimination Act 1991 ("lawful sexual activity"); NT, Anti-Discrimination Act 1992 ("sexuality": heterosexuality, homosexuality, bisexuality, transsexuality); Tas., Anti-Discrimination Act 1998 ("sexual orientation": heterosexuality, homosexuality, bisexuality, transsexuality; "lawful sexual activity"); Vic., Equal Opportunity Act 1995, as amended in 2000 ("lawful sexual activity"; "sexual orientation": homosexuality (including lesbianism), bisexuality or heterosexuality; "gender identity"). See also WA, *Lesbian and Gay Law Reform: Report of the Ministerial Committee* (June 2001), http://www.ministers.wa.gov.au/mcginty/gaylesbian.htm (recommending addition of "sexual orientation" to Equal Opportunity Act 1984). Regulations made under the federal Human Rights and Equal Opportunity Commission Act 1986 give very limited power to conciliate complaints regarding "sexual preference" in employment. See HREOC Regulations, Statutory Rules 1989, No. 407 (21 Dec. 1989). See also Workplace Relations Act 1996 (Cth), s. 170CK ("sexual preference", dismissal only).

[31] See A Chapman and Gail Mason, "Women, Sexual Preference and Discrimination Law: A Case Study of the NSW Jurisdiction", (1999) 21 *Sydney Law Review* 525.

The early NSW case of *Wilson*[32] is notorious and shows that heterosexism (if not homophobia)[33] lies barely beneath the surface of some tribunal decisions. The case involved two gay relationships, where all four men were employed by Qantas Airways. Qantas operated a "married roster" system, under which married and de facto partners could apply to be given the same work schedules. The complainants alleged discrimination over their exclusion from this "married roster". Despite their relationships lying at the heart of their claim, the complainants were defined by the tribunal as "single men" and compared to two "golfing buddies".[34] In other words, a "real" relationship must involve a man and a woman. The tribunal's decision was based on the fact that the men in question could not *legally* be defined as spouses.[35] In one sense, you have to admire the twisted logic of lawyers: the tribunal concluded that refusing a benefit to a gay couple is *neither* discrimination on the basis of homosexuality, *nor* discrimination on the basis of marital status.[36]

I would like to think that *Wilson* could be dismissed as an early aberration, and it was doubted in the later NSW case of *Hope*.[37] It was not, however, overturned. In *Hope*, two gay men and their son challenged their exclusion from the "family" rate by a health insurance fund. Despite ultimately finding in favour of the complainants, the Tribunal refused to include same-sex partners within the term "spouse", following previous decisions in stating that for the purposes of Australian law, a "spouse" can only be of the opposite sex.[38] Instead, the Tribunal decided that the Fund should have admitted the men and their son under a provision of the Fund's rules which allowed it to include, under the definition of dependant (and hence family), "such other person or persons as the Controlling Body may from time to time determine".[39]

Despite the complainants' "success", there is still a refusal to see such relationships as families. According to *Hope*, queer families must be defined in "special" categories, where rights are dependent on discretionary exercises of power. Echoes of the hierarchy are still present in *Wilson*. "Spouse" and "family"

[32] *Wilson & Another* v. *Qantas Airways Limited* (1985) EOC 92-141 (NSW Equal Opportunity Tribunal).

[33] Heterosexism and homophobia are different concepts. By the latter, I mean an irrational fear of lesbians and/or gay men. The former refers to the more subtle and pervasive cultural factors which continually re-inscribe heterosexuality as the only valid form of sexuality.

[34] *Wilson*, *supra* n.32, at 76,395 and 76,398.

[35] *Ibid.*, at 76,395 and 76,397.

[36] The definition of "marital status" in most anti-discrimination legislation in Australia either explicitly excludes same-sex couples, or has been interpreted as doing so. The recent reforms in NSW, discussed by Jenni Millbank below, will not alter this position. The NSWLRC has recommended an amendment explicitly prohibiting discrimination against lesbian or gay couples. See Report 92, *Review of the Anti-Discrimination Act 1977 (NSW)* (Sydney, NSWLRC, 1999), para. 5.60, http://www.lawlink.nsw.gov.au/lrc.nsf/pages/r92toc

[37] *Hope & Another* v. *NIB Health Funds Ltd* (1995) EOC 92–716 at 78,386 (NSW Equal Opportunity Tribunal). After stating its doubts, the Tribunal nevertheless assumed that *Wilson* was correctly decided and then distinguished it.

[38] *Ibid.*, at 78,382, following *Brown*, *supra* n.17.

[39] *Ibid.*, at 78,382 and 78,386.

remain exclusively heterosexual domains. Queer families continue to be defined as "other" and have their difference re-inscribed in *Hope*.

The two cases in the federal jurisdiction have both involved Commonwealth employees challenging their exclusion from partner-defined benefits. In *Muller*,[40] an Australian diplomat claimed that the Department of Foreign Affairs and Trade denied him allowances which were payable to hetero couples (married and de facto). Muller's argument was based on both sexual preference and sex discrimination. The HREOC rejected the latter, largely on the basis of legislative intent behind the Sex Discrimination Act. Mr Muller ultimately withdrew his appeal on this point. The sexual preference argument was accepted by the HREOC, but overturned by the Federal Court on appeal. Again, the Federal Court rejected the case on the basis of the legal definition of "spouse" under Australian law. An identical result was reached in *Kelland*.[41] These cases, like the transsexuality ones, show that the definition of "spouse" in Australia continues to constitute a tightly policed border that sexual outsiders are not permitted to penetrate. This category of privilege has not been opened up to same-sex partners by the courts, as it has in some other jurisdictions such as Canada.[42]

Finally, the overpowering privilege of heterosexual coupledom is seen clearly in the case of *JM* v. *QFG & GK*.[43] In this case, a lesbian in a relationship was denied service at a fertility clinic and brought a claim of sexuality discrimination. The Queensland Anti-Discrimination Tribunal found in her favour, but this was overturned by the Queensland courts, whose decisions are a veritable gold mine of homophobic nonsense. The Tribunal had found that the complainant had been denied a service because she was in a "stable and exclusive" lesbian relationship. The Queensland Court of Appeal, however, overturned this finding on the basis that the evidence could not support it.

In a spectacular exercise of subordination through legal discourse, the Court refused to pay any attention to the lived experience of the complainant, one judge going so far as to imply that she was merely a troublemaker.[44] Instead, and against the stated reasons of the Tribunal, which had the advantage of assessing the witnesses first hand, the Court constructed the situation entirely from the respondent doctor's point of view(lessness). The complainant had not been discriminated against because she was in an "exclusive and stable" lesbian relationship; she had been refused a medical treatment merely because she did not suffer from the condition which the treatment was aiming to correct. The Court accepted the doctor's definition of infertility, i.e. "inability to conceive

[40] *Australia* v. *HREOC & Muller* (1998) EOC 92–931 (Federal Court of Aust.).

[41] *Australia* v. *HREOC & Kelland* (1998) EOC 92–932 (Federal Court of Aust.).

[42] See Casswell, chap. 11, Lahey, chap. 12.

[43] [2000] 1 Qd R 373 (Qld Court of Appeal).

[44] *Ibid.* at 393–4 (Pincus JA): "what prompted the appellant to approach the doctor appears to have been principally a desire to have the point tested; she expected that her approach would be rejected."

after heterosexual intercourse".[45] The judges agreed, therefore, that the complainant was excluded *by definition*, from the class of persons to whom the service was provided. Her lesbianism had nothing to do with it.

The Court conveniently overlooked the highly constructed and discriminatory nature of this very definition, even though the Court was provided with evidence of authoritative contrary definitions which included the complainant. This exclusion by definition is a form of subordination. It is a common legal technology employed in the area of relationship recognition in Australia. Legislatively, "marriage" is *by definition* the union of a man and a woman. Judicially, "spouse" is *by definition* a member of the opposite sex. Now also, by judicial definition (subordination), lesbians are excluded from this form of medical treatment because they do not have sex with men. This was recognised explicitly by the Court. In an extraordinary example of judicial logic, two of the three judges stated: ". . . the evidence of the doctor on which the finding is based makes clear that there was no policy of excluding from services women who engaged in lesbian activity. It was the absence of heterosexual activity which mattered.[46] . . . the true basis of the doctor's refusal to provide services to the patient was not because of her lesbian activity but because of her heterosexual inactivity".[47]

Special Leave to appeal this decision was refused by the High Court, however, as at September 2000 the case was continuing. The Queensland courts sent the case back to the Tribunal for further deliberation on the issue of indirect discrimination. Again, the Tribunal found in favour of the lesbian complainant. Again, this decision has been appealed and is working its way through the Queensland courts.

Regardless of the eventual outcome of this case, the issue of lesbian access to *in vitro* fertilisation (IVF) will continue to cause controversy in Australia. This is because the Prime Minister has recently staked out this site as a primary ideological battleground around the meaning of "family". In July 2000, the Federal Court decided the case of *McBain* v. *Victoria*.[48] Victoria's Infertility Treatment Act 1995 restricted access to IVF technology to women living with their husbands or their male de facto partners. Women not living with a husband or male de facto partner, or living with a female de facto partner, were excluded. This exclusion was challenged by a medical doctor and his unmarried female patient, who was not living with a male de facto partner and wished to be artificially inseminated with donor sperm. The Federal Court held that the Victorian Act was in conflict with the federal Sex Discrimination Act 1984 (Cth) provisions outlawing discrimination on the basis of marital status. This decision was welcomed as a victory for heterosexual women without partners and lesbians. However, the victory may be very short lived.

[45] [2000] 1 Qd R 373 (Qld Court of Appeal) at 396 (Thomas JA).
[46] *Ibid*. at 391 (Pincus JA).
[47] *Ibid*. at 396 (Thomas JA).
[48] (28 July 2000), [2000] FCA 1009 (Federal Court of Aust.).

Immediately after the decision, the Prime Minister personally intervened and announced that the Government would amend the Sex Discrimination Act so that state laws such as those in Victoria would be valid. His stated public defence for overturning *McBain*, was the government's strong belief that "a child has a right to a father".[49] A bill has been drafted and is in the process of making its way through the federal Parliament.[50] The bill faces strong opposition in the Senate and is not expected to pass, although the federal opposition has been wavering over its position, with many in the party agitating for a conscience vote.

The conservative tone of the debate on this controversy is striking. The Prime Minister's determination to preserve a discourse of family fully reminiscent of a 1950s fantasy resonates with the court and tribunal decisions discussed above. The government, like the Courts, exclude lesbians *by definition* from the concept of family, ignoring both reality and human rights. They use anti-discrimination law as a legislative vehicle to reinscribe hierarchies of value associated with different identities. This is clearly shown by the amendment bill.

What is the point of anti-discrimination law if, whenever real and obvious discrimination occurs, the courts and/or government simply deny it, by using their powers of definition to exclude the situation from the range of cases that could even possibly fall within the legal concept of discrimination? Again, the sanctity of heterosexual coupledom and patriarchy[51] are validated by the IVF debate.

Summary: The Cases in Australia

This brief review of case law shows that, partly because of the lack of a constitutional equality guarantee, Australia is falling behind other developed legal jurisdictions when it comes to the judicial recognition of same-sex relationships. When it comes to case law, same-sex relationships continue to be ignored in most areas. All but one of the anti-discrimination claims has failed. The heterosexual preserve that judges have adamantly carved around the term "spouse" so far remains invulnerable. Transsexuals have not been successful in attacking the (biological) hetero-exclusivity of marriage either. The cases in which all the above claims have been made (not to mention the IVF debate) send very clear messages that the privilege of state-sanctioned hetero-coupledom is not to be disturbed.

[49] "PM Ignites Family Row", *The Australian*, 2 Aug. 2000; "Howard Denies IVF Stance Shows He Is Homophobic", *Sydney Morning Herald*, 2 Aug. 2000.

[50] Sex Discrimination Amendment Bill (No.1) 2001 (Cth) (passed by House of Representatives, 3 April 2001; pending before Senate). This bill would allow states to pass laws banning heterosexual women without partners and lesbians from accessing any assisted reproductive technology service.

[51] What sparked off the Queensland case of *JM*, was the fact that the complainant could not provide a consent form from her "male" partner, which was a requirement of the clinic. The Court of Appeal validated this clear expression of patriarchy.

In other words, sexual outsiders in Australia have had little success in even achieving inclusion within the hetero-normative system, let alone challenging that system, at least by judicial means. It is no wonder, then, that the efforts of lobby groups have been focused on legislative reform.

LEGISLATIVE REFORM IN NEW SOUTH WALES: A VICTORY FOR COMMUNITY ACTIVISM

In June 1999, the state government of NSW enacted legislation[52] recognising same-sex relationships across some twenty areas of "public" and "private" law. This legislation is remarkable not just for the result, but for the process by which it was accomplished. The Act had its genesis in a community-based project, and the model it enacts is closely based on that recommended in a community-produced discussion paper. The relative ease of its passage through the NSW Parliament, with unexpected bipartisan support, is also worthy of comment, as is the fact that the government appears to see the Act as the beginning rather than the end of law reform on relationships.

This reform has been both lightning swift and a long hard slog. From the day the Attorney General, Jeff Shaw, announced that he had cabinet approval to introduce such a law, to the passage of the Bill through both houses of Parliament, less than three weeks passed.[53] But this reform was the product of more than six years of consultation, protesting, politicking, legal work and lobbying by the Gay and Lesbian Rights Lobby of NSW (GLRL), a small, unfunded community organisation run entirely by volunteers.[54] In this part, I note how the law was developed and discuss how it embodies, and inevitably dilutes, the wishes and work of our communities. I also want to reflect on the strategies used and what "success" has meant in this context.

The Property (Relationships) Legislation Amendment Act 1999 (NSW) and Its Effects

The legislation changed NSW law in two very substantial ways. It amended the existing definition of "de facto relationship partners" (now "parties to a de facto

[52] Property (Relationships) Legislation Amendment Act 1999 (NSW).

[53] This swift passage was a product of political expediency, which saw the Bill enacted before significant opposition had time to mobilise. The disadvantage of such haste was that there was no opportunity for positive input into the law from community groups—and there are many loose ends which now remain to be fixed.

[54] In addition to GLRL, many other community organisations (such as the AIDS Council of NSW and the Sydney Gay and Lesbian Mardi Gras) contributed time and support to several campaigns waged over the years, hundreds of individuals volunteered their time to organise campaigns, and thousands of lesbians and gay men signed petitions, sent letters and turned up for public rallies and protests. Minor political parties and independent MPs (notably the Australian Democrats, the Green Party and Clover Moore MP) worked to keep the issues alive in Parliament for many years when government and opposition were hostile or disinterested.

relationship") to include same-sex cohabiting couples.[55] The new definition applies to the statutory property regime and various other areas of NSW law, most notably those concerning inheritance, accident compensation, property transfer taxes (stamp duty), and decision-making in illness and after death.[56] As a secondary change, the Act also introduced the concept of "domestic relationships" for the first time in NSW law. "Domestic relationships" are defined to include people who have a cohabiting relationship of interdependence but are not in a couple.[57] This change covers a far smaller number of laws, notably those concerning statutory property division, inheritance, bail, and property transfer taxes (stamp duty).[58]

These changes took effect from July 1999. They do not alter federal Australian law or the laws of other Australian states and territories (though they may influence the progress of developments in other jurisdictions.) It is important to note that many areas which greatly impact upon gay men and lesbians in Australia—including immigration, income taxation, social security, state and private pensions—are matters of federal law and will therefore continue to operate in an exclusory manner.

[55] The Property (Relationships) Act 1984, s. 4(1) (as amended by Sched. 1 of the 1999 Act), now defines a "de facto relationship" as: "a relationship between two adult persons: (a) who live together as a couple, and (b) who are not married to one another or related by family." The amended 1984 Act also includes (in section 4(2)) a non-exhaustive list of factors which a court may take into account when determining the existence of a de facto relationship. The other amended Acts incorporate the new definition into their definitions of "spouse" or "de facto partner". The Attorney General's Second Reading Speech made it clear that the new non-gendered definition of de facto relationship was specifically intended to include lesbian and gay couples: see Parliamentary Debates, Legislative Council of NSW, Hansard, 13 May 1999, Hon JW Shaw at 229. The former definition of "de facto partner" was: "(a) in relation to a man, a woman who is living or has lived with a man as his wife on a bona fide domestic basis although not married to him, and (b) in relation to a woman, a man who is living or has lived with the woman as her husband on a bona fide domestic basis although not married to her".

[56] Legislation which was amended to include same-sex partners includes: De Facto Relationships Act 1984 (now Property (Relationships) Act 1984); Duties Act 1997; Wills, Probate and Administration Act 1898; Family Provision Act 1982; Compensation to Relatives Act 1897; Motor Accidents Act 1988; Guardianship Act 1987; Human Tissue Act 1983; Coroners Act 1980; Mental Heath Act 1990. These Acts are overwhelmingly beneficial in their effects. Legislation which was amended to *maintain* an exclusively heterosexual definition of de facto spouses includes: Conveyancers Licensing Act 1995, Dentists Act 1989, Legal Profession Act 1987, Local Government Act 1993, Retirement Villages Act 1989. Some of these unamended Acts would have required a partner's financial interests to be disclosed, ie required "outing" in the workplace.

[57] The 1984 Act, s. 5 (as amended by Schedule 1 of the 1999 Act), defines a "domestic relationship" as: "(1) . . . (a) a de facto relationship, or (b) a close personal relationship (other than a marriage or a de facto relationship) between two adult persons, whether or not related by family, who are living together, one or each of whom provides the other with domestic support and personal care. (2) . . . a close personal relationship is taken not to exist between two persons where one of them provides the other with domestic support and personal care: (a) for fee or reward, or (b) on behalf of another person or an organisation (including a government or government agency, a body corporate or a charitable or benevolent organisation)." This definition of domestic relationship is distinct from, and narrower than, that in use in some laws in the Australian Capital Territory, see *infra* n.62.

[58] The De Facto Relationships Act 1984 (now Property (Relationships) Act 1984), District Court Act 1973, Duties Act 1997, Family Provision Act 1982, and Bail Act 1978 were amended to include domestic relationships.

The Bride Wore Pink: A Blueprint

The process of developing a model for relationship recognition in NSW was begun by the Lesbian and Gay Legal Rights Service, a project of the GLRL. The Legal Rights Service received numerous inquiries each week regarding sexuality discrimination which it could not solve, because the problems stemmed from legislation, and no means existed of challenging that legislation through litigation. The Legal Rights Service therefore began a process of community consultation in 1992, in order to develop options for law reform which had broad-ranging community support. They held public meetings and canvassed the views of various community groups. In 1993, the Legal Rights Service produced the first edition of the discussion paper which arose from these consultations, *The Bride Wore Pink*.[59] In 1994, after further consideration and consultation, a revised edition was produced.[60] This final edition recommended pursuing a model which included both a "de facto partner" *and* a "domestic partner"[61] regime. That is, the paper recommended that the recognition of both live-in sexual relationships, and other forms of important interdependent relationships, should take place *simultaneously but distinctly*.

Recognition of cohabiting couples through the de facto category was favoured, because it offered breadth and certainty of coverage, as well as the symbolism of formal equality. This was never envisaged as sufficient, however, and the category of domestic relationship, encompassing emotional and financial interdependence in a relationship that need not be sexual nor cohabiting was also proposed.[62] Support for such broader-based, non-couple-focused relationship recognition was very strong within the community. Concerns about who would fall outside the bounds of legal recognition were raised from the very first. Within the GLRL itself, support for broader-based recognition was strongly informed by feminist analysis of marriage and family, and the domestic relationship model was seen as some redress for the traditional legal privi-

[59] H Katzen and M Shaw (for the Lesbian and Gay Legal Rights Service), *The Bride Wore Pink*, 1st ed. (Sydney, GLRL, 1993), reproduced at (1993) 3 *Australian Gay and Lesbian Law Journal* 67.

[60] Katzen and Shaw, *ibid*., 2d ed., 1994, http://www.glrl.org.au. The GLRL shifted from an initial preference for an opt-in registered partnership scheme to a presumption-based de facto relationship scheme because of concerns about practicability and coverage.

[61] Although the 2d ed., *ibid*., used "significant person", "domestic partner" is now used, following reforms in the ACT which had not taken place at that time.

[62] This concept has been developed and implemented in another jurisdiction, the ACT. See Attorney General's Department, *A Proposal for Domestic Relationship Legislation in the ACT*, Discussion Paper (Canberra, 1993). This led to the inclusion of "domestic partners", who need not live together or have a sexual relationship, in three areas of law (property division, intestacy and family provision), as well as the specific inclusion of cohabiting same-sex partners in intestacy and family provision. See the ACT Domestic Relationships Act 1994; Administration and Probate Act 1929 (amended in 1996); Family Provision Act 1969 (amended in 1996). See also Queensland Law Reform Commission, *Shared Property: Resolving Disputes Between People Who Live Together and Share Property*, Discussion Paper 36 (Brisbane, 1991). This paper suggested a property division regime open to all cohabitants, regardless of their relationship.

leging of couples and the privatisation of the family.[63] But these were also bigger questions which extended beyond lesbian and gay relationships and beyond the scope of the GLRL's consultation abilities. *The Bride Wore Pink* therefore recommended that, in addition to implementing de facto and domestic relationship recognition into NSW law immediately, broader questions regarding which relationships the law values and privileges should receive the detailed consideration of an appropriately resourced law reform body.[64]

Both the de facto and domestic model were premised on a presumption-based rather than an opt-in system. This decision was made through consultation, which lead to the evolution of two editions of *The Bride Wore Pink*. I have explained elsewhere in some detail why this method of recognition was favoured,[65] but in brief it was felt that a presumptive regime was likely to cover those who need it the most when they need it the most. Many people do not use opt-in mechanisms when they are made available, and thus it was feared that legal recognition through that avenue would be far more symbolic than real.[66] Australia has extensive recognition of heterosexual couples through presumptive laws for the very reason that declining numbers of heterosexual people were "registering" their relationships through marriage—yet in times of crisis and dispute they still required access to the law. As Australian case law on inheritance shows, few people, including lesbians and gay men, order their affairs in advance through formal documents like wills.[67]

The choice of a presumption-based cohabitee model also turned out to be strategically beneficial. A legal framework of presumptive relationship recognition already existed, was widely accepted, and had spread throughout all Australian jurisdictions over the years without any major opposition. This

[63] See *The Bride Wore Pink*, 2d ed., *supra* n.60 ("Our Agenda"), discussed in Jenni Millbank, "The De Facto Relationships Amendment Bill 1998 (NSW): The Rationale for Law Reform", (1999) 8 *Australasian Gay and Lesbian Law Journal* 1.

[64] Recommendation 5, *The Bride Wore Pink*, 2d ed., *ibid.*, called upon the NSW government to: "allocate funds to an appropriate agency (such as the Law Reform Commission) to consider the question of relationships generally, including: i. The appropriateness or otherwise of bestowing entitlements on the basis of relationships, ii. the focussing on monogamy, exclusivity and blood relations, iii. the need to replace the De Facto Relationships Act 1984 with an Act which bestows rights and entitlements on a broader concept of 'relationships', and iv. the need to ensure that all people with disputes which are based on rights and obligations arising from relationships have access to an inexpensive and accessible forum for the resolution of these disputes. . . ."

[65] See Millbank, *supra* n.63 (discussing the Australian Democrats unsuccessful 1998 bill, which is very similar in form to the 1999 Act).

[66] Overseas experience of registered partnerships shows extremely low rates of registration, with a much lower rate of take-up by women, and a high urban concentration. See Lund-Andersen, chap. 21; Waaldijk, chap. 23.

[67] See e.g. *Ball* v. *Newey* (1988) 13 NSWLR 489 (NSW Court of Appeal); *Benney* v. *Jones* (1991) 23 NSWLR 559 (NSW Court of Appeal); *Bell* v. *Elliott* (1996) NSW LEXIS 3861 (NSW Supreme Court); *Howard* v. *Andrews*, New South Wales Supreme Court, 31 July 1998, Master Macready, unreported (affirmed in *Andrews* v *Howard* [1999] NSWCA 409, NSW Court of Appeal); all discussed in Millbank, *supra* n.12. *Howard* received a great deal of publicity, and numerous references were made in the parliamentary debates on the 1999 Act to Matthew Howard's fight to retain the home he had shared with his late partner for more than a decade.

framework did not need to be created from scratch. It also reflected the pragmatic and appealingly egalitarian premise that the law should reflect and serve the lived realities of people's lives, regardless of the formalities they had, or more likely had not, undertaken.

Secondly, the focus on de facto relationships largely removed the ideological sting of "marriage" from the debate,[68] sidestepped religious questions,[69] and focused on the real issues, the legal ones. The GLRL did not want a symbolic victory or acceptance by the church, or state, for that matter—it wanted to reduce the impoverishment of lesbians and gay men in times of need and increase their access to justice. In choosing this focus, the government was also handed an easy option, as it was then able to argue publicly that this was not a law about marriage or "the family", it was a law about property. The government presented the reforms as changes to the property division regime, which was where the recognition of de facto relationships had begun (but likewise had not been limited to) in NSW in 1984. This discursive sleight-of-hand, although disingenuous in the extreme, was vital to the Bill's parliamentary success, an issue I will discuss below.

Six Years, Three Bills and One Act

In 1995, while still in opposition, leaders of the centre-left NSW Labor Party indicated that they would pursue same-sex relationship recognition in key areas, should they gain office. Labor won the election within months, but no reform was attempted in the three years that followed, and no time-frame proposed in which to do so.[70] Publicly, the government remained silent on any previous commitments, while privately key figures urged patience. The centre-right NSW Liberal Party had offered no support, either when in government or later in opposition, and their coalition partner, the far-right National Party, was actively hostile.

[68] During parliamentary debates, numerous members of the opposition parties did raise the issue of marriage as a bastion of heterosexuality and as a symbol of the church's power (in what is actually a completely secular legal institution). Because marriage is a federal not a state matter in Australian law, even if the NSW government had wished to introduce same-sex marriage—which it repeatedly said it did not—it had no constitutional power to do so. Nonetheless, the amending Act introduced a new s. 62 to the Property (Relationships) Act 1984 providing that: "Nothing in the Property (Relationships) Legislation Amendment Act 1999 is to be taken to approve, endorse or initiate any change in the marriage relationship, which by law must be between persons of the opposite sex, nor entitle any person to seek to adopt a child unless otherwise entitled to by law." This section was the result of an amendment moved by Fred Nile, the leader of an extreme Christian-Right micro-party.

[69] Although the Catholic Education Commission mobilised some opposition, the Anglican Diocese of Sydney was content to support the legislation on the basis that it did not affect marriage or "moral" issues. See Glachan (Liberal), Parliamentary Debates, Legislative Assembly, 26 May 1999, Hansard at 740. This is in marked contrast to religious opposition to lesbian and gay equality rights elsewhere, e.g. anti-discrimination laws in Victoria. See W Morgan, "Still in the Closet: The Heterosexism of Equal Opportunity Law", (1996) 1(2) *Critical InQueeries* 119.

[70] The Attorney General did not table the Domestic Relationships Bill 1996 (NSW).

In 1997, Clover Moore, a progressive independent MP who has been a long-standing supporter of lesbian and gay rights, introduced a private member's Bill into the NSW Legislative Assembly (lower house of Parliament). The Significant Personal Relationships Bill 1997 (NSW) sought to avoid a couple focus, and was centred upon emotional interdependence rather than a sexual relationship as its key concept.[71] The Bill was not debated, and lapsed.

In 1998, a progressive minor party, the Australian Democrats (NSW), offered to introduce a Bill developed by the GLRL. The GLRL, in conjunction with Democrats staff, drafted legislation which attempted to express the vision of *The Bride Wore Pink*, as well as incorporating developments since the paper.[72] The De Facto Relationships Amendment Bill was introduced into the NSW Legislative Council (upper house of Parliament) in June 1998. There was an election approaching in early 1999, with all predictions being that the result would be a very close one. Towards the end of 1998, the government responded to the news that the Bill could pass the upper house, with the support of minor parties and a government conscience vote, by immediately referring the Bill off to a parliamentary committee (the Legislative Council Social Issues Committee). As the Committee was given a reporting deadline some months after the state election, this removed the Bill from parliamentary business for the remainder of the government's first term of office. Lesbian and gay issues were clearly seen as too electorally and politically sensitive to be "out" about.

The government won the 1999 election with ease, achieving an unexpectedly increased majority; thus it took up "controversial" reforms such as drug laws and same-sex relationship recognition very early in its second term. However, the government did not introduce the GLRL/Democrats Bill, preferring a watered-down version with somewhat more traditional relationship definitions and a more limited scope of coverage.[73] The law was titled the Property

[71] See Millbank, *supra* n.63. Clover Moore's Bill utilised a twin model of non-couple relationship recognition: the "recognised relationship", involving an opt-in system, formalised by documents sworn before a solicitor or a local court, and the "domestic relationship", a presumption-based system. A "recognised relationship" could exist even if parties were not members of the same household, did not share finances or have a sexual relationship. A "domestic relationship" was defined as cohabitation, or a somewhat vaguely worded "shared life", and did not require a sexual relationship. Moore's approach, by sidestepping sexual relationships in favour of a focus on emotional connection, in my view also falls prey to the dilemma of de-sexing and thus silencing lesbian and gay relationships, which I discuss in relation to domestic relationships in the section "Success?" below.

[72] The Democrats Bill reflected developments such as the inclusion of domestic relationships in the ACT (see *supra* n.62), and the category of "interdependence" in federal migration law, discussed in Millbank, *supra* n.3.

[73] See J Millbank and K Sant, "A Bride in Her Every-Day Clothes: Same Sex Relationship recognition in NSW" (2000) 22 (2) *Sydney Law Review* 181. Neither the Democrats Bill nor the 1999 Act included joint adoption or second-parent adoption for same-sex couples. See *supra* text accompanying nn.10–11. The GLRL did not attempt to change this situation because of the clear lack of political will (the government had publicly refused to even consider proposals on this issue from its own law reform body in 1997) and because there are only a tiny number of children available for adoption each year in Australia. The 1999 Act did not address the relationships of non-biological parents (co-parents) with the children they raise, which are currently recognised by only a limited

(Relationships) Legislation Amendment Act 1999—a masterful piece of politicking which ensured that very little attention was paid to the Bill by either the media or other politicians. At the last minute, the Liberal-led coalition agreed not to oppose the Bill.

The NSW Parliament Talks About Property

The debate process was an interesting one to witness: a government which had easily enough votes to push the law through pretended that it was not an interesting or important change; and an opposition coalition which previously opposed reform efforts largely pretended that it did not notice.[74] The government was markedly subdued in support of its own legislation. There were few Labor government MPs in attendance, and a carefully orchestrated series of speeches in favour stressed the Bill's property aspects, and did not mention either the history of law reform efforts relating to same-sex relationship recognition or lesbian and gay community involvement in devising the law at hand. Even for parliamentary lawmaking, it was passionless stuff. There was a surprising absence of equality talk or human rights discourse from the debate, and almost no acknowledgment of who was affected by this law and why. Love, emotion, relationships, lesbians and gay men were barely mentioned. When a government MP referred to the previous law as "cruel in its application to those who had lived together in loving and intimate relationships", there was a pause as MPs looked surprised and raised their heads; she stumbled and rejoined, "It was, it was cruel".[75]

The approach of the NSW Parliament is exemplified by statements such as,

> "The legislation . . . recognises the property relationships that people have built up. The law has always worked on the basis that it is important to recognise people's property rights. Our law is founded on recognition of property rights. In fact, law is often expressed in terms of property rights". [76]

The government's discursive strategy of constantly naming the Bill as "about property" and not "about sexuality" or "about marriage", seemed to have an

number of laws. The Act does, however, provide a limited statutory avenue to pursue child support claims by parties to a de facto relationship against one another (regardless of biological parentage) concerning a child for whom the parties have taken joint responsibility. In contrast to federal child support legislation, which provides access to support until the child is 18, this statute only covers children to the age of 12. It is also likely that the category of "domestic relationship" could be used by co-parents and their children.

[74] See generally Parliamentary Debates, Legislative Council, 13, 25, 26 May 1999, Hansard at 228–230, 294–300, 311–322, 393–398 (hereinafter "Upper House"); Parliamentary Debates, Legislative Assembly, 26 May 1999, Hansard at 534, 708–716, 735–744 (hereinafter "Lower House").

[75] Saffin (Labor), Upper House at 298. Her rejoinder is not recorded in Hansard.

[76] Harcher (Liberal), Lower House at 709.

almost hypnotic effect. I had never heard the expression "property relationship" before in my life (as opposed to, say, "sexual relationship" or "cohabiting relationship"), yet it became a frequently used term in the debate—as though gay and lesbian couples had relationships with their property rather than with each other, and that made the reforms okay. The triumph of discourse over substance is well captured by this remark from an opposition MP:

> "If this bill were about sexuality I would not be able to support it. However, as no-one is arguing that this bill is about sexuality, I will not oppose it".[77]

What *actually is in the Bill*, the range of areas that it actually covers, or indeed what the Bill itself actually says (lesbian and gay couples are for instance defined as "spouses") does not matter. What matters is what we all *say* it is about. However, the approach of the opposition was not uniform, with several MPs calling the bluff, especially as time wore on. The almost camp playfulness of this double-talk is nicely expressed in the following interchange between coalition opposition MPs:

> Hon Dr B.P.V Pezzutti: . . . I am keen to support this bill because it does a number of things. It is not simply a property bill. The legislation has been a long time coming. . .
>
> Hon D.J Gay: You are about to talk me out of supporting this bill.
>
> Hon Dr B.P.V Pezzutti: I am not even close.
>
> Hon D.J Gay: The longer you go on, the closer you are getting.[78]

By the time the Bill had reached the lower house, church groups had mobilised and there was much more talk of god, morality, marriage and "the" family. No coalition members voted against the Bill, but many spoke against it, and all of them invoked religion as a reason to do so.[79] Property talk, apparently, will only take you so far when God is involved.

There were some exceptions to the property/god dichotomy, most importantly from the progressive minor parties and independent MPs who discussed the far-reaching effects of the Bill, and connected these developments both to international human rights norms and to the work of local lesbian and gay communities.[80] This was not surprising given their vocal support for lesbian and gay rights in NSW, including in their policy platforms. However, it was deeply ironic that, from the major parties, acknowledgment of the role of the gay and lesbian community came, not from supportive government members, but

[77] O'Doherty (Lib.), Lower House at 739.

[78] Upper House at 321.

[79] See eg Fraser (National Party), Lower House at 736–7: "It disturbs me that the bill does not mention homosexual relationship . . . I am a god-fearing person who does not believe in homosexual relationships. I do not think that God intended us as a race to behave in that way". See also Page (NP), Lower House at 738; Glachan (Lib.), Lower House at 740; Souris (NP), Lower House at 714.

[80] See eg Cohen (Greens), Upper House at 295; Jones (Independent), Upper House at 298; Chesterfield Evans (Democrats), Upper House at 299; Moore (Indep.), Lower House at 710.

instead from a number of conservative opposition MPs; they spoke from GLRL briefing notes, cited individual case studies provided by the GLRL, quoted GLRL spokespeople, and traced the history of the GLRL's efforts to achieve law reform in NSW.[81]

The Bride Wore Pink was undeniably the blueprint for the new law, but the government made no mention of it. Having presented the law as one which tidied up anomalies regarding property, it clearly did not want to acknowledge that it was actually doing something which lesbians and gay men *wanted*. To do so would perhaps open it to claims of bowing to "minority group pressure" and make the law "about" sexuality rather than "about" property. A lack of accreditation in parliamentary records is perhaps a small price to pay for law reform. However the silencing nature of the process was an important aspect of it and sadly accords with conventional political wisdom that to "win" lesbians and gay men must be "discreet".

Success?

This new law, while broad-ranging, was not everything that was required. The government chose a more restricted focus for this Act than earlier Bills. It amended fewer laws to include same-sex de facto partners, and it also used more restrictive definitions of de facto, and particularly domestic, partners than earlier proposals had favoured. Notable omissions, in inclusion of same-sex de facto relationships, were more obviously "public" rights, such as inheritance of a deceased partner's accumulated leave entitlements, and workplace rights such as parental leave.[82] These losses were not felt as sorely as they could have been for two reasons—one is that there is a strong history of piecemeal legal reform in Australia, and many other changes are likely to follow in the guise of "tidying up inconsistencies".[83] The other is that the Attorney General renewed the reference of the original Democrats/GLRL Bill to the Parliamentary Social Issues Committee, suggesting a willingness to extend the ambit of reform.[84] The Attorney General also initiated a broad-based investigation into existing relationships legislation and "other related matters" by the NSW Law Reform Commission.[85] At their very narrowest, these inquiries are expected to discuss

[81] See eg Pezzutti (Lib.), Upper House at 317; Samios (Lib.), Upper House at 294; Turner (NP), Lower House at 740; Richardson (Lib.), Lower House at 715.

[82] In other areas left unamended, formal equality was not seen as appropriate. See *supra* n.56.

[83] Indeed the Opposition Leader characterised the whole Act this way: see Chikarovski (Lib.), Lower House at 713.

[84] *Domestic Relationships: Issues for Reform: Inquiry into De facto Relationships Legislation*, Report 20 (Sydney, Legislative Council Standing Committee on Social Issues, 1999) recommended that immediate steps be taken by the government to eliminate all the "gaps" between the Act and the earlier GLRL/Democrats' Bill, which would mean covering de facto couples and domestic relationships in more Acts, and broadening the definition of domestic relationship to cover non-cohabitees.

[85] See <http://www.lawlink.nsw.gov.au/nswlrc.nsf/pages/refpra>.

the coverage and inclusion of existing laws, while at their broadest, they could reconsider the cohabiting couple paradigm.

In a principled sense, the greatest disappointment of the Act was that it narrowed the definition of domestic relationship to something that more closely resembled cohabiting couples or traditional family relationships. From an original definition (similar to Australian Capital Territory law) which rested on emotional and financial interdependence, it was restricted to only cover cohabitees who "provide care" for each other. In doing so, the government clearly tagged this issue as contentious and pulled it back to be a smaller experiment, although they did not abandon it altogether.

There is a paradox to this legislative go-slow. The new category of domestic relationship is both more radical and less radical than the de facto changes, and the way it has played out in this context is complex and contradictory. The concept of a domestic relationship is radical because it redefines family obligations around love, interdependence and choice, rather than blood and marriage or "marriage-like" relationships, and in doing this destabilises heterosexuality and the hetero-nuclear family. It is dangerously fluid and usurps what some coalition MPs insisted on calling the "natural family" and "normal marriages".[86] Embracing this concept in a whole-hearted way really could be the end of the family as we know it, in a legal sense at least.

But the category is also far less radical than de facto relationships, in a way that I think the government massively miscalculated. It is less radical because it unsexes the dilemma facing the law here; by avoiding sexual relationships, it permits and indeed requires an invisibility of lesbian and gay subjecthood and sexuality. Domestic relationships (like "property relationships") can be seen as about something other than "the other". This process of de-sexing and "normalising" was played out in the lower house debates, where several coalition MPs denounced the Bill in general as leading to the perversion of children, moral decline and so on, but supported the "aspects that relate to carers".[87] These MPs waxed lyrical about daughters caring for their elderly fathers in rural areas of Australia, and what a good thing it was to finally legally recognise such "carer" relationships.[88] In fact, such a woman and her father, ailing or otherwise, were already covered by all of the laws concerned, as they are blood relations—and it is exactly these relationships that are already privileged in current law. But no matter; this woman became an almost mythical presence during the debates,

[86] See eg Page (NP), Lower House at 738; Smith (Lib.), Lower House at 739; Souris (NP), Lower House at 714.

[87] See *supra* n.79.

[88] They appear to have been grasping at a line in the Attorney General's Second Reading Speech, where he gave the example of a domestic relationship being a "woman caring for her elderly father". See Lower House at 229. References to the caring daughter are made by Fraser (NP), Lower House at 736, 737; Page (NP), Lower House at 738; Smith (Lib.), Lower House at 739; Glachan (Lib.), Lower House at 740; Turner (NP), Lower House at 740. Kerr (Lib), Lower House at 742, also drew on maidenly virtue when his example of a non-sexual relationship of interdependence was "two female deacons who are living together".

standing as she did for all that was asexual, altruistic, womanly and supportive of patriarchal control in the family. Indeed, these maidenly virtues of unpaid work in the home for her father could well be seen as quintessential "family values" in the ultra-conservative sense. Yet she did not exist. Her legal dilemma did not exist.[89] Domestic relationships were quickly reconfigured to fit hegemonic notions of the family. This is not to say that they do not have the potential to destabilise the family and heterosexuality. Rather, this episode shows the resilience of those forms, as those in power proceed on the basis of their own universalised experience, and render invisible that which does not conform.

CONCLUSIONS

This brief review of case law and legislation highlights a number of factors concerning same-sex relationships, law reform, and the hierarchies of sexuality and gender which still conspire to render non-conformity invisible.

The strategies which will be most useful to sexual outsiders are those which are sensitive to the local context. In Australia, this has resulted in sites of conflict surrounding the meaning of "de facto relationship" and "spouse", rather than the meaning of "marriage". It has also resulted in legislative reform efforts being shaped in a "de facto" context.[90]

When we look at the Australian cases, however, or even the progressive reforms in NSW, we must be aware of, and analyse, more than just the "outcomes", in the sense of whether sexual outsiders win or lose. Status-quo notions of "proper" (heterosexual and patriarchal) families are validated by law makers subconsciously and routinely. The case law clearly shows identity effects in terms of the continued construction of sexual "otherness"; even in the "progressive" recognition of "domestic relationships" in NSW, identity effects are produced which have profoundly conservative as well as radical tendencies.

The NSW reforms are indeed remarkable and have the potential to lead to a further re-examination of the proper role of law in the variety of human relationships which now exist. Such a broader re-examination is necessary, if we are to challenge the hierarchies of gender and sexuality which lead to our exclusion and invisibility.

[89] A child or other family member is entitled to automatic inheritance in order of the line of descent. A wide range of family members are entitled to make a claim on the property under family provision law, if they have not been adequately provided for. The only area where such a daughter would be excluded is if she wanted to make a claim on the parent's property while they were still alive. In that situation she would have been forced to use the Supreme Court's equitable jurisdiction (as lesbian and gay couples did in NSW prior to the new law).

[90] For the most recent example, see Victoria's Statute Law Amendment (Relationships) Act 2001, which inserted a new non-gendered definition of "domestic partner" in 43 Acts. See also WA, *Lesbian and Gay Law Reform*, *supra* n. 30 (proposing similar reforms); Kirby, chap. 1, n. 26.

15

The New Zealand Same-Sex Marriage Case: From Aotearoa to the United Nations

NIGEL CHRISTIE*

INTRODUCTION

THERE ARE TWO main avenues for legal change—the legislature and the courts. Ironically, both these avenues also present inherent problems when it comes to human rights challenges. The legislature is by nature a majoritarian forum and does not necessarily take account of the views, wishes or needs of any minority. Challenging discriminatory laws through lobbying the legislature may often be futile, unless significant attitudinal changes have already taken place, in which case the formal changes in law may not be so pressing.

A difficulty in striving to effect change through the courts, in an area as contentious as gay rights, is that small degrees of change may be achievable, whereas sweeping change may be seen as threatening to the stability of that with which society is comfortable. Because the courts are "institutionally ill-suited to sweeping social change", they are not always a good forum for rights issues.[1]

It is clear therefore that gays must continue to present rational and coherent arguments to both these forums, in order to attain the full and equal recognition of their relationships. The more aware persons in decision-making positions become of the issues involved, and the logic behind the arguments put forward, the more likely it is that positive change will eventuate.

THE LAW AND HOMOSEXUALITY IN NEW ZEALAND

Homosexuality as a personal characteristic has never been illegal in New Zealand, for men or for women. Lesbian sexual behaviour has never been classed as criminal behaviour. However, all homosexual behaviour between

* Ph.D. Candidate, School of Law, University of Waikato.

[1] M Coles, "The Right Forum, the Right Issue: Initiatives and Family Values", (1993) 8 *Berkeley Women's Law Journal* 180 at 182.

consenting adult males was criminalised by the New Zealand Criminal Code Act 1893.

The New Zealand House of Representatives had already banned anal intercourse in the Offences Against the Person Act 1867. This Act followed the English reform of 1861 and substituted life imprisonment for the death penalty:

> "Whosoever shall be convicted of the abominable crime of buggery committed either with mankind or any animal shall be liable at the discretion of the Court to be kept in penal servitude for life or for any term not less than ten years".[2]

The penalty for attempted buggery remained three to ten years imprisonment.[3]

English law was amended in 1885 to ensure specific criminalisation of all sexual activity between males. This included oral sex and mutual masturbation, as well as anal intercourse. New Zealand attempted, but failed, to make a similar amendment through its Crimes Bill of 1888. However, New Zealand achieved the same result through its Criminal Code Act 1893. The Code included amongst its "Crimes Against Morality" a provision stipulating that:

> "Everyone is liable to imprisonment with hard labour for life, and, according to his age, to be flogged or whipped once, twice or thrice, who commits buggery either with a human being or with any other living creature".[4]

The Code also provided for up to ten years imprisonment, with flogging or whipping,[5] for attempted buggery, assault on another person with intent to commit buggery, or for anyone "who being a male, indecently assaults any other male". In the case of "indecent assault on a male", consent was not a defence.[6]

The buggery laws had been gender-neutral, but now, for the first time, male-to-male sexual activity had been expressly criminalised. Only men could be charged with an indecent assault, and therefore the possibility of female-to-female sexual activity was a legal non-issue.

The penalty of life imprisonment was repealed in 1961, the requirement of flogging in 1941,[7] and the requirement of hard labour in 1954.[8] Following the Crimes Act 1961, male homosexual indecency could earn up to five years imprisonment, and anal intercourse seven years. It is said that such offences were "taken seriously" until the 1980s, with numerous convictions for adult homosexual activity.[9]

Through the 1960s and 1970s, social attitudes were changing. New Zealand had been seen historically as a leader in liberal reform in many social areas.[10] It

[2] Offences Against the Person Act 1867, s. 58.
[3] *Ibid.*, s. 59.
[4] Criminal Code Act 1893, s. 136.
[5] *Ibid.*, s. 137.
[6] *Ibid.*
[7] Crimes Amendment Act 1941, s.3(1).
[8] Criminal Justice Act 1954, s. 54(1).
[9] G Newbold, *Crime and Deviance* (Auckland, Oxford University Press, 1992), at 68 (50 convictions and 14 prison sentences in 1973).
[10] For example, the vote for women was introduced in 1893.

was not extraordinary, therefore, when Parliament was petitioned to decriminalise homosexual activity in 1967. Unfortunately, this petition failed,[11] as did two further attempts in the 1970s (which would have introduced unequal age of consent of 20 or 21).[12] And in 1977, Parliament voted against the inclusion of sexual orientation as a prohibited ground of discrimination in the Human Rights Commission Act.

Even though these reform proposals were unsuccessful, social change was evident. Criminal prosecutions continued but lessened, and by the 1980s were "almost non-existent".[13] By now, homosexuality was no longer seen as a disease or as a psychopathic disorder, except by an insignificant minority. It was now being seen as a difference in sexual identity, as part of a range of sexual norms.[14]

In March 1985, Fran Wilde MP introduced her private member's Bill for the reform of homosexual law. As a result, homosexual activity was decriminalised by a Parliamentary conscience vote in July 1986, although anti-discrimination provisions accompanying the Bill were not enacted. The Homosexual Law Reform Act 1986 decriminalised homosexual behaviour between consenting adult males, with an equal age of consent of 16 years.

Subsequent legislation allowed New Zealand to regain some of its status as one of the more advanced jurisdictions in relation to liberal law reforms. In 1993, Katherine O'Regan MP successfully reintroduced anti-discrimination provisions. As of 1 February 1994, it became illegal, under the Human Rights Act 1993, to discriminate against any person on the basis of their sexual orientation[15] in the areas of employment, housing, education, and the provision of goods and services. By consequential amendment, the prohibition was extended to the legislative, executive and judicial branches of government, as well as other persons or bodies performing public functions, under section 19(1) of the New Zealand Bill of Rights Act 1990. "Sexual orientation" was included in both the 1993 and 1990 Acts as a prohibited ground of discrimination.

During the 1970s and 1980s, the New Zealand Parliament ratified international human rights conventions, such as the International Covenant on Civil and Political Rights.[16] In so doing, New Zealand accepted (in the Preamble) "a responsibility to strive for the promotion and observance of the rights recognized in the present Covenant". New Zealand also acceded to the Optional Protocol to the Covenant,[17] which means that the New Zealand Parliament has

[11] *Supra* n.9, at 69.

[12] H Young, "A Chronicle of Homosexuality in New Zealand: Part 2", http://nzcom.co.nz/NZ/Queer/history/Chronolheads.html.

[13] *Ibid*.

[14] For example, the American Psychiatric Association removed homosexuality from its list of clinical disorders in 1973–74.

[15] S. 21 defines "sexual orientation" as "heterosexual, homosexual, lesbian, or bisexual orientation".

[16] Adopted and opened for signature, ratification and accession by General Assembly resolution 2200A (XXI) of 16 December 1966, and entered into force on 23 March 1976.

[17] New Zealand acceded to the Optional Protocol on 26 May 1989.

accepted the scrutiny of the United Nations Human Rights Committee into the treatment of individuals within the domestic New Zealand jurisdiction, including under Acts of Parliament.

Because of the provisions protecting gays and lesbians from unfair discrimination, it was felt that New Zealand had some of the strongest gay rights legislation in the world. However, as in many other jurisdictions, our work had until recently focused on the rights of individuals. The emphasis had been on liberalising and strengthening the law relating to homosexuality and the treatment of homosexual persons as individuals, rather than on radically changing our status as persons in society. It has only been in the last few years that the legal recognition of same-sex relationships has been placed on the agenda in New Zealand. Gays and lesbians have watched, with interest, variations on the registered partnership theme being formulated and implemented in other countries. We have also watched the marriage cases, such as those in Hawaii and Vermont,[18] and many other significant cases under both national and international law, such as *Toonen* v. *Australia*.[19]

PETITIONING THE COURTS FOR MARRIAGE

Quilter v. *Attorney-General*, the New Zealand same-sex marriage case,[20] was taken not because gays and lesbians are seeking the right to marry per se, but because we are seeking recognition of the right to "full and equal treatment under the law". Currently, we do not have the same choice as opposite-sex couples about whether or not to marry. This means that we do not have the choice of accessing or not accessing, in the way that opposite-sex de facto couples do, the raft of legal protections which opposite-sex married couples take for granted.

There are varying views on what is the best way to achieve the desired result; but it is the contention of those who have been involved in the *Quilter* case that to accept anything less than full and equivalent rights under the law is to accept a second-rate, or even third-rate, citizenship. Access to civil marriage is the only means of achieving equality.

The danger of any legal regime designed specifically for same-sex couples, such as registered partnerships, is that it sets apart same-sex relationships even further. Also, such regimes are often designed to deal with property issues, and tend not to provide fully for personal and family protections, such as next-of-kinship in relation to medical care, death and parenting (issues other than material property). If gays and lesbians accept a "separate but unequal" regime,

[18] See Wolfson, chap. 9; Bonauto, chap. 10.

[19] (Communication No. 488/1992) (31 March 1994) 1 International Human Rights Reports 97 (United Nations Human Rights Committee).

[20] *Quilter* v. *Attorney-General* [1998] 1 NZLR 523 (Court of Appeal), <http://www.brookers.co.nz/legal/judgments>.

they are ignoring a central part of their lives—their core relationships to their partners.

An examination of the legal changes benefitting gays and lesbians in New Zealand would suggest that "broad-brush" changes are generally achieved through the legislature. Examples would include the Homosexual Law Reform Act 1986, the New Zealand Bill of Rights Act 1990, and the Human Rights Act 1993. However, some individual applications to courts in relation to, for example, child custody and access, have been successful, but these are considered on the merits of each case. Over all, the results tend to be inconsistent and have not led to ongoing positive change.[21]

Other changes have resulted from a combination of court actions, whether successful or not, and subsequent pressure for legislative reform. Such a combination removed an inconsistency between the Human Rights Act 1993 and the Accident Compensation Insurance Act 1992. Mary Bramwell's partner, Raewyn Gilmour, died in a horrific car accident. A court denied Mary recognition as the surviving spouse because "spouse" was defined in terms of partners "of the opposite sex".[22] After continued lobbying for change, the definition of "spouse" in a new 1998 Act includes "a person . . . of the same gender".[23]

Having considered the general human rights climate in New Zealand, with a belief that New Zealand's domestic human rights law could require a favourable interpretation of a gender-neutral Marriage Act, and with a realistic recognition of the difficulties ahead, three couples went to court seeking the right to marry. It was hoped that, by placing their story in the socio-legal context of the current human rights climate of New Zealand, the judges involved might recognise, that denying same-sex couples access to the Marriage Act and the right to marry is discriminatory and therefore contrary to New Zealand law.

On 24 April 1996, the three lesbian couples who were the plaintiffs in *Quilter* (hereinafter "the Plaintiffs") appeared before the High Court in Auckland, seeking a declaration that the Registrar-General of Births, Deaths and Marriages was acting in breach of New Zealand law by not issuing marriage licences to same-sex couples who wished to get married. The basic premise of their legal argument was that the Marriage Act 1955 did not stipulate that the parties to a marriage need be a man and a woman, and that officials had acted in breach of New Zealand human rights law by refusing to issue marriage licences to same-sex couples.

[21] See, eg, *VP* v. *PM* (1998) 16 FRNZ 621 (lesbian mother retains custody of two children); *Re an Application by T* [1998] NZFLR 769 (second-parent adoption by lesbian mother of partner's child by donor insemination refused); *A* v. *R* [1999] NZFLR 249 (non-biological mother in *Re an Application by T* held liable for child support payments as a step-parent),

[22] *Estate of Raewyn Gilmour* v. *Accident Rehabilitation and Compensation Corporation* (7 Aug. 1995), Decision No. 104/95 (Judge A. W. Middleton, District Court, Hamilton), applying Accident Compensation Insurance Act 1992, s. 3.

[23] Accident Insurance Act 1998, s. 25.

Justice Kerr declined to issue the declaration sought, holding that, although the law as it stood was discriminatory, the Marriage Act 1955 could not be interpreted as including same-sex couples—any change to that law was a matter for Parliament.

On 3 September 1997, an appeal was heard in the New Zealand Court of Appeal. The bench of five held unanimously that same-sex couples could not marry under existing New Zealand law. Two of the Justices did state that the legislation was discriminatory, but held, like the High Court, that any change to permit same-sex couples to marry must be made by Parliament.

In December 1998, Communication No. 902/1999, *Joslin* v. *New Zealand*, was submitted to the United Nations Human Rights Committee, under Article 2 of the Optional Protocol to the International Covenant on Civil and Political Rights. The Communication urges the Committee to declare that the New Zealand Government, by excluding same-sex couples from the Marriage Act 1955, is in breach of its obligations under Covenant Articles 16, 17, 17 *juncto* 2.1, 23.1 *juncto* 2.1, and 23.2 *juncto* 2.1, and 26. By August 2001, the Committee had begun considering the Communication, and the parties were preparing their final submissions.[24]

THE *QUILTER* PLAINTIFFS' ARGUMENTS BEFORE THE NEW ZEALAND COURTS

In essence, the Plaintiffs submitted that the failure to issue marriage licenses to them, under the provisions of the Marriage Act 1955 as interpreted in light of the discrimination provisions of the New Zealand Bill of Rights Act 1990, was in breach of New Zealand law. The Plaintiffs relied on reading together the relevant provisions of the Marriage Act and sections 19, 6 and 5 of the Bill of Rights Act.

Their argument was that:

(a) the eligibility provisions of the Marriage Act 1955 are gender-neutral and "marriage" is not defined by the Act;

(b) s. 6 of the New Zealand Bill of Rights Act 1990 provides that,

> "[w]herever an enactment can be given a meaning that is consistent with the rights and freedoms contained in this Bill of Rights, that meaning shall be preferred to any other meaning";

(c) s. 19(1) of the Bill of Rights Act provides that "[e]veryone has the right to freedom from discrimination on the grounds of discrimination in the Human Rights Act 1993", which include "sex" (s. 21(a), 1993 Act) and "sexual orientation" (s. 21(m), 1993 Act);

(d) to avoid unjustifiable discrimination on the grounds of sex or sexual orientation, the Marriage Act 1955 must be interpreted as extending eligibility for a marriage license to same-sex couples;

[24] For an analysis of the Communication's prospects before the Committee, see Helfer, chap. 41.

(e) a "male-female only" interpretation would not be a "reasonable limit" on the Plaintiffs' rights under s. 19(1) of the Bill of Rights Act that could be "demonstrably justified in a free and democratic society" under s. 5 of the Bill of Rights Act;
(f) a gender-neutral, non-discriminatory interpretation of the Marriage Act 1955 was supported by obligations which New Zealand had accepted under international human rights instruments.

The Plaintiffs further argued that s. 4 of the Bill of Rights Act ("[n]o court shall . . . (a) hold any provision of [an] enactment . . . in any way invalid . . . or (b) decline to apply any provision of the enactment—by reason only that the provision is inconsistent with any provision of this Bill of Rights") was not relevant, because none of the provisions of the Marriage Act 1955 is expressly or impliedly inconsistent with the Bill of Rights Act. Rather, the 1955 Act can, and must, be interpreted under s. 6 of the Bill of Rights Act in a way that is consistent with s. 19(1) of the Bill of Rights Act.

(a) Gender Neutrality

All legislation dealing with eligibility to marry under New Zealand law is gender-neutral. The Marriage Act 1955 neither defines "marriage", nor uses gender-specific language; instead, it uses words such as "person" or "persons" and "party" or "parties".[25] There are two exceptions, which the Plaintiffs argued did not provide an obstacle to same-sex marriage under the Act. Sections 31(3) and 33(2) use the words "I . . . take you . . . to be my legal wife (or husband), or words to similar effect". The Plaintiffs argued that these provisions do not preclude a man from saying "I take you to be my legal husband", or a woman from saying "I take you to be my legal wife". The second exception is the Act's Second Schedule ("Forbidden Marriages"), which lists the persons a man may not marry (twenty classes of female relatives), and the persons a woman may not marry (twenty classes of male relatives). To eliminate the anomaly of a man being able to marry his brother but not his sister, the Plaintiffs argued that, under the Interpretation Act 1924, "man" and "woman" both include the opposite gender.

The Family Proceedings Act 1980 is also gender-neutral. Section 31(1)(a) of the Act lists the grounds on which a marriage may be declared void ((i) one party is already married; (ii) duress, mistake, insanity or other absence of consent; (iii) marriage within the prohibited degrees found in the Marriage Act's Second Schedule), but does not state that a marriage will be void where the parties to the marriage are of the same gender.

[25] S. 3, for example, states: "The provisions of this Act, so far as they relate to the capacity to marry, shall apply to the marriage of any *person* domiciled in New Zealand at the time of the marriage . . ." (emphasis added).

(b) and (c) Bill of Rights Act

The Plaintiffs argued that a reading together of section 3 ("[t]his Bill of Rights applies only to Acts done—(a) by the legislative, executive or judicial branches of government . . . or (b) by any person or body in the performance of any public function . . ."), section 6 (duty of consistent interpretation), and section 19 (prohibition of sex and sexual orientation discrimination) of the New Zealand Bill of Rights Act 1990, mandated the eligibility of same-sex couples to marry under the Marriage Act 1955.

It was contended that, because the Marriage Act is gender-neutral, it can be interpreted to include same-sex couples, as required by section 6 of the Bill of Rights Act. It was further contended that section 6 obliges the court to *strive* to interpret a statute consistently, and to do so in the context of the late 1990s and the post-Bill of Rights Act era, rather than 1955. The Marriage Act could be, and therefore must be, interpreted to include same-sex couples.

(d) Discrimination

Counsel for the Plaintiffs submitted that:

> "It is not necessary for the Plaintiffs in this case to show that the married status which they are currently denied is objectively better or more advantageous than their current status . . . Secondly, . . . the test as to the link between the unfavourable treatment and the prohibited grounds is objective, and intention and motive are irrelevant". [26]

Counsel then argued that denial of marriage licenses was "less favourable treatment" on the prohibited grounds of "sex" (relying on *Baehr* v. *Lewin*)[27] and/or "sexual orientation".

(e) Justification

It was further contended that the only reason not to accept a gender-neutral, non-discriminatory interpretation of the Marriage Act was where the Government could prove, under section 5 of the Bill of Rights Act, that a "male-female only" interpretation is a "reasonable limit" that can be "demonstrably justified in a free and democratic society". Although the prohibition of marriages between close relatives (in the Marriage Act's Second Schedule) could be justified, a marriage should not be disallowed merely because other persons do not like the fact that the marriage is taking place—essentially the reason given by the Government against the notion of same-sex marriage.

[26] Submission of Plaintiffs, 20.
[27] 852 P. 2d 44 (Hawaii Supreme Court 1993).

(f) International Law

Under international law, New Zealand has accepted obligations to accord its citizens equal protection under the law and to actively promote the removal of discrimination. Relevant international human rights treaties which New Zealand has ratified include the International Covenant on Civil and Political Rights (ICCPR); the International Covenant on Economic, Social and Cultural Rights; the Convention on the Elimination of all forms of Discrimination Against Women (CEDAW); and the Convention on the Rights of the Child.[28] International obligations, even if not incorporated directly into domestic law, are relevant to its interpretation when there are gaps or obscurity in the common law, or ambiguity in statute law.

THE JUDGMENTS OF THE NEW ZEALAND COURTS

Justice Kerr of the High Court in Auckland held that, by not being permitted to marry, same-sex couples are discriminated against, but that it is up to Parliament to change the law. In his application of section 5 of the Bill of Rights Act, Kerr J did not require the Attorney-General to justify the discriminatory limit on the right to marry but rather stated that: "Pursuant to section 5, Parliament is entitled to reasonably limit the persons able to marry so that couples of the same sex are not entitled to go through a marriage ceremony".[29]

Although homosexual behaviour was decriminalised in New Zealand in 1986, there is still a legacy of prejudice. Justice Kerr commented that: "[i]t is no longer an offence for males of 16 years or over to commit indecencies with each other . . ."[30] What he failed to grasp was that homosexual behaviour between consenting adult males is no longer legally an "indecency". This illustrates a failure to understand the legal climate as it affects lesbians and gay men as individuals, and, by implication, our rights in relation to each other and the wider community.

Justice Kerr considered various transgender cases including the New Zealand case *Attorney-General* v. *Family Court at Otahuhu*.[31] *Otahuhu* established that, under New Zealand law, transsexuals can, in fact, choose to marry a person of either gender. A male-to-female transsexual can by law, (a) choose not to register a change of gender and marry a female (both parties "visually" female) or (b) choose to register a change of gender and marry a male (both parties born male). It can be argued that this analysis supports same-sex marriage. However,

[28] The Plaintiffs relied on ICCPR Article 23.2, read together with provisions in CEDAW relating to the right to marry and form a family, and ICCPR Arts. 26 and 2.1, using the *Toonen* statement that "sex" is to be taken as including "sexual orientation". See Helfer, chap. 41.

[29] *Quilter* v. *Attorney-General* [1997] 14 FRNZ 430 at 454 (High Court) (emphasis added).

[30] *Ibid.* at 441.

[31] *Ibid.* at 434 and 435, citing *Otahuhu*, [1995] NZFLR 57.

Kerr J fell short of understanding the intricacies of issues of gender identity, biological/physical gender, legal gender, and sexual orientation. He concluded, incorrectly, that "in New Zealand for a marriage to take place there must be parties who visually at least are male and female".[32]

In the Court of Appeal,[33] there were two key issues: (a) whether gays and lesbians were being unjustifiably discriminated against on the grounds of sex or sexual orientation, contrary to section 19 of the Bill of Rights Act, by being denied the right to marry ("the discrimination issue"); and (b) whether the Marriage Act can be read consistently with section 19 of the Bill of Rights Act, that is, in a gender-neutral way, in order to avoid that discrimination ("the interpretation issue)". For the Plaintiffs to succeed, the answer on both issues had to be "Yes". If the answer on the interpretation issue were "No", the Plaintiffs' claim would fail, because clearly discriminatory legislation prevails over section 19 of the Bill of Rights Act, under section 4 of the Bill of Rights Act. And a negative answer would arguably make it unnecessary to address the discrimination issue.

On the interpretation issue, the five-judge Court held unanimously that the language of the Marriage Act 1955 was sufficiently clear to deny same-sex couples eligibility to marry under that Act. The Court essentially said that, if same-sex couples were to be given the right to marry, that was a policy decision for Parliament. Justice Tipping wrote for the Court on this issue. He referred to the "well-established common law background" against which the Act was passed, and did not use the power granted to the Court under section 3(a) of the Bill of Rights Act to set aside a common law principle where it conflicts with the Bill of Rights Act. His reversion to "the underlying common law meaning of marriage" means that section 6 of the Bill of Rights Act was set aside, rather than the common-law-based interpretation of the Marriage Act, which was inconsistent with the Bill of Rights Act. He also cited the references to "husband", "wife", "man" and "woman" in section 31(3) and the Second Schedule of the Marriage Act (mentioned above), and other gender-specific language in the (post-Bill of Rights Act) Births, Deaths, and Marriages Registration Act 1995.

On the discrimination issue, Richardson P, Gault J and Keith J held that the negative answer on the interpretation question made it unnecessary to decide the discrimination question. But all three went on to state, obiter, that same-sex couples were not being discriminated against by being denied access to legal marriage. President Richardson said only that he was "not persuaded that the right under section 19 of the Bill of Rights Act 1990 to freedom from discrimination requires equal legislative recognition of heterosexual and same-sex marriages".[34]

Gault J argued that there was no discrimination against the Plaintiffs on grounds of their gender or their sexual orientation. "There would have been no

[32] *Quilter* v. *Attorney-General* [1997] 14 FRNZ 430 at 434.

[33] For detailed analysis of each of the judgments, see A Butler, "Same-Sex Marriage and Freedom from Discrimination in New Zealand", [1998] *Public Law* (UK) 396.

[34] *Supra* n.20, at 526.

different reaction had the Plaintiffs been male or if they had been heterosexual and simply seeking a marriage relationship to take advantage of perceived civil benefits".[35] This analysis ignores *indirect* sexual orientation discrimination, that is, differentiation adversely impacting on gays and lesbians as compared with heterosexuals. It also fails to acknowledge the depth of that effect and dismisses it as a matter of "choice": "denial of choice always affects only those who wish to make the choice. It is not for that reason discriminatory".[36] Justice Gault also stated that differentiation is not discrimination and that differentiation in this instance is permissible because it "has long been conventional in the concept of marriage". He also observed that "[j]ustification for differences frequently will be found in social policy resting on community values",[37] but he did not seek to enumerate any "social policy" or other justifications.

Justice Keith found no breach of section 19 of the Bill of Rights Act because "section 19 would not have removed a central element of the accepted definition of marriage . . . Parliament would not have effected such a major change to a fundamental institution . . . in such an indirect way".[38] He also stated that the refusals to issue marriage licences "were not 'on the grounds of' the sexual orientation of each applicant" and "involved no breach of the right to freedom from discrimination on the grounds of the sex of each applicant, since *each and every* individual seeking to marry someone of the same sex would be *equally* refused".[39]

Perhaps the most disappointing element of Justice Keith's reasoning, as a respected international jurist, lies in his blanket rejection of international developments in relation to same-sex marriage. He relied on "the non-acceptance of the world community of any support for a right to same-sex marriage based on the principle of equality or the prohibition on discrimination",[40] a statement which ignored the registered partnership laws of Denmark, Norway, Sweden, Iceland and the Netherlands, as well as the Hawaii Supreme Court's preliminary ruling in *Baehr* v. *Lewin*.

Tipping J agreed that there was no need to decide the discrimination issue, but added, obiter, that:

> "the impact of the prohibition inherent in the Marriage Act against same-sex marriages is much more significant for people with a same-sex orientation that it is for people of heterosexual orientation. . . . Prima facie . . . I see the inability of homosexual and lesbian couples to marry as involving [indirect] discrimination against them on the grounds of their sexual orientation".[41]

Unfortunately, he did not go on to address the question of whether or not this discrimination is justifiable.

[35] *Ibid.*, at 527.
[36] *Ibid.*
[37] *Ibid.*
[38] *Ibid.*, at 555.
[39] *Ibid.*, at 557. See also Koppelman, chap. 35.
[40] *Ibid.*, at 563.
[41] *Ibid.*, at 575–6.

Justice Thomas began by stating that:

"[h]aving regard . . . to the essential thrust of these appeals . . . it would be unduly legalistic to rest the Court's decision on the meaning of the Marriage Act without squarely confronting the question of discrimination".

He then found prima facie discrimination based *both* on sex *and* sexual orientation:

"Whether one adopts the approach urged upon the Court by [the Plaintiffs' counsel, that the female applicant is discriminated against on the grounds of her sex because, being female, she is by law unable to marry another woman], or focuses on the [Plaintiffs'] rights as a couple, the discrimination fairly can be said to be based on their sex. Whatever hesitation may exist to basing the discrimination on the ground of sex, one cannot seriously resist the proposition that gays and lesbians are discriminated against on the ground of sexual orientation. Just as the sexual orientation of heterosexual men and women leads to the formation of heterosexual relationships, so too it is the sexual orientation of gays and lesbians which leads to the formation of homosexual relationships. Sexual orientation dictates their choice of partner in both cases".[42]

He went on to hold that this prima facie discrimination "cannot be qualified by reference to section 5",[43] the justification provision of the Bill of Rights Act. In particular, he rejected the view that "procreation is the sole or major purpose of marriage . . . [T]he essence of the marriage relationship [is instead] cohabitation, commitment, intimacy, and financial interdependence".[44] He also rejected the "circular and question-begging" argument "that gay and lesbian persons are not discriminated against because they are free to marry persons of the opposite sex",[45] and warned of "the danger of looking to the past to determine whether discrimination exists today".[46]

A striking feature of his judgment is his awareness of the consequences to gays and lesbians of exclusion from marriage:

"Based upon [their sexual orientation], gays and lesbians are denied access to a central social institution and the resulting status of married persons. They lose the rights and privileges, including the manifold legal consequences which marriage conveys. They are denied a basic civil right in that freedom to marry is rightly regarded as a basic civil right. They lose the opportunity to choose the partner of their choice as a marriage partner, many again viewing the right to choose as a basic civil right of all citizens. *In a real sense, gays and lesbians are effectively excluded from full membership of society*".[47]

He concluded that the exclusion of gays and lesbians from marriage "inescapably judges them less worthy of the respect, concern and consideration

[42] *Ibid.*, at 536–7.
[43] *Ibid.*, at 540.
[44] *Ibid.*, at 534, 547.
[45] *Ibid.*, at 537.
[46] *Ibid.*, at 550.
[47] *Ibid.*, at 537 (emphasis added).

deriving from the fundamental concept of human dignity underlying all human rights legislation".[48] If it were not for his inability to strike down clear but discriminatory legislation because of section 4 of the Bill of Rights Act (to be discussed below), he might have found for the Plaintiffs.

KEY BARRIERS TO EQUALITY

Tradition

What is being sought, by striving for a re-instatement of rights, is to re-claim a history and an associated rightful place in society. Unfortunately, the story, as re-written over the last few hundred years by the majority culture, is now called "tradition" by the group in power; the hurdle of that inertia must be overcome in order that gay and lesbian voices be heard.

The Plaintiffs argued that it is not logical to justify discrimination by using "tradition". Yet this is precisely what the New Zealand courts and Parliament do. The Plaintiffs also argued that we should not look back to the common-law definition of marriage, which stems from *Hyde* v. *Hyde & Woodmansee* in 1866,[49] to justify a definition of marriage in New Zealand in the 1990s. Yet, before the High Court, the Crown took us back to the case of *Lindo* v. *Bellisario* in 1795.[50] And, in the Court of Appeal judgment of Justice Tipping, we are told that the 1662 version of the *Anglican Book of Common Prayer* says that the first cause for which matrimony was ordained was "procreation".

The message is thus that a tradition of discrimination can be used to justify contemporary discrimination. The courts failed to appreciate that, while traditional values can be positive, there can also be discrimination which stems from the inertia of tradition. Many exciting changes of the past would not have come about had we adhered to certain practices purely on the basis of former and contemporary practice: women would still be the chattels of their fathers or older brothers or husbands; marriage between different racial or ethnic groups would be denied; and women would not now have the right to vote.

The Courts' Inability to Strike Down Legislation

New Zealand has a multi-document constitution which enjoys the status of ordinary law, and the New Zealand Bill of Rights Act 1990 is merely one of

[48] *Ibid.*, at 555.

[49] [1861–73] All ER 175 at 177. Lord Penzance stated that "marriage, as understood in Christendom, may for this purpose be defined as the voluntary union for life of one man and one woman, to the exclusion of all others". The issue in this case was bigamy—the gender of the parties was not at issue.

[50] 161 ER 530: The issue before the Court was the validity of a Jewish marriage, which led the Court to discuss procreation.

those documents. The political decision not to give the Bill of Rights Act any superior status over other legislation is reflected in section 4 of the Bill of Rights Act, quoted above. Section 4 makes it clear that New Zealand courts do not have the ability to strike down legislation which breaches the rights guaranteed by the Bill of Rights Act, including the right in section 19 to freedom from discrimination. This means that a Bill of Rights Act, which purports to "affirm, protect, and promote human rights and fundamental freedoms in New Zealand", and to "affirm New Zealand's commitment to the International Covenant on Civil and Political Rights", is proving to be of no practical use to minority groups.

The power of the Bill of Rights Act lies merely in the ability of judges to interpret legislation that is not absolutely clear in a way that is consistent with the Bill of Rights Act. In *Quilter*, all five judges of the Court of Appeal refused to exercise this power, making it necessary for the Plaintiffs to send their Communication to the United Nations Human Rights Committee. But even if a majority of them had been willing to give the Marriage Act 1955 a gender-neutral interpretation, Parliament could easily have overturned their decision simply by adding a "one man-one woman" definition of marriage to the Act.

New Zealand has built itself a reputation as a leading nation on human rights issues. A speech by Kofi Annan, Secretary-General of the United Nations, in Wellington in March 2000 affirmed New Zealand's significant role in the international human rights community.[51] But in the very same month, Lord Cooke (a judicial member of the British House of Lords and former President of the New Zealand Court of Appeal) expressed his belief that New Zealand had fallen behind, describing the New Zealand Bill of Rights Act 1990 as "one of the weakest affirmations of human rights", because it can be changed by a simple majority in Parliament.[52] And he stated that:

> "[t]here seems something incongruous . . . in expecting the court to engage in an elaborate academic discussion which could not even end in a [non-binding] declaration of incompatibility [as under the British Human Rights Act 1998]".

If New Zealand were to have a stronger human rights regime, our courts would be in a better position to enforce the rights which same-sex couples, amongst others, are claiming.

PROSPECTS FOR LEGISLATIVE REFORM

On 27 November 1999, New Zealand held its general election and a new Labour-led Government was elected. The previous Government, which had been in power for nine years, including the period of the introduction of the

[51] *Council Brief* (Wellington District Law Society), April 2000.

[52] Lord Cooke of Thorndon, "The Role of the Judges", "Building the Constitution" Conference, Wellington, 7–8 April 2000.

New Zealand Bill of Rights Act 1990 and the Human Rights Act 1993, had displayed a lack of commitment to human rights generally and the rights of gay and lesbian couples in particular.

Consistency 2000

The Human Rights Act 1993 contained an exception which enabled the Government to discriminate legally on the new grounds added to the Act in 1993, including sexual orientation, and exempted all other Acts of Parliament. However, a "sunset clause" provided that the exception would expire at the end of 1999.[53] The Act also required the Human Rights Commission to report to the Government by the end of 1998 on all "Acts, regulations, policies, and practices" breaching the anti-discrimination provisions of the Human Rights Act.[54] Reading together sections 5(1)(i), (j), (k), 151, and 152 of the Act, and taking into account the spirit and intent of the Act as expressed by Parliament prior to its passage, it is clear that the Government undertook to ensure that all legislation, regulations, policies and practices of Government were made consistent with the Human Rights Act 1993 by January 2000, unless exemption from compliance was objectively justified and legislated.

In May 1998, the then-Government called an end to the "Consistency 2000" project, citing cost and time as reasons. It then introduced a Bill to amend the statutory provisions requiring the Commission to report, and to exempt the Government permanently from the Human Rights Act, except in areas such as employment and access to buildings, where it would have to act in essentially the same manner as the private sector. But the Bill was not passed by the House of Representatives. The Human Rights Commission met its statutory obligations by presenting a Report to Parliament.[55] The Commission made it very clear in its Report that it was not satisfied with the attempt to stifle its work. A second Bill was introduced and passed in 1999. The Human Rights Amendment Act 1999 effectively extends the old "sunset clause" until the end of 2001, but in the meantime, the work on consistency issues has been seriously delayed.

De Facto Relationships Legislation

The De Facto Relationships Property Bill and the Matrimonial Property Amendment Bill were introduced into Parliament on 24 March 1998. Both Bills proceeded to consideration by a Select Committee and the receipt of public submissions. Despite advice from officials that the exclusion of same-sex couples from the De Facto Bill could raise issues under the Human Rights Act, the Minister of Justice and the Cabinet preferred not to include same-sex couples in

[53] Ss. 151, 152.
[54] Ss. 5(1)(i), (j), (k).
[55] See <http://www.justice.govt.nz/pubs/reports/1998/hrc_consistency/index.html>.

the draft Bill. Submissions on the De Facto Bill were overwhelmingly in favour of the inclusion of same-sex couples.[56] The Bill, which had been before a Parliamentary Select Committee for some twelve months, was then "put on hold", and the Minister of Justice asked his Ministry to prepare a discussion document on the issue of "Same-Sex Couples and the Law". The resulting paper was released in August 1999[57] and invited public comment by 30 April 2000.[58]

The concept of public consultation on human rights issues raises fundamental concerns, and in relation to the Ministry of Justice paper, these concerns were magnified. Firstly, our domestic human rights legislation not only gives Government a mandate to protect minority rights from majoritarian prejudice, but also places on them an obligation to do so. It is arguable, therefore, that it is inappropriate for the Government to then seek the views of New Zealanders at large on what level or levels of protection a minority group should receive. Secondly, the New Zealand Law Commission submitted a study paper to the Ministry of Justice presenting what purport to be the Commission's views.[59] This is not a report of the Commission, is not based on in-depth research, and reflects views contrary to those of many members of the gay and lesbian communities in New Zealand. There is a danger that what are essentially the views of one Commissioner will be given undue weight. Thirdly, the Human Rights Commission, which had previously declined to be an intervening party in the *Quilter* case, also submitted a report to the Ministry of Justice.[60] This report was very light on domestic and international human rights analysis (it did not once mention the New Zealand Human Rights Act), and could also be given undue weight in comparison with individual public submissions.

While the Law Commission study paper does support the recognition of same-sex relationships, it also points in the direction of registered partnerships legislation: "[t]he political reality is that ninety percent of a loaf is better than no bread at all".[61] The Human Rights Commission submission is similar. While it does discuss marriage as a possibility, it does not come out categorically one way or another in terms of what type of recognition should be made available to same-sex couples, but rather speaks of an arrangement whereby "reform should give same-sex couples the option of choosing a legal status which is in all

[57] See <http://www.justice.govt.nz/pubs/reports/1999/same_sex/index.html>.

[58] A draft of the document stated that (former National) Government policy does not allow for same-sex marriage nor the adoption of children by same-sex couples. Cf. Law Commission Report 65, *Adoption and Its Alternatives*, Sept. 2000, <http://www.lawcom.govt.nz> (Publications, Lists, Reports), paras. 350–64. "We recommend that the terminology of a new Act make it clear that de facto (including same-sex couples) may adopt".

[59] Law Commission Study Paper 4, *Recognising Same-Sex Relationships*, Dec. 1999, <http://www.lawcom.govt.nz> (Publications, Lists, Study Papers).

[60] Human Rights Commission, "Same-Sex Couples and the Law", 2 April 2000, <http://www.hrc.co.nz/org/research/index.htm>.

[61] Law Commission, "Editorial: Recognising Same-Sex Relationships", <http://www.lawcom.govt.nz (downloaded 9 December 1999)>.

respects the same as that attaching to marriage".[62] Both submissions are supportive yet conservative, and both circumvent the fundamental premise of "equality under the law", preferring to support political expediency. This is surprising input from two apolitical, independent legal research institutions whose statutory functions require them to, for example, "make public statements . . . promoting understanding of, and compliance with, [the Human Rights] Act".[63]

It appears that the relatively new Labour Government is looking more favourably upon the legal recognition of same-sex relationships. The Prime Minister, Helen Clark, is reported to have stated, "I will support legal recognition of same-sex relationships"[64] and "will not rule out the possibility of same-sex marriage".[65] However, she sees relationship recognition as a conscience issue within Parliament.

In early 2000, the Government announced a proposal to include same-sex couples in the property legislation, and to combine the Matrimonial Property Amendment Bill and the De Facto Relationships Property Bill into one piece of legislation (Supplementary Order Paper No.25). In spite of an initial outcry from the opposition parties about the process, on 4 May 2000, the House voted 64–54 in favour of allowing SOP 25 (renamed the Property (Relationships) Bill 2000) to proceed. Further lobbying by opposition parties resulted in the Bill being referred back to the Justice and Electoral Reform Select Committee for further submissions.

The Select Committee reported to the House on 14 November 2000. The original version of the Bill referred to the Select Committee used the generic term "partner" to cover marriage, de facto heterosexual, and same-sex relationships, which created some consternation amongst opponents. The Select Committee reintroduced the terms "husband" and "wife" in relation to marriage. One of the key advocates of this change was the Leader of the Opposition, Jenny Shipley, who said that "marriage does have a special status in law, and it's different from de facto or same-sex relationships".[66] A de facto relationship is defined as one in which "two people (whether a man and a woman, or a man and a man, or a woman and a woman) are living together in a relationship in the nature of marriage although not married to each other".[67] The substantive treatment within the legislation of "partners", or a "husband" or "wife", remains the same in all instances. The Second Reading debate continued on 21 November 2000 and the House voted 80–39 in favour of the inclusion of same-sex couples in the Bill.

The Bill was finally passed, along with three other bills, on 29 March 2001. In spite of the Select Committee's changes, the four Acts are arguably the first

[62] "Same-Sex Couples and the Law", *supra* n.60, at 12.
[63] Human Rights Act 1993, s. 5(1)(c).
[64] *Evening Post*, Wellington, 7 Dec. 1999.
[65] *Express* (national fortnightly gay and lesbian newspaper), Auckland, 23 December 1999, at 3.
[66] New Zealand National Party, Press Release, 3 March 2000.
[67] Supplementary Order Paper No.25, clause 2A(2).

family-related statutes in New Zealand which are truly compliant with our human rights legislation.[68] The Property (Relationships) Amendment Act 2001 gives same-sex couples and de facto different-sex couples the same property rights (and obligations) as married couples upon the breakdown of a relationship. Subject to a provision which allows for contracting out, there will be a presumption of a fifty-fifty division of property for couples who have been together in a relationship "in the nature of marriage" for a period of three years or more.

The Family Proceedings Amendment Act 2001 will provide for "spousal maintenance" after relationship breakdown (where necessary), in addition to a division of property. The Family Protection Amendment Act 2001 will provide same-sex partners with the same right to make a claim against the estate of a deceased partner where the deceased's will has failed to make provision for the surviving partner. The Administration Amendment Act 2001 will give same-sex partners the same inheritance rights as married partners in relation to the estate of a deceased partner who has not left a will. These four Acts, which come into force on 1 February 2002, give same-sex couples the feeling that our relationships are now being recognised if they come to an end, but are still not being recognised when they begin or throughout their existence.

CONCLUSION

It is true that Parliament's intention when it passed the Marriage Act in 1955 may not have extended to the inclusion of same-sex couples. But Parliament has spoken again since 1955, and its intentions are reflected clearly in the anti-discrimination provisions it has enacted in the New Zealand Bill of Rights Act 1990 and the Human Rights Act 1993.

Those involved in the *Quilter* case believe that there is, in New Zealand, a favourable politico-legal climate for advancing the rights of gay and lesbian couples. An important aspect of the *Quilter* judgments was the acknowledgment by the High Court and by two of the Court of Appeal Justices, that the refusal to allow same-sex couples to marry is discriminatory. We also believe that, through the case, we have been able to ascertain the key points of agreement and disagreement on this issue. Views were strongly expressed on both sides. If nothing else, this meant that the questions were being debated in the gay and lesbian communities and in the wider community.

[68] Before 2001, the only statutes which included same-sex couples were: Electricity Act 1992, s. 111 (definition of a "near relative"); Domestic Violence Act 1995, s. 2 (definition of "partner"); Harassment Act 1997, s. 2 (definition of "partner"); Accident Insurance Act 1998, s. 25 (definition of "spouse"); Housing Restructuring (Income-Related Rents) Amendment Act 2000, s. 5 (definition of "partner"). Same-sex partners are also recognised by the Immigration Service after two years in a "genuine and stable" relationship (as are de facto different-sex partners). See http://www.immigration.govt.nz/migration (Family Category).

One of the huge benefits of the case has been the opportunity to bring our issues before the judiciary, to introduce them to a number of issues which they had never faced before, and to have our issues taken seriously. There was also a large public interest in the case. Contrary to the views of some officials who perceived the exercise as "dangerous", we believe that the case, and the learning that came from it, have been invaluable for the cause of the recognition of same-sex couples, both informally, and formally through the law.

By seeking the right to marry, we are seeking equality under the law. We believe that whatever options are available to opposite-sex couples must also be available to same-sex couples. The recent judgment in the Vermont marriage case has helped to highlight this fact.[69] It is not possible, we believe, to achieve equality under the law by offering a registered partnership regime to same-sex couples in place of marriage. There is no such thing as "a degree of equality". Most importantly, while offering an alternative regime to marriage may assist in relation to property and family rights, it fails to acknowledge the emotional, spiritual, and personal essence of relationships between partners. This element has been described as "the unique meaning-making power of marriage in constructing visions of intimate commitment".[70]

The *Quilter* case, even though unsuccessful in achieving an affirmative outcome for the Plaintiffs on the issue directly before the Court, has been hugely successful in highlighting the issue of same-sex marriage in the New Zealand context. We believe that it has served to expedite a serious examination by our Government of the legal recognition of same-sex relationships.[71]

The fundamental right of marriage, and the fundamental right of freedom of choice of marriage partner, are both enumerated in Article 23 of the International Covenant on Civil and Political Rights. We look to the United Nations Human Rights Committee to stand by the exhortations of that document. It is hoped that a positive response to our Communication to the Committee will send a strong message to the Government of New Zealand that it must comply with the obligations it has assumed, both through its assent to international laws and its enactment of domestic laws. The Government must accept that it has already agreed to equality for gays and lesbians. The only action required by the Government is the removal of barriers that block our access to the rights which already belong to us.

[69] See Bonauto, chap. 10.

[70] W Rountree (University of California, Berkeley) commenting by email on the Vermont same-sex marriage judgment, 4 Jan. 2000.

[71] Tim Barnett MP is leading a campaign for the introduction of a government-sponsored Civil Union Bill (open to same-sex and different-sex couples) in 2002. See http://www.civilunions.org.nz.

16

Brazil's Proposed "Civil Unions Between Persons of the Same Sex": Legislative Inaction and Judicial Reactions

MARCELO DEALTRY TURRA*

INTRODUCTION

On 10 February 1998, the *Superior Tribunal de Justiça* (Superior Court of Justice), Brazil's highest appellate court on non-constitutional matters, acknowledged for the first time an implied partnership between same-sex partners.[1] The Superior Court of Justice decided unanimously that the apartment of a man who died of AIDS complications must be shared, with a 50 per cent interest going to his surviving male partner and a 50 per cent interest to his legal heirs (his brothers and sisters). During the proceedings before the courts of the State of Minas Gerais, it had been proven that the male partner had made financial and other contributions to the acquisition of their joint residence. According to the Superior Court of Justice, "the partnership shall be recognized as a fact, no matter the parties' sexual preferences".

The decision was favourably received in the press, and exposed once again the need for legislation to settle disputes of this kind. The *Jornal do Brasil* newspaper commented as follows:

> "The decision . . . shows how retrograde the Legislature can be, even though it is theoretically more open and in touch with changes in society than the Judiciary. At the end of 1997, the *Câmara dos Deputados* [House of Representatives of the federal *Congresso Nacional* or National Congress] had one of the most shameful sessions in its history, when it was discussing the postponement of a vote on the 'Civil Unions Between Persons of the Same Sex Bill' introduced by Representative Marta Suplicy. Endorsing the audience's jokes and rude insinuations, the leader of the *Partido da Frente Popular*, Inocêncio de Oliveira, said that the mere discussion of the subject was an aberration. But the circumspect gentlemen of the Superior Court of Justice did not

* Lawyer; Adjunct Professor of Law, Universidade Candido Mendes, Rio de Janeiro.

[1] *Milton Alves Pedrosa* v. *João Batista Prearo*, Recurso Especial No. 148897–MG.

think so. This could serve to stimulate the *Congresso Nacional* to deal with the issue with greater seriousness, after the elections, when the Bill will return for discussion".[2]

Since the 1998 decision of the Superior Court of Justice, Mr. José Celso de Mello Filho, President of the *Supremo Tribunal Federal* (Supreme Federal Court), Brazil's highest appellate court on constitutional matters, has publicly declared his support for civil partnership between homosexuals. After a meeting with the *Associação Brasileira de Gays, Lésbicas e Travestis*, he said: "The exercise of freedom requires the practice of tolerance. And the practice of equality requires the recognition of the right to be different".[3]

Brazil is a country in which homosexuals, male or female, have been subjected to great violence. Brutal murders are committed almost daily.[4] The legalisation of civil partnership between same-sex partners would surely improve the acceptance of homosexuality, and diminish homophobia and the violence that results from it. The law, besides accepting and protecting a social fact, would help to remove a source of social disorder.

THE CIVIL UNIONS BILL

Projeto de Lei 1.151 de 1995, introduced in the federal *Câmara dos Deputados* on 26 October 1995 by Representative Marta Suplicy, proposes the legalization of civil unions between partners of the same sex. If the Civil Unions Bill were adopted by the *Congresso Nacional*, it would become the first federal law in Brazil to recognize homosexual rights.[5]

The Bill does not attempt to establish civil marriage for same-sex partners. Instead, it aims to extend certain rights and benefits to same-sex partners that are already granted to married and (in most cases) unmarried heterosexual part-

[2] *Jornal do Brasil* (14 Feb. 1998), at 2.

[3] *O Globo* (5 Dec. 1998), 15. See also <http://www.marta2000.com.br/memoria/mandato/mello.htm>.

[4] L Mott, *Epidemic of Hate: Violations of the Human Rights of Gay Men, Lesbians, and Transvestites in Brazil* (San Francisco, CA, International Lesbian and Gay Human Rights Commission, 1996), <http://www.iglhrc.org/publications/books/index.html>; "Brazil Convicts Skinheads in Death of Gay Man", *Reuters*, 14 Feb. 2001, (twenty-one years in prison for two of "roughly 30 skinheads [who] attacked with chains and brass knuckles two men who were holding hands in a popular downtown São Paulo square"; one died, one escaped).

[5] Prohibitions of discrimination based on sexual orientation (*orientação sexual*) can be found in the Constitutions of two states (Mato Grosso, 1989, Article 10.III; Sergipe 1989, Article 3.II), and in the legislation of around 70 municipalities (see http://www.rolim.com.br/ORSEXUAL.htm). See also R Raupp Rios, "Direitos Fundamentais e Orientação Sexual: O Direito Brasileiro e a Homossexualidade", <http://www.rolim.com.br/Dirhomo.htm>; *Proposta de Emenda Constitucional* (Constitutional Amendment Bill) No. 67/1999, http://www.rolim.com.br/ORSEXUAL.htm, introduced by Deputy Marcos Rolim in the *Câmara dos Deputados* on 30 June 1999, approved by the *Comissão de Constituição e Justiça e de Redação* (Committee on the Constitution, Justice and Drafting) on 13 June 2000. The Bill would add an express prohibition of sexual orientation discrimination to Articles 3(IV) and 7(XXX) of the Federal Constitution, <http://www.uni-wuerzburg.de/law/br00000_.html>.

ners, such as: the possibility of sharing assets if the relationship breaks down, automatic inheritance rights, social security benefits, rights related to health insurance plans, the right to file a joint tax return, the possibility of obtaining a mortgage based on their joint income, the right to open a joint bank account, and the right to residence and nationality (in the case of a foreign partner).

The Bill includes the following provisions:

> "Article 1—There shall be assured to two persons of the same sex the recognition of their civil union [*o reconhecimento da sua união civil*] . . .
> Article 2—The civil union between persons of the same sex is constituted through registration in its own book of the Civil Register of Natural Persons . . . [The partners must present proof that they are unmarried, widows, widowers, or divorced, as well as their contract of civil union.] . . .
> Article 4—The extinction of the civil union occurs: I—on the death of one of the contractants; II—through a judicial decree.
> Article 5—Either of the parties may demand the extinction of the civil union: I—by demonstrating the contractual breach on which the petition is founded; II—by alleging [after two years] that they are not interested in its continuation . . . The parties may demand consensually the judicial homologation of the extinction of the civil union. . . .
> Article 8—It is a crime . . . to maintain the contract of civil union . . . with more than one person . . ."

The Bill goes on to provide for restraint from mortgage over the partners' common dwelling (Article 10), for the non-insured partner to be considered a beneficary of the social security system as the dependant of the insured partner (Article 11), for pensions for the partners of civil servants (Article 12), for employment benefits if one partner is a federal, state or local government employee (Article 13), for each partner to be preferred as guardian if the other is incapacitated (Article 15), and for a non-Brazilian partner to be subject to the same reduced residence requirement as a spouse before claiming naturalisation as a Brazilian national (Article 16).

The civil union contract will determine the division of the assets acquired by the partners during their relationship upon its termination. With regard to inheritance rights, the Bill provides:

> "Article 14—Those contracting a civil union . . . are guaranteed the succession rights established by Law No. 8971 of 29 December 1994".

Law No. 8971 creates rights to financial support[6] and inheritance for unmarried heterosexual couples (after five years of cohabitation). The inheritance rights are:

> "Article 2 . . . I—the surviving partner shall be entitled, if they do not constitute a new union, to the usufruct of one-quarter of the deceased partner's assets, if the deceased has children;

[6] The Civil Unions Bill does not extend these to same-sex couples.

II—the surviving partner shall be entitled, if they do not constitute a new union, to the usufruct of one-half of the deceased partner's assets, if there are no children and no ascendants;
III—in the absence of descendants or ascendants, the surviving partner shall be entitled to the whole estate.
Article 3—If the assets left by the deceased partner are a result of any activity in which the surviving partner has collaborated, the surviving partner shall be entitled to half of the assets".

In her memorandum accompanying the Bill,[7] Marta Suplicy explained its objectives:

"No one can ignore the fact that heterosexuality is not the only form of expression of human sexuality. . . .

This Bill aims to make effective the right to sexual orientation, heterosexual, bisexual or homosexual, as an expression of the rights that are inherent in the human person. Considering that individuals have the right to pursue happiness, . . . there is no reason to keep on denying . . . that many people are happy only when living with someone of the same sex. We have to admit that these people, far from being scandals or anomalies, are only seeking respect for their unions as couples, respect and consideration which are owed to them by society and the State.

Personal relationships based on mutual commitment, family ties and lasting friendships, are part of every human being's life. They fulfil fundamental emotional needs, and provide safety and warmth in times of crisis at various times in life, including old age. They are a powerful instrument against the absence of roots. They protect and maintain the integrity of individuals. With this intention, the permanent and committed relationship between homosexuals must exist as a legal possibility.

At the same time, legal acceptance of same-sex civil unions will encourage more gays and lesbians to accept their sexual orientation. Far from 'creating' more homosexuals, this reality will only make life easier for people who already living this sexual orientation, clandestinely. The possibility of being what one is will diminish anguish and . . . increase the possibility of protecting health, principally in relation to AIDS. What is forbidden produces shame, concealment and, in many cases, fear. The possibility of a stable union, even if it is not exercised, will reduce the problems resulting from the need to hide one's own nature, to not be socially recognised, living in isolation or a lie. . . .

Many homosexual couples feel it is unjust that, even after many years of cohabitation, they are still considered—legally, economically and socially—merely as two persons who share a home. . . .

The possibility of regularising an existing situation of union will make these relationships more stable, because practical, legal, and financial problems would be solved. The social life of homosexual couples would also be affected, making them better accepted by society and even by their own families. . . .

[7] Publication of the Office of Representative Marta Suplicy (PT/SP), "*Projeto de Lei 1.151/95—Um Legítimo Direito de Cidadania*" (26 Oct. 1995) at 6–10. See <http://www.marta2000.com.br/memoria/mandato/projeto.htm> (*Justificativa*) (Portuguese); <http://www.marta2000.com.br/memoria/mandato/ingles.htm> (Justification) (English).

This Bill . . . does not propose to give homosexual couples a status equal to marriage. Marriage has a unique status. The term 'marriage' is reserved for heterosexual marriage, with its ideological and religious implications. . . .

It is understood, however, that all provisions applicable to married couples must also be the right of permanent homosexual couples.[8] . . .

The creation of this new legal institution would be fully compatible with our legal order, both with regard to its form and content. It is an institution in perfect harmony with the fundamental objectives of the Federative Republic of Brazil [set out in Article 3 of the Federal Constitution (*Constituição Federal*) of 1988]: '[I.] building a society of freedom, justice and solidarity'; and '[IV.] promoting the welfare of all, without prejudice as to origin, race, sex, colour, age and any other forms of discrimination'.

A same-sex civil union cannot be confused with either the institution of civil marriage [*o casamento*], regulated by the Brazilian Civil Code, nor with the stable union [between a man and a woman (*a união estável entre o homem e a mulher*)] mentioned in Article 226(3) of the Federal Constitution. It is more a relationship between individuals which, because of its relevance and specificities, deserves the protection of the State and the Law. [9] . . .

Brazilian society is dynamic and contains a diversity of relationships; Brazilian Law must follow the changes in society and take into account, as far as possible, this diversity".

In spite of Marta Duplicy's efforts, her Bill remains mired in the *Câmara dos Deputados* waiting for a vote, even though it has already gone a long way in several Legislative Committees since 1995: Social Security and Family; Labour, Administration and Civil Service; Consumer Protection, the Environment and Minorities; Constitution, Justice and Drafting.[10]

JUDICIAL PROTECTION IN THE ABSENCE OF LEGISLATION

While the Civil Unions Bill languishes in the *Congresso Nacional*, the courts have been forced to fill the legislative vacuum with decisions that creatively interpret existing laws, in order to avoid injustice in individual cases. The 1998

[8] The Bill does not provide for joint adoption by same-sex couples.

[9] See also L Edson Fachin, "Aspectos Jurídicos da Sociedade de Fato Entre Pessoas do Mesmo Sexo (Juridical Aspects of Same-Sex Partnership)" in V Barreto (ed.), *A Nova Família—Problemas e Perspectivas* (*The New Family: Problems and Perspectives*) (Rio de Janeiro, Renovar, 1997) at 123: "The Bill aims to regulate the civil partnership between same-sex partners, and not to guarantee homosexual partnerships a status equal to marriage. Marriage has got a unique status. This Bill deals with . . . 'civil partnership' [*companheiro civil*]." The Civil Unions Bill, Art. 12, would amend *Lei* 8112 of 11 Dec. 1990, Articles 217, 241, by adding to the existing category of different-sex "*união estável como entidade familiar*" ("stable union as a family unit"), the category of "*união civil com pessoa do mesmo sexo*" ("civil union with a person of the same sex"), thus implying that a same-sex civil union is not a family unit.

[10] For the Bill's progress, see <http://www.marta2000.com.br/memoria/mandato/tramite.htm>. A revised version of the Bill, approved by a special parliamentary committee on 10 Dec. 1996, substituted for "civil union" the name "civil registered partnership" ("*parceria civil registrada*"). See <http://www.marta2000.com.br/memoria/mandato/s_1151.htm> (Portuguese); <http://www.marta2000.com.br/memoria/mandato/ingles2.htm> (English); http://www.gaylawyers.rg3.net.

decision of the Superior Court of Justice (in a case from the State of Minas Gerais), mentioned above in the Introduction, was preceded by a 1996 decision of the highest appellate court in the State of Rio de Janeiro, the *Tribunal de Justiça* (Rio Court of Justice). The Rio Court of Justice found an implied partnership between two persons of the same sex, and consequently partitioned the assets acquired during their life together, taking into consideration, above all, the solidarity evidenced by one of the partners towards the other, who was infected with HIV:

> ". . . as for the other existing assets, it has been fully proved, including by a declaration of the deceased partner, the exceptional dedication of the surviving partner, who lived with the deceased partner for five years, caring for him during his illness, and maintaining a joint bank account with him. . . . For these reasons the appeal must be allowed, by declaring the existence of a partnership of fact between the appellant and [X], each one participating equally with 50% shares of their common property". [11]

Prior to this decision, a judicial desire to partition assets, acquired by two persons who had lived together as a couple, collided with the mandatory requirement of proving that both partners had made pecuniary contributions to the acquisition of those assets. Sometimes it was not possible. In the 1996 Rio case, the lawyer for the surviving partner relied on principles of implied partnership in civil and commercial law, whereby two or more persons may combine their efforts or resources to achieve common goals, and in doing so, acquire common property. If the partnership is dissolved, either by mutual consent or because of the death of one of the partners, the common property is shared among the surviving partners and the heirs of the deceased partner.[12]

The surviving partner's lawyer also cited a precedent of the Supreme Federal Court, which established that assets acquired during an unmarried heterosexual couple's life together could be partitioned, once the common effort of both partners has been proven.[13] It is important to note that the "common effort" mentioned in the Supreme Federal Court's decision refers only to a financial contribution to acquiring the assets. But lower courts are not bound by the Supreme Federal Court's interpretation of Article 1363 of the Civil Code: "A contract of partnership is entered into by persons who mutually oblige themselves to combine their efforts or resources to achieve common goals".

Lawyers have attempted to widen the meaning of the expression "common effort" to include, not only financial contributions, but also intangible contributions such as friendship and solidarity. But, in spite of some favourable decisions, they have generally faced resistance from judges who prefer the *status quo*, with its prejudices and stigmas. In the absence of specific legislation, the historical conscience of the Brazilian judiciary remains anchored in the

[11] *Henrique Berbert Silveira* v. *Espólio de Ary Pinto de Mesquita* (27 Feb. 1996), A.C. No. 5717/95, TJRJ, 6th Civil Chamber.

[12] See Brazilian Commercial Code, Article 335.

[13] *Súmula* No. 380, decision of 3 April 1964, published on 11 May 1964.

eighteenth century, with its back turned to the present. Indeed the judiciary goes on giving dead answers to live questions, ignoring the underlying social reality and hiding behind a fortress of formalism.[14]

If existing Brazilian legislation is interpreted in an up-to-date and critical way, a different conclusion can be reached. Law No. 8971 of 29 December 1994, Article 3, supports the argument for a right to have property acquired through the partners' common efforts partitioned, even if they are of the same sex. Article 3 provides: "If the assets left by the deceased partner [*companheiro* or *companheira*] are a result of any activity in which the surviving partner has collaborated, the surviving partner shall be entitled to half of the assets." Although this provision appears in a law granting rights to unmarried male-female partners (who have lived together for five years or more), it could be extended by judicial interpretation to same-sex partners.[15] Such an interpretation might generate some amazement among those who feel threatened by non-traditional relationships, but might be a way to achieve more just results, until more specific legislation is introduced.[16]

Taking a broad view, "collaboration" could involve a material contribution or merely a moral one. Obviously, the mutual cooperation, the understanding between persons who live together, and the psychological support given by one partner to the other in difficult times also contribute to the growth of their common property. For example, in the 1996 Rio case, the surviving partner, by caring for his partner during his AIDS-related illnesses, did the work of doctors, nurses, attendants, and drivers (to transport him to his frequent doctor's appointments), and acted as manager of the common assets. The Rio Court of Justice took these contributions into account in deciding unanimously to partition equally, between the surviving partner and the heirs of the deceased partner, the one-bedroom apartment in which they lived, and which was legally only the property of the deceased partner.

The most important precedent in this area is the case of the photographer Marco Aurélio Rodrigues and his partner, the artist Jorge Guinle Filho, who died of AIDS complications in 1989. Marco struggled to see the common property built up by both of them divided in a fair way. This common property was a result of their "common efforts". These efforts were characterized by Jorge's works of art and lectures, and by Marco's work in choosing and mixing Jorge's paints, taking care of the house, selling paintings, and planning trips, exhibitions, lectures and interviews. One cannot deny that what they did—both of them and not only Jorge—had actually contributed greatly to the growth of their common property. The Rio Court of Justice awarded Marco 25 per cent of Jorge's movable property.[17]

[14] See Fachin, *supra* n.9, at 119–20.

[15] The Civil Unions Bill, Article 14, would expressly extend this right.

[16] See Fachin, *supra* n. 9, at 121.

[17] *Espólio de Jorge Guinle* v. *Marco Aurélio Cardoso Rodrigues* (8 Aug. 1989), A.C. No. 731/89, TJRJ, 5th Civil Chamber.

Despite the absence of legislation ensuring the basic rights of same-sex partners, some everyday conflicts are being resolved individually, either by judicial or administrative decisions. For example, in 1998, the adoption of a nine-year-old child by a homosexual teacher was approved by a trial judge, who found that the petitioner was fully qualified to become an adoptive parent.[18] The trial judge concluded that the Federal Constitution makes every person equal before the law, without any kind of distinction. The Constitution does not allow any kind of prejudice or discrimination in a judicial decision, and even provides that "the law shall punish any discrimination violating fundamental rights and freedoms".[19] Rejecting the concern of a representative of the Public Ministry of the State of Rio de Janeiro that the adoption would provide the child with no real benefits, the trial judge suggested that these advantages must be greater than if the child remained in an institution and later ended up living in the streets or in a juvenile or adult prison.

> "The law does not admit reasons founded on prejudice and discrimination based on origin, race, ethnicity, sex, age, religious belief, political conviction or sexual orientation. Therefore, whatever the law does not forbid, the interpreter cannot innovate [by introducing discrimination not found in the law]".

In 1999, the Rio Court of Justice upheld the lower court's judgment, in a unanimous decision.[20] This was the first such decision by a Brazilian appellate court. The Court's decision was:

> "Adoption—Admitted eligibility due to the adopter's suitability and the real benefits for the adopted. Absurd discrimination based on the petitioner's sexuality, affronting sacred constitutional principles and human and children's rights. Improvident appeal. The judgment of the Childhood and Adolescence Ward is confirmed".

Another decision, in this case administrative (Decree 21670), and also unique in Brazil, was signed on 27 September 1999 by the Secretary of Justice and Citizenship in Recife, capital of the State of Pernambuco. It granted homosexual prisoners the right to intimate visits with their partners in the State's penitentiaries. It was due to the plea of a prisoner who asked for the right to see her female partner privately.

Although the courts are managing to render justice in a few individual cases, legislation on same-sex partners would relieve the judiciary of the burden of dealing with some of these cases.

[18] *Marcelo Cozzolino Gosling* (20 July 1998), No. 98/1/01188–8, State of Rio de Janeiro, First Childhood and Adolescence Ward (*Primeira Vara da Infância e da Juventude*).

[19] Federal Constitution, Art. 5.

[20] *Ministério Público (RJ)* v. *Marcelo Cozzolino Gosling* (21 Jan. 1999), A.C. 14979/98, TJRJ, 17th Civil Chamber.

A FIRST STEP: THE ADMINISTRATIVE CODIFICATION OF A JUDICIAL DECISION

In June 2000, the federal *Instituto Nacional de Seguro Social* (*INSS*) (National Institute of Social Security) enacted an administrative instruction regulating the granting of a pension to the surviving partner where the deceased partner had contributed to the federal social security plan.[21] The administrative instruction, which applies to the whole of Brazil, was enacted because of the decision of a federal court in Porto Alegre (State of Rio Grande do Sul),[22] which held that a pension must be granted to a surviving same-sex partner. According to the administrative instruction, from 25 July 2000, the rules for obtaining this survivor's pension are the same as those for unmarried heterosexual partners.

Article 3 of the instruction provides that the following documents may be used to prove the existence of the partnership and the economic dependency: "an income tax declaration in which the surviving partner is listed as a dependant of the deceased; a will; special declarations made in front of a public notary (a public deed declaring economic dependency); proof of a common residence; proof of shared domestic duties and the existence of a partnership or community in acts of civil life; reciprocally granted powers of attorney; a joint bank account; a registration with a professional association or club on which the surviving partner appears as the deceased's dependent; any notations in the records of the deceased's employer; insurance policies made by the deceased partner and listing the surviving partner as the beneficiary; a medical assistance institute's record in which the deceased partner is listed as responsible for the surviving partner; a real property deed by the deceased in the name of the dependant; any other documents which can confirm the alleged facts".

CONCLUSION

The June 2000 administrative instruction is a good start, even though it requires same-sex partners to formally prove economic dependency, which in practice is presumed in the case of unmarried heterosexual couples. However, it is not a substitute for comprehensive legislation. After the instruction was issued, Marta Suplicy, now Mayor of São Paulo, was reported to have said that the instruction "increases the chances that my bill can be approved after the [October 2000] elections".[23] Opinion polls show that 54 per cent of the people of Brazil support the Civil Unions Bill. It remains to be seen whether the *Congresso Nacional* will have the courage to adopt it.

[21] *Instrução Normativa* No. 25 (7 June 2000).

[22] *Ministério Público Federal* v. *INSS* (17 April 2000), A.C.P. No. 2000.71.00.009347–0, 36th Federal Social Welfare Ward (*36ª Vara Federal Previdenciária*).

[23] R Wockner, *International News No. 320*, 12 June 2000.

Section D—Asia and the Middle East

17

Towards Legal Protection for Same-Sex Partnerships in Japan: From the Perspective of Gay and Lesbian Identity

AKITOSHI YANAGIHASHI*
(translated by KEITH VINCENT)**

NO LEGAL PROTECTIONS exist for same-sex partnerships in Japan. Same-sex marriage is not recognised, nor is there any form of common-law marriage, like that which applies to heterosexual couples.[1] In this chapter, I will introduce some of the debates over legal protection for same-sex partnerships in Japan, and then go on to consider what steps will be necessary to develop a system which would make such partnerships legally viable.

A CONSTITUTIONAL RIGHT TO SAME-SEX MARRIAGE?

Article 24 of the Japanese Constitution provides as follows:

> "(1) Marriage shall be based only on the mutual consent of both sexes and it shall be maintained through mutual cooperation with the equal rights of husband and wife as a basis. (2) With regard to choice of spouse, property rights, inheritance, choice of domicile, divorce and other matters pertaining to marriage and the family, laws shall be enacted from the standpoint of individual dignity and the essential equality of the sexes".[2]

Conventional language usage would clearly suggest that "both sexes" here refers to man and woman, and that the "husband" is assumed to be male and

* Legal Director, Japan Association for the Lesbian and Gay Movement (OCCUR), Tokyo (contact Masaki Inaba, pinktri@kt.rim.or.jp).
** Departments of East Asian Studies and Comparative Literature, New York University. Professor Vincent also provided simultaneous translation for Mr. Yanagihashi and Mr. Inaba at the conference.

[1] There is a great deal of case-law that provides protection for heterosexual couples in common-law marriages. The only difference between marriage and common-law marriage for heterosexual couples is the lack of inheritance rights for partners and the fact that any children born to the couple are considered illegitimate.

[2] For the full text of the Japanese Constitution in English, see <http://www.uni-wuerzburg.de/law/ja00000_.html>.

the "wife" to be female. There is thus little doubt that the term marriage here refers to a specific kind of union between a man and a woman. This common sense interpretation has been so prevalent in Japan that, up until 1990, no legal-scholar or lawyer had ever called it into question.

However, several factors have combined to change this situation. Recent news coverage of the gay and lesbian rights movement in the United States, and the creation of same-sex partnership systems in Scandinavian countries, have increased awareness of the issue. On the domestic front, a 1991 case (*Japan Association for the Lesbian and Gay Movement (OCCUR)* v. *Tokyo Metropolitan Government*) brought the issue of gay and lesbian rights officially into the courtroom for the first time ever in Japan.[3]

Some legal scholars and lawyers have begun to argue that the intent of Article 24 of the Constitution was to reform the family system of pre-World War II Japan, in which women's rights were unfairly limited and the extended family, or "*ie*", was privileged above any individual family member.[4] As such, Article 24's intent was not to confine the definition of marriage to heterosexual couples, but simply to guarantee the rights of individuals and address the inequality of men and women.[5]

Unfortunately, however, the language of Article 24 is not sufficient to justify the extension of the right to marry to same-sex couples. For this reason, legal specialists sympathetic to the idea of legal protection for same-sex partnerships tend to cite the Constitution's stress on "respect for the the individual" and the "pursuit of happiness",[6] as well as the principle of equality,[7] in order to argue that same-sex partnerships should be eligible for protection under the law.[8]

[3] The case involved the Association's exclusion from a City-run youth hostel. The Tokyo Board of Education argued that allowing members of the same sex who are sexually attracted to each other to stay in the same room would contravene the purpose of the facility, but the Tokyo District Court ruled that this was illegal discrimination on 30 March 1994. See *Hanrei Times*, Vol. 45, No.32 (Total No. 859), 1994, at 163; *Hanrei Jihou*, No. 150, 1995, at 80. The City appealed the decision, but the Tokyo High Court affirmed it again on 16 Sept. 1997. See *Hanrei Times*, Vol. 50, No. 1 (Total No. 986), 1999, at 206.

[4] Marriage law in Japan includes a number of laws, mostly found in the Civil Code. In the pre-World War II Civil Code, marriage required the approval of the "head of the household", and wives were almost entirely without rights, including those having to do with property. Individual rights within the family were severely restricted.

[5] Legal experts agree that Article 24 was intended to abolish the pre-World War II family (or "*ie*") system. See Tsunoda Yukiko, *Sei no Horitsu-gaku* (Tokyo, Yuhikaku, 1992), for an example of a legal scholar arguing that the article is not intended to deny same-sex marriage.

[6] These principles are found in Article 13: "(1) All of the people shall be respected as individuals. (2) Their right to life, liberty, and the pursuit of happiness shall, to the extent that it does not interfere with the public welfare, be the supreme consideration in legislation and in other governmental affairs".

[7] The principle of equality is set out in Article 14 in the following terms: "(1) All of the people are equal under the law and there shall be no discrimination in political, economic, or social relations because of race, creed, sex, social status or family origin".

[8] The following texts discuss the possibility of legal protection for same-sex marriage from this perspective: Tanamura Masaaki, "Douseiaisha no kon'in ha kanou ka?" in *Zeminaaru kon'in hou kaisei* (Tokyo, Nihon Hyoron Sha, 1995); Ninomiya Shuhei, *Jijitsukon no gendai teki kadai* (Tokyo, Nihon Hyoron Sha, 1990); Hoshino Shigeru, "Waga kuni ni okeru douseiaisha wo meguru kazoku hou no shomondai", (1997) 69 (Nos. 3–5) *Houritsu ronsou* 237.

Passages relating to the formalities and substance of marriage in Japanese law are found mostly in the Civil Code and the Household Registration Law. Expressions such as "man and wife" and "husband and wife" are used with great frequency in these documents. Here, as in the Constitution, it is evident that a "married couple" refers to a man and a woman and that the husband is a man and the wife a woman. Marriage is defined in Japan as a "legally and socially recognised (spiritual and physical) life-long union between one man and one woman".[9] This definition is accepted even by legal specialists with favorable attitudes towards same sex-marriage.

But many of them argue that since the traditional notion of marriage has begun to change, there is no reason why same-sex marriages and partnerships should not receive legal protection as well. The traditional view of marriage, for example, excludes same-sex partners on the principle that reproduction and child-rearing is an essential component of marriage. These progressive scholars question this logic, by citing the fact that heterosexual couples who do not have children, who do not have a sexual relationship, and who do not even live together, are still eligible for the advantages offered by marriage law.[10]

THE ABSENCE OF LITIGATION AND LOBBYING BY SAME-SEX COUPLES

Of course, the sort of constitutional argument discussed above is still only a minority opinion at this point. It has little sway in the academic world and has not been applied at all to real-life situations in Japan. For the most part, interest in same-sex partnerships is confined to the level of curiosity about what is happening outside Japan.

I myself believe that the question of same-sex marriage and partnership brings up a number of important issues. When the Japanese Constitution states, in relation to marriage and the family, that "Laws shall be enacted from the standpoint of individual dignity and the essential equality of the sexes", what kind of family is being imagined? What is "the family"? What is "individual dignity" in the context of marriage and the family? Serious research and discussion of these questions should prove to be enormously fruitful.

Unfortunately, however, the situation in Japan has yet to reach this level. One reason for this is the lack of concrete action on the part of gays and lesbians to achieve legal recognition of their relationships. We have yet to see any demands

[9] Tanamura Masayuki, "Danjo no arikata: Otoko to On'na", *Jurist* No. 1126 (Tokyo, Nihon Hyoron Sha, 1998), at 25.

[10] Child bearing and rearing is generally cited as one of the functions of heterosexual marriage, and it is also quite common to cite the production and education of the next generation as justification for the state's recognition and protection of, and intervention in, the family as a social system. If we consider, however, that artificial reproductive technologies have made it possible for same-sex couples to have children, this argument has lost much of its import. Arguments against same-sex marriage that rely on the limitation of child bearing and raising to heterosexual couples will have to be analysed from a gay and lesbian perspective for their inherent homophobia.

for the passage of new laws and ordinances recognising same-sex marriage, or any lawsuits brought by same-sex couples who have been refused the right to marry. This situation is clearly the result of a society which makes it very difficult for gays and lesbians to come out and claim their rights. But it is nonetheless true that Japanese gays and lesbians have lacked the power to force society to listen to their claims and to get specialists to take an interest in their issues.[11]

For this reason, getting legal recognition of same-sex partnerships in Japan will require an improvement of the social environment, through theoretically-informed struggle against anti-homosexual discrimination and prejudice. At the same time, however, it will require consciousness-raising and identity formation among gays and lesbians themselves, so that they can live more forward-looking lives. This will mean carving out a psychological environment in which coming out is possible, and forming communities to support those wishing to live their lives as gays and lesbians.

LEGAL ALTERNATIVES TO MARRIAGE OR REGISTERED PARTNERSHIP

As I have mentioned above, there are no laws and no case-law in Japan that would extend any level of protection to same-sex partnerships. Even unmarried heterosexual couples are eligible for certain entitlements,[12] but there is virtually no possibility that same-sex couples would qualify for these. For this reason, many gays and lesbians who share their lives in Japan have chosen other methods to obtain some level of official protection. In some cases, they draw up private contracts or write their wills in such a way as to insure that their partner will receive his or her due after their death. In addition, some have chosen to legally adopt their lovers.

If two people who share their lives together draw up a contract establishing inheritance rights, sharing of living expenses, household labour, and child-rearing responsibilities, the contract will be valid only insofar as if affects the two parties concerned. Unfortunately, however, these contracts have little force when they impinge upon the interests of other parties, such as parents or siblings.

[11] On 30 Aug. 1999, OCCUR testified at an official hearing of a Tokyo Metropolitan Government advisory commission on human rights guidelines for Tokyo. In its Dec. 1999 report, the commission recommended the inclusion of sexual minorities (including lesbians, gays, trans-sexuals and intersexuals). However, the draft guidelines published on 19 June 2000 deleted lesbians and gays. When Tokyo's Governor Shintaro Ishihara was asked about the omission at a press conference, he responded, "In what way are they discriminated against?" See http://www.planetout.com/news/article-print.html?2000/08/16/3. After receiving over 500 protest letters, the Tokyo Metropolitan Government added the following to the final guidelines released on 21 Nov. 2000: "[Over] recent years, various problems faced by homosexuals have been brought to [the public's] attention . . . [D]eeper discussions need to be pursued."

[12] Aside from the heterosexual common-law marriage established by case-law (see *supra* n.1), eligibility for cohabitation in public housing (which is typically permitted only to spouses and family members) and for dependent status in health insurance, can be obtained by a heterosexual couple as long as they are in a marriage-like relationship, regardless of whether they are legally married.

For this reason, the most certain method for gays and lesbians to obtain legal protection is to take advantage of the system of adult adoption, and in fact a small number of couples have done this. Adopting one's lover legally establishes a parent-child relationship, which makes possible certain tax benefits in the event that either party should become unable to work. Companies also provide support for dependents and time off to care for a sick parent or child. Of course, the rights and the obligations of parents and children are different from those obtaining between husband and wife. Moreover, there is always the danger that the adoptive relationship could be annulled as "harmful to public morals", if the court found that it was accompanied by a sexual relationship. Ultimately, this use of the adoption system is merely a temporary substitute for the real legal recognition of same-sex partnerships. Moreover, because it can be implemented without the couple having to come out as gay or lesbian, it does little to advance the larger cause of granting legal protection to gay and lesbian couples.

CONTRACTS V. ADOPTION?

I would argue that private contracts are the most effective way of bolstering gay and lesbian identity, while opening the way toward full legal protection of same-sex partnerships. They would provide in the interim a means of building gay and lesbian identity, by celebrating those who choose to live as out and proud gays and lesbians, and helping to form a supportive community. There are five reasons why this is so.

First, the use of this kind of contract would help to create or bolster our consciousness of living as gays and lesbians. Anyone who is prepared to enter into such a contract must necessarily be committed to living life proactively as a gay or lesbian. As a social ritual with some degree of visibility, the drafting of these kinds of contracts would also help to encourage those who still have doubts about their ability to live as out lesbians and gays. The telephone counseling hotline of OCCUR receives many calls from gays and lesbians dealing with the social pressure to marry someone of the opposite sex. Their problems arise, not only from the social and familial pressure to get married and have children in order to be recognised as a full-fledged adult, but also from their own inability to imagine a stable, long-term relationship with someone of their own sex. There is no question that the lack of role models for same-sex relationships severely hampers the ability of homosexuals in Japan to live their lives as gays and lesbians. It is my opinion that gay and lesbian couples who decide to bring their relationships into the public sphere, through the exchange of legal contracts, also serve as precious role models for the lesbian and gay community at large.

The second reason has to do with the fact that involving third parties in these contractual relationships inevitably means increasing gay and lesbian visibility and giving voice to our thoughts and concerns, possibly even clearing the way for certain institutional protections. For example, it is very hard to find a life insurance company in Japan which will allow a gay or lesbian client to designate his or her partner as the beneficiary, even though the designation of the beneficiary is supposed to be entirely up to the policy holder. It would, however, be very difficult for an insurance company to deny such a request if the couple in question had already made their relationship official through some kind of contractual agreement.

Similarly, there have been several cases in Japan of gays and lesbians whose partners have been hospitalised and who have been refused the right to make decisions about their care when they lost consciousness. In some cases, they have even been refused the right to care for or visit their partners. The best way to prevent this is to draft documents in advance, establishing that the partners in the relationship, as the people most familiar with each other's wishes and preferences, have the right to care for each other, visit each other in the hospital, and make proxy decisions concerning each other's medical treatment.

The third reason is that the contractual approach is useful because it makes room for a large degree of individual variation, thus ensuring the diversity of lesbian and gay relationships. As the restrictive qualities of heterosexual marriage are coming under fire in Japan, it is not at all surprising that gays and lesbians should feel the need to be able to define their own relationships, in the ways that best suit their individual situations and needs. Not all gays and lesbians want simply to be included in the current marriage system, and so the best solution is one which makes room for and encourages serious thought about the kind of life we envision for ourselves as gays and lesbians.

The fourth reason to support the contractual approach is that it would help to create a familiar foundation on which could be based consideration of the kind of formal legal protections gays and lesbians will eventually seek for their relationships. When OCCUR won its suit against the Tokyo Metropolitan Government, a certain university professor bitterly commented that before long the queers would be demanding the right to marry. This comment was typical of the short-sighted view of many homophobes, who assume that marriage along the heterosexual model is the only or the most important right that gays and lesbians want. Many gays and lesbians themselves are not immune to this way of thinking. For this reason, it is absolutely essential that gays and lesbians themselves have the space they need to give serious consideration to what is necessary for them to live their lives out of the closet in every way. There is, of course, a need for the lesbian and gay movement to call either for the extension of marriage to same-sex couples, or for the introduction of a domestic partnership system. But any movement that works solely within the legal system, without consideration of the situation of gays and lesbians themselves, the development of their identity, and the strength of the community, will find itself without the support of its own constituency. It is entirely possible that the community will arrive at the conclusion that marriage is simply not a priority.

The fifth and final reason is that the contractual system, unlike the use of adoption, cannot be criticised as contravening public morals. It may be true that heterosexist society is itself to blame if gays and lesbians are forced to resort to exploiting the adoption system to get the protections they deserve; but we cannot count on that same heterosexist society to be self-reflective enough to understand its own complicity in what it would rather brand the "corruption of public morals". Moreover, the continued use of the adoption system as a substitute for real protections can only impede our efforts to introduce some kind of protection for same-sex relationships, especially since more and more gays and lesbians in Japan are willing to fight for their rights without hiding their identities.

THE FUTURE FOR SAME-SEX COUPLES IN JAPAN

Since the late 1990s, there has been a slow but steady emergence in Japan of gays and lesbians who are committed to finding ways to integrate their sexual orientation with their larger social and political existences. At OCCUR, we receive more and more telephone calls from gays and lesbians who want to include their partners in their wills, or who are concerned about making sure that they or their partners can continue to live in the same house after one of them dies. We have also had calls from people who have been kicked out of their houses by their partners' families after their partners' death. There are also couples who have drawn up contracts guaranteeing that they, and not their respective families, will be primarily responsible for caring for each other in the case of illness, making proxy decisions for each other in case of loss of consciousness, and handling funeral arrangements. One couple even held a commitment ceremony at a local Shinto shrine.

It goes without saying that any attempt to go beyond the level of private contracts and attain official recognition of same-sex marriages will meet with enormous resistance. Indeed, even the existence of out gay and lesbian couples who have made their relationships official through contractual agreements is likely to be perceived as a threat to the heterosexual order. The extent of this resistance is suggested by the fact that it has been impossible in Japan even to change the law requiring married heterosexual couples to share the same surname, for fear of destroying the family and the marital bond. But a strong legal, political, and social movement based on an affirmative gay and lesbian identity should be able to counter that resistance. Such a movement will have to ask tough questions. If the right to partnership is a fundamental human right, exactly what rights is it based upon? How can same-sex partnerships be made equal to heterosexual ones? Can the laws concerning heterosexual marriage be applied directly to same-sex partnerships? If not, why not? Is it possible to apply the case-law on common-law marriages to same-sex couples? If not, why not? All of these legal questions must be considered with reference to the actual lives of lesbians and gay men if we are ever to get the laws that we really need.

At OCCUR, we are currently working with several lawyers to develop a legal consultation service for gays and lesbians. We are particularly interested in finding ways to encourage clients to draft partnership contracts. It is our hope that this practice will contribute to the growth of an affirmative gay and lesbian identity and a greater awareness of the rights to which we all should be entitled. Eventually, we hope that this will help create a basis upon which to argue for the introduction of a legal domestic partner system, while also helping our community through the legal difficulties of daily life as lesbians and gay men.[13]

[13] See generally Pinkerton & Abramson, "Japan" in West & Green (eds.), *Sociolegal Control of Homosexuality* (New York, Plenum Press, 1997); Summerhawk, et al., *Queer Japan: Personal Stories of Japanese Lesbians, Gays, Bisexuals and Transsexuals* (Norwich, VT, New Victoria Publishers, 1998). On 25 May 2001, after hearing submissions by OCCUR and by lesbian and gay individuals, the Council for Human Rights Promotion presented its final report to the Ministry of Justice, specifying (in Section 4-2-2) that "discriminatory treatments based on sexual orientation . . . will be involved in the positive action targets of the National Human Rights Commission" (to be established by 2004).

18

Contextualising the Same-Sex Erotic Relationship: Post-Colonial Tongzhi and Political Discourse on Marriage Law in Hong Kong and Mainland China

CHIU MAN-CHUNG (ANDY CHIU)*

THE STATUS OF marriage brings concrete financial and material benefits to different-sex spouses who engage in marital relationships. Those who are legally married can enjoy a variety of economic benefits provided by employers, government and law: housing allowances, the right to apply for public housing, tax allowances, child custody, the right to adopt children, and the right to have access to artificial reproduction are just a few examples. Put simply, refusing to recognise same-sex partnerships legally can bring about negative consequences to members of such relationships, which in turn would also affect the quality of their relationships.[1] In other words, the refusal would harm the interests of people with same-sex erotic desire.

Same-sex marriage is not currently a political or legal issue in Mainland China,[2] the world's most populous country. Is this because there are no legally recognised lesbian/gay/queer organisations in Mainland China, or because the law in Mainland China discriminates so much against people having same-sex erotic desire that they cannot raise the issue? If it is the result of the absence of a "human rights" concept in Mainland China, then how can we explain the

* Assistant Professor, School of Law, City University of Hong Kong. I would like to thank Dr. Ho Petula Sik-Ying (Department of Social Administration and Social Work, University of Hong Kong), Mr. Shaw Kwok-Wah Roddy (Parents and Friends of Lesbians and Gays in Hong Kong), Mr. Sin Wai-Man (School of Law, City University of Hong Kong) and Mr. Ng Nelson (Ten Percent of Hong Kong) for reading an earlier version of this chap. and giving me invaluable opinions.

[1] 鄭美里 (Cheng Mei-Lei), *女兒圈:台灣女同志的性別、家庭與圈內生活* (*Women's Arena*) (Taipei, Fembooks (女書文化), 1997).

[2] By "Mainland China", I mean every region of the People's Republic of China except for Hong Kong, Macao and Taiwan.

situation in Hong Kong—a former British colony, a predominately Han-Chinese (漢/華人) society[3]—where sodomy was decriminalised in 1991 and a series of human rights protection laws (for example, the Bill of Rights Ordinance,[4] the Sex Discrimination Ordinance,[5] the Disability Discrimination Ordinance[6] and the Family Status Discrimination Ordinance[7]) have been enacted, but anti-discrimination on the ground of sexual orientation is still never an issue, let alone the right to same-sex partnership or marriage. A series of problems therefore arises. Can the concept of rights be applied in a Han-Chinese context? And if we are going to devise an indigenous anti-discrimination strategy and claim the right to same-sex marriage, what kind of considerations should we take into account?

The primary object of this chapter is to emphasise that, in the Han-Chinese context, where a harmonic web of personal relationships is given the prime importance in the socio-legal discourse, even the most intimate associations between individuals are situated within a matrix of social relations—hence simply asking for equal rights in the legal discourse would not help to stop discrimination on the ground of sexual orientation. The crucial issue, as I argue below, is to create a discourse of acceptance, in which the critical importance of interpersonal relationships as a site of self-making and a dimension of human fulfillment can be accented. Only with such a discourse can changes in legal discourse be truly useful and meaningful in the Han-Chinese Confucian (儒) context.

HETEROSEXIST LAW V. SAME-SEX MARRIAGE

Both the Sino-British Declaration and Article 8 of the Basic Law state that the Common Law system of Hong Kong is preserved, and will not be affected by the Civil Law system in Mainland China after 1997. Under the current law in Hong Kong, same-sex marriage is prohibited. Every marriage contracted under the Marriage Ordinance[8] has to be a *Christian* marriage or the civil equivalent of a *Christian* marriage, which means a "formal ceremony recognized by the law as involving the voluntary union for life of *one man and one woman* to the exclusion of all others".[9]

The anti-same-sex-marriage group in the West have identified three basic arguments to support their viewpoint: (1) the definition of the term "marriage" and the procreation intended to result from marriage; (2) a "natural law"/

[3] In Mainland China, there are more than 19 ethnic groups with over 1 million people, and Han is the dominant ethnic group in terms of numbers. Nearly 90% of the population in Mainland China and Hong Kong are Han-Chinese. See Woo Chung-Jin (ed.), *中國民族法學 (Chinese Racial Jurisprudence)* (Beijing, Law Publication (法律), 1991).

[4] Laws of Hong Kong (LHK), Chapter 383.

[5] LHK, Chapter 480.

[6] LHK, Chapter 487.

[7] LHK, Chapter 527.

[8] LHK, Chapter 181.

[9] Marriage Ordinance, s. 40. The principle is again emphasised in the Marriage Reform Ordinance, LHK, Chapter 178, s. 4.

religious argument; and (3) a majoritarian argument that would define same-sex marriages as "odious to the common consent of nations".[10]

The first argument, the idea of promoting heterosexual unions for the purposes of procreation, seems dated and invalid. The contraception and abortion decisions of the Supreme Court in the United States have already suggested that fostering procreation should not be a strong enough public interest to overcome a fundamental right to marry, or a right to be free from discrimination based on sexual orientation or sex.[11] This argument, which was made by the Vermont government, failed to prove a sufficient justification for excluding same-sex couples from the benefits and burdens of marriage in *Baker* v. *State*.[12]

The second argument is illustrated by decisions of courts in the United States invalidating incestuous and polygamous marriages on the grounds that they represent a violation of "natural law". Opponents of same-sex marriage recognition will push for a similar outcome in a same-sex marriage case.[13] The "law of nature" argument seems to transcend all religions but, in fact, has been used almost exclusively in a Judeo-Christian context:

> "The institution of marriage as a union of man and woman, uniquely involving the procreation and rearing of children within a family, is as old as the book of Genesis".[14]

However, this argument has little relevance in Han-Chinese societies, like Hong Kong and Mainland China, where Confucianism also has great influence.

The third argument is the "majoritarian" theory. In 1996, the Government in Hong Kong conducted a survey on sexual orientation and published *Equal Opportunities: A Study on Discrimination on the ground of Sexual Orientation—A Consultation Paper*. 1,535 people were interviewed on the telephone; when asked whether they would accept that homosexuals have the right to use artificial reproduction to form their own families, the answer of the majority was "no". Table 1 indicates their views on same-sex marriage.

Table 1

	Mean Scores of Level of Acceptance*
Two Lesbians Get Married	3.7
Two Gays Get Married	3.3

* Based on a rating scale from 0 to 10, "0" denotes "Totally unacceptable" and "10" denotes "Totally acceptable".[15]

[10] Andrew Griffin, "Another Case, Another Clause: Same-Sex Marriage, Full Faith and Credit and the US Supreme Court's Evolving Gay Rights Agenda" [1997] *Public Law* 315 at 323–324.

[11] *Roe* v. *Wade*, 410 US 113 (1973); *Griswold* v. *Connecticut*, 381 US 479 (1965).

[12] *Baker* v. *State*, 744 A.2d 864 (Vermont Supreme Court 1999).

[13] See David Chambers, "Polygamy and Same-Sex Marriage" (1997) 26 *Hofstra Law Review* 53.

[14] *Baker* v. *Nelson*, 191 NW2d 185 (Minnesota 1971).

[15] *Equal Opportunities: A study on Discrimination on the Ground of Sexual Orientation—a Consultation Paper* (Hong Kong, Government Printer, 1996) at 15, Table 3.3.

The legal prohibition preventing lesbians and gays from getting married therefore seemed to have strong support from the population:

> ". . .since the issue of discrimination is closely associated with personal beliefs and social values, the Association [The Chinese Manufacturers' Association of Hong Kong] believes that . . . [because the] majority of the general public have not changed their prevailing attitudes. . . [and] the cognition and acceptance level of the general public in Hong Kong regarding discrimination on the grounds of . . .sexual orientation is still very low, . . . *it is not appropriate to legislate at this present moment*".[16] (emphasis in original)

However, the "majoritarian" argument has been severely criticised by the Gay Coalition in Hong Kong:

> "'. . . It is necessary to assess carefully the impact of such legislation (Sexual Orientation Discrimination law) on the community so as to ensure that it would command public support. . .' This statement is completely ridiculous because if there was 'public support' of [the] minority, then legislation would be unnecessary".[17]

So, why does the law in Hong Kong and elsewhere still resist same-sex marriage/partnership? The only reason for prohibiting same-sex marriages is the discriminatory attitudes towards same-sex couples that underlie the law. The excuse of the legislature is always that: "permitting same-sex marriage could convey the idea that the Government approves of homosexuality". But, if there is nothing wrong with homosexuality, why would the Government be afraid of accepting it?

QUEER THEORY: LIMITATIONS OF EQUALITY CLAIMS AND IDENTITY POLITICS

In order to pursue the benefits of (heterosexual) marriage, some proponents of same-sex marriage seek legal recognition on the same terms that the law provides for different-sex couples. The equality claims involve a comparison between a chosen relevant aspect of lesbian and gay sexuality (i.e., a person's status as a lesbian or gay man, or her/his participation in same-sex sexual acts) and an equivalent aspect of heterosexuality, if any. Such claims cannot demonstrate the particularities of lesbian and gay sexuality; rather, legal recognition/protection is only available "where—and because—lesbian and gay sexuality is similar enough to heterosexuality".[18]

The equality argument therefore has engaged closely with the conception of lesbian and gay identity. So-called "identity politics" is, however, fatally weak-

[16] *Consultative Documents on Equal Opportunities: Discrimination on the Grounds of Family Status and Sexual Orientation—Compendium of Submissions* (Hong Kong, Government Printer, 1996) at A15.

[17] *Ibid.* at C80.

[18] N Bamforth, *Sexuality, Morals and Justice: A Theory of Lesbian and Gay Rights Law* (London and Washington, Cassell, 1997) at 251.

ened by the problem of essentialism, i.e. the argument has presumed the existence of a universal and fixed sexual identity. Sexuality and gender identity, as William Simon illustrates, are discursive products:

> "Sexuality, more than any other aspect of behaviour, first and foremost, is talk; it is *rooted in discursive formations*; it cannot speak until it is spoken".[19]

In *Postmodern Sexualities*, Simon argues that we have to problematise the stabilities and varieties of the biological substratum and contextualise the examination of sexualities, which are a linguistic product (dis)continuously evolving within human culture and human behaviour. He therefore concludes that:

> "[t]o offer a coherent and explanatory logic, as is perhaps too common to contemporary social science, is to fashion a rhetoric that sustains the *illusion of a corresponding logic inherent in actual practice that is rarely to be found in actual practice*. This tendency is reinforced by the ability of *labels, such as homosexual, heterosexual, or bisexual, to homogenize what are significantly pluralized phenomena*".[20]

It is under this context that Carl Stychin proposes a "queer legal theory". Stychin points out clearly that a queer theory is a resistance towards the identity-based equality claim.[21] Queerness signifies a more fluid conception of subjectivity, a "new elasticity in the meanings of lesbian and gay where the fixity of sexual identity is destabilised".[22] Queerness has successfully challenged the rigid homo/hetero-sexuality binarism by going beyond those categories. According to Stychin, a queer legal theory therefore rests on the tension between law's repressive power and its ability to develop oppositional identities, such as queer. Since

> "[p]erformativity as a concept facilitates an anti-essentialist view of identities by suggesting that it is through *the repetition of actions* alone that all identities come to be naturalised, queer theory, hence, might undermine the dominant performatives of gender and sexuality".[23]

In short, engaging queer legal theory with the claim of same-sex marriage could destabilise the gender specificity of marriage law—marriage is simply a performance by which the subjectivities of heterosexual women/men/couple are constituted. If the gender-specific requirements of marriage are removed, fixation of identity would then be destabilised and the question would arise: how could we define, (not) through marriage, a bisexual/homo/heterosexual woman/man? A further question is: can queer theory simply be adopted in Hong Kong and Mainland China—two predominantly Han-Chinese societies?

[19] W Simon, *Postmodern Sexualities* (London and New York, Routledge, 1996) at 147 (emphasis added).

[20] *Ibid.* at 136 (emphasis added).

[21] C Stychin, *Law's Desire: Sexuality and the Limits of Justice* (London and New York, Routledge, 1995) at 144.

[22] *Ibid.* at 141.

[23] *Ibid.* at 145. See also Judith Butler, *Excitable Speech: A Politics of the Performative* (New York and London, Routledge, 1997).

EROTICS OF CUT SLEEVES[24]

Besides the Judeo-Christian ideology of a heterosexual love-marriage-sex trinity, Han-Chinese convention is another significant force shaping the (homo/hetero)sexuality situation in Hong Kong and Mainland China. It is of course difficult to make a very general statement about the historically extensive Han-Chinese outlook. However, it is quite safe to say that the ideological roots of Han-Chinese views are found mainly in Confucian thinking.

The Confucian school is concerned about the social life of people, but its basic attitude towards sexual intimacy is positive. The interpersonal situation is the starting point of Confucian thinking, and the harmonic familial relationship is considered exemplary of the basic principle of "good being"—"Jen" (仁)[25]—the most important theory of Confucianism. Sexual behaviour is not considered on the basis of good or bad, but instead must be regulated within the ethics of the five relations (emperor/minister, father/son, elder brother/younger brother, husband/wife, and friend/friend) along which the whole community is hierarchically arranged. In this context, sex of whatever kind would be accepted, unless it has an adverse effect on the web of personal relationships—so that is why anal sex is accepted but not rape. The focus is not on the action itself but on its social effect. Confucianism, in short, treated sex(uality) as an essence of life/well-being. In Chinese (as a language), the word "humanity" and the word "sex" share the same character (性).

According to Chinese tradition, homosexuality was therefore not legally marginalised and lesbians and gays were not identified as a group. There was no social or legal hostility related to a person's sexuality. As Matignon wrote in 1889:

> "Public opinion remains completely indifferent to this type of distraction, paying no attention to it at all, except to say that, since it seems to please the dominant partner and the other is willing, no harm is done".[26]

Same-sex eroticism, tolerated in principle, was indeed practised in daily life.[27] Literary sources from the Shang Dynasty (商朝) and Zhou Dynasty (周朝) con-

[24] Chinese people like using metaphors in describing sexual intercourse and "cut sleeves" is used to symbolise same-sex romance. Emperor Ai Ti of the Han Dynasty (漢哀帝) fell in love with a man called Tung Yin (董賢). One day, the emperor was lying on a bed with Tung, and Tung fell asleep on the sleeve of his robe. Since Ai Ti had to get up, Ai Ti preferred to cut the sleeve in two halves rather than disturb Tung. This is how "cut sleeves" came to mean homosexuals.

[25] There is a lot of controversy about the definition of "Jen". But as 楊適 (Yeung Shik) argues, it must be based on the harmonic familial relationship which emphasises obedience towards one's elders. See Yeung Shik, *人倫與自由：中西人論的衝突和前途 (Politics of Human Relationship and Freedom)* (Hong Kong, The Commercial Press (商務), 1991).

[26] Quoted in M Beurdeley, et al. (trans. Diana Imber), *Chinese Erotic Art* (Hong Kong, Chartwell, 1969) at 161.

[27] *Ibid.*

tain examples of open affection between men.[28] The most famous Chinese novel, the *Dreams of the Red Chamber* (紅樓夢), contains descriptions of male homosexuality. In *Jou-pu-tuan* (肉蒲團), the male master also had a homosexual relationship with his servant. The novel, *P'in-hua-pao-chien* (品花寶鑑), describes the customs of actors, all of whom are men, and people who are their friends at the end of the eighteenth and early nineteenth century.[29] As Ambrose King (金耀基) concluded in the *Report on Laws Governing Homosexual Conduct*:

> "Throughout Chinese history, homosexuality seems to have existed openly as a social phenomenon . . . Scholars of comparative cultures and societies felt that the Chinese had a fairly open attitude toward sexual practices. . .Homosexual acts, though generally regarded as repugnant, were tolerated. In the Chinese social setting, people tended to treat it as a private matter. Therefore, a high degree of tolerance toward homosexuality existed, at least in certain periods of Chinese history".[30]

This kind of homosexual-tolerant culture can still be traced in current law—homosexuality was not the subject of law in Mainland China. In Mainland China, the only legal provision which could be used to punish people with same-sex erotic desire was the "crime of hooliganism"[31]—it aimed at maintaining the social order by sanctioning all sorts of hooligan activities, like sexual harassment in a public place, gang fighting and group sex. But this provision was repealed in 1997.

However, it should also be noted that while (male) homosexuality was historically *tolerated*, it did not have a positive image. King has suggested that homosexuality was "certainly *not idealized* in any dynasty of China", and that the punishment a homosexual in traditional China would have received was "public ridicule".[32] This is also why Samshasha (小明雄) thinks that there was a notion of "implicit homophobia" throughout Chinese history, because homosexuality could not bring any offspring naturally and reproduction is emphasised in Han-Chinese culture. There is a Chinese proverb saying: "there are three kinds of disobediences and being without an offspring is the most serious (不孝有三，無後爲大)." Samshasha also forcefully points out that homosexuality is always ignored in history: for example, he says, although the political disturbance which occurred after the death of the (male) Emperor Ai Ti of the Han Dynasty (漢朝) was intensely connected with his romance with Tung Yin (a man), their romance is omitted by Chinese historians.

[28] Pan Kwong-Tan (潘光旦), *Psychology of Sex* (*中國文獻的性變態資料*) (Shanghai, The Commercial Press, 1947).

[29] Bret Hinsch, *Passion of the Cut Sleeve: The Male Homosexual Tradition in China* (Berkeley, University of California Press, 1990).

[30] The Law Reform Commission of Hong Kong, *Report on Law Governing Homosexual Conduct (Topic 2)* (Hong Kong, Government Printer, 1984) at 16–17.

[31] People's Republic of China, Criminal Law, Article 160 (repealed in 1997).

[32] *Supra* n. 30 at 17.

> "Although the disturbance brought by male same sex romance in Chinese history has the same significant status as the coup d'etat caused by women, in history or education, this part of history is always ignored".[33] (trans.)

In short, although homosexuality is not oppressed, there is no positive recognition of legal rights in Han-Chinese society. Chou Wah-Shan (周華山) also writes:

> "But tolerance does not amount to positive support, the decriminalization of sodomy which happened in Hong Kong in 1991 is an example of tolerance, it passively put aside the criminal sanction. But if one wants to ask for the right to apply for public housing, marriage, adoption, succession, or have these rights legalized, she/he would face a lot of pressure".[34](trans.)

TONGZHI THEORY: LOCALISING ANTI-HETEROSEXIST STRATEGY

In Anglo-American legal discourse, where the notion of individual rights[35] and the harm principle are emphasised, the claim to legal recognition of same-sex erotic relationships appeals to fundamental conceptions of political/legal rights. But in a Han-Chinese (legal-)cultural context, the claim goes beyond anti-discrimination arguments, by emphasising human interdependence and situating individual efforts to lead a satisfying life within the context/web of personal/familial relations and responsibilities. Legal decisions on access to same-sex partnership/marriage would have a direct and forceful impact on the intimacies of personal life, like determining the custody of children of lesbian and gay parents, and the rights of partners in caring for sick or dying lovers. The

[33] Samshasha, *History of Homosexuality in China (中國同性愛史錄) Revised edition* (Hong Kong, Rosa Winkel Press (粉紅三角), 1997) at 10.

[34] Chou Wah-Shan, *北京同志故事 (Story of Tongzhi in Beijing)* (Hong Kong, Hong Kong Queer Forum (香 同志出版社), 1996) at 67. The homophobia becomes intensified at the beginning of the 20th century. As argued by Samshasha, *supra* n. 33, and Chou Wah-Shan in *Post-Colonial Tongzhi (後殖民同志)* (Hong Kong, Hong Kong Queer Forum, 1997), when the Ching dynasty (清朝) was defeated several times at the beginning of the 20th century, the Chinese began to think that unless they could have Western culture practiced in China, the nation would not be strong again. Therefore, some of the educated Chinese and young scholars began to advocate the complete desertion of traditional Chinese culture. And when they knew from Western literature that homosexuality was something that people should be ashamed of, they began to criticise same-sex eroticism in China as well. Also, with the introduction of "new" culture, scholars began to write in modern Chinese, and hence, the record of same-sex eroticism in old Chinese writing became less important.

[35] As Elizabeth Schneider writes: "A rights claim can make a statement of entitlement that is universal and categorical. This entitlement can be seen as negative because it protects against intrusion by the state (a right to privacy), or the same right can be seen as affirmative because it enables an individual to do something (a right to choose whether to bear a child). . . Rights claims reflect a normative theory of the person, but a normative theory can see the rights-bearing individual as isolated or it can see the individual as part of a larger social network". See Elizabeth Schneider, "The Dialectics of Rights and Politics: Perspectives from the Women's Movement" in Katharine Bartlett, et al. (eds.), *Feminist Legal Theory: Readings in Law and Gender* (Westview Press, 1991) at 318. In other words, the "discourse of rights" has a very close relationship with individualism.

personal context from which such claims emerge matters enormously to the people affected.

While the concept of individual rights enjoys a significant status in the (legal) context of Hong Kong, the harmonic web of personal relationships also plays a vital role in the Han-Chinese Confucian (legal) culture, where the individual is not an isolated subject but is defined by her/his position within a public order. Hence, King says that the "human is a *relational being*".[36]

This is the context in which "tongzhi" politics is developed.[37] In Chinese, "tongzhi" includes two words—"tong" (同) means the "same" and "zhi" (志) connotes "beliefs (of anti-heterosexism)"; "tongzhi" therefore signifies all people who share and stand up for the destabilisation of heterosexism. As argued by Chou, "tongzhi" politics, like queer politics, transgresses and problematises the boundaries of fixed identities. Chou makes the point explicitly:

> "The interesting part of tongzhi is that we can never accurately distinguish tongzhi from non-tongzhi, and cannot even provide a definition for tongzhi: who is tongzhi? For instance: if two women have same sex erotic desire; but one is very patriarchal, misogynist, classist, racist and ageist, and the other one is a feminist tongzhi, can both of them be called tongzhi? On the other hand, if two men share the same anti-heterosexist belief and work it out thoroughly, but one is straight and the other one is not, are they tongzhi then"?[38] (trans.)

Chou further points out that tongzhi politics, while recognising the discourse of rights (or confrontational politics, as Chou puts it) as tactics of resistance, would also take the harmonic relationship into account. This is where the difference between tongzhi politics and queer theory lies—individual legal rights have to be interpreted within the context of personal relationships. But please note that, by (re)presenting Chinese history and developing "tongzhi" theory, I am not aiming to (re)discover an authentic Chinese homosexual/lesbian and gay politics,[39] but to articulate a localised strategy by questioning the adaptability of queer politics in a Han-Chinese context.

"DOMESTIC COMING OUT"—LOCALISING THE CLAIM OF SAME-SEX MARRIAGE

Claims for the recognition of same-sex couples, in Anglo-American societies, besides relying on the emphasis of rights, are also closely related to the discourse of an increasingly visible queer/lesbian and gay community within which such

[36] A King, *Chinese Society and Culture* (*中國社會與文化*) (Hong Kong, Oxford University Press 1993) at 10.

[37] "Tongzhi" (同志) is a word for comrade in Mainland China and it holds a very precious status in the history of the Chinese Communist Party. The term was first borrowed/used in Hong Kong to mean "lesbian and gay" in 1988.

[38] Chou Wah-Shan, *Post-Colonial Tongzhi* (*後殖民同志*) (Hong Kong, Hong Kong Queer Forum, 1997) at 362, and *Tongzhi: Politics of Same-Sex Eroticism in Chinese Societies* (Binghamton, NY, Harrington Park Press, 2000).

[39] G Spivak, "Can the Subaltern Speak? Speculations on Widow-Sacrifice" (1985) *Wedge* (Winter/Spring) 120.

social choices become feasible: "[t]he personal and political overcoming of the closet has provided the social and historical conditions for reconstructing lesbian and gay intimate associations".[40]

If legal recognition of same-sex marriage *has to be* derived from the "coming out" experience, then the Han-Chinese tongzhi are certain to experience an intense and often difficult time, because coming out places their pre-existing blood or family relationships at risk, as "implicit homophobia" still exists. Mothers, fathers, sisters, brothers, and other relatives/friends may reject a previously beloved relative/friend once they are told of her/his sexual orientation. Thus, if the emotional support needed to survive coming out cannot be derived from the family, the harmonic web of personal relationships would be broken. Therefore, the point is that:

> "A more direct Western way of battling for acceptance and coming out will never win hearts in the Chinese community".[41]

I am *not* suggesting that "coming out" is useless in a Han-Chinese context, or that the claim for legal same-sex marriage should be given up, but that an indigenous strategy should be developed and devised from tongzhi politics in the socio-cultural context of the Han-Chinese. The crucial point is that, when "coming out" is derived from a tongzhi perspective, not only personal identity matters but harmonic (familial) relationships are also a vital consideration. Engaging in a discourse of rights within the Confucian culture, we could then understand why in Hong Kong/Mainland Chinese communities "coming out to one's family" and "asking for the recognition of one's gender identity" are still traumatic today, as this may destabilise the harmonic familial structure, which is the most important unit within the web of relationships. Yuen Pui-Man (阮佩文), a female tongzhi, shares the same feeling in an article "Different style of standing" (不同的站姿):

> "Therefore some people would not tell their families [about their sexual orientation], [but rather they would] spend all days worrying that they may accidentally let their families know [about their sexual orientation], they have to hide everything that would reveal their relationship with their partners, they have to put their romance at the bottom of their hearts. . . Perhaps, *coming out to the family is the last and biggest obstacle*".[42] (emphasis added) (trans.)

Family reaction is still one of the prime concerns for tongzhi. The story of Ah Choy provides a good example:

[40] M Kaplan, *Sexual Justice: Democratic Citizenship and the Politics of Desire* (New York, Routledge, 1997) at 208.

[41] Shaw Kwok-Wah Roddy, a local tongzhi, as quoted in E King, "Ripples on Dragon Boat Day", *South China Morning Post*, 12 June 1999.

[42] Chou Wah-Shan, Anson Mak (麥海珊) and Daniel Kong (江建邦), (eds.), *香港同志站出來 (Hong Kong Tongzhi Standing Out)* (Hong Kong, Hong Kong Queer Forum, 1995) at 94.

"Last year Ah Choy's father died. Ah Choy felt sorry for never revealing himself [his sexual orientation] to his father until his death. He is now struggling to bring this to his mother but being the only son, he is not altogether sure how well she can take it".[43]

It is within this context that I would like to suggest the tactics of a "domestic coming out" in the case of same-sex marriage. The thematic concern of "domestic coming out" is to maintain a harmonic (familial) relationship, and *patience* and *communication* are the keywords. The story of Shaw Kwok-Wah Roddy (邵國華), a tongzhi activist, provides a very good illustration:

"When I first told her (his mother) at the age of 26 that I was gay, like many Chinese people from that generation, she didn't even know what the word meant and she was surprised. Fortunately, we are a family who knew how to *communicate*. . .and so *I talked to her for hours and hours until she understood. The crux of it was related to the ability to explain that I am still her same old son, and the same old brother to my siblings*".[44]

Almond (浪人), a female tongzhi activist in Hong Kong, had a similar experience:

"Coming out to my family is really hard, but now, my sister and brother know that I am a female tongzhi, and get along with my female partner very well. . . When my sister got married and moved out of the apartment, I started to produce *Tongzhi Backtile (同志後浪)* (a tongzhi magazine) at home, perhaps because I have worked for media for years, my family members did not have any strange feeling even when I read materials on homosexuality at home. . .but my brother was very clever, he knew what was happening. So when I told him that I was a lesbian, he did not have any vigourous reaction. . . However, since I kept on producing the *Tongzhi Backtile*, and I was getting close to my partner, my sister also sensed that there was a 'stranger' at home. . . One day, she asked me the true nature of the relationship. I answered her very frankly, by telling her that that friend was my female partner, and our relationship was very close, and it was not a one-night stand. . . My sister at first was very angry, but finally, she could get along with my female partner very well. I suppose my brother and sister could realize that homosexuality is not a strange thing at all".[45]

Drawing on the experience of Shaw and Almond, domestic coming out in the case of a same-sex partnership includes at least 2 steps: (1) the individual must let her/his family know about her/his sexual orientation; and (2) on the basis of step (1), the individual must let her/his family know and accept her/his same-sex partner. From Almond's story, we also know that a tongzhi really has to *plan* a domestic coming out. A domestic coming out does not mean that an individual can go to her/his parents one day and suddenly tell them that she/he is a tongzhi—that could only ruin the relationship given the existence of (implicit)

[43] Comments submitted by Lee Check-Yan et al., in *Consultative Documents on Equal Opportunities: Discrimination on the Grounds of Family Status and Sexual Orientation—Compendium of Submissions*, *supra* n.15 at C154.

[44] *Supra* n.41 (emphasis added).

[45] Almond, "向全世界 come out" ("Come Out to the Whole World") in Chou Wah-Shan et al. (eds.), *supra* n.42 at 102.

homophobia. Take Almond's case as an example: she comes out step by step; she first lets her family members know that she is "interested" in homosexuality, and lets them get used to the fact that she has a close lady friend. Once a rapport is developed, the family members would not have any strong feeling when Almond frankly tells her brother/sister that she is a tongzhi. Also, since her sister has already got used to the company of her close lady friend, she would also understand and accept them as a couple. The whole process takes time and needs a lot of patience, and the theme is communication.

While emphasising the importance of a harmonic familial relationship, I am neither ignoring the significance of legal reform or of legal recognition of same-sex partnerships, nor constructing a Han-Chinese-significant-familial relationship vs. Anglo-American-non-significant-familial relationship dichotomy. *By illustrating a cultural context in which familial relationships are the most treasured personal relationships, I would like to point out that the web of relationships does play an indirect but significant role in legal discourse.* Let us first scrutinise the status of law in Han-Chinese Confucian culture.

While Anglo-American legal tradition emphasises the protection of individual rights and the harm principle, in Han-Chinese culture, law (in Chinese, we call it "*fa*", 法) would only be used when the personal relationship totally collapses. In fact, *qing* (情), *li* (禮) and *fa* exist as a coherent entity. *Qing* generally refers to "the appeal to the other's feeling, emotions, sense of humanity, or common decency",[46] and *li* is similar to rational principle and discursive reasoning of appropriateness. *In other words, qing and li are the concepts abstracted from and in turn responsible for governing the web of personal relationships.*[47] *Fa* is considered as a concept similar to law and is used as a tool to penalise those who act against *li*. The making and interpretation of law must be grounded upon *qing*.[48] Put simply, law is not the most important aspect. What is more important is the context—*qing* and *li, i.e. the web of personal relationships*—where law is executed, interpreted and created. This is why the construction of the discourse of acceptance—a socio-cultural-legal context (i.e. *qing* and *li*) where tongzhi/queer/lesbian and gay/same-sex relationships would be accepted—is so significant, as it has a very important position in the Chinese legal concept. *Domestic coming out is therefore a way to make qing and li accept same-sex relationships. It is only if qing, li and the web of personal relationships accept same-sex erotic relationships that the law could be changed and the change could be executed and accepted.* Simply changing the law, but leaving *qing* and *li* unaddressed is useless. Even if the same-sex partners could get registered legally, if they would still be condemned and isolated by their family members, i.e. their personal relationships web would be destroyed, would that be a useful legal reform? This is why I suggest that a discourse of acceptance plays an

[46] RP Peerenboom, *Law and Morality in Ancient China* (Delhi, SriSatguru, 1993) at 268.

[47] *Supra* n.36 at 17.

[48] Sin Wai-Man (冼偉文) and Chu Yiu-Wai (朱耀偉), "Whose Rule of Law? Rethinking (Post-)Colonial Legal Culture in Hong Kong" (1998) 7(2) *Journal of Social and Legal Studies* 147.

important role in the tongzhi movement in Hong Kong/Han-Chinese society. Without such a discourse, any legal reform would be useless. As Daniel Kong, the spokesman of Horizons—a local tongzhi group, has said:

> "No matter what the law says, if people don't accept gays it will be of no use. . . All we can do is get people to be more open to homosexuality and ourselves be more open within and outside the gay community. I don't see the point in being confrontational".[49]

ENGAGING TONGZHI POLITICS WITH THE SOCIO-LEGAL CONTEXT OF MAINLAND CHINA

Confucianism has an even more influential role in the construction of legal discourse in Mainland China than in Hong Kong, a former British colony. If contemporary Mainland Chinese Law is read within the context of a harmonic web of personal relationships, it becomes easy to understand why refusing to take care of weak, old or infant family members is a criminal offence.[50] Examining the Marriage Law of the People's Republic of China (PRC) from this perspective, the effect of Confucianism can also be easily traced. The familial relationship is regulated by the law: for example, it is stated clearly that husband and wife shall have equal status in the family;[51] parents shall have the duty to bring up and educate their children; children shall have the duty to support their parents.[52] In the legal discourse of Mainland China, there is no liberal private/public split, but an emphasised harmonic web of personal relationships. Because the family is the centre of the web, law (*fa*) has to regulate it.

Under the current Marriage Law, same-sex marriage is not legally recognised in Mainland China, as article 4 provides: "Marriage must be based upon the complete willingness of both man and woman." However, what also matters is the legal/public attitude towards same-sex partnership, which could be shown from the following case (reported in *Sexual Culture and Law* (性文化與法)), in which *qing* and *li* also have a say. In 1991, the local government and police received a "letter of complaint" from a father, stating: (1) that his elder daughter was having a homosexual relationship with another woman from another village; (2) because this was "an extremely immoral phenomenon", if the public authorities would not take action, he would beat the couple to death, no matter what the consequences would be. The police then investigated, and found that everybody knew that the couple were living together. Because there is no law against homosexuality in Mainland China, the legal department could not prosecute the couple. However, as they had to calm down the father, they then sent

[49] D Kong, as quoted in S Oh, "Rift Over Gay Campaign—Homosexuals Split on Pressure Tactics" 6 *Window*, 9 Sept. 1994.

[50] People's Republic of China (PRC), Criminal Law, Art. 261 (1997).

[51] PRC, Marriage Law, Art. 9 (1981).

[52] PRC, Marriage Law, Art. 15 (1981).

the couple to prison for 15 days.[53] The police later said: "we just want to deal with it from *the perspective of morality*."[54]

From this case, we can see that, even in modern Mainland China, the close relationship between law (*fa*) and morality (i.e. *qing* and *li*) still plays a very important role in regulating human behaviour. Within this discourse, harmonic personal relationships are vital to a same-sex relationship—if the family had accepted the daughter's same-sex partner, then the whole incident would not have happened and the police would not have had to punish them under pressure. In other words, domestic coming out, which is derived from a tongzhi perspective, is needed in Mainland China where Confucianism has great influence.[55]

RIGHTS IN HAN-CHINESE CONFUCIANISM: LEGAL RECOGNITION IS STILL IMPORTANT

Domestic coming out and the establishment of a discourse of acceptance are not the end of the story: if domestic coming out is the first step, then what should we do after developing a discourse of acceptance? That is where the Anglo-American discourse of individual rights enters the picture; the tactics that queers/lesbians and gays adopt, and the legal arguments that they propose in the Anglo-American legal discourses would provide a good reference for us. While the significance of a harmonic is emphasised, alongside the concept of individuality, it does not exist in a vacuum, but within a social structure/web of relationships: within such a web, especially if it is a familial web, no individual would insist on her/his (legal) rights, because that may be harmful to the harmony.[56] However, the web itself is not a static concept or entity, and dynamic interaction among individuals can be initiated by individuals themselves. For example, it is a personal choice to be a friend of others or of a government official. In fact, Confucians place a lot of emphasis on individuality and believe

[53] The case report does not state for what sort of offence they were sent to jail.

[54] 談大正 (Tam Tai-Ching), *Sexual Culture and Law* (Shanghai, Shanghai People (上海人民), 1998) at 317–318. See also Ruan Fang-Fu, "China" in West and Green (eds.), *Sociolegal Control of Homosexuality* (New York, Plenum Press, 1997).

[55] *Supra* n.34. While I argue that domestic coming out would be relevant both in the context of Mainland China and Hong Kong, attention should be paid to the different contexts. Although both are Han-Chinese Confucian societies, Hong Kong has been a British colony and separated from Mainland China for 145 years. While Hong Kong is a capitalist and highly industrialised city, in communist Mainland China, the majority of people still live in villages. Differences therefore exist in the familial structure (e.g. the ratio of nuclear families to extended families is not that high), the structure of personal relationships (i.e. people are generally closer), and the degree of knowledge about homosexuality/same-sex eroticism (sex education is not common). Consequently, different strategies of coming out must be devised.

[56] King mentions that the five relationships were considered as the fundamental structure of an ideal/harmonic public order as advocated by the Confucians, and among these five relationships, the father-son(s) relationship/family is the centre of the web and obedience is the keyword. Such a concept is still evident in current Mainland China family law. *Supra* n.36 at 4.

that only if an individual possesses the quality of good being/"Jen" can a harmonic web be built up. As King further illustrates:

> "We should emphasize that, within the web of relationships, the relationship between an individual and others is neither *independent nor dependent*, but relative in nature. Hence, the individual self does not disappear within the web, in contrast, the individual has her/his *space* to take initiative".[57] (emphasis added) (trans.)

Because of this space, the notion of personal rights, which depends on individualism, could engage with Han-Chinese culture, as it influenced contemporary Chinese culture after the May Fourth Movement in 1919.[58] But it is important to note that, although the concept of rights becomes important, its understanding still has to be embedded within the context of personal relationships.[59]

Therefore, though domestic coming out has a lot of positive effects, *legal recognition of same-sex erotic relationships remains an important issue*. One cannot confer on oneself and one's partner the legal status of married couple without statutory authority. Marital status is a positive legal creation, and the rights and duties dependant upon marriage are the clearest signs of commitment our society has. Legal recognition may also "encourage friends and family to support the relationship and take it more seriously".[60] Legal recognition of same-sex partnerships is always important "where [its] presence is necessary as a means of empowerment by combating objectification".[61] Domestic coming out is significant in the sense that it could create the discourse of acceptance, where the harmonic web of personal/familial relationships would be retained.

PROBLEMATISING "DOMESTIC COMING OUT": THE FIGHT FOR GENDER JUSTICE CONTINUES

In this chapter, I have argued that as queer politics and identity politics may not work in a Han-Chinese Confucian culture, an indigenous strategy that claims

[57] *Supra* n.36 at 10.

[58] *Supra* n.33. The May Fourth Movement, which is also known as the New Culture Movement, played a significant role in shaping the socio-political scene of Modern China. "In 1917, China declared war on Germany in the hope of recovering its lost province, then under Japanese control. But in 1918 the Beijing government signed a secret deal with Japan accepting the latter's claim to Shandong. On May 4, 1919, there were massive student demonstrations against the Beijing government and Japan. The political fervour, student activism, and iconoclastic and reformist intellectual currents set in motion by the patriotic student protest developed into a national awakening known as the May Fourth Movement. The intellectual milieu in which the May Fourth Movement developed was known as the New Culture Movement and occupied the period from 1917 to 1923. . .Students returned from abroad advocating social and political theories ranging from *complete Westernization* of China. . ." See L Poon, "History of China", <http://www.chaos.umd.edu/history/republican.html#republic> (2 March 2000).

[59] *Supra* n.38.

[60] M Fajer, "Toward Respectful Representation: Some Thoughts on Selling Same-Sex Marriage" (1997) 15 *Yale Law and Policy Review* 599.

[61] *Supra* n.18 at 266.

the legal recognition of same-sex relationships has to be developed. I have therefore suggested domestic coming out as a necessary step for the construction of a discourse of acceptance, which should be one of the pre-requisites in claiming a right to same-sex marriage.

Questions then arise: if the familial structure under the Han-Chinese Confucian culture is so oppressive, why should tongzhi still respect its prime importance? Why do tongzhi have to take such a passive approach? Why do they not challenge the system? First, family and the web of personal relationships are not oppressive but adopt a toleratant attitude towards homosexuality. Second, since the respect towards a harmonic web of personal relationships and the family are the roots of the Han-Chinese Confucian civilisation, overthrowing such a belief would mean the total desertion of Han-Chinese culture.[62] Domestic coming out needs time, patience and good-planning. It is not passive, as it actively takes part in the construction of a discourse where legal reform could be carried out.

Another problem is: can domestic coming out destabilise the mainstream heterosexist socio-legal system? While pointing out that Confucianism plays an important role in Han-Chinese society, I would also like to claim that it is in fact a very heterosexist-patriarchal system: doctrines like "Men should not let women study" (潘光旦) and "Women should cover up themselves when going out" (出必掩面) are common.[63] Foucault, by deconstructing Enlightenment beliefs, posits the possibility of a resistance politics that relies on the articulation of a discourse which displaces and explodes the discourse of domination. What Foucault means is that, though power is everywhere, it does not mean that domination is universal:

> "An appropriate point from which to proceed is with the statement 'where there is power, there is resistance'. What Foucault meant by this is that resistance is present everywhere power is exercised, that the network of power relations is paralleled by a multiplicity of forms of resistance".[64]

As Foucault suggested, points of local resistance do exist in the discourse of domination and can operate strategically in undermining apparent unities in relations of power. "Domestic coming out" can then be considered as a forum for resistance to the heterosexual hegemony within the Han-Chinese Confucian culture. It explores the space within the dominant Confucian thinking, i.e. the personal relationship, and develops the discourse of acceptance which is vital to the construction of a legal system which would recognise same-sex partnerships and tongzhi.

[62] Yeung Shik, *supra* n.25.

[63] Leng Dong (冷東), "The Position of Women in Traditional Chinese Gender Concept and its Influence" ("婦女在中國傳統性別觀念中的地位及其影響") (1999) 2 *A Collection of Women's Studies* (*婦女研究論叢*) 32.

[64] B Smart, *Michel Foucault* (London, Routledge, 1991) at 132–3.

By suggesting that domestic coming out could be adopted as a strategy, I do not mean that it should be made a legal requirement: "only if all your family members vow to accept your partner before the court, can you apply for same-sex marriage". What I argue is that, under a Han-Chinese Confucian culture, if one would like to maintain a harmonic personal relationship within a family, it is important for the family to accept one's (same-sex) partner before the couple get married. This could also be considered as a step to destabilise the "implicit homophobia" implanted by Chinese tradition (at least in the "domestic" context), and thus problematise this homophobia and make the relevant legal change acceptable and meaningful to all. Without such a discourse, it is nearly impossible to ask for any legal rights for tongzhi people or for same-sex marriage. Even with such a legal change, the broader aim would not be fulfilled, as the personal relationships web would be totally destroyed and tongzhi would still be oppressed in family and society. In the Han-Chinese Confucian culture, I therefore suggest, *a discourse of acceptance* should be constructed at home first, as family is the most important unit in one's harmonic web of personal relationships. Also, because reproduction plays a very important role in Chinese culture, it will be necessary to address related issues, such as artificial reproduction and custody of children. The fight for gender justice will continue.

19

Same-Sex Partnerships and Indian Law: Climate for a Change

POONAM SAXENA*

THE PROBLEM

THE GAY AND lesbian community in India[1] till recently was marginalised to the point of becoming virtually invisible. Discussions and public debates on sexuality and related topics are still considered inappropriate. Consequently, despite their significant numbers in Indian society, the needs and concerns of homosexuals are ignored in the national political arena and in community planning processes. Many of them are isolated and often ignorant of the fact that they are not alone. There are few public forums in which they could gather to seek mutual support, or share their experiences, feelings and questions with others. Moreover, because section 377 of the Indian Penal Code of 1860 designates male homosexuality as a crime, they are discouraged from being open or seeking out others like themselves.

SOCIAL AND CULTURAL ENVIRONMENT AND SEXUAL BEHAVIOUR

India is a country of great diversity, where around seventy-six per cent of the population live in villages. Mostly ridden by the ancient traditions, villagers are usually very conservative, and sharply divided along religious, caste and community (sub-caste)[2] lines. Marriage is a heterosexual relationship. Marriages within the same community are preferred, and arranged marriages are the rule. Parents choose a life partner for their offspring, and the child's showing even a preference for who their partner should be is strictly frowned upon.

* Associate Professor, Faculty of Law, University of Delhi.

[1] Indians still use two different expressions to denote female and male homosexuals. While men involved in same-sex relationships are commonly referred to as homosexuals or gays, women are called lesbians.

[2] Within the four major castes (Brahmins, Kshatriyas, Vaishayas and Shudras), there are numerous sub-castes, which are popularly called communities.

All family laws[3] provide that a girl of eighteen and a boy of twenty-one can validly marry without even consulting their parents. However, such is the pressure from society that adults marrying without the consent of their parents, even within the community, find no place to survive in India. Their parents hunt them with the entire village. Angry parents sometimes even bring false criminal charges of abduction against the husbands of their daughters. Failing to get protection from the police, who sympathise more with the parents than the couple, they have no choice but to give in after living in hiding, and face sanctions imposed by the villagers.

The situation can be judged by an incident which took place in 1999 in Haryana, a northern Indian state. A boy and a girl in the age group of twenty to twenty-four eloped and got married without informing their parents. Though they belonged to the same community, they knew that their parents would not give their consent. The news of their elopement spread like fire and the entire village felt terribly shocked and ashamed of their behaviour. They had just one mission, to find them and produce them before their parents and the village "*panchayat*" (a group of five people elected by the villagers from amongst themselves, whose decisions are obeyed by the whole village). When caught, their own parents and relatives killed them. Ironically, the entire community justified the murder on the basis that, otherwise, other young people's morals would be adversely affected and they might be encouraged to think in this direction. The village had saved its honour by killing these two people, who by their conduct had brought the village into disrepute.

Free mixing of boys and girls in this type of society, therefore, is an absolute taboo. For the 24 per cent of Indians who do live in urban areas, the situation may not be so bad, but it is not happy either. It is only a very small minority of youngsters, living independently in the metropolitan towns and big cities, who may choose their own life partners; otherwise, it is one of the duties of the parents to arrange the matrimonial alliance of their offspring. It may appear strange, but in most of the cases in villages, the husband and wife do not even see each other before their wedding night. In every sense of the term, they are complete strangers to each other.

LIVE-IN OPPOSITE-SEX RELATIONSHIPS

Only a valid marriage, duly solemnised after the completion of all necessary rituals, can give the parties the status of husband and wife. Marriages of minor children, though prohibited by law, are perfectly valid if solemnised with the

[3] There is no uniform family law in India. A separate family law or personal law governs each of the five major religious communities (Hindu, Muslim, Christian, Parsi and Jewish). They vary vastly in their content. Added to these five major laws, numerous Scheduled Tribes are governed by their distinct customary laws, and the states of Jammu and Kashmir, Goa and the Union Territories of Pondicherry, Daman and Diu, have their separate family laws.

consent of their parents.[4] The marriage of a twelve-year-old girl with a sixty-year-old man, solemnised without her consent but with her parents' approval, is perfectly valid. But the voluntary partnership of a thirty-year-old woman with a man of her age would not be recognised by law as valid, or as creating any rights or obligations between the partners. Even a marriage solemnised by actual use of force or fraud is not void, but only voidable, and remains perfectly valid until it is annulled by the court on a petition filed by the aggrieved party. The marriage of a twenty-year-old girl with a twenty-five-year-old man, solemnised at gunpoint, would not be invalid at all. However, if the two on their own voluntarily decide to live with each other, the law would not recognise their relationship.

Living together without getting married is very strongly looked down upon by Indian society. It is not a criminal offence, but the partners do not get the status of "spouse" for any purpose whatsoever and their children are illegitimate. In Gujarat, a western Indian State, people thought of a novel device to give a legal stamp to live-in relationships. Formally called "*maitrey karars*" (friendship contracts), people of opposite sexes would enter into a written agreement to be friends, live with each other, and look after each other. These agreements, which in fact were nothing but live-in relationships (primarily of an already married man with his girlfriend), were declared void by the Gujarat courts, as immoral and exploitative of women. Live-in relationships are virtually absent in rural India, but are found in big cities among all classes, though their number is very small.

SAME-SEX RELATIONSHIPS

The existence of people who have an orientation towards the same sex is almost a universal phenomenon, and India is no exception. Indian history has ample evidence of the existence of same-sex relationships, from ancient to modern times.[5] Examples include: the famous *Kamasutras*; the sculptures at the tenth century Khajuraho temples; the sculptures showing same-sex relationships at the Surya (sun) temple at Konark; and the Yogini temples at Bhedaghat, Khajuraho, Hirapur and Ranipur-Jharial.

It is also believed that, with the advent of Islam in India, cases of homosexuality increased considerably. In fact, history has references to Pathans (Muslim men), known for their lavish lifestyles and constantly seen in the company of young and good-looking boys. Classical poems of even great and famous poets like Mirza Ghalib, and stories of Urdu authors like Ismat Chuglai's "Lihaaf"

[4] Despite the Child Marriages Restraint Act, 1929, which makes it an offence for parents to arrange the marriages of their minor children, it is customary for the vast majority of rural Indians to have their children married before the statutory ages.

[5] See R Vanita & S Kidwai, *Same-Sex Love in India: Readings from Literature and History* (New York, St. Martin's Press, 2000).

(Quilt), give not only references, but base the literature on same-sex relationships. During the regime of the great Mughal king Akbar, historians mention the presence of Ras Khan in his court, who was gay. History has ample evidence of Mughal queens who had relationships with their close female friends. In the time of the Mughal emperors, even the women of the upper middle class were engaged in same-sex relationships. Initially, the predominant reason might not have been their own strong desire, but rather the circumstances in which they lived. In the days when unlimited polygamy was being practised by many Indian men, women were secluded and kept in a place meant only for them called the "harem". No men could visit the harem except the single husband of all these women; when thrown into each other's company, lesbian relationships became not only a necessity but a habit.

Despite the continued existence of same-sex relationships in both rural as well as urban India, they are rarely acknowledged. It is an impossibility for the seventy-six per cent of the population living in villages to openly acknowledge their sexual preference for the same sex.

CLASSIFICATION BY BIOLOGICAL SEX

Indian society acknowledges and classifies people into three broad categories as regards their sexes: males; females; and neuters (who are genitally abnormal males and are popularly called eunuchs). Among eunuchs, there are two distinct groups: Hijiras and Zenana. Both groups dress like women, part and dress their hair like women, wear ornaments, and adopt most tastes and habits of females. Hijira are deprived of their genitalia (penis or testicles or both, congenitally or deliberately, mostly before puberty), while the genitalia of Zenana are abnormal but intact.[6]

The two groups live separately and preserve a line of demarcation between themselves and female sex workers.[7] It is almost an accepted, though self-imposed, stringent rule that the neuters live in groups and not with their families. They make a living by dancing and singing when auspicious occasions (like weddings) take place in the area where they live. Some of them are involved in the sex trade as male sex workers. They are present in every locality and each and every part of India. Singing and dancing is their profession. As a rule, they do not seek ordinary jobs, as being either male or female is mandatory. Neuters ordinarily do not marry outsiders, but may perform a marriage among themselves, with one of them acting as a female and the other as a male. Neuters may even adopt orphans, but a disclosure of their sexual abnormality would debar them from adopting a child validly under the law.

[6] Modi, *Textbook of Medical Jurisprudence and Toxicology*, 17th ed., (1969) at 350.
[7] B Rao, "Eunuchs", *The Antiseptic*, July 1955, at 519–524.

MARRIAGES UNDER HINDU LAW

Marriage under Hindu law is a sacrament, an indissoluble union of flesh with flesh, bone with bone, to be continued in the next world. According to the Hindu texts, a man does not have a material existence until he takes a wife. A man is only half of his self.[8] *The Dharamshastras*, the primary source for Hindu law, provide for the marriage of a maiden with a man. Even in 1999, for a valid Hindu marriage, it is mandatory, not only that the two parties be Hindus and have opposite sexes, but also that they be capable of performing normal sexual intercourse following the order of nature. It is worth noting that, apart from the specific terminology of "bride" and "bridegroom" in section 5, the Hindu Marriage Act, 1955 does not formally say anything about the sexes of the two parties intending to marry under Hindu law. But is often inferred by judges and jurists that Hindu law can recognise only heterosexual marriages.

In the 1976 case of *Moina* v. *Amardeep*, a man and a woman had married under the Hindu Marriage Act. The wife was heterosexual but the man was gay and did not consummate the marriage. The wife sought a declaration that the marriage was void. The Delhi High Court held that, under section 12(1)(a) of the Act, if the marriage was not consummated because the husband was homosexual and could not relate to females generally, the wife was entitled to a decree of nullity.[9]

Marriage between two persons of the same sex, according to Indian jurists, is void *ab initio*, but marriage of a man or a woman with a eunuch or a neuter is not void under our law.[10] In the 1969 case of *Parmaswami* v. *Somathammal*, the wife was a eunuch. The question of the validity of her marriage arose after the death of her husband as a collateral issue. Alagiri Swami J., of the Madras High Court, equated a eunuch wife with an impotent person and held that the marriage was voidable. However, the only person at whose instance it could have been annulled was dead, and therefore the validity of the marriage could not be questioned.[11]

Indian jurists do take into account the need of a person to marry for the purposes of companionship only, and not with a desire to procreate. Indeed, the ancient texts granted a right to eunuchs to marry.[12] But even for companionship, two persons of the same sex are not allowed to have an intimate relationship. Thus two persons born with sexual disabilities are free to marry each other, and a sexually disabled person is allowed to marry a non-disabled person, but two persons of the same sex are not allowed to enter into any intimate relationship under Hindu law.

[8] R K Aggarwala, *Hindu Law* at 31.
[9] All India Reporter, 1976 Delhi High Court 399.
[10] Paras Diwan, *Modern Hindu Law* at 102–37.
[11] All India Reporter, 1969 Madras High Court 124.
[12] *Manu IX*, 203; Kane, *History of Dharamshastras I, Part I* at 431.

A 1982 case suggests that a transsexual marriage might be acceptable. At the age of nineteen, Manju, who had been registered as a female at birth, had surgery to remove her breasts and implant an artificial penis and genital-like structures. She changed her name to the masculine name of Mohan, and declared to the media that she planned to marry a woman, a childhood friend of hers. No hue and cry, and no protests whatsoever. Rather the decision was hailed by some: she was now able to provide much needed security to her parents, as there was no son in the family. This was not treated at all as a case involving a same-sex relationship, although in a sense it was. Manju/Mohan had confided to the press that she had always had a secret admiration and attraction for her friend, and that her feelings were also reciprocated. Nobody protested because they did not want to even think in the direction of lesbianism. Even raising the issue of a same-sex relationship was considered a taboo.

HOMOSEXUALITY AS A CRIMINAL OFFENCE

Homosexuality is both a matrimonial as well as a criminal offence. Nearly all the diverse personal laws of India treat sodomy as matrimonial misconduct and therefore a ground for divorce, available only to the wife. Interestingly, a wife's sexual intimacy with another woman is neither a matrimonial nor a criminal offence.

The Indian Penal Code makes homosexuality a criminal offence even in those cases where it is among consenting adult men in private. Adopted in 1860, the Code is an ancient piece of legislation, section 377 of which makes "carnal intercourse against the order of nature with any man, woman or animal" a criminal offence. The section covers only anal and not oral intercourse. Some amount of penetration is necessary and, accordingly, it has been concluded that in the case of lesbians, the section does not apply, as penetration is not possible. Unlike the other sexual offences, the consent and ages of the parties are totally irrelevant. Two mature, consenting adult men having an intimate sexual relationship would be convicted under section 377, and sent to prison. Boys under the age of sixteen would be sent to juvenile homes. This law (which might never have been passed, but for the British colonisation of India) is a great hindrance in the movement for gay rights.

PERCEPTION OF SAME-SEX RELATIONSHIPS BY SOCIETY AT LARGE

Indian society has always felt shy about discussing any kind of sexuality. However, like any other society, there are and have always been all kinds of relationships existing in India. Same-sex intimate relationships are considered an abnormal behaviour, a deviation from the fixed path, which society has approved and expects every one to follow. A strong prejudice against homosexual men is evident in Indian society. Homosexual men are treated and perceived as nothing other than potential child molesters, AIDS carriers, or deviant sexual perverts. The same prejudice, however, is not not as strong in the case of homosexual women. Until recently, there was no recognised homosexual community in India, as people were afraid to organise themselves for fear of penal action. The trend now is changing, and there are joint as well as scattered attempts by homosexuals to organise themselves and fight for their rightful place in society.

LESBIAN RIGHTS AND THE FILM *FIRE*

As section 377 of the Penal Code does not apply to lesbians, in theory, they do not have any fear of prosecution. Even if they openly declare their preferences and start living with their intimate female friends, the law cannot stand in their way. However, social conditions prevailing in India force an Indian woman to be very discreet about her sexuality. "Sex is not healthy and lesbians are oversexed, which is not how an Indian woman should behave" is the usual response of people towards lesbians.

However, in reality, socially established views are that marriage is essential for a woman, motherhood should be glorified, and women need male protection. Thus, the parents themselves force a girl into marrying a man early in her life. Once married, many women accept as their "fate" being trapped in an unhappy marriage with a violent husband. Few dare to defy social norms and try to live according to their wishes. But all women who revolt against male dominance, either by remaining unmarried or by trying to create a separate path for themselves, are considered a threat to patriarchy and are either subjugated or maligned.

Despite all this, women living independently have often displayed their orientation towards the same sex. Nearly all the boarding schools and colleges, women's hostels, and other institutions where women live together, have consistent cases of lesbian relationships. There were and are still efforts by women's groups to organise lesbians and fight for their rights, but the virtual impossibility of an open discussion about any kind of sexuality has been a big hindrance.

Things did change dramatically in Nov–Dec. 1998. What sparked off the whole debate from an entirely new perspective was Deepa Mehta's film *Fire*, which dealt with the theme of female sexuality and the relationship between two women. It was not a new subject in filmmaking, but it was the first time that a commercial Hindi movie was made with lesbianism as the basic theme. At least two other Indian films (*Umbaratha* in Marathi and *Subah* in Hindi) have fleetingly shown lesbian intimacies. However, in *Fire*, a developing lesbian relationship was shown at length. The film, which was a critique of the institution of "the family" and compulsory heterosexuality, was in itself a rare achievement in a society, embedded with patriarchal and fundamentalist values, in which women's sexuality is striving to find expression.

The film did very well abroad in some Western countries, but faced a very tough time initially in India. The State of Maharashtra, especially Mumbai (Bombay), and Delhi, the capital of India, witnessed some very strong reactions from the self-appointed custodians of the morals of Indians. They first called for a ban on the screening of the film in India, even after the Censor Board of India had passed it with an "Adult" certificate. When that failed, unsatisfied members of the Shiv Sena political party, took to vandalism. The cinema halls where the film was being exhibited were scenes of violence, where protesters went on the rampage, tore down film posters, and destroyed the cinema hall buildings. They tried to prevent people from going inside the cinemas. As a special case, the government sent the film back to the Censor Board again, which passed it without any more cuts. The grounds for the protests ranged from objecting to the names of the two leading characters in the film (Radha and Seeta are the names of two female Hindu deities), to objecting to the theme itself.

Perhaps the best part of Deepa Mehta's film was that it caused people to express their opinions about both the film and the theme of the film in public. For the first time in the history of India, homosexuality and opinions about it appeared in the national daily newspapers. It was amazing how *Fire* gripped the entire nation. Discussions and opinions about same-sex relationships were no longer taboo. Television and the print media took the lead in gathering public opinion, by featuring the subject on talk shows and inviting letters, and by seeking reactions from both known gays and heterosexuals; all this would have been unthinkable before the film. It dawned on Indians that they can now talk about a fourth category of people on the sexual front: besides men and women involved in heterosexual relationships and eunuchs, there are perfectly normal men and women who have an orientation towards people of the same sex. At the same time, the movement for the rights of gays also took a new turn. Encouraged by the support that was expressed by the people of India through newspapers and magazines, people involved in securing the rights of gays began identifying themselves publicly, which strengthened their movement.

POST-*FIRE* REACTIONS FOR AND AGAINST HOMOSEXUALITY

The public debate sparked off by *Fire* and the Shiv Sena vandalism gave an insight into the common people's perception of same-sex relationships. The opinions came through newspapers, magazines, radio, television, public meetings and even the Internet. For nearly two months, discussion of sexuality dominated the media, conferences, workshops, editorials, letters to the editor, and special television talk shows. This was the issue, this was the topic and nobody wanted to lag behind. It was unthinkable, and unbelievable: Indians talking about sexuality openly and not feeling embarrassed about it as they are supposed to. While the discussion was confined to big cities only, *Fire* also did reasonably well in the rural areas. The reactions were for and against the theme, the film and even social expectations. Ironically, the film and the theme could not be separated, as is evident from some of the reactions expressed below.

Actress Shabana Azmi, who played a key role in the film, said:

> "Whenever we talk about minorities and their rights, homosexuals automatically come within its purview, because they . . . constitute a minority group in themselves".[13]

The Toronto-based director, Deepa Mehta, who even received threats to her life for making a film on this forbidden topic, said:

> "If through this film, I am able to organise some scattered and isolated women involved in this kind of relationship, I would consider myself successful".[14]

Others were extremely hostile to the film:

> "An Indian woman needs to be protected from this attempt to corrupt and demoralise her. A majority of women in our society do not even know about lesbianism. Why expose them to it". (Meena Kambli, a deputy of the Shiv Sena leader Mahila Aghadi.)

> "The film is not consistent with normal behaviour and morals". (Ashwin Modi, chief of the Bajrang Dal political party in Surat.)

Mahila Aghadi even filed a petition in court seeking to have the film banned, arguing primarily that:

> "The film was against Indian traditions and should be banned. If women's physical needs get fulfilled through lesbians acts, the institution of marriage will collapse . . . reproduction of human beings will stop".[15]

But there was considerable support from women:

> "This kind of bonding between females isn't all that unusual. It is just that it isn't acknowledged or made public. When Ismat Chuglai, a famous Urdu writer, wrote '*Lihaaf*' (Quilt), she was only writing about what she had seen or observed around her. At that time also, the idealists and the traditionalist custodians of the society had categorised and labelled it as an attack on the basic values of the society. Critics had called it obscene and a large group had called for a ban on the sale and even publication of this story. It however didn't happen".[16]

Reacting very strongly to the vandalism, the National Commission of Women made the following observations:

> "The film with great sensitivity brings out in the open for the first time the poignancy and pathos of women caught in the web of a patriarchal society, which often holds

[13] "*Fire*: Fire in a Society", (Dec. 1998) 5 *Politics India* 45.

[14] *Ibid.*

[15] Other parties to the petition were: the Maharashtra Chief Minister and Cultural Minister, Vibhag Pramukhs of Shiv Shena, and Vahini Samiti of the Jain party.

[16] R Menon, "Shiv Sainiks, Women and Indian Culture: The Fire Within", *Indian Express* (9 Dec. 1998).

them prisoners within the four walls of their matrimonial homes without the slightest concern for their aspirations. The attack is another example of violence against women when they dare break their silence and speak out about their innermost feelings and traumas. We demand that the government demonstrate its belief in the dignity of women's rights of self-expression and take immediate punitive action against the offenders and guarantee that the film could be screened without any threat to life and property of all concerned".[17]

A leading newspaper, the *Times of India*, published a survey on whether there should be a law legalising homosexuality.[18] The response was overwhelming. The cross-section of people who were interviewed were all in favour. Some of the reactions follow:

> "As a homosexual myself, I'd say, once homosexuality is legalised, even the society would be less hypocritical, more acceptable of something that is considered taboo. Looking at the flip side of it legalising homosexuality would also take care of India's population explosion". (Sylvie, a famous male hairstylist in India.)

> "I have a number of homo and heterosexual friends who are living together. They appeared to have made their decision as mature people and no bill is going to make any difference in their opinion or life style. Social sanction could give them security and certain rights". (Sachin Khurana, an actor and model.)

> "Society must respect people's feelings and that people should be free to do what they want in their bedrooms. Sexual preferences of a person are their business alone and nobody should be allowed to interfere in that. If a bill were introduced, legalising homosexuality, it would not change the sexual orientation of people but would help change the society's perceptions about their relationships". (Kusum Sawhney, a writer.)

THE CAMPAIGN FOR GAY RIGHTS

As the survey suggested, support for the gay communities is also growing very rapidly in Indian society. Organisations and individuals working for gay rights are increasingly surfacing in the metropolitan cities of Delhi and Mumbai. Their efforts are paying off and their presence is increasingly felt in society. Many non-governmental organisations are involved in the campaign. Some of them, like "TASHRI" and "ABVA" (*AIDS Bhedbhav Virodhi Andolan*), are working primarily for gay and other persons with HIV/AIDS. Others are working directly on gay rights issues.

One of the remarkable achievers in this area is Ashok Row Kavi, who is attempting to increase the status and security of homosexuals. His work, which was initially confined to Mumbai, is quickly spreading throughout India. By uniting this marginalised group into an organised and vocal community with a

17 "Film Reflects Women's Feelings", NCW *Hindu* (9 Dec. 1998).

18 "Legally Unwedded", *Times of India* (20 Feb. 1999).

common identity, his efforts are bringing pressure on political and social forces in the country. Through social gatherings, outreach programmes, counselling and legal education, he empowers, strengthens and builds self-esteem in the gay community. Drawing upon his journalism background, he uses print media to communicate with and dispense information to gays and lesbians.

His pathbreaking magazine, *Bombay Dost*, is the first legally registered publication to focus exclusively on the issues that confront gays, lesbians and bisexuals, and is also one of the few resources in India for homosexual AIDS education. Upon this foundation, he initiates AIDS education and political actions designed to save lives and create wide public acceptance of homosexuality. *Bombay Dost* provides India's homosexuals a visibility they have not had before, and has helped to create visible gay support groups and networks in many major Indian cities, including Delhi, Lucknow, Calcutta, Hyderabad, Bangalore and Madras. Through networking with gay businesspersons throughout the country, a strong financial support mechanism has been built for *Bombay Dost*.

Ashok has developed nation-wide outreach programmes for homosexuals on safer sex and sexual orientation, and has instituted a gay documentation centre. The programme utilises conventional vehicles, such as publications and workshops, but also has India's first voice-mail helpline. Support groups handle the high response rate of seventy to eighty calls per day, some of which are abusive. Another program uses "drop cards" that are distributed near colleges, parks and other homosexual gathering places. One side of the card has information on services and helpline facilities, and the other side lists safe sex practices. The success of this campaign has led to the creation of a centre for counselling supported by the Mumbai municipal government. In addition, several local and national non-governmental organisations and international agencies have visited the outreach programmes to learn how to create communication channels. Ashok has also been asked to serve as a key consultant on AIDS for the Mumbai Municipal Corporation.

The issue of homosexuality has evoked a mixed response. On the one hand, demands to abolish section 377 of Indian Penal Code are increasing; on the other hand, there is a strong fear persisting in some sections of society. Some people fear that legalisation, and even increased awareness of homosexuality, may have a devastating effect on friendship between Indian men, which is viewed as something special. Jaydeep Ghosh writes:

> "Traditionally friendships between men have always been valued and it is very common to see Indian men hugging or even kissing each other as part of the social greeting . . . But . . . growing awareness of the homosexual relationship makes even a casual fling around the shoulders of a schoolmate by another young boy, look suspicious. Much of the pleasure of even genuine male bonding is thus taken away. Under the shadow of gay relationships. Men thus are finding it difficult to retreat into the Men's world even if for a while. Stag affairs are progressively becoming taboo".[19]

[19] "Brothers in Arms", *Times of India* (10 March 1999).

Ghosh argues that friendship between two men and brotherly love can be a source of great satisfaction. Male bonding is sometimes essential to unwind and derive peer support, and it would be unfortunate if someone were compelled to forego this support and affinity for fear of being branded gay.

In answer to that Joseph Matthews, a gay artist says:

> "Homosexual relationship, too, demands some amount of emotional support from partners rather than just physical intimacy. Even as homosexuals, we are normal human beings with needs and behaviour very similar to that of our heterosexual counterparts. The only difference being that I find love from a man rather than from a woman".[20]

Dr. Rani Dandekar added:

> "Human beings are like isomers. Some are right molecules. Some are left molecules. In the same, way some men are heterosexual and some are homosexual. There is no distinction as normal or abnormal".[21]

However, the approach taken by the Supreme Court is not very encouraging. In the 1983 case of *Fazal Rab Choudhary* v. *State of Bihar*, while convicting a man under section 377, the Court observed:

> "The offence is under Sec. 377 which implies sexual perversity. No force appears to have been used. Neither the notions of the permissive society nor the fact that that in some countries homosexuality has ceased to be an offence has influenced our thinking. However in judging the depravity of the action for determining quantum of sentence, all aspects of the matter must be kept in the mind".[22]

In the absence of an accusation of use of force, the accused was sentenced to rigorous imprisonment for a period of six months, reduced from the three years given by the lower court.

THE MYTH AND THE SURVEYS

The custodians of the society and morals of Indians would have everyone believe that Indians are all heterosexuals, that people voluntarily accept that their parents choose their life partners, and that there is no gay or lesbian community in India. It is a Western concept and Indians need to be saved from it. They would be morally corrupt if they were exposed to any kind of talk on sexuality. This is only a myth; the reality is very different. Indian society just like any other society has had every kind of relationship.

There are various surveys which help to prove that the above-mentioned claims of the custodians of society are totally hollow. Surveys were conducted by two of India's leading English-language magazines: *Debonair* (a more

[20] "Brothers in Arms", *Times of India* (10 March 1999), column 4.
[21] *Ibid.*, column 2.
[22] All India Reporter, 1983 Supreme Court 323.

modest Indian equivalent of *Playboy*) in 1991; and *Savvy* (a magazine catering to more modern women) in 1992. *Debonair*'s survey of 1424 married and unmarried men indicated that one in four adolescents and thirty-seven per cent of all males had had homosexual experiences. *Savvy*'s survey of 500 respondents indicated that 6 per cent of women reported homosexual activity.[23] Narayan Reddy and others conducted a similar study in 1993 in Madras, and recorded the experiences of over ten thousand adult men and women. Three per cent reported having had homosexual experiences.[24] Savera and Sridhar in 1993 conducted a study, using questionnaires and interviews, of English-and Marathi-speaking students and white and blue collar workers and migrant labourers in the Nasik and Thane areas of Maharashtra. Responses were obtained from 1100 males and 1052 females, with 2.4 per cent of all male students and 2.6 per cent of the adult population reporting homosexual contacts.[25]

In spite of these surveys, most Indian men believe proudly, and would like the world to believe, that we are all heterosexuals, and would not accept any arguments to the contrary. Talking about sexuality might corrupt their children and women. In reality, their paranoia is based on a rigid adherence to an ideology that upholds the institutions of marriage and the family. Any departure, or even an attempted departure, from this norm is a violation of the established code they advocate. Undermining the personal choices of people, and making them answerable to society for their intimate actions, is something that conservative Indians by and large would love to do.

It is therefore no wonder that those who have the security of money and power live their lives according to the path they have chosen for themselves. But the common people are very vulnerable. For fear of social stigma, they are unable to come out in public and look for outside support, which is now increasingly made available to them through the gay NGOs, other voluntary organisations, and a few determined individuals. Various surveys indicate that people by and large do not want to interfere with personal choices, and feel that forced sexual behaviour may lead to unpleasantness and problems.

ACCEPTANCE OF GAYS VS. LESBIANS

Although women cannot be punished legally for entering into a same-sex relationship, while a similar relationship involving men would attract penal sanctions, Indian society would generally find it easier to accept gays than lesbians. Women entering into relationships with each other are seen as a threat to the

[23] S J Jejeebhoy, "Adolescent Sexual and Reproductive Behavior: A Review of the Evidence from India", paper presented at the meeting of the World Health Organisation on "Inter-Country Consultation on Development of Strategies for Adolescent Health", New Delhi, 26–29 May 1998.

[24] *Ibid.*

[25] *Ibid.*

patriarchal system and to the very institution of marriage, which is revered by Indians. If there is any commonality amongst the diverse cultures, religions, castes and communities in India, it is that women should not be allowed to exercise their independence in matrimonial matters, and of course in the choice of their partners. Nothing should happen to the institution of marriage, and anything that has the possibility of adversely affecting the superiority of men in a male-dominated society cannot be tolerated by the self-styled protectors of the Hindu religion in India.

The resistance to granting rights to lesbians and gays is therefore completely different. By and large, society does not have any problem with two consenting adult males. What they fear is that legalisation of homosexuality may increase incidents of child molestation. As far as lesbians are concerned, their very existence is symbolic of their independence. Indian history and customs have always leaned towards women's subjugation in a patriarchal society, and any effort by them to liberate themselves from this subordination and establish an identity of their own is always frowned upon. Used to being subjugated from time immemorial, many Indian women toe the line and lack the courage to defy the patriarchal norms. Displaying an inherent weakness, they side with the orthodox elements and try to subdue the independence that few women dare to display.

CLIMATE FOR A CHANGE

The movement has already started. The talks and discussions on sexuality are no longer taboo, but are gaining a seriousness that they deserve. Indians have woken up to the fact that people's choices of their partners, though at variance with the traditional accepted norms, are perfectly normal behaviour. People do not want to be told by others what they should see, and with whom they should share their intimate life. It is primarily their concern, and society must respect the choices they make as mature adults. So long as section 377 exists on the statute books, it will remain a great hindrance to the gay rights movement. The need therefore is to delete it from the statute book.

Though the campaigns led by men have been far more successful than those led by women, joint concerted efforts are needed. Increasingly, Indian women are not only becoming more aware of their sexuality, but are actually taking a lead role in organising themselves; voicing their protests against the negative attitude of society towards them. The NGOs working for persons with AIDS also take care of homosexual rights, but there are very few NGOs who work for them directly. As far as lesbians are concerned, there are a few NGOs working exclusively for their recognition. "Stri Sangam", an organisation looking after and supporting the rights of lesbians, is very active in Mumbai. There is also a helpline for lesbians, "SARGINI", run by the NAZ foundations, and many other efforts on individual levels.

The women's movement is growing and getting stronger day by day. Women's groups have been active in fighting many problems within the family structure in order to work towards women's equality: domestic violence; dowry and bride burning; sati; sex determination and abortion of female foetuses. Numerous notable campaigns have been carried out. In all these campaigns, while the family structure was challenged, sexuality as an issue has hardly been spoken about openly. Of late, the women's movement in India has been open to creating space for discussions on sexuality. Notable in this connection are the national conferences held at Tirupati in 1994 and at Ranchi in 1997.

The national conference of women's movements (*Nari Mukti Sangarsh Sammelan*), held at Ranchi in December 1997, made the following declaration:

> "We seek the right to make choices about our lives, our bodies, our sexuality and our relationships. Some of us are single; some of us are married. Some of us have our primary emotional/sexual/physical/intimate relationship with men. Others with women. Some with both. Some of us do not have sexual relationships. We feel that we must evolve the supportive structures that can make all of these choices a meaningful reality".

The lesbian groups from Delhi and Mumbai, in a press release on 7 December 1998 made the following declaration:

> "We would like to take this opportunity to inform the press and the public that lesbians exist in India. We are here today. We have always been a part of Indian society. Witness the extensive Yogini Temples and lesboerotic sculpture all over India. Women will continue to love women for centuries to come. Lesbianism is not specific to any one culture, religion, society, class, language group, or geography. Lesbianism exists everywhere that women exist—all over the world".

Since the attack on *Fire*, a number of individuals and organisations in Delhi have come together to form "The Campaign for Lesbian Rights" (CALERI). The Campaign seeks: (1) to make lesbianism visible and to dispel the myth that there are no lesbians in India; (2) to dispel misconceptions and prejudices about lesbians; and (3) to achieve public and state recognition of the right of all lesbians to a life of dignity, acceptance, equality and safety. The campaign plans to engage in dissemination of information, public debates on lesbianism, and awareness-raising in the coming years. This is no small achievement, since it is one of the first forums of its kind in Delhi. The homophobia that prevails in some sections of Indian society needs to be confronted, and the need to create space for such discussions and take this issue to the public is imperative.

On 17 January 1999, "Saheli", an NGO based in Delhi, organised a public meeting titled "*Fire*, Lesbianism and Related Issues". The discussion was initiated by three members of the Campaign for Lesbian Rights. The meeting was attended by more than sixty people, including representatives of women's groups, gay rights groups, and democratic and civil rights groups, as well as students and many concerned individuals. It provided a forum for discussion on a wide spectrum of issues, ranging from the film itself to the travails of growing up as a gay person, the need for public recognition of lesbianism, the social harassment faced by lesbians all over the country, the history of the lesbian movement in India and abroad, the role of the women's movement on the issue, and the failure of activists and organisations working on other rights issues to take up or even support the struggle of sexual minorities.[26] The recognition of gay and lesbian rights should be an imperative, not only of the women's movement, but also of the left movement and all democratic forces.

The day is not far off when the homosexual community in India will gain its much-wanted acceptance, and same-sex couples will come out in the open without any fear of penal action. That would be the first step towards recognition of the right of every Indian to live a life of dignity, with the freedom to make choices regarding their lives, their individuality and their partners.[27]

[26] "*Shiv Sena ko gussa kyon aata Hai*" ("The Fire Controversy"), *Saheli Newsletter* at 11–15.

[27] For recent developments, see http://www.tehelka.com/currentaffairs/mar2001/ca030801 lesbians.htm (CALERI excluded from 8 March 2001 International Women's Day march); http://www.iglrhc.org/world/s_asia/index.html (HIV/AIDS prevention workers in Lucknow detained under Penal Code section 377 on 7 July 2001); http://www.Bombay-Dost.com; Conclusion, p. 770.

20

Challenges to Compulsory Heterosexuality: Recognition and Non-Recognition of Same-Sex Couples in Israeli Law

AEYAL M. GROSS*

INTRODUCTION

THE 1990S WERE Israel's "gay decade". Since the decriminalisation of sodomy in 1988, gays and lesbians in Israel have enjoyed more rights and visibility than ever before.[1] The changes that took place during this period can hardly be overestimated. The sight of tens of thousands of people marching in the streets of Tel-Aviv on Gay Pride Parades held since the late 1990s would have been inconceivable only a few years before. One of the pinnacles of this process was a decision of the Israeli Supreme Court in 1994, holding that employers must provide same-sex couples with the same spousal benefits that they give to unmarried heterosexual couples. The decision in *El-Al* v. *Danilowitz* marked an important moment in the transformation of gay visibility in Israel.[2]

* Tel-Aviv University, Faculty of Law. I am grateful to Daphna Barak-Erez, Leora Bilsky, Yishai Blank, Michael Gluzman, Dori Spivak, Yuval Yonay and Amalia Ziv for their helpful comments on a previous draft of this chapter, and to Batya Stein for her editing and language skills.

1 On the criminal prohibition on sodomy and the decriminalisation process, see A Harel, "Gay Rights in Israel: A New Era?", (1996) 1 *International Journal of Discrimination and the Law* 261 at 264–5; Y Yonay, "The Law Regarding Homosexuality—Between History and Sociology", (1998) 4 *Mishpat Umimshal—Law and Government in Israel* 531 at 532–50 (in Hebrew). For a more general discussion of the transformation of gay life in Israel in the 1990s, see L Walzer, *Between Sodom and Eden: A Gay Journey Through Today's Changing Israel* (New York, Columbia University Press, 2000) ; A Sumakai Fink & J Press, *Independence Park: The Lives of Gay Men in Israel* (Stanford, Stanford University Press, 1999).

2 See A Harel, "The Rise and Fall of the Israeli Gay Legal Revolution", (2000) 31 *Columbia Human Rights Law Review* 443 (discussing the political response to *Danilowitz*); A Kama, "From *Terra Incognita* to *Terra Firma*: The Logbook of the Voyage of Gay Men's Community into the Israeli Public Sphere", (2000) 38 *Journal of Homosexuality* 133, 144–5 (how the media response to *Danilowitz* illustrates the growing visibility of gays in Israel).

Danilowitz was decided under Israel's equal employment opportunities statute and, on a narrow reading, may be seen as limited to the sphere of the workplace. Its symbolic effect, however, was to give some official recognition to the lives of gay couples. In this sense, to the extent that legal recognition of same-sex couples does exist in Israel, it has developed in a peculiar way. Israel has not established any mechanism to allow same-sex couples to obtain official recognition of their relationship (eg, a registration system). Nevertheless, as a result of the *Danilowitz* decision, same-sex couples *are* recognised, *de facto*, in the labour area. Moreover, as I show below, the *Danilowitz* holding has paved the way for recognition in other contexts, although this promise has materialised only partly.

In Part 1 of this chapter (pp. 393–401), I discuss the *Danilowitz* decision and show how the reasoning in this case allows both a "narrow *Danilowitz*" and a "broad *Danilowitz*", the latter expanding recognition of same-sex couples beyond the workplace. I also consider how the *Danilowitz* decision, read together with a Supreme Court decision on gender equality, illustrates the links between "compulsory heterosexuality" and patriarchy and the challenges to these institutions. In Part 2 (pp. 401–11), I discuss judicial decisions on same-sex couples given after *Danilowitz*, and show how both the narrow and broad readings of *Danilowitz* exist in the case law. Finally, in Part 3 (pp. 411–14), I point to the dilemma arising from the fact that the arguments for legal recognition of same-sex couples must often rest on a "like heterosexuals" argument, and look into Michel Foucault's proposal for a "new relational right" as a possible new frontier for gay rights that may transcend this type of argument.

In my reading of the case law throughout this chapter, I show the judicial realm as an important arena, in which the battle over the meaning of "heterosexuality" and "homosexuality" is waged, as well as a forum where the content of these identities is constituted.[3] My argument is that, although judicial texts address the issue as if these identities had a fixed, pre-judicial content, these texts actually partake in creating these contents and in granting them meaning. For this reason, I examine not only the legal doctrines established in the case law, but also the discursive strategies that the courts use to explain these doctrines.[4]

[3] I pursue here Janet Halley's insight that, when debating about sexual orientation, we do not just reflect or deliberate about it, but also constitute it and enroll ourselves in it; the role of the law in constituting persons, by providing a forum for their conflict over who they will be understood to be, is deeply material and symbolic. J Halley, "Reasoning About Sodomy: Act and Identity in and after *Bowers* v. *Hardwick*, (1993) 79 *Virginia Law Review* 1721 at 1729–1731.

[4] See K Thomas, "Corpus Juris (Hetero)Sexualis: Doctrine, Discourse, and Desire in *Bowers* v. *Hardwick*," (1993) 1 *GLQ: A Journal of Gay and Lesbian Studies* 33 at 35–36 (on the importance of looking at discursive strategies that the courts use to explain doctrine).

ON PILOTS AND FLIGHT ATTENDANTS: READING *DANILOWITZ*

Alternative Recruiting Slogans

For many years, the Israeli Air Force had used as its recruiting slogan the phrase: "The best men to be pilots". Hebrew is not a gender-neutral language, and the term "pilots" appears in the slogan in its male form. This slogan had a popular, if unofficial, addition: "The best women for the pilots," with the word "pilots" appearing, again, in male form.

The slogan "The best men to be [male] pilots, the best women for the [male] pilots", or at least its official first part, is attributed to Ezer Weizman, Israel's former President, who used to be head of the Israeli Air Force.[5] Jointly, both parts of the recruiting slogan illustrate the link between patriarchy and compulsory heterosexuality, which Adrienne Rich has so convincingly shown:[6] the slogan describes a social order in which only men can hold key positions in society,[7] whereas the main role of women is to be coupled with men.

Speaking at a high school in 1996, President Weizman made some overtly homophobic comments. Homosexuality, he said, "is in my eyes . . . an abnormal phenomenon. . . . I personally do not accept this business of everyone coming out of the closet. It seems to me to be weird".[8] In a demonstration that was held the following day before the President's house, the queer crowd chanted an alternative slogan: "The best women to be [female] pilots , the best men for the [male] pilots". Addressing this slogan at President Weizman was more than fitting. As president and as former air force chief, Weizman had earlier expressed his opposition to the inclusion of women as pilots in the Israeli air force. In fact, one theme recurred in his remarks in these two seemingly different contexts, the issues of women as air force pilots and gays coming out: "I like a man who wants to be a man and a woman who wants to be a woman".[9]

Weizman's longing for men who would be men and women who would be women should probably be read, not only as another expression of the familiar patriarchy/compulsory heterosexuality matrix, but also as representing Zionist ideology. In European tradition, the Jew had often been depicted as feminised

[5] On the history of the air force recruiting slogan, see R Mann, *It's Inconceivable* (Israel, Hed Arzi Publishing House, 1998), at 110 (in Hebrew).

[6] See A Rich, "Compulsory Heterosexuality and Lesbian Existence" in Snitow, Stansell & Thompson (eds.), *Powers of Desire: The Politics of Sexuality* (New York, Monthly Review Press, 1983), at 177–205. Unlike Rich, I will use the term "compulsory heterosexuality" as applying to both men and women.

[7] The air force, and specifically its pilots, enjoy a highly prestigious place in Israeli society.

[8] See "Weizman Calls Gays 'Abnormal," *The Jerusalem Post International Edition* (22–28 Dec. 1996).

[9] *Ibid*. See also "So Said the President", *Ma'ariv* (22 Dec. 1996) (in Hebrew) (quoting May 1996 remarks): "Women should not be pilots. I myself like very much a woman who wants to be a woman, and I do not like so much a man who wants to be a woman."

and sometimes as homosexual.[10] Zionism, as Daniel Boyarin[11] and Michael Gluzman[12] have shown, sought to "cure" the Jewish man by demanding the kind of clear gender lines required by Weizman.

The two cases I will discuss in this section illustrate the two available options: the patriarchal/compulsory heterosexual one of the air force slogan ("The best men to be [male] pilots, the best women for the [male] pilots"), and the alternative offered by the crowd ("The best women to be [female] pilots, the best men for the [male] pilots").

El-Al v. *Danilowitz*: The Flight Attendant Wins

The first case is the "crown jewel" of Israeli gay rights law: the Supreme Court decision in the matter of *El-Al Israel Airlines* v. *Danilowitz.*[13] In a judgment given in 1994, the Israeli Supreme Court upheld a decision by the National Labour Court holding that El-Al Israel Airlines must give the same-sex partner of Mr. Danilowitz, a flight attendant, the same work-related benefits that are granted to the unmarried heterosexual partners of employees. The benefit in question was a free or discounted flight ticket given annually by El-Al to the spouses or "reputed spouses" of its employees.

The *Danilowitz* case came up under Israel's Equal Employment Opportunities Law ("EEO Law"),[14] which was amended in 1992 to include sexual orientation as an explicit category under which discrimination is prohibited.[15] The EEO Law is quite broad, covering not only hiring and firing but also working conditions. The three-judge panel produced two separate majority opinions and a dissent.

Deputy President, Justice Aharon Barak[16]

The first judge in the majority, Justice Barak, described two constructions under which Mr. Danilowitz could claim a free ticket for his partner. The first was the "interpretive construction." Under this construction, the correct interpretation

[10] See G L Mosse, *The Image of Man: The Creation of Modern Masculinity* (Oxford, Oxford University Press, 1996), at 68–72; M Garber, *Vested Interests: Cross-Dressing and Cultural Anxiety* (New York, Routledge, 1992), at 224–233.

[11] D Boyarin, *Unheroic Conduct: The Rise of Heterosexuality and the Invention of the Jewish Man* (Berkeley, University of California Press, 1997).

[12] M Gluzman, "The Zionist Body: Nationalism and Sexuality in Herzl's *Altneuland*," in Biale & Heschel (eds.), *Feminist Readers, Jewish Texts* (Berkeley, University of California Press, forthcoming). See also Mosse, *supra* n.10, at 151–153.

[13] High Court of Justice (HCJ) 721/94, 48(5) *Piskei-Din* (Supreme Court Reports) 749 (1994) (in Hebrew). See also http://metalab.unc.edu/gaylaw/issue2/stein.html (English translation of Barak's opinion; summaries of other opinions). A full translation is posted at http://www.tau.ac.il/law/aeyalgross/legal_materials.htm.

[14] Law of 1988, as amended in 1992, *Israel's Labor Laws* (2d ed.), at 61/1.

[15] See Yonay, *supra* n.1, at 550–5.

[16] Barak now serves as President.

of the El-Al collective bargaining agreement with flight attendants was such that it covered same-sex partners. The context of this construction is that only religious marriage exists in Israel, and people must marry and divorce under their personal religious law. Yet, for many specific purposes, some statutes and some collective agreements also grant spousal rights to a person "commonly known as" or "reputed to be" a spouse.[17] The El-Al collective agreement granted free tickets to someone who is a spouse (husband or wife) and to someone "reputed to be a spouse", which had been applied to unmarried heterosexual partners of employees. The interpretative construction, then, would have meant recognising that, at least for the purposes of the El-Al agreement, the "spouse" or "reputed to be a spouse" clause could cover same-sex partners.[18]

The other possible construction was what Barak called the "statutory construction". Under this construction, the agreement gave the right in question only to heterosexual couples, thereby contradicting the EEO Law's prohibition of discrimination on the ground of sexual orientation. Barak focused on the statutory construction and accepted the argument that the El-Al employment agreement was discriminatory; this discrimination had to be amended through El-Al granting spousal benefits to partners in same-sex couples. In Barak's words: "The Court decides, rather, that by virtue of the principle of equality—and as long as the discriminatory contractual regime is unaltered—a remedy of granting the benefit to the type discriminated against is required, in order to remove the discrimination".[19]

Thus, the *ratio decidendi* of Barak's holding in *Danilowitz* left open the question of whether same-sex partners can be considered as a matter of interpretation as "spouses" or "reputed spouses", at least in this context, but possibly in other contexts as well. In *obiter dicta,* Barak referred to this hypothetical construction as "complex". (The interpretive construction was rejected by the National Labour Court and was not repeated by Mr. Danilowitz in the Supreme Court.)

We see that Barak's holding in *Danilowitz* does not really recognise same-sex relationships as "couples". He does appear to grant some legal recognition to the relationship between Mr. Danilowitz and his partner, however, when he argues that, for the purpose of this matter and as part of the reasoning of why this is a case of prohibited discrimination, there is no difference between "Adam and Eve" and "Adam and Steve".[20] Barak says he is willing to presume that, in certain social contexts, there are differences between same-sex couples and different-sex couples, but argues that "[t]his difference is of no relevance

[17] See A Rosen-Zvi, "Family and Inheritance Law," in Shapira & DeWitt-Arar (eds.), *Introduction to the Law of Israel* (The Hague, Kluwer, 1995), at 75, 97–99.

[18] The El-Al agreement used both the Hebrew equivalents of "husband" or "wife" and "*ben-zug*" (male member of a couple) or "*bat-zug*" (female member of a couple). I will use "spouse" when the Hebrew texts use "*ben-zug*" or "*bat-zug*," although these terms do not mean only "husband" or "wife".

[19] *Supra* n.13, Barak's opinion, para. 20.

[20] Barak referred to "Reuven and Lea" and "Reuven and Shimon".

whatsoever regarding the discussed issue". Barak points out that the benefit is granted because of "the notion of shared life for a certain period . . . which demonstrates a strong social unit, based on cooperative life".

For Barak, then, the relevant question is the following: "Is leaving a same-sex domestic partner easier than leaving a spouse of the opposite sex? Are the shared lives of two persons of the same sex different from those of two persons belonging to opposite sexes?"[21] Given his negative answer to this rhetorical question, he concludes that the distinction in this context is arbitrary and unfair. It amounts to discrimination on the ground of sexual orientation, which is explicitly prohibited by the EEO Law. Barak also notes that the discrimination in this case is also tantamount to sex discrimination. He does admit that it could be claimed that no sex discrimination is involved, since both male and female employees with same-sex partners are denied the benefits, but dismisses this claim as "not convincing". Barak considers himself exempt from deciding this point, because of the EEO Law's explicit prohibition on sexual orientation discrimination.[22]

Barak's discussion of the similarities, between the "shared life" led by two people of the same sex and two people of opposite sexes, shows that his distinction between the "statutory" and the "interpretive" constructions is not so clear-cut. To decide that this is an instance of the arbitrary and unfair discrimination forbidden by the statute, some similarity between same-sex and different-sex couples must be acknowledged. Yet, insofar as this similarity is recognised, we draw closer to the interpretive construction: in order to identify the discrimination, we must view same-sex partners as couples, as each other's "spouse".

By leaving open the question of the interpretive construction, Barak's decision grants legal recognition to same-sex partnerships and simultaneously withdraws it. I show below how this contradiction in *Danilowitz* makes it sufficiently open-textured to allow conflicting results concerning the recognition of same-sex couples in the Israeli legal system. I also discuss below the potential problem involved in the recognition of same-sex couples in terms of their similarity to heterosexual couples.

Justice Dalia Dorner

Justice Dorner concurred with Barak. Her main difference with Barak was that, in her opinion, the general principle of equality in Israeli labour law would have mandated the same result in this case, even without the 1992 amendment to the EEO Law, due to the changes in attitudes toward homosexuality in Israeli society. The amendment did not change the law, by introducing new equal rights for homosexuals, but merely reflected what general labour law principles would

[21] *Supra* n.13, Barak's opinion, para. 15.

[22] Counsel for the United Kingdom Government distinguished *Danilowitz* on this basis when counsel for Lisa Grant relied on the decision before the European Court of Justice in *Grant* v. *South-West Trains*. See Koppelman, chap. 35.

have mandated in any event. According to Dorner, the other side of this coin is that, without these social changes, the EEO Law might have been interpreted narrowly, depriving Mr. Danilowitz of the benefits for which he had sued.

Justice Dorner's decision thus appears the most progressive, arguing for Mr Danilowitz's right to benefits even without the EEO Law. From the perspective of gay rights, however, this claim may seem rather risky, because it makes the legal recognition of gay couples contingent on the social acceptance of homosexuality.[23] Yet, Dorner's decision does entail a potentially broader recognition of same-sex couples. By relying on a general principle of equality incumbent on public authorities and employers in general, she enables the prohibition of discrimination to be extended to gay couples in contexts where the EEO Law does not apply.

Justice Yaakov Kedmi

The third judge, Justice Kedmi, dissented. His dissent is mainly an exegesis on the Hebrew word for couple (*zug*). Kedmi begins by stating that the relevant question is whether the term *ben-zug* (spouse, and, literally, "member of a couple") in labour agreements includes same-sex couples: "My honorable colleague . . . [Barak] concluded that it does. Unfortunately, I cannot concur". Note that Kedmi reads Barak as holding that a same-sex partner is indeed a "spouse" for the purpose of the labour agreement. As I pointed out, however, Barak's reasoning is actually based on the statutory construction, rather than on the interpretive construction as implied by Kedmi. Maybe Kedmi's (mis)reading of Barak illustrates again the difficulty involved in drawing the line between these two constructions. For Kedmi, Barak's reasoning implies recognition of same-sex partners, as "couples", and he is intent on objecting to such recognition.

In his analysis of the word *zug* (couple), Kedmi argues that the word has always indicated a connection between individuals of opposite sexes; a couple is the basis of the family, and there is no family unless the spouses are of opposite sexes. A couple, in principle, has the potential of having children. Two people of the same sex imitating the behaviour of a "couple" do not become a couple. They are, says Kedmi, a "pair of friends". This kind of "couple," according to Kedmi, is not characterised by "the same mutual commitment for stability of the shared life and its continuance". According to Kedmi, "A change in the basic notions of 'couple' and 'family' must involve, primarily, a conceptual change of basic linguistic meanings. . . ."

And he adds:

> "The above mentioned views should not be regarded as stemming from a conservative religious attitude. Religion did not dictate the meaning of the term 'couple' in the linguistic sphere, but life itself has dictated it; and reality, which reflects life, is the basis of the term 'couple' and . . . the source of its social meaning. . . . I wish not to be

[23] See Harel, *supra* n.1, at 266–267.

misunderstood: I do not wish to challenge the increasing recognition of the sexual orientation of persons who wish to live with those of the same sex, and I do not wish to put barriers in the way of those persons toward self-fulfillment, according to their orientation; I wish only to avoid breaking 'a conceptual' barrier, to avoid a linguistic 'chaos' and 'misunderstood' communication, by deviating sharply from the meaning of basic terms, on the basis of which our society exists and operates".[24]

Kedmi's dissent is unusual in more than one way. It is based on an interpretation of the word *zug* (couple), which was not the basis for the majority opinion, and shows an understanding of the Supreme Court as the custodian of the Hebrew language, rather than as the custodian of law and justice.[25] On the one hand, Kedmi asserts that his argument does not rely on a conservative religious attitude. On the other hand, he adduces evidence from one source only, the Bible, referring to events described in Genesis, such as the creation of man and woman and Noah's ark, while ignoring all of Israel's Basic Laws, statutes, or precedents.[26] Mostly, Kedmi assumes that words have essential "social" meanings (or meanings dictated by "life itself"), as if the legal process were not itself a discursive practice shaping the meanings we give to words. His decision is based on an interpretation of the Hebrew word *zug* and its "eternal" meaning. Yet, as Alon Harel has shown, the word *zug* does not appear in any of the biblical quotes cited by the judge, and actually does not appear in the Bible at all.[27]

Another interesting concept in the dissenting opinion is that of "imitation", in the context of characterising the behaviour of two people of the same sex who "imitate" the behavior of a "couple". The underlying assumption here is that one can distinguish a different-sex couple, which is a "real couple", from a same-sex couple, which is not a "real couple". Borrowing from Judith Butler's understanding of the imitative nature of gender,[28] I wish to suggest that a "couple" always exists through imitation: a couple is always an imitation of another thing called a "couple". Kedmi's different-sex couple is a couple only because it imitates another "couple", or tries to approximate the metaphysical ideal of "coupledom" rather than because it follows some "natural" model of what a "couple" is. As Butler says: "Compulsory heterosexuality sets itself up as the original, the true, the authentic; the norm that determines the real implies that 'being' a lesbian is always a kind of miming, a vain effort to participate in the phantasmatic plentitude of naturalised heterosexuality which will always and only fail".[29] But this naturalised heterosexuality, says Butler, is actually an

[24] *Supra* n.13, Kedmi's opinion, paras.1, 7.

[25] Harel is thus correct when he claims that Kedmi's judgment "can be read more as a treatise in etymology than as a judicial decision." Harel, *supra* n.1, at 269.

[26] See also Harel, *supra* n.1, at 268. Compare L Edelman, *Homographesis: Essays in Gay Literary and Cultural Theory* (New York & London, Routledge, 1994), at 99 (use of Genesis by US Supreme Court in *Bowers* v. *Hardwick*).

[27] Harel, *ibid.*, at 268.

[28] J Butler, *Gender Trouble: Feminism and the Subversion of Identity* (New York, Routledge, 1990).

[29] J Butler, "Imitation and Gender Insubordination," in D Fuss (ed.), *Inside/Out: Lesbian Theories, Gay Theories* (New York, Routledge, 1991), at 13, 20–21.

impossible imitation of itself, an imitation that performatively *constitutes itself* as the original.[30]

Kedmi's heterosexual couple should be understood in this light: it presents itself as the "authentic", as the pure source, whereas it is only an imitation of what a "couple" is. Coupling, like all social phenomena, is always imitative, and, therefore, one *imitation* is not ontologically superior to another. Kedmi's decision itself has a share in constituting the heterosexual couple as the "original" and the homosexual couple as "imitation", and, as such, is an act of attempted compulsory heterosexuality.[31]

Alice Miller v. *Minister of Defence*: The Pilot Wins

At this stage, I will briefly discuss another case, ostensibly not a case about gay rights. In *Alice Miller* v. *Minister of Defence*,[32] decided in 1995, the Israeli Supreme Court accepted the petition of Ms Miller, who asked to be considered as a candidate for the air force pilot training course. President Weizman had objected to the inclusion of women in this course, resorting to the same argument he later used in his anti-gay speech, wishing "men to be men and women to be women". Ms Miller asked for President Weizman's help, but he refused to support her and notoriously replied: "*Meidale* ["little girl" in Yiddish], did you ever see a man mending socks?"[33]

Ms Miller took her case to the Supreme Court and won. The two-judge majority held that forbidding women entry to the pilot training course was tantamount to prohibited gender discrimination. Again, Kedmi dissented. One of his arguments for denying the petition was that air force pilots are required to enlist for active reserve duty frequently, and for many years, after the end of their long regular service. Thus, said Kedmi, it would not be fair to force Ms. Miller to choose between dedication to her duties as a pilot and the obligations involved in raising a family, which she would probably assume eventually.[34]

The Recruiting Slogans Revisited

Looking at the cases of Jonathan Danilowitz and Alice Miller together, and especially through the perspective of Kedmi's dissents, the link between the two parts of the original recruiting slogan become more obvious.

[30] *Ibid.*, at 22.

[31] Compare Kedmi's notion of same-sex couples as "imitation" with Local Government Act 1988, s. 28 (England and Wales, repealed for Scotland in 2000), which prohibits "promot[ing] the teaching . . . of the accceptability of homosexuality as a pretended family relationship", discussed in C Stychin, *Law's Desire: Sexuality and the Limits of Justice* (London, Routledge, 1995), at 38–39, 47.

[32] HCJ 4541/94, 49(4) Supreme Court Reports 94 (1995) (in Hebrew).

[33] Mann, *supra* n.5, at 178.

[34] *Miller, supra* n.32, at 117.

The patriarchal social order that requires Ms Miller to care for her family, and thus precludes her becoming a pilot, also demands that Mr Danilowitz and his partner should not be a "couple". The social structure in which it is clear that she will marry a man, have children, and will be responsible for raising them, also requires compulsory heterosexuality. If same-sex couples can exist, the social order in which Ms Miller cannot be a pilot collapses. Patriarchy (and its division of labour within the family) and compulsory heterosexuality are indeed mutually dependent. Once the regime of compulsory heterosexuality is undermined, and a social order in which men can couple with men and women with women becomes possible, the patriarchal regime in which only men can hold key social positions, and the role of women is to be coupled with men and raise the family, becomes untenable.

The recognition of homosexual couples threatens patriarchy in yet another context: homosexuality is often equated with sodomy and with the receptive position in anal intercourse.[35] Recognising homosexual couples thus implies recognising men as the passive, or penetrated, partners in sex, a terrifying image to the patriarchal mind, because it conjures up the image of men in the passive (or female) position. In the psychic economy of the male heterosexual, this entails a horrifying abdication of power.[36] In this sense too, then, the recognition of homosexual relationships discussed in *Danilowitz* threatens the mutually dependent structure of compulsory heterosexuality and patriarchy.[37] It is this threat, and the ensuing anxiety, that could be at the root of Kedmi's unusual opinion in *Danilowitz* and account for its apocalyptic tone: the "chaos" that Kedmi is trying to prevent is not merely linguistic, but rather the "chaos" of a social and sexual order where patriarchy/compulsory heterosexuality cease to be the rule.[38] His opinion thus neglects legal analysis in favour of the Bible and arguments based on the "natural" meaning of words, as if a return to these primordial sources could indeed prevent the feared "chaos".[39]

Kedmi's views did not prevail in the two cases discussed above. Instead, the majority's reasoning opened the possibility of voicing the alternative slogan challenging the compulsory heterosexuality/patriarchy matrix: "The best women to be [female] pilots, the best men for the [male] pilots" or, in the two

[35] See Edelman, *supra* n.26, at 133–134.

[36] See Thomas, *supra* n.4, at 41; L Bersani, "Is the Rectum a Grave?," in D Crimp (ed.), *AIDS: Cultural Analysis, Cultural Activism* (Cambridge, MA, MIT Press, 1988), at 197–222.

[37] See C MacKinnon, *Toward A Feminist Theory of the State* (Cambridge, MA, Harvard University Press, 1989) at 126–154 (centrality of different sexual roles of men and women to male dominance).

[38] The Hebrew term Kedmi uses for "chaos", *"toho vevohu"*, is the term used in Genesis 1:2 to describe the situation on earth at the beginning of creation. Kedmi's fear of a return to such chaos can thus be seen as part of a recurring narrative, identified by Lee Edelman, in which the "passivity" associated with gay male intercourse, and culture's passive acquiescence to male-male anal sex, serve as the "point of origin" for the apocalyptic reversal of Genesis. See Edelman, *supra* n.26, at 99–100.

[39] Compare Thomas, *supra* n.4 (discussing anxiety as explaining the rhetoric used by the US Supreme Court in *Bowers* v. *Hardwick*).

cases read together, "The best women to be [female] pilots, the best men for the [male] [flight attendants]".[40]

DANILOWITZ AND ITS AFTERMATH: THE "NARROW *DANILOWITZ*" AND THE "BROAD *DANILOWITZ*"

Steiner I* vs. *Steiner II

We saw above that, in *Danilowitz,* the Court's reasoning was based on the "statutory construction" (holding that El-Al's collective agreement was discriminatory), rather than on a recognition (the "interpretive construction") that same-sex partners qualify as "spouses" or "reputed spouses". I argued, however, that adopting the "statutory construction" requires a recognition that Mr Danilowitz and his partner are "like" a heterosexual couple; the reasoning in *Danilowitz* thus recognises and fails to recognise same-sex couples at the same time.

Both a narrow and a broad reading of *Danilowitz* are possible. The narrow *Danilowitz* is limited to discrimination in the workplace, without any implications concerning the recognition of same-sex couples beyond that setting. The broad reading relies on Barak's analogy between "Adam and Eve" and "Adam and Steve", and reads *Danilowitz* as implying some kind of general recognition of same-sex relationships, even if the decision was based, not on the interpretive, but rather on the statutory construction.

Interestingly, both these readings of *Danilowitz* appeared in the two divergent decisions in the *Steiner* affair. Mr Steiner was the partner of Colonel Doron Meisel, who died during his military service. Steiner sued for various payments to which family members of deceased army personnel are entitled. These are statutory payments, awarded within the context of military service, and the EEO Law does not apply to them.

Mr Steiner sued under two different statutes, the first involving special payments for families of soldiers who died in service,[41] and the second pertaining to the military service pensions law.[42] The army refused to pay under either statute, and Mr Steiner appealed. In both cases, he asked to be recognised as the person "reputed as the spouse" of Colonel Meisel. The appeals were heard before special appeals panels chaired by judges. The first case (*Steiner I*), which

[40] Following *Danilowitz,* Tel-Aviv University agreed to settle *Uzi Even* v. *Tel-Aviv University,* ND/1712/3. Under the settlement (given the status of a verdict by the Labour Court in Tel-Aviv), the University agreed to give Prof. Even's partner the same benefits it gives to a person "reputed as the spouse" of a faculty member.

[41] Fallen Soldier's Families (Pensions and Rehabilitation) Law, 5710–1950, 4 *Laws of the State of Israel* 115, as amended in 1977, 31 *Laws of the State of Israel* 168.

[42] Israel Defence Forces (Permanent Service) (Benefits) (Consolidated Version), 5745–1985, 39 *Laws of the State of Israel* 152.

Mr Steiner lost, illustrates the narrow *Danilowitz*. The second case (*Steiner II*), which he won, illustrates the broad *Danilowitz*.

Although both decisions lack any significant value as precedents, I will discuss them at some length for two related reasons. First, the *Steiner* decisions illustrate the different alternatives now available in the wake of *Danilowitz*, and show how the arsenal of arguments deployed in *Danilowitz* may be used to produce contradictory results. Second, both decisions, but especially *Steiner I*, are extremely important as social texts warranting close reading. The reasoning in *Steiner I* deploys the arguments often adduced in anti-gay discourse, both inside and outside the courtroom. My hope is that my queer reading of the rhetoric and arguments used in this decision will contribute to the anti-homophobic project.

Steiner I[43]

The first *Steiner* case was heard by an appeals panel adjunct to the Magistrate Court in Tel-Aviv and chaired by Judge Gershon Gherman. The panel rejected the appeal.

The statute invoked in *Steiner I* provides that payments are due to family members of soldiers who died in service. The statute defines "family members" as the wife of the deceased, including a woman who was "reputed" to be his wife, or, in the case of a woman, the husband of the deceased, including a man who was "reputed" to be her husband. Mr Steiner's attorney argued that these gender-specific provisions should be read in light of Israel's Interpretation Law,[44] which states that the male gender shall be interpreted to include the female gender, and vice-versa. Therefore, he argued, the "reputed as" provisions should be interpreted to include a man who was "reputed in public as the husband" of another man.

Gherman rejected this interpretation, relying on the proviso in the Interpretation Law that a rule of interpretation will not apply if something in the relevant context does not accommodate it. To support his conclusion, Gherman made a series of determinations, which I summarise below:

- The statute in question does not use the term "spouse" (*zug*). Although that term might include same-sex couples, the current statute, which includes such terms as "family", "husband," and "wife" cannot include same-sex couples.
- Even in *Danilowitz*, Barak did not use the "interpretive construction" implying that a "spouse" might include a same-sex partner; instead he used the "statutory construction". Thus, following *all* three judges in *Danilowitz*, it is not possible to expand "family member" to include same-sex couples. Furthermore, *Danilowitz* involved an employment case and

[43] Family Appeal 8/94, *Steiner* v. *Pensions Officer* (13 Aug. 1995), unpublished decision (in Hebrew).

[44] Interpretation Law, 5741–1981, 35 *Laws of the State of Israel* 370.

the EEO Law, explicitly forbidding discrimination on the ground of sexual orientation; here, there is no employer-employee relationship, since no such relationships exist in military service.

- The "marriage" between Colonel Meisel and Mr Steiner is not only unrecognised by the laws of the State of Israel but by the laws of nature, on the ground that same-sex couples cannot procreate, and thus, conceptually, cannot form a family.
- There is no violation of equality here, as a sexual relationship between two men does not create a family link, in the absence of the necessary conceptual element of procreation, even if they have a sexual relationship and a deep friendship. Nothing can be done against the laws of nature; there is no similarity between a family and a same-sex couple.
- Recognising Mr Steiner's claim would contradict Israel's Basic Law: Human Dignity and Liberty,[45] which protects the values of the State of Israel as a "Jewish and democratic state". The Bible, which is the fountainhead of Jewish values, prohibits "a man to lie with a man" (Leviticus 18: 22), thus making homosexuality incompatible with Judaism. Although laws may change, the basic values on which a nation establishes its state may not. By defining the State of Israel as a "Jewish state", the Basic Law could be attempting to prevent Israel from straying after the basic values of other nations. According to the literature, these values purportedly include religious values too. Homosexuality, therefore, contradicts the values of Israel as a "Jewish state".[46] The public in Israel is split as to whether a homosexual couple is equal to a heterosexual couple, as Kedmi's dissent in *Danilowitz* shows.
- Non-recognition of Mr Steiner as Colonel Meisel's partner does not contradict the values of the State of Israel as a "democratic state". His rights as a homosexual are not violated. Despite the Jewish position on homosexuals, since 1988, the State of Israel has not enforced a norm prohibiting such relationships. The state does not interfere with the private behaviour of individuals. The correct balance between the values of the state as "Jewish" and "democratic" is manifest in the law's permitting gay individuals to live their private lives according to their sexual orientation, while denying same-sex relationships recognition as families. If the State of Israel wishes

[45] Basic Law: Human Dignity and Liberty, 1992, http://www.israel-mfa.gov.il/mfa/go.asp?MFAH00hi0. On Israel's Basic Laws, see A M Gross, "The Politics of Rights in Israeli Constitutional Law", (1998) 3 *Israel Studies* 80, especially at 88–89. It should be noted that, although the Basic Law serves an important interpretive role, it cannot be used to invalidate a statute passed before the Basic Law was enacted in 1992, even if it contradicts the Basic Law.

[46] See Harel, *supra* n.1, at 271 (Judge Gherman means that excluding same-sex partners is not a violation of the principle of equality under the Basic Law because of the need to interpret it in light of the values of Israel as a "Jewish" state). As I read him, he is implying that, by engaging in homosexual relationships, Mr Steiner and Col Meisel were "violating" the "Jewish" values embedded in the Basic Law.

> to recognise homosexual relationships, it should do so through legislatio
> rather than through an interpretation "more crooked than straight".

The *Steiner I* decision illustrates what I called the "narrow *Danilowitz* Gherman reads *Danilowitz* as narrowly as possible, limiting it to the specif context of employment relationships. The *Steiner I* holding also points to th importance of the reasoning and rhetoric applied by judges in precedent-settir cases. Although the result and some of the reasoning in *Danilowitz* are unequi ocally progressive from a gay rights perspective, Gherman relies partly on th majority opinion in *Danilowitz* to support his own conclusion. A further flaw that he is oblivious to some of the majority statements and, instead, bases h decision on Kedmi's dissent. Gherman's use of the *Danilowitz* rhetoric th illustrates both the importance and the limits of rhetoric, when he arbitrari selects whatever rhetoric will support his conclusion and, at the same tim ignores the egalitarian spirit prevailing in the majority holding.

However, this is not the only flaw in Gherman's reasoning. Three rhetoric moves often used in anti-gay rhetoric in Israel, and outside Israel as well, appe in his decision: the biblical-religious argument, the "laws of nature" argumen and the "privacy" argument, which I analyse below.

The biblical-religious argument

Gherman's argument that homosexual relationships "contradict" the Bas Law: Human Dignity and Liberty because of the clause on "values of a Jewis state" warrants a discussion of this clause that is beyond the scope of this cha ter. I will focus on Gherman's assumption that endorsing Jewish values woul entail a condemnation of homosexuality. To support this assumption, Gherma relies on several Biblical and Talmudic sources, beginning with what h describes as the biblical prohibition on a man lying with a man. Leviticus 18:2 however, words its explicit prohibition as follows: "Do not lie with a man woman's lyings".

Assuming from this prohibition, as Gherman does, that the Bible has an thing to say about "homosexuality" is anachronistic. As many historians of se uality have shown, notably Michel Foucault[47] and David Halperin,[48] th perception of the person as "heterosexual" or "homosexual" is a modern ide related to the development of modern concepts of sexuality. According Foucault, "sodomy", as defined by the ancient civil or canonical codes, was category of forbidden acts, and it was only in the nineteenth-century that th "homosexual" became a person: "[t]he sodomite had been a temporary aberr tion; the homosexual was now a species".[49] Similarly, Halperin shows how th

[47] M Foucault, *The History of Sexuality, Volume 1, An Introduction* (New York, Vintage Book 1990), at 42–44.

[48] D Halperin, *One Hundred Years of Homosexuality* (New York, Routledge, 1990), at 15–40

[49] Foucault, *supra* n.47, at 43.

concept of sexuality as a constitutive principle of the self, and as defined by the gender of the object-choice, is a modern creation.[50]

Using these insights, Daniel Boyarin has suggested that neither the Bible nor the Talmud know the entity we call "sexuality"[51] or, for that matter, homosexuality. Boyarin and others have argued that only anal intercourse is forbidden in the Torah, and that other male-male sexual practices are not. This was the understanding of Leviticus in the Talmud, which itself fails to assume a hetero-homosexuality binary opposition. The Talmud, says Boyarin, sharply distinguishes male-male anal intercourse from other same-sex practices, arguing that only the former is included in the biblical prohibition on male intercourse.[52] Boyarin's conclusion is "that there is no evidence in the Hebrew Bible for a category of homosexuals or homosexuality at all, and whatever explanation is adopted for the prohibition of male anal intercourse, there is as little reason to believe that it extended to other forms of homoerotic practice".[53]

Quite the contrary, Boyarin and other scholars argue that the absence of a "sexuality" category allowed greater scope for other forms of male intimacy, eroticised and otherwise.[54] Nor is there evidence from biblical and talmudic culture that reactions to the violation of this rule differed in any way from those evoked by the breach of other taboos: desecrating the Sabbath was a transgression of the same order as male anal intercourse, and the latter did not constitute a different "species" of human beings.[55] Only after the modern production of a category of sexuality per se, of sexual identity determined by object-choice, does any form of physical intimacy between men become problematic.[56]

Gherman's use of the concept of "homosexuality", as if the Bible had anything to say about it, is thus flawed. He uses the modern understanding of "homosexuality" anachronistically, inserting it into a social order where this understanding did not exist. Gherman then, to use, *mutatis mutandis*, Anne Goldstein's remark on *Bowers* v. *Hardwick*, is obscuring the relative novelty of the distinction between "homosexuality" and "heterosexuality" with a myth

[50] Halperin, *supra* n.48, at 24–25.

[51] D Boyarin, "Are There Any Jews in 'The History of Sexuality'?", (1995) 5 *Journal of the History of Sexuality* 333.

[52] *Ibid.*, at 336–7. Moreover, Boyarin suggests that it is not same-sex eroticism *per se* that worries Leviticus, but rather sex-role reversal, or gender-deviance, which constitutes a prohibited mixing of kinds. *Ibid.*, at 341. See also S M Olyan, "'And with a Male You Shall Not Lie the Lying Down of a Woman': On the Meaning and Significance of Leviticus 18:22 and 20:13," (1994) 5 *Journal of the History of Sexuality* 179, at 185–186, 204–206; M Satlow, "'They Abused Him Like a Woman': Homoeroticism, Gender Blurring, and the Rabbis in Late Antiquity," (1994) 5 *Journal of the History of Sexuality* 1. Satlow says (at 6): "The Hebrew Bible forbids anal intercourse between men and imposes the death penalty on those who commit such an activity. Beyond that almost nothing can be said of any biblical 'view' of homoeroticism".

[53] Boyarin, *supra* n.51, at 353.

[54] Boyarin, *ibid.*, at 354; Satlow, *supra* n.52, at 24–25.

[55] Boyarin, *ibid.*, at 353–55; Satlow, *ibid.* at 24 ("[n]o evidence suggests that the rabbis defined people by the gender of the object of their sexual desire").

[56] Boyarin, *ibid.*, at 355.

about its antiquity.[57] Only through this anachronistic move can Gherman determine that the Torah views homosexuality and Judaism as "incompatible", and arrive at the doctrinal conclusion that an interpretation of the law in light of the values of Israel as a "Jewish and democratic state" requires the denial of Mr Steiner's equality argument. This type of reasoning may be understood as resting on what Janet Halley has called a "manipulation of act and identity":[58] the act forbidden in the Bible is unstably available for characterisation as a species of act *and/or* as an indicator of sexual-orientation personality.[59] In *Steiner I*, it is presented mostly as an indicator of such a personality.[60]

I must stress that, in my critique here and below, I am not arguing that Judaism has one clear position on sexuality, which is more "authentic" than the one adopted by Gherman and which I will follow.[61] Nor am I suggesting that the question of gay rights in Israel should be decided today in the light of Jewish sources. Rather, my discussion attempts to show how Gherman uses a questionable understanding of biblical sources to reinforce a stable, binary heterosexual-homosexual division built around the superiority of the former. Relying on queer theory, and specifically on Boyarin's work on Judaism, I seek to destabilise this binary hierarchy, and thus undermine the foundations of Gherman's reasoning.

"The Laws of Nature"

Gherman relies not only on Jewish sources, but also on the "laws of nature" that, purportedly, dictate that Colonel Meisel and Mr Steiner should not be recognised as a family because they cannot procreate.[62] Homosexuality is often described as "unnatural". As John Boswell has shown, the concept of "unnatural" continues to be used in the context of homosexuality, although it has been abandoned in nearly all others. Together with other "imprecise negations" (e.g. "unenlightened" and "un-American"), it serves today as a rallying point for hostility.[63]

[57] See A B Goldstein, "History, Homosexuality and Political Values: Searching for the Hidden Determinants of *Bowers* v. *Hardwick*," (1998) 97 *Yale Law Journal* 1073, at 1088–1089.

[58] Halley, *supra* n.3, at 1742.

[59] *Ibid.* at 1740. See also J Halley, "*Bowers* v. *Hardwick* in the Renaissance", in J Goldberg (ed.), *Queering the Renaissance* (Durham, Duke University Press, 1994), at 15–39. Halley uses cultural history to dis-authorise *Bowers* v. *Hardwick*. Similarly, I am using Jewish cultural history here to dis-authorise *Steiner I*.

[60] For a discussion of how "sodomy," before its de-criminalisation, was identified with homosexuals in Israeli legal discourse, see Y Yonay & D Spivak, "Between Silence and Damnation: The Construction of Gay Identity in the Israeli Legal Discourse, 1948–1988," (1999) 1 *Israeli Sociology* 257 (in Hebrew).

[61] Judge Gherman's view on "Judaism" and "homosexuality" is indeed resonant of the current Jewish Orthodox position.

[62] Compare *National Coalition for Gay and Lesbian Equality* v. *Minister of Home Affairs* (2 Dec. 1999), http://www.concourt.gov.za/archive.html (Constitutional Court of South Africa) (Ackermann J.), at para. 51 (a view of procreative potential as a defining characteristic of conjugal relationships is demeaning to many couples who for various reasons do not have children).

[63] J Boswell, *Christianity, Social Tolerance, and Homosexuality* (Chicago, University of Chicago Press, 1980), at 15.

Boswell addresses the assumption underlying Gherman's decision, whereby behaviour inherently non-reproductive is "unnatural". He points out that non-reproduction is a feature of celibacy, which was idealised in ancient societies, as well as of masturbation, which is considered "natural" in modern societies. Both these practices, he says, have reproductive consequences identical to those resulting from homosexual activity, and thus, "[t]his objection is clearly a justification rather than a cause of prejudice".[64] Boswell's argument, therefore, is that "[t]he objection that homosexuality is 'unnatural' . . . probably represents nothing more that a derogatory epithet of unusual emotional impact due to a confluence of historically sanctioned prejudices and ill-informed ideas about 'nature' ".[65]

Foucault identifies the "unnatural" as a specific dimension in the field of sexuality, which assumed autonomy regarding other condemned forms of sex, such as adultery. Up until the end of the eighteenth century, there had been no clear distinction between deviations from marriage rules and deviations regarding uses of genitals. In a process that evolved in the eighteenth and nineteenth centuries, "there appeared, on the one hand, infractions against the legislation (or morality) pertaining to marriage and the family, and on the other, offences against the regularity of a natural function".[66] Foucault describes these changes as part of the new persecution of "peripheral sexuality", entailing an incorporation of perversions and a new specification of individuals, which included the creation of the modern "homosexual".[67]

The distinction noted by Foucault is visible in the decision of Gherman, who argues that, from the point of view of "nature", it would be possible to recognise incest. Hence, says Gherman, from the perspective of nature, a daughter, for instance, may be recognised as the "reputed spouse" of her father, and a brother of his sister, because the two can procreate, even if the law does not recognise their marriage. This *dictum* draws the distinction that Foucault had noted between certain condemned forms of sexual behaviour on the one hand, and perversions considered to be "against nature" on the other. Under this distinction, only certain sexual offences are considered "unnatural". This distinction, says Foucault, was developed within the modern concept of sexuality.

Hence, a description claiming that an incestuous relationship would be recognised by the "laws of nature", whereas a relationship between two men would not, should be understood as a manifestation of prejudice incorporating the modern understanding of sexuality, and marking only a certain type of sexual deviance as a "perversion against nature".

[64] *Ibid.*, at 12. I agree with Boswell on this point, while disagreeing with his assumption that "gay people" are a transhistorical category. See also Jeffrey Weeks, *Sexuality and Its Discontents* (London, Routledge, 1985), at 63: "Nature, pure human nature, had very little to do with [the shaping of modern sexuality]".

[65] Boswell, *supra* n.63, at 15.

[66] Foucault, *supra* n.47, at 37–39.

[67] *Ibid.*, at 42–43.

Moreover, given Gherman's insistence that he adopted this interpretation in light of "Jewish values", it is worth noting that, as Daniel Boyarin has shown, "procreation was by no means the sole purpose of sex in rabbinic Judaism".[68] Contrary to a rabbinic perception of sex as meant only for procreation, Boyarin discerns in the Talmud "another view valuing sexual pleasure in its own right".[69] Although procreation was the primary purpose of sex, the rabbis also valorised such dimensions as pleasure, intimacy, and corporeal well-being: "[w]hen for whatever reason sex could not be procreative, its other purposes remained valid and valorised".[70] These insights into the Talmudic concepts of sex further undermine Gherman's reasoning in *Steiner I*.

"Privacy"

Finally, although Gherman's decision cannot be described as "liberal" by any means, it does resort to the liberal rhetoric of "privacy" and shows its impoverishment. Gherman, like Kedmi in his *Danilowitz* dissent, argues that the denial of the equality claim does not infringe on Steiner's right to live his life according to his sexual orientation, and that the State of Israel does not apply a norm prohibiting homosexual relationships. This narrow view of privacy illustrates the problematic nature of arguments for gay rights using this restricted liberal discourse, which is built around a strict public-private distinction.[71] At most, when successful, this argument can serve to decriminalise private sexual behaviour. It is useless, however, for any meaningful recognition of gays in the public sphere, and it may serve to push them back into the closet. In this use of the privacy clause, we hear echoes of the "liberal" argument, whereby what consenting adults do in their bedroom is their business, but "please do not make it mine". The claim that the denial of equality does not violate the right of individuals to live their lives according to their sexual orientation obviously ignores the demand for recognition in the public sphere that is essential to the equality of minorities,[72] and especially of gays.[73]

Looking at *Steiner I*, we see that it shares some traits with Kedmi's dissent in *Danilowitz*: the reliance on biblical sources, the turn to "nature" and reproducibility as indicators of what is "natural", and a clear demarcation of what constitutes a "couple". Kedmi and Gherman establish several hierarchical,

[68] D Boyarin, *Carnal Israel: Reading Sex in Talmudic Culture* (Berkeley, University of California Press, 1993), at 53.

[69] *Ibid*.

[70] *Ibid*., at 72–3.

[71] See K Thomas, "Beyond the Privacy Principle," (1992) 92 *Columbia Law Review* 1431 at 1509–13. For a fascinating attempt to rescue the "privacy" argument, *National Coalition for Gay and Lesbian Equality* v. *Minister of Justice*, (9 Oct. 1998), 1999 (1) SA 6 at 56–62 (Sachs J.), paras. 29–30 (Ackermann J.) (Constitutional Court of South Africa), http://www.concourt.gov.za/archive.html.

[72] See C Taylor, "The Politics of Recognition" in Amy Gutman (ed.), *Multiculturalism and "The Politics of Recognition"* (Princeton, Princeton University Press, 1992), at 25–73.

[73] See N Fraser, *Justice Interrupts* (New York, Routledge, 1997), at 11–39 ("From Redistribution to Recognition").

binary oppositions: "natural" vs. "unnatural", "Jewish" vs. "foreign", "couple" vs. "non-couple", "original" vs. "imitation", "heterosexual" vs. "homosexual".[74] They treat these binary oppositions as if they were some natural given, rather than as concepts the courts had a share in creating. Once we see how judicial texts are constitutive in the creation of these oppositions, we see how both the Kedmi and Gherman opinions are as much about heterosexuality as about homosexuality, and should be read, to use Kendall Thomas's terms, as juridical texts of discursive heterosexual identification and of the processes of homosexual differentiation by which heterosexual identity is secured.[75]

This attempt by both judges to secure heterosexual identity may be understood as a response to the threat that Mr Danilowitz and Mr Steiner pose to the social order of patriarchy. Gherman's identification of Mr Steiner's homosexual identity with the biblical interdiction on the act of "lying with a man a woman's lyings" is significant. It illustrates that what is threatened here is the patriarchal division of labour in the bedroom, which he, like Kedmi, is also intent on preserving.

Steiner II[76]

In contrast to the long argumentation in *Steiner I*, the second case, in which Mr Steiner sued for payment under the army pensions law, was decided in a brief two-page decision. This decision was given by an appeals committee in the Tel-Aviv District Court. Judge Shaul Aloni, who chaired the panel, defined the issue as whether the law applying to unmarried different-sex couples "reputed as spouses" should also apply to same-sex couples. In his answer to this question, Aloni conflated both the "equality" argument and the "recognition of couples" argument.

According to Aloni, equality, as determined in *Danilowitz*, requires that we recognise Mr Steiner as the "reputed spouse" of the late Colonel Meisel, because the purpose of the statute in question is to provide for the relatives of military personnel who died in service. Failing to recognise Mr Steiner's status would amount to discrimination, because had Mr Steiner been a woman he would have received the benefits. Thus, he is being denied the benefits because he is a man. This argument implies that denying Mr Steiner these benefits would amount to sex discrimination, but Judge Aloni also cites Barak's opinion in *Danilowitz*, which is based on the prohibition of sexual orientation discrimination.

Steiner II, then, falls under the rubric of what I have called the broad *Danilowitz*: a reading of *Danilowitz* as mandating equality to gay couples

[74] See J Jakobsen, "Queer Is? Queer Does? Normativity and the Problem of Resistance", (1998) 4 *GLQ: A Journal of Gay and Lesbian Studies* 511 at 523 (homophobic discourse is made up of a set of binaries, which are themselves incoherent).

[75] Thomas, *supra* n.4, at 42.

[76] Various Appeals 369/94, *Steiner* v. *Israel Defence Forces* (8 Jan. 1997), unpublished decision, reproduced in R Ben-Israel, *Equality of Opportunities and Prohibition of Discrimination in Employment* (Tel-Aviv, Open University, 1998), at 1010–12 (in Hebrew).

beyond the context covered by the EEO Law. The two readings are still competing, because *Steiner I* and *Steiner II* were consolidated into one cross-appeal, which ended in an out-of-court settlement granting Mr Steiner a significant proportion of the payment he had requested.[77]

The Family Court in Tel-Aviv vs. the Family Court in Haifa

Two decisions by two different Family Courts in Israel also illustrate the narrow and broad readings of *Danilowitz*. The narrow reading was reinforced in an October 1998 decision of the Tel-Aviv Family Court. The Court rejected a petition for a declaratory judgment holding that a gay couple were "reputed as [each other's] spouse[s]", and that the plaintiff was thus entitled to rights in the respondent's assets. The Court held that it had no jurisdiction to hear the case: the statute establishing the Family Court[78] gave it jurisdiction over litigation brought by a "spouse", which included one "reputed as a spouse". Judge Shtofman noted that *Danilowitz* did not hold that the "reputed as spouse" category includes same-sex couples, because the Supreme Court had relied in that case on the "statutory construction". And the equality principle discussed in *Steiner II* was not relevant to the jurisdiction of the Family Court, only to the determination of rights. Again, as in *Steiner I*, the Court's interpretation of the Family Court Statute follows the narrow reading of *Danilowitz*.[79]

Another Family Court, however, had earlier endorsed the broad *Danilowitz*. In June 1997, the Family Court in Haifa issued a restraining order prohibiting a woman from entering the apartment where her "life partner" lived, and harassing her in any way. The presiding judge noted that the main question before him was whether the word "spouse" in the Law for Prevention of Violence in the Family[80] included same-sex spouses. For this purpose, said Judge Glubinsky, we should look into the majority holding in *Danilowitz*, which "did not deny the possibility of interpreting . . . the term 'spouse' as including a same-sex spouse".[81]

Danilowitz Goes International: House of Lords vs. House of Lords

Recently, the *Danilowitz* holding has been cited in two important gay rights cases decided outside Israel. In the United Kingdom, the House of Lords cited

[77] For a description of the settlement arrangement, see Walzer, *supra* n.1, at 140. See also *Steiner III*, a petition by Mr Steiner for recognition as Colonel Meisel's "spouse" for the purpose of participation in military memorial ceremonies, memorial books, etc. While pending at the Supreme Court, the Minister of Defence settled the case by announcing that, for all non-financial purposes, Mr Steiner would be recognised "as if he were Colonel Meisel's family member".

[78] Family Courts Law 1995, 1995 *Sefer Hukim* 393 (in Hebrew).

[79] Family File 14480/98, *Roe v. Doe*, unpublished decision (in Hebrew).

[80] Prevention of Violence in the Family Law 1991, 1991 *Sefer Hukim* 138 (in Hebrew).

[81] Family File 32520/97, *Roe* v. *Doe*, unpublished decision (in Hebrew).

Danilowitz to support its holding in *Fitzpatrick* v. *Sterling Housing Association Ltd*. on the right of a same-sex partner to succeed to a protected tenancy.[82] And in South Africa, the Constitutional Court cited *Danilowitz* to support its holding that the same-sex partners of gay South African citizens should be granted the same immigration rights as the different-sex spouses of heterosexual South African citizens.[83]

Both cases deployed the *Danilowitz* decision as part of a growing transnational jurisprudence on the recognition of same-sex couples. The international effect of *Danilowitz* thus seems to be that of the broad *Danilowitz*. Nevertheless, within the judgments of the House of Lords one can find both the narrow and the broad *Danilowitz*. The majority of the Law Lords in *Fitzpatrick* held that the same-sex partner of a tenant could not be considered the "spouse" of a tenant under the Rent Act 1977, but could be considered a "member of the . . . tenant's family" under that Act.

Lord Slynn of Hadley deployed the broad *Danilowitz* to support the conclusion that a same-sex partner should be considered a member of the tenant's family, and quoted Barak's discussion in *Danilowitz* of the similarity between the shared life of heterosexual and homosexual couples. Lord Clyde agreed with Lord Slynn, but deployed the narrow *Danilowitz* in holding that the same-sex partner of the tenant would not be considered his spouse: in *Danilowitz* "the respondent . . . did not attempt to challenge the view . . . that a homosexual partner did not qualify as a 'spouse (husband or wife)' nor as a 'cohabitant publicly known as his/her wife/husband'". Both Lord Slynn and Lord Clyde thus used *Danilowitz* to support their identical interpretation of the Rent Act, one using the broad reading of *Danilowitz* and the other using the narrow one.

CONCLUSION: THE "LIKE HETEROSEXUALS" DILEMMA AND FOUCAULT'S "RELATIONAL RIGHT"

We have seen throughout this chapter that, in the aftermath of *Danilowitz*, the question of recognising same-sex couples in the Israeli legal system remains unsettled.[84] In the absence of a clear judicial decision, or of any formal legislative mechanism (such as domestic partnership registration),[85] the battle for

[82] [1999] 4 All England Reports 705. See Bailey-Harris, chap. 34.

[83] *Minister of Home Affairs, supra* n.62.

[84] Recent decisions (in Hebrew) include: HCJ 1799/99, *Berner-Kadish* v. *Minister of Interior*, 54(2) Supreme Court Reports 368 (2000) (permitting lesbian couple to register a California "second-parent adoption") (to be reheard by larger panel); HCJ 293/00, *A. & B.* v. *High Rabbinical Court* (19 March 2001) (rabbinical court had no jurisdiction to order a divorced mother not to be with her female partner in the presence of her children); Labour Case 3816/01, *Patrick Levy* v. *Mivtachim* (Tel-Aviv Regional Labour Court, 25 June 2001) (male partner of deceased man is "reputed spouse" for pension fund purposes).

[85] In the fall of 2000, Israel's then Minister of Justice Yossi Beilin announced that he is going to initiate legislation that will establish the institution of domestic partnership in Israel. However, under his proposed bill, the institution will be open only to different-sex couples.

equality in contexts other than the workplace must be fought on an issue-by-issue basis. Its success depends on the willingness of private parties, government agencies, and courts to adopt the broad reading of *Danilowitz*. In the cases discussed above, and in policy decisions that have not yet reached the courts, practice has not been uniform. In an important rejoinder to *Steiner I*, the Civil Service Commissioner announced in 1998 that it will pay out statutory payments, under a law similar to the military pension law discussed in *Steiner II*, to the partners of deceased civil servants, regardless of their sex.[86] In 2000, the Ministry of the Interior announced that it will recognise same-sex couples for immigration purposes, although to a lesser extent than it recognises married different-sex couples.[87]

Yet, in many other areas such as taxation and inheritance, same-sex couples are not yet granted recognition. Given the clout of religious parties in the Israeli political system, solving the issue through broad legislative recognition seems a difficult cause.[88] Much will thus remain dependent on possible legislative reforms in specific contexts, on the policies adopted by government agencies, and on the courts. In the labour context itself, where the EEO Law and the *Danilowitz* holding do secure equality, the picture remains complex. The *Danilowitz* decision probably helped to open many closet doors, but for many gays the closet is still a bar preventing them from enjoying equality in the workplace (eg, claiming benefits for their partner).[89]

One problem inherent in the litigation of the type discussed in this chapter is that it forces lawyers to argue that gay couples are "like" heterosexual couples.[90] Consider, for instance, the arguments made by Mr Steiner and cited by the judge in *Steiner I*: that Colonel Meisel and Mr Steiner had lived together for eight years, had maintained a joint household, had regular joint meals at home had travelled together, and had maintained a mutual relationship in which "none of the two maintained romantic relationships with a third party". Thi "like heterosexuals" argument did not win for Mr Steiner in *Steiner I*, but a similar one probably did help Mr Danilowitz in his case. Barak mentions in his reasoning that Mr Danilowitz has a "steady and continuous relationship . . with another man", demonstrated, "among other things, by a commo

[86] D Spivak, "The Commissioner of Civil Service: The Partner's Sex Is Not Relevant," *Ha-Zma Ha-Varod (Pink Times)* (May 1998), at 2 (in Hebrew).

[87] [Summer 2000] *Lesbian/Gay Law Notes*, <http://www.qrd.org/www/usa/legal/lgln>.

[88] Harel argues that the public understanding of the *Danilowitz* decision and other legal develop ments as endorsing and accepting homosexuality, as well as the growing visibility of homosexuali as a result of these legal changes, have politicised homosexuality in a way that will make furth progress for gay rights difficult. The conservative forces in Israel now realise that the dominance heterosexist norms is no longer an uncontested axiom of social life, and liberal activists may thus fir the opposition confronting them much more intense than in the past. See Harel, *supra* n.2.

[89] On the permanent presence of the closet in gay life, see E K Sedgwick, *Epistemology of th Closet* (Berkeley, University of California Press, 1990), at 67–90.

[90] On the use of other "like" arguments in litigation for gay rights, see J Halley, "Gay Rights an Identity Imitation: Issues in the Ethics of Representation", in D Kairys (ed.), *The Politics of Law: Progressive Critique*, 3d ed. (New York, Basic Books, 1998), at 115–146.

household and cohabitation in an apartment purchased through shared effort". Recall Barak's rhetorical question: "Is the shared life of two of the same sex different from those belonging to opposite sexes, concerning the cooperative relationships and the operation of the social unit?"[91]

Some may say that the answer to Barak's question should be "no". Others will say that the answer is rather "yes", or at the very least will argue that same-sex shared life is not built around the gendered division of labour typical of different-sex relationships. Still others may argue for other differences, and will want to allow for such differences in any event.[92] It is worth noting that Mr Danilowitz seems to have succeeded because his relationship was sufficiently "like" a heterosexual one.[93] I will not dwell here on whether Barak's rhetoric on this point was inclusive enough of possible varieties among same-sex couples. Although an argument can certainly be made for the claim that it was not,[94] Barak's analogy between heterosexual and homosexual couples does entail a recognition of the equal worth of gay life, albeit as measured by heterosexual standards. It is worth considering whether advocates of gay rights can make equality claims without relying on the "like heterosexuals" argument.

I would suggest that we should ponder whether it is altogether worthy to make the achievement of gay rights contingent on such arguments, and whether a real commitment to equality does not require us to find a way that will not discriminate against those who are not living in relationships of the "like heterosexuals" variety. A further question concerns the potentially problematic effect of reinforcing the "like heterosexuals" norm for unmarried heterosexual couples too, in that it might require them to adopt a certain model of relationship as a qualification for obtaining spousal benefits. Instead of fighting for the recognition of same-sex couples who are sufficiently "like heterosexuals," should we not perhaps be struggling against discrimination based on "relationship status"?[95]

[91] See Harel, *supra* n.1, at 267 (Mr Danilowitz and his partner may be "ideal partners for a test case"; the principle of equality requires the Court to stress their emotional bond, rather than a financial partnership and a shared household). While I agree that the focus should not be shifted away from the financial partnership requirement, focusing on the emotional bond could also be susceptible to the "like heterosexuals" problem.

[92] Compare MacKinnon, *supra* n.37, at 215–234 (sex equality doctrine judges women according to their correspondence to the male standard). Similarly, it might be said that the "like heterosexuals" argument judges gays according to their correspondence to the heterosexual standard. See also B Honig, *Political Theory and the Displacement of Politics* (Ithaca, Cornell University Press, 1993), at 190.

[93] Even when this argument wins, we cannot say that real equality has been achieved: a married heterosexual couple would have received the benefits in question just by the fact of having performed the act of marriage, without any inquiry into the nature of their relationship, which is considered legitimate regarding a gay couple.

[94] See Y Blank in *The Forum for Interdisciplinary Discussion of Law—Meeting No. 1: Thoughts on "El-Al* v. *Danilowitz,"* Tel-Aviv University, Faculty of Law (15 Jan. 1995) (in Hebrew) (Barak takes for granted the heterosexual model of coupledom and implements it on a community different in its sexual behaviour, in a way that benefited Mr Danilowitz and his partner, but would have caused couples not fitting this model to be denied recognition).

[95] In this section, I am sympathetic to Halley's concern that legal reformers, forced to invoke identity in light of the role of law in the building and protecting of identity-generated social

For instance, in a possibly more egalitarian arrangement, each person would be able to designate (an)other person(s) on whom he or she would like to confer certain benefits, regardless of the nature of their relationship(s). This type of arrangement might be fairer to single people, or to all those living in arrangements different from the "like heterosexuals" couple.

Michel Foucault saw the battle for gay rights as "an episode that cannot be the final stage", and spoke of the need for establishing homosexual lifestyles as cultural forms.[96] He did, however, recognise the importance of the first stage: "It is important, first, to have the possibility—and the right—to choose your own sexuality. Human rights regarding sexuality are important and are still not respected in many places",[97] but we must nevertheless go further. One way of doing this is to create new forms of life, relationships, friendships in society, art, culture, and so on:[98] "Rather than arguing that rights are fundamental and natural to the individual, we should try to imagine and create a new relational right which permits all possible types of relations to exist and not be prevented, blocked, or annulled by impoverished relational institutions".[99]

In considering the dilemma I posed above, we could thus turn to Foucault's suggestion. Rather than disparaging the struggle for gay rights, which he considers important, we should look beyond that struggle to the possibility of inventing new rights and establishing new kinds of relationships that might entail their own privileges, duties, and rights.[100] In Foucault's words:

> "We have to reverse things a bit. Rather than saying what we said at one time: 'Let's try to re-introduce homosexuality into the general norm of social relations,' let's say the reverse: 'No! Let's escape as much as possible from the type of relations which society proposes for us and try to create in the empty space where we are new relational possibilities.' By proposing a new relational right, we will see that non-homosexual people can enrich their lives by changing their own scheme of relations".[101]

Foucault is certainly not offering an easy way out of this dilemma. Ensuring success, in obtaining for gay people many rights they are presently denied, may require that we often turn to the "like heterosexuals" argument. Yet, at the very least, I believe we should try to develop modes of argument that will pave the way for recognising, as Foucault has suggested, all types of relationships.

hierarchies, may cross the "dangerous line" between advocacy and coercion. Halley, *supra*, note 90, at 118. Halley's conclusion seems to be that "[w]hen identity can be deployed to harm its own subjects, the search for equal justice also requires that we move beyond identity politics." *Supra*, at 140. But is it possible to challenge those identity-generated social hierarchies while "moving beyond" identity politics?

[96] G Barbedette, "A Conversation with Michel Foucault", (1982) 6 *Christopher Street* 36.

[97] M Foucault, "Sex, Power and the Politics of Identity" (Interview with Bob Gallagher and A Wilson), in P Rabinow (ed.), *Michel Foucault—Ethics—Subjectivity and Truth* (New York, The New Press, 1997), at 163–173.

[98] *Ibid* .

[99] Barbedette, *supra* n.96, at 38.

[100] See D Halperin, *Saint Foucault* (Oxford, Oxford University Press, 1995), at 79–80.

[101] Barbedette, *supra* n.96, at 39.

Section E—Europe

21

The Danish Registered Partnership Act, 1989: Has the Act Meant a Change in Attitudes?

INGRID LUND-ANDERSEN*

INTRODUCTION

IN 1989, DENMARK became a pioneer in the field of family law, as the first country in the world to introduce a Registered Partnership Act for same-sex couples.[1] Under the original 1989 version of the Act, the registration of a same-sex partnership carried the same legal consequences as marriage apart from a few exceptions: the right to a wedding in the state church (the Church of Denmark, which is Lutheran) and the right to adopt children jointly and to have joint custody.[2] Further, provisions of Danish law containing special rules pertaining to one of the parties to a marriage, determined by the sex of that person, did not apply to registered partners. Finally, provisions of international treaties did not apply to registered partnership unless the other contracting parties agreed to such application.

The main purpose of the legislation was political: the only way to achieve full social acceptance of homosexuals was to give homosexual couples almost the same legal framework as married couples. The legislation would be used as an instrument to change attitudes. This aspect was strongly emphasised by the Danish National Association for Gays and Lesbians.

In my opinion, the Registered Partnership Act has fundamentally changed the general opinion of homosexuals in Denmark. I can mention two examples.

* Associate Professor, Faculty of Law, University of Aarhus.

[1] Registered Partnership Act, Law No. 372 of 7 June 1989. The Act was adopted by Greenland (population 55,000) on 26 April 1996, but has yet to be adopted by the Faroe Islands, whose 45,000 inhabitants are the only Danish citizens without access to registered partnerships.

[2] See L Nielsen, "Family Rights and the Registered Partnership in Denmark", (1990) 4 *International Journal of Law and the Family* 297; M H Pedersen, "Denmark: Homosexual Marriages and New Rules Regarding Separation and Divorce", (1991–92) 30 *Journal of Family Law* 289; M Broberg, "The Registered Partnership for Same-Sex Couples in Denmark", (1996) 8 *Child and Family Law Quarterly* 149; I Lund-Andersen "The Legal Position of Homosexuals, Cohabitation and Registered Partnership in Scandinavia" in Eekelaar & Nhlapo (eds.), *The Changing Family: Family Forms and Family Law* (Oxford, Hart Publishing, 1998) at 397.

Firstly, in February 1999, the newly elected Member of the European Parliament, Torben Lund, formerly Minister of Health and a Social Democratic Party Member of the Danish Parliament, was invited to the Danish Queen's party for Members of Parliament. He was invited to attend the royal banquet accompanied by his younger friend, with whom he had lived together for a couple of years. They accepted the invitation, which caused huge—but very positive—media coverage. A month later, their partnership was registered civilly in the Town Hall and among the guests were the Minister of Justice and his wife. Torben Lund and his partner were photographed by the press together with the Mayor of Copenhagen.

Secondly, since 1 July 1999, registered partners have been allowed to adopt each other's children. The initiative came from a Member of Parliament—Yvonne Herløv Andersen—who is also a former Minister of Health and who has recently come out as lesbian. It is remarkable that there was very little debate in Parliament on the question of stepchild adoption.

SOCIAL AND CULTURAL BACKGROUND

The introduction of registered partnership for same-sex couples in Denmark has its background in the social and cultural traditions of the country. Denmark is a modern welfare state based on social democratic ideas. There is a long tradition of associations and interest groups, which often have contacts with one of the political parties represented in the Danish Parliament. The state religion is Protestantism (Church of Denmark), but only a minority of the population is religiously active.

As early as 1948, the Danish National Association for Gays and Lesbians ("LBL") was founded. In the late 1960s, the organisation became more visible when the student movement led to a more liberal attitude to sexuality. In 1984, the organisation put forward a proposal for legislation on homosexual partnership. The same year, two members of the organisation became members of a commission to study the legal, social and cultural conditions of homosexuals. The commission was appointed by Parliament after a proposal by parties outside the Conservative Government.

In 1986, the commission issued a report on inheritance tax suggesting that the surviving partner of a homosexual couple should pay the tax at the same rate as a surviving spouse.[3] A lower tax rate would give the surviving partner—who had been legally unable to marry the deceased partner—better possibilities of maintaining the joint home and continuing at the same standard of living. The same year, an amendment to the law on inheritance tax was passed by Parliament.[4]

[3] Report No. 1065/1986: *Homoseksuelle og arveafgift* (Homosexuals and Inheritance Tax).
[4] Law No. 339 of 4 June 1986.

Before the commission had published its final report,[5] a partnership Bill was introduced in Parliament in January 1988 by the Social Democrats, the Socialist People's Party and the Social Liberals. The commission then completed its report rapidly. The majority—six members—could not support the idea of a registration system. The minority—five members—were in favour of a Registered Partnership Act. In Parliament, the legislators were given a free vote and the bill was passed on 26 May 1989 by seventy-one votes to forty-seven with five abstentions. The debate was emotional, both in the press and in Parliament. The spokesman from the Social Democratic Party stressed: "This bill is an entirely necessary removal of a disagreeable form of discrimination". A member of the Christian Party stated: "The bill is so important for our society that we will put it on the same footing as the introducing of free abortion and of free pornography which have appeared to have many bad consequences. We find that it is a day of sorrow for Denmark".[6]

STATISTICS ON REGISTERED PARTNERSHIPS

Denmark has about five million inhabitants. It is assumed that approximately 5 per cent of the population is purely homosexual (or about 250,000 persons). This means that only a minority of homosexuals have registered their partnerships.

Persons in registered partnerships in Denmark on 1 January 1990–1998 (cumulative)

	Registered partnerships		Dissolved partnerships		Surviving partner		Total
	males	*females*	*males*	*females*	*males*	*females*	
1990	518	122	1	—	1	3	645
1992	1400	491	26	22	61	6	2006
1994	1777	704	105	79	130	14	2809
1996	2050	961	198	147	210	21	3587
1998	2275	1266	322	218	225	31	4337

Statistics Denmark, January 1999

From 1 January 1990 to 1 January 1998, a total of 4337 persons had registered a partnership (which means around 2168 partnerships), 540 persons had dissolved a partnership (which means around 270 partnerships), and 256 partners had died.[7] In comparison, about 31,000 marriages are contracted and about 12,000 marriages are dissolved annually; 18 per cent of marriages contracted in

[5] Report No. 1127/1988: *Homoseksuelles vilkår* (The Conditions of Homosexuals).
[6] *Folketingstidende* (record of debates in Parliament) 1988–89, pp. 10824–39.
[7] Only persons living in Denmark are registered in the statistics.

1990 were dissolved over a period of 6 years and 1 per cent of the spouses had died.

The number of men registering from 1990 to 1998 (2822) was nearly twice the number of women (1515) (registered + dissolved + surviving). However, in recent years more women than men have registered. The reason could be that a great number of men registered their partnership as soon as it was possible, because one or both of them were HIV-positive. Further, the number of registered partnerships with children has been increasing considerably, from 81 partnerships (1 January 1996) to 150 partnerships (1 January 1999) to 176 partnerships (1 January 2000). The children are mainly living in lesbian families, in which the partners are more likely to register when they become a family with a child.

Persons in registered partnerships in Denmark on 1 January 1998

	Registered partnerships		Dissolved partnerships		Surviving partner		Total
Age	*males*	*females*	*males*	*females*	*males*	*females*	
–25	45	30	8	3	1	—	87
25–34	523	321	130	100	28	2	1104
35–44	653	433	101	62	52	4	1305
45–54	606	339	52	35	70	10	1112
55–64	316	102	20	12	40	11	501
65–74	96	32	9	5	22	3	167
75–	36	9	2	1	12	1	61

Statistics Denmark, January 1999

Most of the persons in registered partnerships are aged 25 to 54 years. While 27 per cent of married couples were aged sixty years or more in 1996, only 9 per cent of registered partners were aged sixty years or more. Compared with the rest of the population, there is a higher frequency of well-educated people among registered partners.[8] The well-educated group is often more open to new ideas, and usually has capital from which they wish the surviving partner to benefit.

RECENT LEGISLATIVE DEVELOPMENTS

Adoption of a stepchild

According to the Danish Registered Partnership Act, 1989, section 4, the provisions of the Adoption Act regarding spouses do not apply to registered partners.

[8] See Report on "Registered Partnership, Cohabitation and Blessing", 1997, chap. 2, http://www.folkekirken.dk/udvalg/partnerskab (Danish with English summary).

The legislators considered it best for a child to have a mother and a father, and that children should not be brought up in registered partnerships. However, since 1 July 1999, a registered partner has been permitted to adopt the other partner's child, unless the child is adopted from a foreign country.[9] Stepparent (second-parent) adoption also means that the registered partners have joint custody.

The main reason for this reform is a new understanding of the term "the child's best interests". Firstly, it has been stressed that the child in a registered partnership often has only one known biological parent, because one of the parents is deceased, or the mother has refused to give the identity of the father to the authorities. Therefore, the child has an inferior legal situation to children in marriage, both in the case of inheritance and if the partnership is dissolved. Secondly, it has been pointed out that the new partner in practice provides for the child. When a parent enters into a registered partnership, the social benefits she was receiving as a parent living alone with her child will be stopped. Thus it is inconsistent that her new partner cannot obtain a legal relationship of rights and obligations towards the stepchild. The majority in Parliament found that adoption of a stepchild in a registered partnership was not a question of favouring a new partner, but a question of improving the legal situation of the child. The minority (the Conservative Party, the Christian Party and a small right-wing party) emphasised the child's right to have both a father and a mother.

In May 2000, the Department of Civil Law informed me that the number of stepparent adoptions in registered partnerships is not registered officially. The Department knew about six of those adoptions and found it likely that local authorities had given permission for several more.

Conditions of partnership registration—residence and nationality

Originally, a partnership could be registered only if one of the parties had his permanent residence in Denmark *and* Danish nationality. Since 1 July 1999, it has become easier for foreigners to contract a registered partnership in Denmark. Two persons who do not have Danish nationality may register if they have resided in Denmark for the preceding two years.[10] Moreover Norwegian, Swedish and Icelandic nationality will be treated as equivalent to Danish nationality, because their Registered Partnership Acts are similar to the Danish Act. For other countries with a Registered Partnership Act corresponding to the Danish Act, the Minister of Justice may designate that the nationality of this country will be treated as equivalent to Danish nationality.[11] The first country to be considered will be the Netherlands.

[9] Law No. 360 of 2 June 1999, s. 2, amending s. 4(1) of the 1989 Registered Partnership Act.
[10] *Ibid.*, s. 1, amending s. 2(2) of the 1989 Act.
[11] *Ibid.*, s. 1, amending s. 2(3) of the 1989 Act.

ARTIFICIAL PROCREATION

A Bill on artificial procreation was passed by Parliament in May 1997.[12] One of the main issues was whether women without partners and women with female partners should have access to insemination. After a passionate debate in Parliament, members were given a free vote. The majority voted to limit access to artificial procreation to married couples and cohabitees of opposite sexes (section 3 of the Act on Artificial Procreation). This was the first time in more than twenty-five years that the Danish Parliament had voted against the interests of lesbians and gay men. The view of the majority was that, for lesbians, childlessness is not an illness but the result of a choice of way of life. Further, a child has a right to have both a mother and a father. Thus, access to insemination for lesbians would not be in the best interests of the child, but would only accommodate the wishes of lesbians.

The argument of the "the child's best interests" was also emphasised by the minority. The spokesman from the Social Democratic Party was of the opinion that the "father-mother-child ideal" was too narrow in 1997.[13] The minority also stressed that, because the law does not regulate non-clinical treatment, lesbians cannot be prevented from being inseminated privately with sperm which has not been controlled for dangerous diseases, e.g., HIV. Therefore, the minority in Parliament found that it would be in the best interests of the child to focus on health reasons and not on morality.

Since 1997, there has been an ongoing debate about artificial procreation for lesbians and women living alone. In April 1998, a Bill to repeal section 3 of the Act was introduced in Parliament, but was not passed. The prohibition for lesbians has been bypassed in several ways. Since October 1999, a midwife, who has authorisation to inseminate, has helped twenty-eight lesbian women to become pregnant in her clinic. This practice has not been illegal because the Act on Artificial Procreation only prevents doctors from inseminating lesbians. Furthermore, it is possible for lesbians to order sperm from foreign sperm banks via the Internet. In reality, the prohibition only affects lesbian women who need medical treatment to become pregnant.

In February 2000, the Minister of Health introduced a very limited bill proposing only a longer period for safekeeping frozen eggs (from two years to four years).[14] However, the topic of artificial procreation has a high priority within the political parties. During the spring of 2000, several parties introduced numerous amendments to the Minister's Bill, e.g., repealing section 3 (Social Democrats and two social liberal parties) and, on the other hand, declaring that only doctors may inseminate with sperm so as to prevent lesbians from being inseminated in the midwife's clinic (Liberal Party). The most discussed question

[12] Law No. 460 of 10 June 1997 (in force on 1 October 1997).
[13] *Folketingstidende* 1996–1997, p. 7819
[14] Bill No. 183 of 2 February 2000.

was an amendment permitting payment for artificial procreation in state hospitals (Liberal Party, the Christian Party and a right-wing party).

On 26 May 2000, members of Parliament were given free vote, but most found that they had not had enough time to discuss the consequences of the proposals. As a result, the amendments to the Act on Artificial Procreation were rejected by 95 votes to 71. Some of the bills will be reintroduced and the debate will be reopened in Parliament.

CHURCH CEREMONY

Homosexual members of the Church of Denmark have expressed their wish that persons in registered partnerships might receive a blessing from the Church. The bishops appointed a committee to investigate this question in 1995. The committee published its report "Registered Partnership, Cohabitation and Blessing" on 21 May 1997.[15]

The committee reached the following conclusions:

- As a consequence of changes in family patterns, marriage no longer dominates as a framework for common life and the formation of the family, which the Church of Denmark necessarily must take into account.
- Registered partnership does not constitute any threat to marriage.
- Registered partnership is a new legal status that has not assumed clear contours.
- Marriage and registered partnership are similar, in that they constitute a personal and legally binding relationship between two people.
- Marriage and registered partnership are dissimilar, one of the reasons being that marriage is a relationship between woman and man, while registered partnership is a relationship between two persons of the same sex.
- It is reasonable for an individual member of the church to expect a church service, not merely in general but also in specific important situations during life.
- There is not in principle anything hindering the introduction of new rituals; the Church of Denmark has, however, a well-founded tradition of showing great reticence.
- A blessing in church is aimed at persons and not at institutions.
- The church's blessing is given in the belief that God will bless, and not by virtue of a special clerical authority.
- A ritual for the blessing of a registered partnership would be something totally new in relation to the tradition of the church; it will cause strife and alarm many people.
- The number of persons desiring a blessing in church of their registered partnerships is presumably very small.

[15] See *supra* n.8.

In the opinion of the committee, registered partnerships and homosexual relationships are not in conflict with Christian teaching and morality. The committee considers the biblical statements against the practice of homosexuality as among the Bible's culturally-conditioned historic statements which do not have a normative character. The Bible shall be read in the light of the culture of our time. Consequently, the committee did not find that there are in principle reasons against introducing a ritual for the blessing of registered partnerships.

In October 1997, the twelve bishops in Denmark discussed whether the state church should introduce a new ritual for the blessing of a registered partnership. The bishops had different attitudes to a church ceremony for homosexual couples, and were divided as to the interpretation of the Bible regarding homosexuality. The right wing of the church found that homosexual relationships are in conflict with the Bible's general ethical norms. The outcome of the debate was that the priests were given permission to bless a civilly registered partnership—a possibility which did not require a new authorised ritual. It will be left to the individual priest to decide whether he or she wishes to give a blessing to a homosexual couple.

A DECISION FROM THE SUPREME COURT

As of July 2001, there was only one published court decision about the conditions of partnership registration. In 1993, the Danish Supreme Court found that a registered partnership between two male Russian foreigners, M1 and M2, should not be declared invalid.[16] At the time, according to section 2(2) of the Registered Partnership Act, a partnership could only be registered if one of the partners was a Danish citizen with permanent residence in Denmark.

On 12 June 1991, M1's application for a residence permit was refused by the Department of Foreigners. This decision was upheld by the Refugee Board in April 1992. On 21 June 1991, the Refugee board granted M2 asylum and a residence permit. On 8 November 1991, M1 and M2 had their partnership registered by mistake in Dragør municipality, although neither M1 or M2 was a Danish national. Referring to his registered partnership, M1 applied again for a residence permit. The Department of Civil Law found that the registration of the partnership of M1 and M2 was void under Danish law. The High Court came to the same conclusion. In March 1993, M1 was given a residence permit because of his cohabitation with M2.

On 20 August 1993, the Supreme Court reversed the High Court‘s decision. The Supreme Court stated that, even though the nationality requirement could have been used to refuse to register their partnership, the annulment of an already registered partnership could not be based on the nationality requirement. M1 and M2 had fulfilled the conditions of a marriage: to appear at the

[16] See [1993] *Ugeskrift for Retsvæsen* (Weekly Journal of Law) 849–50.

same time before the competent authority and declare their willingness to enter into a contract of registered partnership with each other. Furthermore, the reason for the Danish nationality requirement was that registration of purely foreign couples was not appropriate, when registration would not have any juridical consequences in their own country.

THE LEGAL SITUATION FOR UNMARRIED DIFFERENT-SEX PARTNERS

In Denmark, around 20 per cent of all different-sex couples are unmarried and 46 per cent of all children are born out of wedlock. The Registered Partnership Act does not allow unmarried cohabitees of different sexes to register, nor is there any general legislation on unmarried different-sex couples. To solve the major problems in property relations that arise upon dissolution of unmarried cohabitation, the courts have introduced a legally-constructed model based on an enrichment principle.[17]

In 1999, the legal situation of the surviving partner was brought into focus. In a February 1999 report ordered by the Minister of Justice, Professor F Taksøe-Jensen of the University of Copenhagen recommended the appointment of a commission to investigate changes in the law of succession. With regard to different-sex cohabitants,[18] he pointed out two possibilities: (a) giving them access to registration solely in order to achieve the same inheritance rules as married couples; or (b) adopting new general legislation for unmarried couples that would apply selected provisions for married couples to different-sex cohabitees. The Minister of Justice has appointed a commission on succession for married and unmarried couples. However, a more general debate on this issue, extending beyond succession, has not yet started in Denmark.

CONCLUSION

The recent amendments to the Registered Partnership Act, and the recent debates about artificial insemination and the question of a church ceremony, have illustrated that the Registered Partnership Act has meant a change in attitudes. The legislation has served its purpose.

Since 1 July 1999, it has been legally possible for a child in Denmark to have two fathers or two mothers. The acceptance of this concept will probably be an important argument in the debate about access for lesbians to insemination, and

[17] See I Lund-Andersen, "Moving Towards an Individual Principle in Danish Law", (1990) 4 *International Journal of Law and the Family* 338–9.

[18] In Denmark, the legal situation for same-sex cohabitees who choose not to register their partnership is the same as for different-sex couples who choose not to marry, unless the legal situation is based on the fact that the partners are of different sexes.

could reopen the debate about registered partners automatically getting joint c
tody of each other's children, without the need for stepparent adoptions. It co
be argued that legislation should regulate the relationship between the perso
who in daily life take care of the child: in other words, the law should ackno
ledge the functional family.

22

"From Society's Point of View, Cohabitation Between Two Persons of the Same Sex is a Perfectly Acceptable Form of Family Life": A Swedish Story of Love and Legislation

HANS YTTERBERG*

THE TURNING POINT IN 1973

HISTORIC DEVELOPMENT IS a continuous process. It is therefore often difficult to identify a single event which radically changes the course of history. But from this rule there are, of course, exceptions. This is the case when we look at the development of the civil and legal rights of gays and lesbians.

Socially and politically, many of us would say that we find such an unusual historical landmark in the so-called "Stonewall uprisings" in New York in the summer of 1969. After years of police harassment in bars and other meeting places, gays, lesbians and transgender people finally decided that enough was enough and that they were not going to accept being bullied any more. That day in late June over thirty years ago, they started to fight back, and the modern political movement for gay and lesbian rights in Western society was born.

In Sweden, there was a corresponding turning point, with regard to law reform, although much less dramatic. Back in 1973, the majority of the Standing Committee on Civil Law Legislation (the "Legislation Committee") of the Swedish Parliament[1] included one and one-half lines in one of its legislative reports. Little did they realise what far-reaching effects their words would have.

* Associate Judge of Appeal. See http://www.homo.se (English versions of some Swedish laws at "This is HomO", "It is the Law"). Ombudsman against Discrimination because of Sexual Orientation (HomO), Stockholm, Sweden.

[1] *Riksdagens lagutskott.*

The Government had presented Parliament with a bill[2] containing proposals for a major reform of Swedish marriage legislation, repealing e.g. the rules on annulment of marriage and legal separation. Some of the older obstacles to marriage were also removed and new, very liberal divorce legislation was introduced. According to the rules of procedure of the Swedish Parliament, when the Government tables a bill, each Member of Parliament has the right to table motions of their own, e.g., suggesting amendments to the tabled bill or taking up subjects in related areas. Thus, in connection with this Government bill, some Members of Parliament tabled a motion[3] dealing with the legal situation of the "sexually deviant", i.e., gay and lesbian couples. More specifically, they submitted that there was also a need for a legal framework for the cohabitation of two persons of the same sex.

Although the Legislation Committee turned down the proposal, it felt the need to express sympathy—genuine or not is difficult to say—for what were perceived as the particular problems of this minority in society. In concluding, it therefore made the following statement:[4] "There are good reasons for taking into account the problems of homosexuals. It is evident that in a lot of ways these people are in a disadvantageous situation compared to cohabitants of different sexes". While declaring itself incapable of solving the problems of this group within the context of the Government bill before it, the Legislation Committee said that it "would like to underline that, *from society's point of view, cohabitation between two persons of the same sex is a perfectly acceptable form of family life*".[5]

Why am I making such a fuss over a line and one-half in a twenty-eight-year-old committee report? The statement certainly did not in itself alter the legal situation of gays and lesbians in Sweden in any way. But it marked a turning point for two different reasons.

Firstly, the statement constituted a declaration of the legitimacy of the issue of gay and lesbian cohabitation on behalf of the highest representative body of the people—i.e. the Parliament. From that day onwards, it was to become politically impossible for politicians, bureaucrats and government representatives alike to refuse to meet with representatives of the gay and lesbian community to discuss whatever problems they felt the need to raise. Certainly, this did not mean that government representatives had to yield to every demand put before them. Nevertheless, they had to engage in discussions with representatives of the gay and lesbian community, who could successfully claim that their legitimacy as partners in these discussions was founded on an official report of Parliament.

Secondly, the statement of the Legislation Committee constituted the first formal recognition in Sweden of the homosexual family. The idea that the capacity in a human being to love, or to be erotically attracted to, someone of their own sex, is a characteristic inherent in the personality of some people but not others

[2] Government Bill (prop.) 1973:3.
[3] Motion (mot.) 1973:1793.
[4] Author's unofficial translation (here and text accompanying n. 5).
[5] Report (bet.) 1973:LU20, p. 116 (emphasis added).

(i.e. the existence of homosexual individuals) had been expressed for around one hundred years. The Committee's statement was, however, the first legal breakthrough for the homosexual family. In that respect, its importance and impact on the development of gay and lesbian rights in Sweden over the next twenty-five years can hardly be overestimated.

THE REFORMS OF 1978–1994

Homosexual relations had been legal in Sweden since 1944. If such relations were not only legal, but from 1973 on also perfectly acceptable, the next natural step in the development was of course to target all remaining discriminatory legislation, whether in family law or in other areas. Two major reforms came quickly. In 1978, the ages of consent for homosexual and heterosexual relations were equalised at the age of 15.[6] In 1979, the medical classification of homosexuality as a mental disorder[7] was officially repealed in Sweden.

In the mean time, in 1977, a special investigating committee had been set up, which included Members of Parliament and was commissioned to look into the situation of gays and lesbians in Swedish society from many different angles.[8] It was to complete its task seven years later in 1984, and its report is still, in 2001, an important source of interesting information. The report shed light on the living conditions of gays and lesbians from a historical, anthropological and legal point of view. It also discussed issues like religion, employment, criminal justice, family law, gays in the armed forces, the educational system, research, gay and lesbian youth, culture, information, and health, and proposed some concrete legal reforms. The Committee noted "that the only certain difference between homosexuals and heterosexuals is that homosexuals are emotionally attracted to persons of the same sex. In the light of this background it is obvious that homosexuals should not be discriminated against".[9]

As a direct consequence of the report, in 1987, a specific provision was introduced in the Penal Code making it a criminal offence to discriminate against anyone on the grounds of his or her homosexuality when providing goods and services,[10] in both the private and the public sectors. Another new Penal Code

[6] Act (*Svensk författningssamling* (SFS) 1978:103), amending chap. 6, s. 4 of the Penal Code (*Brottsbalk*, SFS 1962:700), resulting from Gov't Bill (prop.) 1977/78:69, Standing Committee on Justice Report (JuU) 1977/78:26.

[7] World Health Organisation, Classification of Diseases, 302.00.

[8] *Utredningen om homosexuellas situation i samhället* (Committee on the Situation of Gays and Lesbians in Society).

[9] Report (*Statens offentliga utredningar* (SOU) 1984:63), *Homosexuella och samhället* (Gays and Lesbians and Society). Author's unoffical translation.

[10] Act (SFS 1987:610) amending chap. 16, s. 9 of the Penal Code, resulting from Gov't Bill (prop.) 1986/87:124. The 1987 Act uses the ground "*homosexuell läggning*" or "homosexual inclination". In 1999, specific legislation against employment discrimination was introduced and the Office of the Ombudsman against Discrimination because of Sexual Orientation was established. See SFS 1999:133 (using the ground "*sexuell läggning*" or "sexual inclination").

provision expressly protected gays and lesbians against acts of verbal abuse.[11] And the Homosexual Cohabitees Act[12] was passed. Then, following the examples of Denmark (1989) and Norway (1993), the Registered Partnership Act[13] was passed in 1994, albeit the 1984 report did not call for it. The latter two Acts were of major importance to the homosexual family.

UNREGISTERED COHABITATION

Sweden is the country within the Nordic family which has gone the furthest down the road of introducing specific, civil law, family legislation on non-marital cohabitation. In the case of heterosexual non-married couples, such rules are found in the Cohabitees (Joint Home) Act[14] and in other scattered provisions throughout Swedish legislation. The Homosexual Cohabitees Act[15] extends these rules to gay and lesbian couples, through an exhaustive list enumerating which provisions relating to opposite-sex couples also apply to gay and lesbian couples. The most important of these provisions is the Cohabitees (Joint Home) Act.[16] As a result, to a large extent, the same provisions apply to both unmarried heterosexual couples and to gay and lesbian couples. But it is important to recognise that there are still important exceptions to this rule of equality, which I will discuss below.

The cohabitation provisions presuppose that neither partner has entered into an opposite-sex marriage or a same-sex registered partnership, whether with the other partner or a third party, but that the couple is living together under "marriage-like" circumstances.[17] It is noteworthy that no registration or other special procedure is required for the cohabitation provisions to apply. This has been the main criticism of this set of rules. The application of the rules does not depend on any active choice on the part of the partners, because the legislation seeks to provide minimum protection to the financially more vulnerable party. If the objective criteria are met, and the cohabitation in the individual case is characterised by a certain permanence—no minimum time is stipulated—the rules

[11] Act (SFS 1987:610) amending chap. 5, s. 5 of the Penal Code, resulting from Gov't Bill (prop.) 1986/87:124.

[12] Homosexual Cohabitees Act (*Lag om homosexuella sambor*, SFS 1987:813), resulting from Gov't Bill (prop.) 1986/87:124, Standing Committee on Civil Law Legislation Report (bet.) 1986/87:LU28. The Act came into force on 1 Jan. 1988.

[13] Registered Partnership Act (*Lag om registrerat partnerskap*, SFS 1994:1117), in force on 1 Jan. 1995.

[14] *Lag om sambors gemensamma hem*, SFS 1987:232, resulting from Gov't Bill (prop.) 1986/87:1, Standing Committee on Civil Law Legislation Report (bet.) 1986/87:LU18.

[15] *Supra* n.12.

[16] The Homosexual Cohabitees Act contains a general reference to the whole Cohabitees (Joint Home) Act. This means that all of the provisions of the latter Act apply to gay and lesbian cohabitees.

[17] *Supra* n.14, s. 1; *supra* n.12.

apply. However, an "opt-out clause" permits cohabitees to draw up an agreement in writing stipulating that the rules do not apply to their relationship.[18]

The cohabitation provisions regulate the legal situation between the couple concerning their joint home and their household goods only.[19] Such things as cars, summer houses, and most importantly money in the bank, are not covered by these provisions.[20] Furthermore, only a home and household goods acquired for the couple's common use are covered by the Cohabitees (Joint Home) Act.[21] A home or goods acquired by one partner before the couple started living together, and not for use as or in the couple's joint home, are not covered by the Act.

As long as the couple goes on living together, each partner is still the owner of his or her own property and is still responsible for his or her own debts. However, the Act restricts what a cohabitee can do with the part of his or her property that constitutes a joint home and household goods under the Act, without the consent of his or her partner.[22] This is the same system as the one that applies to married couples. When the cohabitation is interrupted, either because of the death of one of the cohabitees or because of a decision made by the partners to break up, the joint home and household goods are all subject to a division of property.[23] This division—very roughly described—means that each of the cohabitees gets one-half as his or her share, independently of who has been the owner of what.

Cohabitees do not, unlike married or registered couples, inherit from each other if they have not drawn up reciprocal wills to this effect. However, if the cohabitation ends because of the death of one of the cohabitees, the surviving partner has the right to demand division of the property covered by the Act in the same way as if a voluntary breakup had taken place.[24] In this situation, however small the estate, the surviving partner always has the right to a minimum value share of the joint home and household goods (currently a sum approximately equivalent to 7500 USD).[25] This special protection clause can, in practice, lead to the surviving cohabitee walking away with more than half of the value of the joint home and household goods, leaving the legal heirs of the deceased cohabitee with less than half. Although cohabitees are not each other's statutory legal heirs, according to the Inheritance Code, a surviving cohabitee is still a party to the estate and the principally responsible administrator of the estate until such time as it has been distributed among the legal heirs.[26]

[18] *Supra* n.14, s. 15, para. 2; *supra* nn.12, 16.

[19] *Supra* n.14, s. 1, 2.

[20] However, a proposal (see *infra* n.28) to amend the Cohabitees (Joint Home) Act, currently under consideration by the Swedish Government, would provide that motorised vehicles aquired for the common use of the couple would be considered joint household goods.

[21] *Supra* n.14, s. 5, para. 1.

[22] *Supra* n.14, ss. 17–19.

[23] *Supra* n.14, s. 5.

[24] *Supra* n.14, s. 12, para. 1.

[25] *Supra* n.14, s. 12, para. 2.

[26] Inheritance Code (*Ärvdabalk*, SFS 1958:637), chap. 18, s. 1, para. 1.

Contrary to what many cohabitees believe, they do not have any legal obligation to support one another, unlike married or registered couples. But like such couples, cohabitees have no legal obligation to testify against each other in court,[27] and are considered each other's next of kin or nearest relative.

As a consequence of the technical structure of the Homosexual Cohabitees Act, which specifies exhaustively what provisions for unmarried heterosexual couples apply also to gay and lesbian couples, many such provisions have not been included simply by mistake. A recent study report[28] shows that, for no apparent reason, around forty different Acts of Parliament or Government Ordinances still apply differently to same-sex and different-sex couples. Apart from such haphazard discrepancies, there are substantively important exceptions from the principle of legal equality between heterosexual and homosexual cohabitees, important because gay men and lesbians do also have children.

Heterosexual cohabitees can have joint custody of children,[29] or obtain the assistance of the public health care system for the purposes of assisted reproduction.[30] Homosexual couples, so far, cannot.[31] With regard to the adoption legislation, the law does not distinguish between heterosexual common-law couples and gay and lesbian common-law couples, since only married couples are allowed to adopt children jointly.[32] But different-sex couples have the option to marry, whilst a gay or lesbian couple living in a registered partnership are not yet allowed to adopt.[33] Furthermore, statutory law does not make any person ineligible, on the grounds of sexual orientation, to adopt a child *as an individual*. However, in practice, gay and lesbian individuals have been denied permission to receive a child in their home for the purpose of adoption. The reason given has been that such an adoption could never be considered compatible with the best interest of the child.[34]

REGISTERED PARTNERSHIP

The Registered Partnership Act, which came into force in 1995,[35] aims to give gay and lesbian couples a legal framework for their relationships corresponding to that of a traditional marriage.[36] Registration is not open to a different-sex

[27] Penal Code, *supra* n.6, chap. 36, s. 3, para. 1.

[28] Report by the *Samboendekommittén* (Cohabitation Committee), *Nya Samboregler* (New Cohabitation Rules), SOU 1999:104.

[29] Parents and Children Code (*Föräldrabalk*, SFS 1949:341), chap. 6.

[30] Act on Insemination (*Lag om insemination*, SFS 1984:1140), s. 2; Act on *In Vitro* Fertilisation (*Lag om befruktning utanför kroppen*, SFS 1988:711), s. 2.

[31] *Supra* nn.12, 29–30.

[32] *Supra* n.29, chap. 4, ss. 3–4.

[33] *Supra* n.13, chap. 3, s. 2.

[34] See *Regeringsrättens dom* (Supreme Administrative Court ruling) RÅ 1993 ref. 102.

[35] *Supra* n.13.

[36] The Swedish Act is identical to the Danish and Icelandic ones, in the sense that it does not include any requirement with respect to the individual sexual orientations of the partners. It only

couple who do not wish to marry.[37] The obstacles to marriage are also impediments to the registration of a partnership.[38] This means that the same rules regarding the minimum age, the absence of a close blood relationship between the partners, and the ban on bigamy apply both to traditional heterosexual marriages and to registered partnerships. An exception to this rule of equality, however, is that heterosexual couples can be granted permission to marry below the minimum age of eighteen under special circumstances. This is not possible for gay and lesbian couples under the Registered Partnership Act.[39] The legal consequences of a registered partnership are also, with a few important exceptions, the same as those of a traditional marriage. The Act provides that legal provisions concerning a marriage and spouses also apply to a registered partnership and partners.[40] Thus, registered partners have an obligation to support one another.[41] They can take the same surname,[42] and they are each other's statutory legal heirs.[43] In the case of a divorce, they have a statutory right to division of all of their property, and not just their joint home and household goods, unless they have concluded an agreement in writing stating otherwise.[44]

The exceptions from the principle of legal equality all relate to issues concerning the relationships between parents and children. Thus, registered partners cannot adopt children, neither jointly nor individually.[45] Furthermore, registered partners cannot obtain joint custody of children.[46] And lesbian couples in a registered partnership do not have access to programmes for assisted reproduction through the public health services.[47] Swedish family law legislation is thus based on the principle of "separate but equal", or to be accurate, "separate—and not quite equal".

A peculiar thing, though, is that by virtue of Swedish private international law on adoption, a legally valid joint adoption of a child abroad by a same-sex couple, is automatically recognised in Sweden, in spite of the fact that such an adoption would not have been possible under domestic Swedish law. A condition for this is that the adopting parents were citizens of the country in which the adoption took place, or that they had their habitual residence there. If, however, the child was a Swedish citizen or had its habitual residence in Sweden, the

requires them to be of the same sex. This is unlike the Norwegian Registered Partnership Act, which stipulates that two *homosexual* partners of the same sex can have their partnership registered. However, in substance the four Acts do not differ from each other. The purpose of the Norwegian Act in this respect is simply to make its aim clear.

[37] *Supra* n.13, chap. 1, s. 1.

[38] *Ibid.*, chap. 1, s. 3.

[39] *Ibid. Cf.* Marriage Code (*Äktenskapsbalk*, SFS 1987:230), chap. 2, s. 1.

[40] *Supra* n.13, chap. 3, s. 1.

[41] Marriage Code, *supra* n.39, chap. 6, ss. 1–6.

[42] Names Act (*Namnlag*, SFS 1982:670), s. 9.

[43] *Supra* n.26, chap. 3, s. 1.

[44] Marriage Code, *supra* n.39, chap. 9, s. 1.

[45] *Supra* n.13, chap. 3, s. 2.

[46] *Ibid.*

[47] *Ibid.*, chap. 3, s. 2, para. 2.

Government's approval of the adoption decision would be necessary for it to become valid in Sweden.[48] Such an approval can also render legally valid in Sweden a foreign decision on adoption in other situations where the criteria for automatic recognition are not met.[49]

Another anomaly is that, although a registered partner cannot adopt his or her partner's child or obtain joint custody of such a child, under special circumstances that same registered partner can be ordered to pay child support for the partner's child. In exceptional cases, such an obligation continues after the child has moved away from home.[50]

A registered partnership is dissolved in the same way as a traditional marriage, and the consequences of the divorce are also the same.[51] This means, e.g., that there has to be a period of reconsideration of six months before a divorce can be granted, if both partners do not agree to the divorce, or if one of the partners has custody of a child of his or her own who is under sixteen and lives with that partner.[52] And a registered partner can be obliged to pay alimony to his or her ex-partner under the same conditions as a former husband and wife.[53]

The private international law conditions for registration of a same-sex partnership in Sweden currently require that at least one of the partners be habitually resident in Sweden for at least two years, at the time of registration. However, this minimum time requirement with respect to habitual residence is waived when at least one partner is a Swedish citizen habitually resident in the country. Furthermore, Danish, Icelandic, Norwegian and Dutch citizenship is treated in the same way as Swedish citizenship for the purposes of the Registered Partnership Act.[54]

PROPOSALS FOR FUTURE REFORMS

Reforms are being considered primarily in two areas. Firstly, a special investigating committee was given the task of evaluating the provisions on adoption, joint custody and assisted reproduction, to consider whether the legal differences between same-sex couples in registered partnerships and heterosexual married couples are well founded or not, and if they are found not to be, to suggest legal reform.[55] The committee delivered its report in January 2001.[56] In its

[48] Act on International Legal Relations concerning Adoption (*Lag om internationella rättsförhållanden rörande adoption*, SFS 1971:796), s. 3.

[49] *Ibid.*, s. 3, para. 2.

[50] *Supra* n.29, chap. 7, s 5.

[51] *Supra* n.13, chap. 2, ss. 1–2.

[52] *Supra* n.39, chap. 5, s. 1.

[53] *Supra* n.39, chap. 6, s. 7.

[54] *Supra* n.13, chap. 1, s. 2, as amended by SFS 2000:374; in force on 1 July 2000.

[55] Committee on the Situation of Children in Gay and Lesbian Families (*Kommittén* [Ju 1999:02] *om barn i homosexuella familjer*).

[56] *Barn i homosexuella familjer* (Children in Gay and Lesbian Families), SOU 2001:10, http://www.regeringen.se/propositioner/sou/index.htm.

report, the Committee proposes the repeal of all provisions currently in force that prescribe different treatment for registered partners in comparison with heterosexual couples regarding adoption, joint custody and assisted reproduction. The report is currently being considered by the Swedish Government and a legislative bill is expected to be presented to Parliament before the next general elections in the autumn of 2002.

If the proposed legislation is passed, registered partners would be able to adopt each other's children (step-child or second-parent adoption) just like married couples. They would also be eligible for joint domestic or inter-country adoption on the same conditions as married heterosexual couples. However, as is the case for married couples, registered partners could only adopt jointly, not individually. The case-law banning individual adoption by gays and lesbians who do not live in a registered partnership[57] would be overridden. But the proposed amendments would not change the fact that neither unmarried heterosexual couples nor unregistered same-sex couples are eligible for joint adoption.

In the case of joint custody, the proposed amendments would mean that registered and unregistered same-sex couples could be given joint custody of children on the same conditions as heterosexual couples. As for assisted reproduction, the proposed amendments would make public programmes on assisted reproduction available to lesbian couples, whether in a registered partnership or in an unregistered stable relationship, on the same conditions as for heterosexual couples. The proposed amendments also provide for statutory legal parenthood for the female partner of the woman giving birth to the child.

Secondly, the legislation regarding unmarried cohabitees, homosexual and heterosexual, has been evaluated by another special investigating committee in order to identify and eliminate any ill-founded legal differences between the two categories. The Cohabitation Committee presented its report[58] to the Minister of Justice in September 1999. The principal proposal of the Committee is that the two different legal systems of cohabitation be merged into one single Cohabitation Act, valid for both different-sex and same-sex couples, thus eliminating the legal differences between the two categories that are still on the statute book today. The issues of joint custody and assisted reproduction, with respect to same-sex couples, were left untouched by the Committee since they were being looked at by the separate Committee on children in gay and lesbian families.

Finally, will Sweden follow the Netherlands by opening up civil marriage to same-sex couples? In my opinion, neither tradition nor procreative capacity are sufficient reasons for excluding gay and lesbian couples from the possibility of marrying. Traditionally women had no right to vote but that, of course, was no reason to go on denying women the right to vote. The legal consequences of a marriage apply irrespective of whether the married couple has children or not.

[57] *Supra* n. 34.
[58] *Supra* n.28.

And marriage is still allowed for those heterosexual couples who do not want children, or for one reason or another cannot have children. Furthermore—as I have already pointed out—some gay and lesbian couples do have children. Why should these children be denied the allegedly optimal possibility of living in a family where the parents are legally married to each other?

No, objectively justifiable reasons for excluding gay and lesbian couples from the "M-word" institution simply are not there. As a consequence, in my capacity as Ombudsman against Discrimination because of Sexual Orientation, I have requested that the Swedish Government take the necessary legislative measures to amend the Swedish Marriage Code in order to make its provisions gender-neutral, and that the Registered Partnership Act subsequently be repealed. The unofficial response so far has been cautiously positive.

CONCLUSION

Many of the issues that I have touched upon in this chapter are of course the subjects of controversy. But it is also obvious that what was unthinkable in 1973—at least in legal terms—for the Legislation Committee of the Swedish Parliament, is the law today. As I tried to point out in my introduction, historic development is a continuous process. Thus, Swedish law on non-marital cohabitation and same-sex marriage has been and still finds itself in constant evolution. This story of love and legislation will continue, I am sure. To my mind, even countries where the idea of introducing registered partnership legislation similar to that in Sweden may seem very far away, will have to deal with the private international law issues arising from such legislation, i.e., the recognition or non-recognition in many different contexts of registered partnerships or marriages legally contracted abroad between two people of the same sex.

The discipline of private international law could very well prove to be the "Trojan horse" of the homosexual family and its legal recognition in different legal systems around the world. It is my belief that, for gay and lesbian families in Sweden, the rest of Europe, and the rest of the world, what we see now—in the words of Sir Winston Churchill—is certainly not the end, it is not even the beginning of the end, but it may indeed be the end of the beginning.

23

Small Change: How the Road to Same-Sex Marriage Got Paved in the Netherlands

KEES WAALDIJK[1]

INTRODUCTION

THE NETHERLANDS APPEARS to be the first country in the world where a legislative proposal to open up marriage to same-sex couples has become law and come into force. This landmark bill was introduced by the Government on 8 July 1999, passed by the Lower House on 12 September 2000, passed by the Upper House on 19 December 2000, and signed into law by Queen Beatrix on 21 December 2000.[2] The law came into force on 1 April 2001. In every other country where same-sex marriage has become a topic for intense social, political and legal debate, such legislation has yet to be adopted (as of August 2001). Test cases attempting to acquire full marriage rights for same-sex couples were more or less unsuccessful in Germany, Spain, New Zealand, Hawaii, Vermont, and indeed in the Netherlands itself. Legislation introducing a registration system more or less similar to marriage, but not called marriage, has been enacted in Denmark, Norway, Sweden, Greenland, Iceland and the Netherlands, as well as in Vermont. A greater number of jurisdictions has been providing some legal recognition of same-sex *de facto* cohabitation, and/or introducing a registration scheme with far less legal consequences than marriage. But so far the law of most jurisdictions in the world does not recognise the relationships of partners of the same sex at all. This begs the question: Why are the Dutch so fast?

In this chapter, I will try to answer that question, by describing the legal steps that paved the way for this legislation. I will present the Dutch road towards the opening up of marriage as an example of the working of what I call "the law of small change". By doing this, I will implicitly suggest that, and how, and when, same-sex marriage can be achieved in other countries.

[1] LL.M., Ph.D.; Senior Lecturer, E.M. Meijers Institute of Legal Studies, Faculty of Law, Universiteit Leiden, c.waaldijk@law.leidenuniv.nl, http://ruljis.leidenuniv.nl/user/cwaaldij/www/.

[2] See Apps. II, III. (App. means an Appendix to this chapter.)

THE LEGAL AND SOCIAL RECOGNITION OF HOMOSEXUALITY IN THE NETHERLANDS

At the outset, it should be noted that the Netherlands has not always been the leader in the field of legal recognition of homosexuality. Admittedly, homosexual acts were decriminalised as early as 1811, but only because the country was then integrated into the French empire (France having been the first country to decriminalise in 1791, and having exported that decriminalisation to Belgium and Luxembourg in 1792). The Netherlands may have been the first country in Europe where legislation was passed to equalise the minimum ages for homosexual and heterosexual sex (1971), but unequal age limits had never existed in Turkey (which decriminalised homosexual sex in 1858), in Italy (where decriminalisation for the whole of the country was completed in 1889), and in Poland (decriminalisation in 1930).[3] And although implicitly the Dutch Constitution has been prohibiting discrimination on the basis of sexual orientation since 1983,[4] explicit anti-discrimination legislation covering that ground only entered into force in 1992 and 1994, i.e. several years after Norway (1981), Denmark (1987), Sweden (1987), Ireland (1989) and several parts of Australia, Brazil, Canada and the United States had set an example.[5] Registered partnership legislation was invented in Denmark (1989), and first copied in Norway (1993), Sweden (1995), Greenland (1996) and Iceland (1996), before such a marriage-like institution was established in the Netherlands (1998).[6] And finally, as regards second-parent and/or joint adoption by same-sex partners, several parts of Canada and the United States have led the way, recently followed by Denmark (1999).[7] In the Netherlands such adoptions only became possible on 1 April 2001, when the law of 21 December 2000 on adoption by persons of the same sex came into force.[8]

[3] For a detailed overview of the history of the criminalisation and decriminalisation of homosexual sexual activity, see H Graupner, *Sexualität, Jugendschutz und Menschenrechte*, Teil 2 (Frankfurt, Peter Lang, 1997), and "Sexual Consent: The Criminal Law in Europe and Overseas", (2000) 29 *Archives of Sexual Behavior* 415.

[4] In 1983, a new Article 1 was inserted into the Dutch Constitution: "discrimination on the grounds of religion, belief, political opinion, race, sex or any other ground whatsoever is prohibited". The words "or any other ground whatsoever" were added with the explicit intention of covering homosexual orientation. See K Waaldijk, "Constitutional Protection Against Discrimination of Homosexuals", (1986/1987) 13 *Journal of Homosexuality* 57 at 60.

[5] See R Wintemute, *Sexual Orientation and Human Rights* (Oxford, Oxford University Press, 1997) at xi and 266 (updated at App. II to this book, pp. 781–88).

[6] Years in which the legislation came into force. See p. 462; Lund-Andersen, chap. 21; Ytterberg, chap. 22.

[7] See Polikoff, chap. 8; Casswell, chap. 11; Lahey, chap. 12; Lund-Andersen, chap. 21; N Maxwell, A Mattijssen & C Smith, "Legal Protection for All the Children: Dutch-United States Comparison of Lesbian and Gay Parent Adoptions", (2000) 17 *Arizona Journal of International and Comparative Law* 309, (1999) 3.1 *Electronic Journal of Comparative Law* (http://law.kub.nl/ejcl/general/archive.html). See also N Maxwell, "Opening Civil Marriage to Same-Gender Couples: A Netherlands-United States Comparison", (2000) 4.3 *Electronic Journal of Comparative Law*.

[8] See Apps. IV, V. The proposal for this law was prepared and approved parallel to that on the opening up of marriage.

Although not always first, the Netherlands can certainly be ranked as one of the most gay/lesbian-friendly societies and jurisdictions in the world. Is there any other country where, since the early 1980s, the percentage of the population agreeing that homosexuals should be as free as possible to live their own lives, and should have the same rights as heterosexuals in such fields as housing, pensions and inheritance, has been 90 per cent or more?[9] Or where anti-homosexual discrimination in the armed forces was declared unlawful by the highest court as early as 1982?[10]

All this can be attributed to various social characteristics of the Netherlands. For example, it seems that no other country is as secular as the Netherlands: no country in the world has a less religious population. The Netherlands prides itself on a firm tradition of accommodating all kinds of minorities. And it has often been claimed that the interaction between the various minorities, especially through their political, social and academic elites, is faster and more productive than in most other countries. Furthermore, the Netherlands has a less direct, and therefore less populist, democratic system (no referendums, no district-based elections) than many other countries.[11] The combination of these factors may have made the Netherlands the country most likely to be the first to lift the heterosexual exclusivity of marriage. However, this lifting has been a very slow process. Before describing that process, I shall first sketch the general trends of legal recognition of homosexuality in Europe. Against the background of these trends, it becomes apparent that the Dutch opening up of marriage is not out of step with the rest of Europe. The Netherlands is following the same trends as most other European countries. In that light, the opening up of marriage to same-sex couples is only natural.

THE PATTERN OF LEGAL RECOGNITION OF HOMOSEXUALITY IN EUROPE

If you look at the legislative history of the recognition of homosexuality in European countries, it seems that this process is governed by certain trends, that can tentatively be formulated as if they were "laws of nature". At the very least, there is a clear pattern of *steady progress* according to *standard sequences*. Since the early 1970s, hardly any European countries have introduced new anti-homosexual legislation. On the contrary, in almost all European countries legislative progress has been made in the legal recognition of homosexuality. And where progress has taken place, it seems to be following *standard sequences*: legislative recognition of homosexuality starts (most probably after some form

[9] *Sociaal en Cultureel Rapport 1992* (Rijswijk, Sociaal en Cultureel Planbureau, 1992) at 465; Martin Moerings, "The Netherlands" in D J West and R Green (eds.), *Sociolegal Control of Homosexuality* (New York, Plenum Press, 1997) 299 at 300.

[10] Centrale Raad van Beroep, 17 June 1982, (1982) *Militair Rechtelijk Tijdschrift* 300.

[11] I will leave it to sociologists and political scientists to substantiate these generalisations about my country.

of association of homosexuals and information on homosexuality has becom legal) with (1) decriminalisation, followed or sometimes accompanied by th setting of an equal age of consent, after which (2) anti-discrimination legislatio can be introduced, before the process is finished with (3) legislation recognisin same-sex partnership and parenting.[12]

The "law of standard sequences" implies two things. Firstly, that normall the next step only becomes possible after the previous step has been take (although this might sound tautological). For example, you could not logicall outlaw employment discrimination on the basis of homosexual orientatio while you preserve the criminal punishability of homosexual acts.[13] Secondly and more importantly, each step seems to operate as a stimulating factor for th next step.[14] For example, once a legislature has provided that it is wrong to trea someone differently because of his or her homosexual orientation, it becomes a the more suspect that the same legislature is preserving rules of family law tha do precisely that.

I have argued before that each step in this standard sequence is in fact sequence in itself.[15] Decriminalisation normally is a process consisting of severa legal steps, the equalisation of ages of consent often being the last step (which i turn may be split into two steps, as has happened in France, Germany and th United Kingdom, where the age difference was first reduced, before being abo ished several years later).[16] The same can be said about anti-discrimination (i Ireland, Denmark and Sweden, for example, employment discrimination wa only covered, fully or at all, by later supplementary legislation),[17] as well a about partnership and parenting legislation. And it is precisely in those mor detailed sequences that I perceive the working of what I would like to call th *"law of small change"*, which could be formulated as follows:

> "Any legislative change advancing the recognition and acceptance of homo sexuality will only be enacted,
> - if that change is either perceived as small, or
> - if that change is sufficiently reduced in impact by some accompanying leg islative 'small change' that reinforces the condemnation of homosexuality"

[12] For a few exceptions to these "laws" of steady progress and of standard sequences, se Waaldijk, chap. 23.

[13] There have been a few exceptions outside of Europe, e.g., Minnesota.

[14] K Waaldijk, "Civil Developments: Patterns of Reform in the Legal Position of Same-Se Partners in Europe", (2000) 17 *Canadian Journal of Family Law* 61 at 85. For political analysis, se Adam, Duyvendak & Krouwel, *The Global Emergence of Gay and Lesbian Politics* (Philadelphia Temple University Press, 1999) at 345; J Donnelly, "Non-Discrimination and Sexual Orientation Making a Place for Sexual Minorities in the Global Human Rights Regime" in Baehr, Flinterman & Senders, eds., *Innovation and Inspiration: Fifty Years of the Universal Declaration of Human Righ* (Amsterdam, Royal Netherlands Academy of Arts and Sciences, 1999) at 93–110.

[15] K Waaldijk, "Standard Sequences in the Legal Recognition of Homosexuality—Europe's Pas Present and Future", (1994) 4 *Australasian Gay & Lesbian Law Journal* 50.

[16] See Graupner, *supra* n.3.

[17] See Wintemute, *supra* n.5.

Clear examples of the working of the "law of small change" can be found in the process of decriminalisation of homosexual acts in countries like Bulgaria, the United Kingdom, Cyprus and Romania;[18] and in the piecemeal development of anti-discrimination policies and legislation with limited fields of application, with various exceptions and with limited enforcement structures all over Europe.[19] But let me now present, as a prime example of the operation of this "law of small change", the extremely gradual and almost perversely nuanced (but highly successful) process of legislative recognition of same-sex partnership in the Netherlands.

THE RECOGNITION OF SAME-SEX COHABITATION

Since 1979, Dutch cohabiting couples have increasingly been given legal rights and duties similar to those of married couples.[19a] One after the other, changes were introduced in rent law, in social security and income tax, in the rules on immigration, state pensions and death duties, and in many other fields. In none of these fields was any distinction made between heterosexual and homosexual cohabitation. Therefore, there was never a need for any specific law on same-sex cohabitation: all recognition was given as part of the recognition of non-marital cohabitation in general, and usually in the context of a more general overhaul of the rules of a specific field. Simultaneously, cohabitation contracts and reciprocal wills became common (among different-sex and same-sex partners), and were fully recognised by the courts. This evolution was more or less completed when it was made illegal for any employer, and for any provider of goods or services, to distinguish between married and unmarried couples.[20] The Netherlands seems to be one of very few countries in Europe where such discrimination on the basis of civil status has been forbidden.

With regard to parenting (a field where rights and duties traditionally were strongly linked to marriage), some gradual improvements were also made. In the 1970s, fostering children became a possibility for gay and lesbian and other unmarried couples. Having a homosexual orientation or relationship ceased to be a bar to child custody or visitation rights after a divorce. And providing

[18] In all these countries the decriminalisation of sexual activity between adult men (and women) was accompanied by the maintenance or introduction of various specifically homosexual offences, including bans on homosexual activity "in public" (United Kingdom and Romania), or leading to "public scandal" (Bulgaria, Romania and formerly Spain), as well as on "proselytism" for it (Austria, Cyprus and Romania). See Graupner, *supra* n.3; Scott Long, *Public Scandals: Sexual Orientation and Criminal Law in Romania* (New York, Human Rights Watch/International Gay and Lesbian Human Rights Commission, 1998) at 37–8.

[19] See Wintemute, *supra* n.5, and K Waaldijk, "The Legal Situation in the Member States" in Waaldijk & Clapham (eds.), *Homosexuality: a European Community Issue* (Dordrecht, Martinus Nijhoff Publishers, 1993) 71 at 81, 108–10.

[19a] See p. 777.

[20] General Equal Treatment Act of 2 March 1994, *Staatsblad* (Official Journal) 1994, nr. 230, Articles 1, 5, 6, 7 (in force since 1 Sept. 1994).

artificial insemination and other means of medically assisted reproduction to lesbian or other unmarried women, was never legally banned in the Netherlands—although four of the thirteen clinics for *in vitro* fertilisation have been refusing this service to women in lesbian relationships.[21]

Nevertheless, there are still certain differences between the position of married spouses and cohabiting partners. Normally, the latter will have to demonstrate that they have been living together for a certain period (three months, two years, five years). Some private pension funds still do not pay pensions to unmarried surviving partners, although unmarried employees generally pay exactly the same premiums as their married colleagues.[22] In the immigration rules, until 1 April 2001, a higher income was required of an unmarried person before his or her foreign partner would be given a residence permit. In the fields of tax, property, inheritance and death duties, it can be difficult and sometimes impossible to obtain (through contracts and wills) the same advantages as married couples. And numerous other small differences between married and unmarried partners can be found throughout Dutch legislation.

Until recently, the difference between marriage and unmarried cohabitation remained especially large in the field of parenting: a child born to a married mother automatically has the mother's husband as its legal father, who then automatically shares the mother's authority and responsibilities over the child.[23] An unmarried male partner of a mother can only become the legal father by acknowledging the child as his own.[24] (A female partner does not have that possibility.) Until 1986, unmarried partners could not have joint authority over their children. When the Supreme Court finally did allow unmarried parents to have joint authority over their children (until then a privilege of properly married parents), the Court withheld this new possibility from same-sex couples, thus introducing a rare inequality between unmarried same-sex couples and unmarried different-sex couples.[25] And until 1998, only a married couple (and neither an individual nor an unmarried couple) could adopt a child.[26]

Thus, although cohabitation had been recognised to a large degree in the Dutch legal order, there remained a variety of reasons why the exclusion of same-sex couples from marriage was seen as discriminatory and disadvantageous to the persons involved.

[21] According to the Equal Treatment Commission (opinion of 7 February 2000, nr. 2000–04 http://www.cgb.nl) such a refusal is prohibited by Art. 7 of the General Equal Treatment Act. In answering a parliamentary question about that opinion, the Minister for Health agreed with the Commission (*Aanhangsel* Parliamentary Debates II 1999/2000, nr. 930).

[22] This form of discrimination is specifically permitted by Art. 5(6) of the General Equal Treatment Act.

[23] Civil Code, Book 1, Art. 199 (a), (b).

[24] *Ibid.*, Art. 199(c).

[25] Hoge Raad, 24 Feb. 1989, (1989) *Nederlandse Jurisprudentie* nr. 741; *Kerkhoven v Netherlands* (No. 15666/89), declared inadmissible, 19 May 1992 (European Commission of Human Rights), http://www.echr.coe.int/hudoc. See Wintemute, chap. 40.

[26] Civil Code, Book 1, Art. 227.

FIGHTING THE HETEROSEXUAL EXCLUSIVITY OF MARRIAGE

As in some other countries, the exclusion of same same-sex couples from marriage and from certain marriage-related rights and duties, led to several test cases in the 1980s and 1990s. Some of these focused on particular privileges of marriage, such as joint parental authority, adoption, partner immigration, widow's pensions, or specific tax benefits. These cases were generally unsuccessful. In two other test cases, admission to marriage itself was claimed. In the case of two men, the Amsterdam District Court did not want to rule whether their human rights were violated, because it considered it to be up to the Government and Parliament to remedy any discrimination that might exist.[27] Two women lost their parallel case three times, finally in the Supreme Court on 19 October 1990.[28] It ruled that the exclusion of same-sex couples from marriage was not unjustified (and therefore not discriminatory under Article 26 of the International Covenant on Civil and Political Rights), because one of the legal consequences of marriage was that the spouse of a woman giving birth was legally considered to be the father of her child.[29] However, in an *obiter dictum*, which has since been interpreted as a clear signal towards the legislature, the Supreme Court referred to the "possibility" that there might be insufficient justification for the fact that specific other consequences of marriage are unavailable in law for same-sex couples in a lasting relationship.

The publicity around the two marriage cases (especially the men's case, which was actively supported by a popular gay magazine) ensured that the legislature was in fact listening when the Supreme Court spoke. Within two weeks after the judgment, the Minister of Justice, having been pressed to do so by a majority in Parliament, asked the Advisory Commission for Legislation to report on the issue. Further political pressure resulted from the decisions of over one hundred Dutch local authorities to start offering semi-official registration of lesbian and gay partnerships. In the absence of parliamentary legislation on this subject, these registrations had only political and symbolic, but no legal, significance. In the meantime, in 1989, Denmark had become the first country to enact legislation introducing registered partnership. Not surprisingly, the Advisory Commission for Legislation produced a report in 1992, recommending the introduction of registered partnership, more or less along the lines of the Danish model.[30]

[27] Rechtbank Amsterdam, 13 Feb. 1990, (1990) *NJCM Bulletin* 456.
[28] Hoge Raad, 19 Oct. 1990, (1992) *Nederlandse Jurisprudentie* nr. 129.
[29] See *supra* n.23.
[30] Parliamentary Papers (*Kamerstukken*) II 1991/1992, 22300–VI, nr. 36.

THE INTRODUCTION OF REGISTERED PARTNERSHIP AND SOME PARENTING RIGHTS

A bill on registered partnership was introduced in Parliament in 1994, togeth with a bill on joint authority and joint custody. Both bills were heavily amend on their way through Parliament, before they became law in 1997 and too effect in 1998.

The original 1994 partnership bill (introduced under a coalition government Christian Democrats and Social Democrats) still provided for many differenc between marriage and registered partnership. It proposed to offer the possibili of partnership registration not only to same-sex couples, but also to close relativ who were not permitted to marry each other (like brother and sister, parent ar child, grandparent and grandchild).[31] A new coalition government (Soci Democrats, Liberals and Social-Liberal Democrats) changed the bill in 1995 ar 1996 so as to base the formalities and consequences of registered partnership mo on the marriage model. The close relatives were thrown out of the bill, but t scope of the bill was increased considerably by also allowing (not closely relate different-sex couples to choose to be registered as partners.[32] Thereby, the Dut legislation diverged from the examples from Denmark, Norway, Swede Greenland and Iceland, where only same-sex partners can register.

The partnership bill was approved and entered into operation on 1 Janua 1998,[33] and together with the Registered Partnership Adjustment Act effect changes to more than one hundred existing statutes.[34] In many hundreds of pr visions, registered partnership is now put on the same footing as marriage. spite of this cumbersome method of amending legislation, registered partne ship is almost a clone of marriage. Unlike (unregistered) cohabitants, register partners do not have to wait for three months or more to get most of the righ and duties attached to marriage. And in the fields of tax, property, inheritan and death duties, partners that register are now in exactly the same position married spouses.

However, using registered partnership as a means to realise full equali appeared to be too big a step for the Dutch legislature. As a result, some aw ward exceptions were included in the partnership legislation. The three ma exceptions related to parenting, foreigners and pensions:[35]

[31] Parliamentary Papers II 1993/1994, 23761, nr. 2.

[32] Parliamentary Papers II 1994/1995, 23761, nr. 5, and idem 1995/1996, nr. 8.

[33] Act of 5 July 1997 providing for the amendment of Book 1 of the Civil Code and of the Co of Civil Procedure, concerning the introduction therein of provisions relating to registered partn ship (*Staatsblad* 1997, nr. 324). See App. I; W Schrama, "Registered Partnership in the Netherlands (1999) 13 *International Journal of Law, Policy and the Family* 315.

[34] Act of 17 Dec. 1997 providing for the adjustment of legislation to the introduction of register partnership in Book 1 of the Civil Code (Registered Partnership Adjustment Act; *Staatsblad* 199 nr. 660).

[35] The other differences between registered partnership and marriage (apart from numerous m takes and oversights in the partnership legislation) are minimal and include the following: (1) t

Parenting

The existence of a registered partnership generally does not affect the position of the children of either partner. For example, the registered (female or male) partner of a woman who gives birth is not deemed to be the second parent of the child.[36] Consequently, the partner will not automatically have any authority over, or maintenance duties towards, the child. The maintenance duties that married spouses have towards their stepchildren[37] do not apply to registered partners. However, for the purposes of tax law, all children of a taxpayer's spouse or registered partner are deemed to be the taxpayer's children, as are the spouses and registered partners of the taxpayer's children.[38]

Foreigners

Since 1998, registered partners have had the same immigration rights as married partners. However, until 2001, foreigners did not have the same right to partnership registration. A foreigner without a "residence entitlement" was not allowed to take part in a registered partnership—neither with a Dutch citizen, nor with another foreigner.[39] So each foreigner wishing to register as a partner first had to acquire a residence entitlement on other grounds.[40]

parties to a marriage marry each other through their declarations (Civil Code, Book 1, Art. 67), whereas the parties to a registered partnership are registered by the registrar (Art. 80a(5)); (2) a church "wedding" (which has no legal consequences in Dutch law) can only take place after the marriage has taken place at the registry office (Art. 67), whereas the parties to a registered partnership can go to church before the partnership registration takes place; (3) the King or Queen, or a person in line for the throne, does not need permission by Act of Parliament before entering into a registered partnership (Art. 28 of the Constitution requires such permission for a marriage); (4) even in the case of mutual consent of the married spouses, a divorce can only be obtained in court (Arts. 150–165), whereas in the case of mutual consent, a registered partnership can be dissolved through a contract (Art. 80c(c)); (5) the rules on separation (Arts. 168–183) do not apply to registered partnerships; (6) most rules of private international law, and rules based on international or European law, that apply to marriage have not been declared applicable to registered partnership; (7) some rules of Dutch secondary legislation might not yet have been made applicable to registered partnership; (8) in law, words like "marriage", "spouse", "divorce", "widow", etc., remain the exclusive domain of married persons (including married lesbians and gays since 1 April 2001).

[36] The paternity rule, *supra* n.23, still only applies to married husbands.

[37] Civil Code, Book 1, Arts. 392, 395, 395a. See *infra* pp. 450–51, for further developments.

[38] General Act on National Taxes, Art. 2, as amended by the Registered Partnership Adjustment Act.

[39] Civil Code, Book 1, Art. 80a (1), (2). It should also be remembered that in the case of two foreigners, at least one of them needs to be officially residing in the Netherlands; the same condition applies to heterosexual marriage (Art. 43).

[40] Parliamentary Papers II 1996/1997, 23761, nr. 11, p. 7; Parliamentary Debates (*Handelingen*) II 1996/97, p. 3143. It was not quite clear what exactly amounted to a "residence entitlement". A residence or settlement permit, or recognition as a refugee, would be enough, but a mere tourist visa certainly would not, according to parliamentary statements of the State-Secretary for Justice. See *infra* pp. 450–51 for the end to this confusing bit of discrimination.

Pensions

The surviving registered partner is entitled to a pension, but that pension may be much smaller than that paid out to a married widow or widower. Pension funds which had not yet extended their payments to non-married partners were allowed to calculate the pension of a surviving registered partner on the basis of only those premiums that were paid after 1997.[41]

In these three main areas of discrimination between marriage and cohabitation, the introduction of registered partnership did not end the discrimination, but only reduced it slightly. However, in the field of parenting, the differences between (same-sex) cohabitation and (different-sex) marriage were further reduced by two other laws that came into effect in 1998.

On 1 January 1998, legislation introducing joint authority and joint custody where one partner is not a legal parent came into operation.[42] A parent and his or her (same-sex or different-sex) partner can now obtain a court order giving the couple joint authority over the child of the parent.[43] Similarly a (same-sex or different-sex) couple of foster parents can now obtain a court order giving them joint custody over their foster child.[44] Such joint authority or joint custody entails a maintenance duty for both partners towards the child, and may be accompanied by a change of family name for the child. It also reduces the inheritance tax to be paid when the child benefits from the will of the "non-parent". Other parental rights and duties have so far not been attached to it.

A further change in parenting law came into operation on 1 April 1998. Adoption ceased to be a privilege of married couples.[45] Since that date, a child can also be adopted by a heterosexual cohabiting couple, or by an individual (even if that individual is living with a partner of the same sex).[46]

DEBATING THE OPENING UP OF MARRIAGE TO SAME-SEX COUPLES

After the 1998 reforms relating to parenting, the number of *legal* reasons why a same-sex couple could prefer marriage to registered partnership became almost zero (see above).[47] By 1998, a very great proportion of the (traditionally marriage-related) special rights of heterosexual couples had also become available

[41] Pension Funds Act, Art. 2c, inserted by the Registered Partnership Adjustment Act. This Act applies to collective pension schemes for public and private sector employees. Most Dutch employees are covered by such a scheme. See *infra* pp. 650–51, for further developments.

[42] Act of 30 Oct. 1997, *Staatsblad* 1997, nr. 506

[43] Civil Code, Book 1, Arts. 253t–253y.

[44] *Ibid.*, Arts. 282–282b.

[45] Act of 24 Dec. 1997, *Staatsblad* 1997, nr. 772.

[46] Civil Code, Book 1, Art. 227.

[47] See also *supra* n.35. And, although "marriage" is a universal status (recognised in all countries), it is hardly likely that Dutch same-sex marriages will get more (or less) recognition abroad than Dutch same-sex registered partnerships. Foreign authorities inclined to reject a same-sex marriage

to same-sex couples. However, this did not silence the call for the opening up of marriage. On the contrary, the social and political pressure increased. In retrospect, it seems that the whole legislative process leading to the introduction of registered partnership and joint custody, served to highlight the remaining discrimination caused by the exclusion of same-sex couples from marriage: the awkward exceptions listed above, and the *separate and unequal social status* of registered partnership as compared to marriage. With the introduction of the very marriage-like institution of registered partnership (alongside joint authority and joint custody, and individual adoption), the number of legal reasons *not* to open up marriage to same-sex couples was of course also approaching zero.

Politically, the time was right for it too. Since 1994, the Netherlands has been governed, for the first time in eighty years, by a coalition not including Christian Democrats. The current, so-called "purple" coalition, renewed in August 1998, consists of Social Democrats, right-of-centre Liberals and Social-Liberal Democrats. And they have quickly found out that family law reform is an area in which they can reach agreement fairly easily (as opposed to areas like the economy or the environment). Against that background, it became possible for some very "out" and skilful gay and lesbian and gay-friendly members of Parliament (in all three governing parties) to effectively push for fuller equality for same-sex partners and their children. Their efforts led to the adoption by the Lower House of the Dutch Parliament, in April 1996, of (non-binding) resolutions demanding the opening up of marriage and adoption to same-sex couples.[48] The Government responded by establishing an advisory commission of legal experts, the "Commission on the opening up of civil marriage to persons of the same sex" (the "Kortmann Commission"), which reported in October 1997.[49]

The Commission recommended unanimously that same-sex couples be allowed to adopt (either jointly or as stepparents), and that other parental rights and duties be extended to them. The Commission made this unanimity possible by simultaneously recommending that the conditions for adoption be made somewhat stricter. On top of the existing requirement that the adoption is "in the evident interest of the child",[50] it should become a requirement "that the child has nothing to expect anymore from its parent or parents".[51] That

(registered partnership), could pretend that it is not a "marriage" (that a registered partnership is not largely equivalent to a marriage), or they could invoke the public policy exception of private international law. See *D.* v. *Council*, discussed in Bell, chap. 37; Waaldijk, chap. 36; and at pp. 767–69.

[48] On 16 April 1996, the marriage resolution obtained a majority of 81 against 60, and the adoption resolution a majority of 83 against 58: Parliamentary Papers II 1995/1996, 22700, nrs. 18 and 14; Parliamentary Debates II 1995/1996, 4883–4884.

[49] The Kortmann Commission consisted of eight members (including this author) and was chaired by Professor S C J J Kortmann, who teaches private law at the Catholic University of Nijmegen. (i.e. the brother of Professor C A J M Kortmann, who teaches constitutional law at the same university, and who chaired the Advisory Commission for Legislation that recommended the introduction of registered partnership in 1992).

[50] Civil Code, Book 1, Art. 227(3).

[51] *Rapport Commissie inzake openstelling van het burgerlijk huwelijk voor personen van hetzelfde geslacht* (Den Haag, Ministerie van Justitie, 1997) at 24.

condition would, of course, always be met in the case of artificial insemination with semen from an anonymous donor.

By proposing this extra condition, the Commission accommodated a prevalent ambiguity in the current opinions about adoption (which is in fact a two-sided institution, both creating and severing parental ties). On the one hand, a great number of people would support the idea of adoption being used to give a child the security and benefit of one or two new fully responsible parents; on the other hand, many people are critical of adoptions being used to sever whatever links the child might still have with its original parent(s). It seems to me that this ambiguity, which surrounds the issue of adoption in general (and post-divorce stepparent adoption in particular), is central to the whole debate about the specific issue of adoption by same-sex partners.

By a majority of five against three, the Commission also recommended that same-sex couples be allowed to marry, the majority (including this author) considering it discriminatory to exclude gay men and lesbian women from this legal institution and its symbolic importance. The Commission was able to reach this majority conclusion by first agreeing (unanimously) that the presumed paternity of the spouse (see above) should not apply in the case of two (married) women. A child born to a married lesbian couple would therefore only have its biological mother as its legal mother. However, the Commission also recommended that the two married women would automatically acquire joint authority over the child (plus a maintenance duty towards the child).[52] Full legal parenthood for both women would only be available through the adoption procedure (during which the biological father, if known, could be heard).[53]

By thus removing the paternity issue (which had been the deciding factor for the Supreme Court when denying same-sex couples the right to marry, see above), the Commission further reduced the number of issues involved in the debate about same-sex marriage. And by simultaneously recommending that—in a lesbian marriage—the most important parental rights and responsibilities should be acquired at birth, and that the status of legal parent should be available to the mother's female partner through adoption, the majority of the Commission could nevertheless maintain that it was proposing full equality.

In February 1998, the Dutch Cabinet decided how it would act on the recommendations of the Kortmann Commission. It promised to prepare legislation giving effect to the unanimous recommendations on parenting, but not to the majority recommendation on marriage. As far as the question of same-sex marriage was concerned, the Government agreed with the minority of the Commission. The Government considered that the new law on registered partnership, together with the extended possibilities for joint authority/custody and adoption, offered virtual equality of rights for homosexual couples. The main reason why the Government was not prepared to create a fully equal status for

[52] For two women wishing to have joint authority, it would thus no longer be necessary to go to court. See *supra* n.43.

[53] *Rapport*, *supra* n.51, at 23–4.

homosexual couples, seemed to be that same-sex marriage would not generally be recognised abroad.[54] (The Commission had in fact carried out a survey of governmental family law experts in the Council of Europe. The outcome had suggested that same-sex registered partnership would be met with only marginally more recognition abroad than same-sex marriage).[55]

Parliament was not happy with the Government's response to the Kortmann Commission. In April 1998 (just before the national elections in May), the Lower House of Parliament passed new resolutions demanding legislation to open up marriage and adoption.[56] After the elections, the three governing parties renewed their coalition, and committed themselves in the coalition government manifesto of August 1998 to introducing (and passing) bills to open up marriage and adoption to same-sex partners.[57]

ALMOST THERE

The introduction of registered partnership in January 1998 had been welcomed by such large numbers of same-sex and different-sex couples that a real demand for same-sex marriage was to be expected. Anecdotal evidence suggested that many same-sex couples were not registering their partnerships, because they preferred to wait for real marriage. Nevertheless, during the first years of the possibility of registered partnership, a greater number of male couples, and a far greater number of female couples, chose to register than in any Nordic country.[58] In 1999 and 2000, the number of same-sex partnership registrations in the Netherlands was 1761 and 1600 respectively.[59] If you compare that to a total of around 87,000 marriages annually in the Netherlands, it seems that there have been *two* same-sex registrations for every hundred different-sex weddings. This is not a low percentage, because the number of persons enjoying a homosexual preference tends to be estimated as somewhere around 5 per cent of the total population, and many of them do not have the same reasons to formalise their relationship as many heterosexuals (most same-sex couples do not have, or plan on having, children; and if they do, having their partnership registered would hardly make a difference). And in comparison with Denmark, the percentage is quite high.[60]

[54] Parliamentary Papers II 1997/1998, 22700, nr. 23, p. 7

[55] *Rapport*, *supra* n.50, at 17–9.

[56] On 16 April 1998, the resolutions were adopted with the slightly larger majorities of 81 against 56 for marriage, and of 95 against 42 for adoption: Parliamentary Papers II 1997/1998, 22700, nrs. 26 and 27; Parliamentary Debates II 1997/1998, 5642–5643. See *supra* n.48.

[57] Parliamentary Papers II 1997/98, 26024, nr. 9, p. 68.

[58] See App. VI.

[59] The number for 1998, the first year that the Dutch partnership law was in force, was 3010.

[60] Since 1991 (the second full year the Danish partnership law was in force), the annual number of same-sex registrations has varied between 178 (1997) and 258 (1991), i.e. 0.8% or less of the annual number of marriages of 31,000. See J Eekelaar, "Registered Same-Sex Partnerships and Marriages—A Statistical Comparison", (1998) *Family Law* 561 at 561 ("the take up of the institution seems to be very low" in Denmark).

In a survey commissioned by the Ministry of Justice, it was found that eight per cent of the same-sex partners who did register would have chosen to marr if that option had been available. And 62 per cent of them said that they woul like to convert their partnership into a marriage, once that would be possible As their main reason for that desire, most respondents gave "full equality" o the notion that "marriage has more significance".[61]

Similarly, the interest of heterosexual couples in registered partnership (i 1999 and 2000, heterosexuals were almost as big a user-group as lesbians an gays together)[62] indicates that there is at least socially a significant differenc between marriage and registered partnership. According to the same survey, th reasons given by different-sex couples for preferring partnership over marriag include not only an "aversion to marriage as a traditional institution", but als the notions that "registered partnership is less binding than marriage" and tha it can be arranged more quickly and at a lesser cost.[63] These reasons cannot b referring to the *legal* aspects of registered partnership (in law, marriage and reg istered partnership are equally binding and cost exactly the same amounts o money and time), but presumably to the symbolic value socially attached to get ting married (as evidenced by the amounts of time and money required for tra ditional wedding parties). This is support for the argument that full equality fo gays and lesbians has not been accomplished by the introduction of registere partnership. This in turn explains why many lesbians and gays would rather ge married.

In the meantime, the continued push for full equality had led the Governmen to promise and prepare legislation to remedy the three main areas of differenc between marriage and registered partnership (indicated above):

Parenting

- Firstly, legislation was prepared to allow same-sex couples to jointly adopt a Dutch child, including the adoption of the child of one partner by his or he same-sex partner. This 1999 bill was signed into law in 2000 and entered int force on 1 April 2001. It contains the extra condition proposed by th Kortmann Commission.[64]
- Secondly, amendments to the rules on registered partnership were prepared t give registered partners exactly the same duties towards each other's childre as married spouses have towards their stepchildren.[65]

[61] Y Scherf, *Registered Partnership in the Netherlands. A quick scan* (Amsterdam, Van Dijk, Va Someren en Partners, 1999) at 22.

[62] See App. VI.

[63] Scherf, *supra* n. 61, at 21.

[64] See Apps. IV, V.

[65] These amendments were attached to the bill on the opening up of marriage for persons of th same sex, and therefore took effect on 1 April 2001. See App. II.

- Thirdly, a bill was drafted to provide for automatic joint authority over the children born in a registered partnership (of two women, or of a man and a woman). This bill was introduced in March 2000 and approved by the Lower House of Parliament on 27 March 2001.[66]
- Fourthly, there is talk of attaching further legal consequences to the joint authority that a parent and his or her partner may have acquired over a child.[67] It is uncertain whether this will lead to more than the introduction of certain provisions regulating *testate* inheritance.

Foreigners

In October 1999, a bill was introduced to allow a foreigner without a valid residence entitlement to enter into a registered partnership with a Dutch citizen, or with a foreigner who is a legal resident of the Netherlands. The bill was signed into law on 13 December 2000.[68] This law, which entered into force on 1 April 2001, makes the position of foreigners wishing to register a partnership identical to the position of foreigners wishing to marry under Dutch law: only one of the partners needs to have either Dutch citizenship or his or her domicile in the Netherlands.

Pensions

In July 1999, a bill was introduced to abolish the exception for registered partners in the Pension Fund Act. The resulting law entered into effect on 23 June 2000.[69] However, full equality was not achieved here, because a transitional provision allows pension funds to continue using the exception when calculating the payment to a surviving registered partner whose partner died, retired or changed to another pension scheme before the effective date of the law. This means that, for the next thirty years or more, a few dozen surviving registered partners will receive a lesser pension than surviving married spouses in similar situations. Such was the legislative "small change" which was necessary to break the opposition of the pension funds to full equality. An end to this small-scale scandal could come once the lesser pension is recognised (by the relevant pension fund, by a Dutch court, or by the European Court of Human Rights) as a discriminatory restriction of the property and privacy rights of the gay men and lesbian women involved.

[66] Parliamentary Papers II 1999/2000, 27047. After approval by the Upper House (expected in Oct.), it could take effect later in 2001. This bill also provides (in a new Art. 253sa in Book 1 of the Civil Code) for automatic joint authority over the children born in a same-sex *marriage* (i.e. a lesbian marriage).

[67] See App. III, para. 2.

[68] See App. I. (The same law contains a list of corrections of minor errors made in the legislation introducing registered partnership.)

[69] Act of 25 May 2000 (*Staatsblad* 2000, nr. 256). See *supra* pp. 445–46.

THE FINAL STEP

As a result of these bills equalising the position of (registered) same-sex partners and (married) different-sex partners, only one national rule of marriage law remained an issue: the presumption of paternity of the husband of the woman who gives birth. Not surprisingly, that presumption became the one exception in the field of national family law, when in July 1999 the Dutch Government finally introduced a bill concerning the opening up of marriage for persons of the same sex.[70] (The only other differences foreseen between same-sex marriage and different-sex marriages are in the area of private international law[71]).

The possible application of the presumption of paternity to lesbian marriages proved too controversial. This, in itself, should not be seen as the continuation of discrimination, because the Dutch rules on paternity are aimed at settling in law who is most probably the biological father. However, the second function of the presumption of paternity is making sure that, from the moment of birth, most children have *two* legal parents. This result could have been reached for children born in lesbian marriages by a rule which would merely state that the female spouse of a woman who gives birth will in law be deemed the second parent (or second mother) of the child.

This rule, too, seemed too big a step for many. This is strange if you take into account that it will soon be possible, through adoption, for a child to have two parents of the same sex. However, the compromise reached, first in the Kortmann Commission,[72] and then also in politics, is a useful one. This one legal difference between same-sex and different-sex marriage has been considered by most advocates of same-sex marriage as a tiny bit of "small change", which we would gladly pay for this important increase in equality. (The difference is indeed tiny, because from the moment of birth, both women will have parental authority over, and maintenance duties towards, the child, with full parental status being obtainable after a little while through adoption). On the other hand, the same legal difference can also be used to present the opening up of marriage to same-sex couples as really only a "small change" in the law. In line with what I have labelled the "law of small change", this perception must have improved the bill's chances.[73]

But even small changes take time. Originally the Government's aim was to let the marriage and adoption bills of 8 July 1999 become law by the end of 2000, so that they would enter into force in January 2001. The committee stages and plenary debates in both houses of Parliament took a little more time than anticipated. The final vote in the Lower House was on 12 September 2000. The

[70] See App. II.

[71] The Royal Commission on Private International Law is expected to report in 2001 on the question of which changes in this area of law are necessary as a result of the opening up of marriage.

[72] See *supra* nn.49, 51.

[73] See *supra* p. 440.

proposal to open up marriage was approved with a majority of 109 against 33 votes, and the adoption proposal with a similar but uncounted majority.[74] On 19 December 2000, both bills gained an (uncounted) majority in the Upper House, and two days later the Queen and her State-Secretary for Justice, Mr M J Cohen, signed them into law.[75]

In the meantime, a separate law was needed to adjust the language of other legislation to the opening up of marriage.[76] This Adjustment Act introduces gender-neutral language into provisions that formerly used gender-specific words for parents and spouses (e.g. in the definitions of polygamy and half-orphans). The Act replaces the old rule, that the child benefit to which all parents are entitled is paid to the mother in the event of a disagreement between father and mother, by a gender-neutral rule; now the benefit office will decide to whom to pay the benefit in such circumstances. And the Act also specifies that an intercountry adoption will only be possible by different-sex married couples or by one individual (this is so because the authorities in the original country of the child would not allow it to be adopted by Dutch same-sex partners).

The Act on the Opening Up of Marriage, the Adoption Act and the Adjustment Act took effect on 1 April 2001. At the stroke of midnight the first four same-sex couples had their registered partnerships converted into full civil marriages. Later that month, 300 registered same-sex couples did likewise, and 82 unregistered same-sex couples married.

The passage of the marriage and adoption bills became possible because of the constant reduction in the Netherlands of the number of issues involved in the opening up of marriage, which made it into a topic that could be discussed in an orderly and reasonable fashion. In such an orderly discussion, it could more easily be established that there is hardly a reasonable argument against it. In fact, the debate could focus on whether there were any acceptable arguments against reducing the legal distinctions between same-sex and different-sex partners *a little further*.

The difference between the Netherlands and other jurisdictions in the world is that the debate in other jurisdictions remains burdened with all kinds of issues that really should be divorced from the notion of marriage: the position of churches, tax revenues, the burdens of social security, the influx of foreigners, the finances of pension funds, the upbringing of children, the plight of adoptive children, the integrity of family trees, etc. So what to mankind may seem a giant step—the opening up of the institution of marriage to same-sex couples—is, for the Dutch, only a small change.

[74] Parliamentary Debates II 1999/2000, pp. 6468–6469. All but two members of the opposition Christian Democrat Party voted against both bills, as did the small strict Protestant parties. All liberal and left-of-centre parties voted in favour.

[75] See Apps. II, IV.

[76] *Staatsblad* 2001, nr. 128, resulting from Parliamentary Papers II 1999/2000, 27256, nr. 2 (introduced on 22 Aug. 2000, approved by the Lower House on 30 Jan. 2001, approved by the Upper House on 6 March 2001, signed into law on 8 March 2001).

APPENDIX I

TEXT OF THE KEY ARTICLES ON REGISTERED PARTNERSHIP IN THE DUTCH CIVIL CODE[77]

The incorporation of the new civil status of "registered partner" into Dutch legislatio has been effected by a series of Acts. The two most important acts are the Act of 5 Jul 1997 amending Book 1 of the Civil Code and of the Code of Civil Procedure, concernin the introduction therein of provisions relating to registered partnership (*Staatsblad* 199 nr. 324); and the Act of 17 December 1997 providing for the adjustment of legislation t the introduction of registered partnership in Book 1 of the Civil Code (Registere Partnership Adjustment Act; *Staatsblad* 1997, nr. 660). Both laws came into operation o 1 January 1998, and effected changes in more than one hundred existing statutes. In Boo 1 of the Civil Code several new articles were introduced, especially articles 80a to 80 These and other articles have since been amended by the acts opening up marriage an adoption for persons of the same sex (see Appendices II to V), and by the Act of 1 December 2000 (*Staatsblad* 2001, nr. 11). All three acts entered into force on 1 April 200 The resulting text of the key articles is as follows:

"Article 80a
(1) A person can simultaneously be in a registered partnership with one other perso only.
(2) Those who enter into a registered partnership, may not already be married to some one.
(3) Registration of partnership is effected by a document of registration of partnershi drawn up by a registrar. . . ."

The further paragraphs of Article 80a declare applicable almost all provisions on the for malities of contracting a marriage. Article 80b declares applicable all provisions on th mutual rights and duties of married spouses and on matrimonial property.

"Article 80c
The registered partnership ends:
(a) by death;
(b) by disappearance of one partner followed by a new registered partnership or by marriage of the other partner . . .;
(c) with mutual consent by the registrar's recording . . . of a dated declaration, signed b both partners and by one or more advocates or public notaries, stating that, and a what moment, the partners have concluded a contract relating to the termination c the registered partnership [as specified in Article 80d];

[77] All the translations in Apps. I to V to this chapter are unofficial translations by this autho who is not a professional translator. Regularly updated versions can be found at http://ruljis leidenuniv.nl/user/cwaaldij/www/. Before publishing any of these translations elsewhere please con sult with: c.waaldijk@law.leidenuniv.nl. Text between square brackets or in footnotes is not translation, but additional information.

(d) by [judicial] dissolution at the request of one partner [as specified in article 80e, which declares applicable the provisions on marital divorce];
(e) by conversion of a registered partnership into a marriage [as specified in article 80g]."

The hundreds of other new or amended articles merely state that certain (groups of) provisions relating to the procedures and/or consequences of marriage are also applicable to registered partnership. Thus, registered partnership is almost identical to marriage.[78] If a private law document (such as a contract or a will) attaches significance to someone's being married, and the document dates from before 1998, then the transitional provision of Article V of the Act of 5 July 1997 provides that the same significance will be attached to someone's being registered as partner. But if the document dates from after 31 December 1997, then such equality can only be based on the General Equal Treatment Act, which not only prohibits direct and indirect discrimination based on sexual orientation, but also discrimination based on civil status. The status of being a registered partner is now considered to be a new civil status. Because the General Equal Treatment Act only applies to employment and the provision of goods and services, private discrimination between married and registered partners in other fields might not always be unlawful.

APPENDIX II

TEXT OF DUTCH ACT ON THE OPENING UP OF MARRIAGE FOR SAME-SEX PARTNERS

Staatsblad van het Koninkrijk der Nederlanden
(Official Journal of the Kingdom of the Netherlands), 2001, nr. 9 (11 January)

Act of 21 December 2000 amending Book 1 of the Civil Code, concerning the opening up of marriage for persons of the same sex (Act on the Opening Up of Marriage)[79]

We Beatrix . . . considering that it is desirable to open up marriage for persons of the same sex and to amend Book 1 of the Civil Code accordingly;
Article I . . .
(D)
Amendment of Article 28.[80] . . .
(E)
Article 30 shall read as follows: "Article 30 (1) A marriage can be contracted by two persons of different sex or of the same sex. (2) The law only considers marriage in its civil relations".[81]

[78] See *supra* pp. 445–46, 450–51 and n. 35 for the remaining differences.
[79] *Wet openstelling huwelijk, Staatsblad* 2001, nr. 9, http://www.eerstekamer.nl/9202266/d/w26672st.pdf. The Act resulted from a Bill introduced by the Government on 8 July 1999 (Parliamentary Papers II 1998/1999, 26672, nr. 2), amended by the Government on 3 May 2000 and 4 August 2000, adopted by the Lower House of Parliament on 12 Sept. 2000 and by the Upper House on 19 Dec. 2000, and signed into law on 21 Dec. 2000. It entered into force on 1 April 2001. See also *supra* nn.76, 77.
[80] This article lists the conditions to be fulfilled if a transsexual wishes the sex on his or her birth certificate to be changed. The condition of not being married is now deleted.
[81] New Art. 30(2) was previously the whole text of Art. 30.

(F)
Article 33 shall read as follows: "Article 33 Through marriage a person can at the same time only be linked with one person".[82]
(G)
Amendment of Article 41.[83]
(H)
A new Article 77a shall be inserted: "Article 77a (1). When two persons indicate to the registrar of the domicile of one of them that they would like their marriage to be converted into a registered partnership, the registrar can make a record of conversion to that effect. . . . (3) A conversion terminates the marriage and starts the registered partnership on the moment the record of conversion is registered in the register of registered partnerships. The conversion does not affect the paternity over children born before the conversion". . . .
(J)
Amendment of Article 80a.[84] . . .
(L)
A new Article [80g] shall be inserted: "Article [80g] (1).When two persons indicate to the registrar of the domicile of one of them that they would like their registered partnership to be converted into a marriage, the registrar can make a record of conversion to that effect. . . . (3) A conversion terminates the registered partnership and starts the marriage on the moment the record of conversion is registered in the register of marriages. The conversion does not affect the paternity over children born before the conversion". . . .
(N)
Article 395 shall read as follows: "Article 395 Without prejudice to article 395a, a stepparent is obliged to provide the costs of living for the minor children of his spouse or registered partner, but only during his marriage or registered partnership and only if they belong to his nuclear family".[85]
(O)
Article 395a(2) shall read as follows: "(2) A stepparent is obliged to provide [the costs of living and of studying] for the adult children of his spouse or registered partner, but only during his marriage or registered partnership and only if they belong to his nuclear family and are under the age of 21".[86] . . .
Article III
Within five years after the entering into force of this Act, Our Minister of Justice shall send Parliament a report on the effects of this Act in practice with special reference to the relation to registered partnership.

[82] Previously, Art. 33 only outlawed heterosexual polygamy.
[83] Insertion of the words "brothers" and "sisters" into the provisions that previously only outlawed marriages between siblings if they were of different sexes (and between descendant and ascendant).
[84] The minimum age for marriage and registered partnership is eighteen, but it is reduced to sixteen if the woman is pregnant or has given birth. Previously, this reduction was only possible for marriage.
[85] Previously, Arts. 395 and 395a only applied to marriage, not to registered partnership.
[86] *Ibid.*

Article IV
This Act shall enter into force on a date to be determined by royal decree.[87]
Article V
This Act shall be cited as: Act on the Opening Up of Marriage.
. . . Given in The Hague, 21 December 2000: Beatrix
The State-Secretary for Justice: M.J. Cohen

APPENDIX III

EXPLANATORY MEMORANDUM ACCOMPANYING THE ORIGINAL BILL ON THE OPENING UP OF MARRIAGE FOR SAME-SEX PARTNERS[88]

". . . 1. History

. . . From the government's manifesto of 1998 (Parliamentary Papers II, 1997/1998, 26024, nr. 9, p. 68) it appears that the principle of equal treatment of homosexual and heterosexual couples has been decisive in the debate about the opening up of marriage for persons of the same sex.

2. Equalities and differences between marriage for persons of different sex and marriage for persons of the same sex

. . . As to the conditions for the contracting of a marriage no difference is made between heterosexuals and homosexuals . . .[89]

The differences between marriage for persons of different sex and marriage for persons of the same sex only lie in the consequences of marriage. They concern two aspects: firstly the relation to children and secondly the international aspect. . . .

[According to Civil Code Article 199, the husband of the woman who gives birth during marriage is presumed to be the father of the child.] It would be pushing things too far to assume that a child born in a marriage of two women would legally descend from both women. That would be stretching reality. The distance between reality and law would become too great. Therefore this bill does not adjust chapter 11 of Book 1 of the Civil Code, which bases the law of descent on a man-woman relationship. Nevertheless, the relationship of a child with the two women or the two men who are caring for it and who are bringing it up, deserves to be protected, also in law. This protection has partly been

[87] 1 April 2001 (*Staatsblad* 2001, nr. 145). Just after midnight on the night of 31 March to 1 April 2001, Mr J Cohen (now Mayor of Amsterdam) conducted the world's first legal same-sex marriages in the council chamber of Amsterdam City Hall. One female-female and three male-male couples converted their registered partnerships to civil marriages. See http://news.bbc.co.uk/hi/english/world/europe/newsid_1253000/1253754.stm.

[88] Parliamentary Papers II 1998/1999, 26672, nr. 3 (8 July 1999). This is a lengthy text (signed by Mr J Cohen, State-Secretary for Justice), of which some brief passages have been translated here. See *supra* n.77.

[89] For example, only one of the persons wishing to marry needs to have either his or her domicile in the Netherlands, or Dutch nationality.

realised through the possibility of joint authority for a parent and his or her partner (Articles 253t ff.) and will be completed with a proposal for the introduction of adoption by same-sex partners [see Appendix IV to this chapter], with a proposal for automatic joint authority over children born in a marriage or registered partnership of two women [introduced 15 March 2000, Parliamentary Papers II 1999/2000, 27047],[90] and with a proposal to attach more consequences to joint authority [not yet introduced]. . . .

As far as the law of the European Union is concerned, the Kortmann Commission concluded that it is certainly not unthinkable that the rules of free movement of persons relating to spouses will not be considered applicable to registered partners or married spouses of the same sex (report, p. 20).[91] A recent judgment of the Court of Justice in Luxembourg strengthens this conclusion (see Court of Justice of the EC 17 February 1998, *Grant* v. *South-West Trains*, case C-249/96). . . .

Treaties relating to marriage are almost all dealing with private international law. . . . An interpretation of these treaties based on a gender-neutral marriage seems improbable. Just Because of this it will be necessary, when opening up marriage for persons of the same sex in the Netherlands, to design our own rules of private international law. The Royal Commission on private international law will be asked to advise on this, as soon as this bill will have been approved by the Lower House of Parliament [report expected after the summer of 2001].

3. Relation to registered partnership; evaluation

Registered partnership was introduced in the Netherlands on 1 January 1998. In 1998 4556 couples (including 1550 different-sex couples) have used the possibility of contracting a registered partnership . . . Compared to other countries with registered partnership legislation the interest in registered partnership in the Netherlands is relatively high.[92] . . .

The relatively high number of different-sex couples that contracted a registered partnership in 1998 and the results of a quick scan evaluation research[93] make it plausible that there is a need for a marriage-like institution devoid of the symbolism attached to marriage.

Therefore the government wants to keep the institution of registered partnership in place, for the time being. After five years the development of same-sex marriage and of registered partnership will be evaluated. Then . . . it will be possible to assess whether registered partnership should be abolished. . . .

4. International aspects

. . . As the Kortmann Commission has stated (p. 18) the question relating to the completely new legal phenomenon of marriage between persons of the same sex concerns the interpretation of the notion of public order to be expected in other countries. Such interpretation relates to social opinion about homosexuality. The outcome of a survey by the

[90] See *supra* n.66.
[91] See *supra* nn.49, 51.
[92] See also App. VI.
[93] See Scherf, *supra* n.61.

said Commission among member-states of the Council of Europe was that recognition can only be expected in very few countries. This is not surprising. . . .

Apart from the recognition of marriage as such, it is relevant whether or not in other countries legal consequences will be attached to the marriage of persons of the same-sex. . . .

As a result of this spouses of the same sex may encounter various practical and legal problems abroad. This is something the future spouses of the same sex will have to take into account. . . . However, this problem of "limping legal relations" also exists for registered partners, as well as for cohabiting same-sex partners who have not contracted a registered partnership or marriage. . . .

7. Explanation per article

. . . Article I . . . The principle of gender-neutrality of marriage is expressed by [new Article 30(1)]. . . ."

APPENDIX IV

TEXT OF DUTCH ACT ON ADOPTION BY PERSONS OF THE SAME SEX

Staatsblad van het Koninkrijk der Nederlanden
(Official Journal of the Kingdom of the Netherlands), 2001, nr. 10 (11 January)

Act of 21 December 2000 amending Book 1 of the Civil Code (adoption by persons of the same sex)[94]

We Beatrix . . . considering that it is desirable to amend the rules on adoption and related provisions in Book 1 of the Civil Code as regards the introduction of the possibility of adoption by persons of the same sex; . . .

Article I (D)

Article 227 shall be amended as follows:

(a) The first paragraph shall read as follows:
"(1) Adoption is effected by a decision of the district court at the joint request of two persons or at the request of one person alone.[95] Two persons cannot make a joint adoption request if according to Article 41 they are not allowed to marry each other."[96]

[94] *Wet van 21 december 2000 tot wijziging van Boek 1 van het Burgerlijk Wetboek (adoptie door personen van hetzelfde geslacht), Staatsblad* 2001, nr. 10, http://www.eerstekamer.nl/9202266/d/w26673st.pdf. The Act resulted from a Bill introduced by the Government on 8 July 1999 (Parliamentary Papers II 1998/1999, 26673, nr. 2), amended by the Government on 3 May 2000 and 4 August 2000, adopted by the Lower House of Parliament on 12 Sept. 2000 and by the Upper House on 19 Dec. 2000, and signed into law on 21 Dec. 2000. It entered into force on 1 April 2001. See also *supra* nn.76, 77.

[95] After the words "two persons", the words "of different sex" have been deleted.

[96] See *supra* App. II.

(b) A second sentence is added to the second paragraph, which shall now read as follows:

"(2) The joint request by two persons can only be done, if they have been living together during at least three continuous years immediately before the submission of the request. The request by an adopter who is the spouse, registered partner or other life partner of the parent, can only be done, if he has been living together with that parent during at least three continuous years immediately before the submission of the request".

(c) The third paragraph shall read as follows:

"(3) The request can only be granted if the adoption is in the evident interest of the child, if at the time of the adoption request it is established, and for the future it is reasonably forseeable, that the child has nothing to expect anymore from its parent or parents in his/her/their capacity of parent(s), and if the conditions specified in Article 228 are fulfilled as well".[97] . . .
Article III
This Act shall enter into force on a date to be determined by royal decree.[98]
. . . Given in The Hague, 21 December 2000: Beatrix
The State-Secretary for Justice: M.J. Cohen

APPENDIX V

EXPLANATORY MEMORANDUM ACCOMPANYING THE ORIGINAL BILL ON ADOPTION BY PERSONS OF THE SAME SEX[99]

". . . 1. Introduction

. . . A child being cared for and brought up in a lasting relationship of two women or two men, has a right to protection in that relationship, including legal protection. Both women or both men have taken on the responsibility for the care and upbringing of the child and readily want to have that responsibility. In the interest of the child this relationship with these adults deserves protection.

Instead of through changing the law of descent, such protection shall be offered in the form of the adoption possibilities provided for in this bill, in accordance with the advice of the Kortmann Commission,[100] as well as in the forms of joint authority for a parent and his partner and of joint custody (both introduced by legislation taking effect on 1 January 1998). An important difference between descent and adoption is that adoption

[97] One of the conditions (Art. 228(1)(f)) is the minimum period of pre-adoption care and upbringing. In case of individual adoption by someone who is not a stepparent, the minimum is three years. In case of joint adoption by two persons, the minimum is one year. In case of adoption by the spouse, registered partner or other life partner of the child, the minimum is also one year, unless the child is born in the relationship of the mother with another woman. Then there is no minimum period.

[98] 1 April 2001 (*Staatsblad* 2001, nr. 145).

[99] Parliamentary Papers II 1998/1999, 26673, nr. 3 (8 July 1999). This is a lengthy text (signed by Mr J Cohen, State-Secretary for Justice), of which some brief passages have been translated here. See *supra* n.77.

[100] See *supra* nn. 49, 51.

always is an abstraction from descent. . . . Because parenting by two persons of the same sex always involves a form of non-biological parenting, we have opted for a change of the law of adoption and not of the law of descent. . . .

2. Scope of the legislative proposal

The bill relates to adoption of children in the Netherlands. In recent years not more than sixty to one hundred Dutch children have been adopted annually under the Dutch law of adoption [not counting stepparent adoptions], for in the Netherlands only rarely does a mother not bring up her own child.

The bill primarily aims to make adoption by persons of the same sex possible. Probably this will mostly take the form of adoption by the female partner of the mother of the child, or of adoption by the male partner of the father of a child. This form is similar to the existing form of stepparent adoptions.

The reason why we do not propose to extend the possibilities for intercountry adoption, is that in that context other facts need to be taken into account. In 1997 the Ministry of Justice studied the legislation on intercountry adoption, and its application in practice, in six countries from which children come to the Netherlands, and in six other countries where such children are adopted. The study showed that in practice there is a strong preference for intercountry adoption by a married couple. . . .

3. The new condition for adoption

It is being proposed that adoption—apart from the already existing conditions—will only be possible if the child has nothing to expect anymore from its original parent or parents. This criterion is being proposed irrespective of whether it is adoption by persons of the same sex or adoption by persons of different sexes. . . .

The words "parent or parents" refer to legal parents as well as to biological parents. . . .

The criterion that the child has nothing to expect anymore from its original parent or parents, relates to the parent-child relationship. Therefore the question is not whether the child has not or will not have any de facto contact with its original parents. The relevant issue is whether the child can expect that its parents are capable of giving substance to their parenthood. Only if it is certain that the child has nothing to expect from its original parents as parents, the new condition for adoption will be fulfilled. . . .

There will be cases in which this question can easily be answered, as in the case of duo-mothers where a child has been conceived through artificial insemination with semen of an anonymous donor. Since the ties with the legal mother, who has given birth to the child, will not be severed by the adoption, and because no other—biological—parent can be indicated, the new criterion shall be fulfilled.

The balancing may be different if the child is conceived with the semen of an acquaintance of the mother and/or of her partner. . . .

5. The relation to joint authority

. . . Since in the Netherlands joint authority is available as an adequate alternative for adoption, aimed at protecting the family life of a child with its de facto carers/upbringers, it may be stated that adoption in many cases is not really necessary anymore. . . .

7. Consequences for private international law

The bill, intending to allow adoption by persons of the same sex, only relates to adoptions of children with their habitual residence in the Netherlands. To these, as to adoptions in the Netherlands by persons of different sexes, Dutch law is applicable. So problems relating to the applicability of foreign substantive laws that do not know adoption by same-sex partners, will hardly arise. . . .

The question whether adoptions by persons of the same sex, decided upon in the Netherlands, will be recognised in other countries is of a different nature. Since the legal developments abroad with respect to this form of adoption, have not progressed as far as in the Netherlands, it may be expected that, for the time being, the family ties created by such adoptions will not be recognised abroad. . . . Possibly, the parental authority linked to these adoptions could be recognised in some countries". . . .

APPENDIX VI

NUMBERS OF PARTNERSHIP REGISTRATIONS IN FIVE EUROPEAN COUNTRIES[101]

Since 1989, several European countries have introduced legislation creating the marriage-like institution of registered partnership for same-sex couples (in the Netherlands also for different-sex couples). In these countries, partnership registration has almost all the consequences of marriage, with the exception of most rights and duties of parents and children. Partnership registration became possible in Denmark on 1 October 1989, in Norway on 1 August 1993, in Sweden on 1 January 1995, in Iceland on 27 June 1996, and in the Netherlands on 1 January 1998.[102]

The table below gives an overview of the absolute numbers of partnership registrations,[103] and the relative frequencies of persons who register as partners.

- Female-female partnerships are indicated with "ff", male-male with "mm", and female-male with "fm".

[101] At http://ruljis.leidenuniv.nl/user/cwaaldij/www/, a regularly updated version will be available. Corrections and additions are always welcome (c.waaldijk@law.leidenuniv.nl).

[102] It also became possible in Greenland (1996), but no figures from there could be found. Registrations in France, Belgium and (certain regions of) Spain have not been included, because of their having far less legal consequences than marriage.

[103] Sources: Statistics Denmark; Statistics Sweden; Statistics Iceland; Statistics Norway (http://www.ssb.no/english/subjects/02/02/30/, updated each year); Statistics Netherlands (http://statline.cbs.nl/statweb/index_ENG.stm, Population, Monthly Statistics; updated each month).

- The absolute numbers are for partnership *registrations*. The number of persons that registered their partnership will therefore be twice as high.
- The frequencies are an indication of the number of registered *partners* per 100,000 inhabitants over a twelve-month period. For periods longer than twelve months, the numbers have first been reduced to the average number per twelve months. For shorter periods no frequency has been calculated.

Partnership registrations in five countries

Country	Period	Absolute numbers				Frequency	
Population		total	ff	mm	fm	ff	mm
Denmark	1989 (three months)	340	70	270	—		
5.3 million (1997)	1990	450	120	330	—	5	12
	1991	280	90	190	—	3	7
	1992	240	80	160	—	3	6
	1993	220	70	150	—	3	6
	1994	230	100	130	—	4	5
	1995	230	80	150	—	3	6
	1996	220	100	120	—	4	5
	1997	190	110	80	—	4	3
	1998	210	120	90	—	5	3
	1999	298	137	161	—	5	6
	Total	2908	1077	1831	—		
	First 15 months	*790*	*190*	*600*	—	*6*	*18*
Norway	1993 (five months)	158	42	116	—		
4.4 million (1998)	1994	133	47	86	—	2	4
	1995	98	34	64	—	2	3
	1996	127	47	80	—	2	4
	1997	117	43	74	—	2	3
	1998	115	44	71	—	2	3
	1999	144	62	82	—	3	4
	Total	892	319	573	—		
	First 17 months	*291*	*89*	*202*	—	*3*	*6*
Sweden	1995	333	84	249	—	2	6
8.8 million (1998)	1996	160	59	101	—	1	2
	1997	131	52	79	—	1	2
	1998	125	46	79	—	1	2
	1999	144	67	77	—	2	2
	2000	179	70	109	—	2	2
	Total	1072	378	694	—		
	First 12 months	*333*	*84*	*249*	—	*2*	*6*
Iceland	1996 (six months)	21	11	10	—		
0.27 million (1997)	1997	12	7	5	—	5	4
	1998	13	7	6	—	5	4
	1999	11	5	6	—	4	4
	Total	57	30	27	—		
	First 18 months	*33*	*18*	*15*	—	*9*	*7*
Netherlands	1998	4626	1324	1686	1616	17	21
15.7 million (1998)	1999	3256	864	897	1495	11	11
	2000	2922	785	815	1322	10	10
	Total	10,804	2973	3398	4433		
	First 18 months	*6132*	*1740*	*2098*	*2294*	*15*	*18*

- Frequencies have been calculated by me using the given population number for 1997 or 1998.
- Some absolute numbers given may be a little too small, because of occasional non-reporting, and because Denmark, Sweden and Norway do not include all non-residents in their statistics. The numbers given for Denmark for 1989 to 1998 are only estimates; for 1999, actual numbers were available.[104]
- To facilitate comparability, frequencies have also been calculated over the initial period of 12 to 18 months after the entering into force of the legislation.

SOME CONCLUSIONS FROM THE COMPARATIVE FIGURES

- If you add up the totals of the five countries, it can safely be said that by the end of 2000, more than 30,000 Europeans had obtained the civil status of being a registered partner.
- In the initial period after its introduction (i.e. the first twelve to eighteen months), registered partnership tends to be more popular than in later years. This contrast is sharpest with regard to men in Denmark and Sweden, and weakest with regard to different-sex couples in the Netherlands.
- During the initial periods, registered partnership has been much more popular in the Netherlands than in any other country. Partnership registration between women was eight times as popular as in Sweden, five times as popular as in Norway, and three times as popular as in Denmark (the difference with Iceland was much less). Partnership registration between men was more than three times as popular as in Sweden, and more than twice as popular as in Norway or Iceland (the difference with Denmark was small).
- After the initial period, the numbers of partnership registrations tend to stabilise. In Sweden, these numbers remain at much lower frequencies than in Norway, Denmark and Iceland. In the Netherlands, the frequencies are much higher.
- In all countries but Iceland, partnership registration has so far been more popular among men than among women. In recent years, however, this difference between men and women has become smaller in all countries.

[104] For the years 1989–1998, Statistics Denmark does not have the numbers of registrations, but only the numbers of people who were living as registered (or ex-registered) partners in Denmark on 1 January of the following year. On the basis of these numbers, I have made an estimate of the likely numbers of registrations. This means that registrations of partners living abroad are not included.

24

"Statutory Cohabitation" Under Belgian Law: A Step Towards Same-Sex Marriage?

OLIVIER DE SCHUTTER and ANNE WEYEMBERGH*

"LES CONCUBINS SE *passent de la loi, la loi se désintéresse d'eux*". ("Concubines do without the law, the law takes no interest in them".) These famous words of Napoléon describe, quite accurately, the indifference of the French Civil Code of 1804, still the basis of Belgian family law, towards cohabitation, when those living together are not bound by marriage. However, things have been changing in Belgium in recent years, perhaps at an accelerated pace since the European Court of Human Rights held that a difference in treatment between children born out of wedlock and children born to married couples constitutes discrimination,[1] and since the decriminalisation of adulterous male-female sexual activity (1987) and the equalisation of the age of consent to male-male sexual activity (1985). These changes are twofold.

First, the case-law on different-sex cohabitation outside marriage has evolved. Generally speaking, it has moved from a firm moral condemnation of cohabitation outside marriage—especially when it was of an adulterous character—to a position of relative tolerance. For example, it has become possible for different-sex cohabitees to receive gifts from each other without these gifts being declared void as having an immoral foundation, as was the case before 1977.[2] Similarly, a different-sex cohabitant may now seek damages from the person liable for the loss of his or her companion, the required "legally cognisable interest" being considered to exist since 1989–1990 in the case-law of the Court of Cassation.[3] These changes in the case-law bear witness to the fact that

* See p. xii.

[1] *Marckx* v. *Belgium* (13 June 1979), Series A, No. 31 (Eur. Ct. H.R.). For its effect on progress towards a diversity of ways of family life, see P Senaeve, "Het personen- en familierecht, de Grondwet en het E.V.R.M". in *Gezin en recht in een postmoderne samenleving—Twintig jaar post-universitaire cyclus* Willy Delva (Gent, Mys en Breesch, 1994), at 348–50.

[2] Cass. (1st ch.), 23 June 1977, *Pas.*, 1977, I, p. 1083.

[3] Cass. (2nd ch.), 1 Feb. 1989, *Pas.*, 1989, I, p. 582, *R.G.A.R.*, 1989, n°11.517, note R.O. Dalcq, *J.T.*, 1989, p. 354. See also Cass. (1st ch.), 15 Feb. 1990, *Pas.*, I, 1990, p. 694 ("the person responsible for a homicide may not invoke the adulterous character of a relationship, which is a state of affairs which belongs to the private life of the other party").

Belgian judges have agreed to recognise, to some extent, that different-sex cohabitation outside marriage may be assimilated to a "*de facto* marital relationship", including the *affectio maritalis*—the special, sentimental affection partners have for one another, very much like spouses within marriage.

However, this evolution of the judicial legal consciousness and consequent recognition in Belgian case-law of the fact of different-sex cohabitation outside marriage has but very seldomly benefited same-sex partners. Indeed, because the recognition of the legal effects of cohabitation has been justified by the analogies between cohabitation and marriage, these effects have been mostly denied to same-sex partners. Indeed, same-sex partners have not been seen as living "as if married", i.e., as leading a marital way of life.[4]

The second evolution, a legislative rather than judicial one, requires a longer discussion. On 23 November 1998, legislation was enacted creating a new institution of "statutory cohabitation" ("*cohabitation légale*").[5] This law, which came into force on 1 January 2000, creates a "third way" between marriage, on the one hand, and the few and rather uncertain legal consequences of *de facto* cohabitation, on the other hand. The principle of the law is simply stated. Any two natural persons having full legal capacity, whether of different sexes or the same sex, may declare their choice to live under this status of "statutory cohabitation". This declaration, made before a public officer ("*officier de l'état civil*"), is then officially registered. This status has only a few material consequences. The common residence of the cohabitees is protected, as well as their furniture. The debts incurred by each cohabitant, either for the needs of the household or for the care of their children, are owed by both cohabitees. Just like spouses within marriage, the contribution of both cohabitees to the common expenses is proportionate to their means. Whenever the relationship between the cohabitees is seriously damaged, a judge—the justice of the peace ("*juge de paix*")—may order urgent and provisional measures, concerning for instance the occupation of their common residence, or the custody and care of their children.

Two features of this legislation are especially noteworthy. First, although its principal purpose was to offer legal protection to the weakest partner in a relationship outside marriage, the regime of "statutory cohabitation" in fact offers only a very faint protection, because of the ease with which each of the partners can put an end to the status. Indeed, not only does the "statutory cohabitation" end with the death of one of the partners, or with the marriage of the two partners together or of either partner with a third person, it may also be terminated by a simple, joint or unilateral declaration. In some instances, a unilateral declaration that the "statutory cohabitation" has ended will amount to a form of repudiation of one partner by the other—the declaration being immediate in its

[4] See the French Court of Cassation's interpretation of the concept of "*concubinage*": Cass. fr., 17 Dec. 1997, *Rec. Dall.*, 1998, II, p. 88, note J.-L. Aubert; Borrillo, chap. 25.

[5] *Loi du 23 novembre 1998 instaurant la cohabitation légale, Moniteur belge*, http://194.7.188.126/justice/index_fr.htm,12 Jan. 1999, p. 786 (over 14,000 declarations by 4 Aug. 2001).

effects and requiring no justification whatsoever. In other words, not only does the "statutory cohabitation" end when a partner disappears, it can also be ended by the unilateral will of either of the parties. No wonder that one of the most authoritative commentators has recently completed his analysis of the regime on "statutory cohabitation" by concluding: "Herein lies, perhaps, . . . the particularly serious dead-end to which we are led, because of the choice to institutionalise a couple relationship under a legal form which has been devised, under the pretext of 'rescuing' the institution of marriage, as an empty shell—a shell, indeed, empty of any real legal and human bond".[6]

Second, the parliamentary discussion of the law on "statutory cohabitation" had as its departure point both proposals to create a form of "civil union" ("*union civile*"), resembling in many respects marriage, and proposals to outlaw all forms of discrimination based on sexual orientation.[7] Yet it would require a stretch of the imagination to think that the legislation finally adopted responds to the demands of the gay and lesbian community, or even modestly satisfies their needs, with respect to access to marriage or to an institution resembling marriage. It is true that, initially, one of the objectives of the proposal which led to the law on "statutory cohabitation" was to respond to the needs of same-sex partners. Indeed, the Law of 23 November 1998 originated in a bill (*proposition de loi*) of 23 October 1995 suggesting the creation of a "contract of common life" ("*contrat de vie commune*"). This contract had as its objective, according to its drafters, to "make concrete from a social point of view a link uniting two natural persons wishing to establish between themselves a community of life (*communauté de vie*) and to ensure themselves reciprocally a material security".[8] Among the reasons why such an institution was felt necessary, the drafters of the bill mentioned "the existence of specific social categories like homosexuals, in need of a specific legal framework for the protection of their couple".

However, the intent of the legislative bill, even then, was not to create a sort of quasi-marriage for the benefit of same-sex partners: the aim was rather to guarantee a limited material security to non-married partners, through the possibility given to courts to grant financial support to the partner in need after a separation, or to allow one partner or the surviving partner to stay in the common residence of the couple after a separation or the death of one of the

[6] J-L Renchon, "Mariage, cohabitation légale et union libre" in J Pousson-Petit (ed.), *Liber amicorum Marie-Thérèse Meulders-Klein: Droit comparé des personnes et de la famille* (Bruxelles, Bruylant, 1998), at 572–3.

[7] *Proposition de loi relative à la protection contre les discriminations fondées sur le sexe et les tendances sexuelles ou relationnelles*, 31 May 1996, *Doc. parl., Chambre* (Ch.), sess. 1995–1996, n°600/1; *Proposition de loi modifiant le Code pénal, abrogeant la loi du 30 juillet 1981 tendant à réprimer certains actes inspirés par le racisme ou la xénophobie et modifiant la loi du 15 février 1993 créant un Centre pour l'égalité des chances et la lutte contre le racisme*, 24 June 1997, *Doc. parl.*, Ch., sess. 1996–1997, n°1089/1.

[8] *Proposition de loi concernant le contrat de vie commune*, 23 Oct. 1995, *Doc. parl.*, Ch., sess. 1995–1996, n°170/1.

partners. In fact, the assimilation of the partners bound by the proposed "contract of common life" to a married couple was complete only with regard to some aspects of social security legislation.

Subsequent changes to the initial bill moved it even further from the idea of guaranteeing an alternative to marriage to those excluded from the institution. On 7 January 1998, four Members of the Chamber of Representatives (*Chambre des Représentants*), representing the three main political parties of the country (Social Christian, Socialist, Liberal), amended the initial bill.[9] The amendment introduced the concept of "statutory cohabitation"—an innovation which would lead, later on, to a change in the title of the legislation—and accentuated further the purely patrimonial character of the organisation of the "common situation of life" ("*situation de vie commune*"), which organisation is chosen by the couples making the declaration in the prescribed form ("*déclaration de cohabitation légale*"). Significantly perhaps, the institution of "statutory cohabitation" was then moved from Book I of the Civil Code ("*Des personnes*") to Book III ("*Des différentes manières dont on acquiert la propriété*"). And while the initial bill imposed on the partners declaring a "statutory cohabitation" an obligation of mutual aid and assistance, which is perhaps a natural consequence of the *affectio maritalis* presumed to exist within a married couple, such an obligation disappeared with the new amendment. Moreover, the amended bill of January 1998 attached no consequences whatsoever, in the areas of taxation and social security, to the status it introduced.

The limits of the regime of "statutory cohabitation" are manifold. A few examples will suffice to show how unsatisfactory it remains. This is of particular concern to those—same-sex couples—who are currently barred from marriage. Indeed, the justification for these limits (the partners have chosen to remain outside the institution of marriage[10] and thus ought not to be protected beyond their will) simply does not apply to same-sex couples.

1. According to the initial bill instituting the "contract of common life", in case of separation, the partner in need could be granted by the judge a form of financial support. There is no such provision in the Law of 23 November 1998. There is in fact only one protection in case of separation: during a limited period, a justice of the peace may order some urgent measures, provisionally organising the separation, which may remain in force for a maximum of one year.
2. In case of the death of one of the "legal cohabitees", no inheritance rights are recognised to the surviving partner (unlike in the case of a spouse). It is true that the "legal cohabitees" may to a certain extent compensate for this legislative gap by organising the consequences of their death through a will; however, this concerns only the portion of the succession which is not reserved to heirs designated by

[9] *Proposition de loi concernant le contrat de vie commune*, Amendment n°1, 7 Jan. 1998, *Doc. parl.*, Ch., sess. 1997–1998, n°170/2.

[10] It is perhaps significant that the original bill which led to the Law of 23 November 1998 had among its objectives to meet the situation of couples who, although they could decide to marry, have expressed a preference for a "*concubinage de revendication* . . . seeking a total rejection of any legal institution which has the object of organising the life of a couple". See *supra* n.8, pp. 1–2.

law as "*héritiers réservataires*", and even then, the estate is subject to a very high rate of taxation.

3. Apart from providing for the termination of the"statutory cohabitation", the Law of 23 November 1998 does not organise the consequences of the death of one of the partners. One aspect of this failure to regulate is particularly serious: the surviving partner has no right to remain in the common residence of the couple, if he or she is neither an owner nor a tenant of the residence. While both partners are alive, the Law of 23 November 1998 extends to them the protection of Article 215 of the Civil Code, which applies to marriage and provides for the protection of each of the spouses against the sale of the couple's residence by one of the spouses, and for the automatic extension to each spouse of the rights which the other spouse has over the residence. But for a "statutory cohabitation" couple, this protection ends immediately after the death of one of the members of the couple. Whilst the surviving spouse is guaranteed some rights affording at least minimal material security, the surviving "statutory cohabitee" has no legal rights whatsoever after the death of his or her partner.
4. Unlike a surviving spouse, a surviving "statutory cohabitee" has no *automatic* right to compensation for the damage suffered as a result of the loss of his or her partner, when the death of the partner was caused by the negligence of a third party. At most, the "statutory cohabitation" might establish a presumption that the relationship, albeit outside marriage, was a legally cognisable one, that some form of *affectio maritalis* was present between the partners, and that the loss suffered by the surviving partner is therefore a loss deserving compensation. But it is uncertain whether this presumption, borrowed *mutatis mutandis* from the case-law concerning heterosexual couples living outside marriage in a state of "*concubinage*", will also apply to same-sex partners living under "statutory cohabitation".
5. A "statutory cohabitation" produces no consequences in the field of filiation or adoption. Under Belgian law, joint adoption is possible only for married couples.[11] Although this restriction was questioned during the debates in Parliament about the "statutory cohabitation" law, because it prevents non-married heterosexual couples from adopting jointly, the consensus appeared to be that the right to joint adoption should not be extended to same-sex partners.[12] However, some judges have recognised, more or less explicitly, that "family life" may come to exist between same-sex partners raising a child in common, especially when the consequences of a separation of the couple must be organised with respect to the child of one of the partners.[13]

[11] Art. 346 of the Civil Code.

[12] Note, however, that Art. 1477, para. 4, of the Civil Code, introduced by the Law of 23 Nov. 1998, mentions the debts incurred by one of the partners living under "statutory cohabitation" for the care of the children raised by the couple. To some extent, the fact that children are raised within the couple is thus recognised; but the effects of this recognition remain confined to the patrimonial sphere.

[13] See Ghent Appeals Court, 10 Dec. 1982 (note J. Pauwels), *R.W.*, 1984–1985, 2135, annulling Brugge (First Instance Court), 15 April 1981, *J.T.*, 1982, p. 36; Leuven Minors' Court (*Tribunal de la jeunesse*), 23 March 1994 (note L. Versluys), *Journal des procès*, 1994, n°261, pp. 30–1; Brussels Appeals Court, 2 March 1987, *R.T.D.F.*, 1991, p. 219. See also Kortrijk Minors' Court, 18 March 1997 (note L. Versluys) , *Journal des procès*, 1997, n°334, p. 16. See generally K Dekelver, "Homofiel huwelijk en homofiel gezin: juridische, filosofische et beleidsmatige kanttekeningen", [1996/2] *Revue générale de droit civil* 82, at 82–4.

6. Although the initial bill of October 1995 would have granted Belgian citizenship the foreign (non-married) partner of a Belgian national, this proposal was later aba doned, the risk of abuse being rated too high. Instead, on 30 September 1997, t Minister of the Interior adopted an administrative regulation (under the legal for of a "*circulaire*") stating that a right to reside in Belgium would be recognised whomever lives in a stable relationship with a person authorised to stay in the cou try for a period of more than three months.[14] The regulation ends the previous inab ity of same-sex partners to benefit from the right to family reunion in Belgiu However, this right to residence is subject to a series of conditions, notably th within a period of six months, the couple must bind itself through a "contract common life" organising legally their cohabitation outside marriage. Despite the conditions, the very existence of a right to family reunion is, of course, of cruc importance to same-sex partners, to whom marriage is currently inaccessible.

Surely, the symbolic meaning of the Law of 23 November 1998 must not underestimated. As noted by Louis-Léon Christians, by defining as "legal" t cohabitation which this law organises, the legislator underlines "the distinctic between different forms of cohabitation, with only some cohabiting coupl acceeding to the new legal regime. . . . Although some legal effects have be recognised progressively to *concubinage* and cohabitation, especially in the fie of social security law, neither in fact benefited from a specific institution recognition. They were taken into account in their purely factual reality, but o could not, by individual will, have access to any form of 'civil status' ('*ét civil*'). Thus, well beyond the creation of a new legal regime, the bill . . . inn vates through the 'public' recognition which it offers to the relationships organises. . . . That the concepts used are void of any matrimonial connotatic does not mean that we are to conclude that there has been an abandonment any symbolic background".[15]

As Christians points out, "statutory cohabitation" is not, and should not interpreted to be, a substitute for marriage. "Statutory cohabitation" is, in fac just a legal framework which two persons living together may choose to use organise their relationship, instead of opting either for *de facto* cohabitatio with all the legal uncertainty this choice implies, or for a cohabitation contrac i.e., the contractual definition of the rights and duties of each of the cohabite ("statutory cohabitees" may also enter into such a contract). An analysis of t debates in Parliament prior to the adoption of the Law of 23 November 19 shows, in fact, that most amendments to the initial bill on the institution of form of "civil union" were motivated precisely by the concern not to create a institution which could threaten the institution of marriage, by constituting credible alternative to it, especially at a time when the institution of marriage going through an unprecedented crisis.

[14] *Circulaire du 30 septembre 1997 relative à l'octroi d'une autorisation de séjour sur la base de cohabitation dans le cadre d'une relation durable*, *Moniteur belge*, *supra* n.5, 14 Nov. 1997, p. 30,3

[15] "Les nouvelles tensions du concept de mariage: Enjeux du pluralisme pour une théologie d droits civil et canonique", (1998) 120 *Nouvelle revue théologique* 564, at 576–7.

Perhaps tellingly, the political compromise which permitted the adoption of the Law of 23 November 1998 included an agreement to make a systematic study of the discrimination existing, in the field of taxation, between married couples and unmarried cohabitees, with a view to its elimination.[16] The fear was that marriage would become less attractive if a parallel institution were created, which would offer many of the same guarantees and symbolic endorsement as marriage, but which would be somewhat more flexible and more advantageous from the fiscal point of view.

As a result of the compromise made in Parliament between the main political groups, a status has been introduced in Belgian law—that of "statutory cohabitation"—which is best characterised by its fragility and by the fact that it produces no effects after the death of one of the partners or the separation of the cohabitees. This result strikes us as rather paradoxical. Indeed, same-sex couples, who currently have no access to marriage, suffer most from this unwillingness to create an institution paralleling marriage, perhaps capable even of competing against it. Same-sex couples, of course, are prohibited from marrying. Their only choices are "statutory cohabitation", *de facto* cohabitation, or some form of cohabitation contract, i.e., contractual organisation of their cohabitation within the limits authorised by law. For them, therefore, the differences still separating "statutory cohabitation", which is available to same-sex couples, from marriage, which is not, count most. The paradox is that, to some extent, same-sex couples are made to pay for the crisis of the institution of marriage—an institution, however, which they would be eager to rescue from its allegedly impending ruin, should they be given a chance to do so.

Two paths may be followed in the future. The first is that of registered partnership. A bill introduced early in 1998 would create such an institution,[17] which is inspired by the laws in Denmark, Iceland, the Netherlands, Norway and Sweden, and which Patrick Senaeve, in particular, has been active in promoting.[18] The purpose is, insofar as is possible, to put the "registered partners" (two persons of the same sex) in a position equivalent to that of married spouses. The registration of the partnership would assimilate the partners to spouses (e.g., the conditions for the dissolution of the registered partnership

[16] The coming into force of the Law of 23 Nov. 1998 was postponed until 1 Jan. 2000 because the reform of tax legislation had not been accomplished. An action for annulment of the Law was filed with the *Cour d'arbitrage* (Constitutional Court) on 10 Feb. 1999 (Case No. 1616, *Moniteur belge*, 4 March 1999). In a judgment of 23 Feb. 2000 (Case n°23/2000), the *Cour d'arbitrage* concluded from a description of the legal regime introduced by the Law of 23 Nov. 1998 that statutory cohabitees are not in a situation comparable to that of legally-married spouses. Indeed, the law on "statutory cohabitation" "only creates a limited patrimonial protection which seeks a partial inspiration from the clauses applicable to marriage". (See part B.1.5. of the judgment.) Thus, the applicants, who considered that, as married persons, they were treated less favourably than statutory cohabitees in the field of taxation, could not seek the annulment of the legislation on "statutory cohabitation". According to the Court, such an annulment would not remedy the discrimination between married couples and non-married couples which was the object of their complaint.

[17] *Proposition de loi organisant le partenariat enregistré, Doc. parl.*, Ch., sess. 1997–1998, No. 1417/1.

[18] P Senaeve & E Coene, *Geregistreerd Partnerschap* (Maklu, Antwerpen/Apeldoorn, 1998).

would be as demanding as they are in the case of marriage) in all respects, except in the fields of filiation and adoption.

The other path, more radical on its surface but also simpler, would be to open civil marriage to persons of the same sex. As it appears from the debates leading to the Law of 23 November 1998, the political consensus was based then on two contradictory principles: first, that of tolerance towards different forms of private life deserving, in a pluralistic society, equal respect, the choice between these different forms of life being a private choice of the individual; second, that of the refusal to grant any public recognition to the union of individuals having the same sex, or at least of any recognition which could lead to a confusion with the institution of marriage. Indeed, to recognise a form of partnership between individuals of the same sex, it was generally agreed, would threaten the institution of marriage, understood in a somewhat tautological fashion as "an act of will by which a man and a woman choose to have a common life project".[19]

The position thus summarised is based on a curious understanding of the neutrality of the State with respect to the diversity of the forms of private life coexisting under its jurisdiction. The present political consensus, insofar as it tolerates other forms of cohabitation between persons (including persons who have the same sex) but denies to same-sex partners access to marriage or an alternative institution open to any two natural persons wishing to live together, produces three series of consequences. First, it makes it, if not impossible, at least more difficult, for same-sex partners to maintain a life-long relationship, insofar as the legal organisation of a relationship has an influence on how it is understood and lived through by the parties to the relationship. Secondly, insisting that same-sex partnership is not deserving of marriage may lead some homosexuals to deny their homosexuality, for fear of being marginalised. Thirdly, the inaccessibility of marriage to same-sex partners may lead those individuals whose preferences are more fluid to prefer a heterosexual life leading to marriage, rather than a same-sex partnership.
The first two consequences are sufferings inflicted upon gays and lesbians, which although they are mainly psychological, are no less real. The last consequence may seem easier to defend, but we are left to wonder, nevertheless, whether the desire to encourage heterosexual marriage may long justify the perpetuation of such an invidious discrimination based on the sexual preference of individuals.[20]

In early April 2001, within days of the first same-sex marriages in the Netherlands, some Belgian Government ministers appeared ready to envisage

[19] Speech of M-T Meulders before the Justice Committee of the Chamber of Representatives, *Rapport fait au nom de la commission de la justice par MM. D. Vandenbossche et F. Lozie*, 11 March 1998, *Doc. parl.*, Ch., sess. 1997–1998, n°170/8, p. 45.

[20] See K A Appiah, "The Marrying Kind", *New York Review of Books* (20 June 1996), p. 48 at 51 : "After all, if you really want to encourage straight people to stay married, why not toughen the divorce laws and increase tax advantages? Taking it out on homosexuals is not merely mean; it is ineffectual."

opening the institution of marriage to same-sex couples. This was a remarkable development, especially in view of the extreme cautiousness that marked the debates on the Law of 23 November 1998: the consensus was, only three years ago, that in no circumstances should the assimilation of same-sex couples to different-sex couples be complete, and there was hardly even a minority to be found to defend a less orthodox view. Yet on 22 June 2001, on the initiative of Marc Verwilghen (the Minister of Justice and a leading figure in the Flemish Liberals), the Cabinet ("*Conseil des Ministres*") approved a draft bill ("*avant-projet de loi*") that would amend the Civil Code so as to treat same-sex and different-sex couples equally in relation to marriage, except with regard to filiation and joint adoption. According to the Government's press release:

> " . . . In our contemporary society, marriage is lived and felt as a (formal) relationship between two persons, having as its main object the creation of a lasting community of life. Marriage offers to the two partners the possibility of publicly affirming their relationship and the feelings that they have for each other. Mentalities having evolved, there is no longer any reason not to open marriage to persons of the same sex. . . . The bill's starting point is . . . equality of treatment, in relation to marriage, of homosexual and heterosexual couples. The bill removes, consequently, a discrimination found in our legislation because of an historical context. Marriage has nevertheless a great symbolic value and a legal impact on the status of a person. If two persons want to commit themselves to such a relationship, no discrimination based on sex or sexual affinities [*affinités sexuelles*] can be an obstacle to their intention. This means that the rules relating to . . . marriage . . . should, as far as possible, be applicable to a marriage between persons of the same sex. However, there also exist differences. Thus, the marriage of two persons of the same sex has no effects with regard to filiation. . . . The distance between reality and the law would become . . . too great. . . . The opening of marriage does not involve the possibility for two spouses of the same sex to adopt [jointly]. The limitation of the possibility of adopting to persons of different sexes will prevent potential problems with respect to recognition outside Belgium and the establishment of adoptions that would be considered 'irregular' under private international law. . . . [To marry in Belgium, t]he national law of the two future spouses must permit marriage between two persons of the same sex". . . .[21]

After approval by the Council of State ("*Conseil d'Etat*") and final approval by the Cabinet, the bill will be published and introduced in Parliament. If it is passed by Parliament and receives royal assent, it could come into force in 2002. It will be very interesting to see whether Belgium will be able to make the leap from "statutory cohabitation" to same-sex marriage in such a short time.

In one of its most famous cases, the United States Supreme Court defined marriage as "an association that promotes a way of life, not causes; a harmony in living, not political faiths; a bilateral loyalty, not commercial or social projects.

[21] Translation of extracts from French original: *Communiqué de presse*, "Mariage de personnes du même sexe", 22 June 2001, http://194.7.188.126/justice/index_fr.htm (Communiqués). On the same day, the Cabinet also approved a draft bill opening up joint and second-parent adoption to different-sex cohabitants. *Communiqué de presse*, "Adoption", 22 June 2001 (same URL).

Yet it is an association for as noble a purpose as any involved in our prior decisions".[22] The legal organisation of "statutory cohabitation" provides a limited number of material guarantees to those who choose this form of relationship; but it seems to assume that any possibility of *affectio maritalis* is absent from the relationship, as appears most clearly from the ease with which either of the partners may end, unilaterally and without having to offer any justification, the "statutory cohabitation" which both entered. To deny access to marriage to persons who have the same sex constitutes a discrimination against these persons in their private and family lives. To suppose that the "statutory cohabitation" established by the Law of 23 November 1998 could constitute for these persons a satisfactory alternative, and to justify by the existence of such an alternative the prohibition of same-sex marriage, not only perpetuates this discrimination, but is also an insult to the institution of marriage itself. Of course, marriage cannot be restricted to the possibility of procreation; marriage rather constitutes, in the words of the US Supreme Court, a harmony between two human beings uniting their destinies, having made the choice to promise to one another a "bilateral loyalty". The empty shell of "statutory cohabitation" is thus a poor version of marriage offered to a category of the population characterised by the sexual orientation of its members.

[22] *Griswold* v. *Connecticut*, 381 U.S. 479, 486 (1965).

25

The "Pacte Civil de Solidarité" *in France: Midway Between Marriage and Cohabitation*

DANIEL BORRILLO*

FOLLOWING IN THE footsteps of Denmark (1989), Norway (1993), Sweden (1994), Iceland (1996), the Netherlands (1997), Belgium (1998) and Spain (Catalonia 1998 and Aragon 1999), France has introduced a new form of conjugal relationship into its law. In November 1999, the campaign for legal recognition of same-sex partnerships in France, which began after the passage of the Danish law on registered partnerships in 1989, culminated in the adoption of a law creating a new legal institution, the *Pacte civil de solidarité* (PaCS or "Civil Solidarity Pact").[1] Before the PaCS, there were only two types of legal recognition of partnerships in France, civil marriage and *concubinage* (cohabitation), and both were limited to different-sex partners. While civil marriage requires a formal expression of the will of the parties, through a marriage ceremony, *concubinage* involves the legal recognition of the fact that two persons are living together as spouses, and does not depend on the will of the parties. The PaCS aims to introduce an intermediate status for non-marital unions, in between civil marriage and *concubinage*, thereby permitting, in particular, the recognition of non-marital homosexual unions.

Premised like marriage on a voluntarist approach, the PaCS is an act of will that immediately creates a legal situation and produces juridical consequences, rather than a situation of fact to which juridical consequences are attached. Although the PaCS is open to two and only two individuals, it does not modify the civil status of the parties, who remain "single". And the conditions governing the formation and termination of a PaCS are much more flexible than those applicable to civil marriage. There is no obligation to publicise the existence of the PaCS, it is not subject to medical requirements, and as will be seen below, its termination is much easier than a divorce. Even though the French legislature

* Maître de conférences en droit privé, Université de Paris X (Nanterre); Centre National de la Recherche Scientifique (laboratoire CERSA, Université de Paris II (Panthéon-Assas)).

[1] *Loi no. 99–944 du 15 novembre 1999 relative au pacte civil de solidarité*, http://www.legifrance.gouv.fr/html/frame_jo.html.

wanted to differentiate strongly between the PaCS and civil marriage, it did not go so far as to create a special form of contract reserved to same-sex couples. As a result, unlike Scandinavian registered partnerships, the PaCS is open to all couples, regardless of gender. The French traditions of "equality" and "universality of legal rules" preclude special laws applying only to minority groups.[2]

THE PROPOSALS THAT PRECEDED THE PACS LAW

From 1989 to 1999, a political and social movement whose stated aim was to reform the law concerning conjugal life inspired many parliamentary bills and two government-commissioned reports.[3] Despite the generality of its stated aim, this movement's primary goal was the legal recognition of the union between two persons of the same sex. Indeed, it was mainly groups concerned with defending the rights of homosexuals and/or active in the fight against AIDS who articulated law reform claims and who rallied around the various parliamentary bills.[4] The HIV epidemic dramatically brought to the fore the precarious legal position of people with AIDS, both as individuals and as members of couples. In 1997, in *Vilela* v. *Weil*, the highest civil court in France, the *Cour de cassation*, held that the doctrine of *concubinage* cannot be applied to homosexual

[2] Only the sociologist Irène Théry publicly proposed a special status for same-sex couples. In so doing, she departed paradoxically from the republican tradition she had previously always advocated. See I Théry, "Le CUS en question", [1997] *Notes de la fondation Saint Simon* 26, and also in [Oct. 1997] *Revue Esprit*.

[3] The parliamentary bills are: *Proposition de loi* n° 422 on the *Contrat de partenariat civil*, Senate, 25 June 1990 (Socialist); *Proposition de loi* n° 3066 on the *Contrat d'union civile*, National Assembly, 25 Nov. 1992 (Socialist); *Proposition de loi* n° 880 on the *Contrat d'union civile*, National Assembly, 23 Dec. 1993 (Movement of Citizens); *Proposition de loi* n° 3315 on the *Contrat d'union sociale*, National Assembly, 23 Jan. 1997 (Socialist); *Proposition de loi* n° 3367 relating to the rights of non-married couples, National Assembly, 20 Feb. 1997 (Communist); *Proposition de loi* n° 88 on the *Contrat d'union civile et sociale*, National Assembly, 23 July 1997 (Radical, Movement of Citizens, Green); *Proposition de loi* n° 94 on the *Contrat d'union sociale*, National Assembly, 23 July 1997 (Socialist); *Proposition de loi* n° 249 on the rights of unmarried couples, National Assembly, 30 Sept. 1997 (Communist); *Proposition de loi* n° 138 on unmarried couples, Senate, 1 Dec. 1997 (Communist). From the collaboration between J-P Michel (Movement of Citizens sponsor of *Proposition* n° 88), J-M Ayrault (Socialist sponsor of *Proposition* n° 94, an amended version of which became the Socialist version of the *Pacte civil de solidarité* on 29 May 1998), and G Hage (Communist sponsor of *Proposition* No. 249) arose the first common MOC-Socialist-Communist version of the *Pacte civil de solidarité* (Rapport n° 1097, 23 Sept. 1998; Opinion n° 1102, presented to the National Assembly on 1 Oct. 1998). The subsequent versions of the PaCS bill had the numbers 1118, 1119, 1120, 1121 and 1122, as a result of amendments by the Assembly and the "shuttles" to the Senate. The two reports are: J Hauser, *Comité de réflexion sur les conséquences financières de la séparation des couples. Le projet de pacte d'intérêt commun* (Ministry of Justice, April 1998); I Théry, *Couple, filiation et parenté aujourd'hui, le droit face aux mutations de la famille et de la vie privée* (Ministry of Justice & Ministry of Employment and Solidarity, May 1998; Paris, O Jacob, June 1998) (see particularly the chapter concerned with *concubinage*).

[4] In Nov. 1999, all of the major associations concerned with AIDS and/or the rights of gays and lesbians created an umbrella group called "*L'observatoire du PaCS*" ("PaCS Watchdog Group"), in order to monitor the law's application and to fight for civil marriage for same-sex couples. For the 1999 Report of "*L'observatoire du PaCS*", see http://www.chez.com/obspacs.

unions.[5] According to the Court, cohabitation is modelled on the institution of marriage and thus can only concern heterosexual couples. Having decided that there is no legal equivalent to heterosexual *concubinage* for same-sex couples, the Court held that when one member of such a couple dies from AIDS, the lease of an apartment, in the name of the deceased, cannot be assigned to his surviving partner. The bereaved survivor, after losing his partner, can therefore legally be evicted from his home. In reaching this decision, the Court rejected the opinion of the *Avocat Général*: "Without waiting for the legislature to intervene, mere statutory interpretation permits you to adapt your case-law to the reality of society today".[6]

Concubinage is merely a legal recognition of an existing situation of fact. All the *Cour de cassation* had to do was recognise the *de facto* situation of two people of the same sex living together under the same roof, enjoying both a sexual and economic relationship. Even polygamy, where it exists in fact, may generate social welfare rights in France.[7] But the union of two people of the same sex, with a view to a communal life together based on reciprocal affection and support, was completely ignored by the legislature and the courts.[8]

The refusal of the *Cour de cassation* to recognise same-sex *concubinage* in 1997 was consistent with the first two same-sex couple cases the Court decided in 1989. In *Secher* v. *Air France*, a male steward sought a reduced price air ticket for his male partner. The Court held that the applicable regulations made the benefit available to a "spouse living in a free union" ("*conjoint en union libre*"),

[5] *Cour de cassation, Chambre civile 3e*, 17 Dec. 1997, Bull. civ. 1997.III.151, No. 225, Dalloz.1998.Jur.111. The trial court, the *Tribunal d'instance* of the 4th *arrondissement* in Paris, in an unpublished judgment of 5 Aug. 1993, had ruled that leases could be transferred, as "the legislation identifies an acknowledged partner in a totally neutral and general manner, the only condition being the stability of the union. The evidence . . . shows that the homosexual partnership between Mr W and Mr X had been acknowledged and stable for several years". The judge's ruling went even further, however, stating that "owing to changes in social behaviour, the term *concubinage* now signifies cohabitation as a couple, and no longer requires the partners to be of different genders as was previously the case". The *Cour d'appel de Paris* (court of appeal) disagreed, in a judgment of 9 June 1995, [1995] *Revue trimestrielle de droit civil* 607, holding that the *Loi no. 89–462 du 6 juillet 1989* "authorising the transfer of a lease to a *concubin notoire* (well-known or manifest partner) who had been living with the deceased for at least one year at the time of death" did not apply to same-sex couples. An eviction order was therefore issued. The *Cour de cassation* affirmed, in its judgment of 17 Dec. 1997, *supra*, holding that "*concubinage* can only result from a stable and continuous relationship having the appearance of marriage, therefore between a man and a woman".

[6] Dalloz.1998.Jur.111 at 113.

[7] Both French legislation and case law are tolerant with regard to polygamy: a female spouse and a female concubine can simultaneously be beneficiaries of the social security of the same insured man (*Code de la sécurité sociale*, Arts. L313–3, L164–14); gifts by a married man to his female concubine are valid (*Cour de cassation, Chambre civile 1re*, 28 Jan. 1997, [1997] *Droit de la famille*, No. 184).

[8] Several decisions by lower courts, not reversed on appeal, have recognised same-sex couples: *Tribunal d'instance de Bobigny*, 11 May 1992, unpublished, RG 4255/92 (assignment of lease to partner following death of tenant); *Tribunal correctionel de Belfort*, 25 July 1995, *La Semaine Juridique* (J.C.P.).1996.II.3903 at 60 (claim for compensation after death of partner in road accident); *Tribunal d'instance d'Aubervilliers*, 12 Sept. 1995, unpublished, RG 1195584 (assignment of lease); *Tribunal d'instance de Toulouse*, 20 Sept. 1996, unpublished (assignment of lease).

and that living like spouses outside marriage "can only concern a couple consisting of a man and a woman".[9] In *Ladjka* v. *Caisse primaire d'assurance maladie de Nantes*,[10] a woman was denied the benefit of her female partner's (public) health and maternity insurance coverage. Again, the Court held that the concept of "marital life" ("*vie maritale*") used in the applicable social security legislation could only apply to an unmarried different-sex couple.

In view of the repeated refusal of the French courts to recognise same-sex partnerships, new legislation seemed the only way to find a suitable solution. Since 1989, there have been many proposals for legislation. The first bill was presented by Senator Jean-Luc Mélenchon on 25 June 1990,[11] approximately one year after the passage of the Danish registered partnership law. It proposed a *Contrat de partenariat civil* (CPC or "Civil Partnership Contract") and was inspired by suggestions from homosexual groups such as *Gays pour les libertés* ("Gays for Freedoms") and *Homosexualité et Socialisme* ("Homosexuality and Socialism"). The CPC aimed to be universal, in that it would have been open to any two persons regardless of their sexes, or of the nature of their relationship. Thus, the CPC would have been open, not only to couples, but also to siblings or mere pairs of friends or two persons who decided to live together. The CPC bill did not make the headlines and did not benefit from a parliamentary debate.

In 1992, certain *députés* in the National Assembly, among them Jean-Yves Autexier, Jean-Pierre Michel, and Jean-Pierre Belorgey presented a new bill proposing a *Contrat d'union civile* (CUC or "Civil Union Contract").[12] An unmarried individual could enter into a CUC with any unmarried person, whether related or not. The only exception was for the individual's ascendants and descendants (parents, grandparents, children, grandchildren, etc.). The bill thus extended a certain number of rights, not only to unmarried different-sex or same-sex couples, but potentially also to every person living under the same roof with another person and, of course, not covered by the exception. This was to avoid attaching any personal identity labels to the parties to a CUC (e.g., two women who entered into a CUC would not be assumed to be lesbian). Although the bill was never debated in its entirety, two provisions were voted on: one concerned the availability of social welfare benefits to a dependent cohabitee regardless of sex; the other dealt with the possibility of assigning a lease to a cohabitee regardless of sex. Only the first provision was finally adopted in 1993,[13] and effectively overruled the 1989 *Ladjka* decision of the *Cour de cassation*.[14] The second was declared unconstitutional in 1993 by the *Conseil constitutionnel* (Constitutional Court) on procedural grounds.[15] The victory of the

[9] *Cour de cassation, Chambre sociale*, 11 July 1989, Bull. civ. 1989.V.311, No. 514.
[10] *Cour de cassation, Chambre sociale*, 11 July 1989, Bull. civ. 1989.V.312, No. 515.
[11] *Proposition de loi* n° 422, *supra* n.3.
[12] *Proposition de loi* n° 3066, *supra* n.3.
[13] *Loi no. 93–121 du 27 janvier 1993.*
[14] See *supra* n.10.
[15] Decision No 92–317 DC, 21 Jan. 1993, [1993] *Recueil des décisions du Conseil constitutionnel* 1240.

Right in the legislative elections of 1993 discouraged the homosexual community. Only a few activists associated with the *Collectif pour le CUC*, which had originally proposed the CUC, continued the struggle timidly.

In the face of public apathy, the HIV/AIDS organisation "*Aides*" (established by Daniel Defert in 1985, one year after the death from AIDS of his partner, the philosopher Michel Foucault), took a central role in the new debate. Trying to combat various forms of discrimination linked to the AIDS epidemic which the association witnessed daily, in 1995, *Aides* proposed a new bill creating a *Contrat de vie sociale* ("Social Life Contract"), limited to couples. Later that year, this bill was merged with the CUC to give rise to the proposed *Contrat d'union sociale* (CUS or "Social Union Contract"). On 1 March 1996, a group of intellectuals, including Pierre Bourdieu, Jacques Derrida, Didier Eribon, Michelle Perrot and Pierre Vidal-Naquet, signed a manifesto in the newspaper *Le Monde* advocating the recognition of same-sex couples. On 19 June 1996, Socialist senators introduced a bill in the Senate (*Proposition de loi* no. 454) that would broaden the right to transfer a lease after the death or desertion of the tenant to any person who had lived with the tenant for at least one year. Three days later, *Le Monde* published a new appeal ("Towards a Better Citizenship: The CUS") cosigned by a former Prime Minister, Michel Rocard, and six future Ministers, Elisabeth Guigou, Catherine Trautmann, Dominique Voynet Daniel Vaillant, Bernard Kouchner and Martine Aubry, as well as numerous well-known intellectuals and artists.

On 23 January 1997, the CUS was introduced in the National Assembly for the first time (*Proposition de loi* no. 3315) ("CUS I"). Socialist senators introduced a similar bill in the Senate on 19 March. On 24 April, the President of France dissolved the National Assembly and called early elections, which the Left won. During the electoral campaign, the parties of the Left all supported the CUS. On 23 July, after the Euro Gay Pride in Paris in June, attended by nearly 300,000 people, National Assembly *député* Jean-Pierre Michel, with his colleagues from the Radical, Movement of Citizens and Green parties, introduced a bill (*Proposition de loi* no. 88) that would have created a *Contrat d'union civile et sociale* (CUCS or "Civil and Social Union Contract"). On the same day, the Socialists introduced for the second time the CUS bill (*Proposition de loi* no. 94) ("CUS II"). The main difference between the CUS on the one hand, and the CUCS and the CUC on the other hand, was that the CUS excluded all close family members and focussed on couples, whereas the CUCS and the CUC could apply to any two persons (except between ascendants and descendants), including brothers and sisters. The reasoning behind the restriction of the CUS to couples was not explained. It is also surprising that the CUCS and the CUC, which did not purport to regulate the life of a couple, were limited to two persons. And if the relationship did not have to be sexual, why were ascendants and descendants excluded from such a contract? The answer is probably that these restrictions were a political manoeuvre to avoid shocking public opinion, which was considered chilly with regard to homosexuality.

On 30 September, the Communist Party introduced a bill on the rights of unmarried couples (*Proposition de loi* no. 249). In contrast with its predecessors (CPC, CUC, CUS I, CUCS, CUS II), the Communist text sought to put civil marriage and *concubinage* legally on the same level, without giving rights of filiation to same-sex couples. A consensus of sorts developed among the parties of the Left whereby the legal notion of "couple" would be opened to same-sex unions, while closing or at least not mentioning the delicate question of parental rights. At this time, an association which had been very discreet until then began to emerge in the public arena: the *Association des parents et futurs parents gays et lesbiens* (APGL).

None of the CUCS, CUS II and Communist bills was passed. The following spring of 1998 saw the publication of two reports, commissioned by government ministries, which proposed different solutions to the problems experienced by couples living in a free union outside marriage. The first report, prepared by Professor Jean Hauser, had been requested by the former conservative Justice Minister, Jacques Toubon. The Hauser Report[16] proposed a *Pacte d'intérêt commun* (PIC or "Common Interest Pact"), open to any two persons, of different sexes or the same sex. The PIC avoided the question of emotional and sexual relationships, seeking instead to resolve questions of property law, and provide certain social welfare and tax rights to regulate the economic aspects of the parties' daily lives. This was to be achieved by inserting new articles into the Civil Code between the sections concerning the setting up of a business and joint ownership.

The second report, by Irène Théry on "Couples, Filiation and Kinship Today",[17] which was presented to the government a few weeks after the Hauser Report, was more ambitious in its analysis. It aimed to go beyond property issues and touched upon an individual's relationships without, however, examining issues of family law for homosexual couples. Indeed, the author refused not only the right to a civil marriage for homosexuals, but also any possibility of joint parental rights for a same-sex couple. She did so in defence of the "symbolic order"[18] of western culture! However, the author suggested recognising *concubinage* for homosexuals (by means of an article in the Civil Code's section on personal rights), and at the same time strengthening certain tax benefits and welfare rights. Indeed, she devoted a specific chapter to cohabitation, with a spe-

[16] J Hauser, *Comité de réflexion sur les conséquences financières de la séparation des couples. Le projet de pacte d'intérêt commun* (Ministry of Justice, April 1998).

[17] I Théry, *Couple, filiation et parenté aujourd'hui, le droit face aux mutations de la famille et de la vie privée* (Ministry of Justice & Ministry of Employment and Solidarity, May 1998; Paris, O Jacob, June 1998).

[18] In France, anti-homosexual discrimination has been justified less by a religious discourse of a "natural order" than by a "learned" discourse of a "symbolic order" informed by a specific use of anthropology and psychoanalysis. For a criticism of this notion, see M Iacub, "Le couple homosexuel, le droit et l'ordre symbolique", (Oct. 1998) 12–13 *Revue Le Banquet* 111; Fassin (*Témoin*), *infra*, p.492.

cial section on homosexual cohabitation. The Théry Report went beyond questions of property, proposing to insert the following article into the section on personal rights in the Civil Code: "Cohabitation consists in the existence of a natural couple, irrespective of whether the cohabitees are of the same sex or not". Putting aside the problems of proof, it was an interesting approach.

However, althought the proposals in the Théry Report responded to the urgent needs identified by the associations concerned with fighting AIDS, it was only a small step towards the recognition of homosexual couples. The acceptance of *de facto* cohabitation does not imply legal recognition of the union. Just as occupation without title does not imply the recognition of a property right, cohabitation is nothing more than a precarious union which does not automatically presuppose its legal stability. The sole legal institution in France today which recognises a union is civil marriage. A proposal to recognise cohabitation between homosexuals should be within the context of enlarging the institution of marriage. Because Irène Théry's proposal categorically refuses the right to marriage for homosexuals, it loses all credibility.

PASSAGE OF THE PACS LAW

By ignoring both the Hauser Report and the Théry Report, the government abandoned the idea of introducing a government bill (*projet de loi d'initiative gouvernementale*). This clearly demonstrated the embarrassment of the Socialist Party, which continued to support the project very tentatively. Catherine Tasca, President of the Parliamentary Law Commission, asked National Assembly *députés* Patrick Bloche and Jean-Pierre Michel to prepare a report on a new bill synthesising the preceding bills. Their report led to the first version of a bill that would ultimately become law: the *Pacte civil de solidarité* (PaCS or "Civil Solidarity Pact"). This new bill, supported by all the parties of the Left, was presented in the National Assembly on 1 October 1998. By introducing an obligation of mutual financial support and liability between partners, by prohibiting a union between ascendants, descendants and close relatives, and by excluding married individuals and those already united by an earlier PaCS, the bill covered "couples" and not merely two persons living under the same roof. In this, it resembled the "couples-only" CUS, and differed from the "any two persons" CUC, CUCS and PIC.

The bill was first presented for debate in the National Assembly on Friday, 9 October 1998, and enjoyed the theoretical support of the governing Socialist Party and other parties of the Left holding a majority of seats in the Assembly. However, only 16 per cent (50 out of 320) of the Socialist, Communist, Radical, Movement of Citizens, and Green deputies were in the Assembly that day. Parties of the Right, even though feebly represented (60 deputies), were thus able to win a vote ruling that the bill was inadmissible because the text violated the Constitution (a rare procedure, used for only the second time in the Fifth

Republic). As *Le Monde*'s headline astutely observed on 10 October, "[t]he Socialist members were ashamed of the PaCS". Their lukewarm support was difficult to understand as the PaCS had become an extremely timid proposal, and according to a survey carried out by Iftop-Libération on 8 September 1998, 57 per cent of unmarried different-sex couples were for it.[19]

The Right's rout of the Left on 9 October 1998 permitted them to rediscover an ephemeral union and a common enemy: the "homosexual lobby" and its allies on the Left. The Right's attitude radicalised the debate by obliging the Left to strengthen its support for the PaCS. One month later, a slightly modified text was presented in the National Assembly once again. The debates on the new bill lasted nearly 70 hours between 3 November and 9 December. Christine Boutin, a conservative *député* and an advisor to the Vatican's "Pontifical Council for the Family", opened the first debate with a speech of five and one-half hours, during which she brandished a bible. After discussions that were fierce and sometimes insulting towards homosexuals,[20] and despite more than a thousand obstructive amendments proposed by the Right, the bill's first reading ended on 10 December with the majority of *députés* voting in favour.

On 31 January 1999, nearly 100,000 persons demonstrated in Paris against the bill, with Christine Boutin in the lead.[21] Among the thousands of signs, one could read slogans such as "The homosexuals of today are the paedophiles of tomorrow", "*Pas de neveux pour les tantouzes*" ("No nephews [young lovers passed off as nephews] for the big aunties [a very pejorative term for older gay men considered 'effeminate']"), or "*Jospin fais gaffe à tes arrières!*" ("[Prime Minister Lionel] Jospin take care of your behind!"). Several family associations and representatives of every religious community (Catholic, Protestant, Muslim, Jewish) marched beside representatives of the Right and the extreme

[19] The poll used a representative sample of 407 unmarried different-sex couples. Support varied as follows: women (59%), men (55%); persons aged 25 to 49 (more than 60%); a majority in all professions except retired persons; Paris (62%), provinces (56%); Green supporters (66%), supporters of parties of the Right (53%). A more recent poll, by Sofres for the magazine *Têtu* on 1–2 Sept. 2000, found that 70% of adults in France were in favour of the PaCS, 48% were in favour of same-sex marriage, and 29% were in favour of adoption by same-sex couples.

[20] On 7 Nov., in response to *député* A Touret's statement that "it is up to Parliament to legislate once social evolution has crystallised", conservative *député* J Myard shouted: "There are zoophiles too!". On 8 Nov., when the Minister of Justice stated that the PaCS would not give rise to adoption rights for same-sex couples, conservative *député* P Lalouche shouted: "So sterilise them!" Conservative catholic *député* P de Villiers added: "your innovation, this PaCS, is simply a return to barbarism".

[21] The demonstration was only the visible part of the iceberg. In April 1998, as the PaCS was being discussed, the signatures of 12,000 French mayors against "*le mariage homo*" were collected. In Sept. 1998, a Christian sect, *Avenir de la Culture* (Future of Civilisation) flooded the Prime Minister's office with nearly 100,000 letters against "the unspeakable and repugnant proposal for homosexual marriage", while the Conference of (Catholic) Bishops of France declared that the PaCS is a "useless and dangerous law". Meanwhile, the very active Association of Catholic Families and the powerful association Families of France were running an extremely organised campaign against the alleged "homosexual lobby". For an in-depth analysis, see C Fourest & F Venner, *Les anti-PaCS ou la dernière croisade homophobe* (Paris, ProChoix, 1999).

Right. When they passed a sign saying "Homophobes", held up by Act-Up Paris, the crowd let loose with: *"Sales pédés! Brûlez en enfer!"* ("Filthy fags! Burn in hell!"), and *"Arrêtez de nous faire chier avec votre sida"* ("Stop making us shit [annoying us] with your AIDS"). The euphoric mob shouted throughout the march: *"Les pédés au bûcher!"* ("Burn the fags at the stake!").

It was in this context, and after several public hearings,[22] that the bill reached the Senate. The majority in the Senate rejected the PaCS (by 216 to 99) but, to avoid having too conservative an image, adopted a proposal for a new Civil Code article dealing with *concubinage*, while declining to state expressly that *concubinage* could also involve a same-sex couple.[23] This manoeuvre by the Senate introduced the question of *concubinage* into the parliamentary debate. Thus, when the bill returned to the National Assembly, a new Civil Code article was added defining *concubinage* as "a union of fact, characterised by a common life presenting a character of stability and continuity, between two persons, of different sexes or of the same sex, who live as a couple".[24] On second reading, the National Assembly also amended the bill by excluding the possibility of a PaCS between an individual and their brother, sister, uncle, aunt, nephew or niece. When the bill returned to the Senate for a second reading, the Senate simply refused to discuss it. Faced with this impasse, a *"commission mixte paritaire"* (joint National Assembly-Senate commission) was established in May 1999 in order to find a compromise. The commission could not reach an agreement and sent the bill to the National Assembly for a third reading. On 30 June, the final day of the parliamentary session, the Senate refused to adopt the bill on third reading and, through delaying tactics, stopped the National Assembly from finally adopting it.[25]

Finally, on 13 October 1999, during a new parliamentary session, the decisive vote took place. The National Assembly adopted the PaCS law by 315 votes for (Socialist, Communist, Green, Movement of Citizens, and one conservative *député*, Roselyne Bachelot), 249 votes against (the RPR, UDF and other parties of the Right), and 4 abstentions. The same day, 213 *députés* and 115 senators of the Right filed an application with the *Conseil Constitutionnel*, arguing that the Left had not followed proper parliamentary procedures, and that the PaCS law contained numerous violations of the French Constitution (provisions on equality, division of powers, the national government's budget, etc.).[26] On

[22] Senate, *Rapport* n° 258, by Senator P Gélard in the name of the *Commission des Lois constitutionnelles*, ordinary session, 1998–1999.

[23] The Senate also proposed a Civil Code amendment defining marriage as "the union of a man and a woman celebrated by a civil status officer".

[24] *Code civil*, Art. 515–8.

[25] After three *navettes* (shuttles) between the National Assembly and the Senate, the National Assembly has the final say under Art. 45 of the French Constitution.

[26] Under Arts. 61–62 of the French Constitution, an ordinary law can only be declared unconstitutional by the *Conseil Constitutionnel* if it has been referred to the *Conseil* within the 15-day period before the President would normally promulgate it. Once it has been promulgated by the President, after having been upheld by the *Conseil*, or if there was no reference, no court in France can declare it unconstitutional.

9 November 1999, the *Conseil* declared the law consistent with the Constitution.[27] The law was promulgated by President Jacques Chirac on 15 November 1999, and published in the *Journal Officiel* on 16 November 1999,[28] with the first PaCSs contracted a few days later. The PaCS law inserts a new Title XII, consisting of two chapters, "Of the civil solidarity pact" (Articles 515–1 to 515–7), and "Of *concubinage*" (Article 515–8), into Book I ("Of persons") of the Civil Code. It also amends the Social Security Code, the Labour Code, the rules regarding the right of foreigners to reside in France, the General Tax Code, and several laws dealing with the civil service. The *décrets d'application* providing more detailed rules on the procedures for applying the law, were published on 21 December 1999 (Nos. 99–1089, 99–1090, 99–1091) and 3 February 2000 (Nos. 2000–97, 2000–98). The fruit of a veritable national debate, the PaCS is the result of numerous negotiations and compromises, and reveals the degree of tolerance or recognition of French society with regard to homosexuality.

THE CONTENT OF THE PACS LAW

Midway between civil marriage and *concubinage*, the PaCS creates a third type of union. For heterosexual couples who already have the choice between the two types already mentioned, the PaCS may be considered as a less formal alternative to marriage, or a more formal version of *concubinage*. A PaCS is "a contract concluded between two adult individuals, of different sexes or of the same sex, to organise their life in common (*vie commune*)".[29] Although "life in common" does not necessarily imply a sexual relationship, the *Conseil Constitutionnel* upheld the PaCS law as constitutional subject to its interpretation of "life in common" as meaning "life as a couple (*vie de couple*)":

> "the notion of life in common does not involve only a community of interests and is not limited to a requirement of simple cohabitation between two persons; . . . the life in common mentioned in the referred law supposes, beyond a common residence, a life as a couple, which is all that justifies the legislature's providing for certain causes of the nullity of a pact which, either reproduce the obstacles to marriage aimed at preventing incest [no PaCSs between close relatives], or avoid a violation of the obligation of fidelity resulting from marriage [a married person may not enter into a PaCS]".

This interpretation is binding on all courts and other public authorities under Article 62 of the French Constitution, and would seem to render the celebration of a PaCS between two persons who are merely friends and not a couple fraudulent and void. "Common residence" does not necessarily mean a single resi-

[27] Decision No. 99–419 DC, http://www.conseil-constitutionnel.fr/decision/1999/99419/index.htm.

[28] See *supra* n. 1.

[29] Code civil, Art. 515-1.

dence. If a PaCS is treated like a civil marriage, under Civil Code Article 108, partners joined by a PaCS will be able to have two separate residences, but a "common life" including "life as a couple" will remain essential. Through its restrictive interpretation of the PaCS law, the *Conseil Constitutionnel* clearly wanted to avoid "PaCSs of convenience".

Your proposed partner must be 18 years old and capable of entering into contracts, must not be married or a party to another PaCS, and cannot be your parent, grandparent, child, grandchild, parent-in-law, child-in-law, brother, sister, uncle, aunt, nephew or niece, but can be your cousin.[30] In France, the union must be declared at the registry of the *Tribunal d'instance* (county court) of the area in which the partners establish their common residence.[31] Two non-European Union nationals can sign a PaCS, as long as one of them has a residence permit. Outside France, at least one partner must be a French national, and the PaCS is registered with the French consular officials of the country in which the partners have their common residence.[32] Partners joined by a PaCS undertake to help one another "mutually and materially", and they are jointly liable to third parties for debts contracted by either of them "for the necessities of their daily life and for expenses relating to their common residence".[33] Unless otherwise agreed, movable and immovable (real and personal) property purchased by the partners after the conclusion of the PaCS is presumed to be jointly owned with 50 per cent shares and no right of survivorship (*indivision par moitié*).[34] The partners may choose another regime, either in the PaCS agreement they submit to the county court (in the case of future purchases of furniture and appliances), or in each document granting them title to each item of property (in the case of future purchases of other property).

The partners are subject to joint taxation of their combined incomes in the year of the third anniversary of the registration of their PaCS.[35] However, joint taxation of their combined wealth begins immediately, and the partners are jointly and severally liable for the wealth tax.[36] If one partner dies without making a will, the other partner has no automatic inheritance rights. However, two years after their PaCS, the first 375,000 French francs in testamentary and *inter vivos* gifts between partners will be exempt from gift taxes.[37] If one partner is the official tenant of the partners' common residence and abandons the residence or dies, the lease continues for the benefit of, or is transferred to, the other partner.[38] (This provision effectively reverses the 1997 *Vilela* v. *Weil* decision of

[30] Code civil, Art. 515-2.
[31] Code civil, Art. 515-3.
[32] *Ibid.*
[33] Code civil, Art. 515-4.
[34] Code civil, Art. 515-5.
[35] *Code général des impôts*, Art. 6(1).
[36] *Ibid.*, Arts. 885 A,1723 ter-00 B.
[37] *Ibid.*, Art. 779(III).
[38] *Loi no. 89–462 du 6 juillet 1989*, Art. 14.

the *Cour de cassation* mentioned above.[39]) If one partner cannot claim social security benefits in any other capacity, he or she can benefit from the other partner's (public) health and maternity insurance coverage.[40] Partners enjoy the same rights as spouses to request a transfer for the partner left behind when the other partner is transferred to another city for professional reasons (if both partners are civil servants),[41] to simultaneous vacations (if they are working in the same company), to two days of bereavement leave if one partner dies,[42] and to the return to the surviving partner of the capital of certain social security contributions made by a deceased partner.[43]

As for non-European Community nationals, unlike the previous proposals, the PaCS does not grant the automatic right to a residence permit. However, the existence of a PaCS is an "element" to be considered in deciding whether the non-EC national partner's "personal" (not "family") ties with France are such that "the refusal to authorise residence would violate his or her right to respect for his or her private and family life in a manner disproportionate to the reasons for the refusal".[44] A non-EC national joined by a PaCS to a French or other EC national must show a "life in common" in France of at least three years, regardless of the date the PaCS was contracted. A non-EC national joined by a PaCS to another non-EC national must show five years of cohabitation in France, or the PaCS must have existed for at least three years.[45]

As with the registered partnerships of Scandinavian countries, a PaCS does not permit the partners to adopt a child jointly (only married heterosexual couples may do so),[46] or to have joint parental authority over the child of one of the partners (married and cohabiting heterosexual couples may obtain it),[47] or to have access to medically assisted procreation (infertile married and cohabiting heterosexual couples have access).[48] It is clear from the text of earlier bills, and from the parliamentary debates on the PaCS bill, that parental rights are not covered. Nor will the reform of family law have any provisions on same-sex couples who are, or would like to be, parents.[49]

A PaCS is terminated with immediate effect if (i) both partners agree to file a declaration with the *Tribunal d'instance*, (ii) one partner marries, or (iii) one partner dies. Otherwise, one partner may terminate the PaCS by notifying the other partner. A unilateral termination takes effect three months after the notice

[39] See *supra* n.9.

[40] *Code de la sécurité sociale*, Art. L 161-14.

[41] *Loi no. 99–944 du 15 novembre 1999*, Art. 13.

[42] *Loi no. 99–944 du 15 novembre 1999*, Art. 8; *Code du travail*, Arts. L 223-7, L 226-1.

[43] *Code de la sécurité sociale*, Art. L 361-4.

[44] *Loi no. 99–944 du 15 novembre 1999*, Art. 12; *Ordonnance no. 45–2658 du 2 novembre 1945*, Art. 12bis(7).

[45] *Circulaire du Ministère de l'intérieur du 10 décembre 1999* (Nor/Int/D/00251 C.).

[46] *Code civil*, Art. 343.

[47] *Ibid.*, Arts. 371–387.

[48] *Code de la santé publique*, Art. L152-2.

[49] See D Borrillo, "La protection juridique des nouvelles formes familiales : le cas des familles homoparentales", (March-April 2000) *Mouvements* n° 8, p. 54.

is delivered to the other partner, provided that a copy of the notice has been sent to the registrar of the *Tribunal d'instance*. Rights to property and financial support may be determined by the partners when they sign their PaCS. If their PaCS is silent on these matters, and they are unable to agree on them, a court may determine the proprietary and financial consquences of the breakdown of their PaCS.[50]

Before the PaCS law, different-sex couples had two choices as to the law governing their relationship: civil marriage or *concubinage*. Same-sex couples had neither choice and were not legally recognised. After the PaCS law, different-sex couples can choose civil marriage, a PaCS or *concubinage*, and same-sex couples can choose a PaCS or *concubinage*, but not civil marriage. Same-sex couples who enter into a PaCS will not enjoy all the advantages of marriage. Their relationship will not be recognised outside of France, except possibly in certain countries with registered partnership institutions similar to the PaCS. Nor does a PaCS resolve the question of recognising a family unit, because the partners are still considered "single". Partners joined by a PaCS must wait several years to enjoy certain rights that married couples are granted immediately, receive a less generous tax deduction in relation to gifts, cannot adopt jointly or have access to medically assisted procreation, do not receive social security allowances for widows and widowers or resulting from accidents in the workplace, and cannot represent each other judicially or extra-judicially. All this shows that, instead of granting equality, the PaCS confirms the inequality of same-sex couples.

Despite these limitations, the PaCS has been relatively successful. By May 2000, six months after the promulgation of the law, more than 15,000 PaCSs had been signed. Thus, it would appear that, in the first year of the PaCS, over 30,000 or 7 per cent of the 450,000 cohabiting couples formed in France each year, according to the *Institut d'études démographiques*, could be expected to opt for a PaCS. Although it is much too early to attempt a sociology of the PaCS, the majority of those contracting a PaCS would seem to be same-sex couples from the urban middle class.[51]

THE ONGOING STRUGGLE FOR THE EQUALITY OF COUPLES

Now that the debate on the PaCS is over in France, a new question arises: why should civil marriage, and with it the right to adopt children jointly and to use assisted reproduction techniques, not be made available to same-sex couples?[52]

[50] *Code civil*, Art. 515-7.

[51] See "*Les petits ratés du Pacs*", *Le Monde* (26 April 2000), at 10.

[52] I have developed arguments for marriage between people of the same sex in "*Homosexualité et liberté matrimoniale*", (May 1998) 12 *Revue Témoin* 75 (Editions Balland, Paris); "*Les unions de même sexe : entre mariage impossible et concubinage improbable*", (Oct. 1998) 12–13 *Revue Le Banquet* 125 (*Centre d'études et de réflexion pour l'action politique*, Paris); "*Le mariage homosexuel : vers une égalité radicale*", (March 1999) *La Mazarine* G030 (*dossier Homosexualité et famille*)

If love, affection and the wish for a child are the same irrespective of whether the couple is of the same sex or of different sexes, why should the law treat the same-sex couple differently? The PaCS is a cowardly project,[53] resulting from the difficulty facing gays and lesbians in achieving equal rights, either through the legislature or the courts. But for this difficulty, how can it be explained that people were excited by a law that confines homosexual couples to a form of sub-standard marriage, while giving the false impression that their union is recognised in the same way as a civil marriage? The PaCS fails to comply with the European Parliament's 1994 "Resolution on equal rights for homosexuals and lesbians in the EC", which called on the Commission of the EC to draft a Recommendation seeking to end "the barring of lesbians and homosexuals from marriage or from an equivalent legal framework, and . . . guarantee the full rights and benefits of marriage, allowing the registration of partnerships", and to end "any restrictions on the rights of lesbians and homosexuals to be parents or to adopt or foster children".[54]

Far from banishing discrimination, or providing "an equivalent legal framework", the PaCS restricts same-sex couples to an inferior status compared to different-sex couples. (See the table at the end of this chapter.) In choosing between civil marriage, a PaCS and *concubinage*, a different-sex couple must decide whether to emphasise liberty or security. Yet, it is difficult to imagine why a heterosexual couple, who preferred liberty, would want to confine themselves to a PaCS, a union which, if ended non-consensually, would submit the partners to considerable constraints. On the other hand, if security is a priority, why would they choose a PaCS, a status which gives rise to rights only after a certain number of years and which, moreover, does not give full social welfare protection to the couple. By creating an intermediate status between *concubinage* and civil marriage, which is likely to be of interest mainly to same-sex couples, the PaCS further institutionalises the exclusion of homosexuals from the marriage contract. The PaCS is an extraordinary indication of the impossibility for Western democracies to implement fully their frequently proclaimed values such as equality and non-discrimination.

I am not concerned here with taking a position vis-à-vis the institution of marriage, but rather to defend the legitimacy of the claim to a right to marriage. Regardless of what one thinks of the institution, it remains the best legal instrument for the protection of the couple, both at the international and the national level. For example, the right to marry is a fundamental freedom mentioned in international human rights instruments, such as the Universal Declaration of

(Paris); "*Le mariage homosexuel : hommage de l'hérésie à l'orthodoxie*", in Borrillo, et al., *La sexualité a-t-elle un avenir?* (Paris, Presses Universitaires de France, 1999); "*Uniones del mismo sexo y libertad matrimonial*", (July 1999) 35 *Jueces para la democracia* 15 (Madrid) and (Nov. 1998) 15 *Revista de Sociología del Derecho* 22 (La Plata, Argentina).

[53] See D Borrillo, E Fassin & M Iacub (eds.), *Au-delà du PaCS : l'expertise familiale à l'épreuve de l'homosexualité* (Paris, Presses Universitaires de France, 1999).

[54] Resolution A3–0028/94, [1994] Official Journal C 61/40.

Human Rights (Article 16), the International Covenant on Civil and Political Rights (Article 23), and the European Convention on Human Rights (Article 12). And European Community law fully recognises only legally married non-EC national "spouses" as having the right to move freely with an EC national throughout the European Union.[55] The PaCS gives homosexuals a poor substitute for marriage, the only status which—nationally and internationally—grants full legal recognition. Juridical doctrine has never offered a single legal reason why the choice of marriage, and the rights and obligations that accompany it, should not be open to same-sex couples. The arguments offered in opposition to extending the right to marry or to the PaCS are based on individual prejudices or explicit homophobia.[56]

Would we find it normal for the law to exclude homosexuals from property rights, only allowing them to benefit from occupation without title (mere possession of land) or from usufruct (a life estate in land), but not full ownership (freehold title to land)? Likewise, as far as the right to vote is concerned, would we accept a law which states that gays and lesbians may only vote in regional elections but not in national ones? If this is absurd in other areas of law, why should such an exclusion be acceptable in the area of family law? The PaCS creates a specific form of sub-standard citizenship for same-sex couples. Its acceptance by many in the lesbian and gay minority suggests that they have accepted the dominant argument, which consists in making them believe that they cannot have equal rights and that their exclusion is, therefore, justified. The PaCS reveals the extraordinary political difficulties linked to homosexuality. "Between an old-fashioned Right and a faint-hearted Left", to quote *Le Monde*'s editorial of 14 November 1998, same-sex couples in France found themselves, throughout the PaCS debate, in the middle of a disturbing spectacle which humiliated them and threw scorn upon their fight for equality.

[55] See Regulation 1612/68, Art. 10(1); Dir. 68/360, Art. 1; E Guild, chap. 38.

[56] See D Borrillo, "Fantasmes des juristes vs. *Ratio juris* : la *doxa* des privatistes sur l'union entre personnes de même sexe" in Borrillo, Fassin et Iacub, *supra* n.53.

COMPARISON OF CIVIL MARRIAGE, THE PACS AND *CONCUBINAGE*[57]

Right or obligation	**Civil marriage**	**PaCS**	***Concubinage***
place of registration	*Mairie* (town hall)	*Tribunal d'instance* (county court)	no registration
minimum age	16 for women, 18 for men (or 16 if emancipated)	18	18
obligation of fidelity	Yes	No	No
mutual support obligations	Yes	Yes	No
liability to third parties for debts of partner	Yes	Yes	No
ownership of property	presumed 50% joint ownership, (*communauté*) unless agreed otherwise	presumed 50% joint ownership (no right of survivorship) (*indivision par moitié*), unless agreed otherwise	separate ownership, according to who purchased asset
voluntary termination	after divorce procedure before *Tribunal aux affaires familiales*	immediate if bilateral, 3 months if unilateral	immediate in all cases
joint taxation	from date of marriage	in year of 3rd anniversary of PaCS	none
health and maternity insurance of partner	Yes	Yes	Yes, if "effectively, totally and permanently" dependent on partner
joint job transfers (civil service) and simultaneous vacations (same employer)	Yes	Yes	No
bereavement leave	Yes	Yes	No
damages claim where partner's death caused by third party's negligence	Yes	Yes	Yes

[57] See also S Dibos-Lacroux, *PACS: Le guide pratique* (Paris, Editions Prat, 2000) at 97–135.

Right or obligation	**Civil marriage**	**PaCS**	***Concubinage***
inheritance on intestacy or in spite of will	surviving spouse receives a life interest in at least 25% of estate, regardless of willinheritance tax	none first 500,000 francs	none first 375,000 francs
first 10,000 francs			
	exempt	exempt	exempt
transfer of lease upon death of partner	Yes	Yes	Yes, after one year of living together
survivor's pension and widow or widower's allowance (social security)	Yes	No	No
return of capital of social security contributions	Yes, if no dependant invokes priority	Yes, if no dependant invokes priority	No, unless can invoke priority as dependant
residence permit for non-EC national partner	automatic	discretionary; PaCS is an "element" to be considered	discretionary; *concubinage* is an "element"
nationality for non-French national partner	automatic after one year of marriage	after five years of residence in France, if "assimilation" shown; PaCS is evidence	after five years of residence if "assimilation" shown; *conc.* is evidence
judicial or extra-judicial representation of one partner by the other	Yes	No	No
civil status	married	single	single
joint adoption of unrelated child	Yes	No	No
second-parent adoption of partner's child	Yes	No	No
joint parental authority over partner's child	Yes	different-sex—Yes same-sex—No	different-sex—Yes same-sex—No
access to medically assisted procreation	Yes	infertile different-sex—Yes (after two years) same-sex—No	infertile different-sex—Yes (after two years) same-sex—No

BIBLIOGRAPHY (NOT CITED IN FOOTNOTES)

Aoun, Alia, *Le PACS: Vos droits en 100 questions-réponses* (Paris, Delmas, 2000)

Borrillo, Daniel, *Vers la reconnaissance des couples de même sexe: Analyse et propositions* (with Marianne Schulz), 2d ed. (Paris, Documents Aides Fédération National, 1997)

—— "Droit et sida" (with Jean-Luc Dupuy) (1998) 71 *Informations sociales* 90 (Caisse nationale des allocations familiales)

—— "Adoption et homosexualité: analyse critique de l'arrêt du Conseil d'Etat du 9 octobre 1996" (with Thierry Pitois) in *Homosexualités et droit: De la tolérance sociale à la reconnaissance juridique* (ed.), 2d ed. (Paris, Presses Universitaires de France, 1999)

—— *L'homophobie. Que-sais je ?* (Paris, Presses Universitaires de France, 2000)

—— "L'orientation sexuelle en Europe : esquisse d'une politique publique antidiscriminatoire", (June-Aug. 2000) 609 *Les Temps Modernes* 263

Bourdieu, Pierre, *La domination masculine* (Paris, Liber, Seuil, 1998)

De la Pradelle, Géraud, and Mecary, Caroline, *Les droits des homosexuel(le)s. Que sais-je?* (Paris, Presses Universitaires de France, 1998)

Dubreuil, Eric, *Des parents de même sexe* (Paris, Odile Jacob,1998)

Eribon, Didier, *Réflexions sur la question gay* (Paris, Fayard, 1999)

Fassin, Eric, "PaCS socialiste: la gauche et le 'juste milieu'", (1998) 12–13 *Revue Le Banquet* 147 (Centre d'études et de réflexion pour l'action politique, Paris)

—— "L'illusion anthropologique: homosexualité et filiation, (May–June 1998) 12 *Revue Témoin*. [no page available]

—— "Homosexualité et mariage aux Etats-Unis: histoire d'une polémique", (January 1999) *Actes de la Recherche en Sciences Sociales* ("Homosexualités")

Fourest, Caroline, and Venner, Fiametta, *Les Anti-PaCS ou la dernière croisade homophobe* (Paris, Prochoix, 1999)

Lecuyer, Hervé, ed., *Le PACS, Droit de la famille, Les mensuels spécialisés du Juris-Classeur*, n° 12, December 1999.

Leroy-Forgeot, Flora, *Histoire juridique de l'homosexualité en Europe* (Paris: Presses Universitaires de France, 1997)

—— *Les enfants du PaCS: Réalités de l'homoparentalité* (Paris, L'Atelier de l'Archer, 1999)

Leroy-Forgeot, Flora and Mécary, Caroline, *Le PACS. Que sais-je?* (Paris, Presses Universitaires de France, 2000)

—— *Les unions légales des personnes de même sexe* (Paris, Odile Jacob, 2000)

Mécary, Caroline, *Droit et homosexualité* (Paris, Dalloz, 2000)

Moutouh, Hugues, "La question de la reconnaissance du couple homosexuel: entre dogmatisme et empirisme", (1998) 39 *Recueil Dalloz (cahier chronique)*

—— "L'esprit d'une loi: Controverses sur le Pacte civil de Solidarité", (March-April 1999) 603 *Les Temps Modernes* 189

Thouret, Sylvain, "Le PACS: Techniques de rédaction et esquisse de contrat", (10 March 2000) *Les Petites Affiches*, No. 50, pp. 4–7

Welzer-Lang, Daniel et al. (eds.), *La peur de l'autre en soi: Du sexisme à l'homophobie* (Montréal, Vib Editeur, 1994)

26

Spain: The Heterosexual State Refuses to Disappear

NICOLÁS PÉREZ CÁNOVAS*

INTRODUCTION

MORE THAN TWO decades since the promulgation of the Spanish Constitution of 1978,[1] homosexual relationships have ceased to be an illicit behaviour, prosecuted and punished by the State, but they still do not receive the same legal treatment as heterosexual relationships. The persistence of old homophobic prejudices in dominant academic writing, in the legislature and, ultimately, in the *Tribunal Constitucional* (Constitutional Court), is a major factor in the maintenance of the Heterosexual State. The Constitution's guarantee of the right of every person to the free development of their personality (Article 10(1)), and prohibition of discrimination based on race, sex, religion, opinion, or any other personal or social condition or circumstance (Article 14),[2] have been interpreted restrictively by the *Tribunal Constitucional* when applied to relationships between persons of the same sex. The *Tribunal* has upheld as constitutional legal rules that exclude such relationships from the recognised constitutional rights to contract a marriage (Article 32(1))[3] and to constitute a family (Article 39(1))[4].

* *Profesor titular de Derecho Civil* (Civil Law), *Universidad de Granada*. Author of *Homosexualidad, Homosexuales y Uniones Homosexuales en el Derecho Español* (Granada, Ediciones Comares, 1996); "Homosexualité et unions homosexuelles dans le droit espagnol" in Daniel Borrillo, *Homosexualités et droit*, 2d ed. (Paris, Presses Universitaires de France, 1999); "La heterosexualidad en el discurso jurídico sobre el matrimonio y la familia", (2000) 1 *Orientaciones* 83; "La Crisis del Estado Heterosexual: Del derecho a la vida privada al derecho a la vida familiar de las parejas homosexuales", [2001] 4 *Revista de la Facultad de Derecho de la Universidad de Granada*. [no page available]. Translated from Spanish to English by R Wintemute.

[1] See http://alcazaba.unex.es/constitucion/ (Spanish); http://www.uni-wuerzburg.de/law/sp00000_.html (English).

[2] From its first judgments (*sentencias*, Ss), the *Tribunal Constitucional* (TC) held that, because of the final category, Art. 14 should not be seen as expressing an intention to enumerate exhaustively and exclude any ground not mentioned in the text. See SsTC 22/1981 (2 July), 75/1982 (3 Aug.).

[3] "*El hombre y la mujer tienen derecho a contraer matrimonio en plena igualdad jurídica*". ("Man and woman have the right to contract a marriage in full legal equality".)

[4] "*Los poderes públicos aseguran la protección social, económica y jurídica de la familia*". ("Public authorities assure the social, economic and legal protection of the family.")

REFORMS IN CRIMINAL, ANTI-DISCRIMINATION AND MILITARY LEGISLATION

Recognition that the right of every person to the free development of their emotionality (*afectividad*) and sexuality is unquestionably included in the constitutional right to free development of personality, inevitably led to a series of anti-discrimination reforms in the criminal law. In 1979, the law that considered homosexuals as "social dangers" ("*peligrosos sociales*") was amended.[5] In 1988, the offence of "public scandal" ("*escándalo público*") in Article 431 of the old Penal Code (*Código Penal*), which had been used to punish homosexual sexual behaviour, was repealed.[6] In 1995, the new Penal Code[7] went beyond decriminalisation and extended the protection of the criminal law to persons who had suffered discrimination because of their sexual orientation (*orientación sexual*), in employment (Article 314) or in the exercise of their constitutional rights (Articles 510–12).

In military law, progress was more limited. The new Military Penal Code[8] dropped the old offence of "dishonest acts with individuals of the same sex" ("*actos deshonestos con individuos del mismo sexo*") ("old Article 352"),[9] which was punishable by up to six years in prison and discharge from the military. However, such conduct was included as deserving of disciplinary sanctions in the Organic Law on the Disciplinary Regime in the Armed Forces.[10] In 1991, the *Tribunal Constitucional* held that homosexual relationships in the armed forces had ceased to be criminal but had become, at least in certain circumstances, an administrative infraction.[11] In the mid-1980s, the Tribunal had upheld old Article 352 as constitutional, suggesting that the legislature would be free to reintroduce it at any time.[12] However, a 1999 decision of the European Court of Human Rights would preclude this.[13]

[5] *Decreto-ley* (Decree-Law) of 11 Jan. 1979 amending the *Ley de peligrosidad y rehabilitación social* (Law on Dangerousness and Social Rehabilitation) of 4 Aug. 1970.

[6] *Ley Orgánica* (Organic Law) of 9 June 1988. Before and after the Constitution of 1978, the *Tribunal Supremo* (TS) (Supreme Court) frequently used Art. 431 to criminalise sexual relations, even though they were between consenting adults and in the most absolute privacy. See, e.g., SsTS (*Sala Segunda*) (Second Chamber) of 2 Nov. 1943, 18 Feb. 1978, 13 May 1985. A challenge to the vagueness of the offence was rejected by the *Tribunal Constitucional*. See STC 62/1982 (15 Oct.).

[7] *Ley Orgánica* of 23 Nov. 1995.

[8] *Código penal militar* of 27 Nov. 1986.

[9] *Código de justicia militar* of 17 July 1945, Art. 352.

[10] *Ley Orgánica del régimen disciplinario de las fuerzas armadas* of 27 Nov. 1985. Art. 9.20 prohibited, as a serious fault, "having sexual relations in barracks, ships, bases or other military establishments in a way that harms military dignity". Art. 59.3 treated "conduct seriously contrary to discipline, service and military dignity" as a reason for the imposition of extraordinary disciplinary sanctions, including demotion and discharge (Art. 61). The terminology used in these provisions has been criticised as excessively subjective and contrary to the sexual freedom of individuals. The 1985 law was replaced by the *Ley Orgánica del régimen disciplinario de las fuerzas armadas* of 2 Dec. 1998, Articles 8.24, 17.2.

[11] STC 196/1991 (17 Oct.).

[12] *Auto* (Order) TC 446/1984 (11 July); STC 33/1985 (7 March).

[13] *Smith & Grady* v. *United Kingdom*; *Lustig-Prean & Beckett* v. *UK* (27 Sept. 1999). See Wintemute, chap. 40.

CONSTITUTIONAL PROTECTION OF MARRIAGE AND THE FAMILY

Based on the express constitutionalisation of marriage in Article 32(1) of the Constitution, the case-law of the *Tribunal Constitucional* has given marriage an institutional value from which the Tribunal has deduced that, between spouses, there exists automatically a family-like cohabitation deserving the protection of Article 39(1) of the Constitution.[14] But this access route to the scope of family relations has so far been barred to homosexual couples. Academic writing on civil law has deduced, from the reference to "man and woman" in Article 32(1) of the Constitution,[15] that a difference in the sexes of the contracting parties is a requirement for marriage. This conclusion is based, not on a literal interpretation of Article 32(1), which does not say "man *with* woman" or define marriage as "*between* man and woman", but on an historical interpretation, mainly supported by the debates of those who adopted the Constitution, and on a comparison with sex-neutral terms used elsewhere in the Constitution, such as "citizens", "Spaniards" and "everyone".

In my opinion, to continue insisting on this interpretation of Article 32(1) means ignoring the transformations experienced by Spanish society, which have been promoted by the values system of the Constitution. The legality of emotional and sexual relationships between persons of the same sex has made possible their visibility and the public expression of demands to equality of rights with heterosexual relationships.[16] This has had a remarkable impact on the pace of change in social attitudes, whereby acceptance has gradually gained ground on intolerance,[17] as the fallacy of age-old homophobic prejudices has been shown. These social changes have made it an urgent necessity that public authorities interpret Article 32(1) in a way that effectively realises constitutional values and principles which, through their legitimating and hermeneutic function, fulfill an evolutive and dynamic role in the legal order. Yet, the legislator accepted the dominant academic interpretation (opposite-sex marriage only) in amending the marriage provisions of the Civil Code (*Código Civil*) so as to bring them into conformity with the Constitution.[18]

The *Tribunal Constitucional* supported this interpetation in a decision of 11 July 1994, in which a man claimed a widower's pension under the General Law on Social Security,[19] after the death of his male partner of eleven years. The

[14] STC 222/1992 (11 Dec.) ("the constitutional concept of family, without doubt, includes the case of a marriage without children or dependent relatives").

[15] *Supra* n.3.

[16] Associations of lesbian women and gay men were legalised for the first time on 16 July 1980.

[17] See "Nuevas familias", (Oct. 1997) *Boletín del Centro de investigaciones sociológicas* (57% said yes and 33% no when asked: "should homosexual couples who live together in a stable way be granted the same rights (e.g., to pensions and social security) and obligations as married couples?").

[18] *Ley* of 13 May 1981; *Ley* of 7 July 1981. See eg Civil Code, Arts. 44 ("*El hombre y la mujer . . .*", "Man and woman . . ."), 66, 67 ("*El marido y la mujer . . .*", "Husband and wife . . .").

[19] *Ley General de la Seguridad Social*, Art. 160.

TC rejected the claim, citing judgments of the European Court of Human Rights on marriages by transsexual persons[20] in finding no violation of the constitutional principle of equality. "[T]he union between persons of the same biological sex is not a legally regulated institution, nor is there a constitutional right to establish it; unlike marriage between man and woman which is a constitutional right . . . [T]he full constitutionality of the heterosexual principle as qualifying the marital link must be accepted, as our Civil Code provides . . ."[21]

Because this access route to the constitutional scope of the family has been blocked for homosexual couples, it is a constitutional necessity that they be considered at least as *de facto* couples on the same footing as heterosexual *de facto* couples. The *Tribunal Constitucional* has held that a heterosexual de facto couple constitutes a family relationship, albeit that it may receive less favourable legal treatment, within reasonable limits, than the family unit based on marriage.[22] Yet in its 11 July 1994 decision, the *Tribunal Constitucional* went on to hold that "public authorities may grant a privileged treatment to the family union consisting of a man and a woman compared with a homosexual union. This does not preclude the legislator from establishing an equivalent system permitting homosexual cohabitants to enjoy the full rights and benefits of marriage, as proposed by the European Parliament".[23]

[20] *Rees* v. *United Kingdom*, *Cossey* v. *United Kingdom*. See Wintemute, chap. 40.

[21] *Auto* TC 222/1994 (11 July). See also *Resolución de la Dirección General de los Registros y del Notariado* (Resolution of the Directorate General of Registers and Notaries) of 21 Jan. 1988, denying the registration of a male-male couple as a marriage in the *Registro Civil*. The Directorate General held that "marriage has always been understood as an institution in which different sexes are essential" and found no discrimination contrary to Art. 14 of the Constitution. There was no sex discrimination, because the two men could each marry a woman, while the difference in treatment between heterosexual and homosexual unions had an objective and reasonable justification. The *Tribunal Supremo* has refused to permit post-operative transsexual persons to marry a person of their birth sex. See, e.g., SsTS (*Sala Primera*) (First Chamber) of 27 July 1987, 19 April 1991. A bill passed by the *Senado* on 7 March 2001 (*Proposición de Ley sobre el derecho a la identidad sexual*) would overturn this case-law.

[22] In STC 184/1990 (15 Nov.), the *Tribunal Constitucional* held that Art. 39(1) "does not establish an equality of treatment in every aspect between marital and non-marital unions". Art. 39(1) permits measures of public authorities that "grant different and more favourable treatment to the family unit based on marriage than to other cohabitation units", or "facilitate or favour the exercise of the constitutional right to contract a marriage [Art. 32], so long as they do not restrain or impede unreasonably a man and a woman who decide to live together *more uxurio* [in the manner of a wife]". Applying this doctrine, the *Tribunal Constitucional* has upheld, as consistent with the prohibition of discrimination in Art. 14 of the Constitution, the exclusion of the surviving member of a *de facto* couple from the survivor's pension that legislation grants exclusively to a spouse (see e.g. SsTC 184/1990 (15 Nov.), 66/1994 (28 Feb.)), and the exclusion of *de facto* couples from the right to a subsidy for unemployment because of family responsibilities enjoyed by married couples (see *Autos* TC 1021/1988, 1022/1988 (both 26 Sept.)). However, the *Tribunal Constitucional* found a violation of Art. 14 where legislation excluded *de facto* couples from the right of a surviving spouse to subrogation *mortis causa* to a lease contracted by the deceased spouse, and held that the right must be extended to those cohabiting *more uxorio*. See SsTC 222/1992 (11 Dec.), 6/1993 (18 Jan.), 47/1993 (8 Feb.), 66/1994 (28 Feb.).

[23] *Auto* TC 222/1994 (11 July). See also European Parliament, "Resolution on equal rights for homosexuals and lesbians in the EC", OJ [1994] C 61/40 (adopted on 8 Feb. 1994).

It follows from this statement that the legislator has the power to decide whether, and to what extent, to apply the constitutionally proclaimed principle of equality to eliminate the discriminatory treatment that gay and lesbian couples receive compared with *de facto* heterosexual couples, with regard to being considered a family-like cohabitation. For the *Tribunal Constitucional*, the principle of equality is thus not a constitutionally applicable principle with a direct and immediate effect that abolishes this different legal treatment. Instead, anti-discrimination policies are left to the discretion of the different political opinions and ideologies that govern from time to time. In other words, this constitutional doctrine opens a wide margin of constitutionality, which would permit the total exclusion of homosexual couples from the family rights extended to heterosexual couples, or the complete opposite. This converts the Constitution into a neutral instrument before one legislative option or the other.

The doctrine of the *Tribunal Constitucional* leaves no constitutional doubts as to the full effectiveness at the individual and private level of the relations between members of a homosexual couple, and thus as to the validity of the agreements and contracts relating to property rights that they establish between themselves, both to regulate their cohabitation and to determine the consequences of its termination. But when it comes to considering this type of relationship as a family, the Constitution is silent as a grave, leaving the decision to recognise or not, totally or partially, to the legislature. Under this approach, with regard to measures of social protection in family law and their public and institutional dimension, the legislature faces no constitutional obstacles in deciding with absolute freedom. A homosexual couple is therefore not a family that is protected constitutionally, but instead one that is protected only to the extent that the legislature chooses. If the legislature provides protection, the couple will be a stautorily protected family, but will lack the constitutional guarantees that restrict legislative power, and thus be "deconstitutionalised".

NATIONAL LEGISLATION RECOGNISING HOMOSEXUAL AND HETEROSEXUAL *DE FACTO* COUPLES

What has the Spanish national legislature[24] done about this situation? On the one hand, it has left in place an express and unequivocal prohibition of the joint adoption of a child by a homosexual couple.[25] On the other hand, it has treated *de facto* couples, without regard to the couple's sexual orientation, in the same

[24] The Spanish national legislature is known as the *Cortes Generales* and consists of two chambers, the *Congreso de los Diputados* and the *Senado*.

[25] *Ley de Adopción* of 11 Nov. 1987, *disposición adicional* 3: "References in this Law to the capacity of spouses to adopt a child simultaneously will also be applied to a man and a woman who make up a couple united in a permanent way by an emotional relationship analogous to that of spouses". Even though no similar provision exists with regard to fostering children, most academic writers have defended an analogous interpretation of Articles 172–3 of the Civil Code that prevents homosexual couples from fostering children jointly.

way as married couples in three statutes: the Law on Urban Leasing,[26] the Law on Limits on Real Property Rights to Eliminate Architectural Barriers to Persons with Disabilities,[27] and the Law on Assistance for Victims of Violent or Sexual Crimes.[28] At the local level, the 1994 decision of the Mayor of the City of Vitoria[29] to establish the first municipal register of *de facto* couples, without regard to the couple's sexual orientation, had an enormous impact on public opinion. The example of Vitoria was followed by hundreds of municipalities and by several regions (*comunidades autónomas*).[30]

These timid advances in the equal legal treatment of homosexual and heterosexual couples, with regard to the protection of family relationships, have had the perverse effect of establishing an interpretative criterion that permits courts to exclude homosexual couples from other legislation where the provision extending rights of married couples to *de facto* couples does not include the phrase "without regard to [the relationship's] sexual orientation" ("*con independencia de su orientación sexual*") or a similar expression.[31] Courts have begun to use this intepretation to deny the right to compensation to the surviving member of a homosexual couple for the death of their partner in a motor vehicle accident. Until the promulgation of the 1995 Law on the Regulation and Supervision of Private Insurance,[32] the right to compensation was based on the concept of an adversely affected person (*perjudicado*) under Article 1902 of the Civil Code (right to compensation for damage caused by negligence), which case-law had interpreted as not requiring the existence of a family relationship or a right to inherit. Because the Insurance Law (unlike the three other Laws cited above which were passed shortly before or after the Insurance Law) does not include a similar phrase regarding sexual orientation when referring to *de facto* couples, it has been assumed that only heterosexual *de facto* couples are covered.[33]

[26] *Ley de Arrendamientos Urbanos* of 24 Nov. 1994, Arts. 12, 16, 24, *disposición transitoria segunda* B(7), giving effect to the 1992–94 judgments of the *Tribunal Constitucional*, *supra* n.22 (references to a person cohabiting "in a permanent way in an emotional relationship analogous to that of spouses, without regard to its sexual orientation").

[27] *Ley de límites del dominio sobre inmuebles para eliminar las barreras arquitectónicas a personas con discapacidad* of 30 May 1995, Art. 2.

[28] *Ley de ayuda y asistencia a las víctimas de delitos violentos o contra la libertad sexual* of 11 Dec. 1995, Art. 2.3.

[29] *Decreto de la Alcaldía* (Mayoral Decree) of 28 Feb. 1994.

[30] See the *Decretos de los Gobiernos autonómicos* (Regional Government Decrees) establishing de facto union registers in the regions of Valencia (7 Dec. 1994), Asturias (29 Dec. 1994), Madrid (20 April 1995), Andalucía (9 Jan. 1996), and Extremadura (18 March 1997).

[31] *Supra* nn.26–28. Since the PP was elected in 1996, see *infra*, no such expressions have been included in legislation.

[32] *Ley de ordenación y supervisión de los seguros privados* of 8 Nov. 1995, *Anexo*, *Tabla* I, (basic compensation for death), *Grupo* I (victims with spouses): "established *de facto* conjugal couples ("*las uniones conyugales de hecho consolidadas*") are treated in the same way as legal situations".

[33] Although it is a rare exception, the judgment of the *Tribunal Superior de Justicia de Cataluña, Sala de lo Contencioso-Administrativo, Sección 2* (Superior Court of Justice of Catalonia, Administrative Litigation Chamber, Section 2) of 4 July 1996 is worth mentioning. The *Tribunal* recognised as a family grouping, for the purpose of the right to obtain a residence permit, a male Colombian citizen who had maintained, for two years in Colombia, a stable cohabiting relationship

After the elections of 3 March 1996 brought the conservative PP (*Partido Popular*, People's Party) into power, the PSOE (*Partido Socialista Obrero Español*, Spanish Socialist Workers Party), which had been in power since 1983, abandoned its vague unfulfilled promises and continual playing to the gallery regarding *de facto* couples.[34] Instead, the PSOE twice introduced bills on *de facto* couples without regard to the sexual orientations of their members, but both were rejected. Two similar attempts by the IU-IC (*Izquierda Unida-Iniciatives per Catalunya*, United Left-Initiatives for Catalonia) met the same fate.[35] Although the socialist (PSOE) bills were less generous in their extension of equal treatment than the communist (IU-IC) bills, all of them expressly recognised *de facto* homosexual couples as families.[36]

Paradoxically, through a series of incredible circumstances, on 27 May 1997 the *Congreso de los Diputados* gave preliminary approval to a bill presented by the CC (*Coalición Canaria*, Canary Islands Coalition), which contained about 90 per cent of the provisions of the PSOE bill which had been rejected earlier that day. However, the CC bill made no progress and, by the dissolution of the legislature for the 12 March 2000 elections, remained mired in the parliamentary committee charged with addressing the many amendments that had been submitted.[37] Even the CC had abandoned it.

as a *de facto* couple with a male Spanish citizen. The *Tribunal* had to interpret the expression "spouse" ("*cónyuge*") in Art. 7.2(a) of the *Reglamento de ejecución* (Implementing Regulation), approved by the *Real Decreto* (Royal Decree) of 26 May 1986, which implemented the *Ley Orgánica de derechos y libertades de los extranjeros en España* (Organic Law on the Rights and Liberties of Foreigners in Spain) of 1 July 1985 (since replaced by a similarly-named law of 11 Jan. 2000). The *Tribunal* held that "spouse" had to be enlarged to include "the person who cohabits in a stable and permanent way, in an emotional relationship equivalent to that of a spouse, without regard to the person's sexual orientation, so as not to ignore the essential content of the right to equality guaranteed by Art. 14 of the Constitution". The TS took a different approach in STS (*Sala de lo Contencioso-Administrativo, Sección* 6) of 6 May 2000 (discussed in EuroLetter No. 83, Oct. 2000), in holding that the residence permit of a South American man in a *de facto* union with a Spanish woman for three years must be extended. The TS interpreted the "sufficient cause" in the 1985 Law and the "exceptional circumstances" in the 1986 Decree, necessary to justify a discretionary extension, as including the "irreparable damage" resulting from "the interruption of . . . a stable *de facto* union between two persons" ("*la unión de hecho estable entre dos personas*").

[34] See the non-binding Resolution (*Proposición no de Ley*) presented by the socialist group and approved by the *Congreso de los Diputados* on 29 Nov. 1994, calling on the Government to "submit to the [*Congreso*] a bill on the regulation of de facto unions, without regard to their sexes", without specifying a date or the content of the bill. See [1994] 110 *Diario de sesiones del Congreso de los Diputados* 5884.

[35] The PSOE and IU-IC bills were rejected by the *Congreso de los Diputados* on 18 March 1997 and 27 May 1997.

[36] Both proposals recognised, *inter alia*, the rights to support, to inheritance upon intestacy, to survivor's pensions, to compensation after the death of a partner in an accident at work, and to the same fiscal treatment as married couples. The communist proposal added, *inter alia*, the rights to acquire Spanish nationality, to adopt jointly, to represent an incapacitated partner, and to be granted a "wedding leave" by the partners' employers, as well as the presumption of paternity.

[37] The PP organised a filibuster to block the normal unfolding of the procedures necessary for the CC bill's approval, thus gaining sufficient time to negotiate with the CC a change of approach, and increasing the chance that the legislative session would expire without action being taken. Among other dilatory tactics, one worth noting is the fact that the time limit for submitting amendments to the bill was extended a record (for the *Congreso de los Diputados*) of ten times, finally ending on 27 Oct. 1997.

The PP, seeking to prevent the adoption of a law on *de facto* couples that would include homosexual couples by granting them a family status, counterattacked by presenting, as an alternative to the CC bill, a confused bill proposing a "civil union contract".[38] Surmounting its first procedural hurdle in the *Congreso* on 29 Oct. 1997, the PP bill purported to leave *de facto* couples outside the institutional scope of the family, so as to situate them in the area of contract,[39] by placing them in a general category of non-matrimonial cooperative cohabitations and diluting the significance of their recognition. The PP bill thus hid what characterises *de facto* couples, and founds their claims for equal treatment with married couples: not that they involve a business transaction through which the contracting parties exchange exclusively economic contributions, but that they involve an alternative form of marital cohabitation and constitute a framework of solidarity and dependence based on sexual affection between the members of the couple.

Because of the PP's obsessive refusal to recognise something as obvious as the fact that two persons of the same sex can love each other, the PP's bill ran into a contradiction. It granted certain effects of marriage to non-marital cohabitation, making it plain that the bill was essentially about regulating *de facto* couples. Yet, in seeking to ensure that it did not grant the status of "family" to homosexual couples, the bill had the unrequested, and juridically undesirable effect, of extending the same rights to other forms of cohabitation that have nothing in common with marriage (e.g. persons living together in a non-sexual relationship), and who logically require different legal treatment. In any case, the PP bill, like the CC bill, was not acted upon before the 2000 elections.

On 12 March 2000, the PP won majorities of the seats in both the *Congreso de los Diputados* and the *Senado*. In the new legislative session, history repeated itself. On 19 September 2000, the PP took advantage of its majority in the *Congreso* to defeat four *de facto* couple bills introduced by the IU, the PSOE, the CIU (*Convergència i Unió*, a Catalan party), and the *Grupo Parlamentario Mixto*,[40] and announced its intention to introduce a new version of its "civil union contract" bill.[41] The right to "family life", a conservative and almost

[38] *Proposición de Ley orgánica de contrato de unión civil*, [29 Sept. 1997] *Boletín Oficial de las Cortes Generales* (*VI Legislatura, Serie B*, 117–1), http://www.congreso.es(*Publicaciones*) ("*Congreso* Bulletin"). Lesbian and gay organisations expressed their opposition to this bill in the manifesto "Different Families, Equal Rights" ("*Familias diversas, iguales derechos*").

[39] The bill would have modified several laws in which rights are granted to spouses and to persons living in analogous cohabiting relationships, sometimes adding "without regard to [the relationship's] sexual orientation".

[40] See IU, *Proposición de Ley de medidas para la igualdad jurídica de las parejas de hecho*, [8 May 2000] *Congreso* Bulletin (VII, B, 37–1); PSOE, *Proposición de Ley por la que se reconocen determinados efectos jurídicos a las parejas de hecho*, [25 April 2000] *Congreso* Bulletin (VII, B, 27–1); CiU, *Proposición de Ley sobre uniones estables de pareja*, [8 May 2000] *Congreso* Bulletin (VII, B, 40–1); *Grupo Parlamentario Mixto*, *Proposición de Ley sobre igualdad jurídica para las parejas estables*, [29 May 2000] *Congreso* Bulletin (VII, B, 58–1). See also Parliament of Navarra (author), *Proposición de Ley para la igualdad jurídica de las parejas estables*, [19 July 2000] *Congreso* Bulletin (VII, B, 81–1) (rejected on 3 April 2001);

[41] See [2000] 24 *Diario de sesiones del Congreso de los Diputados* 1065: "[W]e have a point of departure, which is the civil union contract. . . . The People's Party wishes to legislate on this

assimilationist concept, will continue to be a privilege of heterosexual couples. The PP will try by any means to impede the extension of this concept to homosexual couples, aligning itself with the position maintained by the Roman Catholic Church and its political arm, the Opus Dei. This impasse, which runs counter to the legislative trend in other European countries, has provoked the displacement of the issue to regional parliaments in which the PP does not have a sufficient majority to prevent the adoption of legislation.

REGIONAL LEGISLATION RECOGNISING HOMOSEXUAL AND HETEROSEXUAL *DE FACTO* COUPLES

Spain has nineteen regions (*comunidades autónomas*): Andalucía, Aragón, Asturias, the Balearic Islands, the Canary Islands, Ceuta, the Basque Country (*País Vasco*), Cantabria, Castile-La Mancha, Castile and León, Catalonia, Extremadura, Galicia, La Rioja, Madrid, Melilla, Murcia, Navarra, and Valencia. Of these, four have enacted legislation on *de facto* couples, which has been the subject of polemical academic writing. Commentators have argued that the regional legislatures have exceeded their constitutional powers, and that the new laws violate the Spanish Constitution by granting to cohabitants a quasi-matrimonial status.

Catalonia

On 30 June 1998, the *Parlament de Catalunya* passed the Law on Stable Unions of Couples,[42] with every political party supporting it except the PP. The Law was both the first in Spain to regulate *de facto* couples, and the first to include homosexual unions. Because of constitutional limits on the competences of the Catalan Parliament, the Law does not cover questions of criminal law, labour law and social security law.[43] The Preamble to the Law also acknowledges that it is an exercise of Catalonia's competence over civil law, "apart from the reserve of exclusive competence to the Spanish State with regard to the forms of marriage, because the regulation of heterosexual or homosexual *de facto* couples implies the recognition of situations that are not necessarily comparable to marriage, as constitutional case-law has expressly recognised".[44] Under Article 149.1(8) of the Constitution, the Spanish State has exclusive competence over civil legislation, "without prejudice to the maintenance, modification or

subject, wishes to speak of emotionality, wishes to speak of de facto couples, without doubt any person is capable of loving . . ."

[42] *Llei 10/1998, de 15 de juliol, d'unions estables de parella*, (10 July 1998) 309 *Butlletí Oficial del Parlament de Catalunya* (BOPC) 24738, http://www.parlament-cat.es/porta.htm (*Publicacions, Textos aprovats, V Legislatura*).

[43] See Constitution, Arts. 149.1(6), (7), (17).

[44] (10 July 1998) 309 BOPC at 24776.

development by the regions of regional or special laws, where they exist", but with the exception of, *inter alia*, "juridical-civil relations relating to the forms of marriage" ("*las formas de matrimonio*"). Thus, the six regions of Aragón, the Balearic Islands, the Basque Country, Catalonia, Galicia, and Navarra have some competence over civil law, including family law, but not "the forms of marriage".

The Catalan Law, which is discussed in detail in chapter 27, has been criticised for granting heterosexual but not homosexual *de facto* couples the right to adopt children jointly, for not creating a public register of *de facto* couples, and for recognising *de facto* couples in a special law, outside the Family Code. The latter feature indicates the refusal of the Catalan Parliament to recognise that between the members of a *de facto* couple there is a cohabitation of a family-like character.

Aragón

The region of Aragón followed Catalonia on 12 March 1999, when the *Cortes de Aragón* approved the Law Relating to Unmarried Stable Couples,[45] with the support of all political parties except the PP. The law applies to "an unmarried stable couple in which there exists an emotional relationship analogous to that of spouses" ("*una pareja estable no casada en la que exista relación de afectividad análoga a la conyugal*") (Article 1). Unlike the Catalan law, the Aragón law establishes a mandatory administrative register for *de facto* couples (Article 2), applies to both heterosexual and homosexual *de facto* couples either after two years of marital cohabitation ("*convivencia marital*") or the execution of a public deed (Article 3), and provides that "the rights and obligations of spouses in Aragón public law, which do not have a fiscal character, will apply equally to the members of a stable unmarried couple" (Article 18). However, it does not provide for any intestate succession rights. Like the Catalan law, the Aragón law limits joint adoption of children to heterosexual *de facto* couples (Article 10), and is a special law, outside the body of Aragón family law contained in Aragón's *Compilación de Derecho Civil*. Indeed, Article 14 stresses that "an unmarried stable couple does not generate any relationship of kinship between either of its members and the relatives of the other".

Navarra

On 22 June 2000, the *Parlamento de Navarra* adopted the Regional Law for the Legal Equality of Stable Couples,[46] which goes well beyond the Catalan and

[45] *Ley relativa a parejas estables no casadas*, (26 March 1999) 255 *Boletín Oficial de las Cortes de Aragón*, http://www.cortesaragon.es (BOCA, *Legislaturas anteriores*, IV).

[46] *Ley Foral 6/2000, de 3 de julio, para la igualdad jurídica de las parejas estables*, [7 July 2000] 82 *Boletín Oficial de Navarra*, http://www.cfnavarra.es/BON/007/00707003.htm.

Aragón laws. Article 1 establishes a non-discrimination principle and clearly classifies *de facto* couples as "families": "[N]o one can be discriminated against by reason of the family group of which they form part, whether it has its origin in kinship, marriage or the union of two persons who cohabit in an analogous emotional relationship, without regard to its sexual orientation [*la unión de dos personas que convivan en análoga relación de afectividad, con independencia de su orientación sexual*]". A stable couple is established either by one year of cohabitation or by the execution of a public document (Article 2(2)). Its members can adopt children jointly with the same rights and obligations as married couples (Article 8(1)). The Law adds several provisions to Navarra's *Compilación del Derecho Civil Foral* stating that the members of a stable couple are considered as spouses for a number of purposes, including inheritance rights (Article 11), taxation (Article 12), and civil service employment benefits (Article 13). It also provides for a voluntary Register of Stable Couples (*Disposición adicional*).

The Law is currently the subject of a *recurso de inconstitucionalidad* before the *Tribunal Constitucional*, brought by eighty-three PP members of the Parliament of Navarra on 6 October 2000, who argue that it is inconsistent with Navarra's legislative powers and with Articles 9.(3), 10.(1), 14, 18.(1), 32, 39, and 149.1(1) of the Spanish Constitution. The TC's judgment[47] could affect all of Spain's regional laws on *de facto* couples.

Valencia

On 28 March 2001, the *Cortes Valencianas* adopted the Law to Regulate De Facto Unions.[48] Because Valencia does not have the same competence over civil law as Catalonia, Aragón and Navarra, and because the law resulted from a government bill (*proyecto de ley*) introduced by the PP, it is the least generous of the four regional laws to date. The Law applies to "persons who are cohabiting as couples, in a free, public and obvious manner [*las personas que convivan en pareja, de forma libre, pública y notoria*], linked in a stable way, for at least an uninterrupted period of twelve months, in an emotional relationship" (Article 1(1)). The phrase "analogous to that of spouses", used in Aragón, has been omitted. A *de facto* union is constituted only by registration in the Administrative Register of De Facto Unions (*Registro Administrativo de Uniones de Hecho*), and not merely by fulfilling the requirement of twelve months' cohabitation (Article 1(1)–(2)). To prove that their cohabitation complies with Article 1(1), the *de facto* couple must provide two witnesses (Article 3(2)). The Law cannot affect civil law matters governed by the Civil Code, such

[47] *No. de Registro* 5297–2000 (filed by Alvaro Lapuerta Quintero), http://www.tribunalconstitucional.es.

[48] *Ley por la que se regulan las uniones de hecho*, (9 April 2001) 93 *Boletín Oficial de las Cortes Valencianas* 12404, http://www.corts.gva.es/esp (Publicaciones, BOCV).

as inheritance rights or adoption. However, the members of a *de facto* union will be treated like spouses in Valencian public law and with regard to civil service employment benefits (Articles 8 and 9).

Proposals in Other Regions

As of April 2001, bills on *de facto* couples were being drafted, had been introduced, or were about to be reintroduced (after elections), in the legislatures of six regions: Andalucía, Asturias, the Balearic Islands, the Basque Country, the Canary Islands, and Castile-La Mancha.[49] Because only the Balearic Islands and the Basque Country, of these six regions, have some competence over civil law (excluding "the forms of marriage"), any laws enacted in the other four regions will necessarily be more limited, as in Valencia.

CIVIL MARRIAGE

Given the opposition of the PP in the national legislature, and the lack of competence of regional legislatures, the opening up of civil marriage to homosexual couples is not imminent in Spain. However, on 5 April 2001, inspired by the first homosexual marriages in the Netherlands four days before, the IU introduced a bill[50] that would amend Article 44 of the Civil Code so that it would read: "Any person has the right to contract marriage in conformity with the provisions of this Code". ("*Cualquier persona tiene derecho a contraer matrimonio conforme a las disposiciones de este Código*").

[49] See http://www.fundaciontriangulo.es/temporal/prensa/parejas.htm.

[50] *Proposición de Ley para la modificación del Código Civil en materia de matrimonio*, [20 April 2001] *Congreso* Bulletin (VII, B, 132–1). The bill would also substitute "spouses" ("*los conyuges*") for "husband" ("*el marido*") and "wife" ("*la mujer*") in Arts. 66 and 67. Four similar bills have been introduced. See *Congreso* Bulletin (VII, B) at 135–1 (PSOE) and 137–1, 138–1, 154–1 (*Grupo Parlamentario Mixto*).

27

The Law on Stable Unions of Couples in the Catalonia Autonomous Community of Spain

FRANCESC JAURENA I SALAS*

INTRODUCTION

CATALONIA IS A nation with its own private law. Over the course of Catalonia's history, this body of private law has survived several attempts to abolish it. In 1713, after the War of the Spanish Succession, the Treaty of Utrecht was drawn up between Great Britain (along with Austria, Holland, Portugal and Savoy) and the Bourbons of France. The Treaty awarded, among other things, Gibraltar and Minorca to Great Britain. Despite the fact that Great Britain had promised to defend the Catalan Constitution, they allowed Catalan public law to be replaced by that of Castile. The British, and afterwards the Austrians, left the Catalans in the hands of the Bourbon monarchy in Madrid, who immediately imposed their own public and penal law, and brought Catalan civil law to a standstill by abolishing the Catalan Parliament.

It was not until the end of the nineteenth century, a time of codification all over Europe, that the first attempt was made to codify Catalan private law. In the 1930s, at the time of the Second Spanish Republic in Madrid and the Republican Generalitat in Catalonia, Catalan public law was established, and Catalan private law was reformed and modernised by the Parliament of Catalonia (1932–1939). After the Spanish Civil War, General Franco's dictatorship (1939–1975) abolished the Parliament of Catalonia and Catalan public law. Catalan private law was partly tolerated because it could not be amended, and was expected to die because of lack of reform.[1] In 1982, as part of the post-Franco reforms in Spain, Catalonia was granted the status of an Autonomous Community (*Comunidad Autónoma*) and the Parliament of Catalonia was reestablished. Although public law (including criminal, labour and social security law) is still regulated by the central legislature (*Cortes Generales*) in

* Lawyer, Assistant to a Member of the Catalan Parliament, Barcelona.

[1] On 21 July 1960, the central legislature in Madrid passed a bill which only partially compiled those aspects of Catalan private law which still subsisted.

Madrid,[2] the Catalan Parliament's restored powers have led to a renaissance of Catalan private law, which differs from Spanish private law and has its own principles, institutions and solutions to legal problems.

Prime examples of the Parliament of Catalonia's exercising its right to develop its own legislation are the Family Code[3] and the Law on Stable Unions of Couples ("Stable Unions Law"),[4] which were both passed on 30 June 1998 and came into force on 23 October 1998. These two laws form the cornerstone of Catalan family law. They are also part of a much wider process of reform, development and updating, which has been occurring within Catalan civil law over the past few years and should lead to the publication of the Catalan Civil Code.

The Stable Unions Law made Catalonia the world's sixth country to systematically regulate homosexual couples, after Denmark, Norway, Sweden, Iceland and the Netherlands. More importantly, Catalonia was the first predominantly Roman Catholic country to do so.[5]

The Law consists of two chapters. The first sets out the rules applicable to unmarried heterosexual couples (*la unió estable heterosexual*), while the second regulates homosexual couples (*la unió estable homosexual*). Although the Law deals with the two types of couple separately, a thorough reading reveals that many of the regulations are the same for both types of couple. For example, the patrimonial (property) effects of cohabitation, of the termination of the union during the couple's joint lifetime, and of the death of one of the partners are the same for both types of couple. On the other hand, the regulations differ when it comes to inheritance. Certain inheritance rights are guaranteed for homosexual couples, while the law excludes unmarried heterosexual couples from all inheritance rights. Other differences include the definition of what actually constitutes a stable union, and the fact that unmarried heterosexual couples may jointly adopt a child or individually adopt their partner's child. Homosexual couples have been denied these two possibilities.

[2] See, e.g., *Código penal, Ley orgánica del 23 de noviembre de 1995*, No. 10/1995, Arts. 12, 22(4), 510–12, 515(5), prohibiting various forms of sexual orientation discrimination.

[3] *Llei 9/1998, de 15 de juliol, del Codi de família*, (10 July 1998) 309/V *Butlletí oficial del Parlament de Catalunya* (BOPC) 24738, http://www.parlament-cat.es/porta.htm (*Publicacions, Textos aprovats, V Legislatura*).

[4] *Llei 10/1998, de 15 de juliol, d'unions estables de parella*, (10 July 1998) 309/V BOPC 24775. See Francesc Jaurena i Salas, *La llei d'unions estables de parella a través del dret civil català i constitucional* (Barcelona, Llibres de l'Índex, 2000); Pedro Talavera Fernández, "Les unions homosexuals en la llei d'unions estables de parella: Aproximació crítica", [2000] 2 *Revista Jurídica de Catalunya* 333; Juán López Burniol, "La ley catalana de uniones estables de pareja", [1999] 3 *Revista Jurídica de Catalunya* 642; Miguel López-Muñiz Goñi, *Las uniones paramatrimoniales ante los procesos de familia* (Madrid, Colex, 1999); Encarna Roca i Trias, *Familia y cambio social* (Madrid, Civitas Ediciones, 1999).

[5] Since the Catalan law, similar laws have been passed in the Aragon (1999), Navarra (2000) and Valencia (2001) autonomous communities of Spain (see Pérez Cánovas, chap. 26), as well as in Belgium (1998) (see De Schutter & Weyembergh, chap. 24), France (1999) (see Borrillo, chap. 25), and Portugal (2001) (see p. 762).

CONSTITUTING A STABLE UNION WITH JURIDICAL EFFECT

The requirements for the validity of a stable union are set out in Articles 1–2 (heterosexual couples) and 19–21 (homosexual couples). For both types of couple, the Stable Unions Law establishes two main criteria determining who may lawfully constitute a stable union with juridical effect.

First, the Law prohibits certain people from forming a stable union. The following groups of people may not constitute a stable union with juridical effect: (i) minors; (ii) individuals who already bound to a third party in some other way, whether through marriage or another stable union; and (iii) couples who are too closely related by blood or adoption to enter into a marriage. It is important to note that the requirement that one member of the couple not be bound by an unextinguished stable union with a third party cannot currently be enforced. This is because the Law has not set up any kind of centralised or interconnected administrative register that would permit existing stable unions to be detected.[6] Such a register could be established provisionally by the Parliament of Catalonia, but only the central legislature in Madrid has the constitutional power to incorporate Catalan stable unions into the Spanish Civil Register Law.

Second, the Law requires that at least one of the members of the couple is a citizen of Catalonia. It must be remembered that matters relating to the personal statutory rights of the individual (family law, succession, etc.) are regulated through personal law, e.g., through nationality in the case of international conflicts, and through citizenship in the case of conflicts within the Spanish State (i.e., between the laws of different Autonomous Communities, or between a law of an Autonomous Community and a law of the Spanish State). Therefore, the application of the Law is personal rather than territorial. In this way, the Law may be enforced outside of Catalonia, or even outside of Spain. One of the problems facing the Law will be its enforcement outside of Catalonia.

Although the substantive requirements for the validity of a stable union are the same for heterosexual and homosexual couples, the formal means of acquiring this legal status differ. In the case of a heterosexual couple, Article 1 provides three possibilities:

(i) the couple draw up a public deed stating that they wish to be subject to the law;
(ii) the couple have lived together as though they were married (*maritalment*) for an uninterrupted period of two years; or
(iii) the couple have common children and are living together.

It must be pointed out that, in cases (ii) and (iii), the legal status of stable union is imposed on the couple whether or not they have expressed their willingness to

[6] This is not possible even where the stable union is constituted by a public deed executed before a notary, who retains a copy.

accept the framework created by the Law. This imposition is arguably incompatible with the negative freedom not to marry in Articles 32 and 17 of the Spanish Constitution.

In contrast, the only way to constitute a homosexual stable union with juridical effect is through a public deed (Article 21). Although Article 19 contemplates that the homosexual couple live together *maritalment*, there is no minimum period of cohabitation before they can execute the public deed, and the Law will only apply to them if they do execute it, no matter how long they cohabit. The advantage of this treatment is that, unlike in the case of heterosexual couples, it guarantees the homosexual couple's willingness to be subject to the Law.

REGULATION OF THE STABLE UNION

Common Expenses and Mutual Support Obligations

Articles 3–4 (heterosexual) and 22–23 (homosexual) establish the obligation to contribute to common expenses, and define these expenses. The couple are permitted to enter into an agreement on how each partner shall contribute to common expenses. If they do not do so, the law sets out a number of different ways of contributing: through domestic work; through work without salary or with reduced remuneration in their partner's profession or company; or through the resources derived from their activities or from their possessions in proportion to their income, and, if this is not sufficient, in proportion to their patrimonies (individual net worth).

Under Articles 8 (heterosexual) and 26 (homosexual), the members of a stable union are obliged to provide financial and other support (*aliments*) to each other, with preference over any other person (including children, parents or siblings).

Liability for Debts Owed to Third Parties

Articles 5 (heterosexual) and 24 (homosexual) provide that, in the case of common expenses, if they are affordable in terms of the couple's means and standard of living, both partners are jointly liable to pay a debt to a third party (i.e., the partner who did not incur the debt may be obliged to pay the totality of the debt to the third party). Whoever pays the totality of the debt has the right to claim a contribution from their partner. If the debt does not relate to a common expense, or relates to a common expense that is not affordable in terms of the couple's means and standard of living, then the partner who incurred the debt is liable for its payment.

Guardianship in the Event of a Partner's Incapacity

According to Articles 7 (heterosexual) and 25 (homosexual), if one of the members of the couple is rendered incapable of looking after themselves, due to a physical or mental illness or disability, it is necessary to juridically incapacitate them and appoint a guardian to protect their person and property. Every Catalan may appoint someone to act as their guardian, or even exclude people from this position, as a precaution in the event of their ever being incapacitated. If they have not appointed a guardian by public deed, then a judge will select the guardian in accordance with the order of preference stipulated by the Stable Unions Law and the Family Code. Within this list of people, it is the partner who holds first place in the order of preference.

Economic Structure of the Cohabiting Couple

Articles 3 (heterosexual) and 22 (homosexual) of the Stable Unions Law contemplate two possibilities: (i) the cohabiting couple wish to enter into an agreement regulating their economic structure; or (ii) they do not enter into any such agreement. In the first case, the Law grants the cohabiting couple a great deal of leeway. Their agreement may be made orally or in a private or public document, but if they are dealing with real property (e.g., interests in a house or land, including a usufruct), the agreement will have to take the form of a public deed (witnessed by a notary).

The couple may choose from an infinite number of possibilities when regulating the financial and property aspects of their relationship. For example, they could decide:

- (i) to establish common ownership of their property;
- (ii) to create a civil partnership;
- (iii) to form a "pact on economic structure", until now only seen in the realm of matrimony under the Family Code or another law.

They could also decide to share their earnings. If the rules in the pact are not sufficient, then complementary legal rules would have to be applied. If the members of the couple have not drawn up any agreement, then Articles 3 and 22 provide that each member of the couple maintains the dominion, enjoyment and administration of his or her own property.

Disposal of the Common Residence

Under Articles 11 (heterosexual) and 28 (homosexual), the partner who is the owner, tenant or lessee of the couple's common residence or furniture of ordinary use, may not alienate (e.g. sell or exchange), make money from (e.g. mortgage), or in general make any other decisions compromising their use (e.g. renting them out), without the consent of the other partner or judicial authorisation.

If one partner commits any of these acts without obtaining the other partner's consent, or without judicial authorisation, then the other partner (or any common children living with them in the common residence) can seek the cancellation of this act within a period of four years of becoming aware of it, or from its inclusion in the Property Register. Cancellation is not permitted if the third party acted in good faith and provided consideration (*de bona fe i a títol onerós*), and the partner committing the act represented that the residence was not a common residence, even if the representation was obviously false. If cancellation is barred, the only thing that the defrauded partner may demand from the partner committing the act is compensation, under ordinary tort law, for the damage they have suffered as a result of the act to which they did not consent.

EXTINCTION OF THE STABLE UNION DURING THE COUPLE'S JOINT LIFETIME

Articles 12 (heterosexual) and 30 (homosexual) provide that stable unions are extinguished for the following reasons:

(i) mutual agreement;
(ii) the unilateral decision of one partner, certifiably notified to the other, for example, through a notary;
(iii) the death of one partner;
(iv) separation for more than one year;
(v) the marriage of one partner (which must be understood as including an intention to marry).

The extinction of the stable union during the couple's joint lifetime has five main civil effects. First, in accordance with Articles 17 (heterosexual) and 29 (homosexual) of the Stable Unions Law, each partner is prohibited from entering into another stable union with a third party by means of a public deed (any such union is void) until six months have passed since the couple have fulfilled their legal obligation (Articles 12(2), 30(2)) to invalidate the public deed corresponding to their extinguished union. This deed can be invalidated either jointly or separately. Second, extinction revokes any powers granted by one partner to the other (Articles 12(3), 30(3)).

The third civil effect is that one partner may claim economic compensation for unjust enrichment (*un enriquiment injust*) from the other under Articles 13 and 31(1). The partner who has worked for the common home or for the other partner, for no remuneration or for insufficient remuneration, has the right to receive compensation if the result is a situation of inequality between the net assets of the two parties that implies an unjust enrichment. Work for the common home or for the other partner (e.g. in a company or business) will only be compensated if it went beyond what is necessary for the fulfilment of the legal obligation of the complaining partner to contribute towards family or common expenses.

The fourth civil effect is that either partner may claim alimony (*una pensió alimentària*) from the other if they need it in order to adequately maintain themselves (Articles 14, 31(2)), if:

(i) the cohabitation has diminished the applicant's earning capacity; or (only in the case of a heterosexual couple)
(ii) if the applicant has custody of the couple's common children in circumstances in which the applicant's earning capacity has been diminished.

In case (i), the obligation to pay ceases to exist if the receiving partner marries or cohabits with a third party, ceases or is reduced if the imbalance between the partners ceases or is reduced, and ceases, regardless of the circumstances, if three years have passed since the payment of the first instalment (Articles 16(4)–(5), 32(4)–(5)). In case (ii), the obligation to pay ceases when the receiving partner stops caring for the child for whatever reason, or when the child becomes an adult or is emancipated, unless the child is disabled (Article 16(4)). The rights to economic compensation and to alimony are compatible with each other, but must be requested at the same time, so that any overlap between the two claims can be considered (Articles 16(1), 32(1)).

The fifth civil effect is the right to transfer a lease from the tenant to the other partner in accordance with Articles 12(1), 12(3) and 12(4) of the Spanish Urban Leasing Law,[7] which recognises the right of the partner whose name is not on the lease to replace their partner as tenant if the latter should decide to sever the lease (*inter vivos*). However, the Urban Leasing Law only recognises stable unions which, independently of their sexual orientation, have cohabited for two years or have children together, and not those formed by public deeds. Stable unions validly formed by public deed under the Catalan Stable Unions Law have no right to subrogation under the Urban Leasing Law until they have been cohabiting for two years. Conversely, homosexual couples not formed by public deed who have cohabited for two years have rights under the Urban Leasing Law, but not under the Stable Unions Law.

EXTINCTION OF THE STABLE UNION UPON THE DEATH OF ONE PARTNER

The juridical protection guaranteed by Catalan civil law for the surviving member of a stable union (as well as a marriage) can be divided into two large categories of rules or guarantees. The first category of protection deals with the so-called "*post-mortem* effects" of the union. This first category consists of rules

[7] *Ley 29/1994, del 24 de noviembre, de Arrendamientos Urbanos.*

relating to legal property rights that were not renounced during the couple's joint lifetime and belong to family law. These rules, the object of which is to immediately protect the survivor, are almost identical for the surviving member of a stable union and for a surviving spouse. The second category of protection deals with the "succession (inheritance) effects" of the union. The fundamental aim of these rules is to establish who is entitled to the property of the deceased in the long term.

The surviving members of both heterosexual and homosexual stable unions have access to the first category of protection. However, the second category of protection is only applicable to the surviving members of homosexual stable unions. Heterosexual couples are excluded and must make reciprocal wills if each partner wants the other partner to inherit their estate. The Catalan legislator's decision to differentiate between heterosexual and homosexual stable unions in this respect stems from the assumption that the former have willingly rejected their legal right to contract a marriage, whereas homosexual couples are denied the right to marry, whether or not they want to do so.

Post-Mortem Effects

The four main post-mortem effects are the same for both homosexual and heterosexual stable unions (and for married couples). First, the death of one partner entails the termination and liquidation of the cohabiting couple's economic structure, if one had been agreed upon (see Part 3(d) above). The surviving partner receives the net profit from this liquidation, which is exempt from inheritance tax, as it is not an inherited profit.

Second, Articles 18(1) (heterosexual) and 33(a) (homosexual) provide for the right to retain the adornments of the common or family home. There exists a whole range of possessions that might have been especially vital in the everyday life of the couple, and so are necessary for the surviving partner to be able to continue living in the common home, at least temporarily. These possessions include the linen, furniture and utensils that constitute the adornments of the common home. The Stable Unions Law particularly endeavours to protect these goods and ensure that they remain in the possession of the surviving partner, by (i) establishing the direct transfer of ownership of these goods to the surviving partner; and (ii) providing that these goods are not part of the bequeathed estate. This means that they are not subject to the inheritance process, and therefore may not be claimed by the heirs or debtors of the deceased partner. They are also exempt from inheritance and gift tax.

Third, Articles 18(2) (heterosexual) and 33(b) (homosexual) entitle the surviving partner to a year of mourning, which means the right to receive all they need during the period of one year after the death of their partner, to maintain the standard of living enjoyed before the bereavement within the limits of the estate. All necessary expenses will be charged to the estate. It also means the right to live in the common home for a period of one year after their partner's death.

Fourth, if the deceased partner was the tenant of the common home, Articles 18(3) (heterosexual) and 33(c) (homosexual) provide that the surviving partner has the right to be subrogated to the rights of the deceased under the Urban Leasing Law.[8]

Succession Effects

Article 34 of the Stable Unions Law stipulates that the patrimonial rights of the surviving member of a homosexual stable union depend on whether the deceased has any surviving relatives. There are three possibilities.

First, if a partner dies leaving descendants (children, grandchildren, great-grandchildren, etc.) or ascendants (parents, grandparents, great-grandparents, etc), the surviving partner has the right to claim up to one-quarter of the deceased's estate from the deceased's heirs for the survivor's own personal maintenance (Article 34(1)(a)). This claim can only be made if the survivor cannot maintain the standard of living that they had known before the partner's death, either through their own means or earnings, or through property inherited from the deceased partner. The surviving partner has this right whether or not the deceased partner made a will (Article 35), but the survivor will lose it if they marry or enter a heterosexual or homosexual stable union before claiming it (Article 34(2)(c)). This right is very similar to the share of the estate awarded to a surviving spouse by the Code of Succession.[9]

Second, if a partner dies leaving only siblings, or if the partner's siblings have died and left children (nieces or nephews of the deceased partner), the surviving partner has the right to one-half of the estate (Article 34(1)(b)). Third, if a partner dies leaving none of the aforementioned relatives, the totality of the estate goes to the surviving partner (Article 34(1)(c)).

ADOPTION OF CHILDREN

Article 6 of the Stable Unions Law states that the members of a heterosexual stable union may adopt a child jointly. This means that, in accordance with the Family Code, they can both adopt an unrelated child, or that one partner can adopt the other partner's child (a second-parent adoption).[10]

The Stable Unions Law and the Family Code deliberately exclude homosexual couples from both joint adoption and second-parent adoption, which means

[8] *Ibid.*

[9] See *Llei 40/1991, de 30 de desembre, del Codi de successions per causa de mort en el Dret Civil de Catalunya,* (31 Dec. 1991) 333/III BOPC, Art. 379 et seq.

[10] *Supra* n.3, Arts. 115(2), 117(1)(a).

that they cannot jointly share the custody of a minor. However, the Family Code does permit one member of a homosexual couple to adopt as an individual. The applicant, just like any other citizen wishing to adopt a child, must fulfil the requirements set out in the Family Code: they must be at least twenty-five years old and there must be an age difference of at least fourteen years between the adoptive parent and the child.[11] Still, it must be noted that, in practice, hetero-sexual couples (married or in stable unions) who wish to adopt are prioritised over individual applicants.

ASSISTED REPRODUCTION

The Family Code provides that the filiation of a baby born via assisted reproduction is independent of whether the gametes (ovum and sperm) come from an interested party or are donated, of the actual techniques employed, and of whether the mother is married or cohabiting with her male partner. What is of supreme importance in the eyes of the law for the determination of who is the child's father is the consent of the husband or the man with whom the woman lives.[12] There is no legal impediment preventing a woman without a male partner (e.g. a lesbian couple) from making use of assisted reproduction techniques. In these cases, the baby only has a mother, and a maternal single-parent family is created.

In the case of a gay male couple employing a surrogate mother, maternity is legally determined by birth and not by the source of the ovum or the agreement of the parties. Therefore, surrogate motherhood contracts do not alter the fact that the woman who gives birth is the child's mother, even where a donated ovum is used.

NON-PRIVATE ASPECTS OF THE STABLE UNIONS LAW

Articles 9 (heterosexual) and 27 (homosexual) grant many of the benefits that up until now were enjoyed only by the married partners of people working for the *Generalitat* (the Government of Catalonia), to the stable union partners of civil servants, including the right to leave or reduced hours in the event of the death or illness of the civil servant's partner. One exception is the fifteen days' leave awarded to couples that have just married.

Final Provision One (*Disposició Finals, Primera*) of the Stable Unions Law states that the *Generalitat* must regulate by law the specific fiscal treatment of heterosexual and homosexual stable union couples with regard to income tax and inheritance and gift tax. To date, the Parliament of Catalonia has only done

[11] *Supra* n.3, Art. 115(1).
[12] *Ibid.*, Art. 97(1).

so with regard to inheritance and gift tax. Since 1 January 1999, the surviving member of a stable union receives the same rights as a surviving spouse, but only in relation to inheritance and gift tax.[13] Before this date, the surviving partner was considered as a stranger in relation to the deceased, and therefore always had to pay double the tax paid by a surviving spouse in the same circumstances.

A JURIDICAL CONCEPT OF FAMILY?

Unlike other constitutions that define family and marriage (e.g. the Italian Constitution),[14] the Spanish constitution has systematically disconnected the concept of family from that of marriage. Both institutions are regulated by different rules (marriage by Article 32 and family by Article 39), and neither set of rules depends on the other. Both institutions are constitutionally guaranteed, but marriage is not a requirement for the formation of a family.

This has two consequences for homosexual couples. First, homosexual marriage is not a constitutional, but rather a legal question: the legislator may permit homosexual marriage because it is not constitutionally prohibited, but is not constitutionally obliged to do so.[15] Second, it is juridically possible to consider a homosexual couple as a family, and therefore extend to them the juridical and social protection that families receive. The concept of family has not been constitutionally determined, and can therefore be juridically extended to non-traditional families.

CONCLUSION

The Stable Unions Law aims to regulate the relationships between cohabiting couples (horizontal relationships), but not the relationships between parents and children (vertical relationships). The rules applied to horizontal relationships between married couples, as well as to vertical relationships between parents and children (within or outside marriage), are contained in the Family Code.

If all children (vertical relationships) are generally equal in the eyes of the law, couples (horizontal relationships) are legally different from one another. This occurs because Catalan legislation wishes to differentiate between the civil and juridical effects of homosexual and heterosexual stable unions. When it comes to horizontal relationships, Catalan law has opted to award more civil and

[13] See *Llei 25/1998, de 31 de desembre, de mesures administratives, fiscals i d'adaptació a l'euro,* (31 Dec. 1998) 360A/V BOPC A-2, Article 31.

[14] See Scappucci, chap. 28.

[15] It would be the central legislature in Madrid, rather than the Parliament of Catalonia, that would have competence over this question under Art. 149.1(8) of the Spanish Constitution. The Family Code in Catalonia currently contemplates marriage between the husband (*el marit*) and the wife (*la muller*). See *supra* n.3, Art. 1.

juridical effects to homosexual stable unions than to heterosexual stable unions. The former, as seen above, are granted certain inheritance rights. The key reason for this differentiation is set out in the Preamble to the Stable Unions Law: "If a cohabiting heterosexual couple does not marry, it is of their own free will. Homosexual couples cannot marry even if they want to".[16]

On the other hand, when it comes to vertical or hierarchical relationships (between parents and children), Catalan legislation has opted for the opposite solution: the members of a heterosexual stable union may share the custody of a child through joint or second-parent adoption, whereas these possibilities have been denied to homosexual stable unions. Denying in all cases the possibility that a homosexual couple may adopt a child together, or that one of its members may adopt the child of the other partner, goes directly against the most fundamental principle of Catalan child law, i.e., the preeminence of the child's interest over any other. For example, if a woman has custody of a child from a previous, dissolved heterosexual relationship, and forms a stable union with another woman, the Family Code prevents the mother's partner from adopting the child, even if the father has died. If the mother dies, her female partner, with whom the child might have cohabited for a long time, will be treated as a legal stranger and, if the father has died or been legally deprived of custody, guardianship will normally be granted to the child's grandparents.[17]

In Catalonia, there are now several different types of couple with different legal rights and obligations. This situation is very similar to the image of a train with three carriages, and a fourth group of passengers making their journey on foot. Going from those whose relationship has the greatest juridical effects to those whose relationship has the least, we have the following four different types of couple in Catalonia.

In the first carriage, travelling first class, we have married heterosexual couples, who enjoy the maximum juridical effects. Gay and lesbian couples may not board this carriage.

The second carriage is for second-class passengers, which is exclusively reserved for homosexual couples who have decided to constitute a stable union. Here the ticket inspectors and their ways of working are different. Instead of God's workers, we can only find public notaries who, almost in a clandestine way and without ceremony, open the doors of this carriage to homosexual couples who have tickets: a deed stating that they have constituted a stable union. The marriage ceremony for this type of couple is invisible in the eyes of society. However, it is illegal to travel second class accompanied by children for some reason still not clarified by the rail authorities.

The third class carriage is another world. We yet again are facing a reserved zone, this time for heterosexual couples. They are passengers who could have travelled first class, but have decided not to do so. For this reason, the services

[16] *Supra* n.4, at 24775.

[17] *Supra* n.3, Art. 179(1)(b).

offered in this carriage are considerably lower in standard. However, they may travel with children.

But the three aforementioned groups of couples are not the only possibilities. We must not forget the fourth group, which is not mentioned in the Stable Unions Law. If we follow the train metaphor, these couples are the only passengers travelling on foot.

This fourth group is made up of the following couples:

(i) homosexual couples who willingly have not constituted a stable union through public deed, no matter how long they have cohabited;
(ii) either heterosexual or homosexual couples in which one member is married and therefore unable to constitute a stable union; and
(iii) heterosexual couples during the first two years of cohabitation.

The fact that there are no specific regulations for this group does not mean that they are completely ignored by the law. In the event of termination of the relationship, they can invoke general legal principles relating to unjust enrichment, or compensation for moral or economic damage.

Catalan legislation has managed completely and obstinately to avoid any connotation of family for homosexual and heterosexual stable unions. The term "family" is only used when regulating families based on marriage. Instead, the Stable Unions Law uses concepts such as "cohabitation" ("*convivència*"), "couple" ("*parella*") and "common" ("*comú*, *comunes*, etc."), e.g., when referring to the common home or common expenses rather than the family home or family expenses.

Despite this terminology, the Catalan Parliament, perhaps somewhat subconsciously, has dealt with stable unions as though they were families. First, the Stable Unions Law requires of both heterosexual and homosexual couples that which is essential for a family: solidarity. This is the basis of all mutual aid and help between family members, and is found in the the mutual obligation to provide support (Articles 8, 26), and the preference for appointment as guardian in the event of one partner being rendered incapacitated (Articles 7, 25).

Second, the legislation deals with both types of stable unions, not as simple contracts between two parties, but rather as families. Family law is characterised by a large number of obligatory rules. Such rules, which endeavour to protect the weaker member of the couple, are found throughout the Stable Unions Law, and do not leave the couple with much room to formulate their own agreements. For heterosexual couples, the legislator wished to accentuate even further the institutional character of a stable union by imposing the law on them after two years of cohabitation, or if they have children. On the other hand, homosexual couples are granted the freedom to decide whether or not they wish to be subject to the law, which does make their stable union seem more voluntary and contractual.

Yet once the couple is subject to the Stable Unions Law, regardless of how they qualify, the Law imposes a whole range of obligations typical of family law, which the members of the couple may not denounce (without terminating the union) because they are considered the minimum. This series of mandatory rules reveals something that the legislator did not wish formally and willingly to recognise: stable unions are an institution of family law that is not based on a simple contract.

The appearance of contractual freedom (Articles 3.(1), 22(1)) is more like a mermaid's chant trying to deceive sailors. In fact, stable union couples have little room for manoeuvre. For example, the members of a stable union, whether it is homosexual or heterosexual, will never be able to exclude: joint liability for debts incurred by one of the partners (Articles 5, 24); the mutual and preferential obligation to provide support (Articles 8, 26); the obligation to contribute to joint expenses (Articles 4, 23); the restriction on disposing of the common residence without the consent of the other partner (Articles 11, 28); economic compensation and alimony in the event of the termination of a union (Articles 13, 14, 31); the right to retain the adornments of the common dwelling (Articles 18(1), 33(a)); the year of mourning (Articles 18(2), 33(b)); the transfer of the lease of the common residence in the event of the termination of the union, whether in the couple's joint lifetime, or after the death of one partner (Articles 18(3), 33(c)); the limitations to the freedom to draw up a will (homosexual couples only, Article 34).

Most of these rights and obligations are shared with the economic structure of marriage. This structure is what the Family Code imposes on all marriages, independently of any agreement between the members of the married couple. Married couples, along with stable unions, may not avoid these juridical effects of their legal relationship.

The constitutional differentiation between marriage and family, the existence of new families outside wedlock, and the constitutional obligation for public authorities to protect the family, require further changes to family law. The Legislator has a crucial choice: either to follow the long path of full recognition for homosexual couples as families using the technique of creating special laws for stable unions, or directly opening the door of the institution of marriage to homosexual couples. The first option is available to the Parliament of Catalonia, whereas the second is currently in the so far tightly closed hands of the Spanish Parliament.[18]

[18] *Supra* n.15.

28

Italy Walking a Tightrope Between Stockholm and the Vatican: Will Legal Recognition of Same-Sex Partnerships Ever Occur?

GIOIA SCAPPUCCI[1]

IN RECENT YEARS, issues such as prohibiting discrimination on the basis of sexual orientation, as well as legally recognising same-sex partnerships, have been on and off the Italian political agenda. On the one hand, Italy appears attracted by the Nordic countries' model of recognition of same-sex partnerships. On the other, it is restrained by the weight and value attached to the traditional interpretation of "family" by the Roman Catholic Church.

This vacillating attitude finds its roots in Italy's particular social and legal context. To understand the issues and challenges with regard to legal recognition of same-sex partnerships in Italy, it is necessary to start by presenting its complex social context and its strong constitutional framework.[2] The picture would not be complete if it did not also portray the *de facto* situation of same-sex couples and the symbolic initiatives taken to protect them at the local level. Indeed, local municipalities have proven much more determined to act than the national legislature. Using their anagraphic powers,[3] many municipalities have granted same-sex partners the possibility of registering their "civil unions" in the municipality's public register. The working of such systems will be outlined, in explaining their influence on the state of the legislative debate.

[1] PhD candidate, Faculty of Laws, University College, University of London. This chapter is a result of the author's academic research. It thus does not reflect, in any way, the point of view of her employer. The author would like to thank Franco Grillini, Director of NOI *(Notizie omosessuali italiane*, http://www.gay.it/noi), for having provided her with useful documentation.

[2] To the author's knowledge, same sex-relationships have not given rise to any case-law in Italy. Until Italian anti-discrimination law is reformed to include a reference to sexual orientation, it seems unlikely that legal recognition of same-sex partnerships will occur through judicial interpretation of existing law. The explanatory statement to DLG No. C.6582, *infra* n.5, seems to confirm this reasoning. The role of the Italian judiciary in the legal recognition of same-sex partnerships will thus not be covered by this chapter.

[3] See *Regolamento Anagrafico,* d.p.r. 30/05/89, no. 223, establishing who is considered a resident of a particular municipality and how to classify the population.

The main arguments for and against legal recognition of same-sex partnerships will then be presented by analysing the most recent bills[4] on legal recognition of "affective unions" and non-discrimination on the ground of sexual orientation. Finally, the status of the question of legal recognition of same-sex partnerships (in March 2001) will be considered by referring to the debate which preceded and followed the approval on 8 October 1999, for submission to Parliament, of a Government bill on measures to combat discrimination and promote equal opportunities (DLG No. C.6582)[5].

It seems that the issue of legally recognising same-sex partnerships has so far been put aside, considered as less urgent and less controversial than the adoption of anti-discrimination legislation specifically covering the ground of sexual orientation. The latter issue, which has been deadlocked since the approval of DLG No. C.6582, will be pushed back on the parliamentary agenda by the obligation to implement (by 2 December 2003) the European Community Directive prohibiting sexual orientation discrimination in employment.[6] As to the former issue, after the heated reactions to the European Parliament's most recent (16 March 2000) resolution[7] calling for legal recognition of same-sex partnerships, one wonders whether this will ever occur in Italy.

A COMPLEX SOCIAL CONTEXT

Attempting to grasp an "Italian" homosexual culture and lifestyle is problematic.[8] It has been said that the North/South division of the country mirrors quite well the coexistence in Italy of both the Scandinavian and the Mediterranean homosexual culture and lifestyles.[9] Such heterogeneity is counterproductive

[4] The text of most bills cited in this chapter can be found at http://www.parlamento.it/att/ddl/home.htm (*Senato* or S.), http://www.camera.it/index.asp (*Progetti di legge*) (*Camera dei Deputati* or C.), or http://www.gay.it/noi (*Archivio legislativo* or *Proposte di riforma*).

[5] DLG (*Disegno di legge governativo*) No. C.6582, *Misure contro le discriminazioni e per la promozione delle pari opportunità*, introduced by the *Ministero per le pari opportunità* in the *Camera dei Deputati* on 23 Nov. 1999, was based on two earlier bills (C.2551, C.5865). See *infra* nn.28, 29.

[6] Council Directive 2000/78/EC of 27 Nov. 2000, OJ [2000] L 303/16 (see Bell, chap. 37). The Italian versions of both the Dir. and Art. 13 of the EC Treaty refer to "*le tendenze sessuali*" ("sexual tendencies"), whereas DLG No. C.6582 refers to "*orientamento sessuale*" ("sexual orientation").

[7] Resolution on respect for human rights in the European Union (1998–1999), Document A5–0050/00, http://www.europarl.eu.int/plenary/default_en.htm (Texts Adopted by Parliament), paras. 56–7. See also p. 725, n.70.

[8] See Biagini, Bertozzo & Ravaioli, "Italy" in Beger, Krickler, Lewis & Wuch (eds.), *Equality for Lesbians and Gay Men: A Relevant Issue in the Civil and Social Dialogue* (Brussels, ILGA-Europe, 1998), http://www.steff.suite.dk/report.pdf, for an in-depth account of the social and political climate for lesbians and gay men in Italy. See also F Brunetta d'Usseaux & A D'Angelo (eds.), *Matrimonio, matrimonii* (Milan, Giuffrè Editore, 2000); Emanuele Calò, *Le Convivenze Registrate in Europa: Verso un secondo regime patrimoniale della famiglia* (Milan, Giuffrè Editore, 2000); Ezio Menzione, *Diritti omosessuali* (Rome, Enola, 2000).

[9] Biagini, et al., *ibid.* at 67.

when it comes to advocacy for the affirmation of one's rights. The Italian homosexual movement was indeed not very active until the 1990s.

The low profile of homosexual militancy in Italy has also been explained by referring to another Italian particularity, i.e. the acceptance of a sort of "tacit pact" between the homosexual community and the Italian State at the end of the nineteenth century.[10] According to this "pact", the State abrogated all provisions criminalizing homosexuality in exchange for renunciation of homosexual advocacy for the right to be different. Another consequence of this "pact" was the withdrawal of the State from the sexual realm, which was left to the Roman Catholic Church. This Church has been and still is an important actor in the moulding of the social and moral context in Italy. Its heavy influence even shapes the strategies chosen by those in favour of same-sex partnership recognition, who tend to highlight the fact that the recognition of same-sex partnerships will not encroach on the traditional concept of "the family".

This social context would favour the maintenance of the *status quo* if other factors did not come into play. It is particularly important to understand the constitutional framework in which advocacy for legal recognition of same-sex partnerships has to be placed. A brief overview of this framework is thus essential to understand why arguments of a constitutional and European Community nature have recently become the main instruments used to fight for change.

A STRONG CONSTITUTIONAL FRAMEWORK

Article 29 of the Italian Constitution explicitly protects the family, which it defines as a "natural society based on marriage". The existence of this explicit reference to the "traditional" understanding of the notion of family (the so-called *favor familiae*) has been used as a strong argument to rule out any protection of other forms of relationships. The majority of commentators consider Article 29 as a legal obstacle to the recognition of any form of cohabitation outside marriage—be it homosexual or heterosexual.

Article 2 of the Italian Constitution "recognises and guarantees the inviolable rights of the person, whether as an individual or in the social formations where he/she develops his/her personality". This is the so-called "personality principle" ("*principio personalista*") which constitutes one of the founding principles of the Italian constitutional framework. To understand its potential, one should read it in combination with two other fundamental constitutional principles: the "social pluralism principle" ("*pluralismo sociale*", Article 2) and the "equality and social dignity principle" ("*principio di uguaglianza e dignità sociale*", Article 3). According to the "personality principle", "social formations" between the individual and the State (all sorts of "communities, societies and organisations") should be encouraged and protected, as they serve the purpose

[10] *Ibid.*

of the free development of each human being's personality as well as the realisation of solidarity. According to the "social pluralism" and "equality and social dignity" principles, the State has to remove "all obstacles of an economic and social nature that in practice limit the equality of citizens thus encroaching on the full development of their personality" (Article 3).

The combination of these three principles has been invoked by the supporters of legal recognition of same-sex partnerships.[11] Indeed, the explanatory statement accompanying the 1998 Soda Bill,[12] on legal recognition of "affective unions" and non-discrimination on the ground of sexual orientation, strongly emphasised the role of these principles in eliminating the discriminatory situation in which same-sex couples have to live, because their relationships continue to be disregarded by the law.

As far as non-discrimination is concerned, "sexual orientation" ("*orientamento sessuale*") is not a category expressly mentioned in the Constitution[13] or in legislation. The fate of three recent bills that sought to change this situation will be discussed below.

To complete the legal framework in which advocacy for the legal recognition of same-sex partnerships and the abolition of discrimination on sexual orientation takes place, one must also note that, according to the standard interpretation of the Italian Civil Code (*Codice Civile*), marriage is between two persons of different sexes. As for adoption, although there are exceptional cases in which an unmarried individual (heterosexual, lesbian or gay) can theoretically adopt a child, in most cases only married couples may adopt.[14] This excludes *a priori* unmarried same-sex and different-sex couples, as well as unmarried individuals without partners. However, if a judge so rules, the institution of custody (*affido familiare*) may be granted to unmarried individuals, and in some cases homosexuality has not been regarded as an obstacle.[15] As far as criminal law is concerned, as mentioned above, all "anti-homosexual" provisions were deleted from the Penal Code (*Codice Penale*) at the end of the nineteenth century. At that time, the age of consent was equalised at fourteen for both heterosexual and homosexual relations.[16]

[11] The reference to Arts. 2 and 3 of the Constitution as a legal argument against those who invoke Art. 29 will be explained in more detail below.

[12] See *infra* n.27.

[13] See http://www.senato.it/funz/cost/home.htm (Italian), http://www.uni-wuerzburg.de/law/it00000_.html (English). Two *Proposte di legge costituzionale*, PDL No. C.3934 (Pisapia, 1 July 1997) and DDL (*Disegno di legge*) No. S.1521 (Salvato, 22 Oct. 1996) have sought to amend the Constitution by adding sexual orientation to the list of grounds in Art. 3 (sex, race, language, religion, political opinion, personal and social conditions). DLG No. C.6582 would not have done so.

[14] See Law No. 149 of 28 March 2001, Arts. 6, 25 (amending Law No. 184 of 4 May 1983); *Di Lazzaro* v. *Italy* (No. 31924/96) (10 July 1997), 90-B Decisions & Reports 134 (European Commission of Human Rights).

[15] Biagini, et al., *supra* n.8, at 66.

[16] Penal Code, Art. 609 ter.

A SIGNIFICANT *DE FACTO* SITUATION

Out of fifteen million heterosexual couples in Italy, more than 300,000 are not married. In a population of approximately fifty-eight million, there are probably about three million homosexuals,[17] many of whom establish relationships based on engagements of mutual assistance and solidarity.[18] Both heterosexual and homosexual *de facto* couples are not recognised by law. Indeed, the 1975 reform of family law included recognition of children born outside marriage, but did not provide for any kind of rights and obligations for *de facto* couples.

On 20 April 1999, Deputy De Luca introduced a bill in the Italian Parliament aiming at some kind of legal recognition of *de facto* couples.[19] The bill, which was withdrawn on 26 May 2000, defined a *de facto couple* as two persons (no sex specified) who have lived together for at least four years, and covered only inheritance rights, with the aim of protecting the economically weaker partner in the relationship.

While in Parliament bills are being put forward, discussed and then shelved, local authorities ("*comuni*") have taken practical initiatives to recognise the reality of *de facto* couples[20] They have created a form of recognition of same-sex couples by granting them the possibility of registering their "civil union" in the public local registers (*registro comunale*). The *delibera comunale* (decision of the municipality) to establish "civil union" registers (*Registro dei Patti di Convivenza*) is based on the acknowledgement that society has evolved, and that relations other than traditional marriage exist and should thus be taken into consideration. Accordingly, numerous Italian municipalities allow two persons (same-sex or opposite-sex) to register their partnership.

The working of such a system can be explained by taking the case of the municipality of Rome as an example. To have one's relationship registered, a few conditions have to be fulfilled. Firstly, one of the partners has to be resident in Rome. The nationality of the partners is irrelevant: it is not even required that one of the two be Italian. Secondly, the partners have to prove that they have been living together for at least two years and that no blood relation exists between them. Thirdly, they need to demonstrate that they are not married or in any other similar relationship with anybody else. If they were married or in a similar *de facto* situation, at least one year must have passed since divorce or the dissolution of the other relationship. Registration does not in itself create any

[17] See De Luca Bill, *infra* n.19; 1998 Soda Bill, *infra* n.27.

[18] According to F Grillini (reported by ANSA on 16 March 2000), there are 50,000 same-sex couples living together in Italy.

[19] *Disciplina successoria della convivenza giuridicamente rilevante*, PDL (*Proposta di legge*) No. C.5933 (the "De Luca Bill").

[20] In addition to the local registers, some regional laws provide that cohabitants (without specifying their sexes) who have lived together for at least two years are families and must be admitted to public housing. See e.g. *Legge Regionale* No. 10 of 3 March 1994 (*Regione Liguria*), Art. 6(4) (the "*nucleo familiare*" includes a "*convivente more uxorio* [like a wife]" after two years of cohabitation).

legal consequences. Such "civil unions" may be dissolved at any time, if both partners declare that they no longer are in a relationship. If one of the two partners disagrees, the "civil union" will cease to exist one year after the manifestation of the other partner's desire to put an end to it.

The *delibera comunale* establishing the *Patti di Convivenza Civile* does not create any rights or duties for the partners. It merely provides that the free choice of registering one's union should be treated with respect. Nonetheless, the symbolic value of such *de facto* recognition should not be underestimated. The municipalities' decisions have been harshly criticised by the opponents of legal recognition of same-sex partnerships. They have also been attacked by the body that determines the conformity with national laws of municipal decisions in each region (the *Comitato regionale di controllo*). These bodies have stressed the local authorities' lack of competence over establishing the civil status of citizens. The Regional Administrative Tribunal of Tuscany has held that,[21] by creating a register for civil unions, the local municipality of Empoli exceeded its anagraphic competences. It could not classify the population on the basis of a criterion—that of engaging in a civil union—which was not recognised by Italian law.

THE ARGUMENTS FOR AND AGAINST LEGAL RECOGNITION IN ITALY

The arguments for and against legal recognition of same-sex partnerships are intimately linked with the particular social and legal context described above. The opponents of legal recognition of same-sex partnerships have essentially two sets of arguments: one is of a constitutional nature, while the other draws upon considerations of "morality".

According to the first set of arguments (the *favor familiae* argument based on Article 29), the Constitution has clearly opted for a special protection of the family based on marriage. This means that legal recognition and protection of any form of relationship between individuals which is not marriage is ruled out *a priori*. It is commonly said that, if two persons of the same sex want to live together in a marriage-like way, they are obviously free to do so as long as it is within the sphere of their private life.

As mentioned above, the decisions taken by local municipalities to set up "civil union" registers are also attacked using supplementary constitutional arguments. Article 128 of the Constitution, concerning the division of competences between the twenty regions and the Italian State, and Law No. 142 on the autonomy of local authorities,[22] are invoked to demonstrate that local municipalities do not have the power to modify the understanding of the notion of "family" by recognising other forms of relationships.

[21] *TAR per la Toscana; sezione I, sentenza 9 febbraio 1996, n. 49* (Decision No. 49 of 9 Feb. 1996); *Comune di Empoli c. Regione Toscana.*

[22] *Ordinamento delle autonomie locali* (8 June 1990).

The second set of arguments used by the opponents of legal recognition of same-sex partnerships are of a more "ideological and moral" nature. It is assumed that the recognition of forms of relationships not founded on marriage is an attack on the institution of marriage which would deprive it of its unique value. Recognition of non-marital relationships is characterised as the establishment of a "second-hand" alternative to marriage: the engagement between partners is viewed as weaker than between spouses given that—according to the proposals tabled—its dissolution would be much easier than a divorce. As will be explained below, the 1998 Soda Bill was rather superficial as to the conditions required to engage in an "affective union", as well as to the protection against its expedient dissolution.

The supporters of legal recognition of same-sex partnerships have two main sets of counter-arguments; both are of a legal nature. The first set of counter-arguments is a response to the *favor familae* argument. It consists in emphasising that legal recognition of same-sex partnerships would not constitute an attack on the traditional family. The idea is not to abolish the institution of marriage, but to create alongside it other institutions reflecting today's societal and moral evolution.

Apart from the family, the Constitution also explicitly protects the "social formations" in which the individual develops his/her personality. The relationship of mutual assistance and solidarity between two persons of the same sex wanting to live together may fall into this category. Moreover, deciding to share one's life with somebody else is considered as a manifestation of each individual's choice to develop his/her personality alone or with their beloved. Thus, legal recognition would be in full accordance with the Constitution: it would eliminate an unjustified discrimination among individuals which Article 3 of the Constitution forbids.

The second set of counter-arguments used to push for legal recognition of same-sex partnerships relies on European Community decisions. It is not important whether such a decision is a resolution of the European Parliament which is not legally binding, or whether it is a new Article of the European Community Treaty.[23] What counts is that the supranational decision reflects a common European understanding of the issue that goes beyond Italian internal controversies and should therefore be taken into due consideration.[24]

Indeed, the 1994 European Parliament (EP) "Resolution on equal rights for homosexuals and lesbians in the EC"[25] provided the impetus needed to launch

[23] Art. 13 of the EC Treaty ("the Council may . . . take appropriate action to combat discrimination based on . . . sexual orientation"). See Bell, chap. 37.

[24] On 16 March 2000, the presidents of the Italian national organisations Arcigay and Arcilesbica—Sergio Lo Giudice and Titti De Simone—greeted the European Parliament's resolution calling for recognition of same-sex partnerships (*supra* n.7) as "an historic event, a civil answer to a retrograde Italy, to the anti-democratic forces which today are still hostile to the evolution of our society" (ANSA).

[25] OJ [1994] C 61/40 (adopted on 8 Feb. 1994).

the debate on recognition of same-sex partnerships in Italy.[26] Leftist parties, with the support of some *Forza Italia* deputies, introduced various bills into the Italian Parliament using the EP Resolution as a strong argument for political support. Nonetheless, these did not succeed, probably because of the Roman Catholic mentality, which still strongly determines Italian policy-making, especially in areas touching upon the notion of "family".

The aim of these early bills was to legally recognise same-sex partnerships and thus accord same-sex partners more or less the same rights and duties as "spouses". The reference model chosen was the Scandinavian one: legal recognition was sought only for same-sex couples. Some proposals were even more far-reaching than the Scandinavian model, as they also provided for the application to same-sex couples of the provisions concerning adoption. The legal protection of heterosexual non-married couples (so called *de facto* families) was not covered by these proposals.

On 12 March 1998, legal recognition of same-sex partnerships was, once again, on the Italian political agenda. Deputies Soda, Melandri, Iotti, Folena, Colletti and Taradash presented to the *Camera dei Deputati* a bill entitled *Disciplina dell'unione affettiva* (the "1998 Soda Bill").[27] It aimed to legally recognise same-sex partnerships (which it denominated "*unioni affettive*" or "affective unions"), as well as to introduce sexual orientation as a category for non-discrimination legislation. It drew upon the experience of the obstacles encountered by all previous bills, and tried to iron out some of the most controversial issues. The result was an attempted compromise between embracing the Stockholm model and surrendering to the Vatican. One really gets the impression that Italy is walking a tightrope: if it loses its balance and falls it will develop vertigo and give up.

The 1998 Soda Bill is composed of two chapters. The first one provides for the establishment and recognition of "affective unions". Article 1 defines them as a union between two adult persons of the same sex, whose relationship is based on affection, solidarity and an engagement of mutual moral and material assistance. It also states that such a union is recognised by the law and that the rights and duties of the partners are thus regulated by the law.

Keeping in mind the existing registers in many local municipalities, Article 2 of the 1998 Soda Bill provides that affective unions are recognised through registration in public registers held by local municipalities. The dissolution of an

[26] In Dec. 1993, while the EP resolution was still under discussion, Deputies Cioni, Vendola and Taradash (belonging to the leftist and radical parties) tabled the first bill on legal recognition of same-sex partnerships, but no action was taken on it.

[27] PDL No. C.4657. Deputy Soda had the support of other deputies of the left (*Democratici della sinistra)*, as well as of some deputies of the centre-right (*Forza Italia)*. Earlier partnership bills include PDL No. C.1020 (Vendola, 17 May 1996), DDL No. S.935 (Manconi, 11 July 1996), DDL No. S.1518 (Salvato, 22 Oct. 1996), PDL No. C.2870 (Buffo, 11 Dec. 1996), DDL No. S.2725 (Cioni, 30 July 1997). A more recent one is PDL No. C.7297 (Paissan, 15 Sept. 2000), *Norme sulle unioni civili*. The *Ministero per le pari opportunità* has also prepared a *Schema di disegno di legge*, "*Disciplina degli accordi di convivenza*" ("Regulation of Cohabitation Agreements"), dated 14 Sept. 2000.

affective union must also be communicated to the public register. Contrary to the precision of the local municipalities' systems, the 1998 Soda Bill does not set out the conditions for registering or dissolving an "affective union". No requirement of nationality or residence in Italy is mentioned. The partners do not even have to provide proof of their relationship.

Article 3 of the 1998 Soda Bill assimilates the relationship between same-sex partners who have contracted an "affective union" to that between "spouses". Indeed, it states that all civil and criminal code provisions applicable to marriage apply to "affective unions". Nonetheless, it excludes application of any provision whose aim is to favour "the natural family based on marriage". Several exceptions are listed, including the provisions concerning adoption or artificial insemination, legal effects of the union on the children of either partner, and application of the provisions of international treaties concerning marriage without the consent of the other State.

The second chapter of the 1998 Soda Bill provides for non-discrimination on the ground of sexual orientation. Articles 5 and 6 refer to existing non-discrimination legislation and provide for its amendment by including sexual orientation alongside race, religion and sex. Article 7 guarantees a right of sexual privacy (*riservatezza sessuale*). It explicitly forbids public authorities to make inquiries regarding the sexual life or sexual orientation of citizens without due justification. Article 8 covers non-discrimination at school during sexual education classes and forbids any statement of intolerance towards homosexuals. Articles 9 and 10 concern discrimination based on sexual orientation in matters relating to health insurance. Whenever the 1998 Soda Bill forbids certain specific manifestations of discrimination, it also provides sanctions by referring to specific articles of the Criminal Code.

Although the 1998 Soda Bill tried to find a compromise between the two contrasting forces pulling Italy towards or away from legal recognition of same-sex partnerships, it did not succeed and, like earlier proposals, was shelved.

DISCRIMINATION PROTECTION BEFORE PARTNERSHIP RECOGNITION?

In 1999, two bills aiming at the inclusion of sexual orientation alongside other grounds of non-discrimination were discussed in the Constitutional Affairs Committee of the Italian Parliament. Both bills were entitled *Proposta di legge antidiscriminatoria*. The first bill had already been presented to the *Camera dei Deputati* by Deputy Vendola on 24 October 1996 (the "Vendola Bill").[28] The second bill was a revised version of the 1998 Soda Bill, containing only its non-discrimination provisions and nothing on legal recognition of same-sex unions (the "Revised Soda Bill").[29] Both the Vendola Bill and the Revised Soda Bill

[28] PDL No. C.2551.

[29] PDL No. C.5865 was presented to the *Camera dei Deputati* by Deputies Soda and other others on 26 March 1999. Earlier anti-discrimination bills include DDL No. S.1810 (Pieroni, 28 Nov. 1996),

sought to amend existing non-discrimination legislation by including the ground of sexual orientation. The Revised Soda Bill also specifically provided for non-discrimination at school, in the workplace, and with regard to health insurance, as well as for the same right to "sexual privacy" as the 1998 Soda Bill.

Even though the subject covered by these two bills does not appear to be that controversial, in Italy it gave rise to a fierce debate. Newspapers such as *L'Avvenire* (Roman Catholic) and *Il Corriere della Sera* (liberal) reported the clashes between those who supported these bills and those who opposed them. The situation was more complicated than with the reactions to the proposed recognition of same-sex partnerships. The non-discrimination issue is not viewed in the same way by Catholics who are on the centre-left of the political spectrum (*PPI—Partito Popolare Italiano*), and those who are on the centre-right (*CCD—Cristiano democratici*). The former support these bills. The latter are allied with the right (*AN—Alleanza Nazionale*) in harshly opposing any reference to sexual orientation in the law.

The arguments for and against the adoption of these bills differ from the ones examined above for legal recognition of same-sex partners. The supporters of the bills focus on issues of equality, the right to be different, the need to positively foster tolerance and solidarity. Those who oppose the bills instead claim that "sexual orientation" should be considered as a "behaviour" of the individual and that as such it should not be regulated by law.[30] Moreover, the Vatican[31] reiterates its arguments of morality to justify its opposition to an explicit protection against discrimination on the basis of sexual orientation.

Because of this public debate on the issue of protection against sexual orientation discrimination, discussions in the Constitutional Affairs Committee of the *Camera dei Deputati* were deadlocked until October 1999 when the Government approved its anti-discrimination bill, DLG No. C.6582. When the minister for equal opportunities, Laura Balbo, presented the bill, she declared that "with this provision, we are conforming ourselves with the European situation, notwithstanding the polemics". She also stressed that it was the task of Parliament to do its part and transform DLG No. C.6582 into a comprehensive anti-discrimination law.

According to Article 1 of DLG No. C.6582, its aim is to provide for a complete application of both Article 3 of the Italian Constitution and Article 13 of the EC Treaty. The prohibited grounds of discrimination included in the bill are therefore all the grounds protected by Article 3 (sex, race, language, religion,

DDL No. S.2147 (Salvato, 25 Feb. 1997). The Pieroni and Salvato bills also provided that same-sex couples should be treated in the same way as cohabiting heterosexual couples (Art. 2, DDL No. S.1810; Art. 4, DDL No. S.2147: "*la condizione del convivente more uxorio omosessuale è parificata a quella del convivente more uxorio eterosessuale*").

[30] "*Non ho niente contro i gay ma è inutile tutelarli per legge*", interview with I Montanelli, *Oggi* (29 Sept. 1999).

[31] Interview with E Tonini, Cardinal of Ravenna, *L'Avvenire* (14 Sept. 1999). See also Introduction to this book. p. 4, n.12.

political opinion, personal and social conditions), and four grounds found in Article 13 but not in Article 3 (ethnic origin, age, disability, sexual orientation). DLG No. C.6582 would allow every individual who has suffered discrimination on any of the above-mentioned grounds in any economic-social context to seek a judicial remedy against such discrimination. Reactions to the Government's bill were along the same lines as those which followed the presentation of the Vendola Bill and the Revised Soda Bill.

On 11 January 2001, DLG No. C.6582, the Vendola Bill and the Revised Soda Bill were referred to the Constitutional Affairs Committee of the *Camera dei Deputati* for examination. By March 2001, no debate on any of them had taken place. Since Parliament was dissolved on 7 March 2001, all three bills lost their chance of becoming law. None of them can be carried forward automatically to the new Parliament. It will be up to the new government to decide whether similar legislative initiatives in the field of non-discrimination should be pursued. If the centre-right's candidate for Prime Minister, Deputy Berlusconi, wins the elections on 13 May 2001, it is not likely that such an initiative will be amongst his priorities. Consequently, the implementation of Council Directive 2000/78/EC will probably be the only measure taken against sexual orientation discrimination.

CONCLUSIONS

The three recent anti-discrimination bills provoked a very animated debate in Italy. The debate became even more heated on 16 March 2000 when the European Parliament adopted another resolution calling for the recognition of same-sex partnerships. The Vatican clearly voiced its opinion[32] against the appeal from Strasbourg. The debate in the Italian Parliament on sexual orientation discrimination was negatively influenced by the reactions, highly reported by the media, to the EP's resolution. Thus, at the end of March 2001, there were no pending proposals to prohibit sexual orientation discrimination. However, EC law obliges Italy to implement Council Directive 2000/78/EC by 2 December 2003. Italy will therefore have to adopt legislation prohibiting sexual orientation discrimination in the field of employment. This will constitute an important first step. Nonetheless, the implementation of this Directive will fall short of the ambition of DLG No. C.6582, which would have applied to any economic-social context ("*qualsiasi contesto economico-sociale*"),[33] not just employment. Given the problems that DLG No. C.6582 encountered, one has to admit that adding sexual orientation to other prohibited grounds of discrimination in all economic-social areas (other than employment) will not be an easy objective to

[32] See Introduction, *ibid*.

[33] See the *Relazione* (explanatory statement) accompanying DLG No. C.6582.

achieve. If this target is not reached, the issue of legal recognition of same-sex partnerships will not be tackled in the near future. Priorities might change if further legislative action is taken at the EC level.[34]

[34] Deputy Franco Grillini (elected, like new Prime Minister Berlusconi, on 13 May 2001) introduced three bills on 7 June 2001: PDL No. C.605 would add sexual orientation and other grounds to Art. 3 of the Constitution (see similar bills, *supra* n.13); PDL No. C.606 would prohibit sexual orientation discrimination in employment, schools and health insurance, and grant an express right of asylum to those persecuted because of their sexual orientation; PDL No. C.607 would create an institution of "*unione domestica registrata*" for same-sex couples, allowing them to acquire all the rights and obligations of married different-sex couples, except with regard to adoption. See also his bill PDL No. C.977 (21 June 2001), which would make 28 June "Dignity Day" in Italy, "to remember the victims of centuries of persecution, discrimination and hate against homosexuals, bisexuals and transsexuals".

29

At the End of the Fairy Tale, Will Heidi Stay Single? Same-Sex Partnerships in Switzerland

FRANÇOIS E BAUR[1]

INTRODUCTION

FOR DECADES, THE Heidi image of Switzerland as an unspoiled world, held by many foreigners, also applied to the situation of homosexuals and lesbians. In the nineteenth century, which saw England sentence one of its greatest poets to two years forced labour for "gross indecency", a resident of Switzerland from the Canton of Glarus was publishing one of the first manifestos on the acknowledgement of love between man and man.[2] As early as 1942, Switzerland decriminalised same-sex sexual activity between adults,[3] and cantonal law was likewise no longer permitted to subject it to penalties.[4] This was a reflection of a tolerant attitude on the part of the state and society, according to which it cannot be the duty of the state to regulate the sexual behaviour of the mature citizen, as long as it causes neither damage nor a significant nuisance to others.

During the Second World War, when men were sent to concentration camps for homosexual activities in Germany, homosexuals and lesbians could pursue a peaceful private life in Switzerland, largely free from repression by the state authorities. As a result, a lively social life developed in Zürich, for instance, around the discrete Swiss friendship association known as the "League for Human Rights". In the course of the 1940s and 1950s, the monthly magazine "Der Kreis", published in three languages in Switzerland, became one of the most important homosexual publications in Europe, and was even

[1] Vice-Director, Legal Department, Swiss Federal Office of Culture; President, Pink Cross (Swiss Gay Federation), Bern, http://www.pinkcross.ch/german/index.shtml (or /french/index.shtml).

[2] H Hössli, *Eros—die Männerliebe der Griechen, ihre Beziehungen zur Geschichte, Erziehung, Literatur und Gesetzgebung aller Zeiten* (Berlin, Verlag Rosa Winkel, 1996), reprinting (Glarus, 1836).

[3] Cantonal penal laws generally only banned male-male sexual activity.

[4] Decisions of the Swiss Federal Supreme Court (*Bundesgerichtsentscheide, Arrêts du Tribunal fédéral*), BGE 81 IV 124. See G Stratenwerth, *Schweizerisches Strafrecht, Besonderer Teil I: Straftaten gegen Individualinteressen*, 4th ed. (Bern, Stämpfli, 1995), at p. 137 et seq.

distributed in the United States.[5] However, despite an attitude that was tolerant in comparison with other countries, homosexuals and lesbians, and in particular same-sex couples, did not benefit from legal recognition on the part of Swiss state institutions. Moreover, Swiss penal law included the crime of unnatural indecency, which penalised male-male and female-female sexual activity with persons under the age of twenty, compared with the age of sixteen for male-female sexual activity, until it was repealed in 1992.[6] Mother Helvetia was sleeping as deeply as the Sleeping Beauty, and there was no one there to kiss her awake.

THE RIGHT TO MARRY AS A CONSTITUTIONAL GUARANTEE

The Freedom to Marry Pursuant to New Federal Constitution Article 14

Like the entire civil law, matrimonial law is regulated in Switzerland at the federal level. Swiss marital law knows no other form of partnership or cohabitation than marriage. According to Article 14 of the new Federal Constitution,[7] "[t]he right to marriage and [to marriage and family] family is guaranteed". The wording gives no indication that the guarantee of marriage refers only to a relationship between a man and a woman, for the text itself is neutral.

In the view of the Federal Council (the Swiss federal government),[8] and according to prevailing doctrine, the institution of marriage in Switzerland and in Western culture generally is interpreted, on the basis of Roman Law and Christianity, as a relationship between two people of different sexes.[9] According to this historic construction, the guarantee of marriage extends "neither to marriages between transsexuals nor to homosexual marriages. . . . The institution of marriage was always based on the traditional couple. An extension to all forms of cohabitation would today conflict with the fundamental concept of the institution of marriage".[10] However, this view is not undis-

[5] W Catrina, "Als Zürich ein Schwulen-Eldorado war", *Tages-Anzeiger* (4 May 1999).

[6] Art. 194, old Penal Code, Classified Compilation of Federal Law (*Systematische Sammlung des Bundesrechts, Recueil systématique du droit fédéral*), SR Nr. 311.0.

[7] Federal Constitution of the Swiss Confederation, SR 101 (adopted 18 April 1999, in force 1 Jan. 2000), http://confinder.richmond.edu(French, German, Italian, English).

[8] Message of the Federal Council concerning a new Federal Constitution dated 20 Nov. 1996, *Bundesblatt* (official journal), BBl 1997 I 154.

[9] Federal Office of Justice (*Bundesamt für Justiz, Office fédéral de la justice*), *Die rechtliche Situation gleichgeschlechtlicher Paare im schweizerischen Recht: Probleme und Lösungsansätze, La situation juridique des couples homosexuels en droit suisse: Problèmes et propositions de solution* (June 1999), http://www.bj.admin.ch/themen/glgpaare/vn-ber-d.pdf (or /vn-ber-f.pdf) (the "FOJ Report"), at p. 27.

[10] *Ibid.* See also Bräm & Hasenböhler, *Kommentar zum Schweizerischen Zivilgesetzbuch (Zürcher Kommentar)*, 3rd ed. (Zürich, Schulthess, 1993), Note 12 on Art. 159 of the Civil Code (same-sex marriage cannot be achieved without an amendment to the Federal Constitution in light of the unspoken prevalent opinion that marriage is a community between two heterosexual persons).

puted. Jean-Francois Aubert, in a legal opinion for the Federal Office of Justice, denies the existence of an institutional guarantee, and concludes that the legislature could make marriage available to same-sex couples even without an amendment to Article 14 of the new Federal Constitution.[11]

According to the Federal Supreme Court (*Bundesgericht, Tribunal fédéral*), marriage between two persons of the same sex infringes Swiss *ordre public*.[12] In 1993, the Court had to decide on a case in which a Brazilian male-to-female transsexual, who had married a non-transsexual man in Denmark, requested the registration of the marriage in the Register of Births, Marriages and Deaths in Switzerland. The legislation in effect in Brazil prevented the applicant from amending his civil status there after his gender reassignment. In the opinion of the Federal Supreme Court, there is a breach of *ordre public* if fundamental legal principles are infringed, i.e., if the act in question is absolutely incompatible with the Swiss system of law and values. According to this point of view, the concept of *ordre public* is based on the general sense of justice and the moral values of the citizens.

On the basis of the last representative opinion poll dated 8 May 1999,[13] according to which 53 per cent of the Swiss population are of the opinion that gay and lesbian couples should be allowed to marry, as compared with 37 per cent opposed to such a measure, the question may be raised whether the general sense of justice still corresponds with the Federal Supreme Court's interpretation of *ordre public*. The fact that the general sense of justice has gradually changed in Switzerland is also detectable among academic lawyers, not always renowned for their progressive thinking; a growing number favour changing the law and granting legal recognition to same-sex partnerships.[14]

In one case, moreover, a same-sex marriage was implicitly recognised at the local level: the St. Gallen District Court allowed the registration in the Register of Births, Marriages and Deaths, as a woman under her female given name after a gender reassignment, of a male-to-female transsexual who had married a non-transsexual woman before the reassignment. The wife of the transsexual had confirmed her consent to this measure. The court came to the conclusion that the interests of the married transsexual in the recognition of her reassignment and the continuation of her marriage, and hence the public interest in the protection of a functioning conjugal partnership, was clearly greater then the public interest in

[11] Unpublished opinion requested by the FOJ on 5 May 1998, at p. 17, quoted in FOJ Report, *supra* n.9, at p. 62, n.246.

[12] BGE 119 II 266.

[13] Representative opinion poll dated 3–8 May 1999, by the *Institut für Markt- und Sozialforschung* in Lucerne for the lesbian organisation LOS and Pink Cross.

[14] I Schwenzer, "Familienrecht im Umbruch", [1993] *Zeitschrift des Bernischen Juristenvereins* 274; T Geiser, "Gleichgeschlechtliche Lebensgemeinschaften in der Schweiz aus rechtlicher Sicht", in H Puff (ed.), *Lust, Angst und Provokation: Homosexualität in der Gesellschaft* (Göttingen & Zürich, Vandenhoeck & Ruprecht, 1993) at 233; Hegnauer & Breitschmid, *Grundriss des Eherechts*, 4th rev. ed. (Bern, Stämpfli, 1993), Note 2.32b; I Schwander, "Sollen eheähnliche und andere familiäre Gemeinschaften in der Schweiz gesetzlich geregelt werden?", [7/1994] *Aktuelle Juristische Praxis* 918 at 920.

the protection of the institution of marriage, and for this reason the (legally and physically) same-sex marriage was to be tolerated.[15] In its decision, the District Court emphasised that the recognition of an originally different-sex marriage, which only became same-sex after a gender reassignment, could not be used to draw conclusions with respect to marriage between persons who are of the same sex at the time of the marriage.[16] But the Court also justified its decision by referring to the changed social values with respect to same-sex partnerships.[17]

The Prohibition on Discrimination in New Federal Constitution Article 8(2)

Article 8(2) of the new Federal Constitution expressly forbids discrimination against any person by reason of his or her "way of life" ("*Lebensform*", "*mode de vie*", "*modo de vita*"). The debates in the Federal Assembly (the Swiss federal parliament) on this Article make it clear that "way of life" is intended to refer above all to homosexuality.[18]

This apparently small addition could be of greater importance in future than the Federal Administration today admits.[19] This has been shown in cantons whose cantonal constitution includes a prohibition on discrimination based on "way of life".[20] Thus, the Canton of Bern has extended the right to refuse to testify in criminal procedural law to "persons living together in a marriage-like manner with the defendant".[21] In addition, persons in the Canton of Bern who have lived together for at least ten years in a family household (*Hausgemeinschaft*) or common household (*Wohngemeinschaft*) are now subject to a lower inheritance tax rate in the event of inheritance than other non-related persons. This concession benefits heterosexual and homosexual partners equally.[22]

In a recent publication, Hangartner claims that, because "way of life" is expressly mentioned in Article 8 of the Federal Constitution, same-sex partner-

[15] (1997) 93 *Schweizerische Juristenzeitung* 442 et seq.

[16] *Ibid.* at 445.

[17] *Ibid.* at 444.

[18] *Amtliches Bulletin Nationalrat, Bulletin officiel Conseil national*, AB NR, 18 March 1998. The concept of "way of life" was only introduced by the National Council (lower chamber) as a result of the lobbying work of the homosexual umbrella organisations Pink Cross and LOS.

[19] The FOJ Report, *supra* n.9, at 61, rejects the idea that specific legal claims can be derived by same-sex couples from Art. 8(2) of the new Federal Constitution, on the remarkable grounds that this claim also applies for other ways of life such as heterosexual cohabiting couples. In fact, Art. 8(2) permits no discrimination whatsoever on the basis of ways of life, i.e. neither those of same-sex couples nor those of heterosexual cohabiting couples. Thus, this provision in no way excludes both ways of life having to be treated as equal with marriage (the traditional way of life).

[20] Cantonal Constitutions of Bern, Appenzell Outer Rhodes; draft Cantonal Constitutions of Neufchatel, St. Gall and Schaffhausen.

[21] Str.V BE, Art. 113, Para. 1, No. 1. Corresponding provisions are to be found in the codes of criminal procedure of the Cantons of Schwyz, Solothurn, Schaffhausen and Ticino, and the codes of civil procedure of the Cantons of Lucerne, Uri, Schwyz and Thurgau.

[22] Act concerning Inheritance and Gift Tax, Art. 10, Para. 1, No. 2; practice of the Cantonal Taxation Administration of Bern. See M Bertschi, *Schützt die Rechtsordnung vor Diskriminierung aufgrund der sexuellen Orientierung?* (Bern, Pink Cross, 1997) at 15 et seq.

ships enjoy the same constitutional protection as married couples under Article 14. To prevent discrimination against same-sex partnerships compared to married couples, the state is obliged to provide a legal status for same-sex partners equal to that of married couples. Differences in the rights and duties attached to the two marital statuses may only be introduced for substantial reasons (for instance due to a distinctive sex characteristic).[23]

NO STATUTORY REGULATION OF COHABITATION

Unlike other countries such as Sweden,[24] Switzerland has no statutory regulation or definition of cohabitation as a way of life. This ought to lead to the conclusion that same-sex and unmarried different-sex couples must be treated equally under the law as a matter of principle.

However, the Federal Supreme Court defines cohabitation in the narrow sense as a partnership, between two persons *of different sexes,* of a fundamentally exclusive character intended for a long period of time if not for life, involving intellectual, spiritual, sexual and economic components, or "a common home, table and bed".[25] It is distinguished from other living together (the broad sense) by the stability of the exclusive intellectual, spiritual, sexual and economic relationship between the partners. Usually, it is sufficient to prove a five-year duration for the relationship to qualify as cohabitation in the narrow sense.

Despite the fact that cohabiting couples are not covered by statutes, cohabitation can still have legal effects. Thus, unmarried couples (both different-sex and same-sex) can regulate individual aspects of their cohabitation within the framework of contracts, e.g., concerning maintenance or inheritance rights. If no contracts are made, if the unmarried couple is different-sex and not same-sex, the provisions concerning ordinary partnerships in the Code of Obligations are applied as a substitute, e.g., to regulate the consequences of the termination of the partnership or payment for work carried out for the partnership.[26]

However, cohabitation generally has no effects against third parties. Thus, for instance, there is no statutory right to represent the cohabitation partner, which would have to be agreed by contract. Nor can cohabitation partners rely on Article 272 of the Code of Obligations, according to which a tenant may request the extension of a lease if its termination would result in hardship for his/her family.[27] Likewise, cohabitation has no effects whatsoever with respect to the state, such as in the fields of taxation law, social insurance law, and

[23] See I Hangartner, "Verfassungsrechtliche Grundlagen einer registrierten Partnerschaft für gleichgeschlechtliche Paare", [2001] *Aktuelle Juristische Praxis* 252.

[24] FOJ Report, *supra* n.9, at 10.

[25] BGE 118 II 238. See B Pulver, *L'union libre—Droit actuel et réformes nécessaires* (Lausanne, Editions Réalités, 1999), *Unverheiratete Paare—Aktuelle Rechtslage und Reformvorschläge* (Basel, Helbing & Lichtenhahn, 2000).

[26] FOJ Report, *supra* n.9, at 27.

[27] BGE 105 II 199; FOJ Report, *ibid.*, at 27 et seq.

immigration law.[28] Nor do cohabiting couples as yet enjoy a right to refuse to testify in most cantons.[29] But the principle of a lack of external effect has some exceptions. Thus, a spouse who is seeking a divorce and has begun a cohabitation in the narrow sense could be barred from claiming maintenance from their spouse.[30]

The Federal Supreme Court's definition of cohabitation in the narrow sense could without difficulty also be applied to same-sex couples. Since the legal problems of heterosexual and homosexual cohabiting couples are largely the same, their relationships should have the same legal consequences.[31] However, a major difference is that different-sex cohabitating couples can at any time improve their legal status, and remove the associated discrimination as compared with married couples, by themselves contracting a marriage, while this option is denied to same-sex couples. For this reason, it appears improper to demand the same five-year period of cohabitation for same-sex couples, and under certain circumstances a shorter period should be sufficient for qualification as a stable same-sex cohabitation.[32] Nevertheless, the opinion is also held in legal circles in Switzerland that the relationship of a same-sex couple is not to be defined as cohabitation,[33] with a resulting tendency—as we will see below—to discriminate against same-sex couples as compared with heterosexual cohabiting couples.

THE LEGAL CONSEQUENCES OF MARRIAGE

The June 1999 report of the Federal Office of Justice concerning the legal situation of same-sex couples under Swiss law[34] contains a detailed list of the discrimination against same-sex couples under statutory regulations based on the existence of a marriage, ranging from residence rights to family, inheritance and contractual law, and from social insurance law to penal and administrative law. The following sections present a number of less obvious examples of subtle discrimination resulting from the prohibition on marriage for same-sex couples.

[28] FOJ Report, *ibid.*, at 28.

[29] But see *supra* n.21.

[30] FOJ Report, *supra* n.9, at 28. In BGE 118 II 225, the Federal Supreme Court denied a wife who was fully supported by her cohabitation partner a claim to maintenance in divorce proceedings.

[31] R D Dussy, *Ausgleichsansprüche für Vermögensinvestitionen nach Auflösung von Lebensbeziehungen nach deutschem und schweizerischem Recht* (Basel, Helbing & Lichtenhahn, 1994) at 3; FOJ Report, *ibid.*

[32] See Schwander, *supra* n.14 at 920, who would accept a cohabitation in the narrow sense after only one year.

[33] BGE 118 II 238; Hegnauer & Beitschmid, *supra* n.14, Notes 1.08, 2.25 and expressly Note 3.32b; FOJ Report, *supra* n.9, footnote 107.

[34] *Supra* n.9.

Immigration Law

According to Swiss law, foreigners have in principle no right to the grant or prolongation of a residence permit. An exception applies for the spouses of Swiss nationals. Pursuant to Article 7 of the Federal Act concerning Residence and Settlement of Foreigners (ANAG),[35] they are entitled at any time to the grant of a prolongation of their residence permit and, after an uninterrupted five-year stay in Switzerland, are entitled to a settlement permit, which is a precondition for the exercise of a profession in Switzerland. According to the opinion of the Federal Office of Justice, same-sex couples cannot rely on this provision.[36] But the wording of Article 8(2) of the new Federal Constitution, which prohibits any discrimination by the state on the basis of "way of life", makes it doubtful whether this situation can continue in the future. Heterosexual and same-sex partnerships corresponding to the Federal Supreme Court's definition of a cohabitation in the narrow sense must logically also be able to rely on the exception in Article 7 of the ANAG.

Immigration law also distinguishes between foreigners in employment and foreigners not in employment. For foreigners in employment, the Federal Council periodically lays down maximum limits for permits for annual residents, seasonal residents and short-stay residents. However, "serious personal cases of hardship" are excluded from these quotas.[37] A similar exception also applies for foreigners not in employment.[38] The existence of hardship is determined by reference to the facts of the individual case. Since this is an exception, the Federal Supreme Court applies the regulation strictly and requires a personal emergency on the part of the person concerned. In the opinion of the Federal Supreme Court, this was the case for a homosexual relationship between a Swiss citizen and a foreigner. Alongside the fact that the refusal of the permit would have broken up an almost four-year partnership, the decisive factor for the Court was that the foreign partner was integrated in the family of the Swiss partner, who was obliged to and in fact did provide financially for his friend. This, in the view of the Court, proved the closeness of the relationship.[39]

In contrast, the Government Council of the Canton of Zürich dismissed a request for a residence permit, based on the hardship clause, by the New Zealand-national member of a lesbian couple resident in Zürich.[40] Relying on the practice of the Federal Supreme Court, the Government Council held that

[35] SR 142.20.

[36] FOJ Report, *supra* n.9, at 30.

[37] Art. 13f of the Regulation concerning the Restriction of the Number of Foreigners (BVO, SR 823.21).

[38] Art. 36, *ibid.*, provides for the possibility of a residence permit "if it is required for important reasons", subject to the same criteria as an exceptional permit pursuant to Art. 13f, *ibid.*

[39] Federal Supreme Court Decision, 2nd Public Law Division, 22 May 1992, i.p. R & S c. EJPD, quoted in FOJ Report, *supra* n.9, at 31.

[40] Extract from the Minutes of the Government Council of the Canton of Zürich, Session dated 11 Nov. 1998.

the difficulty or even impossibility of maintaining a four-year, stable, marriage-like, same-sex partnership over the distances involved did not establish a case of hardship. Additional reasons for the refusal were that:

- all other same-sex couples including a foreign partner were in the same situation, and for this reason the case in question could not be described as a personal emergency;
- thanks to her additional British nationality, the applicant could settle in the United Kingdom or in a European Union member state close to the Swiss border;
- there was no justification for benefiting same-sex partnerships as compared with heterosexual cohabitating couples that include a foreign partner (the Government Council naturally ignored the fact that the latter—unlike same-sex partners—can at any time establish a claim to a settlement permit by marrying each other).

The Government Council's decision was upheld by the Administrative Court of the Canton of Zürich and only partly revised by the Federal Supreme Court in its decision of 25 August 2000.[41] The Court refused to grant the non-Swiss partner a right of residence, reasoning that the partners had lived their relationship mainly outside of Switzerland and therefore could not claim a special attachment to the country. The Court also explained its reticence to rule in favour of the couple by stating that it is up to the legislator to decide under which circumstances it is justified, in view of Swiss foreign and immigration policy, to grant a right of residence to non-Swiss homosexuals. This decision has been widely criticised by the media and academic commentators.[42] Although the Federal Supreme Court denied same-sex couples the right to be treated equally with married heterosexual couples, it acknowledged that stable partnerships of same-sex couples are to be considered more intensive than a usual social relationship, and therefore may—under certain circumstances—justify a right of residence for the non-Swiss partner under Article 8 ("private life") of the European Convention on Human Rights.[43]

The Right of Asylum

The spouses and minor children of refugees recognised as such in Switzerland are in principle also recognised as refugees, unless particular reasons argue to

[41] BGE 126 II 425.

[42] See e.g. I Handgartner, [3/2001] *Aktuelle Juristische Praxis* 361.

[43] Some academic commentators consider it merely a question of time until same-sex partners can rely in full on Art. 8 (including the right to respect for "family life"). See Schwander, *supra* n.14, at 920, citing S Breitenmoser, "Das Recht auf Achtung des Privat- und Familienlebens in der schweizerischen Rechtsprechung zum Ausländerrecht', [1993] 20 *Europäische Grundrechte-Zeitschrift* 537; L Wildhaber, *Internationaler Kommentar zur Europäischen Menschenrechtskonvention, Komentierung des Art. 8 EMRK* (Cologne, C. Heymanns, 1992) at 144–51; Bertschi, *supra* n.22; Handgartner, *supra* n.23.

the contrary.[44] The Federal Office for Refugees (BFF) goes beyond the clear wording of the Asylum Act and also applies the provision to cohabiting partners and their children. In contrast, a same-sex partner of a recognised refugee would not be recognised as a refugee, and would no doubt be deported. The different application of the Act is justified by the BFF by reference to the practice of the Federal Supreme Court, which forbids same-sex marriage as being in conflict with *ordre public*.[45]

Matrimonial Law

Swiss matrimonial law regulates the mutual rights and obligations of spouses to each other and to their families, specifically the mutual right of representation, and the mutual rights and obligations to provide maintenance and care for the family. In addition, it regulates spouses' financial relationships and their reciprocal claims in the event of a termination of the marriage, as a result of divorce or the death of a spouse. Given the impossibility of marriage, all these provisions naturally are inapplicable to same-sex couples. If they wish to regulate their cohabitation under the law, they must have recourse to detailed contractual agreements between themselves.[46]

Of particular importance for same-sex couples is without doubt the power of one partner to represent the other in the event of an illness or an accident suffered by the other. This only applies if the partners have granted each other the right of representation and issued a comprehensive power of attorney,[47] although it then also applies against relatives. Moreover, the law does not, as is often alleged, authorise unequal treatment of same-sex couples in the field of the medical duty to provide information. Article 321 of the Swiss Penal Code[48] forbids doctors from giving information to unauthorised persons concerning the state of health of their patients. This medical confidentiality applies to family members just as much as to same-sex partners. However, in the case of family members, there is a greater tendency to assume the patient's consent to the revocation of medical confidentiality. Here too, to prevent any misunderstandings, it is sufficient to issue reciprocal declarations in which medical personnel are expressly authorised to provide information to the partner.[49]

[44] Art. 3(3) of the Asylum Act (AsylG, SR 142.31).
[45] BGE 119 II 264; FOJ Report, *supra* n.9, at 32.
[46] See FOJ Report, *ibid.*, at 33 et seq.
[47] Arts. 31 et seq. of the Code of Obligations (OR, SR 220).
[48] StGB, SR 311.0.
[49] FOJ Report, *supra* n.9, at 42.

Adoption and Artificial Procreation

Swiss family law recognises both joint and individual adoption. Joint adoption, however, is only available to married couples.[50] Likewise, the adoption of a stepchild is only possible if the adopting person is married to the biological parent.[51] On the other hand, individual adoption is also open to anyone who lives in a same-sex partnership, provided that the statutory conditions are satisfied, namely that the adopting person has reached the age of 35, that there is an age difference of at least 16 years between the adopting person and the adopted child, and that the biological parents have consented to the adoption.[52] However, the same-sex partner of the adopting person—like a stepparent—has no custody rights with respect to the adopted child. In contrast, where the custody claim is by a biological parent, the parent's sexual orientation is not allowed to play a role. Thus, the Federal Supreme Court has expressly refused to deny custody of the children to the mother in a divorce case because she was living in a same-sex relationship.[53]

Since the new Federal Constitution only permits artificial insemination if "the infertility cannot be remedied in any other way",[54] with infertility understood in the narrow sense, which excludes absence of a male partner, medically assisted insemination is legally denied to lesbian couples.[55] On the other hand, Swiss law does not provide any sanction where a fertile woman obtains a child by artificial insemination.

Inheritance Law

Same-sex partners do not enjoy the same statutory inheritance rights with respect to each other, but can mutually appoint each other as heirs by contract. However, strict statutory regulations must be complied with.[56] In addition, the partner must take account of their relatives' inheritance rights. Children, spouses and, in the absence of these, parents enjoy a claim to a compulsory portion against the testator, which cannot be revoked by contract without their consent. For instance, a divorced man with children can leave to his same-sex partner a maximum of one-quarter of his estate, and must leave the rest to his children. In contrast, a spouse with children is entitled to half the estate in principle, and can at most be reduced to one-quarter of the estate.[57] If the surviving

[50] Art. 264a of the Civil Code (ZGB, SR 210).
[51] Art. 264a(3), *ibid*.; FOJ Report, *supra* n.9, at 35.
[52] Art. 264b et seq., *ibid*.
[53] BGE 108 II 371 et seq.
[54] Art. 119(2c).
[55] FOJ Report, *supra* n.9, at 35.
[56] Civil Code, Art. 498 et seq.
[57] *Ibid*., Art. 471.

partner nevertheless does inherit, he/she will be made to pay heavily depending on the canton. Since he/she is neither related nor married to the testator, inheritance tax rates of up to 40 per cent are applied, while in many cantons married spouses are exempt from inheritance tax. The Canton of Bern is an exception, and here a reduced rate of tax is applied in the case of partnerships lasting more than ten years.[58] In addition, the surviving spouse's right to demand that the marital home and household goods be included in his or her inheritance is denied to the same-sex partner.[59]

Social Insurance Law

In the field of social insurance law, same-sex couples, as well as different-sex cohabiting couples, are at a disadvantage as compared with married couples, particularly with respect to occupational pension provisions. Alongside old-age and survivor's pension insurance (AHV), Switzerland also has a system of occupational pensions. In principle, employee and employer pay contributions for the duration of the employment into a fund for the benefit of the employee. The insured person is entitled to the assets thus accumulated upon retirement. If the insured person dies, he can transfer these tied assets to certain persons. The Federal Occupational Pensions Act would also permit non-marital partners as beneficiaries.

However, the Federal Taxation Administration (EStV)—without being able to rely on a sufficient statutory basis—is threatening pension funds with the withdrawal of their tax exemptions if the circle of beneficiaries is extended.[60] As a rule, the circle of beneficiaries permitted by the EStV does not include unmarried partners. To understand the significance of this exclusion, one needs to know that in practice, when matrimonial goods or estates are distributed upon divorce or death, social security benefits often exceed all other matrimonial property, and indeed often represent the only assets to which the survivors are entitled upon the death of the fund beneficiary.[61] In addition, the inclusion of same-sex partners amongst the beneficiaries would be one of the few ways of allowing them to obtain assets free of inheritance tax.

[58] See *supra* n.22.

[59] Civil Code, Art. 612a; FOJ Report, *supra* n.9, at 37.

[60] Circular No. 1, 30 Jan. 1986, "Federal Act to Harmonise the BdBST to the Federal Act concerning Occupational Pensions", in *Archiv für schweizerisches Abgaberecht* (ASA) 54, p. 501 et seq., amended by Circular No. 1a, 20 August 1986, in ASA 55, p. 199 et seq.

[61] T Koller, "Begünstigtenordnung zweite und dritte Säule: Gutachten zuhanden des Bundesamtes für Sozialversicherung", in *Beiträge zur sozialen Sicherheit* (Bern, Federal Social Insurance Office, 1998) at 6.

Taxation Law

According to the principle of family taxation prevailing in the field of direct federal taxes in Switzerland, married couples are taxed jointly, i.e., their incomes are added together. As a result, because of progressive taxation rates on higher incomes, dual-income couples are at a disadvantage compared with unmarried partners, despite certain corrective measures.[62]

In order to eliminate these disadvantages, a Commission of Experts has drafted a report on the existing system of family taxation for the Federal Finance Department, setting out the present defects and putting forward proposals for a new approach.[63] One of the fundamental decisions taken by the Commission was that married and cohabiting couples in the same financial conditions should be submitted to the same tax burden. This once again brought up the question of the definition of cohabitation. However, in its report, the Commission takes as its starting point a lasting partnership between man and woman, and despite a motion in the Federal Assembly,[64] fails to take account of same-sex couples.[65] Consequently, same-sex couples will be systematically disadvantaged as compared with heterosexual cohabiting couples in all three taxation models proposed to the Federal Council by the Commission. However, this procedure is a clear infringement of the prohibition on discrimination in Article 8(2) of the new Federal Constitution. The Federal Supreme Court has repeatedly held that new statutory regulations in the field of taxation law should not generally lead to a significantly increased, and systematically less favourable, burden on individual groups of taxpayers,[66] such as might become the case here.

THE CAMPAIGN FOR LEGAL REGULATION OF SAME-SEX PARTNERSHIPS

The initial goal of the Homosexual Working Parties of Switzerland (*Homosexuelle Arbeitsgruppen Schweiz*, HACH) was an amendment to the criminal law abolishing all direct discrimination against same-sex sexual activity and providing for a uniform age of consent of sixteen. This amendment entered into force on 1 October 1992. HACH first examined the legal situation of same-sex

[62] Hegnauer & Breitschmid, *supra* n.14, Note 2.32; FOJ Report, *supra* n.9, at 43.

[63] *Report of the Commission of Experts on the Examination of the Swiss System of Family Taxation* (Bern, 1998) (the "Locher Report").

[64] Motion by the Legal Affairs Committee of the National Council, "Same rights for same-sex couples", 27 February 1996, requesting the Federal Council to examine "what forms must be created to eliminate the legal problems of same-sex couple relationships and what rights and obligations would be associated with such an institution".

[65] The Commission sees no need for action as long as civil law does not regulate this question. See Locher Report, *supra* n.63, at 38 et seq.

[66] Cf. ASA 63, p. 749.

partnerships in a report[67] published in 1991. In April 1991, HACH held a conference in Solothurn on the topic of "Clear rights for homosexual and lesbian partnerships", at which various solutions were discussed with a number of politicians. It became apparent that there was considerable disagreement amongst homosexuals and lesbians regarding the route to be taken, and the discussions culminated at times in proposals to abolish the institution of marriage altogether.[68] On the basis of the relatively new possibility of registered partnerships in Denmark, two proposals were launched in the Federal Assembly for the first time in 1994 to deal with the question of the protection of same-sex couples.[69]

On 9 January 1995, the "Same Rights for Same-Sex Couples" Committee submitted a petition bearing 85,181 signatures requesting the the Federal Assembly to eliminate legal discrimination against same-sex couples. In a motion from the National Council (the lower chamber of the Federal Assembly, the upper chamber being the Council of States), the Federal Council was invited on 13 June 1996 to examine "what forms must be created to eliminate the legal problems of same-sex couple relationships and what rights and obligations would be associated with such an institution".[70] After further moves in the Federal Assembly, and a number of promises on the part of the Federal Council to submit the report soon, a number of members of the National Council lost patience. On 30 November 1998, a parliamentary initiative, signed by twenty-two National Councillors, was submitted in the form of a general proposal[71] that two persons who intended to establish a permanent cohabitation should be given the possibility of registering their partnership. A further parliamentary initiative[72] demanded that civil marriage be made available to same-sex couples.

On 21 June 1999, the Legal Affairs Committee of the National Council, by eighteen votes to three with one abstention, supported the initiative for the creation of registered partnerships, and recommended that it be accepted by the National Council. This very clear decision was justified by the President of the Committee on the grounds that the model of a partnership registered at the Registry of Births, Marriages and Deaths appeared capable of achieving consensus and of being rapidly implemented.[73]

[67] *Neue Lebensformen oder Ehe für Schwule und Lesben? Eine Analyse der heutigen rechtlichen Situation und Materialien für eine zukünftige Lebensformenpolitik* (Bern, HACH, 1991).

[68] See T Bucher, *Lebensformenpolitik für gleichgeschlechtliche Partnerschaften in der Schweiz*, Beiträge der Koordinationsstelle Homosexualität & Wissenschaft Nr. 7 (Zürich, 1992).

[69] Simple request by Member of the Council of States Petitpierre to the Federal Council to consider the problem of same-sex couples (94.1027); motion by National Councillor Grendelmeier on the establishment of legal protection for same-sex couples (94.3439).

[70] AB NR (*supra* n.18) 1996, 911 et seq. A petition from the Swiss Democratic Union (EDU), resisting equal treatment of same-sex couples with heterosexual couples, was dismissed by the National Council.

[71] 98.443, initiative by National Councillor J-M Gros (Liberal Party, Geneva).

[72] 98.453, initiative by National Councillor R Genner (Green Party, Zürich).

[73] *Schweizerische Depeschen Agentur* (SDA) report on the press conference of the Legal Affairs Committee of the National Council, 21 June 1999. This opinion was confirmed by the representative opinion poll of 8 May 1999, *supra* n.13, according to which 68% of Swiss citizens were in favour of registered partnership for homosexuals and lesbians.

On 23 September 1999, the National Council ordered its Law Committee to draft a registered partnership bill, applying only to same-sex partners, and excluding adoption of children and artificial insemination. But the Committee has yet to start, because the Federal Council announced on 25 October 2000, that it would publish its own registered partnership bill by the summer of 2001.[74] Unlike the Scandinavian partnership laws, the Federal Council's bill will not refer by analogy to existing matrimonial regulations, but will regulate rights and obligations between the same-sex partners independently of matrimonial law. In her press conference, the Minister of Justice, Federal Councillor Ruth Metzler, justified this separate treatment by referring to the special situation and needs of same-sex partners. She argued that, as a rule, same-sex partners are both working and have no common children. The Swiss media commented on this explanation with amusement, as the Minister of Justice is in a "double income, no kids" relationship herself.

The Federal Council has yet to say what the differences between matrimonial law and same-sex partnership regulation will be. However, it is quite clear already that the the federal government's bill will not allow same-sex partners to adopt children and will exclude them from artificial procreation. Once published, the bill will be put out for consultation, which will allow all interest groups to comment on it, before it is presented to the Federal Assembly. It must then be discussed and adopted by both chambers. The whole procedure will take three to four years before a registered partnership bill can become law. The parliamentary initiative on making civil marriage available to same-sex couples has been suspended, but not yet abandoned.

On 15 February 2001, the Canton of Geneva adopted a law granting certain rights under cantonal law to unmarried same-sex and different-sex partners who obtain a certificate of partnership.[75] Article 1(3) provides that partners shall be treated in the same way as spouses in their relations with the public administration of the Canton (excluding taxation and social welfare benefits). Article 7 provides that partners enjoy the same rights as spouses in the civil service (except with regard to retirement pensions). However, as civil law (including matrimonial, family and adoption law) is governed by federal law, the Geneva legislation will mainly have a symbolic effect.

LEGISLATIVE PROPOSALS BY THE FEDERAL OFFICE OF JUSTICE (FOJ)

The developments in the National Council discussed above were in line with the report published by the FOJ in June 1999: *The Legal Situation of Same-Sex Couples Under Swiss Law: Problems and Proposed Solutions*. The three sections

[74] FOJ press release (25 Oct. 2000), http://www.bj.admin.ch/themen/glgpaare/ve-com-d.htm (or /ve-com-f.htm).

[75] *Loi sur le partenariat du 15 février 2001* (7611), (RSG E 1 27), http://www.geneve.ch/rechercher/welcome.asp(partenariat).

of the report cover the development of the law abroad, a detailed analysis of the legal situation in Switzerland, and finally four possible solutions:

(1) specific legislative intervention;
(2) a partnership contract under the law of obligations with external effect;
(3) a registered partnership law with two alternative versions, and
(4) making civil marriage available to same-sex couples.

Specific Legislative Intervention[76]

The proposal by the FOJ provides that adjustments be made to individual statutes so as to achieve the legal equality of same-sex couples. However, the amendment of individual statutes involves considerable legislative effort. Given the long, drawn-out Swiss legislative process, it could under certain circumstances take decades until all laws had been adjusted to such an extent that one could speak of the equal treatment of same-sex couples. Nor would this solve the problem of the definition of a same-sex partnership. The authorities could attach conditions to the recognition of such a partnership that would still disadvantage the couples affected as compared with married couples. In addition, certain inequalities of treatment, for instance in the taxation system, cannot be remedied by the Federal Council and Federal Assembly alone, because the twenty-six cantons must also amend their legislation.

A Partnership Contract with External Effect[77]

The second proposal is a partnership contract between two persons of the same sex who are not married, who are not bound by another partnership agreement, and who are not related to each other in the direct line and are not siblings. In order to be valid, the agreement would have to be officially recorded, and could be dissolved with a particular notice period. The agreement would be regulated by the private law of obligations, but would have certain public law effects in the fields of income and inheritance tax, social insurance and immigration, a feature that would be unusual in the Swiss legal system. In addition, certain public law legislation would still have to be adjusted.

A Registered Partnership Law[78]

In the case of registered partnership, the FOJ is thinking of the model already established by statute in the Scandinavian countries. Registration would take

[76] Alternative 1, FOJ Report, *supra* n.9, at 54 et seq.
[77] Alternative 2, FOJ Report, *ibid.*, at p. 55 et seq.
[78] Alternatives 3a and 3b, FOJ Report, *ibid.*, at p. 56 et seq.

place before a state authority, the same obstacles would apply as for marriage, and for reasons of simplicity, dissolution would be subject *mutatis mutandis* to the provisions concerning divorce. With respect to the effects of a registered partnership, the FOJ proposes two alternatives. Under alternative 3a, the effects that only make sense in matrimonial law, such as with respect to the care of the couple's children, the common family name, certain matrimonial property regimes, and certain inheritance law provisions, would not apply to same-sex partnerships.

However, this would also mean that the legislature would have to regulate the effects of the registered partnership in more detail than would be the case for alternative 3b, which, as in the Scandinavian countries, applies the provisions of marital law by means of a system of references *mutatis mutandis* to the institution of registered partnership. The only exclusions under alternative 3b are the rights to joint adoption and medically assisted procreation. Of course, the FOJ cannot support these restrictions by scientific studies that would show that the personal development of children growing up in a same-sex family is at risk. For this reason, the prohibition on artificial insemination and adoption are justified by the child's claim to be legally associated with a father and a mother. Alternative 3b has the undisputed advantage that it could be implemented simply and rapidly through legislation. In addition, it would achieve widespread equality between married couples and same-sex partners, without allowing unintended scope for conflicting interpretations of different statutory regulations.[79]

Making Civil Marriage Available to Same-Sex Couples[80]

Making civil marriage available to same-sex couples would certainly be the simplest solution, but also the most radical. The justification in the parliamentary initiative for making civil marriage available to same-sex couples is that it is the only solution that achieves absolute equality between same-sex couples and different-sex couples.[81] Nevertheless, in the opinion of the FOJ there are also reasons for not making marriage available. Swiss law provides special constitutional protection to marriage and the family because, from the point of view of the state, marriage is not primarily the legal recognition of associations between two adult persons, but rather the creation of suitable structures to promote the further development and continued existence of the community.[82] From the

[79] This corresponds with the legislative proposal by T Geiser, "Draft for a Federal Act concerning Registered Partnerships", requested by Pink Cross and LOS, Bern 1997.

[80] Alternative 4, FOJ Report, *supra* n.9, at p. 60 et seq.

[81] Justification of the parliamentary initiative by Genner, *supra* n.72. See also A Ramsauer, *Alternativentwurf zum Eherecht: Einführung der gleichgeschlechtlichen Ehe ins schweizerische Zivilgesetzbuch* (Bern, Pink Cross & LOS, 1997).

[82] FOJ Report, *supra* n.9, at 60.

point of view of the FOJ, a major aspect of marriage is to secure the sequence of generations. Since, however, same-sex couples are denied the right to joint adoption and artificial insemination, the Federal Office regards making civil marriage available to same-sex couples as problematic.[83]

This legal approach, based on the Roman understanding of the law of a certain Emperor Augustus,[84] must be criticised as thoroughly antiquated. Moreover, the adherents of this point of view have not provided an answer to the question why heterosexual couples, who do not want children, are infertile, or are no longer of child-bearing age, should not also be denied the right to marry. However, it is true that making marriage available would encounter strong resistance, above all in conservative religious circles.[85] Moreover, a number of homosexuals and lesbians express their difficulties with the institution of marriage, which in their opinion continues to reflect strongly religious and moral concepts of the church tying together man and woman, and which represents the incarnation of social exclusion for them.

RESULTS OF THE CONSULTATION PROCEDURE

In August 2000, the FOJ released the results of the consultation that followed the publication of its report in June 1999.[86] As is the custom in Switzerland, all interested groups (i.e., the twenty-six cantons and the political parties) were invited to comment on the proposals of the federal government. But ordinary citizens could also give their opinion. Twenty-five cantons, ten parties, twenty-five non-governmental organisations, and 178 individuals answered the questions of the FOJ. Twenty-four of twenty-five cantons, all parties except for two religious conservative ones, and all NGOs acknowledged the need to improve the legal status of same-sex partnerships.

Concerning the different proposals of the FOJ, alternative 1 (Specific Legislative Intervention) and alternative 2 (Partnership Contract with External Effect) were rejected by the majority of the respondents, as being ineffective and unfamiliar to the existing legal system of Switzerland. They therefore favoured alternative 3 (Registered Partnership Law). Only the Social Democratic Party, the Ecologists Party (the Greens), and the Swiss Unions Federation, together with the gay and lesbian groups, supported alternative 4 (Civil Marriage) as the

[83] *Ibid.*, at 61.

[84] Gaius Julius Caesar Octavianus, known as Augustus Caesar, first Roman Emperor from 63 BC to 14 AD, as a part of a major reform of the law, introduced an obligation to marry for free and freed Roman citizens. The *lex Papia Poppaea* demanded the existence of legitimate children: in the case of free born citizens at least three; in the case of freed citizens, at least four. See H Honsell, *Römisches Recht*, 4th ed. (Berlin, Springer, 1997) at 165.

[85] *Supra* n.69. The Legal Affairs Committee of the National Council would also like to suspend the initiative concerning the opening up of marriage to same-sex couples, to avoid the development of an opposition coalition. See SDA Communication, 21 June 1999.

[86] *Vernehmlassungsergebnisse, Résultats de la procédure de consultation* (Bern, FOJ, August 2000), http://www.bj.admin.ch/themen/glgpaare/ve-ber-d.pdf (or /ve-ber-f.pdf).

only way to realise absolute equality between same-sex and different-sex couples. As for alternatives 3a and 3b, they where equally favoured by the supporters of a registered partnership law. Cantons with big cities, moderate and liberal parties, and most NGOs supported the Scandinavian model (3b), whereas rural cantons and more conservative parties preferred regulation independent of matrimonial law (3a).

As mentioned above, the Federal Council responded to the consultation by announcing on 25 October 2000 that it had chosen alternative 3a, and would present its own registered partnership bill (for same-sex couples only) by the summer of 2001.[87] The federal government gave as a reason the fact that interest groups opposed to any legal regulation of same-sex couples had to be taken into consideration. It remains to be seen how the registered partnership bill will differ from matrimonial law, and whether it will infringe the prohibition of discrimination in Article 8(2) of the new Federal Constitution.[88]

SUMMARY

Same-sex partnerships have hitherto not been recognised under Swiss law. Swiss law only knows marriage as the sole statutorily regulated form of partnership. As a result, same-sex couples are discriminated against in all aspects of civil and public law where legal consequences are tied to the existence of a marriage. However, the most recent developments give rise to hope that the position of same-sex couples in Switzerland will be assimilated to that of married couples, through the creation of an institution of registered partnership, which will not follow the Scandinavian model, but will provide rights and obligations to same-sex couples independently of matrimonial law. By doing so, the most important forms of discrimination should disappear.

As we can see, Heidi is applying all her efforts to struggle through the thorns and reach the Sleeping Beauty in order to kiss her awake. Let us hope that she will soon succeed.

[87] *Supra* n.74.

[88] Text accompanying nn.18–23, *supra*.

30

The First Will Be The Last: Legal Recognition of Same-Sex Partnerships in Austria

HELMUT GRAUPNER*

AUSTRIA WAS THE first country in the world to abolish its death penalty for homosexual relations. In 1787, Emperor Joseph II, in his new Penal Code,[1] reduced the offence of "carnal knowledge" of a person of the same sex (lumped together in the same provision with "carnal knowledge" of an animal) from a felony[2] to a misdemeanor,[3] triable at the political authority rather than the criminal court. He also mitigated the sanction from decapitation and subsequent burning of the corpse[4] to a maximum of just one month's imprisonment.[5] This reform applied to the whole territory of his dominion, which encompassed not only today's Austria but also today's Czech Republic, Slovak Republic, Hungary, Slovenia, Croatia, and Bosnia-Herzegovina, as well as parts of today's Poland, Ukraine, Romania, Serbia and Italy.

DASHED HOPES

Hopes that this reform would lead to complete decriminalisation of homosexuality—as happened in the course of the French Revolution in France and a

* *Rechtsanwalt* (lawyer); Doctor in Law, University of Vienna; Vice-President, Austrian Society for Sex Research (ÖGS); President, Rechtskomitee LAMBDA, an Austrian lesbian and gay rights organisation, http://www.RKLambda.at; member, Expert Committee for the Revision of the Law on Sexual Offences, appointed by the Austrian Minister of Justice in 1996; Vice President for Europe, International Lesbian and Gay Law Association (ILGLaw); http://www.graupner.at.

1 *Constitutio Criminalis Josephina* (CCJ). See H Graupner, *Sexualität, Jugendschutz und Menschenrechte: Über das Recht von Kindern und Jugendlichen auf sexuelle Selbstbestimmung* (Frankfurt/M., Peter Lang, 1997) at Vol. 1, 133.

2 Art. (*Paragraph*) 74, *Constitutio Criminalis Theresiana* (CCT) 1768. See Graupner, *ibid.*, at 131; H Graupner, "Austria" in D J West & R Green (eds.), *Sociolegal Control of Homosexuality: A Multi-Nation Comparison* (New York, Plenum, 1997) at 270.

3 Art. 71, 2nd Part, CCT 1787.

4 Art. 74, CCT 1768.

5 Arts. 10, 72 2nd Part, CCT 1787.

number of other European states over the next decades[6]—were rapidly dashed when Joseph II died in 1790. His successors not only refused to pursue his reforms, but instead even continuously stiffened the law, so that by the middle of the 19th century, homosexual relations (between men and between women) incurred punishment of "severe dungeon" for six months to five years.[7]

This remained the state of the law long into the twentieth century. Only as late as 1971 did Austria finally repeal its total ban on homosexuality.[8] However, instead of introducing full equality of treatment in the criminal law—as many other European jurisdictions did—Austria enacted four new special offences for homosexuals (two of them for gay men only).[9] One of these special offences is still in force. In addition to the traditional general minimum age limit for sexual relations of fourteen years,[10] gay males are bound by a second age limit of eighteen years.[11] So while consensual heterosexual and lesbian relations with adolescents between fourteen and eighteen years of age are completely legal, consensual male homosexual relations with that age-group are a felony, liable to imprisonment of half a year minimum and up to five years maximum.[12] According to information given by the Austrian Minister of Justice, currently about a dozen men are jailed under this discriminatory statute;[13] nearly one thousand have been convicted since its enactment in the year 1971.[14]

Against this background of continuing discrimination in the criminal law, one would suppose that not much has been achieved with regard to the recognition of same-sex partnerships by the civil law. This is indeed the case.

[6] See H Graupner, "Von 'Widernatürlicher Unzucht' zu 'Sexueller Orientierung': Homosexualität und Recht" in Hey, Pallier & Roth (eds.), *Que(e)rdenken: Weibliche/männliche Homosexualität und Wissenschaft* (Innsbruck, Studienverlag, 1997) at 204ff.

[7] Arts. 113ff, Criminal Code (*Strafgesetzbuch*, StGB) 1803 (felony punishable from 6 months to 1 year); Art. 129, StGB 1852 (felony punishable from 6 months to 5 years). See Graupner *supra* n.1, at Vol. 1, 134, 137; Graupner, *supra* n.2 at 271.

[8] Criminal Law Amendment Act 1971.

[9] Arts. 129–30 ("Same-Sex Lewdness" with a person under eighteen; applied only to males), 500a (ban on "Commercial Same-Sex Lewdness"; applied only to the prostitute), 517 ("Propagation of Same-Sex Lewdness and Lewdness with Animals"), 518 ("Associations Promoting Same-Sex Lewdness"), StGB 1852, which later became Arts. 209, 210, 220, 221, StGB 1975. Art. 210 was repealed in 1989, Arts. 220 and 221 in 1996. See Graupner *supra* n.1, at Vol. 1, 141; Graupner, *supra* n.2, at 272ff; Graupner, *supra* n.6, at 209.

[10] Arts. 206, 207, StGB 1975.

[11] Art. 209, StGB 1975.

[12] See Graupner, *supra* n.1, at Vol. 1, 156ff; Graupner, *supra* n.2, at 273ff; H Graupner, *Homosexualität und Strafrecht*, 8th ed. (Vienna, Rechtskomitee LAMBDA, 2001) at 19.

[13] H Graupner, "Österreichs 11 politische Gefangene", (1999) 2 *Ius Amandi* 2.

[14] Graupner, *ibid.*; Graupner, *supra* n.2, at 273; Graupner, *supra* n.13, at 13ff. On 30 Jan. 2001, the European Court of Human Rights communicated three applications challenging the discriminatory age of consent to the Austrian government: *S.L.* v. *Austria* (No. 45330/99), *G.L.* v. *Austria* (No. 39392/98), *A.V.* v. *Austria* (No. 39829/98).

"*FORNICATIONES SIMPLICES*" AND "*CONCUBINATUS*"

Sexual intercourse between the unmarried ("*fornicationes simplices*") and *concubinage* ("*concubinatus*") were criminal offences in Austria until 1787.[15] In the Middle Ages, however, the effects of these laws had been mitigated by the institution of "marriage by consensus", which was marriage engaged in simply by sexual intercourse with the intent to marry. In everyday life, *concubinage* could not easily be distinguished from "marriage by consensus", the only difference being the presence or absence of an intent to stay together for life.

After the reform of matrimonial law by the Council of Trent in the year 1563, the offenses of "*fornicationes simplices*" and "*concubinatus*" did gain increased practical importance. With this reform, the Roman Catholic Church repealed the institution of "marriage by consensus" and prescribed that henceforth a valid marriage could only be contracted in a formal ceremony before a priest. From then on, intercourse between the unmarried and *concubinage* could readily be identified and sanctioned without involving major practical evidentiary problems. In the sixteenth century, the offences came under the jurisdiction of the secular courts.[16] In 1787, Joseph II repealed them, along with the offences of masturbation,[17] "lewdness against the order of nature" between man and woman,[18] incest,[19] and intercourse between Christians and non-Christians (so-called "unbelievers").[20]

Though *concubinage* was no longer expressly mentioned in the Criminal Code, nevertheless it was still considered illegal. Consequently, the partners could be held liable under decrees making it an offence to commit acts that were "declared illegal by law or decree without establishing a certain penalty for contraventions".[21] For such acts, a fine or short-term detention for up to two weeks could be sanctioned by the political authority. Domestic servants, journeymen, apprentices, and day-labourers could also be subjected to beating with a stick (men over eighteen), or to caning (men under eighteen and women).[22] It also seems highly probable that intercourse between the unmarried (simple fornication) and *concubinage* could be punished under the decrees. However, case-law was not uniform in this area. Sometimes authorities applied the decrees only to "acts conflicting with public morals" which gave rise to a public nuisance.[23]

[15] Art. 81, CCT 1768. For details of the historical development, see Graupner, *supra* n.1, at Vol. 1, 126ff; Graupner, *supra* n.2, at 278.

[16] Police Regulations of the Reich 1548.

[17] Art. 74, CCT 1768.

[18] *Ibid.*

[19] Art. 75, CCT 1768. Resistance to the decriminalisation of incest had been underestimated. Only nine months after the promulgation of the CCJ 1787, the offence was re-introduced by imperial decree (*Justizgesetzsammlung* 744). See Graupner, *supra* n.1, at 133.

[20] Art. 82, CCT 1768.

[21] Decree of 30th September 1857 (RGBl No. 198).

[22] Graupner, *supra* n.1, Vol. 1 at 138ff; Graupner, *supra* n.2, at 278ff.

[23] The Supreme Political Authority, 1828. See *ibid.*

The decrees were abolished in 1925,[24] which meant that criminalisation of intercourse between the unmarried and *concubinage* had finally ceased: a man and a woman copulating or living together without being married could not be punished anymore. On the contrary, over the next decade, non-marital partnerships between a man and a woman increasingly gained legal recognition and support. Legislation in the 1920s and 1930s placed unmarried heterosexual partners (the law called them "household-keepers") on the same footing as spouses regarding some areas of social security rights. This mitigated the social problems of couples who could not marry because one partner had already been married. For the large Roman Catholic majority of the Austrian population, divorce was unavailable at that time. With the (general) introduction of divorce in 1938, the social need for recognising unmarried heterosexual partners decreased; correspondingly, legal development in this area slowed down.[25]

In 2001, while unmarried different-sex couples enjoy the same rights and obligations as married couples in a quite considerable range of areas—mostly as a result of the legal developments in the 1920s and 1930s—same-sex couples do not. The law by and large does not recognise them as a couple, instead treating them as strangers, with fatal consequences regarding social protection.

RIGHTS ENJOYED ONLY BY MARRIED DIFFERENT-SEX COUPLES

Testimony in Civil Courts and Administrative Procedures

The right to refuse to testify against one's partner in civil courts[26] and before administrative authorities[27] is not available to same-sex partners. This is even true in administrative penal procedures.[28]

Inheritance

If no will is made, a same-sex partner does not inherit anything.[29] If a will is made, he/she has to pay inheritance tax at a rate that is up to a seven times higher than that paid by a surviving married partner.[30]

[24] Art. II par. 2 lit. 10, Introductory Law to the Laws on Procedure in Administrative Proceedings (EGVG) 1925.
[25] F Schneider, "Die rechtliche Stellung der Lebensgefährten", (1965) 7 *Österreichische Juristenzeitung* 174.
[26] Art. 320, Code of Civil Procedure (ZPO).
[27] Art. 49, Act on Administrative Procedure (AVG).
[28] Art. 24, Act on Administrative Penal Procedures (VStG).
[29] Art. 758, General Civil Code (ABGB).
[30] Arts. 7–8, Donations and Inheritance Tax Act (ErbStG).

Freehold Flats

Common ownership of a freehold flat by a same-sex couple is not available.[31]

Assignment of a Tenancy

There is no right to assign a tenancy to a same-sex partner without the consent of the lessor.[32]

Unification of Families

Facilitated entry and immigration of the same-sex partner of an Austrian citizen or a foreigner legally residing in Austria is not available.[33]

Assignment of Citizenship

Facilitated assignment of citizenship to the same-sex partner of an Austrian citizen is not available.[34]

Dependents' Rights

Surviving same-sex partners are not entitled to dependents' rights in the social insurance system (e.g., widows' and widowers' pensions).[35] The same is true in the law of torts, for instance when a same-sex partner has been killed in a car accident.[36]

Funerals

Relatives of the deceased partner legally can exclude the surviving same-sex partner from funeral arrangements and grave-yard matters.[37]

[31] Arts. 8ff, Act on Freehold Flats (WEG).

[32] Art. 12, Tenancy Rights Act (MRG).

[33] Arts. 7 par. 4 lit. 3, 18 par. 1 lit. 2–3, 19 par. 2 lit. 4, 20, 21, 37, 46 par. 2 lit. 4, 47, 49, Foreigners Act (FrG).

[34] Art. 11a, Citizenship Act (StbG).

[35] General Act on Social Insurance (ASVG); Act on Social Insurance of Tradespeople (GSVG); Act on Social Insurance of Independent Professions (FVG); Act on Social Insurance of Farmers (BSVG); Act on Social Insurance of Notaries (NVG); Act on Health and Accident Insurance of Civil Servants (B-KUVG).

[36] Art. 1327, ABGB.

[37] Graupner, *supra* n.2, at 281.

Pictures, Letters, Confidential Records

The surviving same-sex partner has no right whatsoever to prohibit the publication or public distribution of pictures (e.g., photographs) and confidential records of the deceased partner, as well as letters sent or received, even if the survivor has a well-justified interest in non-publication or non-distribution.[38]

Adoption

Adoption is available for unmarried individuals and married couples only. Joint adoption by same-sex partners is impossible.[39]

RIGHTS ENJOYED ONLY BY MARRIED AND UNMARRIED DIFFERENT-SEX COUPLES

Leave to Nurse

Homosexual employees cannot claim paid leave to nurse a same-sex partner who is ill. Heterosexual employees can claim paid leave of up to forty hours per year to nurse their different-sex partner who has fallen sick.[40]

Artificial Insemination

Artificial insemination is available for married and unmarried different-sex partners only. Women living in a lesbian partnership are not entitled to it. If they nonetheless obtain it, they (and the physician carrying out the insemination) can be punished with an administrative fine of up to Euro 36,000 or, in default of payment, with detention of up to fourteen days.[41]

Insurance Law

Claims by an insurance company against the married or the unmarried different-sex-partner of the insured are prohibited. As a result, an insurance company cannot have recourse against the partner to whom the insured lent his car and who caused an accident damaging the car. In the case of a same-sex partnership, the company can claim its money back from the partner.[42]

[38] Arts. 77–78, Act on Copyright Law (UrhG).
[39] Art. 179, ABGB.
[40] Art. 16, Vacations Act (UrlG).
[41] Arts. 3(2), 22–23, Act on Reproductive Medicine (FMedG).
[42] Art. 67 par. 2, Act on Insurance Treaties (VersVG).

Psychiatric Confinement

If a court orders the psychiatric confinement of a person, his married or unmarried different-sex partner can appeal against the decision. Partners of the same sex cannot do so.[43]

Public Sector Housing

Unmarried different-sex couples are put on a par with married couples regarding the distribution of public sector houses and flats. Persons living in a same-sex partnership can obtain such houses or flats only as unmarried individuals.[44]

Health Insurance Benefits

One same-sex partner cannot claim public health insurance benefits for the other. Heterosexual partners can do so. Social insurance companies are even restrained by law from granting benefits to the non-insured same-sex partners of their insureds.[45]

Unemployment Benefits

Unemployed persons who live in a "community of life" (*lebensgemeinschaft*) with a partner of the opposite sex who is dependent on them can claim a supplement to their unemployment benefit, but an unemployed person living with a dependant partner of the same sex cannot.[46] On the other hand, the income of a same-sex partner reduces an unemployed person's "emergency aid" (relief after expiration of unemployment benefits).[47] Occasionally, benefits from unemployment insurance can even be claimed directly by the heterosexual partner of an unemployed person in lieu of the insured person himself.[48] Same-sex partners are never allowed to do so.

[43] Placement Act (UbG).

[44] J Stabentheiner, "Die nichteheliche Lebensgemeinschaft: ein Überblick", (1995) 127 *Österreichische Notariatszeitung* FN 160 at 3.

[45] Art. 123, ASVG; Arts. 10, 83, GSVG; Art. 3, FVG; Art. 56, BSVG; NVG; B-KUVG. See *supra* n.35.

[46] Art. 20, Act on Unemployment Insurance (AlVG).

[47] Art. 36, *ibid.*

[48] Art. 2, Act on Exceptional Relief (SUG).

Tax Privileges

According to the Act on Income Tax, married and unmarried different-sex partners can claim a range of tax reductions.[49] Same-sex partners cannot.

Public Welfare

In most of the nine Austrian states, the presence of a needy cohabiting different-sex partner increases public welfare benefits.[50] A partner of the same sex is not recognised.

In 1996, a fairly typical case of discrimination caused a sensation. The Regional Court of Leoben sentenced a man to six months imprisonment for driving the car of his male partner without authorisation. Had his partner been female, whether or not they were married, no crime would have been committed. On appeal, the Upper Regional Court of Graz reduced the sentence to two months. The case prompted an outcry by the Austrian lesbian and gay movement. Due to massive lobbying by Rechtskomitee LAMBDA and other organisations, the Austrian federal president finally pardoned the convicted man and reduced the sentence to a fine.[51] This was the first, and so far the only, case in which an Austrian president pardoned a person convicted under a statute discriminating against homosexuals.

The most striking example of denial of equality for same-sex partners is Austria's tenancy law. Article 14(3) of the Tenancy Act (*Mietrechtsgesetz*, MRG) grants the right of succession to the surviving partner (*Lebensgefährte*) if he/she has been living with the deceased tenant "in a household community [domestic partnership] that is arranged, in the economic sense, like a marriage" ("*in einer in wirtschaftlicher Hinsicht gleich einer Ehe eingerichteten Haushaltsgemeinschaft*"). Traditionally, the courts have held—in sharp contradiction with the wording of the law—that only partners of different sexes can economically arrange their partnership like a marriage. This traditional case-law has recently been challenged in a case involving the request of a landlord to remove a surviving same-sex partner from the flat of his deceased tenant. Both the Vienna County Court and the Vienna Regional Court for Civil Affairs expressed the opinion that, in view of the increasing tolerance and acceptance of homosexuality in society, the traditional case-law had to be reversed. Both courts cited the 1994 resolution of the European Parliament.[52] However, the Supreme Court reversed the decision of the Vienna Regional Court for Civil

[49] Art. 106 Act on Income Tax (EstG).

[50] Stabentheiner, *supra* n.44, at 3.

[51] H Graupner, "Als erster Präsident: Klestil begnadigt Homosexuellen", (1996) 5 *Ius Amandi* 1.

[52] "Resolution on equal rights for homosexuals and lesbians in the EC", OJ [1994] C 61/40 (adopted on 8 Feb. 1994).

Affairs and granted the request of the landlord.[53] The Court held that the legislature intended to put only heterosexual relations on the same footing as marriage, not also homosexual ones, and that it would be for the Austrian Parliament only, not the courts, to reverse this state of the law. The European Parliament resolution is not binding and merely calls on national parliaments to act on its suggestions. Thus, the Supreme Court handed the ball over to the legislature. But the Austrian Parliament has failed to act, with only one notable exception, caused by exceptional circumstances.

MINOR REFORMS

In July 1998, Austria for the first time took over the Presidency of the Council of the European Union. Exactly at this time, the Austrian Parliament was debating the Criminal Law Amendment Act 1998. On this occasion, opposition parties forced a vote on the abolition of the discriminatory age of consent law mentioned above. As a result, the Conservative Party (ÖVP), a member of the coalition government, was put in a rather embarrassing situation. This party for years had vigorously opposed the repeal of the law, despite the resolution of the European Parliament, while presenting itself as the pro-European party of the country, taking pride in Austria's EU Presidency, and stressing Austria's open-mindedness, tolerance and commitment to human rights.

Fearing that they would be labeled backward discriminators against homosexuals at such a crucial historical moment, the Conservative Party proposed a deal to the Social Democratic Party (SPÖ), their coalition partner: while maintaining their opposition to the repeal of the discriminatory age of consent for gay men, they would accept the equalization of the rights of same-sex couples in all other areas of the criminal law. On 17 July 1998, the deal was executed. The Austrian Parliament, while again rejecting a motion for the repeal of the special minimum age limit for gay men, passed the Criminal Law Amendment Act 1998, which substituted the broader phrase "persons living with each other in a community of life" ("*Personen, die miteinander in Lebensgemeinschaft leben*")[54] for the prior definition, which had been explicitly restricted to different-sex couples. With the notable exception of the minimum age limit, same-sex couples are now put on the same footing as unmarried different-sex couples in the whole of the criminal law and the law on criminal procedure. And in this field—with some minor exceptions—both same-sex and unmarried different-sex couples are put on the same footing as married couples.

[53] Supreme Court (*Oberste Gerichtshof*, OGH), 5 Dec. 1996 (6 Ob 2325/96x), http://www.ris.bka.gv.at/auswahl. In Dec. 2000, the surviving partner's application to the European Court of Human Rights was communicated to the Austrian government: *Karner* v. *Austria* (No. 40016/98). See Wintemute, chap. 40.

[54] Art. 72 par. 2, StGB 1975.

RIGHTS ENJOYED BY ALL COUPLES, MARRIED OR UNMARRIED, DIFFERENT-SEX OR SAME-SEX

Since 1975, the following privileges have been granted not only to marriage, but also to heterosexual non-marital relationships. Since 1 October 1998, they have been available to same-sex partnerships.

Testimony in Criminal Courts

One same-sex partner now also has the right to refuse to give testimony against the other in a criminal court.[55]

Aiding and Abetting

The same-sex partner of a person who has committed an offence no longer faces punishment for aiding and abetting their partner.[56] The same is true for non-prevention of the commission of a criminal offence, if the reason for not preventing the offence is to protect the partner from damage.[57]

Offences Against the Property of the Partner

Offences against the property of the partner without violence cannot be prosecuted by the public prosecutor, but only by the victim (with a strict six-week time limit), and the offender is liable to imprisonment of not more than six months regardless of the value of the possessions taken or damaged.[58] For example, theft with damage of more than Euro 36,000 is normally punishable by imprisonment from one to ten years.[59] However, one married or cohabiting partner can steal millions from, or defraud, the other partner, and is not liable to more than six months imprisonment; if the other partner does not file a prosecution within six weeks of knowledge of the deed, the guilty partner cannot be punished at all. Moreover purloining (i.e. theft with minor damage committed out of destitution, thoughtlessness or to satisfy a desire),[60] fraud with minor damage out of destitution,[61] and unauthorised use of motor vehicles[62] are not punishable at all if committed between cohabiting partners.

[55] Art. 152, Act on Criminal Procedure (StPO); Art. 290, StGB 1975.
[56] Art. 299 par .3, StGB 1975.
[57] Art. 286, StGB 1975.
[58] Art. 166, StGB 1975.
[59] Art. 128, StGB 1975.
[60] Art. 141, StGB 1975.
[61] Art. 150, StGB 1975.
[62] Art. 136, StGB 1975. This reverses the result in the 1996 Regional Court of Leoben case. See *supra* n.51 and accompanying text.

Other Offences

The offence of negligently causing minor bodily harm is also not punishable between cohabiting same-sex partners anymore.[63] And the offence of threatening the partner with a violation of his bodily integrity, liberty, honour or property can only be prosecuted with the authorisation of the partner.[64] To prosecute rape and sexual coercion between cohabiting partners, a complaint by the victim is now required.[65]

REFORMS OUTSIDE THE CRIMINAL LAW

Equality provided by the Austrian Parliament has so far been confined to the criminal law. And outside the legislature, equality measures also remain the exception. In 1993, the Minister of the Interior issued a decree ordering that the police must abstain from behaviour that could be perceived as discrimination on the basis of (inter alia) sexual orientation.[66] This is the first, and so far the only, antidiscrimination provision protecting homosexuals in Austrian law. Austria was the third country in Europe to enact a regulation banning discrimination on the basis of sexual orientation that covers the police forces. However, the question remains: how can the police enforce the anti-homosexual age of consent law while not creating the impression that they are discriminating on the basis of sexual orientation?

In 1998, the City of Vienna, Austria's biggest landlord, announced that, not only will it lease flats to same-sex couples under the same conditions as for married and unmarried heterosexual couples, but it will also grant succession rights to the same-sex partners of deceased tenants. Moreover, both the City of Vienna and the State of Styria announced that they will grant their employees paid leave to nurse their same-sex partners when they fall ill.[67] On 20 March 2001, the Styrian parliament (*Landtag*) called on the government of Styria to ask the Austrian federal government to take action to equalise the legal status of same-sex and opposite-sex non-marital partnerships (*Lebensgemeinschaften*) in the areas of tenancy law and labour law.[68]

[63] Art. 88, StGB 1975.

[64] Art. 107, StGB 1975.

[65] Art. 203, StGB 1975 (as amended by the Criminal Law Amendment Act 1989).

[66] Art. 5, Decree of Guidelines (RLV).

[67] H Graupner, *Keine Liebe zweiter Klasse: Partnerschaft und Diskriminierungsschutz für gleichgeschlechtlich L(i)ebende*, 3rd ed. (Vienna, Rechtskomitee LAMBDA, 1999) at 35. The City of Vienna has established an *Antidiskriminierungsstelle für gleichgeschlechtliche Lebensweisen* (same-sex lifestyles). See http://www.wien.at/queerwien.

[68] See http://www.gleichvielrecht.at.

PROSPECTS FOR FUTURE REFORM

Apart from these sporadic examples of progress, the overall legal situation of same-sex couples in Austria remains bleak. It is true that the Constitutional Court in 1989 held that the Austrian Constitution protects the basic right of homosexuals to respect for their private life, and to freedom from discrimination on the basis of sexual orientation. However, in the same decision, the Court declared the higher minimum age provision for male homosexual conduct not to constitute discrimination on the basis of sexual orientation, because it is justified on objective and reasonable grounds.[69] So not much protection can be expected from the Constitution. And—with the sole exception of one isolated and insignificant administrative law provision on the refusal to supply goods and services[70]—Austrian non-constitutional law enshrines anti-discrimination protection on the ground of sex only, and not even on the basis of race, ethnic origin or religion.[71]

Comprehensive legal recognition and equality for same-sex couples are still a long way off in Austria. Apart from some motions on equalisation of rights in a few specific areas (e.g., succession rights in tenancy legislation), no proposals for a registered partnership law or a similar regulation have been tabled in Parliament. However, this is probably at least partly a result of the split in the Austrian lesbian and gay movement over the right model. While *Rechtskomitee LAMBDA* (RKL) favours the Scandinavian model, *Österreichisches Lesben- und Schwulenforum* (ÖLSF) promotes the French one, and *Homosexuelle Initiative* (HOSI) *Wien* prefers a modified Scandinavian model: a registered partnership law for same-sex partners only (as in Scandinavia), which would not incorporate all or most of the regulations of marriage, but instead would introduce special, less restrictive regulations (i.e., on dissolution and the mutual obligations of the partners). Only recently, in October 2000, most of Austria's lesbian and gay associations agreed on common demands for equal partnership rights[72] to be presented in a petition to Parliament in the spring of 2001. However, it seems highly unlikely that a parliamentary majority currently can be found to support these demands. To date, such a majority has not even been found for ending the criminal persecution of gay men, a persecution that in most other European states ended a long time ago, in some almost 200 years ago.[73]

[69] Constitutional Court (*Verfassungsgerichtshof*, VfGH), 3 Oct. 1989 (G 227/88, 2/89).

[70] Art. IX par. 6, EGVG.

[71] EC Council Directives 2000/43 and 2000/78 will require Austria to introduce prohibitions of employment discrimination based on racial or ethnic origin (by 19 July 2003), religion or belief and sexual orientation (by 2 Dec. 2003), and disability and age (by 2 Dec. 2006). See Bell, chap. 37.

[72] These demands include: (a) access of same-sex partners to the full range of rights and obligations associated with marriage; (b) complete legal equality between opposite-sex and same-sex non-marital partnerships. See http://www.gleichvielrecht.at.

[73] See Graupner, *supra* n.6, at 204ff.

A recent opinion poll showed that 55 per cent of Austrians favour complete equalisation of the rights and duties of heterosexual cohabitation and marriage (36 per cent against), but only 29 per cent of the population support the opening-up of marriage to same-sex couples (60 per cent against). Opinion leaders seem a little bit more open-minded: 63 per cent favour equalisation of heterosexual cohabitation with marriage (30 per cent against) and 40 per cent support lesbian/gay marriage (55 per cent against).[74] This poll suggests that Austrians are substantially more conservative than their German-speaking neighbours. According to recent polls, 54 per cent of Germans (37 per cent against)[75] and 53 per cent of the Swiss favour the opening-up of marriage to same-sex partners.[76] Among Germans under thirty-four years of age, 77 per cent support lesbian/gay marriage.[77] Among the Swiss, 68 per cent of all ages answered in favour of registered partnership for same-sex couples (21 per cent against; Germans and Austrians were not asked about registered partnership).

The state of public opinion in Austria is not so surprising if one remembers that, in polls some years ago, more than one-fourth (27 per cent) of the Austrian population still favoured a reintroduction of the total criminal law ban on homosexual relations. On the other hand, details of these polls also give cause for hope. Among pensioners, 45 per cent favoured such a measure, but only 6 per cent of teenagers did so.[78] The considerable amount of tolerance among young people was also shown in another study, which found that only 29 per cent of 16 to 24-year-olds, as opposed to 44 per cent of the adults, placed homosexuality among things one is not allowed to do under all circumstances. Only killing in self-defence and divorce were treated as less taboo.[79] Among Viennese teenagers, 78 per cent agreed that, for some people, homosexuality is as important and normal as is love between man and woman for others.[80]

This in some way nurtures the hope that my country, which once stood at the forefront of legal progress in this field, and which subsequently fell so blatantly behind, will once again meet European legal standards. Hopefully, it will not take too much time.

[74] "Partnerschaften: Es muß nicht immer Ehe sein", (1999) 36 *Format* 7.

[75] Austria Press Agency (APA), 106 5 CA 0092 (15 May 1999).

[76] APA, 455 5 CA 0207 AA (22 June 1999).

[77] According to a recent EMNID poll, 72% of German heterosexual women and 61% of German heterosexual men support "same-sex marriage". *Die Welt*, 29 March 2001.

[78] S Fritsch & K Langbein, *Land der Sinne: Die große Analyse: Liebe, Sex und Partnerschaft in Österreich* (Vienna, Orac, 1991) at 159.

[79] Österreichische Institut für Jugendkunde, *Österreichische Jugendwertestudie* (Vienna, Österreichisches Institut für Jugendkunde, 1991).

[80] W Dür & S Haas, *Aids-Aufklärung und sexuelle Kommunikation bei Jugendlichen* (Vienna, Ludwig-Boltzmann-Institut für Medizin- und Gesundheitssoziologie, 1991).

31

Nice on Paper: The Aborted Liberalisation of Gay Rights in Hungary

LILLA FARKAS*

THE REVISION OF the Hungarian Constitution in 1989 introduced a general anti-discrimination clause, which provides as follows: "The Republic of Hungary shall respect the human rights and civil rights of all persons in the country without discrimination on the basis of race, colour, gender, language, religion, political or other opinion, national or social origins, financial situation, birth or on any other grounds whatsoever".[1] Sexual orientation is covered by the reference to "any other grounds whatsoever".[2]

In 1992, the constitutional anti-discrimination clause was supplemented by a similar anti-discrimination provision in the Labour Code.[3] Article 5 provides that: "In connection with employment, no employee shall be discriminated against on the basis of gender, age, race, national origin, religion, political views or membership in employee advocacy organisations or activities connected therewith, as well as any other circumstances not related to employment. Any differentiation clearly and directly required by the character or nature of the work shall not be construed as discrimination".

Hungary also has a number of other piecemeal anti-discrimination regulations, ranging from Article 7 of the Act on Public Health,[4] which provides for health care without discrimination on the ground of "sexual orientation" ("*szexuális irányultság*") to Article 7 Sub. 4 of the Act on Public Education,[5] which prohibits discrimination on the ground of the "birth or other status" of

* Hungarian Helsinki Committee; Legal Defence Bureau for National and Ethnic Minorities, Budapest.

[1] Art. 70/A, Act No. 20 of 1949, http://www.uni-wuerzburg.de/law/hu00000_.html (English translation). Where no source is cited, translations are by the author.

[2] In 20/1999 (VI.25.) AB *határozat* (decision), the Constitutional Court confirmed for the first time that sexual orientation may be a ground calling for protection against discrimination.

[3] Act No. 22 of 1992.

[4] Act No. 154 of 1997.

[5] Act No. 79 of 1993.

the pupil or his/her relatives.[6] Here again, sexual orientation may come under the protection provided for on the ground of "other status".

The impact of these legislative provisions is, however, questionable in the absence of an efficient system of sanctions against those violating the law. As a result of a recommendation by the Parliamentary Commissioner for National and Ethnic Minorities, the protection against employment discrimination under Article 5 of the Labour Code has been strengthened. Since 1 January 1999, under the Code on Civil Procedure,[7] the discriminatory denial of employment may now also give rise to civil actions. But in other areas, victims of discrimination can only invoke general civil law remedies,[8] and must be inventive, as discrimination on the grounds of sexual orientation is not expressly prohibited by the Civil Code.[9]

Because of the weakness of Hungarian anti-discrimination legislation, the Constitutional Court, generally known in Central and Eastern Europe for its pro-active attitude, seems to have taken the lead in shaping lesbian and gay rights with a more or less progressive attitude. The Court has done so in spite of the unfriendly social climate. For example, in 1995, homosexuals were thought to be the second least sympathetic marginalised group, more sympathetic than drug addicts but less sympathetic than skinheads or Roma.[10] Notwithstanding the general obligation under Article 70/H of the Constitution of citizens to defend the country, open homosexuals are not in practice drafted into the army,[11] and recent incidents suggest that they are not welcome among professional soldiers either.[12]

CRIMINAL LAW

As early as 1961, Hungarian legislation decriminalised same-sex sexual acts between two consenting adults if they were both aged twenty or more.[13] The age

[6] Further examples include Art. 25 of Act No. 1 of 1978 (discrimination in internal trade) and Art. 6 of Act No. 43 of 1996 (service relations).

[7] Art. 349, Sub. 2 lin. a, of Act No. 3 of 1952.

[8] Art. 84 of Act No 4 of 1959 (findings of violations, injunctions against current and future violations, public declarations, restitution, damages, and public fines resembling exemplary or punitive damages).

[9] Arts. 75–85 of Act No. 4 of 1959. Under Art. 76, any discrimination against individuals on the grounds of gender, race, nationality or religion is a violation of civil rights (rights attached to persons).

[10] Zoltán Fábián, "Tekintélyelvűség és előítéletek", *Új Mandátum*, [not available] 1999 (95% of those polled would not let their children befriend homosexuals and 98% would not let them in their flat).

[11] Under 7/1996 (VII.30.) HM-NM *együttes rendelet* (joint decree, Ministry of Defence and Ministry of Health), homosexuality comes under the same heading as infantility and severe personality disorder.

[12] The situation will have to be reconsidered following the European Court of Human Rights' judgments in the *Lustig-Prean & Beckett* v. *United Kingdom* and *Smith & Grady* v. *United Kingdom* (27 Sept. 1999).

[13] Art. 279 of Act No. 5 of 1961 on the Penal Code. Under Art. 279, lin. b, unnatural sexual conduct between two consenting same-sex partners above twenty remained a crime if it was committed

of consent for male and female homosexuals was reduced to eighteen years of age in 1978 and has remained there ever since, compared with fourteen for heterosexuals.[14] There have been a number of efforts to remedy this discriminatory situation, with all initiatives aiming primarily at the overall reform of legislation on sexual offences, and viewing the regulation pertaining to the age of consent as part and parcel of this reform.[15]

Lobbyists have been persistent in drawing attention to the European Parliament's relevant resolutions. One of the most recent, on 17 September 1998,[16] stated that in a number of countries seeking membership of the European Union, the criminal law still contains several provisions that severely discriminate against homosexuals. The Parliament's commitment not to accept, as members, countries whose legislation or official measures violate the rights of gays and lesbians was reinforced, and countries seeking accession—such as Hungary—were called upon to revoke legal regulations that discriminate with regard to the age of consent.

The day after this resolution was adopted, a first instance court in Budapest suspended proceedings[17] against a homosexual man on the count, *inter alia,* of "unnatural sexual conduct", and requested the Constitutional Court to review and quash as unconstitutional Article 199 of the Penal Code, which criminalises sexual acts between same-sex partners where one is above and the other below the age of consent of eighteen. The court found that "the age of consent is defined in an utterly arbitrary and unconstitutional fashion". It was satisfied that one cannot decide whether or not an adult's sexual relationship with an underage partner of the same sex might be more disadvantageous to the latter's sexual development than a relationship with an adult of different sex. Unusually for a first instance court, the introduction of a comparative outline of the age of consent in European countries was allowed, and the outline was considered in favour of the defendant. The Constitutional Court is presently considering the court's request for a ruling.

Since the Budapest case, the Town Court in Eger has also suspended proceedings in a similar case. However, in each of 1998 and 1999, six men were convicted and three were imprisoned under Article 199. In 2001, one man is in pre-trial detention charged with the same offence.[18]

"in a scandalous manner". The reason for decriminalisation was that therapy could not help even those willing to rid themselves of homosexuality. See *Országgyűlési Irományok* (1961), at 270.

[14] See Act No. 4 of 1978 on the Penal Code, Arts. 199, 201–202. No reasons for the reduction were given.

[15] Draft amendments submitted by members of Parliament László Donáth (Socialist) and Ferenc Kőszeg (Liberal); the 1996 petition of Géza Juhász, gay rights activist, and founder of the Rainbow Association (*infra*) (pending before the Constitutional Court).

[16] "Resolution on equal rights for gays and lesbians in the EC", OJ [1998] C 313/186.

[17] Case No. 1.B.II.82009/98/14, Budapest 2–3 District Court.

[18] This information is based on a communication from defence counsel Csaba Fenyvesi concerning his client, J V.

In a recent decision,[19] the Constitutional Court addressed the constitutionality of the present criminal provision regulating incest.[20] It was found that the penalisation of unnatural sexual conduct between same-sex siblings (above the age of consent) constituted discrimination on the grounds of other status, which in the given case "had no objective and reasonable ground". As a result of the judgment, only different-sex siblings engaged in sexual intercourse may face punishment for incest.

In 1998, the gay rights group Habeas Corpus Working Party (*Habeas Corpus Munkacsoport*) reported[21] that the police had abused their powers in dealing with a number of the group's clients. On 22 February 1997, a young man alleged to the police operating in the area of a railway station that a gay man had been following him. Two policemen asked the gay man for his identity card and took him to a room belonging to the Budapest Metro. One of them asked him whether he was gay.[22] He said "yes" and was then asked to go into a little room, where the contents of his pockets were checked. The policeman inquiring about his sexual preferences came in and punched him in the stomach. More policemen arrived and gave him blows and kicks all over his body. At the end of the incident, another policeman told him: "You can go now".[23]

In 2000, the group reported another case[24] in which criminal law provisions affected employment. On 19 October 1996, R.E. and B.F., both off-duty policemen, were having sex in R.E.'s car in a remote area known among locals as a meeting place for secret lovers. Their colleagues patrolling in the area spotted the car and arrested them. The following day B.F., a married man, told the police captain that he had been so drunk that he had in fact been sexually assaulted by R.E. without his knowledge or consent. The captain accused R.E. of "forcible unnatural conduct"[25] and immediately fired him from the police force. R.E. brought an action challenging his dismissal (but did not invoke Article 5 of the Labour Code prohibiting discrimination). His action was rejected by the first instance court. Although R.E. had not been convicted of a crime, the court found that "regardless of the hetero- or homosexual nature of the relationship, the person who engages in sexual intercourse in daytime in a public space is unworthy of official service", because by doing so he "seriously endangers the public confidence necessary to the operation of an armed body", under the Act on

[19] 20/1999 (VI.25.) AB *határozat*.

[20] Art. 203 of Act No. 4 of 1978.

[21] *Fundamentum*, 1998/3, p.174.

[22] Under Art. 2, para. 2, of Act No. 63 of 1992 on the Protection of Personal Data, information relating to one's sexual life is sensitive data and can only be handled pursuant to the written permission of the person concerned. But under Act No. 125 of 1995 on the National Security Services, high-ranking officials (e.g. ambassadors, state secretaries, national commanders of the police forces, etc.) can be asked questions relating to their different-sex or same-sex partners outside of marriage.

[23] *Fundamentum*, 1998/3, pp.174–5.

[24] *Fundamentum*, 2000/1, pp.163–7.

[25] Art. 200 of Act No. 4 of 1978. Criminal proceedings in this situation can be instituted by anybody; rape of a woman over eighteen is punishable only as a result of a report by the victim. See Art. 209 of the Act.

Service Relations.[26] This decision was later upheld by the second instance court, as well as the Supreme Court. B.F. was later transferred to another workplace and consequently decided to leave the police force. R.E. committed suicide.

SAME-SEX PARTNERSHIPS

Although individuals do not yet seem to be ready to vindicate their rights in test cases, advocacy groups have used litigation before the Constitutional Court as a force for change. The gay group *Homérosz-Lambda* brought a case before the Constitutional Court concerning a law on different-sex partnerships outside marriage. They petitioned the Court to find, not only that the law on civil partnerships was unconstitutional because it excluded same-sex partnerships, but also that the law on civil marriage was unconstitutional for the same reason.

With regard to marriage,[27] the Court held on 13 March 1995[28] that "in our culture and in law the institution of marriage is traditionally the union of a man and a woman. This union is typically aimed at giving birth to common children and bringing them up in the family in addition to being the framework for the mutual taking care and assistance of the partners. The ability to procreate and give birth to children is neither the defining element nor the condition of the notion of marriage, but the idea that marriage requires the partners to be of different sexes is a condition that derives from the original and typical designation of marriage. The institution of marriage is constitutionally protected by the State also . . . [because] it promotes the establishment of families with common children".[29]

Apart from Article 15 of the Constitution ("The Republic of Hungary protects the institutions of marriage and family"), the Court concluded that, "from the wording of the most important international human rights documents,[30] it can also be derived that the family is conceived of as the union of a man and a woman: the right to get married is defined as the right of men and the right of women, while in relation to other rights, the subjects of rights are 'persons' . . .".[31] It also invoked the judgment of the European Court of Human Rights in the *Rees* case[32] to support this interpretation of marriage. The Court recognised that "[i]n recent decades . . . homosexuality has been decriminalised,. . . movements have been

[26] Under Art. 56 of Act No. 43 of 1996, a person is unworthy of official service if: "(a) he is sentenced to imprisonment . . ., (c) through his off-duty conduct he seriously endangers the public confidence necessary for the operation of an armed body".

[27] Art. 10(1), Act No. 4 of 1952 on Marriage, Family and Guardianship.

[28] 14/1995 (III.13.) AB *határozat*. See L Sólyom & G Brunner, *Constitutional Judiciary in a New Democracy: The Hungarian Constitutional Court* (Ann Arbor, Univ. of Michigan Press, 2000), at 316–21 (English translation).

[29] Sólyom & Brunner, *ibid.*, at 318.

[30] Universal Declaration of Human Rights, Art. 16; International Covenant on Civil and Political Rights, Art. 23; European Convention on Human Rights, Art. 12.

[31] *Supra* n.28.

[32] *Rees* v. *United Kingdom* (17 Oct. 1986).

started to protest against negative discrimination with respect to homosexuals . . . [and] changes can be observed in the traditional family model . . . [But] [a]ll these are not reasons for the law to diverge from the legal concept of marriage . . . preserved in traditions to this day, . . . common in today's laws and . . . in harmony with the notion of marriage according to public opinion and in everyday language".[33]

As to the duties of the state, the Court found that it "can offer different legal options for traditional and currently exceptional communities", and that "it can maintain and support traditional institutions, as well as creating new legal forms for acknowledging new phenomena", thereby "extend[ing] the boundaries of 'normality' in public opinion". However, "the right of the affected person is not that the same institutions be available to everybody; instead, the constitutional requirement is that those affected are handled as . . . persons of equal human dignity, that is, their points of view are evaluated with like . . . attention, impartiality and fairness". The Court concluded that the challenged provision, which "prohibits men and women equally from marrying persons of their own sex", "does not discriminate either in terms of sex or . . . other conditions" and does not violate Articles 70/A (discrimination on grounds including gender) and 66(1) (equality of men and women) of the Constitution.[34]

With regard to partnerships outside of marriage,[35] however, the Court reached a different conclusion: "An enduring union for life of two persons may constitute such values that it should be legally acknowledged on the basis of the equal personal dignity of the persons affected, irrespective of the sex of those living together. . . . The cohabitation of persons of the same sex, which in all respects is very similar to the cohabitation of partners in a [different-sex] domestic partnership—involving a common household, as well as an emotional, economic and sexual relationship . . . —gives rise today, albeit to a lesser extent, to the same necessity for legal recognition as it did in the 1950s for those in a [different-sex] domestic partnership. . . . The sex of partners . . . may be significant when the regulation concerns a common child or . . . a marriage with another person. However, if these exceptional considerations do not apply, the exclusion from regulations covering . . . [different-sex] domestic partnership . . . is arbitrary and violates human dignity; therefore it is discrimination contrary to Article 70/A . . . The benefits (social and social security) that can be given only on the basis of a domestic partnership cannot depend only on the sex of the two people living together".

The Court found that the legalisation of same-sex partnership and the introduction of unmarried different-sex partnership into statutory law[36] were both

[33] *Supra* n.28.

[34] *Ibid.*, at 318–9.

[35] Prior to the amendment following the decision of the Constitutional Court, Art. 578/G, Act No. 4 of 1959 on the Civil Code (as amended in 1977), defined partnership as "a woman and a man living together in a common household in an emotional and economic community outside a marriage".

[36] The Penal Code in 1961 and the Civil Code in 1977.

motivated by similar practical needs. The Court left several options to the legislature—including a registered partnership law like the one in Denmark—and the case was suspended to allow time for amendments to the law. Following a heated parliamentary debate in May 1996, Act No. 42 of 1996 extended the scope of the provision of the Civil Code regulating the property relations of people living in the same household to same-sex partners, by a vote of 283 to 22 with one abstention, so as to comply with the Constitutional Court's decision.[37]

The following summary of the speech[38] delivered by the state secretary of the Ministry of Justice reflects the careful balance the government attempted to strike. The speaker stressed that "the lasting communion of two people may constitute values that are worthy of legal recognition, regardless of the sex of the persons thus cohabiting". Without elaborating on why a separate legal form providing for the equal status of same-sex partners with their unmarried different-sex counterparts was not proposed, and discarding for reasons of practicality amendments to already existing provisions relating to partners, she put forth the May 1996 amendment. She then explained that, given the existing legal framework, under which unmarried partners did not have the right to jointly adopt children, and that only married women could ask for artificial insemination (with the consent of their husbands), whether or not partners were of the same sex had no legal relevance. She stressed that the draft was supported by the Parliamentary Commissioner for Human Rights and a gay advocacy group, Rainbow Association for the Rights of Gays and Lesbians (*Szivárvány társulás a melegek jogaiért*) ("Rainbow Association"). And she invoked the European Parliament's 8 February 1994 "Resolution on equal rights for lesbians and homosexuals in the EC".[39] But she reiterated the government's unrelenting efforts to strengthen and protect families, because "parents living in a harmonious marriage can best ensure the peaceful development of their children. The legal recognition of same-sex partnership is not contrary to these efforts, because it enforces other interests".

Partnership is an institution of civil law. Partners are included among relatives under the Code on Civil Procedure,[40] but are not kin in terms of family law. Partnership is a factual relationship, being effective without registration, which in turn entails evidentiary problems. For example, under the Act on Social Security Pensions,[41] unmarried widowed partners are eligible for survivor's

[37] Art. 578/G, Act No. 4 of 1959 on the Civil Code: "(1) Partners shall acquire joint property rights in proportion to their contribution to the acquisitions while cohabiting. If the ratio of contributions cannot be determined, it shall be considered equal. Work done in the household shall be construed as contributing to acquisitions. (2) These provisions shall also be applied to the financial relationship of other relatives, with the exception of spouses, living in the same household". Act No. 42 of 1996 adds to the Civil Code a new Art. 685/A: "Partners—if not stipulated otherwise by law—are two people living in an emotional and economic community in the same household without being married".

[38] *Parlamenti Jegyzőkönyv* 1996, pp.18854–18856.

[39] OJ [1994] C 61/40.

[40] Art. 13, sub. 2, of Act No. 3 of 1952.

[41] Art. 45 of Act No. 81 of 1997.

pensions if they had continuously lived together with their deceased partners and given birth to a common child, or if they had continuously cohabited for ten years prior to death. In addition to the different treatment of surviving partners with common children in contrast to those with no children, the government decree implementing the May 1996 Act[42] creates further evidentiary problems, by requiring partners to prove their eligibility for a survivor's pension by an official certificate stating that they had lived at the same address as the deceased. If the length of cohabitation is otherwise proven, differing addresses do not effect eligibility.

What needs to be proven is the existence of a common household where unmarried partners live together in an emotional and economic communion. Unmarried partners gain common property rights over acquisitions, according to their share of input. As opposed to married couples, who gain common property rights over profits from any of their separate properties and assets, unmarried partners are entitled to a proportionate share of the profits from the other's separate property only if they take part in its accumulation.[43] In case of a dispute arising between them with regard to the division of their common property, same-sex partners are entitled to settle their disputes in court in the same way as different-sex partners. Partners are expected to settle property disputes along the principles of justice and fairness.[44]

Unmarried partners may inherit from each other on the basis of a will, but they are not listed among the statutory heirs.[45] Tenancy in local authority housing can be shared and continued by the partners with the local authority's written permission.[46] However, if the lease is in one partner's name, there is no automatic right for the other partner to continue living in the flat (e.g., after the death of the tenant). The local authority is quite unlikely to grant permission, given evidentiary problems and the shortage of local authority housing. Problems of this kind have arisen both for same-sex and different-sex partners. Similarly, the death of a partner renting a private flat terminates the right previously allowed to the other partner to use it.[47] As for immigration, only married spouses, dependent children, parents and grandparents are given the benefit of family (re)unification, i.e. the law does not provide for exemption from general immigration rules for Hungarian nationals who wish to sponsor their same or different-sex partners.[48]

Unmarried partners are not listed among relatives obliged under family law to support each other.[49] Under the Act on Social Administration,[50] however,

[42] 168/1997 (X. 6.) *Korm. rendelet* (government decree).
[43] Judgment No. BH1980.245.
[44] Judgment No. BH1984.225.
[45] Arts. 607–610 of Act No. 4 of 1959.
[46] Act No. 78 of 1993
[47] Judgment No. BH1999.113.
[48] Art. 17 of Act No. 86 of 1993 on Entry, Stay and Immigration in Hungary.
[49] Arts. 60–69 of Act No. 4 of 1952 on the Family Code.
[50] Act No. 3 of 1993, Art. 4, lin. c, "'family': close relatives cohabiting in a household on a permanent basis"; lin. d, "'close relatives': . . . partners if not stipulated otherwise under this Act"; lin f, "'household': persons cohabiting in a flat on a permanent basis" .

partners are defined as family members and may, under certain conditions, be obliged to support people cohabiting with them in a common household.[51] Partners are eligible for nursing fee (the cost of a partner's caring for their ill partner),[52] and can become beneficiaries under the national pension scheme, private pension schemes,[53] voluntary mutual insurance schemes,[54] or other insurance schemes.[55] No case has been publicly reported yet as to unlawful discrimination against same-sex partners by any of the above schemes. The government's housing programme, which primarily supports families and single persons with dependent family members (among whom partners are not included according to family law), may disqualify as ineligible for support applicants whose partners own or lease housing.[56]

There is no mention of adoption in the Constitutional Court's 1995 decision, apart from a suggestion that the Court considered a same-sex partnership to be a unit without children over whom both partners shared parental authority. Only married couples, and not unmarried partners (different-sex or same-sex) can jointly adopt a child. A child adopted by a single person who later marries can be adopted by that person's spouse,[57] but not by her/his partner. Since 1997, the suitability of parents wishing to adopt has been examined by the Child Protection Service, and adoptions have been approved by the State Guardian Office.[58] Under the Act on Public Health,[59] only married couples and different-sex partners (neither of whom is married) can undergo artificial insemination. To establish the existence of their partnership for this purpose, different-sex partners are required to sign a document before a public notary.

At a conference on adoption by foreign nationals, held in Budapest on 9–10 September 1999,[60] the issue of adoption by gays and lesbians arose, triggering a heated debate which revealed that some officials had known of a number of cases in which they had suspected the parent adopting (as an individual) to be gay or lesbian. The idea of giving children up for adoption by gays and lesbians was opposed by the majority of participants. Draft government policy guidelines on family matters envisaged the restoration of the traditional Christian family and confirmed that homosexual values shall not be promoted. Following a debate in professional circles, the Ministry of Social and Family

[51] For example, under Art. 114 of Act No. 3 of 1993, one partner may be obliged to pay fees for personal care provided to the other partner by the state.

[52] Arts. 41–44 of Act No. 3 of 1993.

[53] Act No. 82 of 1997.

[54] Act No. 96 of 1993.

[55] Act No 4. of 1959, Art. 536–567.

[56] 106/1988 (XII.26.) *MT rendelet* (government decree).

[57] Art. 47 of Act No. 4 of 1952.

[58] Arts. 62 and 112 of Act No. 31 of 1997 on the Protection of Children.

[59] Arts. 167–168 of Act No. 154 of 1997.

[60] L Mocsonaki, president of Background Support Society for Gays and Lesbians (*Háttér Baráti Társaság Egyesület a Melegekért*) later gave an oral account of the events. He said that some officials feared that children adopted by Danish or Dutch parents could "end up" being raised by same-sex couples.

Matters carefully deleted all supposedly derogatory references from the guidelines, which are still not final.

FREEDOM OF ASSOCIATION

On 17 May 1996, the Constitutional Court delivered a much-debated decision[61] in the so-called "Rainbow Case". The Rainbow Association (see p. 569) sought to be registered as an association in 1994 but was refused by the Metropolitan Court, which held, *inter alia*, that the word "gay" did not pass the test of authenticity, i.e., only words commonly used in Hungarian may feature in names of organisations seeking registration. The main issue, however, was the Metropolitan Court's finding that persons under eighteen were not allowed to become members of an organisation advocating for the rights of homosexuals. In this regard, the Metropolitan Court argued that the Association's objective, i.e. to create an infrastructure necessary for institutionalised homosexual life, bore the risk of causing the crime of "unnatural sexual conduct" (same-sex sexual activity with a person under eighteen) to be committed. The Rainbow Association refused to accept this restriction as a condition of registration. On appeal, the Supreme Court suspended the case and requested a decision from the Constitutional Court with regard to the legality of restrictions on membership based on age.

Measuring the right to freedom of association (Constitution, Article 63(1)) against the state's duty to protect children's well-being (Article 67), the Constitutional Court held that "the child's membership in associations relating to homosexuality can be excluded or restricted in laws or in court decisions". Claiming not to "form a moral judgment about homosexuality",[62] the Court noted the "ambiguous boundaries of homosexuality" and observed that "individual decision plays an important role in homosexual behaviour . . . whether one wants to remain hidden . . . or wants militantly to go public. . . . Publicly assuming homosexuality . . . is an existentially decisive decision . . . because of the current social reception of homosexuality by contemporary Hungarian society; . . . later any change is difficult.[63] . . . It might prove helpful for a minor under eighteen years of age struggling with homosexuality if he/she can find company . . . where there are people with similar problems and where he/she can receive . . . counselling . . .. But an association of adult, practising homosexuals, one which is part of the homosexual subculture is different. . . . [T]here is a possibility that a minor whose homosexuality has not yet been fixed and who has not chosen a role excludes his/her options by a premature decision".[64]

[61] 21/1996 (V.17.) AB *határozat*. See Sólyom & Brunner, *supra* n.28, at 333–45 (English translation).

[62] Sólyom & Brunner, *ibid.*, at 344.

[63] *Ibid.*, at 343.

[64] *Ibid.*, at 345.

Philosopher János Kiss has argued[65] that, by finding that immature homosexual coming out was risky, the Constitutional Court had departed from its self-declared principle of neutral argument. In his view, neutrality should not have permitted the Court to consider negative social attitudes, because these were contrary to the principles of equal treatment and non-discrimination. In a democratic state, discrimination should not only be impermissible but also fought against, including by the courts. A further peculiarity of the decision was that it did not entertain the possibility of granting parents the right to instruct their children as to membership, nor did it explain why the restriction could be justified in the case of a gay organisation, as opposed to a heterosexual organisation.

As a result of the Constitutional Court's decision, the Rainbow Association's request for registration was refused. In 1997, the Association filed an application[66] with the European Commission of Human Rights. On 12 May 2000, the European Court of Human Rights—sitting as a committee of three judges, who did not even communicate the application to the Hungarian government—declared the complaint relating to Article 11 of the European Convention "manifestly ill-founded", reasoning that "[t]he condition for registration that the applicant association should exclude minors from membership pursued the legitimate aims of the protection of morals and the rights and freedoms of others. The Court finds that the interference was proportionate to the aims pursued and could, therefore, reasonably be regarded as necessary in a democratic society". The Court also declared the remainder of the applicant's complaints, under Articles 8 and 14, inadmissible as they did not "disclose any appearance of a violation of the rights and freedoms set out in the Convention and its Protocols". In the context of further dismissed applications—mainly those dealing with police ill-treatment of Roma in Hungary[67]—one may conclude that there seem to be cases displaying clear violations of Convention rights which the Court—for reasons as yet unknown—is unwilling to take on.

The Constitutional Court seems to have been more at ease with allowing freedom for homosexuals in a matter that primarily concerned adults (the partnerships case), but more restrictive when it came to one concerning adolescents (the Rainbow Case). Yet the fact that adult homosexuals have not been granted complete liberty was revealed by the Court when it further explained its partnership decision in the Rainbow Case. The Court said that it had found constitutional protection for "[t]he relationship between persons of the same sex—in its durable and publicly assumed form and confined to certain aspects of life".[68]

[65] See J Kiss, "A Szivárvány-teszt", *Beszélő*, July 1996, pp. 26–36; G Halmai & K Lane Scheppele, "Decision 21 of 1996 (V.17.) AB from the Constitutional Court of Hungary", [1997] 3 *East European Human Rights Review* 17.

[66] *Szivárvány társulás a melegek jogaiért* v. *Hungary*, No. 35419/97 (12 May 2000) (unpublished).

[67] See e.g. *Géza Farkas* v. *Hungary*, No. 31561/96 (2 March 2000).

[68] Sólyom & Brunner, *supra* n.28, at 342.

Because action from the legislature is unlikely, the resolution of the age of consent issue will probably fall to the Constitutional Court. As witnessed in previous cases,[69] the Court might feel compelled to follow the majority trend in Europe, especially because of the possibility of an application to the European Court of Human Rights.[70] However, it will be interesting to see whether the Constitutional Court will take the road of its partnerships decision, or the Rainbow Case.

[69] 23/1990 (X.31.) AB *határozat* on the abolition of the death penalty, 64/1991 (XII.17.) on abortion, 30/1992 (V.26.) on freedom of expression.

[70] See *Sutherland* v. *United Kingdom*, No. 25186/94, European Commission of Human Rights, Report of 1 July 1997.

32

The Legal Situation of Same-Sex Partnerships in Germany: An Overview

ROLAND SCHIMMEL* and STEFANIE HEUN**

INTRODUCTION

THE MAIN OBSTACLE to the legal recognition of same-sex couples is not practical problems raised by couples who live together outside of marriage. Rather, it is the fact that the legal rules governing cohabitation of couples are based on the assumption that only socially useful and desirable couple relationships should be recognised. Although these rules could be applied to any form of relationship as a couple between two human beings, the current legal situation in Germany is that these rules are generally applied only to married couples of different sexes. In the first part of this chapter, the rules governing human partnerships and their application by administrative and judicial authorities will be outlined. This will include an overview of the reasons either for confining the application of these rules to partnerships of different sexes, as is the majority opinion, or, as some dissenting views propose, for extending their application to same-sex partnerships. In the second part of this chapter, recent proposals for legislative reform, as well as the reform enacted in 2001, will be discussed.

LEGAL RECOGNITION OF SAME-SEX PARTNERSHIPS UNDER EXISTING LAW

Any survey of the legal situation of same-sex partnerships must take into account both the relevant provisions of constitutional law and Statute Law. To formulate a legal framework for same-sex partners to organise their cohabitation, several options are conceivable. On the one hand, same-sex partners willing to establish a legally binding relationship could be allowed to marry. This would give them access to the established legal regime for a marriage, which contains defined rights and obligations, as well as legal alternatives for arranging the relationship. If this position were rejected for legal reasons,

* *Rechtsanwalt* (Lawyer), Schimmel Buhlmann, Frankfurt am Main.

** Legal Counsel, Legal Affairs Department, *Deutsche Börse* (German Stock Exchange), Frankfurt am Main.

same-sex partnerships could instead be treated as a kind of common-law marriage, i.e., a partnership (deemed) for life, and granted some degree of legal recognition and protection. This would raise the questions of how much recognition, and whether this would be sufficient as a substitute for the legal framework of marriage.

As will be seen below, there is certainly reason to call for legislative activity. Exclusion from the institution of marriage causes same-sex partners a variety of legal difficulties and disadvantages. Admittedly, the partners can avoid some of these by making binding declarations or undertakings, either among themselves or towards third parties, thereby setting up a contractual or testamentary regime. However, this entails expense in drafting such legal arrangements, which couples of different sexes are not obliged to incur. Moreover, even the most diligently drafted "design" for such a regime will necessarily leave out some of the legal consequences of marriage, in particular as regards matters governed by rules of a public law character. The formal legal status of marital partner or descendant, which is established through the legal act of marriage or the legal concept of affiliation, entails a variety of legal consequences, and is referred to in various other legal regimes, cannot be entirely replaced by mere contractual agreements.

For instance, the rate of inheritance tax will be much higher for a person who is not married or otherwise related to the deceased than is the case for a spouse, despite all kinds of contractual undertakings. Even carefully tailored notarial deeds, containing reciprocal appointments as each other's heir, cannot confer on one partner the privilege of refusing to give evidence against the other in a trial, as is the case for spouses. A particularly drastic example may be found in immigration law. If one partner is likely to be expelled or summarily deported as an undesirable alien, this will normally threaten the whole relationship, without giving rise to any special legal remedy[1]. Moreover, apart from these material disadvantages, there may also be a symbolic burden resulting from the far-reaching denial of legal recognition and protection for same-sex partnerships.

Constitutional Law

The German Constitution of 23 May 1949, the *Grundgesetz* (GG) or Basic Law,[2] does not expressly mention same-sex couples or even sexual orientation. However, the Constitution's part on fundamental rights contains three relevant provisions: Articles 6(1), 2(1) and 3(1) GG.

[1] See Hailbronner, [1997] *Neue Zeitschrift für Verwaltungsrecht* (NVwZ) 460.

[2] See http://www.bundestag.de/gesetze/gg(German); http://www.uniwuerzburg.de/law/gm 00000_.html (English).

Article 6(1) GG

The most specific provision is Article 6(1) GG: "Marriage and family are under the special protection of the State". It is probably undisputed among German constitutional lawyers that this provision has three different aspects: protecting individual liberty in relation to marriage, establishing an institutional foundation for marriage, and protecting the institution of marriage against competition.

Individual Liberty

First, the freedom to conclude a marriage is guaranteed by Article 6(1) without reservation. This means that the State may only interfere with this freedom by stipulating specific requirements for concluding a marriage, or prohibitive restraints on particular marriages, but must not prohibit marriage as such.[3] Such interferences (normally through statutes that are inferior to the GG) are subject to judicial review of their constitutionality by the German Federal Constitutional Court (*Bundesverfassungsgericht*, BVerfG). The Court has developed rather severe criteria, welcomed by academic commentators, which oblige public authorities (including the legislature and courts) to be as inobtrusive as possible in stipulating specific requirements or prohibitive restraints.[4] Moreover, the Court has clearly held that any rule without a reasonable foundation must not be an impediment to marriage.[5] Consequently, there is an established line of judgments quashing prohibitions on marriage that could not be justified.[6]

These constitutional standards must be applied to determine the validity of the exclusion of same-sex couples from civil marriage. The partners' being of the same sex could be seen as a prohibitive restraint on marriage, or the partners' being of different sexes could be seen as a specific requirement for marriage. Either understanding would have to be justified by explaining why the policy reasons for placing marriage under specific constitutional protection necessitate the exclusion of same-sex partnerships from this protection. Different lines of argument may be followed.

First, one could look to the historical foundations of Article 6(1) GG in Article 119 of the Weimar Constitution of 1919, but protection of marriage received little attention during the political debates. One reason might be the spirit and mood of that period, which reflected the rather conservative sociology

[3] See e.g. *Entscheidungen des Bundesverfassungsgerichts* (BVerfGE) 29, 166, 174; BK-Pirson, *Randziffer* (Rz.) 89 on Art. 6.

[4] See BVerfGE 36, 146, 163; 49, 286, 300; Seifert/Hömig, Rz. 8 on Art. 6; MüKo-Müller-Gindullis, Rz. 22 on *Ehegesetz* (EheG), para. 1.

[5] See BVerfGE 49, 286; 300, 36, 146, 163. For the opposite point of view, see Böhmer, [1991] *Das Standesamt* (StAZ) 125, 127.

[6] See e.g BVerfGE 36, 146, 163 (prohibition of marriage between two partners, one of whom had had a sexual relationship with one of the other partner's parents or children, declared unconstitutional).

of the family of the late nineteenth century, and a perceived need to protect against (alleged) signs of decay in the established patterns of family and marriage. Similarly, during the deliberations on the GG, no particular attention was given to the reasons for a specific legal protection of marriage.[7]

Second, one could propose a contemporary interpretation of Article 6(1) GG. Opponents of same-sex marriage commonly refer to the meaning of marriage as "the founding of a family", which is itself the nucleus of society, and thus deserving of special protection.[8] This, however, is highly disputable reasoning which leads to erroneous results. At the outset, it is doubtful whether marriage has a purpose either for the parties to it or for society as a whole.[9] When constitutional protection of individual freedoms is granted, any interference by the State will require a special justification; this also applies when the interference results from legal formulation of defined purposes of marriage. According to current developments in the academic study of family law, it is almost impossible, and certainly more and more difficult, to identify any specific purposes of marriage. Instead, it should be left to the partners themselves to determine the purposes of their marriage.

Even if specific purposes can be identified by the legislature, they cannot include a duty to conceive and raise children. This interpretation follows from the wording of Article 6(1) GG, which makes it clear that family and marriage are protected separately and independently by constitutional law. It follows that family and marriage cannot be the same, neither from a sociological perspective nor in legal terms. In fact, there are several functions of marriage which justify special legal protection independent of any link to family:[10]

- Marriage is the smallest entity in society that serves to guarantee its stability. A relationship between two persons consciously created to last indefinitely is a value in itself, for it preserves and realises values and rules in society.
- A further purpose of marriage is to channel, and provide with a social regime, any form of sexual activity.
- Just as importantly, marital relationships often provide relief to publicly funded social security schemes: a conjugal relationship is not only an emotional one, but also requires financial support which would otherwise have to be provided by the community as a whole.

It is not evident that same-sex partnerships are incapable of accomplishing these functions of marriage in the same way as different-sex partnerships.

[7] See von Campenhausen, *Veröffentlichungen der Vereinigung Deutscher Staatsrechtslehrer* (VVDStRL) 45, 8, 13.

[8] See BVerfG, [1993] *Neue Juristische Wochenschrift* (NJW) 3058.

[9] See e.g. Berghahn, [1993] *Kritische Justiz* (KJ) 397, 417.

[10] See Coester, *Stenographische Berichte der Gemeinsamen Verfassungskommission* (SBdGV), 6. *öffentliche Anhörung* (10 Dec. 1992) at 3; Otto, SBdGV, 14. *Sitzung* (14 Jan. 1993) at 8. Cf. the functions of marriage listed by K Zoras, *Ehe und Familie unter dem besonderen Schutz der verfassungsmäßigen Ordnung* (Freiburg, 1978) at 52: "Reproduction of society, education of children, economic functions, emotional stability".

Moreover, it is undisputed that marriages are permitted between older persons, or those otherwise incapable of reproduction, even though the future creation of a family is clearly not the foundation of the marriage. Likewise, there is no obstacle to a marriage between fertile partners who, as has become more frequent, do not intend to have children but nonetheless wish to enjoy the legal benefits of marriage. In current social reality, marriage and family have become more and more distinct concepts: the number of cohabiting partners with children has increased considerably over the last few decades, while more and more married couples remain childless, deliberately or not. Thus, on an empirical basis, there is no longer a foundation for any postulated identity between family and marriage. The legal recognition of a family, in turn, is not confined to those founded on a marriage between the parents of a child.

Even if the traditional link between family and marriage is retained, same-sex couples can be the joint social (if not legal or genetic) parents of children from an earlier heterosexual relationship of one of the partners, as well as of children fostered and later adopted by one partner. And scientific progress could cast doubt on the assumption that two same-sex partners cannot both be the genetic parents of a child.

The individual liberty aspect of the constitutional protection of marriage points in favour of the integration of same-sex couples into the concept of marriage. It is not a compelling counter-argument that those who adopted the 1949 Constitution took a different position. The purpose of a constitutionally granted freedom is open to change by way of further development of the reading of the Constitution. Such a constitutional development has a reasonable foundation with regard to same-sex partnerships: the social meaning of marriage is significantly different from that of 1949, as is the social and legal recognition of homosexuality and same-sex partnerships.

In the case of marriage, the introduction of the obligatory civil (registry-office) marriage in 1875 separated private law marriage from the ecclesiastical act of matrimony. Since then, the meaning of marriage has largely changed from a religious or metaphysical concept to a much more individualistic one. At the same time, concepts of conjugal life have become more diverse, giving marriage a more varied appearance from the perspective of legal sociology, and the relationship between family and marriage has changed.

In the case of same-sex partnerships, both the parties to them and the public have—sometimes reluctantly—come to accept them as a social normality. For example, almost every soap opera on German television features a sympathetic gay or lesbian couple. And after so many years of discussion, the position that no form of "gay marriage" is necessary has become almost untenable in television discussions of the matter. Even if this does not mark the end of the development, it can still be said that the social climate in Germany towards same-sex partners has never been more open and tolerant than it is now. This is even reflected in case-law. Although the courts have yet to accept same-sex marriages as a legally valid concept, all standard arguments against the mere acceptability of a same-sex partnership have by now disappeared. In fact, no court would nowadays still consider the nomination of a same-sex partner as an heir as contrary to public morals and therefore an unconscionable act.

One might thus argue that, both in terms of social reality and in terms of the social meanings of the concepts, same-sex relationships and marriage are approaching each other. Developments to date may still be insufficient to require constitutional change, in the sense of extending the meaning of marriage to same-sex couples. However, there is a clear tendency, and there may be even more cogent reasons within the next few years.

Institutional Foundation

A second meaning of Article 6(1) GG is that it protects marriage against abolition or compulsory annulment, i.e., it is an institutional foundation or safeguard for the existence of the legal and social concept of marriage as such. Seen from this perspective, the recognition of same-sex couples might be doubtful at first sight, because it would abolish a firmly established feature of marriage, namely the diversity of the sexes of the partners. But recourse to this meaning of Article 6(1) GG as precluding same-sex marriage is subject to several reservations.

First, it is highly doubtful whether this understanding is in conformity with the principle enshrined in Article 1(1) GG, according to which human dignity is deemed to be the supreme constitutional value; this understanding is likely to place formal juridical interpretation above the interests of human beings, for whose sake law exists. Moreover, it is hard to say what disadvantages (if any) will follow, either for the individual or for society as a whole, from admitting same-sex couples to marriage. The institutional foundation of marriage could thus be seen as a device to prevent a liberalisation of established concepts, and therefore considered obsolete. It is not surprising that courts have drawn remarkably disparate conclusions when relying on this institutional principle,[11] the argumentative value of which should thus not be overestimated. It must be borne in mind that permitting marriages between same-sex partners would not abolish marriage between different-sex couples, but would only lead to some degree of "dilution" both in terms of numbers and of meaning. Consequently, the institutional foundation of marriage in the Constitution should not be seen as of particular relevance.

Protection Against Competition

Some authors have inferred from Article 6(1) GG a constitutional obligation on the State to protect marriage against alternative models of living together as a couple. But given that sexual preferences and inclinations are not at the disposition of the person having them, and are in this sense "irreversible", there is no room for their "bearer" to freely opt for either a same-sex partnership or an

[11] See Bosch, *Familienrechtsreform*, 45. For the opposite point of view, see BVerfGE 31, 58, 83; 53, 224, 245; Zuleeg, [1986] NVwZ 800, 805, each referring to the "institution of marriage".

"ordinary", different-sex marriage. Consequently, if one attaches importance to Article 6(1)'s individual liberty aspect, in accordance with its position in a list of individual liberties in the Constitution, and if the social functions of marriage mentioned above are taken into consideration, one will come to the result that Article 6(1) GG should be interpreted as requiring the recognition of marriages between same-sex partners.

Article 2(1) GG

Also of relevance is Article 2(1) GG, which reads as follows: "Everyone has the right to free development of his personality insofar as he does not violate the rights of others or offend against the constitutional order or against morality". Although Article 6(1) GG is the specific provision on freedom to marry, and as such will normally have priority over Article 2(1), the latter norm is nonetheless applicable to unmarried cohabitation resembling a common-law marriage, which is constitutionally protected only by the universal liberty of action contained in Article 2(1). Given that Article 6(1) has priority over Article 2(1), the reservation for non-compliance with morality in Article 2(1) is inapplicable. In any case, standards of morality have become highly uncertain in the political and cultural pluralism of recent times. Any legal objection to same-sex partnerships disappeared with the repeal of Paragraph 175 of the Penal Code (*Strafgesetzbuch*) in 1994, which established a higher age of consent for male-male sexual activity. Public opinion, as derived from opinion polls and press articles, is probably still not free from bias. But it is no longer possible to recognise a general view that same-sex couples violate moral principles.

Article 3(1) GG

The equality provision of the Constitution is Article 3 GG: "(1) All humans are equal before the law. (2) Men and women are equal. . . . (3) No one may be disadvantaged or favoured because of his sex, his parentage, his race, his language, his homeland and origin, his faith, or his religious or political opinions. No one may be disadvantaged because of his handicap". Article 3(1) contains both a command for equality of treatment of essentially similar sets of facts, as well as a prohibition of discrimination between essentially similar cases. Article 3(3) provides for some specific prohibitions of discrimination, which do not include sexual orientation. The question of adding sexual orientation was raised during debates on constitutional reform immediately following German reunification in 1990, but no action was taken.[12] Same-sex partnerships could therefore only fall under Article 3(3) if sexual orientation is part of the sex of a person, which is obviously not the case.[13]

[12] Cf. the Constitutions of the *Länder* (states, regions) of Berlin (1995), Article 10(2) ("*sexuelle Identität*"); Brandenburg (1992), Article 12(2) ("*sexuelle Identität*"); Thuringia (1993), Article 2(3) ("*sexuelle Orientierung*").

[13] But see Koppelman, chap. 35.

It can be argued that couples formed of partners (that is individuals) of the same or of different sexes are essentially similar sets of fact. In both cases, the members of the couple are willing to establish an officially recognised, durable commitment towards each other. This bond is equally deserving of protection in both cases. Failing to treat same-sex couples in the same way as different-sex couples (e.g., by refusing to permit them to marry) is discrimination contrary to Article 3(1) unless there are justified grounds or a legitimate reason for a differentiation. Although such a purpose could at first sight be found in encouraging "the founding of a family", it was shown earlier that this is not a valid argument. Otherwise, it would be very difficult to show compliance with the principle of proportionality.

Given that persons with a homosexual orientation do not have a proper choice to marry somebody of the other sex, the prohibition of same-sex marriage is hardly suitable to further the founding of families by such persons. Nor should such a prohibition be upheld without any compensation by way of advantages otherwise granted by the public system. It is true that, under German constitutional law, the legislator is free to categorise and generalise, even if this will lead to a certain degree of inequality of treatment. The right to marry could therefore be confined to partners who are biologically capable of having children, and able to contribute to the preservation of the people constituting the State by founding a family.

However, such a legislative generalisation must not exceed certain limits. According to both courts[14] and legal writings,[15] a margin of error reaching 10 per cent is considered excessive. Given the number of married couples without children, such a generalisation appears unacceptable. Moreover, it has to be noted that the extent of a discrimination resulting from such a generalisation will also be of relevance; the higher the degree of inequality, the less acceptable the legal regime will be. Applying the principle of non-discrimination, the prohibition of marriage for same-sex couples is subject to serious reservations. Therefore, from the perspective of constitutional law, the extension of marriage to same-sex partnerships is in any event conceivable, and possibly even mandated.

From a pragmatic perspective, however, this conclusion is insufficient. In legal reality, the Constitution only grants such rights as are recognised by the Federal Constitutional Court, or are added by express constitutional amendments. Since an amendment expressly permitting same-sex marriage is not on the agenda of any of the political parties in Germany, the Court currently has the last word on the matter. On 4 October 1993, the Court held that same-sex marriages are not mandated by Articles 6(1), 3(1) and 2(1) GG.[16] According to the Court, Article 6(1) only provides access to marriage for partners of different

[14] See BVerfGE 63, 119, 128; *Entscheidungen des Bundesverwaltungsgerichts* (BVerwGE) (Federal Administrative Court) 68, 36, 41.

[15] See von Münch/Kunig-Gubelt, Rz. 26 on Art. 3; Jarass/Pieroth, Rz. 20a on Art. 3.

[16] See BVerfG, [1993] NJW 3058.

sexes; no change had been introduced by the development of social attitudes. Even changes in statute law will not necessarily influence the meaning of marriage in constitutional law. Marriage is still founded, the Court held, to provide protection for the partners as a legal framework for founding a family.

However, the Court added that various forms of unequal treatment of same-sex couples, compared with "ordinary" different-sex marriage, could possibly constitute an infringement of the principle of equality of treatment in Article 3(1). This could require the legislature to provide for a remedy. But it was not necessary for the Court to decide this issue, because the case only concerned access to marriage. The Court also left open the question of whether ordinary statute law requires the recognition of same-sex marriages. The only finding by the Court was that the Constitution does not require it.

Statute Law

It is certainly possible to bring same-sex partnerships within the statutory meaning of marriage. Like the Constitution, the relevant statutory provisions do not contain any express references to same-sex couples. Nor is the term "marriage" defined in the Civil Code (*Bürgerliches Gesetzbuch*, BGB), the Law on Personal Status (*Personenstandsgesetz*), or the Marriage Law (*Ehegesetz*, repealed in 1998). Thus, the relevant provisions are to be construed according to the applicable rules of statutory interpretation. Provisions referring to "man" and "woman" are obviously not meant to serve as a statutory definition. They only describe the legal consequences of marriage, but not its prerequisites.

Nonetheless, until recently, the understanding of the term "marriage" as a legally recognised bond between two persons of different sexes was obvious and a matter of course in all respects, both in everyday language and in specific legal terminology. Consequently, there was no reason for legislation to refer to diversity in the sexes of the partners as an element of marriage, be it a specific requirement or a prohibitive restraint.

It can be argued that the term "marriage" has become rather uncertain in its meaning since same-sex couples started to claim a right to marry. Although a "gay marriage" ("*Homo-Ehe*") was a contradiction in terms only a few decades ago, the term—with or without quotation marks—has almost become commonplace, through frequent use in the media and in political debate for legal reform. In particular, both legislative activity (in the Scandinavian countries, the Netherlands and France)[17] and progressive judicial opinion (the Supreme Court of Hawaii)[18] have contributed to this development. Similarly, since the 1977 divorce reform, a lifelong bond between the partners is no longer an element of marriage; even the requirement of monogamy may be set aside in

[17] See Lund-Andersen, chap. 21; Ytterberg, chap. 22; Waaldijk, chap. 23; Borrillo, chap. 25.
[18] See Wolfson, chap. 9.

certain circumstances under private international law. The meaning of the statutory term "marriage" has thus become far more ambiguous.

However, when interpreting the relevant provisions in the light of their historical background (a recognised tool of statutory interpretation in Germany), it is without any doubt that the legislature intended marriage to be construed solely as a community between woman and man. As far as the BGB is concerned, this is obvious from parliamentary debates and the published reports of the drafters (*Motive* and *Protokolle*). There is no indication whatsoever of an intention to deviate from this concept. Yet according to a widely accepted opinion, this is by no means an insurmountable obstacle to a different interpretation, especially given the time elapsed since the adoption of the BGB in 1900. It is therefore argued that a change in social and even legal reality may justify a departure from the original legislative intention or understanding.

Little may be derived from an analysis of the context in which the norms governing marriage are embedded. As far as the law governing engagement is concerned, the former Paragraph 1300 BGB (repealed in 1998) referred somewhat more clearly to man and woman (the premarital sexual act—coitus—sanctioned in that provision can, from its wording, only be performed by man and woman). But because engagement necessarily refers to marriage, which it is meant to precede, there is a danger of a circular reasoning. Also, it is of little significance that many of the provisions of family law concerning child care would not apply to many or most same-sex marriages: childless married different-sex couples are no longer an exception; and same-sex couples could well raise children through adoption or donor insemination. Moreover, since the 1994 amendment to the Penal Code, mentioned above, it can no longer be argued that homosexual partnerships could have as their purpose criminal offences. However, there is an indication contained in Paragraph 8.1.2 of the Law on Transsexuality (*Transsexuellengesetz*), according to which it is necessary to dissolve a transsexual person's existing marriage before a change of legal sex after gender reassignment surgery is allowed to be entered in the public civil status register. This precludes the conversion of a different-sex marriage into a same-sex marriage as a result of the surgery.

If the relevant provisions on marriage are interpreted, not according to their legislative history or statutory context, but according to their purpose (a method which is available in German law), the question becomes what a contemporary legislator should understand by "marriage" today. A decisive factor is the obligation to interpret statute law in conformity with the requirements of the Constitution. As mentioned above, the position that the constitutional freedom to marry will be best realised by extending the concept of marriage to include same-sex partnerships appears to be not only tenable, but also the most persuasive.

Same-Sex Marriage Litigation

Following the American example, in the early 1990s, the German gay and lesbian movements began to consider claiming same-sex marriage through litigation. An "*Aktion Standesamt*" ("action at the registry office") was initiated in 1992, during which several hundred homosexual couples sought marriage, and which led to legal action before the family courts, and eventually the Federal Constitutional Court. The couples made the constitutional law and statute law arguments discussed above. However, the action did not have the support of a majority of public or judicial opinion. Only one single district court (*Amstgericht*, AG), in a comprehensively reasoned judgement, affirmed the applicability of the relevant provisions of family law to same-sex partnerships.[19] This position was eventually quashed on appeal,[20] and was rejected by every higher district court (*Landgericht*, LG)[21] and higher regional court (*Oberlandesgericht*, OLG).[22] Some couples finally referred the matter to the Federal Constitutional Court. However, the Court did not find the constitutional actions grounded on Articles 6(1), 3(1), 2(1) GG admissible (arguable), for the reasons mentioned above, and dismissed them without holding a hearing on the merits.[23]

This, of course, largely ended the attempt to establish the availability of marriage for same-sex couples through litigation. Some litigation did follow, challenging various inequalities in the treatment of same-sex couples compared with different-sex couples (other than in relation to marriage). But the line of argument provided by the Federal Constitutional Court largely determined the reasoning adopted by courts considering other issues. They held that there are important differences between marriage (or other different-sex partnerships) and same-sex partnerships, which justify different legal treatment.[24]

In parallel, but also following the 1992 action, the subject of same-sex marriage has gained increasing prominence in legal writings. The majority of authors[25] continue to support the already dominant opinion, both in constitutional

[19] See AG Frankfurt/Main, [1993] NJW 940 f., [1993] *Monatsschrift für Deutsches Recht* (MDR) 116, [1993] *Zeitschrift für das gesamte Familienrecht* (FamRZ) 557, [1993] StAZ 48, 149.

[20] See LG Frankfurt/Main, [1993] NJW 1998.

[21] See LG Osnabrück, [1993] FamRZ 327; LG Bonn, [1993] StAZ 13; LG Gießen, [1993] NJW 942; LG Neubrandenburg, [1993] MDR 871; LG Münster, [1993] StAZ 320.

[22] See OLG Köln, [1993] StAZ 147; *Bayerisches Oberstes Landesgericht* (BayObLG) (Bavaria), [1993] NJW 1996; OLG Celle, [1993] FamRZ 1082; *Kammergericht* (KG), [1994] StAZ 220; OLG Köln, [1994] FamRZ 1107.

[23] See BVerfG, [1993] NJW 3058.

[24] See e.g. *Bundessozialgericht* (BSG) (Federal Social Insurance Court), [1997] NJW 2620 (claim for unemployment insurance, *Arbeitslosengeld*); BSG, [2000] NJW 2038 (civil servant's claim for pension for a surviving dependant, *Hinterbliebenenrente*); *Bundesarbeitsgericht* (BAG) (Federal Labour Court), [1997] *Arbeit und Recht* (AuR) 3184 (employee's claim for additional payment based on a wage agreement, *Tarifvertrag*).

[25] See B Verschraegen, *Gleichgeschlechtliche "Ehen"* (*Same-Sex "Marriages"*) (Vienna, Medien und Recht, 1994); Pauly, [1997] NJW 1955.

law[26] and family law,[27] of the unavailability of marriage for homosexual couples, although quite often they provide no detailed analysis of the issue. However, some authors now strongly endorse the opposite position.[28] Even so, the case-law of the higher courts makes it quite unlikely that homosexual couples will try to achieve marriage through litigation in the near future.

Invoking the Rights and Obligations of Unmarried Different-Sex Cohabitants

In German law, there is no parallel to a common-law marriage, or any marriage of inferior legal status. Although unmarried different-sex cohabitants are a permanent social reality in Germany, this has yet to lead to legislative action, or even a legal definition. The current legal situation is that unmarried different-sex cohabitants are bound by some legal duties, but have few legal rights. This is due to the rule contained in Article 6(1) GG according to which there is an obligation upon the State to promote marriages, which almost invariably entails a prohibition on affording to any other form of cohabitation any treatment more favourable than, or similar to, that received by married couples. For example, unmarried different-sex cohabitants have to accept, in the law relating to social assistance, that the income of the unmarried partner of the claimant is taken into account, as in the case of a married couple.[29]

In general, courts are rather reluctant—despite the obvious similarity in fact—to apply norms applicable to married couples even partially to unmarried different-sex cohabitants. Usually, courts attempt to find a solution in contract,

[26] See AK-GG-Richter, Rz.15 on Art. 6; vonMünch/Kunig-E.M.vonMünch, Rz. 4; M/D/H/S-Maunz, Rz. 15; Jarass/Pieroth, Rz. 2; Schmidt-Bleibtreu/Klein, Rz. 6; Seifert/Hömig, Rz. 5; Pieroth/Schlink, Rz. 720, 723; Stein, *Staatsrecht*, § 35 II.1.a) (S.291); Lecheler, [1986] *Deutsches Verwaltungsblatt* (DVBl.) 905–6; Zippelius, [1986] *Die öffentliche Verwaltung* (DÖV) 805–6; Friauf, [1986] NJW 2595, 2601; von Campenhausen, VVDStRL 45, 8, 26; Zoras, *supra* n.10, at 31.

[27] See Wacke, [1990] FamRZ 347, 350; Neuhaus, *Ehe und Kindschaft in rechtsvergleichender Sicht*, § 4 IV. (S.25 f.); Dölle, *Familienrecht I*, § 5 I 1. (S.524); Gernhuber, *Familienrecht*, § 5 I 2. (S.37); Ramm, *Familienrecht*, § 5 2.a) (S.47), § 53, III.7. (S.443 f.); Tschernitschek, *Familienrecht*, Rz.23 f.; Beitzke-Lüderitz, *Familienrecht*, § 5 I 2. (S.30); Palandt-Diederichsen, Rz. 14 on EheG, para. 11; MüKo-Müller-Gindullis, Rz. 17 on EheG, para. 11; Soergel-Heintzmann, Rz. 1 on EheG, para. 11; AK-BGB-Lange-Klein, Rz. 6 at paras. 1353 ff.; Erman-Aderhold, Rz. 1 on EheG, para. 1; Müller-Manger, *Art. 6 Grundgesetz: Wandel familiärer Lebensmuster*, 132; Kissel, *Ehe und Ehescheidung* 45; Hepting/Gaaz, Rz. 97 on EheG, paras. 3 ff., Rz. 9 on EheG, para. 11.

[28] See R Schimmel, *Eheschließungen gleichgeschlechtlicher Paare?* (*Marriages for Same-Sex Couples?*) (Berlin, Duncker & Humblot, 1996); S Grib, *Die gleichgeschlechtliche Partnerschaft im nordischen und deutschen Recht* (*Same-Sex Partnerships in Nordic and German Law*) (Neuried, ars una, 1996); J Risse, *Der verfassungsrechtliche Schutz der Homosexualität* (*The Constitutional Protection of Homosexuality*) (Baden-Baden, Nomos, 1998); S Heun, *Gleichgeschlechtliche Ehen in rechtsvergleichender Sicht* (*Same-Sex Marriages from a Comparative Law Perspective*) (Berlin, Duncker & Humblot, 1999). See also J Wegner, *Die nichteheliche Lebensgemeinschaft im deutschen Ausländerrecht* (*Unmarried Cohabitation in German Law on Foreigners*) (Berlin, VWB, 1997); Wegner, [1995] *Zeitschrift für Rechtssoziologie* (ZsfRSoz) 170; Trimbach/Webert, [1998] *Neue Justiz* (NJ) 63; von Renesse, [1996] *Zeitschrift für Rechtspolitik* (ZRP) 212; Ott, [1998] NJW 117; Hochroter, [1998] NJW 3677.

[29] Federal Social Assistance Law (*Bundessozialhilfegesetz*), para. 122.

restitution (quasi-contract), or the law relating to unincorporated partnerships. Given the number of issues to be resolved, it is doubtful whether such a piecemeal legal framework applicable to unmarried different-sex cohabitants is a sufficient substitute for the legal framework of marriage. Needless to say, no difficulty will arise for unmarried different-sex cohabitants who reject marriage, for whatever reason, and strive to be bound by as few rules as possible. For those, however, who wish to marry and are unable to do so, or are the weaker partner and in need of legal protection, the rules applicable to unmarried different-sex cohabitants will not be sufficient.

It cannot be assumed that extending to same-sex couples the rights and obligations of unmarried different-sex cohabitants will allow them to profit from at least some of the legal "perks" provided to married couples. It is certainly true that the applicability of the rules on marriage to unmarried different-sex cohabitants is under constant debate and regularly raised before the courts. And, although the case-law is not entirely clear and coherent, certain strands of reasoning are nonetheless discernible. Yet, the inclusion of same-sex couples has been a difficult task. While courts and legal writers have over the years applied almost interchangeably the concepts of "non-marital cohabitation" and "quasi-marital live-in partnership", it has by now become clear that same-sex partnerships are "non-marital" but not "quasi-marital".

This distinction results from the definition of quasi-marital partnership provided by the Federal Constitutional Court: ". . . a live-in community for life (to last for an indefinite period of time) between a man and a woman, not allowing a similar partnership alongside it, characterised by inner feelings reaching beyond a mere household community or a budgetary partnership in that the partners will stand in for each other".[30] The Federal Supreme Court (*Bundesgerichtshof*, BGH, the highest court on civil law matters) supported this position fairly soon thereafter.[31] In an obiter dictum, it stated that Paragraph 569a.2.1 BGB, providing for the continuation of a landlord-tenant relationship beyond the death of the tenant for the benefit of a "family member" (*Familienangehöriger*) living in a "joint household" (*gemeinsamer Hausstand*) with the tenant, is inapplicable even by way of analogy to ". . . same-sex partnerships and such live-in communities which are entered into for a limited period of time only . . .".[32] This was new reasoning for the Supreme Court which, only a few years before, still referred to ". . . the living together of unmarried persons of the same or of different sexes in a quasi-marital

[30] See BVerfGE 87, 234, 264.

[31] See *Entscheidungen des Bundesgerichtshofes in Zivilsachen* (BGHZ) 121, 116; Stintzing, [1994] *Juristische Schulung* (JuS) 550; Heinz, [1994] *Juristische Rundschau* (JR) 89, 91. See also *Verwaltungsgerichtshof* (VGH) Mannheim (Administrative Court of Appeal), [1993] NJW 2888; AG Berlin-Wedding, [1994] NJW-RR (*Rechtsprechungs-Report*) 524; LG Hannover, [1993] FamRZ 547; AG Nürnberg, [1994] *Streit* 185.

[32] This reasoning was applied by the German courts in the case that became *Röösli* v. *Germany* (No. 28381/95) (15 May 1996), 85 D.R. 149 (European Commission of Human Rights) (inadmissible). See Wintemute, chap. 40.

partnership . . .".[33] However, the more recent "different-sex only" interpretation, which has been supported[34] and criticised[35] in legal writings, has been followed by other courts.[36]

As a matter of substance, it is submitted, the Supreme Court's new approach is less convincing, and inconsistencies can be found in social welfare law. For example, it is said that the income of a claimant's same-sex partner also has to be taken into account in assessing a claim for social assistance, because otherwise same-sex partners would receive preferential treatment compared with married couples. This would be contrary to the principle of protection of marriage against competing forms of partnership. A similar approach could apply to obligations imposed by private law. An obvious example may be found in Paragraph 1579.7 BGB, under which financial support after termination of marriage may be excluded if the beneficiary is living together with a new partner in a non-marital partnership. Certainly, it should not make a difference if, for instance, the divorced wife entitled to support is now in partnership with another woman instead of a man, if the partner is providing her subsistence. Inconsistencies with regard to social welfare and private law *obligations* could then be used to argue that the few social welfare and private law *rights* of unmarried different-sex cohabitants should apply to same-sex partners.

LEGISLATIVE REFORM

After the substantial failure of attempts to achieve improved treatment or comprehensive legal recognition for same-sex partnerships through litigation, the focus has necessarily shifted to possibilities for legislative reform. In Germany's federal system, most of the matters of concern to same-sex partners fall within the legislative power of the Federation. This means that legislation by a German *Land* (state, region) would be of little significance. For example, the so-called "Hamburg marriage", introduced by a statute of the German *Land* of Hamburg in 1999,[37] and open only to same-sex couples, has mainly symbolic value. Registration under the Hamburg law does not create legal consequences similar to marriage.

At the federal level, all bills introduced in the *Bundestag* (the lower house of the German Parliament) during the Christian Democrat-Free Democrat coalition government from 1982 to 1998 failed to secure the necessary parliamentary majority. This was the case for bills by the Greens to open marriage to same-sex

[33] See BGHZ 92, 213, 219.

[34] See Medicus, [1993] *Juristenzeitung* (JZ) 952–3.

[35] See Schumacher, [1994] FamRZ 857, 860; Merschmeier, [1994] *Zeitschrift für Miet- und Raumrecht* (ZMR) 13.

[36] See e.g. BSG, [1997] NJW 2620.

[37] *Gesetz über die Eintragung gleichgeschlechtlicher Partnerschaften* of 14 April 1999, [1999] *Gesetz- und Verordnungsblatt Hamburg* 69.

couples,[38] and by the Greens[39] and the Social Democrats[40] to create a new institution of registered partnership or prohibit discrimination based on sexual orientation. But the sponsors of these bills, a small group of politicians who are either homosexual themselves, or heterosexual and sensitive to the difficulties encountered by homosexual couples, managed to gain lasting political attention for the subject, thus paving the way for future legislation.

After the September 1998 elections, a coalition of Social Democrats and Greens formed the new federal government. During their respective election campaigns, both parties had emphasised their commitment to policies of concern to gay and lesbian voters. In particular, both had promised to initiate legislative activity to establish equal treatment for same-sex partnerships. A first bill, drafted by the Federal Ministry of Justice under its head, Ms Herta Däubler-Gmelin, was launched in early January 2000. It was criticised by interest groups of gays and lesbians for not going far enough.[41] This led to a new proposal by both the Social Democrats and the Greens in the summer of 2000, which was split into two bills, one containing provisions that could constitutionally be adopted by the *Bundestag* on its own, and the other containing provisions requiring the assent of the German Parliament's upper house, the *Bundesrat*.

The *Bundestag* adopted both bills on 10 November 2000. The first bill became law on 16 February 2001 as the *Gesetz zur Beendigung der Diskriminierung gleichgeschlechtlicher Gemeinschaften: Lebenspartnerschaften*[42] (Law on Ending Discrimination Against Same-Sex Communities: Life Partnerships), and entered into force on 1 August 2001.[43] The Law provides for the creation of a new concept ("legal institute") of family law, a "life partnership" (*Lebenspartnerschaft*), open only to same-sex couples and requiring registration. Life partnerships are governed by a combination of rules in Article 1 of the Law, known as the *Gesetz über die Eingetragene Lebenspartnerschaft* (*Lebenspartnerschaftsgesetz*–LPartG) (Law on Registered Life Partnership, or Life Partnership Law); amendments to the Civil Code in Article 2 of the Law; and amendments to sixty-one other federal statutes and decrees in Article 3 of the Law. Many of these amendments insert the new category "life partner" ("*Lebenspartner*") after the existing category "spouse" ("*Ehegatten*").

The combination of rules in these three Articles cover the requirement of official registration, the family name used by the partners, the applicable matrimonial property regime, separation of the couple, mutual financial support obligations, limited rights of care and custody of children in such a partnership

[38] BT-Drs. 11/7197, BT-Drs. 12/7885, BT-Drs. 13/2728.

[39] BT-Drs. 11/7197, BT-Drs 13/7228, BT-Drs. 13/9706.

[40] BT-Drs. 13/100081.

[41] See *Die Tageszeitung* (6 Jan. 2000), pp. 1, 12.

[42] [2001] 9 *Bundesgesetzblatt* 266 (22 Feb. 2001), http://www.bundesanzeiger.de/bgbl1f/b1findex.htm; [2001] FamRZ 399.

[43] For a first review, see Schwab, [2001] FamRZ 385. See also K Muscheler, *Das Recht der Eingetragenen Lebenspartnerschaft* (Bielefeld, Erich Schmidt Verlag, 2001).

(without creating a right to second-parent or joint adoption), and even the creation of a family relationship both between the partners and between each partner and the other partner's family (thus creating parents- and siblings-in-law). These rules also remove any existing forms of legal discrimination in relation to the law of tenancy, the legal regime for succession (inheritance), the law concerning immigration of non-German partners, and benefits under the public health insurance and nursing care insurance schemes.

The second bill, the *Lebenspartnerschaftsgesetzergänzungsgesetz* (LPartGErG) (Life Partnerships Law Amendment Law),[44] contains those provisions that require the assent of the *Bundesrat* under German constitutional law. This is the case in particular for provisions on use of the same registry offices as for marriage; on income tax, real estate transfer tax, and inheritance tax; on amendments to the civil service law, including benefits provided by the State to civil servants in case of illness or certain other events; and on social assistance and public housing benefits. As was to be expected, the second bill was rejected by the more conservative *Bundesrat* on 1 December 2000, and must now be renegotiated in the inter-parliamentary mediation committee, the *Vermittlungsausschuß*.

Academic writers almost without exception, both in constitutional and in family law, take a highly critical view of the Law passed by the *Bundestag*.[45] Needless to say, it is also highly disputed politically. While it is considered by the relevant interest groups and associations to be a first step in the right direction, three *Länder* (Bavaria, Saxony and Thuringia) have launched actions in the Federal Constitutional Court, seeking a declaration that the *Bundestag*'s Law is unconstitutional and therefore invalid. The main issue for the Court will be whether Article 6(1) GG requires the federal legislature to preserve a legal difference (or, as it is called in the debate, a "distance") between different-sex marriage and same-sex life partnerships.

As long as the provisions of the second bill before the *Bundesrat*, which would award essential legal benefits to same-sex life partnerships, have not been enacted, there will obviously exist such a "distance" between life partnerships and marriage. If the second bill is passed, there will still remain differences between life partnerships and marriage, greater than those between registered partnerships and marriage in the Scandinavian countries. For example, second-parent or joint adoption of children will not be possible for life partners, donor insemination will not be available to lesbian life partners, and life partners will not receive the same tax benefits as married partners. These differences could still be sufficiently great to permit the Court easily to reject the *Länder*'s argument.[46]

[44] See http://www.lsvd.de/recht/index.html (*Lebenspartnerschaftsgesetz*).

[45] See Diederichsen, [2000] NJW 1841; Scholz/Uhle, [2001] NJW 393; Finger, [2001] MDR 1999; Sachs, [2001] JR S. 45; J Braun, [2001] ZRP 14.

[46] The Court refused (5-3) to enjoin the entry into force of the 16 Feb. 2001 law on 1 Aug. 2001 (*Urteil* of 18 July 2001, 1 BvQ 23/01, 1 BvQ 26/01), and (3-0) to hold that Bavaria's intention not to implement the law until the autumn of 2001 violated the Constitution (*Beschluss* of 9 August 2001, 1 BvR 1262/01). See *supra* n.44 or http://www.bverfg.de.

33

From Individual Protection to Recognition of Relationships? Same-Sex Couples and the Irish Experience of Sexual Orientation Law Reform

LEO FLYNN*

WITHOUT BEING WILDLY optimistic, it is clear that the legal situation of same-sex couples in Ireland is on the cusp of major change. In October 1999, a new Equality Authority was established in order to enforce the Employment Equality Act, 1998, which prohibits discrimination in public and private employment relating to nine protected statuses, including that of sexual orientation. Six months later, the Authority was empowered to enforce the Equal Status Act, 2000, which prohibits discrimination on the same grounds in the public and private provision of goods, services, housing and education. Yet, sexual activity between males had only been decriminalised in 1993, and "sexual orientation" had first appeared in Irish legislation only in 1989, in the Prohibition of Incitement to Hatred Act. In the decade which followed that first step towards equality of social and economic participation in Irish life for all persons, regardless of their sexual orientation, a rolling programme of legislative and policy reform has made the legal position of lesbian, gay and bisexual individuals stronger than would have seemed imaginable. As of 2001, only a few of these changes have effected same-sex couples, rather than their individual members, but the status of such couples is now on the agenda, both for groups lobbying for legal and political reform, and for policy-makers and legislators. This chapter will examine this evolution and attempt to identify the pressure points where future change may come about.

* Legal Secretary, Court of Justice of the European Communities, Luxembourg; Lecturer, School of Law, King's College London. I am very grateful to Christopher Robson for his comments and for the information which he supplied. All views expressed are personal to the author.

AN UNPROMISING CONSTITUTIONAL FRAMEWORK

What makes the recent developments in Irish law all the more extraordinary is that one starts from what appears to be, in legal terms, rocky ground. The 1937 Constitution of Ireland, *Búnreacht na h-Éireann*, was in many ways a progressive document for its time. Almost alone among the European States revising their basic laws in the 1930s, it enshrined a separation of powers, instituted judicial review of legislation's constitutionality, and entrenched a bill of personal rights. The most important of the latter provisions, for present purposes, are those regarding non-discrimination (Article 40.1),[1] personal rights (Article 40.3) and the family (Article 41).

Article 40.1 is the first provision in the Constitution dealing with fundamental rights and provides that:

> "40.1 All citizens shall, as human persons, be held equal before the law. This shall not mean that the State shall not in its enactments have due regard to differences of capacity, physical and moral, and of social function".

Constitutional litigation based on this equality guarantee has achieved relatively little. There are positive decisions, such as *de Búrca* v. *Attorney General*[2] (finding the exclusion of women from obligatory jury service unconstitutional) and *O'G.* v. *Attorney General*[3] (striking down legislation precluding widowers but not widows from adopting children). However, these rulings are more than off-set by the approach taken under the Constitution to other equality claims, for example, disability discrimination in *Draper* v. *Attorney General.*[4] The Constitution's limited effect is the result of the "thin" nature of the equality guarantee contained in Article 40.1, which has been held to cover only essential aspects of the human personality, as opposed to incidental activities in which individuals may be engaged,[5] and also of the substantial weight which the Constitution gives to competing interests such as property.[6]

The personal rights of the individual are dealt with by Article 40.3 which states that:

> "40.3.1 The State guarantees in its laws to respect, and, as far as practicable, by its law to defend and vindicate the personal rights of the citizen.

[1] The May 1996 *Report of the Constitution Review Group* recommended (at p. 230) that a list of prohibited grounds of discrimination, including sexual orientation, be added to Art. 40.1.

[2] [1976] Irish Reports (IR) 38. (All decisions are of the Irish Supreme Court unless otherwise indicated.)

[3] [1985] Irish Law Reports Monthly (IRLM) 61 (High Court).

[4] [1984] IR 277, finding no unconstitutional discrimination in the non-existence of special provisions enabling physically incapacitated persons to vote in *Dáil* (parliamentary) elections.

[5] See, generally, T Murphy, "Economic Inequality and the Constitution", in Murphy & Twomey (eds.), *Ireland's Evolving Constitution: 1937–1997* (Oxford, Hart Publishing, 1998) at 163.

[6] See, e.g., *In the matter of Article 26 of the Constitution and in the matter of the Equal Status Bill 1997*, [1997] 2 IR 387.

> 40.3.2 The State shall, in particular, by its law protect as best it may from unjust attack and, in the case of injustice done, vindicate the life, person, good name, and property rights of every citizen".

Courts have used this Article to identify a series of personal rights which are not expressly enumerated in the Constitution's text,[7] amongst which is that of individual privacy.[8]

The fundamental rights provision of the Constitution which most closely reflects the ethos of the period when it was adopted is Article 41:

> "41.1.1 The State recognises the Family as the natural primary and fundamental unit group of Society, and as a moral institution possessing inalienable and imprescriptible rights, antecedent and superior to all positive law.
> 41.1.2 The State, therefore, guarantees to protect the Family in its constitution and authority, as the necessary basis of social order and as indispensable to the welfare of the Nation and the State.
> 41.2.1 In particular, the State recognises that by her life within the home, woman gives to the State a support without which the common good cannot be achieved.
> 41.2.2 The State shall, therefore, endeavour to ensure that mothers shall not be obliged by economic necessity to engage in labour to the neglect of their duties in the home.
> 41.3.1 The State pledges itself to guard with special care the institution of Marriage, on which the Family is founded and to protect it against attack. . .".

While the family protected by the Constitution is not specifically defined therein, its contours can be fairly readily determined by looking at the provision as a whole. It is unsurprising therefore that, in *Murray* v. *Ireland*,[9] Costello J considered that the constitutional meaning of marriage was derived from the Christian notion of "a partnership based on an irrevocable personal consent given by both spouses which establishes a unique and very special life-long relationship". The same approach was taken in *Murphy* v. *Ireland*,[10] where Hamilton J stated:

> "[T]he pledge of [Article 41.3.1] to guard with special care the institution of marriage is a guarantee that this institution in all its constitutional connotations, including the pledge given in Article 41.2.2 as to the position of the mother in the home, will be given special protection so that it will continue to fulfil its function as the basis of the family and as a permanent, indissoluble union of man and woman".[11]

It seems that the State is required to ensure that there is at least neutrality between marital and non-marital families, and is permitted to take positive action in favour of the former.[12] The existing constitutional provisions embody,

[7] *Ryan* v. *Attorney General*, [1965] IR 294.
[8] *Kennedy* v. *Ireland*, [1987] IR 587.
[9] [1985] IR 532 (High Court).
[10] [1982] IR 241.
[11] These references to the indissolubility of marriage must be read in light of the constitutional prohibition of divorce, formerly contained in Art. 41.3.2 but removed in 1995.
[12] See *The State (Nicolaou)* v. *An Bord Uchtála*, [1966] IR 567; *G.* v. *An Bord Uchtála*, [1980] IR 32; *O'B.* v. *S.*, [1984] IR 316.

moreover, static and essentialist conceptions of both femininity and masculinity, making them of, at best, limited use in any litigation or lobbying strategy concerned with same-sex couples.[13]

Against this background, it is not surprising to learn that the 1984 challenge to the constitutionality of Victorian-era legislation criminalising all forms of male-male sexual activity in *Norris* v. *Attorney General* was unsuccessful.[14] A minority of the Supreme Court was prepared to accept the challenge, based on the individual's right to privacy and to equality before the law with other individuals, such as fornicators and adulterers, whose behaviour, although immoral and inimical to the institution of marriage, is not penalised. The majority of the Court's members, however, took the view that to permit such behaviour would be to undermine directly the position of marriage. The Supreme Court, ruling by a three to two majority, accordingly found that these rights to privacy and equality could not be successfully invoked against sodomy and indecency legislation which penalised male-male sexual activity only.[15]

PIECE MEAL LEGISLATIVE REFORM

Following the failure of his action in the Irish courts, David Norris submitted an application against the State to the European Commission of Human Rights, claiming that the criminalisation of sexual activity between men under Irish law infringed the European Convention on Human Rights. He was ultimately successful in 1988, with the European Court of Human Rights ruling eight to six that his right to privacy under Article 8 had been infringed.[16] The result was unsurprising, as the same legislation had been found to violate the Convention in an earlier case brought regarding the Northern Irish legal system.[17] Notwithstanding this ruling, the criminal law remained unchanged in Ireland until 1993, and it is arguable that, in the ultimate decision to repeal that legislation and establish a partly equal age of consent, the Convention played a relatively minor role.[18] While this assertion may seem surprising, in that the

[13] See Y Scannell, "The Constitution and the Role of Women", in Farrell (ed.), *De Valera's Constitution and Ours* (Dublin, Gill & McMillan, 1988) at 123; A Connelly, "The Constitution", in Connelly (ed.), *Gender and the Law in Ireland* (Dublin, Oak Tree Press, 1993) at 4; L Flynn, "To Be an Irish Man: Constructions of Masculinity Within the Constitution", in Murphy & Twomey *supra* n.5, at 135.

[14] [1984] IR 36, rejecting the argument that legislation penalising sexual conduct between males, but not sexual conduct between females, was an unconstitutional discrimination.

[15] See further L Flynn, "The Irish Supreme Court and the Constitution of Male Homosexuality", in Herman and Stychin (eds.), *Legal Inversions: Lesbians, Gay Men and the Politics of Law* (Philadelphia, Temple University Press, 1995) at 29.

[16] *Norris* v. *Ireland* (26 Oct. 1988), Series A, No. 142, 13 European Human Rights Reports (EHRR) 146.

[17] *Dudgeon* v. *United Kingdom* (22 Oct. 1981), Series A, No. 45, 4 EHRR 149.

[18] See L Flynn, "Ireland", in Conor Gearty (ed.), *European Civil Liberties and the European Convention on Human Rights* (Dordrecht, Kluwer Law International, 1997) at 200–2.

Council of Europe would eventually have required repeal (while permitting a clearly unequal age of consent), it is more easily understood when one points out that, by 1993, legislative measures had already been adopted, or were about to be adopted, making sexual orientation a protected status in several fields, including that of dismissal. These measures made decriminalisation and a partly equal age of consent much less controversial. In addition, David Norris had become a member of the upper house of the Irish parliament, the *Seanád*, elected from the university constituency of Trinity College, Dublin, where he was a lecturer in English.

The presence of Senator Norris was undoubtedly of assistance in procuring legislative changes. For example, in 1989 he proposed amendments to include sexual orientation as one of several protected grounds in legislation which prohibited hate speech, and regulated the sale and showing of video recordings which would incite hatred.[19] However, he was not acting alone. In 1988, as the Strasbourg judgment was being handed down in *Norris*, the umbrella group GLEN ("Gay and Lesbian Equality Network") was formed in order to coordinate the response of the lesbian and gay community to the judgment, and to campaign for wider reforms giving the community equality of opportunity, participation and outcome within Irish society.[20] GLEN had a relatively simple agenda, to achieve equality, but it devised a long-term strategy to achieve this goal, based on individual measures and specific advances, as well as coalition-building with trade unions, non-governmental organisations, political parties and lobbying groups representing other disadvantaged groups, such as women, the disabled community, and the travelling community. This desire to present a common front did not, however, prevent the formation of LOT ("Lesbians Organising Together"), a group whose activities are directed at celebrating lesbian difference and addressing the social, economic and legal problems experienced by lesbians; nor did the creation of this group diminish the sense of shared interest in the outcome of GLEN's activities.

While obtaining an appropriate implementation of the *Norris* judgment was an immediate goal, one of the leading figures in GLEN commented that the move to equal protection in labour law was a more important development, and would have been the first choice of GLEN, if a choice had to be made.[21] In fact, the two objectives were realised more or less simultaneously. In July 1993, the Criminal Justice (Sexual Offences) Act abolished all legal rules, both legislative and common law, criminalising sexual activities between men, so that consensual sexual activity between all persons above seventeen years is lawful. There is still, however, not full equality in this field, in part because the age of consent for marriage is fifteen years, and consensual sexual activity within marriage is

[19] See Prohibition of Incitement to Hatred Act, 1989, ss. 2, 3; Video Recordings Act, 1989, s. 3(1)(a)(ii).

[20] See C Robson, "Anatomy of a Campaign", in O'Carroll & Collins (eds.), *Lesbian and Gay Visions of Ireland: Towards the Twenty-First Century* (London, Routledge, 1995) at 47–59.

[21] *Ibid.*, at footnotes 19, 54.

lawful.[22] The Unfair Dismissals (Amendment) Act, adopted in July 1993 only a week after the criminal law reform, made it unautomatically unfair to dismiss a worker on grounds of their sexual orientation, with sexual orientation being one of several protected statuses, including gender, age, disability, race and membership of the travelling community.[23] The scope of this protection will be examined in greater detail in the context of the more recent prohibition of such discrimination in all aspects of the employment relationship. A final measure which is worth mentioning at this point is the Immigration and Asylum Act, 1997, as a result of which sexual orientation is recognised as a protected status in respect of asylum.

The legislation adopted between 1989 and 1997 was intended to extend protection for individuals; to the extent that the partners in a same-sex relationship are protected, it is only as individuals. There are two exceptions: the Domestic Violence Act, 1995, and the Powers of Attorney Act, 1995. Lesbian and gay couples are recognised, as are all non-marital couples, for the purposes of domestic violence legislation, which allows a Safety Order or an Interim Protection Order to be granted to an applicant who "resides with respondent in a relationship the basis of which is not contractual".[24] They are similarly implicitly incorporated with other non-marital couples for the purpose of nominating another person to have the power of attorney. However, in relation to fiscal and social welfare matters, housing rights and family law rights in general, there is no specific recognition given to non-marital couples at present. Lone parents, whether married or unmarried, have certain rights in relation to custody, guardianship and state support, but their unmarried partners have no statutory family rights. And while there is no reported case-law which indicates a bias against, for example, lesbian mothers in child custody disputes against their husbands, former husbands or former male partners, there is a strong perception amongst such women that any public manifestation of their sexual orientation, especially the presence of a female partner, may jeopardise the conditions on which they have custody.

THE EMPLOYMENT EQUALITY ACT, 1998

The piece meal reform of the early and mid-1990s has been succeeded by more comprehensive and far-reaching legislation on equality. Two linked bills were passed by the Irish parliament in 1996 and 1997, the first on employment equality and the second on "equal status" (the provision of goods, services, housing

[22] See further J Kingston, "Sex and Sexuality under the European Convention on Human Rights" in L Heffernan (ed.), *Human Rights: A European Prospective* (Dublin, Round Hall Press, 1994) at 186–8.

[23] In fact, those working in the public sector were already protected against such discrimination under the HIV and Sexual Orientation Protection Codes for Public Workers adopted in 1988.

[24] Domestic Violence Act, 1996, s. 2(1)(iv).

and education).[25] This legislative package expanded the number of protected grounds from two, sex and marital status, to nine, including sexual orientation. At the same time, its material scope was expanded as much as its personal scope, from only public and private employment, in the case of the two original grounds, to the public and private provision of goods, services, housing and education. However, both bills were referred to the Supreme Court by the President, exercising her powers under Article 26 of the Constitution, to determine if any of their provisions were unconstitutional. The Supreme Court subsequently declared that certain aspects of the Employment Equality Bill were repugnant to the Constitution.[26] It constituted an unjust attack on employers' property rights, requiring them to bear the cost of special treatment or facilities for people with disabilities, unless the employer could show that this burden caused it undue hardship. It also violated employers' rights in the manner that it imposed vicarious liability for the criminal conduct of their employees. The Equal Status Bill was later struck down because of its analogous provisions.[27]

Both bills were later re-introduced with the amendments necessary to ensure that they would survive constitutional scrutiny.[28] The constitutional difficulties having been resolved, the Employment Equality Act was adopted in June 1998 and came into effect in October 1999. The Equal Status Bill was adopted in April 2000. As the first broad equality measure to come into force, the provisions of the Employment Equality Act will be examined in relation to sexual orientation and the situation of same-sex couples.

The 1998 Act contains seven parts: Parts 1 and 2 deal with technical and definitional matters, Parts 3 and 4 with the substantive provisions prohibiting discrimination on gender and non-gender grounds respectively, and Parts 5, 6 and 7 with the establishment of an Equality Authority and new procedures, remedies and enforcement. The specific provisions as to equality between women and men are dealt with in a different Part of the Act (Part 3) from those concerned with the other protected statuses (Part 4). This separation is the consequence of the decision to give a lower standard of protection to the other grounds than that which is necessitated by European Community legislation on sex discrimination. For example, there is no limit on the amount of compensation which can be awarded for gender discrimination, while a cap is placed on other forms of discrimination, unless they constitute indirect gender discrimination.[29] Similarly, while a complaint based on gender may be taken directly to

[25] Prior to the Equal Status Act, 2000, special arrangements to ensure non-discrimination in relation to sexual orientation in the provision of services existed only for health insurance. See Health Insurance Act, 1994, ss. 7, 8.

[26] *In the matter of Article 26 of the Constitution and in the matter of the Employment Equality Bill 1996*, [1997] 2 IR 321.

[27] *Supra* n.6.

[28] The necessary adjustments have led to critical comments on the adequacy of the legislation, in particular as concerns disability discrimination. See D O'Connell, *Equality Now: The SIPTU Guide to the Employment Equality Act, 1998* (Dublin, SIPTU, 1999) at 11, 34.

[29] S. 88.

the courts, where the complaint is based on the other grounds it must be pursued initially through the Director of Equality Investigations, unless that complaint arises from a dismissal.[30] Because of these advantages, there may be good reason in some circumstances to attempt to frame a sexual orientation discrimination claim in terms of direct or indirect sex discrimination, although given the precedents from the Court of Justice of the European Communities,[31] and from national decisions,[32] such arguments are unlikely to be successful.

The 1998 Act creates an entitlement to equal pay for the same work, equal work or work of equal value, irrespective of the worker's sexual orientation.[33] Sexual orientation is defined as "heterosexual, homosexual or bisexual orientation".[34] The Act also introduces an equality clause related to non-gender issues, including sexual orientation, into all employment contracts, whether individual or collective, in respect of all matters other than pay.[35] The Act also precludes indirect discrimination on grounds, *inter alia*, of sexual orientation by employers and professional regulatory bodies.[36] However, for non-gender grounds, it is possible for an employer to show that a practice is not indirectly discriminatory, notwithstanding its adverse impact, if the practice in question is "reasonable in all the circumstances". To defeat a claim of indirect gender discrimination, it must show that the practice "cannot be justified by objective factors unrelated to [. . .] sex" (the EC law test).[37] The Act also specifically outlaws harassment in the workplace based on sexual orientation.[38] While positive action is permitted to facilitate workplace integration for older people, people with disabilities and members of the travelling community, sexual orientation is not a basis for positive action, although the Act provides that the State is not precluded from directing training programmes or work experience schemes towards specific disadvantaged groups.[39]

The Act contains a number of savings and exceptions which are of relevance to sexual orientation, and specifically to same-sex couples. Section 34(1) provides that the prohibition of non-gender discrimination does not make it unlawful for an employer to provide: (i) a benefit to an employee in respect of events related to members of the employee's family or any description of those members; (ii) a benefit to or in respect of a person as a member of an employee's

[30] S. 77.

[31] See Case C-490/96, *Grant* v. *South-West Trains Ltd*, [1998] ECR I-621. See further L Flynn, "Equality Between Men and Women in the Court of Justice", (1999) 19 *Yearbook of European Law* 259 at 280.

[32] See Employment Equality Officer Recommendation (EEO)12/1993, *Brookfield Leisure Centre* v. *A Worker*. See further L Flynn, "No Gay People Need Apply", (1994) 16 *Dublin University Law Journal* 180.

[33] S. 29.

[34] S. 3(1).

[35] S. 30.

[36] S. 31.

[37] S. 22(1)(c).

[38] S. 32.

[39] S. 33.

family; (iii) a benefit to an employee on or by reference to an event occasioning a change in the marital status of the employee; or (iv) to an employee who has a family status, a benefit intended directly to provide or assist in the provision, during working hours, of care for a person for whom the employee has responsibility. The final element of section 34(1) saves measures which are designed to allow employees holding a family status in relation to another person to take time off work; in essence, this allows for flexible work arrangements for carers in relation to children or people with disabilities requiring continuing, regular or frequent care. It could be used by an employer to offer an employee the opportunity to look after her or his same-sex partner, if the latter has a disability.

However, the first three exceptions in section 34(1) are directed at the traditional family and are less responsive to the needs of same-sex couples. Employers are, for example, entitled to provide marriage gratuities, provided that there is no gender discrimination, or to offer benefits to the children of employees. "Members of the family" is narrowly defined in the legislation as a person's spouse or the brother, sister, uncle, aunt, nephew, niece, lineal ancestor or lineal descendant of that person or their spouse.[40] It was proposed during the parliamentary debates that the definition of family member be expanded to include partners, or at least co-habiting partners, but this suggestion was not accepted. Because a same-sex partner is not, therefore, a member of the family, it would not be possible to argue that the denial of a spousal benefit to such a partner constituted impermissible discrimination on grounds of sexual orientation. Indeed, section 34 reverses the situation under the previous legislation, under which a refusal to give spousal benefits to the opposite-sex partners of unmarried employees had been held to be unlawful discrimination on grounds of marital status.[41] Moreover, the legislation does not define what is meant by a "benefit", which may lead to interpretation problems in cases where a person in a same-sex relationship is treated less favourably than a married co-worker.

The other exception which may prove to be significant for members of same-sex couples is section 37(1)(a), which provides that a religious, educational or medical institution which is under the direction or control of a body established for religious purposes, or whose objectives include the provision of services in an environment which promotes certain religious values, shall not be taken to discriminate if it takes action which is reasonably necessary to prevent an employee or prospective employee from undermining the religious ethos of that institution. The scope of this provision (which seems to have influenced the equivalent exception in the 2000 EC Directive on sexual orientation discrimination in employment)[42] is not clear. Given the traditionally extensive involvement of religious groups, primarily from the larger Christian denominations, in the provision of education and medical services in Ireland, its impact could be widespread. Section 37(1)(b) could, for example, permit a refusal to employ a

[40] S. 2(1).
[41] See EEO 12/1995, *Doyle* v. *Eagle Star Insurance Ltd.*
[42] See Bell, chap. 37.

prospective employee by an institution with a religious ethos because she or he is living with a same-sex partner, although the compatability of this approach with the constitutional rights to privacy and to earn a livelihood has been called into question.[43] This scenario assumes that some forms of homosexual conduct, including establishing a relationship with someone of the same sex, are incompatible with the religious ethos of certain institutions. However, it is unclear whether the status of an individual, that is the fact that they are lesbian, homosexual or bisexual untranslated into conduct of any kind, can similarly be the basis of action by an employer under section 37.

There is already case-law under the pre-1993 unfair dismissals legislation to the effect that "an employee's conduct in sexual matters outside the place of employment may justify dismissal if it can be shown that it is capable of damaging the employer's business".[44] While this approach can be criticised as an unnecessarily wide statement going beyond the authorities on which it is based,[45] it would permit an employer to argue that to dismiss an individual whose lifestyle was disapproved of by customers or fellow employees was based, not on sexual orientation, but on the conduct of the individual, which is a potentially fair ground of dismissal. However, this argument, even taken on its own terms, would require the employer to provide evidence that similar action would have been taken against another worker of a different sexual orientation engaging in the same conduct. Moreover, the status/conduct distinction is usually artifical and tends to dilute the scope of protection offered to individuals, making it incompatible with an interpretation permitting the Act's effective implementation.

FURTHER LEGISLATIVE REFORMS AND SAME-SEX COUPLES

The Equal Status Act, 2000 complements the Employment Equality Act in relation to the the public and private provision of goods, services, housing and education. A few of its provisions are worthy of comment. It is interesting to note that one of the services which is covered by the Act is becoming an adoptive or foster parent. The only exemption is for an age requirement,[46] so that sexual orientation discrimination is, by necessary implication, precluded in that field. There is no provision in Irish law for joint adoption by couples, other than married couples, but an unmarried individual could adopt a child.[47] If they have a

[43] O'Connell, *supra* n.28, at 70. However, because the Unfair Dismissals Act 1977, as amended in 1993, makes dismissal on the basis of sexual orientation automatically unfair, and provides no exception analogous to s. 37(1)(b), it seems that such an institution would be precluded from dismissing the individual *on that ground only*. Whether a person could be dismissed for misleading the employer by not disclosing their sexual orientation is a question which may have to be examined.

[44] *Flynn* v. *Sister of the Holy Faith*, [1985] ILRM 336 at 341 (Costello J, High Court).

[45] See L Flynn, "Discrimination on grounds of sexual orientation", (1993) 4 *Employment Law Reports* xxvii at xxviii.

[46] S. 5(2)(j).

[47] Adoption Act, 1991, s. 10(2).

same-sex partner, their partner would have no parental rights or duties in relation to the child. However, the possibility of individual adoption is of limited practical importance, given the low number of children adopted or fostered in Ireland. The Act contains a provision which parallels section 34(1) of the 1998 Act by permitting the imposition of "a reasonable preferential fee, charge or rate in respect of anything offered or provided to or in respect of persons together with their children, married couples, persons in a specific age group or persons with a disability".[48] Thus, while it is possible to have, for example, special discounts for married couples, no similar obligation would arise in respect of partners, including same-sex partners.

However, to look at equality questions primarily through the prism of partnership issues is problematic in the Irish context. As articulated through GLEN, the focus of reform efforts is currently on the experiences of poverty and exclusion and the health concerns of lesbians and gay men. This agenda has had some success in placing issues of exclusion and their links to disadvantage and poverty on the agenda of policy-makers, both nationally and locally. Government-funded research and development work carried out through groups such as GLEN and LOT has identified a series of problems and strategies for tackling them. Moreover, legal recognition of partners has not been a significant item for discussion by lesbians and gay men to date. There is little sign at present of a consensus within the lesbian and gay community that same-sex couples should be seeking the right to contract marriages, or the right to register their relationships, or recognition in a functional fashion where specific difficulties arise. Indeed, debate on these questions has been rather muted to date. A forum on this question was organised by the Equality Authority early in 2001 as part of a process which will lead to proposals from it to the government later this year. However, it remains far from clear that marriage, registered partnership, or some other regime to recognise same-sex relationships is a generally agreed goal in Ireland.

Where strategic initiatives to obtain equality can be undertaken, the lack of a defined goal as to the overall legal position of same-sex couples has not been a hindrance. In part, this may be because such couples in Ireland can be readily compared with many opposite-sex couples who are unable to marry each other, even if willing to do so. Divorce only became possible in Ireland in 1995, and the legislation governing termination of marriage is restrictive, requiring that the spouses be separated for five years before proceedings may be initiated. As a result, there are many heterosexual long-term relationships where one or both partners are already married to someone else, for whom divorce may not be an immediate prospect. By making common cause with this group, and seeking to obtain benefits currently confined to married couples, it is possible for same-sex couples to improve their legal situation.

[48] S. 16(1).

A good example of this strategy can be seen in relation to Capital Acquisition Tax. Where on the death of one partner ownership of the home is transferred to the other, the survivor takes the first 12,700 Euros tax-free, and is subject to 40 per cent tax on the value of the property above that amount. Because of urban asset-inflation over recent years, particularly in Dublin, this system means that the death of a partner requires the survivor to sell the home to pay the tax debt which arises. In contrast, a surviving spouse takes the home without incurring any tax liability. Following lobbying and some debate in the *Séanad*, the Minister of Finance made a commitment to revise the relevant legislation in order to change this situation, and thereby improve the position of all unmarried cohabiting couples.[49] As a result, in the 2000 Budget, the Minister introduced the Principal Residence Benefit, which allows an individual to receive a gift or inheritance of a residential property free from capital acquisition tax on certain conditions, chiefly that the premises were the beneficiary's principal private residence for three years prior to the gift or inheritance.

EXTERNAL SOURCES OF CHANGE

The sources of change traced and examined above have been, for the most part, internal to the Irish legal and political system. However, as a small, English-speaking island on the edge of Europe, Irish society is perhaps particularly susceptible to external influence. At a very basic level, the changing demographic situation of the State may well create the conditions in which pressure for the recognition of alternative family forms grows. Unlike the experience of constant emigration for most of the twentieth century (with the exception of a brief period between 1965 and 1980), net immigration to Ireland has run at some 22,000 per annum since 1990. Moreover, since 1970, emigration has been a less permanent experience than was previously the case, and many Irish people who go to work abroad return to Ireland. This is equally true (if not more so) of lesbians and gay men, whose experiences abroad influence the formation of expectations and aspirations within Ireland. Moreover, as more of the State's European partners permit the registration of same-sex partnerships, the chances increase that Irish nationals will be involved in such relationships, or that couples who have registered their partnerships will immigrate.

These social factors aside, the international legal obligations of the State are also a potential source of change. One of the factors which led to decriminalisation of male-male sexual activity was the ruling of the European Court of Human Rights condemning Ireland's maintenance of legislation penalising such activity.[50] However, the ruling merely set a floor for legal reform, and left open

[49] See *Irish Times* (16 Sept. 1999). For a thorough survey of the legal status of same-sex couples in Irish Law, see J Mee & K Ronayne, *Report on Partnership Rights of Same-Sex Couples* (Dublin, Equality Authority, June 2000), http://www.equality.ie/pdf/SAMESEX.PDF.

[50] *Supra* n.16.

the possibility of a higher male-male age of consent, such as the age of twenty-one that prevailed in the United Kingdom in 1993. Instead, the domestic reform movement was able to achieve a partly equal age of of seventeen. In 2001, given that the European Court of Human Rights is unlikely to go beyond the existing legislative position in Ireland, the European Convention on Human Rights will probably not be a source of change in the medium-term.[51] The same could also be true of the machinery established under the International Covenant on Civil and Political Rights.[52]

There are some prospects of reform visible on the European Community horizon. It is worth noting that, during the periods it has held the Presidency of the Council, Ireland has pushed forward important measures making sexual orientation a Community issue. Ireland held the Presidency in 1990 when the Council adopted a "Resolution on the Protection of the Dignity of Women and Men at Work", which recognised that sexual orientation-based harassment at work might violate Community law.[53] More significantly, the first inclusion of sexual orientation in the draft of what became Article 13 of the EC Treaty, was achieved during the Irish Presidency during the 1996–97 Intergovernmental Conference.[54] The European Commission proposals to reform Community legislation on free movement of persons, so as to remove discrimination on grounds of sexual orientation, could provide a basis for the recognition of same-sex partnerships for the purposes of residence and employment rights for non-EEA-national partners of nationals of other Member States, and Irish nationals who have exercised their personal mobility rights.[55] The Directive on sexual orientation discrimination in employment, adopted on 27 November 2000,[56] does not go much beyond the framework established by the current Irish legislation, although on specific points, such as enforcement mechanisms and limits on monetary remedies, it could constitute an improvement.

CONCLUSION

The developments in the Irish legal system in relation to sexual orientation since 1989 are little short of phenomenal. The formal rules relating to lesbians, gay men and bisexuals are designed to engender public discourse in which homophobia is not permitted, and to foster respect and dignity for all persons, irrespective of their sexual orientation, in the workplace and in public and private transactions. However, where the relationships of lesbians and gay men

[51] But see Wintemute, chap. 40.
[52] But see Helfer, chap. 41.
[53] Official Journal [1990] C 157/3.
[54] See L Flynn, "The Implications of Article 13 EC: After Amsterdam, Will Some Forms of Discrimination Be More Equal than Others?", (1999) 36 *Common Market Law Review* 1127 at 1131–2; Bell, chap. 37.
[55] See Guild, chap. 38.
[56] See Bell, chap. 37.

encounter the law, they remain vulnerable in a way which is not true for married couples. As this chapter has tried to indicate, this is not necessarily direct sexual orientation discrimination, because all unmarried couples are equally poorly served. Moreover, the effective absence of divorce means that many unmarried heterosexual couples are, like lesbians and gay men, unable to marry the partner of their choice immediately. This failing in the legal system thus does not have such an obviously disparate impact as in other jurisdictions. However, unmarried heterosexual couples are faced with "marriage postponed", rather than "marriage denied", unlike their homosexual counterparts. Even if this shared disadvantage currently facilitates coalition-building to lobby for legal reform, it is, in the long-term, no real substitute for recognition of the relationships of same-sex couples.

It is hard to escape the feeling that such recognition will come in the Irish legal system in the medium-term. The dynamics of legal reform which have been described above are unlikely to settle down with the status quo. It may be that the example of other European States will eventually make it seem desirable to legislators and policy-makers that this step be taken. However, in view of the past record, it is more likely that the impetus for reform will be domestic.

34

Same-Sex Partnerships in English Family Law

REBECCA BAILEY-HARRIS*

INTRODUCTION

THE MERITS AND defects of the current law in any field must be measured by reference to the purposes which legal regulation is designed to achieve in that context. Hence the essential preliminary question is: why should the law regulate same-sex partnerships? The answer to that question in turn depends on the identification of the interests of the "stakeholders" concerned, namely the State and the family members themselves.

The State has a multiplicity of interests in the regulation of same-sex relationships, which include (in no particular order):

- the promotion of pluralism and party autonomy
- the promotion of equality[1] and equal access to legal rights
- the encouragement of stability in family life
- the safeguarding and promotion of the welfare of any children involved
- the achievement of economic justice between parties on the breakdown of a relationship
- the protection of the public purse through the effective enforcement of individual obligation

Any child brought up in a same-sex relationship has an unarguable right to the protection and promotion of his or her welfare and best interests. Adults who form relationships with members of the same sex have rights to:

- free choice and self-determination
- equal access to legal protection and to the law's institutions
- the enjoyment of mutual support in a stable family relationship
- protection from exploitation where a relationship is or was characterised by a power imbalance

* Professor of Law, University of Bristol.

[1] For an original and penetrating analysis of the nature of sex discrimination, see R Wintemute, "Recognising New Kinds of Direct Sex Discrimination: Transsexualism, Sexual Orientation and Dress Codes", (1997) 60 *Modern Law Review* 334.

- fairness in the resolution of the consequences of relationship breakdown.

It is not suggested that the interests of the State and of individual family members are antithetical, for a high degree of congruence is readily apparent. The extent—and limitations—on the right of individuals to choose their family life in a pluralist society were well encapsulated by the Australian Law Reform Commission:

> ". . . the law should not inhibit the formation of family relationships and should recognise as valid the relationships people choose for themselves. Further, the law should support and protect those relationships. However, the law should restrict a person's choice to the extent that it is necessary to protect the fundamental rights and freedoms of others . . ."[2]

Where there is internal conflict between the interests outlined above—reflecting a fundamental tension between party autonomy and State paternalism—social policy choices have to be made by lawmakers. The present writer has argued elsewhere[3] that the interests identified above do not differ according to the marital status or the sexual orientation of the couple in question. Whether this "mainstreaming" approach to the regulation of same-sex relationships is politically or ideologically acceptable to others is a question which will be raised later.

This chapter will present a critical analysis of the current law in England and Wales[4] on the regulation of same-sex partnerships, with a primary focus on family law.[5]

THE OPTIONS FOR LEGAL REGULATION

Three main models[6] for the statutory regulation and recognition of same-sex partnerships may be identified:

[2] ALRC Paper No 47, *Multiculturalism and Family Law* (Australian Government Printing Service, Sydney, 1991), para. 24.

[3] "Property Disputes in Unmarried Relationships: Can Equity Still Play a Role?" in M Cope (ed.), *Equity: Issues and Trends* (Federation Press, Sydney, 1995); "Law and the Unmarried Couple: Oppression or Liberation?", (1996) 8 *Child and Family Law Quarterly* 137; "Lesbian and Gay Family Values and the Law", [1999] *Family Law* 560.

[4] Scotland and Northern Ireland have separate legal systems; domestic statutes in the family law field are similar though, particularly in the case of Scotland, by no means identical. It is possible that devolution will lead to greater divergence in social policy. The Scottish Parliament enacted the first express statutory recognition of same-sex partnerships in 2000. See Adults with Incapacity (Scotland) Act 2000, section (s.) 87(2) ("nearest relative" includes "a person of the same sex . . . [who] has been, for a period of not less than six months, living with the adult in a relationship which has the characteristics, other than that the persons are of the opposite sex, of the relationship between husband and wife").

[5] On the difficulties of defining the boundaries of "family law", see John Dewar, "Concepts, Coherence and Content of Family Law", in P Birks (ed.), *Examining the Law Syllabus: Beyond the Core* (Oxford, Oxford University Press, 1993).

[6] For a full discussion of recognition models, see J Millbank, "Lesbian and Gay Families", (1998) 12 *Australian Journal of Family Law* 99 at 128.

(a) *Same-sex marriage*,[7] with all (or virtually all) the legal consequences of marriage.
(b) *The "opt-in" system of registered partnership*,[8] with defined consequences in particular areas of law. The nature and content of those consequences is a question of social policy for the legislature, in particular how closely they mirror those of marriage. The registration option may also be made available to heterosexual partners.[9] A variant on this model is to permit the parties to determine for themselves the consequences of the recognised relationship.[10]
(c) *A statute-defined qualifying relationship*: legal regulation imposed by operation of law, through definition of a qualifying relationship to which legal consequences in defined areas are attached.[11] As a precondition, a minimum duration for the relationship or the presence of a child of the family may be required. There are two sub-models for defining the qualifying relationship:
(i) the cohabitation model (e.g. 'living together as . . .'); and
(ii) a definition which does not imply the need for a sexual relationship (although one may in fact exist), e.g. "domestic relationship",[12] "associated person",[13] "homesharer",[14] "close personal relationship".[15]

Each of the two sub-models for defining the qualifying relationship has both ideological and practical merits and defects in the context of same-sex relationships.[16] The cohabitation model has traditionally drawn a close analogy with the *consortium vitae* of marriage, and so an extension to same-sex partners may be unacceptable both to the partners themselves and to a conservative

[7] See Waaldijk, chap. 23.

[8] L Nielsen, "Family Rights and the 'Registered Partnership' in Denmark", (1990) 4 *International Journal of Law and the Family* 297; M Broberg, "The Registered Partnership for Same-Sex Couples in Denmark", (1996) 8 *Child and Family Law Quarterly* 149; C Lind "Pretended Families and the Local State in Britain and the USA", (1996) 10 *International Journal of Law, Policy and the Family* 134; I Andersen, "Registered Personal Relationships", [1997] *Family Law* 175; J Eekelaar, "Registered Same-Sex Partnerships and Marriages—A Statistical Comparison", [1998] *Family Law* 561; I Lund-Andersen, "The Legal Position of Homosexuals, Cohabitation and Registered Partnership in Scandinavia" in Eekelaar & Nhlapo (eds.), *The Changing Family: Family Forms and Family Law* (Oxford, Hart Publishing, 1998).

[9] As in the Netherlands since 1 Jan. 1998. See Waaldijk, chap. 23.

[10] E.g. the *Pacte Civil de Solidarité* in France. See Borrillo, chap. 25. In "Reforming the Rights of Cohabitants—Lessons from Across the Channel", [1999] *Family Law* 477 at 478–479, A Barlow and R Probert criticise the PACS for failing to impose adequate minimum standards as to the content of a couple's mutual rights and obligations.

[11] See e.g. Property (Relationships) Act 1984 (New South Wales), as amended by Property (Relationships) Legislation Amendment Act 1999; Domestic Relationships Act 1994 (Australian Capital Territory); Millbank & Morgan, chap. 14.

[12] Australian Capital Territory, *ibid*.

[13] See e.g. Family Law Act 1996 (UK), s. 62(3).

[14] M Harpum, "Cohabitation Consultation", [1995] *Family Law* 657; R Probert, "Homesharing: Widening the Debate", [1999] *Family Law* 153.

[15] Property (Relationships) Act 1984 (New South Wales), as amended in 1999, s. 5(1)(b).

[16] See Millbank, *supra* n.6, at 134–6; Millbank & Morgan, chap. 14.

legislature.[17] On the other hand, this definition best expresses the notion of a couple. The more general definition inevitably encompasses a wide range of different relationships, whose sheer variety may render it difficult to define the content of the legal rights and consequences to be attached. Of course, there is nothing to prevent a legislature adopting both sub-models simultaneously, as illustrated by recent developments in New South Wales.[18] Where legal consequences are attached to unmarried relationships by operation of law, the interests of party autonomy can be protected through the provision of a contractual "opt-out" facility.

THE CURRENT STATE OF THE LAW IN ENGLAND AND WALES

Presenting the current state of the law in England and Wales on the legal recognition of same-sex relationships is an unenviable task, and one fit only for an apologist by nature. It is ironic that there is such a dramatic mismatch[19] between community acceptance of lesbian and gay lifestyles and the pattern of formal legal regulation in this country. As will be shown, current English legislation in the family context does not permit same-sex marriage nor registered partnership, nor does it, in general, recognise same-sex cohabitation as such. In some limited contexts, a same-sex partner is included—together with a range of other relationships—within the wider definition under sub-model (c) (ii) *supra*.[20] In others, a same-sex partner's rights are recognised only in his or her individual capacity as a single person.[21] Thus family law in England and Wales has created a hierarchy of family forms with differing levels of legal recognition and protection: in descending order, marriage, heterosexual cohabitation, and same-sex partnerships. Recognition of same-sex partnerships as such is very limited.

The explanation for this approach lies in the persistence of conservative family values ideology in the Government and Parliament. It is notable that the notorious section 28 of the Local Government Act 1988 remains unrepealed at the time of writing, and that controversy continues to surround its existence both in political debate and the pages of the popular press. The courts of England and Wales are strictly constrained by the interpretation of existing legislation. Nevertheless, within those constraints, they have in recent years shown themselves increasingly willing to recognise the authenticity of commitment within the same-sex family. Nor have judges been slow in pointing up the distinction between interpretation of an existing statutory provision and accep-

[17] But see *supra* n.11 (New South Wales), and the Property Law Amendment Act 1999 (Queensland), both of which extend the definition to same-sex relationships.

[18] *Ibid.*

[19] A mismatch commented on by many of the overseas delegates to the conference in London in July 1999 on which this book is based.

[20] See e.g. Family Law Act 1996, s. 61(2) ("associated person") and Rent Act 1977, as amended, Sch. 1, para. 2(2) ("member of . . . the family . . . residing. . .in the dwelling-house").

[21] See e.g. Adoption Act 1976, s. 15.

tance of the social policy which underpins it.[22] Moreover, there is an increasing groundswell of consistent support for law reform in the field of cohabitation, including same-sex partnerships, from judges, academics and practitioners alike.[23]

Parental Rights: Creating the Family

In current English adoption law, only spouses are permitted to adopt jointly,[24] i.e. as a couple. An unmarried partner (whether homosexual or heterosexual) may adopt in the capacity of a single person,[25] and a joint residence order may be used to confer parental responsibility on the other partner.[26] However, single-person adoptions are not generally regarded as favourably by agencies as adoption by a married couple, and tend to be utilised for children with special needs who are otherwise difficult to place. The legislative restriction on joint adoption is based on the unreasoned assumption (crudely articulated in the White Paper, *Adoption: The Future*, in 1993 and not revisited since) that marriage is the preferred institution for the upbringing of children.[27]

Nevertheless, the approach of recent case-law has, within the constraints of restrictive legislation, been increasingly enlightened in emphasising the parenting commitment of same-sex adopters, particularly in relation to children with special needs, and has moreover stressed the need to interpret current adoption legislation in a non-discriminatory way. Examples are *Re W (Adoption: Homosexual Adopter)*[28] and *AMT (Known as AC) (Petitioner For Authority to Adopt SR)*.[29] In *AMT*, an adoption order was made in favour of a gay man living in a long-term stable relationship. The judgment of the Court of Session was notable for its rejection of homophobic preconceptions, and for the taking of judicial notice of the lack of evidence on negative aspects of same-sex parenting, i.e. the lack of substantiation for assertions that children will be stigmatised by peers,

[22] See most recently *Fitzpatrick* v. *Sterling Housing Association Ltd*, [1999] 3 WLR 1113, discussed in detail *infra*.

[23] See e.g. Thorpe LJ and R Bailey-Harris, chaps. 1 and 5 in R Bailey-Harris (ed.), *Dividing the Assets on Family Breakdown*, (Bristol, Family Law, 1998); Mark Harper, "Cohabitation Law: The Way Forward", [1999] *Family Law* 435; R Bailey-Harris (1999), *supra* n.3; *Cohabitation Committee Report*, Solicitors' Family Law Association, April 1999; *Cohabitation: Proposals for Reform of the Law*, Family Law Committee of the Law Society, Sept. 1999.

[24] Adoption Act 1976, s. 14. Clauses 41–43 of the Adoption and Children Bill (published on 15 Mar. 2001) would not change this, but would provide for step-parent adoptions (one spouse alone adopting the child of the other spouse).

[25] *Ibid.*, s. 15.

[26] Children Act 1989, s. 8; *Re AB (Adoption: Joint Residence)*, [1996] 1 Family Law Reports (FLR) 27.

[27] See "Law and the Unmarried Couple", *supra* n.3, at 144, and "Lesbian and Gay Family Values and the Law", *supra* n.3, at 565, for criticism by the present writer.

[28] [1997] 2 FLR 406. See also *Re E (Adoption: Freeing Order)*, [1995] 1 FLR 382.

[29] [1997] *Family Law* 225; [1997] *Scots Law Times* 724 (interpeting Scottish legislation that is identical for present purposes).

that they are more likely themselves to be homosexual, or that same-sex families are intrinsically less stable or supportive than their heterosexual counterparts.

In current social conditions in the United Kingdom, as elsewhere in the Western world, very few young children become available for adoption, and a childless couple may well turn to the option of reproductive technology. The principal regulatory statute is the Human Fertilisation and Embryology Act 1990, which does not deny same-sex partners access to reproductive technology services, but in section 13(5) requires account to be taken of "the need of [the] child for a father". Since 1995, the Code of Practice of the Human Fertilisation and Embryology Authority has been liberalised to focus on a clinic's assessment of each particular couple's parenting commitment and capacity. This is undoubtedly a step forward, but much still depends in practice on the clinic's exercise of discretion at the local level. In other words, a same-sex couple's access to reproductive technology services is permitted but not guaranteed.

What of other methods of conferring parental rights? In English law at the moment, only the unmarried biological father may apply for a parental responsibility order *per se*.[30] Other persons (including the biological parent's partner, heterosexual or homosexual, married or unmarried) must resort to the strategy of an application for a joint residence order,[31] which will confer parental responsibility during minority, but will not create a legal parent-child relationship for life (e.g., for inheritance purposes). There are currently no government proposals to extend the category of those who may apply for parental responsibility *per se*.

Post-Separation Parenting

When it comes to a continuing parental role following family breakdown, section 1(1) of the Children Act 1989 makes the welfare of the child the paramount consideration. A range of orders regulating post-separation parenting are available under section 8 of the Act: residence, contact, specific issue, and prohibited steps.[32] Recent reported case-law and anecdotal evidence of unreported court practice suggests that courts are increasingly more willing to recognise the parenting capacity of lesbian and gay parents than they were in the past,[33] and here too to avoid a discriminatory application of the legislation. A reported illustration in point is the decision of Bracewell J, *G* v. *F (Contact and Shared Residence)*,[34] in which a child was born through assisted reproduction to two

[30] Children Act 1989, s. 4.

[31] *Ibid.*, s. 8.

[32] S. 1(5) requires a court to be satisfied that the making of an order will be more beneficial to the child than making no order at all. This provision reflects a policy favouring resolution by settlement over that by adjudication.

[33] For illustrations of earlier homophobic assumptions in applications relating to children, see e.g. *S* v. *S (Custody of Children)*, [1980] FLR 143; *Re P (A Minor)(Custody)*, (1983) FLR 401; *B* v. *B (Minors)(Custody, Care and Control)*, [1991] 1 FLR 402; *C* v. *C (A Minor: Custody Appeal)*, [1991] FLR 223.

[34] [1998] 2 FLR 799.

committed lesbians who had lived in an established relationship for five years. In granting the non-biological parent's post-separation applications for leave to apply for both contact and shared residence, Bracewell J commented that it would be wholly wrong and unsustainable for the nature of the relationship to reflect against her.

Dividing Money and Property on Family Breakdown

In England and Wales, no statutory jurisdiction exists for the reallocation of assets between an unmarried couple on the breakdown of their relationship; there is no equivalent for the unmarried (whether homosexual or heterosexual) of Part II of the Matrimonial Causes Act 1973, which operates on divorce. On the breakdown of an unmarried relationship, a party who desires a distribution of property must invoke general principles of property law, including the equitable doctrines of trust and proprietary estoppel. The legal situation is particularly unsatisfactory where property is not held in joint names and there is no written deed of trust. The fundamental problem is that, in default of a statutory adjustive regime, a jurisdiction which is declaratory in nature is used as the vehicle for dispute resolution. Common-law legal and equitable doctrines are directed strictly to the ascertainment of existing proprietary interests, and were simply not designed to achieve a fair allocation of assets on family breakdown. Moreover, in ascertaining what the parties' existing proprietary interests are, equitable doctrines seek to give effect to agreements and common understandings.[35] Where there is no written declaration of trust, nor evidence of oral discussions or representations as to the sharing of the beneficial interests,[36] the English models of resulting and constructive trusts place undue emphasis on financial contributions to the acquisition of property as evidence of the required common intention, and fail to give proper consideration to the wide range of different contributions made to family welfare in the course of a relationship.[37]

Equitable doctrines are complex and expensive to access, and give rise to common misconceptions in the public mind. Nor does the current law permit consideration of the whole range of a couple's assets. There is no provision for an award of maintenance (income provision), and no facility for the earmarking

[35] See M Howard & J Hill, "The Informal Creation of Interests in Land", [1995] 15 *Legal Studies* 356. With the English model of constructive trust based on common intention, contrast the remedial models developed in other jurisdictions to remedy unfair conduct: *Pettkus* v. *Becker*, (1980) 117 DLR (3d) 257; *Baumgartner* v. *Baumgartner*, (1987) 164 CLR 137; *Gillies* v. *Keogh*, [1989] 2 NZLR 327.

[36] Express discussions are the foundation of express trusts of personalty (*Rowe* v. *Prance*, [1999] 2 FLR 787), and of constructive trusts of realty under the second branch of the formulation of Lord Bridge in *Lloyd's Bank plc* v. *Rosset*, [1991] AC 107. In such cases, the courts also arguably take a more liberal view of detriment.

[37] *Burns* v. *Burns*, [1984] Ch. 317; *Rosset*, *ibid.*; the liberalisation effected by *Midland Bank* v. *Cooke*, [1995] 2 FLR 915, applies only where an initial contribution to the purchase price has been made.

or division of pension entitlements between unmarried partners. Although the general law principles have the supposed merit of formal equality in their application, since they are neutral as to sexual orientation,[38] the reality is that same-sex and heterosexual couples are equally disadvantaged under the current law in comparison with their married counterparts.

Despite frequent criticisms of the current law and consistent calls for reform by judges, practitioners and academics alike,[39] the current government is curiously reluctant to address the issue, and the Law Commission's long-awaited discussion paper on the property rights of homesharers has yet to appear. However, 1999 saw the publication of two significant reform proposals by two of the principal professional organisations: the Solicitors' Family Law Association (SFLA),[40] and the Law Society's Family Law Committee.[41] The reports have much in common. Both propose the enactment of a statutory adjustive regime providing increased protection for the unmarried, without equating their rights precisely with those of the married. Both propose wide powers for the courts to deal with the whole range of the parties' assets on relationship breakdown. Both recommend principles for determining capital distribution and maintenance entitlement drawn from the provisions of the Family Law (Scotland) Act 1985,[42] as well as a contacting-out facility subject to safeguards. As to the definition of the relationship, the Law Society proposes the adoption of a cohabitation model framed in language both gender- and sexuality-neutral, whereas the SFLA's first preference[43] is for the "personal relationship" model, similarly inclusive of same-sex relationships. It remains to be seen whether these important reports will provide the spur for government action.

Protection From Violence

Non-molestation[44] and occupation[45] orders are available under Part IV of the Family Law Act 1996, which provides an interesting illustration of English law's reluctance to recognise the same-sex partnership as cohabitation, and more generally exemplifies the hierarchical approach to legal regulation of family forms. Central is the concept of "associated persons". This term includes[46]—

[38] Examples of the use of equitable doctrines by former same sex-partners include *Tinsley* v. *Milligan*, [1993] 2 FLR 693; *Wayling* v. *Jones*, [1995] 2 FLR 1029. See generally J Mee, *The Property Rights of Unmarried Cohabitants* (Oxford, Hart Publishing, 1998).

[39] See *supra* n.23; District Judge Taylor, "Section 25: Quick, Cheap and Conciliatory", [1995] *Family Law* 403.

[40] See *supra* n.23.

[41] *Ibid*.

[42] S. 9. The Act governs the breakdown of marriages.

[43] The SFLA acknowledged the political sensitivity of including same-sex partners, and recommended, as a "second best", a definition based on the heterosexual cohabitation model: see *SFLA Review Issue* 79, June 1999, p 6.

[44] Family Law Act 1996, s. 42.

[45] *Ibid*., ss. 33–41.

[46] *Ibid*., s. 62(3).

significantly, as separate categories—"cohabitants" (heterosexually defined[47]) and persons who "live or have lived in the same household". The statute thus declines to extend the cohabitation model to same-sex couples. Moreover, it confines the right to claim transfer of protected tenancies on family breakdown to heterosexual cohabitants.[48] The Act's hierarchical approach to the protection of different family forms is illustrated by the different factors governing the grant of occupation orders to spouses, former spouses or cohabitants who have no proprietary or contractual rights respectively, and through distinctions as to the duration of the orders which can be made.[49] Whether these distinctions are as apparent in court practice as on the face of the statute, is an entirely different question.

Family Rights on Death

English law also evidences an unwillingness to recognise the same-sex couple as cohabitants upon the death of one partner. The Inheritance (Provision for Family and Dependants) Act 1975 permits an application for provision from the deceased's estate by a party who has lived as the deceased's cohabitant in the same household for at least two years.[50] To date, this provision has been interpreted as confined to heterosexual cohabitation.[51] Similarly, only a heterosexual cohabitant may claim compensation under the Fatal Accidents Act 1976 where the death of their partner was caused by the negligence of a third party.[52] However, a same-sex partner is now permitted to bring a claim under the Criminal Injuries Compensation Scheme where the death was caused by a criminal act,[53] and same-sex partners (and heterosexual partners who are legally unable to marry) are now recognised for the purpose of immigration.[54]

[47] *Ibid.*, s. 62(1); see also the interpretation of para. 2(2) of Schedule 1 to the Rent Act 1977.

[48] *Ibid.*, s. 53 and Sch. 7.

[49] *Ibid.*, ss. 33– 41.

[50] See s. 1(1)(ba).

[51] See A Barlow, *Cohabitants and the Law*, 2d ed. (Butterworths, 1997) at 92–6. A same-sex partner may only claim, under s. 1(1)(e) of the Act, as a person who "was being maintained wholly or partly by the deceased".

[52] S. 1(3)(b). The Law Commission has recommended that this right be extended to "any person wholly or partly maintained by the deceased", and that the right to claim damages for bereavement be extended to heterosexual cohabitants and "any person of the same gender as the deceased who has lived with the deceased for [two years] in a relationship equivalent to [living as husband and wife]". See *Claims for Wrongful Death*, LAW COM No. 263, Nov. 1999, http://www.lawcom.gov.uk/library/menu_reports.htm. See also *Liability for Psychiatric Illness*, LAW COM No. 249, Mar. 1998 (recommending that the plaintiff be "conclusively taken to have had a close tie of love and affection", for the purpose of a "nervous shock" negligence claim, if he or she was "the immediate victim's cohabitant", including a same-gender cohabitant in a relationship equivalent to "liv[ing] together as man and wife").

[53] See Criminal Injuries Compensation Scheme 2001, http://www.cica.gov.uk. Para. 38(a)(i) defines "partner of the deceased" as "a person who was living together with the deceased as husband and wife or as a same sex partner".

[54] Immigration Rules, paras. 295A-295O (2 Oct. 2000 changes), http://www.ind.homeoffice.gov.uk/default.asp?PageId=1193 ("living together in a relationship akin to marriage which has subsisted for two years or more").

Most recently, the context of succession to an assured private sector tenancy has provided the opportunity for consideration at the highest judicial level of the classification of a same-sex partnership. In *Fitzpatrick* v. *Sterling Housing Association Ltd*,[55] the applicant had lived with his same-sex partner for eighteen years in a flat of which the partner was the protected tenant. On his partner's death, he applied for a declaration to the effect that he was entitled to succeed to the tenancy under the Rent Act 1977 as amended. The First Schedule to the Act confers succession rights on a person who was "living with the original tenant as his or her wife or husband" (para. 2(2)), and on "a member of the original tenant's family . . . residing with him in the dwelling-house at the time of and for the period of two years immediately before his death" (para. 3(1)). The first category was the result of a 1988 amendment[56] directed to the recognition of unmarried cohabitation. The second had existed since 1920.

In the Court of Appeal (of England and Wales), Waite and Roch LJJ, held that the applicant did not qualify under either limb of the schedule; Ward LJ in a vigorous dissent held that he qualified under both.[57] The House of Lords was unanimous in rejecting the claim under para. 2(2), but by a three to two majority[58] held that the applicant was a member of the deceased tenant's "family" at the relevant time under para. 3(1). The decision of the House of Lords was much vaunted by the media for its liberal interpretation of the concept of the family and its implications for gay rights generally, but, as will be explained, a careful reading of the speeches of their Lordships reveals the limitations of the decision. On the other hand, the speeches do make it clear that a judicial ruling on an issue of statutory interpretation does not necessarily imply acceptance of the social policy underpinning the provision in question.

The first notable aspect of the decision of the House of Lords is the repeated insistence[59] that the case concerned only a narrow issue of statutory interpretation and nothing more. For example, Lord Clyde observed that:

> "It would be wrong to regard the present case as one about the rights of homosexuals. It is simply a matter of the application of ordinary language to this particular statutory provision in the light of current conditions".[60]

Only Lord Hutton (dissenting) regarded the implications of the decision as more far-reaching.[61] As to the date on which the intention of Parliament is to be ascertained, there was orthodox consensus that this is the date of enactment of the

[55] [1999] 3 WLR 1113 (House of Lords).

[56] Housing Act 1988, s. 39(2), Sch. 4, Part 1, paras. 2, 3.

[57] [1998] 1 FLR 6. The dissent of Ward LJ was strongly criticised by Lord Hobhouse for overstepping the legitimate bounds of the judicial function in relation to statutory interpretation: [1999] 3 WLR 1113 at 1152.

[58] Lord Slynn of Hadley, Lord Nicholls of Birkenhead and Lord Clyde, with Lord Hutton and Lord Hobhouse of Woodborough dissenting.

[59] [1999] 3 WLR 1113 at 1118 (Slynn), 1129 (Hobhouse), 1136, 1138 (Clyde).

[60] *Ibid.* at 1136.

[61] *Ibid.* at 1148.

relevant provision,[62] although Lord Nicholls and Lord Clyde considered it legitimate to undertake the ascertainment exercise in the light of social developments which Parliament is deemed to have contemplated.[63]

The outcome of the case reveals the problems for same-sex partnerships inherent in the statutory definition used for the traditional cohabitation model, and an unwillingness to recognise same-sex cohabitation as a *de facto* equivalent of the *consortium vitae* of marriage. There was no support in the House of Lords for recognition of the applicant's claim to recognition under para. 2(2). In the views of all their Lordships, the 1988 amendment was intended to cover persons who, although not legally husband and wife, lived together as such without being married. The terminology employed—"his or her wife or husband"—was gender-specific and indicated cohabitation between persons of opposite sexes.[64] Their Lordships' unanimous view was that Parliament in 1988 had not intended that terminology to include "my same-sex partner"; if it had, it would have spelled it out.

The assumption in the House of Lords that the terminology of para. 2(2) is gender-specific, and that the *de facto* union must resemble the *de jure* one (marriage), contrasts sharply with the approach of Ward LJ in the Court of Appeal.[65] His Lordship's judgment was underpinned by a functionalist, as opposed to formalistic, approach to the question of statutory construction:

> "The trend in the cases, as I see them, is to shift the focus, or the emphasis, from structure and components to function and appearance—what a family does rather than what a family is, or putting it another way, a family is what a family does . . . If . . .there is doubt about the ordinary meaning of the words of the statute, I would strain to place upon them that construction which produces a dignified result. . . . To exclude same-sex couples from the protection of the Rent Act proclaims the inevitable message that society judges their relationship to be less worthy of respect, concern and consideration than the relationship between members of the opposite sex. The fundamental dignity of the homosexual couple is severely and palpably affected by the impugned distinction. . . . 'As' means 'in the manner of' and suggests how the couple functioned, not what they were . . . That [sexual] activity takes place between members of different sexes or of the same sex is a matter of form not function . . . I would say that there is no essential difference between a homosexual and a heterosexual couple".[66]

However, the unanimous view of the House of Lords in *Fitzpatrick* leaves the same-sex partnership outside the scope of recognition as a *de facto* equivalent of the *consortium vitae*. In the present writer's opinion, this shortcoming of English law is only imperfectly remedied by the recognition by the majority of the House of Lords of the alternative claim under the Rent Act 1977; to acknowledge a longstanding homosexual monogamous union under the wider rubric of

[62] *Ibid.* at 1122 (Slynn), 1147 (Hutton).

[63] *Ibid.* at 1129 and 1133 respectively.

[64] *Ibid.* at 1118 (Slynn), 1127 (Nicholls), 1131 (Clyde), 1140 (Hutton), 1153 (Hobhouse).

[65] For comments on the Court of Appeal decision, see N Wiley, (1998) 10 *Child and Family Law Quarterly* 191; R Bailey-Harris, [1997] *Family Law* 784.

[66] [1998] 1 FLR 6 at 38–40.

"family" (which also includes relationships of a quite different nature) is inevitably a second best. Interestingly, this shortcoming was recognised by Lord Hobhouse and Lord Hutton (both dissenting), who asked why Parliament in 1988 had not extended the definition of the cohabitation model to the same-sex couple.[67]

By a narrow majority of three to two in the House of Lords, it was held that the applicant qualified under para. 3(1) as a member of the deceased tenant's "family" at the relevant time.[68] The majority emphasised that the interpretation of "family" which they were required to give was (i) confined to the context of the Rent Act 1977, and (ii) within that context, purposive. Hence it would be quite wrong to treat this decision as binding authority for the interpretation of "family" in other statutes, where it may be given a wider or narrower meaning as appropriate.

There was unanimity of view that the interpretation question in a given case is one of mixed law and fact. The first stage is to construe the meaning which the term "family" is capable of bearing; the second is to determine whether an applicant in fact satisfies the relevant criteria.[69] The majority considered that Parliament had deliberately left the term "family" undefined in the Rent Act 1977, and had intended the term to be interpreted broadly and flexibly.[70] The purpose[71] of the statutory provision was to provide a measure of security for those who shared their lives with the tenant on the premises in a way which characterises a family unit. That unit is characterised by mutual interdependence, sharing, caring, affection, commitment and support between the members, and can be brought into existence by choice as well as by virtue of kinship.[72]

Lord Hutton and Lord Hobhouse (both dissenting) adopted a narrower construction of the term "family" in this context. Thus, according to Lord Hobhouse, the 1988 extension was intended to:

> "cover those who are in a legal or *de facto* relationship to the tenant of blood or affinity . . . Living together as homosexual lovers is not a familial relationship. It is a different relationship: for present purposes . . . no better and no worse—no more or less meritorious, just different".[73]

Lord Hutton's conclusion was the same:

> "I consider that the plaintiff does not qualify as a member of [the deceased's] family because he had no relationship with [the deceased] by marriage or blood or adoption

[67] [1999] 3 WLR 1113 at 1141, 1151–3, 1155–6.

[68] See S Cretney & F Reynolds, "Limits of the Judicial Function", (2000) 116 *Law Quarterly Review* 181.

[69] *Ibid.* at 1119, 1123, 1142.

[70] *Ibid.* at 1119 (Slynn), 1124–5 and 1129 (Nicholls), 1132 and 1138 (Clyde).

[71] *Ibid.* at 1125–7 (Nicholls), 1132 (Clyde).

[72] *Ibid.* at 1122 (Slynn), 1127 (Nicholls), 1135 (Clyde).

[73] *Ibid.* at 1153, 1155.

and no link with him which was broadly recognisable as creating *de facto* such a relationship".[74]

Neither was prepared to accept that a family relationship could be brought into existence by parties of the same sex choosing to enter into an intimate relationship. Their Lordships were clearly perturbed by the "floodgate" argument, namely that an open-ended interpretation of "family" is capable of embracing a wide range of relationships, and that it becomes "difficult to discern what criterion would include one person residing with the tenant and exclude another".[75] An implicit preoccupation was the need to identify a mirror-image *de jure* family in order to establish a *de facto* family, of which there was allegedly none on the facts of the present case. The authority of the decision in *Carega Properties SA* v. *Sharrat*[76] on the interpretation of para. 3(1) weighed heavily with the minority.[77] In that case, a close platonic relationship between the elderly tenant and a young man, who were not related but considered themselves as aunt and nephew, was held not to be capable of qualifying. It is interesting to note that, by contrast, the majority treated the earlier decision as not binding on them, Lord Slynn and Lord Clyde holding that it turned purely on its own facts,[78] Lord Nicholls that there was no sexual relationship involved.[79]

In the view of the present writer, the outcome of *Fitzpatrick*, despite representing some advance in the legal recognition of the same-sex partnership, nevertheless is unsatisfactory, because is fails to recognise same-sex cohabitation *per se*, but only under the umbrella of a far wider classification of familial link.[80] Given the nature of the statutory provisions in question, a different result could scarcely have been expected. However, a particular judicial interpretation of a statutory provision should not be mistaken for approval of the social policy concerned. The judicial effort made to distinguish the two issues in *Fitzpatrick* is striking.[81] Those campaigning for increased rights for same-sex partnerships should not be downcast by the restrictive interpretations adopted in some of the speeches in this case. They merely reflect a judicial view of the incapacity of courts to formulate new social policies where the words of a statute are considered to be unambiguous.

[74] *Ibid.* at 1144.
[75] *Ibid.* at 1147 (Hutton). See also at 1155 (Hobhouse).
[76] [1979] 1 WLR 928.
[77] [1999] 3 WLR 1113 at 1144 (Hutton), 1155 (Hobhouse).
[78] *Ibid.* at 1121 and 1134 respectively.
[79] *Ibid.* at 1128.
[80] *Fitzpatrick* would not assist an applicant in a public sector housing case. The Housing Act 1985, ss. 87, 113, defines "family members" exhaustively as spouses, persons "living as husband and wife", and certain relatives by blood or marriage. The Housing (Scotland) Act 2001, s. 108, treats as "family members", or in some cases as "spouses", persons who are living together "in a relationship which has the characteristics of the relationship between husband and wife except that the persons are of the same sex".
[81] *Ibid.* at 1117 (Slynn), 1140, 1149 (Hutton), 1150–2, 1156 (Hobhouse).

CONCLUSION: WHITHER IN THE FUTURE?

This chapter has demonstrated the limitations which current English legislation imposes on the recognition of the same-sex partnership, and the constraints within which an increasingly enlightened judiciary is forced to operate. At the time of writing, the government continues to be highly ambivalent about the degree of legal protection to be given to family relationships other than marriage. This was evidenced in the Green Paper *Supporting Families* (1998) and in the Lord Chancellor's speech to the UK Family Law Conference at the Inner Temple in London on 25 June 1999. No White Paper on *Supporting Families* has been published. Moreover, the Law Commission has still not delivered its discussion paper on the property rights of homesharers. This reluctance contrasts strongly with the increasing calls by practitioners and academics for the reform issue to be addressed.[82]

In delivering the *Third Stonewall Lecture* on 25 March 1999,[83] and in other writings,[84] the present writer has been strongly critical of legislative inaction in relation to same-sex partnerships, and in relation to unmarried cohabitation generally. The *Third Stonewall Lecture* advocated three strategies for the promotion of the family law rights of lesbian and gay men in this country:

- a reformulation of family values ideology to recognise the authenticity and commitment of a wide range of family forms;
- a revival of functionalist analysis of family law to identify the law's true purpose in a particular context, freed from discriminatory distinctions based on marital status or sexual orientation;
- a robust interpretation of the Human Rights Act 1998 by the UK judiciary, departing where necessary from conservative Strasbourg jurisprudence on the interpretation of respect for family life in Article 8, and discrimination in relation to family life under Article 14.[85]

But to which of the three models of legal regulation of same-sex partnerships outlined earlier in this chapter does the application of these strategies lead us?

In the *Third Stonewall Lecture*, the author applied the three strategies to argue for model (c), the statute-defined qualifying relationship, i.e., inclusion of same-sex partnerships in a broad definition of unmarried relationship, with statutory amendments in *inter alia* the fields of adoption law, acquisition of parental responsibility, and distribution of assets on breakdown of the relation-

[82] *Supra* n.23.

[83] "Lesbian and Gay Family Values and the Law", [1999] *Family Law* 560.

[84] *Supra* n.3 (1996), n.23 (1998).

[85] In force since 2 Oct. 2000, s. 3(1) of the Act requires UK courts to interpret UK legislation "so far as it is possible to do so" in a way that is consistent with the European Convention. This could require the House of Lords to revisit its interpretation of "living as husband and wife" in *Fitzpatrick*. See R Wintemute, "Lesbian and Gay Inequality 2000: The Potential of the Human Rights Act 1998 and the Need for an Equality Act 2002", [2000] *European Human Rights Law Review* 603.

ship. This approach arguably has the advantage of "mainstreaming" lesbian and gay family rights. The same-sex marriage model was rejected as politically unrealistic in view of the current government's policy towards family law reform. The registered partnership model (an "opt-in" model)[86] was also rejected as providing inadequate protection to the vulnerable partner, where the stronger partner refuses to register, and a system of regulation imposed by operation of law was preferred.

However, the views expressed at the *Third Stonewall Lecture* were not without controversy. To "mainstream" same-sex partnerships into unmarried cohabitation arguably fails to "mainstream" them into marriage. It is an essential theme of the author's argument that the significance of marriage as a legal institution is greatly diminished. But is it correct to deny lesbians and gay men the right, from a position of equality with heterosexuals, to opt for any institution? Thus the author's favoured model, while politically expedient, can arguably be seen as violating the principle of equality of access to family rights recognised in Articles 8 and 14 of the European Convention, and therefore as being vulnerable to attack now that the Human Rights Act 1998 has come into operation. Ultimately, the debate as to the future direction of reform of same-sex family rights is a finely-balanced one, and this chapter aspires to stimulate rather than to conclude discussion.

[86] On 6 Aug. 2001, the Greater London Authority began accepting applications for the mainly symbolic London Partnerships Register, which is open to same-sex and unmarried heterosexual couples where one partner is a London resident. See http://www.london.gov.uk/mayor/partnerships/index.htm. In their manifesto for the 7 June 2001 elections, the Liberal Democrats promised to "[e]stablish a scheme for the civil registration of partnerships . . . giv[ing] two unrelated adults . . . legal rights . . . at present only available to married couples". See http://www.libdems.org.uk (Policy, Manifestos). Lord Lester of Herne Hill QC, a Liberal Democrat member of the House of Lords (the upper house of the UK Parliament), plans to introduce a private member's bill establishing such a scheme (in England and Wales at least) in the autumn of 2001. See http://www.parliament.the-stationery-office.co.uk/pa/pabills.htm.

PART III

EUROPEAN LAW

Section A—European Community Law

35

The Miscegenation Analogy in Europe, or, Lisa Grant meets Adolf Hitler

ANDREW KOPPELMAN[1]

ANTIDISCRIMINATION LAW RESTS on the memory of crimes against humanity. In the United States, the interpretation of the Civil War Amendments and the Civil Rights Act of 1964 always takes place in the shadow of slavery and segregation. In Europe, every human rights instrument carries with it the memory of fascism, preeminently the fascism of Nazi Germany. We can argue about the extension of the antidiscrimination norm to new cases, but history places a limit on the range of arguments that can be made. What you may never do is make an argument that implies that the crimes that generated the norm were not wrong at all. Their wrongness provides an anchor for all subsequent legal argument.

This constraint, I will here argue, was violated by the European Court of Justice (ECJ) in *Grant* v. *South-West Trains*,[2] which rejected the claim that discrimination against a lesbian was a form of sex discrimination. The *Grant* decision is a major defeat for lesbians and gay men, but they are not the only losers. Human rights law has been damaged at its core. At the level of practice, *Grant* implies that quite a lot of discrimination is henceforth no longer to be understood *as* discrimination. At the level of theory, it would legitimate at least one of the notorious Nuremberg Laws of Nazi Germany, and would make problematic some unquestionably correct decisions, such as *Brown* v. *Board of Education*[3] and *Loving* v. *Virginia*.[4]

I

The basic sex discrimination argument is simple. Any action that singles out homosexuals facially classifies on the basis of sex. If a business fires Ricky, or if

[1] Associate Professor of Law and Political Science, Northwestern University. Thanks to D Cassel, W Eskridge, Jr, and J Gardner for helpful conversations, and to M Lehr and R Wintemute for their assistance.

[2] Case C-249/96, [1998] ECR I-621, http://europa.eu.int/jurisp/cgi-bin/form.pl?lang=en.

[3] 347 US 483 (1954).

[4] 388 US 1 (1967).

the state prosecutes him, because of his sexual activities with Fred, while these actions would not be taken against Lucy if she did exactly the same things with Fred, then Ricky is being discriminated against on the basis of his sex.

This connection between sexual orientation and sex is neither a coincidence nor a lawyer's trick. The link between heterosexism and sexism is common knowledge if anything is. I won't presume to speak of Europe, but most Americans learn no later than high school that one of the nastier sanctions that one will suffer if one deviates from the behaviour traditionally deemed appropriate to one's sex is the imputation of homosexuality. The two stigmas, sex-inappropriateness and homosexuality, are virtually interchangeable, and each is readily used as a metaphor for the other. Moreover, both stigmas have gender-specific forms that imply that men ought to have power over women. Gay men are stigmatised as effeminate, which means, insufficiently aggressive and dominant. Lesbians are stigmatised as *too* aggressive and dominant; they appear to be guilty of some kind of insubordination. As was true in *Brown*, the findings of scholarship reinforce what common sense already tells us. Numerous studies by social psychologists have found that support for traditional sex roles is strongly correlated with (and, in some studies, is the best single predictor of) disapproval of homosexuality. Historians chronicling the rise of the modern despised category of "the homosexual"—and here I *am* talking about Europe—have found similar connections with sexism.[5]

This argument has been accepted by a few courts, rejected by many more.[6] The ones that have rejected it have always done so on the basis of the same argu-

[5] I have developed the claims made in this paragraph at much greater length in "Why Discrimination Against Lesbians and Gay Men is Sex Discrimination", (1994) 69 *New York University Law Review* 197.

[6] The only final appellate decision that fully adopts the argument and remains good law is *Baehr* v. *Lewin*, 852 P.2d 44 (Hawaii Supreme Court 1993), http://www.lambdalegal.org/cgi-bin/pages/library?class=4 ("Lambda URL") (same-sex marriage) (see Wolfson, chap. 9). Even in that case, the argument was initially only accepted by two out of five judges; a supplementary opinion after a change of personnel made it effectively a majority opinion. See *Baehr*, 852 P.2d at 74; Koppelman, *ibid.*, at 204–5. The argument was accepted by intermediate appellate courts in *Engel* v. *Worthington*, 23 Cal.Rptr.2d 329 (California Court of Appeal 1993), review denied and opinion withdrawn from publication in official reports, No. S036051, 1994 Cal. LEXIS 558 (California Supreme Court, 3 Feb. 1994) (denial of service to same-sex couple); *Lawrence* & *Garner* v. *State of Texas*, Lambda URL, *supra*, 2-1 panel decision (8 June 2000), reversed, 7-2, by *en banc* court, 41 S.W.3d 349 (Texas Court of Appeals, 14th District, 15 March 2001), Lambda URL, *supra* (same-sex sodomy); and *MacDonald* v. *Ministry of Defence*, [2000] Industrial Relations Law Reports (IRLR) 748 (Scottish Employment Appeal Tribunal) (3-0), http://wood.ccta.gov.uk/eat/eatjudgments.nsf (Search, homosexual, 06/10/2000), reversed, [2001] IRLR 431 (Court of Session, Inner House) (2-1), http://www.scotcourts.gov.uk/opinions/XA172_00.html (military employment). The argument was intimated, but its implications were not fully articulated, in *Nabozny* v. *Podlesny*, 92 F.3d 446, 454-5 (7th Circuit 1996), Lambda URL, *supra* (sex discrimination where state school tolerated violent harassment of openly gay student "because both the perpetrators and the victims were males"; it was "impossible to believe that a female lodging a similar complaint would have received the same response"). The argument was accepted by one judge of a final appellate court in two same-sex marriage cases: *Baker* v. *State*, 744 A.2d 864 at 904–907 (Vermont Supreme Court 1999) (Johnson, J), Lambda URL, *supra* (see Bonauto, chap. 10); and *Quilter* v. *Attorney-General*, [1998] 1 NZLR 523, 535-36 (New Zealand Court of Appeal) (Thomas, J), http://www.brookers.co.nz/legal/judgments (see Christie, chap. 15). In *Pearce* v. *Governing Body of Mayfield School* (English [intermediate]

ment: both sexes are treated alike by sanctions against homosexuality, because no one of either sex may engage in sexual conduct with another person of the same sex.[7] Ricky can't marry Fred, it's true, but Lucy likewise can't marry Ethel. This is the argument that was adopted by the Court in *Grant*.

II

The facts of the *Grant* case were as follows. South-West Trains Ltd. granted travel concessions, which were a combination of free and discounted train passes, to its employees' opposite-sex unmarried partners. Article 119 (now 141) of the EC Treaty provides that men and women must receive equal pay, and it has been settled that benefits such as the travel concessions constitute "pay" for the purposes of Article 119. Lisa Grant, an employee of the company, applied for the benefit and was denied it; her male predecessor in the job had also lived with a woman, but he had received the concession. She sued, arguing that the only reason she was denied the benefit was that she was a woman.

The Court rejected her claim, in spite of her argument that "her employer's decision would have been different if the benefits in issue . . . had been claimed by a man living with a woman, and not by a woman living with a woman".[8] Instead, the Court accepted her employer's argument that men and women are treated the same by the rule:

> "[T]ravel concessions are refused to a male worker if he is living with a person of the same sex, just as they are to a female worker if she is living with a person of the same sex. Since the condition imposed by the undertaking's regulations applies in the same

Court of Appeal, 31 July 2001, see IRLR or LEXIS) (student harassment of lesbian teacher), Hale, LJ, appeared willing to accept it, but for the binding precedent of *Gardner Merchant*, *infra* n.7 (both *Pearce* and *MacDonald*, *supra*, could go to the House of Lords). The argument was adopted by trial judges in *Brause* v. *Bureau of Vital Statistics*, Lambda URL, *supra* (Alaska Superior Court, 27 Feb. 1998) (same-sex marriage) (constitutional amendment rendered appeal moot); and *Picado* v. *Jegley*, Lambda URL, *supra* (Arkansas Circuit Court, 23 March 2001) (same-sex sodomy). In *Toonen* v. *Australia* (Communication No. 488/1992) (31 March 1994), 1 International Human Rights Reports 97 at 105, para. 8.7, http://www.unhchr.ch (Treaty Bodies Database Search, Toonen) (ban on all male-male sexual activity), the United Nations Human Rights Committee declared that the prohibition of sex discrimination in the International Covenant on Civil and Political Rights includes sexual orientation, but did not state its reasoning. See also Gross, chap. 20, pp. 396, 409 (Israel).

[7] See *Singer* v. *Hara*, 55 P.2d 1187 (Washington Court of Appeals 1974); *Smith* v. *Liberty Mutual Insurance Co.*, 395 F.Supp. 1098, 1099 n.2 (Northern District of Georgia 1975), aff'd, 569 F.2d 325, 327 (5th Circuit 1978); *DeSantis* v. *Pacific Tel. & Tel. Co.*, 608 F.2d 327, 331 (9th Circuit 1979); *State* v. *Walsh*, 713 S.W.2d 508, 510 (Missouri Supreme Court 1986); *Phillips* v. *Wisconsin Personnel Comm'n*, 482 N.W. 2d 121, 127–28 (Wisconsin Court of Appeals 1992); *Dean v. District of Columbia*, 653 A.2d 307, 363 n.2 (District of Columbia Court of Appeals 1995) (Steadman, J, concurring); *Baker*, *ibid.* at 880 n.13; *X & Y* v. *UK*, (1983) 5 European Human Rights Reports 601 (Commission); *R.* v. *Ministry of Defence, ex parte Smith* (1995), [1996] QB 517 (English Court of Appeal); *Smith* v. *Gardner Merchant*, [1998] 3 All ER 852 (English Court of Appeal); see also *Valdes* v. *Lumbermen's Mutual Casualty Co.*, 507 F.Supp. 10 (Southern District of Florida 1980) (discrimination against lesbians may constitute actionable "sex-plus" discrimination, but employer can rebut charge by showing that it discriminates equally against gay men); *Gardner Merchant*, *supra* (same reasoning applied to harassment of gay male employee).

[8] *Grant*, *supra* n.2, at para. 16.

> way to female and male workers, it cannot be regarded as constituting discrimination directly based on sex".[9]

The Court's reasoning has troubling analogues in American law. It echoes an 1883 decision, *Pace* v. *Alabama*,[10] in which the United States Supreme Court considered for the first time the constitutionality of "miscegenation" laws—laws prohibiting interracial sex or marriage. The statute in question in *Pace* prescribed penalties for interracial sex that were more severe than those imposed for adultery or fornication between persons of the same race. The Court unanimously rejected the equal protection challenge to the statute, denying that the statute discriminated on the basis of race:

> "[The section prohibiting interracial sex] prescribes a punishment for an offence which can only be committed where the two sexes are of different races. There is in neither section any discrimination against either race. . . . Whatever discrimination is made in the punishment prescribed in the two sections is directed against the offence designated and not against the person of any particular color or race. The punishment of each offending person, whether white or black, is the same".[11]

The structure of *Grant*'s reasoning is identical to that of *Pace*: the employer's rule excludes only certain relationships "which can only [take place] where the two [participants] are of [the same sex]", and it is directed against those relationships "and not against the person of any particular [sex]".

In the United States, *Pace* is no longer good law. It was repudiated by the Supreme Court in the next miscegenation case it considered, *McLaughlin* v. *Florida*.[12] In the wake of the unanimous decision condemning segregated public schools in *Brown* v. *Board of Education*,[13] the *McLaughlin* Court, again unanimously, invalidated a criminal statute prohibiting an unmarried interracial couple from habitually living in and occupying the same room at night. "It is readily apparent", wrote Justice White for the Court, that the statute "treats the interracial couple made up of a white person and a Negro differently than it does any other couple".[14] In response to the state's reliance on *Pace*, White declared that "*Pace* represents a limited view of the Equal Protection Clause which has not withstood analysis in the subsequent decisions of this Court".[15] Racial classifications, he concluded, can only be sustained by a compelling state interest. Since the State had failed to establish that the statute served "some overriding statutory purpose requiring the proscription of the specified conduct when engaged in by a white person and a Negro, but not otherwise",[16] the

[9] *Ibid.*, at paras. 27–28.
[10] 106 US (16 Otto) 583 (1883).
[11] *Ibid.*, at 585.
[12] 379 US 184 (1964).
[13] 347 US 483 (1954).
[14] *McLaughlin*, 379 US at 188.
[15] *Ibid.*
[16] *Ibid.*, at 192.

statute necessarily fell as "an invidious discrimination forbidden by the Equal Protection Clause".[17]

McLaughlin thus stands for the proposition (which should be obvious even without judicial support) that if penalised conduct is defined by reference to a characteristic, the penalty is not neutral with reference to that characteristic. Hence, in *Grant* it should have been dispositive that, had Lisa Grant been a man in exactly the same situation, she would have received the benefit. To paraphrase *McLaughlin*, it is readily apparent that the law treats the same-sex couple differently than it does any other couple. "Such a practice does not pass the simple test of whether the evidence shows 'treatment of a person in a manner which but for that person's sex would be different'".[18]

Now, it may reasonably be asked what any of this has to do with the ECJ. While decisions of the US Supreme Court may be of interest, and have some advisory weight, in a European context, they certainly are not binding precedent in Europe. So, with *Pace* in mind, let us turn to some European precedent that *is* relevant.

The Law for the Protection of German Blood and Honour, one of the infamous Nuremberg Laws of 1935, declared that "marriages between Jews and nationals of German or kindred blood are forbidden" and that such marriages were void and criminal. The law also criminalised "relations outside marriage between Jews and nationals of German or kindred blood".[19]

Did the Nazi law discriminate on the basis of race?

The question was a silly one before *Grant*. It is no longer silly. Imagine that the validity of such a law came before the European Court of Human Rights. That is not impossible; the sort of racialism that begot the Nazis is not dead in Europe. Such a law would be subject to challenge under the European Convention on Human Rights, which declares the rights "to respect for . . . private . . . life" and "to marry and to found a family", and requires that the rights that it enumerates "shall be secured without discrimination on any ground such as . . . race, . . . religion, . . . national or social origin . . ."[20]

The argument for upholding the law would be structurally identical to that of *Grant*. Compare the following with the quotation from *Grant*, above:

> "Punishment is imposed on a German if he has sexual relations with a Jew, just as it is on a Jew if he has sexual relations with a German. Since the condition imposed by

[17] *Ibid*., at 192–93.

[18] *Los Angeles Dept. of Water & Power* v. *Manhart*, 435 US 702, 711 (1978) (quoting "Developments in the Law, Employment Discrimination and Title VII of the Civil Rights Act of 1964", (1971) 84 *Harvard Law Review* 1109 at 1170, in holding that Title VII prohibits assessment of larger pension fund contributions from female than from male employees, even though as a class women do live longer than men).

[19] Law for the Protection of German Blood and German Honour of 15 Sept. 1935, partial translation by Office of US Chief of Counsel, in J Mendelsohn (ed.), *The Holocaust: Selected Documents, vol. 1: Legalizing the Holocaust, The Early Phase, 1933–39* (New York, Garland Publishing, 1982), at 24–25.

[20] Council of Europe, Convention for the Protection of Human Rights and Fundamental Freedoms, Arts. 8, 12, 14.

the law applies in the same way to Germans and Jews, it cannot be regarded as constituting discrimination directly based on race".

Similarly, an employer's denial of travel concessions to mixed Jewish-German couples, but not to "racially pure" Jewish-Jewish or German-German couples, could be subject to challenge before the ECJ under EC directives prohibiting discrimination in employment based on "racial or ethnic origin" or "religion".[21] Again, compare the following with the quotation from *Grant*, above:

> "[T]ravel concessions are refused to a German worker if he or she is living with a Jewish worker, just as they are to a Jewish worker if he or she is living with a German worker. Since the condition imposed by the undertaking's regulations applies in the same way to German and Jewish workers, it cannot be regarded as constituting discrimination directly based on racial or ethnic origin or religion".

If *Grant*'s definition of discrimination is accepted, then it is hard to see how to avoid these results.

III

Grant has been treated too respectfully by its commentators, who treat the problem it presents in a way that makes it seem harder than it really is. That commentary has focused, much more than American discussions of the sex discrimination argument had, on the question of how to decide the appropriate similarly-situated person of the other sex with whom to compare the plaintiff. "In order to establish that there is discrimination, a relevant comparator is normally invoked to establish that less favourable treatment has been afforded as a consequence of the use of the sex-derived criteria".[22] The problem is that of selecting the relevant comparator, as Kenneth Armstrong notes:

> "Clearly, Lisa Grant received less favourable treatment when compared with a heterosexual male. But, this is where a difficulty creeps in. In order to establish that a female is treated less favourably than a male then all conditions should remain the same other than the fact of being of one sex or another. To compare Lisa Grant to a heterosexual male is to change two conditions: biological sex and sexual orientation. Thus, it can be argued that the correct comparator must be a homosexual male in order for biological sex to be the determining factor. In which case one finds that Lisa Grant is treated no less favourably then a male with a same-sex partner. This was the approach taken by the ECJ".[23]

[21] See Bell, chap. 37.

[22] K A Armstrong, "Tales of the Community: sexual orientation discrimination and EC law", (1998) 20 *Journal of Social Welfare & Family Law* 455 at 460.

[23] *Ibid*. A number of commentators have been persuaded by this reasoning. See R Bailey-Harris, "Comment: *Grant* v. *South-West Trains Ltd*.", (1998) 28 *Family Law* 392; C Barnard, "The Principle of Equality in the Community Context: *P*, *Grant*, *Kalanke* and *Marshall*: Four Uneasy Bedfellows?", (1998) 57 *Cambridge Law Journal* 352 at 364–65; C Barnard, "Some Are More Equal Than Others: The Decision of the Court of Justice in *Grant* v. *South-West Trains*", in A Dashwood & A Ward (eds.), 1 *Cambridge Yearbook of European Legal Studies* (Oxford, Hart Publishing, 1999), at 153–4.

Robert Wintemute has objected that this argument "avoids a finding of direct sex discrimination by changing not only the sex of the man but also the sex of his partner. Yet for a valid sex discrimination analysis, the comparison must change only the sex of the complaining individual and must hold all other circumstances constant".[24] Armstrong objects that the ECJ's approach makes sexual orientation an additional variable, but no one in *Grant* made that a variable. If Lisa Grant, while remaining a lesbian, had taken up living quarters with a man, she would have been entitled to the benefits. Her predecessor in the job who lived with a woman was entitled to the benefits even if he was gay.[25]

The most sophisticated defence of the reasoning of *Grant* (written, however, before the Court's decision was handed down) has been made by John Gardner.[26] I will end this discussion of the commentators by considering his argument in some detail. Gardner attempts to defend the logic followed by *Grant*, but what he actually accomplishes is to reveal, more explicitly than the court's opinion does, the bankruptcy of that logic.

Professor Gardner argues that sexuality discrimination is not sex discrimination because, although such discrimination does take sex into account, it does so as a minor or auxiliary rather than a major or operative premise of the discriminator's reasoning.

The distinction between major and minor premises is integral to the syllogism, which is the basic unit of deductive reasoning. In a syllogism, two premises entail a conclusion. The major premise attributes a predicate to a category. The minor premise states that an individual is a member of that category. The conclusion attributes the predicate to the individual named in the minor premise. Thus, from the major premise "all men are mortal" and the minor premise "Socrates is a man" follows the conclusion, "Socrates is mortal".

Gardner's objection to the sex discrimination argument turns on the fact that, in practical reasoning, only the major premises have motivating force.

> "I reason: (1) I need to be home by seven; (2) it's now six; (3) the bus sometimes takes as much as an hour; so (4) I'd better leave now. Only (1) is an operative premiss, while (2) and (3) are auxiliary, leading to conclusion (4). Premisses (2) and (3) simply supply the information which allows me to derive one injunction to action from another, to work out the means I must use, (4) from the end I must achieve, (1). That 'it's now six'

[24] R Wintemute, "Recognising New Kinds of Direct Sex Discrimination: Transsexualism, Sexual Orientation and Dress Codes", (1997) 60 *Modern Law Review* 334 at 344. Wintemute's analysis has been quoted with approval by two commentators on *Grant*. L R Helfer, "International Decisions: *Grant* v. *South-West Trains Ltd.*", (1999) 93 *American Journal of International Law* 200 at 202; M Bowley, "A Pink Platform", (13 March 1998) 148 *New Law Journal* 376. As will be seen, I agree with Wintemute.

[25] In both hypothetical cases, "a statutory declaration . . . that a meaningful relationship has existed for a period of two years or more" had to be signed. See *Grant*, *supra* n.2, at para. 5. The policy did not make clear whether it could be satisfied if the parties were in a *celibate* meaningful relationship.

[26] For clarity, it should be noted at the outset that Gardner is a strong supporter of legal equality for gays. My disagreement with him here is confined to our differing assessments of the strength of the sex discrimination argument.

> or 'the bus sometimes takes as much as an hour' is motivationally inert by itself, without some premiss like (1) to give it some significance for my action. That's what makes these premisses auxiliary".[27]

Gardner thinks that the distinction between these two kinds of premises is crucial to the proper understanding of antidiscrimination law. "There is no such thing as an auxiliary premiss which one is right to believe but wrong to act on; since an auxiliary premiss has only an informational and not a motivational role in one's thinking, the only question which arises is whether one is right to believe it".[28] The core case of discrimination that Gardner seems to have in mind is one in which the desire to discriminate is what motivates the discriminator: "(1) I hate Wallonians. (2) John is a Wallonian. (3) I hate John". One cannot be motivated by a minor premise, because minor premises merely state what is the case and are motivationally inert. Therefore, if the sex of the person discriminated against figures into the discriminator's reasoning only as a minor premise, it cannot be sex that is motivating the discriminator.

One should be able to see immediately that something has gone wrong here. If someone is being treated in a way that would have been different but for her sex, then sex is certainly figuring into the discriminator's reasoning. The fact of her sex is itself motivationally inert, but if her sex is the but-for cause of the discrimination, the thing but for which the discrimination would not have occurred, then something in the discriminator's major premises is making her sex relevant.

Gardner's argument depends for its force on a failure to unpack the supposedly neutral major premise. Consider the defendant's rule of decision in *Grant*. The rule does not discriminate on the basis of sex in the same way as, say, a rule that only male employees get free passes for their girlfriends. But it does require the decisionmaker to look for auxiliary premises that discriminate on the basis of sex. It expressly makes the sex of the employee relevant to her opportunities.

One could unpack the company's reasoning in the following way:[29]

(1) every employee gets a free pass for a person of the opposite sex with whom the worker has a stable relationship.
(2) not all of our employees' stable relationships are with persons of the opposite sex.
Therefore
(3a) Of employees who have stable relationships with women, males will get the benefit and females will not.
(3b) Of employees who have stable relationships with men, females will get the benefit and males will not.

[27] J Gardner, "On the Ground of Her Sex(uality)", (1998) 18 *Oxford Journal of Legal Studies* 167 at 180.
[28] *Ibid.*, at 182.
[29] The following syllogism is modeled on one that Gardner lays out at p. 181 in an attempt to show the failure of the sex discrimination argument.

(4) Lisa Grant has a stable relationship with a woman.
(5) Lisa Grant is female.
Therefore
(6) She doesn't get the benefit.

Suppose we were to concede, for the sake of the argument, that the starting premise, (1), does not discriminate among men and women. But just for that reason, it cannot operate as a working rule of decision. In the reasoning necessary to apply the rule, (3a) becomes a new operative premise, to which (4) and (5) are auxiliary. (3a) expressly discriminates on the basis of sex. It doesn't seem to me that this conclusion is changed by the fact that there is an analogue of (3a) in (3b).

The larger point is that, in order for sex to figure as a relevant auxiliary premise in anybody's reasoning, there must be some operative premise that is making it relevant. Thus, it appears to me that Gardner's attempted distinction between the "operative premise" test, which he endorses, and the "but-for" test, which asks whether the discriminator would have acted differently but for the victim's sex, collapses. Where discriminations of a parallel nature are going on, then it is perhaps possible to state the reasoning while suppressing the operative premise that is doing this work, but it will always be possible to dig out that operative premise.

One might reach the same conclusion more directly by asking why the "but-for" test is not always preferable to the subtleties of Gardner's "operative premise" test, which makes many obvious cases of discrimination seem hard to invalidate. Gardner's approach would reach only those kinds of discrimination where only one race or sex is burdened, such as when a law excluded blacks and only blacks from juries.[30] And this seems to be the core case of discrimination that he has in mind. But his argument would render deeply problematic the US Supreme Court's decision in *Brown* v. *Board of Education* against racially segregated schools, since all races were equally forbidden to attend the schools of the other race. It would revive the Southern states' defence of the miscegenation laws, already discussed above. As we have seen, it could even be invoked in defence of the Nuremberg laws. Indeed, I wonder whether there is *any* discrimination that could not be recharacterised in race- or sex-neutral terms, so that the victim's race or sex would only figure as an auxiliary premise. In the jury example mentioned above, one could have a rule that "no one may serve on a jury who belongs to a race that did not serve on juries in 1850." This rule would, of course, apply equally to both races. Would anything at all be left of antidiscrimination law if one allowed discriminators this safe harbour?[31]

[30] See *Strauder* v. *West Virginia*, 100 US 303 (1879).

[31] Gardner could reply that, in the hypothetical case, the law would be a sham, existing only to protect discrimination. In practice, however, judges are exceedingly reluctant to attribute bad motives to legislatures. See K L Karst, "The Costs of Motive-Centered Inquiry", (1978) 15 *San Diego Law Review* 1163 at 1164–65. That is one of the strengths of an approach to antidiscrimination law that applies the but-for test, instead of attempting to reconstruct the reasoning process of the

IV

One can nonetheless appreciate what led the European Court of Justice to do what it did. From a political standpoint, the sex discrimination argument proves too much. The sex discrimination argument has great logical power, but paradoxically, this very strength is its often-fatal weakness. If accepted, the argument would cast into question *all* laws discriminating against gays.

The Court's caution can be usefully contrasted with an earlier decision in which it was bolder. In *P.* v. *S. and Cornwall County Council*,[32] the Court held that discrimination against transsexuals was contrary to the 1976 Equal Treatment Directive. The Court noted in *P.* that discrimination based on gender reassignment was "based, essentially if not exclusively, on the sex of the person concerned".[33] This conclusion appeared to give Lisa Grant an unbeatable case, but the *Grant* court declared without explanation that the holding of *P.* "is limited to the case of a worker's gender reassignment and does not therefore apply to differences of treatment based on a person's sexual orientation".[34]

P. and *Grant* are logically indistinguishable. As Mark Bell shrewdly notes, however, they are very different politically. Because gay people are so much more numerous than transsexuals, a decision in Lisa Grant's favour would have had a much greater impact than *P.* did. And because of the smaller numbers, there was little public awareness of *P.*, while a decision in favor of Grant would have been highly visible and controversial.[35] Moreover, the public status of homosexuality is an emotionally charged and salient issue. Prudence dictates that the Court keep its distance from this minefield.[36]

The Court's reticence may have been reinforced by the limitations of its traditional mission and of the central ambition of the law that it was interpreting. The EC Treaty did not begin as a human rights instrument. Its function is primarily to create a single market in Europe, and its equal pay provision is an ancillary device whose original purpose was to prevent businesses in states permitting lower pay for women from having a competitive advantage in the single market. The primary human rights instrument in Europe is the European Convention on Human Rights, and the authoritative interpreter of the Convention is the European Court of Human Rights (ECtHR), whose lead the ECJ generally follows when applying the Convention in cases involving EC law.

discriminator to see whether the forbidden category figured in a major or a minor premise of the discriminator's reasoning.

[32] Case C-13/94, [1996] ECR I-2143.

[33] *Ibid.*, at para. 21.

[34] *Grant*, *supra* n.2, at para. 42.

[35] M Bell, "Shifting Conceptions of Sexual Discrimination at the Court of Justice: from *P* v. *S* to *Grant* v. *SWT*", (1999) 5 *European Law Journal* 63 at 74–76.

[36] In *Grant*, *supra* n.2, at paras. 47–48, the Court passed the issue to the EC legislature by referring to the possibility of new legislation prohibiting sexual orientation discrimination in employment under Art. 13 of the EC Treaty. See Bell, chap. 37.

Thus, in *Grant*, the ECJ cited decisions of the European Commission of Human Rights (the tribunal that formerly screened cases for the ECtHR) holding that less favourable treatment of same-sex couples, compared with unmarried opposite-sex couples, does not violate the Convention.[37] The European Court of Human Rights has an explicit "margin of appreciation" policy which allows states some discretion to depart from the human rights norm based on local conditions. The margin of appreciation is broadest with respect to matters of social policy, and where there is not yet any "European consensus" on the particular issue.[38] If the tribunals charged with enforcing the Convention were not yet willing to protect same-sex couples against discrimination, the ECJ was not going to jump ahead.

None of these considerations could have easily been written into the opinion, but all of them probably influenced the outcome in *Grant*. This analysis diminishes the weight of *Grant* as a precedent in other human rights decisions. Perhaps the damage done by *Grant* was unavoidable, but that damage should not be permitted to spread any further.[39]

[37] See *Grant*, *ibid*., at para 33. On the Convention, see Wintemute, chap. 40.

[38] See, eg, *Petrovic* v. *Austria* (28 Feb. 1998), http://www.echr.coe.int/hudoc (ECtHR), at paras. 38–43; Case C-317/93, *Nolte* v. *Landesversicherungsanstalt Hannover*, [1995] ECR I-4625 (ECJ), at para. 33. All of these points were made in conversation by my colleague at Northwestern University, Prof. Douglass W Cassel Jr.

[39] *Grant* did not affect the decisions of the ECtHR in *Lustig-Prean & Beckett* v. *United Kingdom*, *Smith & Grady* v. *United Kingdom* (27 Sept. 1999), http://www.echr.coe.int/hudoc, holding that the British ban on gays in the military violated the Convention.

36

Towards the Recognition of Same-Sex Partners in European Union Law: Expectations Based on Trends in National Law

KEES WAALDIJK[1]

INTRODUCTION

IN THE FINAL third of the last century (i.e. since the 1960s), an increase in the legal recognition of homosexuality could be seen in almost all European countries. Four trends appear to be characteristic of this process of legal recognition *at the national level:* (i) steady progress; (ii) standard sequences; (iii) small change; and (iv) symbolic preparation. The purpose of this chapter is to assess how these trends might also operate *at the supranational level* of the European Union. The assumption is that a comparative analysis of national legislation may provide useful guidance about what recognition of same-sex partners to expect (and to demand) from the legislative bodies of the European Community—and when.

COMPARATIVE OVERVIEW

For thirty-six member states of the Council of Europe, I have summarised the process of legal recognition of homosexuality by listing (in the Appendix, Tables 1 and 2, pp. 649–50) the years of the main *legislative* steps in that process. The structure of both tables is based on my perception of the trends of *steady progress* and of *standard sequences* (see below). The idea is that almost all (European) countries go, at different times and paces, through a standard sequence of steps recognising homosexuality. After decriminalisation (followed or accompanied by an equalisation of the ages of consent), more or less specific anti-discrimination

[1] LL.M., Ph.D.; Senior Lecturer, E.M. Meijers Institute of Legal Studies, Faculty of Law, Universiteit Leiden, c.waaldijk@law.leidenuniv.nl, http://ruljis.leidenuniv.nl/user/cwaaldij/www/.

legislation will be enacted, to be followed by legislation institutionalising same-sex partnership (and parenthood).[2]

Table 1 ranks the fifteen member states of the European Union according to the number of steps they have taken in their legislation, and according to how long ago a particular country legislated its last step. Table 2 gives a ranking, based on the same criteria, of twenty-one other member states of the Council of Europe. By presenting these two groups of countries separately, it becomes evident that the pattern of legal reform among EU countries is similar to that among non-EU countries.

Both tables are of course a gross simplification. Judicial, administrative, local and non-governmental forms of (legal) recognition have not been incorporated. In the two columns on criminal law, no distinction has been made between laws only applying to sex between men, and laws also applying to sex between women. Earlier periods of equality in criminal law have not been taken into account.[3] Legislative recognition of unregistered same-sex cohabitation (eg Hungary) is absent from this overview, as are the possibilities for same-sex couples to have joint authority over the children of one of the partners (eg United Kingdom, the Netherlands, Iceland).

FOUR TRENDS

The four trends characteristic of the process of legislative recognition of different aspects of same-sex love, can be witnessed in so many (European) countries that it is tempting to formulate them as "laws". In the absence of falsification so far, I will indeed speculatively formulate the third and fourth trends as "laws".[4] The notable exceptions to the first two trends, however, prevent me from phrasing them as general truths.

The Trend of Steady Progress

Since the 1960s, almost all European countries have made some legislative progress in the legal recognition of homosexuality. The tables in the Appendix show four exceptions to this trend of steady progress. In Greece, the last round of progressive legislation relating to homosexuality took place a little earlier (in 1950). And the other three exceptions (Turkey, Italy and Poland) happen to be

[2] K Waaldijk, "Standard Sequences in the Legal Recognition of Homosexuality—Europe's Past, Present and Future", (1994) 4 *Australasian Gay and Lesbian Law Journal* 50; "Civil Developments: Patterns of Reform in the Legal Recognition of Same-Sex Partners in Europe", (2000) 17 *Canadian Journal of Family Law* 61.

[3] The most recent example of such a period was in Portugal from 1945 until 1995. See H Graupner, *Sexualitaet, Jugendschutz und Menschenrechte*, Teil 2 (Frankfurt, P Lang, 1997) at 597–8.

[4] I hope to challenge readers to try to falsify my hypotheses.

the three European countries with by far the longest uninterrupted history of full equality in criminal law.[5] In most countries, one step of legislative recognition of homosexuality was followed some years later with one or two other steps in the same direction.

Furthermore, since the 1960s, hardly any country has introduced new anti-homosexual legislation. Luxembourg did so in 1971 by introducing a higher minimum age for homosexual sex,[6] and Portugal did it (inadvertently) in 1995 by introducing a lower minimum age for heterosexual sex.[7] The only other example that I know of is the (ineffective) British law of 1988 prohibiting local authorities from "promoting" homosexuality.[8]

The Trend of Standard Sequences

A *standard sequence* may be seen in the typical order of the changes in those countries that do make progress. Legislative recognition of homosexuality starts (most probably after some form of association of homosexuals and information on homosexuality has become legal) with (1) decriminalisation, followed or sometimes accompanied by the setting of an equal age of consent, after which (2) anti-discrimination legislation can be introduced, before the process is finished with (3) legislation recognising same-sex partnership and parenting. This trend is quite strong, both inside and outside the European Union. This can be seen in Tables 1 and 2 in the Appendix:

- In only thirteen of the thirty-six countries was the decriminalisation of homosexual acts accompanied by the setting of an equal age of consent.[9] In most countries, the step of decriminalisation was (or will have to be) followed by a later step of equalising the age limits.
- With the exceptions of Ireland and Finland, all countries that have so far enacted anti-discrimination provisions, had decriminalised homosexual activity and had established equal ages of consent at least three years before.[10] Furthermore, only four of the twelve countries with equal ages of consent for

[5] Turkey and Italy lead in this way (with 143 and 112 years respectively). Poland (with 69 years) is also far ahead of countries like the Netherlands and Norway.

[6] From 1971 until 1992, the minimum age for sex between women or between men was eighteen, whereas the heterosexual age limit was fourteen; since 1992, it has been sixteen for all. See Graupner, *supra* n.3, at 531.

[7] In 1995, the minimum age for heterosexual sex was lowered from sixteen to fourteen, whereas the homosexual age limit was left at sixteen; Graupner, *supra* n.3, at 597–8.

[8] Local Government Act 1988, s. 28 (now only England and Wales; repealed for Scotland in 2000).

[9] However, in five of these countries (Netherlands, France, Belgium, Luxembourg and Portugal), different age limits were introduced many years after the initial decriminalisation.

[10] Finland equalised its age limits three years *after* the introduction of specific anti-discrimination legislation.

more than a decade, have so far *not* enacted anti-discrimination provisions: Belgium, Poland, Italy and Turkey.

- All twelve countries with some form of national or regional registered partnership legislation in force or in preparation have already equalised their ages of consent in criminal law. And ten of them also have in force national constitutional or legislative anti-discrimination provisions intended to cover sexual orientation. The two apparent exceptions are Belgium and Germany (but see p. 767, and note the provisions in four German *Länder*). Furthermore, only three of the thirteen countries with such anti-discrimination provisions do not have some form of national or regional registered partnership legislation in force or in preparation: Ireland, Luxembourg and Slovenia.

The "Law of Small Change"

A *"law of small change"* can be formulated to capture the fact that legislative change on homosexuality is seldom big; legislation advancing the recognition and acceptance of homosexuality only gets enacted if it is perceived as a small change to the law, or if it is sufficiently reduced in impact by some accompanying legislative "small change" that reinforces the condemnation of homosexuality.[11]

The "Law of Symbolic Preparation"

Finally, I would submit, the process is governed by a *"law of symbolic preparation"*. A legal system that has been oppressing homosexuality, will only move to legislation that actually protects and supports lesbian women and gay men, after first passing some symbolic legislation reducing the condemnation of homosexuality (e.g. by advancing its acceptance). The main examples of the working of this law are decriminalisation (which seldom is more than the repeal of criminal rules that were hardly ever applied, because almost all forbidden acts take place in private, or because the authorities had already decided to no longer prosecute under these rules) and anti-discrimination legislation (which mostly consists of rules that are hardly ever applied, because the forbidden grounds often remain undetected and unprovable in the mind of the discriminator, or because the victims of the discrimination frequently have good reasons *not* to start proceedings).

This is not to say that criminal and anti-discrimination provisions do not have any practical effects: in certain individual cases they will be used, and they will serve generally to deter or justify certain behaviour. It seems that only after decriminalisation and anti-discrimination legislation have been enacted, will national law-makers pass legislation that is of more direct practical importance to the lives of greater numbers of lesbian women, gay men and their children.

[11] For illustrations of this "law" at work in the Netherlands, see Waaldijk, chap. 23.

The primary importance of the intermediate symbolic legislation may well lie in its paving the way for such practical legislation on partnership and parenting. Jurisdictions (and their judges, legislators, and electorates) seem to need time to get used to the idea that homosexuality is neither a crime, nor a good reason for refusing employment or housing.

PREDICTING DEVELOPMENTS IN EUROPEAN UNION LAW

I will now try to use these four trends and "laws" to predict the process of legal recognition of homosexuality, and especially same-sex partnership, in the European Union as such.

Steady Progress in the European Union

If most EU countries are making progress in the legal recognition of homosexuality, then it may be assumed that the EU as such will make similar *steady progress*. Furthermore, the European Parliament repeatedly,[12] the Commission and Council occasionally,[13] and the collective of member states once,[14] have given some evidence that homosexuality is slowly getting more favourable treatment in EC law. All this is not surprising, given the fact that the EU is becoming very much like a European state. The most recent example is Article 21 (Non-discrimination) of the (non-binding) Charter of Fundamental Rights of the European Union (the "EU Charter"): "Any discrimination based on any ground such as sex, race, colour, ethnic or social origin, language, genetic

[12] See eg "Resolution on sexual discrimination at the workplace", Official Journal (OJ) [1984] C 104/46; "Resolution on equal rights for homosexuals and lesbians in the EC", OJ [1994] C 61/40 (calls on the Commission to draft a Recommendation seeking to end "the barring of lesbians and homosexual couples from marriage or from an equivalent legal framework" and guaranteeing "the full rights and benefits of marriage, allowing the registration of partnerships"); "Resolution on respect for human rights in the European Union (1998–1999)", 16 March 2000, A5–0050/00, http://www.europarl.eu.int/plenary/default_en.htm ("57. . . . calls on the Member States . . . to amend their legislation recognising registered partnerships of persons of the same sex and assigning them the same rights and obligations as exist for registered partnerships between men and women; . . . to amend their legislation to grant legal recognition of extramarital cohabitation, irrespective of gender; . . . rapid progress should be made with mutual recognition of the different legally recognised non-marital modes of cohabitation and legal marriages between persons of the same sex in the EU"). See also p. 725, n. 70.

[13] Notably by including anti-homosexual harassment in the notion of sexual harassment in the non-binding "Commission Recommendation of 27 Nov. 1991 on the protection of the dignity of women and men at work", endorsed by a Council Declaration of 19 Dec. 1991 (OJ [1992] L 49/1, C 27/01). See A Byrne, "Equality and Non-Discrimination" in Waaldijk & Clapham (eds.), *Homosexuality: A European Community Issue* (Dordrecht, Martinus Nijhoff Publishers, 1993) 211 at 214–5; M Bell, "Equal Rights and EU Policies", in K Krickler (ed.), *After Amsterdam: Sexual Orientation and the European Union* (Brussels, ILGA-Europe, 1999) at 30–1, http://www.ilga-europe.org (Policy Documents). See also *infra* n.24.

[14] By including the ground of "sexual orientation" in the new Art. 13 of the EC Treaty, which empowers the Council to combat discrimination on various grounds.

features, political or other opinion, religion or belief, membership of a national minority, property, birth, disability, age or *sexual orientation* shall be prohibited".[15] Just like other European states, the EU is gradually recognising homosexuality in law.

Following the Standard Sequence?

If the EU then may be following the trend of steady progress, the expectation should be that it will also follow the standard sequence. Here, the problem is that the EU as such has no history of anti-homosexual criminal law, because criminal law has generally been a competence of the member states. So for the first steps, we have to look at the individual member states. All have decriminalised. Eleven have equalised their ages of consent. Four member states still have unequal age limits,[16] and at least one of them, Austria, is still actively using the higher age limit for gay sex to imprison people.[17] This may not be a total bar to any anti-discrimination or indeed partnership legislation by the EC; after all, Ireland and Finland have shown that anti-discrimination legislation may be enacted before full equality in criminal law has been reached.[18] Furthermore, the age limit discrimination in the criminal law of two countries is limited (to oral and manual sex in Ireland and to seduction in Greece), and in Portugal the age limit for gay sex is not higher than it is for heterosexual sex in most other countries.[19]

Hopefully, a future ruling of the European Court of Human Rights will establish that age limits in criminal law must not discriminate on the basis of sexual orientation. Such a ruling (most likely in a future case against Austria)[20] would probably result in a further reduction of the number of member states with discriminatory age limits. And that in turn would help to pave the way for more comprehensive anti-discrimination measures being unanimously adopted by the Council of the EU.

With a majority of the member states having national anti-discrimination legislation covering sexual orientation by 1997,[21] the time had come for the

[15] Solemn Proclamation, signed by the Presidents of the European Parliament, the Council, and the Commission in Nice on 7 Dec. 2000, OJ [2000] C 364/1 (emphasis added).

[16] See App., Table 1.

[17] See H Graupner, "Austria", in D West & R Green (eds.), *Sociolegal Control of Homosexuality: A Multi-Nation Comparison* (New York, Plenum Press, 1997) 269 at 273.

[18] See p. 637.

[19] See App., Table 1.

[20] In *Sutherland* v. *UK* (No. 25186/94), the European Commission of Human Rights has already reached this conclusion (Report of 1 July 1997, http://www.echr.coe.int/hudoc). That the European Court of Human Rights will follow the Commission seems likely, given three cases recently decided by the Court: *Smith & Grady* v. *UK* and *Lustig-Prean & Beckett* v. *UK* (27 Sept. 1999); *Salgueiro da Silva Mouta* v. *Portugal* (21 Dec. 1999); *A.D.T.* v. *UK* (31 July 2000). Three challenges to an unequal age limit, *S.L.* v. *Austria* (No. 45330/99), *G.L.* v. *Austria* (No. 39392/98), and *A.V.* v. *Austria* (No. 39829/98), were communicated by the Court to the respondent on 30 Jan. 2001. See Graupner, chap. 30.

[21] See App., Table 1.

adoption of EC rules outlawing at least certain forms of discrimination. These could be based on the new Article 13 in the EC Treaty (added in October 1997 and in force since May 1999), which enables the Council (acting unanimously) to prohibit discrimination on eight grounds, including *sexual orientation*.[22] The Commission did not waste much time in preparing some implementation of Article 13: on 25 November 1999, it presented a "Proposal for a Council directive establishing a general framework for equal treatment in employment and occupation",[23] which would prohibit employment discrimination on all Article 13 EC grounds (including sexual orientation, but excluding sex, already covered by other directives). The proposal made swift progress and was adopted by the Council on 27 November 2000.[24]

This new "Framework Directive" could (together with the no doubt growing number of countries with some sort of same-sex partnership legislation) greatly help to prepare the ground for later EC legislation recognising same-sex partnership, in such diverse fields as freedom of movement or the EC staff regulations. The Directive could also provide the much needed extra justification for the Court of Justice to interpret the numerous references in EC law to "spouses" in a less traditional way.[25] One of the key dynamics of the standard sequence seems to be, that once a jurisdiction has prohibited others (e.g. employers) from distinguishing on the basis of sexual orientation, the legislature and judiciary will have to ask themselves whether it is justifiable that the law itself continues to distinguish on the same, now suspect ground.[26]

Small Change in the EU

That the EU in this field is following the *"law of small change"* is only too evident. The first mention of homosexuality in a legal anti-discrimination document can be found in the *explanatory* part of the *non-binding* "Commission Recommendation of 27 November 1991 on the protection of the dignity of

[22] See M Bell, "The New Article 13 EC Treaty: A Sound Basis for European Anti-Discrimination Law?", (1999) 6 *Maastricht Journal of European and Comparative Law* 5; L Flynn, "The Implications of Article 13 EC—After Amsterdam, Will Some Forms of Discrimination Be More Equal than Others?", (1999) 36 *Common Market Law Review* 1127. See also Krickler, *supra* n.13.

[23] COM (1999) 565, OJ [2000] C 177 E/42. See Bell, chap. 37.

[24] Council Dir. 2000/78/EC of 27 Nov. 2000 establishing a general framework for equal treatment in employment and occupation, OJ [2000] L 303/16. Two grounds (racial or ethnic origin) were deleted because they were covered by a separate directive. See *infra* n.33.

[25] At the very least, any distinction between married heterosexual spouses and homosexual registered partners should be classified as a distinction based on sexual orientation. The first chance for the Court of Justice to rule on this point came when it had to decide *D. v. Council*, Cases C-122/99 P, C-125/99 P (appeals from a 28 Jan. 1999 decision of the Court of First Instance in Case T-274/97; in his Opinion of 22 Feb. 2001, Advocate General Mischo urged the Court of Justice to dismiss the appeals; the Court of Justice agreed in its Judgment of 31 May 2001; see Conclusion, pp. 767–69). See also Bell, chap. 37; L Flynn, "Equality between Men and Women in the Court of Justice", in Eeckhout & Tridimas (eds.), (1998) 18 *Yearbook of European Law* 259 at 285–26.

[26] See Waaldijk (2000), *supra* n.2, at 85.

women and men at work".[27] What followed were facilities for same-sex partners of European Parliament staff to use restaurants and language courses.[28] And the new anti-discrimination clause in the Staff Regulation does indeed include the ground of sexual orientation.[29] However, the clause renders itself virtually meaningless with regard to the partners of gay and lesbian staff by providing that distinctions based on marital status are unaffected.[30]

These small changes indicate that it is more than probable that EC legislation protecting or supporting lesbian women and gay men will take relatively short steps, reflecting the caution or prejudice of perhaps only a few of the many individuals and countries involved in producing EC rules. The new Article 13 of the EC Treaty itself, although politically important, is already an example of that: it is only an enabling clause, it has no direct effect, it can only be implemented by a unanimous Council, and the ground of sexual orientation is not accompanied by that of civil status.[31] Similarly, Article 21 of the new EU Charter is not binding.

Of the first two directives adopted by the Council on the basis of Article 13 EC, only the Framework Directive deals with sexual orientation discrimination, and that directive only covers the field of employment.[32] That restriction is in sharp contrast with the much wider directive prohibiting racial discrimination in employment, social security, healthcare, education, and the provision of goods and services, including housing (the "Race Directive").[33] And the potential impact of the Framework Directive may be further reduced by the following pieces of "small change":

- As to the ground *sexual orientation*, the Commission's explanatory memorandum claims that "a clear dividing line should be drawn between sexual orientation, which is covered by this proposal, and sexual behaviour, which is not".[34] This is of course a nonsensical claim: no such dividing line can be made, because in most cases of anti-homosexual discrimination, the difference of treatment is based on *the sexual orientation of certain behaviour*. Hardly anyone will be denied employment because he or she has had sex (or lives) with another person, nor because of his or her unexpressed sexual preferences: the denial of employment will far more often be based on the sexual orientation of the sexual activity or on the sexual orientation of the

[27] See *supra* n.13.

[28] On 25 Feb. 2000, a similar measure was adopted at the Court of Justice: non-pecuniary spousal benefits are now available to unmarried (same-sex or different-sex) partners of employees of the Court. A more generous scheme, including pecuniary benefits such as pension entitlements, was adopted on 17 Aug. 1995 at the European Monetary Institute in Frankfurt, and subsequently at the European Central Bank.

[29] Council Regulation 781/98 of 7 April 1998, OJ [1998] L 113/4, Art. 1a.

[30] See Bell, *supra* n.13, at 31.

[31] See *supra* n.22.

[32] See *supra* n.24.

[33] Council Dir. 2000/43/EC of 29 June 2000 implementing the principle of equal treatment between persons irrespective of racial or ethnic origin, OJ [2000] L 180/22, Art. 3.

[34] *Supra* n.23, para. 5 at Art. 1.

cohabitation, i.e. on the fact that the person's behaviour was oriented towards someone of the same sex.[35] Nevertheless, the statement in the explanatory memorandum could be (wrongly) interpreted (at the national level) as implying that employers will be allowed to continue discrimination against *practising* homosexuals. Fortunately, the Court of Justice does not use explanatory memoranda when interpreting directives.

- The explanatory memorandum also claims that "this proposal does not affect marital status and therefore it does not impinge upon entitlements to benefits for married couples".[36] Preambular paragraph 22 repeats this claim: "This Directive is without prejudice to national laws on marital status and the benefits dependent thereon." This claim is in direct contradiction to the proposed prohibition of indirect discrimination. It is evident, in the words of Article 2(2) of the Directive, that the "apparently neutral" criterion of marital status "puts . . . at a particular disadvantage" gay and lesbian couples, because they are barred from marriage. Of course, neither the explanatory memorandum nor the preamble can introduce an exception to the operative part of the Directive. Nevertheless, these statements could be (wrongly) interpreted as implying that employers will be allowed to continue the most common form of *indirect* anti-homosexual discrimination—even if there is no objective justification for it.
- Article 4(2) of the Directive allows for an exception for "public or private organisations the ethos of which is based on religion or belief". Under certain conditions such organisations would then be permitted to base a difference of treatment on "a person's religion or belief" (but not another ground),[37] and "to require individuals working with them to act in good faith and with loyalty to the organisation's ethos." Applying the "loyalty to the ethos" requirement, certain religious organisations could claim to have the freedom to continue discriminating against lesbians and gay men.

These three, dangerously vague, potential restrictions of the proposed prohibition of sexual orientation discrimination in employment seem to have been politically necessary to achieve the unanimous adoption of the directive as a whole.

[35] In view of *Grant* v. *South-West Trains*, Case C-249/96, [1998] European Court Reports I-621, it will be difficult to deny that to discriminate between same-sex and different-sex partners is indeed sexual orientation discrimination. Under the Dutch General Equal Treatment Act, the main problems of anti-homosexual discrimination are in fact related to the non-availability for same-sex couples of marital status and marital advantages: since 1994, two-thirds of the more than thirty-five "homosexual cases" brought before the Equal Treatment Commission have been about such partner-discrimination. See http://ruljis.leidenuniv.nl/user/cwaaldij/www/ (overview in Dutch).

[36] *Supra* n.23, para. 5 at Art. 1.

[37] The Commission's original proposal permitted discrimination based on a "relevant characteristic related to religion or belief", which seemed capable of being interpreted as covering sexual orientation. *Ibid.*, para. 5 at Art. 4.

Symbolic Preparation for Further Reforms in EU Law

As far as the *"law of symbolic preparation"* is concerned, the question must be whether the EU can properly be called a legal system that has been oppressing homosexuality. I think it can. Firstly, the EU is mainly the continuation, in a growing number of fields, of national legal systems that have oppressed homosexuality in many ways, and that are only slowly replacing the oppression with some recognition. Secondly, the directives and regulations of the EC are full of references to "marriage" and "spouse", thus excluding all homosexual partners from various advantages in many fields, especially that of free movement.[38] In a sense, the EC has its own—very traditional and therefore exclusively heterosexual—family law. Therefore, it may well be necessary to get some symbolic preparation enacted, before this legal system is up to the task of replacing its oppression with recognition.

As mentioned above, some such symbolic legislation has already been enacted in the context of the EC. Article 13 of the EC Treaty "stands out as conspicuously and deliberately neutered".[39] Nevertheless, the process of adopting the text of Article 13, including the words "sexual orientation", may have served to get the member states used to the idea that in the context of the EC they will occasionally have to address the rights of lesbian women and gay men. Thus, Article 13 "which at present stands as a rhetorical gesture may unexpectedly give additional content to the concept of (European) citizenship".[40] The rather limited Framework Directive on employment discrimination, and the non-binding Article 21 of the EU Charter, will serve as further symbolic legislation, preparing the field for more practically relevant laws. For example, it remains to be seen whether enough political power can be mobilised to make the Framework Directive as strong as the Race Directive, and whether the Framework Directive will (some day) be interpreted as prohibiting indirect discrimination via the so-called "neutral" criterion of marital status.[41]

For the European Union itself, opening up marriage or introducing registered partnership is not an option, because it has no competence relating to civil status in particular or family law in general, which is left to the member states.[42]

[38] The Dutch Government's "Commission on the opening up of civil marriage to persons of the same sex" made an inventory of EC regulations and directives explicitly referring to "marriage" or "spouse". In its report (*Rapport Commissie inzake openstelling van het burgerlijk huwelijk voor personen van hetzelfde geslacht*, The Hague, Ministry of Justice, Oct. 1997, at 34), it produced a list of seventeen such regulations and twenty-four such directives from very diverse fields, including the free movement of persons (notably Council Regulation 1612/68/EEC), social security, tax law, employment, agriculture (including Commission Regulation 2568/91/EEC on olive oil), fisheries (including Council Dir. 78/659/EEC on water quality for fish), transport (including Commission Dir. 91/662/EEC on the behaviour of the steering wheel), and insurance.

[39] Flynn, *supra* n.22, at 1133.

[40] *Ibid.*, at 1151–2.

[41] See p. 643.

[42] The institutions of the EU cannot provide EU citizens with a civil status (more or less equivalent to marriage). However, as employers, the institutions of the EC could establish a register of staff

Therefore, there are three forms of partner-discrimination which can be eliminated by—and in—EC law:

(1) discrimination between unmarried different-sex partners and unmarried same-sex partners (direct discrimination on the basis of sexual orientation);
(2) discrimination between married different-sex spouses and registered same-sex partners (direct or indirect discrimination on the basis of sexual orientation);[43]
(3) discrimination between married different-sex spouses and unmarried same-sex partners (indirect discrimination on the basis of sexual orientation).

The third form represents the biggest problem in most countries. However, if full equality (in employment) between unmarried same-sex couples and married different-sex couples remains too big a step for the Court of Justice, in interpreting the Framework Directive, then at least the other two forms of partner-discrimination need to be included in it. Both inclusions will be only of limited application in most member states (because they do not recognise unmarried different-sex partners or do not have registered partnership for same-sex partners), but they would be highly relevant as symbolic preparation for adjusting EC legislation to the existence of same-sex couples. This would lead to two principles to be incorporated in the interpretation of the Framework Directive:

- *Principle 1 (Employment). Where an employer provides spousal benefits to the unmarried different-sex partner of an employee, this employer should provide the same benefits to the unmarried same-sex partner of an employee.*

  (This of course is the principle that the Court of Justice refused to adopt, applying EC sex discrimination law, in *Grant* v. *South-West Trains*.[44]) This principle would only affect employers who are both too modern to deny the existence of heterosexual cohabitation, and too traditional to recognise gay and lesbian cohabitation. The huge majority of employers in Europe are

who have registered their unmarried partner for the purposes of claiming "spousal" rights and obligations under the Staff Regulations. See chap. III.i, Commission's consultative document of 29 Nov. 2000, SEC(2000)2085/4, discussed in *Egalité Newsletter*, Issue 31, Winter 2001, pp. 3–4). The EC has also entered the field of "free movement of civil status" through Council Regulation 1347/2000/EC of 29 May 2000 on jurisdiction and the recognition and enforcement of judgments in matrimonial matters and in matters of parental responsibility for children of both spouses.

[43] A fourth form of discrimination could emerge, if any national body or an EC institution refused to recognise a same-sex marriage (e.g., one contracted in the Netherlands) as equivalent to a different-sex marriage.

[44] *Supra* n.35. The Court misstated the issue in that case when it: "considered the position of unmarried same-sex couples in relationship to unmarried *and married* opposite-sex couples, where in fact, the only circumstance directly relevant to this case was the position of unmarried opposite-sex and unmarried same-sex couples. Lisa Grant's claim was centred on the fact that other *unmarried* couples enjoyed the travel concession". M Bell, "Shifting Conceptions of Sexual Discrimination at the Court of Justice: From *P* v. *S* to *Grant* v. *SWT*", (1999) 5 *European Law Journal* 63 at 72.

probably either more modern, or more traditional than that.[45] So they would not be bothered by this interpretation of the Framework Directive.[46]

- *Principle 2* (*Employment*). *Where an employer provides benefits to the married different-sex partner of an employee, this employer should provide the same benefits to the registered (or married) same-sex partner of an employee.*

  (This of course is the issue which the Court of Justice had to address in *D.* v. *Council*.[47]) This principle would only affect employers who happen to employ persons who have already registered with (or married) their same-sex partners, e.g. in a Nordic country or the Netherlands.[48] For most employers in other countries, it will be some time before this will be the case. However, given the *Grant* judgment, it can hardly be denied that to distinguish between different-sex marriage and same-sex registered partnership (or marriage) is (direct) discrimination on the basis of sexual orientation.

Then at some later stage the third principle could be added:

- *Principle 3* (*Employment*). *Where an employer provides benefits to the married different-sex partner of an employee, this employer should provide the same benefits to the partner of an employee who cannot marry the employee because they are of the same sex, and cannot register with the employee because there is no registered partnership legislation.*

It will then be up to the employer whether or not to provide the same benefits also to the unmarried different-sex partner of an employee who *has chosen* not to marry. Alternatively, employers could be required (by European or national law) to give equal treatment to married and *all unmarried* couples (i.e. including different-sex cohabitants).

Once Principles 1 and 2 (and perhaps 3) have been incorporated into the interpretation of the Framework Directive, the time will definitely have come to start amending (or re-interpreting) all the EC regulations and EC directives that favour married spouses. Because there are no EC rules that favour different-sex cohabitees over same-sex cohabitees, it will not be necessary to first apply Principle 1 to those regulations and directives. The incorporation of Principle 1 into the interpretation of the Framework Directive should make it politically possible to prevent spousal benefits in EC rules from being extended to *heterosexual* unmarried partners only.

In the absence of a move towards full equal treatment of married and unmarried partners (Principle 3), the process of amending or interpreting all those EC

[45] See pp. 642–43.

[46] For this reason (and because *Grant* was only about equal pay and not about other aspects of employment), I would disagree with M Bell (*supra* n.44, at 75, 79) and L Helfer ((1999) 93 *American Journal of International Law* 200 at 203), who have both argued that *Grant* may have been lost because the Court was asked to do too much.

[47] *Supra* n.25.

[48] For numbers of registered partners, see Waaldijk, chap. 23, App. VI.

rules could therefore cautiously start with Principle 2 (countering the second form of partner-discrimination):

- *Principle 2 (All EU Law). Where a directive or regulation provides for a benefit for married spouses, it should be interpreted as applying to same-sex married spouses, and interpreted or amended so as to make that benefit available to registered partners.*

That principle will probably be first applied to the staff regulations of the EC, because there the parallel with the Framework Directive is most evident. After that, the various directives and regulations in the economic field could be adjusted.[49] Obviously, such an extension of partnership rights would be more controversial in some fields of EC law than in others. The immigration rights of the registered same-sex partners of EU citizens (and especially of non-EU citizens) may well be the last to be recognised.[50]

Until Principle 2 is incorporated into most EC rules, it would seem unlikely that Principle 3 would be applied to them. Principle 2 is far less controversial, because it simply reflects and respects changes in national family law, which are taking place as and when a member state feels ready to make a quasi-marital civil status available to same-sex couples. The recognition of same-sex registered partnerships (and marriages) in EU law would be a good incentive for other countries to create such a status for their own citizens, without encroaching on the competence of the Member States in the field of family law. However, because it seems improbable, in the next ten years, that every member state will legislate some form of partnership registration, the third principle will remain necessary to guarantee full equality for all European citizens in same-sex relationships. So the final step in recognising same-sex partners would need to be the incorporation of Principle 3 in all fields of EU law:

- *Principle 3 (All EU Law). Where a directive or regulation provides for a benefit for married spouses, it should be interpreted or amended so as to make that benefit also available to partners who cannot marry each other because they are of the same sex, and cannot register as partners because there is no equivalent-to-marriage registered partnership legislation.*

Obviously one way to incorporate that principle would be to extend the benefits to all (same-sex and different-sex) cohabitants.

CONCLUSION: RECOGNISING THE RECOGNITION OF SAME-SEX PARTNERSHIPS

One of the many ways in which the European Union resembles its member states is in its tradition of having numerous special rights for heterosexual couples.

[49] See *supra* n.38.

[50] See K Waaldijk, "Towards Equality in the Freedom of Movement of Persons", in Krickler, *supra* n.13, 40 at 46–7.

However, the EU also mirrors those member states in having slowly started to legally recognise homosexuality. The fact that four member states have not yet fully completed the decriminalisation of homosexual activity could slow down progress in the EU. Nevertheless, like the majority of member states, the EU has started on the road of explicit prohibition of anti-homosexual discrimination. An important, but largely symbolic step, was the inclusion of sexual orientation as a non-discrimination ground in Article 13 of the EC Treaty. The first directive implementing the non-discrimination principle of Article 13 with respect to sexual orientation, the Framework Directive, is only a small step because of its limited scope (although it is certainly of great symbolic importance). Whether the Directive will be interpreted by the Court of Justice as covering all direct and indirect discrimination between same-sex and different-sex partners is uncertain. If not, amending directives will be necessary to extend its scope to equality between same-sex and different-sex cohabitants, between married spouses and registered partners, and eventually between married spouses and unmarried/ unregistered same-sex partners.

Full recognition of same-sex partners in fields other than employment seems even further away, especially with respect to free movement of persons. It seems likely that here, too, the EU will follow the standard sequence followed by the member states: only after making it unlawful for (private) employers to discriminate on the basis of sexual orientation will the legislative bodies start to scrutinise their own products for distinctions on the same ground. Almost all anti-homosexual discrimination contained in EC regulations and directives takes the form of special benefits for married spouses. It is submitted that these numerous regulations and directives could first be extended, by interpretation or amendment, to cover registered (and married) same-sex partners; in other words, *the EU should first recognise any national recognition of same-sex partnerships*. Thus, the EU would be merely reflecting the changes that are taking place in the family law of a growing number of member states. And then at a later stage, a more comprehensive revision of EC regulations and directives could become feasible: extending all spousal benefits to all partners who cannot marry each other because they are of the same sex, and cannot register as partners because there is no equivalent-to-marriage registered partnership legislation.

APPENDIX

HISTORICAL OVERVIEW OF THE MAIN LEGISLATIVE STEPS IN THE LEGAL RECOGNITION OF HOMOSEXUALITY IN EUROPEAN COUNTRIES

This overview is based on the hypothesis that almost all countries go, at different times and paces, through a standard sequence of legislative steps recognising homosexuality.[51]

Symbols Used

1993 = year in which the legislation came into force
(1993) = limited or implicitly worded legislation
[1993] = legislation applying in part(s) of the country only
i.p. = legislation in preparation or not yet in force

Table 1 EU Member States

	Decriminalisation of male (+ female) homosexual acts	Equalisation of age limits in sex offences	Specific anti-discrimination legislation	Registered partnership legislation	Joint or second-parent adoption	Civil marriage
Netherlands	1811	1971	(1983), 1992, 1994[53]	1998[52]	2001	2001
Denmark	1930	1976	1987, 1996[54]	1989	1999	—
Sweden	1944	1978	1987, 1999[55]	1995[56]	i.p.	—
France	1791	1982	(1985, 1986), i.p.[57]	(1999)	—	—
Germany	[1968], 1969[58]	[1989], 1994	[1992, 1993, 1995, 1997][59]	(2001)	—	—
Spain	1822	1822[60]	1995	[(1998, 1999, 2000, 2001)] [62]	[i.p.][61]	—
Finland	1971	1998	1995	i.p.	—	—
Luxembourg	1792	1992	1997	—	—	—
Ireland	1993	—[63]	(1989), 1993, 1998, 2000[64]	—	—	—
Belgium	1792	1985	—	(2000)	—	i.p.
Italy	1889[65]	1889	—	—	—	—
UK	[1967, 1980], 1982[66]	2001	—	—	—	—
Portugal	1945	—[67]	—	—[68]	—	—
Greece	1950	—[69]	—	—	—	—
Austria	1971	—	(1993)	—	—	—

Table 2 Other Council of Europe Member States[70]

	Decriminalisation of male (+ female) homosexual acts	Equalisation of age limits in sex offences	Specific anti-discrimination legislation	Registered partnership legislation	Joint or second-parent adoption	Civil marriage
Iceland	1930[71]	1992	1996	1996	2000[72]	—
Norway	1972	1972	1981, 1998	1993	—	—
Slovenia	1977	1977	1995	—	—	—
Czech Rep.	1961	1990	2001	i.p.	—	—
Switzerland	1942[73]	1992	(1999) [74]	[(2001)],[75] i.p.	—	—
Turkey	1858	1858	—	—	—	—
Poland	1932	1932	—	—	—	—
Malta	1973	1973	—	—	—	—
Slovakia	1961	1990	—	—	—	—
Ukraine	1991	1991	—	—	—	—
Russia	1993	1997	—	—	—	—
Latvia	1992	1998	—	—	—	—
Estonia	1992	i.p.	—	—	—	—
Lithuania	1993	i.p.	i.p.	—	—	—
Hungary	1961	—	(1997)	—[77]	—	—
Romania	1996	—	(2000)[76]	—	—	—
Bulgaria	1968	—	—	—	—	—
Croatia	1977	—	—	—	—	—
Moldova	1995	—	—	—	—	—
Albania	1995	—	—	—	—	—
Cyprus	1998	—	—	—	—	—

[51] See *supra* n.2 and pp. 637–38. A general source for the information in this table is the *World Legal Survey* of the International Lesbian and Gay Association, http://www.ilga.org, as well as ILGA-Europe's monthly *EuroLetter*, http://inet.uni2.dk/~steff/eurolet.htm. See also Graupner, *supra* n.3, at 361–759, and "Sexual Consent: The Criminal Law in Europe and Overseas", (2000) 29 *Archives of Sexual Behavior* 415 (decriminalisation); R Wintemute, *Sexual Orientation and Human Rights* (Oxford, Oxford University Press, 1997) at viii, xi, 265–6 (anti-discrimination legislation) (updated in Appendix II to this book); the other chapters in this book (partnership and adoption). Corrections and additions are always welcome (c.waaldijk@law.leidenuniv.nl).

[52] Unregistered cohabitation has received legislative recognition since the late 1970s. See Waaldijk, chap. 23.

[53] In the prohibition of discrimination in Art. 1 of the Dutch Constitution, which entered into force in 1983, the words "or any ground whatsoever" were added with the explicit intention of covering discrimination based on homosexual orientation (see K Waaldijk, "Constitutional Protection Against Discrimination of Homosexuals", (1986/1987) 13 *Journal of Homosexuality* 57 at 59–60). In 1992, "hetero- or homosexual orientation" was inserted in several anti-discrimination provisions of the Penal Code. In 1994, the General Equal Treatment Act came into force, covering several grounds including "hetero- or homosexual orientation" (see Appendix II, p. 786).

[54] Anti-discrimination legislation extended to cover employment discrimination in 1996.

[55] Anti-discrimination legislation extended to cover employment discrimination in 1999.

[56] Legislation on unregistered cohabitation came into force in 1988. See Ytterberg, chap. 22.

[57] With the intention of covering sexual orientation discrimination, the word "*moeurs*" (morals, manners, customs, ways) was inserted in several anti-discrimination provisions of the Penal Code (1985) and of the Labour Code (1986). "Sexual orientation" is expected to be added in 2001. See Appendix II, p. 784.

[58] In the former German Democratic Republic (East Germany), homosexual acts between men were decriminalised in 1968, and the age limits were equalised in 1989. In the pre-unification Federal Republic of Germany (West Germany), the dates were 1969 and 1994. See Graupner, *supra* n.3, at 407–10.

[59] Anti-discrimination provisions specifically referring to sexual orientation have been included in the constitutions of three *Länder* (states): Brandenburg (1992), Thuringia (1993) and Berlin (1995). Anti-discrimination legislation has been enacted in at least one *Land*: Saxony-Anhalt (1997).

[60] Although the formal age limits for heterosexual and homosexual acts were equalised at the time of decriminalisation of homosexual acts in 1822, in practice homosexual acts with minors continued to be penalised until 1988 under a general provision against "serious scandal and indecency" (see Graupner, *supra* n.3, at 665–6).

[61] The provisions on joint adoption by unmarried different-sex and same-sex couples have been suspended pending a challenge to the constitutional power of Navarra (vs. the national government) to enact them. See Pérez Cánovas, chap. 26.

[62] Limited registered partnership legislation has so far only been enacted in four regions: Catalonia (1998), Aragon (1999), Navarra (2000) and Valencia (2001).

[63] For oral and non-penetrative sex, the age limit is higher for male homosexual acts (17) than for heterosexual and lesbian acts (15). Since decriminalisation in 1993, the age limit for male homosexual anal sex and for heterosexual vaginal and anal sex is equal at 17. See Graupner, *supra* n.3, at 481, 487.

[64] In 1989, only incitement to hatred was prohibited. Discriminatory dismissal became unlawful in 1993, other employment discrimination in 1998, and discrimination in education, housing, goods and services in 2000.

[65] In several parts of Italy decriminalisation of sex between men took place before 1889 (e.g. in 1861 in the Neapolitan province). See Graupner, *supra* n.3, at 505, and F Leroy-Forgeot, *Histoire juridique de l'homosexualité en Europe* (Paris, Presses Universitaires de France, 1997) at 66.

[66] Decriminalisation of most sex between two men over 21 took place in England and Wales in 1967, in Scotland in 1980 and in Northern Ireland in 1982 (see Graupner, *supra* n.3, at 711, 727, 739).

[67] See *supra* n.3.

[68] Legislation on unregistered cohabitation came into force in 2001. See p. 762.

[69] In the case of "seduction", the age limit for sex between men is higher (17) than for lesbian or heterosexual sex (15). See Graupner, *supra* n.3, at 466.

[70] Table 2 does not include Andorra, Armenia, Azerbaijan, Georgia, Liechtenstein, Macedonia and San Marino, as well as three European states which have yet to join the Council of Europe (Belarus, Bosnia-Herzegovina, Serbia-Montenegro).

[71] Graupner (*supra* n.3, at 491) assumes that decriminalisation took place in the same year as in Denmark (1930). From 1918 until 1944, Iceland was an independent Kingdom in personal union with the Kingdom of Denmark.

[72] On 8 May 2000, the Icelandic Parliament passed an amendment allowing a person in a registered partnership to adopt the child of his or her registered partner. See *EuroLetter*, *supra* n.51 (No. 80, June 2000).

[73] In five Swiss cantons, sex between men had been decriminalised before the entering into force of the first national Penal Code in 1942. See Graupner, *supra* n.3, at 640.

[74] Since 1999, the Swiss Constitution has included "way of life" ("*mode de vie*", "*Lebensform*", "*modo di vita*") in the list of grounds in its non-discrimination clause, which is intended to cover "sexual orientation".

[75] The canton of Geneva adopted a limited registered partnership law in 2001.

[76] Executive ordinance only.

[77] Hungary does have legislation on unregistered same-sex cohabitation. See Farkas, chap. 31.

37

Sexual Orientation Discrimination in Employment: An Evolving Role for the European Union

MARK BELL[1]

INTRODUCTION

THE PROBLEMS CONFRONTED by lesbians and gay men in the workplace have been made manifest in recent years through a combination of litigation and research. In terms of litigation, three such cases have reached the European Court of Justice: *Grant* v. *South-West Trains*,[2] *D.* v. *Council*,[3] and *Perkins*.[4] The first two cases concerned denial of benefits in respect of a same-sex partner, where the same benefits were provided to married or unmarried opposite-sex

[1] Lecturer, Faculty of Law, University of Leicester. Many thanks to Maurice FitzGerald, Barry Fitzpatrick, Mia Hunter and Lisa Waddington for generous assistance in the preparation of this chapter, which is an expansion of Mark Bell, "Article 13 EC: The European Commission's Anti-Discrimination Proposals", (2000) 29 *Industrial Law Journal* 79. See also M Bell, *Anti-Discrimination Law and the European Union* (Oxford, Oxford University Press, forthcoming in 2002); O De Schutter, *Discriminations et marché du travail: Liberté et égalité dans les rapports d'emploi* (Brussels, Peter Lang, 2001).

[2] Case C-249/96, [1998] European Court Reports (ECR) I-621. See, *inter alia*, K Armstrong, "Tales of the Community: Sexual Orientation Discrimination and EU law", (1998) 20 *Journal of Social Welfare and Family Law* 455; T Connor, "Community Discrimination Law: No Right to Equal Treatment in Employment in Respect of Same-Sex Partner", (1998) 23 *European Law Review* 378; K Berthou & A Masselot, "La CJCE et les couples homosexuels", (1998) 12 *Droit social* 1034; Koppelman, chap. 35.

[3] Case T-264/97, [1999] Reports of European Community Staff Cases (ECR-SC) II-1. See C Denys, "Homosexuality: A Non-Issue in Community Law?", (1999) 24 *European Law Review* 419 at 421; G Scappucci, "Court of First Instance refuses to recognize Swedish 'Registered Partnership' rights and duties", (2000) 6 *European Public Law* 355. The judgment of the Court of First Instance was appealed to the Court of Justice (Joined Cases C-122/99 P, C-125/99 P), with the Swedish, Danish and Dutch governments intervening on the side of D. In his Opinion of 22 Feb. 2001, Advocate General Mischo urged the Court to dismiss the appeals. The Court agreed in its Judgment of 31 May 2001 (see Conclusion, pp. 767–69).

[4] *R.* v. *Secretary of State for Defence, ex parte Perkins*, [1997] Industrial Relations Law Reports (IRLR) 297, registered at the Court of Justice as Case C-168/97, but subsequently withdrawn by the English High Court following *Grant*. See *Perkins (No. 2)*, [1998] IRLR 508; J Dunhill de La Rochère & N Grief, "Orientation sexuelle; directive 76/207/CEE; retrait d'une question préjudicielle", (1998) 34 *Revue trimestrielle de droit européen* 622.

couples. The third case concerned the exclusion of all homosexuals from the workplace—in that case, the UK armed forces.[5] At the same time, social research has demonstrated the frequency with which lesbians and gay men encounter discrimination in employment. For example, in Sweden, a 1997 survey of 650 gay, lesbian and bisexual employees found that 36 per cent had experienced discrimination at work.[6]

Against this background, on 25 November 1999, the European Commission proposed, as part of a package of anti-discrimination measures, a new directive forbidding discrimination on grounds of sexual orientation in employment, which was adopted by the Council on 27 November 2000. The purpose of this chapter is to look in some depth at the directive, and to evaluate how effective it will be in dealing with the various expressions of homophobia in the workplace. In keeping with the overall theme of this book, special attention will be paid to the impact of the directive on the rights of same-sex partners. However, before turning to the substantive content of the directive, it is essential to introduce the context to this package of law reforms.

THE CONTEXT TO THE EUROPEAN COMMISSION PROPOSALS

European Union law-making is often characterised by its incremental nature, reflected in the length of time it can take for a proposal to reach final adoption. Occasionally though, moments of dynamism occur—for example, the stock of sex equality legislation built in the mid-1970s.[7] Similar momentum has been clearly detectable in anti-discrimination law since the mid-1990s. Various non-governmental organisations, principally supported by the European Parliament, had been campaigning for the European Union to extend its anti-discrimination law beyond the existing focus on sex and nationality.[8] This led, in 1997, to the fifteen Member States agreeing to amend the Treaty establishing the European Community, by inserting a new Article 13 EC:

> "Without prejudice to the other provisions of this Treaty and within the limits of the powers conferred by it upon the Community, the Council, acting unanimously on a proposal from the Commission and after consulting the European Parliament, may

[5] The ban was subsequently held to be contrary to Art. 8 of the European Convention on Human Rights in *Lustig-Prean & Beckett* v. *UK*, *Smith & Grady* v. *UK* (27 Sept. 1999), http://www.echr.coe.int/hudoc (European Court of Human Rights).

[6] B Skolander, "Sweden" in Beger, Krickler, Lewis & Wuch (eds.), *Equality for Lesbians and Gay Men: A Relevant Issue in the Civil and Social Dialogue* (Brussels, ILGA-Europe, 1998) at 87, http://www.steff.suite.dk/report.pdf. See also A Palmer, *Less Equal Than Others: A Survey of Lesbians and Gay Men at Work* (London, Stonewall, 1993).

[7] See generally C Hoskyns, *Integrating Gender: Women, Law and Politics in the European Union* (London, Verso, 1996).

[8] See M Bell & L Waddington, "The 1996 Intergovernmental Conference and the Prospects of a Non-Discrimination Treaty Article", (1996) 25 *Industrial Law Journal* 320.

take appropriate action to combat discrimination based on sex, racial or ethnic origin, religion or belief, disability, age or sexual orientation".[9]

Keen to build upon the existing momentum, the European Commission swiftly committed itself to proposing anti-discrimination legislation[10] founded on the new legal competence. To this end, a lengthy consultation process took place during 1998 and 1999, culminating in the publication of the Commission's anti-discrimination package on 25 November 1999. This was characterised by three central elements:

1. a "Proposal for a Council directive establishing a general framework for equal treatment in employment and occupation",[11] prohibiting employment discrimination on the grounds of racial or ethnic origin, religion or belief, age, disability or sexual orientation;
2. a "Proposal for a Council directive implementing equal treatment between persons irrespective or racial or ethnic origin" (the "Race Directive"),[12] prohibiting racial discrimination in employment, social protection, education and access to goods and services;
3. a "Proposal for a Council Decision establishing a Community Action Programme to combat discrimination, 2001–2006".[13] This seeks to combat discrimination on grounds of racial or ethnic origin, religion or belief, age, disability or sexual orientation through non-legislative avenues. In particular, funding will be provided for activities to develop understanding of issues related to discrimination, to promote exchange of information and good practice, and to "disseminate the values and practices underlying the fight against discrimination".[14]

Unfortunately, a degree of confusion was introduced by the release of an incorrect version of the proposals through the Employment and Social Affairs Directorate-General's website.[15] The initial version released was a draft dated 25 October 1999. This was subsequently annulled and replaced with the final 25 November 1999 version on 2 December 1999. Whilst the overall nature of the package remained the same, important amendments were made of special relevance to sexual orientation discrimination.

[9] See L Waddington, "Testing the Limits of the EC Treaty Article on Non-Discrimination", (1999) 28 *Industrial Law Journal* 133; L Flynn, "The Implications of Article 13 EC—After Amsterdam, Will Some Forms of Discrimination Be More Equal Than Others?", (1999) 36 *Common Market Law Review* 1127.

[10] Commission, "An action plan against racism", COM (1998) 183 (25 April 1998), at para. 2.2.2.

[11] COM (1999) 565 (25 Nov. 1999), Official Journal (OJ) [2000] C 177 E/42. "Racial or ethnic origin", also covered by Proposal 2, was later dropped from Proposal 1.

[12] COM (1999) 566 (25 Nov. 1999), adopted as Council Directive 2000/43/EC of 29 June 2000 implementing the principle of equal treatment between persons irrespective of racial or ethnic origin, OJ [2000] L 180/22.

[13] COM (1999) 567 (25 Nov. 1999), adopted as Council Decision of 27 Nov. 2000 establishing a Community action programme to combat discrimination (2001 to 2006), OJ [2000] L 303/23.

[14] Art. 3, *ibid*.

[15] See now http://europa.eu.int/comm/dgs/employment_social/index_en.htm. Many thanks to R Wintemute for clarifying this situation.

The most crucial element of the package, from the perspective of sexual orientation discrimination, is what began as proposal 1. above (the "Framework Directive").[16] The main body of this chapter will examine this Directive in detail—its scope, effects and limitations. Following this discussion, the chapter shall conclude by returning to a broader look at the overall direction which EU anti-discrimination law is now taking.

THE SCOPE OF THE FRAMEWORK DIRECTIVE

The *material* scope of the Framework Directive is set out in Article 3. This provides that the Directive will apply, *inter alia*, to recruitment, promotion, working conditions, dismissals, and vocational training and guidance, as well as "membership of, and involvement in, an organisation of workers or employers, or any organisation whose members carry on a particular profession". This appears to be a comprehensive coverage of all aspects of employment. It is especially relevant to gays and lesbians that Article 3 is unequivocal as to its application to wages and other forms of remuneration. Paragraph (c) specifies that the Directive covers "employment and working conditions, including dismissals and *pay*".[17] Paragraph (d) states that it also applies to the "benefits" provided by worker, employer and professional associations.

Existing EU law on sex equality has established that "pay" should be defined broadly. The European Court of Justice has held that "the concept of pay . . . comprises any other consideration, whether in cash or in kind, whether immediate or future, provided that the worker receives it, albeit indirectly, in respect of his employment from his employer".[18] For example, this includes employee benefits, such as free travel allowances,[19] and contracted-out occupational pension schemes.[20] It even extends to compensation for unfair dismissal.[21] Therefore, the full variety of benefits which employers may provide in respect of employees' partners fall within the scope of the Directive.

Alongside the material scope, it is important to consider the *personal* scope of the Framework Directive. The principal issue here is whether the Directive will apply to all persons resident on Union territory, or only to European Union citizens.[22] The status of third country nationals is a constant difficulty in EU law,

[16] Council Directive 2000/78/EC of 27 Nov. 2000 establishing a general framework for equal treatment in employment and occupation, OJ [2000] L 303/16. Art. 18 sets an implementation deadline for Member States of 2 Dec. 2003.

[17] Emphasis added. But see Art. 3(3) (not payments from social security, social protection or other state schemes).

[18] Case C-167/97, *R.* v. *Secretary of State for Employment, ex parte Seymour-Smith & Perez* [1999] ECR I-623, para. 23.

[19] Case C-12/81, *Garland* v. *British Rail Engineering*, [1982] ECR 359, para. 9.

[20] Case C-262/88, *Barber* v. *Guardian Exchange Assurance Group*, [1990] ECR 1889.

[21] See *supra* n.18, para. 28.

[22] It seems reasonable to assume that a significant number of lesbians and gay men in the EU are also third-country nationals—given that at least twelve million third-country nationals are now

given the lack of clarity in the founding treaties on this point. Certain provisions, specifically those granting rights to free movement within the Union, have been interpreted as not applying to third-country nationals.[23] At the same time, it has been argued that other areas of EU legislation apply to all persons resident in the Member States.[24]

This analysis is reinforced by the decision in *Awoyemi*.[25] The case concerned a Nigerian national in possession of a UK driving licence who was charged with driving in Belgium without being in possession of a Belgian driving licence. The Court of Justice held that Mr Awoyemi could *not* challenge such laws on the basis that they constitute obstacles to the free movement of persons, because third-country nationals cannot rely on the free movement provisions of the EC Treaty.[26] Nevertheless, the Court found that this did not prevent third-country nationals from invoking the rights in Directive 80/1263/EEC[27] on the introduction of a Community driving licence, as the directive applied irrespective of nationality.[28] The principle emerging from *Awoyemi* appears to be that third-country nationals can rely on EU law, except where it concerns rights which are specifically restricted to EU citizens. This approach is confirmed in the Framework Directive. Recital 12 in the preamble to the Directive states "this prohibition of discrimination should also apply to nationals of third countries". Therefore, a national of a non-EU state who suffers sexual orientation discrimination when present in the Union should be able to have recourse to the protection provided by the Directive. However, it should be noted that the Directive does not "cover differences of treatment based on nationality".[29]

The final dimension to the scope of the Framework Directive relates to the scope of the grounds of discrimination. Article 1 states that the Directive lays down "a general framework for combating discrimination on the grounds of religion or belief, disability, age or sexual orientation". No further definition is provided for any of these grounds, but, in its commentary on Article 1 of the Directive, the Commission states that "a clear dividing line should be drawn between sexual orientation, which is covered by this proposal, and sexual behaviour which is not".[30] The foundation for this statement is not completely evident. None of the other grounds in the Directive is defined. Moreover, the annulled October 1999 version of the proposals did not contain this "clarifying" statement on sexual orientation, so it would seem this was a late addition. The most likely

long-term residents of the Union. See A Geddes, *Immigration and European Integration: Towards Fortress Europe?* (Manchester, Manchester University Press, 2000) at 11.

[23] Case C-230/97, *Awoyemi*, [1998] ECR I-6781, para. 29.

[24] See eg Commission, "Communication from the commission on the social situation and employment of migrant women", COM (1988) 743 (15 Dec. 1988), at 1.

[25] *Supra* n.23.

[26] *Ibid.*, paras. 27–9.

[27] OJ [1980] L 375/1.

[28] *Supra* n.23, para. 23.

[29] Art. 3(2).

[30] *Supra* n.11, at 8.

explanation is the concern that a ban on sexual orientation discrimination could extend to cover all forms of sexual behaviour, most notably paedophilia.

Whilst this fear is understandable, it is misplaced. Nothing in the Framework Directive would in any way affect the criminal law in relation to the sexual abuse of children. Furthermore, prejudicial treatment of an individual in employment on the grounds of a prior criminal conviction is not directly affected by the Directive. There is also no evidence that this has caused a problem under national laws on sexual orientation discrimination, both inside and outside of the European Union. Indeed, if it was necessary to define sexual orientation, a more appropriate model would be Ireland's Equal Status Act, 2000.[31] Section 2 states that "sexual orientation means heterosexual, homosexual or bisexual orientation".

The difficulty created by the introduction of a distinction between sexual behaviour and sexual orientation is the risk that employers will seek to rely on this as a defence to a claim of discrimination. The Commission does not even limit its comment to *unlawful* sexual behaviour. This creates a real prospect that employers will attempt to justify discrimination against lesbians or gays who are sexually active on the grounds of their sexual behaviour. This will be especially possible where the discrimination is against a same-sex couple. The argument could be made that the discrimination is not against an individual's personal orientation, but against their sexual behaviour by virtue of being in a same-sex relationship.

The impression is left that this was a statement added in haste without clear thought being given as to its full meaning and potential implications. Ultimately, any dispute as to what "sexual orientation" means in law will have to be dealt with by national courts and the European Court of Justice. The Commission's opinion in the explanatory memorandum is not binding, therefore, it must be hoped that the courts will eschew the establishment of such a distinction, with the attendant dangers it would create for the efficacy of the law.

THE DEFINITION OF DISCRIMINATION

Article 2 sets out what constitutes unlawful discrimination for the purposes of the Framework Directive. Discrimination is divided into four dimensions: direct discrimination, indirect discrimination, harassment, and instructions to discriminate.

Direct discrimination

Article 2(2)(a) provides that "direct discrimination shall be taken to occur where one person is treated less favourably than another is, has been or would be

[31] No. 8 of 2000, http://www.irlgov.ie/bills28/acts/2000/default.htm.

treated in a comparable situation, on any of the grounds referred to in Article 1". Less favourable treatment in the case of sexual orientation will normally require a comparison between the treatment of gay men or lesbians, and the treatment accorded to heterosexuals. For example, the former ban on homosexual persons serving in the UK military would be an obvious example of direct discrimination—persons of a homosexual orientation were treated less favourably than those of a heterosexual orientation.

The Framework Directive does not specifically comment on whether and when direct discrimination may be justified. This question has also never been fully resolved in EU sex equality law,[32] but the consistent approach of the Court has been that only an express exception in the Treaty or secondary legislation can be relied upon to justify direct discrimination.[33] Based on this principle, direct sexual orientation discrimination will only be permitted by reason of the exceptions provided for in the Directive; namely, genuine occupational requirements, positive action schemes, and "necessary in a democratic society" exceptions.[34] The scope of these exceptions shall be examined later in this chapter. However, it seems evident that the views of customers or other staff, or the fact that the position involves working with children, will not constitute sufficient grounds to justify sexual orientation discrimination.[35]

Indirect discrimination

The experience of EU law on sex and nationality discrimination has been that, as states and employers become more aware of the penalties for unlawful discrimination, overt prejudice migrates into more covert forms of discrimination, referred to as indirect discrimination. This is prohibited by Article 2(2)(b) of the Directive, which provides:

> "indirect discrimination shall be taken to occur where an apparently neutral provision, criterion or practice would put persons having a . . . particular sexual orientation at a particular disadvantage compared with other persons unless: (i) that provision, criterion or practice is objectively justified by a legitimate aim and the means of achieving that aim are appropriate and necessary . . ."

This is a particularly strong aspect of the proposed Framework Directive—as is revealed by a comparison with the equivalent definition for the purposes of EU sex equality law:

[32] Flynn, *supra* n.9, at 1140.

[33] See Opinion of Advocate General Elmer in *Grant*, *supra* n.2, at I-632. For example, in Case C-224/97, *Ciola* v. *Land Vorarlberg*, [1999] ECR I-2517, para. 16, the Court held that discriminatory national rules in relation to the free movement of services "are compatible with Community law only if they can be brought within the scope of an express derogation, such as Art. 56 of the EC Treaty".

[34] Arts. 4, 7 and 2(5).

[35] See R Wintemute, "Sexual Orientation Discrimination" in McCrudden & Chambers (eds.), *Individual Rights and the Law in Britain* (Oxford, Clarendon Press, 1994) at 505 (decisions accepting and rejecting these justifications).

> "indirect discrimination shall exist where an apparently neutral provision, criterion or practice disadvantages a substantially higher proportion of the members of one sex unless that provision, criterion or practice is appropriate and necessary and can be justified by objective factors unrelated to sex".[36]

The crucial difference lies in the requirement in sex equality law to establish that the rule or practice affects *a substantially higher proportion* of women than men, or vice versa. Naturally, this tends to require a statistical approach to demonstrate the existence of indirect discrimination. Even where the relevant statistics are available, further problems can emerge concerning the relevant point in time for the statistical comparison, and the relevant groups to compare.[37]

In relation to sexual orientation, obtaining any reliable statistical data would be very difficult indeed. First, individuals can and do conceal their sexuality (especially in employment). Second, collecting statistics creates a potential conflict with the privacy rights of individual employees. Therefore, a requirement to show that a particular provision or rule affected a substantially higher proportion of homosexuals than heterosexuals would be quite challenging to meet in practice. Article 2(2)(b) avoids this problem by only requiring evidence that a given measure or practice would put persons of a particular sexual orientation at a "particular disadvantage".

A concrete example of indirect discrimination on grounds of sexual orientation is in the area of employers' dress codes. A rule that women must wear skirts potentially discriminates against lesbian employees. Whilst such a rule applies irrespective of sexual orientation, it could be argued that it is liable to adversely affect lesbians, for whom trousers may be an important expression of sexual identity.[38] In recognition of the wider range of rules which may be challenged as indirect discrimination, the law also permits greater flexibility in the range of permissible justifications. Article 2(2)(b) of the Framework Directive allows indirectly discriminatory rules or practices where they are "objectively justified by a legitimate aim and the means of achieving that aim are appropriate and necessary". Therefore, an employer could argue that a dress code was necessary to create a particular professional image of the company.

Harassment

The third form of discrimination forbidden in the Framework Directive is harassment. This represents significant progress beyond all existing EU anti-

[36] Council Dir. 97/80/EC on the burden of proof in cases of discrimination based on sex, OJ [1998] L 14/6, Art. 2(2).

[37] *Supra* n.18. See C Barnard and B Hepple, "Indirect Discrimination: Interpreting *Seymour-Smith*", (1999) 58 *Cambridge Law Journal* 399.

[38] P Skidmore, "Dress to Impress: Employer Regulation of Gay and Lesbian Appearance", (1999) 8 *Social & Legal Studies* 509.

discrimination law, in which harassment has not previously been explicitly forbidden. In relation to sex discrimination, a 1991 Recommendation on dignity at work did express the view that harassment "may, in certain circumstances, be contrary to the principle of equal treatment".[39] However, this depends heavily upon national courts and tribunals interpreting the Equal Treatment Directive[40] in conformity with the Recommendation.

Not only does Article 2(3) of the Framework Directive include a ban on harassment, but it defines harassment in a broad fashion as "unwanted conduct . . . with the purpose or effect of violating the dignity of a person and of creating an intimidating, hostile, degrading, humiliating or offensive environment". This makes it clear that unlawful harassment is not merely *quid pro quo* actions—for example, where the employer makes promotion conditional on sexual favours. On the contrary, any behaviour which damages the working environment will be potentially in breach of the Framework Directive. For instance, homophobic remarks or jokes should constitute actions contributing to an offensive environment. The definition of harassment is also strengthened by the fact that there is no requirement to show that the harasser *intended* to create a hostile environment—it is sufficient that their actions have had that effect. Furthermore, the provision is phrased in sufficiently broad terms as to include harassment from persons other than the employer, such as other members of staff or customers. This is particularly important when one considers that in the Swedish survey mentioned above, 27 per cent had experienced harassment, and the greatest source was co-workers.

Despite its strength, two aspects of Article 2(3) remain in need of further clarification. First, it does not indicate the standard to be used in determining whether a given action creates a hostile environment. An important difference exists between whether this is to be judged according to what a reasonable person would view as constituting a hostile environment, or whether it depends simply on the perception of the victim. A third way would be to assess the behaviour based on the perception of a reasonable person possessing the characteristics of the victim. The second issue left unresolved is the liability of the employer for harassment caused by other employees or customers. Arguably, employers should be under a duty to take all reasonable steps to prevent harassment at work.[41]

Article 2(3) additionally provides that "the concept of harassment may be defined in accordance with the national laws and practice of the Member States". This implies that those aspects of the concept of harassment not otherwise specified in Article 2(3) are left to national discretion. However, if widely

[39] Commission Recommendation on the dignity of women and men at work, adopted 27 Nov. 1991, OJ [1992] L 49/1, Art. 1.

[40] Council Dir. 76/207/EEC of 9 Feb. 1976 on the implementation of the principle of equal treatment for men and women as regards access to employment, vocational training and promotion and working conditions, OJ [1976] L 39/40.

[41] See eg Ireland, Employment Equality Act, 1998, No. 21 of 1998, s. 32, http://www.irlgov.ie/bills28/acts/1998/default.htm.

divergent approaches to issues such as employers' liability for harassment are permitted, this could undermine the effectiveness of the Directive's provisions in certain states. One means of establishing minimum standards would be to elaborate more detailed rules through non-binding instruments. These could specify precisely what steps employers would be expected to take in fulfilling their obligations under the Framework Directive—for example, the establishment of a "confidential counsellor" to whom complaints of harassment can be addressed.[42] In this context, it is valuable that the Directive imposes an obligation on Member States to promote the development of further anti-discrimination instruments by the social partners.[43]

Instructions to discriminate

Article 2(4) provides that "[a]n instruction to discriminate against any persons on any of the grounds referred to in Article 1 shall be deemed to be discrimination . . .". This is particularly valuable in the context of employment agencies. Employers may seek to circumvent the ban on discrimination by instructing employment agencies only to provide workers of a particular ethnic origin or age, for instance. Article 2(4) provides protection from such behaviour. Therefore, a hypothetical advertising producer who instructed an agency for actors not to send any gay men or lesbians would have committed unlawful discrimination.

EXCEPTIONS TO THE BAN ON DISCRIMINATION

Having established what constitutes unlawful discrimination under the Framework Directive, it is necessary to turn now to the exceptions. Three specific exceptions are provided in respect of all grounds of discrimination covered by the Directive: genuine occupational requirements, positive action schemes, and "necessary in a democratic society" exceptions.

Genuine occupational requirements (GORs)

GORs are a commonly recognised justification for discrimination. In the context of sex discrimination, Article 2(2) of the Equal Treatment Directive[44]

[42] European Parliament, "Report of the Committee on Women's Rights on a new post of 'confidential counsellor' at the workplace" [Segarra], A3–43/94, 27 Jan. 1994.

[43] Art. 13(1) states: "Member States shall . . . take adequate measures to promote the dialogue between the social partners with a view to fostering equal treatment, through the monitoring of workplace practices, collective agreements, codes of conduct and through research or exchange of experiences and good practices".

[44] *Supra* n.40.

provided Member States with the option to exclude from the "field of application" of the directive "those occupational activities and, where appropriate, the training leading thereto, for which, by reason of their nature or the context in which they are carried out, the sex of the worker constitutes a determining factor". This exception is, however, intended to be subject to close control. Article 9(2) requires Member States to keep such exceptions under periodic review with regard to their necessity, and to notify the Commission of the results of these assessments.

The Court of Justice has also emphasised the need for any exceptions to be limited. In *Sirdar* v. *Army Board*,[45] the Court was called upon to consider the legitimacy of the exclusion of women from the UK Royal Marines. Considering the scope of Article 2(2) in the Equal Treatment Directive, the Court stressed that "as a derogation from an individual right laid down in the directive, that provision must be interpreted strictly".[46] As a result, any derogation created had to comply with the principle of proportionality—that is, it must be necessary and appropriate and must not go beyond the least restrictive means possible of achieving the given objective.[47]

Article 4(1) of the Framework Directive provides an exception from the ban on discrimination where:

> "by reason of the nature of the particular occupational activities concerned or of the context in which they are carried out, such a characteristic constitutes a genuine and determining occupational requirement, provided that the objective is legitimate and the requirement is proportionate".

An example of the application of this provision could be the provision of welfare services in the gay and lesbian community, where it is believed necessary that the individuals employed actually are gay or lesbian. However, this must be verified on a case-by-case basis, and the exception does not apply to general categories of occupation.

Article 4(2) goes further:

> "Member States may maintain [existing] national legislation . . . or provide for future legislation incorporating [existing] national practices . . . pursuant to which, in the case of occupational activities within churches or other public or private organisations the ethos of which is based on religion or belief, a difference of treatment based on a person's religion or belief shall not constitute discrimination where, by reason of the nature of these activities or the context in which they are carried out, a person's religion or belief constitute a genuine, legitimate and justified occupational requirement, having regard to the organisation's ethos. This difference of treatment . . . should not justify discrimination on another ground.
>
> . . . [T]his Directive shall thus not prejudice the right of churches and other public or private organisations, the ethos of which is based on religion or belief, . . . to require

[45] Case C-273/97, [1999] ECR I-7403. See also Case C-285/98, *Kreil* v. *Germany* [2000] ECR I-69.
[46] *Ibid.*, paras. 23, 25.
[47] *Ibid.*, para. 26. However, in relation to public security measures, Member States enjoy a "a certain degree of discretion" (para. 27).

individuals working for them to act in good faith and with loyalty to the organisation's ethos".

Making sense of this complex provision is challenging, however, it seems essentially to build on the general exception for genuine occupational requirements in Article 4(1). This additional paragraph clearly intends to provide the Member States with the option of maintaining legislation whereby churches, and other bodies with an ethos based on religion or belief, can accord preferences to persons sharing their particular religion or belief. Nonetheless, there still needs to be a justification of any difference of treatment by reference to the specific occupational activity. Whilst it may be relatively easy for a church, mosque, synagogue or other religious institution to establish that the nature of the activity requires religious leaders and teachers to possess a particular religion or belief, this will be more controversial in respect of other positions in such organisations where the main activity would not, at first sight, appear to demand the possession of a particular belief. A common example is the maths or chemistry teacher in a school with a religious ethos. It remains open though for the school to argue that all teaching staff also have responsibilities for the general welfare of specific groups of students (which can involve personal counselling or advice), and hence holding a particular belief is relevant for all teaching positions. In such cases, judges at both the national and European level will have to strike a delicate balance between the rights of the organisations and the rights of the individuals concerned.

Importantly, Article 4(2) explicitly provides that it is not an alibi for discrimination on other grounds. Some of the lobbying surrounding this provision specifically referred to the desire of certain organisations not to employ lesbian or gay individuals for reasons of religious belief.[48] Article 4(2) will not permit organisations to reject applicants purely on the basis of their sexual orientation. A lesbian or gay applicant who actually shares the religion or belief of the organisation cannot be rejected on the basis of Article 4(2), unless the organisation can successfully argue that it is impossible to be homosexual *and* share their beliefs. The difficulty for lesbian and gay employees in such organisations stems, however, from the "good faith" and "loyalty" obligations found in the final sentence of Article 4(2). These are broad terms with no further definition in the Directive. For example, can a school require a teacher to refrain from revealing any information which might disclose their sexual orientation? To what extent do these "good faith" requirements extend into the private life of the employee? Again, the ambiguity of the Directive leaves future dilemmas for the judiciary and national legislatures to resolve.

[48] See e.g. *European Threat to Religious Freedom: A Response to the European Union's Proposed Employment Directive* (Newcastle, Christian Institute, 2000).

Positive action

The second exception from the ban on discrimination which applies to the sexual orientation ground is found in Article 7 of the Framework Directive:

> "With a view to ensuring full equality in practice, the principle of equal treatment shall not prevent any Member State from maintaining or adopting specific measures to prevent or compensate for disadvantages linked to any of the grounds referred to in Article 1".

Reconciling positive action schemes with the general rule of non-discrimination has proven one of the more difficult aspects of EU sex equality law.[49] The explanatory memorandum to the Framework Directive explains the Commission's view that "as positive action measures are a derogation from the principle of equality, they should be interpreted strictly, in the light of the current case law on sex discrimination".[50]

This approach could affect some existing positive action measures, notably for ethnic minority communities.[51] But it is unlikely to create problems with regard to sexual orientation discrimination, where positive action measures are less common. Existing examples of positive action on this ground tend to be initiatives such as the inclusion of sexual orientation in employers' equal opportunities policies,[52] or targeted recruitment through the lesbian and gay press.[53] Such programmes seem quite compatible with Article 7 of the Directive. The major difficulties will be encountered in respect of preferential recruitment practices, but there is no evidence of these ever being applied in respect of homosexuals.

"Necessary in a democratic society" exceptions

Article 2(5) states: "This Directive shall be without prejudice to measures laid down by national law which, in a democratic society, are necessary for public security, for the maintenance of public order and the prevention of criminal offences, for the protection of health and for the protection of the rights and

[49] See G F Mancini and S O'Leary, "The new frontiers of sex equality law in the European Union", (1999) 24 *European Law Review* 331 at 341–6.

[50] *Supra* n.11, at 11.

[51] See the Race Dir. Art. 5, *supra* n.12. The Netherlands has experimented with hiring preferences for ethnic minorities similar to the hiring preferences for women held unlawful by the Court of Justice in Case C-450/93, *Kalanke* v. *Bremen*, [1995] ECR I-3051. See M Gras and F Bovenkerk, *Preventing Racism at the Workplace: The Netherlands*, Working Paper No. WP/95/49/EN (Dublin, European Foundation for the Improvement of Living and Working Conditions, 1995) at 39.

[52] "Equality for Lesbians and Gay Men in the Workplace", (July-Aug. 1997) 74 *Equal Opportunities Review* 20.

[53] For example, South Yorkshire Police and Sussex Police have advertised vacancies in the gay press, and specifically welcomed applications from gay persons, so as to improve police relations with the gay community (*ibid*., at 27).

freedoms of others". This general exception to the principle of equal treatment is unique in EU anti-discrimination law and the text has been imported from the European Convention on Human Rights.[54] It is not evident what motivation lies behind this addition to the Directive. For example, is this designed to protect laws restricting the activities of certain religious movements and their adherents? Alternatively, it may be another mechanism though which to guarantee that the ban on sexual orientation discrimination does not inadvertently provide protection for persons engaging in unlawful sexual behaviour. As discussed earlier, these concerns seem misplaced and it is to be hoped that national and European courts will interpret the exception in Article 2(5) restrictively. This would be consistent with the general approach of the Court of Justice to exceptions to the principle of equal treatment.[55]

DISCRIMINATION AND THE RIGHTS OF SAME-SEX PARTNERS

Having identified the rules governing what will constitute unlawful discrimination, this section applies these rules to the specific situation of same-sex partners. As illustrated by the cases of *Grant* and *D.* v. *Council*, non-recognition of same-sex partners is a common form of discrimination confronted by lesbian and gay employees. At one level, it constitutes a symbolic representation of disapproval of same-sex relationships.[56] By rendering same-sex partners invisible, these relationships are devalued in comparison with married (and often unmarried) opposite-sex partnerships, which are deemed worthy of reward. At a more practical level, this is a simple question of remuneration. The effect of non-recognition of partners can be quite substantial in monetary terms. Lisa Grant was deprived of benefits worth around 1000 British pounds (1500 Euros) *per annum* in free rail travel for her partner.[57] Therefore, the value and effectiveness of the Framework Directive for lesbians and gay men will be directly related to its ability to address the issue of partner recognition in the workplace.

Deciphering how the Directive will affect same-sex couples requires precision as to the circumstances of the case. Waaldijk has identified four variants of discrimination which can arise in this context:[58]

(a) between unmarried opposite-sex couples and unmarried same-sex couples;
(b) between married opposite-sex couples and married same-sex couples;

[54] In particular, Arts. 8(2), 9(2), 10(2) and 11(2).

[55] For example, Case C-222/84, *Johnston* v. *Chief Constable of the RUC*, [1986] ECR 1651 a[t] 1687.

[56] This may be regarded as an element of what Skidmore, *supra* n.39, at 523, describes as th[e] workplace "(re)production of heterosexuality".

[57] *Supra* n.2, at I-629.

[58] K Waaldijk, "Towards Equality in the Freedom of Movement of Persons" in K Krickler (ed.) *After Amsterdam: Sexual Orientation and the European Union* (Brussels, ILGA-Europe, 1999) at 41 http://www.steff.suite.dk/ilgaeur.htm (Policy Documents).

(c) between married opposite-sex couples and unmarried same-sex couples;
(d) between married opposite-sex couples and registered same-sex partners.

This classification provides an excellent basis upon which to analyse the Framework Directive and therefore the following discussion will address each of these categories.

Discrimination between unmarried opposite-sex couples and unmarried same-sex couples

This is the scenario present in the *Grant* case and constitutes *direct* discrimination, as the only relevant difference between the couples is sexual orientation. As stated earlier, this is likely only to be justifiable by reference to the specific exceptions in the Framework Directive. The Article 7 positive action exception is obviously not relevant to this situation. The Article 4 exception is mainly concerned with *access* to certain occupational activities, therefore it is difficult to apply in this context. As a result, the Framework Directive will forbid this form of discrimination between couples, unless it can be justified under Article 2(5) as "necessary in a democratic society" for the protection of "the rights and freedoms of others". This will require the employer to establish that they have a right to distinguish between homosexual and heterosexual partnerships—an argument considered further below.

Discrimination between married opposite-sex couples and married same-sex couples

The Netherlands has become the first jurisdiction in the world to open marriage to same-sex couples.[59] As in the preceding scenario, any unequal treatment will be direct discrimination, as the only relevant difference between the couples is sexual orientation.

Discrimination between married opposite-sex couples and unmarried same-sex couples

This form of discrimination is the most common across the European Union, because there are many situations in which all unmarried couples (same-sex or opposite-sex) are denied a benefit. In its explanatory memorandum on the Framework Directive, the Commission stated:

> "[I]t should be underlined that this proposal does not affect marital status and therefore it does not impinge upon entitlements to benefits for married couples".[60]

[59] See Waaldijk, chap. 23.
[60] *Supra* n.11, at 8.

This statement found its way into the preamble of the Framework Directive as Recital 22: "This Directive is without prejudice to national laws on marital status and the benefits dependent thereon".

In a number of respects, this is a surprising provision. Nothing in the operative text of the Framework Directive refers to married couples' entitlements. Such benefits fall within the scope of the Directive,[61] hence there is no legal barrier to their being challenged as unlawful sexual orientation discrimination. Recital 22 certainly provides highly persuasive evidence for the courts that the Member States did not intend the Directive to affect benefits reserved to married couples. However, the actual wording of the Recital restricts this to benefits "dependent" on national laws on marital status. Whilst benefits provided in public sector employment may be conceivably linked to national marriage laws, it is doubtful if private sector benefits for married couples can be really described as being "dependent" on national laws on marital status, except in the most general sense. Therefore, space remains for an eventual decision by the Court of Justice that Recital 22 does not exclude all employment benefits provided to married couples from the scope of the Directive. If these benefits can be challenged as sexual orientation discrimination, it remains to be considered whether the courts would regard such discrimination as justifiable.

It could be argued that distinctions between married opposite-sex couples and unmarried same-sex couples are an example of *direct* sexual orientation discrimination. This would be founded on the reasoning that marriage is a sexual orientation-specific criterion. As only opposite-sex couples can get married, any difference in treatment on the grounds of marriage is, by definition, direct discrimination on grounds of sexual orientation. In this respect, an analogy could be made with discrimination on grounds of pregnancy which is treated as direct sex discrimination as only women can become pregnant.[62] Nonetheless, many gay men and lesbians do get married, even though they cannot marry each other. Therefore, it is not clear that this form of discrimination would be regarded as direct discrimination.

The more likely approach is that discrimination between married and unmarried couples will be regarded as indirect sexual orientation discrimination. This approach is likely to appeal to the Court of Justice on "policy" grounds.[63] *Prima facie* indirect discrimination is open to a wide range of justifications, under Article 2(2)(b)(i) of the Directive, which depend on the interpretation of the Court. This will allow it to exercise a close degree of control over the circumstances in which spousal benefits must be extended to same-sex partners.

[61] Arts. 3(1)(c) and 3(1)(d).

[62] Case C-177/88, *Dekker* v. *VJV-Centrum*, [1990] ECR I-3968, 3973. For a critique of this approach, see R Wintemute, "When Is Pregnancy Discrimination Indirect Sex Discrimination?" (1998) 27 *Industrial Law Journal* 23.

[63] V Harrison, "Using EC law to Challenge Sexual Orientation Discrimination at Work" in Hervey & O'Keeffe (eds.), *Sexual Equality in the European Union* (Chichester, John Wiley & Sons, 1996) at 280.

An indirect discrimination analysis proceeds from the assumption that rules providing benefits to employees' spouses apply irrespective of sexual orientation. However, such rules clearly put lesbians and gay men "at a particular disadvantage compared with other persons", as they cannot marry their same-sex partners and are therefore unable to receive the benefits. At this stage, attention turns to the possible justifications for this *prima facie* indirect discrimination. In particular, the employer must establish under Article 2(2)(b)(i) that the practice "is objectively justified by a legitimate aim and the means of achieving that aim are appropriate and necessary". There are at least three potential justifications for denying unmarried partners access to spousal benefits: (i) the fundamental difference in the social value attached to opposite-sex and same-sex relationships; (ii) economic reasons—that is, the cost implications for employers; and (iii) the risk of abuse by fraudulent partnerships.

Social value attached to opposite-sex and same-sex relationships

This justification was presented in the *Grant* case, where South-West Trains (the employer) argued that its policy of not recognising same-sex partners was legitimate because such partnerships (unlike unmarried opposite-sex partnerships) "are not generally regarded by society as equivalent to marriage".[64] Advocate General Elmer addressed the issue in his Opinion and firmly rejected this reasoning:

> "[It] amounts, in reality, to nothing more than saying that on the basis of its own private conceptions of morality that employer wishes to set aside a fundamental principle of Community law [non-discrimination] in relation to some people because it does not care for their lifestyle. . . .
>
> Under the Treaty it is the rule of law in the Community that the Court must safeguard; it is not its task to watch over questions of morality either in the individual Member States or in the Community . . ."[65]

Nonetheless, the Court's judgment in *Grant* provides support for the position of South-West Trains. In particular, the Court's assessment that "in the present state of the law within the Community, stable relationships between two persons of the same sex are not regarded as equivalent to marriages . . .",[66] seems to create a legal foundation for the argument that employers would be entitled to continue to distinguish between opposite-sex and same-sex couples.

The Court's verdict in *Grant* relied heavily on the non-recognition of same-sex couples under the European Convention on Human Rights (ECHR).[67] Yet, it is important to keep in mind the rapid evolution of the ECHR case law since

[64] *Supra* n.2, at I-642.

[65] *Ibid.*, at I-633.

[66] *Ibid.*, at I-648. For a similar approach, see Case C-59/85, *Netherlands* v. *Reed*, [1986] ECR 1283, paras. 10–11.

[67] *Ibid.*, at I-647 ("stable homosexual relationships do not fall within the scope of the right to respect for family life under Art. 8 of the Convention").

Grant. First, in its decision on military employment in *Lustig-Prean* v. *UK*, the Court of Human Rights signalled a new rigour in respect of homophobia, which it compared to "similar negative attitudes towards those of a different race, origin or colour".[68] It continued, "the Court cannot overlook the widespread and consistently developing views and associated legal changes to the domestic laws of Contracting States on this issue".[69] Second, in *Salgueiro da Silva Mouta* v. *Portugal*,[70] the Court expressly confirmed that Article 14 ECHR on non-discrimination was to be interpreted as including sexual orientation,[71] and that distinctions based on sexual orientation "cannot be tolerated under the Convention".[72]

Returning to the Court of Justice, how should these ECHR decisions influence its attitude to the non-recognition of same-sex partners by employers? The Court should certainly take account of the general direction of the Convention case law, which is firmly towards the rejection of discrimination on grounds of sexual orientation.[73] The analysis of the Convention in *Grant* is arguably no longer applicable, and the Court of Justice must at least reconsider its statements there. Nonetheless, Harrison points out that "Community case law indicates that the Court will avoid making far-reaching decisions which challenge important institutions such as marriage and the family".[74] This assessment is supported by the Opinion of Advocate General Mischo in *D.* v. *Council*, where he dismisses arguments in favour of a revision of the approach in *Grant*.[75]

Ultimately, the Court will need to balance conflicting influences in deciding whether to require employers to recognise same-sex couples. A fundamental rights perspective, drawing on the trends in ECHR law, should incline the Court towards equal treatment for same-sex partners. However, the principle of subsidiarity[76] suggests greater deference to the Member States. Indeed, the Court has acknowledged that where "moral, religious and cultural considerations" are at stake, the Member States should be extended a "sufficient degree of latitude".[77] Perhaps the most likely outcome is that the Court will wait for a consolidation of national laws on the recognition of same-sex partners before making any far-reaching decisions for the whole of the European Union.

Economic reasons

Extending spousal benefits to cover same-sex partners will naturally impose some economic costs on employers. This is unlikely to succeed as a justification

[68] *Supra* n.5, para. 90 (*Lustig-Prean*).
[69] *Ibid.*, para. 97 (*Lustig-Prean*).
[70] (21 Dec. 1999), http://www.echr.coe.int/hudoc.
[71] *Ibid.*, para. 28.
[72] *Ibid.*, para. 36.
[73] See Wintemute, chap. 40.
[74] Harrison, *supra* n.63.
[75] *Supra* n.3, paras. 96–97.
[76] Art. 5(2) EC.
[77] Case C-124/97, *Läärä* v. *Kihlakunnansyyttäjä (Jyväskylä)*, [1999] ECR I-6067, paras. 13–14.

for denying same-sex partners equal treatment, because of the proportionality requirement. In other words, if the same objective can be achieved in a less restrictive fashion, then the existing measure is disproportionate.[78] For instance, if the costs were genuinely substantial, it would always remain open to the employer to reduce the overall range of benefits available. For example, in the *Grant* case, South-West Trains could have replaced the free rail travel concession with a scheme where employees' partners received rail tickets at a discounted price. From the perspective of the Court, the nature of the benefits provided is not relevant—simply that they are provided without discrimination. Finally, it will always be open to the Court to limit the retroactive effect of its judgment, so as to cushion the economic impact on the State and employers.[79]

The risk of abuse by fraudulent partnerships

Certainly it is more difficult for employers to organise partners' benefits where national law does not provide any recognition of same-sex partners. Again, proportionality indicates that this does not seem a sufficient ground for total non-recognition. For example, employers could require evidence of sustained cohabitation as a means of avoiding fraudulent claims. It is also persuasive that some companies do recognise non-marital partnerships, and that there has been little or no evidence of fraud being a significant problem. For example, South-West Trains have now finally decided voluntarily to recognise the same-sex partners of their employees.[80]

Discrimination between opposite-sex married couples and registered same-sex partners

In an increasing number of Member States, various forms of legal recognition for same-sex partnerships have been created. The new dimension this creates to discrimination against same-sex couples was demonstrated in *D.* v. *Council*.[81] This case concerned the denial by the EU Council of Ministers (as an employer) of spousal benefits to a Swedish employee in respect of his same-sex registered partner. Unlike in *Grant*, the benefits were not available to unmarried opposite-sex partners. The case was initially heard at the EU Court of First Instance (CFI). Relying principally on the decision in *Grant*, the CFI rejected the arguments that this was unlawful sex discrimination or a breach of fundamental rights.[82]

[78] See eg Case C-350/96, *Clean Car Autoservice GmbH* v. *Landeshauptmann von Wien*, [1998] ECR I-2521 at paras. 35–7.

[79] See eg *Barber*, *supra* n. 20.

[80] "Partners of Gay Train Staff Get Equal Rights", *Stonewall Press* Release (5 Oct. 1999).

[81] *Supra* n.3.

[82] *Ibid.*, paras. 43 and 39 respectively. The CFI also refused to take into account the amended EU Staff Regulations on the basis that these were adopted subsequent to the decision by the Council to

The aspect of the CFI judgment which seems most vulnerable to criticism is its assertion that persons in a registered partnership need not be regarded as married for the purposes of the Staff Regulations.[83] Marriage is not defined in the regulations, therefore, it was for the CFI to interpret the full scope of this term. The CFI argued that the EU Council was free to develop an autonomous definition of marriage, without any need to refer to the laws of the Member States.[84] Consequently, the Council was at liberty to choose not to include registered partnerships in its definition of marriage. The CFI then erroneously cited the ECHR case law and the *Grant* decision in support of this conclusion.[85]

The CFI's reasoning ignored the facts that the *Grant* case did not concern registered partners, and that the Strasbourg Court has never had an opportunity to comment on the legal status of registered partnerships. Denys argues persuasively that, as marriage is a status conferred only through *national* law, the Court should have accorded more importance to the relevant national law in this case—the Swedish partnership law.[86] This would also seem more consistent with the requirement in Article 6(3) of the EU Treaty that "[t]he Union shall respect the national identities of its Member States". Including registered partnerships in the definition of marriage would not interfere with the choices of those Member States which do not have registered partnership laws. However, it would ensure respect for the social and legal choices made by those states where a registered partnership law has been established.

Nonetheless, Advocate General Mischo's Opinion in the appeal of the decision in *D.* v. *Council* to the ECJ provides support for a definition of marriage as only between persons of opposite sexes. He argues that the principles in *Grant* represent a general rule in Community law that there is no requirement to treat equally homosexual and heterosexual partnerships, because same-sex partnerships are different "in nature".[87] This is a surprisingly overt defence of discrimination against same-sex couples, justified principally by reference to the fact that the partners are homosexuals.

deny benefits to D. in respect of his partner: "Officials shall be entitled to equal treatment under these Staff Regulations without reference, direct or indirect, to race, political, philosophical or religious beliefs, sex or sexual orientation, without prejudice to the relevant provisions requiring a specific marital status". Council Regulation (EC, ECSC, Euratom) No. 781/98 of 7 April 1998 amending the Staff Regulations of Officials and Conditions of Employment of Other Servants of the European Communities in respect of equal treatment, OJ [1998] L 113/4, Art. 1a. However, the exception for provisions "requiring a specific marital status" suggests that the new regulations might make no difference. Similar cases before the CFI include: Case T-96/99, *Fleurbaay* v. *European Investment Bank* (Netherlands registered partnership); Case T-102/99, *Van Hamme* v. *Commission* (same); Case T-167/00, *D.* v. *Commission* (same-sex stable union registered in Catalonia, Spain).

[83] Case T-264/97, *supra* n. 3, paras. 29–30. The CFI extended *Grant* by holding that an employer is not required to treat a same-sex partnership, "even having been officially registered by a national administration", as equivalent to a traditional marriage.

[84] *Ibid.*, para. 27. The CFI had previously refused to bring unmarried opposite-sex cohabitation within the definition of marriage in the Staff Regulations. Case T-65/92, *Arauxo-Dumay* v. *Commission*, [1993] ECR II-597, para. 30.

[85] *Ibid.*, para. 28.

[86] Denys, *supra* n.3, at 421.

[87] Mischo Opinion, *supra* n.3, para. 87.

Notwithstanding this Opinion, there remained an opportunity for the Court to reject the narrow interpretation of marriage adopted by the CFI.[88] This would not only have achieved a more satisfactory outcome in *D.*, but would also have clarified the legal situation in advance of the implementation of the Framework Directive by Member States. Discrimination against same-sex registered partnerships (in comparison with married opposite-sex couples) would then have been regarded as direct sexual orientation discrimination, as civil marriage and registered partnership would both have been viewed as valid forms of marriage for the purposes of EU law.

However, because the Court sustained the approach of the CFI, registered partners will have to challenge unequal treatment as indirect sexual orientation discrimination, as discussed in the previous section. Again it will fall to the Court to determine whether an employer was justified in not recognising same-sex partnerships. Arguably, there will be an even weaker foundation for such discrimination, as the law will have already conferred a degree of social recognition upon registered partners. Moreover, the risk of fraudulent claims will not be relevant, as there will be a legal basis upon which to extend benefits.

In summary, the protection of marital benefits in Recital 22 cannot be regarded as conclusive. The full impact of the Directive upon marital benefits will only be revealed through litigation. Such benefits potentially constitute indirect (if not direct) discrimination, and their legality will depend upon the Court's assessment of their justification. Furthermore, even if the Court of Justice is initially cautious in extending same-sex partners' rights, this will remain open to re-evaluation in the light of legal and social change in the European Union.[89]

ENFORCING EQUAL TREATMENT

The experience of EU sex equality law has confirmed that enforcing anti-discrimination law is extremely difficult. Individual victims face a wide variety of barriers in bringing a case—such as the financial and emotional costs, difficulties in gathering sufficient evidence, and possible negative consequences for existing or future employment relationships.[90] Sensibly, the Commission has attempted to build on this experience in the Framework Directive. Whilst this chapter does not permit a full and exhaustive analysis of these provisions, their value should not be under-estimated. Wedderburn highlights that even "the best

[88] See *supra* n.3. The Court declined to consider the argument that non-recognition of registered partners forms an unlawful obstacle to the free movement of persons. See Guild, chap. 38.

[89] *Supra* n.2, at I-648.

[90] See Blom, et al., *The Utilisation of Sex Equality Litigation in the Member States of the European Community*, V/782/96–EN, Report to the Equal Opportunities Unit of [former] DG V (Brussels, Commission, 1995).

of labour laws is effective only when matched by adequate procedures and sanctions".[91]

There are several key aspects to the provisions of the Directive dealing with enforcement. First, organisations deemed to have a "legitimate interest" in enforcing the provisions of the Directive are given legal standing to bring cases on behalf or in support of a complainant (with their approval).[92] Second, there is provision for a shift in the burden of proof where the complainant establishes "facts from which it may be presumed that there has been direct or indirect discrimination".[93] Third, victimisation of complainants is forbidden.[94] Finally, the sanctions for violations of the Directive must be "effective, proportionate and dissuasive".[95]

To demonstrate how important these provisions are, it is worth considering further the first aspect—legal standing for NGOs. Article 9(2) states:

> "Member States shall ensure that associations, organisations or other legal entities, which have . . . a legitimate interest in ensuring that the provisions of this Directive are complied with, may engage, either on behalf or in support of the complainant, with his or her approval, in any judicial and/or administrative procedures provided for the enforcement of obligations under this Directive".

In practical terms, this allows lesbian and gay organisations to act legally on behalf of an individual victim of discrimination. It also permits trade unions to represent individuals in discrimination cases. This is especially valuable given the resources of the trade union movement, and their accumulated expertise in dealing with workplace disputes. At the same time, it is disappointing that organisations may only act on behalf of individuals, and not in their own name. In this way, the law still requires an individual to suffer discrimination before any action can be taken.

NGOs and trade unions will certainly be a useful source of support for victims of discrimination, but the assistance they can provide is constrained by their resources. This point is recognised in the Race Directive. Article 13(1) places an obligation on Member States to "designate a body or bodies for the promotion of equal treatment of all persons without discrimination on the grounds of racial or ethnic origin".[96] Article 13(2) requires that "the competences of these bodies include: . . . providing independent assistance to victims of discrimination in pursuing their complaints about discrimination, conducting independent surveys concerning discrimination, publishing independent reports and making recommendations on any issue relating to such discrimination". It is difficult to understand why these bodies are not regarded as also

[91] Lord Wedderburn, *Employment Rights in Britain and Europe* (London, Lawrence & Wishart, 1991) at 381.

[92] Art. 9(2).

[93] Art. 10(1).

[94] Art. 11.

[95] Art. 17.

[96] *Supra* n.12.

necessary to support the fight against discrimination on grounds of religion or belief, age, disability or sexual orientation (or indeed sex). The absence of any comparable requirement in the Framework Directive (or the Equal Treatment Directive) leaves an impression that some grounds of discrimination are not of the same priority as discrimination based on racial or ethnic origin. This is reinforced when one considers that the Commission has already proposed an amendment to the Equal Treatment Directive to require the establishment of independent bodies to assist victims of sex discrimination.[97]

CONCLUSION

Overall, there can be no doubt that the adoption of the Framework Directive is a significant advance for lesbian and gay rights within European Union law. It offers considerable benefits at the national level, especially for those Member States where there is no national legislation expressly prohibiting sexual orientation discrimination in public and private employment—Austria, Belgium, Germany, Greece, Italy, Portugal and the United Kingdom.[98] Nonetheless, it is impossible to ignore the remaining points of concern within the new Directive—such as the treatment of partners' benefits or the protection of lesbian and gay employees in religious organisations. These weaknesses in the Directive probably reflect the requirement in Article 13 EC that all legislation based on this provision must be adopted by unanimity in the Council. Decision-making by unanimity inevitably requires the accommodation of specific national concerns.

Lesbian and gay law reform is often difficult and even divisive. The problems faced in France in adopting the civil solidarity pact law,[99] or the controversies in the United Kingdom over reform of the age of consent and removal of the ban on local authorities "promoting homosexuality",[100] demonstrate the potential for conflict in this area. The European Union needs to be especially careful, as not only will there be differences in views as to the merits of the measures, but some will argue that this is unwarranted intervention in matters best left to the discretion of the Member States.

Strengthening the human rights dimension of European Union law is often justified in terms of enhancing the legitimacy of the Union in the eyes of its citizens.[101] Through the guarantee of individual rights, citizens will perceive a

[97] "Proposal for a Directive of the European Parliament and of the Council amending Council Directive 76/207/EEC . . .", COM (2000) 334 (7 June 2000).

[98] See R Wintemute, *Sexual Orientation and Human Rights: The United States Constitution, the European Convention and the Canadian Charter* (Oxford, Clarendon Press, 1997) at xi, 265–7; Beger, et al, *supra* n.6. Appendix II, pp. 781–88.

[99] See Borrillo, chap. 25.

[100] Local Government Act 1986, s. 2A (as amended by Local Government Act 1988, s. 28). See eg "Ministers suffer heavy defeat on Section 28", *The Guardian*, 8 Feb. 2000.

[101] C Barnard, "*P.* v. *S.*: Kite Flying or a New Constitutional Approach" in Dashwood & O'Leary (eds), *The Principle of Equal Treatment in European Community Law* (London, Sweet & Maxwell, 1997) at 67.

direct stake in the integration process, and a sense of commitment and loyalty will be generated. Yet, the achievement of these goals depends heavily upon the degree of consensus surrounding the values underpinning the rights.[102] Where values are contested rather than shared, then EU intervention has as much potential to alienate as to promote stronger bonds.

Lesbian and gay rights are a prime example of how developing human rights protection may be a double-edged sword for the Union. From the human rights perspective, this is an opportunity for the Union to reaffirm its democratic credentials and to demonstrate the added value it can bring to human rights law in the Member States. However, from the perspective of subsidiarity, and the avoidance of intervention in issues of national sensitivity, then lesbian and gay rights seem fraught with the potential for controversy. Ultimately, an incremental approach seems the most likely to secure progress without major opposition from the national level. One of the important lessons from the negotiation of Article 13 EC is the possibility of advancing sexual orientation issues when placed in the context of wider anti-discrimination law reform. By shifting the focus towards discrimination in general, it becomes more difficult for critics to single out specific grounds of discrimination.

The European Union's first legislative initiatives adopted under Article 13 EC contain a mixed message as to the direction of anti-discrimination law. On the one hand, the Framework Directive is founded upon a common approach to tackling diverse forms of discrimination.[103] On the other, the adoption of a separate Race Directive[104] sends out a confusing signal. This is accentuated by informal commitments to bring forward an additional proposal in 2003 specifically addressing disability discrimination.[105] This may be an advantageous approach from the perspective of racial or disability discrimination, but it makes further progress on sexual orientation discrimination more difficult to foresee. In this light, the adoption of the Framework Directive was imperative, not only to enhance protection against employment discrimination, but also to establish firmly a foundation stone upon which further lesbian and gay law reform at the EU level can be built.[106]

[102] G de Búrca, "The Language of Rights and European Integration" in Shaw & More (eds.), *The New Legal Dynamics of European Union* (Oxford, Clarendon Press, 1995) at 46.

[103] *Supra* n.11, at 6.

[104] *Supra* n.12. See L Waddington & M Bell, "More Equal Than Others: Distinguishing European Union Equality Directives", (2001) 38 *Common Market Law Review* 587.

[105] "Article 13 Package Adopted", *European Disability Forum Press Release* (25 Nov. 1999).

[106] See Waaldijk, chap. 36.

38

Free Movement and Same-Sex Relationships: Existing EC Law and Article 13 EC

ELSPETH GUILD*

IN THIS CHAPTER, I will consider the right of free movement of persons in European Community law[1] and the consequences that this right has for persons in same-sex relationships. The central question here will be: what are the rights of a same-sex couple (consisting of two Community nationals, two third-country nationals, or one of each) when the partners have decided to exercise the free movement right in European Community law to go to, live in, and exercise economic activities in, another Member State?

INDEPENDENT RIGHTS OF FREE MOVEMENT: ECONOMIC ACTIVITIES AND RESIDENCE

Article 3 of the EC Treaty sets as an objective of the Community the abolition of obstacles to free movement of persons within the territory of the Union. Articles 39–55 EC give particularity to that objective. However, these Articles of the Treaty require that those exercising the free movement right be doing so for the purpose of economic activity. Nationals of the Member States are entitled to travel to, enter, and reside in another Member State for the purposes of employment (Article 39), self-employment (Article 43), and provision or receipt of services (Article 49).[2] The right to move and reside for economic activities can only be denied by a Member State on the basis that its exercise is not genuine and effective,[3] or on the basis that the individual is a threat to public policy,

* CPO Professor of European Migration Law, Katholieke Universiteit Nijmegen (Netherlands); Partner, Kingsley Napley, London.

[1] See generally, E Guild, *Immigration Law of the European Community* (The Hague, Kluwer, 2001); E Guild (ed.), *The Legal Framework and Social Consequences of Free Movement of Persons in the European Union* (The Hague, Kluwer, 1999); E Guild & C Harlow (eds.), *Implementing Amsterdam: Immigration and Asylum Rights in EC Law* (Oxford, Hart Publishing, 2001).

[2] Case 286/82, *Luisi*, [1984] European Court Reports (ECR) 377.

[3] Case 66/85, *Lawrie-Blum*, [1984] ECR 2121.

public security or public health.[4] These concepts have been very narrowly defined by the Court of Justice, which has given them an autonomous and uniform Community meaning.[5]

In 1990, the European Community extended the right to move and reside to economically inactive but self-sufficient persons. Three Directives were adopted, entitling persons with sufficient resources, pensioners, and students to move and reside in another Member State.[6] In 1992, the Treaty of Maastricht inserted what is now Article 17 EC, which established citizenship of the Union. Article 18 EC grants every citizen of the Union the right "to move and reside freely within the territory of the Member States", but has yet to be interpreted as adding anything to the three Directives and Articles 39, 43 and 49 EC.

What does this mean for same-sex couples? Where the parties to a same-sex relationship both hold the nationality of one Member State and seek to travel and reside in another Member State, normally they will be able to do so on the basis of an exercise of a Community law right by each of them individually. Therefore, for instance, a same-sex couple in which both partners are German nationals (or a mixed German-Italian couple) who travel to Spain to retire will each be able to do so on the basis of Directive 60/364, which gives a right of entry and residence to pensioners, provided that they are economically self-sufficient and covered by private health insurance. The fact that one of the parties is moving and exercising (or not) an economic activity exclusively because he or she wants to be with the other partner, rather than on the basis of an economic or other need, is irrelevant.[7]

In practice, what often occurs is that one same-sex partner is transferred by his or her employer from one Member State to another. The other partner chooses to accompany the employee. The right of residence of the transferred employee is based on economic activity—usually Article 39 EC, the right of free movement of workers. The other partner moves in exercise of his or her right of residence, showing economic self-sufficiency and health insurance. Subsequently, the other partner often also engages in an economic activity once settled in the host Member State. In law, what is happening is that the other partner is exercising an independent right of residence and then an independent right to economic activity. Although the principal reason for the exercise of these rights is in order to enjoy family life, the legal framework is the exercise of independent rights accruing to each partner by virtue of his or her nationality of a Member State.

[4] Art. 39(3) EC; Council Dir. 64/221/EEC of 15 Feb. 1964 on the co-ordination of special measures concerning the movement and residence of foreign nationals, Official Journal (OJ) [1963–4] Sp Ed 117.

[5] Case 30/77, *Bouchereau*, [1977] ECR 1999.

[6] Council Dir. 90/364/EEC of 28 June 1990 on the right of residence, OJ [1990] L 180/26; Council Dir. 90/365/EEC of 28 June 1990 on the right of residence for employees and self-employed persons who have ceased their occupational activity, OJ [1990] L 180/28; Council Dir. 93/96/EEC of 29 Oct. 1993 on the right of residence for students, OJ [1993] L 317/59.

[7] Case 53/81, *Levin*, [1982] ECR 1035.

The traditional rights of movement, residence and economic activity only apply to nationals of the fifteen Member States of the European Union.[8] Under the 1992 Agreement creating the European Economic Area (EEA), nationals of Iceland, Liechtenstein and Norway enjoy the same free movement rights as Community nationals. However, these rights do not extend to other third-country nationals,[9] whether already lawfully within the territory of the Union or seeking to come to the Union. Where a same-sex couple includes, for instance, a Thai national, that partner will not have an independent right in Community law to enter, reside in, and exercise economic activities in any Member State. It is, therefore, to this group that I will now turn.

DERIVED RIGHTS OF FREE MOVEMENT: FAMILY MEMBERS

A Community national exercising a free movement right to go to, reside in, and exercise economic activity in a Member State, other than that of his or her nationality, is entitled to do so in freedom and dignity. Regulation 1612/68 in its preamble stresses that the exercise of a free movement right must include the right to be accompanied or joined by family members.[10]

As discussed above, the right of free movement for economic purposes is limited to nationals of the fifteen Member States (or the EEA).[11] Although the European Court of Justice (ECJ) has indicated that there is a potential competence to extend at least some of these rights to third-country nationals residing within the Union, this has not been done.[12] However, family members of Community nationals exercising free movement rights are entitled to accompany their Community national principal, and exercise economic activities, anywhere in the Union, irrespective of the nationality of those family members. Therefore, the Thai spouse of a German national going to Spain to retire is entitled to accompany the German spouse to Spain; should the Thai spouse wish to take employment or otherwise engage in economic activities, this must be permitted under Community law.[13] Without the relationship with a Community national, the Thai national would not have a right from Community law to travel to the host Member State and to work and reside there.

[8] Austria, Belgium, Denmark, Finland, France, Germany, Greece, Ireland, Italy, Luxembourg, Netherlands, Portugal, Spain, Sweden, United Kingdom.

[9] In this chapter, the term "third-country national" means a national of any state outside the fifteen Member States of the European Union.

[10] Council Regulation 1612/68/EEC of 15 October 1968 on freedom of movement for workers within the Community, OJ [1968] L 257/2 (as amended).

[11] By virtue of other agreements with third countries, for example, Turkey and some Central and Eastern European countries, nationals of those states have some rights of entry, residence and economic activity, but all are more circumscribed than the rights of Community nationals.

[12] C-369/90, *Ayowemi*, [1998] ECR I-6781.

[13] Dir. 90/365, *supra* n.6, Arts. 1, 2.

The circle of family members permitted to join or accompany a Community national moving to another Member State may have any nationality whatsoever. They are defined, however, as a spouse, children under the age of twenty-one, and dependent relatives of the Community national and/or their spouse in the ascending and descending lines (including dependent children aged twenty-one and over or dependent parents).[14] There is a further obligation to facilitate or favour the admission of any member of the family (such as an aunt, brother, niece or cousin) not coming within the above definition, but who either is dependent on the Community national or living under his or her roof in the country whence he or she comes.[15]

Can one then argue in respect of the same-sex couple that the third-country national partner is the equivalent of a spouse, and therefore entitled to accompany the Community law national to another Member State? In 1986, in *Netherlands* v. *Reed*, this question was answered by the ECJ in the negative. The term "spouse" in Community law has so far been limited to persons who have formally contracted a civil marriage recognised by the law, and has not yet been interpreted as including an unmarried partner living with a Community national as if he/she were a spouse.[16]

It has been suggested that, even if a same-sex partner is currently excluded from the definition of a "spouse" for the purposes of accompanying a Community national to another Member State, nonetheless such a person ought to qualify as a "member of the family" for whom there is a duty to "facilitate" admission. Nicholas Blake argues that the concept of a "member of the family" should be wide enough to include a same-sex partner, particularly when taken in the light of the Community's obligation to respect the European Convention on Human Rights, including its Article 8 right to respect for "family life":[17]

> "Given the regard had to the standards of the ECHR in developing the meaning of Community legislation there may be scope for argument as to the non-Community national partner of a Community national. This argument would be strongest in circumstances where there are children or other cogent evidence of the enjoyment of family life together; such as the adoption of married names, joint tenancies, and ownership of property. If this line of reasoning proves admissible one could work backwards down the line from extra-marital children, extra-marital partner, to same-

[14] Regulation 1612/68, *supra* n.10, Art. 10(1) (workers); Council Dir. 73/148/EEC of 21 May 1973 on the abolition of restrictions on movement and residence within the Community for nationals of Member States with regard to establishment and the provision [or receipt] of services, OJ [1973] L 172/14, Article 1(1).

[15] Regulation 1612/68, *supra* n.10, Art. 10(2); Dir. 73/148, *ibid.*, Art. 1(2).

[16] Case 59/85, *Netherlands* v. *Reed*, [1986] ECR 1283; Case T-65/92, *Arauxo-Dumay* v. *Commission*, [1993] ECR II-597. In Case C-65/98, *Eyüp* v. *Vorarlberg*, Advocate General La Pergola concluded that an unmarried opposite-sex "*concubin . . . vivant en union libre*" is a "member of the family", in connection with the EC–Turkey association agreement. However, the ECJ avoided the issue in its judgment of 22 June 2000 (paras. 32–38). The question is presented again in Case C-407/99, *Pathminidevi* v. *Landeskreditbank*.

[17] See N Blake QC, "Family Life in Community Law: The Limits of Freedom and Dignity" in Guild (1999), *supra* n.1, at 7–19. See also Wintemute, chap. 40.

sex relationships that the Strasbourg Court has hitherto considered only relevant to private life, to conclude that Community law must advance with society and contemporary modes of living if it is to fulfil its objective of removing obstacles to free movement".

This argument has yet to be adopted by the European Court of Justice.[18] However, the chance that it may receive a more favourable hearing has been increased by the inclusion in the EC Treaty of Article 13, which creates an explicit Community competence to prohibit discrimination on the basis of, *inter alia*, sexual orientation. I will return to this point below, and will also consider the alternative argument that recognition of the right of a Community national to cohabit with a same-sex partner in a host Member State is part of the duty of the Member States to abolish "obstacles" to free movement.

DERIVED RIGHTS OF FREE MOVEMENT: POSTED WORKERS

A right of entry and economic activity for third-country nationals in the Community may also arise by virtue of an individual's relationship with an employer.[19] For instance, a Community-based employer who wishes to send employees to another Member State to provide services is entitled to do so, without being hindered as regards the nationality of the employees to be sent. For instance, a Belgian employer wishing to send a Moroccan national employee to France to provide services for the employer is entitled to do so without having to obtain a work permit in advance, and without fear of fines for employing the Moroccan in France without a work permit.[20]

Unfortunately, this right of Community nationals to send third-country national staff around the Union, in exercise of economic activities for the employer, is still subject to substantial administrative obstacles in many Member States. The Commission has prepared a report and proposed directives to simplify and give effect to the rights.[21] Service provision is generally accepted to be a short-term activity, and duration is one of the dividing lines between services and establishment.[22] Further, the right to move third-country national staff to provide services has yet to be recognised to extend also to the right to

[18] An English judge recently rejected this argument, without referring the question to the ECJ. R. v. *Secretary of State for the Home Department, ex parte McCollum* (24 Jan. 2001), Case No. CO/569/99 (High Court, Queen's Bench Division, Administrative Court, Mr. Justice Turner) (Brazilian male partner of Irish man denied permission to enter the United Kingdom).

[19] See J Onslow-Cole, "The Right of Establishment and Provision of Services: Community Employers and Third Country Nationals" in Guild (1999), *supra* n.1, at 63–72.

[20] Case C-43/93, *Vander Elst*, [1994] ECR I-3803.

[21] Proposal for a Directive on the posting of workers who are third-country nationals for the provision of cross-border services, and Proposal for a Directive extending the freedom to provide cross-border services to third-country nationals established within the Community, COM (1999) 3 (26 Feb. 1999), OJ [1999] C 67/12, 17.

[22] Case C-55/94, *Gebhard*, [1995] ECR I-4165.

send a third-country national to set up a commercial presence on behalf of the employer (i.e. exercise the freedom of establishment right for the enterprise).

What does this mean for a same-sex couple seeking to move to, and reside in, a host Member State? As discussed above, the problem of exercising a free movement right as a couple arises only where one of the parties is not a national of a Member State (or the EEA). If the third-country national partner is already lawfully resident in one Member State, and is being sent by his or her employer to another Member State to provide services, the Community national will be able to accompany him or her in exercise of the Community national's independent free movement rights. If it is the Community national who is being moved, then there is always the possibility that the third-country national's employer could be convinced that the third-country national should also be sent to the same host Member State at the same time to provide services. However, service provision is normally of short duration. If the Community national takes long-term employment in another Member State, or needs to move to a host Member State for some reason, even the most flexible employer will have difficulty sending the third-country national partner on a service provision contract which repeats itself continuously, so as to provide a way for the couple to continue living together.

THE FREE MOVEMENT RIGHT: ABOLISHING INTRA-COMMUNITY BORDER CONTROLS

The Single European Act (1986) amended the EC Treaty by introducing, in what is now Article 14 EC, the deadline of 31 December 1992 for the abolition of intra-Community border controls on persons. The objective was not achieved within the time-frame, as a result of the failure of the Council to adopt flanking legislation needed for its implementation.[23] The failure to adopt the necessary legislation was not least because of resistance from the United Kingdom. This resistance continued until the Treaty of Amsterdam (1997) allowed the UK to opt out of the common measures altogether, while introducing into the EC Treaty a new Title IV (Visas, Asylum, Immigration and Other Policies Related to Free Movement of Persons). Title IV (Articles 61–69 EC) relaunches the objective of the abolition of intra-Community border controls on persons. In so doing, it inserts into the EC Treaty the so-called "Schengen *acquis*", the intergovernmental agreement of five Member States, signed at Schengen in 1985 (subsequently joined by all Member States except Ireland and the UK) which provides the nuts and bolts on movement of persons across external EU borders, so as to pave the way for the abolition of intra-Community border controls. Denmark (a Schengen member), Ireland and the UK opted out of Title IV by specific protocols to the Treaty of Amsterdam, thereby letting the other Member States go

[23] Case C-378/97, *Wijsenbeek*, [1999] ECR I-6207.

forward with the abolition of border controls on persons, and other measures on immigration and asylum, using the procedures of the EC Treaty.

The new Article 62(1) EC, applicable to the twelve participating Member States, specifically states that the abolition of border controls among the Member States (to be achieved by 1 May 2004) will apply both to Community nationals and third-country nationals. Under the Schengen *acquis*, third-country nationals resident in one Member State, or lawfully admitted to one Member State, are entitled to travel for up to three months within the territory of the Union. Thus, the three-month travel rule is now a rule that is incorporated in EC law along with the rest of the defined Schengen *acquis*. This free movement right is the only one which a third-country national may exercise without being dependent on a Community national principal.

The same-sex couple who wish to exercise only a short-term free movement right, for instance, to go on holiday to another Member State, will be able to rely on Title IV rights. For once, the fact that one of the partners is a third-country national does not change the quality of the right to travel. Each party to the relationship will have an independent right to travel for three months within the territory of the Member States participating in Title IV. However, the Community law right is one to move, not to stay for a period beyond three months, nor to exercise economic activities.

FREE MOVEMENT AND NATIONALITY DISCRIMINATION

Article 12 of the EC Treaty guarantees that, "[w]ithin the scope of application of this Treaty, and without prejudice to any special provisions contained therein, any discrimination on grounds of nationality shall be prohibited". This general right to non-discrimination finds particularity in the free movement provisions of Articles 39–55 EC. But what is discrimination for these purposes? The ECJ has held that this means that similar situations shall not be treated differently, unless differentiation is objectively justified.[24] What is a similar situation for a same-sex couple?

Same-sex partners are in a struggle for equality with married and unmarried opposite-sex partners. The critical question, with regard to the principle of equality in Community law, is whether the two situations are similar. If they are not categorised as similar, then it would offend Community law for them to be treated equally. The decision that same-sex partnerships are similar situations to marital and non-marital opposite-sex partnerships is both a judicial and, more importantly, political decision. So far, as discussed above, marriage and non-marital relationships (opposite-sex or same-sex) have been treated as different situations for the purposes of Community free movement rules. The next question, then, is whether non-marital opposite-sex relationships and same-sex relationships are treated by Community law as similar situations.

[24] Case 117/76, *Ruckdeschel*, [1977] ECR 1753.

Community law prohibits both direct and indirect discrimination against nationals of other Member States: "inequality of treatment on the basis of nationality must be considered as a form of [direct] discrimination prohibited by Article [12] of the Treaty if it occurs in an area to which the Treaty applies".[25] Indirect discrimination is discrimination which, by the application of criteria of differentiation other than nationality, leads in fact to the same result of unequal treatment.[26] Because the prohibited ground of discrimination is nationality, the relevant comparison is between the position of a migrant Community national and that of a national of the host Member State. Article 7(2) of Regulation 1612/68 requires that migrant Community nationals enjoy the same "social and tax advantages" as national workers.

In 1986, in *Netherlands* v. *Reed*, the ECJ also held that, where a Member State permits its own nationals to enjoy family life with unmarried third-country national partners, then it must allow nationals of other Member States to enjoy such family life, and must give the same residence (and work) rights to the unmarried third-country national partner of a national of another Member State as it gives to the partners of its own nationals.[27] *Reed* involved a heterosexual couple, but by extension it should also apply to a homosexual couple. Although the ECJ held in 1998, in *Grant* v. *South-West Trains*, that "in the present state of the law within the Community, stable relationships between two persons of the same sex are not regarded as equivalent to marriages or stable relationships outside marriage between persons of opposite sex",[28] the issue in *Grant* was discrimination based on sex or sexual orientation. Where the discrimination is based on nationality, as in *Reed*, the issue of the equivalence of marital and non-marital opposite-sex relationships (or non-marital opposite-sex and same-sex relationships) does not arise. The host Member State has voluntarily decided to establish such an equivalence for its own nationals, in relation to their unmarried third-country national partners, and cannot withhold this "social advantage" from nationals of other Member States.

Of course, the protection against nationality discrimination that *Reed* provides is limited. Unless the host Member State has voluntarily decided to admit the third-country national same-sex partners of its own nationals, the State is under no obligation to extend such a right to nationals of other Member States. If a German national and his or her same-sex Thai partner chose to move to the Netherlands, the partner would be eligible to reside and engage in economic activities, but only because the German partner is entitled to rely on his or her Community right to be treated in the same way as a Dutch national. Because a Dutch national is entitled to be joined by a third-country national same-sex

[25] Case 283/83, *Gravier*, [1985] ECR 593.

[26] Case 152/73, *Sotgiu*, [1974] ECR 153.

[27] *Supra* n.16.

[28] Case C-249/96, [1998] ECR I-621, para. 35. See also Koppelman, chap. 35; Waaldijk, chap. 36; Bell, chap. 37.

partner, non-discrimination on the basis of nationality requires the same treatment for the German national and his or her Thai partner.

The conditions surrounding the exercise of the right of the partner to enter are entirely in the hands of the host Member State. The conditions which may be placed on the family life of same-sex partnerships may be more or less restrictive at the discretion of the host Member State, as the existing right does not extend beyond that of non-discrimination based on nationality. Indeed, should the Member State decide not to permit immigration rights to same-sex partnerships at all (while allowing them to marital and non-marital opposite-sex partnerships), there will be no breach of the Community prohibition of nationality discrimination. As nationals of the host Member State are denied the possibility of family life with their same-sex partners, there is no discrimination against nationals of another Member State.

FREE MOVEMENT AND "OBSTACLES"

The right of free movement of persons goes further than a right of access to the territory and a right to non-discrimination. An express objective of the Community, in Article 3(1)(c) EC, is "the abolition . . . of obstacles to the free movement of . . . persons". The concept of "obstacles" (or "restrictions") and their abolition has been much more fully developed in Community law in the fields of free movement of goods and, to some extent, free movement of services. In the area of free movement of persons, its most famous application was as regards transfer fees for professional footballers.[29] An obstacle is a provision or practice which precludes or deters a national of a Member State from leaving his or her country of origin (or going to or remaining in a host Member State) in order to exercise a right of freedom of movement.[30] The ECJ has held that obstacles are unlawful (unless they can be justified), even if they apply without regard to the nationality of the worker concerned.[31] When an obstacle is identified and found to be inhibiting the free movement right of (eg) a worker, it is not necessary for the Court to go on to consider whether discrimination on the grounds of nationality has occurred.

What does this mean for same-sex couples? It may be argued that, where a same-sex couple wish to move to another Member State, and the third-country national partner is unable to join and remain with his or her Community national partner in the host Member State, there is an obstacle to the Community national's right of free movement. The obstacle consists of the lack of a national immigration rule permitting the same-sex partner to accompany and reside with the migrant Community national, which makes the exercise of

[29] Case C-415/93, *Bosman*, [1996] ECR I-4921.
[30] Case C-10/90, *Masgio*, [1991] ECR I-1119.
[31] Case C-18/95, *Terhoeve*, [1999] ECR I-345.

the Community national's free movement right less attractive, or indeed unacceptable to the Community national.[32]

According to the ECJ, there are various justifications which a Member State can assert for creating or maintaining an obstacle to free movement. However, to be consistent with Community law, an obstacle (or restriction) must fulfil four conditions:

1. It must be applied in a non-discriminatory manner;
2. It must be justified by imperative requirements in the general interest;
3. It must be suitable for securing the attainment of the objective pursued;
4. It must not go beyond what is necessary to achieve it.[33]

Where a Member State does not recognise same-sex partnerships at all for immigration rights, there will be no discrimination with regard to the position of its own nationals if it refuses to admit the same-sex partner of a Community national. Yet, certainly in such circumstances the exercise of a free movement right by the Community national is hindered and made less attractive. Can the Member State argue that the refusal to permit the third-country national same-sex partner to reside and engage in economic activities in the State is justified by imperative requirements in the general interest? It would be for the Member State to establish that the policy pursues a legitimate objective. The sanctity of marriage and the social mores of the Member State are possible legitimate objectives.

However, a ban on same-sex partner immigration might go beyond what is necessary to achieve these objectives. Recognition of same-sex partnerships for the limited purpose of allowing the partners to live in the same country would not undermine the sanctity of marriage and the social mores of the Member State, and would prevent the severe emotional harm the partners would suffer if their relationship could not continue. The ECJ's decision whether or not to accept this justification would probably be strongly influenced, as in *Grant*, by the case law of the European Court and Commission of Human Rights on same-sex couples at the time of the ECJ's decision.[34]

FREE MOVEMENT AND SEXUAL ORIENTATION DISCRIMINATION: ARTICLE 13 EC

The Treaty of Amsterdam broke new ground when it amended the EC Treaty by inserting an explicit anti-discrimination competence (Article 13 EC):

[32] In *D.* v. *Council*, discussed in Bell, chap. 37, the non-recognition of the applicant's Swedish same-sex registered partnership, for the purpose of an employment benefit, caused the applicant to give up his job with the Council in Brussels and return with his male partner to Sweden.

[33] *Supra* n.22.

[34] See Wintemute, chap. 40. In *D.* v. *Council*, the ECJ declined to consider the obstacle to free movement argument. See pp. 767–69.

"Without prejudice to the other provisions of this Treaty and within the limits of the powers conferred by it upon the Community, the Council, acting unanimously on a proposal from the Commission and after consulting the European Parliament, may take appropriate action to combat discrimination based on sex, racial or ethnic origin, religion or belief, disability, age or sexual orientation".

This provision clearly lacks sufficient clarity, precision and unconditionality to have direct effect in the legal orders of the Member States, and therefore requires implementing legislation. Nonetheless, it is an extremely important step forward and will provide a legal basis both (a) for enacting new legislation on discrimination against same-sex partners, and (b) for interpreting existing EC law as providing rights to same-sex partners.

With regard to new legislation, the Council has recently adopted, on the basis of Article 13 EC, a directive prohibiting sexual orientation discrimination in employment, which Mark Bell discusses in chapter 37.[35] However, the Commission has yet to invoke Article 13 EC as the legal basis of any proposals for legislation on free movement of same-sex partners. A proposal under Article 40 EC, later abandoned because of opposition from Member States, would have added the following provisions to Regulation 1612/68:[36]

Recital (5): "Whereas discrimination on grounds of . . . *sexual orientation* represents an obstacle to the free movement of workers and their families";
Article 1a: "Within the scope of this Regulation, all discrimination on grounds of . . . *sexual orientation* shall be prohibited".
Article 10:
"1. The following shall, irrespective of their nationality, have the right to install themselves with a worker who is a national of one Member State and who is employed in the territory of another Member State:
(a) his spouse or *any person corresponding to a spouse under the legislation of the host Member State*, and their descendants";

The proposed amendment to Article 10 would have been more helpful had it referred to "the Member State whence he comes", thereby requiring Member States to recognise registered same-sex partnerships from other Member States, even if the host Member State has no such legislation. The same objection can be made against a more recent Commission proposal (under Article 63(3)(a) EC) for a directive on family reunification (in relation to third-country nationals and Community nationals who have not left their own Member States), Article 5(1) of which would require Member States to "authorise the entry and residence . . . of the following family members: (a) the applicant's spouse, or an unmarried partner living in a durable relationship with the applicant, if the legislation of

[35] Council Dir. 2000/78/EC of 27 Nov. 2000 establishing a general framework for equal treatment in employment and occupation, OJ [2000] L 303/16. See also Waaldijk, chap. 36.

[36] *Supra* n.10. See Proposal for a European Parliament and Council Regulation amending Council Regulation 1612/68/EEC on freedom of movement for workers within the Community, OJ [1998] C 344/9.

the Member State concerned treats the situation of unmarried couples as corresponding to that of married couples . . ."[37]

With regard to interpretation of existing EC law, Article 13 EC could strengthen the "obstacle" to free movement argument (discussed above), as well as the argument that a same-sex partner is "a member of the family" (discussed above).[38] Indeed, an applicant could rely on Article 13 EC and ask the ECJ to reconsider its judgment in *Reed* that non-marital partners are not "spouses" in EC free movement law. As this book demonstrates, there has been a substantial increase in the legal recognition of unmarried opposite-sex couples and same-sex couples by Member States since *Reed* was decided in 1986. If the ECJ is still able to hold that an unmarried and unregistered same-sex partner is not a "spouse", and that the discrimination is based on marital status (because unmarried opposite-sex partners do not qualify) rather than sexual orientation, it will be harder to exclude a registered same-sex partner,[39] and even harder to exclude a same-sex partner who is married to a Dutch national in the Netherlands.[40] To exclude a married same-sex partner, the ECJ would have to adopt a Community definition of "spouse" as a married opposite-sex partner only.

CONCLUSIONS

I have looked in some depth at Community law and how its provisions on free movement of persons and non-discrimination could affect same-sex partnerships. A same-sex partner can have an independent free movement right (as a Community national or as a third-country national under Title IV EC), or a right derived from a Community national as a family member or a posted worker. The right to non-discrimination on the basis of nationality can help same-sex partners who are moving to a host Member State whose own nationals are entitled to immigration rights for their third-country national same-sex partners. However, this right cannot help where no such immigration rights exist for nationals of the host Member State. In such cases, the Community national must argue that the host Member State's refusal to admit their same-sex partner is an "obstacle" to the exercise of their free movement right. The

[37] Proposal for a Council Directive on the right to family reunification, COM (1999) 638, a amended by COM (2000) 624, OJ [2001] C 62E/99. The Commission's Explanatory Memorandur makes it clear (at p. 14, COM (1999) 638) that an unmarried partner "may be of the same sex".

[38] Additional support could be found in Art. 21(1) of the (non-binding) Charter of Fundamenta Rights of the European Union, OJ [2000] C 364/1: "Any discrimination based on . . . sexual orien tation shall be prohibited".

[39] See *supra* nn. 32, 34.

[40] See Waaldijk, chaps. 23 and 36; K Waaldijk, "Towards Equality in the Freedom of Movemer of Persons" in K Krickler (ed.), *After Amsterdam: Sexual Orientation and the European Unio* (Brussels, ILGA-Europe, 1999), http://www.steff.suite.dk/ilgaeur.htm (Policy Documents A Elman, "The Limits of Citizenship: Migration, Sex Discrimination and Same-Sex Partners in E Law", (2000) 38 *Journal of Common Market Studies* 729.

host Member State can, however, attempt to justify an obstacle to free movement on the basis of imperative requirements in the general interest. The Community national can also argue that, in light of Article 13 EC, such Community concepts as "member of the family" and "spouse" must be interpreted as including a same-sex partner, so as to avoid direct or indirect sexual orientation discrimination. Although same-sex partners have a number of arguments at their disposal, it may take not only time, but also lobbying and litigation, before progress is made to achieve an acceptance in Community law that they are entitled to the same protection as unmarried, and indeed married, opposite-sex partners[41].

[41] Two recent Commission proposals do not invoke Art. 13 EC and include "unmarried partners" subject to the same conditions as COM (2000) 624, *supra* n.37: Proposal for a Council Directive concerning the status of third-country nationals who are long-term residents, COM (2001) 127, Art. 2(e); Proposal for a European Parliament and Council Directive on the right of citizens of the Union and their family members to move and reside freely within the territory of the Member States, COM (2001) 257, Art. 2(2) (would repeal and consolidate Arts. 10 and 11 of Reg. 1612/68, *supra* n. 10, and nine Dirs., including those cited *supra* in nn. 4, 6, 14). See also Art. 4 (both proposals, *supra*, and COM (2001) 388): "Member States shall give effect to the provisions of this Directive without discrimination on grounds of [on the basis of] . . . sexual orientation".

Section B—European Convention on Human Rights

39

Sex: Has It Any Place in Modern Marriage?

STEPHEN WHITTLE*

MANY TRANSSEXUAL PEOPLE seek marriage in their new gender role. Like others, transsexual people want the opportunity publicly to declare their commitment to and love for their partners. But marriage is not just a religious or spiritual ceremony; it is also a civil contract under which the parties acquire various responsibilities, rights and social benefits. Transsexual people also want to be able to provide economic and emotional protection for their families. Yet at the moment, they are uniquely placed in British law in being unable to contract a legally secure marriage with a partner of either sex. In a recent submission to the the Government's "Interdepartmental Working Group on Transsexual People" (the "Press For Change Submission"), the leading campaigning groups in this area said:

> "In many cases, transsexual people have already been economically disadvantaged due to lengthy periods of time in which career aspirations had to be put on hold, as medical treatment was sought and undergone. For many of us, social pressures will have meant our education has suffered. Job insecurity, or failure to get a job due to prejudice, will mean that we will have spent time being unemployed. Finally, as we achieve some sort of social acceptance, we then discover that without the right to contract a marriage, [we are denied] many of the financial benefits that accrue on marriage [such as survivor's pensions] . . . [B]ecause only spouses and legally related children can benefit . . . [w]e find ourselves having to buy extra financial security for our families, and yet we are invariably already financially worse off than our peers for all of the other reasons, such as entering a career late, or having missed out on formal education".[1]

* Reader, School of Law, Manchester Metropolitan University, s.t.whittle@mmu.ac.uk.

[1] Change, FTM Network, G & SA, The Gender Trust, GIRES, Liberty, Press For Change, *Meeting the Needs of Transsexual People: A Presentation to the Interdepartmental Working Group on Transsexual Issues*, 19 Jan. 2000, http://www.pfc.org.uk/workgrp/jan2000.htm. On 26 July 2000, the Home Office published the April 2000 *Report of the Interdepartmental Working Group on Transsexual People*, http://www.homeoffice.gov.uk/ccpd/wgtrans.pdf. Having been asked "to consider, with particular reference to birth certificates, the need for appropriate legal measures to address the problems experienced by transsexual people, having due regard to scientific and societal developments, and measures undertaken in other countries to deal with this issue", the Working Group did not actually make any recommendations, merely identifying three options to put out to public consultation: "to leave the current situation unchanged; to issue birth certificates showing the

CIRCUMSCRIBING MARRIAGE I

Marriage confers an enhanced form of citizenship; in United States federal law, there are an estimated 1049 legal rights and responsibilities associated with civil marriage.[2] Marriage is not, as is often thought, simply a recognition of one contractual relationship, that between the respective contractors. It is also a mechanism whereby a far more complex set of relationships are put in place. These relationships are not just between the marriage partners themselves, but also between the marriage partners and the children brought into or resulting from the marriage, between the state and the marriage partners, and between the state and the children of the marriage.

Marriage delineates the extent of the dependency claims between the partners, and in relation to the state. For example, in effect, marriage partners agree to forego the enhanced levels of state welfare benefits afforded to single people when they are, for whatever reason, unable to work or to provide for themselves. In return, the state in effect pledges to ensure that the marriage partners will be able to transfer their pension rights to each other in the event of the death of one partner. Whilst marriage still affords these sorts of benefits—which exist within our modern welfare state primarily to ensure that children and spouses are not left seeking welfare benefits—it is a strange aberration that people who want to provide for their families, by entering the institution that confers these automatic rights, are excluded from doing so. It is even more of an anomaly at a time when state welfare benefits continue to be eroded in the name of "protection of the public purse".

CIRCUMSCRIBING MARRIAGE II

In the United Kingdom, the definition of a valid and legal marriage is contained in the *ratio decidendi* of the nineteenth century case, *Hyde* v. *Hyde*[3]:

> "marriage is a voluntary union for life of one man and one woman to the exclusion of all others".

new name and, possibly, gender; and to grant full legal recognition of the new gender subject to certain criteria and procedures" (para. 5.5). With regard to marriage, the Working Group noted: "Legal recognition of a change of sex would have implications for pre-existing marriages. If a subsisting marriage continued after one of the partners had changed sex, this would conflict with the current legal position that a person can be married only to someone of the opposite (legal) sex. It might therefore be necessary to require, as in most countries which allow marriage after a change of sex that any previous marriage should be dissolved before a change of sex could be legally recognised" (para. 4.17.).

[2] See Report No. OGC-97–16 (31 Jan. 1997), http://www.gao.gov (GAO Reports, Find GAO Reports).

[3] [1866] Law Reports Vol. 1 (Probate & Divorce Cases) 130 at 133.

It is easy to criticise this historical definition as no longer being "good law". Of the four components contained within the decision (a voluntary union, for life, the exclusion of all others, a "man and . . . woman"), three are no longer needed for a legal and valid marriage.

Consider the voluntary nature of the union. In *Kaur* v. *Singh*,[4] a Sikh was forced by his parents to marry a woman in India. His petition for nullity was rejected; respect for the cultural traditions which practise arranged marriage seemed to be a major policy factor in the decision.[5] Under the Matrimonial Causes Act 1973, section 12(c), an involuntary union will render a marriage voidable rather than void, so it will not be void until the court exercises its discretion and declares it so. Therefore, an involuntary union could, given the right circumstances, be a valid marriage, apparently contrary to the definition in *Hyde*.

As regards the requirement that a marriage is for life, the availability of divorce would indicate that this requirement is no longer taken literally. In England and Wales, there are approximately 150,000 divorces per year, two for every three marriages that take place. Peter Pace, citing the case of *Nachimson* v. *Nachimson*,[6] claims that this requirement is satisfied if the couple, at the time of celebration, intend their marriage to last for life.[7] This intention often falls short of an actual life-long union. A divorce does not mean that the marriage is void, it simply ends the marriage, the marriage was valid whilst it lasted.

Similarly, the requirement that a marriage is to the exclusion of all others is no longer an essential aspect of the contract as far as the courts and marriage are concerned. Although adultery accounts for almost 30% of all divorces,[8] it does not make a marriage void, and the parties are not required to seek a divorce when they discover that their partner has committed adultery. Many married people no longer see monogamy as an essential requirement for marriage. Furthermore, polygamous marriages are recognised in UK law for some purposes, although they cannot be contracted here. Pace cites *Radwan* v. *Radwan (No. 2)*,[9] in which a polygamous marriage that was not contracted in the UK was held to be valid for the purpose of temporary residence rights in the UK, as the parties intended to reside permanently in Egypt where polygamy was permitted. This, along with the adultery statistics, shows that often a marriage is not to the exclusion of all others.

When considering the obstacles to marriage for transsexual people, the fact that three of these components are no longer, or not always, requirements for the validity of a contemporary marriage is indicative of the changing nature of

[4] [1981] *Family Law* 152 (Court of Appeal).

[5] See A Bainham, "Family Law in a Pluralistic Society", (1995) 22 *Journal of Law and Society* 234 at 242.

[6] [1930] P. 217 (Court of Appeal).

[7] *Family Law* (London, Pitman Publishing, 1992) at l6.

[8] See Bainham, *supra* n.5, at 237.

[9] [1972] All ER 967.

marriage. It could be said to have become a civil contract of aspirations reflecting contemporary social mores. It is a mechanism whereby family life can be regulated and contained, in which responsibilities and rights within the nation-state are delineated and in which citizenship is improved, but it is not a static concept and has historically undergone frequent changes.

Despite these changes, a marriage between two people who are not respectively male and female is still void, *ab initio*, under the Matrimonial Causes Act 1973, section 11(c). Such marriages were also void before the Act. One example was *Talbot* v. *Talbot* (1967),[10] concerning the voiding of a marriage between two women. The most infamous case was *Corbett* v. *Corbett*.[11] The husband of a (male-to-female) transsexual woman sought a decree of nullity, alleging that the respondent was biologically male and that the marriage had not been consummated. It was not in dispute that marriage is a heterosexual union between a man and a woman. What was in dispute was whether one of the parties was in fact a woman for the purposes of marriage.

I have argued, elsewhere, that a major criticism of Ormrod J's decision in *Corbett* must be that he

> "constantly mixed the notions of 'male and female' with those of 'man and woman' . . . He argues that marriage is a relationship based on sex rather than gender, so he really needed to consider her to be a 'man' . . . [A]lmost certainly Ormrod was faced with a dilemma that arose from his being unable to define the person in front of him as a man yet he felt unable, in law and because of the test he had devised, to call her a woman".[12]

I would consider this to summarise many of the problematic issues surrounding the determination of the sex of the transsexual person for the purposes of marriage. How do we decide who is a man or a woman, and should such a decision be based solely on biological factors?

In 1977, a mere seven years after the decision in *Corbett*, the evolving medical evidence surrounding the complexities of determining sex was recognised in the case of Renee Richards. In *Richards* v. *US Tennis Association*,[13] a transsexual woman was determined to be exactly that, a woman, for the purpose of playing sport. Yet as regards marriage, the courts have continued in many cases to refuse to take on board the new scientific and medical knowledge in these areas. Is that because marriage is considered to be predominately a matter of biology?

There has been a retreat over the years, in many courts and jurisdictions, from Ormrod's decision in *Corbett*. But we can see, in the recent case of *Littleton* v. *Prange* in the Texas Court of Appeals,[14] the social stigma that surrounds trans-

[10] [1967] 111 SJ 213 (Ormrod J).

[11] [1970] 2 All ER 33. See also *Bellinger* v. *Bellinger* (17 July 2001), http://www.courtservice.gov.uk/judgments/judg_frame.htm (Search) (Court of Appeal, 2–1).

[12] S Whittle, "An Association for as Noble a Purpose as Any", *New Law Journal* (15 March 1996), 366–7.

[13] 400 N.Y.S.2d 267 (Supreme Court, New York County 1977).

[14] *Littleton* v. *Prange*, 9 S.W.3d 223 (Texas Court of Appeals, 4th District, 1999), http://www.4thcoa.courts.state.tx.us/opinions/9900010.htm.

sexual people to this day, and the inability of some courts to recognise what marriage actually is: a social and contractual arrangement which has little to do with sex, sexuality, sexual orientation or sexual activity. Rather, as long ago as 1965, marriage was defined by the US Supreme Court in *Griswold* v. *Connecticut*[15] as:

> "a coming together for better or for worse, hopefully enduring, and intimate to the degree of being sacred. It is an association that promotes a way of life, not causes; a harmony in living, not political faiths; a bilateral loyalty, not commercial or social projects. . . It is an association for as noble a purpose as any".[16]

Despite *Griswold*, courts determining the validity of marriages continue to be trapped in discussions of biology and hence sexual activity, even though this is not the primary aim or motivation of many marriages.

CIRCUMSCRIBING SEX I

Ormrod J set out in *Corbett* how sex is to be determined for the purposes of marriage. He considered sex to be decided through three factors: chromosomal, genital and gonadal characteristics at birth. His reasoning can be criticised. According to Yatoni I Cole-Wilson,[17] there was general agreement among the expert medical witnesses in *Corbett* that there was a fourth factor (which Ormrod J disregarded), ie, psychological characteristics. This factor had in fact proven to be crucial in an earlier case, *John Forbes-Semphill* v. *The Hon. Ewan Forbes-Semphill*,[18] in which a question of title inheritance depended upon the sex of the petitioner (who would almost certainly nowadays be classified as a transsexual man). Lord Hunter held that the predominance of "masculine attributes, behaviour and desires" was instrumental in his decision that Ewan Forbes-Semphill was a man. However, in *Corbett*, Ormrod excluded psychological characteristics, justifying his exclusion on the ground that marriage was essentially heterosexual in character, by which he meant that "physical characteristics" were what counted.

There is now evidence that transsexuality is in fact related to biological factors, which may in themselves be determined by, or determine, the form taken by chromosomes, genitals and gonads.[19] The scientific evidence to date is inconclusive as to the "cause" of transsexuality, but it is also becoming increasingly inconclusive as to the biological determinants that will result in chromosomes, genitals and gonads being congruently of the male or female form. For example,

[15] 381 U.S. 479 (1965).

[16] *Ibid*., at 486.

[17] "*Corbett* v. *Corbett*: Is It Still Good Law", paper presented at the Third International Congress on Sex and Gender, Oxford, Sept. 1998, at 4.

[18] (1967), unreported (Scottish Court of Administration).

[19] Zhou, Hoffman, Gooren & Swaab, "A Sex Difference in the Human Brain and Its Relation to Transsexuality", (2 Nov. 1995) 378:6552 *Nature* 68.

the Intersex Society of North America estimates that one in five hundred people have a karyotype (sex chromosome pattern) other than XX (female) or XY (male).[20] The sex chromosomes determine whether the gonads will be ovaries or testes. When the pattern is not XX or XY, the result is intersexuality (hermaphroditism). An example of one such condition is Androgen Insensitivity Syndrome (AIS), where the body's cells are unable to respond to the "male" hormone androgen. Testes develop, but due to the lack of response to androgen, the genitals "differentiate in the female, rather than the male pattern".[21] So the gonads are male, but the genitals are female. According to Ormrod's criteria, would a person with AIS be male or female? This condition causes as many problems for his criteria as April Ashley did in *Corbett*, with the added factor here that the chromosomes, genitals and gonads have never been congruent.

Corbett has not been followed in other jurisdictions, because of the distinction that was made between biological (physical) sex and psychological gender. In *M.T.* v. *J.T.*,[22] the New Jersey Superior Court (Appellate Division) agreed with Ormrod J that marriage must be between a man and a woman, but they used a dual test of anatomy and gender identity to determine the sex of a person:

> ". . .for marital purposes if the anatomical and genital features of a genuine transsexual are made to conform to the person's gender, psyche or psychological sex, then identity by sex must be governed by the congruence of these standards".[23]

In *Attorney General* v. *Family Court at Otahuhu* (1994),[24] Ellis J was "unable to accept the decision in *Corbett*'s case" because "the law of New Zealand has changed to recognise a shift away from sexual activity and more emphasis being placed on psychological and social aspects of sex, sometimes referred to as gender issues".[25] Ellis felt that if society allows a person to undergo surgery to change their sex, then it ought to allow them to "function as fully as possible in their reassigned sex, and this must include the capacity to marry".[26] In addition, there was no social advantage to not recognising such a marriage, and no "socially adverse effects . . . or harm to others, particularly children".[27] Even in the United Kingdom, Ward LJ has recently suggested in *S.-T.* v. *J.*[28] that, in the light of "new insight into the aetiology of transsexualism", it may be appropriate that *Corbett* should be re-examined.

However, recent developments have not all been "anti-*Corbett*". In *Littleton* v. *Prange*,[29] the Texas Court of Appeals asked:

[20] See http://www.isna.org/index.html (FAQ).
[21] *Ibid.*
[22] 355 A.2d 204 (1976).
[23] *Ibid.*
[24] [1995] NZFamLR 57, http://www.pfc.org.uk/legal/ellisj.htm.
[25] *Ibid.*
[26] *Ibid.*
[27] *Ibid.*
[28] [1998] 1 All ER 431 at 447.
[29] *Supra* n.14.

> "Can there be a valid marriage between a man and a person born as a man, but surgically altered to have the physical characteristics of a woman?"

In holding that, for the purposes of marriage, a (male-to-female) transsexual woman was male and therefore any marriage to a man was invalid, the court relied on a chromosomal test and expressly referred to *Corbett*. However, in her dissenting judgment, Lopez J hits at the nub of the matter:

> "Particularly material to this case, the legislature has not addressed whether a transsexual is to be considered a surviving spouse under the Wrongful Death and Survival Statutes".

Christie Lee Littleton is a transsexual woman who, from a very early age, had felt extreme discomfort at living the life of a boy and a male. At the age of twenty-three, she started treatment to undergo gender reassignment. Upon completion of her treatment, Christie had to petition a court to get her birth certificate amended. After hearing expert opinions, the court granted an amendment on the grounds that there was now satisfactory evidence to show that the original birth certificate was inaccurate. In 1989, Christie married Jonathon Littleton in the state of Kentucky, and lived with him until his death in 1996. Jonathon was fully aware of her background and the fact that she had undergone gender reassignment surgery. In 1996, whilst undergoing surgery, Jonathon died on the operating table. Christie filed a medical malpractice suit under the Texas Wrongful Death and Survival Statute in her capacity as Jonathon's surviving spouse.

The sued doctor, Dr Prange, filed a motion for summary judgement in the trial court. This motion challenged Christie's status as a proper wrongful death beneficiary, asserting that Christie is a man and cannot therefore be the surviving spouse of another man. The trial court agreed and granted summary judgment, having only discovered that Christie was a transsexual woman when she had to answer the deposition question "Have you ever been known by another name"? Christie appealed to the Texas Court of Appeals. However, their judgment concluded: that, at the time of birth, Christie was a male, both anatomically and genetically; that the facts contained in the original birth certificate were true and accurate; and that the words contained in the amended certificate were not binding. The Court went on to state:

> "There are some things we cannot will into being. They just are. . . . [A]s a matter of law, Christie Littleton is a male. As a male, Christie cannot be married to another male. Her marriage to Jonathon was invalid, and she cannot bring a cause of action as his surviving spouse".

The Texas Supreme Court refused to review the case, as did the US Supreme Court.[30]

Dr Greer and Dr Mohl, who had psychiatrically assessed Christie, testified that true (male-to-female) transsexual women are, in their opinion, psychologically

[30] See http://christielee.net/main2.htm.

and psychiatrically female, both before and after the sex reassignment surgery, and that Christie is a true transsexual woman. Dr Greer served as a principal member of the surgical team that performed the gender reassignment surgery on Christie. In Dr Greer's opinion, the anatomical and genital features of Christie, following that surgery, are such that she has the capacity to function sexually as a woman. Both Dr Greer and Dr Mohl testified that, in their opinions, following the successful completion of Christie's gender reassignment treatment, Christie was medically a woman.

Christie had suffered years of pain growing up as a boy and as an adolescent, and further years of trauma participating in medical and psychiatric treatment, trying to persuade doctors and medical experts to believe her and correct her anatomy to coincide with her deep psychological conviction that she is a woman. Despite those same medical experts' testifying in court that, as far as medical opinion was concerned, Christie is a woman, at law she is still a male, at least for the purposes of marriage. Hence, her seven-year marriage to her husband Jonathon was reversed at a stroke and made void, as was the validity of her gender reassignment surgery and her new identity as a woman. She may still be able to drive or travel abroad as a woman, but that does not compensate if she is called a man in other areas of her life, such as relationship formation, or employment. The undeniable tragedy of this case is that the questions surrounding Jonathon Littleton's death may now go unanswered, with nobody having to take responsibility, and the wife he cared and provided for throughout the years of their marriage being left unprovided for, despite all their efforts as a married couple to the contrary.

CIRCUMSCRIBING SEX II

The second issue in *Corbett* was whether the marriage had been consummated—what were the requirements as regards sexual activity in marriage. Ormrod J decided that a post-operative (male-to-female) transsexual woman and a non-transsexual man would not be able to have "normal" intercourse. In reaching this conclusion, he distinguished *Sy* v. *Sy*,[31] where a woman was capable of marriage, despite suffering from a vaginal defect which prevented what Ormrod referred to as "normal" intercourse. There is, in fact, little difference between a wholly artificial vagina (as in *Corbett*) and an extended one (as in *Sy*), both medically and sexually. Indeed, on the basis of modern medical knowledge:

> "It is very likely that [Sy] would have been diagnosed as a case of testicular feminisation and accordingly been discovered to be a chromosomal male".[32]

Therefore, Ormrod J misdirected himself in distinguishing *Corbett* from *Sy*.

[31] [1962] 3 All ER 55 (Court of Appeal).
[32] *Supra* n.12, at 367.

A separate criticism comes from Pace,[33] who argues that by stressing the capacity for heterosexual intercourse as a requirement for marriage, Ormrod J would also render void the marriage of a person without such capacity due to age or injury. Yet, incapacity for these reasons is no longer considered a ground for automatically voiding a marriage:

> "Marriage has also long moved beyond the point of being little more than consummation, procreation and property transfer. As a society we would not dare to consider refusing the right to marry to a person with a disability that meant they could not consummate the marriage through penetrative sexual intercourse".[34]

The Press for Change Submission argues that:

> "to protect spouses, failure to consummate could lead to the dissolution of a marriage, just as it can in other marriages where there has been *prior deceit as to the ability to consummate*. As the law stands, failure to give material information to a spouse, such as *implying that procreation is possible*, is a material fact that can lead to the dissolution of any marriage".[35]

This would mean that a spouse of a transsexual person would have a legal recourse if, for example, a transsexual man implied prior to marriage to a non-transsexual woman that he had the ability to participate in ordinary sexual intercourse when he had, in fact, not undergone any genital reconstruction.[36]

Moreover, sexual intercourse and procreation are no longer considered the primary purpose of, or perhaps even essential to, the modern concept of marriage. As Inge Lauw has said:

> "There has never been any attempt to prohibit unions between a sterile woman and a fertile man, or vice versa. Nor does legislation exist which 'requires' a married couple to have children. If procreation—or the lack thereof—were a real concern of the legislature, it is probable that there would be legislation regulating marriages by sterile and handicapped persons. The fact that the laws do not do this suggests that procreation is not a primary concern".[37]

Nevertheless, as the law is currently understood, Ormrod J ruled out marriage for the majority of transsexual people (and hence factually same-sex couples) on two counts: firstly, that the partners must have had, at their birth, chromosomal, genital and gonadal congruent male and female features respectively; and secondly, that the couple must be able to consummate the marriage through "normal" heterosexual intercourse. However, though there have been many criticisms of *Corbett*, and many other jurisdictions have chosen not to follow it, none of the criticisms suggest that factually same-sex couples should be

[33] *Supra* n.7, at 36.

[34] *Supra* n.1, at 10.

[35] *Ibid.*

[36] Few transsexual men actually undergo genital reconstruction, as such surgical procedures are life-threatening and rarely successful.

[37] "Recognition of Same-Sex Marriage: Time for Change?", 1994, http://www.murdoch.edu.au/elaw/issues/v1n3/lauw2.txt.

able to marry. So while *Corbett* may have been rejected, in some jurisdictions, it has not been done in a way that would allow factually same-sex couples to marry, including homosexual or lesbian transsexual people and their factually same-sex partners. There is a certain irony to this though; in those jurisdictions where transsexual people cannot marry in their new gender role, they can marry in their "old" gender role. Thus, we see a situation in which legally different-sex but factually same-sex marriages are contracted, as gay transsexual men marry their male partners, and lesbian transsexual women marry their female partners. Some of these marriages may be voidable under the consummation requirements for "normal" heterosexual intercourse, but by no means all of them.

It has also been said that:

> "As *Hyde* was a reflection of mid-nineteenth century morality, it may be questioned whether, and if so why, public policy should prevent post-operational transsexuals from contracting a valid marriage".[38]

The moral values of the mid-nineteenth century, thankfully, no longer prevail in most walks of life. We would be horrified if there was any suggestion that they should, therefore we must ask whether those values are still pertinent to modern-day marriage.

CIRCUMSCRIBING RIGHTS, CIRCUMSCRIBING BENEFITS

Civil marriage provides legal benefits which thousands of people take for granted. It is important to remember that marriage also brings obligations, such as spousal support on the breakdown of the marriage. A marriage is not only a commitment between the couple, but also a contract with the state. In looking at how the law affects transsexual people and their partners who are unable to marry because they are considered, in effect, to be "same-sex" couples, there are three areas I wish to examine briefly: 1. the couple themselves during their relationship; 2. the couple's conceiving children and their responsibilities as parents; and 3. the couple's separation, either through death or breakdown of the relationship. It is impossible to list all of the legal benefits and obligations of civil marriage because there are too many.[39]

The Couple

Firstly, with regard to immigration, a non-European Community national, whose partner is a British national whom they are legally unable to marry, cannot claim residency in the UK until they have lived for two years in a relation-

[38] *Supra* n.7, at 16–7.
[39] Text accompanying n.2, *supra*.

ship "akin to marriage" with their British partner.[40] In many cases, the couple have no right to live in the foreign partner's country either. For example, in the United States, the Immigration and Naturalization Service does not recognise legally "same-sex" relationships, no matter how longstanding they are. This causes problems in satisfying the "akin to marriage" requirement, because the foreign partner is not allowed residency in the UK, and the British partner is often not allowed residency in the foreign country. Even though the UK Government's current policy is a huge improvement over the pre-1997 policy, it is still much easier for a non-transsexual person to get a visa by marrying a person of the opposite sex, having met them two weeks before, than it is for a transsexual person in a ten-year, long-distance relationship with their factually opposite-gender partner.

In many countries, transsexual people can solve their immigration problems by marrying. At least 22 of 43 Council of Europe countries,[41] every Canadian province, much of the USA, Israel, South Africa, Namibia, and New Zealand provide mechanisms whereby transsexual people can be recognised in their new "sex" as regards civil registration procedures. This does not guarantee that their marriages to their opposite-gender partners are entirely secure, but any marriages they contract are recognised for many purposes, including immigration. The fact that a transsexual person can marry in many US states, but not in the UK, means that the UK immigration service would recognise the immigration rights of a US non-transsexual woman who had contracted a marriage, in the US, to a US transsexual man who had residency rights in the UK. Yet, they would not recognise the immigration rights of a US transsexual man who had married a British non-transsexual woman, wherever their marriage had been contracted.

An example of British non-recognition of a transsexual person's marriage, validly contracted outside the UK, was cited to the European Court of Human Rights in *Sheffield & Horsham* v. *UK*.[42] Rachel Horsham had been registered as a "boy" at her birth in the UK. She had undergone gender reassignment in the Netherlands, and had become a Dutch citizen through naturalisation. In the Netherlands, she had received a "Certificate of Reassignment", which had allowed the Dutch authorities to issue her with a "new" birth certificate showing her sex as female. This allowed her full rights as a woman in Dutch society, including the right to contract a marriage to a non-transsexual man, which would be recognised throughout the world for immigration purposes. However, if she contracted a marriage with a non-EC national, that marriage would not

[40] Immigration Rules, paras. 295A-295O, http://www.ind.homeoffice.gov.uk/default.asp?PageId=1193. See also http://www.stonewall-immigration.org.uk.

[41] See http://www.pfc.org.uk/legal/liba-all.htm (Liberty, 1997): 22 yes, 13 unclear (including Spain), 4 no (Albania, Andorra, Ireland, UK), 4 not surveyed (Armenia, Azerbaijan, Bulgaria, Georgia). A bill passed by the Spanish Senate on 7 March 2001 would allow a transsexual person to change their civilly registered "sex", rather than just their first name. See p. 496, n.21; EuroLetter No. 87 (March 2001).

[42] (30 July 1998), http://www.echr.coe.int/hudoc.

be recognised if they chose to move to the UK. Because her original birth certificate would be that used for immigration purposes, her marriage would be considered void, i.e., as having never existed.

The second detriment to transsexual people and their partners (who are often viewed in law as "same-sex" couples) is in relation to fringe benefits and employment. In *Grant* v. *South-West Trains*,[43] the European Court of Justice (ECJ) held that Article 119 (now 141) of the EC Treaty, which prohibits sex discrimination in relation to pay, was not violated by a refusal to grant travel concessions to a lesbian employee's female partner. The decision was based on three grounds: (a) the employer's requirement that the partner be of the opposite sex applied regardless of the sex of the worker because travel concessions were also refused to gay male employees; (b) EC law has not yet adopted rules stating that same sex relationships are equivalent to marriages or stable opposite-sex relationships; and (c) *P.* v. *S. & Cornwall County Council*[44] where the ECJ held that dismissal "for a reason related to a gender reassignment" was sex discrimination contrary to the Equal Treatment Directive,[45] could be distinguished from *Grant*.

This decision is considered bad law by many commentators,[46] as there is a potential inconsistency between *P.* and *Grant*. If it is contrary to EC sex discrimination law to discriminate against a person because they are undergoing or have undergone gender reassignment, then would it still be sex discrimination if a transsexual employee were denied a benefit for their legally "same-sex" partner? Or would it be the same sort of legal discrimination that Lisa Grant and her female partner suffered, if Lisa Grant had instead been a transsexual man called Liam Grant? The ECJ will have to answer this question in *Bavin* v. *NHS Trust Pensions Agency*,[47] which concerns the denial of a survivor's pension provided to "widows" and "widowers" to a transsexual man who is the partner of a non-transsexual female employee, who is legally unable to marry him. The Employment Appeal Tribunal had doubts about the law as it is at present in relation to non-traditional partnerships, saying:

> ". . . we can and do invite those who are responsible for such matters to consider whether it is sensible in modern times for eligibility to any concession or benefit to depend upon the marital status of the people concerned. It is the experience of the members of this court that many if not most pension schemes give trustees a discretion to make payments where relationships outside marriage are stable. We can think of no good social reason why travel facilities or derived pension benefits should not be available where there is a stable long-term relationship between two unmarried people, whatever the reasons for not being married. Such a change would not have to address the more complicated and

[43] Case C-249/96, [1998] ECR I-621.

[44] Case C-13/94, [1996] ECR I-2143. See also Sex Discrimination (Gender Reassignment) Regulations 1999, SI 1999 No. 1102 (amending Sex Discrimination Act 1975).

[45] Council Dir. 76/207/EEC of 9 Feb. 1976, OJ [1976] L 39/40.

[46] See Koppelman, chap. 35; Bell, chap. 37; Waaldijk, chap. 36.

[47] [1999] ICR 1192 (Employment Appeal Tribunal); referred to the ECJ by the Court of Appeal (England and Wales) on 4 Oct. 2000; registered as Case C-117/01, *KB* v. *National Health Service Pension Agency*.

difficult question as to whether persons of the same sex should be permitted to marry or transsexuals be permitted formally to change their birth certificates".[48]

I would argue that, since the interpretation of *P.* v. *S.* by the EAT in *Chessington World of Adventures* v. *Reed*,[49] there is no need for a specific comparator in cases concerning gender reassignment under the Sex Discrimination Act 1975 (Great Britain). Instead the courts, in the light of *P.* v. *S.*, should determine what "feature" caused the discrimination, i.e., the court should consider what position the plaintiff would have been in, if she had not had that feature, compared to the position she is in now. For Bavin, the feature was that she was a non-transsexual woman with a transsexual male partner. The discrimination must be based on sex, because if her partner were a non-transsexual male, she would have been able to contract a lawful marriage to him, which would have qualified him for the survivor's pension benefits. Alternatively, if she had been a non-transsexual man with a transsexual male partner, they could have contracted a valid marriage and the partner would again have qualified. Therefore, the discrimination against Bavin was based on sex and, because it relates to pay, violated both Article 141 EC and the Equal Pay Act 1970 (Great Britain). In *Bavin*, the ECJ will have to decide whether to apply *P.* v. *S.* or *Grant*. If the ECJ applies *Grant*, then British couples where one partner is transsexual will have to look to any protection for legally "same-sex" partners provided by the EC directive prohibiting sexual orientation discrimination in employment.[50]

The Couple's Children

Transsexual men and their (non-transsexual) female partners often form families by bringing children into their domestic unit. Sometimes they are the biological children of the transsexual man, born prior to his transition to his new gender role, and sometimes the children of the female partner from a prior relationship. On occasion, though, female partners have children within their relationship with the transsexual man. These children are conceived by the female partner either having an "affair" with a non-transsexual male, or by donor insemination. Many partners of transsexual men now seek the help of donor insemination services provided through licensed fertility clinics. Clinics are bound to keep as their paramount concern the welfare of any child who is born by the treatment they provide.

A prospective transsexual father cannot keep his status a secret in this process. Many clinics will not treat unmarried women at all,[51] because of the

[48] [1999] ICR 1192 at para. 19.

[49] [1997] IRLR 556, http://www.pfc.org.uk/legal/chess.htm.

[50] Council Dir. 2000/78/EC of 27 Nov. 2000, OJ [2000] L 303/16. See Bell, chap. 37; Waaldijk, chap. 36.

[51] Douglas, Hebenton & Thomas, (1992) "The Right to Found a Family", 142 *New Law Journal* 488.

requirement in section 13(5) of the Human Fertilisation and Embryology Act 1990 that:

> "a woman shall not be provided with treatment services unless account has been taken of the welfare of any child who may be born as a result of the treatment (including the need of that child for a father)".

Hence the transsexual man needs to be involved in the application for treatment in order for the first barrier to be crossed. Then the male partner will be investigated as to whether he is the cause of the infertility within the relationship. This requires the giving of sperm samples, etc. It is far easier for the transsexual man to be open about the situation from the beginning. Indeed, if a transsexual man has to consider keeping his status "secret", it implies that being transsexual would somehow make him less able as a parent. I have argued elsewhere that:

> "Just as in the history of negative eugenics it becomes illogical to discuss the 'best interests' of the child, if the child can never be born, if the claim is made that transsexual people are not suitable for parenthood, then they are refused access to parenthood, . . . this supports the claim because there is no evidence to the contrary".[52]

In these cases, the consultant often refers the matter of the treatment of the partner of a transsexual man to his Ethical Committee, which advises doctors on whether certain treatments or experimental work they may do are within ethical boundaries. The role of the Ethical Committee in fertility treatment cases is merely advisory; it is not a decision-making body and it is doubtful whether a committee could veto the decision of a doctor to provide fertility treatment. Furthermore, *R.* v. *Ethical Committee of St Mary's Hospital, ex parte H.* held that a decision by an Ethical Committee could be reviewed where, for example, there was a policy of refusing treatment to anyone who, for example, was Jewish or Black.[53]

Once treatment is obtained and a child conceived and born, the transsexual man is not in a position to be registered as the child's father.[54] The mother of the child can choose to give the child her partner's surname, and this will be entered upon the child's birth certificate (the short form has no space for details of the child's parents, so may be preferred by such a family as documentary evidence of the child's birth; however, the full certificate has a space for the completion of the father's details). Undoubtedly, many transsexual men ignore the law and, with their partner's consent, register themselves as the father of the child, just as many other non-biological fathers do. However, unlike other social fathers, the transsexual man is committing an offence under the Registration of Births and Deaths Act 1953. This would be on the grounds that

[52] Change, FTM Network, G & SA, The Gender Trust, GIRES, Liberty, Press For Change, *The Problems of Gender Re-Registration: A Consultation Paper to the Interdepartmental Working Group on Transsexual People's Issues*, 16 Feb. 2000, http://www.pfc.org.uk/workgrp/feb2000.htm

[53] [1987] 137 New L.J. 1038.

[54] See *X,Y & Z* v. *UK* (22 April 1997), http://www.echr.coe.int/hudoc.

he is not entitled to be treated as the father of the child under section 28 of the Human Fertilisation and Embryology Act 1990, even though he is compelled to agree to be the child's father in order that his partner will receive treatment. Section 28 provides that, if treatment using donated sperm is provided for a woman together with a man, and although the embryo was not created using the sperm of that man, that man will be treated as the father of the child for all purposes. As the transsexual man is not a "man" under English law, he cannot become the father of the child, though he will be allowed to share parenting under the provisions of the Children Act 1989.

Various legal anomalies appear. The transsexual man may claim the additional tax allowance that is available to the parent of a child if he can show that he maintains the child. At the same time, for all welfare benefits purposes, the child's mother will remain legally a single parent and the income of the child's transsexual father will be ignored. This means that the mother may claim the additional single parent's allowance and, if she is not working, or working only part-time, she will qualify to claim income support for herself and the child, or family credit.[55] The Child Support Agency is obliged to ask mothers who are claiming benefits for details of the child's father, in order that maintenance may be claimed from him. But children who are born through donor insemination, provided by a licensed clinic to a transsexual man's female partner, currently have no legal father. In practice, the mother merely needs to inform the CSA of the nature of the child's conception, and any further action is dropped.

There is no reason why a transsexual parent cannot apply to adopt a child, as an unmarried individual. The attitudes of some local social services in London and elsewhere have recently changed their views towards gays and lesbians adopting a child, and the courts have confirmed their eligibility.[56] However if a transsexual person's partner is of the same natal sex (i.e. a transsexual woman lives with a non-transsexual male, or a transsexual man lives with a non-transsexual female), and that partner is the parent of a child, the transsexual person would not be able to adopt that child without the biological parent losing their parental rights. The Adoption Act 1976, section 14, states that a joint adoption order may be made only on the application of a married couple. As the transsexual person and their partner cannot get married, it is not possible for them to be joint parents, though it may be possible for them to share parental rights and duties under the Children Act 1989.

After the child has been born, there are legal obstacles for the family, including the child. The partner who is not the legal parent of the child does not, in the eyes of the law, bear parental responsibility as a married partner would. The most that can be done by the co-parent is to apply (jointly with the legal parent) for a residence order in both of their names. In law, the transsexual man and his

[55] Letter from V Bottomly, Secretary of State for Health, to G Kaufman, MP, 4 July 1992.

[56] See eg *Re W (a minor) (adoption: homosexual adopter)*, [1997] 3 All ER 620.

non-transsexual female partner are currently treated as if they were two cohabiting women, which makes case law on lesbian couples relevant. In Manchester High Court on 24 June 1994, a lesbian couple obtained joint legal recognition as parents of a two-year-old baby, through a "joint residence order". The judge held that the child's welfare was his first and paramount consideration, and that the evidence in the case overwhelmingly pointed to the making of such an order.[57]

A joint residence order would be available to a transsexual man and his partner, but it has limitations. It allows the transsexual parent to make decisions with the legal parent, for example, to authorise medical treatment.[58] However, it is not the same as a parental responsibility order, which only unmarried biological fathers can obtain. A joint residence order only exists whilst the partners cohabit and disappears immediately on the separation of the couple, or the death of one of the partners. Potentially therefore, the birth parent could die and leave the children of the family "parentless" and hence "homeless" in law. It is also important that a transsexual man write a will leaving his property appropriately, because his partner and children (if not his own biological children) are not covered by the intestacy rules that provide for family dependants. The Stonewall lobbying and litigation group in London are arguing that same-sex co-parents should be entitled to seek parental responsibility orders, and that a child should be allowed to inherit from a co-parent who has a joint residence order or a parental responsibility order.

These orders (and wills) would not be necessary if transsexual people and their factually opposite-gender partners were able to marry: the married (or unmarried) transsexual male partner of the mother of children conceived by donor insemination would automatically be their legal father; either partner's children from a prior relationship could be adopted by the other partner; and unrelated children could be adopted jointly. The right to marry would also force an end to the presumption that transsexual people do not form meaningful relationships, and therefore do not provide a suitable environment for children.

The Couple's Separation

When a transsexual person and their opposite-gender partner separate, they do not have the protection of the Matrimonial Causes Act 1973, Part II. They are treated as though they were strangers by the law and must rely on, for example, property law to determine ownership of land. There is no legal duty to support a partner who is economically dependent during the relationship, as there is when a marriage breaks down. This is also the case for children; there is no

[57] News Release, Otten & Skemp Solicitors, 28 June 1994.

[58] See generally Barlow et al., *Advising Lesbian and Gay Clients* (London, Butterworths, 1999) at 52–5.

obligation to pay child maintenance and no right of access for the non-birth parent of the children.

Since *Fitzpatrick* v. *Sterling Housing Association*,[59] a longstanding same-sex relationship (including a transsexual person and their opposite-gender partner) does give the surviving partner a right of succession to a tenancy under the Rent Act 1977, but as a "family member" and not as a "spouse". In the Act, protection given to a family member is not as great as that given to spouses.[60] Nor does the Act apply to public sector tenancies.

Despite the *Fitzpatrick* decision, transsexual people and their partners generally do not qualify as next of kin, unlike married couples. This means that if their partner is ill, or dies, they do not have the rights and responsibilities that a spouse would have in relation to hospital visits and consultation, and funeral arrangements. Some of these rights and responsibilities can, however, be obtained by using Powers of Attorney between the partners.

There are also financial disadvantages to not being a surviving spouse. For example, in relation to inheritance, there are three problems. Firstly, if there is no will, the rules of intestacy mean that the estate will pass to the nearest blood relative, not the unmarried partner. Secondly, if there is a will, and the estate is worth more than £234,000,[61] it is subject to inheritance tax. Married couples are exempt from this. Thirdly, where a pension scheme provides for a survivor's pension if the scheme member dies before his or her spouse, it generally does not apply to an unmarried partner.

It is true that there are some benefits to transsexual people and their partners in not having their relationships recognised by the state, because the partners' incomes will not be combined in relation to social security and eligibility for legal aid. But these advantages do not outweigh the disadvantages. Additionally, the advantages to these couples of non-recognition of their relationships are disadvantages to the state. Therefore, it is not beneficial, either to these couples or (in a more limited way) to the state, to refuse to recognise their relationships.

CIRCUMSCRIBING HUMAN RIGHTS

Three Articles of the European Convention on Human Rights are relevant to marriage. Firstly, Article 12 states that:

> "Men and women of marriageable age have the right to marry and to found a family, according to the national laws governing the exercise of this right".

[59] [1999] 4 All ER 705.

[60] A surviving family member of the original tenant is entitled to a life interest (an assured tenancy), but a surviving spouse becomes the statutory tenant and can pass on the tenancy to a family member or subsequent spouse.

[61] Limit for the 6 April 2000 to 5 April 2001 tax year.

This confers a right to marry on all people of marriageable age. However, the European Court of Human Rights has held that it does not apply to transsexual men and women. In *Rees* v. *UK*, the Court indicated that the primary purpose of Article 12 is to "protect marriage as the basis of the family".[62] Therefore, the inability of Rees to procreate entitled the UK to refuse the right to marry. Even though many married couples cannot procreate, the Court concluded that "the right to marry guaranteed by Article 12 refers to the traditional marriage between persons of opposite biological sex" and that the challenged rule was not such that "the very essence of the right is impaired".[63]

In 1991, the Court followed *Rees* in *Cossey* v. *UK*.[64] However, four dissenting judges strongly criticised the court's view that procreation is the basis of marriage. Katherine O'Donovan[65] notes in particular the dissenting opinion of Judge Martens based on "humanistic principles of dignity, freedom and privacy". Mirroring the decision of the US Supreme Court in *Griswold*,[66] Judge Martens argued that marriage is:

> "far more than a union which legitimates sexual intercourse and aims at procreating . . .it is a societal bond . . . a species of togetherness in which intellectual, spiritual and emotional bonds are at least as essential as the physical one".[67]

The second relevant Article of the European Convention of Human Rights is Article 14. It provides that:

> "The enjoyment of the rights and freedoms set forth in this Convention shall be secured without discrimination on any ground such as sex, race, colour . . . or other status".

Although one might presume that gender identity is included in this list as an "other status",[68] the Court ruled in *Sheffield & Horsham* that:

> "not every difference in treatment will amount to a violation of [Article 14]. Instead, it must be established that other persons in an analogous or relatively similar situation enjoy preferential treatment, and that there is no reasonable or objective justification for this distinction".[69]

Clearly opposite-sex couples enjoy preferential treatment because they have access to the benefits of civil marriage. Cohabiting opposite-sex couples also have more of these benefits available to them than cohabiting couples who are considered in law to be of the same sex. According to Simon Foster,[70] the

[62] (17 Oct. 1986), http://echr.coe.int/hudoc, para. 49.
[63] *Ibid.*, at paras. 49–50.
[64] (27 Sept. 1990), http://echr.coe.int/hudoc.
[65] *Family Law Matters* (London, Pluto Press, 1993) at 50.
[66] *Supra* n.15.
[67] *Supra* n.64, at para. 4.5.2 (Judge Martens).
[68] See *Salgueiro* v. *Portugal* (21 Dec. 1999), http://echr.coe.int/hudoc, para. 28.
[69] *Supra* n.42, at para. 75.
[70] "Transsexuals, Sexual Identity and the European Convention", (1998) 32 *Law Teacher* 323 at 328.

"objective justification" for the difference in treatment can be "administrative or other inconveniences". These reasons are hardly an adequate justification for restricting civil liberties.

The third provision of the European Convention of Human Rights of relevance is Article 8, which provides a right to respect for private and family life. Article 8(2) allows a state to interfere with this right if the interference is in accordance with the law and necessary in a democratic society. In 1997, in *X, Y & Z* v. *United Kingdom*, the Court confirmed that "family life" in Article 8 could include de facto family relationships, other than those joined by marriage. The Court identified a number of factors which evidenced a de facto relationship: "whether the couple live together, the length of their relationship and whether they have demonstrated their commitment to each other by having children together or by any other means".[71] On the facts of *X, Y & Z*, the Court found that there was a de facto family relationship.[72] However, the UK's refusal to allow legal recognition of the relationship between X (a female-to-male transsexual man) and Z (his child conceived through donor insemination) was held not to amount to a breach of Article 8. The Court weighed "the disadvantages suffered by the applicants" against the "general interests" of the "community as a whole" (the community interest in maintaining a coherent system of family law; uncertainty as to whether amendments to the law would be to the advantage of children such as Z; the implications that amendments would have in other areas of family law) and found that the general interests prevailed.[73] As there was no common ground between the member states of the Council of Europe, and "X is not prevented in any way from acting as Z's father in the social sense", the UK had to be given a wide margin of appreciation.[74]

In 1998, in *Sheffield & Horsham*, the court rejected a claim by two (male-to-female) transsexual women of a violation of Article 8[75] for two main reasons. Firstly, "the applicants have not shown that [since *Cossey*] there have been any findings in the area of medical science which would settle conclusively the doubts concerning the causes of the condition of transsexualism". [76] In addition, "it continues to be the case that transsexualism raises complex scientific, legal, moral and social issues, in respect of which there is no generally shared approach among the Contracting States".[77] Secondly, the Court was not persuaded that "the failure of the authorities to recognise their new gender gives rise to detriment of sufficient seriousness as to override the respondent State's margin of appreciation in this area". However, in a dissenting judgement, Judge van Dijk expressed the view that "the very existence" of a legal system that "keeps treating post-operative transsexuals . . . as members of the sex which

[71] *Supra* n.54, at para. 36.
[72] *Ibid.*, at para. 37.
[73] *Ibid.*, at paras. 47–48.
[74] *Ibid.*, at paras. 44, 50.
[75] They also claimed violations of Arts. 12, 13 and 14.
[76] *Supra* n.42, at para. 56.
[77] *Ibid.*, at para. 58.

they have disowned psychically and physically as well as socially . . . must continuously, directly and distressingly affect their private life".[78]

Will the UK's Human Rights Act 1998, in force since 2 October 2000, be any more helpful with regard to giving transsexual people, their partners and their families the benefits of civil marriage? It is seems unlikely because, although UK courts are not bound by decisions of the European Court of Human Rights, they must take these decisions into account and will probably follow *Rees*, *Cossey*, *X, Y & Z* and *Sheffield & Horsham*. The European Community's Equal Treatment Directive, as interpreted in *P.* v. *S. & Cornwall County Council*, is more likely to provide protection.[79]

Whatever the legal source of protection, as the Press For Change Submission noted:

> ". . . the remaining steps to enhance our social inclusion are, we believe, not only necessary, but can be done easily, . . . They would make a massive difference in the quality of life not just for the many transsexual people who are citizens of these islands, but also for the friends, family and colleagues with whom we share our lives and who also suffer through our lack of recognition.
>
> . . . Any nation which legitimises, even unintentionally, the social exclusion of any of its citizens simply because of a condition, increasingly recognised in scientific medicine as one of the many possible intersex conditions that exist, and which has no bearing at all on their ability to participate fully in society cannot be a nation worthy of the name.
>
> Whether it is one person, or as in this case, maybe 5000 people, this social exclusion must not continue. Many other nations have successfully responded to the needs of the transsexual people in their societies. . . .
>
> . . . As our knowledge of all sorts of . . . conditions grows, as medicine increasingly admits to there being a significant number of births in which it is impossible to guarantee that the sex designation given is unquestionable, and as our society increasingly removes the barriers to equality between the sexes, it may be that 'sex' is no longer something that we should record about the individual".[80]

"Sex" may also become something that is no longer relevant to the modern concept of marriage, as we increasingly recognise the true worth and value of marriage to our society. It is a matter of contractual relationships and agreements of dependency "for richer or poorer, in sickness and in health" based upon mutual respect; an "association for as noble a purpose as any", in which sex, whether chromosomal or an act, is increasingly nothing more than the icing on some people's cakes.

[78] *Ibid.*, para. 5 (Judge van Dijk's dissent).

[79] *Supra* nn.44–45. See App. III, pp. 789–90.

[80] See also *In re Estate of Gardiner*, 22 P.3d 1086, http://www.kscourts.org/kscases (No. 85030) (Kansas Ct. of Appeals, 11 May 2001) (birth sex not conclusive as to whether transsexual woman's marriage was valid for the purposes of intestate succession).

40

Strasbourg to the Rescue? Same-Sex Partners and Parents Under the European Convention

ROBERT WINTEMUTE*

INTRODUCTION

WHEN THE EQUALITY claims of same-sex partners and same-sex parents[1] in the forty-three member states of the Council of Europe[2] are rejected by their national legislatures or courts, or (in fifteen of those member states) by the European Community (EC) legislature or the European Court of Justice (ECJ), they often turn as a last resort to the European Court of Human Rights in Strasbourg. There, they can invoke their rights under the European Convention on Human Rights[3] to "respect for [their] private and family life [and] home" (Article 8), "to marry and to found a family" (Article 12), and to enjoy their Article 8 and 12 rights "without discrimination on any ground" (Article 14).[4] In this chapter, I will consider how the very promising text of the Convention has been interpreted to date by the European Court and Commission of Human Rights, in cases involving same-sex partners and parents, and how the case-law of the Court could develop in the future.

* Reader, School of Law, King's College, University of London.

[1] At first, "same-sex parents" sounded awkward to me. But the expression highlights the difficulty that the law and society have in dealing with a family consisting of a child with two mothers or two fathers, and in treating such a family in the same way as a family where one or both of a child's different-sex parents are not genetic parents. See Polikoff, chap. 8.

[2] See http://www.coe.int (About the COE).

[3] European Treaty Series (ETS) No. 005, http://conventions.coe.int (Search) (opened for signature 4 Nov. 1950, in force 3 Sept. 1953). Except where a paper-published version is mentioned, every judgment (J.), report (R.) or admissibility decision (A.D.) of the European Court (Ct.) and Commission (Com.) of Human Rights cited in this chapter is available in English or French (often both) at http://www.echr.coe.int/hudoc (Access HUDOC, tick appropriate box(es) at top, type applicant's name (after Title), or type application number).

[4] The prohibition of discrimination in Art. 14 can only be invoked in conjunction with another Convention right. See R Wintemute, *Sexual Orientation and Human Rights: The United States Constitution, the European Convention, and the Canadian Charter* (Oxford, Oxford University Press, paperback edition, 1997), at 91, 119–21.

CASE-LAW OF THE EUROPEAN COURT OF HUMAN RIGHTS ON SAME-SEX PARTNERS AND PARENTS

It is important to note at the outset that, as of August 2001, the European Court of Human Rights[5] has not decided a single case clearly raising the rights and obligations of a same-sex couple (i.e., a couple consisting of two non-transsexual men or women who are legally, physically and psychologically of the same sex), in relation to each other, any children they are raising together, or a third party.[6] The first such case to reach the Court, *Karner* v. *Austria*,[7] was communicated to the Austrian Government in December 2000, but has not yet been declared admissible (arguable) or inadmissible (usually "manifestly ill-founded"). *Karner*, to be discussed below, involves Austrian legislation on tenancies which the Austrian Supreme Court interpreted as granting a succession right to the unmarried different-sex partner of a deceased tenant, but not to the deceased's same-sex partner.[8] This case will give the Court the opportunity to decide for the first time whether a same-sex couple has a "family life" under Article 8, and whether differences in treatment between unmarried different-sex couples and same-sex couples are unjustifiable discrimination based on sexual orientation, contrary to Articles 8 and 14, in relation to the applicant's "private life" or "family life" or "home".

CASE-LAW OF THE FORMER EUROPEAN COMMISSION OF HUMAN RIGHTS ON SAME-SEX PARTNERS AND PARENTS

The former European Commission of Human Rights, which screened all cases until it was effectively merged into the Court on 1 November 1998,[9] declared inadmissible, as "manifestly ill-founded", at least seven applications it received from same-sex partners or parents. The Commission adopted a line of reason-

[5] See http://www.echr.coe.int.

[6] *Craig* v. *United Kingdom* (UK) (No. 45396/99) (21 March 2000) (Ct. A.D.) is technically such a case, because it concerned a court-approved agreement by a lesbian mother (L), settling custody litigation with her former husband, that their four children would spend alternate weeks with each parent, and that "she would not permit the children to come into contact with . . . the applicant [C, her female partner] or . . . any other person known to L to be lesbian". The Court declared the application inadmissible, finding any interference with C's private and family life justifiable under Article 8(2), especially because L had agreed to the restrictions and had not sought a court order varying them. The decision is thus confined to the standing of C to complain about restrictions, involving sexual orientation discrimination, on L's shared care of L's children. Because C and L did not agree about whether to challenge the restrictions, the Court gave priority to L's view. In light of *Salgueiro infra* n.36, a complaint by L about the restrictions would almost certainly have been declared admissible.

[7] Application No. 40016/98.

[8] See Graupner, chap. 30.

[9] The date on which Protocol No.11 to the Convention came into force.

ing in the first case, *X and Y* v. *United Kingdom* (UK) in 1983,[10] which it followed, and did not seriously question, over the next thirteen years.

In *X & Y*, the Commission held that the UK's refusal to permit a Malaysian-national man to remain in the UK with his UK-national male partner (causing them to leave for Sweden after the Malaysian partner was convicted of over-staying and ordered deported) did not violate their rights under Articles 8 and 14. In one sentence, the Commission concluded that the applicants were not a family: "Despite the modern evolution of attitudes towards homosexuality, the Commission finds that the applicants' relationship does not fall within the scope of the right to respect for family life". Instead, their relationship was "a matter of their private life". Because they were both "professionally mobile", and had not shown that there was no country in the world apart from the UK in which they could live together, the deportation order did not even constitute an "interference" with their Article 8 right to respect for their private lives, and therefore required no justification. [11]

In an immigration case, a finding that the applicants had a "family life" would not have made much difference, because Article 8 does not guarantee even married different-sex partners a right to live together in a particular country.[12] Their stronger argument was that, in relation to their private life, they had suffered discrimination "on the basis of their sex" compared with an unmarried different-sex couple in their situation,[13] contrary to Article 14 combined with Article 8. However, the Commission held that, because they did not have "family life", "no comparison can be made with the differential treatment afforded to relationships classified as family life". They could only compare themselves with a lesbian couple, who would have been treated in the same way.[14]

In 1986, in *Simpson* v. *UK*,[15] the Commission considered the same facts as *Karner*. A woman faced eviction from her local-authority-owned house after the death of her female partner, the only legal tenant of the house. UK legislation granted a succession right to the person who "live[d] together as husband and wife" with the tenant, but the Court of Appeal (of England and Wales) had interpreted this phrase as meaning "unmarried different-sex partner".[16] Because the Commission reached the same conclusion as in *X & Y*, that the applicant did not have a "family life" with her deceased partner, her strongest argument was that she had suffered discrimination in relation to her "home", contrary to

[10] (No. 9369/81) (3 May 1983), 32 Decisions & Reports (DR) 220, 5 European Human Rights Reports (EHRR) 601 (Com. A.D.).

[11] *Ibid.*, 32 DR at 221–2.

[12] See e.g. *Abdulaziz* v. *UK* (28 May 1985) (Ct. J.); *Shebashov* v. *Latvia* (No. 50065/99) (9 Nov. 2000) (Ct. A.D.).

[13] As will be seen below, the discrimination argument is more difficult in member states that limit immigration to married different-sex partners.

[14] *Supra* n.10, 5 EHRR at 602.

[15] (No. 11716/85) (14 May 1986) (Com. A.D.).

[16] *Harrogate Borough Council* v. *Simpson*, [1986] 2 Family Law Reports 91. See also Bailey-Harris, chap. 34.

Articles 8 and 14, "for no other reason than that she was of the wrong sex".[17] Unlike in *X & Y*, the Commission permitted her to compare herself and her deceased partner with a different-sex couple, and accepted that she had been treated differently. However, the Commission found an objective and reasonable justification for the difference in treatment, meaning that it was not "discrimination", because "the family (to which the relationship of heterosexual unmarried couples can be assimilated) merits special protection in society and [the Commission] sees no reason why a [government] should not afford particular assistance to families".[18]

From 1986 to 1996, the Commission merely applied the reasoning developed in its first two decisions in four subsequent cases: three immigration cases resembling *X & Y*,[19] and a housing case, *Röösli* v. *Germany*,[20] identical to *Simpson* and *Karner*. Indeed, *Röösli* is almost word-for-word the same decision as *Simpson*, and gives no indication that anything had changed in Europe over the intervening ten years (such as the enactment of same-sex registered partnership laws in Denmark, Norway and Sweden). The Commission found no reason to depart from *Simpson*, having regard to the German courts' reasoning: "[V]iews on marriage and family had changed in society and justified the extension of the [statutory term 'family member'] to [unmarried] heterosexual couples. However, homosexual or lesbian couples were not similarly accepted in society".[21]

Does the presence of children make a difference? In one of the three subsequent immigration cases, *C. & L.M.* v. *UK*,[22] the fact that the applicants were an Australian-national woman and her daughter by donor insemination, whom the first applicant and her UK-national female partner were raising together, did not affect the Commission's conclusion that the two same-sex partners did not have a "family life". However, in the seventh unsuccessful case, *Kerkhoven* v. *Netherlands*,[23] concerning an application by two lesbian partners for joint parental authority over the genetic child by donor insemination of one of the partners, the Commission wavered. It held both that they did not have a "family life",[24] and that there had been no interference with their Article 8 right to

[17] *Supra* n.15, at Complaints.

[18] *Ibid.* at The Law, para. 7.

[19] *W.J. & D.P.* v. *UK* (No. 12513/86) (11 Sept. 1986) (Com. A.D.); *C. & L.M.* v. *UK* (No. 14753/89) (9 Oct. 1989) (Com. A.D.); *B.* v. *UK* (No. 16106/90) (10 Feb. 1990) (Com. A.D.), arising from *R.* v. *Secretary of State for the Home Department, ex parte Binbasi*, [1989] Immigration Appeals Reports 595.

[20] (No. 28318/95) (15 May 1996) (Com. A.D.).

[21] *Ibid.* at Facts.

[22] *Supra* n.19.

[23] (No. 15666/89) (19 May 1992) (Com. A.D.).

[24] In *X, Y & Z* v. *UK* (No. 21830/93) (27 June 1995) (Com. R.), paras. 53–59, the Commission later distinguished *Kerkhoven*, holding that a transsexual man (born female), his non-transsexual female partner and their child by donor insemination enjoyed "family life", noting that "[t]o all appearances, . . . the first applicant is the third applicant's father". The Commission made the physical appearance of being a father (absent in *Kerkhoven*) a condition for the non-genetic co-parent of a genetic mother to claim "family life" with the mother and child and a Convention right to legal

respect for their "family life": the Dutch legislation "[did] not prevent the three applicants from living together as a family", and the Dutch government's positive obligation to respect their "family life" did not require joint parental authority.[25] It also held that there was no discrimination, contrary to Articles 8 and 14, even though unmarried different-sex partners with a child by donor insemination could claim joint parental authority for the genetic mother and the non-genetic father: "as regards parental authority over a child, a homosexual couple cannot be equated to a man and a woman living together".[26]

No application presented to the Commission appears to have involved a claim by a same-sex couple (as defined above) that they have a Convention right to contract a civil marriage under Article 12, alone or together with Article 14. In *C. & L.M.*, the first applicant argued that deportation would interfere with her Article 12 "right to found a family" with her female partner, which was not dependent on the Article 12 "right to marry". The Commission replied, citing case-law on attempts by transsexual persons to marry, that "the first applicant's relationship with her lesbian cohabitee does not give rise to a right to marry and found a family within the meaning of Article 12".[27]

The negative decisions of the Commission discussed above are "frozen", in the sense that the Commission no longer exists, and are in no way binding on the Court, which is free to depart from them without citation or explanation. The Court has held that "the Convention is a living instrument which, . . . must be interpreted in the light of present-day conditions".[28] Because the legal treatment of same-sex partnerships in Council of Europe countries has changed dramatically since the Commission's first decision in 1983 (which it essentially followed in the next six cases), the Court can easily reach different conclusions than the Commission. Thus, the Court's case-law could be described as a "blank slate".

However, until the Court issues a positive judgment in a case involving same-sex partners or parents, the Commission's negative case-law can continue to have harmful effects when it is cited by national or EC courts. The Commission's decisions that same-sex couples do not have to be accorded the same treatment as unmarried different-sex couples influenced the judgment of the ECJ in *Grant* v. *South-West Trains*, and the Opinion of the Advocate General in *D.* v. *Council*.[29] Because the EC courts do not specialise in human

parenthood (or parental authority). Thus, according to the Commission, only factually (if not legally) different-sex parents, and not same-sex parents, have a Convention right to both be recognised as legal parents of their child. The Court agreed as to "family life", but found no positive obligation under Art. 8 to grant legal parenthood to a non-genetic parent. See *X, Y & Z* v. *UK* (22 April 1997) (Ct. J.); Whittle, chap. 39.

[25] *Supra* n.23, at The Law, para. 1. *M.* v. *Netherlands* (No. 16944/90) (8 Feb. 1993), 74 DR 120 (Com. A.D.), provided some respect to a family like that in *Kerkhoven* by denying a sperm donor's claim that he had a family life with the lesbian couple's daughter.

[26] *Supra* n.23, at The Law, para. 2.

[27] *Supra* n.19, at The Law, para. 3.

[28] *Tyrer* v. *U.K.* (25 April 1978) (Ct. J.), para. 31.

[29] See *Grant* (Case C-249/96), para. 33, *D.* (Case C-122/99 P), paras. 109–10 (Opinion), http://europa.eu.int/jurisp/cgi-bin/form.pl?lang=en. See also Koppelman, chap. 35; Bell, chap. 37.

rights issues, and spend most of their time on economic issues relating to the functioning of the single EC market, they tend to defer to the case-law of the European Court and Commission of Human Rights, where a particular human rights issue has already been considered by those tribunals. In view of the fact that the Commission had not extended any protection to same-sex couples, and that the Court had not had an opportunity to do so, it was unlikely that the EC courts would take the lead in protecting them against discrimination in *Grant* or *D.* v. *Council*.

FACTORS LIKELY TO INFLUENCE THE COURT'S FUTURE CASE-LAW ON SAME-SEX PARTNERS AND PARENTS

The Court's Recent Case-Law on Other Sexual Orientation Issues

One of the most important factors influencing the Court's first decisions on same-sex partners or parents will be its recent case-law on other forms of sexual orientation discrimination. From 1981 to 1999, the Court had only been asked to consider one form of sexual orientation discrimination: blanket criminalisation of all sexual activity between persons of the same sex.[30] It held in *Dudgeon* v. *UK*[31] and two subsequent cases[32] that such criminalisation violates the right to respect for private life in Article 8. Because no other cases clearly presenting other issues of sexual orientation discrimination had reached the Court (generally because the Commission had declared them inadmissible), it was not clear whether, given the opportunity, the Court would be willing to extend the principle of *Dudgeon* beyond criminalisation. However, from 1 November 1998, the Court took on the role of deciding whether all new and pending applications were admissible. It declared three sexual orientation discrimination cases admissible, and found violations of the Convention in all three cases over a ten-month period from September 1999 to July 2000.

The first case, on the British ban on lesbian, gay and bisexual military personnel, yielded two judgments: *Smith & Grady* v. *UK* and *Lustig-Prean & Beckett* v. *UK* (the "*Armed Forces Judgments*").[33] In finding that the ban violated the right to respect for private life in Article 8, the Court held that, because "the sole reason for the investigations . . . and . . . discharge was their sexual orientation[,] . . . a most intimate aspect of an individual's private life, particularly serious reasons by way of justification were required".[34] The Court also rejected the hostility of heterosexual members of the armed forces as a justification for

[30] See generally Wintemute, *supra* n.4, chaps. 4 and 5.

[31] (22 Oct. 1981) (Ct. J.).

[32] *Norris* v. *Ireland* (26 Oct. 1988) (Ct. J.); *Modinos* v. *Cyprus* (22 April 1993) (Ct. J.).

[33] (27 Sept. 1999) (Ct. J.). The Court did not cite the Commission's admissibility decision findin[g] no violation: *Bruce* v. *UK* (No. 9237/81) (12 Oct. 1983), 34 DR 68.

[34] *Ibid.*, *Smith* at para. 90, *Lustig-Prean* at para. 83.

the blanket ban on lesbian, gay and bisexual members: "To the extent that they represent a predisposed bias on the part of a heterosexual majority against a homosexual minority, these negative attitudes cannot, of themselves, be considered by the Court to amount to sufficient justification for the interferences with the applicants' rights . . ., any more than similar negative attitudes towards those of a different race, origin or colour".[35] Thus, the *Armed Forces Judgments* established that "particularly serious reasons" are required to justify sexual orientation discrimination challenged under Article 8 (including in public sector employment), and drew an explicit analogy between prejudice against members of racial or ethnic minorities and prejudice against lesbian, gay and bisexual persons.

The second case, *Salgueiro da Silva Mouta* v. *Portugal*,[36] was the first in which the Court has considered the rights of individual lesbian, gay and bisexual parents, without reference to the rights of any same-sex partner they may have.[37] The Lisbon Court of Appeal had treated a gay father's sexual orientation as a negative and determining factor in reversing a trial court's decision to award him custody of his (genetic) daughter from a prior marriage, and granting custody instead to her heterosexual (genetic) mother. The Strasbourg Court found discrimination violating Articles 8 and 14 in relation to his "family life" with his daughter. "There was a difference of treatment between the applicant and [the child's] mother which was based on the applicant's sexual orientation, a concept which is undoubtedly covered by Article 14 of the Convention . . . [T]he list [of grounds in Article 14] is illustrative and not exhaustive, as is shown by the words 'any ground such as' ".[38] Moreover, "the applicant's homosexuality was a factor which was decisive in the final decision", especially as the Lisbon Court of Appeal had "warned him not to adopt conduct which might make the child realise that her father was living with another man 'in conditions resembling those of man and wife'".[39]

In deciding that the difference in treatment was disproportionate to the legitimate aim of protecting the health and rights of the child, and therefore "discrimination", the Strasbourg Court observed that the Lisbon Court of Appeal had "made a distinction based on considerations regarding the applicant's sexual orientation, a distinction which is not acceptable under the Convention (see, *mutatis mutandis*, the *Hoffmann* judgment cited above, p. 60, para. 36)".[40] In

[35] *Ibid.*, *Smith* at para. 97, *Lustig-Prean* at para. 90.

[36] (21 Dec. 1999) (Ct. J.).

[37] Although *Salgueiro* is clearly about a gay parent, I would not classify it as a same-sex partner r parent case, because the Court was not asked to the grant the father's male partner any rights, or npose any obligations on him, in relation to the child.

[38] *Supra* n.36, at para. 28.

[39] *Ibid.*, at para. 35. The Court's statement about "her father . . . living with another man" implies at a grant of custody or visitation rights conditioned on a lesbian or gay parent's not having any ntact with their same-sex partner while the child is present would violate Arts. 8 and 14. This nfirms that *Craig*, *supra* n.6, decided after *Salgueiro*, must have turned on standing.

[40] *Salgueiro*, *ibid.* at para. 36.

Hoffmann v. *Austria*,[41] the Strasbourg Court had held that the decision of the Austrian Supreme Court to overturn a trial court's decision and deny a Jehovah's Witness custody of her daughter, because she might not consent to a blood transfusion (even though a court could override her decision), violated Articles 8 ("family life") and 14. "Notwithstanding any possible arguments to the contrary, a distinction based essentially on a difference in religion alone is not acceptable".[42] Thus, by citing *Hoffmann* in *Salgueiro*, the Strasbourg Court drew an implicit analogy between freedom from discrimination based on religion and freedom from discrimination based on sexual orientation.

The third case, *A.D.T.* v. *UK*,[43] concerned British statutes providing that sexual activity between consenting adult men in private is illegal if "more than two persons take part or are present". The Court had no trouble finding a violation of Article 8 ("private life"), and did not even find it necessary to consider the fact that the statutes discriminated on the basis of sexual orientation, by not applying the same rule to male-female or female-female sexual activity. *A.D.T.* suggests that all sexual orientation discrimination in the criminal law, including unequal ages of consent to sexual activity, is likely to violate either Article 8 on its own, or Article 8 with Article 14.[44]

In light of these three recent cases, the Court's case-law appears to be evolving towards a general principle that all differences in treatment based on sexual orientation without a strong justification violate the Convention, either as an unjustifiable interference with "private life" (and possibly at some stage "family life") under Article 8, or as "discrimination" in relation to these areas under Articles 8 and 14. The Court has adopted a "particularly serious reasons" standard in sexual orientation cases under Article 8, and has said that "elements such as gender identification, name and sexual orientation and sexual life are important elements of the personal sphere protected by Article 8". . . .[45] Moreover, the Court's statements in *Salgueiro* and *Hoffmann* that distinctions based on sexual orientation or religion are "not acceptable" under the Convention, could lead it at some stage to hold that "very weighty reasons" are required to justify such distinctions, as is the case for distinctions based on sex,[46] birth out of wedlock,[47] and nationality.[48]

[41] (23 June 1993) (Ct. J.).

[42] *Ibid.* at para. 36.

[43] (31 July 2000) (Ct. J.). The Court did not cite the Commission's admissibility decision findin[g] no violation: *Johnson* v. *UK* (No. 10389/83) (17 July 1986).

[44] Because the UK Government settled the case by agreeing to amend the offending legislatio[n] the Court has not yet had a chance to confirm the Commission's finding, in *Sutherland* v. *UK* (N[o.] 25186/94) (1 July 1997) (Com. R.), that unequal ages of consent violate Arts. 8 and 14. Three cha[l]lenges to the unequal age limits in Austria are awaiting admissibility decisions by the Court: *S.L.* v. *Austria* (No. 45330/99), *G.L.* v. *Austria* (No. 39392/98), *A.V.* v. *Austria* (No. 39829/98).

[45] *Bensaid* v. *UK* (6 Feb. 2001) (Ct. J.), para. 47.

[46] *Abdulaziz* v. *UK* (28 May 1985) (Ct. J.), para. 78.

[47] *Inze* v. *Austria* (28 Oct. 1987) (Ct. J.), para. 41.

[48] *Gaygusuz* v. *Austria* (16 Sept. 1996) (Ct. J.), para. 42.

The Court's Case-Law on Transsexual Marriage

Same-sex partners or parents contemplating applications to the Court must consider both its sexual orientation case-law and its gender identity case-law. The Court has decided three cases where a post-operative transsexual individual was seeking to marry a person of their birth sex, i.e., of the opposite sex physically and psychologically, but of the same sex chromosomally (and therefore legally in the UK). In each of these cases, the Court said that the right to marry in Article 12 of the Convention refers "to the traditional marriage between persons of opposite biological sex".[49] However, in the most recent case, *Sheffield & Horsham* v. *UK* in 1998, nine of twenty judges dissented, holding that the right to respect for private life in Article 8 requires the UK to allow transsexual individuals to have their sex on their birth certificates changed (from which legal sex, the right to marry a person of the opposite legal sex, and the right of a legally male person to be considered a legal father[50] generally follow). At any time, the Court could decide that there has been sufficient evolution with regard to the treatment of transsexual persons in Council of Europe countries that denying them the right to change their birth certificates is no longer consistent with the Convention.[51] And it is important to note that the Court has yet to consider a case in which a transsexual individual with a legally (but not factually) "same-sex" partner was seeking, not the right to marry itself, but some other right or benefit enjoyed by legally and factually different-sex couples, married or unmarried.[52]

The Court's Case-Law on Unmarried Different-Sex Couples

Same-sex partners or parents also need to be aware of the Court's case-law on unmarried different-sex couples. The Court has clearly held that "family" in Article 8 "is not confined to marriage-based relationships and may encompass other de facto 'family' ties where the parties are living together out of wedlock".[53] Similarly, in deciding that a woman was a "victim" with an Article 34 right to complain that her unmarried male partner had been killed by the police, the Court said: "a couple who have lived together for many years constitute a

[49] *Rees* v. *UK* (17 Oct. 1986) (Ct. J.), para. 49; *Cossey* v. *UK* (27 Sept. 1990) (Ct. J.), para. 43; *Sheffield & Horsham* v. *UK* (30 July 1998) (Ct. J.), para. 66. See also *Fretté*, *infra* n. 71.

[50] A major reason why the Court rejected the transsexual father's claim in *X, Y & Z* v. *UK* (22 April 1997) (Ct. J.), para. 47, was that the majority could not imagine X being a legal father for the purpose of parental rights and obligations, yet female for all other purposes. See Whittle, chap. 39.

[51] At least two applications declared admissible by the Commission are now pending before the Court: *I.* v. *UK* (No. 25680/94) (27 May 1997); *Goodwin* v. *UK* (No. 28957/95) (1 Dec. 1997).

[52] Such a case is pending before the ECJ. See Case C-117/01, *KB* v. *National Health Service Pension Agency*, referred by the Court of Appeal (England and Wales), 4 Oct. 2000; *Bavin* v. *NHS Trust Pensions Agency*, [1999] ICR 1192 (Employment Appeal Tribunal); Whittle, chap. 39.

[53] *Elsholz* v. *Germany* (13 July 2000) (Ct. J.), para. 43.

'family' for the purposes of Article 8 . . . and are entitled to its protection notwithstanding the fact that their relationship exists outside marriage".[54] Statements of this kind certainly cover unmarried different-sex partners, whether or not they have children,[55] and do not preclude the inclusion of same-sex partners.

However, the Court tends to find violations of Article 8, or Articles 8 and 14, when a distinction between unmarried different-sex couples and married different-sex couples adversely affects the children of an unmarried different-sex couple.[56] When unmarried different-sex partners challenge the denial to themselves of legal rights against third parties or each other, the Court has often been less sympathetic. In 1986, in *Johnston* v. *Ireland*, the Court did not "consider that it is possible to derive from Article 8 an obligation on the part of Ireland to establish for unmarried couples a status analogous to that of married couples".[57] In 1999, in *Saucedo Gómez* v. *Spain*, a woman who had lived with her male partner for eighteen years would arguably have had a legal right to occupy their common home after the relationship ended, if she had been married to him. The Court declared her application inadmissible, finding no violation of Articles 8 and 14: "[S]ocial reality demonstrates the existence of stable unions between men and women based on ties of solidarity and mutual support, constituting a full common life emotionally, economically and socially, which do not however come within the legal framework of a marriage. Nevertheless, it is not up to the Court to dictate, or even to indicate, the measures to take in this situation, because the question falls within the margin of appreciation of the respondent State, which has a free choice of the means to be employed [subject to Article 8]".[58]

Saucedo Gómez shows that the Court is currently very reluctant to decide what distinctions between married and unmarried different-sex couples are discriminatory. But this does not mean that the Court would automatically reject any claim by a same-sex couple for equal treatment with (i) an unmarried different-sex couple, or even (ii) a married different-sex couple. In the first situation, of which *Karner* is an example, it is the national legislature or courts that have decided to extend a particular right or benefit of married different-sex partners to unmarried different-sex partners. The Court need only decide whether it is sexual orientation discrimination, contrary to Articles 8 and 14, to deny a right or benefit enjoyed by unmarried different-sex partners to unmarried same-sex partners. This issue is much easier than the one in *Saucedo Gómez*.

[54] *A.V.* v. *Bulgaria* (41488/98) (25 April 1999) (Ct. A.D.), The Law, para. 1.

[55] See *Kroon* v. *Netherlands* (27 Oct. 1994) (Ct. J.), para. 30 ("family life" may generally require cohabitation, but "exceptionally other factors", such as the couple's having had children together, may suffice).

[56] See e.g. *Camp & Bourimi* v. *Netherlands* (3 Oct. 2000) (Ct. J.); *Mazurek* v. *France* (1 Feb. 2000) (Ct. J.); *Kroon, ibid.*; *Keegan* v. *Ireland* (26 May 1994) (Ct. J.); *Johnston* v. *Ireland* (18 Dec. 1986) (Ct. J.), paras. 70–76.

[57] *Johnston, ibid.* at para. 68.

[58] (No. 37784/97) (26 Jan. 1999) (Ct. A.D.), *En droit* (author's translation from French). See also *Nylynd* v. *Finland* (No. 27110/95) (29 June 1999) (Ct. A.D.).

In the second situation, *Saucedo Gómez* can also be distinguished. Where a same-sex couple seeks a right or benefit enjoyed by married different-sex couples (apart from the right to marry),[59] in all Council of Europe member states other than the Netherlands (as of August 2001), same-sex couples do not have the option of marrying to obtain this right or benefit, unlike most unmarried different-sex couples. In *Saucedo Gómez*, the Court stressed that the applicant had lived with her partner for over ten years, after divorce was legalised in Spain, without seeking a divorce from her husband and marrying her partner. "The applicant could have regularised her situation with her partner so as to enjoy all the economic advantages inherent in the status of spouse. However, she freely chose not to do so".[60]

"European Consensus" on Equal Treatment of Same-Sex Partners

My statement above about evolution towards a "general principle" in relation to sexual orientation discrimination must be tempered by acknowledging a particular feature of the Court's approach to interpreting the Convention. One of the most important factors in the Court's decisions as to whether an interference with "private life" or "family life" can be justified as "necessary in a democratic society" under Article 8(2), or whether a difference in treatment is "discrimination" under Article 14 combined with Article 8, is the degree of "consensus" within the forty-three member states of the Council of Europe as to the need for the challenged practice. The higher the degree of "consensus" that the practice is not necessary, the more likely it is that the Court will find a violation, and vice versa.[61] As the Court observed recently, "consensus" is an integral part of the Court's "living instrument" approach to interpreting the Convention, whereby its interpretation of the Convention evolves with changing social and legal conditions in Europe: "[The Court] should not depart, without good reason, from precedents laid down in previous cases. Since the Convention is first and foremost a system for the protection of human rights, the Court must however have

[59] See e.g. *Gay Times* (Oct. 2000), p. 46 (case of Ron Strank and Roger Fisher relating to a survivor's pension restricted to a "widow" or "widower"; same UK pension scheme as in *KB*, *supra* n.52).

[60] *Saucedo*, *supra* n.58, *En droit* (author's translation from French). See also *Quintana Zapata* v. *Spain* (No. 34615/97) (4 March 1998) (Com. A.D.) (survivor's pension denied after sixty-five years' cohabitation because woman could have married her male partner).

[61] See e.g. *Petrovic* v. *Austria* (27 March 1998) (Ct. J.), para. 38 ("one of the relevant factors [in deciding whether a difference in treatment is justified] may be the existence or non-existence of common ground between the laws of the Contracting States"); *Chapman* v. *UK* (18 Jan. 2001) (Ct. J.), paras. 93–94. See also Wintemute, *supra* n.4, at 138–40; L Helfer, "Consensus, Coherence and the European Convention on Human Rights", (1993) 26 *Cornell International Law Journal* 133; Laurence Helfer, "Finding a Consensus on Equality: The Homosexual Age of Consent and the European Convention on Human Rights", 65 New York University Law Review 1044 (1990) (this article probably helped inspire the late Peter Duffy QC to propose the applications that led to *Sutherland*, *supra* n.44, and ultimately to the equalisation of the age of consent in the UK by the Sexual Offences (Amendment) Act 2000).

regard to the changing conditions in Contracting States and respond . . . to any emerging consensus as to the standards to be achieved . . ."[62]

The negative case-law of the Commission, discussed above, was based on its perception of "European consensus" regarding the treatment of same-sex couples in 1983. As this book demonstrates, there has clearly been a dramatic change in this consensus over the last eighteen years. In 1983, only the Netherlands had adopted legislation providing some form of legal recognition of same-sex partnerships. By August 2001, legislation creating some kind of formal registration procedure, or granting a significant package of rights and obligations to same-sex couples (or both), had been passed at the national level in Belgium, Denmark, France, Germany, Hungary, Iceland, the Netherlands, Norway, Portugal, and Sweden, as well as in four regions of Spain and one canton of Switzerland.[63] Legislation providing recognition in one or a few specific areas had been adopted at the national level in Austria and Spain, and in Scotland in the United Kingdom.[64]

Developments in national law have both influenced and been influenced by an emerging consensus in the Parliamentary Assembly of the Council of Europe (PACE), and the EC's European Parliament (EP). In 2000, the PACE expressed its opinion "that the enumeration of grounds in Article 14 is, without being exhaustive, meant to list forms of discrimination which [the PACE] regards as being especially odious. Consequently the ground 'sexual orientation' should be added"[65] to Protocol No. 12 to the Convention (the new general prohibition of discrimination).[66] The PACE also recommended: (a) that the forty-three Council of Europe member states "review their policies in the field of social rights and protection of migrants in order to ensure that homosexual partnership[s] and families are treated on the same basis as heterosexual partnerships and families" and "take such measures as are necessary to ensure that bi-national lesbian and gay couples are accorded the same residence rights as bi-

[62] *Chapman*, *ibid.* at para. 70. See also *Mazurek*, *supra* n.56, para. 52: "With regard to the situation in other member States . . ., the Court notes . . . a distinct tendency in favour of eradicating discrimination against adulterine children. It cannot ignore such a tendency in its—necessarily dynamic—interpretation of the relevant provisions of the Convention. . . . [T]he reference made by the Government to the *Rasmussen* v. *Denmark* [1984] judgment . . . is not convincing, since the factual and temporal circumstances have now changed".

[63] See chaps. 21–27, 29, 31–32, 36.

[64] See chaps. 26, 30, 34.

[65] Opinion No. 216 (2000) on "Draft Protocol No. 12 to the European Convention on Human Rights", http://stars.coe.fr/ta/ta00/eopi216.htm (26 Jan. 2000), based on the Report of the Committee on Legal Affairs and Human Rights, Document (Doc.) 8614 (Rapporteur: Mr Erik Jurgens), http://stars.coe.fr/doc/doc00/edoc8614.htm (14 Jan. 2000). The Committee of Ministers of the Council of Europe rejected the Opinion of the PACE and declined to change the text. Although express inclusion would have had important symbolic benefits (cf. Art. 21 of the Charter of Fundamental Rights of the European Union, Waaldijk, chap. 36, pp. 639–40), sexual orientation is still implicitly included in Protocol No. 12 and Art. 14. See *Salgueiro*, *supra* n.36.

[66] ETS No. 177, http://conventions.coe.int (Search) (opened for signature 4 Nov. 2000; will enter into force after ten ratifications, only in ratifying member states). Protocol No. 12 will eliminate the need under Art. 14 to show that a specific case of discrimination falls "within the ambit" of another Convention right. See *supra* n.4.

national heterosexual couples";[67] and (b) that these member states "adopt legislation which makes provision for registered partnerships".[68]

The EP addressed the rights of same-sex partners and parents for the first time in 1994, when it called on the Commission to draft a recommendation: (i) seeking to end "the barring of lesbians and homosexual couples from marriage or from an equivalent legal framework, [and guarantee instead] the full rights and benefits of marriage, allowing the registration of partnerships"; and (ii) seeking to end "any restrictions on the rights of lesbians and homosexuals to be parents or to adopt or foster children".[69] In 2000, the EP urged the fifteen EC member states "to amend their legislation recognising registered partnerships of persons of the same sex and assigning them the same rights and obligations as exist for registered partnerships between men and women" and "to amend their legislation to grant legal recognition of extramarital cohabitation, irrespective of gender". The EP also called for "rapid progress . . . with mutual recognition of the different legally recognised non-marital modes of cohabitation and legal marriages between persons of the same sex in the [European Union]".[70]

PENDING AND POTENTIAL FUTURE CASES ON SAME-SEX PARTNERS AND PARENTS

Fretté v. *France*

In *Fretté* v. *France*,[71] the Court has been asked to determine whether, under Articles 8 and 14 of the Convention, a gay man can be denied an "approval" (*agrément*) as eligible to adopt a child as an unmarried individual (which is permitted in France), solely because of his sexual orientation. The rejection of Philippe Fretté's application was upheld by the *Conseil d'État*, the highest administrative court in France, because of his "*choix de vie*" ("choices of life") or "*conditions de vie*" ("conditions of life").[72] The *Conseil d'État* reversed the

[67] Recommendation 1470 (2000) on the "Situation of gays and lesbians and their partners in respect of asylum and immigration in the member states of the Council of Europe", http://stars.coe.fr/ta/ta00/erec1470.htm (30 June 2000), based on the Report of the Committee on Migration, Refugees and Demography, Doc. 8654 (Rapporteur: Mrs R-G Vermot-Mangold), http://stars.coe.fr/doc/doc00/edoc8654.htm.

[68] Recommendation 1474 (2000) on the "Situation of lesbians and gays in Council of Europe member states", http://stars.coe.fr/ta/ta00/erec1474.htm (26 Sept. 2000), based on the Report of the Committee on Legal Affairs and Human Rights, Doc. 8755 (Rapporteur: Mr C Tabajdi), http://stars.coe.fr/doc/doc00/edoc8755.htm.

[69] "Resolution on equal rights for homosexuals and lesbians in the EC" (8 Feb. 1994), OJ [1994] C 61/40 at 42, para. 14.

[70] See p. 639, n.12 (16 March 2000). See also Resolution A5-0223/2001, paras. 84-85 (5 July 2001), http://www.europarl.eu.int/plenary/default_en.htm (Texts adopted).

[71] (No. 36515/97) (12 June 2001) (Ct. A.D.) (admissible, Arts. 8 and 14, not 12 and 14).

[72] *Département de Paris* v. *Fretté*, *Conseil d'État*, 9 Oct. 1996, *Recueil des décisions du Conseil d'État*.1996.391.

decision of the *Tribunal administratif de Paris*, which had interpreted "*choix de vie*" (the reason given by the social services department for the rejection) as a euphemism meaning "homosexuality".[73]

The issue in *Fretté* is essentially the same as that in *Salgueiro*. Did the *Conseil d'État* make "a distinction [affecting the applicant's 'potential family life' or 'private life'] based on considerations regarding the applicant's sexual orientation, a distinction which is not acceptable under the Convention"? The only way in which *Fretté* would extend the case-law of the Court is that, whereas *Salgueiro* involved an existing parent-child relationship between a gay father and his genetic daughter, *Fretté* involves an attempt to create a new parent-child relationship between a gay man and his prospective adoptive child. But like *Salgueiro*, *Fretté* is not a same-sex parent case, in the sense that the applicant is not seeking to establish a legal relationship between the child and a same-sex partner, thereby giving the child simultaneously two legal parents who are both male or both female.

Fretté concerns an "individual adoption" rather than a "second-parent adoption" or "joint adoption". With regard to individual adoptions, very few Council of Europe member states that permit adoption by unmarried individuals (at least in some cases, instead of confining adoption in all cases to married different-sex couples) have found it necessary to impose a blanket ban on adoption by lesbian, gay or bisexual individuals, either through an express prohibition in legislation, or a decision of a final appellate court interpreting non-discriminatory adoption legislation.[74] Second-parent adoptions by same-sex couples are currently permitted only in Denmark, Iceland and the Netherlands, and joint adoptions by same-sex couples (excluding inter-country adoptions) are permitted only in the Netherlands.[75] Thus, a same-sex parent case, i.e., an application to the Court by a same-sex couple legally unable to adopt each other's children, or to jointly adopt an unrelated child, would probably encounter a considerable problem of lack of "European consensus". More member states would probably have to permit second-parent and joint adoptions[76] before the Court would consider sexual orientation discrimination in relation to such adoptions as a violation of Articles 8 and 14.

[73] 25 Jan. 1995, Dalloz.1995.Jur.647. See also *La Semaine Juridique* (J.C.P.).1997.II.22766 (*Conclusions du Commissaire du Gouvernement*) (16 Sept. 1996).

[74] I am not aware of any express legislative prohibitions. As for decisions of final appellate courts, apart from France, the only exception of which I am aware is Sweden, where a government committee has recommended legislation overriding the decision. See Ytterberg, chap. 22, nn. 34, 56.

[75] See Lund-Andersen, chap. 21; Waaldijk, chap. 23; Euro-Letter No. 80 (June 2000), http:// www.steff.suite.dk/eurolet.htm.

[76] Art. 6(1) of the European Convention on the Adoption of Children, ETS No. 058, http://conventions.coe.int (Search), presents an obstacle in the seventeen ratifying member states (as of 18 Aug. 2001) (except Denmark which made a reservation excluding Art. 6(1)): "The law shall not permit a child to be adopted except by either two persons married to each other, whether they adopt simultaneously or successively, or by one person". These states include Germany, Italy, Norway, Sweden and the United Kingdom, but not Finland, France, Iceland, Spain or the Netherlands.

Karner v. *Austria*

The *Karner* case, as mentioned above,[77] is the first same-sex partner or same-sex parent case to reach the Court. If the application were declared admissible, and a judgment ultimately rendered in favour of Siegmund Karner, it would mark an extension of the Court's protection against sexual orientation discrimination beyond protection for lesbian, gay and bisexual individuals in the criminal law (*Dudgeon* and *A.D.T.*), employment (the *Armed Forces Judgments*), and family law on the rights of individual genetic parents (*Salgueiro*). The Court would recognise that unmarried different-sex couples and unmarried same-sex couples are in comparable situations, and that the Austrian Supreme Court's granting a tenancy succession right to an unmarried different-sex partner, while permitting the eviction of an unmarried same-sex partner, made "a distinction based on considerations regarding the applicant's sexual orientation, a distinction which is not acceptable under the Convention". The Court would not have to depart in any way from its case-law on transsexual marriage or unmarried different-sex couples, because Karner is not seeking the right to marry, or a right that Austria has confined to married different-sex couples.

The Court could find sexual orientation discrimination in *Karner*, contrary to Articles 8 and 14, in relation to Karner's "private life" or "home". But it could also determine that, in view of the evolution in social attitudes, national legislation, and European parliamentary resolutions since 1983, same-sex couples must now be considered as having "family life". As the Court said in *Mazurek* v. *France*, "the institution of the family is not fixed, be it historically, sociologically or even legally".[78] Whatever basis the Court used to find a violation, it would join the New York Court of Appeals,[79] the Supreme Court of Israel,[80] the Constitutional Court of Hungary,[81] the Supreme Court of Canada,[82] the United Kingdom's House of Lords,[83] and the Constitutional Court of South Africa[84] in holding that, at least in some circumstances, a same-sex partner must be treated like an unmarried or even married different-sex partner, whether as a member of their partner's "family" or otherwise.

[77] *Supra* n.7.

[78] *Supra* n.56, para. 52.

[79] *Braschi* v. *Stahl Associates Co.*, 543 N.E. 2d 49 (1989) (tenancy succession); *Levin* v. *Yeshiva University* (2 July 2001) (student housing). See Leonard, chap. 7, pp. 137, 139–42, 152.

[80] *El Al Airlines Ltd.* v. *Danilowitz*, High Court of Justice 721/94, 48(5) *Piskei-Din* (Supreme Court Reports) 749 (1994) (employment benefits). See Gross, chap. 20.

[81] (13 March 1995), 14/1995 (III.13.) (all rights of unmarried different-sex couples). See Farkas, chap. 31.

[82] *M.* v. *H.*, [1999] 2 S.C.R. 3 (financial support after relationship breakdown). See L'Heureux-Dubé, pp. 211–13; Casswell, chap. 11; Lahey, chap. 12.

[83] *Fitzpatrick* v. *Sterling Housing Association Ltd.*, [1999] 4 All E.R. 705 (tenancy succession). See Bailey-Harris, chap. 34.

[84] *National Coalition for Gay & Lesbian Equality* v. *Minister of Home Affairs* (2 Dec. 1999), 2000 (2) SA 1 (immigration). See Lind, chap. 13.

A Same-Sex Marriage Case?

It can be argued that exclusion of same-sex couples from civil marriage is sex discrimination,[85] which can only be justified by "very weighty reasons" under Article 14, in relation to the "right to marry" in Article 12. Although the English text of Article 12 grants this right to "men and women", and the French text grants it to "*l'homme et la femme*", neither text says that a man can only marry a woman, or that a woman can only marry a man. It is likely that, at some point in the future, the Court will be willing to accept this argument, in keeping with its "living instrument" approach to interpreting the Convention, and will modify its "opposite-sex only" interpretation of Article 12 in its transsexual marriage case-law,[86] so as to recognise an "emerging consensus" that restricting civil marriage to different-sex couples is discriminatory.[87]

However, if this argument were presented to the Court in August 2001, when only one of forty-three Council of Europe member states has opened up civil marriage to same-sex couples, it is extremely unlikely that the Court would accept it. The absence of "European consensus" would almost certainly be fatal. As an international tribunal, the Court is not in a position effectively to order forty-two member states to end the exclusion of same-sex couples from civil marriage. If a same-sex couple were to decide in 2001 to begin a discrimination case in their national trial court, it could take five to ten years before they had exhausted their domestic remedies, submitted an application to the Court, and (if their application were declared admissible) argued the merits of their case at a hearing in Strasbourg. By that time, "European consensus" will certainly have changed, and more countries are likely to have opened up civil marriage to same-sex couples. But it still might not be enough. Although it is extremely frustrating for same-sex couples who would like to be able to marry now, rather than in ten or twenty years, they might be best advised to wait a few more years before starting down the road to Strasbourg.

CONCLUSION

Initially, the main source of increased equality for same-sex couples in Europe will be the national legislatures and courts. Only when sufficient change has occurred in the member states, with respect to a particular issue, will the Court

[85] See *Baehr* v. *Lewin*, 852 P. 2d 44, clarified, 852 P.2d 74 (Supreme Court of Hawaii 1993); Wolfson, chap. 9; Koppelman, chap. 35.

[86] This case-law may have deterred the litigants in the Dutch, German and Hungarian same-sex marriage cases from filing applications with the European Commission of Human Rights. See Waaldijk, chap. 23; Schimmel & Heun, chap. 32; Farkas, chap. 31.

[87] See *W.* v. *UK* (No. 11095/84) (7 March 1989) (Com. R.) (Mr HG Schermers, dissenting, *obiter* in a transsexual marriage case): "In my opinion the fundamental human right underlying Art. 12 should also be granted to homosexual and lesbian couples".

identify a "European consensus" and require dissenting member states to comply with it. For this reason, the Convention will be of little relevance in the most progressive member states, such as the Nordic countries and the Netherlands. However, the Court could be said to be a mirror that reflects the light of human rights consensus into the darker corners of Europe. Same-sex partners and parents in countries that lag behind an "emerging consensus" on legal recognition of same-sex partnerships (such as Austria or the United Kingdom) could find that Strasbourg will, eventually, come to the rescue.

PART IV

INTERNATIONAL LAW

41

Will the United Nations Human Rights Committee Require Recognition of Same-Sex Marriages?

LAURENCE R HELFER*

INTRODUCTION

SINCE DENMARK BECAME the first nation in the world to enact a registered partnership law in 1989, same-sex couples in more than a dozen countries have achieved, if not the right to marry, then at least some meaningful slice of the rights, privileges, and responsibilities that married and unmarried heterosexual couples have long enjoyed.[1]

These newly-acquired rights have been achieved in one of two ways. First, by national legislatures (as in the Scandinavian countries) enacting new statutes that recognise partnership rights for same-sex couples. And second, by national court judges (as in Canada and South Africa) using constitutional equality norms to overturn existing laws that grant benefits only to married or unmarried heterosexual couples.

Within the last few years, however, a new form of advocacy for same-sex relationships has arisen: the use of an international litigation strategy based on treaty norms to compel governments to reform their domestic laws. It is this strategy that I will address in this chapter. I will focus in particular on the international petition that two lesbian couples recently filed before the United Nations Human Rights Committee (UNHRC or "the Committee").[2] In that petition, known as *Joslin* v. *New Zealand*,[3] the two couples assert that New

* Professor of Law, Loyola Law School, Los Angeles, California, United States.

[1] For a recent survey see, International Gay and Lesbian Human Rights Commission, *IGLHRC Fact Sheet: Registered Partnership, Domestic Partnership, and Marriage* (San Francisco, IGLHRC, Nov. 1998), http://www.iglhrc.org.

[2] This chapter presumes a familiarity with the monitoring and adjudicatory functions of the UNHRC. For a detailed discussion of those functions, see L R Helfer & A-M Slaughter, "Toward a Theory of Effective Supranational Adjudication," (1997) 107 *Yale Law Journal* 273 at 338–43.

[3] Communication No. 902/1999 to the UN Human Rights Committee under the Optional Protocol to the International Covenant on Civil and Political Rights against the Government of New Zealand (hereinafter "*Joslin* Communication") (filed Dec. 1998). See Christie, chap. 15, p. 322.

Zealand's failure to recognise marriage rights for same-sex couples violates the International Covenant on Civil and Political Rights (ICCPR or "the Covenant"), a UN-based human rights treaty ratified by 146 nation states.[4]

The *Joslin* petition raises a cluster of related strategic questions concerning the struggle for same-sex marriage and partnership rights. First, is an international litigation strategy an effective way to achieve broad-based and lasting recognition for same-sex marriages or partnerships? Second, what are the limits of that strategy given the current contours of the global legal landscape and the capabilities of international human rights tribunals? Finally, what would be the consequences of a decision in favor of the *Joslin* petitioners for lesbians and gay men who seek alternatives to same-sex marriage, or who seek to change the institution of marriage more fundamentally?

THE TENSION BETWEEN TWO ADJUDICATORY FUNCTIONS OF THE UNHRC

Why would the two lesbian couples in the *Joslin* case take their case to the UNHRC, after their unsuccessful efforts to achieve recognition for same-sex marriages in New Zealand's courts?[5] In part, the answer to that question is found in *Toonen* v. *Australia*, a 1994 decision of the Committee. In *Toonen*, the UNHRC unanimously concluded that a criminal ban on same-sex consensual sodomy by the Australian state of Tasmania violated the ICCPR's privacy and non-discrimination rights. Responding to pressure from Tasmanian lesbian and gay rights organisations and the Australian federal government to implement the *Toonen* decision, Tasmania repealed its sodomy laws in 1997.[6]

In light of *Toonen*, the UNHRC appears to be quite a sympathetic forum for lesbian and gay rights claims. I believe, however, that the same-sex marriage claim in *Joslin* raises far more problematic issues for the Committee and for the petitioners.[7] In particular, *Joslin* highlights the tensions between two distinct

[4] 999 United Nations Treaty Series 171, 301 (1967) (adopted 16 Dec. 1966, entered into force 23 March 1976) (hereinafter "ICCPR"). As of 16 July 2000, there were 147 states parties to the ICCPR. Of those states, 97 had ratified the First Optional Protocol to the ICCPR, which authorises the UNHRC to receive petitions from individuals alleging violations of the treaty.

[5] The named plaintiff in the New Zealand proceeding was Lindsay Quilter. *See Quilter* v *Attorney-General*, [1998] 1 NZLR 523 (Court of Appeal), http://www.gaylawnet.com/cases/quilter_judgment.txt. For a discussion of the *Quilter* litigation in New Zealand's courts, see Christie, chap. 15.

[6] (Communication No. 488/1992) (31 March 1994) 1 International Human Rights Reports 97 (hereinafter "*Toonen* v. *Australia*"), http://www.unhcr.ch (Treaty Bodies Database Search (Toonen). For a discussion of the *Toonen* case and its implications for lesbian and gay human rights advocacy, see L R Helfer & A M Miller, "Sexual Orientation and Human Rights: Toward a United States and Transnational Jurisprudence", (1996) 9 *Harvard Human Rights Law Journal* 61 at 67–77.

[7] These issues are also likely to arise, albeit in a somewhat more muted form, in *Young* v *Australia*, a communication submitted to the Committee on 26 April 2000. The communication alleges that Australia's refusal to pay pension benefits to Edward Young, the same-sex partner of a deceased veteran, under the Veterans' Entitlements Act 1986 is discrimination on the ground of sexual orientation in violation of ICCPR article 26. Under the Act, both a married heterosexual spouse of a veteran and an unmarried heterosexual partner of a veteran are entitled to pension benefits

adjudicatory functions exercised by the UNHRC when reviewing individual petitions: first, providing justice to aggrieved individuals on an individualised, case-specific basis; and second, expounding the meaning of the Covenant for all states parties to the treaty.[8] The tension between these two functions makes the outcome of the *Joslin* case extremely difficult to predict.

Consider first the Committee's "individualised justice" function. When exercising this role, the Committee acts as the arbiter of a fact-specific dispute focused on the national laws of a single state. The Committee's finding that such laws are incompatible with the Covenant is not aimed principally at clarifying the treaty's text, but rather is designed to urge the government to provide a specific remedy to the aggrieved individual.

Seen from this perspective, a decision in favor of the two lesbian couples in *Joslin* would be a logical result. New Zealand already provides a high level of discrimination protection to lesbians and gay men.[9] The failure of New Zealand courts to extend marriage rights to same-sex couples is based, in part, on a rather backward-looking provision of the New Zealand Bill of Rights Act that prevents judges from declaring invalid any legislation that is inconsistent with the Act.[10] And the Human Rights Commission, a domestic governmental body, has concluded that the New Zealand Marriage Act discriminates against same-sex couples.[11] Given these developments, the UNHRC could readily conclude that New Zealand has violated the Covenant's non-discrimination clauses by unjustifiably excluding same-sex couples from the rights and responsibilities of marriage.

In tension with this "individualised justice" role, however, is a second and distinct function exercised by the Committee: to act as the interpreter of a global human rights treaty. It is this "interpretive or expositive function" that may give the Committee pause before ruling in favor of the lesbian couples. When the Committee interprets a clause in the Covenant in one case, it is aware that its reasoning has presumptively persuasive force for all treaty parties. Viewed from this second vantage point, a decision by the UNHRC against New Zealand would have profound implications for both lesbian and gay advocacy and for international human rights law generally. This would be particularly so if *Joslin* generated a fresh set of petitions challenging the failure of other treaty parties to recognise same-sex marriages.

whereas no benefits can be awarded to a veteran's same-sex partner. See *Sydney Star Observer*, Issue 506, 4 May 2000, http://www.ssonet.com.au (Search, Edward Young).

[8] For an insightful analysis that draws similar conclusions about the Committee's functions, see H J Steiner, "Individual Claims in a World of Massive Violations: What Role for the Human Rights Committee?" in P J Alston & J Crawford (eds.), *The Future of UN Human Rights Treaty Monitoring* (Cambridge, Cambridge University Press, 2000) at 15–54.

[9] Human Rights Act 1993, s. 21(1)(m) (prohibiting discrimination on the ground of sexual orientation in employment, housing, education, and the provision of goods and services).

[10] New Zealand Bill of Rights Act 1990, s. 4.

[11] Human Rights Commission, *Consistency 2000 Project Report*, http://www.justice.govt.nz/pubs/reports/1998/hrc_consistency/index.html, s. 9.10 (31 Dec. 1998).

Two important points are worth stressing here. First, the Committee's decisions are only recommendations to states parties, not interpretations of the Covenant that are legally binding on states parties.[12] Thus, the Committee's ability to alter national legal landscapes is only as good as the quality of its reasoning, and its ability to cajole or shame states into taking action. The Committee itself is very much aware of this. In a 1995 study, it lamented the fact that its decisions were not legally binding, and it estimated that states implemented its recommendations in less than 30 per cent of its cases finding for petitioners.[13] Thus, unlike the European Court of Justice or the European Court of Human Rights, the UNHRC is still very much in the early stages of inculcating a legal culture of voluntary compliance with its decisions.

The second point is that a state's initial decision to ratify a human rights treaty, or participate in human rights adjudication, should not been seen as a blanket guarantee of continued respect for human rights norms or institutions. As recent actions by Caribbean states opposed to human rights limitations on the death penalty have made painfully clear, some nations are willing to formally denounce human rights treaties if they feel that a tribunal's case law is too far out of sync with national law concerns.[14] A decision by an international human rights tribunal requiring the recognition of same-sex marriages probably would not create the same friction as the death penalty issues that precipitated the treaty denunciations by these Caribbean nations. The denunciations do suggest, however, that the many states which have historically been hostile to sexual minorities within their populations may simply ignore decisions by the UNHRC favouring lesbian and gay petitioners.

In sum, the Committee's individualised justice function is likely to favour a ruling for the lesbian petitioners, while its interpretive or expositive function is likely to favour a contrary decision. The uncertain question is whether the Committee can find a way to reconcile the tension between these two competing functions when it decides the *Joslin* case.

RECONCILING THE TENSION IN *JOSLIN*: EMPHASISING THE LEGAL SITUATION FACING SAME-SEX COUPLES IN NEW ZEALAND

I start by examining the assumption that the Committee will want to build upon the *Toonen* case and extend the ICCPR's protections to lesbian and gay couples This is by no means a foregone conclusion. References to the "family" and to marriage between "men and women" can be found in the Covenant and

[12] See Helfer & Slaughter, *supra* n.2, at 351.

[13] See *Follow-Up Activities Under the Optional Protocol*, UN General Assembly, Human Right Commission, 50th Session, Supplement No. 40, at 96, UN Document A/50/40 (1995).

[14] For a discussion of these denunciations and their significance, see L R Helfer, "Forum Shopping for Human Rights" (1999) 148 *University of Pennsylvania Law Review* 285 at 389–91.

throughout international human rights law and practice.[15] And, as Kristen Walker has observed, "it is clear that the form of the family in international law is . . . heterosexual".[16]

In Europe, those urging more expansive definitions of family have met with significant resistance, and only now are a few tentative cracks in the traditional definition beginning to appear in the regional case law.[17] Moreover, most states recognising lesbian and gay couples have not fully assimilated same-sex unions into their national marriage laws, but instead have created separate and not entirely equal registered partnership statutes. Thus, there is a risk that the Committee, faced with a petition seeking full-fledged marriage, could adopt a "heterocentric" reading of the ICCPR's equality and family life provisions.

Assuming, however, that the Committee believes that a decision for the lesbian couples in *Joslin* is appropriate, can it expand the principles of *Toonen* without alienating the more culturally conservative states parties to the ICCPR? The most prudent approach the Committee could take would be to issue a narrow ruling focused on the discriminatory nature of New Zealand's marriage laws in light of the significant *de facto* legal protections already provided to lesbian and gay couples in New Zealand.

Specifically, the Committee should find that New Zealand has violated only the ICCPR's non-discrimination provisions without deciding the remaining legal claims alleged by the petitioners.[18] Such a decision defers to future cases more difficult and controversial issues such as comprehensive definitions of the terms "family" and "marriage" in the ICCPR. And it implicitly grants to other states parties some leeway to choose the pace at which they afford legal protection to same-sex relationships.

There are at least three advantages to this narrow approach. Consider first the persuasiveness to a hostile audience of a decision focusing on the anomalous

[15] See Universal Declaration of Human Rights, article 16(3), ICCPR, Art. 23(1) ("The family is the natural and fundamental group unit of society and is entitled to protection by society and the State."); UDHR, Art. 16(1), ICCPR, Art. 23(2), European Convention on Human Rights, Art. 12 ("men and women" have the right "to marry and to found a family").

[16] See K Walker, "Capitalism, Gay Identity and International Human Rights Law", (2000) 9 *Australasian Gay and Lesbian Law Journal* 58.

[17] See, e.g., *X, Y and Z* v. *United Kingdom* (1997) 4 European Human Rights Reports 143, paras. 35, 37.

[18] The petitioners in *Joslin* have alleged violations of the following ICCPR articles: Art. 26 (guaranteeing the right to "the equal protection of the law" and prohibiting discrimination on the grounds of, *inter alia*, "sex" and "other status", which arguably includes sexual orientation); Art. 16 (guaranteeing "the right to recognition everywhere as a person before the law"); Art. 17 (prohibiting arbitrary or unlawful interference with privacy and family); and Art. 23(1) and 23(2) (obligating states to protect the family and to recognise the "right of men and women of marriageable age to marry and to found a family"). The petitioners have also alleged violations of Arts. 17 and 23 together with Art. 2(1), which requires each treaty party to "respect and ensure" the other rights recognised in the Covenant without discrimination, *inter alia*, on the grounds of "sex" and "other status". For each of their discrimination claims, the petitioners allege that New Zealand's marriage laws discriminate against same-sex couples on the basis of sex and sexual orientation. They rely in part on *Toonen*, in which the Committee expressed the view that the word "sex" in Art. 2(1) "is to be taken as including sexual orientation". *Toonen*, *supra* n.6, para. 8.7.

legal situation facing same-sex couples in New Zealand. Although lesbian and gay couples are denied the right to marry, other national laws and court decisions already provide significant recognition of same-sex relationships and undermine procreation-based arguments against gay marriage. For example: (a) New Zealand immigration policies permit the long-term same-sex partner of a national or permanent resident to be admitted into the country; (b) a variety of statutes, including the Domestic Violence Act 1995 and Accident Insurance Act 1998, protect the rights of same-sex couples; (c) artificial insemination is available to lesbian couples; (d) in February 1999, a New Zealand High Court judge ordered a lesbian to pay child support to her former partner; (e) in 1995, the High Court issued a ruling permitting a transsexual woman, who was born male but had undergone gender reassignment surgery to become female, to marry a man; and finally, (f) the New Zealand Human Rights Commission has stated that excluding same-sex couples from public benefits and services is unlawful under the Human Rights Act 1993.[19]

Yet even these steps toward legal recognition of same-sex couples are inadequate, many government officials acknowledge.[20] Seen from this perspective, New Zealand has already recognised in principle that same-sex couples are near equivalents to married heterosexuals and that further changes in the law are necessary.[21] It is but a short and logical step to a conclusion that New Zealand, given the extent to which its laws have evolved, has engaged in discrimination by denying formal legal recognition to same-sex unions.[22]

A second virtue of a narrow ruling is that it comports with the Committee's existing jurisprudence on marriage and family rights. In its 1990 general comment, the Committee stated that, because "the concept of the family may differ in some respects from State to State", it was "not possible" to give a "standard definition" of what a family is for all treaty parties.[23] The Committee invited states to submit information "on how the concept and scope of the family is construed or defined in their own society and legal system". And it stressed that "when a group of persons is regarded as a family under the legislation and practice of a State, it must be given the protection referred to in Article 23"—which

[19] These legal developments are documented in the *Joslin* petition and in the *Consistency 2000 Project Report*, *supra* n.11.

[20] For example, the New Zealand Human Rights Commission recently concluded that same-sex couples continue to experience discrimination precisely because they are excluded from statutory benefits conferred only on couples defined as married under New Zealand law. *Ibid.*, at s. 9.10.

[21] Ministry of Justice, *Discussion Paper: Same-Sex Couples and the Law* (Aug. 1999), http://www.justice.govt.nz/pubs/reports/1999/same_sex/index.html (summarising ways in which same-sex couples are treated differently from married and cohabiting opposite-sex couples).

[22] The petitioners in *Joslin* have emphasised this point. They argue that their legal claims should be considered in the light of conditions prevailing in New Zealand, and should not be seen as prescribing marriage rules for other states parties to the ICCPR. See *Joslin* Communication, *supra* n.3, at para. VI(1)(vi)(b). As I note above, however, the Committee's interpretive function may make it difficult to adopt a ruling limited to New Zealand, unless the Committee restricts its analysis to the Covenant's non-discrimination clauses.

[23] General Comment 19/39 of 24 June 1990 on Marriage and Family.

includes the right to marry. These statements suggest that the Committee will grant states some discretion to shape family definitions to fit the evolving needs of their societies, but will limit that discretion to bar discriminatory distinctions among similarly situated groups.

A third benefit of the approach I suggest is that it avoids the danger of privileging a particular model of lesbian and gay relationships. As several other contributors to this book have noted, one potentially problematic aspect of current rights claims surrounding same-sex marriage is the way in which they can constrain lesbians and gay men to conform to identities that mirror idealised heterosexual relationships. This trend is apparent in the *Joslin* case. Consider the following description of two of the petitioners:

> "Juliet Joslin and Jennifer Rowan have been in a lesbian relationship since January 1988. . . . Since commencing their relationship, both [women] have jointly assumed full responsibility for the support and care of all [five] children [conceived during previous marriages to men]. . . . In addition . . . they have pooled their respective finances, operating a joint banking account out of which have come mortgage payments, all household expenses, and all educational, care and support expenses for the children. Their current home is owned jointly . . . in equal shares. There is a joint mortgage over the home. They maintain sexual relations".[24]

This description presents the relationship of these two women as exemplars of fidelity, longevity, equality, and financial interdependence. There is nothing wrong with an advocacy strategy which frames their union in this way, to emphasise the irrationality of denying them the benefits and burdens of marriage. There *is* a danger, however, that the Committee could use this sympathetic narrative framing to exclude less idealised same-sex (and heterosexual) relationships from international protection.

For example, the Committee might adopt a ruling that applies to all signatories of the ICCPR, but that conditions international recognition of same-sex relationships on indicia of committedness similar to those demonstrated by these two petitioners. In effect, the Committee could, conscious of the need to justify a controversial decision to a potentially hostile audience of conservative states, signal that recognition of same-sex marriages is required *only* if the individuals involved can show a level of commitment that even many heterosexual couples cannot satisfy.[25] By contrast, a ruling principally affecting governments

[24] *Joslin* Communication, *supra* n.3, at para. IV(1).

[25] Arguably, the Committee could avoid this problem by issuing a decision that requires New Zealand simply to grant same-sex couples access to marriage on whatever terms apply to heterosexual couples. If the Committee were to adopt this approach, then same-sex couples need only go through a valid marriage ceremony under New Zealand law and need show no indicia of committedness at all. Such a ruling would place same-sex couples on an equal footing with opposite-sex couples, but allow states discretion to alter the qualifications for marriage applicable to *all* unions.

It is also possible, however, that the Committee could conflate the issue of (1) using indicia of committedness to prove that lesbian and gay couples are similarly situated to heterosexual couples for purposes of granting them access to the institution of marriage as an initial matter, with (2) using indicia of committedness as a condition of awarding a marriage license to a particular same-sex

that have already granted some legal protections to same-sex couples will allow the Committee to preserve its authority for future cases, in which states seek to impose unrealistic and inflexible standards for recognising same-sex unions.

There is, of course, an obvious objection to the proposal I have just advanced. By tailoring the obligation to recognise same-sex marriages to the evolution of legal developments within a particular nation state, it could be argued that states seeking to avoid any legal recognition of lesbian and gay relationships can do so simply by choosing never to undertake the initial steps in the law reform process.

Perhaps this is true in the short term. But a combination of national law advocacy and international litigation will, I believe, eventually create the conditions necessary for the formation of lesbian and gay civil societies within different nations that can then advocate for more extensive legal reforms. Kees Waaldijk has documented the sequence of legislative steps that governments in Europe and elsewhere have followed in the legal recognition of homosexuality.[26] Registered partnerships and same-sex marriage laws are the last stage in that sequence, and many nations of the world have not even taken the first step—repeal of consensual sodomy laws.

I might add to this continuum two additional steps. First, a step that precedes any gay or lesbian-specific law reforms, namely, a commitment by government officials to the core elements of the rule of law and the protection of individual rights. And second, the application of laws of general application, such as those protecting freedom of expression and association, to lesbians and gay men.

Both of these events create the conditions for safer public manifestations of non-traditional sexualities and interest-group advocacy. Significantly, it is in both of these areas that international human rights tribunals and review bodies can play a regular and important role by holding governments, on a case-by-case basis, to the commitments they made when ratifying human rights treaties. Thus, lesbian and gay rights advocates can expect international jurists to intercede in their favor in cases of gross human rights abuses (such as extra-judicial killings of or state-sponsored violence against sexual minorities), and in cases involving violations of clearly recognised civil and political rights (such as bans on lesbian or gay publications, associations, meetings or parades). Unlike same-sex marriage cases, decisions on these issues are more likely to be heeded by national governments, particularly those who have complied with international decisions in the past. At a minimum, such cases create sites for advocacy interventions that will attract broad-based international attention and support.

couple. Although this conflation fails to respect the principle of equality, it may be more politically palatable than a decision that denies member states any discretion to treat both groups as anything other than entirely equal.

[26] See Waaldijk, chap. 23.

CONCLUSION

The most effective and lasting legal advances for lesbians and gay men will be achieved, not by adopting an aggressive international litigation strategy imposing human rights norms from above, but rather by a selective use of international litigation together with non-litigation approaches and active domestic advocacy of sexual orientation issues. Advocates must remember that lesbians and gay men are only very recent claimants within human rights systems outside of Europe. As a result, international human rights litigation is most likely to succeed once advocates have laid sufficient groundwork, both through consensus-building and political advocacy at the national level, and through monitoring and fact-finding efforts that raise the visibility of lesbian and gay human rights issues internationally. Advocates should not, therefore, place too much weight on the UNHRC's decision in the *Joslin* case, even if, as I hope, the lesbian couples do win the right to marry under New Zealand law.

42

United Nations Human Rights Law and Same-Sex Relationships: Where to from Here?

KRISTEN L WALKER*

INTRODUCTION

SAME-SEX RELATIONSHIPS HAVE to date received little attention in the United Nations human rights system. That will change when the UN Human Rights Committee considers the communication under the First Optional Protocol to the International Covenant on Civil and Political Rights (ICCPR) concerning New Zealand's refusal to allow same-sex marriage,[1] although the outcome of that case is by no means clear. In this chapter, however, I wish to direct our attention to aspects of the UN human rights system other than the ICCPR: the International Covenant on Economic, Social and Cultural Rights (ICESCR), the Convention on the Elimination of All Forms of Discrimination Against Women ("the Women's Convention") and the Convention on the Rights of the Child ("the Children's Convention").[2] These instruments are, I argue, overlooked in arguments about the impact of international human rights law on the recognition of same-sex relationships.

The ICCPR lends itself to a fairly straightforward argument around relationship recognition, which proceeds as follows. Article 23(2) of the ICCPR recognises "the right of men and women of marriageable age to marry and to found a family". Article 26 provides that states shall not discriminate on the basis of, *inter alia*, "sex" or "other status", and Article 2(1) provides for non-discrimination in the application of the rights protected by the ICCPR. In the *Toonen* case, the Human Rights Committee held that "sex" in Articles 26 and 2(1) includes

* LLB (Hons), BSc, LLM (Melbourne), LLM (Columbia). Senior Lecturer in Law, University of Melbourne; Adjunct Professor, Columbia Law School (1998–2000). I would like to thank Alice Miller and Miranda Stewart for their invaluable insights into this project; all errors remain, of course, my own.

[1] See Christie, chap. 15; Helfer, chap. 41.

[2] One could also include the International Labour Organisation Conventions, but for reasons of space I will not address those here.

sexual orientation;[3] even if this is controversial, it is strongly arguable that "other status" includes sexual orientation.[4] On this basis, a state may not deny the right to marry based on someone's sex or sexual orientation; denial of same-sex marriage violates the ICCPR. Further, to the extent that a state recognises unmarried heterosexual relationships, it must also recognise unmarried same-sex relationships, again on the basis of equality.

The focus of this argument is on achieving equality of treatment: gay men and lesbians ought to be permitted access to the same state privileges granted to heterosexuals. I suggest, however, that this argument is problematic, as it fails to unpack and analyse the various functions marriage performs in society, and the different kinds of state structures that support these functions, some of which we should be fighting for and some of which we should not. As an alternative, I suggest that we look to human rights instruments other than the ICCPR (though we need not abandon the ICCPR). My use of these treaties is in part informed by my view that same-sex marriage is not something we should be seeking, whether through national or international human rights law.

My argument is structured as follows. First, I will outline some of the functions of marriage and the ways that states support these functions. I give examples from Australia and a range of other countries, however a full survey is beyond the scope of this chapter. Second, I will briefly outline some of the reasons why pursuing the right to marry at the international (or national) level is problematic. Third, I will offer an alternative way to think about relationship recognition. Fourth, I will link this alternative back to the UN human rights system, focusing on the ICESCR, the Women's Convention and the Children's Convention.

THE FUNCTIONS OF MARRIAGE AND FAMILY

"Marriage" and "the family" are social institutions that perform a variety of functions in society. They are regulated and constructed both legally and socially, in particular through religion. It is unhelpful to simply address questions of same-sex marriage, family and relationship recognition, without first considering what functions those institutions perform in society, and which of those functions ought to be supported by the state. This functional analysis is not intended to reify marriage as some essential, unchanging institution. In addition to performing the functions outlined below, marriage is also a discursive category that influences our ideas about relationships and what they can be and mean. I return to this in my critique of marriage below.

[3] *Toonen* v. *Australia*, (Communication No. 488/1992) (31 March 1994) 1 International Human Rights Reports 97 (United Nations Human Rights Committee). See also E Heinze, *Sexual Orientation: A Human Right* (Dordrecht, Martinus Nijhoff, 1995) at 216–220.

[4] See Heinze, *ibid.*, at 215–6, 224–5; L Helfer, "Finding a Consensus on Equality: The Homosexual Age of Consent and the European Convention on Human Rights", (1990) 65 *New York University Law Review* 1044 at 1089.

Of course, the particular forms of marriage and family relationships, and the norms that govern them, vary from society to society. However, at least some common functions may be identified. These include:

Regulation of sexual behaviour: marriage must (at least in theory) be for an indefinite period,[5] heterosexual[6] and—in most, but not all countries—between two people.[7] In many societies, transgression of these rules constitutes a crime,[8] or at least a basis for divorce.[9]

Regulation of women: Marriage has traditionally been, and still is in many societies, a way to continue male control over women's behaviour, sexual and otherwise.[10] This occurs through violence and economic coercion, as well as through social norms.

[5] Marriage for a defined term is generally not permitted in Western societies. See, eg, Australia, Marriage Act 1961 (federal), s. 46. Nor is it permitted in many non-Western societies, such as Algeria. It is permitted in Iran. See N M Mahieddin, "Marriage: Its Formation and Effects in Algerian Substantive Law" in A Bainham (ed), *The International Survey of Family Law 1994* (The Hague, Martinus Nijhoff, 1994) at 6.

[6] As of August 2001, same-sex marriage is permitted only in the Netherlands (see Waaldijk, chap. 23). In various European countries relationship recognition through a system of registered partnerships has been created exclusively or primarily for same-sex couples. See, eg, Lund-Andersen, chap. 21; Ytterberg, chap. 22; Waaldijk, chap. 23. Such registration systems are often (though in my view mistakenly) referred to as systems for "civil marriage".

[7] In most countries, marriage must be between two people. See eg Australia, Marriage Act 1961 (federal), ss. 23, 23B; I Zhilinkova, "The Marriage Relationship in Ukraine" in Bainham, *supra* n.5, at 468. In some non-Western societies, polygamous marriage, where a man may take more than one wife (polygyny) is permitted. In Algeria, a man may have up to four wives under certain circumstances, but monogamy is the norm. See Mahieddin, *supra* n.5, at 16. Polygyny is also permitted under some Australian Aboriginal customary laws, but such relationships are not recognised as legal marriages by the Australian legal system. See P Parkinson, "Multiculturalism and the Regulation of Marital Status in Australia" in N Lowe & G Douglas (eds), *Families Across Frontiers* (The Hague, Martinus Nijhoff, 1996) at 312.

[8] For example, adultery is illegal in many US states and in Iran (where the penalty may include death by stoning). See M Siegel, "For Better or Worse: Adultery, Crime and the Constitution", (1991/92) 30 *Family Law Journal* 45 at 50, especially n.36; K Miller, "The Human Rights of Women in Iran: The Universalist Approach and the Relativist Response" (1996) 10 *Emory Law Journal* 779 at 794. Bigamy is also illegal in countries adhering to the monogamy requirement. See Australia, Marriage Act 1961 (federal), s. 94 (up to five years in prison for bigamy); A Michaels, "Constitutional Innocence", (1999) 112 *Harvard Law Review* 828 at 835, 953–4 (US position on bigamy).

[9] For example, in the US and India, adultery is a basis for divorce: see J Biondi, "Who Pays for Guilt? Recent Fault-Based Divorce Reform Proposals, Cultural Stereotypes and Economic Consequences", (1999) 90 *Boston College Law Review* 611; S Garg, "Law and Religion: The Divorce Systems of India", (1998) 6 *Tulsa Journal of Comparative and International Law* 1 at 11, 17. Bigamous marriages are usually considered void. See eg Australia, Marriage Act 1961 (federal), ss. 23, 23B.

[10] S Moller Okin has argued that, in the United States, marriage is "the pivot of a societal system that renders women vulnerable to dependency, exploitation and abuse". See S Moller Okin, *Justice, Gender and the Family* (New York, Basic Books, 1989), chap. 7. In Algeria, the Family Code provides that the wife must "obey her husband". See Mahieddin, *supra* n.5, at 24. In the UK, it was only in 1992 that the House of Lords held that a man could be convicted of raping his wife. See *R* v. *R* [1992] 1 AC 599. In the African context, "one school of thought regards African customary [family] law as a patriarchal, male dominated system which is highly discriminatory towards women and incompatible with human rights". J de Koker, "African Customary Family Law in South Africa: A Legacy of Many Pasts" in Eekelaar & Nhlapo (eds.), *The Changing Family* (Oxford, Hart Publishing, 1998), at 321.

Care of children: in most societies, though by no means all, care of children occurs within the biological family. Day-to-day care of children is often the responsibility of the mother, or of extended family members, usually women. As Davina Cooper noted in chapter 4, this involves the privatisation of care.

Care of other dependents: in addition to the care of children, caring for elderly parents or sick or disabled family members is also often privatised within families.

Nurturing of family members: physical and emotional intimacy and support between family members occurs within many families, although it must be noted that this ideal is not realised for many women and children in many families.[11]

Sharing of economic resources: families provide a way to pool economic resources and to share economic costs. However, it is often assumed that *all* families operate in this way, in spite of recent work that shows that such intrafamily sharing is often incomplete or absent.[12]

Joining of extended families: in many societies, marriage signifies the social joining of two previously unrelated families. This may have political, legal, economic and social consequences for those involved.

Of course, many of these functions are performed by relationships other than marriage, too, such as unmarried cohabitation, friendship and kinship networks. But this does not negate the fact that marriage and extended family structures offer a clear, socially accepted way to fulfil these functions within society. In many circumstances, they also offer a way to privatise functions that the state might otherwise need to perform, such as care of elderly, young, sick or unemployed individuals.

The state provides support for these functions through rules of recognition and the provision of a variety of benefits. These benefits are numerous and vary from state to state, thus it is impossible to list them exhaustively. However, for the purposes of my argument, I have divided them into the following categories

The basic rule of recognition: the state recognises only some relationships between individuals. Primary among these is marriage. Broader family relationships are also recognised for some purposes, extending to children, parents grandparents, cousins and so on—the common feature being a biological relationship or legal adoption. The rules of recognition privilege these relationships in a symbolic manner as well as in more tangible ways (outlined below).

Financial benefits for couples: States offer a variety of financial benefits to recognised sexual relationships (usually married couples, but sometimes also unmarried heterosexual couples). These may include tax benefits,[13] survivor pensio

[11] The Canadian Supreme Court has noted that "the family is often a very dangerous place fo children". *B(R)* v. *Children's Aid Society*, [1995] 1 SCR 315, para. 219.

[12] See, eg, P Blumstein & P Schwartz, *American Couples* (New York, Morrow, 1983); Jan Pah *Money and Marriage* (Basingstoke, Macmillan, 1989).

[13] In the US, a married couple is treated as a tax unit; that is, married couples are taxed jointl instead of each individual being taxed separately. This has offered a financial advantage to marri

benefits,[14] and automatic inheritance rights on intestacy (or the right to challenge an inadequate will).[15]

Non-financial benefits for couples: The state offers various non-financial benefits to recognised sexual relationships (usually married couples, but sometimes also unmarried heterosexual couples). These may include preferential immigration rights for a partner, and the facilitation of recognition by non-state actors (eg employers and hospitals, especially where the partner is unable to consent to medical treatment).

Financial benefits for those caring for children: These may include provision of child care,[16] paid maternity or parental leave,[17] tax benefits,[18] or direct cash payments.[19]

Non-financial recognition of relationships involving children: for example, provision of child care, child custody and visitation arrangements,[20] adoption[21] and access to reproductive technologies.[22]

couples where one spouse earns no income, or where the spouses earn significantly different incomes; it has also resulted in what is known as the "marriage penalty" for couples who each earn a similar amount of income. See Federal Public Law No. 107–16, Title III (2001); E McCaffery, *Taxing Women* (Chicago, University of Chicago Press, 1997) at 16–21, 25–26; Hugh Ault, *Comparative Income Taxation* (The Hague, Kluwer Law International, 1997) at 270–272. Germany also permits joint tax filing by married couples. See Ault, *supra*, at 272–273. In many countries, husband and wife can transfer property to each other free of income, estate and gift taxes; on divorce, property transfers and some support arrangements may be tax-free, or the tax treatment can be negotiated between the spouses. And employer fringe benefits for spouses of employees, such as health insurance, are often tax exempt. See P Cain, "Same-Sex Couples and the Federal Tax Laws" (1991) 1 *Law and Sexuality* 64 at 98–99.

14 See, eg, Lind, chap. 13; Millbank & Morgan, chap. 14; Casswell, chap. 11.

15 See J Millbank, "If Australian Law Opened Its Eyes to Lesbian and Gay Families, What Would It See?", (1998) 12 *Australian Journal of Family Law* 99 at 108–11.

16 In France, free public nursery schools are provided for children aged two to six; before and after school hours care and creches for children under three are subsidised. See B Bergman, "Government Support for Families with Children in the United States and France", (1997) 3 *Feminist Economics* 85 at 87.

17 In France, the government provides paid maternity leave for mothers. See Bergman, *ibid.*, at 88.

18 In the US, a special "head of household" rate schedule (midway between the individual and married schedules) and other tax benefits were introduced for an unmarried person living with a dependant or a child. See B Bittker, "Federal Income Taxation and the Family" (1975) 27 *Stanford Law Review* 1389 at 1391, 1417; A Alstott, "The Earned Income Tax Credit and the Limitations of Tax-Based Welfare Reform" (1995) 108 *Harvard Law Review* 533.

19 In the US, examples are the food stamps and Temporary Assistance to Needy Families programmes. See J Nice & L Trubek, *Cases and Materials on Poverty Law: Theory and Practice* (St Paul, West Publishing, 1997) at 94, 624–8. In France, family allowances are provided for families on an income-tested basis. See Bergman, *supra* n.16, at 89.

20 These arrangements are rarely extended to non-biological parents, but some US courts have begun to grant rights to a biological mother's same-sex partner. See Polikoff, chap. 8; K Markey, "An Overview of the Legal Challenges Faced by Gay and Lesbian Parents", (1998) 14 *New York Law School Journal of Human Rights* 721 at 750–3; Millbank, *supra* n.15, at 125–6.

21 See, eg, Polikoff, chap. 8; Millbank & Morgan, chap. 14; Casswell, chap. 11.

22 Assisted reproduction is often restricted to married couples or, sometimes, to heterosexual couples, to the exclusion of lesbians or single women. See L A Minot, *Conceiving Parenthood* (International Gay & Lesbian Human Rights Commission, San Francisco, 2000), at 134–9. Once a child is born to a married couple via assisted reproduction, it is generally recognised as the child of the couple, notwithstanding any donated sperm or ova, or the use of a surrogate mother. Thus, the

As Janet Halley observed in chapter 5, the state also imposes burdens (or responsibilities) on recognised relationships, primarily on separation. One such burden is the difficulty of terminating a marriage (or other biological family relationships) in many states. Once a marriage is terminated, marital responsibilities are often ongoing, involving child support and/or spousal support.

An equality-based approach to same-sex relationship recognition challenges only the heterosexual restriction in this scheme, by seeking entry into the system. It does not address the question of whether these various functions and benefits of marriage and family are just. Pursuing a right to equality focuses solely on getting the same rights as others; it does not challenge the status quo or consider broader questions of justice and ordering of society.

A CRITIQUE OF THE MARRIAGE STRATEGY

In this section I briefly outline some of the arguments against pursuing same-sex marriage, building on rather than repeating the various critiques of marriage offered earlier in the book, especially by Davina Cooper and Janet Halley.

First, seeking same-sex marriage is a fundamentally conservative strategy. Seeking marriage seeks entry to a system of privileges for those who conform to a particular model (apart from the sex of their partner). This does not broaden our approach to relationship recognition. Furthermore, marriage has a normalising effect—that is, it operates as an "optimum towards which one must move" to use Foucault's words.[23] This leaves little space for the negotiation or invention of alternative forms of relationship. And those who do not marry may have their relationships downgraded in status and significance.

Second, seeking entry into marriage or family does not challenge the economic status quo. Presently, the state confers economic benefits on certain members of society, those who conform to the required model, to the exclusion of others. We need to address the question of whether the current redistributive consequences of marriage and relationship recognition are appropriate, rather than simply accept those consequences.

Third, the current push for same-sex marriage is culturally biased towards a Western model of relationship recognition. In particular, this model is couple based and does not recognise extended family or other kinship structures.[24] T

husband (or unmarried male partner) of a woman who receives donated sperm is recognised in law as the child's father, but the female-to-male transsexual partner or the non-transsexual female partner is not. See UK, Human Fertilisation and Embryology Act 1990, section 28; Whittle, chap. 3 C Lind, "Fatherhood and the Unmarried Infertile Man" (1997) 147 *New Law Journal* 196; N Elste "Who Is the Parent in Cloning?" (1999) 27 *Hofstra Law Review* 533 at 538.

[23] M Foucault, *Discipline and Punish* (New York, Vintage Books, 1995), at 182–3. See als M Fineman, "Our Sacred Institutions: The Ideal of the Family in American Law and Society", [199 *Utah Law Review* 387.

[24] See, eg, P Letuka & A Armstrong, "Which Law? Which Family? Which Women?" in Lowe & Douglas, *supra* n.7, at 212; B Atkin & G Austin, "Cross-Cultural Challenges to Family Law Aotearoa" in Lowe & Douglas, *supra*, at 332.

use Carl Stychin's words, there is a danger of "colonisation by an Anglo-American model".[25]

Fourth, feminist scholars have exposed the institution of marriage as thoroughly gendered and a place where many women and children experience violence and oppression.[26] In many societies, men and women play different and unequal roles within marriage. The gendered nature of marriage is often overlooked by those seeking same-sex marriage; or, if it is addressed, proponents of same-sex marriage assert that same-sex marriage will break down the gendered nature of the institution.[27] Yet it is by no means clear that simply seeking entry into an institution, without taking other concrete steps to alter its nature, can fundamentally alter the nature of the institution.[28] Further, seeking a right to same-sex marriage ignores other problematic aspects of marriage in many societies, such as child marriages,[29] involuntary marriage,[30] difficulty or impossibility of divorce[31] and severe punishment of adultery.[32] Supporting marriage at the international level thus shores up support for a problematic and oppressive institution.

Fifth, arguments for same-sex marriage often ignore the class effects of marriage. In many societies, where marriage offers financial benefits many (though not all) of these benefits accrue to wealthier, middle-class couples who own property, have jobs with spousal benefits, have access to other benefits such as private health insurance or retirement benefits, or have one income earner and

[25] C Stychin, *A Nation by Rights: National Cultures, Sexual Identity Politics, and the Discourse of Rights* (Philadelphia, Temple University Press, 1998) at 196.

[26] See R Bailey-Harris, "Equality or Inequality Within the Family? Ideology, Reality and the Law's Response" in Eekelaar & Nhlapo, *supra* n.10, at 251; Moller Okin, *supra* n.10; C Tinker & S Pimentel, "Violence in the Family: Human Rights, Criminal Law and the New Constitution in Brazil" in B Stark (ed), *Family Law and Gender Bias: Comparative Perspectives* (Greenwich, JAI Press, 1992) at 85.

[27] T Stoddard, "Why Gay People Should Seek the Right to Marry" in S Sherman (ed), *Lesbian and Gay Marriage: Private Commitments, Public Ceremonies* (Philadephia, Temple University Press, 1992) at 18–19; N Hunter, "Law and Gender: A Feminist Inquiry", (1991) 1 *Law and Sexuality* 9 at 18–19.

[28] See, eg, N Polikoff, "We Will Get What We Ask For: Why Legalizing Gay and Lesbian Marriage Will Not 'dismantle the legal structure of gender in every marriage'", (1993) 79 *Virginia Law Review* 1535; P Ettelbrick, "Since When Is Marriage a Path to Liberation?" in Sherman, *ibid.*, at 20.

[29] Over thirty countries permit marriage of children under fifteen, including the US. See L Askari, "The Convention on the Rights of the Child: The Necessity of Adding a Provision to Ban Child Marriage", (1998) *ILSA Journal of Comparative and International Law* 123 at 125.

[30] See, eg, A Macklin, "Cross-Border Shopping for Ideas: A Critical Review of US, Canadian and Australian Approaches to Gender-Related Asylum Claims", (1998) 13 *Georgetown Immigration Law Journal* 25 at 39, 44; J Chuang, "Redirecting the Debate Over Trafficking in Women: Definitions, Paradigms and Contexts", (1998) 11 *Harvard Human Rights Journal* 65.

[31] In Malta, divorce is not possible (although foreign divorces are recognised). See R Farrugia, "The Impact of CEDAW and the Aftermath" in Bainham, *supra* n.5, at 329, 333. The institution of the "*get*" in Jewish law makes divorce difficult for many Jewish women, in whatever jurisdiction they may reside. See M Freeman, "Law, Religion and the State: The *Get* Revisited" in Lowe and Douglas, *supra* n.7, at 361.

[32] See *supra* n.8.

one breadwinner.[33] This can be contrasted with the effects of marriage on low income earners and people on welfare, who will not gain from changes to tax, inheritance and property laws, and whose financial position may be negatively affected by relationship recognition.

AN ALTERNATIVE APPROACH TO RELATIONSHIP RECOGNITION

I argue that we need to examine the functions of marriage and family and the ways in which the state supports those functions, outlined above, and seek only some of these for same-sex relationships. In particular, we should challenge marriage because of its function as a mechanism for the regulation of sexuality. More concretely, of the benefits provided by the state for recognised relationships, I argue that our strategy should be to proceed as follows.

First, we should seek to remove public financial preferences for certain forms of sexual relationships. While these relationships perform important functions within society, it is not clear to me why the state should offer financial support for only some sexual relationships and not others. Our choice of sexual partner(s) should not be something for which we are financially rewarded, particularly when there are many more deserving claims on the public purse.

However, the state should provide financial and material support for relationships of care and dependence. Here I include parents or other adults caring for children, those caring for older people, those caring for sick people (this is especially relevant with respect to AIDS and caring relationships between lovers and friends), and those caring for people with disabilities. These are relationships that need support and thus ought to be afforded special protection and benefits. As Martha Fineman has argued, taking care of someone is work, represents a major contribution to the society, and should be explicitly recognised as such.[34] We are all dependent at some point in our lives, thus state support for caring does not value some people's choices over others. Further, it recognise the importance to society of caring for those who cannot care for themselves.

Although I argue against the provision of financial benefits to particular sexual relationships, I do not argue against all forms of relationship recognition. We should seek state recognition of people's intimate and important relationships (of whatever form) in non-financial areas, such as medical visitation and care, care and custody of children, employers' recognition of employees' relationships for compassionate leave, and for immigration purposes. However this recognition should be based, not on a state assumption of the appropriat form of relationship, but on the individual's decision as to the importance of the relationship.

[33] See McCaffery, *supra* n.13.

[34] M Fineman, "The Nature of Dependencies and Welfare 'Reform' ", (1996) 36 *Santa Clara La Review* 287 at 305, 308.

Finally, I argue that, at a broader level, we should seek changes to the economic conditions that make it so important for gay men and lesbians to seek marriage. For example, we should pursue rights to universal health care, so that access to private health insurance is no longer a crucial issue in our lives (eg in the USA or South Africa). We should pursue rights to social security and unemployment benefits. We should pursue rights to old age pensions, so that access to a private pension fund is no longer a crucial concern. And we need to pursue basic economic rights for those in countries where poverty, not private health insurance and private pension funds, is the main issue. This does not mean that we should abandon the quest for equality; but I argue that the equality argument is too narrow and that we need to fight more generally for social justice, not just for access to systems of privilege.

RELATIONSHIP RECOGNITION AND THE UN HUMAN RIGHTS REGIME

When assessing the potential of international human rights law to advance same-sex relationship recognition, we need to bear in mind the variety of international instruments available. While the ICCPR offers an obvious and accessible route, we ought to look to other international instruments as well in seeking recognition of same-sex relationships whilst avoiding some of the problems outlined above. There are two strategies I advocate here. The first is to use what we have. The second is to seek development of new international law in this area.

Using What We Have

Using what we have may seem like an obvious suggestion; yet to date, there have been no suggestions or strategies involving use of existing UN human rights instruments other than the ICCPR. This may in part be due to the constraining, discursive effect that marriage has on our approach to relationship recognition. In using what we have, however, we need to be careful in our choices. Our practical next step must not foreclose or compromise important principles.

First, although I argue that we ought not to pursue same-sex marriage, we can and should use the notion of "family" in international human rights law. "The family" is already recognised in many international instruments,[35] and this needs to be built upon, reclaimed and reworked so that our understanding of "family" in international law embraces a diversity of models, and does not assume that there is one "natural" form (based on the sexual couple with or

[35] See, eg, Universal Declaration of Human Rights, Art. 16; ICCPR, Art. 23; ICECSR, Art. 10; the Children's Convention, Preamble para 5; European Convention on Human Rights, Art. 12; American Convention on Human Rights, Art. 17; African Charter of Human and People's Rights, Art. 18.

without a child). Our approach here must be flexible enough to include culturally diverse family forms, such as extended families, non-biological and non-sexual family forms.[36] Furthermore, we should not simply focus on same-sex relationships; rather, gay and lesbian lawyers and activists should embrace relationship recognition generally, forging coalitions with other excluded groups, such as unmarried heterosexuals.

Such a reworking of the concept of "the family" will not be easy. But no work around sexuality and international law is easy, as events at the 1995 Fourth World Conference on Women in Beijing indicate.[37] International human rights law provides us with a site of intervention and contestation over meaning and values, and we need to seize this opportunity, rather than simply concede the field or participate only on the limited basis of marriage.

In addition to using existing references to "family" in the ICCPR, we must also consider the provisions of various other rights documents, in particular the ICESCR, the Children's Convention and the Women's Convention. These treaties are under-utilised generally in human rights law, and especially with respect to sexuality, which (as Janet Halley points out in chapter 5) is generally not seen as being about redistributive issues. My argument is that we can use these three instruments to achieve recognition and benefits in certain areas: recognition of diverse family forms; provision of non-financial benefits for important relationships—sexual and non-sexual; and state support for those caring for dependents.

The ICESCR

There are various provisions in the ICESCR that could be used to advance relationship recognition both internationally and domestically:

Article 7 provides for "equal remuneration for work of equal value without distinction of any kind". This provision offers a strong argument for challenging policies and practices that deny benefits to lesbians and gay men that are provided to heterosexual couples. The argument is straightforward: if lesbians and gay men are doing the same work as their heterosexual counterparts, then they should receive the same remuneration, which includes benefits provided to one's spouse. This argument could also be used for broader relationship recognition extending to permit all individuals to select a beneficiary for benefits provided to an employee's spouse or "significant other". After all, if the work is the same there is no reason why a married person or person in a sexual relationship should effectively be paid more than an unmarried or single person.

[36] On the formation of non-biological kinship relationships in gay and lesbian communities, s[ee] K Weston, *Families We Choose: Lesbians, Gays, Kinship* (New York, Columbia University Pres[s] 1991).

[37] See, eg, D Otto, "Holding Up Half the Sky, But for Whose Benefit? A Critical Analysis of t[he] Fourth World Conference on Women", (1996) 6 *Australian Feminist Law Journal* 7.

Article 9 provides for "the right of everyone to social security, including social insurance". Article 11 provides for "the right of everyone to an adequate standard of living for himself and his family, including adequate food, clothing and housing, and to the continuous improvement of living conditions". These provisions should be used to work towards a basic, minimum standard of living so that reliance on access to one's partner's benefits ceases to be crucial.

Article 10 of the ICESCR states that "the widest possible protection and assistance should be accorded to the family, which is the natural and fundamental group unit of society, particularly for its establishment and while it is responsible for the care and education of dependent children". It goes on to provide that "special measures of protection and assistance should be taken on behalf of all children and young persons without any discrimination for reasons of parentage or other conditions". This reverence for "family" must be used cautiously, with appropriate attempts to broaden the definition of family, as discussed above. However, this provision can be usefully used to argue for state financial benefits for those caring for dependent children, whatever their sexuality.

Article 12 provides for "the right of everyone to the enjoyment of the highest attainable standard of physical and mental health" including "the creation of conditions which would assure to all medical service and medical attention in the event of sickness". This provision is of particular relevance to those people living with HIV/AIDS or caring for people with HIV/AIDS. It is also more generally relevant to our community and to other communities, particularly poorer communities without access to private health insurance. We should use this obligation to seek to develop a system of health care accessible to all, so that health is recognised as a right and not something which must be bought.

Finally, Article 2(2) provides for non-discrimination in the enjoyment of these rights. As the UN Human Rights Committee recognised in *Toonen* (in relation to the very similar Article 2(1) of the ICCPR), this provision includes sexual orientation; thus none of the rights protected by the ICESCR may be denied to an individual on the basis of his or her sexuality.

The Children's Convention

The Children's Convention has extensive provisions that are relevant to ecognition of caring for children, rather than to relationship recognition more enerally:

Article 5 provides that "States Parties shall respect the responsibilities, rights nd duties of parents or, where applicable, the members of the extended family r community as provided for by local custom, legal guardians or other persons egally responsible for the child, to provide, in a manner consistent with the volving capacities of the child, appropriate direction and guidance in the exerise by the child of the rights recognised in the present Convention". This proision could be particularly useful in the battle for recognition of alternative family structures, as it expressly goes beyond the narrow, Western concept of family that focuses on two parents and their biological child(ren).

Article 9 provides that "a child shall not be separated from his or her parents against their will, except when competent authorities subject to judicial review determine, in accordance with applicable law and procedures, that such separation is necessary for the best interests of the child". It goes on to state that "States Parties shall respect the right of the child who is separated from one or both parents to maintain personal relations and direct contact with both parents on a regular basis, except if it is contrary to the child's best interests". While the concept of the "best interests of the child" has been used against lesbians and gay men in domestic family law in many countries,[38] Article 9 offers the opportunity to challenge traditional and homophobic approaches to the child's best interests and to seek to preserve gay and lesbian families. Article 16 may be of additional assistance here, providing that "no child shall be subjected to arbitrary or unlawful interference with his or her privacy, family, home or correspondence".

Several articles in the Children's Convention recognise the duty of the State to provide financial and other support for those caring for children. Article 18 provides that States Parties shall render appropriate assistance to parents and legal guardians in the performance of their child-rearing responsibilities and shall ensure the development of institutions, facilities and services for the care of children. Article 23 recognises the "right of the disabled child to special care and shall encourage and ensure the extension, subject to available resources, to the eligible child and those responsible for his or her care, of assistance". Article 26 provides that States Parties shall recognize for every child the right to benefit from social security, including social insurance, and Article 27 provides that States Parties shall "recognize the right of every child to a standard of living adequate for the child's physical, mental, spiritual, moral and social development and . . . shall take appropriate measures to assist parents and others responsible for the child to implement this right and shall in case of need provide material assistance and support programmes". These provisions can be used to argue for a redistribution of state financial benefits to those caring for children.

Finally, just as in the ICESCR, Article 2(1) of the Children's Convention provides for non-discrimination in the enjoyment of these rights; applying *Toonen* this should include discrimination on the basis of sexuality.

[38] In the US and South Africa, the "best interests of the child" standard has been used to deny ga or lesbian parents custody of, and visitation with, their children. See, eg, Markey, *supra* n.20; Lis Pooley, "Heterosexism and Children's Best Interests: Conflicting Concepts in *Nancy S* v. *Michel* G", (1993) 27 *University of San Francisco Law Review* 477; T Mosikatsana, "Children's Rights ar Family Autonomy in the South African Context: A Comment on Children's Rights Under the Fin Constitution", (1998) 3 *Michigan Journal of Law and Race* 341 at 391.

The Women's Convention

Article 5 of the Women's Convention provides that:

> "States Parties shall take all appropriate measures . . . to modify the social and cultural patterns of conduct of men and women, with a view to achieving the elimination of prejudices and customary and all other practices which are based on the idea of the inferiority or the superiority of either of the sexes or on stereotyped roles for men and women".

This offers a general tool to attack state laws, policies and practices that are based on traditional assumptions about male and female behaviour, including the sex of one's partner.[39]

Like the Children's Convention, the Women's Convention is also concerned with care of children. Article 11 provides that states shall "encourage the provision of the necessary supporting social services to enable parents to combine family obligations with work responsibilities and participation in public life, in particular through promoting the establishment and development of a network of child-care facilities". This can be used in combination with provisions of the Children's Convention to seek greater state support for those caring for children.

The ICESCR and the Children's Convention do not yet have the same individual complaints mechanism as the ICCPR, and the Women's Convention only acquired one in late 2000.[40] This may make them seem less attractive as tools for change, but we must also remember that, even with such a complaints mechanism, UN human rights law is not really an enforceable system (and is certainly less enforceable than the European Convention on Human Rights). There is no UN police force, and States do not usually go to war or impose economic sanctions (with UN support or otherwise) over human rights issues such as gender equality and racial equality, except in the face of human rights violations on a massive scale.[41] Nonetheless, UN human rights law remains binding on states, and can be used by activists on the ground to advance their cause in the domestic arena. As Eric Heinze has noted in the context of the ICCPR, UN human rights law has important "political, moral, symbolic and didactic" functions.[42] The ICESCR, the Women's Convention and the Children's Convention can offer us important law and rhetoric for our domestic battles; after all, states parties do have obligations under these treaties, even if they do not all permit us to obtain a pronouncement in a particular case.

[39] See Heinze, *supra* n.3, at 217–8.

[40] An Optional Protocol providing an individual complaints mechanism for CEDAW was adopted by the UN General Assembly on 6 Oct. 1999, and entered into force on 22 Dec. 2000. See http://www. un.org/womenwatch/daw/cedaw/protocol/history.htm.

[41] The international response to apartheid is one example of state action in the face of massive racial discrimination; there is no such example with respect to gender equality.

[42] Heinze, *supra* n.3, at 92–104.

Development of New International Law

None of the Conventions discussed above will give us everything we are seeking. Thus we need to consider the development of new international human rights instruments.[43] This is a task that cannot be undertaken lightly;[44] it will involve much debate, discussion and hard work before a Convention dealing with sexuality or relationship recognition—or both—is even ready for consideration by States. Yet it should not therefore be dismissed. If existing UN human rights law is inadequate to address fundamental issues of equality and justice, then the development of new instruments is appropriate. It is also important if we are to challenge the dominant norms around sexuality and relationships. As Eric Heinze has suggested,[45] this could begin with a "bottom-up" approach—a Beijing-type process that enables participants from diverse states and cultures to participate and consider how best to approach these issues.

CONCLUSION

I have argued that to use the UN human rights system to simply seek inclusion in the existing structures of relationship recognition is inadequate and inappropriate. Rather, we need to use international law to challenge both the economic and social status quo around these issues. This involves using all the UN human rights instruments available to us, including the ICCPR, the ICESCR, the Women's Convention and the Children's Convention. It involves challenging the definition of family in international law, and seeking a redistribution of financial benefits from sexual couples to those caring for dependents. It also involves seeking recognition of non-normative sexual relationships in non-financial areas.

In addition to focusing on relationship recognition, we also need to look more broadly at sexual rights in the international arena. In this regard, some scholars have begun to articulate a right to sexuality[46] or to sexual self-determination.[47] Discussion of this is beyond the scope of this chapter, but suffice it to say that I

[43] For an example of a draft, see E Heinze's "Model Declaration of Rights Against Discrimination on the Basis of Sexual Orientation", *ibid.*, at 289–303. While this draft is, in my view too limited, it provides a useful starting point for discussion.

[44] P Alston, "Conjuring Up New Human Rights: A Proposal for Quality Control", (1984) 7 *American Journal of International Law* 607.

[45] Presentation to the King's College London same-sex partnerships conference, 3 July 1999.

[46] See A Miller, "Human Rights and Sexuality: First Steps Towards Articulating a Right Framework for Claims to Sexual Rights and Freedoms", (1999) *American Society of Internationa Law: Proceedings of the 93rd Annual Meeting* 288.

[47] See K Walker, "Capitalism, Gay Identity and International Human Rights Law", (2000) *Australasian Gay and Lesbian Law Journal* 58.

see relationship recognition and sexual rights as fundamentally connected; if we are to explore and develop one, we must explore and develop the other. Ultimately, however, we need to ensure that any actions around sexuality, relationships and international human rights law recognise the diversity of queer lives around the world.

Conclusion

ROBERT WINTEMUTE*

> "The past provides many instances where the law refused to see a human being when it should have. See, e.g., *Dred Scott*, 60 U.S. [(19 How.) 393] at 407 [(1857)] (concluding that African slaves and their descendants had "no rights which the white man was bound to respect"). . . . The extension of the Common Benefits Clause to acknowledge plaintiffs as Vermonters who seek nothing more, nor less, than legal protection and security for their avowed commitment to an intimate and lasting human relationship is simply, when all is said and done, a recognition of our common humanity". *Baker* v. *State*, 744 A.2d 864 at 889 (Supreme Court of Vermont, 20 December 1999).

WHERE, THEN, do we stand in 2001 with regard to legal recognition of same-sex partnerships? In concluding this book, I will attempt to distill from the preceding forty-two chapters, three introductions and one foreword: (i) the current state of legal recognition of same-sex partnerships throughout the world; (ii) the patterns that can be seen in this recognition; (iii) examples of how "portability of legal recognition" is already becoming an issue; and (iv) the relevance of reforms in "Western", "developed" countries to "non-Western" or "developing" countries. Finally, I will suggest what economic, political, legal and social factors in a particular jurisdiction make reform more likely, and where we can expect to see further reforms over the next five to ten years.

CURRENT STATE OF LEGAL RECOGNITION OF SAME-SEX PARTNERSHIPS

Twenty-three years ago, in 1978, it would appear that not a single legislature (above the level of a city, county or other local government), whether national, federal, state, provincial, regional or cantonal, had passed a law that was intended to extend to same-sex couples a right, benefit or obligation previously only enjoyed by, or imposed on, married or unmarried different-sex couples. The first such law was perhaps the law passed by the Netherlands in 1979

* Reader, School of Law, King's College, University of London.

granting a succession right to the different-sex or same-sex cohabitant of a deceased tenant.[1] By August 2001, the number of jurisdictions with laws effecting reforms of this kind (whether national, federal, state, provincial, regional or cantonal, and whether providing very limited or very extensive recognition) had risen to at least thirty-eight. Tables 1 and 2 (pp. 761–62) illustrate the explosive growth in these laws since 1979, and especially since 1997.

The year indicated is the year the jurisdiction's first law recognising same-sex partnerships was enacted (vs. came into force), even if it was only in one specific area[2] and was later followed by a much more comprehensive reform (e.g., a registered partnerships law; a few subsequent laws have been added in square brackets). Thus, the year for Denmark is 1986 rather than 1989. Table 1 indicates the jurisdictions passing their first laws in each year, while Table 2 is a chart depicting the growth in cumulative recognition. Official citations, and often Internet sources for the text, have been listed in Appendix I to this book, which also details the wide range of terminology these laws employ: "common-law partners", "common law spouses", "*de facto* partners", "*de facto* spouses", "domestic partners", "eligible partners", "life partners", members of or parties to a "civil union" or "community of life" or "confirmed cohabitation" or "*de facto* relationship" or "*de facto* union" or "domestic relationship" or "lasting joint household" or "stable couple" or "stable union", "partners", persons cohabiting "as spouses" or "in a spousal relationship", "reciprocal beneficiaries", "registered partners", "same-sex partners", "spouses", and "statutory cohabitants".

The huge variety of forms that legal recognition has taken, reflected in the diverse vocabulary mentioned above, can be roughly divided into four categories: (1) civil marriage; (2) registered partnership; (3) registered cohabitation; and (4) unregistered cohabitation. These four categories also correspond, even more roughly, to "levels" of recognition: rights and obligations decrease going from (1) to (3) (if not always to (4), which can be similar to (2) in some cases, such as in some provinces of Canada), and the practical and symbolic benefits of the public registration procedures in (1), (2) and (3) disappear at level (4). By "registered partnership", I mean a law that is intended to be a substitute for civil marriage for same-sex couples (or exceptionally an alternative for different-sex couples), providing all or substantially all of the rights and obligations of civil marriage. By "registered cohabitation", I mean a law that is intended to provide a package of rights and obligations that is substantially inferior to civil marriage. By "unregistered cohabitation", I mean laws (or regulations or policies of employers) that grant rights or impose obligations on unmarried couples, different-sex or same-sex, after a minimum period of cohabitation and without requiring any formal registration with a public official or execution of a public deed. Table 3 (pp. 764–65) shows which jurisdictions have provided which lev

[1] Act of 21 June 1979, *Staatsblad* 1979, nr. 330, introducing Art. 1623h of the Civil Code (in force on 1 July 1979). See Waaldijk, chap. 23.

[2] See p. 779, n.3.

els of recognition (some provide more than one), and whether they have been extended to different-sex partners only, to same-sex partners only (or mainly), or to both different-sex and same-sex partners. Within each category, jurisdictions are listed alphabetically, and no attempt has been made to rank them according to the rights and obligations they provide (which vary widely, especially in categories (3) and (4)).

Table 1 – Cumulative Statutory Recognition of Same-Sex Partnerships (Number of Jurisdictions) (Data Table)

Year	Cumulative Total	Total for Year	Jurisdictions
1979	1	1	Netherlands
1986	2	1	Denmark
1987	3	1	Sweden
1989	3	0	[Denmark – registered partnerships]
1992	6	3	British Columbia (Canada), District of Columbia (USA), New Zealand
1993	7	1	Norway (registered partnerships)
1994	9	2	Australian Capital Territory, Spain (national), [Sweden – registered partnerships]
1996	12	3	Hungary, Iceland (registered partnerships), South Africa
1997	13	1	Hawaii (USA), [Netherlands—registered partnerships]
1998	17	4	Austria, Belgium, Catalonia (Spain), Yukon Territory (Canada)
1999	24	7	Aragón (Spain), California, France, New South Wales (Australia), Ontario (Canada), Québec (Canada), Queensland (Australia)
2000	31	7	Canada (federal), Navarra (Spain), New Brunswick (Canada), Newfoundland (Canada), Nova Scotia (Canada), Scotland (UK), Vermont (civil unions) (USA)
2001 (Jan.–Aug.)	38	7	Geneva (Switzerland), Germany, Manitoba (Canada), [Netherlands – civil marriage], Portugal, Saskatchewan (Canada),Valencia (Spain), Victoria (Australia); bills pending in at least 3 jurisdictions

Table 2—Cumulative Statutory Recognition of Same-Sex Partnerships (Number of Jurisdictions) (Chart)

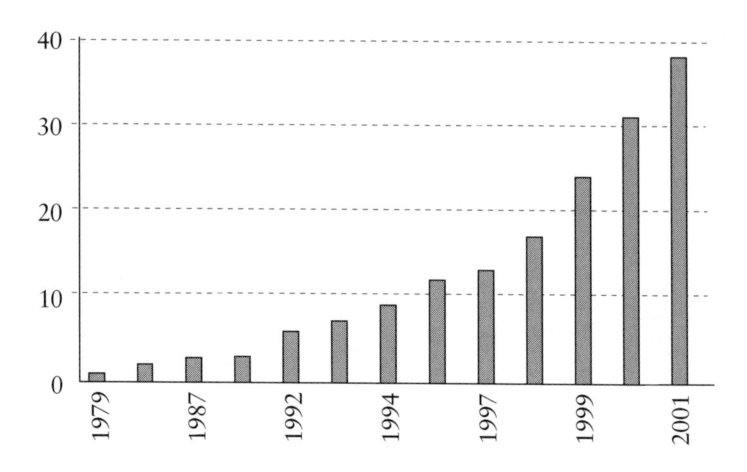

Each law in Table 3 is discussed or mentioned in the relevant chapter of this book. Exceptions are the registered partnership laws in Norway and Iceland,[3] which are very similar to those in Denmark and Sweden, and the "Law of 11 May 2001 adopting measures of protection for *de facto* unions" in Portugal.[4] As of August 2001, bills are pending before the legislatures of Brazil,[5] the Czech Republic,[6] and Finland,[7] and are expected soon in Western Australia and Alberta (Canada).[7a] A bill in Latvia was rejected by a parliamentary committee in 1999.[8]

[3] See App. I. Iceland (like Denmark) permits second-parent adoption, whereas Norway (like Sweden) does not.

[4] *Lei No. 7/2001 de 11 de Maio, Adopta medidas de protecção das uniões de facto*, [2001] 109 (I-A) *Diário da República* 2797, http://www.portugalgay.pt (*Entrar, Espaço Aberto, Política*). The Portuguese law applies to "two persons, regardless of sex, who live in a de facto union for more than two years", and provides for, *inter alia*, certain occupancy or succession rights in relation to a joint residence owned or leased by the deceased partner, spousal benefits for partners of civil servants and certain other employees, and joint taxation. Art. 7 expressly limits joint adoption to "persons of different sexes living in a *de facto* union".

[5] See Turra, chap. 16.

[6] For the background to the current bill, see M Kotisová, "The Czech Republic" in T Greif & A Coman (eds.), *Equality for Lesbians and Gay Men: A Relevant Issue in the EU Accession Process* (Brussels, ILGA-Europe, March 2001), http://www.steff.suite.dk/ee-report.pdf.

[7] See *EuroLetter* http://www.steff.suite.dk/eurolet.htm, No. 85 (Jan. 2001).

[7a] See p. 316, n.90 and p. 265, n.45.

[8] On 30 Nov. 1999, the Human Rights and Public Affairs Commission of the Latvian *Saeima* (Parliament) rejected the bill "On registered partnership between persons of the same gender" submitted by the National Human Rights Office. See J L Lavrikovs, *EuroLetter*, *Ibid.*, No. 74 (Oct. 1999) (text of bill), 77 (Feb. 2000).

PATTERNS IN LEGAL RECOGNITION

In the great diversity of forms of legal recognition discussed in this book, what patterns can be seen?[9] The four common issues faced by all jurisdictions considering the legal recognition of same-sex partnerships are: (A) the *package* of rights and obligations to be provided, and whether the difference between the package and that of civil marriage is to be very large (only a few rights and obligations will be extended to same-sex couples), substantial (a significant number of rights and obligations are withheld), relatively small (only three or four rights or obligations, such as joint adoption of children and access to donor insemination, are withheld), or non-existent (the package is identical to that of civil marriage);[10] (B) whether or not to provide a procedure for *registration* of partnerships, thereby allowing same-sex partners to acquire an official legal status and legal rights and obligations immediately, or instead to require only a minimum period of cohabitation; (C) whether or not to restrict the new legal institution to same-sex couples, or to open it up to *unmarried different-sex couples* as well; and (D) what *name* to attach to the legal institution made available to same-sex couples, i.e., civil marriage or something else. The different responses of jurisdictions to these issues account for the variety of outcomes in Table 3.

Issues (A) and (C) are linked. The closer the package of same-sex partners is to that of married different-sex partners, the more likely it is that any new institution created for same-sex partners (as a substitute for civil marriage) will be closed to unmarried different-sex partners, so that the new institution will not compete with civil marriage. This is the general pattern with registered partnership laws, the Netherlands being the only exception. If there is a substantial difference between the package attached to the new institution and that of civil marriage, so that different-sex couples still have an incentive to marry, they are far more likely to be granted access to the new institution. This is the general pattern with laws on registered cohabitation or unregistered cohabitation.

The current law in Germany (the first part of the reform that could be adopted by the *Bundestag* on its own) appears to be an exception. It provides a package that it is substantially inferior to civil marriage, yet is limited to same-sex partners. It will cease to be an exception if the second part of the reform is

[9] An extended comparison is not possible in a multi-author work like this one. For thorough single-author comparisons, see C Forder, "European Models of Domestic Partnership Laws: The Field of Choice", (2000) 17 *Canadian Journal of Family Law* 371; C Forder, *Transforming Family Relationships* (Dordrecht, NL, Kluwer, forthcoming in 2002); Y Merin, *Equality for Same-Sex Couples: A Comparative Study of the Legal Recognition of Gay Partnerships in Europe and the United States* (Chicago, Univ. of Chicago Press, forthcoming in 2002).

[10] Measuring and comparing the gap between the packages of same-sex partners and married different-sex partners in various jurisdictions can be difficult, both because it is not easy to determine exactly which of hundreds of rights or obligations have been omitted, and because people will disagree about what weight to attach to particular omissions.

Table 3 – Levels of Statutory (or Other) Recognition of Different-Sex and Same-Sex Partnerships

Level of Recognition	Different-Sex Partners Only	Same-Sex Partners Only (or Mainly)	Different-Sex and Same-Sex Partners
(1) Civil Marriage	– all jurisdictions except Netherlands		– Netherlands
(2) Registered Partnership		– Denmark – Iceland – Germany (if *Bundesrat* approves second part of reform) – Norway – Sweden – USA (Vermont)	– Netherlands
(3) Registered Cohabitation		– Germany (first part of reform approved by *Bundestag*) – USA (California, Hawaii) (mainly same-sex)	– Belgium – Canada (Nova Scotia) – France – Spain (Aragón, Catalonia, Navarra, Valencia) – Switzerland (Geneva) – USA (District of Columbia and local domestic partnership laws)
(4) Unregistered Cohabitation (exhamples, not comprehensive)	– Austria (statute challenged before Eur. Ct. H.R. in *Karner* v. *Austria*) – Canada ("spouse" definitions not yet amended after *M.* v. *H.*)	– UK (immigration for partners legally unable to marry) (mainly same-sex) – USA (some public and private sector employers' benefit plans only	– Australia (Australian Capital Territory, New South Wales, Queensland, Victoria) – Canada (federal B.C., Sask., Man.,

Level of Recognition	Different-Sex Partners Only	Same-Sex Partners Only (or Mainly)	Different-Sex and Same-Sex Partners
	– UK ("living as husband and wife" statutes currently interpreted as different-sex only)	recognise same-sex partners and not unmarried different-sex partners of employees)	Ontario, Québec, Nova Scotia) – France (*concubinage*) – Hungary – Netherlands – Portugal – Spain (Navarra) – Sweden

adopted by the *Bundesrat*, because the combination of the two parts will provide a package closer to those of the Nordic and Dutch registered partnership laws than to, e.g., the *pacte civil de solidarité* in France. Other exceptions are laws or policies that require different-sex (but not same-sex) couples either to marry to qualify for the right or benefit, or to show that they have a specified "good reason" for not marrying. Examples include California's domestic partnership legislation (different-sex partners must both be aged sixty-two and eligible for social security benefits, which would be reduced if they married), Hawaii's reciprocal beneficaries legislation (they must be legally unable to marry), the United Kingdom's immigration rules (same as Hawaii), and some public and private sector employers' benefit plans in the USA (they must marry).[11]

Issues (A) and (D) are also linked. The greater the difference between the package of same-sex partners and that of married different-sex partners, the easier it will be to justify attaching a name other than "civil marriage" to the package. As the difference shrinks and eventually disappears (as a result of legislation or equality litigation), it becomes much harder to justify different names for legally identical institutions. The debate then shifts to the realm of symbols. Same-sex couples argue that being admitted to the same institution as different-sex couples is essential for true equality. Without access to civil marriage, they will be stigmatised as inferior. Some heterosexual opponents respond by trivialising the claim: "You have all the rights and obligations. Why do you need the name? It's only a name". Yet, these opponents simultaneously argue that the name has great value to different-sex couples, and would be tarnished

[11] See *Irizarry* v. *Board of Education of City of Chicago*, 251 F.3d 604, http://laws.findlaw.com/7th/003216. html (7th Circuit, 15 May 2001) (Posner, CJ) (upholding as rational under the Equal Protection Clause the exclusion of unmarried different-sex partners from "domestic partner" health insurance benefits).

or degraded, causing them emotional harm, if it had to be shared with same-sex couples. ("It's our institution. Get your own.") At this point, defence of the heterosexual exclusivity of civil marriage begins to sound like an attempt to exclude a racial minority from a private club (or more appropriately here, a public museum), because the place would not be the same if "they" were let in. The Dutch concept of "opening up" marriage to same-sex partners captures very well the idea of civil marriage as a public institution "for heterosexuals only".

Issue (B), registration, contains a tension between a desire for legal certainty (it substitutes a formal act of registration for a case-by-case determination of whether particular relationships qualify as "cohabitation"), and a desire to avoid creating new institutions that resemble civil marriage. Unregistered cohabitation, triggering rights and obligations after a minimum period of cohabitation, has the advantage of addressing the situation of couples who fail, because of a mutual or unilateral decision or mere inertia, to exercise whatever registration options are available to them. Canada, for example, developed an extensive system of recognition of unmarried different-sex cohabitation during the 1970s and 1980s, one rationale being the granting of rights and the imposition of obligations where a woman might suffer from a man's refusal to marry. This system is gradually being extended to same-sex partners.

Two final patterns can be noted. First, jurisdictions seem to choose between "subtraction" and "enumeration" methods of allocating rights and obligations to same-sex couples. The Nordic registered partnership laws specify (more or less) that "registered partners have all the rights and obligations of married different-sex partners, *minus* the following". The Dutch and German laws, and all the registered cohabitation and unregistered cohabitation laws in Table 3, opt for the "enumeration" method. The result in some cases is very long lists, and the risk of unintended omissions when particular rights or obligations are overlooked. The Vermont civil unions law uses both methods, but subtracts nothing from the general statement of equality, and then enumerates for greater certainty.[12]

Second, in every jurisdiction, the question arises whether same-sex couples should seek legislation recognising their relationships if a law prohibiting sexual orientation discrimination in employment, housing, services, etc. has not yet been adopted. In most of the jurisdictions in Table 3, a broad anti-discrimination law had already been passed, or was passed around the same time as the legislation on same-sex partners (see Appendix II). This makes sense, both because equal treatment for same-sex couples tends to be more politically controversial than equal treatment for lesbian, gay and bisexual individuals, and because an individual could be deterred from publicly registering their partnership at the town hall, or asking their employer to recognise it, if they could face discrimination as a result. Arguably there are a few exceptions: the Netherlands, Hungary, Belgium, Germany, Portugal, and Geneva (Switzerland). But in a

[12] See 15 Vermont Statutes Annotated s. 1204, http://www.leg.state.vt.us/docs/2000/acts/act09 htm.

these jurisdictions, the partnership legislation coincided more or less with a breakthrough in anti-discrimination law.[13] Even so, in some countries, many members of the lesbian, gay and bisexual community see anti-discrimination legislation as abstract and difficult to enforce, and registered partnership legislation as responding more concretely and effectively to their practical and emotional needs for legal recognition of their relationships.

PORTABILITY OF LEGAL RECOGNITION

We live in an increasingly mobile and globalising world, in which (subject to immigration laws) couples are more and more likely to relocate voluntarily, or to find that one partner has been transferred by a multi-national corporation or a government to another jurisdiction. Now that some form of legal recognition of same-sex partnerships has been achieved in a significant number of jurisdictions, the question will increasingly arise as to whether other jurisdictions will recognise the legal status granted to the same-sex couple by their home jurisdiction, either voluntarily, or because of a federal, European or international law obligation to do so. This question is beyond the scope of this Conclusion and this book, and will almost certainly be addressed in a few years in a book entitled *Same-Sex Partnerships and Private International Law*.

However, a few recent examples of this problem can be cited. On 31 May 2001, the European Court of Justice (ECJ) decided *D. & Sweden* v. *Council*.[14] The case concerned the refusal by the Council to treat the Swedish same-sex registered partnership of a Council employee as equivalent to a marriage in relation to an employment benefit. After the dismissal of D's annullment action by the Court of First Instance (CFI), both D. and the Swedish government appealed to the ECJ, and the Danish and Dutch governments intervened on the side of D. The ECJ agreed with the CFI and Advocate General Mischo, giving five main reasons for dismissing the appeals.

First, the provision of the European Community (EC) Staff Regulations providing for the payment of a household allowance to a "married official" could not be interpreted as covering an official who had contracted a registered partnership. The ECJ noted that: (a) unregistered same-sex cohabitation (as in *Grant*

[13] The 1979 Dutch legislation on unregistered same-sex cohabitation coincided with the process of adding the "or any other ground whatsoever" category to the equality provision of the Dutch Constitution (see Waaldijk, chap. 23). Hungary's 1996 legislation was required by a 1995 Constitutional Court finding of discrimination violating the 1989 Constitution (see Farkas, chap. 1). Belgium's 1998 legislation followed the 1997 signing of the Treaty of Amsterdam (inserting Art. 3 into the EC Treaty), and Germany and Portugal's 2001 legislation followed the adoption of an employment discrimination directive under Art. 13 in 2000 (see Bell, chap. 37). The implicit prohibition of sexual orientation discrimination in Switzerland's 1999 Federal Constitution preceded Geneva's 2001 legislation (see Baur, chap. 29).

[14] Joined Cases C-122/99 P, C-125/99 P, http://europa.eu.int/jurisp/cgi-bin/form.pl?lang=en. See Waaldijk, chap. 36; Bell, chap. 37; Guild, chap. 38.

v. *South-West Trains*) was "not necessarily equivalent to a registered partnership under a statutory arrangement" with legal effects "akin to those of marriage" (meaning that *Grant* was not conclusive);[15] (b) "according to the definition generally accepted by the Member States, the term 'marriage' means a union between two persons of the opposite sex";[16] and (c) "since 1989 an increasing number of Member States have introduced, alongside marriage, statutory arrangements granting legal recognition to various forms of union between partners of the same sex or of the opposite sex", which arrangements "are regarded in the Member States concerned as being distinct from marriage".[17]

The ECJ thus concluded: "the Community judicature cannot interpret the Staff Regulations in such a way that legal situations distinct from marriage are treated in the same way as marriage", given the above-mentioned circumstances and the fact that, "in a limited number of [the fifteen] Member States, a registered partnership is assimilated, although incompletely, to marriage".[18] (At the time of the judgment, only Denmark, the Netherlands and Sweden had full, almost-identical-to-marriage registered partnership laws; Iceland and Norway are not EC member states.) The ECJ left the issue of recognition to the EC legislature, stressing that a 1998 request by the Swedish government, that the Staff Regulations be amended to expressly provide for the equivalence of marriage and registered partnership, had been rejected by the Council and referred to the Commission for study.[19]

Second, this interpretation of the Staff Regulations did not involve any sex discrimination with regard to pay, contrary to Article 141 (formerly 119) of the EC Treaty, because a woman with a female partner would have been treated in the same way (the same faulty reasoning as in *Grant*).[20] Third, this interpretation did not involve any sexual orientation discrimination (potentially prohibited for EC institutions and member states implementing or derogating from EC law through the unwritten and open-ended "general principle of equal treatment" in EC law), because "it is not the sex of the partner which determines whether the household allowance is granted, but the legal nature of the ties between the official and the partner".[21]

Fourth, this interpretation did not violate the general principle of equal treatment as "nature of legal ties" (or implicitly "marital status") discrimination, because the principle "can only apply to persons in comparable situations . . The existing situation in the Member States . . . as regards recognition of partnerships between persons of the same sex or of the opposite sex reflects a grea[t] diversity of laws and the absence of any general assimilation of marriage an[d]

[15] *D., ibid.*, para. 33.
[16] *Ibid.*, para. 34.
[17] *Ibid.*, paras. 35–6.
[18] *Ibid.*, paras. 37, 39.
[19] *Ibid.*, paras. 32, 38.
[20] *Ibid.*, para. 46. See Koppelman, chap. 35.
[21] *Ibid.*, para. 47. The ECJ did not cite Art. 13 of the EC Treaty or Art. 21 of the Charter [of] Fundamental Rights of the European Union. See Waaldijk, chap. 36; Bell, chap. 37.

other forms of statutory union . . . In those circumstances, the situation of an official who has registered a partnership . . . cannot be held comparable . . . to that of a married official".[22] (Because comparison was not permitted, the Council did not have to provide any justification for the difference in treatment.) Fifth, this interpretation is not "capable of constituting interference in private and family life within the meaning of Article 8 of the European Convention".[23]

The ECJ declared inadmissible (as raised only on appeal) a sixth argument, that the marriage-only interpretation of the Staff Regulations constitutes nationality discrimination, or an obstacle to the free movement of workers, violating the EC Treaty, i.e., Danish, Dutch and Swedish workers who had registered their partnerships would be deterred from moving to other member states to work (including to Brussels to work for an EC institution) if their registered partnerships were not treated as equivalent to marriages. Just as *Grant* was overruled by the combination of a 1997 amendment to the EC Treaty and a subsequent Directive,[24] a solution to the problem of non-recognition of registered partnerships by EC institutions and in other member states will probably require new legislation. However, if the EC legislature does not act, and the number of member states with registered partnership laws continues to grow, in a few years another applicant could ask the ECJ to reconsider the arguments made by D. (including the free movement argument).

The decision in *D. & Sweden* highlights the importance of the "name" attached to the legal institution same-sex partners are permitted to join. Although the few differences between registered partnership and marriage in Swedish law made it easier for the ECJ to conclude that they were not the same, it is not clear that removing the remaining differences in rights and obligations would have changed the ECJ's conclusion, as long as the difference in the "name" remained. Where the "name" is "civil marriage", legislatures and courts in other jurisdictions can, of course, still assert public policy reasons for not recognising civil marriages between persons of the same sex. However, use of a different "name" greatly facilitates their task. They can simply say: "Registered partnership? What's that? We've never heard of it. It doesn't exist here".

An intermediate appellate court in the US state of Georgia will soon consider, in the context of a restriction on a lesbian mother's having her children visit while cohabiting with anyone other than a marriage partner or a relative, whether the mother's Vermont "civil union" with her female partner counts as a marriage.[25] The "name" will certainly be one issue in that case, in contrast

[22] *Ibid.*, paras. 48–51.

[23] Here, the ECJ seems to have focussed on D.'s argument that the Council's notifying Belgian authorities that he was "single" was an interference with his Art. 8 rights, rather than on whether there was discrimination in relation to his "private life" or "family life" contrary to Art. 8 and 14. Nor, unlike in *Grant*, did the ECJ cite any decisions of the European Court or Commission of Human Rights. See Wintemute, chap. 40.

[24] See Bell, chap. 37.

[25] See *Burns* v. *Freer*, [May 2001] *Lesbian/Gay Law Notes*, http://www.qrd.org/www/usa/legal/lgln.

with the case of two Australian residents of Amsterdam (Thomas Lexmond and Darren Reynoldson), who were planning to contract a "civil marriage" there, and then seek recognition upon their return to Australia.[26]

RELEVANCE TO "NON-WESTERN" OR "DEVELOPING" COUNTRIES?

Reading the list of legislation recognising same-sex partnerships in Appendix I to this book, one cannot help but notice that, although the list has grown from nothing in 1978, it contains only nineteen countries (in which the thirty-eight jurisdictions listed above are found) out of the one hundred eighty-nine members of the United Nations (as of 2000) plus Switzerland. Almost all of the nineteen countries are both "Western" (in the sense that a majority of the population, or of the political elite, is of European descent) and "developed". The only exception is post-apartheid South Africa (which stands as a beacon for other African countries, such as Namibia and Zimbabwe).[26a] The world's two most populous countries, China and India, and the world's second largest economy, Japan, are not represented. Does this mean that the issue of legal recognition of same-sex partnerships is relevant only to countries that are "Western" in their history, culture and values, and "developed" in the sense that the majority of people have a "developed world" standard of living?

I would argue that it does not. The majority of the world's potential same-sex partners (i.e., individuals who, in the absence of cultural and economic constraints, would ideally like to cohabit in a stable relationship with a same-sex partner) live in countries that are "non-Western" or "developing" or both. As the chapters in this book on China, India and Japan demonstrate, the lesbian, gay, bisexual and transgendered (LGBT) equality movements in these countries (where individual rights are sometimes a relatively new and foreign concept, and traditional heterosexual family values may be very strong) are at an earlier stage, often still struggling to achieve social acceptance of the right of LGBT individuals to be open about their sexual orientations or gender identities, without fear of criminal prosecution or violence or police harassment, and to form associations to improve their social and legal situations. Legal recognition of same-sex partnerships is therefore not a priority in most of these countries. However, as demonstrated by the recent attempt of two lesbian women in India to register their Hindu marriage,[27] judicial decisions in Colombia[28] and

[26] See http://www.expatica.com/main.asp?pad=34,35,&item_id=8713 (April 2001).

[26a] See E Cameron, "Constitutional Protection of Sexual Orientation and African Conceptions of Humanity", (2001) 118 *South African Law Journal* (forthcoming).

[27] See http://www.the-week.com/21may20/events5.htm (Woman and wife) (May 2001).

[28] See Constitutional Court of Colombia, *Sentencia* No. C-098/96 (7 March 1996). Germán Humberto Rincón Perfetti challenged the constitutionality of Law No. 54 of 1990 (29 Dec.) on "*uniones maritales de hecho*" ("de facto marital unions"), defined as being between one man and one woman. The Court held that the exclusion of same-sex partners was not discriminatory, citing *inter alia* the "weakness of the female cohabitant" (in relation to her male partner) and the need o

Namibia,[29] and actual or proposed bills in Argentina,[30] Brazil[31] and Mexico's Federal District (Mexico City),[32] the issue will gradually become more important. One does not need money to fall in love.

PREDICTING FUTURE DEVELOPMENTS

What economic, political, legal and social factors make legal recognition of same-sex partnerships more likely in one jurisdiction than another, and affect the form and the source (legislative or judicial) of the recognition? This is a broad and difficult question,[33] but I will present a short, tentative list of factors here:

1. the degree of economic development ("developed world" *vs.* "developing world");
2. the strength of democracy and respect for human rights ("democratic world" *vs.* "non-democratic world");
3. the strength of the influence of religion on politics (e.g., the Netherlands or Canada *vs.* Italy or the southern United States);
4. the self-image of the jurisdiction as a small one that distinguishes itself in the world (or its country) by being a leader on human rights issues (e.g., the Netherlands, Canada or Vermont *vs.* Germany, the USA or Texas);
5. the degree of legal and social acceptance of unmarried different-sex couples (e.g., Sweden or Canada *vs.* Italy or the USA);
6. the position of the political party in power in national government on the political spectrum (the closer to the centre or left, the more likely there will be reform) (e.g., in 2001, France or Germany *vs.* Spain, at the national level, or Austria);
7. the ability of courts to declare discriminatory legislation constitutionally invalid when legislatures refuse to amend it (e.g., Canada, Vermont or South Africa *vs.* Australia or the United Kingdom);
8. the legal, political and social acceptability of "separate but equal (or almost equal)" treatment (e.g., the Scandinavian countries, Germany or Vermont *vs.* France).

the legislature to tackle one injustice at a time. Many thanks to Esteban Restrepo (doctoral candidate, Yale Law School) for telling me about this decision.

[29] *Chairperson of the Immigration Selection Board* v. *Frank*, Case No. SA 8/99 (Supreme Court of Namibia, 5 March 2001) (reversing trial decision ordering that German female partner of Namibian woman be granted permanent residence).

[30] *Proyecto de ley de Unión Civil para parejas del mismo sexo "parteneriato", Diputada* L C Musa, *Cámara de Diputados*, 11 Dec. 1998, No. 7816-D-98, http://www.sigla.org.ar (*Derechos Civiles*).

[31] See Turra, chap. 16.

[32] See http://www.mundogay.com/magazine/semana54/mexico.htm (proposed bill on *uniones solidarias* announced by Deputy Armando Quintero on 13 Dec. 2000).

[33] For a compelling analysis of these factors, especially in Europe, see Waaldijk, chaps. 23, 36.

In what countries or jurisdictions will these factors interact so as to produce legal recognition, further legal recognition, or full legal equality for same-sex partnerships over the next five to ten years? Unregistered cohabitation laws will continue to spread or be strengthened in Canada, Australia and New Zealand. More and more European countries will adopt some form of registered partnership or registered cohabitation law, countries with registered cohabitation laws will be pressured to improve them, and countries with registered partnership laws will be asked to remove the remaining differences with civil marriage. The Nordic countries' "friendly human rights competition" with the Netherlands and with each other, could lead to the opening up of civil marriage to same-sex couples through legislation in Denmark, Norway, Sweden and Iceland. In the United States, state legislatures will consider bills proposing Vermont-style "civil unions". But it is not clear whether any state legislature would yet be willing to enact one in the absence of a constitutional obligation, like the one identified by the Supreme Court of Vermont.[34]

As has been seen throughout this book, the process of legislative reform will often be accelerated by positive[35] judicial decisions interpreting equality guarantees in national, European or international bills of rights. Several same-sex marriage cases will reach the Supreme Court of Canada in about five years,[36] and by that time, the 55 per cent majority of Canadians who support same-sex marriage[37] will probably have grown. A same-sex marriage suit has recently been filed in Massachusetts.[38] The judicial decisions in Canada and Massachusetts, as well as other judicial or legislative deliberation regarding civil marriage[39] and other forms of legal recognition, will be strongly influenced by the Netherland's historic "opening up" of civil marriage to same-sex couples on 1 April 2001. The legislation that made this possible was a legal watershed for the world, comparable to Vermont's becoming (in 1777) the first US state to abolish slavery,[40] and New Zealand's becoming (in 1893) the first country in the world to grant the vote in national elections to women.[41] It is no longer possible for any jurisdiction to say that we cannot have same-sex marriages because

[34] See Bonauto, chap. 10.

[35] See especially *M.* v. *H.* (Supreme Court of Canada), discussed by L'Heureux-Dubé pp. 211–13, Casswell, chap. 11, Lahey, chap. 12. Negative decisions can also accelerate the process by clearly putting the onus on the legislature to act, as in the Netherlands. See Waaldijk, chap. 23.

[36] See Lahey, chap. 12, n.21.

[37] Environics Research Group, 5–24 April 2001 opinion survey, *National Post Online* (10 May 2001).

[38] *Hillary Goodridge & Julie Goodridge, et al.* v. *Dep't of Public Health* (Massachusetts Superior Court, Suffolk County, filed 11 April 2001), http://www.glad.org.

[39] I used to think that joint adoption of children was the "final frontier" for lesbian, gay and bisexual equality. This may still be the case in Europe, in view of the Netherlands' introducing same-sex civil marriage while excluding inter-country joint adoption. See Waaldijk, chap. 23. But in jurisdictions in the USA and Canada where same-sex partners can already adopt jointly (including children from other countries, if the sending country permits it), civil marriage has become the "final frontier". See Polikoff, Chapter 8; Casswell, Chapter 11; Lahey, chap. 12; Ytterberg, p. 435.

[40] Vermont Constitution of 1777, Art. 1.

[41] Electoral Act 1893, s. 6.

no country has them, and that "one man and one woman" is the universal and inalterable definition of marriage.

Within a few years, once it has become clear that the sky has not fallen, the rest of the world will be able to piggyback on the courage of the Netherlands.[42] Just as the collapse of the Berlin Wall and the Iron Curtain began with a trickle of East German refugees crossing the Hungarian-Austrian border in the summer of 1989, the global wall separating different-sex and same-sex partners now has a crack. The crack will gradually be widened, and ultimately the wall will be demolished. As the Supreme Court of Vermont said, "recognition of our common humanity" will allow legislators, judges and ordinary citizens to see that love is love, regardless of the sexual orientation of the couple.

[42] Belgium could be the first country to follow the Netherlands. See p. 473. Cf. the amendment to 1e US federal Constitution proposed by the Alliance for Marriage on 12 July 2001: "Marriage in the 'nited States shall consist only of the union of a man and a woman. Neither this constitution or the onstitution of any state, nor state or federal law, shall be construed to require that marital status r the legal incidents thereof be conferred upon unmarried couples or groups".

APPENDIX I—SAME-SEX PARTNERSHIPS[1]

NATIONAL (FEDERAL, STATE, PROVINCIAL, REGIONAL, LOCAL) LEGISLATION RECOGNISING SAME-SEX PARTNERSHIPS[2]

Australia

Australian Capital Territory—Domestic Relationships Act 1994, http://www.austlii.edu.au/au/legis/act/consol_act/dra1994253 ("parties to a domestic relationship"); Administration and Probate (Amendment) Act 1996, http://www.austlii.edu.au/au/legis/act/num_act/aapa1996339 ("eligible partners"); Family Provision (Amendment) Act 1996, http://www.austlii.edu.au/au/legis/act/num_act/fpa1996289 ("eligible partners")

New South Wales—Property (Relationships) Legislation Amendment Act 1999, http://www.austlii.edu.au/au/legis/nsw/consol_act/plaa1999490 ("parties to a *de facto* relationship")

Queensland—Property Law Amendment Act 1999, http://www.legislation.qld.gov.au/LEGISLTN/ACTS/1999/99AC089.pdf ("*de facto* spouses"); Industrial Relations Act 1999, Schedule 5, definition of "spouse", http://www.legislation.qld.gov.au/LEGISLTN/ACTS/1999/99AC033.pdf ("*de facto* spouses")

Victoria—Statute Law Amendment (Relationships) Act 2001, http://www.dms.dpc.vic.gov.au (Statute Book) ("domestic partners")

Austria

Criminal Code (*Strafgesetzbuch*) 1975, *Paragraph* 72, as amended in 1998, http://www.ris.bka.gv.at/bundesrecht ("*Personen, die miteinander in Lebensgemeinschaft leben*"; "persons living with each other in a community of life")

Belgium

Loi du 23 novembre 1998 instaurant la cohabitation légale, Moniteur belge, http://194.7.188.126/justice/index_fr.htm,12 Jan. 1999, p. 786("*cohabitants légaux*"; "statutory cohabitants")

Canada

Federal Level—Modernization of Benefits and Obligations Act, Statutes (S.) of Canada 2000, chapter (c.) 12, http://www.parl.gc.ca/common/Bills_House_Government.asp?Language=E&Parl=36&Ses=2 (C-23, Royal Assent) ("common-law partners", "*conjoints de fait*")

[1] To facilitate consultation of the texts, Apps. I, II and III will be posted at http://www.ilga.org. World Legal Survey).

[2] Legislation dealing only with second-parent or joint adoption of children by same-sex partners ot included.

British Columbia—Medical and Health Care Services Act, S.B.C. 1992, c. 76, http://www.legis.gov.bc.ca/1992/3rd_read/gov71-3.txt (repealed in 2000) ("spouses"); Family Relations Amendment Act, 1997, S.B.C. 1997, c. 20, http://www.legis.gov.bc.ca/1997/3rd_read/gov31-3.htm ("spouses"); Definition of Spouse Amendment Act, 1999, S.B.C. 1999, c. 29, http://www.legis.gov.bc.ca/1998-99/3rd_read/gov100-3.htm ("spouses"); Definition of Spouse Amendment Act, 2000, S.B.C. 2000, c. 24, http://www.legis.gov.bc.ca/2000/3rd_read/gov21-3.htm ("spouses")

Manitoba—An Act to Comply with the Supreme Court of Canada Decision in *M.* v. *H.*, http://www.gov.mb.ca/leg-asmb/bills/37-sess2/b041e.html (6 July 2001) ("common-law partners")

New Brunswick—Family Services Act, N.B. Acts, c. F-2.2, section (s.) 112(3), as amended in 2000, http://www.gov.nb.ca/acts/acts/f-02-2.htm (spousal support obligations of unmarried persons living in a family relationship)

Newfoundland—An Act to Amend the Family Law Act, S.N. 2000, c. 29, http://www.gov.nf.ca/hoa/sr (Annual Statutes) ("partners")

Nova Scotia—Law Reform (2000) Act, S.N.S. 2000, c. 29, http://www.gov.ns.ca/legi/legc/index.htm ("common-law partners", "[registered] domestic partners")

Ontario—Amendments Because of the Supreme Court of Canada Decision in *M.* v. *H.* Act, S.O. 1999, c. 6, http://www.ontla.on.ca/ Documents/StatusofLegOUT/b005ra_e.htm ("same-sex partners")

Québec—An Act to amend various legislative provisions concerning *de facto* spouses, S.Q. 1999, c. 14, http://publicationsduquebec.gouv.qc.ca (*Lois et règlements*, *Projets de loi*, 1st session, 36th legislature, No. 32) ("*conjoints de fait*", "*de facto* spouses")

Saskatchewan—Miscellaneous Statutes (Domestic Relations) Amendment Acts, 2001, S.S. 2001, cc. 50–51, http://www.legassembly.sk.ca/bills/default.htm ("common-law partners", or persons "cohabiting as spouses" or "cohabiting in a spousal relationship")

Yukon Territory—Dependant's Relief Act, Revised (R.) S.Y. 1986 (Vol. 1), c. 44, s. 1, as amended by S.Y. 1998, c. 7, s. 116 ("common law spouses"); Family Property and Support Act, R.S.Y. 1986 (Vol. 2), c. 63, ss. 1, 30, 31, as amended by S.Y. 1998, c. 8, s. 10 ("spouses"); Estate Administration Act, S.Y. 1998, c. 7, ss. 1, 74 ("common law spouses"); texts at http://legis.acjnet.org/Yukon/index_en.html (Republished Statutes)

Denmark

Law of 4 June 1986, nr. 339 (inheritance tax reform), repealed by Law on Registered Partnership (*Lov om registreret partnerskab*), 7 June 1989, nr. 372, http://www france.qrd.org/texts/partnership/dk/denmark-act.html (English) ("*registrerede partnere*"; "registered partners")

France

Loi no. 99-944 du 15 novembre 1999 relative au pacte civil de solidarité, http://www legifrance.gouv.fr/html/frame_jo.html ("*partenaires*"; "partners")

Germany

Law of 16 Feb. 2001 on Ending Discrimination Against Same-Sex Communities: Li Partnerships (*Gesetz zur Beendigung der Diskriminierung gleichgeschlechtlich*

Gemeinschaften: Lebenspartnerschaften), [2001] 9 *Bundesgesetzblatt* 266, http://www.bundesanzeiger.de/bgbl1f/b1findex.htm ("*Lebenspartner*"; "life partners")

Hungary

Civil Code, Article 685/A, as amended by Act No. 42 of 1996: "Partners—if not stipulated otherwise by law—are two people living in an emotional and economic community in the same household without being married".

Iceland

Law on Confirmed Cohabitation (*Lög um stadfesta samvist*), 12 June 1996, nr. 87, http://www.althingi.is/lagas/126a/1996087.html,http://www.france.qrd.org/texts/partnership/is/iceland-bill.html (English) ("parties to a confirmed cohabitation")

Netherlands

Act of 21 June 1979 amending the Civil Code [Art. 7A:1623h] with respect to rent law, *Staatsblad* 1979, nr. 330 ("*duurzame gemeenschappelijke huishouding*"; "lasting joint household"); Acts of 17 December 1980 (*Staatsblad* 1980, nr. 686) and 8 November 1984 (*Staatsblad* 1984, nr. 545) amending the Inheritance Tax Act 1956 ("*gemeenschappelijke huishouding*"; "joint household"); Act of 5 July 1997 amending Book 1 of the Civil Code and the Code of Civil Procedure, concerning the introduction therein of provisions relating to registered partnership (*geregistreerd partnerschap*), *Staatsblad* 1997, nr. 324 ("*geregistreerde partners*"; "registered partners"); Act of 21 December 2000 amending Book 1 of the Civil Code, concerning the opening up of marriage for persons of the same sex (Act on the Opening Up of Marriage), *Staatsblad* 2001, nr. 9, http://ruljis.leidenuniv.nl/user/cwaaldij/www (English) ("*echtgenoten*"; "spouses"); Dutch texts (since 1995) at http://www.overheid.nl/op (*Starten*, 1. *Staatsblad*, 3. *jaar* (year) and *Publicatienummer, Zoek*)

New Zealand

Electricity Act 1992, s. 111 ("near relatives"); Domestic Violence Act 1995, s. 2 ("partners"); Harassment Act 1997, s. 2 ("partners"); Accident Insurance Act 1998, s. 25 ("spouses"); Housing Restructuring (Income-Related Rents) Amendment Act 2000, s. 5 ("partners"); Property (Relationships) Amendment Act 2001 ("*de facto* partners"); Family Proceedings Amendment Act 2001 ("*de facto* partners"); Family Protection Amendment Act 2001 ("*de facto* partners"); Administration Amendment Act 2001 ("*de facto* partners"); all Acts at http://rangi.knowledge basket.co.nz/gpacts/ actlists.html

Norway

Law on Registered Partnership (*Lov om registrert partnerskap*), 30 April 1993, nr. 40, http://www.lovdata.no/all/nl-19930430-040.html,http://www.france.qrd.org/texts/partnership/no/norway-en.html (English) ("*registrerte partnere*"; "registered partners")

Portugal

Lei No. 7/2001 de 11 de Maio, Adopta medidas de protecção das uniões de facto, [2001] 109 (I-A) *Diário da República* 2797, http://www.portugalgay.pt (*Entrar, Espaço Aberto, Política*) ("*uniões de facto*"; "*de facto* unions")

South Africa

See, e.g., Special Pensions Act (No. 69 of 1996), s. 31(2)(a) ("spouses"); Basic Conditions of Employment Act (No. 75 of 1997), s. 27(2)(c)(i) ("life partners"); Employment Equity Act (No. 55 of 1998), s. 1 (definition of "family responsibility") ("partners"); Medical Schemes Act (No. 131 of 1998), s. 1 (definition of "dependant") ("partners"); texts at http://www.parliament.gov.za/acts/index.asp (see also pp. 288–9, nn. 30, 35)

Spain

National Level—see, e.g., Law on Urban Leasing (*Ley de Arrendamientos Urbanos*) of 24 Nov. 1994, Articles 12, 16, 24, *disposición transitoria segunda* B(7): housing rights granted to a person cohabiting "in a permanent way in an emotional relationship analogous to that of spouses, without regard to its sexual orientation [*con independencia de su orientación sexual*]"

Catalonia—*Llei 10/1998, de 15 de juliol, d'unions estables de parella*, (10 July 1998) 309 *Butlletí Oficial del Parlament de Catalunya* (BOPC) 24738, http://www.parlament-cat.es/porta.htm (*Publicacions, Textos aprovats, V Legislatura*) ("*unions estables de parella*"; "stable unions of couples")

Aragón—*Ley relativa a parejas estables no casadas*, (26 March 1999) 255 *Boletín Oficial de las Cortes de Aragón*, http://www.cortesaragon.es (BOCA, *Legislaturas anteriores*, IV) ("*parejas estables no casadas*"; "unmarried stable couples")

Navarra—*Ley Foral 6/2000, de 3 de julio, para la igualdad jurídica de las parejas estables*, [7 July 2000] 82 *Boletín Oficial de Navarra*, http://www.cfnavarra.es/BON/007/00707003.htm ("*parejas estables*"; "stable couples")

Valencia—*Ley por la que se regulan las uniones de hecho*, (9 April 2001) 93 *Boletín Oficial de las Cortes Valencianas* 12404, http://www.corts.gva.es/esp (Publicaciones, BOCV) ("*uniones de hecho*"; "*de facto* unions")

Sweden

Homosexual Cohabitees Act (*Lag om homosexuella sambor*), SFS 1987:813; Law on Registered Partnership (*Lag om registrerat partnerskap*), 23 June 1994, SFS 1994:1117, http://www.france.qrd.org/texts/partnership/se/sweden-act.html (English) ("*registrerade partner*"; "registered partners"); Swedish texts at http://www.notisum.se (*Författningar, SLS, kronologiskt register*)

Switzerland

Geneva (Canton of)—*Loi sur le partenariat du 15 février 2001* (7611) (RSG E 1 27), http://www.geneve.ch/rechercher/welcome.asp (partenariat) ("*partenaires*"; "partners")

United Kingdom

Scotland—Adults with Incapacity (Scotland) Act 2000, s. 87(2) ("nearest relative"); Housing (Scotland) Act 2001, s. 108 ("family members" or "spouses"); texts at http://www.scotland-legislation.hmso.gov.uk/legislation/scotland/s-acts.htm

United States[3]

California—Cal. Statutes (Stat.) 1999, chapter 588, http://www.leginfo.ca.gov/statute.html ("domestic partners")

District of Columbia—see, e.g., D.C. Code section (s.) 36-1401 (11 June 1992, D.C. Law 9-114, s. 2, 39 D.C. Register 2861) ("domestic partners")

Hawaii—Hawaii Revised Stat., e.g., s. 572C-4 (1997), http://www.capitol.hawaii.gov/site1/archives/docs2001.asp#hrs ("reciprocal beneficiaries")

Vermont—An Act Relating to Civil Unions, 2000 Vermont Stat. No. 91 (26 April 2000), http://www.leg.state.vt.us/baker/baker.cfm ("parties to a civil union", included in "spouse", "family", etc.)

Local Level— see, e.g., New York City Administrative Code, s. 3-241 (added by Local Law No. 27 of 1998, http://leah.council.nyc.ny.us/law98/int0303a.htm, s. 2); City of San Francisco Administrative Code, http://www.amlegal. com/sanfran/viewcode.htm, Chapters 62 ("domestic partners") (adopted 6 Nov. 1990), 12B, 12C (City contractors must agree not to discriminate on the basis of "domestic partner status"); see also Wayne van der Meide, *Legislating Equality: A Review of Laws Affecting Gay, Lesbian, Bisexual, and Transgendered People in the United States* (Washington, DC, Policy Institute of the National Gay & Lesbian Task Force, Jan. 2000), http://www.ngltf.org/downloads/legeq99.pdf.

[3] For US states, specific statutory references to "domestic partners", not part of a law providing a package of rights to "domestic partners", have not been included.

APPENDIX II—SEXUAL ORIENTATION

EUROPEAN TREATIES AND LEGISLATION AND NATIONAL CONSTITUTIONS AND LEGISLATION EXPRESSLY PROHIBITING DISCRIMINATION BASED ON SEXUAL ORIENTATION[1]

EUROPEAN TREATIES AND LEGISLATION

European Union

Treaty establishing the European Community, Rome, 25 March 1957, Article 13 (inserted as Article 6a and renumbered as Article 13 by the Treaty of Amsterdam, 2 October 1997), http://europa.eu.int/eur-lex/en/treaties/index.html ("sexual orientation") (in force on 1 May 1999; authorises a legislative prohibition; is not itself a prohibition)

Council Directive 2000/78/EC of 27 November 2000 [adopted under Article 13 of the EC Treaty] establishing a general framework for equal treatment in employment and occupation, Official Journal [2000], series L, issue 303, p. 16, http://europa.eu.int/eur-lex/en/lif/dat/2000/en_300L0078.html ("sexual orientation") (must be implemented by 2 December 2003 in all fifteen European Union member states, and especially in Austria, Belgium, Germany, Greece, Italy, Portugal and the United Kingdom, which did not have any such national legislation as of August 2001)

NATIONAL (FEDERAL, STATE) CONSTITUTIONS

Brazil

Mato Grosso—Constitution, 1989, Article 10.III ("*orientação sexual*")
Sergipe—Constitution, 1989, Article 3.II ("*orientação sexual*")

Ecuador

Constitution, 1998, Article 23(3), http://www.georgetown.edu/pdba/Constitutions/Ecuador/ecuador98.html ("*orientación sexual*")

Fiji Islands

Constitution Amendment Act 1997, section (s.) 38(2)(a), http://confinder.richmond.edu/FijiIslands.htm ("sexual orientation")

[1] Or a similar or broader ground which is intended to cover sexual orientation (or same-sex sexual orientation).

Germany

Berlin—Constitution, 1995, Article 10(2), http://www.datenschutz-berlin.de/gesetze/berlin/verfass/verfass.htm ("*sexuelle Identität*")

Brandenburg—Constitution, 1992, Article 12(2), http://www.landtag.brandenburg.de/rand_6e.htm ("*sexuelle Identität*")

Thuringia—Constitution, 1993, Article 2(3), http://www.thueringen.de/de (*Verfassung*) ("*sexuelle Orientierung*")

South Africa

Constitution of the Republic of South Africa Act (No. 200 of 1993), Section 8(2) (transitional Constitution) ("sexual orientation"); Constitution of the Republic of South Africa (No. 108 of 1996), Sections 9(3), 9(4) (final Constitution) ("sexual orientation"); texts at http://www.parliament.gov.za/acts/index.asp

Switzerland

Federal Constitution, adopted on 18 April 1999, Article 8(2), http://www.admin.ch/ch/f/rs/101/index.html ("*Lebensform*", "*mode de vie*", "*modo de vita*"; "way of life")

NATIONAL (FEDERAL, STATE, PROVINCIAL, TERRITORIAL, LOCAL) LEGISLATION

Argentina

Buenos Aires (Autonomous City of)—Constitution, 1 Oct. 1996, Article 11, http://www.legislatura.gov.ar/1legisla/constcba.htm#_Toc0 ("*orientación sexual*")

Australia

Federal (Commonwealth) Level—Workplace Relations Act 1996, s. 170CK, http://www.austlii.edu.au/au/legis/cth/consol_act/wra1996220 ("sexual preference"; dismissal only)

Australian Capital Territory—Discrimination Act 1991, s. 7(1)(b), http://www.austlii.edu.au/au/legis/act/consol_act/da1991164 ("sexuality")

New South Wales—Anti-Discrimination Act 1977, Part 4C, http://www.austlii.edu.au/au/legis/nsw/consol_act/aa1977204 ("homosexuality" added in 1982)

Northern Territory—Anti-Discrimination Act 1992, s. 19(1)(c), http://www.austlii.edu.au/au/legis/nt/consol_act/aa204 ("sexuality")

Queensland—Anti-Discrimination Act 1991, s. 7(1)(l), http://www.legislation.qld.gov.au/Legislation%20Docs/CurrentA.htm ("lawful sexual activity")

South Australia—Equal Opportunity Act, 1984, ss. 5(1), 29(3), http://www.austlii.edu.au/au/legis/sa/consol_act/eoa1984250 ("sexuality")

Tasmania—Anti-Discrimination Act 1998, http://www.thelaw.tas.gov.au/search, ss. 3, 16 ("sexual orientation", "lawful sexual activity")

Victoria—Equal Opportunity Act 1995, ss. 4, 6, http://www.austlii.edu.au/au/legis/vic/consol_act/eoa1995250, as amended by Equal Opportunity (Gender Identity and

Sexual Orientation) Act 2000, http://www.dms.dpc.vic.gov.au (Statute Book) ("lawful sexual activity", 1995; "sexual orientation", 2000)

Austria

See European Union, Council Directive 2000/78/EC ("*sexuelle Ausrichtung*"); *Richtlinien-Verordnung* (Guidelines-Ordinance for Police Forces, not legislation), [1993] *Bundesgesetzblatt* Nr. 266, *Paragraph* 5(1), http://www.ris.bka.gv.at/bundesrecht ("*sexuelle Orientierung*")

Belgium

See European Union, Council Directive 2000/78/EC ("*seksuele geaardheid*", "*orientation sexuelle*")

Brazil

For a list of around seventy municipalities with legislation prohibiting sexual orientation discrimination, including São Paulo and Rio de Janeiro, see http://www.rolim.com.br/ORSEXUAL.htm ("*orientação sexual*")

Canada[2]

Federal Level—Canadian Human Rights Act, Revised Statutes of Canada (R.S.C.) 1985, chapter (c.) H-6, ss. 2, 3(1), http://laws.justice.gc.ca/en/H-6/index.html ("sexual orientation" added in 1996)

British Columbia—Human Rights Code, R.S.B.C. 1996, c. 210, ss. 7–11, 13–14, http://www.qp.gov.bc.ca/statreg/stat/H//96210_01.htm ("sexual orientation" added in 1992)

Manitoba—Human Rights Code, R.S.M. c. H175, s. 9(2)(h), http://www.gov.mb.ca/chc/statpub/free/legdbindexeng-m.html ("sexual orientation" added in 1987)

New Brunswick—Human Rights Code, R.S.N.B. c. H-11, ss. 3–7, http://www.gov.nb.ca/acts/acts/h-11.htm ("sexual orientation" added in 1992)

Newfoundland—Human Rights Code, R.S.N. 1990, c. H-14, ss. 6–9, 12, 14 http://www.gov.nf. ca/hoa/statutes/h14.htm ("sexual orientation" added in 1997)

Nova Scotia—Human Rights Act, R.S.N.S. 1989, c. 214, s. 5(1)(n), http://www.gov.ns.ca/legi/legc/index.htm (Statutes, Consol.) ("sexual orientation" added in 1991)

Ontario—Human Rights Code, R.S.O. 1990, c. H.19, ss. 1–3, 5–6, http://www.e-laws.gov.on.ca/tocStatutes_E.asp?lang=en ("sexual orientation" added in 1986)

Prince Edward Island—Human Rights Act, R.S.P.E.I. 1988, c. H-12, s. 1(1)(d), http://www.gov.pe.ca/law/statutes/index.php3 ("sexual orientation" added in 1998)

Québec—*Charte des droits et libertés de la personne*, R.S.Q. c. C-12, s. 10, http://www.cdpdj.qc.ca/htmfr/htm/4_4.htm ("*orientation sexuelle*" added in 1977)

[2] "Sexual orientation" was "read into" Alberta's Human Rights, Citizenship and Multiculturalism Act, http://www.qp.gov.ab.ca/display_acts.cfm, by the Supreme Court in *Vriend v. Alberta*, [1998] 1 S.C.R. 493, http://www.lexum.umontreal.ca/csc-scc/en/index.html. *Vriend* should also apply to the Northwest Territories' Fair Practices Act, http://legis.acjnet.org/TNO/Loi/_en.html, and Nunavut Territory's Fair Practices Act (Nunavut), http://legis.acjnet.org/Nunavut/Loi/index_en.html.

Saskatchewan—Saskatchewan Human Rights Code, S.S. 1979, c. S-24.1, ss. 9–19, 25, 47, http://www.gov.sk.ca/shrc ("sexual orientation" added in 1993)

Yukon Territory—Human Rights Act, S.Y.T. 1987, c. 3, ss. 6, 34, http://legis.acjnet.org/cgi-bin/folioisa.dll/e_stats.nfo/query=*/doc/{t43523}? ("sexual orientation")

Costa Rica

Law No. 7771 (*Ley General Sobre el VIH-SIDA*), *La Gaceta* No. 96 (20 May 1998), Article 48, http://www.pasca.org/cd/pasca/Dialogo/cr_ley.pdf ("*opción sexual*"; "sexual option")

Czech Republic

Law 155/2000 of 18 May 2000 (amending Labour Code, Law 65/1965, Art. 1(4), and Law on Soldiers, Law 221/1999, Art. 2(4)), [21 June 2000] 49 *Sbírka Zákonu* (Law Gazette) 2290, 2318, http://www.mvcr.cz/sbirka/2000/sb049-00.pdf ("*sexuální orientace*")

Denmark

Law of 9 June 1971, nr. 289, as amended by Law of 3 June 1987, nr. 357; extended to private employment by Law of 12 June 1996, nr. 459 ("*seksuelle orientering*" added in 1987)

Finland

Penal Code (as amended by Law 21.4.1995/578), c. 11, para. 9, c. 47, para. 3 ("*sukupuolinen suuntautuminen*"; "sexual orientation")

France

Nouveau Code pénal, arts. 225-1, 225-2, 226-19, 432-7; *Code du travail*, arts. L. 122–35, L. 122-45, http://www.legifrance.gouv.fr (*Codes*) ("*moeurs*", "morals, manners, customs, ways", added by *Loi* No. 85-772, 25 July 1985, *Loi* No. 86–76, 17 January 1986; "*orientation sexuelle*" expected to be added in 2001 by *Proposition de loi relative à la lutte contre les discriminations*, http://www.senat.fr/leg/tas00-124.html.

Germany

Federal Level—see European Union, Council Directive 2000/78/EC ("*sexuelle Ausrichtung*")

Saxony-Anhalt—*Gesetz zum Abbau von Benachteiligungen von Lesben und Schwulen* (Law on Reducing Discrimination Against Lesbians and Gay Men), 22 Dec. 1997 (public sector only) ("*sexuelle Identität*")

Greece

See European Union, Council Directive 2000/78/EC ("*γενετήσιος προσανατολισμος*"; "genetisios prosanatolismos"; "sexual orientation")

Hungary

Act on Public Health, Act No. 154 of 1997, art. 7 ("*szexuális irányultság*"; "sexual orientation")

Iceland

General Penal Code, No. 19/1940, s. 180, as amended by Act No. 135/1996, s. 1, http://www.althingi.is/altext/stjt/1996.135.html ("sexual orientation")

Ireland

Unfair Dismissals Act, 1977, No. 10, s. 6(2)(e), as amended by Unfair Dismissals (Amendment) Act, 1993, No. 22, s. 5(a); extended to other aspects of employment by Employment Equality Act, 1998, No. 21, s. 6(2)(d), http://www.irlgov.ie/bills28/acts/1998/a2198.pdf; extended to education, goods, services, housing by Equal Status Act, 2000, No. 8, s. 3(2)(d), http://www.irlgov.ie/bills28/acts/2000/a800.pdf ("sexual orientation" added in 1993)

Israel

Equal Opportunities in Employment Act 1988, as amended by Book of Laws, No. 1377 of 2 Jan. 1992 ("*neti'ya minit*"; "sexual orientation")

Italy

See European Union, Council Directive 2000/78/EC ("*tendenze sessuali*")

Lithuania

Penal Code, art. 169, Law of 26 September 2000, Nr. VIII-1968 ("*seksualine orientacija*") (not yet in force)

Luxembourg

Code pénal, arts. 454-457, added by Law of 19 July 1997, http://www.etat.lu/memorial/T97_a/tablechr.html (*Juillet 1997*) ("*orientation sexuelle*", "*moeurs*")

Mexico

Aguascalientes—Penal Code, art. 205 *bis* (as amended on 11 March 2001), http://www.congresoags.gob.mx (*Legislación, Código Penal*) ("*orientación sexual*")
Federal District (Mexico City)—Penal Code, art. 281 *bis* (as amended on 2 Sept. 1999), http://www.asambleadf.gob.mx/princip/Enl-06.htm (*Códigos, Código Penal, Libro Segundo*) ("*orientación sexual*")

Namibia

Labour Act, 13 March 1992, No. 6, s. 107, http://natlex.ilo.org/scripts/natlexcgi.exe?lang=E (Namibia, General provisions, 1992-03-26) ("sexual orientation")

Netherlands

Penal Code, arts. 137f, 429 *quater* (inserted by Act of 14 Nov. 1991, *Staatsblad* 1991, nr. 623); General Equal Treatment Act, arts. 1, 5–7 (Act of 2 March 1994, *Staatsblad* 1994, nr. 230); Dutch and English texts at http://ruljis.leidenuniv.nl/user/cwaaldij/www/NHR/transl-anti-discr.htm or http://www.cgb.nl ("*hetero- of homoseksuele gerichtheid*"; "hetero- or homosexual orientation")

New Zealand

Human Rights Act 1993, s. 21(1)(m), and s. 145, Second Schedule (amending New Zealand Bill of Rights Act 1990, s. 19), http://rangi.knowledge-basket.co.nz/gpacts/actlists.html ("sexual orientation")

Norway

Penal Code, para. 349a as amended by Law of 8 May 1981, nr. 14, ("*homofile legning, leveform eller orientering*"; "homophile inclination, lifestyle or orientation"); extended to employment by *Lov om arbeidervern og arbeidsmiljø m.v.*, Law of 4 Feb. 1977, nr. 4, para. 55A, as amended by Law of 30 April 1998, nr. 24 ("*homofile legning eller homofile samlivsform*"; "homophile inclination or form of cohabitation"); texts at http://www.lovdata.no/all/index.html (*Søk*, *Hele teksten*, *homofile, Søk*, documents 2, 3)

Portugal

See European Union, Council Directive 2000/78/EC ("*orientação sexual*")

Romania

Ordinance on Preventing and Punishing All Forms of Discrimination, 31 August 2000 ("*orientarii sexuale*") (executive order, not legislation)

Slovenia

Penal Code (Law of 29 Sept. 1994, published in *Uradni list*, 13 Oct. 1994), art. 141 ("*spolni usmerjenosti*"; "sexual orientation")

South Africa

Labour Relations Act (No. 66 of 1995), s. 187(1)(f) (dismissal); extended to other aspects of employment by Employment Equity Act (No. 55 of 1998), s. 6, and to hate speech and harassment by Promotion of Equality and Prevention of Unfair Discrimination Act (No. 4 of 2000), ss. 1(1)(xxii)(a), 10–11; texts at http://www.parliament.gov.za/acts/index.asp ("sexual orientation" added in 1995)

Spain

Penal Code, Organic Law of 23 Nov. 1995, No. 10/1995, arts. 314, 511–12 (see also arts 22(4), 510, 515(5)) ("*orientación sexual*")

Sweden

Penal Code (*Brottsbalk*), SFS 1962:700, c. 16, para. 9, as amended by Law of 4 June 1987, SFS 1987:610, http://justitie.regeringen.se/propositionermm/ds/pdf/Penalcode.pdf (English) ("*homosexuell läggning*"; "homosexual inclination"); extended to employment by Law of 11 March 1999, SFS 1999:133 ("*sexuell läggning*"; "sexual inclination"); Swedish texts at http://www.notisum.se (*Författningar, SLS, kronologiskt register*); see also http://www.homO.se

United Kingdom

See European Union, Council Directive 2000/78/EC ("sexual orientation")

United States[3]

California—e.g., Government Code, ss. 12920, 12921, 12940, 12955, http://www.leginfo.ca.gov/calaw.html ("sexual orientation" originally added to Labor Code in 1992)

Connecticut—Conn. General (Gen.) Statutes (Stat.), e.g., ss. 4a–60a, 45a–726a, 46a–81b to 46a–81r, http://prdbasis.cga.state.ct.us/BASIS/TSAMDHP/LIN1/AMD/MSF (Text: sexual orientation, Database: Statutes K) ("sexual orientation" added in 1991)

District of Columbia—D.C. Code, e.g., ss. 1-2501 to 1-2533 ("sexual orientation" originally added in 1973)

Hawaii—Haw. Revised (Rev.) Stat., e.g., ss. 378-1, 378-2, http://www.capitol.hawaii.gov/site1/archives/docs2001.asp#hrs ("sexual orientation" added in 1991)

Maryland—2001 Laws of Maryland chapter (ch.) 340, http://mlis.state.md.us/2001rs/billfile/SB0205.htm ("sexual orientation") (possible repeal referendum in 2002)

Massachusetts—Mass. Gen. Laws, e.g., ch. 151B, ss. 3, 4, http://www.state.ma.us/legis/laws/mgl/mgllink.htm ("sexual orientation" added in 1989)

Minnesota—Minn. Stat., e.g., ss. 363.01(subdivision 41a), 363.03, http://www.revisor.leg.state.mn.us/forms/getstatute.shtml ("sexual orientation" added in 1993)

Nevada—Nev. Rev. Stat., e.g., s. 613.330, http://www.leg.state.nv.us/NRS/NRS-613.html ("sexual orientation" added in 1999)

New Hampshire—N.H. Rev. Stat., e.g., ss. 21:49, 354-A:7, 354-A:10, 354-A:17, http://sudoc.nhsl.lib.nh.us/rsa/search.htm ("sexual orientation" added in 1997)

New Jersey—N.J. Stat., e.g., ss. 10:5-5.hh.-kk., 10:5-12, http://www.njleg.state.nj.us/html/statutes.htm (Search) ("affectional or sexual orientation" added in 1991)

Rhode Island—R.I. Gen. Laws, e.g., ss. 11-24-2 to 11-24-2.2, 28-5-2 to 28-5-7.3, 28-5-41, 34-37-1 to 34-37-5.4, http://www.rilin.state.ri.us/Statutes/Statutes.html (Search) ("sexual orientation" added in 1995)

Vermont—Vt. Stat., e.g., title 1, s. 143; title 21, s. 495, http://www.leg.state.vt.us/statutes/statutes2.htm ("sexual orientation" added in 1991)

Wisconsin—Wis. Stat., e.g., ss. 111.31 to 111.36, http://www.legis.state.wi.us/rsb/stats.html (1999-2000 Wis. Stat., Search) ("sexual orientation" added in 1982)

[3] Oregon Statutes s. 659.030 prohibits employment discrimination "because of the . . . sex . . . of any other person with whom the [employee] associates", which has been interpreted as providing some protection to lesbian, gay and bisexual employees. See *Tanner* v. *Oregon Health Sciences University*, 971 P.2d 435 (Oregon Ct. of Appeals 1998); Leonard, Chapter 7.

US cities or counties (outside the twelve states listed above) with prohibitions of sexual orientation discrimination extending to private sector employment include Arlington County (VA), Austin (TX), Chicago (IL), Cleveland (OH), Denver (CO), Detroit (MI), Kansas City (MO), Louisville (KY), Miami-Dade County (FL), New Orleans (LA), New York (NY), Philadelphia (PA), Phoenix (AZ), Pittsburgh (PA), Portland (OR), Raleigh (NC), Saint Louis (MO), Seattle (WA) and Tampa (FL). See Wayne van der Meide, *Legislating Equality: A Review of Laws Affecting Gay, Lesbian, Bisexual, and Transgendered People in the United States* (Washington, DC, Policy Institute of the National Gay & Lesbian Task Force, January 2000), http://www.ngltf.org/downloads/legeq99.pdf.

APPENDIX III—GENDER IDENTITY

EUROPEAN TREATIES AND LEGISLATION AND SELECTED NATIONAL LEGISLATION EXPRESSLY OR IMPLICITLY PROHIBITING DISCRIMINATION BASED ON GENDER IDENTITY[1]

EUROPEAN TREATIES AND LEGISLATION

European Union

Treaty establishing the European Community, Rome, 25 March 1957, Article 141 (formerly 119, renumbered in 1997), http://europa.eu.int/eur-lex/en/treaties/index.html ("[e]qual pay without discrimination based on sex")

Council Directive 76/207/EEC of 9 February 1976 on the implementation of the principle of equal treatment for men and women as regards access to employment, vocational training and promotion, and working conditions, Official Journal [1976], series L, issue 39, p. 40, http://europa.eu.int/eur-lex/en/lif/dat/1976/en_376L0207.html ("no discrimination . . . on grounds of sex")

Case C-13/94, *P.* v. *S. and Cornwall County Council*, [1996] ECR I-2143 (interpreting Council Directive 76/207/EEC, and implicitly Article 141, as prohibiting discrimination "for a reason related to a gender reassignment")

(The national legislation or case-law of Austria, Belgium, Denmark, Finland, France, Germany, Greece, Ireland, Italy, Luxembourg, the Netherlands, Portugal, Spain, Sweden and the United Kingdom must give effect to *P.* v. *S. and Cornwall County Council*. Only the legislation doing so in the United Kingdom is indicated below.)

NATIONAL (FEDERAL, STATE, LOCAL) LEGISLATION

Australia

Australian Capital Territory—Discrimination Act 1991, section (s.) 7(1)(c), http://www.austlii.edu.au/au/legis/act/consol_act/da1991164 ("transsexuality")

New South Wales—Anti-Discrimination Act 1977, Part 3A, http://www.austlii.edu.au/au/legis/nsw/consol_act/aa1977204 ("transgender grounds" added in 1996)

[1] Any international, European or national treaty or constitution or legislation prohibiting discrimination based on "sex" or "sexual orientation" (including those listed in Appendix II), and not defining these grounds, can arguably be interpreted as prohibiting discrimination based on "gender identity", i.e., against transsexual or transgendered persons. Grounds such as "civil status", "disability" and "personal appearance" have also been invoked.

Northern Territory—Anti-Discrimination Act 1992, s. 4(1), http://www.austlii.edu.au/au/legis/nt/consol_act/aa204 ("sexuality" defined as including "transsexuality")
South Australia—Equal Opportunity Act, 1984, ss. 5(1), 29(3) http://www.austlii.edu.au/au/legis/sa/consol_act/eoa1984250 ("sexuality" defined as including "transsexuality")
Tasmania—Anti-Discrimination Act 1998, ss. 3, 16, http://www.thelaw.tas.gov.au/search ("sexual orientation" defined as including "transsexuality")
Victoria—Equal Opportunity Act 1995, ss. 4, 6, http://www.austlii.edu.au/au/legis/vic/consol_act/eoa1995250, as amended by Equal Opportunity (Gender Identity and Sexual Orientation) Act 2000, http://www.dms.dpc.vic.gov.au (Statute Book) ("gender identity")

South Africa

The constitutional prohibition of discrimination based on "sexual orientation" (see Appendix II) was interpreted as covering "persons who are . . . transsexual" in *National Coalition for Gay and Lesbian Equality* v. *Minister of Justice* (9 Oct. 1998), 1999 (1) SA 6 (Constitutional Court), para. 21, http://www.concourt.gov.za/archive.html (Justice Ackermann).

United Kingdom

Sex Discrimination (Gender Reassignment) Regulations 1999 (SI 1999, No. 1102, Great Britain; SR 1999, No. 311, Northern Ireland), http://www.hmso.gov.uk/legis.htm (employment and vocational training only) ("intend[ing] to undergo, . . . undergoing or ha[ving] undergone gender reassignment")

United States

Minnesota—Minn. Statutes, e.g., ss. 363.01(subdivision 41a), 363.03, http://www.revisor.leg.state.mn.us/forms/getstatute.shtml ("sexual orientation", added in 1993, includes "having . . . a self-image or identity not traditionally associated with one's biological maleness or femaleness")

"Gender identity" has been used an an independent ground of discrimination in local legislation in such cities as Ann Arbor (MI, 1999), Atlanta (GA, 2000), Louisville (KY, 1999), San Francisco (CA, 1994), Seattle (WA, 1999), Tucson (AZ, 1999), and West Hollywood (CA, 1998), and has been included in the definition of "sexual orientation" in, e.g., Toledo (OH, 1998). "Gender identification" has been used in New Orleans (LA, 1998), and "gender variance" in Boulder County, Colorado (CO, 2000). Minnesota-style definitions of "sexual [or affectional] orientation" can be found in, e.g., Minneapolis (MN, 1975) and St. Paul (MN, 1991). Seattle's 1986 definition of "sexual orientation" included "transsexuality" and "transvestism". In Santa Cruz (CA, 1992), "'gender' has the same meaning as 'sex' . . . and shall be broadly interpreted to include . . . persons who are . . . transgendered". In Pittsburgh (PA, 1997), "'sex' means the gender of a person . . . including those who are changing or have changed their gender identification". See Paisley Currah & Shannon Minter, *Transgender Equality: A Handbook for Activists and Policymakers* (Washington, DC, Policy Institute of the National Gay & Lesbian Task Force, June 2000), http://www.ngltf.org/downloads/transeq.pdf, at pp. 49-53, and n.72.